THE ATLAS OF WINTERING BIRDS IN NORTHUMBRIA

EJ STEELE '02

THE ATLAS OF WINTERING BIRDS IN NORTHUMBRIA

Compiled and Edited

by

John C. Day & Mike S. Hodgson

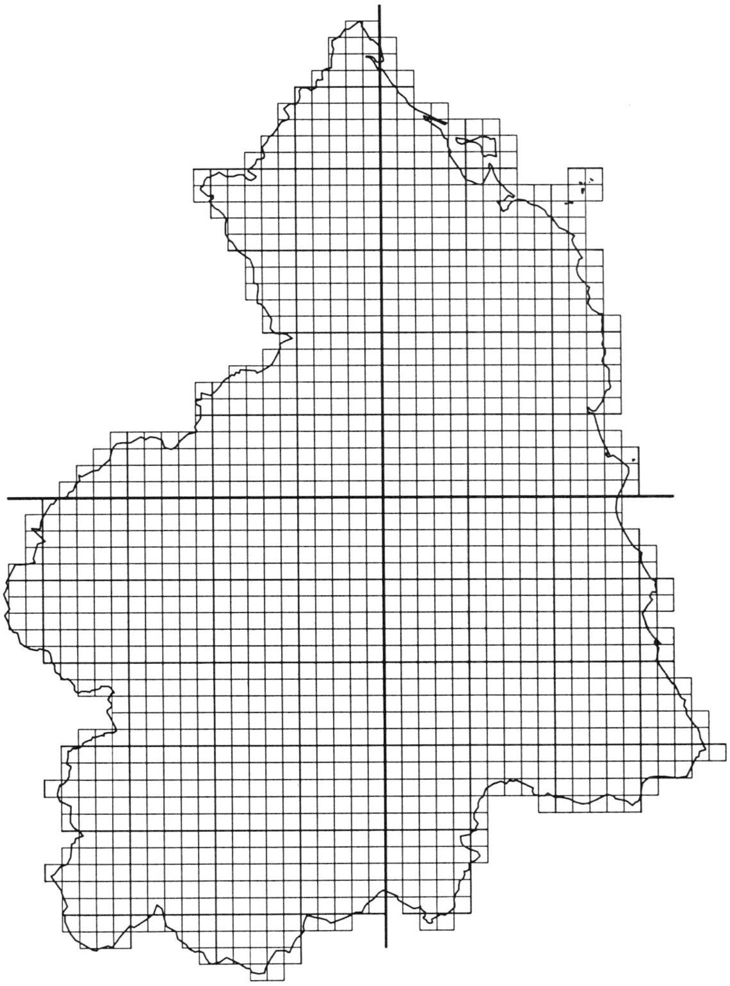

Northumberland & Tyneside Club
2003

This publication has been supported by

English Nature

North of England Raptor Conference

NORTHUMBRIAN WATER

NEWCASTLE AIRPORT

Geoff Macfarlane Memorial Trust

Newcastle City Council

Henry Bell Trust

Sinden Optics

Forest Enterprise

Northumberland National Park

Northumberland County Council

Donations in memory of the late Sandy Bankier

Legacies bequeathed by the late Alan Blackett and the late Josie Forster

Donations from Kathleen Barratt and Mary & James Howat

Donation from the estate of the late Mike Bell

Published by the Northumberland & Tyneside Bird Club 2003
Registered Charity No. 517641

ISBN 0-9538839-4-9

Design and DTP by Mike S. Hodgson and John C. Day

All maps were produced using DMAP software

Cover Painting by John Steele

Printed by Pattinson & Sons, Newcastle upon Tyne
Bound by John Joyce & Son, Gateshead

CONTENTS

List of Plates

List of Maps in the Introduction

List of Tables in the Introduction

List of Figures in the Introduction

INTRODUCTION

The publication of the *Atlas of breeding birds in Northumbria* in December 1995 was a landmark event for everyone involved in the collection, analysis and presentation of the relevant data. It proved to be the biggest single survey organised by the Northumberland & Tyneside Bird Club (NTBC), and it would be fair to say that many local birdwatchers actually missed the fieldwork that the survey entailed once it was completed.

All ornithological data, accrued systematically or otherwise and stored in an appropriate archive, can benefit our understanding of the birds we watch and the ecosystems that they inhabit, and hopefully assist with conservation initiatives. Whilst quantitative breeding information is vitally important, it should be remembered that this may only refer to a third or so of a bird's year and, with this in mind, the NTBC decided, during 1996, to embark on a full survey based on tetrads (2 x 2 km squares) of the species spending the winter months in its recording area.

The organisation and execution of a winter atlas survey is very different from that required for a breeding survey. Many of the birds are not tied to a specific territory and may move as a reaction to harsh weather conditions and the availability of food, while others choose different areas in which to spend their winter each year. For fieldworkers too there are added problems in surveying remote areas in sometimes inhospitable weather.

Nevertheless, once again club members, together with other local birdwatchers, rallied to support a survey whose data had not only the potential to establish a baseline for future work but, to a certain extent, could also be compared with the results of the national winter survey of 1981-1984 and, for some species, against the local breeding atlas data. A small Winter Atlas Committee was formed to plan and co-ordinate the fieldwork, produce and supply all necessary stationery, and to collect, check and collate the results. At an early stage it was also apparent that a fuller introductory section would be desirable for this new atlas. The original accounts in *The atlas of breeding birds in Northumbria* relating to the geographical environment and local habitats and to the region's climate merited considerable expansion, not least because of their impact on wintering species. To enhance the geographical section, a series of aerial photographs was obtained from the extensive library maintained by AirFotos Ltd and a number of 'land-based' habitat photographs around the county were also taken during the three winter seasons. A specialised paper on the climate in Northumberland has also been included.

The whole project had three main aims which were described as a) to collate all data as a permanent record in the county archive, hopefully to be utilised for conservation purposes, b) to map, as accurately as possible, the winter distribution of all species in the county and c) to provide, in conjunction with the distribution maps, an estimate of the potential winter population of all species in the county.

The publication of the local breeding atlas and subsequent income from sales gave the Northumberland & Tyneside Bird Club Committee the opportunity to create a special Development Fund. This fund exists to promote the development of ornithological studies and other aspects of our natural heritage, primarily in the club's recording area. A number of grants have been made to a variety of causes over recent years and the funding of this winter atlas is, in large part, from the Development Fund. Other monies have been raised by the sale of the atlas data and by direct grants from interested organisations as well as from generous bequests to the Bird Club.

We must again acknowledge our debt to the sterling efforts and boundless enthusiasm shown by everyone committed to this project. As a rather ambitious survey, its success or otherwise must be judged by the contents of this volume and full credit should be given to all who have been involved. The fieldworkers, the authors of individual species accounts and the artists have again given unstintingly of their time and services.

John C. Day and Mike S. Hodgson
Editors

WINTER ATLAS SURVEY COMMITTEE

MEMBERSHIP 1996 - 1999

The following Bird Club members served on the small Winter Atlas Committee throughout the survey period between 1996 and 1999 :

Muriel L. Cadwallender, Tom A. Cadwallender, John C. Day, Mike S. Hodgson and Margaret Macfarlane.

THE AREA COVERED BY THE WINTER ATLAS SURVEY

While the title of this Atlas incorporates the name Northumbria, the editors are aware that historically this relates to an ancient kingdom which initially stretched from the Forth to the Humber. It has been chosen because the geographical area covered during the winter survey extends beyond the administrative boundaries of the County of Northumberland to include the Metropolitan Boroughs of Newcastle upon Tyne and North Tyneside. These three geographical areas correspond with the Northumberland and Tyneside Bird Club's recording area and also those covered by the standard county ornithological accounts and *The atlas of breeding birds in Northumbria.* Throughout this volume, therefore, all references to Northumbria, Northumberland, the county, recording area, region or survey area should be taken to refer to the geographical/political divisions defined above.

The area for which the Bird Club maintains records falls across four 100,000 metre British National Grid squares (NT, NU, NY & NZ - see Map 1), comprising all or part of 75 ten kilometre squares. More detail can be found on the Ordnance Survey Landranger (1:50 000 scale) maps, in particular sheets 74, 75, 80, 81, 86, 87 and 88. The boundaries of the area surveyed do not fall neatly along the boundaries of the national grid lines and, for the purposes of this survey, any tetrad (two kilometre square) which has ten percent or more of its area within the county was visited by fieldworkers. For those tetrads bisected by the recording area boundary, only the portion within the recording area was included in the survey. This resulted in data being received from a total of 1,432 tetrads during the survey period, including a number of coastal squares in which the open sea constituted a large proportion of the recording area.

This compilation, like the earlier local breeding atlas, complements *Northumberland's birds*, which had become the standard retrospective ornithological account for the area. It was compiled by Bryan Galloway and Eric Meek and issued in three parts between 1978 and 1983 by the Natural History Society of Northumbria. Extensive references and acknowledgements to that work have been made throughout the individual species accounts. Some also make reference to the more recently published *Northumbrian birds* by Ian Kerr (2001), which serves to update Galloway and Meek by extending the retrospective coverage to the end of the twentieth century.

Grey Partridges in stubble and snow by Martin Eccles

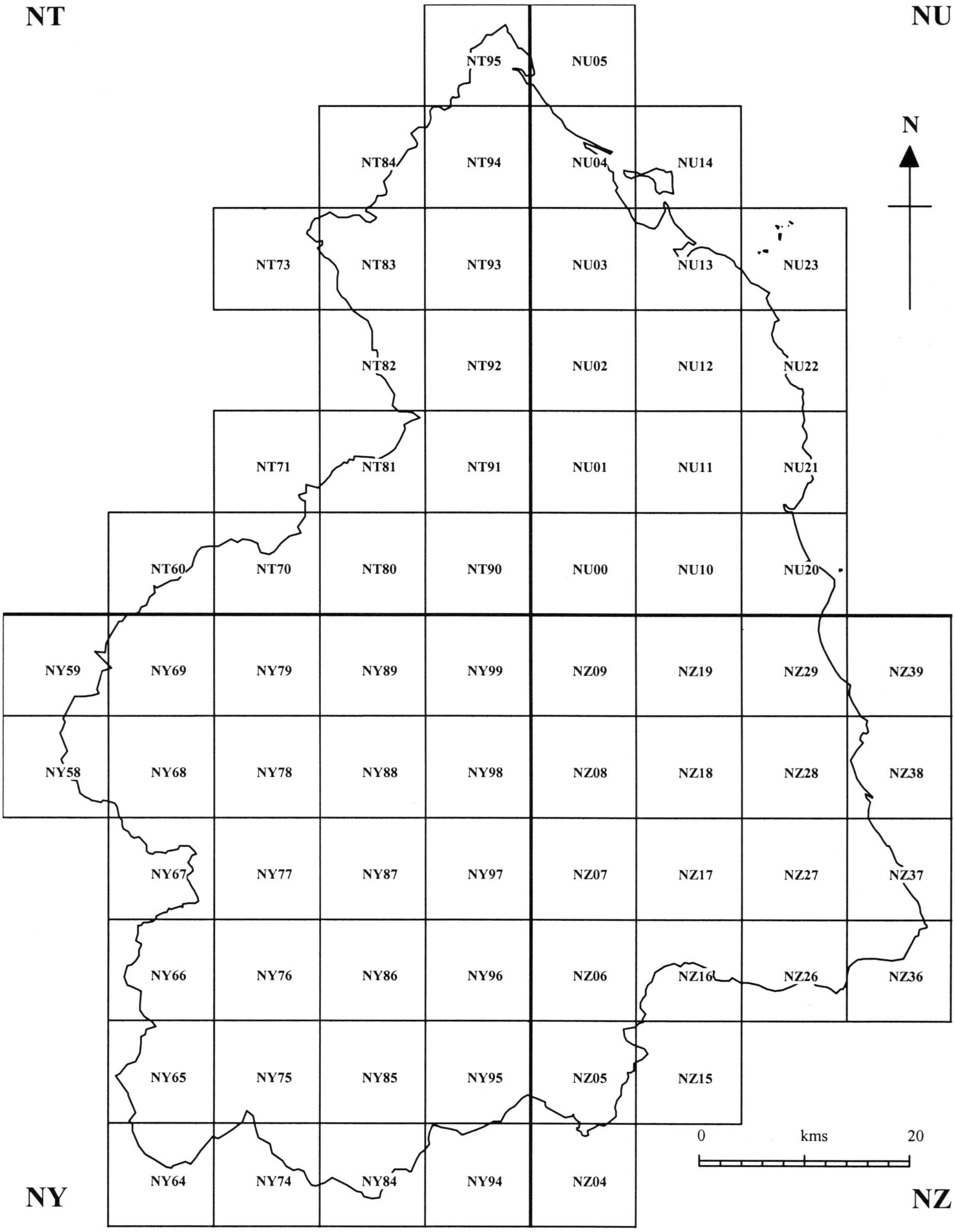

Map 1 Ordnance Survey 10km squares for Northumberland and Tyne & Wear (North)

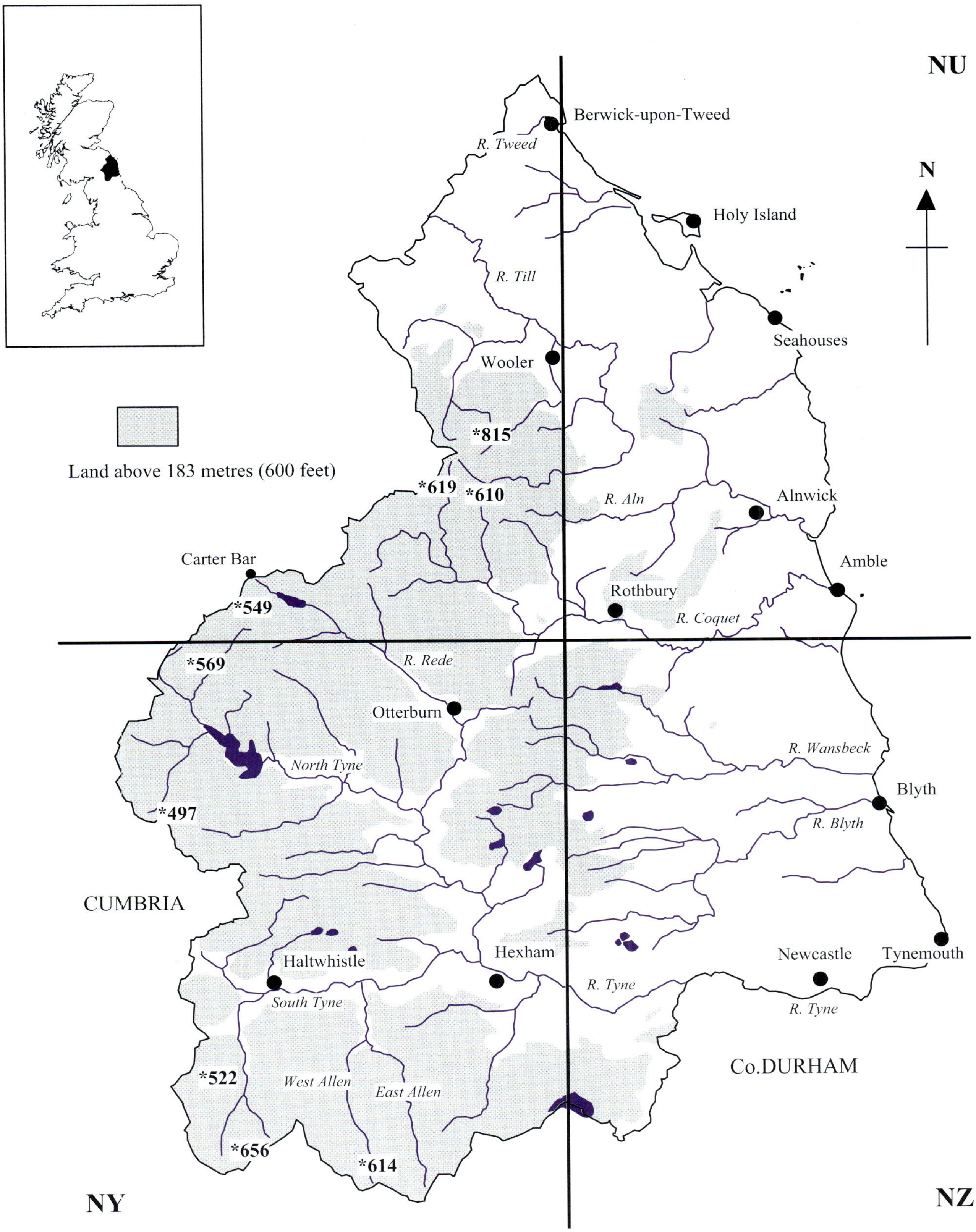

Map 2 Topographical map of Northumberland and Tyne & Wear (North)
(Spot heights are shown in metres a.s.l.)

Plate 1 The North Pennines in winter (1996) *(Copyright AirFotos)*
This area, around Nenthead and Coalcleugh (NY74/NY84), highlights the exposed, rounded hilltops of the bleak upland plateau at an altitude over 550m a.s.l. The importance of small plantations, whether of coniferous or mixed woodland, in providing food and shelter is essential for several avian species.

GEOGRAPHICAL BACKGROUND OF NORTHUMBERLAND

The total area encompassed by this latest county atlas survey is in excess of half a million hectares (Northumberland 502,644 ha; the boroughs of North Tyneside and Newcastle upon Tyne 19,564 ha, plus a number of largely open sea areas), making it one of the largest ornithological recording regions in England. It also corresponds to the Watsonian floral vice-counties of South Northumberland (67) and Cheviot (68), although the two vice-counties, which are delineated by a combination of administrative boundaries and physical features, do not accurately reflect the diverse range of ornithological habitat types that they enclose (Swan, 1993).

Along much of its northern and western boundaries Northumberland abuts with Scotland along the 'Border fence', although the summit ridge of the Cheviot Hills is a rather indistinct divide. This is not the case to the east, however, as the North Sea clearly forms an abrupt natural boundary. South of the Tyne-Irthing gap (the Newcastle to Carlisle corridor), the boundary of the recording region is partly delineated by the rivers Tyne and Derwent, although further west, in the Allendales and South Tyne Valley, the higher land of the northern Pennine Hills forms the boundary with both Co. Durham and Cumbria (Map 2). The western hills reach a height of 815m (2,674 ft) above sea level on the summit of the Cheviot (Plate 35), with many other tops exceeding 549m (1,800 ft), whilst south of the River Tyne heights of up to 673m (2,208 ft) are recorded along the Co. Durham and Cumbrian borders (Plate 1). These uplands are deeply incised by the main river systems creating a number of enclosed valleys flanked by hills with rounded summits, the results of earlier glacial activity (Plates 2 & 3). Nearly half of the area covered by this atlas lies above the 183m (600 ft) contour with the remainder forming an agricultural plain and coastal belt which varies in width from 19 to 40 kilometres (12 to 25 miles), being narrowest in the north and widest across the south eastern sector.

The atlas area therefore straddles a number of distinct faunal habitats that have been fully described in *Northumberland's birds*. It is, nevertheless, necessary to provide a brief synopsis of that data to appreciate the significance of some of the distribution maps in the main body of the text. With this purpose in mind the provision of a transparent overlay accompanying this volume should also facilitate the location of the main river systems and other salient features.

Galloway and Meek (1978) recognised a number of different habitats including the following.

1. Extensive heather moorland and acid grassland (Map 3), which lies predominantly in the west of the county and is often associated with crags (Plates 4 & 5). These rock outcrops may be sandstone, as in the Simonside Hills (Plate 6), volcanic lava and screes as in the Cheviots (Plate 7), or the Whin Sill escarpment (Plate 33) which extends westwards from the Farne Islands to the Roman Wall and into Cumbria (Johnson, 1995). The moorland can be divided into three distinct types. The most fertile is that which supports poor quality grassland and Bracken *Pteridium aquilina* on the lower and drier flanks of the hills. The second category of moorland tends to be in areas of higher rainfall and poor soils where acid grasslands, dominated by Purple Moor-grass *Molinia caerulea* or Mat-grass *Nardus stricta*, are dominant. Heather *Calluna vulgaris* is also much in evidence in the drier areas and it is in this habitat that it is managed on some estates by rotational burning (Plate 8). The third type of moorland contains peat bogs, which tend to be the wettest upland habitat, usually occurring over 450m above sea level. Cottongrass *Eriophorum* sp., Cross-leaved Heath *Erica tetralix* and Heather predominate. The atlas maps in this volume highlight land over 183m (600 feet) a.s.l., and this corresponds closely to the junction between the moorland edge and the extent of enclosed upland grazing (Plate 9).

2. Woodland forms the next major habitat. Much of it in Northumberland is man-made, with vast expanses of spruce and pine planted by both the Forestry Commission and by private economic forestry groups, some of it in the early 1920s. The accompanying map (Map 4) based on data collected by atlas fieldworkers, clearly shows the extent of this habitat (in excess of 66,000 ha), although the coniferous woodland is no longer the mono-culture one might expect as the current practice of creating open areas, clear felling, re-planting and the retention of former native woodland is providing a much more diverse vegetational mosaic (Plate 10). Deciduous woodland on the other hand is much more fragmented in its distribution. It survives in upland areas where the valley sides of many rivers and tributaries retain some native hardwoods (Plates 11 & 12). It has been estimated that approximately 550-600 hectares of upland oak woodland still survive in Northumberland (Brodin, 2001). Mature deciduous woodland and mixed woodland, sometimes including exotic species, can also be found on the agricultural plain around many farmsteads and particularly in the parkland setting of a number of country houses, such as those at Cragside (Plate 13). Some of the former industrial sites in the south east of the recording area, now being reclaimed as nature reserves and recreational land, are also being replanted with coniferous or mixed woodland, as well as by much spontaneous re-growth of natural scrub.

3. The extensive agricultural lowland and coastal plain is also a very important habitat, particularly in winter. It begins in the Tweed and Till basin in the north of the county, expands southwards around Alnwick (Plate 15) to the coastal plain near Morpeth, and then skirts the Tyneside conurbation on its western flank, to extend into the Tyne Valley and Hexhamshire (Map 5). The relatively small agricultural field units allow for a diversity of crops and livestock, and the retention of hedgerows and shelter-belts provides food and sanctuary for many winter species (Plate 14). Much of the agricultural land of what was the north east corner of the former coalfield has suffered from the inroads of extensive

opencast mining and, when the areas are unimaginatively reconstituted, often becomes a flat, hedgeless panorama, interspersed with small coniferous plantations and shelter-belts (Plate 19).

4. Freshwater lakes, rivers and ponds form another important habitat (Map 6). They may be natural lakes or loughs like those at Broomlee and Sweethope (Plate 16), subsidence ponds in the former coalfield (e.g. Arcot Pond, Big Waters, Wallsend Swallow Pond) or man-made reservoirs including those at Whittle Dene (Plate 32), Catcleugh, Fontburn, Derwent or, largest of all, Kielder (Plate 36). To these should be added artificially created pools on nature reserves at coastal sites like Low Hauxley, Linton, Druridge Bay Country Park, East Chevington (Plate 17) and inland at sites such as Caistron (Plate 18) and Cragside. Some very small man-made farm ponds also provide an interesting habitat. It has been calculated that there are approximately 2,290 ha of standing open water in Northumberland. The reservoirs total 1,724 ha with Kielder Reservoir alone accounting for 65% of that figure. The remaining ponds and lakes cover about 560 ha (Feige, 2000).

Major riparian habitat can be found along the many rivers and their tributaries that rise in the Cheviots or the North Pennines to the south of the Tyne-Irthing gap. The middle and upper reaches often run through native deciduous woodland and the presence of shingle banks and 'carrs' (i.e. low-lying wet areas of alder, willow and birch) provide valuable habitat for many species. The lower reaches too, as pollution decreases, are becoming a more important habitat, particularly in winter. The major rivers are the Tweed, Till, Breamish, Aln, Coquet, Wansbeck, Rede, the East and West Allen and, of course, the North and South Tyne which merge near Hexham to form the River Tyne (Map 7). Most flow in an easterly or south-easterly direction.

5. The coastline is particularly significant in Northumberland, extending for some 97 kilometres, with large colonies of breeding seabirds on suitable mainland cliffs and on offshore sites like the Farne Islands and Coquet Island. In winter the coastal waters continue to attract numerous species, particularly in the northern half of the county. There are also considerable areas of sand dunes, with their associated vegetation, along the whole length of the coastline (Plates 25-30). A further sub-zone on the coast is the intertidal mudflats that occur on the Lindisfarne National Nature Reserve (Plates 22, 26 & 27) and in the estuaries of the rivers Tweed (Plate 25), Coquet (Plates 20 & 29), Aln (Plate 23), Wansbeck, Blyth (Plates 21 & 31) and Tyne. The county's intertidal habitat exceeds 3,000 hectares, with 2,713 of them constituting a large part of the Lindisfarne NNR (Brodin, 2001). Whilst the other estuaries enclose much smaller amounts (see below), all feature prominently in the national Wetland Bird Survey (WeBS) counts (see Appendix H).

Locality	Area in hectares
Tweed Estuary	68
Lindisfarne NNR (including Budle Bay)	2,713
Aln Estuary	87
Coquet Estuary	30
Wansbeck Estuary	37
Blyth Estuary	90
Tyne Estuary	57
Total	3,072

6. The last important habitat is that of the urban and suburban areas (Plate 24) where the previous increase in derelict colliery and industrial wasteland is now being partly alleviated by rejuvenation. Not only is the vegetation on new-town trading estates, such as that at Cramlington, maturing but there has been a gradual spread of suburban leisure areas like those along the banks of the rivers Wansbeck and Tyne. Whilst the greenbelt around the fringes of the Tyneside conurbation has been eroded by the development of new trading estates and housing projects, the planting of trees and shrubbery has partly reduced its loss. So too, on many of the private housing estates, has the suburban garden. Here, in an artificial environment, with its peanut and fat-feeders during the winter months, the spread, and even increase, of a number of avian species has been encouraged.

Plates 25-36

In addition to the Northumberland National Park and the existence of the LNNR, many sites in the club's recording area have some form of environmental or conservation-based protection, with over 120 SSSIs alone being listed by English Nature in 2002. A significant move was the implementation of the Northumberland Coast Management Plan (1993) and a series of on-going legislative applications. Plates 25 to 36 consist of more aerial photographs of sites and habitats of ornithological significance in the county with a particular relevance for wintering species. Coastal locations are depicted by Plates 25-31, all of which have a range of special protection measures including Ramsar, SSSI, SPA and SNCI status, with many currently being considered for the new European designation of Special Area of Conservation (SAC). The remaining five (Plates. 32-36) attempt to illustrate further the wide diversity of inland habitat types in the recording area with photographs of the central agricultural plain, the Tyne Valley, the Cheviot massif and the Kielder Reservoir and Forest.

Plate 2 Chillingham (*M. S. Hodgson*)
Improved grassland near Chillingham (NU02T), with a number of mature mixed woodland shelter-belts. A snow-capped Hedgehope (714m) and Cheviot (815m) are visible in the background.

Plate 3 The Cheviot foothills (*J. C. Day*)
The 'white-lands' of the Cheviot foothills taken from near Ridlees Cairn (NT80H/NT80M), over 400m a.s.l. The thin soils, over peat, support large areas of Mat-grass *Nardus stricta*, the deeper soils Purple Moor-grass *Molinia caerula*. In the middle distance are economic conifer plantations.

Plate 4 Houx Hill, Redesdale (*J. C. Day*)
Houx Hill (450m) in Redesdale (NT70S) showing montane heathland dominated by mosses, Crowberry *Empetrum nigrum* and Bilberry *Vaccinium* sp.

Plate 5 Cross Cleugh, Upper Redesdale (*J. C. Day*)
Cross Cleugh (450m) in Upper Redesdale (NT70), looking westwards towards the Scottish border on Carter Fell. A typical scene in upland Northumberland where impeded drainage on peaty gleys has created the tussock formation of Purple Moor-grass *Molinia caerula*.

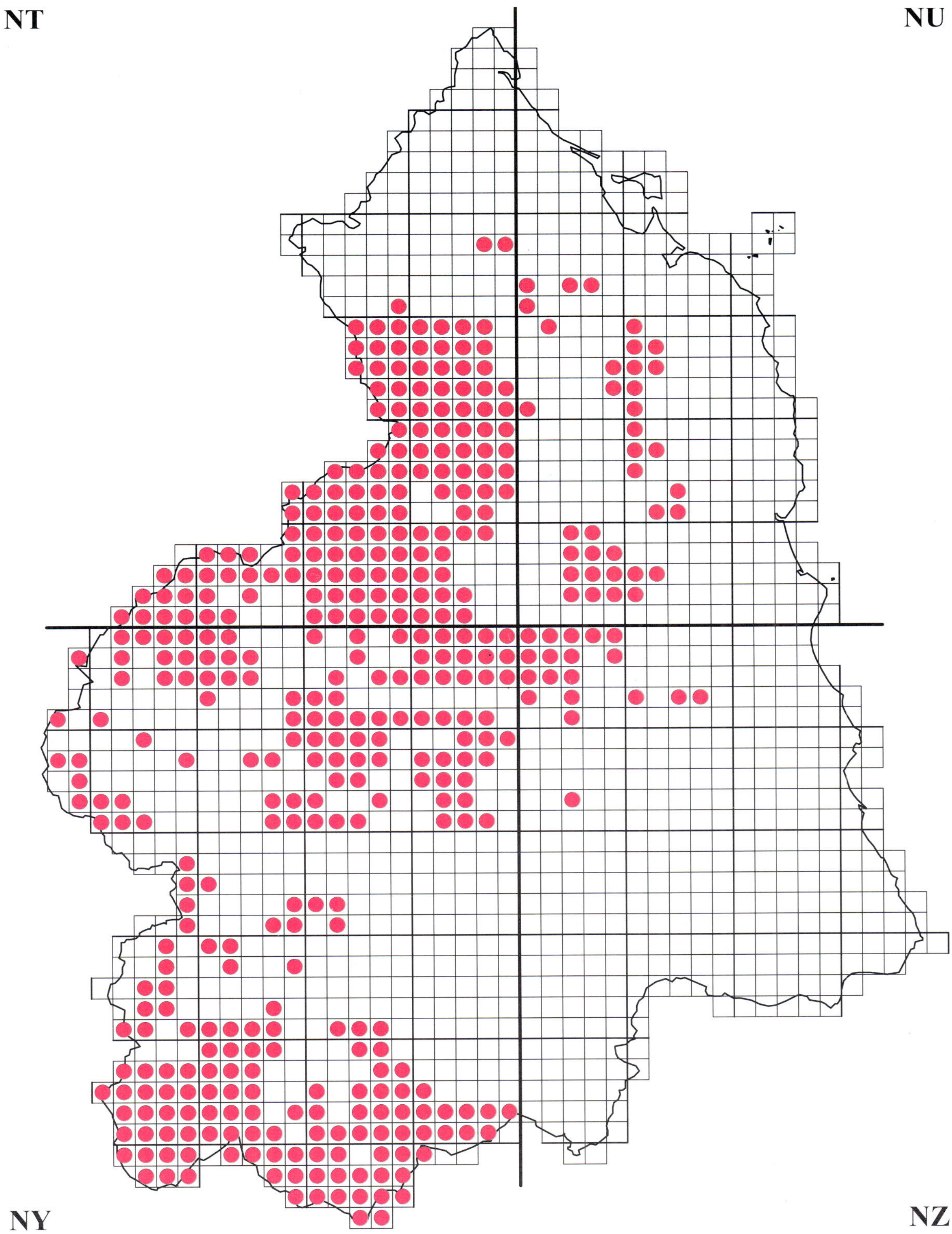

Map 3 Distribution of Moorland as a significant habitat within tetrads
The tetrad data on which this map is based were collected and recorded by atlas fieldworkers during timed visits. Fuller details appear in the section dealing with fieldwork methodology.

Plate 6 Heather moorland, Simonside Hills (*J. C. Day*)
Dense and widespread Heather *Calluna vulgaris* moorland in the Simonside Hills (NY09B), some 370m a.s.l.

Plate 7 The Harthope Valley near Langlee (*M. S. Hodgson*)
River terracing in the Harthope Valley, near Langlee (NT92), with remnant Birch *Betula* sp. to the left, and Gorse *Ulex europaeus* on the shingle beds. The steep andesitic scree slopes of the valley sides are typical in the Cheviot Hills.

Plate 8 The Ottercops (*J. C. Day*)
Managed Heather *Calluna vulgaris* moorland at the Ottercops (NY99K), some 300m a.s.l., with improved grassland in the foreground.

Plate 9 Plashetts near Kirkwhelpington (*J. C. Day*)
Unimproved upland grassland at c.220m a.s.l. at Plashetts near Kirkwhelpington (NY98W). The results of attempted drainage nevertheless increase the potential for greater diversity of floral and avian species such as Snipe *Gallinago gallinago*.

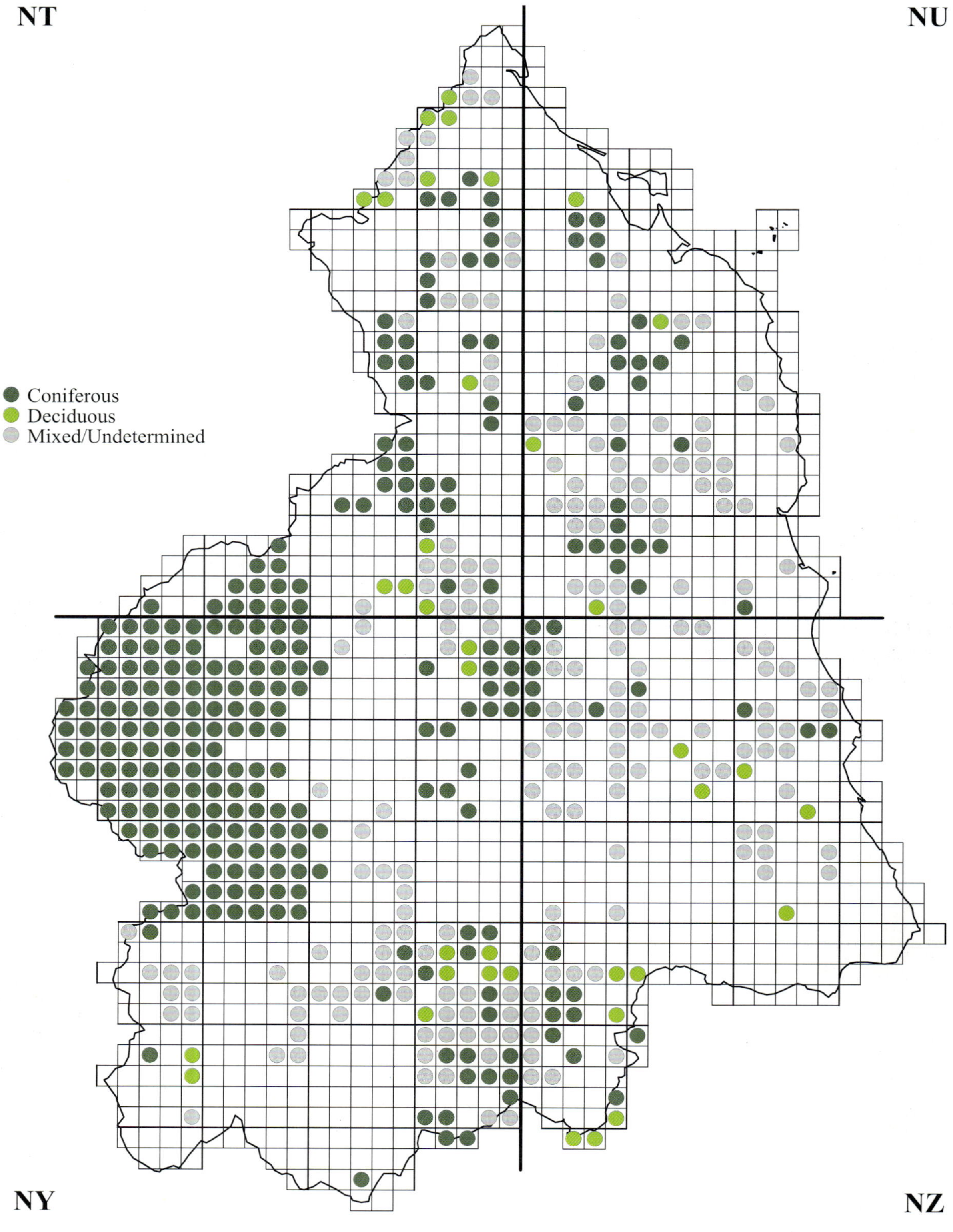

Map 4 Distribution of Woodland as a significant habitat within tetrads

The tetrad data on which this map is based were collected and recorded by atlas fieldworkers during timed visits. Fuller details appear in the section dealing with fieldwork methodology.

Plate 10 Kielder Forest (*M. S. Hodgson*)
Upland Sitka *Picea* sp. plantations in Kielder Forest showing tracts of older growth (c.40 years old), replanted areas (c.5 years old) and some cleared sections. The Heather *Calluna vulgaris* moorland on the skyline delineates the height (c.400m) above which conifer growth is restricted.

Plate 11 Fallowlees (*J. C. Day*)
Remnant semi-natural woodland near Fallowlees (NY09G), 230m a.s.l. Many of Northumberland's upland valleys still retain considerable tracts of Oak *Quercus* sp., Alder *Alnus* sp., Hazel *Corylus avellana*, and Birch *Betula* sp., most of which date from the end of the First World War.

Plate 12 Allendale (*M. S. Hodgson*)
Near Sinderhope in south west Northumberland (NY85). An area of mature semi-natural woodland with, at lower altitudes, substantial base-rich pasture land.

Plate 13 Cragside, Rothbury (*Copyright AirFotos*)
A largely 'Victorian landscape' of ornamental woodland in central Northumberland (NU00), created in the nineteenth century. Its position in the plain of the River Coquet, to the east of the Cheviot massif, and adjacency to heather moorland, makes the whole area an important wintering ground for many species.

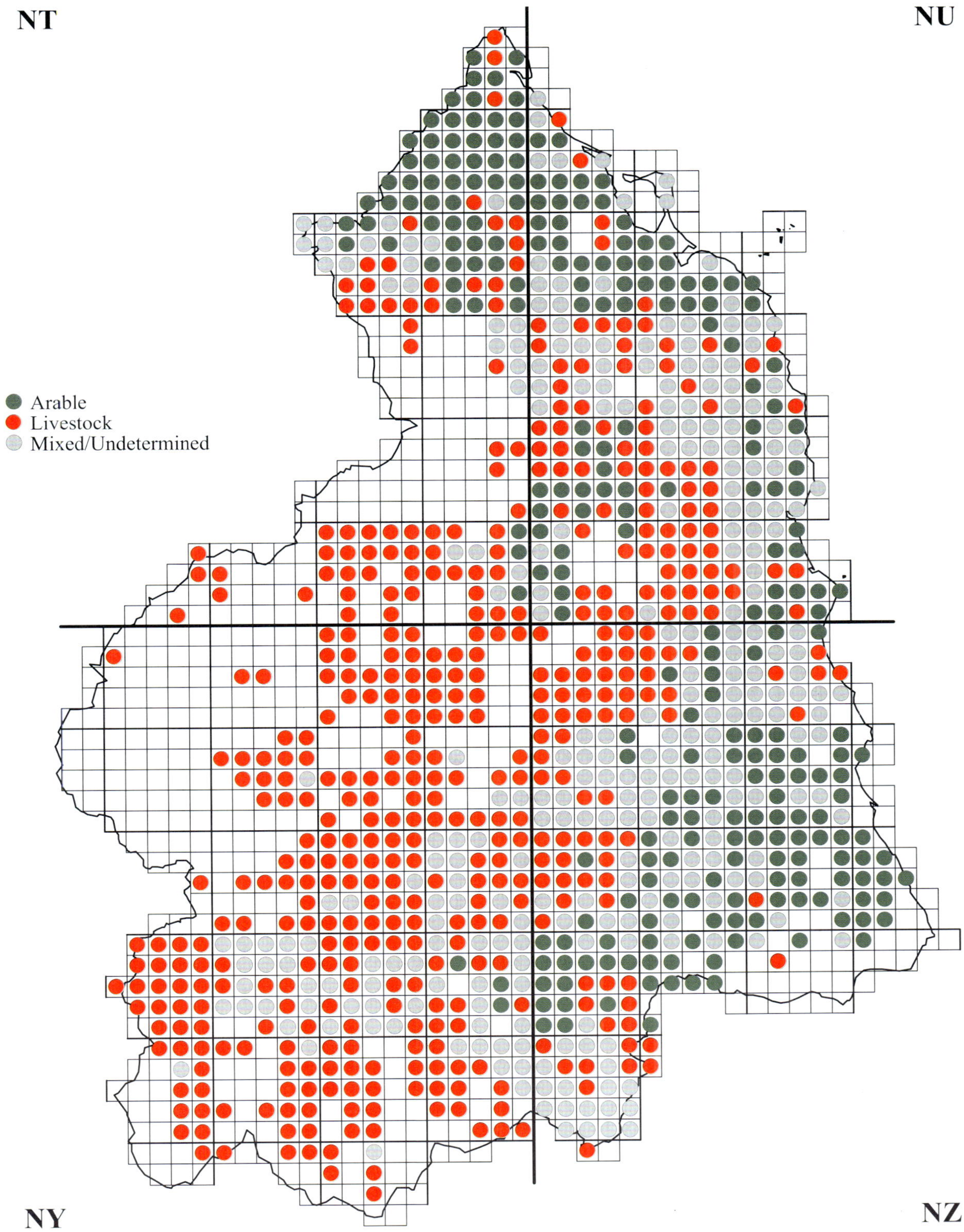

Map 5 Distribution of Farmland as a significant habitat within tetrads
The tetrad data on which this map is based were collected and recorded by atlas fieldworkers during timed visits. Fuller details appear in the section dealing with fieldwork methodology.

Plate 14 The agricultural plain (*J. C. Day*)
The snow-covered Northumberland agricultural plain from the east coast, near Blyth, looking towards the Cheviot Hills. It shows the traditional pattern of small agricultural units with many hedgerows and ancient field boundaries still intact.

Plate 15 The coastal plain near Alnwick (*Copyright AirFotos*)
The coastal plain in the north of the county near Alnwick (NU11W). The photograph shows a complex mosaic of different field sizes with many old hedgerows, field boundaries and 'dene' woodland.

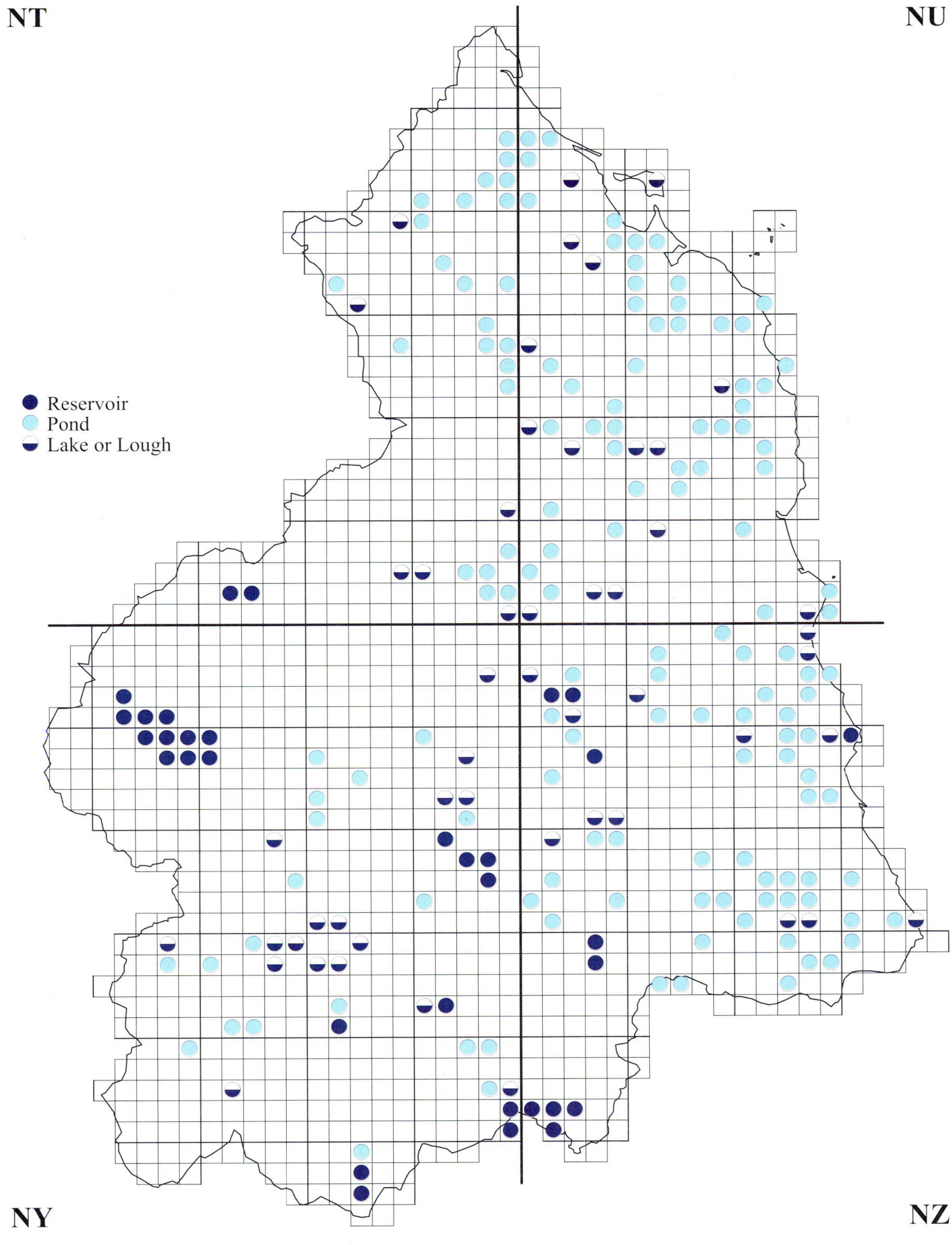

Map 6 Location of Reservoirs, Lakes, Loughs and Ponds in Northumberland

The tetrad data on which this map is based were collected and recorded by atlas fieldworkers during timed visits. Fuller details appear in the section dealing with fieldwork methodology.

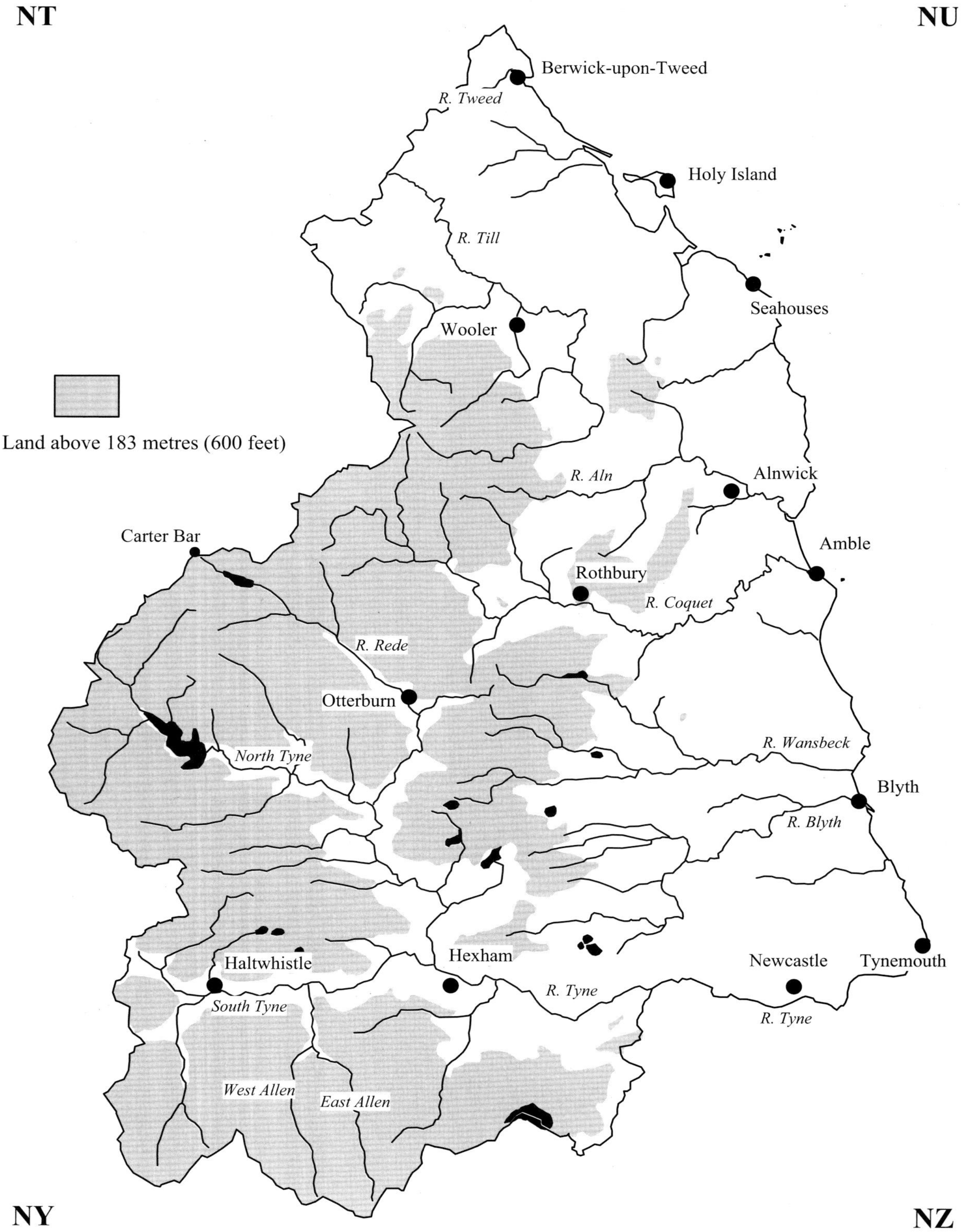

Map 7 Main Rivers in Northumberland and Tyne & Wear (North)

Plate 16 Sweethope Loughs (1996) (*Copyright AirFotos*)
Sweethope Loughs (NY98G/L) in central Northumberland, some 250m a.s.l. In addition to the extensive conifer plantations, the 'black' Heather *Calluna vulgaris* moorland in the foreground contrasts with the 'white' rough-grazing grassland to the north of the Loughs. Within the heather moorland is a drained raised mire. In winter the Loughs attract wildfowl and host a gull roost.

Plate 17 Druridge Bay Country Park and East Chevington (2000) (*Copyright AirFotos*)
The coastal plain near Broomhill (NU20K). The area in the foreground at Druridge Bay Country Park includes Ladyburn Lake (NU20Q), whilst to the left of it lies the somewhat more recent north pond at East Chevington Nature Reserve (NZ29U). Both were created after extensive opencast mining during the 1980s and 1990s. In the Country Park are mixed and conifer shelter-belts, but the newly planted hedgerows and plantations at East Chevington have still to mature. Only the coastal dunes in this photograph have survived industrial exploitation.

Plate 18 Mid-Coquetdale (*J. C. Day*)
An extensive area of mixed farming with many secondary plantations and shelter-belts. In the centre of the photograph, former gravel extraction pits constitute a private nature reserve. During the winter atlas data collection period, this site at Caistron (NU00A) recorded more species than any other far-inland location.

Plate 19 Reclaimed opencast site near Widdrington (*M. S. Hodgson*)
The rather featureless panorama of a reclaimed coastal opencast site near Widdrington (NY29I). In the foreground is a rye grass/clover ley for silage, with a large new conifer plantation in the centre of the photograph. In the background, the retaining banks of the ongoing deep opencast workings can be seen.

Plate 20 The Coquet Estuary (*M. S. Hodgson*)
The Coquet Estuary (NU20S) is an area of local and national importance for wintering waders and wildfowl. It includes sites with SSSI status and forms a significant section of the Northumberland coastal protection area.

Plate 21 The Blyth Estuary (*M. S. Hodgson*)
The Blyth Estuary (NZ38B). An estuarine habitat with a small remnant of a dune system in the foreground. The area is of local and national significance as both a winter feeding area and roost site, particularly for waders.

Plate 22 Holy Island and Fenham Flats (1995) (*Copyright AirFotos*)
Taken from the north west, this view shows the causeway from the mainland across the intertidal area of Fenham Flats. The causeway passes round the southern edge of The Snook and continues to the village and castle at the south east corner of the island. To the right of the causeway lies part of Beal Sands, along the edge of which is a bed of *Spartina*, fringed by a slightly darker coloured bed of Eelgrass *Zostera* sp. Lying within the Lindisfarne NNR, the whole area teems with birds during the winter months. It holds internationally and nationally important numbers of some species of wildfowl and waders The Svalbard population of pale-bellied Brent Geese *Branta bernicla hrota* winters here and is now joined by numbers of dark-bellied Brent *B. b. bernicla*. The saltmarsh and dune areas are also important habitats for species such as Skylark *Alauda arvensis*, Twite *Carduelis flavirostris* and Snow Bunting *Plectrophenax nivalis*.

Plate 23 Alnmouth (2001) (*Copyright AirFotos*)
The estuarine mudflats at the mouth of the River Aln, Alnmouth (NU21K). The Alnmouth Dunes and the saltmarsh of Low Buston, which can attract species such as Twite *Carduelis flavirostris* and Snipe *Gallinago gallinago*, lie to the south and to the north, at Boulmer (NU21R/S), there are large areas of coastal rock formations which are exposed at low tide. To the north west of Alnmouth village can be seen the haugh-lands at Foxton and the final meander of the River Aln. The area can hold good numbers of wintering wildfowl and waders.

Plate 24 The Tyne Estuary (2002) (*Copyright AirFotos*)
The mouth of the River Tyne (NZ36U) from the west, with North Shields and Tynemouth in the background. The extensive industrial wasteland holds a limited number of species, but in the foreground, to the left of the storage tanks, is the new Northumbrian Water nature reserve at Howdon Sewage Treatment Works (NZ36N). It is already attracting large numbers of waders, waterfowl and gulls.

Plate 25 Berwick-upon-Tweed and the Tweed Estuary (1988) (*Copyright AirFotos*)
In the foreground are the important shingle bars at Berwick Little Beach (NU05B) and, behind the breakwater, the intertidal area on the north side of the estuary with Yarrow Slake beyond the Royal Border Bridge. All are important areas for waders. The whole of the estuary holds very significant numbers of Mute Swan *Cygnus olor* and Goldeneye *Bucephala clangula* together with Goosander *Mergus merganser* and other wildfowl. There can be variable numbers of these birds in the estuary depending on the time of day and the state of the tide. The inshore waters here can hold good populations of seabirds including Red-throated Diver *Gavia stellata*, Red-breasted Merganser *Mergus serrator* and Shag *Phalacocorax aristotelis*.

Plate 26 Holy Island (1982) (*Copyright AirFotos*)
The view from the east looking over the southern half of Holy Island (NU14G), with Fenham Flats (NU14A) in the distance. The coastal waters, particularly in the area of Holy Island harbour and the open sea immediately south and east, can be excellent for the three species of diver *Gavia* sp., Red-necked *Podiceps grisegena* and Slavonian Grebe *P. auritus*, Eider *Somateria mollissima*, Common Scoter *Melanitta nigra* and Long-tailed Duck *Clangula hyemalis*. The fields on the island itself are important for wintering flocks of finches and also for feeding and resting groups of waders. A number of high-tide roosts occur around the Lindisfarne NNR and are monitored under the WeBS counts organised by the BTO.

Plate 27 Budle Bay and Ross Back Sands (1995) (*Copyright AirFotos*)
This photograph of Budle Bay (NU13M/N) shows the tidal mudflats of the extensive shallow bay where many wildfowl and waders feed and roost in winter. In the foreground is the mixed woodland at Spindlestone (NU13L) and immediately above the northern edge of Budle Bay lie the sand dunes of Ross Links. On the seaward side, the area forms part of 'Skate Road' much favoured by grebes, divers and sea duck. Budle Bay is part of the Ramsar-designated Lindisfarne NNR and the Heugh at Spindlestone is an SSSI.

Plate 28 The Farne Islands (1995) *(Copyright AirFotos)*
The Farne Islands (NU23) from the mainland, with Inner Farne in the foreground, Brownsman and Staple Island in the centre and Longstone, with its lighthouse, furthest out to sea. The Farnes now belong to the National Trust and have both SSSI and SPA status. In most winters the sea around the islands holds large numbers of duck, including Common Scoter *Melanitta nigra,* Long-tailed Duck *Clangula hyemalis* and Eider *Somateria mollissima* with divers and grebes also regularly recorded.

Plate 29 Amble Harbour and the River Coquet (1989) (*Copyright AirFotos*)

The photograph shows the tidal estuary of the River Coquet (NU20M/S) with Warkworth in the background. To the north of the seawall are important sand dunes, a saltmarsh and the 'Gut'. It is a wintering area of significance, not only for waders, gulls and wildfowl, but also for flocks of Twite *Carduelis flavirostris* and other small passerines. The Warkworth dunes and saltmarsh are specifically designated as an SSSI, the coastal section itself being part of the Northumberland Coast Ramsar protected area.

Plate 30 Druridge Bay and Cresswell Pond (1991) *(Copyright AirFotos)*
Druridge Bay (NZ29) holds large numbers of sea duck and divers during the winter months. To the south can be seen the promontory of Snab Point (NZ39B) and to the north, in the haze, is Coquet Island (NU20X). In between is Cresswell Pond (NZ29X), important for wintering duck and waders, and further north it is possible to make out Druridge Pools (NZ29T) and beyond that Ladyburn Lake (NU20Q). The rich flat agricultural plain favoured by flocks of Whooper Swan *Cygnus cygnus* and geese *Anser* sp. is clearly shown. Various conservation measures protect most of the Druridge Bay sites with the National Trust, the Northumberland Wildlife Trust and Northumberland County Council all involved.

Plate 31 The Blyth Estuary (1995) (*Copyright AirFotos*)
According to the WeBS count statistics the Blyth Estuary (NZ38) is the second most important estuary for wintering species in the county, the first being that of the River Tyne. It is particularly important for flocks of roosting waders, including Purple Sandpiper *Calidris maritima*, as well as Cormorant *Phalacrocorax carbo* and Shelduck *Tadorna tadorna*. Because of its importance much of the estuary and adjacent coast has varying degrees of protection provided by a combination of SSSI, SPA, SNCI and Ramsar status.

Plate 32 Whittle Dene Reservoirs (1997) *(Copyright AirFotos)*
The central agricultural plain near Whittle Dene Reservoirs (NZ06T/U). The dominant crop is spring-sown Oil-seed rape *Brassica napus* and there is a noticeable lack of shelter-belt plantations. Many hedges have also been removed creating an 'open' situation favoured by flocks of wintering geese. The Reservoirs hold many wildfowl during the winter months.

Plate 33 Roman Wall country (1983) (*Copyright AirFotos*)
The Roman Wall near Housesteads (NY76Z) and the Whin Sill escarpment with extensive rough grazing on either side of the Wall. Around the farm of Hotbank, in the foreground, is some richer improved grazing, and in the top left corner the fresh water lough at Broomlee. A number of coniferous and mixed shelter-belt plantations are also visible. All lie within the Northumberland National Park and both the lough and the escarpment have SSSI status. Swans, geese, wildfowl and birds of prey are amongst the more interesting wintering species in this bleak marginal upland area.

Plate 34 Plenmeller Common (2000) (*Copyright AirFotos*)

This photograph of Plenmeller Common (NY76), in the Tyne Valley, clearly shows 'the greening of the uplands'. There is a distinct encroachment of improved grassland on former Heather *Calluna vulgaris* moorland. What little moorland is left is rapidly disappearing because of winter feeding *in situ*, resulting in a much depleted habitat. Opencast working for coal is also in evidence in the top right corner of the moorland. The area is adjacent to a designated moorland SSSI, with large populations of Red Grouse *Lagopus lagopus* and some Black Grouse *Tetrao tetrix*. Wintering birds of prey are also a feature of the area with occasional records of Red Kite *Milvus milvus* and Hen Harrier *Circus cyaneus*, as well as a rapidly expanding resident population of Common Buzzard *Buteo buteo*.

Plate 35 College Valley and The Cheviot (1999) (*Copyright AirFotos*)
This view shows the College Valley (NT82) dominated by the summits of Coldburn Hill (484m) and Preston Hill (525m) on its east side, with the massive bulk of The Cheviot (815m) behind. These rounded and glaciated hilltops have Heather *Calluna vulgaris* on their summits with economic coniferous plantations along their flanks. Remnant Alder *Alnus glutinosa* and Birch *Betula* sp. woodland is visible on the valley floor, with an important mature Oak *Quercus* sp. wood in the lower left-hand corner of the photograph. The valley also contains extensive patches of Gorse *Ulex europaeus* along the river shingle. Wintering birds are to be found primarily in the sheltered valley bottom, although Red Grouse *Lagopus lagopus*, Raven *Corvus corax* and Common Buzzard *Buteo buteo* are also present.

Plate 36 Kielder Reservoir and the Border Forest (1987) (*Copyright AirFotos*)
Surrounded by extensive coniferous forestry plantations Kielder Reservoir (NY68/69) is a bleak area in winter. As the trees mature, however, what once seemed a rather sterile mono-culture is becoming a much more varied series of habitats as felling takes place and some clear-felled areas are left unplanted. The development of natural hardwoods along the valley sides and a more aesthetic approach to the landscape is creating a much more bird-friendly area. The Border Forest Park also contains some important areas of Heather *Calluna vulgaris* moorland. During the winter months, the coniferous plantations and remnant alder and birch woodlands usually hold good numbers of Goldcrest *Regulus regulus*, Coal Tit *Parus ater*, Siskin *Carduelis spinus* and, in good cone crop years, breeding Crossbill *Loxia curvirostra*. The forest is also home to Common Buzzard *Buteo buteo*, Goshawk *Accipiter gentilis*, Tawny Owl *Strix aluco* and occasionally wintering Great Grey Shrike *Lanius excubitor*.

THE CLIMATE OF NORTHUMBERLAND DURING THE WINTERS OF 1996/97, 1997/98 & 1998/99

Dennis Wheeler

INTRODUCTION

One of the features that characterises the physical environment of the British Isles is its variability from one location to another. Regions, districts, even valley floors and nearby hilltops, often stand in marked contrast to one another. Such differences are rarely more apparent than in day-to-day weather and its longer-term counterpart, climate. Physiography, soils, water bodies and, more recently, extent of built-up area, all contribute to this rich variety. Of these elements, few are of greater significance than altitude and the unwary hill-walker is well-advised to note that nowhere on our planet does climate deteriorate - if by this one means increases in rainfall and wind speed, and decreases in temperature and sunshine - as rapidly with height as it does in the British Isles.

It is against this background that the climate of Northumberland is best understood. Indeed, it might be argued that in its extent (502,000 hectares) and its altitudinal range (sea level to 815 metres at the Cheviot) it would be wrong to presuppose any climatic unity within the county. This view has some justification, yet some aspects provide at one and the same time for a degree of consistency within the county and for a contrast with other regions. The principal factors in these respects are latitude, eastward aspect and proximity to the North Sea.

As England's most northerly county it is also one of the coolest and rarely enjoys the summer maxima of southerly areas that are more regularly exposed to the advances of tropical air from the Azores anticyclone, or to the yet warmer summer air streams that reach the south east of England from France or the Mediterranean. Heatwave conditions can occur, however, but require particular arrangements of weather systems with a well-developed anticyclone centred over the Midlands or southern England. An example is described in Wheeler (1988) when the region was, exceptionally, the warmest in the country. Other climatic characteristics are a response to geographic situation. The North Sea exercises a powerful influence in this respect and cools coastal districts by as much as 5 °C or more during the summer (Wheeler, 1984) but, conversely, may warm them relative to inland locations during the winter. When coastal sea breezes are fully developed the summer cooling influence can extend several kilometres inland across the undulating topography of the eastern half of the county. These local circulations, paradoxically, occur when warm and settled conditions dominate the rest of the country. In their worst manifestations they also bring one of the region's most characteristic weather elements; the curiously thick and chilling sea fogs known as 'haars', 'rokes' or 'frets'. They are usually confined to a narrow coastal belt overland, but can extend for several kilometres over the North Sea. The haars are a direct consequence of humid air, often from mainland Europe, drifting across the North Sea where it encounters the coldest waters to be found anywhere around the British Isles (Manley, 1935). Even in summer the sea surface temperatures will struggle to rise above 13°C whilst in winter 4°C is commonplace (Evans, 1967). This peculiarity results from the difficulty that the warm waters of the North Atlantic Drift find in penetrating the shallow North Sea basin.

During winter, in contrast, the North Sea is often warmer than the sub-zero air streams that sweep southwards from above the Arctic Circle or reach our shores as damp and raw winds from eastern Europe or beyond. As a consequence, coastal minima are moderated to a notable degree and locations such as Boulmer and Tynemouth experience relatively few frosts. This moderating influence soon diminishes with distance from the coast and, more particularly, with altitude. The more remote valleys of upper Tynedale and Coquetdale will consequently have lower mean winter temperatures and far greater frost frequencies, the annual average rising from about 25 at the coast to nearer 100 on the highest ground. The collective influence of proximity to the sea and of altitude leads to a marked temperature gradient at all times of the year from the coast, becoming cooler inland as height is gained (Figure 1). There are no high level data for Northumberland but those from Great Dun Fell (Cumbria, 848m) are included in this figure as being representative of all such exposed high altitude sites in the Northern Pennines and Cheviots.

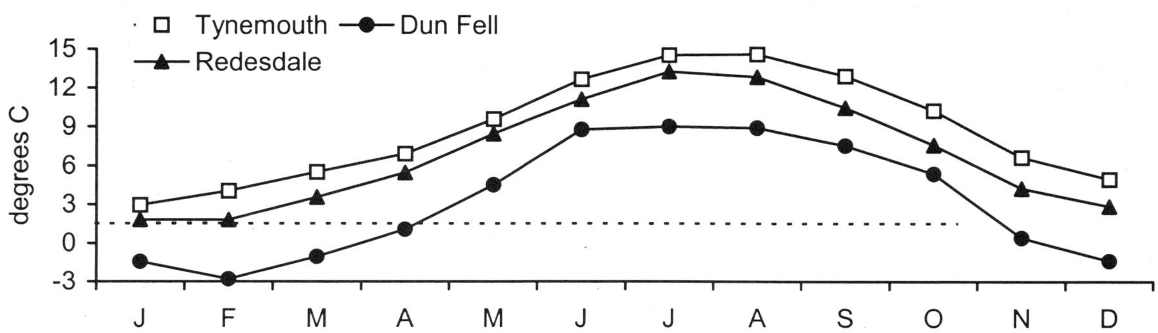

Figure 1 Monthly mean temperatures (in degrees Celsius) for sites in North East England

Precipitation presents a similarly ordered picture with a west-to-east decrease that reflects the general fall in altitude in that same direction. One of the county's more marked climatic features is the relatively low level of precipitation that results from the rain shadow cast not only by the high ground that marks its western boundary but also by the yet higher peaks of the Lake District and South West Scotland. So marked is the rain shadow cast by these barriers that coastal districts of North East England have some of the lowest mean annual rainfall totals in Britain, and are often less than 600mm. Even in the wettest locations mean annual totals are a relatively modest 1,500mm, a figure scarcely comparable with places at similar altitudes in the Lake District where 2,500mm is typical. This contrast is accounted for by the westerly character of much British weather, a direction from which Northumberland enjoys notable shelter. On the other hand the county is exposed to the less frequent, but by no means unusual, winds from between north and south-east. Many eastern areas therefore receive significant proportions of their rain and snow from winds of those directions which only slightly offsets the rain shadow effect. Figure 2 demonstrates that the west-to-east gradient persists throughout the year. It also reveals the weak seasonality of the annual rhythm of rainfall. Nevertheless, spring and early summer are clearly shown to be the driest of the seasons, and late autumn and early winter the wettest.

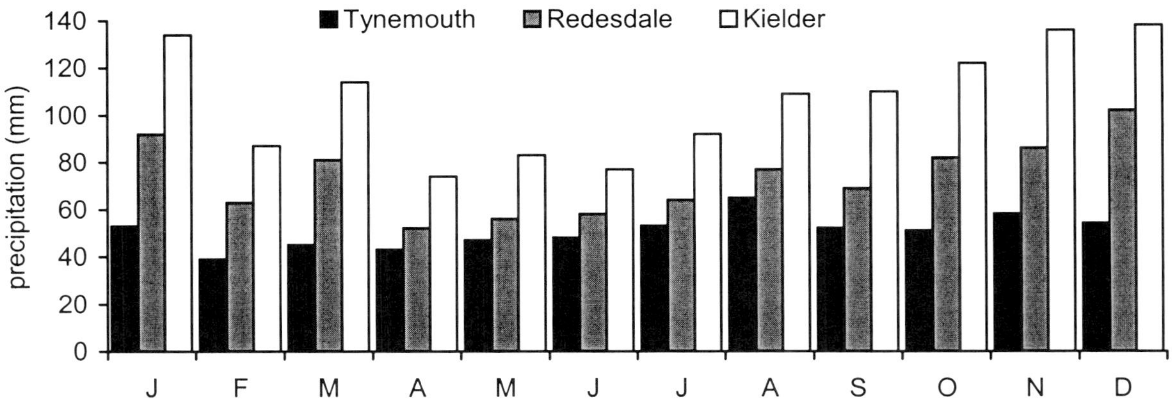

Figure 2 Monthly mean precipitation (in millimetres) for sites in Northumberland

The geographical distribution of snowfall across the region does not perfectly replicate that of rainfall. This is because the county's most abundant falls occur with cold northerly outbreaks that leave coastal areas every bit as vulnerable as high ground. Thus the steep west-to-east gradient in average annual rainfall disappears when examining snowfall and Tynemouth, with an annual average of 26.9 snow days, differs little from inland sites such as Haydon Bridge with 24.5 days. A contrast is, however, provided by the number of days on which the snow lies. The colder conditions required for the latter lead to an annual mean of 20.1 such days at Haydon Bridge decreasing to only 7.6 at Tynemouth. On high ground the number of days of snow lying rises to over 50. Most snow falls in late winter and January and February are more likely to witness it than November or December. Falls at other times of the year are by no means uncommon and one of the features of the local climate is the lateness of the spring that can see snow falling often in April, occasionally in May and, on very rare occasions, in June (most recently on 2nd June 1975).

The county's northerly latitude leads to a poverty of sunshine when compared with favoured south coast resorts. Nowhere between Tyne and Tweed can approach the 1,700 annual mean sunshine hours of the Channel coast resorts. Tynemouth, one of county's sunnier locations, enjoys only 1,385 hours annually and, a little further south, Sunderland's annual average is just over 1,500 hours. By northern standards, such totals are high and the same rain shadow effect that reduces precipitation totals also disperses cloud cover, giving greater scope for bright conditions especially along the coast, a potential only marginally offset by the sea fogs noted above. On high ground the annual totals are closer to 1,000 hours but reliable data are hard to come by in such remote areas (a short period of study on Dun Fell gave an annual mean of 817 hours).

The region's often sheltered situation also reduces the risk of frequent gales and the regular winter storms, with gusts in excess of 80 knots that are so much part of the climate of exposed western districts of Scotland, are exceptional in Northumberland. They do, however, occur from time to time. Few stations have the machinery for accurate wind observation but at Newcastle the severe storm of 16th/17th January 1984 brought gusts that were recorded to have exceeded 90 knots (Sharp, 1993). Winds of such ferocity over low-lying ground occur only about once a decade but become much more frequent on higher ground where they are near-annual in frequency of incidence.

THE CHANGING CLIMATE

Generalisations of the type outlined above suggest that climate has some permanence of character. A little over half a century ago few scientists would have argued against such stability. This is not the arena in which to engage in the 'global warming debate' but it serves as an important reminder that climate can undergo change beyond its day-to-day capricious behaviour. Of singular importance in this respect is the marked tendency over the past fifteen years for winters to be milder

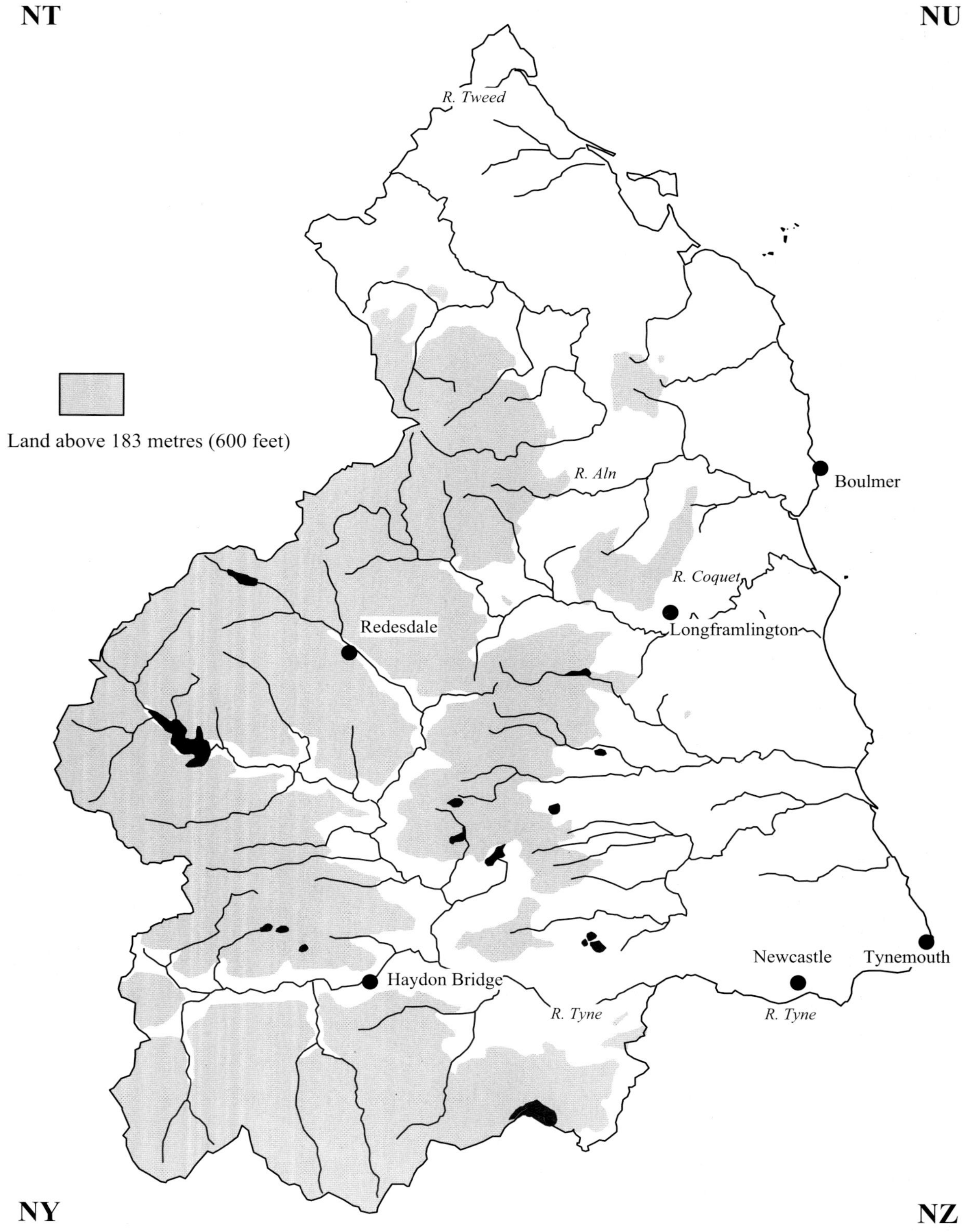

Map 8 Localities recording meteorological data in Northumberland and Tyne & Wear (North)

and shorter. Thus, when undertaking the task of reviewing the winters of 1996/97, 1997/98 and 1998/99, it needs to be recalled to mind that all parts of Britain are experiencing similar conditions of unprecedented warmth. Figure 3 demonstrates the character of temperature changes in winter over the past century for a site within the north east of England that possesses a period of record long enough to give a true measure of regional climatic change. This graph draws attention to a number of important aspects regarding winter temperatures. Firstly, and to a degree not found in the other three seasons, conditions vary a great deal from year to year. Secondly, and despite this variability and a cooling tendency in the 1970s, the trend since 1980 has been inexorably upwards. By coincidence, the early 1980s marks also the last occasion when wintering activity of British birds was reviewed in detail (Lack, 1986). It is important to note that the winter averages for 1981/82, 1982/83 and 1983/84 were respectively 1.9°C, 3.5°C and 3.4°C, whilst those for the winters currently under review were significantly warmer: 1996/97 (3.6°C), 1997/98 (5.7°C) and 1998/99 (4.6°C). Indeed, the winter of 1981/82 was one the coldest of the century in the region, and the December of 1981 was the coldest since 1878.

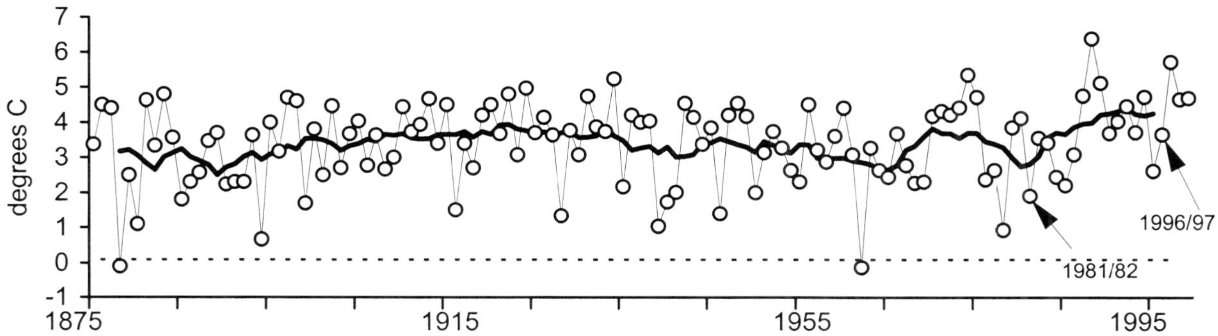

Figure 3 Mean winter temperatures (in degrees Celsius) for the site at the University of Durham. The darker line indicates the smoothed ten-year running mean value

Rainfall or, to be more precise, precipitation (which includes water depth equivalents of snowfall) reveals no corresponding trends. Precipitation is, however, much more variable from place to place and depends upon a host of local factors related to aspect and shelter. This caveat notwithstanding, the data in Figure 4 are representative of the region as a whole. Variability is still, however, a feature of this climatic element and the dry years of the late 1980s and early 1990s have been followed by a run of wet years.

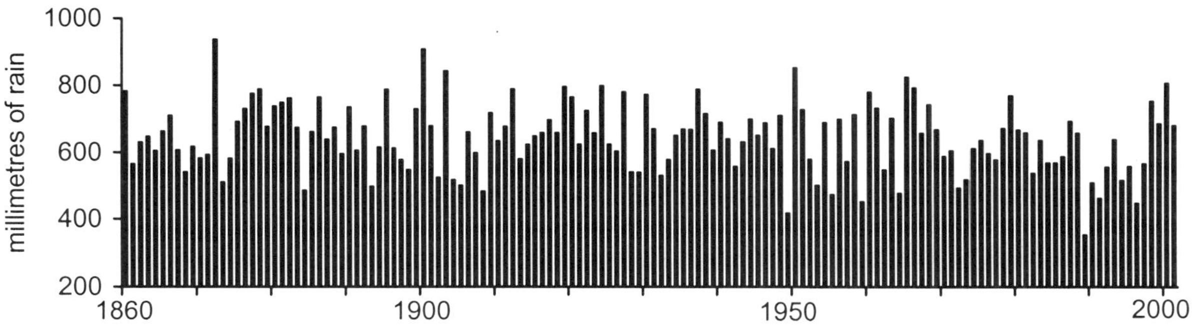

Figure 4 Annual precipitation recorded at the University of Sunderland

In contrast with the temperature data, there were no significant differences in the winter precipitation totals for 1981/82, 1982/83 and 1983/84 and those currently under review. It must, however, be added that a much greater proportion of the precipitation in the former winters fell as snow.

RECENT WINTER WEATHER

Given the characteristics displayed in Figure 3, it is scarcely surprising that the winters of 1996/97, 1997/98 and 1998/99, whilst notably warmer than the early 1980s, should have been quite different from one another. Comprehensive data for the various climatic elements of precipitation, sunshine, temperatures and snowfall are available from only a very few sites in the county. Table 1 draws these data together and provides a summary of the three winters. There is an unavoidable bias towards low-ground sites but the general picture is sufficiently representative of the wider region to permit some preliminary conclusions to be drawn. All three winters were above average with regard to temperatures, but the winter of 1997/98 is the most notable in this respect and was the second warmest winter of the century. The first two winters were slightly wetter than normal and that of 1998/99 drier. Finally, the winters of 1996/97 and 1998/99 were both sunnier than normal, but that of 1997/98 was exceptionally dull.

Season	mean max. (deg. C)	diff. from average	mean min. (deg.C)	diff. from average	precipitation (mm)	% of normal	sunshine (hours)	% of normal
1996/97	6.8	0.1	1.9	0.4	264.8	104.5	260.0	106.8
1997/98	8.7	2.0	4.2	2.7	275.5	110.1	180.2	73.7
1998/99	7.7	0.9	2.2	0.7	218.3	87.7	298.7	123.5

Table 1 Aggregated statistics derived from data recorded at Newcastle, Haydon Bridge, Longframlington, Tynemouth, Redesdale and Boulmer. N.B. Sunshine is not recorded at Haydon Bridge, Longframlington and Tynemouth

The winter of 1996/97

The latter part of November 1996 was dominated by the passage of several active depressions. Rainfall was frequent but rarely heavy, even on high ground and the highest daily total was a modest 19 mm at Haydon Bridge on 19th. There was, however, heavy snowfall on 25th with up to 25cm in some exposed areas. It was not, despite this outbreak, an exceptionally cold month. In absolute terms, December was much cooler. This was partly the natural response to the declining year, but was accentuated by a run of cold easterlies in the latter part of the month. Even under the normally temperate regime at Tynemouth, five air frosts were recorded. Redesdale registered 19 air frosts with an absolute minimum of -6.3°C on 26th. Alone of the English regions, the North East experienced above average rainfall in December - a consequence of the high frequency of easterlies, the only direction from which it has no protection (Table 2). Some of the precipitation fell as snow, particularly towards the end of the month when temperatures were at their lowest. Indeed, the months of November and December 1996, and January 1997 were collectively, and by a substantial margin, the snowiest of the three winters under review. The snow fell in distinct periods in the last ten days of November and again at the end of December, the latter spell extending into early January.

Month	mean max. (deg.C)	diff. from average	mean min. (deg.C)	diff. from average	precipitation (mm)	% of normal	sunshine (hours)	% of normal
Nov. 1996	8.0	-0.9	3.7	-1.1	79.1	136	87.9	121
Dec. 1996	5.5	-1.4	2.3	-1.1	74.9	142	40.6	82
Jan. 1997	6.1	0.0	1.8	-0.5	18.6	35	51.9	92
Feb. 1997	9.0	+2.7	4.6	+2.5	54.0	136	107.2	146

Table 2 Monthly statistics (1996/97) averaged across the region and based on data from the sources used for Table 1.

January was nationally the driest such month since 1880, a feature reflected in the region's rainfall of only 18.6mm. It is all the more remarkable therefore to note that it was the snowiest month of the twelve in this review. Most of the snow fell in a cold spell of easterly winds that embraced the first ten days of the New Year but rarely amounted to a cover of more than a few centimetres in depth. Although conditions became warmer in the following weeks, in southern England it was the coldest January since 1987. Fortunately, Northumberland's conditions were by no means so severe and the month, unusually, was warmer than the immediately preceding December. The dry conditions were not matched by brightness and the often anticyclonic weather brought with it a typical wintery picture of overcast skies with falls of light snow. The season's most remarkable month was, however, February. The settled conditions of January were replaced by unsettled, cyclonic and westerly weather. Whilst it was exceptionally mild (nationally it was the fourth warmest February of the century) rainfall was plentiful. To the west of the Pennines it was three times the normal, but the shelter from the prevailing westerly winds that was enjoyed by Northumberland ensured that the local conditions were by no means so inclement. In these westerly situations the rainfall contrast between the high ground in the west and coastal areas is at its greatest and well-exemplified by Redesdale's monthly total of 176mm compared with Tynemouth's 49mm.

The winter of 1997/98

With the exception of February, the abiding feature of this winter was its warm but dull and wet weather. November was a cloudy month in the region, as it was nationally. Temperatures were high for the time of year and cold spells almost entirely absent. Redesdale recorded only two air frosts in the month, whilst coastal areas were entirely frost-free. In general, the overnight minima were notably mild, reflecting the degree of cloud cover which limits nocturnal heat losses. December opened with a short spell of cold weather but was mild thereafter and south-easterly winds in advance of the passage of a series of active fronts brought rain to many parts of eastern England. So frequently did this situation occur that at the month's conclusion it was eastern and not western Britain that recorded the highest totals. Snowfalls were light and restricted to the month's early cold period when air frosts were also widespread. On 2nd minima varied between -1.6°C at Tynemouth and -4.5°C in Redesdale. The same cloudy conditions that brought the rain also account for the low hours of sunshine. The month's most notable event was the severe storm that caused widespread damage on Christmas Eve when winds gusted to over 70 knots even in the relatively sheltered north east of England. The stormy and unsettled weather continued until late January and ensured the persistence of dull but mild weather into the New Year. Snow was again limited to a short period around 19th and 20th and was restricted to higher ground. The outbreak of cold northerly weather that brought the snow also marked the end of the milder, unsettled weather. The month's final ten days were characterised by a more anticyclonic and settled regime that lasted through February to give the much drier and sunnier conditions noted in Table 3.

Month	mean max. (deg.C)	diff. from average	mean min. (deg.C)	diff. from average	precipitation (mm)	% of normal	sunshine (hours)	% of normal
Nov. 1997	10.6	+1.7	7.1	+2.4	78.2	132	39.6	54
Dec. 1997	7.8	+0.9	5.0	+1.7	86.0	163	31.4	64
Jan. 1998	6.9	+0.8	3.5	+1.2	79.7	150	44.1	78
Feb. 1998	10.9	+4.6	6.7	+4.6	39.6	45	88.9	121

Table 3 Monthly statistics (1997/98) averaged across the region and based on data from the sources used for Table 1.

Persistent anticyclonic weather at this time of year usually brings intensely cold weather but the month's temperature anomaly was the highest of the three winters under consideration. Frosts were confined to sheltered situations and recorded on the first four nights of the month with none thereafter until the final night. The coastal areas were frost-free. Nationally it was the third warmest February of the past three hundred years (only those of 1869 and 1779 had been warmer). This behaviour was the result of the dominant high pressure system being centred to the west of Britain, in which situation it sustained a mild westerly airflow over the British Isles. The more usual arrangement at this time of year would find a cold anticyclone over Scandinavia and the Baltic drawing freezing air from as far east as Russia. It was also the driest February in Britain since 1993 and nationally the totals were less than one-third of normal. Snow in the region was recorded in only scattered locations in the month's coldest period at its very start and conclusion.

The winter of 1998/99

This winter got off to a cool start in Northumberland, the coldest weather coming shortly after mid-month when Redesdale recorded minima close to -5°C on 17th and 18th November. This cold spell was widespread across the region and air frosts were also recorded at Boulmer and Newcastle. Looking more widely across the country, much of eastern England was colder than normal but the national picture was slightly warmer. The statistics suggest November was unusually wet (Table 4). This was not the case and it was relatively dry for much of the month following an opening wet spell when nearly half of the 30-day total fell on 2nd at which time heavy rain was widespread with most places recording between 25 and 40mm in 24 hours. Such wet periods in early winter are a feature of the local climate (Wheeler, 1985).

Month	mean max. (deg.C)	diff. from average	mean min. (deg.C)	diff. from average	precipitation (mm)	% of normal	sunshine (hours)	% of normal
Nov. 1998	8.3	-0.6	3.9	-0.8	81.0	137	79.5	108
Dec. 1998	7.7	+0.8	3.9	+0.6	29.1	55	39.9	81
Jan. 1999	7.8	+1.7	3.8	+2.5	27.3	51	72.4	128
Feb. 1999	7.8	+1.5	3.3	+1.2	25.3	64	109.1	148

Table 4 Monthly statistics (1998/99) averaged across the region and based on data from the sources used for Table 1

December saw a return of relatively mild conditions with cyclonic, westerly weather dominating the climatic picture. By a remarkable coincidence, the stormy nature of the month reached a peak, as it did in 1997, around Christmas time, with strong gales and local damage on 26th and 27th. Rainfall was about half the normal for the time of year and in complete contrast to the more exposed districts to the west of the Cheviots and Pennines where the month's totals were all above normal. Snow was not abundant and light falls only were noted around 5th and 6th with further flurries on 21st. It was, nonetheless, a dull month with plentiful cloud on fronts advancing from the Atlantic. Whilst having lost much of their power to produce rainfall, these fronts were sufficiently active to maintain overcast skies and bring frequent, if light, rain. Haydon Bridge, for example, recorded rain on no less than twenty four days. January continued these mild conditions; the rainfall was again light but much heavier to the west of the Pennines. Further afield, flooding was widespread in the Midlands. On this occasion enough energy and moisture had been dissipated by weather systems in the west to provide for much clearer skies in the east. The dry conditions of February, seemingly a continuation of the trend of the preceding two months, were in fact the result of a stronger anticyclonic influence. Winds veered from south west to west and north west to give slightly cooler conditions although it was still a mild month. The region's shelter from the often north-westerly winds made it one of the sunniest in Britain. Unsettled outbreaks nevertheless occurred, the most notable of which was on 4th when gale force winds swept across the region with gusts in excess of 70 knots. On balance, and despite the cold spells of north westerlies, the month was warmer than normal. The first week was exceptionally warm with maxima of over 12°C on the coast and approaching 10°C further inland. The month's coldest spell was between 5th and 12th when northerly winds from above the Arctic Circle bathed the country in polar air. Frosts, though not sharp, were frequent and widespread across the region with Redesdale recording -4.1°C on 9th. That same night Newcastle registered -1.8°C. More significantly, the daytime maxima were also low (Redesdale's maximum on 9th was only 0.9°C). Temperatures recorded after this date were higher and frosts were less in evidence even on high ground.

CONCLUSION

This review presents a picture that is contrasting in detail, but broadly familiar to climatologists in all parts of the British Isles. The tendency to winter warmth is undeniably the most important feature. The salient question is: will it last into the future? The indications are that it will. More recent observations show no significant decrease in the warming trend, and long-range computer predictions are unanimous in suggesting that it may continue for the next few decades at least. The influence on rainfall and on sunshine are harder to predict, as, significantly, are its wider environmental consequences.

ACKNOWLEDGEMENTS

Data for this chapter were provided by the Newcastle Weather Centre, the University of Durham, the University of Sunderland and the Climatological Observer's Link.

----------oOo----------

FIELDWORK METHODOLOGY

The Survey Period

The 'winter period' for undertaking the fieldwork was determined as being from 15th November to 28th February in each of the three seasons in which the base data were to be collected. The years in question were the winters of 1996/97, 1997/98 and 1998/99, although, in order to complete the county-wide coverage desired, data for a small number of remaining tetrads were not obtained until the winter of 1999/2000. The winter period dates were based on those used by fieldworkers in collecting data for *The atlas of wintering birds in Britain and Ireland* (Lack, 1986) and in addition, locally, they relate to the main winter period for most species, as the autumn migration has generally ended by mid-November and the return migration has barely begun by late February. It was hoped that by using the same time periods over the three winter seasons the data from the earlier national atlas and those collected for this local winter atlas would allow for some direct comparison to be drawn at the 10km scale between the two sets.

General

For each of the four Ordnance Survey 100 kilometre grid squares into which the recording area falls specific survey co-ordinators were appointed. For the NT, NU and NY squares M. L. and T. A. Cadwallender undertook responsibility, with J. M. Macfarlane co-ordinating the data collection in the NZ sector (Map 9).

The co-ordinators contacted potential fieldworkers and identified individuals who would take responsibility for each ten kilometre square. In practice, groups of observers, and occasionally single fieldworkers, covered several ten kilometre squares throughout the three seasons of the survey. At the beginning of each winter period the co-ordinators distributed relevant guidelines and recording forms. They likewise ensured, at the end of each season's work, that completed record cards were returned to the editors for checking and analysis prior to the data being entered into a computer database.

Timed visits

As had been the pattern of data collection for *The atlas of breeding birds in Northumbria* (Day *et al.*, 1995), fieldworkers were asked to visit every tetrad in their designated ten kilometre square(s) during the three winter periods. A minimum of nine tetrads was to be covered in each of the first two seasons of the survey with the remainder to be completed in the final season. A single tetrad visit, between 15th November and 28th February, was to be of two hours duration, with any additional sightings beyond the formal visit period to be recorded as supplementary records.

To standardise data recording, the editors produced a detailed instruction sheet. Essentially, fieldworkers were to record all species encountered during the two-hour visit and provide a count or estimate for each species. Birds that were flying over and not obviously 'using' the tetrad (i.e. for feeding, etc.) were not to be included in the species count, although any that had been flushed into flight, or were hunting or loafing, were to be recorded. A 'common-sense' approach was expected by each observer although there was provision made on the recording form for fieldworkers, if they thought fit, to note over-flying birds. For counting large concentrations of birds, e.g. gull roosts, corvid flocks, etc., additional time beyond the two-hour period was allowed.

All fieldworkers were provided with a Winter Atlas Record Card (Figure 5) for each tetrad to be covered together with a supply of Supplementary Record Cards, as well as an introductory letter to be shown to farmers and other landowners in cases where permission was needed to carry out the survey. Prior to embarking on the survey, observers were asked to refer to the 1:50 000 scale Ordnance Survey map to determine the exact boundaries of the tetrads they intended to visit and were provided with a transparent overlay (Figure 7) showing a grid with each of the 25 tetrad letters in a typical ten kilometre square, to facilitate correct tetrad identification.

In addition to the basic species data the editors felt that some general information relating to each tetrad would be beneficial in interpreting winter bird distribution in the recording area. Therefore instructions regarding weather conditions and on types of habitat and the existence of lakes, ponds, rivers etc., were incorporated in both the general guidance notes and on the Winter Atlas Record Card. Whilst information on the weather and the existence of water bodies and rivers was straightforward, that referring to habitat was more complex. It was well known that the overall recording area contained much land over 300m and that there were vast swathes of coniferous forest on the Cumbria/Scottish border to the west, but all observers were asked to provide an indication of the predominant habitat in every tetrad in the county. In particular they were instructed to note those types of habitat that made up more than 33% of the total area in each tetrad. At its simplest, in most rural tetrads, this might be any combination of Farmland, Woodland and Moorland, with the opportunity for fieldworkers to break these down into secondary habitat types. Further habitat categories were identified for coastal and suburban and urban areas. Table 5 below shows the Major and Second level habitat designations.

Major habitat type.	**Second level habitat type**
Farmland	Arable Livestock Undetermined (or mixed)
Woodland	Deciduous Coniferous Mixed deciduous/coniferous
Moorland	
Coastal	
Urban	
Suburban	
Estuary	
Island	

Table 5 Habitat types used during the Winter Atlas Survey

Five weather-related factors were requested on the timed visit record card and data were received for 1,425 visits in respect of visibility, rain, wind and ground condition and 1,424 in respect of snow cover. Although a comprehensive review of the local weather during the three winter periods is provided earlier in this introduction, it is interesting to review the observer results presented in Table 6.

Visibility		**Rain**		**Snow Cover**		**Wind**		**Ground condition**	
Good	1,188	None	1,224	None	1,283	Calm/Light	842	Not Frozen	1,153
Moderate	215	Light	178	Light	117	Moderate	448	Frozen	272
Poor	22	Heavy	23	Heavy	24	Strong	135		

Table 6 Observer-recorded weather conditions during timed visits to tetrads

'Control' Tetrad timed visits

The impact of severe winter weather on bird distribution, both locally and nationally, is a well-documented phenomenon. It was therefore decided during the course of collecting the first season's data (1996/97) to introduce timed visits to a number of 'control' tetrads in the succeeding winter periods. For the 1997/98 and 1998/99 seasons, fieldworkers were asked to select a typical tetrad in their allocated area, which they had covered in the 1996/97 period, and re-visit it for a second standard two-hour period in 1997/98 and again for a third visit in 1998/99. It was recommended that these additional visits should be at approximately the same date as the original visit and that the same route should be covered. Appropriate forms for recording control tetrad data were supplied to fieldworkers during the second and third winter seasons.

Winter Survey work

It was felt necessary to provide a word of warning for fieldworkers, indicating the potential dangers of undertaking winter survey work, and to supply some guidelines on personal safety. As the least populated county in England, many areas of Northumberland are remote and in hard winters are often difficult to gain access to. On higher land weather conditions can deteriorate rapidly and many areas are still outside the range of mobile telephones. The provision of adequate supplies of food and suitable clothing, informing other people of the proposed route and checking the weather forecast beforehand were all regarded as basic, but advisable, precautions to be followed by all observers visiting the more isolated areas.

Initial tetrad data

Fieldworkers visited 1,432 whole or part tetrads during the primary data collection stage. As for the earlier local breeding atlas, in which data from 1,410 tetrads were amassed, a part tetrad was deemed one that contained 10% or more of the recording area. The discrepancy between the 1,410 'breeding' tetrads and the 1,432 'wintering' ones is explained by the additional 'open sea' tetrads along the length of the Northumberland coast which were successfully covered during this survey.

Supplementary data

The timed visits to tetrads were designed to collect the bulk of the data required on the presence of wintering species, but it was recognised that some might be overlooked. To cater for this, fieldworkers were encouraged to submit supplementary records made outside timed visits for any tetrad that they revisited or passed through during any of the three winter periods. It was hoped this would reveal any species that may have been missed on a timed visit and also provide the potential for higher counts for particular species.

It was recognised that few areas would give specific problems but, because of the geographical nature of the Lindisfarne NNR, it was felt that some duplication of counts of wildfowl and waders was probable as large numbers of birds were known to move extensively between their roosting and feeding sites. Therefore, two synchronised counts (timed visits of two hours each) by a co-ordinated group of observers were undertaken in the winters of 1997/98 and 1998/99. The full results of these counts have been incorporated into the dataset and have been reproduced in Appendices F and G.

Club record cards

The NTBC has a large number of members who contribute their observations monthly, throughout the year, for publication in a monthly bulletin and the county annual report *Birds in Northumbria*. These records include a relatively wide selection of observations with many from birdwatchers not involved with the winter fieldwork. For the periods covering the winter atlas survey these cards were diligently searched for any additional information that could be accurately assigned to a specific tetrad.

Control Tetrad data

A total of 60 widely distributed control tetrads (Map 10) received timed visits three times during the survey period (a further two receiving one additional timed visit only). The data from this source were primarily used for comparative purposes in the individual species accounts (see Appendices D & E for further details). On occasion, however, these second or third visits produced higher totals for specific species and have therefore been incorporated into the statistical and descriptive analysis. The importance of long-term information from this type of survey has encouraged the bird club to continue with this project and, although the winter atlas data have been utilised, the control tetrads project is now entering its sixth year.

----------oOo----------

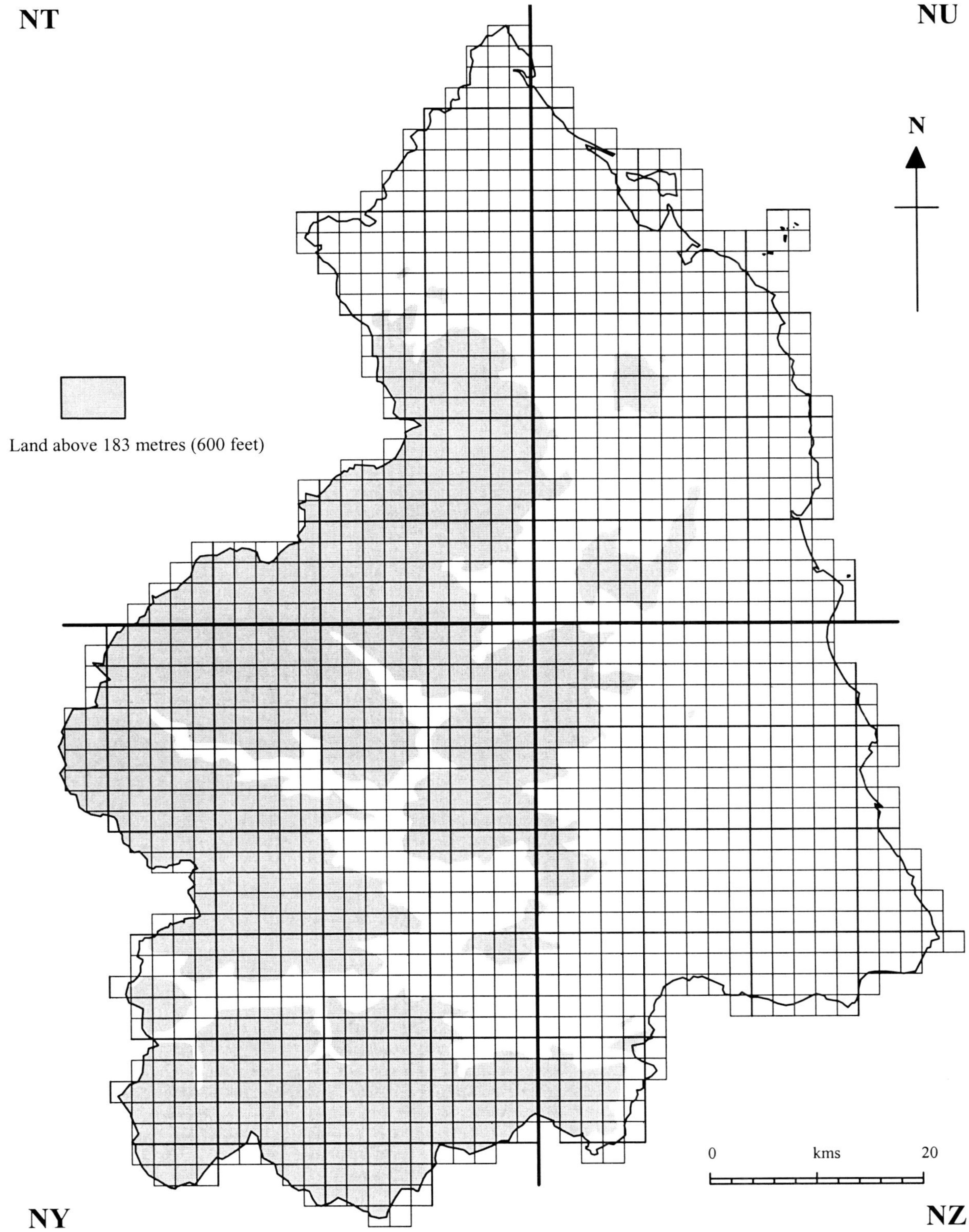

Map 9 Tetrads (2km x 2km squares) for Northumberland and Tyne & Wear (North) covered by this Atlas Survey

NORTHUMBERLAND & TYNESIDE BIRD CLUB
WINTER ATLAS RECORD CARD

Name & Address (BLOCK LETTERS) : Mike S. Hodgson 31 Uplands Whitley Bay Telephone No.	Ten KM Square	NU13
	Tetrad Letter	M
	Date of Visit	02/01/98
	No. of different species seen	58
	CARD NUMBER	781
Name of largest village/town in Ten KM Square	BELFORD	

Comments : (Please complete weather boxes as appropriate)
Main Budle Bay tetrad. Waren Burn flows into bay.

VISIBILITY	1	RAIN	1	SNOW	1	WIND	1	GROUND	1

Major Habitat Type		Second Level (if applicable)	Major Habitat Type		Second Level (if applicable)
F FARMLAND			W WOODLAND		
M MOORLAND			O COASTAL	O	
U URBAN			S SUBURBAN		
E ESTUARY	E		I ISLAND		
X WATER BODY			R RIVER/STREAM	Z	

SPECIES	Code	Count	SPECIES	Code	Count
Red-throated Diver	RH		Common Scoter	CX	
Black-throated Diver	BV		Velvet Scoter	VS	
Great Northern Diver	ND		Goldeneye	GN	1
Little Grebe	LG		Smew	SY	
Great Crested Grebe	GG		Red-breasted Merganser	RM	6
Red-necked Grebe	RX		Goosander	GD	
Slavonian Grebe	SZ		Ruddy Duck	RY	
Fulmar	F.		Hen Harrier	HH	
Gannet	GX		Goshawk	GI	
Cormorant	CA		Sparrowhawk	SH	1
Shag	SA		Buzzard	BZ	
Grey Heron	H.		Kestrel	K.	3
Mute Swan	MS	2	Merlin	ML	
Whooper Swan	WS		Peregrine	PE	
Bean Goose	BE		Red Grouse	RG	
Pink-footed Goose	PG		Black Grouse	BK	
White-fronted Goose	WG	24	Red-legged Partridge	RL	
Greylag Goose	GJ	341	Grey Partridge	P.	6
Canada Goose	CG		Pheasant	PH	2
Barnacle Goose	BY	1	Water Rail	WA	
Brent Goose	BG	8	Moorhen	MH	
Shelduck	SU	357	Coot	CO	
Wigeon	WN	629	Oystercatcher	OC	72
Gadwall	GA		Ringed Plover	RP	114
Teal	T.	426	Golden Plover	GP	
Mallard	MA	151	Grey Plover	GV	112
Pintail	PT		Lapwing	L.	196
Shoveler	SV	2	Knot	KN	271
Pochard	PO		Sanderling	SS	3
Tufted Duck	TU		Purple Sandpiper	PS	
Scaup	SP	2	Dunlin	DN	362
Eider	E.	5	Ruff	RU	
Long-tailed Duck	LN		Jack Snipe	JS	

Figure 5 Example of a Timed Visit Record Card (front side only)

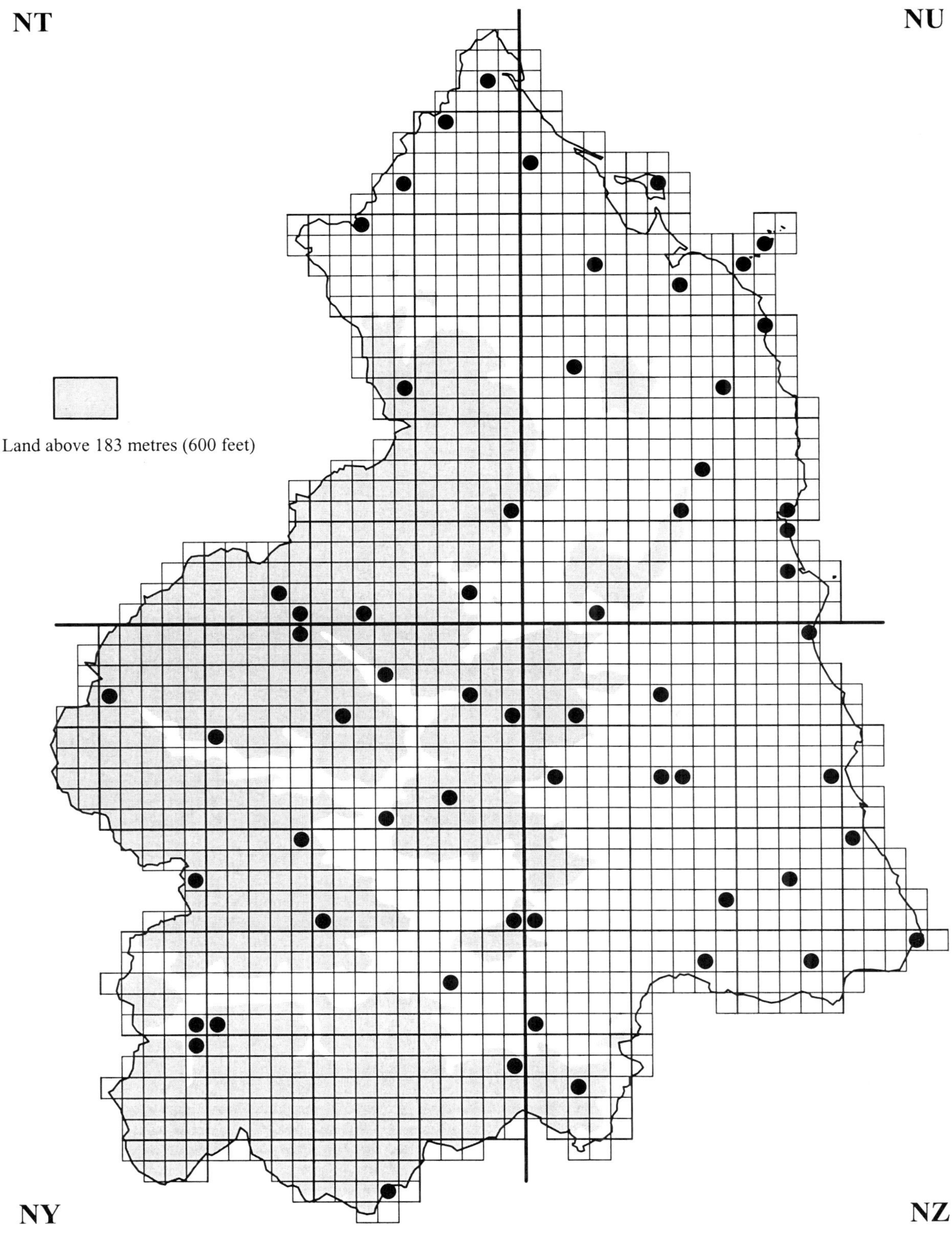

Map 10 Location of the Control Tetrads visited during the winters of 1996/97-1998/99

DATA COLLATION

Computerisation

As with the data from the earlier *Atlas of breeding birds in Northumbria*, those from the Winter Atlas Record Cards, the Supplementary Cards and the Club's monthly bulletins and annual reports were stored in a computer database. In this instance, however, the editors retained total control of the records and were solely responsible for entering data into the specially created database. All details relating to weather, habitats, etc. were additional to those collected for the breeding survey and it was felt important that appropriate reports should be produced to allow for the maximum analysis and interpretation of all aspects of the information collected. At the same time, there was a need to ensure that detailed distribution maps could be produced from the data held by passing it directly to suitably compatible software.

The database software used was Microsoft Access, a well-known user-friendly package. A number of database tables were specified to contain details of header information and species count data obtained from both timed visit and supplementary record cards. Each record card was allocated a unique reference number as it was received which, together with other fields such as ten kilometre/tetrad and species code, enabled easy linking of the various tables. A number of special reference tables were also created to ensure that data entered through a variety of specifically designed screens would have at least some first level validation. Examples of this were the validation of species codes and allowable tetrad letters on data input. When all data had been entered then tables holding the species counts were merged and several update queries utilised to sort and remove any multiple entries in a ten kilometre/tetrad/species grouping, leaving only the record with the highest count. In this way only 'unique' records were made available for use in exporting the data for mapping purposes and also for creating the reports to be used for cross-checking the data and production of species accounts.

Manual records

In addition to the summation of the wintering records into an easily accessible computer database, it was necessary to carry out a similar exercise in manual format to allow for the accurate cross-checking of all data received. With this in mind, a 'master' tetrad record card was designed on which the species and numbers could be entered after the rationalisation of any duplication of timed counts and supplementary records had been made. The rules for creating final counts on the 'master' cards were the same as for the computerised files and, in this way, two independent sets of data were available to assist with the inevitable checking and cross-checking that was necessary. In addition, on the 'master' card, habitat data were collated and for each tetrad an estimate of the average metric height above sea level was calculated and recorded from the relevant Ordnance Survey maps.

Accuracy checks

Immediately following the receipt of data from fieldworkers and its keying into the database at the end of each survey season, various Club members laboriously checked the original Record Card details against the newly created computer input. After all data for the atlas period had been received and assembled, the tetrad 'master' cards were used to compare species and totals produced from the computer database. This was carried out both on a tetrad basis and by individual species breakdown. The use of the two data sets, although very time consuming, allowed immediate identification of any anomalies in data entry and/or misinterpretation of figures, etc. Both sets of data were updated as necessary and a complete match was achieved. This ensured the accurate production of statistics and that distribution maps could be produced with confidence.

Statistics

The Winter Atlas Survey generated a total of 40,497 species records (Tables 7, 8 & 9), 22% less than the 52,144 records amassed during the local three-year breeding atlas project. They included records from timed visits, supplementary sightings (including control tetrad data) and extracts from both monthly club bulletins and annual county bird reports. An analysis of the totals arranged by the main Ordnance Survey grid areas of the recording area is given below.

Area	Number of records	Number of Unique records	Number of ten km squares	Number of tetrads
NT	5,017	4,425	15	257
NU	10,877	8,780	15	300
NY	10,959	9,162	26	525
NZ	13,644	11,079	19	350
Totals	**40,497**	**33,446**	**75**	**1,432**

Table 7 Summary of records received

The number of records received is that submitted or obtained from all sources, while the number of unique records is that calculated after the removal of duplicate counts of species in a tetrad by the merging process to show maximised occupancy status.

A further analysis of the sources of the data shows the following distribution :

	1996/97	1997/98	1998/99	1999/2000	Total
Timed Visits	550	461	409	12	1,432

Table 8 Breakdown of timed visits

	1996/97	1997/98	1998/99	1999/2000	Total
Timed Visit Records	11,811	8,268	7,430	365	27,874
Supplementary Records	3,497	3,117	4,068	0	10,682
Other club records	629	700	610	2	1,941
Totals	**15,937**	**12,085**	**12,108**	**367**	**40,497**

Table 9 Breakdown of records received by winter period

It should be remembered that the records contained on atlas cards relate to multiple species, whilst those on bird club record cards refer to only one species. Nevertheless, in order to extract supplementary data from bird club record cards it was necessary to evaluate and then eliminate many thousands of records in order to determine which entries were relevant and therefore suitable for inclusion.

----------oOo----------

DISTRIBUTION MAPS - PRODUCTION AND INTERPRETATION

All of the distribution maps which accompany the individual species accounts and those in this introductory section were produced using DMAP software. The use of a compatible relational database package facilitated the export of the various source data, in a format suitable for DMAP, ensuring consistency between the database tables and the map data. Dedicated digitising software in the DMAP package was used to create the county boundary outline and also the shaded high ground areas and various 10km and 2km grids with which it was to be overlaid.

The distribution maps presented here are arguably the most important result of the winter atlas survey. As with the earlier county breeding atlas, species distribution on the tetrad maps is shown using three different sized dots but whilst those in the breeding atlas related to the three categories of confirmed, probable or possible breeding status, those in this winter atlas refer to maximum counts. That is to say each of the three dot sizes represents a different numerical grouping of birds. In determining the correct groupings, and hence how many of the three dot sizes in each category should be used on a specific map, the total number of individuals recorded for that species was broken down into three divisions with a percentage ratio of 50% : 30% : 20%. The smallest size dot (50%) therefore represents the lowest number of birds (e.g. 1-12), the medium sized dot (30%) the next grouping (e.g. 13-40) and the largest dot (20%) the greatest number of birds (e.g. 41+). This follows the methodology used in *The atlas of wintering birds in Britain and Ireland* (Lack, 1986), which was adopted in order to reduce spatial distortion on the distribution maps. As the numbers of each species recorded during the survey differ, the values of the three dots from map to map vary considerably, and it is imperative that prior to interpreting the distribution pattern of each species the key, printed to the left of each tetrad map, is consulted.

Following the practice used in *The atlas of breeding birds in Northumbria*, the county tetrad maps are reproduced in black and white as this was felt to present the individual species' distribution pattern most effectively. Similarly a 'plain' tetrad map was thought to be of limited value but the inclusion of too many physical features on each map would detract from its prime purpose of conveying winter distribution. A decision was therefore made to include shading to represent higher ground over 183m (600 ft) above sea level in the recording area. This feature not only delineates the upland area but also indicates the major river valleys and coincides with most blanket afforestation and the edge of moorland and rough grazing and, perhaps importantly, was also included on the local breeding atlas maps and may therefore facilitate, for some species, a direct comparison.

The Bird Club was again fortunate, through Margaret Macfarlane, in having access to the archives of the late L. G. Macfarlane which contained details of the winter survey carried out in the county between 1981-1984. This was primarily information gathered for the first national wintering atlas survey organised by the BTO, which culminated in *The atlas of wintering birds in Britain and Ireland*. However, that survey was based on ten kilometre squares, and the area covered was slightly different on the periphery from the current survey, so a direct comparison with the newly produced tetrad maps was difficult. A second ten kilometre square distribution map, based directly on the current tetrad map, was therefore produced for most species to allow immediate comparison to be made. It should be noted that the 1981-1984 ten kilometre square maps for several species reproduced in this volume differ slightly from those produced by Lack (1986). In this atlas the dots relate only to those species known to have been found within the Club's recording area whereas the national atlas maps can show dots for those species also found in adjacent areas of Co. Durham, Cumbria and the Scottish Borders. The two ten kilometre square maps are reproduced for each species on the same page as the tetrad map.

The computer-produced maps were checked by both the individual account authors and by the editors. This was regarded as an essential further check on the data, both in the positioning of each dot in the appropriate tetrad and also the overall number and size of dots on each map. In the case of geographical features that occurred in more than one tetrad, e.g. smaller reservoirs and lakes, records for waterbirds were normally recorded in only one tetrad unless it was relatively straightforward to assign them to a specific tetrad (e.g. Kielder Reservoir).

Dot sizes

Whilst the designation of confirmed, probable and possible status for the dots used in *The atlas of breeding birds in Northumbria* was clear and unambiguous, the use of dots to record abundance in the winter atlas creates a number of problems. Essentially, in both the national atlas (Lack, 1986) and this local atlas, the figures used for each bird species in all the squares surveyed, which were later translated into different dot sizes, were those of the 'best-day count'. For example, over the three-season survey, if a count of Blackbirds *Turdus merula* was given as 16 on a timed tetrad visit on 10th December 1996, with supplementary records in the same tetrad of 13 birds on 3rd January 1997, and 18 on 15th February 1998, then the 'best-day count' of 18 was the one used in compiling both the map and the statistics. In the national atlas, where there was a considerable range of time spent by observers in each ten kilometre square, it was necessary to produce a regression coefficient of 'numbers of birds seen' on a 'time spent in the field' calculation to bring all sightings up to a six-hour average. Apart from a few of the very common species, the calculation did not appear to be a significant factor in producing the final distribution maps. As the Northumberland fieldwork was based on a standard two-hour visit to each tetrad, plus occasional supplementary data, it was not felt necessary to produce a similar table of assessment.

Map interpretation

Lack (1986) noted that winter atlasing creates a number of problems of interpretation not present in undertaking the analysis of breeding species data. The same problems occur whether the survey is a national or a local one, and relate to duplicate counting, the over-recording of less common species and exaggeration of total numbers as a result of using maximum counts.

Duplicate counting

Winter patterns of bird distribution are more fluid and variable than those in the breeding season. Not only do many species move from higher ground to lowland areas in the colder months, but there may also be additional influxes from outside the local area due to more severe weather conditions in other parts of the UK or on the continent. Some species automatically flock each winter, but others congregate only as weather conditions deteriorate. Availability of food each winter will also determine where flocks gather to feed and roost. Increasingly, as winters appear to be getting milder, some species are remaining inland nearer to their breeding areas, whilst others, like the Blackcap *Sylvia atricapilla*, that did not winter here previously, are now becoming commoner in the UK in that season.

This mobility may result in duplicate counting particularly for species that form large winter flocks e.g. corvids, gulls, pigeons, waders, thrushes, wildfowl and, to a lesser extent, finches. Depending on food availability, flocks may move from one tetrad to another, or from one ten kilometre square to another, virtually overnight. An observer visiting a tetrad one weekend and an adjacent one the following weekend could encounter, and unwittingly record, the same flock twice. Gulls near roost sites, movements of Fieldfare *Turdus pilaris* and Redwing *Turdus iliacus* through the county, and coastal parties of Lapwing *Vanellus vanellus* and Golden Plover *Pluvialis apricaria* are particularly difficult to assess. The situation is further aggravated as regular wintering flocks (e.g. corvids and pigeons) may winter in the same ten kilometre square each year, but in different tetrads from year to year, as their food sources follow local crop rotation patterns.

The editors could find no simple solution to accurately eliminate the above forms of duplication. Nevertheless, an attempt was made to check the data for flocks of all species and, when bird numbers were nearly identical and reporting dates virtually the same, editorial licence was invoked and one flock eliminated. But, as the species in question was using the tetrad, then other records had to be checked to see if smaller parties of birds in different years had been present and, if so, that lower figure was then incorporated in the data.

Less common species

Whilst Lack (1986) found that there was little distortion on maps showing the distribution of the commoner species, this was not the case for the less common birds. A series of dots in adjacent tetrads gives the impression that a species is more widespread than it really is, particularly in the case of highly mobile birds. Likewise, if the species in the following winter utilises neighbouring squares then the distribution pattern can be even more misleading. Examples of both potential distortion and the use of adjacent tetrads is provided by records for wintering Hen Harrier *Circus cyaneus*, Raven *Corvus corax* and Waxwing *Bombycilla garrulus*. Lack uses Great Grey Shrike *Lanius excubitor* as an example, where he found that in three winters it was recorded in a total of 238 ten kilometre squares. However, when the statistics are broken down into individual winters, this represented occupancy in 71 squares in 1981/82, 124 in 1982/83 and 86 in 1983/84. In fact the species was only present in 44 squares in more than one winter. He also drew attention to the possibility of over-recording some species e.g. Raven, Dipper *Cinclus cinclus*, and Robin *Erithacus rubecula*, as they become more evident when they begin their territorial breeding displays in February and March.

Maximum counts

The use of maximum counts i.e. 'best-day counts', for each species using a tetrad, has the potential for distorting overall numbers. In using the numbers given in the written accounts it should be remembered that the figures were collected over three seasons, and only the highest number was recorded for atlas purposes. Again, if consistency in using the 'best-day counts' was to be observed, eliminating this problem was virtually impossible. Discrepancies are evident for example when comparing 'best-day counts' and totals for waders over the three seasons with the data from WeBS counts, although the atlas figures may well include inland squares not covered by the WeBS survey. Nor would it be correct to divide the winter season 'best-day counts' by three to create an average annual figure, as, with the exception of the widely diverse control tetrads, totally different unrelated tetrads were visited each season. Support for the accuracy and justification of 'best-day counts' is provided by the data from the control tetrads where similar numbers for some species were recorded on each of the three visits. It should also be remembered that a timed two-hour tetrad visit does not cover the whole square, and for many birds the total numbers recorded, particularly of the commoner species, may be an under-estimation.

Some potential bias was also suspected by Lack in squares where enthusiastic observers had sent in large numbers of records for their areas, although he later found it to be a comparatively insignificant factor. There were certainly four or five tetrads in this winter survey where over-exuberance occurred, but 'best-day counts' eliminated the majority of superfluous sightings.

----------oOo----------

THE SPECIES ACCOUNTS

The editors were keen to encourage as many people as possible, who had taken part in the survey, to be further involved in the production of the Atlas. As a result, fieldworkers who had indicated an interest in analysing the collated species data and subsequently producing one or more written accounts were approached with a potential list of species. In addition, the editors felt that a winter overview of four groups of birds might be particularly useful and informative. These accounts relate to wildfowl, birds of prey, waders and gulls and have been included in the main body of the text to serve as an introduction before the accounts of the individual species in each of the four groups. In all four instances either the winter distribution pattern or the sheer number of birds wintering in Northumberland was thought to be worth emphasising.

Although authors were encouraged to write accounts with an individual interpretation, a number of guidelines had to be provided. They were asked to include, or consider including, a brief historical statement of the wintering status of each species, perhaps comparing it with any national data or trends where this was relevant, and utilise wherever possible previously published local survey data. Obviously the results of the current survey and any possible trends were to be highlighted. Each author was provided with a print-out of the appropriate species data, a draft distribution map and, where necessary, a number of references from local surveys and publications. The editors undertook to assist in the tracing of more obscure references and were also available for advice and guidance.

For many years now the compilers of the county annual report, *Birds in Northumbria*, have used a classification table of the number of occurrences recorded in the county as an indication of abundance for each species in the Club's recording area. Although this does not specifically relate to wintering records, it has allowed a reasonably accurate assessment of a species' abundance to be made, albeit with much emphasis placed on local knowledge of contributors and compilers alike. Galloway and Meek (1978-1983), in *Northumberland's birds,* and later Kerr (2001), also employed a similar table of abundance. The classification used is outlined in Table 10. In keeping with the publications noted above, authors were asked where possible to place all species recorded during the winter atlas survey in one of the above categories. This would hopefully maintain a standardisation of descriptive terms and also assist the county bird report compilers in assessing any changes in wintering status in future years.

Term	Number of occurrences
Abundant	more than 10,000 per annum
Common	1,001 to 10,000 per annum
Well-represented	101 - 1,000 per annum
Uncommon	11 - 100 per annum
Rare	1 - 10 per annum, but more than 10 in total
Extremely rare	up to 10 in total

Table 10 Classification of a species' abundance

The species accounts broadly follow the order compiled by Professor K. H. Voous (1977), in his *List of recent Holarctic species*, although a few are slightly out of sequence in order to facilitate the layout of text and maps. It should be noted that English bird names are those used in the county annual reports, *Northumberland's birds*, *Northumbrian birds* and *The atlas of breeding birds in Northumbria*. The decision to use these names has been made in order to preserve continuity and also to reflect those which seem to remain in current usage by British birdwatchers. It was felt that the situation regarding any 'new' English bird names, proposed in the last few years, has still not yet been satisfactorily resolved.

Two statistical summaries have been included with most species accounts. The first, like that in the county breeding atlas, is an analysis of the total number of tetrads in which wintering birds were observed with, in parentheses, the same figure expressed as a percentage of the tetrads surveyed. In the example provided 609 = 43% of the total of 1432 tetrads surveyed.

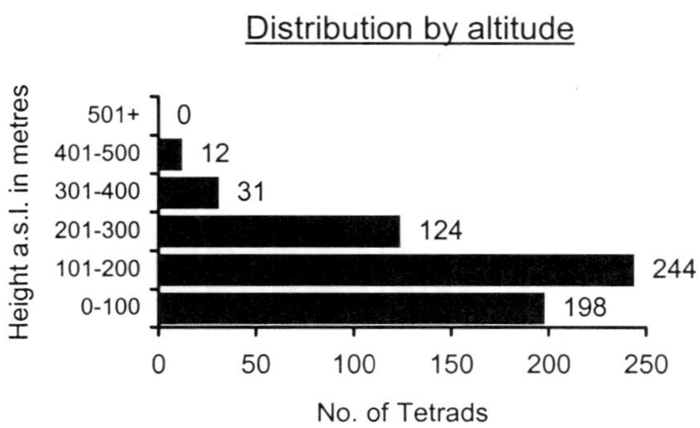

No. of tetrads in which recorded		609 (43%)
Tetrad Analysis	No. of tetrads	
1-30 birds	297 (49%)	
31-100 birds	190 (31%)	
101+ birds	122 (20%)	
Total No. of birds counted		43,977

Figure 6 Example of statistical tables featured in individual species accounts

The figure of 609 is further broken down according to the three dot sizes used on the accompanying tetrad map. Thus, in the example used, the smallest dot, covering the lowest numerical grouping of 1 to 30 birds, occurs on the map in 297 tetrads. The medium sized dot (31 to 100 birds) occurs in 190 tetrads, and the largest dot is present in 122 tetrads where 101 or more birds were recorded. The numbers 49, 31 and 20 in parentheses are the closest percentage calculations possible to the 50% : 30% : 20% formula described in the Map Production methodology section, which has been used to create a representative optical distribution pattern hopefully free from distortion. The final figure in the analysis (43,977) is the total number of birds reported from 'best-day counts' from all tetrads over the three winter seasons.

The other statistical table takes the form of an horizontal bar chart. It is divided into six bands, based on the average height in metres above sea level of each tetrad, and shows the number of surveyed squares in each band in which the species was observed. As perceived movement of many species in winter is regarded as significant it was felt important to try to illustrate whether this occurred in a simple tabular format.

The accurate counting of all wintering birds of a particular species, even in a survey of this magnitude, is rarely possible. Nevertheless, the counts made during the exercise provide a base-line for estimating current wintering populations and will also be of great use in providing comparisons with any future surveys, although the limitations noted in the Map Interpretation section should be borne in mind, and some of the figures used with caution.

Throughout this atlas, and in particular in the species accounts, there are many references to specific localities. However, as fieldworkers were operating on two kilometre square tetrads, grid references incorporating the relevant tetrad letter have been quoted rather than a four, six or eight figure OS grid reference. This means that following the 10km square grid reference, e.g. NY89, more precise reference is provided by adding the standard alphabetical tetrad letter A to Z. In interpreting both the written accounts and the maps users of the atlas should therefore familiarise themselves with the A to Z grid reproduced below. The use of this form of reference facilitates comparison with *The atlas of breeding birds in*

NORTH ↑

E	**J**	**P**	**U**	**Z**
D	**I**	**N**	**T**	**Y**
C	**H**	**M**	**S**	**X**
B	**G**	**L**	**R**	**W**
A	**F**	**K**	**Q**	**V**

Figure 7 Layout of tetrads in a ten kilometre square (not to scale)

Northumbria, and provides continuity for the on-going control tetrad project that has emanated from this winter atlas survey.

The data presented in Appendix K have a particular relevance to this section and allow a comparison with the results from the county breeding atlas survey. Arrangement by tetrad provides comparative figures for the number of species present in each surveyed square in both the breeding season and in winter between mid-November and the end of February. An analysis of this data clearly demonstrates that many upland breeding species move away from the area once that season is over.

In all a total of 188 species were recorded during the winter survey, which compares with 165 species in the breeding atlas. Of the 188 in this atlas 171 have received comparatively full write-ups and usually an accompanying tetrad map. Brief notes are also provided on a further 17 scarce or rare wintering species. Another seven species have been categorised as escapes or other exotica.

It is interesting to note that a total of 12 species (albeit mainly rare visitors) were recorded on more than one occasion in Northumberland during the preceding 16 winter periods but not during the current survey. These were Sooty Shearwater *Puffinus griseus* (5 records), Manx Shearwater *Puffinus puffinus* (15), Ring-necked Duck *Aythya collaris* (3), Avocet *Recurvirostra avosetta* (4), Little Stint *Calidris minuta* (2), Grey Phalarope *Phalaropus fulicarius* (4), Ring-billed Gull *Larus delawarensis* (4), Hoopoe *Upupa epops* (3), Bearded Tit *Panurus biarmicus* (2), Arctic Redpoll *Carduelis hornemanni* (5), Parrot Crossbill *Loxia pytyopsittacus* (2) and Pine Bunting *Emberiza leucocephalos* (2).

----------oOo----------

WINTER ATLAS SURVEY FINDINGS

Whilst detailed descriptions for each species are contained in the individual accounts it is interesting to compare the local Northumberland findings with those of Lack (1986). He found that there was a scarcity, even an absence, of birds on higher ground in winter, but a marked concentration of species in coastal areas. Good numbers of birds were also to be found in areas of mixed farming, although fewer were present where there were large tracts of arable land or grassland. All of his findings were confirmed in the Northumberland survey and are particularly well shown in Map 11 where the numbers of species per tetrad are recorded. Dots representing less than 20 species per tetrad are most evident on land above 183 metres (600 ft) a.s.l. Those representing 21 to 60 species dominate the agricultural lowlands and the upland river valleys of the Tyne, North Tyne and Rede, whilst those recording 61 to 100 species are along the coastal plain, with the exception of one inland site. The distinction between mixed farmland and arable land is less obvious although quite a number of dots in the lowland plain that fall into the less than 20 species category are in areas where there is a large proportion of arable land. The inland site referred to above lies in the Coquet Valley at Caistron (NU00A) and, during the winter fieldwork, was still a large active private nature reserve created from former gravel workings. Unfortunately, at the time of writing, the future of the Caistron Reserve is in the balance.

Lack also stated that urban areas were low in the number of species and this appeared to be true in the Northumberland survey. However, if the suburban areas, with their parkland and housing estate gardens are included, then 21 to 40 species per tetrad was common, with some registering between 41 to 60 species. The table below provides a breakdown of the number of species per tetrad.

Number of species	NT	NU	NY	NZ	TOTAL
0	2	0	2	0	4
1 - 20	158	76	327	64	625
21 - 40	87	180	173	218	658
41 - 60	10	27	21	51	109
61 - 80	0	12	2	14	28
81 - 100	0	5	0	3	8
Number of Tetrads	257	300	525	350	1,432

Table 11 Analysis of number of species per tetrad

Bearing in mind that the survey was undertaken over three mild winters, the findings contained in the accounts for most species confirm many known wintering trends. For example, of the resident breeding species, Grey Heron *Ardea cinerea*, Grey Partridge *P. perdix*, Moorhen *Gallinula chloropus*, Collared Dove *Streptopelia decaocto*, Dipper *C. cinclus*, Dunnock *Prunella modularis*, Blue Tit *Parus caeruleus* and Jackdaw *Corvus monedula* appear to remain near their breeding areas throughout the year. Movement from the uplands to the lowland agricultural areas was most marked in species such as Skylark *Alauda arvensis*, Meadow Pipit *Anthus pratensis*, Grey Wagtail *Motacilla cinerea*, Song Thrush *Turdus philomelos*, Chaffinch *Fringilla coelebs* and Yellowhammer *Emberiza citrinella*, with almost all the waders concentrated on the coastal strip in winter. For some species there is a wider county distribution in winter than in the breeding season, although again, the higher ground is avoided. This is the case for species such as Barn Owl *Tyto alba*, Goldcrest *R. regulus*, Coal Tit *Parus ater*, Jay *Garrulus glandarius*, Goldfinch *C. carduelis*, Siskin *Carduelis spinus* and Bullfinch *P. pyrrhula*. Numbers for breeding species are of course much higher in the early part of the winter as they are swollen by the surviving young from the breeding season while, for some species in this last category, numbers may be increased by autumn and occasionally mid-winter influxes of 'foreign' birds. Others may simply be less secretive in colder winter weather than in the breeding season or feeding strategies make them more obvious. Of some of the species which come to winter in the area it was noticeable that both Redwing *Turdus iliacus* and Brambling *Fringilla montifringilla* pass through on a wide front but, in both instances, seem to avoid high ground. Fieldfare *Turdus pilarus* on the other hand, whilst distributed throughout the county, do not avoid the uplands.

Since the county breeding atlas was published, the new wintering maps show that the distribution of some resident species may have undergone considerable expansion. This is the case for both Magpie *Pica pica* and Nuthatch *Sitta europaea*, although the most spectacular increase is probably that of the Common Buzzard *Buteo buteo*. The Stonechat *Saxicola torquata* has also increased in numbers, but this is perhaps due to better survival rates in milder winters rather than steady colonisation.

Two of the most frequently asked questions about an ornithological survey such as this Winter Atlas are which species is most abundant and which species is most widespread. The two questions, of course, rarely have the same answer. Tables 12 and 13 show the top ten most widely distributed species and those with the largest counts as indicated by this latest winter survey. It should be remembered that in respect of distribution, only one bird needed to be seen in a particular tetrad to produce a registration while the largest counts could well include a degree of duplication.

Species	Number of Tetrads
Carrion Crow	1,180
Wren	1,068
Chaffinch	1,048
Blue Tit	1,004
Robin	966
Blackbird	963
Coal Tit	881
Rook	880
Jackdaw	866
Woodpigeon	849

Table 12 Top ten most widely distributed species in the Winter Atlas

Species	Number of birds counted
Woodpigeon	117,165
Starling	108,207
Rook	99,737
Common Gull	61,880
Jackdaw	56,117
Black-headed Gull	51,759
Fieldfare	43,977
Golden Plover	42,586
Lapwing	42,360
Chaffinch	31,621

Table 13 Top ten species with the largest counts in the Winter Atlas

Of other county or area winter atlases, comparison with *The birds of North-East Scotland* (Buckland *et al.*, 1990) proved difficult. It was an all-year survey i.e. covering a whole calendar year, with fieldwork undertaken from January 1981 to December 1984. Extensive use was also made of casual records from 1975-1984 and, for some species, data from 1985-1988. It was based on habitat types within the Ordnance Survey ten kilometre grid squares, creating 395 'sites'. Areas of analysis included breeding statistics, occupied habitat types and brief details on wintering patterns, involving the use of a twelve-month 'clock' to indicate occupancy and height above sea level, at various times of the year. Within the species accounts, winter data on movement and feeding habits compare favourably with the Northumberland findings. A separate paper on wintering wildfowl is particularly relevant as the north east Scottish coast, like Northumberland, has a National Nature Reserve and a number of SPAs that are sites of national importance for a range of species.

Likewise, the Northumberland winter survey findings have little in common with the Kent Ornithological Society's *Winter bird survey* (Tardivel, 1984). Their survey was undertaken during the winters of 1977/78-1979/80 but, while based on the tetrad unit, no attempt was made to collect numerical data. The published findings consist almost entirely of maps in which three dot sizes relate to the number of winters in which each species was recorded in the individual tetrads. The coastal distribution of wintering waders and wildfowl is as expected, but the lack of high land and bleak moorland in Kent, and the incomplete coverage for some areas, makes comparative analysis with the Northumberland data for many species almost impossible.

Whilst this section is an attempt at providing a brief overview of the Northumberland winter atlas findings, full details for all the named species should be sought in the individual accounts. Nevertheless the maps for three species are worthy of mention. For the first time there is now a clearer picture of the numbers and distribution pattern of both wintering Blackcap *Sylvia atricapilla* and Chiffchaff *Phylloscopus collybita* and one of the surprises of the survey, although long alluded to by historical authors, was the number of Snow Bunting *Plectrophenax nivalis* wintering in the uplands of Northumberland. Interestingly the 'conservation value' of many areas is often based on the variety and numbers of breeding species. It is perhaps time that wintering distributions of species, other than waders and wildfowl, should also be taken into account in future biodiversity and conservation planning programmes.

----------oOo----------

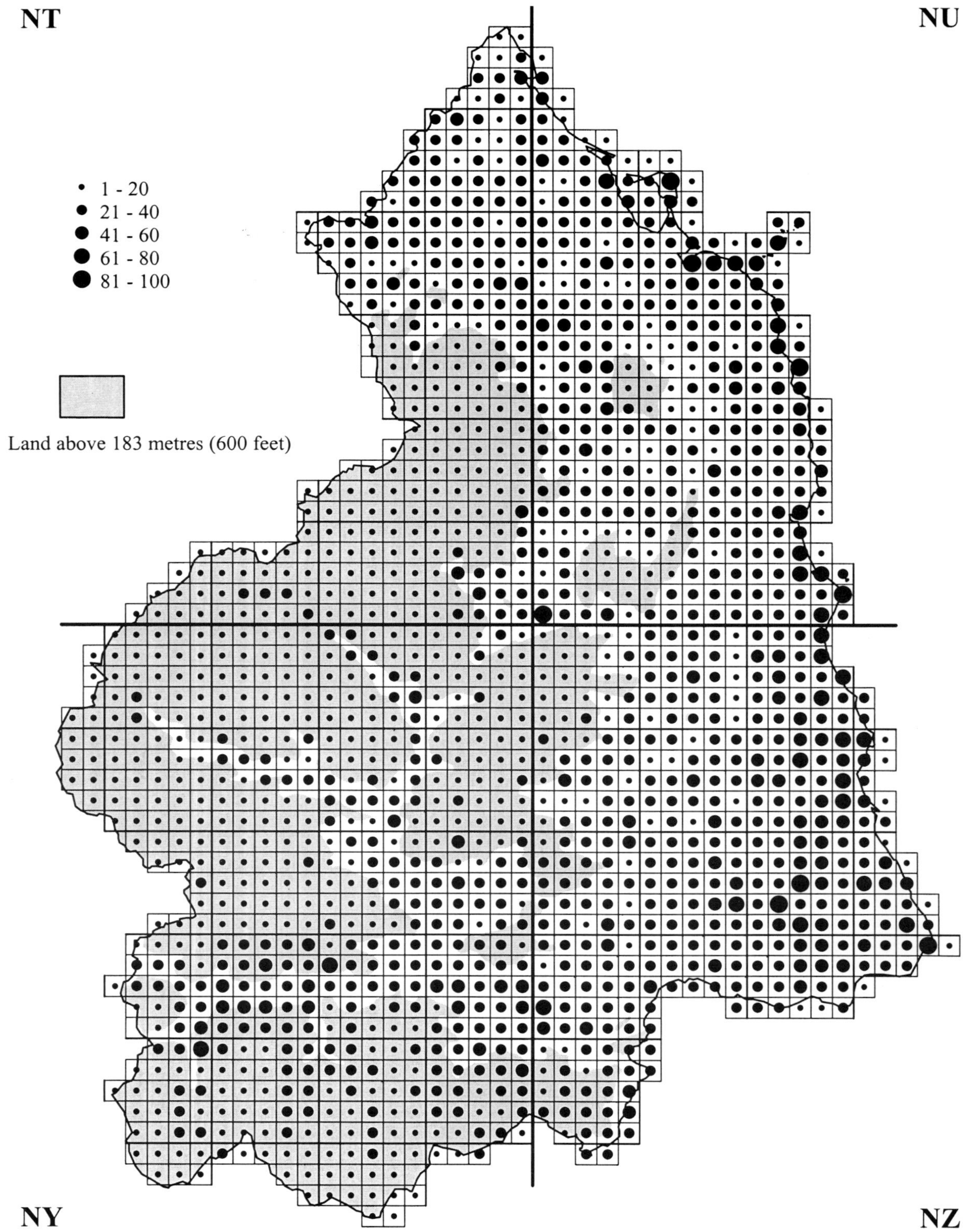

Map 11 Number of species recorded in each tetrad

LIST OF ABBREVIATIONS

a.s.l.	(height) above sea level
BBS	The Breeding Bird Survey - organised annually by the British Trust for Ornithology
BOURC	The British Ornithologists' Union Records Committee
BTO	British Trust for Ornithology
CBC	The Common Bird Census - organised annually by the British Trust for Ornithology
cf	compare
e.g.	for example
et al.	and others
ft	feet
ha	hectare(s)
km	kilometre(s)
m	metre(s)
MOD	Ministry of Defence
n.b.	note
NNR	National Nature Reserve
NR	Nature Reserve
OS	Ordnance Survey
pers. comm.	personal communication
pers. obs.	personal observation
q.v.	which see
Ramsar site	A specific site designated under The Ramsar Convention on Wetlands of International Importance.
RSPB	Royal Society for the Protection of Birds
SAC	Special Area of Conservation
SNCI	Site of Nature Conservation Importance
SPA	Special Protection Area
SSSI	Site of Special Scientific Interest
viz.	namely
WeBS	The Wetland Bird Survey - organised by the BTO, Wildfowl & Wetlands Trust, RSPB and the Joint Nature Conservation Committee

----------oOo----------

ACKNOWLEDGEMENTS

An undertaking such as this atlas survey cannot be anything other than a tremendous team effort and we sincerely thank the large number of people who have given advice and assistance in so many ways. We are especially indebted to Muriel and Tom Cadwallender and Margaret Macfarlane who acted as liaison officers with fieldworkers. They not only ably organised fieldworkers and supplied them with the appropriate stationery but also collected and checked the completed record cards as they were returned. Both Michael Holmes and Keith Brooks cross-checked the bulk of the timed visit record cards against the computer database for accuracy while Alan Curry cross-checked all of the Control tetrad record cards. Ian Fisher and Nick Rossiter, the current and previous County Recorders respectively during the atlas survey period, gave valuable assistance with the club's monthly record cards. Roger Norman kindly provided data extracts from the county coastal WeBS counts and, together with Graeme Bowman, also checked various items in the manuscript. Wardens from both the National Trust and English Nature provided assistance with counts and records at the Farne Islands and Lindisfarne NNR. Graeme Bowman, Bryan Galloway, Roger Norman and Nick Rossiter provided the short introductory papers for four species groups while Dennis Wheeler of the Geography Department of Sunderland University produced the comprehensive and most readable review of the local climate during the survey years. Professor A. J. Richards freely gave his time to assist with various habitat queries and commented on the relevant sections. Dr. Alan Morton, who developed and maintains the DMAP software, also provided much advice and helped to overcome a number of technical problems. The staff at AirFotos Ltd were very helpful in providing a wide selection of excellent aerial photographs for possible inclusion, although space and cost sadly limited our final choice.

Mention must be made of all the very talented local and not-so-local artists namely Mike Carr, Alan Hart, Stewart Sexton, Chris Gibbons, Mark Cornish, Ian Fisher, Martin Eccles, George Miller, Mike Henry and John Steele, who produced a fine array of varied and interesting illustrations which grace the following pages. A special mention should go to John Steele who, once again, produced a magnificent painting capturing the flavour of the whole endeavour for the cover. Mike Smith carried out an invaluable task by painstakingly reading and commenting on the entire text. He made many useful suggestions and his eye for detail in the English language has improved much of the 'flow'.

Finally the editors wish to thank their wives, Joan and Ann, for their understanding and patience (well, some of the time) during the long and often fraught hours when they probably should have being doing something far more domesticated.

----------oOo----------

Illustrators

Michael Carr pages 78, 80, 82, 84, 96, 98, 100, 102, 104, 132, 140, 152, 156, 160, 168, 184, 216, 226, 232, 236, 238, 241, 244, 248, 250, 252, 254, 258, 260, 262, 264, 280, 294, 296, 298, 302, 304, 308, 310, 312, 316, 326, 348, 358, 374, 376, 410, 416, 418
Mark Cornish pages 192, 230, 266, 268, 270, 272, 274, 344, 354, 360, 362, 364, 390, 408
Martin Eccles page 138 and colour painting page 9
Ian Fisher page 196
Chris Gibbons pages 124, 150, 154, 202, 204, 208, 212, 214, 366, 404, 406
Alan Hart pages 86, 88, 90, 92, 126, 134, 146, 158, 198, 200, 206, 210, 228, 276, 278, 330, 332, 334, 336, 338,
Mike Henry pages 162, 172, 180, 182
George Miller page 136
Stewart Sexton pages 72, 74, 76, 106, 108, 110, 112, 114, 116, 120, 148, 161, 186, 218, 234, 284, 286, 288, 290, 292, 300, 314, 340, 352, 382, 384, 388, 396, 398, 400
John Steele pages 142, 166, 170, 174, 176, 178, 222, 378

Colour cover paintings by John Steele

----------oOo----------

LIST OF FIELDWORKERS

M. G. Anderson
N. Anderson
E. Bagshaw
A. Baker
H. Baker
S. Barratt
S. Barrett
Mrs S. Beech
The late M. Bell
S.A. Bell
M. Bentley
M. Bickmore
R. & C. Bluck
J. S. Booth
A. I. Bowman
G. Bowman
D. Boyd
K. V. Brooks
J. Brown
A. & L. Brunt
K. Buchanan
A. H. Burgess
M. L.& T. A Cadwallender
M. J. & E. F. Carr
P. Charleton
T. Charman
J. W. Clark
J. Coleman
A. Copland
The late N. R. Cox
E. Crabtree
W. M. Crawford
T. L. Crilley
J. Cummings
A. Curry
P. R. Davey
I. S. Davidson
A. J. Davis
M. Davison
K. Dawson
J. C. & J. M. Day
R. Dickinson
W. Dickson
J. L. Doleman
J. Dutton
J. Eccles
S. Eccles
M. E. Eccles
K. Eccles
P. R. Fairhurst
Mrs E. M. Fish
I. Fisher
N. Foggo
S. Foley
R. Forster
M. P. Frankis
A. Furness
R. Gadjus
B. Galloway
S. Gilmour
T. P. Goodwin
Mrs L. S. Goodwin
M. Greene
J. Hallowell
D. F. & S. M. Hamilton
A. Hart
R. Harvey
M. Henry
S. J. Hingston
M. S. Hodgson
M. K. Hodgson
S. Holliday
R. M. Holmes
Mrs S. Inness
C. Irvine
R. Jackson
A. Janes
C. Jewitt
A. J. Johnston
Lord J. Joicey
P. & G. Jones
I. Kerr
M. Kitching
C. Knox
S. Laing
S.& I. Lavelle
G. Linkleter
R. Lockwood
D. Lockwood
W. T. Logan
L.J. McDougall
J. McKee
D. McKeown
A. McLevy
A. Middleton
F. D. Middleton
S. Moffitt
G. W. Moon
A. Mossop
M. Nattrass
L. Naughton
D. W. Nichol
R. Norman
N. F. Osborne
J. D. Parrack
Miss E. J. Pattinson
G. C. Pollinger
B. R. Pollinger
K. Redgrave
R. Reid
J. Richardson
M. R. Richardson
D. Robinson
K. Robson
L. Robson
B. N. Rossiter
K. & L. Russell
J. W. Rutter
S. Sexton
D. R. Shannon
E. Slack
M. R. Smith
J. G. Steele
E. J. Steele
The late A. Stimpson
B. & M. Sykes
M. L. Taylor
D. M. Turner
S. C. Votier
The late R. Walton
J. Walton
T. Watson
S. & A. Westerberg
C. H. L. Westmacott

With apologies for any accidental omissions

Key to scales and symbols on the distribution maps

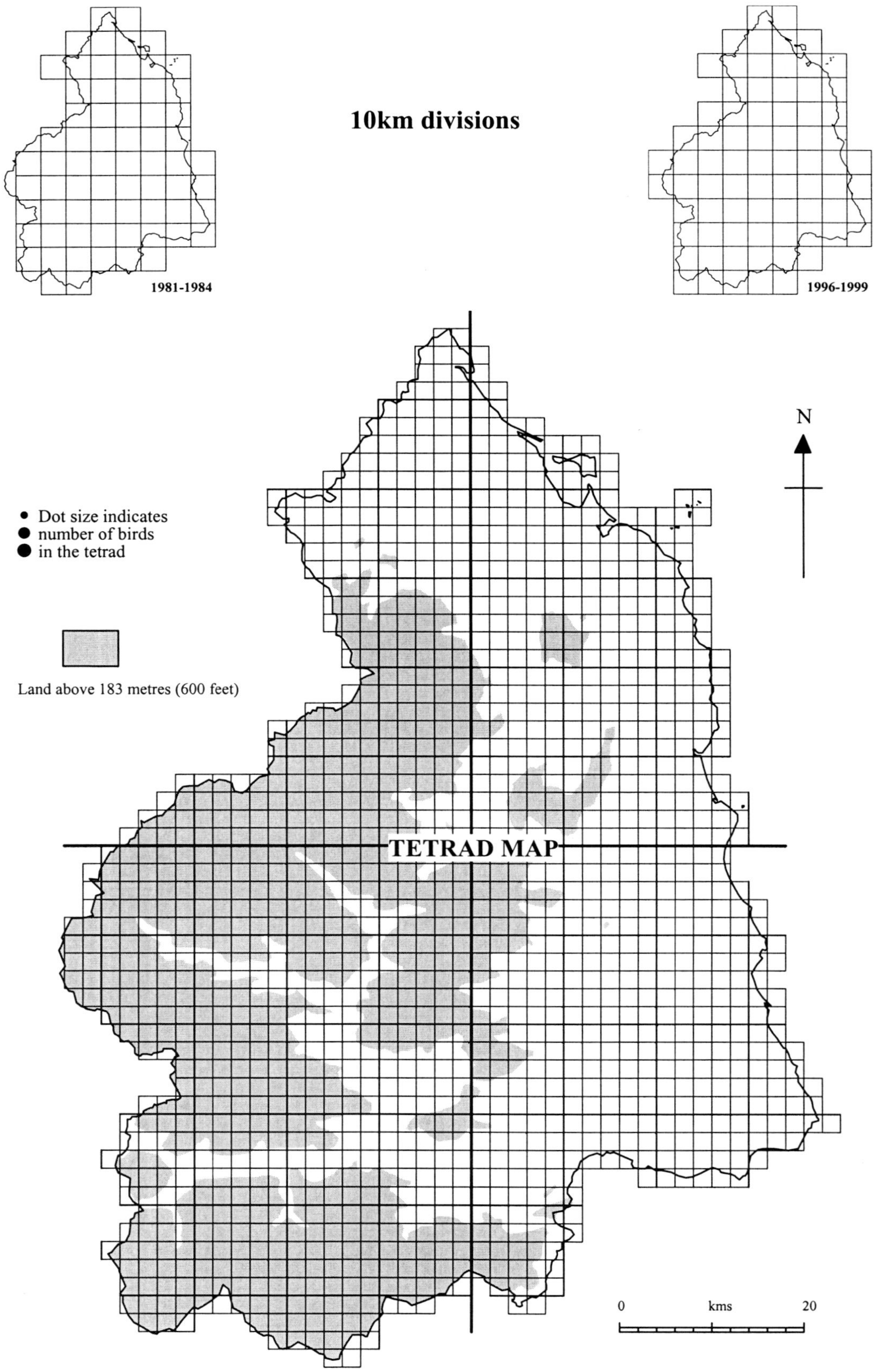

For the majority of species, the distribution maps accompanying the species account are presented as in the above layout where the two smaller maps are overlaid with a grid representing 10km squares and the larger tetrad map with a grid representing 2km squares. For a small number of species only the 10km square maps are given.

SPECIES ACCOUNTS AND DISTRIBUTION MAPS

RED-THROATED DIVER *Gavia stellata*

The Red-throated Diver is the commonest of the three members of the genus regularly wintering in the county. Bolam (1932) said it was 'a winter visitant, fairly common along the coast, sometimes even numerous, and more given to trusting itself inland, both on lakes and our larger rivers, than either of its congeners'. Galloway and Meek (1978) indicated that it was a common winter visitor with favoured stretches at Holy Island-Bamburgh and Alnmouth and Druridge Bays. They also said in the preceding ten years about 20 had been noted inland on lakes and rivers as far west as Catcleugh and Hallington Reservoirs and that these sightings were usually as a result of severe weather or oiling incidents. Between 1985 and 1996 the county annual bird reports show that one or two birds have occurred about 17 times on mainly coastal ponds or rivers within a few kilometres of the sea although one was on the River Tyne at Wylam in February 1986.

Red-throated Divers arrive in Northumberland waters from September, sometimes building up to quite large concentrations during October, before a proportion move on and the remainder settle in wintering areas. Large coastal passage of presumably non-wintering birds also regularly occurs in both spring and autumn and occasionally during the winter. Two recoveries, at Cullercoats in February 1983 and the Wansbeck Estuary in February 1989, of pulli ringed in Shetland in 1980 and Orkney 1973, indicate that at least some of the birds wintering in Northumberland probably originate from the relatively small Scottish breeding population.

The current survey indicates its status and distribution remain largely unchanged since the earlier reviews. The tetrad map clearly demonstrates that it is distributed along almost all of the coastline although larger concentrations were mainly in the northern third of inshore waters. Most reports, about 80%, were of singles or gatherings of less than ten birds. This is typical of the species and confirms its preference for shallow bays and waters which provide adequate feeding. The few areas displaying an apparent lack of birds, however, may merely be as a result of unfavourably rough sea conditions masking their presence during survey visits or perhaps tidal or feeding conditions moving the birds further offshore. The largest counts were recorded off Spittal (NU05A & NU05B) where about 100 were seen in early January 1999, concentrated in the outflow from the River Tweed, presumably attracted there as a result of unusual feeding opportunities. Both Druridge and Alnmouth Bays continue to attract reasonable numbers with gatherings of 43 (NZ29T), 13 (NZ29U) and ten (NU20N) while in the favoured area between Bamburgh and Cheswick four tetrads produced maximum counts of 27, 25, 21, and 19 (NU13T, NU04N, NU13N & NU13P respectively). The only other site with more than ten birds was Beadnell Bay (NU22N). Odd birds were also recorded on several coastal ponds although one bird was further inland at Killingworth Lake (NZ27Q) in January/February 1997.

The main wintering areas in Europe are the Atlantic and North Sea coasts around Britain and Ireland and from western Norway at least south to Brittany, with smaller numbers in the Kattegat and Baltic, Black and Caspian Seas and a small minority penetrating south to the Bay of Biscay and the Mediterranean (Cramp & Simmons, 1977). Lack (1986) said they were 'well-represented along the east coast of Britain' and that 'numbers fluctuate widely in response to weather conditions and other factors which may affect the available food supply'. He gave a wintering population in Britain and Ireland of 12,000-15,000 birds and indicated that the arrivals along the east coast from mid-September suggested immigration from Scandinavia. However, Batten *et al.* (1990) gave a British wintering population of perhaps 10,000 in the light of estimates made by Tasker *et al.* (1987) of 3,100-4,200 on the east coast of Britain while more recently Stone *et al.* (1997) gave an estimated wintering population of 4,850 in Great Britain.

During the three winters of the survey period the species was located in 50 tetrads in the county and a total of 374 birds counted. The numbers present during any winter period can vary considerably from year to year depending on weather and feeding conditions in both this and other areas but an average population of between 150-400 birds seems realistic.

MIKE S. HODGSON

No. of tetrads in which recorded — 50 (3%)

Tetrad Analysis	No. of tetrads
1-2 birds	25 (50%)
3-10 birds	15 (30%)
11+ birds	10 (20%)

Total No. of birds counted — 374

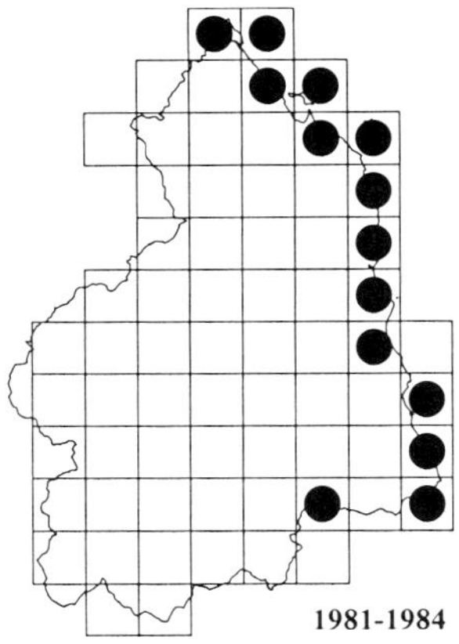

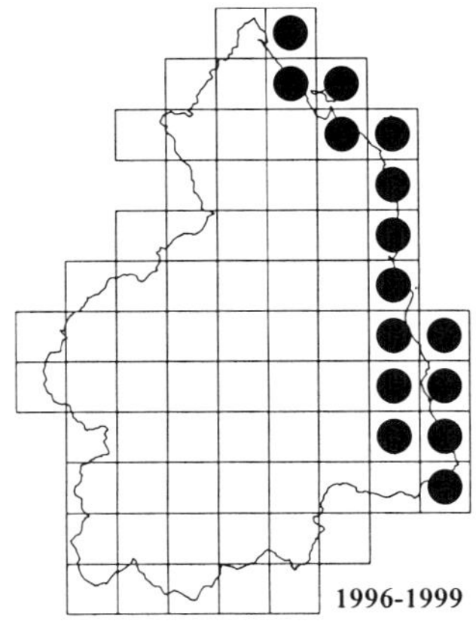

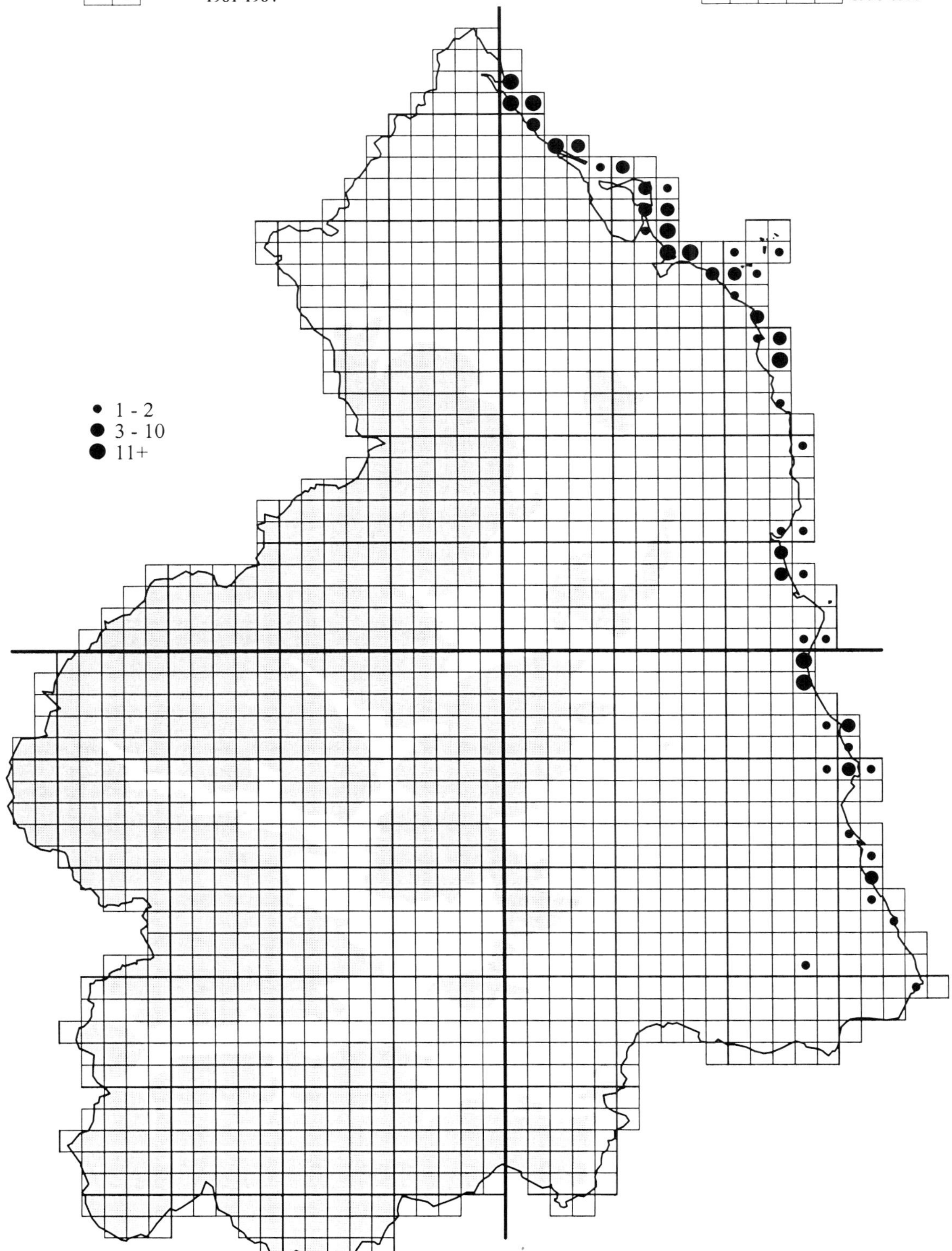

Red-throated Diver

BLACK-THROATED DIVER *Gavia arctica*

It would appear that the Black-throated Diver has been much less common in Northumberland than Red-throated Diver *G. stellata* and perhaps also Great Northern Diver *G. immer* for many years. Chapman (1889) said it was 'by far the most scarce' and that 'I have only met with it on two or three occasions', while Bolam (1932) reported it as 'a winter visitant, not rare, but more numerous in some years than in others, and always much scarcer than the next (viz. Red-throated Diver)'. This situation prevailed and Galloway and Meek (1978) considered it an uncommon winter visitor and thought that it was probably the least numerous of the divers. Like the previous species, they said that offshore between Holy Island and Bamburgh was an important area but inland they knew of only eight records, the furthest west being at Broomlee Lough, and in their *Supplement* (1986) could add only one other, at Whittle Dene Reservoirs in November 1984. Since then records in the county annual bird reports for 1986-1995 inclusive have mentioned about six individuals on coastal or near-coastal pools and others further inland on the River Tyne between Newburn and Ryton in 1986 and again on Whittle Dene Reservoirs in 1994.

The tetrad map for the current winter atlas survey confirms little change in both distribution and numbers for this species. The largest gatherings were, as expected, along the northern part of the coastline with a maximum count of eight off Cocklawburn (NU04J) although up to seven were feeding with other divers and seabirds off Spittal (NU05A) in January 1999. Smaller counts of two-three were made at Redshin Cove (NU05F), Holy Island (NU14F), Budle Point (NU13T), Bamburgh (NU13X), off Warkworth Beach (NU20N) and at Newbiggin (NZ38D). There was a scattering of singles at various localities along the coast including birds in the Tyne Estuary, on the Long Nanny (NU22I) and just inland at the Queen Elizabeth II Country Park (NZ28Z). Another was again found well inland on Whittle Dene Reservoirs (NZ06U), this bird circling and flying off to the south east on its second day. Because of the relatively small numbers wintering in the county it is possible that some birds were overlooked during the survey period and others may have been missed due to difficulties in identification at long ranges and in adverse conditions. Passage numbers are rarely exceptional in spring and autumn but Galloway and Meek mentioned a mid-winter movement involving 36 moving south at Seaton Sluice-St. Mary's Island in early January 1974, these birds clearly reacting to gales and probably to feeding conditions in the North Sea.

Cramp and Simmons (1977) indicated that outside the breeding season most birds resort to sheltered coastal and marine waters and the winter visitors in the North Sea were probably Norwegian breeders. As a result of the national winter atlas of 1981-1984, Lack (1986) said it was the rarest of the three divers around the shores of Ireland, western Britain and on inland waters, and that numbers increased slightly and steadily around the south east coast of Britain and up the east coast to the Firth of Forth and the Moray Firth. The peak numbers were found along the coastline of western Scotland. At that time a wintering population of about 1,300 birds was suggested. Tasker *et al.* (1987) estimated that about 100 wintered along the east coast of Britain.

The total of 39 birds located in 19 tetrads over the three winter periods probably means that, on average, some ten-25 would be a 'normal' wintering population off the Northumberland coast although, as noted by previous authors, numbers can be much higher in some years. These figures probably represent a not inconsiderable percentage of the total wintering along the east coast.

MIKE S. HODGSON

No. of tetrads in which recorded 19 (1%)

Tetrad Analysis	No. of tetrads
1 birds	11 (58%)
2 birds	5 (26%)
3+ birds	3 (16%)

Total No. of birds counted 39

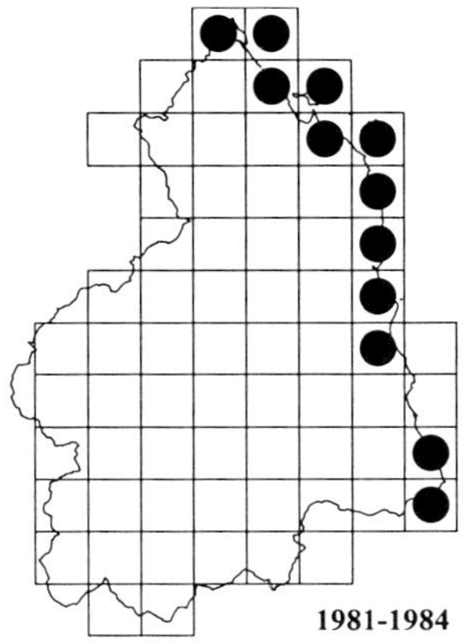

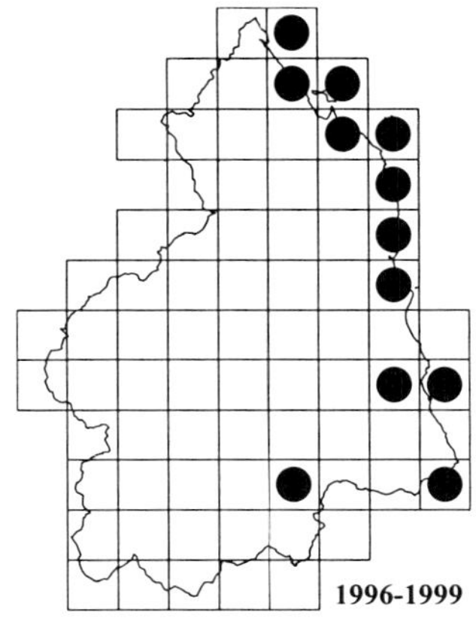

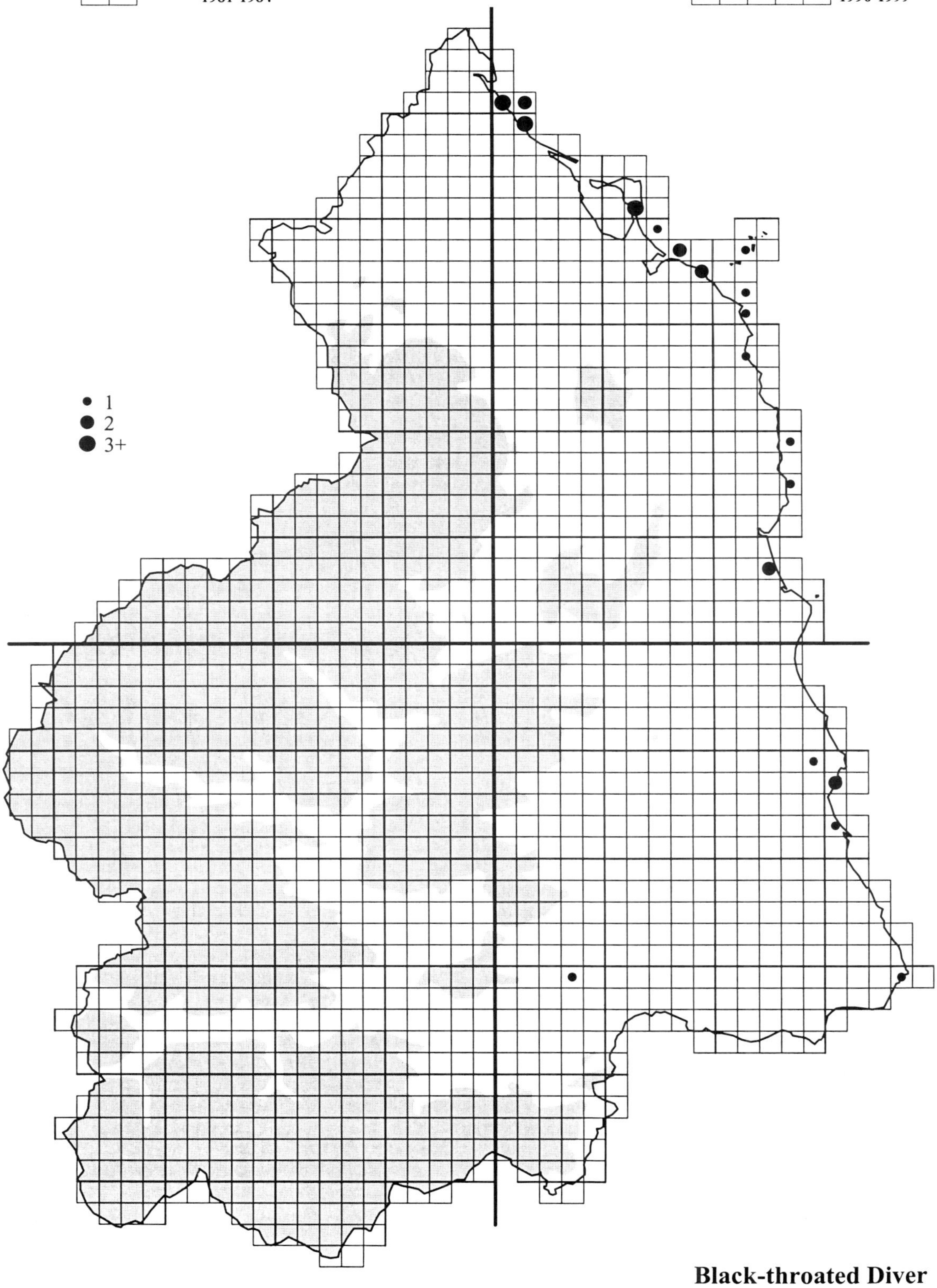

Black-throated Diver

GREAT NORTHERN DIVER *Gavia immer*

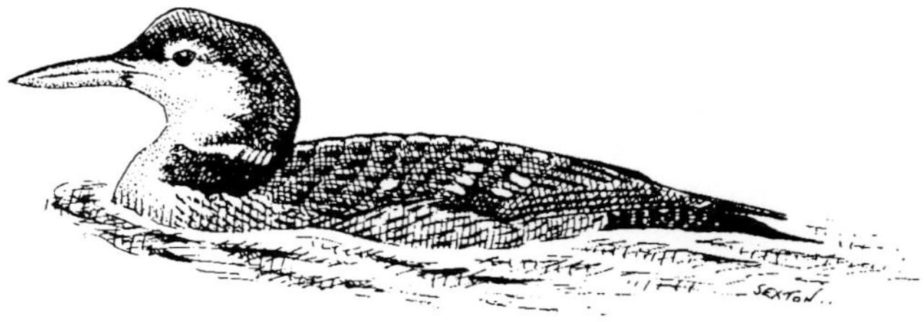

The Great Northern Diver seems never to have been a particularly numerous species in the county but, nevertheless, has been regularly reported along the coastline for over a century. Chapman (1889) said that they were 'not infrequently met with on the Northumberland coast, a few occurring almost every winter' while over 40 years later Bolam (1932) could say they 'were not uncommon along the coast from about the end of October till March or April'. Galloway and Meek (1978) classified it as an uncommon winter visitor and said passage was usually inconspicuous. In common with the preceding two diver species, they mentioned that it regularly occurred in the Holy Island-Bamburgh and Druridge Bay areas where up to eight may be seen. A much larger total of about 20, many badly oiled, were in the Holy Island area in January 1952. Birds are occasionally encountered on coastal ponds but there were only a handful of documented inland records up to 1968 with the furthest west at Catcleugh Reservoir.

The tetrad distribution map confirms that the situation remains almost unchanged with small numbers wintering mainly along the northern half of the county coastline. Peak counts during the three winter periods of the survey were 11 off Spittal (NU05F) in November 1998 and six off nearby Scremerston (NU04J) in January 1997. Other areas favoured by wintering birds, shared with both Red-throated *G. stellata* and Black-throated Divers *G. arctica*, are clearly indicated around the Holy Island (NU14C/F/H) / Ross Back Sands / Stag Rocks area (NU13P/T/X), the Farne Islands and the adjacent shore (NU23C/D/I/N), and Beadnell (NU22N) and Alnmouth Bays (NU20N). Numbers, however, were typically quite low with three tetrads holding three birds, three holding two birds and 13, some 65% of the occupied tetrads, having only a single bird. There was one inland record, a well-watched bird on Killingworth Lake (NZ27Q) in November 1996. A comparison of the two 10km square maps shows it was recorded in two fewer squares during this latest winter survey but this is entirely in keeping with the fact that they are more numerous in some years than others.

Great Northern Divers winter regularly around Britain and Ireland and in the North Sea, although numbers are relatively small. After breeding they usually move to marine waters, often off rocky and exposed coasts but also in bays, channels and sheltered inlets (Cramp & Simmons, 1977). Following the fieldwork for the national winter atlas in 1981-1984 a wintering total of 3,500-4,500 was suggested in Britain and Ireland with the bulk of these along the west coast of Ireland, western Scotland and the Orkney and Shetland Islands. Along the North Sea coasts of Scotland and England they were only thinly distributed (Lack, 1986). However, as the main European breeding population of about 300 pairs is currently confined to Iceland (Hagemeijer & Blair, 1997), it would seem, as suggested by Lack, that the British and Irish wintering population must derive from somewhere further west.

The species is known to be capable of wintering further offshore than the smaller divers and this, together with variable sea conditions, will mean that a small number at least were probably missed during the current survey. Even so, the total of 45 counted over three winter periods is probably an overestimate, a more realistic 'average' winter total being in the range of 20-30 birds. As already noted, their fluctuating numbers will be much higher in certain years.

MIKE S. HODGSON

No. of tetrads in which recorded	21 (1%)

Tetrad Analysis	No. of tetrads
1 bird	13 (62%)
2 birds	3 (14%)
3+ birds	5 (24%)

Total No. of birds counted	45

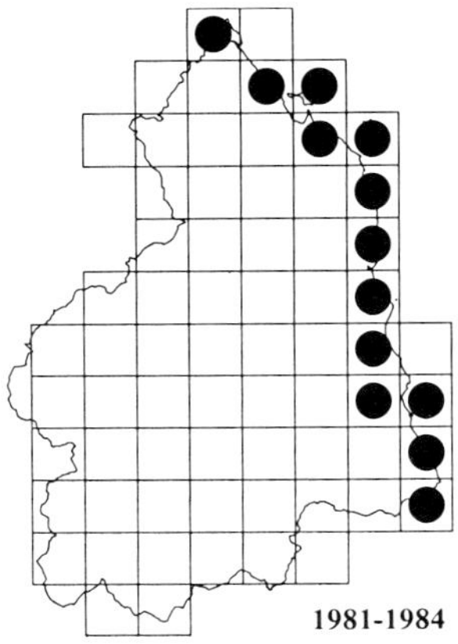

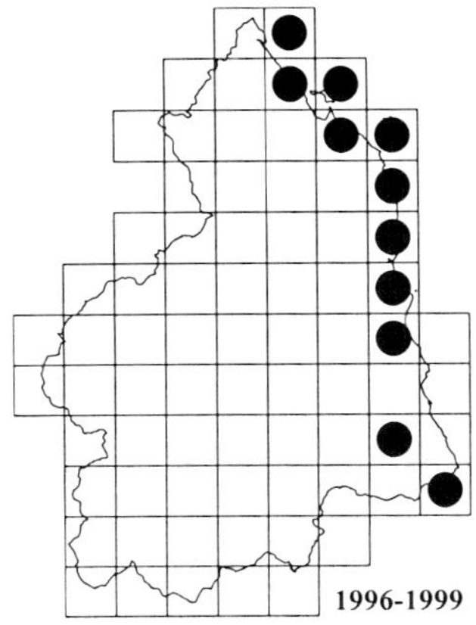

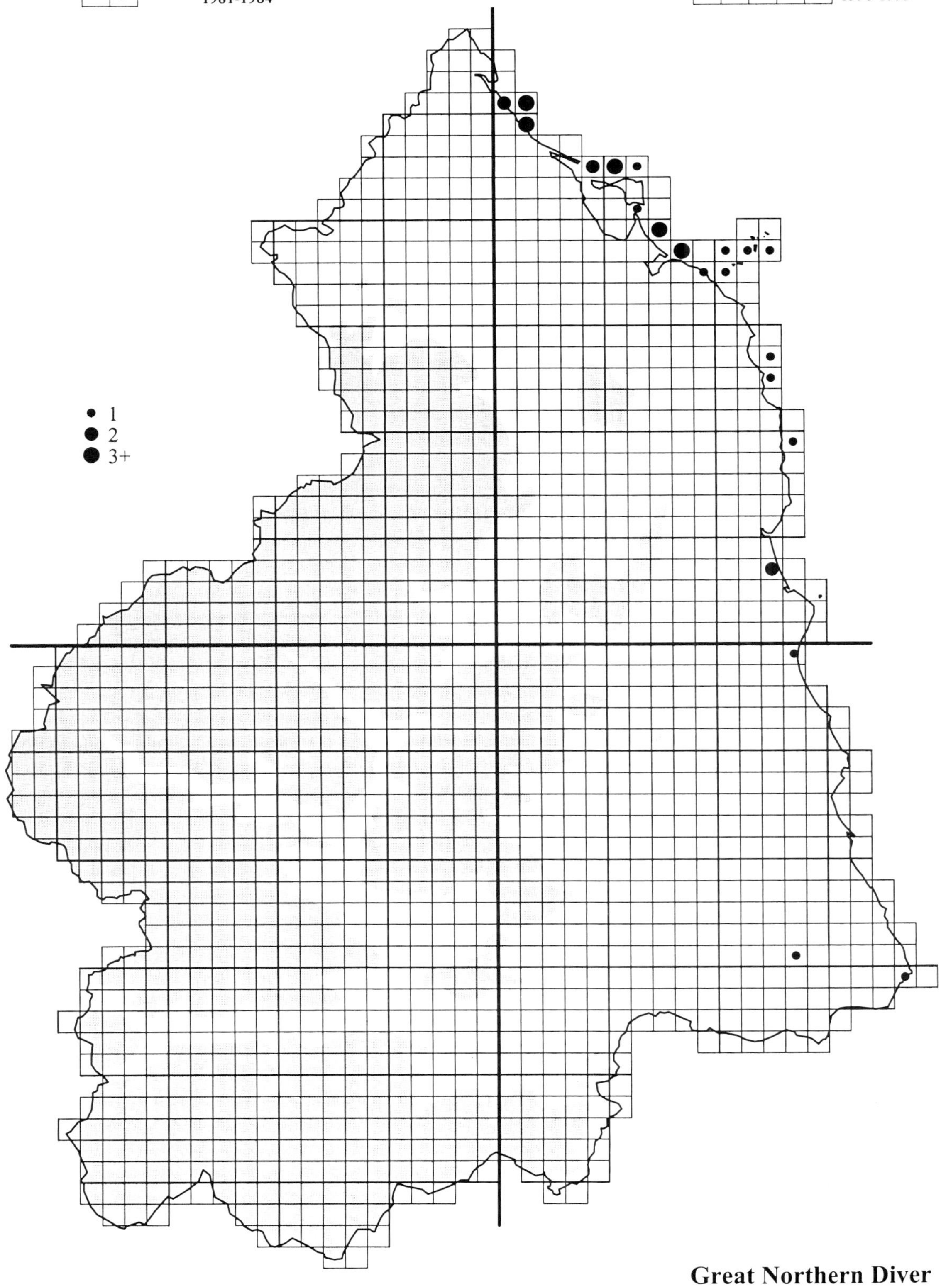

Great Northern Diver

LITTLE GREBE *Tachybaptus ruficollis*

Bolam (1932) wrote that the Little Grebe in winter was 'frequently seen along the coast, especially off estuaries'. Over 50 years later Galloway and Meek (1978) observed that 'he recorded flocks of 20 to 30 around Holy Island' adding that 'such numbers are no longer recorded anywhere along the coast'. This assertion is upheld by the counts made during the current winter survey when the largest groups recorded were of 14 at Cresswell Pond (NZ28X), the regular favoured site for large concentrations, and ten at the Aln Estuary (NU21K). However, it should be noted that Bolam's 'winter' might not be totally in line with the definition of winter as used by the current survey. Flocks similar in numbers to the Bolam figures do occur just outside the period of the winter atlas survey with a county record peak of 46 noted at Cresswell Pond in October 1999. However *Birds in Northumbria 1999* confirms the fact, endorsed by the atlas, that there is 'a sharp decline evident in the final two months (of the year) when peak counts were of eight at Cresswell Pond and four-five at Hartburn and Lilburn Pond', a pattern noted in each year of the survey.

Little Grebes are traditionally regarded as a sedentary species and the winter map is very similar to the one in *The atlas of breeding birds of Northumbria* (Day *et al.*, 1995). This correlation was also noted by Lack (1986) when he compared national breeding and winter distribution maps. Both local maps show the species' aversion to high ground, a fact well borne out by 51 of the 67 occupied tetrads noted lying between 0-100 metres a.s.l. with only one occupied tetrad being found between 201-300 metres a.s.l. One major difference between the maps is the number of records in the north of the county during the winter survey. Little Grebes resorting to the River Tweed during winter can explain this, a fact noted by Galloway and Meek (1978) when they wrote 'rivers further inland are also frequented in winter; for example, up to six on the Tyne at Hexham and small numbers may be seen on the Tweed'.

Cramp and Simmons (1977) stated that there is a 'less marked shift to the coast or large lakes for winter than other European grebes', maintaining that some adults remain on their territories throughout the winter, others, perhaps mainly juveniles, disperse or are forced to move by cold weather. This is not the case in Northumberland where each year there is a general retreat to the coast from inland areas regardless of winter conditions (*Birds in Northumbria*). Sightings usually come from between ten to 15 mainly coastal localities during the winter period. This is in keeping with Lack (1986) who noted that 'recent population studies in Avon and Gwynedd, however, clearly demonstrated a widespread autumn exodus from their breeding areas'. This is confirmed by sightings during this atlas survey and amplifies the statement by Galloway and Meek that 'birds usually desert breeding waters in November and one to two are often noted in such places as Budle Bay and the estuaries of the Long Nanny, Aln and Coquet'.

Of the 67 tetrads where Little Grebes were recorded only 21 sightings were made during timed visits, the remainder being supplementary records, thus emphasising the species' secretive nature, which although less marked in winter when 'they become readily visible and often gathering in small flotillas when feeding' (Lack, 1986), is still apparent when trying to census a relatively small population. It is likely that the total of maximum counts of 172 individuals during the survey period is an inflated figure for the normal winter population. However, it would seem that a population of 50-100 individuals is more realistic in any one winter, keeping the species' status somewhere between the higher end of the uncommon and lower end of the well-represented categories.

ALAN J. JOHNSTON

Distribution by altitude

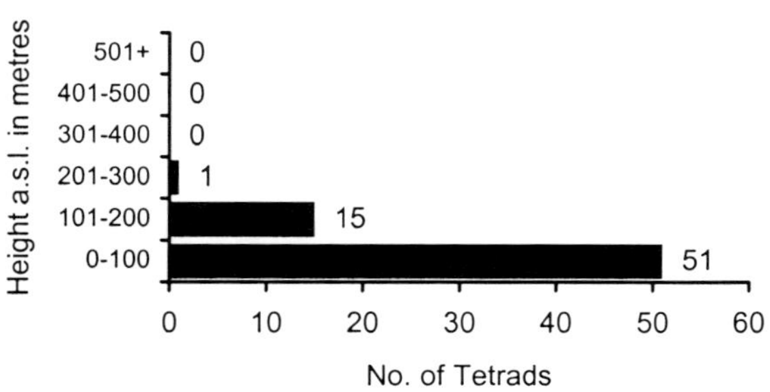

No. of tetrads in which recorded 67 (5%)

Tetrad Analysis	No. of tetrads
1 bird	30 (45%)
2-3 birds	23 (34%)
4+ birds	14 (21%)

Total No. of birds counted 172

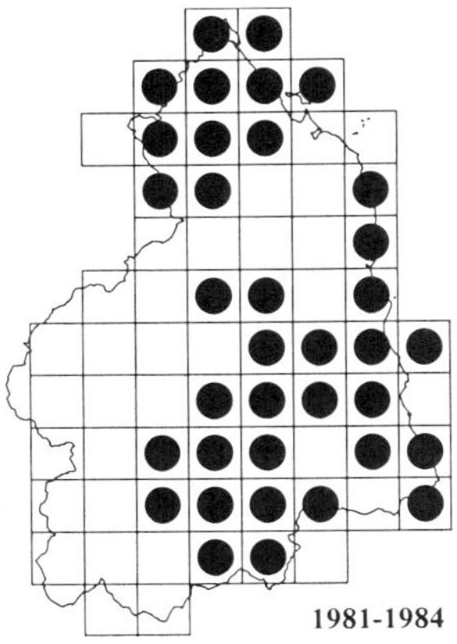

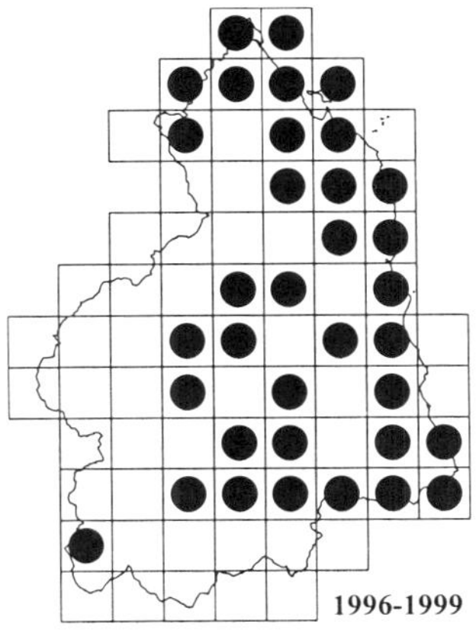

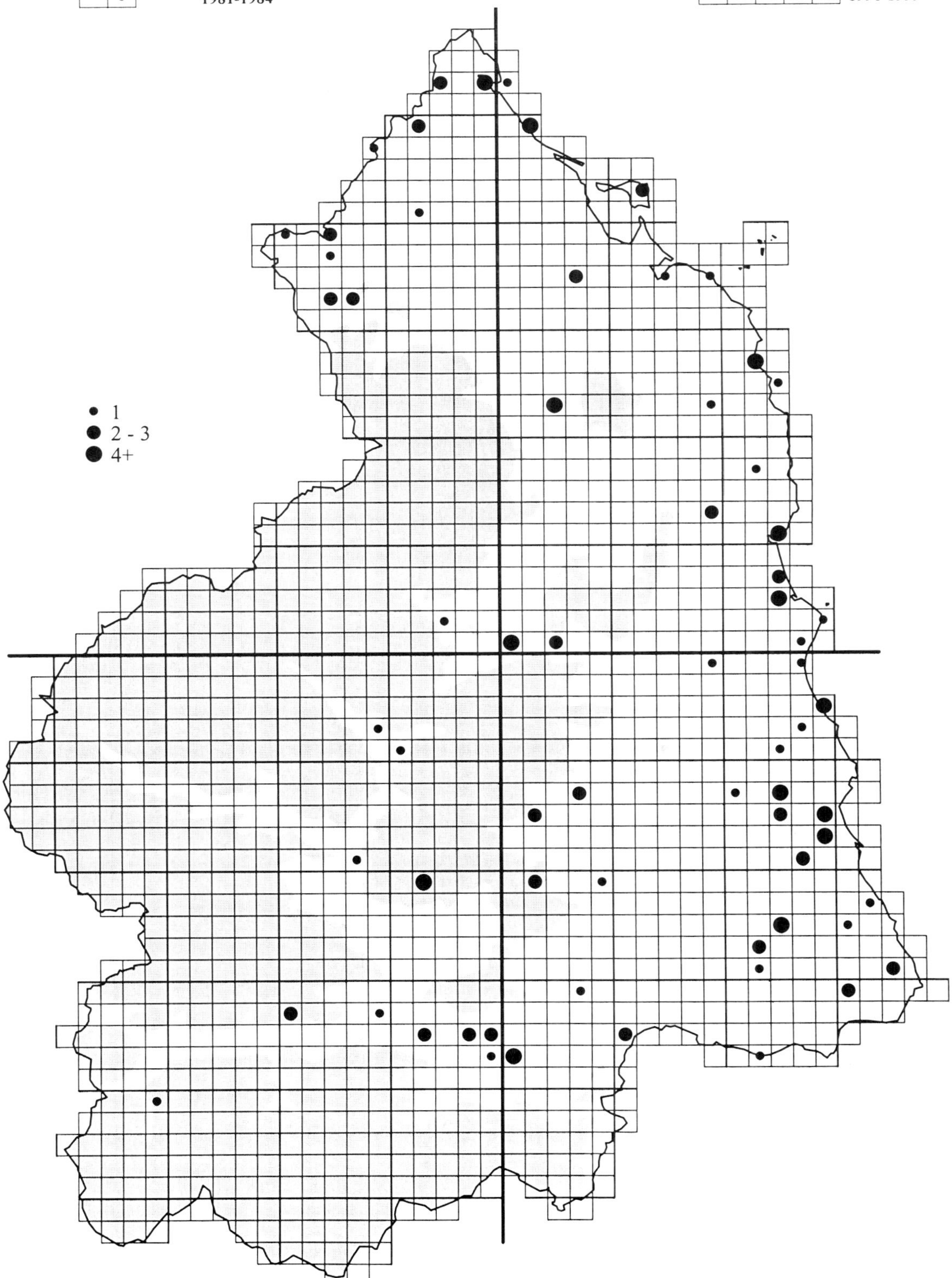

Little Grebe

GREAT CRESTED GREBE *Podiceps cristatus*

Bolam (1912) stated that it was 'an annual winter visitor ... by no means uncommon on the coast ... with an increasing tendency to appear on inland waters' and he was hopeful that it would become a resident. Galloway and Meek (1978) chronicled its rise as a breeding species and showed that it had become an uncommon resident that frequented the coast in winter, as it did in Bolam's day.

Cramp and Simmons (1977) stated that 'movements away from nesting areas begin July-August' and in autumn 'many smaller waters are deserted'. They also indicated that there were 'marked shifts from inland waters to the sea in winter'. This is confirmed by the findings of the winter survey as the tetrad map shows clearly that the winter distribution of this graceful bird is almost exclusively on the coast and lowland subsidence ponds of the south east of the county, with grebes being recorded in only four tetrads away from these areas. Birds can remain throughout the winter at breeding sites such as Big Waters, Arcot and Holywell Ponds unless, or until, the water freezes. This was reported in 1999 when up to five were at Big Waters until a cold spell around 19th November forced them to leave (*Birds in Northumbria 1999*).

Following its severe persecution in Victorian times, the species' recovery and subsequent expansion is one of the success stories of the twentieth century. *The atlas of wintering birds in Britain and Ireland* (Lack, 1986) reported 'distribution is also more coastal in winter'. Generally they show a preference for lowland localities: when breeding sites freeze they desert them sometimes for the remainder of the winter. Lack also considered that 'Britain and Ireland clearly receive a large influx of winter visitors from western Europe'. This large influx is not apparent in our region where numbers dwindle in December with concentrations rarely reaching double figures. The origin of these birds is not known, however, but Galloway and Meek surmised 'they probably include continental immigrants and their numbers have changed little since Bolam's time'.

Of the 29 tetrads where the species was reported 25 (86%) were at 0-100 metres a.s.l. The low winter numbers of this species is confirmed by the recording of singles in 16 of the occupied tetrads, especially in the period between December to January. Despite being a bird of open water and easily observed during the winter period, the fact that grebes were only reported on three timed visits shows the scarcity of the species in winter in the region. The distribution map relies greatly on supplementary records for its completeness. Peak concentrations were of 12 between Birling Carrs and Alnmouth (NU20P), seven at Big Waters (NZ27M) and on the sea off Druridge Pools (NZ29T) with five at Holywell Pond (NZ37C). An additional large count of ten, covering a number of tetrads, in the Chevington-Cresswell stretch of Druridge Bay, is also noted in *Birds in Northumbria 1998*.

Pair formation begins in mid-winter, often before the return to breeding areas. In mild conditions display is frequently reported, for example as early as late January at Big Waters (*Birds in Northumbria 1999*).

The status of Great Crested Grebe in the region is described in the annual county bird reports as 'an uncommon resident and passage visitor'. The results of the survey confirm this and, with the grand total of maximum counts standing at only 68 individuals, it will need a great change in the species' fortunes to move it into a higher category. Indeed it would seem that no more than a maximum of ten-20 birds spend the winter in our recording area.

ALAN J. JOHNSTON

Distribution by altitude

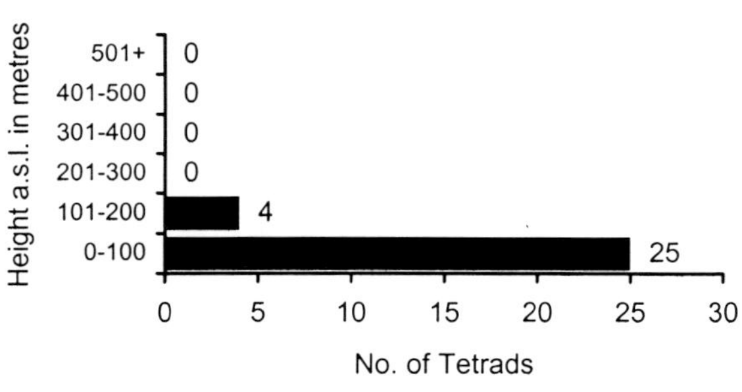

No. of tetrads in which recorded		29 (2%)
Tetrad Analysis	No. of tetrads	
1 bird	16 (55%)	
2 birds	6 (21%)	
3+ birds	7 (24%)	
Total No. of birds counted		68

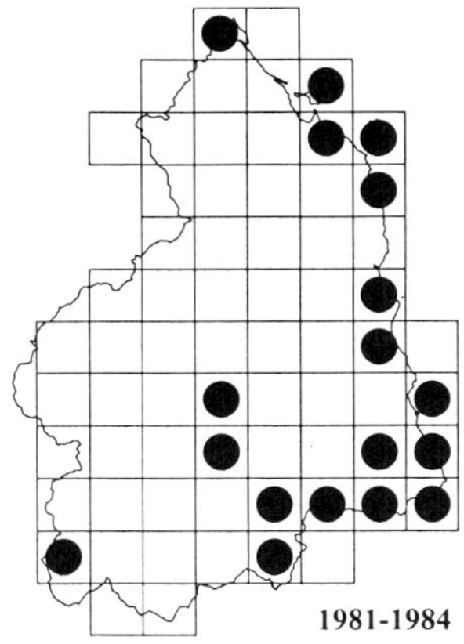

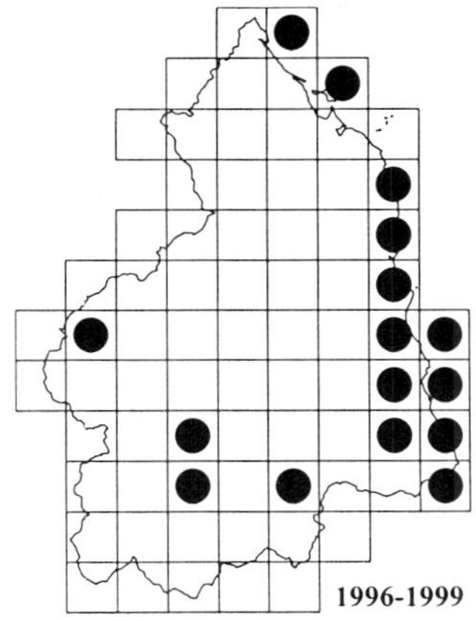

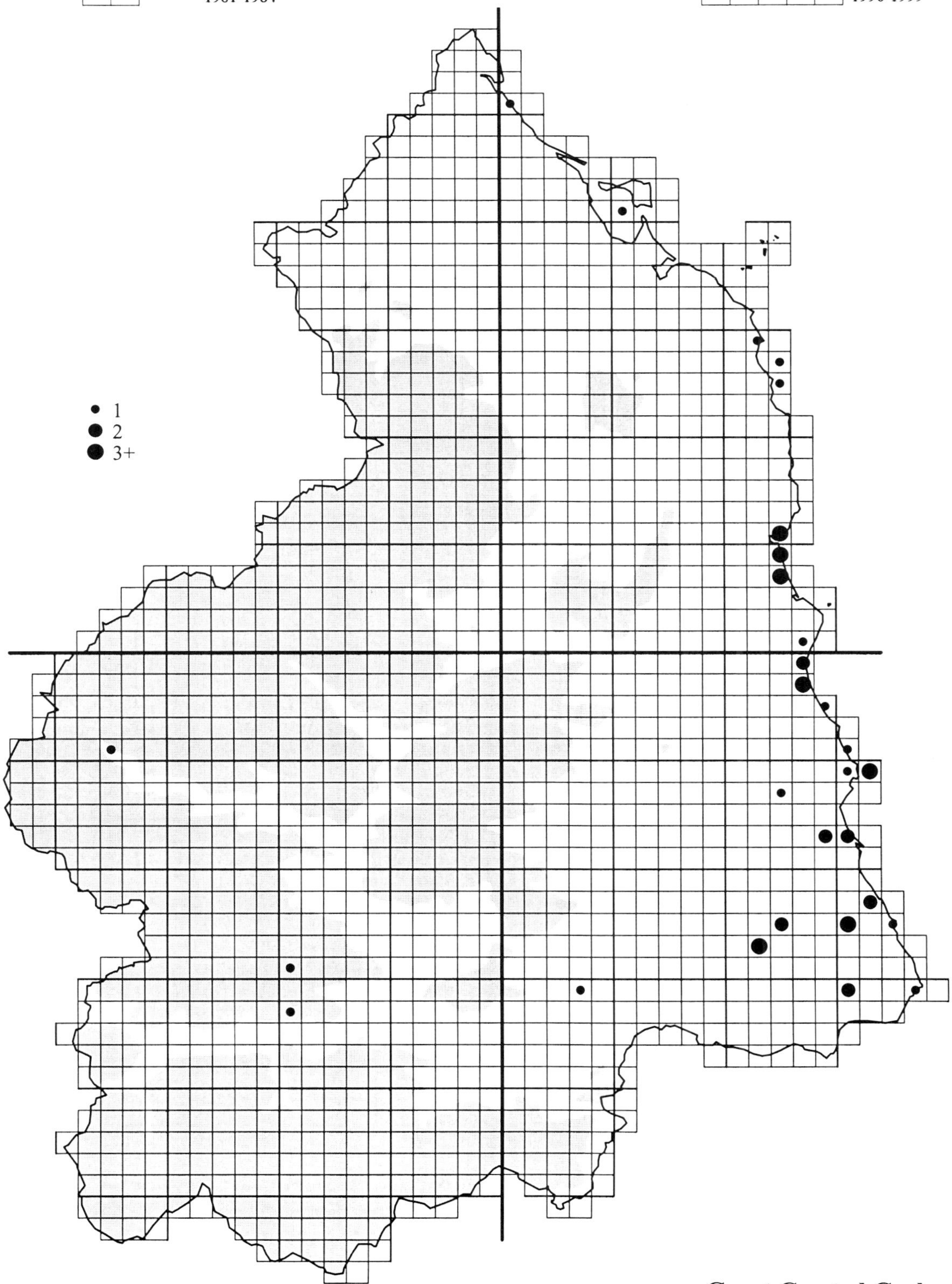

Great Crested Grebe

RED-NECKED GREBE *Podiceps grisegena*

Bolam (1912) described the species as 'an irregular winter visitant ... usually only appearing in hard weather, when ... it sometimes arrives in considerable numbers'. He also stated that it didn't usually arrive 'till after the New Year'. Over 60 years later Galloway and Meek (1978) declared that the Holy Island-Bamburgh area was still the favourite location, 'with up to 15 occurring between January to early April'. Larger gatherings have occurred with 27 on 8th February 1964 and 43 on 26th January 1968. These 'modern' day highs pale into insignificance when compared to a count made sometime between 1936 and 1943 when about 100 were counted (Perry, 1946).

In western Europe, Red-necked Grebes winter along the coasts of south west Norway, Germany, Denmark, Holland and the Swedish Baltic coast (Chandler, 1981) and may be more susceptible to hard weather in their wintering quarters than are other members of the family. There have been notable influxes in 1891, 1897, 1899 and 1922 as well as that noted above by Perry. The most recent influx occurred in the winter of 1978/79 when there was a two-phased arrival. The first was at the end of 1978 and peaked when 43 birds were found on 26th January 1979. The second arrival took place between 21st January-26th April when 'birds were noted close inshore all along the coast. At least 20 perished and several ventured onto fresh water' (*Birds in Northumbria 1979*). Monthly totals during this influx involved 30 in February, 40 in March and 17 in April.

Red-necked Grebe is an inshore bird which tends to favour shallow sandy bays. The distribution of records during the current winter survey period demonstrates this habitat preference with birds being found in the shallow bays of Newbiggin, Druridge, Alnmouth and Beadnell, as well as the favoured area of Holy Island/Ross Back Sands/Stag Rocks. Usually about 20 to 30 birds are recorded most winters, although there must be some duplication of records in the inshore waters between Holy Island and Stag Rocks.

During the current winter survey, Red-necked Grebes were second in abundance only to Slavonian Grebe *P. auritus* with a total of 72 birds being counted in 26 coastal tetrads. This represents 13 ten kilometre squares and compares favourably with the 1981-1984 national winter atlas survey when birds were found in 11 ten kilometre squares (Lack, 1986). Most, as usual, were seen in the north of the county in the favoured Holy Island to the Farne Islands stretch of coastline, reaffirming the status described by earlier authors. Five or more birds were recorded in five tetrads (one as far south as the Blyth area), with two to four birds recorded in another seven and single birds in the remaining 14 tetrads.

Inland records are rare. Discounting sightings on the coastal ponds, there have been about 29 inland records since 1970, some as far west as Bakethin Reservoir, Kielder. Some, such as birds at an inland locality between 1993-1996 and at Big Waters and Arcot Pond between 1998/99 (both during the breeding season), may refer to returning birds. Of the 29 records, only nine were during the November to February winter period. One at Big Waters (NZ27G) on 1st-2nd January 1998 was the only inland occurrence during the current survey period. There was also one inland record during the earlier survey, a bird present at Whittle Dene Reservoirs between 13th-20th February 1982.

IAN FISHER

No. of tetrads in which recorded	26 (2%)

Tetrad Analysis	No. of tetrads
1 bird	14 (54%)
2-4 birds	7 (27%)
5+ birds	5 (19%)

Total No. of birds counted	72

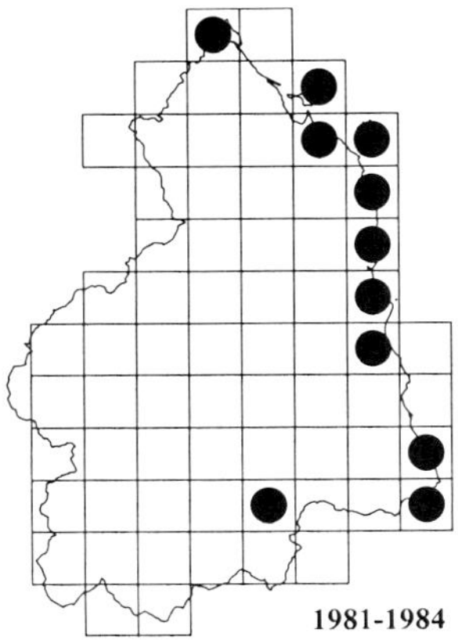

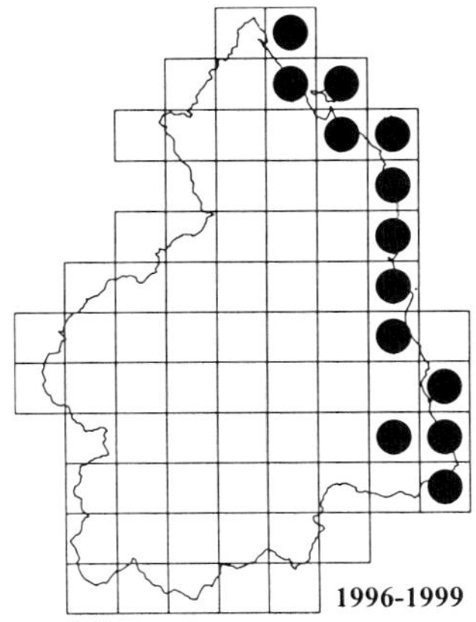

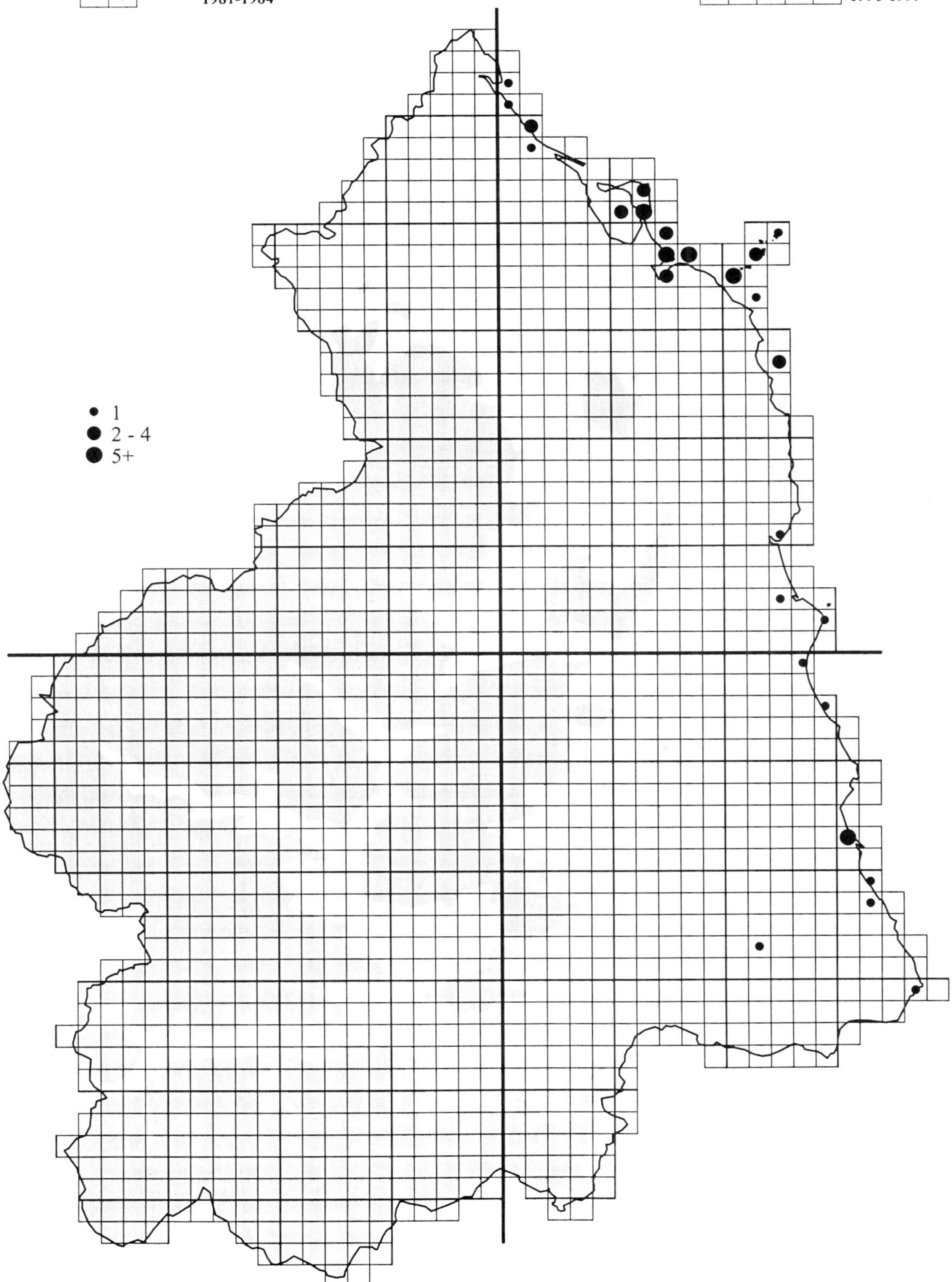

Red-necked Grebe

SLAVONIAN GREBE *Podiceps auritus*

The Slavonian Grebe, with its distinctive appearance (appropriately in winter tones of black and white) is a regular visitor to north Northumberland during the winter period. It favours inshore sandy bays, particularly around the Lindisfarne/Skate Road/Bamburgh area. Bolam (1932) described it as 'common along the coast in moderate numbers, appearing from October onwards, but usually most numerous after the New Year'. Nearly fifty years later Galloway and Meek (1978) stated that 'it is the most numerous of the winter grebes and Skate Road attracts the largest numbers' and they go on to say that 'up to 40 are present regularly ... although occasionally much larger numbers are recorded, at least a hundred on 24 February 1963, and seventy-eight on 24th March 1968, being the maxima in recent years'. Today the Lindisfarne/Skate Road/Bamburgh (NU14F/K, NU13P/T) area is still the favoured locality with some of the more sheltered bays to the south regularly attracting one to three birds.

Since the *Supplement* to Galloway and Meek (1986) annual wintering numbers have rarely exceeded 20 birds. Years in which large numbers do occur, although still nowhere near the 100 in 1963, are few and probably coincide with severe conditions in the Baltic area. Such an influx occurred in 1987 when 40 were present in the Skate Road/Stag Rocks area on 31st January with 53 present on 20th February rising to over 80 by 27th March. This last count probably included birds from further south on their northwards migration back towards the breeding grounds. Another influx occurred in 1999 when 35 were in the same area on 7th January with 54 being present at the end of the month.

During the current winter survey a total of 90 birds was counted, mainly in the species' winter stronghold of the Lindisfarne/Bamburgh area. They were found in 12 tetrads in nine 10 km squares. The total of 10 km squares is slightly lower than that of the 1981-1984 national winter atlas survey (Lack, 1986) when birds were recorded in 12 ten kilometre squares. There was only one coastal record (compared with two inland occurrences) in the south east of the county, at St. Mary's Island on 13th January 1998, with all others being along the northern half of the coastline, ranging between Hauxley and Cocklawburn.

During the current winter survey there were two inland occurrences when singles were seen at Queen Elizabeth II Country Park (NZ28Z) near Ashington on 24th November 1996 and at Whittle Dene Reservoirs (NZ06U) on 2nd January 1998. In previous years other inland records were also scarce. Just outside the survey dates a bird was recorded at Druridge Bay Country Park on 7th November 1998. Overall there have been about 70 records in all months, with nearly half in the November to February period (*Birds in Northumbria*; Galloway & Meek, 1978). Most have been on the coastal ponds of Cresswell, Druridge and Holywell but several have ventured as far west as the Bakethin Reservoir, Kielder.

It has been suggested that the slowly expanding Scottish breeding population, with 53 pairs in 1997 (Murray, 1999) but decreasing to 31 pairs in 2000 (Benn, 2001), may account for some of our wintering birds (Lack, 1986), though with the species' breeding grounds including Iceland, Scandinavia and Russia, it is more likely that these areas provide most of our winter visitors. Indeed, a bird ringed near Vologda (NW Russia) in July 1962 was recovered in Yorkshire in April 1963 (Hudson 1964).

IAN FISHER

No. of tetrads in which recorded	12 (<1%)
Tetrad Analysis	**No. of tetrads**
1 bird	6 (50%)
2-8 birds	3 (25%)
9+ birds	3 (25%)
Total No. of birds counted	90

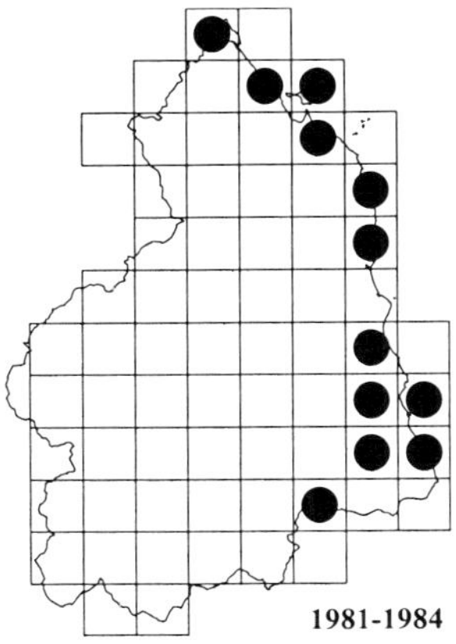

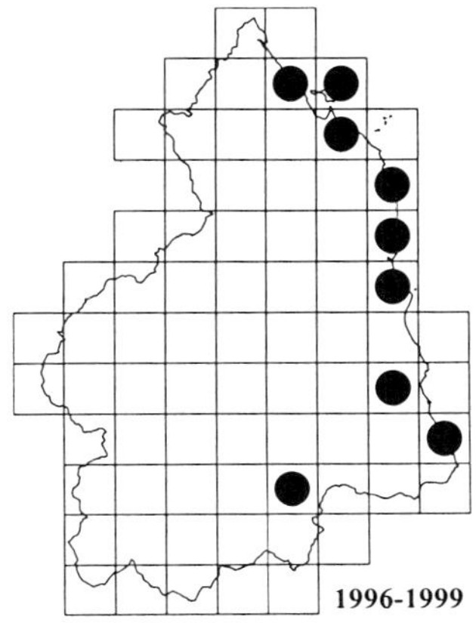

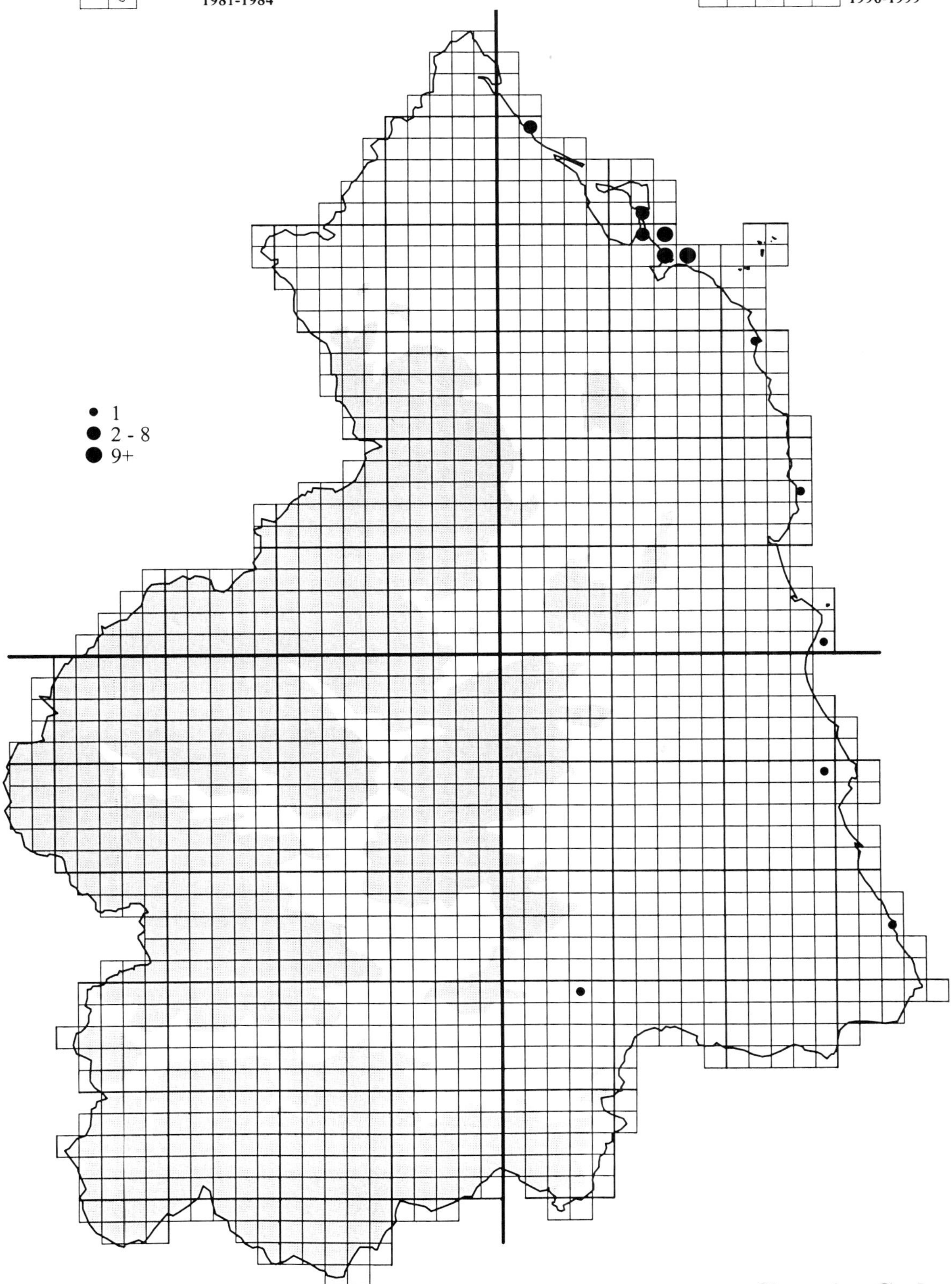

Slavonian Grebe

FULMAR *Fulmarus glacialis*

The Fulmar is essentially a maritime species and this is reflected in its almost exclusive coastal distribution during the three years of this atlas fieldwork. The species was recorded in a total of 29 tetrads ranging from Berwick (NT95W) in the north to Tynemouth (NZ36U) in the south with concentrations around Holy Island (NU14G) and the Farne Islands (NU23). It is nevertheless interesting that comparison between the earlier 10km distribution map for the period 1981-1984 and the current 10km map indicates some gaps in the coastal pattern.

Without doubt the status of Fulmar both as a wintering and breeding species has clearly changed since the days of Hancock (1874) and Bolam (1912). The former described it as a rare casual visitant and the latter simply as a casual visitant, but it was not until 1928 that breeding occurred for the first time (Galloway & Meek, 1978). Since then the breeding population has increased rapidly reflecting a marked range expansion southwards that has occurred throughout the British Isles. *The atlas of breeding birds in Northumbria* (Day *et al.*, 1995) indicates that approximately 1,100 pairs were breeding in the county by 1992. As expected perhaps, for this species, both the breeding and wintering distribution maps show considerable similarities.

However, inland sightings are increasing, presumably birds prospecting for potential nest sites as much of the available coastal habitat becomes occupied. This is reflected in records from two near-coastal tetrads during the study period at Ratcheugh Quarry, Alnwick (NU21H) and East Sleekburn (NZ28W), although the former is a long-standing breeding site.

Following the breeding season, birds disperse out to sea with some young travelling considerable distances but adults are present within feeding range of the breeding colonies during the winter (Snow & Perrins, 1998). It is the norm for some of the Northumberland Fulmar population to move out to sea, usually in September, their return often being dependent on weather conditions. This may mean that breeding sites are not re-occupied until the turn of year. It is also feasible that some coastal observations in late February/early March relate to passage birds moving to more northerly breeding sites. Examples of birds returning early to their nest sites during the winter atlas period included about 230 around the Farne Islands from mid-November 1996 (Walton, 1997). That territories can be occupied throughout the winter, with periodic dispersal only during poor weather, was also commented on in *The atlas of wintering birds in Britain and Ireland* (Lack, 1986).

With the British breeding population of the species still increasing at around 3%-4% per year (Mead, 2000), the future for this species seems secure and further increases in both the breeding and wintering populations in Northumberland can be expected.

ROBIN HARVEY

No. of tetrads in which recorded	29 (2%)

Tetrad Analysis	No. of tetrads
1-20 birds	14 (48%)
21-65 birds	10 (35%)
66+ birds	5 (17%)

Total No. of birds counted	1,062

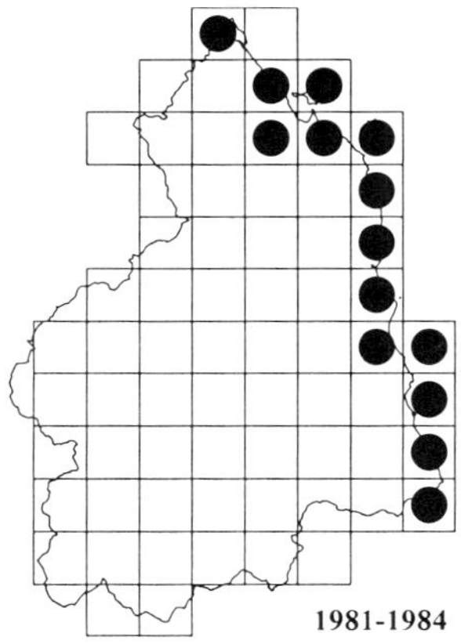

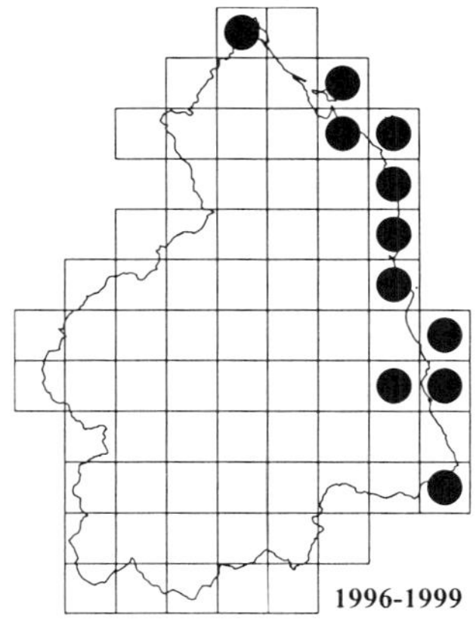

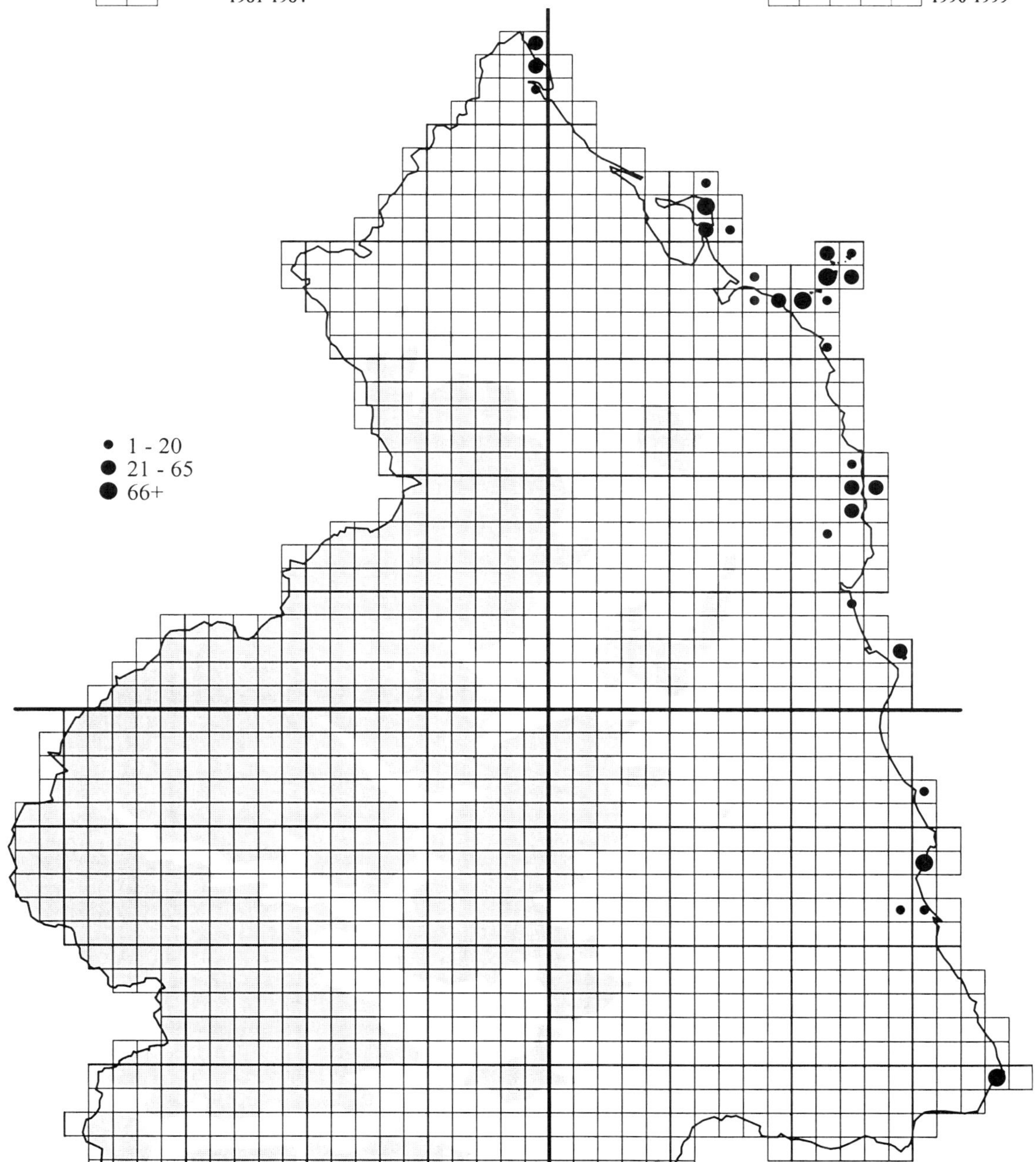

Fulmar

GANNET *Morus bassanus*

Gannets were only recorded in four tetrads during the three winters of fieldwork for this atlas with a total of only 16 individuals noted. Birds breeding in British colonies migrate south for the winter with some reaching as far as the tropical waters off West Africa (Snow & Perrins, 1998). Although a few remain in British waters, most do not return until January so a paucity of records in the winter months is to be expected. Despite this, the species is commoner off the Northumberland coast in winter than the atlas data suggest. *Birds in Northumbria 1995-1999* list the species as 'well represented' in winter with records from popular sea-watching localities such as Holy Island (NU14G), Newton Point (NU22M), Newbiggin (NZ38J) and Seaton Sluice (NZ37I) regularly recording small numbers of birds. Sightings are usually weather-dependent with the largest numbers seen during or after strong northerly or on-shore winds. Numbers are frequently in single figures in late November and through December but increase, sometimes substantially, in late January and February as birds begin to return to their more northerly breeding grounds. Examples of such passage movements during the atlas period included 50 or more birds flying north on various dates in February 1997 at St. Mary's Island (NZ37M), Newton Point and Holy Island where over 50 birds per hour moved north in late February 1998 and 25 north off Stag Rocks (NU13S) in February 1999. These records however are excluded from the tetrad distribution map because of the methodology adopted for this winter atlas survey.

With the closest breeding colonies some distance away, at Bass Rock, Lothian, with 34,000 pairs and Bempton Cliffs, Yorkshire with in excess of 1,600 pairs (Mead, 2000), there is no reason to expect a change in the species' status of abundant passage visitor (Galloway & Meek, 1978). It seems set to remain a winter scarcity in Northumberland.

ROBIN HARVEY

No. of tetrads in which recorded 4 (<1%)

Tetrad Analysis	No. of tetrads
1-4 birds	3 (75%)
5+ birds	1 (25%)

Total No. of birds counted 16

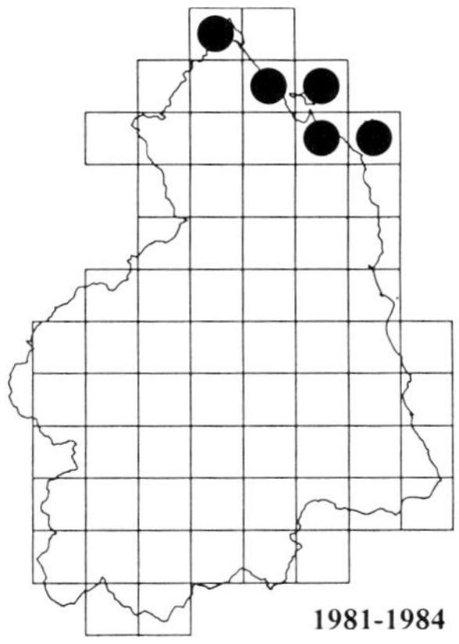

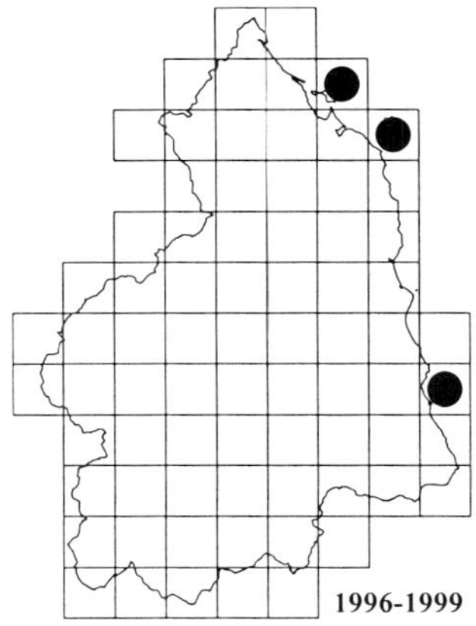

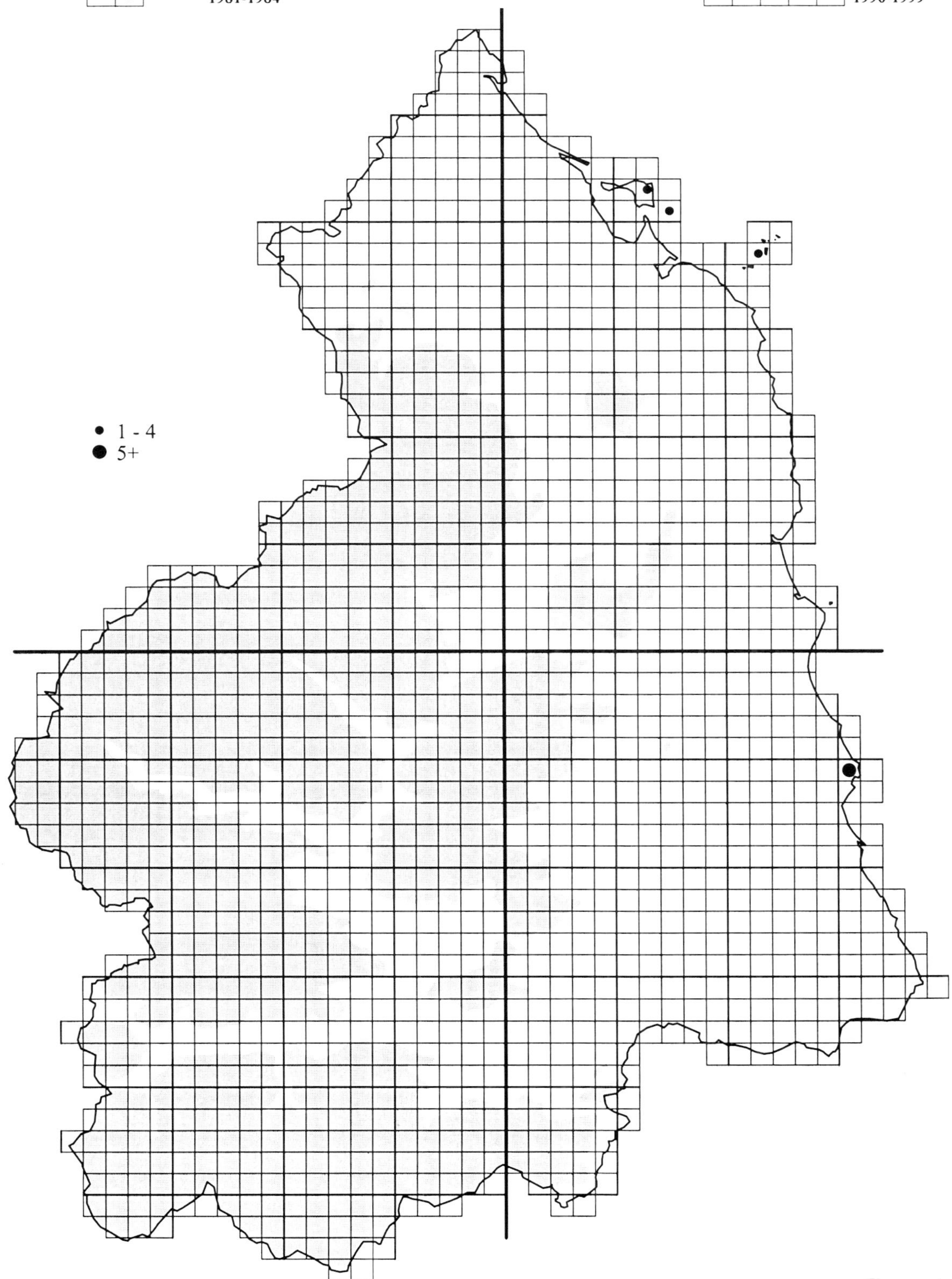

Gannet

CORMORANT *Phalacrocorax carbo*

Bolam (1912) described the Cormorant as 'a common resident on the coast', while Galloway & Meek (1978) noted it as 'a well-represented winter visitor and breeding species'. It still retains the winter status of well-represented in the county.

The tetrad distribution map shows a strong coastal spread from the north to the south, with additional obvious presence along the Rivers Tyne and Tweed and association with the loughs and reservoirs in the south west quarter of the county. There is little difference in distribution between the 10km square maps of 1981-1984 and 1996-1999. The earlier map records the species in 35 ten kilometre squares, while the later map notes its presence in 40. Of the 141 tetrads occupied during the current winter survey, 116 (82%) were below 100 metres a.s.l., 14 (10%) were from 101-200 metres a.s.l. with the remaining 11 (8%) between 201-300 metres a.s.l.

Table 1 below provides data for some of the most regularly occupied sites from the current winter survey period. In addition maximum numbers at other important inland county locations provide evidence of a substantial wintering population with 60 at Corbridge (NY96X), 20 at Hallington (NY97T), 15 at Sweethope Loughs (NY98G, NY98L) and 23 at Whittle Dene Reservoirs (NZ06T, NZ06U). There was a very large coastal count of 450 at Berwick Little Beach (NU05B) on 3 January 1999.

Winter	Tyne Estuary	Blyth Estuary	Coquet Estuary	Lindisfarne	Berwick	Colt Crag
1996/97	82	67	84	37	not known	13
1997/98	61	36	76	63	43	28
1998/99	72	66	80	77	450	not known

Table 1 Maximum counts at some feeding, resting and roosting Cormorant sites in Northumberland during the winter survey period. Data from the Northumberland & Tyneside Bird Club and additional records from Turner (unpublished).

On ringing evidence, wintering birds in Northumberland would appear to include some originating from Scottish, English and European populations as well as birds which have bred locally. A definite example of a bird of the continental race *P. c. sinensis* with a green colour ring was recorded at Blyth Harbour and Cresswell from September to October 1999 and at Blyth Harbour again in October-November 2000, having been ringed as a chick in Denmark in June 1999. Small numbers of birds showing characteristics of the *sinensis* race have been reported in the county in winter and early spring for many years although the County Records Committee does not feel that this race is identifiable in the field on present knowledge.

Lack (1986) mentioned that 'Cormorants are recorded inland mostly during the winter' and calculated a wintering population in Britain and Ireland of 20,000-25,000 birds, based on a population of 8,000 breeding pairs recorded during Operation Seafarer. Since then Lloyd *et al* (1991) have increased the earlier estimates to 11,700 pairs in 1985-1987 giving a total population of between 31,000-35,000 birds. This indicates that the count of 1,175 birds in Northumberland during this winter atlas survey represents a significant percentage of the UK population.

DANIEL M. TURNER

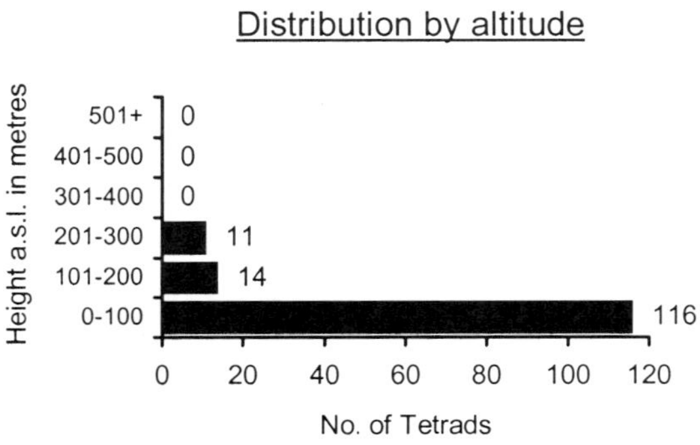

No. of tetrads in which recorded	141 (10%)
Tetrad Analysis	**No. of tetrads**
1-2 birds	71 (50%)
3-8 birds	41 (29%)
9+ birds	29 (21%)
Total No. of birds counted	1,175

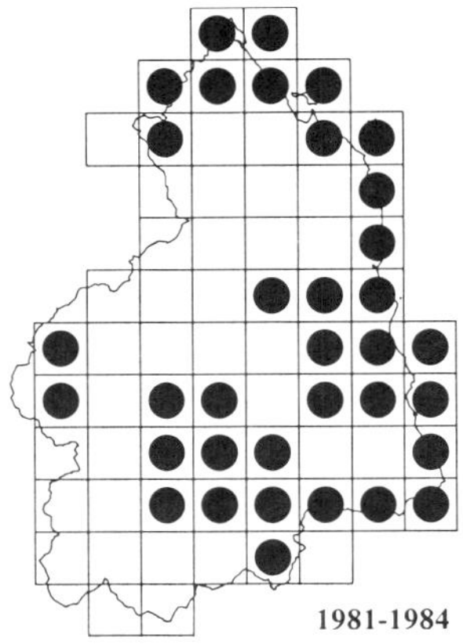

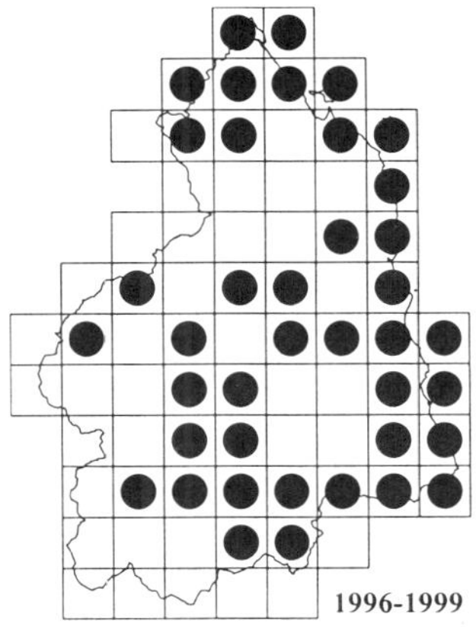

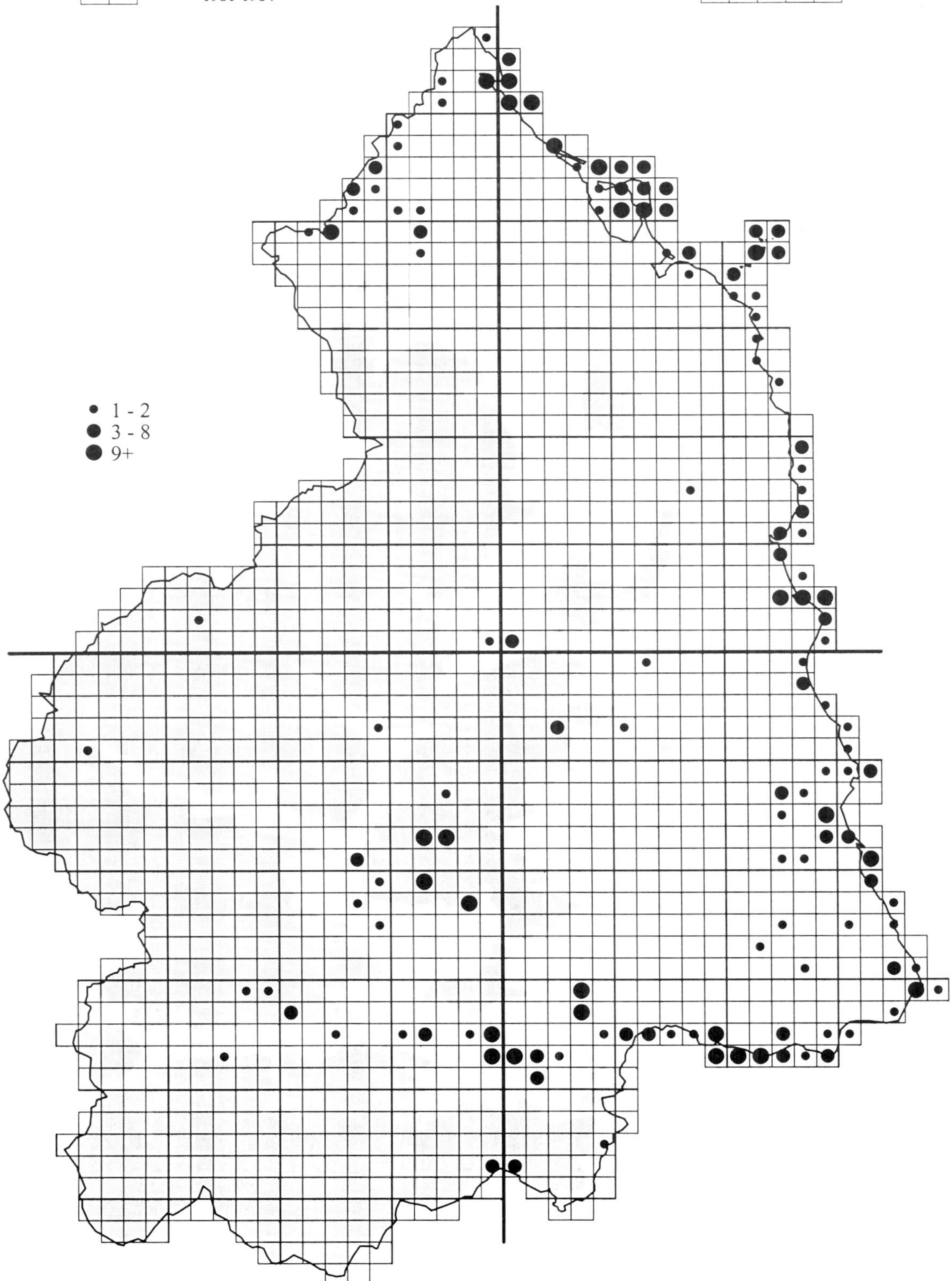

Cormorant

SHAG *Phalacrocorax aristotelis*

The Shag is a well-represented breeding species in the county with almost the entire population concentrated at one locality, the Farne Islands. During the breeding seasons immediately preceding the three winter periods of the current survey the colonies on these islands held 994, 1,060 and 1,000 nesting pairs respectively. Cramp and Simmons (1977) mentioned that adult Shags were present all year on the Farnes with juveniles dispersing by mid-October when an influx of juveniles from other colonies occurred. In addition, Hawkey (1991) also said that they were present all year with large numbers feeding around the islands during the winter months and included the total of about 2,500 birds in November and December 1988. It is not surprising, therefore, that the largest numbers during the winter atlas period came from tetrads in this area, between two-six kilometres offshore, with four providing counts of between 193 to 514 (NU23C/I/N/P). Two of these squares were the subject of 'control' visits in each of the winter periods and, although numbers were lower in the middle winter, gave an average of 242 and 303 birds. It should perhaps be noted that these counts were in the very early part of the winter before early December when the seasonal wardens vacate the islands.

The tetrad map shows that the bulk of the rest of the wintering population is present along the northern half of the county's coastline with particular concentrations northwards away from the Farnes past Bamburgh, Ross Back Sands, Holy Island and the Tweed Estuary. Indeed the next largest count was some 300 concentrated with other seabirds off Spittal (NU05A & NU05B) in early January 1999 as a result presumably of good feeding conditions. Numbers seem to decrease southwards from the Farnes and distribution along the coast becomes patchy. A comparison between the two 10km square maps would appear to show a similar distribution in the two surveys but this masks an indication of some recent increase in the numbers wintering along the southern half of the coastline including as many as 23 in Blyth Bay (NZ37J) in February 1999.

It was not until the early part of the twentieth century that large numbers of Shags began to winter off the North Northumberland coast (Bolam, 1932; Galloway & Meek, 1978) with the latter authors showing from ringing studies that many arrived during September, including an appreciable proportion of immatures from the Firth of Forth colonies. In addition, in their 1986 *Supplement* they quoted a very large total of 5,174 around the Farnes on 4th December 1984. This pattern fits in nicely with the national perspective reported by Lack (1986) who said that very few British or Irish Shags leave the country during the winter and there is little evidence of birds arriving from the continent. In most years, adults remain within 100km of their breeding colonies while immatures move up to 200km. He put the British and Irish mid-winter population at between 100,000 and 150,000 birds.

During the three winter periods of the current survey there was no indication of abnormal numbers present along the county's coastline and no 'wrecks', to which this species is occasionally prone, occurred. It seems likely that some birds will have been missed particularly during timed visits depending on such factors as how far from the shore they were feeding and tidal and weather conditions at the time but, with total counts of 2,155 being made, it would be reasonable to suggest that the wintering population might be in the range of 2,000-4,000 birds.

MIKE S. HODGSON

No. of tetrads in which recorded 52 (4%)

Tetrad Analysis	No. of tetrads
1-3 birds	26 (50%)
4-30 birds	16 (31%)
31+ birds	10 (19%)

Total No. of birds counted 2,155

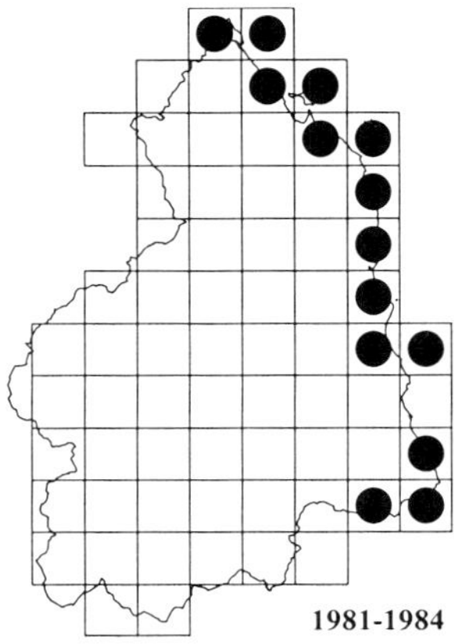

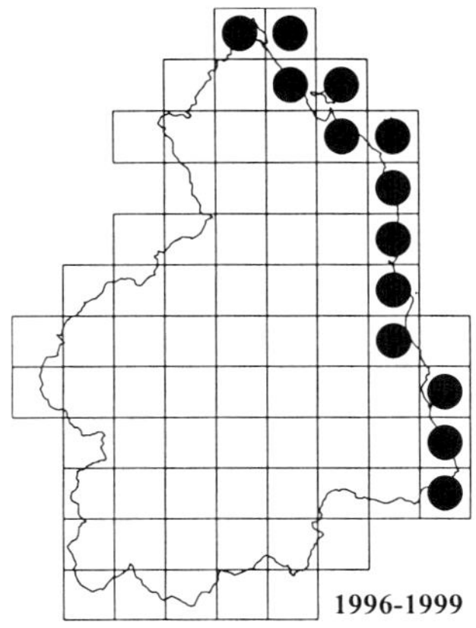

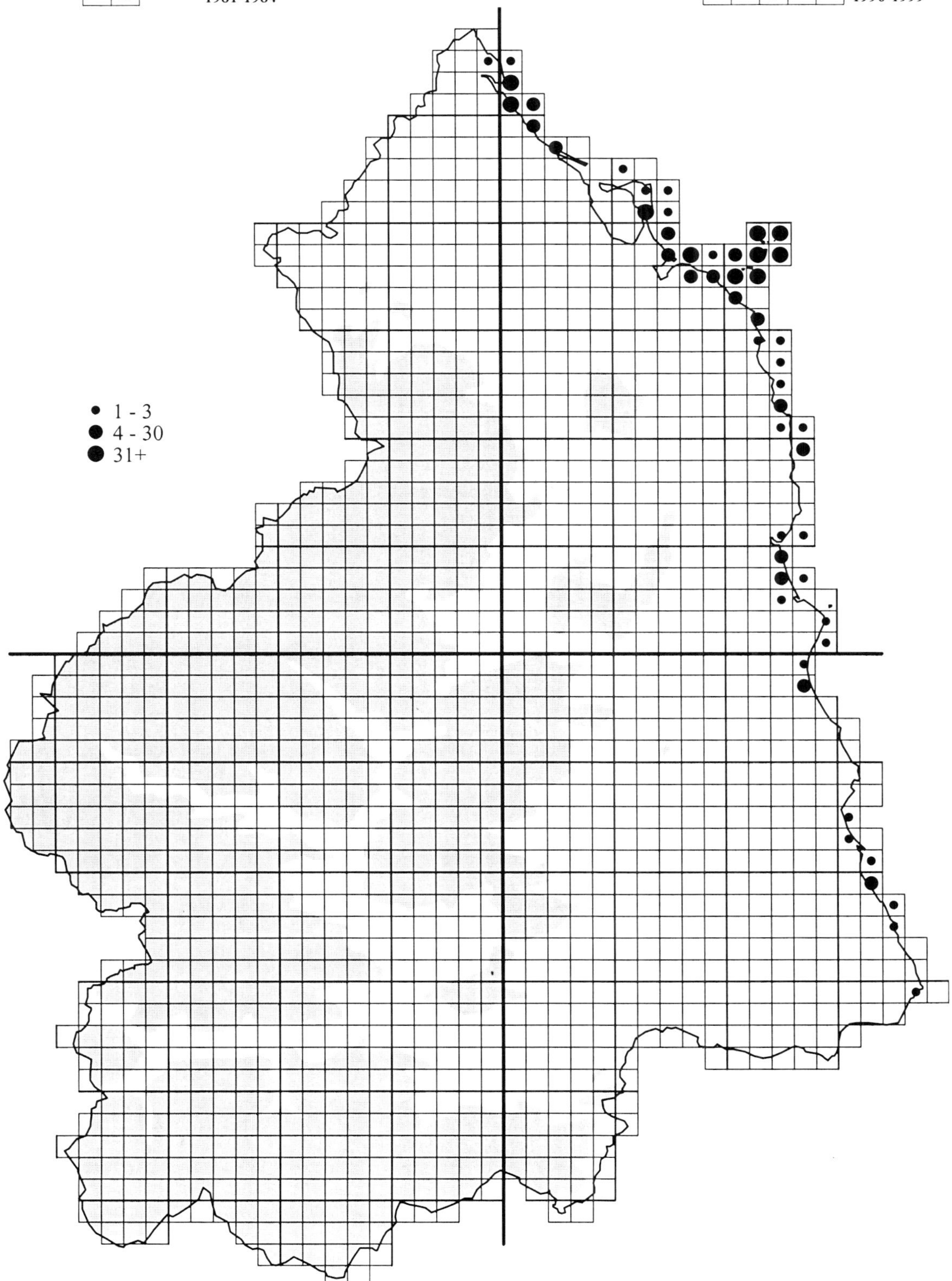

Shag

BITTERN *Botaurus stellaris*

At the end of the nineteenth century Bolam (1912) regarded the Bittern as 'once a common resident ... now reduced to the rank of only a casual visitor ... though a year seldom passes without one'. By the 1930s he felt that its status had declined to that of 'an irregular winter visitant' (Bolam, 1932), and Galloway and Meek (1978) concurred with this view. Lack (1986), in *The atlas of wintering birds in Britain and Ireland* stated that the majority of wintering Bittern in the UK were of north west European origin, although he noted that numbers each year depended on the severity of continental winters. It was estimated that nationally between 50 and 150 individual birds might winter here, the majority being found south of a line from the Humber to the Mersey. Nevertheless, single birds and occasionally two visit Northumberland in many winters. In the last decade of the twentieth century birds were present in the winters of 1990/1, 1993/4, 1996/7, 1998/9 and 1999/2000. Specifically during the winter survey period single individuals were at Cragside (NU00R) in December 1996, Big Waters (NZ27G) in January 1999 and Caistron (NU00A) in February 1999, with two present at Holywell Pond in January 1997. The Big Waters bird was found dead at the site, a not uncommon fate for emaciated birds in hard weather. Whilst there does not seem to be any wintering pattern within the recording area, Holywell Pond and Caistron Reserve have more Bittern sightings than any other locality, although the latter is well inland and Holywell virtually within sight of the sea. Earlier Bittern records in the 1980s show an equally diverse distribution pattern with almost as many birds on inland waters as at coastal sites.

JOHN C. DAY

No. of tetrads in which recorded 4 (<1%)

Tetrad Analysis	No. of tetrads
1 bird	3 (75%)
2 birds	1 (25%)

Total No. of birds counted 5

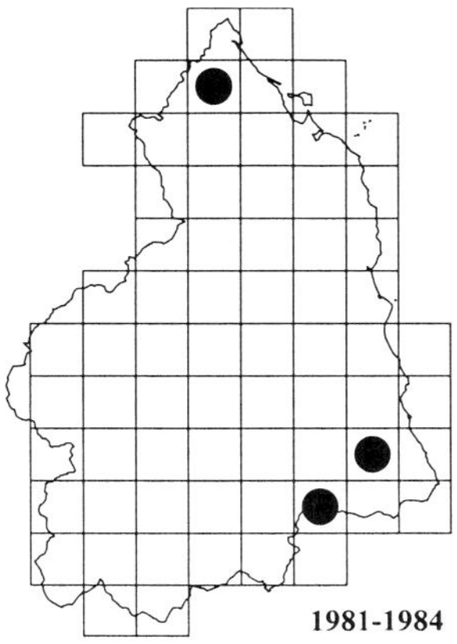

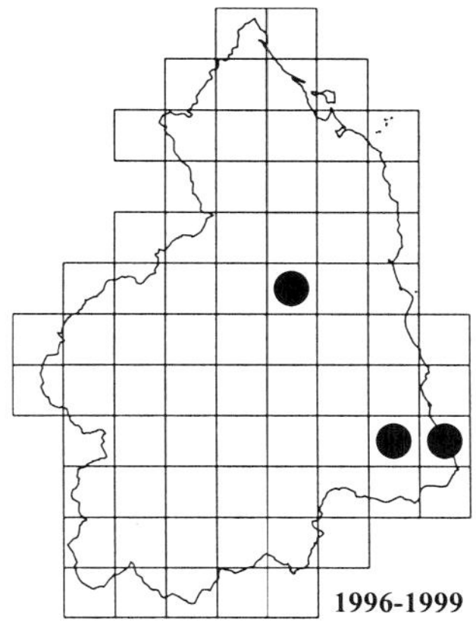

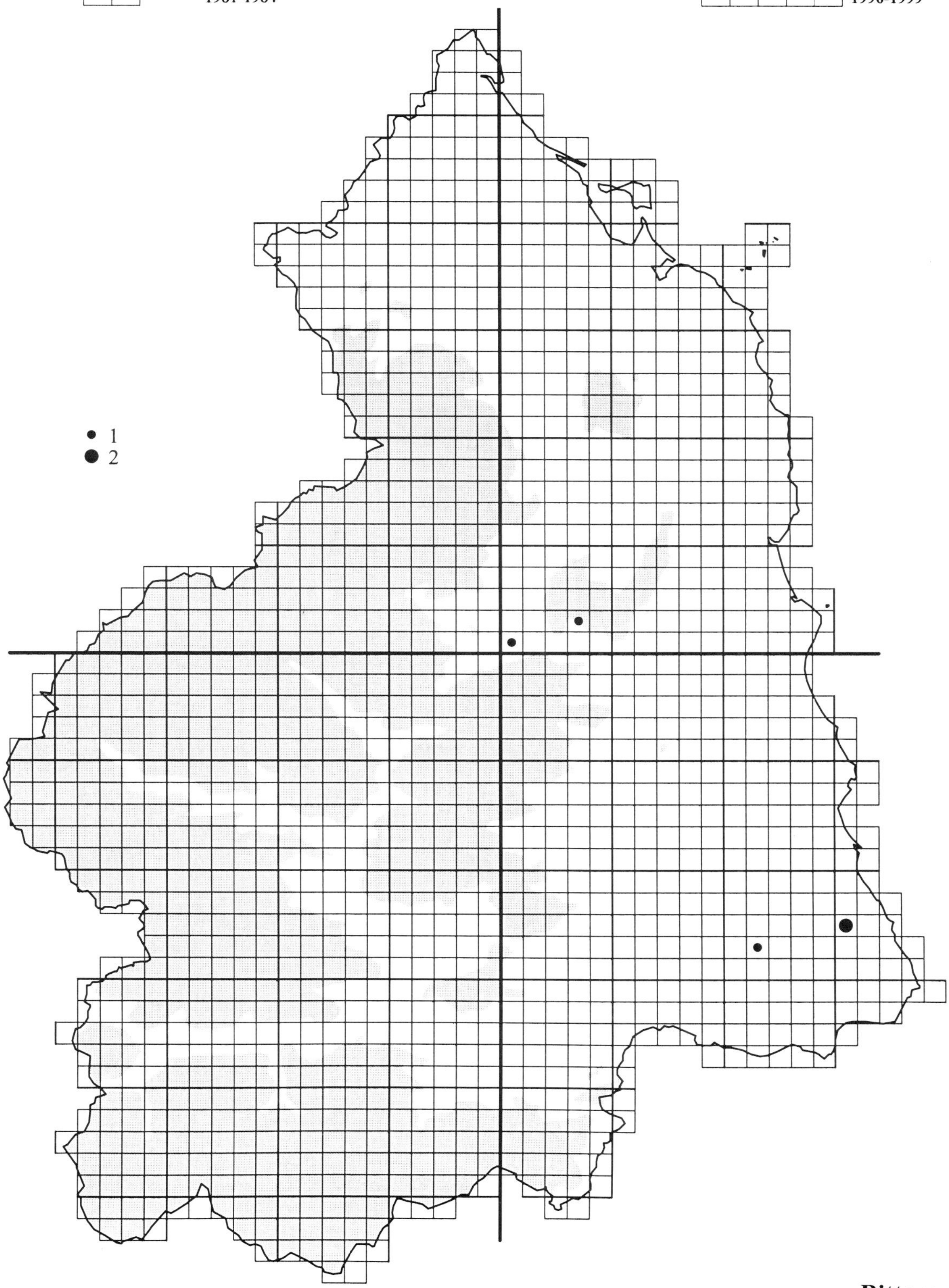

Bittern

GREY HERON *Ardea cinerea*

The BTO has undertaken research on the Grey Heron over a longer period of time than for any other species in the British Isles. Although there have been problems at times in carrying out survey work, due to difficulty of access, this has resulted in the accumulation of an enormous amount of data on the species. Historically, both Hancock (1874) and Bolam (1932) described it as a common but declining resident in Northumberland. However, BTO data collected in 1928 indicated a steeper decrease in the county population than appreciated by Bolam (Galloway & Meek, 1978). Declines were attributed to the destruction by felling of the large trees used by nesting colonies, and was accelerated during and immediately after the Second World War. This, coupled with the very severe winter of 1962/63, lead to the species reaching its lowest ebb in the county (in common with the rest of the country) during the mid-1960s. Since then numbers have recovered throughout the UK. Hagemeijer and Blair (1997) estimated that the British breeding population was in excess of 10,000 pairs while Snow and Perrins (1998) described the British and Irish breeding birds as the sole non-migratory population within Europe, showing only nomadic movements mainly within 150 km of natal heronries.

In total, a maximum of 561 birds was counted during fieldwork for this winter survey which compares closely with the 234 breeding pairs located during fieldwork for *The atlas of breeding birds in Northumbria* (Day *et al.*, 1995). This correlation is interesting given the evidence, afforded by the recovery of ringed nestlings from Norway and Sweden, that Scandinavian Grey Herons swell the wintering population in the recording area. Other recoveries have also indicated that dispersal from other parts of Britain has occurred post-breeding with, for example, birds ringed in Suffolk being recorded in the county. Conversely locally bred birds have been recovered from Ayrshire, Glamorganshire, Leicestershire and Lincolnshire (Galloway & Meek, 1978).

Unsurprisingly, the survey demonstrated that the population is more widely dispersed during winter with birds recorded in 327 tetrads (23% of the 1,432 surveyed) than in the breeding season when only 176 tetrads (13% of 1,410 surveyed) were occupied. They were located mainly in the lowland areas of the county with 83% of the records in tetrads below 200 metres a.s.l. Single birds accounted for 70% of the records with a further 17% representing only two birds. Gatherings of ten or more birds were recorded on only five occasions with the largest being 20 at a roost site on the Blyth Estuary (NZ28W) in January 1999, and two gatherings of 13 birds on the Tweed Estuary (NT95W) and at North Sunderland (NU23A). These results may appear contrary to those given in *Birds in Northumbria* which consistently highlight the Tweed Estuary as being a favoured wintering location in the county throughout the 1990s with gatherings well in excess of 20 birds annually between November and February. As the three winters of the survey were comparatively mild, perhaps the Grey Herons on the Tweed were more widely dispersed.

The species was recorded in 31 control tetrads although only four (13%) held birds in all three survey seasons, 11 (35%) during two seasons and 16 (52%) in one season only. Again, interestingly, a control tetrad adjacent to the River Tweed (NT95R) contained birds in only two seasons, seven in 1997/98 and ten in 1998/99. These records serve to demonstrate the difficulties of census work, the influence of methodology on results and the caution necessary in drawing conclusions from data obtained. It is, however, appropriate to describe the Grey Heron in Northumberland as well-represented in winter.

BRIAN SYKES

Distribution by altitude

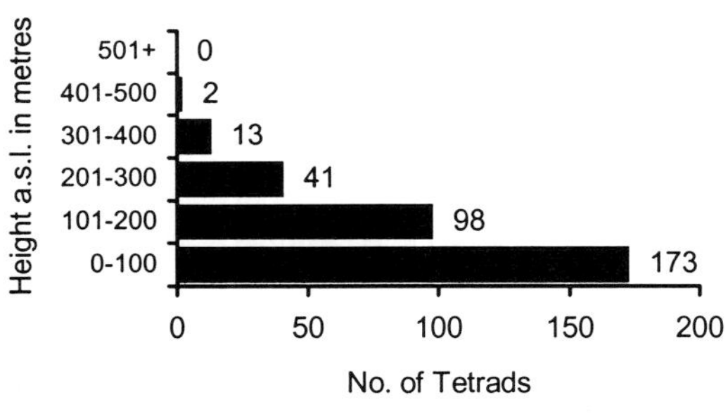

No. of tetrads in which recorded 327 (23%)

Tetrad Analysis	No. of tetrads
1 bird	230 (70%)
2 birds	56 (17%)
3+ birds	41 (13%)

Total No. of birds counted 561

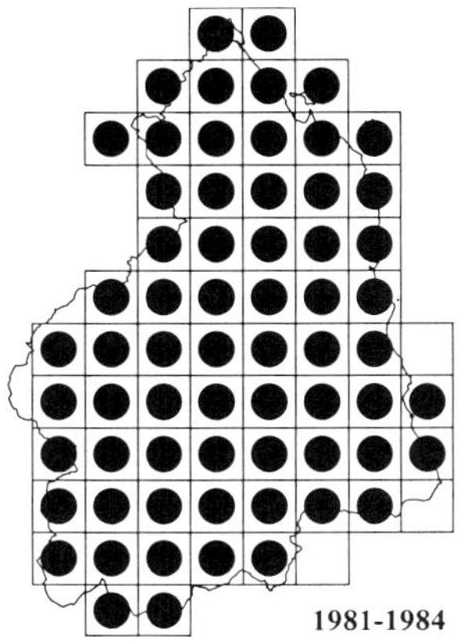

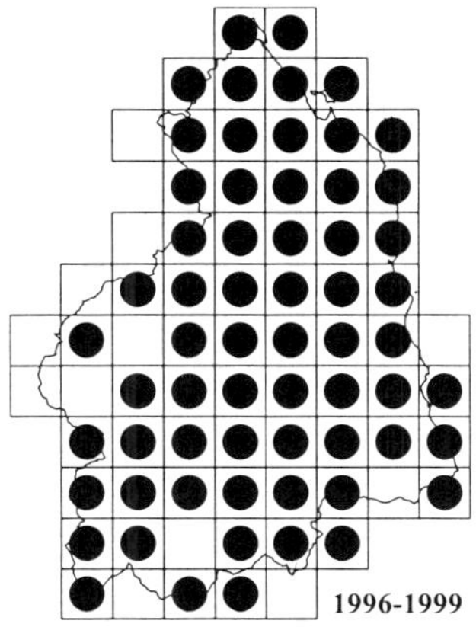

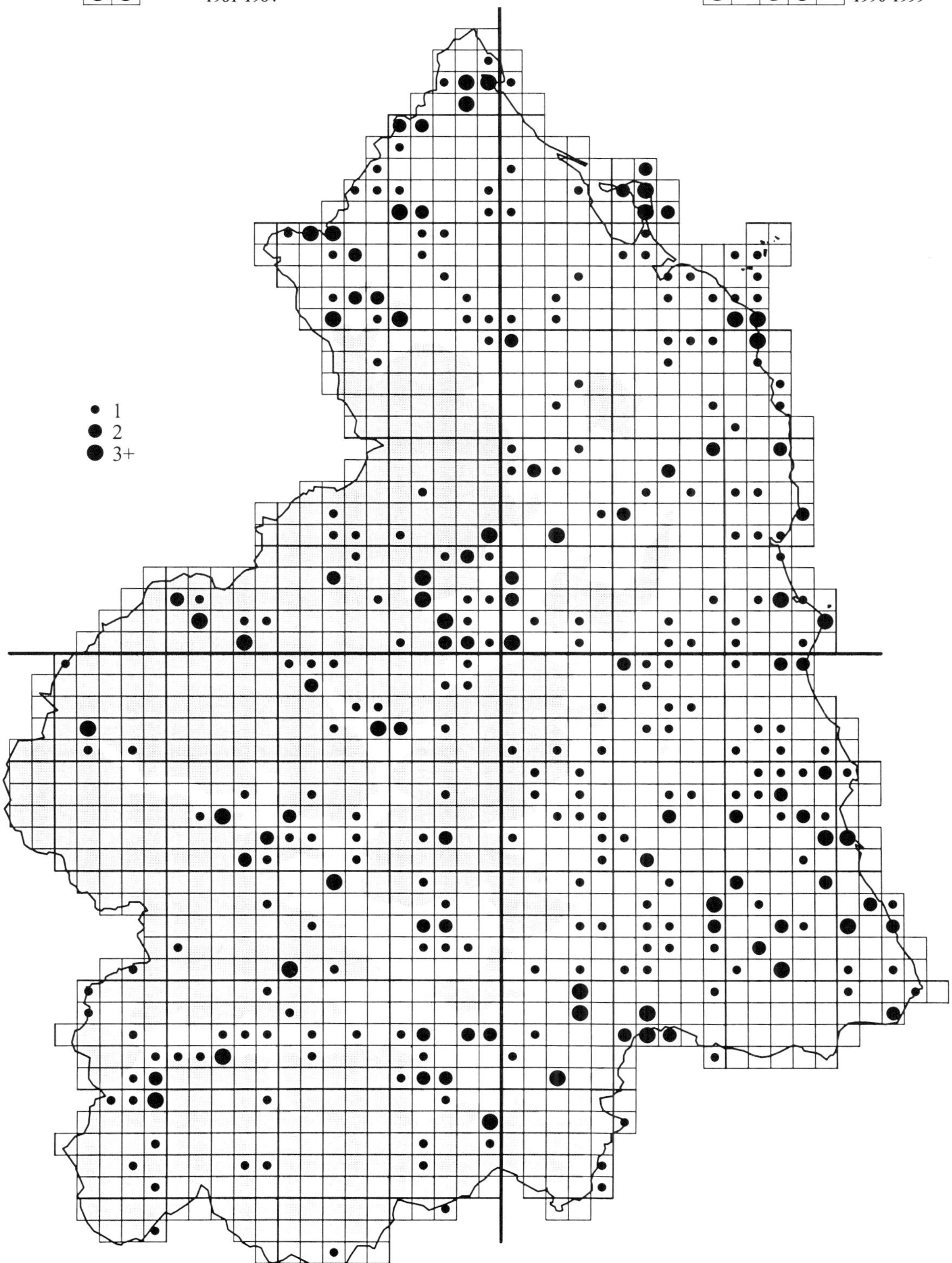

Grey Heron

WINTERING WILDFOWL IN NORTHUMBERLAND

Graeme Bowman

A total of 29 species of wildfowl can typically be found in the county during the winter period. This involves three species of swans, six of geese and 20 of ducks. Amongst the scarcer species in this total are Bewick's Swan *Cygnus columbianus*, White-fronted Goose *Anser albifrons*, Mandarin *Aix galericulata*, Scaup *Aythya marila*, Velvet Scoter *Melanitta fusca*, Smew *Mergellus albellus* and Ruddy Duck *Oxyura jamaicensis*. In addition, Bean Goose *Anser fabalis* is erratically recorded most winters, although it has no consistently regular wintering site. Several rarer wildfowl species occur occasionally. Examples recorded over this atlas period were Snow Goose *Anser caerulescens*, American Wigeon *Anas americana*, Green-winged Teal *Anas carolinensis* and Blue-winged Teal *Anas discors*.

The importance of key areas for wildfowl (and wading birds) is demonstrated by the designation of the Lindisfarne NNR, Holburn Lake and Moss and the Northumbria Coast as Ramsar sites and Special Protection Areas (SPAs), which include many SSSIs. During the period of the atlas fieldwork many coastal areas also became candidates for consideration as Special Areas of Conservation (SACs), under the Natura 2000 European Habitats Directive. Such designations are based on several criteria including waterbird counts undertaken for the Wetland Bird Survey (WeBS). A summary table of important sites and species numbers appears in Appendix I.

The single most important locality within the county for wildfowl in general is the Lindisfarne NNR. This extensive site holds several thousand birds during the winter period and over 10,000 at peak times. Internationally important numbers of pale-bellied Brent Geese *Branta bernicla hrota* can be found with, for example, a peak of 4,092 in January 1997 representing almost the entire Svalbard population of this race. Shelduck *Tadorna tadorna*, Wigeon *Anas penelope*, Eider *Somateria mollissima* and Common Scoter *Melanitta nigra* are also present in nationally important numbers whilst, within a county context, Lindisfarne also holds significant populations of Greylag Geese *Anser anser*, Teal *Anas crecca*, Mallard *Anas platyrhynchos*, Pintail *Anas acuta* and Long-tailed Duck *Clangula hyemalis*. The vast majority of Pintail can be found in the Fenham Flats area of Lindisfarne with only a few being found elsewhere in the county.

Pink-footed Geese *Anser brachyrhynchus* have become more numerous since the early 1990s and numbers in the Lindisfarne-Holburn Moss-Milfield Plain area are now of international importance with a WeBS peak count at Holburn Moss for winter 1997/98 of 4,500. Whooper Swans *Cygnus cygnus* are present in nationally important numbers in up to five distinct areas at Caistron-Thropton, Druridge Bay, Hartburn, Lindisfarne and the Tweed Valley. Numbers at specific sites within these broad areas vary from year to year according to factors such as crop availability and disturbance.

Other important sites can be broadly divided into open coast, estuaries, rivers, lowland lakes and ponds, and upland waters such as loughs and reservoirs.

Typical coastal species, such as Eider, Long-tailed Duck, Common Scoter and Red-breasted Merganser *Mergus serrator*, are generally found in greater concentrations in the northern half of the county. The most productive stretches for Eider are Seahouses-Budle Point, the Farne Islands and, to a lesser extent, the Amble and North Blyth areas. The coastline from Seahouses north to Spittal (including Lindisfarne), and in particularly the Stag Rocks-Ross Back Sands stretch, is generally more productive for marine ducks than that to the south. Exceptions include the Druridge Bay area and North Blyth-Cambois, which can attract notable counts of Common Scoters and Red-breasted Mergansers. Localised and temporary food abundance can attract above average numbers. An evident concentration of fish off Spittal in January 1999, for instance, produced counts of 100 Red-breasted Mergansers and 74 Goosanders *Mergus merganser*.

Of the major estuaries, the Blyth, Coquet and Tweed are most significant. The latter is particularly important for Goldeneye *Bucephala clangula* with 804 in January 1997, the largest concentration ever recorded in the county, and to a lesser extent also holds smaller numbers of Goosanders. Away from Lindisfarne, the Blyth Estuary is the next most favoured site for Shelduck. The major estuaries can act as a refuge for a variety of wildfowl during periods of prolonged hard weather.

The rivers Tyne, Tweed and Wansbeck are also important for certain species. Large counts of Goldeneye and Goosanders occur along the Tyne, particularly between Newburn and Wylam, and the tidal mudflats in the Scotswood area are attracting increasing numbers of Teal. The Tweed Valley also holds important numbers of Goldeneye and Goosanders, whilst the Castle Island section of the Wansbeck sometimes holds large gatherings of Goldeneye. This latter flock appears to commute between the river and the offshore sewage outfall at Cambois. The 'clean-up' of this outfall is expected to lead to a reduction in rich feeding conditions and may see a decline in bird numbers, particularly Goldeneye. Other river systems, such as the Till, can attract high counts of wildfowl like Mallard, although they may be scattered over a wide area. The often flat and relatively lush land bordering rivers can be good for grazing birds, such as Whooper Swans along the Tweed Valley.

As a combined unit the many ponds, lakes and reservoirs within the region hold more wildfowl in total than the Lindisfarne NNR. Amongst the most important locations for these wildfowl totals are Caistron and the recently created pools at East Chevington, both sites regularly holding in excess of 1,000 birds. The latter site is likely to become less significant for wildfowl as a planned *Phragmites* reedbed takes shape. Other noted sites include Big Waters, Bothal Pond, Capheaton Lake, Colt Crag Reservoir, Cresswell Pond, Druridge Pools, Gosforth Park, Grindon Lough and Holywell Pond. It is worth noting the benefit that the coal mining industry has had for wildfowl with major sites, such as the Druridge Bay nature reserves, being created following the end of opencast mining operations, and many other ponds elsewhere formed through mining subsidence.

The largest water body in the county, Kielder Water, is negligible in terms of attractiveness to wintering wildfowl. Grindon Lough regularly hosts large numbers of Canada Geese *Branta canadensis*, Wigeon and Teal, and occasionally small numbers of Pintail, but the loughs at Broomlee and Greenlee are, by comparison, less important. The reservoirs at Colt Crag, Hallington and Whittle Dene are also attractive to wildfowl to varying degrees, the last named holding a regular Goosander roost.

Favoured sites for fresh water diving ducks, such as Pochard *Aythya ferina* and Tufted Duck *Aythya fuligula*, include East Chevington, Holywell Pond, Marden Quarry, and Ladyburn Lake and Queen Elizabeth II Country Park. Smew can be found at inland haunts such as Whittle Dene or Colt Crag but are more frequent on waters along the coastal strip with the Druridge Pools-East Chevington-Ladyburn Lake-Hauxley area being especially favoured. This conglomeration along the length of Druridge Bay between Cresswell Pond and Hauxley Nature Reserve, together with the immediate hinterland and the offshore waters, can often be the best general area in the county for concentrating the greatest variety of wintering wildfowl species, followed by the Lindisfarne NNR.

Winter weather, both in the county and outside it, can have a dramatic effect on wildfowl populations and movements. Prolonged hard weather with sub-zero temperatures often forces birds away from inland waters as they freeze over. Diving species, such as Pochard and Tufted Ducks, are regularly the first to abandon in search of unfrozen waters, and may resort to rivers and estuaries under such circumstances. Surface feeding wildfowl, Wigeon, Teal and Mallard for example, are more likely to remain until a thaw occurs. Severe weather on the continent can result in an influx of various wildfowl in above average numbers. Typical examples include White-fronted Goose, Scaup and Smew.

Populations of the various wildfowl species are not constant throughout the winter period. A pattern revealed by WeBS counts at Lindisfarne, and mirrored at inland sites, sees a peak in total numbers in December and a gradual decline through January and into February. It is also worth noting that for some species, such as Wigeon at Lindisfarne NNR, the temporary influx of birds in September-October greatly outnumbers those that remain to over-winter.

General trends show increases in the populations of Pink-footed Goose, Canada Goose, Mandarin and Gadwall *Anas strepera*, and decreases for Pochard, Tufted Duck, Scaup and Velvet Scoter. Peak concentrations for Pochard and Tufted Duck are becoming noticeably smaller and three figure counts at any one site for either species are quite uncommon.

The impact of controlled hunting of those species on the quarry list is uncertain. Its effect on Wigeon may be detrimental as mean counts of this main target for wildfowlers at Lindisfarne have declined over the 1990s. However, while the Lindisfarne count has fallen, numbers at sites free from shooting disturbance have increased. The introduction of a temporary refuge on part of the reserve, denying access to all, between September 1997 and February 2000 produced a small change in fortunes. Mallard figures at some inland sites may also be exaggerated by the release of hand-reared birds.

Increasingly mild winter weather may have the effect of discouraging long-distance movement to former wintering areas, and encouraging birds to stay closer to their breeding sites. What is certain is that wildfowl distribution and population size are dynamic and constantly changing. One example of this has been the withdrawal of regular Whooper Swan flocks in the south east of the county, away from the Druridge Bay area. The former strongholds of Big Waters, Prestwick Carr, and Holywell Pond have been completely abandoned and any records at all from these sites are now considered noteworthy.

MUTE SWAN *Cygnus olor*

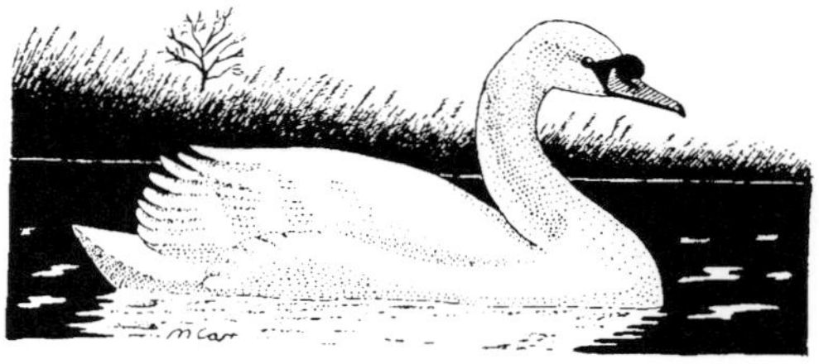

The Mute Swan is Britain's largest bird and the only common resident of the three species of wild swan recorded in Britain. Its large size and readiness to associate with man has made it one of the most popular and well known birds in the country despite some conflicts with fishing and agricultural interests. Data collected over the three winters for this atlas survey show that the Mute Swan is a well-represented winter resident. Records in the early part of the 1900s suggested the Mute Swan was a relatively common species. Galloway & Meek (1978) highlighted a decline at Lindisfarne NNR in the 1970s. Since then, however, the population has increased through to the present day. The evidence in Northumberland is reflected nationwide with the 1955/56 survey providing a national estimate of 21,000 birds decreasing to 18,000 birds in 1978 and increasing to an estimated 25,000 in the 1990 census (Kirby *et al.*, 1994). The recent expansion has been attributed to milder winter weather allowing greater survival of juveniles and the provision of more breeding habitat as a result of man-made water bodies (Coleman *et al.*, 2001).

In winter, non-breeding birds are normally gregarious and from October onwards juveniles leaving their natal sites augment the numbers of birds in the wintering herds. Most juveniles disperse in October and November of their year of hatching but some leave the natal site as late as March and April. By contrast many breeding pairs remain on their territories throughout the winter, only leaving in the most severe weather conditions (pers. obs.). Many of the smaller concentrations of birds shown on the tetrad map probably refer to individual pairs and siblings on or near their territories. The Mute Swan shows a preference for low altitudes, with birds avoiding land over 300 metres a.s.l. (Lack, 1986), and this is reflected in the local winter distribution. Most flock sites are on the coastal plain with some flocks occurring further inland along the main river valleys. Those few sites occurring over 200 metres a.s.l. are closely associated with river valleys, and no birds were recorded above 300 metres a.s.l. Indeed, 79% of all occupied tetrads were below 100 metres a.s.l.

Most flocks occur on either estuaries such as the Tweed (NT95W/NU05B) and Coquet (NU20S) or on still water sites such as Killingworth Lake (NZ27Q) which are traditionally used each year. Gatherings normally number less than 50 birds, the exception being the Tweed Estuary where upwards of 100 may often be seen. Birds on these sites often take advantage of artificial feeding by the general public to supplement their natural vegetarian diets, although some flocks do remain remote from human habitation. In cold weather, numbers in tame flocks increase significantly as birds become more dependent on handouts. By contrast, a number of flocks also occur on agricultural land. Although always close to water for roosting, the birds in these flocks spend their daylight hours grazing on winter crops. The favoured crop is oil seed rape and flocks often change location between winters, following the crop as it is rotated between fields. These birds, in contrast to their more aquatic counterparts, normally remain wild throughout the winter. Field-feeding flocks are particularly common along the Tweed Valley but also occur along the Coquet Valley and in the Druridge Bay area. Often they associate with wintering Whooper Swans *C. cygnus* forming mixed flocks that exceed 100 individuals. Combined with the population increase in Mute Swans this field-feeding behaviour is causing increasing concern among farmers. Winter movements, as established through extensive colour ringing in the region, indicate that most are of relatively short distance with birds in the north normally moving along the Tweed Valley and those further south moving between local flocks throughout the winter.

Birds were recorded in a total of 143 tetrads during the three year period with the total of maximum counts indicating a population of 1,224. However, due to the mobile nature of field-feeding flocks this is likely to be an overestimate. The counts in control tetrads give some indication of the mobile nature of swans in winter with only three of 17 squares containing swans in every year. Independent winter surveys, undertaken each year, suggest an average population over the three winter periods of 702 birds. This is further confirmed by independent spring surveys, of all flocks and breeding locations, which suggest an average over the three years of 775 (Coleman, unpub. data). The maximum count of 1,224 therefore is likely to be an overestimate of between 37%-43% for the region.

JON COLEMAN

Distribution by altitude

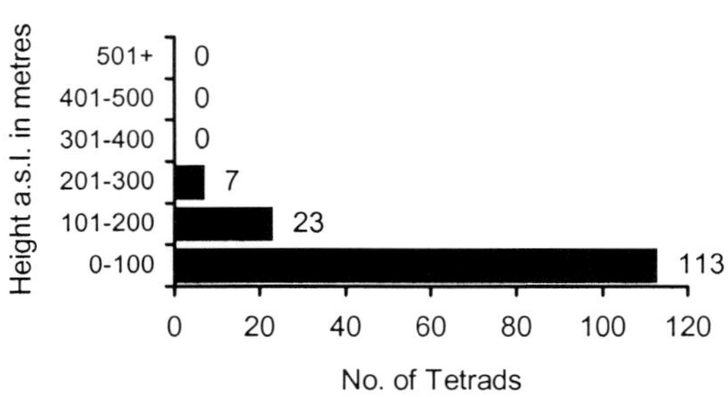

No. of tetrads in which recorded 143 (10%)

Tetrad Analysis	No. of tetrads
1-2 birds	67 (47%)
3-9 birds	46 (32%)
10+ birds	30 (21%)

Total No. of birds counted 1,224

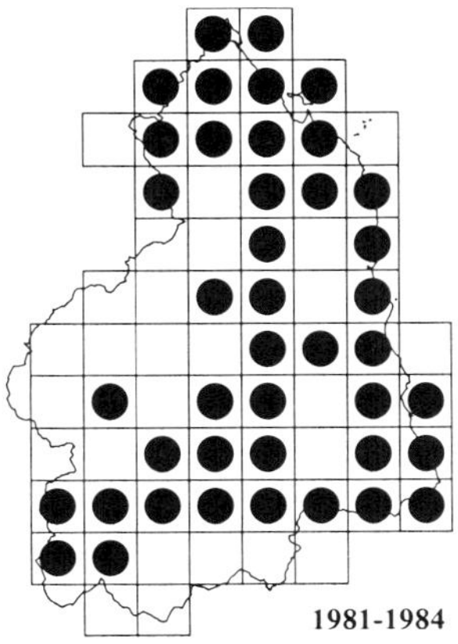

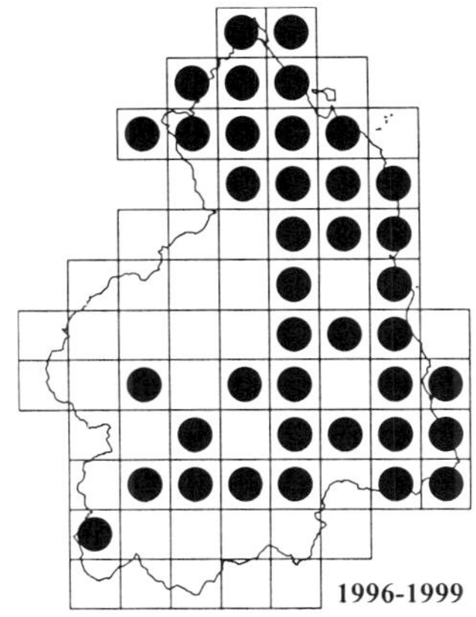

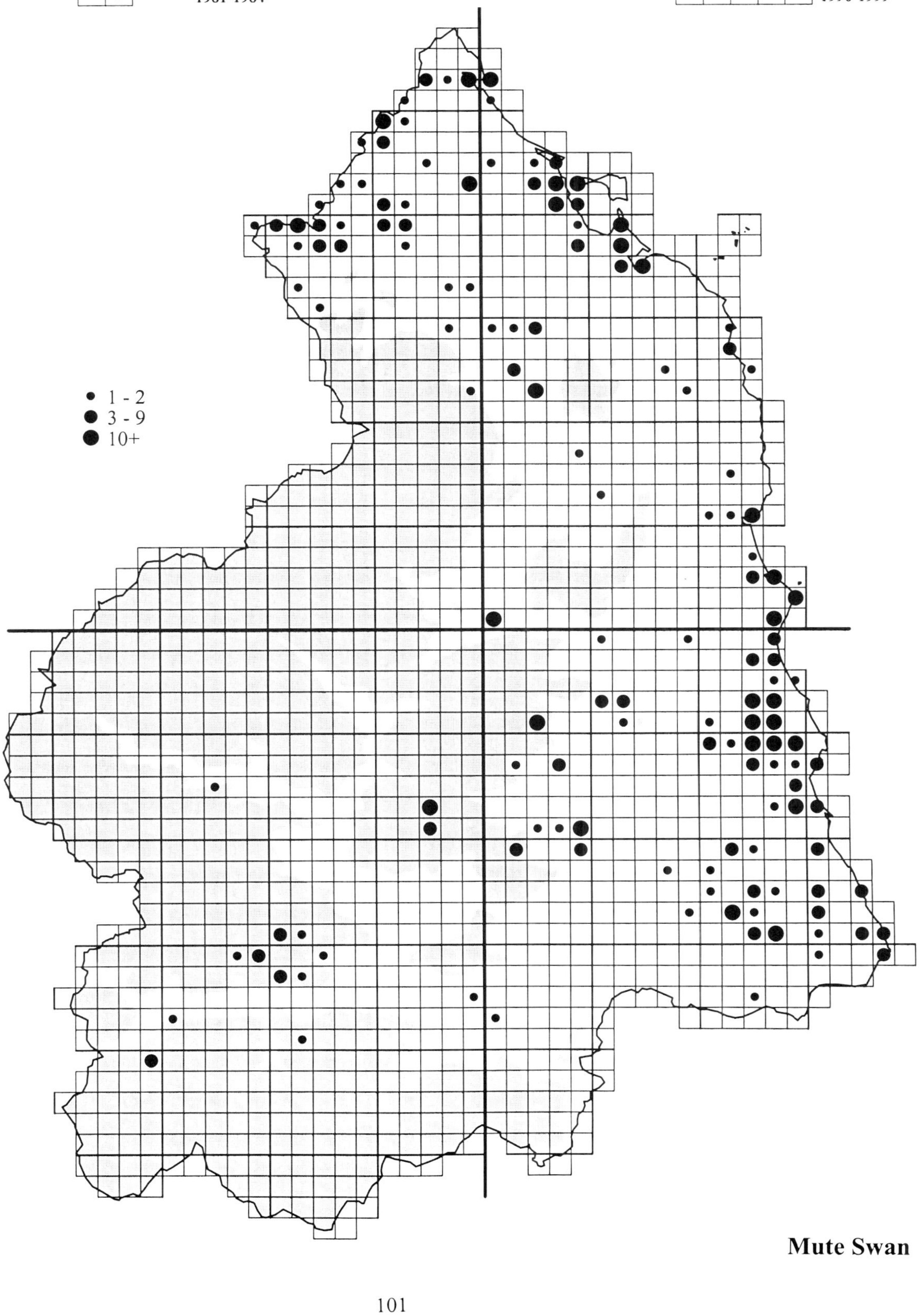

Mute Swan

BEWICK'S SWAN *Cygnus columbianus*

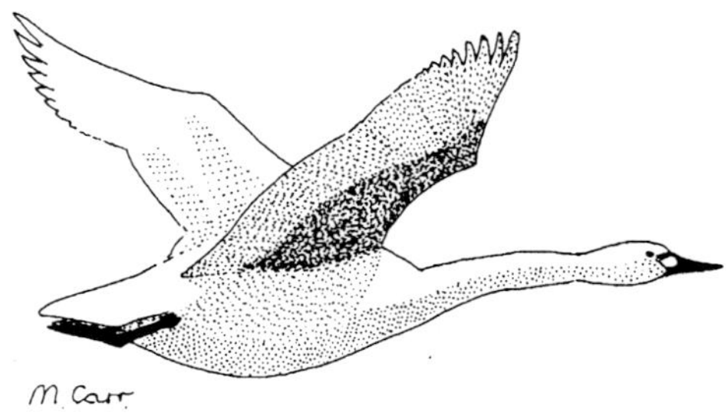

The winter atlas survey, undertaken over three winters, revealed a maximum total of 84 birds located in 12 tetrads. Galloway and Meek (1978) quoted Hancock as saying that the Bewick's Swan is 'quite as common as the Whooper'. Bolam (1932), however, considered it much the rarer of the two species describing it as 'a winter visitant ... but a good deal less numerous'. Galloway and Meek added that the species 'is seen in small numbers every winter', and in the county annual bird report its status is currently described as an uncommon passage and winter visitor.

Separated from the Whooper Swan in 1829, and named after the renowned Tyneside wood engraver Thomas Bewick (1753-1828), the Bewick's Swan arrives in November and usually remains until March. Favoured localities in the county have been the Lindisfarne NNR and the Northumbrian Loughs but the most regular sites used have been near the coast in south east Northumberland including Longhirst, Cresswell, Warkworth Lane and Holywell Ponds. Traditionally Bewick's Swans have shown a preference for natural wetland habitats with shallow freshwater lakes and ponds and slow-moving rivers near grasslands which are liable to flooding. Since the early 1970s, however, the species has also taken to foraging on waste root crops, grain stubbles and winter cereals.

During this survey three quarters of all the records of Bewick's Swan were from the Ellington/Warkworth Lane/Druridge area of south east Northumberland (NZ28/29). Of the 12 occupied tetrads, ten were below 100 metres a.s.l. indicating that altitude is not a factor in preventing larger numbers occurring in the county. The other two tetrads were inland at Caistron (NU00A) and Grindon Lough (NY86D) and the records relate to single birds which presumably had accompanied herds of Whooper Swans *C. cygnus*.

The origin of the population reaching the United Kingdom is western Russia from as far east as the Taimyr Peninsula although those wintering in Northumberland are a tiny proportion of the 7,000 or more that reach England each winter. It is surprising that Northumberland should maintain such small, yet regular, numbers of a species which winters in large numbers in the Netherlands and southern Britain. Small numbers have also regularly reached the Camargue in southern France since the mid-1960s. Ringing records are rare in the county so a family party at Warkworth Lane in February 1994, which had all been ringed at the Nenetski State Game Reserve in north east European Russia in 1993, confirms the origin of some of our small wintering population.

Given that Bewick's Swans mix with Whooper Swans in the same favoured localities each year in Northumberland, and that there is much suitable habitat available to support larger numbers, competition or lack of habitat does not influence the numbers of Bewick's Swans wintering in the county. The largest flock ever recorded appears to be 30 at Holywell Ponds in November 1983 (Kerr, 2001). All recent local authors have indicated that only small numbers are seen annually and this would seem to be borne out by the counts made during the current survey when a maximum of 20 was at Druridge (NZ29T) in February 1997. To put this count into perspective, the maximum for Great Britain in February 1997 was 8,443 birds after cold weather on the continent brought an influx of birds (Waters *et al.*, 1998).

The total of 84 birds over the three seasons is almost certainly an overestimation of the wintering population within the county as some double-counting, due to the mobile nature of the species between feeding sites in favoured areas, seems inevitable. The more southerly distribution in Britain will ensure, for the moment, that Bewick's Swan will remain an uncommon winter visitor to Northumberland.

TIM WATSON

Distribution by altitude

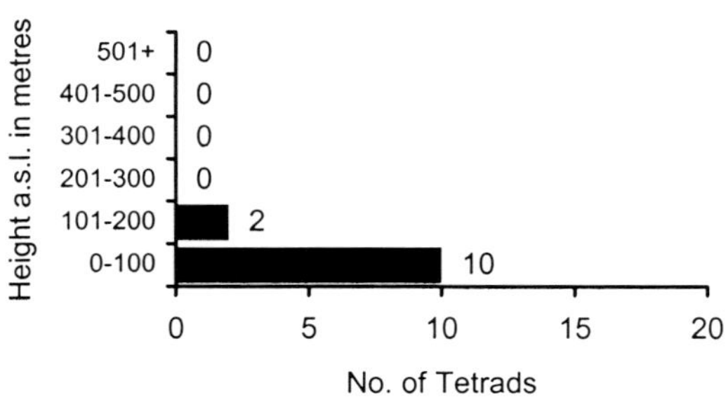

No. of tetrads in which recorded 12 (<1%)

Tetrad Analysis	No. of tetrads
1-5 birds	6 (50%)
6-10 birds	3 (25%)
11+ birds	3 (25%)

Total No. of birds counted 84

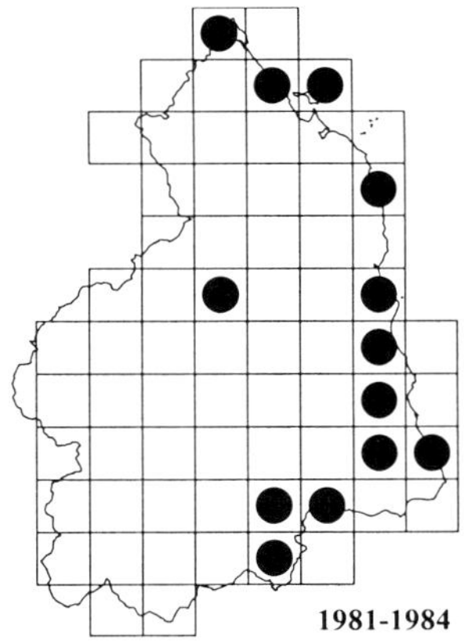

1981-1984

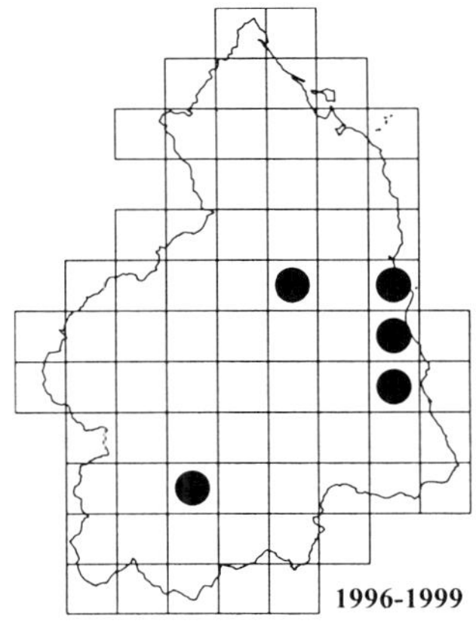

1996-1999

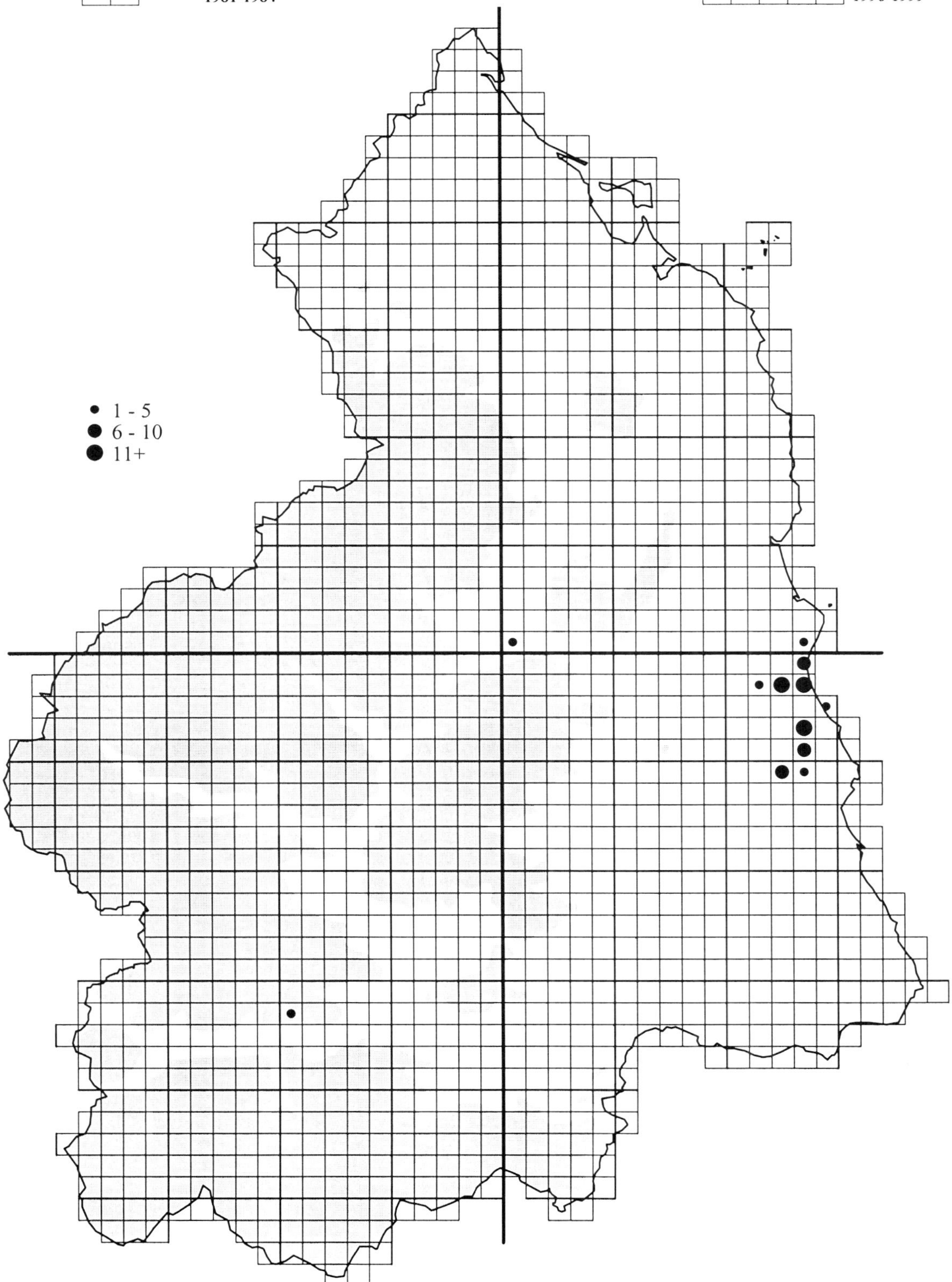

Bewick's Swan

WHOOPER SWAN *Cygnus cygnus*

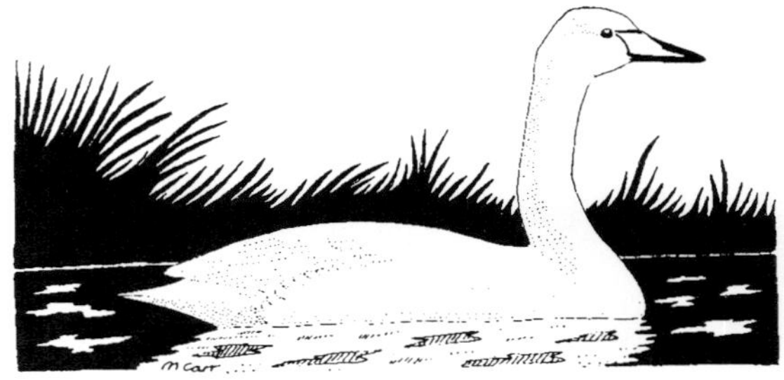

The current atlas survey revealed a maximum total of 1,332 Whooper Swans counted within 47 tetrads over the three winters. Selby (1831) regarded the Whooper Swan as 'an occasional winter visitant' but, by 1912, Bolam indicated that the species was 'a pretty regular winter visitant, in limited numbers'. By the 1970s the Whooper Swan had become more numerous and Galloway and Meek (1978) described it as 'a well-represented passage and winter visitor'. Whilst that status remains true today, there have been changes in numbers and distribution influenced by relatively new agricultural practices, urban encroachment and, possibly, the feeding policies at reserves outside the area.

Bolam (1932) suggested that large flocks were more usual on the loughs in the county than on the coast, where 'it has been much harassed by punt gunners and others'. By the 1970s, however, sites close to, or at, the coast, were more commonly used, although wildfowling continued to take place, and still does, at the Lindisfarne NNR. After the usual arrivals from mid-October onwards, as many as 440 were present in fields adjoining Fenham Flats on the Reserve in December 1980, then the largest flock in England, while over 200 were present at Holywell Pond, a favoured site, in December 1983 (Galloway & Meek, 1986). During the 1980s, early ploughing and re-seeding, together with urban spread reduced the availability of stubbles, resulting in some favoured haunts being deserted and smaller totals being seen in the county. In 1980 at least 700 birds wintered in the county, but by 1989, Holywell Ponds ceased to hold a wintering herd and the total in 1991 for the county was only 200. Also, the autumn arrivals at Lindisfarne NNR which had always featured in the county annual report, *Birds in Northumbria*, were not present in autumn 1992. These reductions compare with the increases at the Wildfowl and Wetlands Trust Reserves at Martin Mere and the Ouse Washes. The Ouse Washes held 'just a handful of birds in the 1960s', but the numbers recorded at each of these sites 'more than doubled to over 1,000 birds between 1987 and 1997'. During 1999/2000, a massive 2,120 were present at the Ouse Washes (Musgrove *et al.*, 2001). The International Swan Census has shown that the Icelandic population was at 18,035 in 1991, dropping to 15,840 in 1995, but then increasing to 20,655 in 2000. Thus, the Northumberland county population remains stable, but reduced, from earlier years, while national numbers are increasing.

In winter the species is locally restricted to areas of suitable habitat where they eat a variety of emergent and submergent water plants, and on land where they can graze grass and stubbles and nibble at potatoes. On intertidal mudflats, they favour eelgrass *Zostera*. Despite some loss of habitat in Northumberland, there remain sufficient areas to support a larger population. The species favours lowland areas with 75% of tetrads used by Whooper Swans being below 100 metres a.s.l. and the remaining tetrads between 101 to 300 metres a.s.l. Parties of over 100 Whooper Swans were recorded in the autumn at Ellington/Warkworth Lane and East Chevington areas (NZ28/29), the Tweed Valley (NT83/94) and the Lindisfarne NNR (NU04). There can be a general westerly movement during the winter to the Northumbrian loughs, Scotland and Ireland, although the East Chevington herd still numbered 114 in February 1999 and 100 were at Wark-on Tweed (NT83J). By early April, the remaining birds have left for Iceland.

The Northumberland wintering population is thought to originate exclusively in Iceland where about 6% remain all year round moving to geothermally warmed waters. Colour ringing and neck collars have shown that individual birds move between sites within Europe and the UK during different winters, and, locally, move widely within our county during the same winter. During July 1980 46 birds were fitted with neck collars at Lake Myvatn in northern Iceland and in 1981 four of these were in the county, with two at Lindisfarne NNR and two in the Holywell area. Three of these birds were also seen at Ellington and near Capheaton. Another, ringed at Anavatn in eastern Iceland, spent the winter of 1988/89 in Denmark and the winters of 1990-1994 in the Druridge area and the winter of 1995/96 at Welney, Norfolk.

TIM WATSON

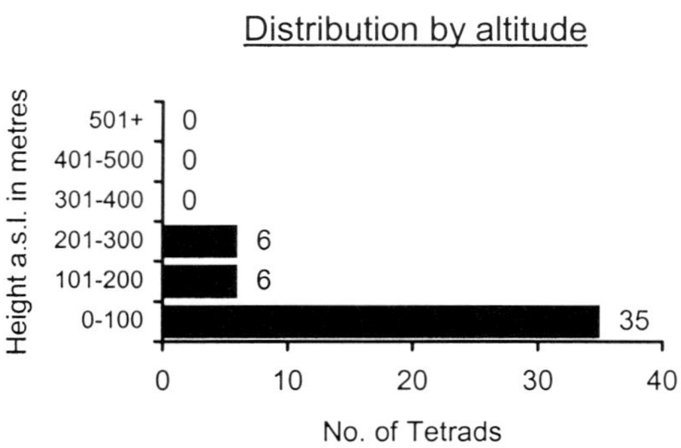

No. of tetrads in which recorded 47 (3%)

Tetrad Analysis	No. of tetrads
1-11 birds	27 (57%)
12-61 birds	10 (22%)
62+ birds	10 (21%)

Total No. of birds counted 1,332

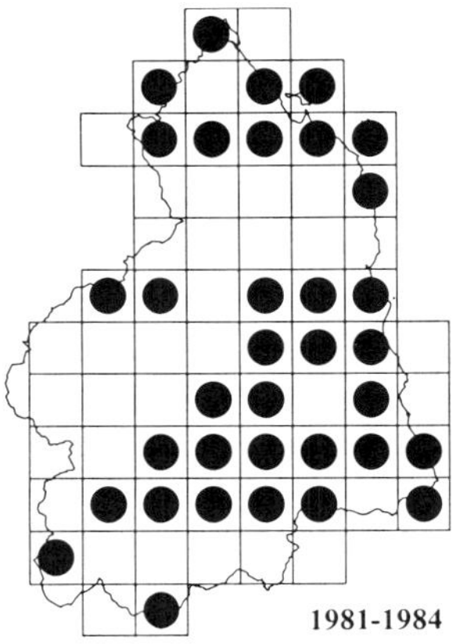

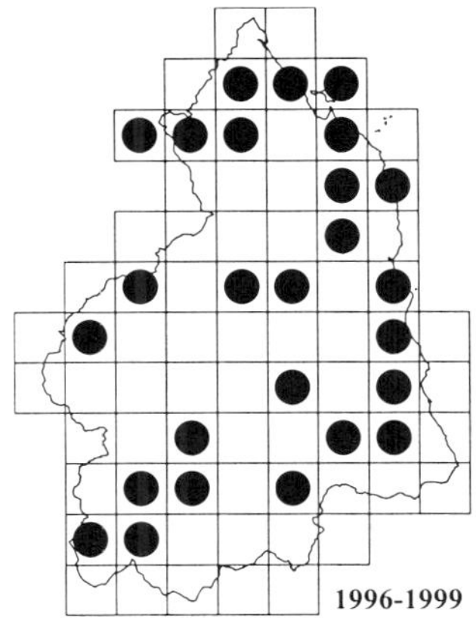

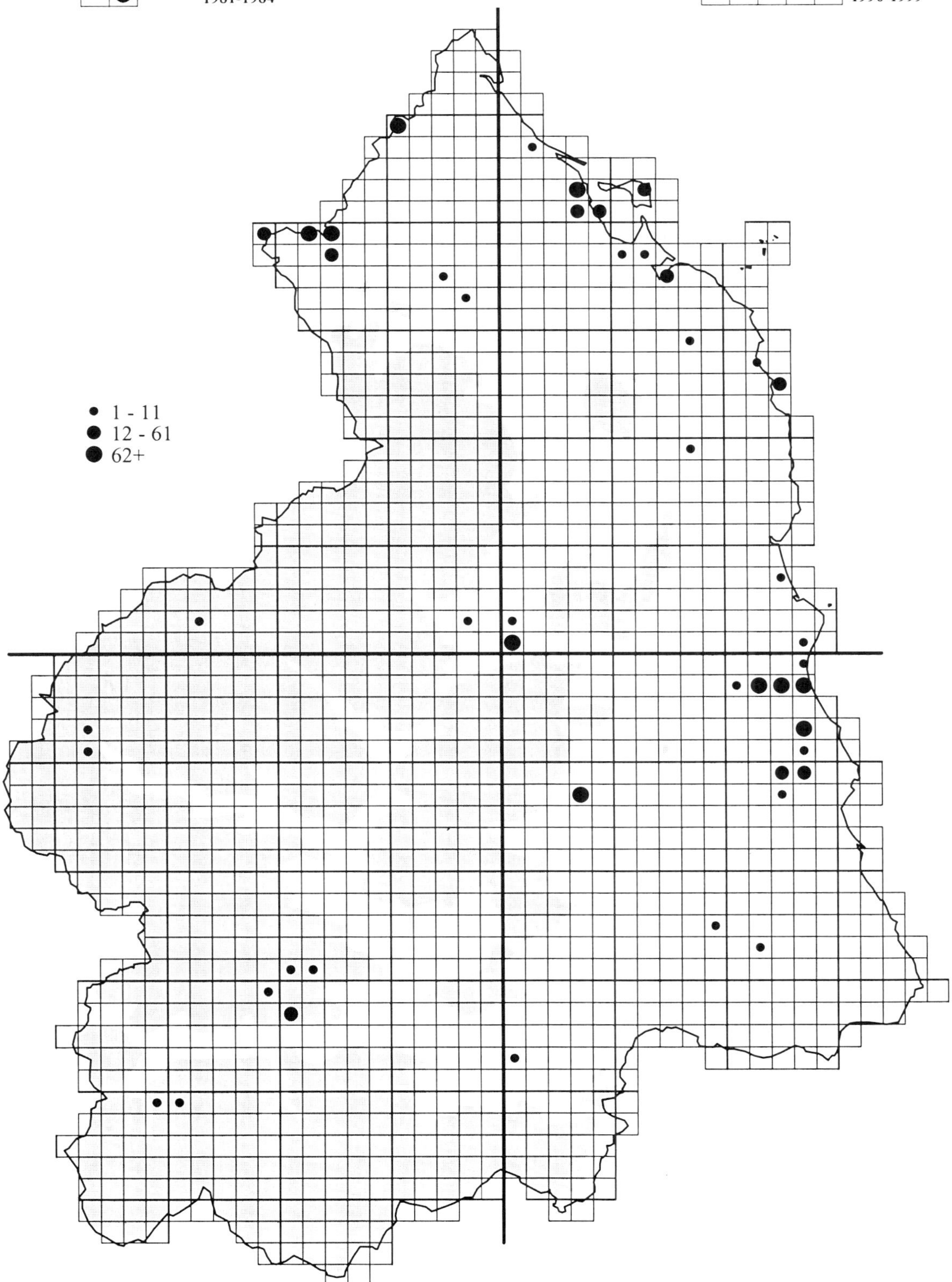

Whooper Swan

BEAN GOOSE *Anser fabalis*

Rather surprisingly perhaps, in view of its current status, the Bean Goose was by all accounts the commonest grey goose to visit the county from the eighteenth century to the mid-nineteenth century (Rossiter, 1999). Large flocks of this species were noted in the River Tweed and Till areas by Wallis (1769) and at Prestwick Carr by Maddison (1830). Selby (1831) also regarded it as very numerous and in large flocks as did Hancock (1874) who also suggested that the Bean Goose was our commonest grey goose in autumn and winter, usually seen in considerable flocks, with Berwick Hill being a favoured locality. The position seems to have changed somewhat by the end of the nineteenth century. Bolam (1912) wrote that, after the Pink-footed Goose *A. brachyrhynchus*, the Bean Goose is our commonest grey goose. Chapman (1889) supported Bolam's statement from his observations of specimens secured from mid-winter shooting and the final years of plenty for the Bean Goose appear to have been the early 1930s when it was noted as the most frequent inland at localities such as Greenlee Lough (Bolam, 1932).

Locally, a rapid decline then followed. By the 1960s and 1970s Grindon Lough was favoured, with 80 in February 1961 and 39 in March 1970, but parties seldom exceeded 20 (Galloway & Meek, 1978). This decline was associated with persecution and changes in forest habitats in its Scandinavian breeding areas (Cramp & Simmons, 1977). Since the late 1970s the species has continued to be very scarce with only two years in which flocks have reached double figures. In 1985, 16 were at Druridge Bay and Holywell in February and March and, in 1995, 14 were at East Chevington in November (Kerr, 2001).

The current atlas data show how scarce the species has become, with records in the three winters from only seven tetrads and maximum counts of nine at Budle Bay (NU13N) on 6th January 1998 and three at Beal (NU04R) on 9th January 1999. All the peak counts were from supplementary records and were from the coast or within two kilometres of the coast, with none from the formerly favoured Grindon Lough area.

Two races of Bean Goose are recognized, nominate *fabalis* from the Scandinavian range and *rossicus* from the tundra across Eurasia. There have been moves to consider these races as separate species but here the BOURC approach of considering them as subspecies is followed. The traditional large flocks visiting the county were presumably nominate *fabalis* (Bolam, 1932) and it appears that this form predominates today. Records of *fabalis* include the nine at Budle Bay and three at Beal mentioned above and one at Warkworth Lane (NZ29R) in December 1997. Records of *rossicus* include two at East Chevington (NU29U) in November and December 1996. Not all individuals were identified to the subspecific level.

Lack (1986) estimated that the wintering population in Britain was now between 200 and 300 birds, although in severe winters numbers might double with influxes from Denmark, northern Germany and the Netherlands. The overall wintering population in the county represents a tiny fraction of the world population. Sadly, in Northumberland, with only small numbers occurring each year, the Bean Goose looks set to remain no more than a rare winter visitor.

B. N. ROSSITER

No. of tetrads in which recorded	7 (<1%)
Tetrad Analysis	**No. of tetrads**
1 bird	3 (43%)
2 birds	2 (29%)
3+ birds	2 (28%)
Total No. of birds counted	19

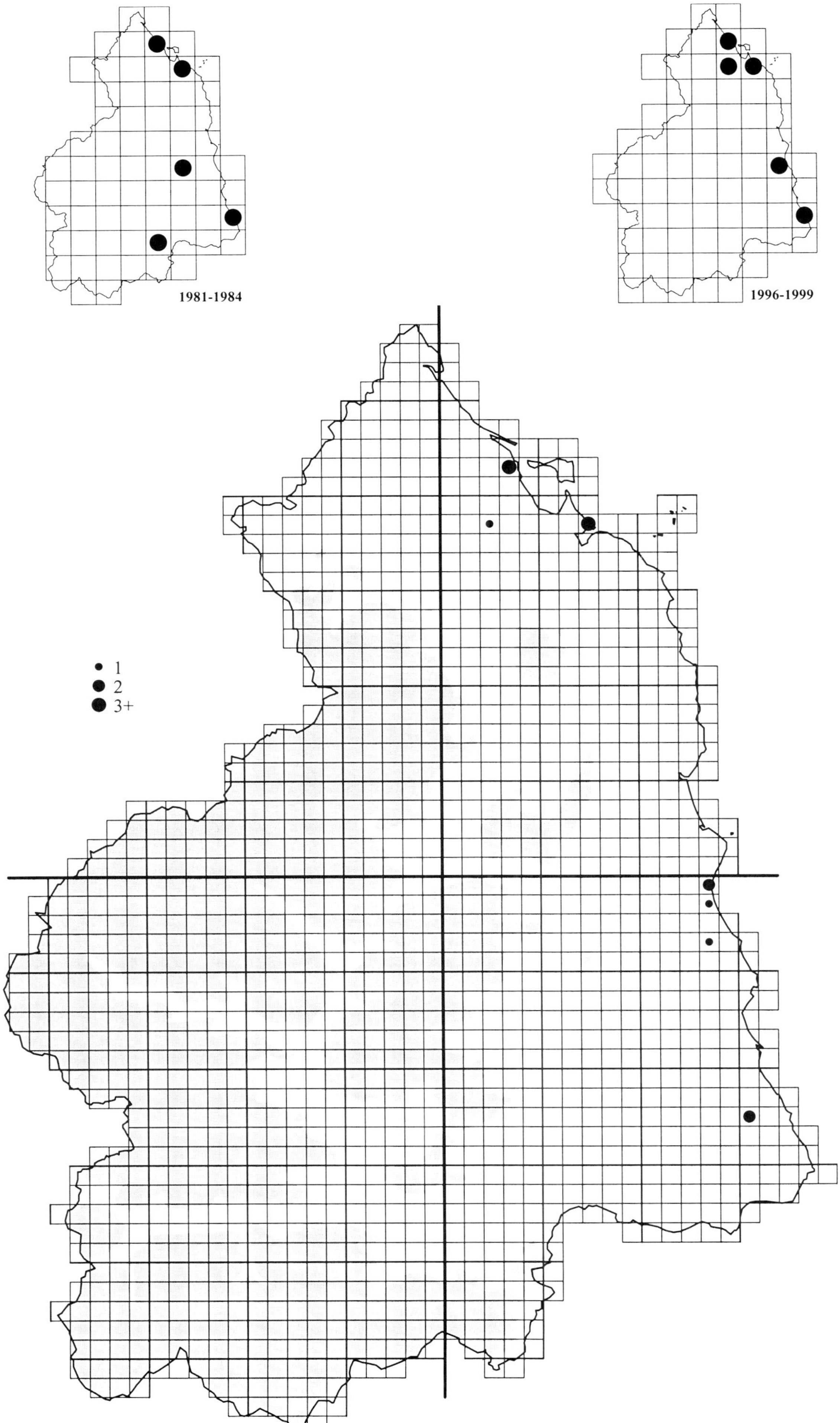

Bean Goose

PINK-FOOTED GOOSE *Anser brachyrhynchus*

Like other geese, this species has undergone major population fluctuations in the past. Evidently less common that the Bean Goose *A. fabalis* from the time of Wallis (1769) to that of Hancock (1874), it appeared to become the commonest grey goose in the county from the late nineteenth century (Chapman, 1889) to the mid-twentieth century. It was noted in a *Guide to the birds of Holy Island* (1909) that the Pink-footed Goose was found in very large numbers. Bolam (1932) reported flocks of 3,000-4,000 on Ross Links and large flocks were still occasionally noted in the mid-twentieth century with 1,500-2,000 at what is now the Lindisfarne NNR in 1948 and 1951. However, numbers then declined dramatically with concentrations of no more than 200 in the 20 years up to the publication of *Northumberland's Birds* (Galloway & Meek, 1978). Although in October 1979 an exceptionally large flock of 1,200 was in the Tweed Valley (Galloway & Meek, 1986) it was not until the 1990s that this goose again became more common (Kerr, 2001).

The recent increase in numbers and distribution is reflected in the expansion from 15 occupied 10km squares in the 1981-1984 winter atlas to 29 in the current survey as shown by the two smaller maps. The range occupied today is mainly lowland with 37 (69%) out of the total of 54 occupied tetrads lying at 100 metres a.s.l. or less, 13 (24%) between 101-200 metres a.s.l. and only four (7%) over 200 metres a.s.l. The distribution map at the 10km level appears to show that the species is widely distributed but examination of the tetrad map shows a marked preference for the north east of the county and the Druridge Bay area. The counts made show that by far the highest numbers are found in the north east with 3,000 at Doddington (NT93W) on 15th January 1997 and 1,600-2,500 in four tetrads in NU03 and NU04, the area inland from Lindisfarne NNR, over the three winter periods. The highest count at Druridge Bay was 375 at Druridge Pools (NZ29T) on 12th December 1997. Numbers well inland were generally much smaller with the highest counts of 102 at Grindon Lough (NY86D) on 25th February 1998 and 100 in the Whaup Moss area (NY98N) in January 1999.

All of the birds visiting Britain breed in either Iceland or east Greenland. By far the greatest number are from Iceland (Lack, 1986) and it was from here that two birds, seen at Holywell Pond on 12th April 1997, had been colour-ringed as goslings in July 1996 (*Birds in Northumbria 1997*).

It is likely that the increased population in Northumberland results from a range expansion of the wintering population in eastern Scotland. This increase is attributed to changes in farming practices such as larger fields and the greater availability of food in winter (Lack, 1986). The mobile nature of flocks between favoured roosting and feeding sites together with probable ongoing movements into and out of the county as winter progresses, means that the maximum total of 13,621 is an over-estimate of the average wintering population. However, the currently large numbers of Pink-footed Geese arriving in the county during the late autumn to start their winter sojourn means the species' status remains that of a common winter visitor to Northumberland.

B. N. ROSSITER

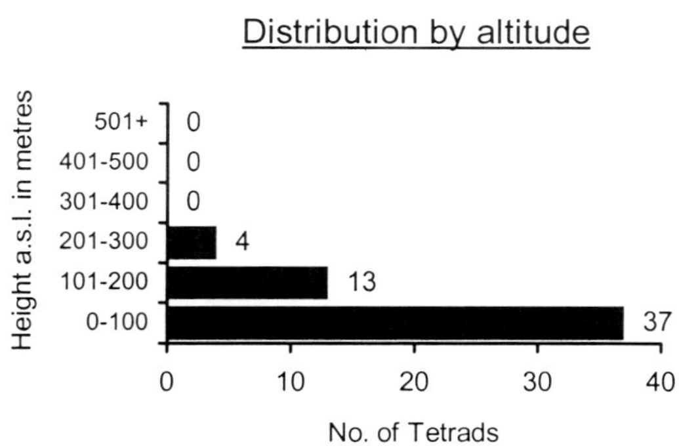

No. of tetrads in which recorded 54 (4%)

Tetrad Analysis	No. of tetrads
1-25 birds	27 (50%)
26-100 birds	16 (30%)
101+ birds	11 (20%)

Total No. of birds counted 13,621

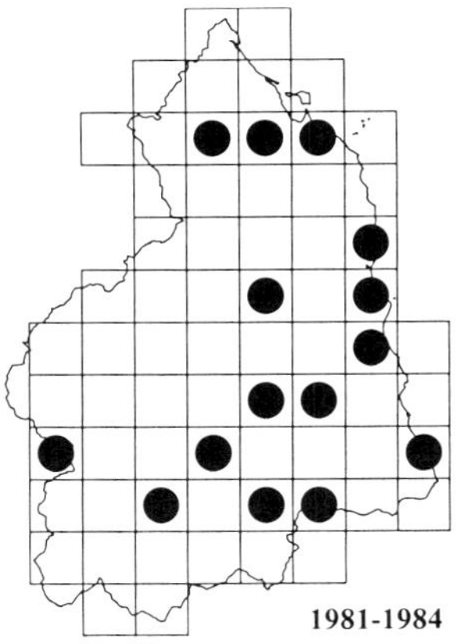

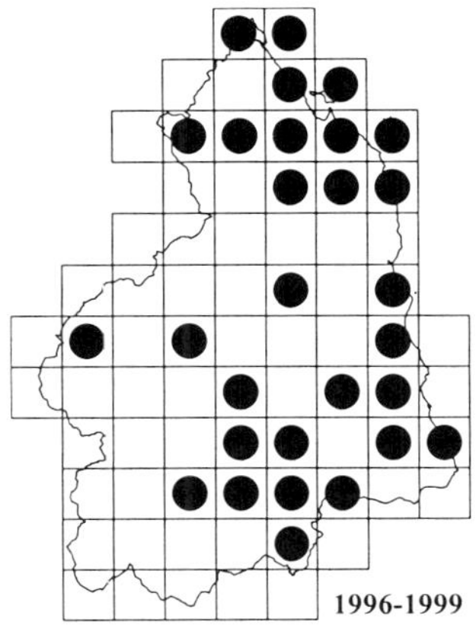

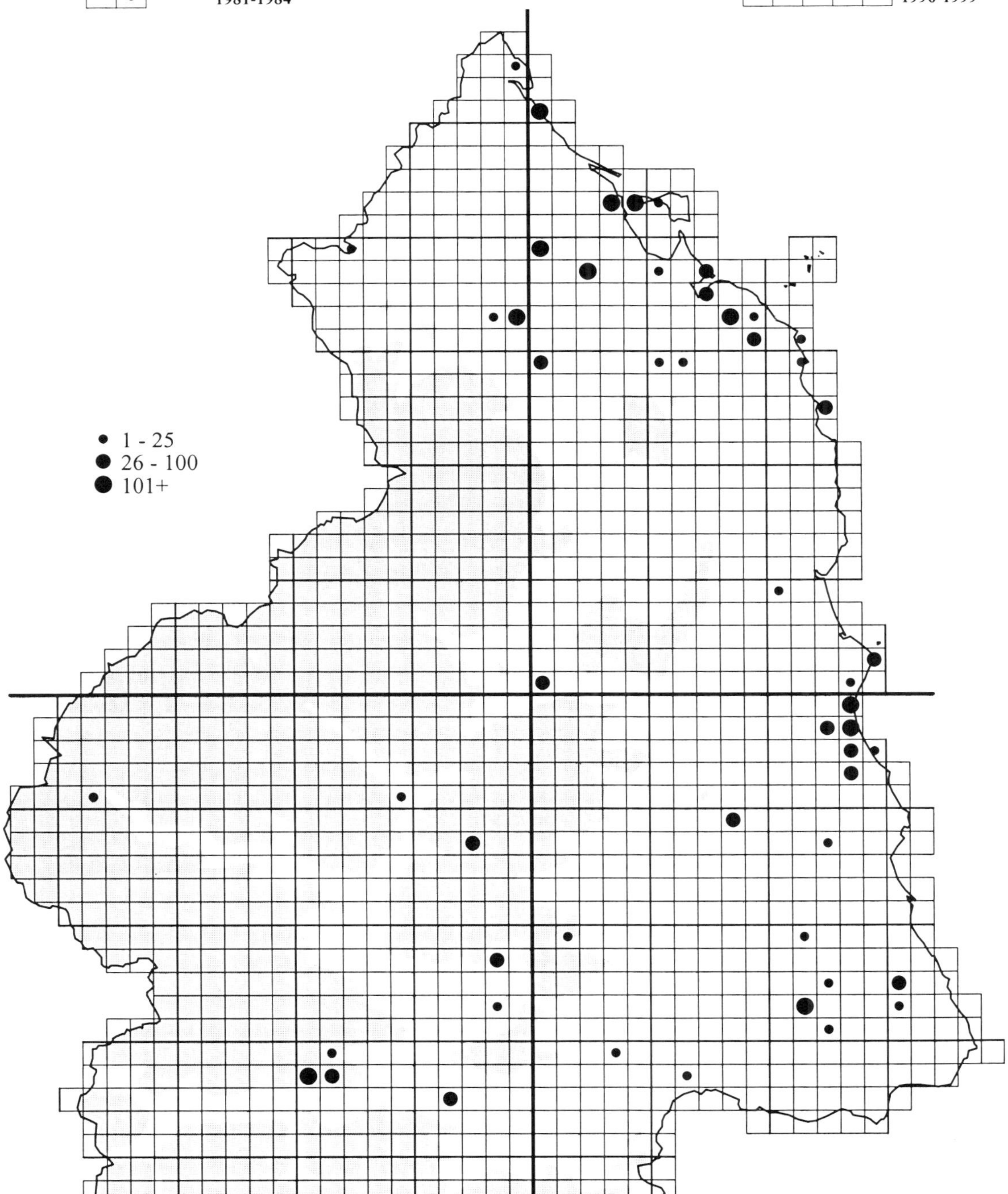

Pink-footed Goose

WHITE-FRONTED GOOSE *Anser albifrons*

Unlike the Bean Goose *A. fabalis* and indeed the other grey geese found in the winter atlas survey, this species has never been common. The earliest mention is by Selby (1831) who recorded it as a winter visitor, not as numerous as the Bean Goose. Later Hancock (1874) noted it as an autumn and winter visitor and Bolam (1932) as an irregular winter visitor, mainly to the coast. Since the 1970s, when Galloway and Meek (1978) reported it as being a scarce winter visitor from November-January, numbers have increased. The most favoured areas have been on or near the coast at the Lindisfarne NNR, Druridge Bay and Holywell Pond areas and well inland, at 200 metres a.s.l., at Grindon Lough. Notable flocks in the 1980s were 60 flying north over Bamburgh in December 1984 and 25 at Druridge Pools in March 1986. In the early 1990s, 23 were at Linton Pond in February and March 1993 and 21 near Big Waters in February 1991. The largest flocks to date were found in early 1996 with 106 at Goswick on 23rd February, 44 at Holywell Pond in March and 16 at Grindon Lough in March and April.

In the current winter atlas the distribution is similar to that in 1981-1984, as shown by a comparison of the two 10km square maps, with most records from the north of the county, or the coastal area from Backworth to East Chevington, and the loughs and reservoirs of the south west. A total of only 21 tetrads was occupied over the three winter periods with few records outside the main roosting areas. Indeed in only one 10km square was it recorded in more than two tetrads, namely the Druridge Bay area (NZ29) in five tetrads. All the peak counts were from supplementary records, the highest being 44 at Budle Bay (NU13M) on 31st January 1998, 32 at nearby Elwick (NU13D) in February 1998 and 27 at East Chevington (NZ29U) in November 1997. In the south west, 14 were at Derwent Reservoir (NZ05G) in February 1999 and 11 at Grindon Lough (NY86D) in January 1999. The county population appears to have been about 50 in recent winters. The Grindon Lough flock typically returns in October but the main influxes in coastal areas have been in January and February, with departures in March.

Two races of White-fronted Goose are recognized, nominate *albifrons* from Europe and *flavirostris* from Greenland, both of which occur in the county. In the current atlas survey, the Greenland race predominated inland with the flocks at Grindon Lough and Derwent Reservoir being of this form. However, two at Caistron (NU00A) in February 1997 were of the nominate form. On the coast, flocks of 18 at Cresswell (NZ29X) and 11 at Backworth (NZ37B) in February 1999 were thought to be *flavirostris*. However, the 32 at Elwick in February 1998 and five at Bell's Pond, near Cresswell (NZ29S) in February 1999 were thought to be of the nominate form. Nationally the Greenland form very much predominates in western Scotland and Ireland and the European form in southern England and South Wales (Lack, 1986). In Northumberland the Greenland form is likely to predominate in the south west as an outlier of the Scottish wintering population but on the coast the more populous European form may predominate, particularly in hard winters. With no regular large-scale increase in numbers during the winter months the species remains an uncommon visitor to Northumberland.

B. N. ROSSITER

Distribution by altitude

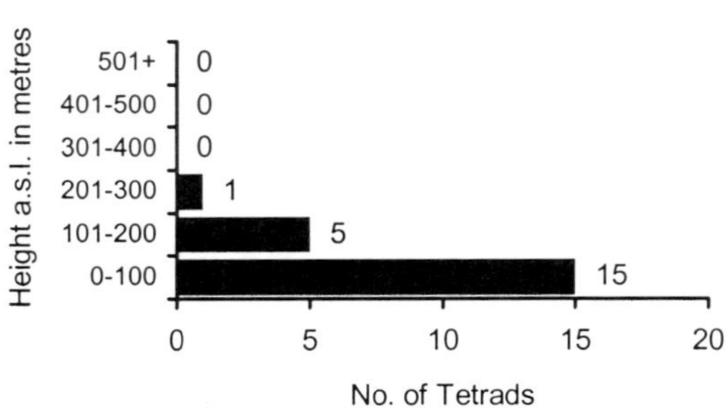

No. of tetrads in which recorded	21 (2%)
Tetrad Analysis	**No. of tetrads**
1-6 birds	12 (57%)
7-20 birds	5 (24%)
21+ birds	4 (19%)
Total No. of birds counted	232

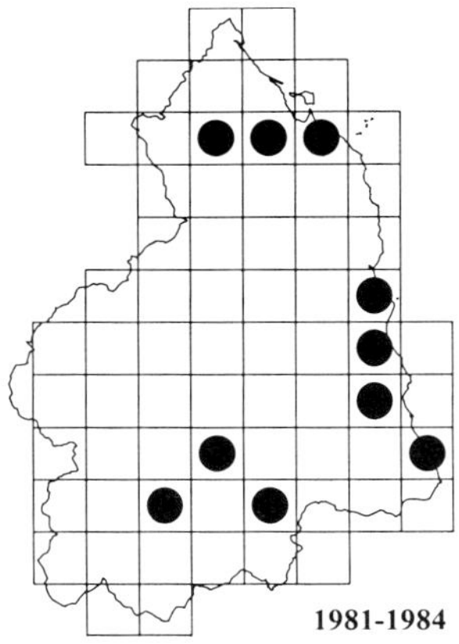

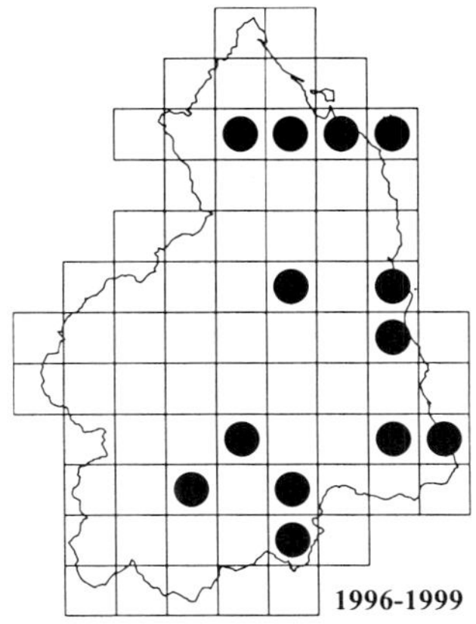

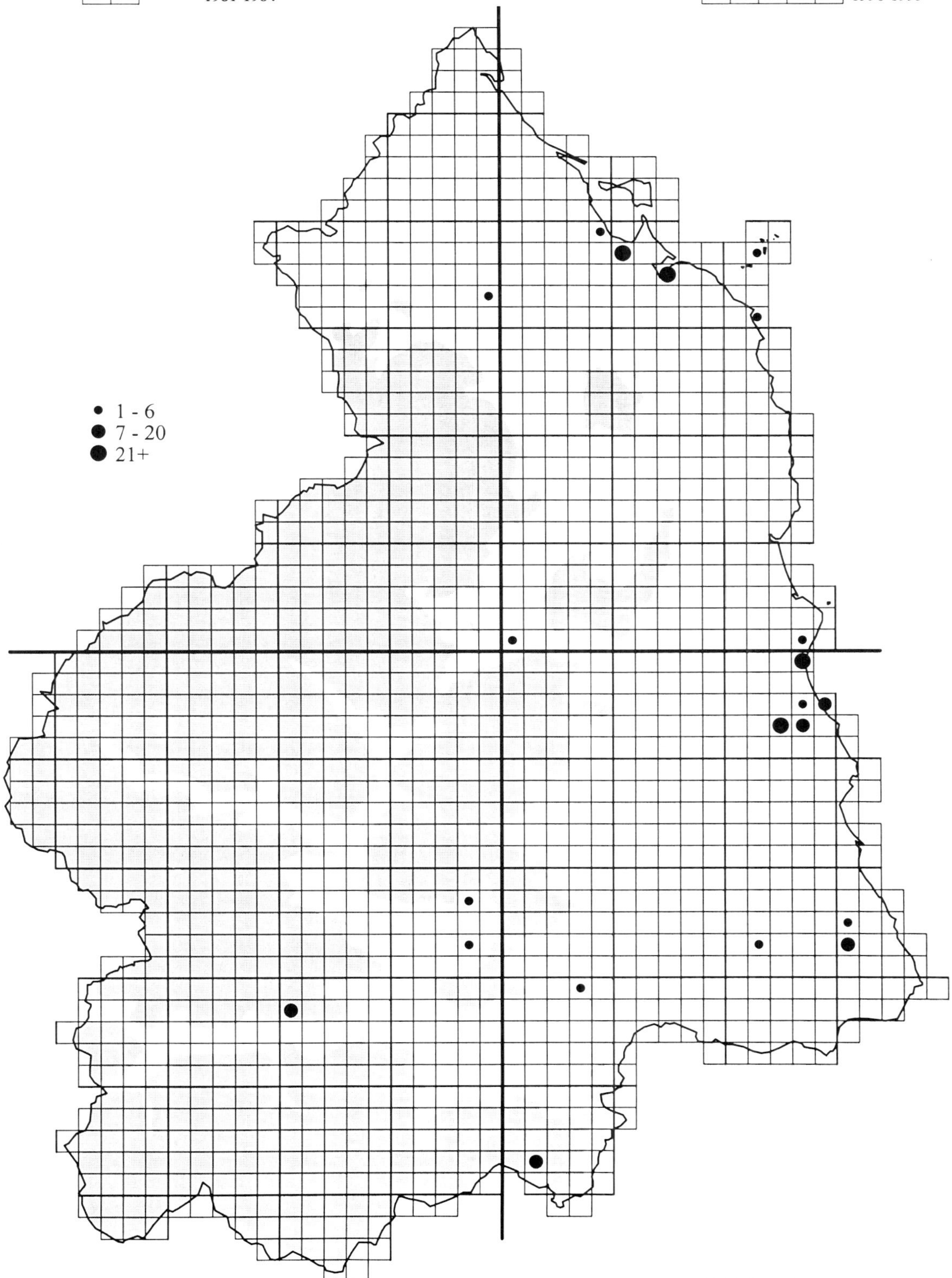

White-fronted Goose

GREYLAG GOOSE *Anser anser*

This goose is thought to be the grey goose that used to breed in Britain and much of continental Europe and was the precursor of the domestic goose (Lack, 1986). Selby (1833) said in Britain it appears that this species was formerly very abundant and was also a presumed resident, breeding annually in great numbers. Loss of habitat and excessive hunting probably led to its decline. Today a large and increasing feral breeding population has spread into the county from further south with a population of 36 pairs recorded during fieldwork for *The atlas of breeding birds in Northumbria* (Day *et al.*, 1995) and 34 broods with at least 185 young noted in 1999 (*Birds in Northumbria* 1999). Such birds appear to remain on site for most of the year including the winter period.

Despite its former national abundance in the nineteenth century this goose was a rare visitor to Northumberland. Selby (1831) noted it as by no means a common species and Hancock (1874) recorded it as a casual visitor. Bolam (1932) said that its numbers may have been increasing for the past two decades and, by 1946, 300 were wintering at Lindisfarne (Galloway & Meek, 1978). Numbers continued to increase and this species has been the most numerous of the grey geese visiting the county since the mid-twentieth century with peaks of 6,000 at the Lindisfarne NNR in January 1982 and November 1985, 5,000 in the Tweed Valley in December 1979 and 2,500 at Thropton in February 1996 (Kerr, 2001).

A comparison of the two 10km square distribution maps indicates that the current winter atlas shows a slight decrease from 45 to 40 occupied 10km squares since 1981-1984. There appears to have been a contraction of distribution in the centre and extreme south east of the county and an expansion in the west and south west. During the current survey, compared to the Pink-footed Goose *A. brachyrhynchus*, the Greylag is more widespread, occupying 103 tetrads across the county rather than the Pink-foot's 54 in a localized area. It also occupies, to a greater extent, upland areas being found in a total of 44 tetrads (43%) over 100 metres a.s.l. including 15 (15%) over 200 metres a.s.l. Although widespread, the Greylag does show a tendency to concentrate around some favoured localities. These include Howburn, near Hoselaw Loch (NT83C) with 1,600 birds on 14th December 1996, Caistron (NU00A) with 1,590 on 18th January 1998, Derwent Reservoir (NZ05B) with 1,400, Holburn Moss (NU03N) with 1,200, Budle Bay (NU13M) with 1,000 and in the Backworth/Holywell Pond area (NZ37B) with 900. Other large counts at favoured sites included 700 at the Whittle Dene Reservoirs area (NZ06U), 637 in Druridge Bay at East Chevington (NZ29U), 600 on the Milfield Plain south of Doddington (NT93V) and 352 at Grindon Lough (NY86D).

Adding up the maximum counts at the main concentrations gives a total of about 10,000 birds over the three winter periods. However, some movement occurs between these sites and the wintering population in a typical winter is likely to be substantially lower, perhaps in the range 5,000-6,000, making this still the commonest grey goose visiting Northumberland.

The entire Icelandic population visits Britain in winter, with other breeding populations believed to concentrate elsewhere in Europe (Lack, 1986). One at Backworth in spring 1999, ringed in Iceland in 1997, fits this pattern while another at Newton Pool in March 1997 and March 1998, ringed in Sweden during June 1990, is perhaps less expected.

B. N. ROSSITER

Distribution by altitude

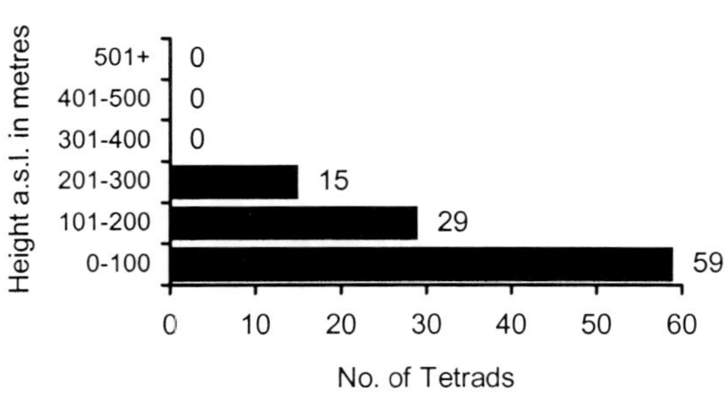

No. of tetrads in which recorded 103 (7%)

Tetrad Analysis	No. of tetrads
1-60 birds	51 (50%)
61-400 birds	30 (29%)
401+ birds	22 (21%)

Total No. of birds counted 24,198

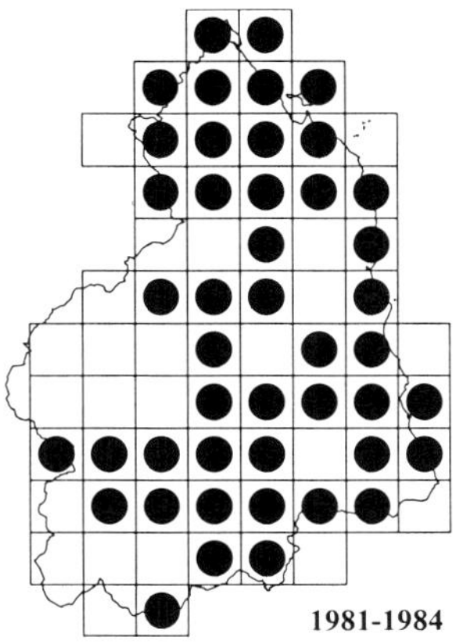

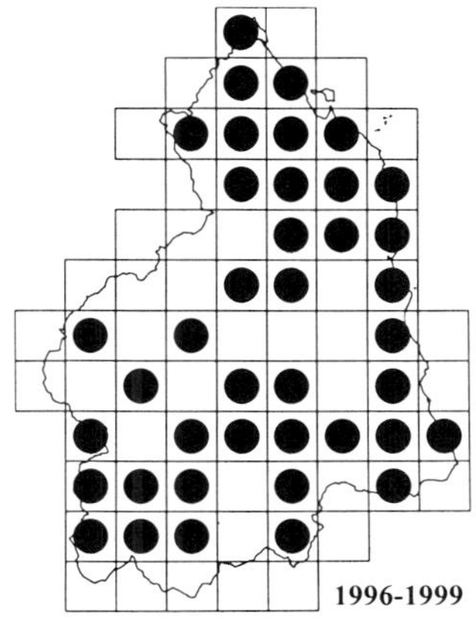

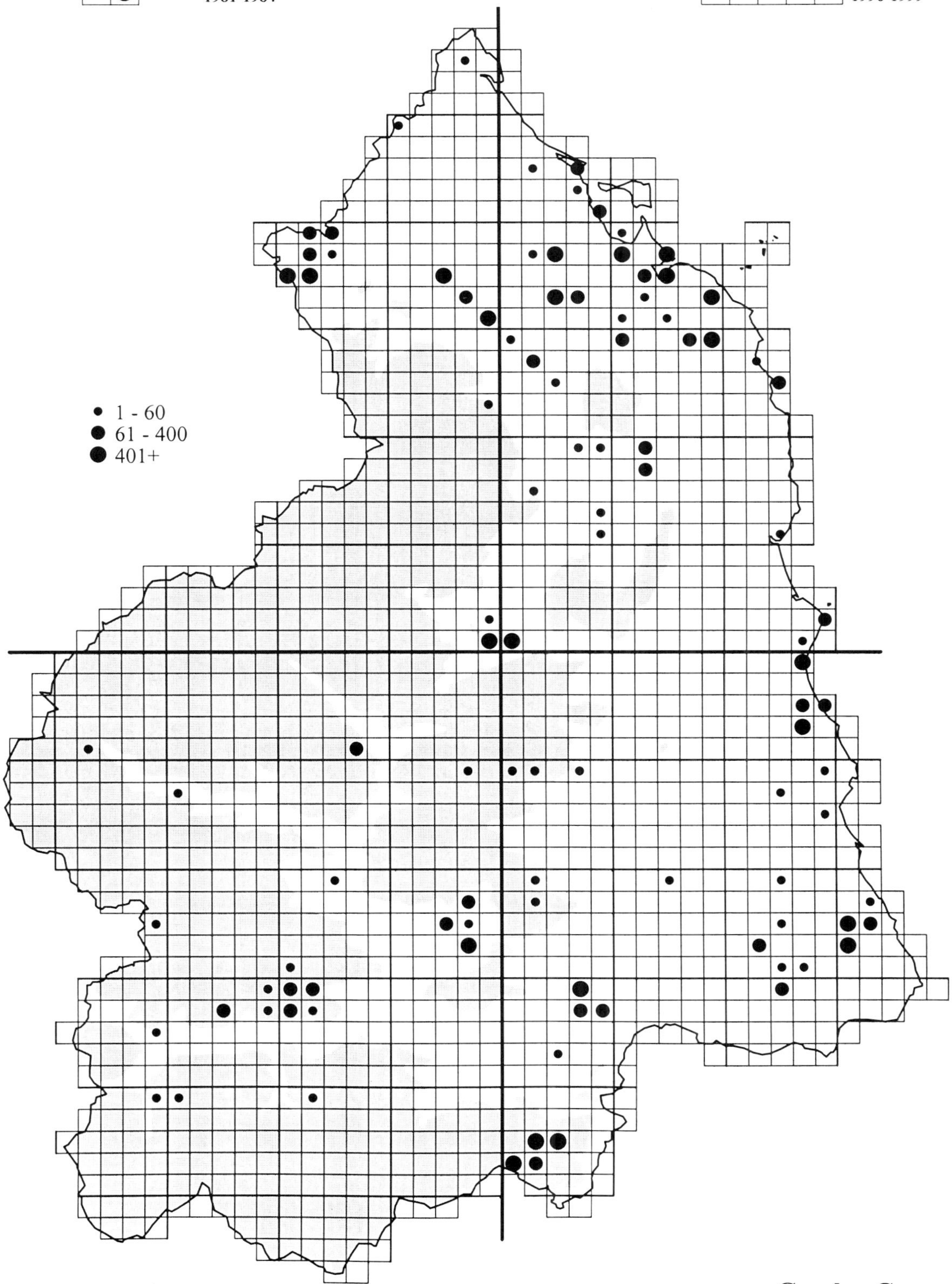

Greylag Goose

CANADA GOOSE *Branta canadensis*

There are no definite records of birds of North American origin in the county, although Bolam (1912) thought that, though most records referred to escapes from captivity, it was not advisable to ignore the species altogether. In the early 1930s, however, he did not include the species in his *Catalogue* suggesting that, in his opinion, no records to date referred to genuinely wild birds (Bolam, 1932).

In the late 1950s about 50 free-flying birds were introduced to Sweethope Lough. These quickly became established with a few pairs breeding annually from at least the mid-1960s. Numbers grew steadily with a peak of 150 at Colt Crag Reservoir in September 1975 (Galloway & Meek, 1978). Since then the breeding population has slowly increased with 20 confirmed pairs in 1988-1992 (Day *et al.*, 1995) and 16 broods with 99 young noted in 1999 alone (*Birds in Northumbria 1999*). The highest numbers in the county have been found in autumn when large flocks of geese occur, particularly in the Hallington Reservoirs area, moving between breeding areas further south (Yorkshire and the Midlands) and the moulting grounds in the Beauly Firth. For instance 800 were at Hallington in late August 1999. Confirmation of the origins of these flocks comes from three individuals, ringed in Yorkshire and Leicestershire, and noted in the county in October and November (Kerr, 2001).

The current atlas survey shows a fairly stable range over time with records from 14 ten kilometre squares as against 12 in the 1981-1984 winter atlas. The range in winter is very similar to that shown in *The atlas of breeding birds in Northumbria*, concentrating upon the loughs of the south west, the reservoirs north of the Roman Wall and Caistron. This suggests that the local population is very sedentary. Indeed records were received from only 23 tetrads, indicating a very localised distribution. Their distribution by altitude shows that they were found in 14 tetrads (61%) between 101-300 metres a.s.l. and only nine tetrads (39%) below 101 metres a.s.l. This goose remains scarce in the north of the county with only one bird recorded, near Norham (NT94E), in the entire winter atlas period.

The highest numbers found in the current atlas in particular areas were 390 at Grindon Lough (NY86D) on 21st January 1999, 180 at Hallington Reservoirs (NY97T) on 27th November 1996, 87 at Capheaton (NZ07J) in February 1999, 83 at Caistron (NU00A) in February 1997 and 60 at Bothal Pond (NZ28N) in December 1998. The count at Grindon is the highest recorded in winter to date, suggesting that the local population is steadily increasing. Although the number of broods is relatively low in relation to the overall population, the breeding data for 1999 above shows that a high productivity of 6.2 young per brood is probably driving the population higher.

The total count of 1,546 over the three winter periods of this survey is likely to be an overestimate largely due to local movement of the winter flocks. A more realistic county population in winter is now likely to be about 600 birds. Mead (2000) suggested that although the rate of population increase in England may now be slowing down in some areas, their concentration of numbers may well be considered a nuisance. Hopefully this situation will not arise in Northumberland.

B. N. ROSSITER

Distribution by altitude

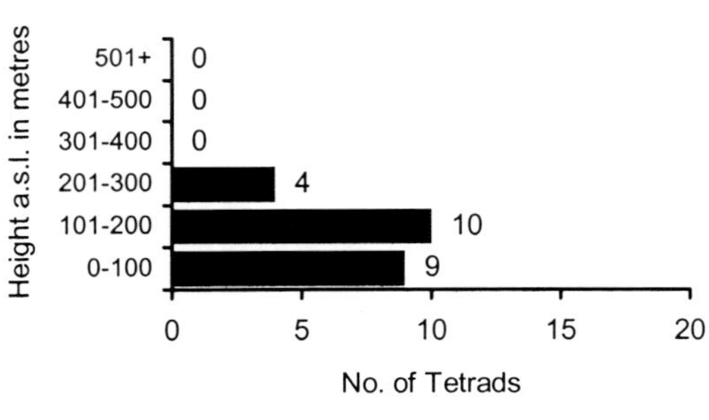

No. of tetrads in which recorded 23 (2%)

Tetrad Analysis	No. of tetrads
1-12 birds	12 (52%)
13-87 birds	7 (31%)
88+ birds	4 (17%)

Total No. of birds counted 1,546

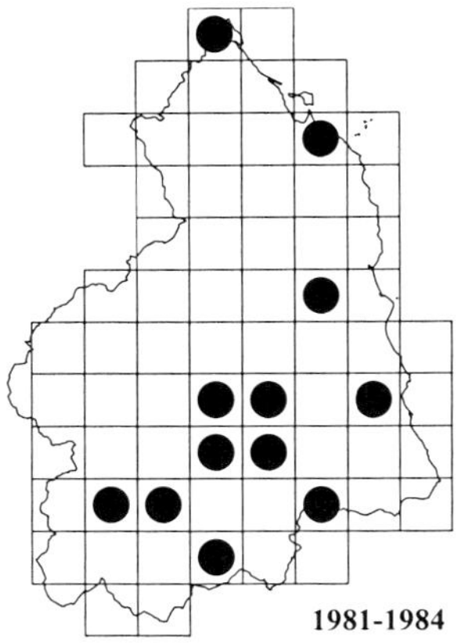

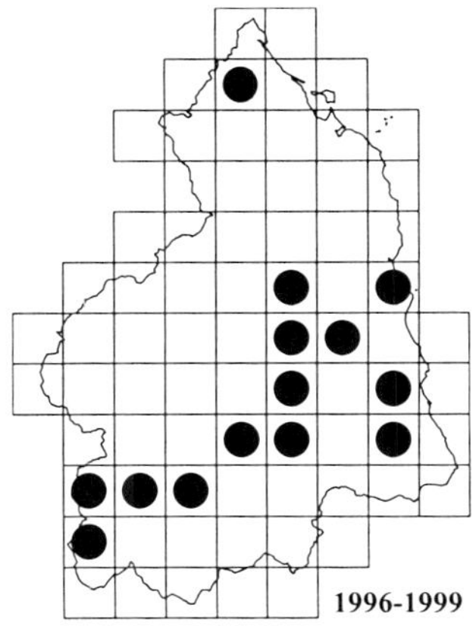

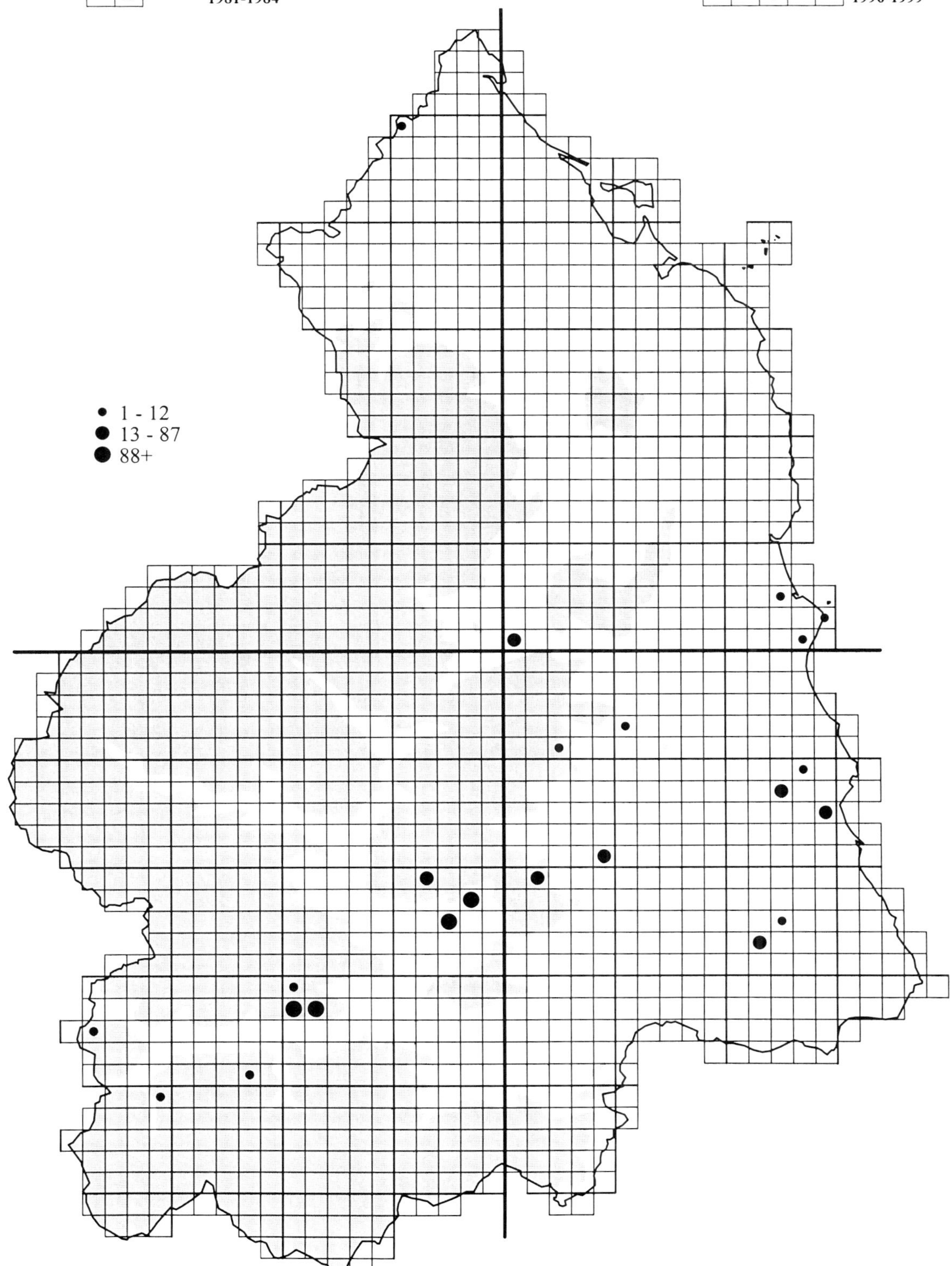

Canada Goose

BARNACLE GOOSE *Branta leucopsis*

The Barnacle Goose is one of the most attractive of all the geese which winter in Britain, the pied plumage making it instantly recognisable, causing none of the identification problems associated with some of the grey geese. The distant barking call of passing flocks gives away its presence long before birds come into view. Historically, its winter status does not appear to have changed much since Bolam's day for he described it as 'a winter visitant, not by any means common' (Bolam, 1912). Likewise Galloway and Meek (1978), although acknowledging that it was a little more frequent during September and October, described single birds associating with other goose flocks as being the norm in winter.

There are three separate breeding populations in the world, two of which winter exclusively in Britain and Ireland. Birds breeding in Greenland winter along the west coast of Scotland, from the Outer Hebrides in the north, to Islay, where the bulk of the population is centred. Islay alone supports over 30,000 birds in winter. Breeding birds in the Svalbard (Spitsbergen) group of islands winter entirely on the inner Solway Firth at Caerlaverock NNR, Dumfries and Galloway, and Rockcliffe marshes in Cumbria. Ringing recoveries tend to confirm it is this latter population which is responsible for the bulk of records in Northumberland particularly during the main migration periods in late September-October and April-early May. There are, however, at least two records of Greenland birds in the county. The first was a bird shot at Cresswell in October 1970 which had been ringed in Greenland in 1961 (*Birds in Northumbria 1980*) and the second at the Farne Islands in April 1997, this bird having been ringed at Loch Gruinard, Islay in November of the previous year (*Birds in Northumbria 1999*).

The Solway population continues to increase, reaching a peak of 26,040 in December 1998 (Pollitt *et al.*, 2000). Accordingly, the number of passage birds in Northumberland has also increased, raising its status from that of well-represented to common passage migrant, although still uncommon in winter. Both the current winter atlas results and *The atlas of wintering birds in Britain and Ireland* (Lack, 1986) confirm this uncommon winter status in our area. By the end of October passage through the region has virtually ceased, leaving behind odd stragglers, who manage to attach themselves to the wintering flocks of Greylag Geese *Anser anser*. Small groups occasionally begin to appear again in February, as birds move away from their traditional wintering sites.

Analysis of the current winter atlas figures reveals an average of seven occupied tetrads per season with maximum counts of 39 birds in the first winter (1996/97), 69 in the second winter (1997/98) and only 12 in the final winter (1999/98). The winter of 1997/98 included two sizeable flocks in February, with 35 at the Long Nanny (NU22I) and 21 well inland at Caistron gravel works (NU00A). Apart from one other notable flock of 28 in Budle Bay in December 1996, all other records refer to one-five birds. The 10km square maps for both winter atlas surveys in 1981-1984 and 1996-1999 each show 13 occupied squares, with almost identical distribution. The coastal bias is apparent, as are the sparsely distributed records in the Tyne Valley, where two-three birds were at Grindon Lough (NY86D) and four at Whittle Dene Reservoirs (NZ06U). Both these localities support large numbers of wintering Greylag Geese which may attract passing groups of Barnacle Geese moving between the Solway and the east coast. This may also account for the record at Caistron, in the Coquet Valley, as both are recognised overland flyways.

Given that this species has consistently remained faithful to traditional wintering sites, it is highly unlikely the Barnacle Goose will be anything other than a regular passage migrant in Northumberland, remaining uncommon in winter.

MICHAEL RICHARDSON

Distribution by altitude

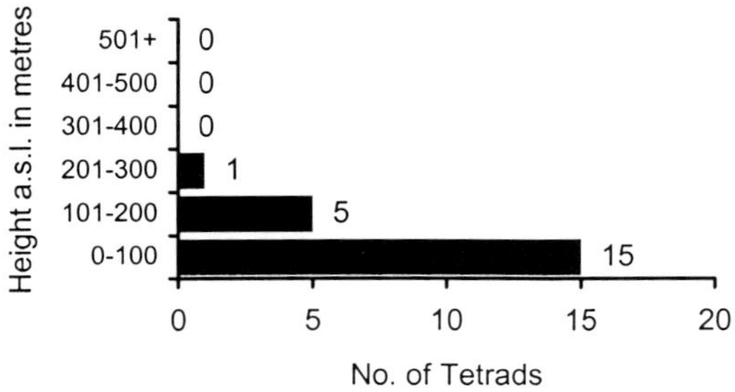

No. of tetrads in which recorded 21 (1%)

Tetrad Analysis	No. of tetrads
1-2 birds	14 (67%)
3-5 birds	4 (19%)
6+ birds	3 (14%)

Total No. of birds counted 120

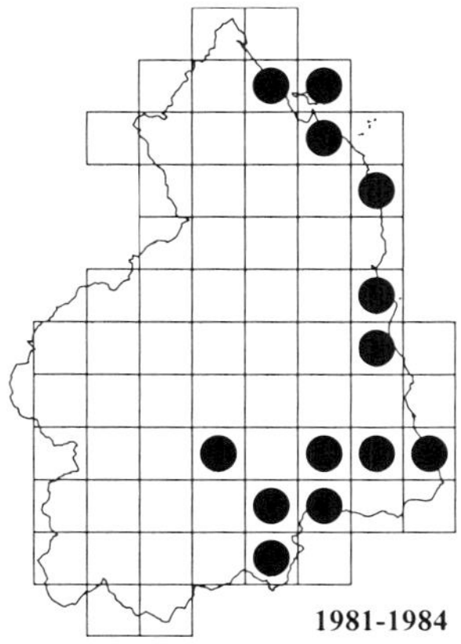

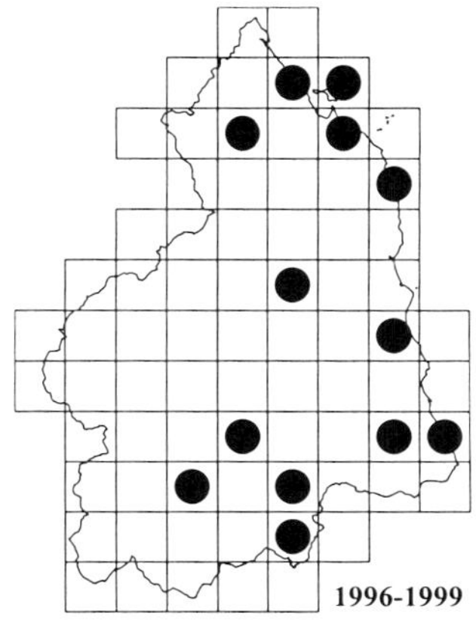

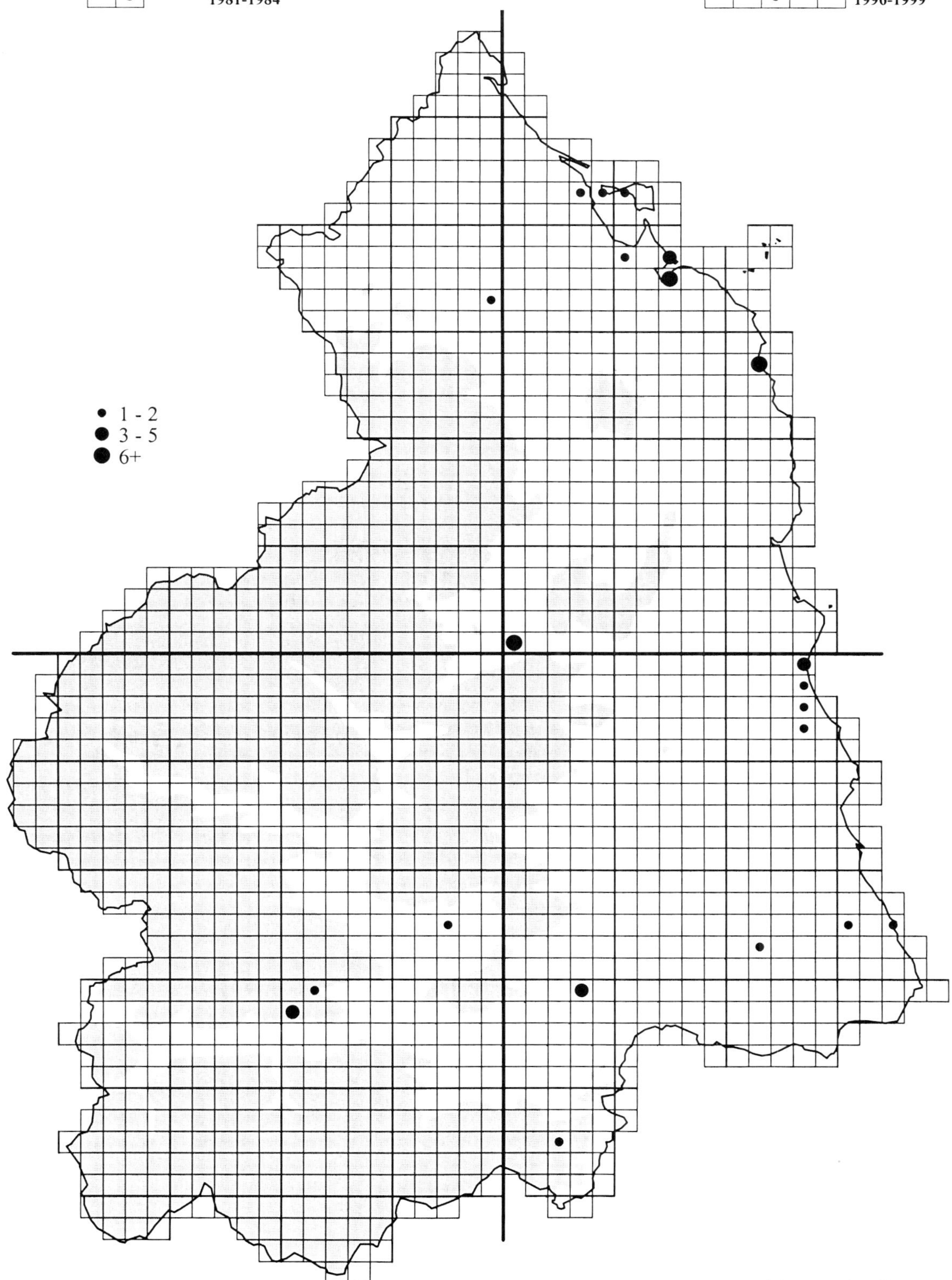

Barnacle Goose

BRENT GOOSE *Branta bernicla*

Bolam (1912) described this species as 'a regular winter visitant ... which come to the slakes at Holy Island during the first months of the year, often numbering many thousands'. This included the largest flock ever recorded in Britain of at least 30,000 in 1886 (Chapman, 1889), but the average number was about 6,000 and the great majority were of the dark-bellied race, *B. b. bernicla,* (Galloway & Meek, 1978). Numbers dwindled in the 1950s and 1960s but have increased since then.

The main site for the species wintering in the county remains the Lindisfarne NNR and, during the last two decades, numbers have consistently reached an annual peak of 2,500-3,000, mostly of the pale-bellied race, *B. b. hrota,* (Clausen *et al.*, 1998). Clausen and Percival (1998) noted that 'in 1973-1988 very few dark-bellied Brent Geese were seen amongst the pale-bellied Brent Geese, with annual peak counts ranging from 5 to 39 geese, but during 1989-1995 annual peaks ranged from 280 to 453 geese'. Latterly there has been a peak count of 600 dark-bellied Brent Geese on Holy Island sands on 11 Nov 1999 (Denny, unpublished data). At Lindisfarne, Brent Geese feed mainly on the intertidal *Zostera* beds (Percival *et al.*, 1996), and to a lesser extent on saltmarsh (Anderson, 1999). Since 1995, they have frequently fed on agricultural land adjacent to the estuary (Percival & Anderson, 1998), with consistent feeding on winter wheat and barley crops from December onwards in the 2000 and 2001 seasons (Denny, unpublished data). Favoured winter cereal fields have been at Beal Road Ends, Goswick and Elwick, and pasture at Elwick. However, for most of the winter period feeding birds were distributed across the *Zostera* bed on the muddier mainland side of the intertidal area. The two main roosts were at Elwick and The Snook. Since the implementation of a shooting-free refuge in 1997 at the southern end of the site, around Elwick, the geese have increased their use of this area for both feeding and roosting (Denny, 2001). Prior to the 1980s, Brent Geese arrived at Lindisfarne from October, peaking in January/February and leaving in March/April. Since then birds have arrived and peaked earlier, with a correspondingly earlier leaving date in some years, a pattern that has been driven mainly by a change in food supply at the Danish wintering sites with less *Zostera* encouraging greater dispersal to alternative sites (Clausen & Percival, 1998).

During the current survey period the majority of records, and by far the largest flocks, were observed at Lindisfarne. The largest single count of Brent Geese from a tetrad during the survey was 1,000 pale-bellied birds on arable land at Beal (NU04R). Non-survey counts include a maximum of 4,092 (98% pale-bellied birds-85% of the total population) in January 1997 when the Danish feeding grounds were frozen over (Percival & Anderson, 1998), constituting the largest count in Northumbria in recent decades. To give an idea of the day-to-day use of Lindisfarne, the number of bird-days each winter over the last decade have been calculated (see Appendix B) and show a fluctuation annually of between 15,000 and 45,000.

Since the 1980s, the Brent Geese at Lindisfarne have been the subject of an intensive colour-ringing programme, and latterly a satellite telemetry study. The results from these have proven the close link between Lindisfarne and the Danish wintering areas: together they hold over 99% of an isolated population of pale-bellied Brent Geese (Clausen *et al.*, 1999). Until recently, this population was assumed to breed only on Svalbard and Frans Josef Islands, however, satellite telemetry has shown that approximately 20% of the population breed in north east Greenland (Clausen & Bustnes, 1998), resulting in the current name of East-Atlantic pale-bellied Brent Goose. Lindisfarne-ringed pale-bellied birds have also been seen at scattered sites from Aberdeenshire to northern France during cold weather movements. Ringed dark-bellied birds have been re-sighted at wintering grounds in south east England and the Netherlands. The East-Atlantic population of pale-bellied Brent Geese, despite growing in recent years, still only numbers about 6,000 individuals, making it one of the most threatened goose populations in the world (Madsen *et al.*, 1996). Although this population seems to be mainly limited by breeding success, survival rates are severely affected by cold weather (Clausen *et al.*, 2001). Lindisfarne, being the most important cold weather refuge and regularly holding over half of the population, has a critical role to play in the conservation of this globally threatened population.

The county's first Black Brant, *B. b. nigricans,* was present on Holy Island Sands, and associating with dark-bellied Brent Geese, during the current survey period from 11th-27th November 1999 (Denny, 2000).

MATTHEW DENNY

No. of tetrads in which recorded 25 (2%)

Tetrad Analysis	No. of tetrads
1-20 birds	12 (48%)
21-344 birds	8 (32%)
345+ birds	5 (20%)

Total No. of birds counted 5,326

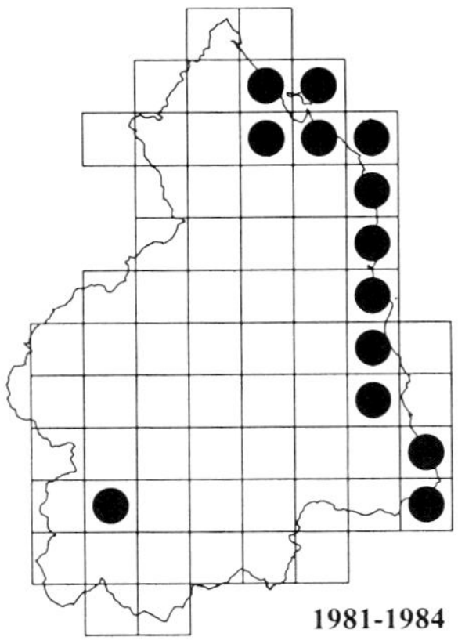

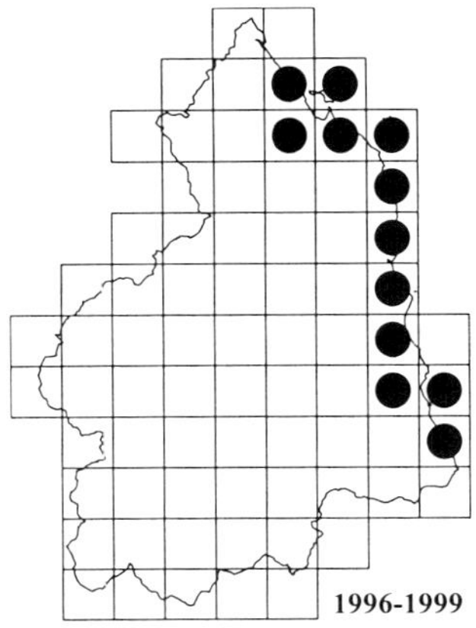

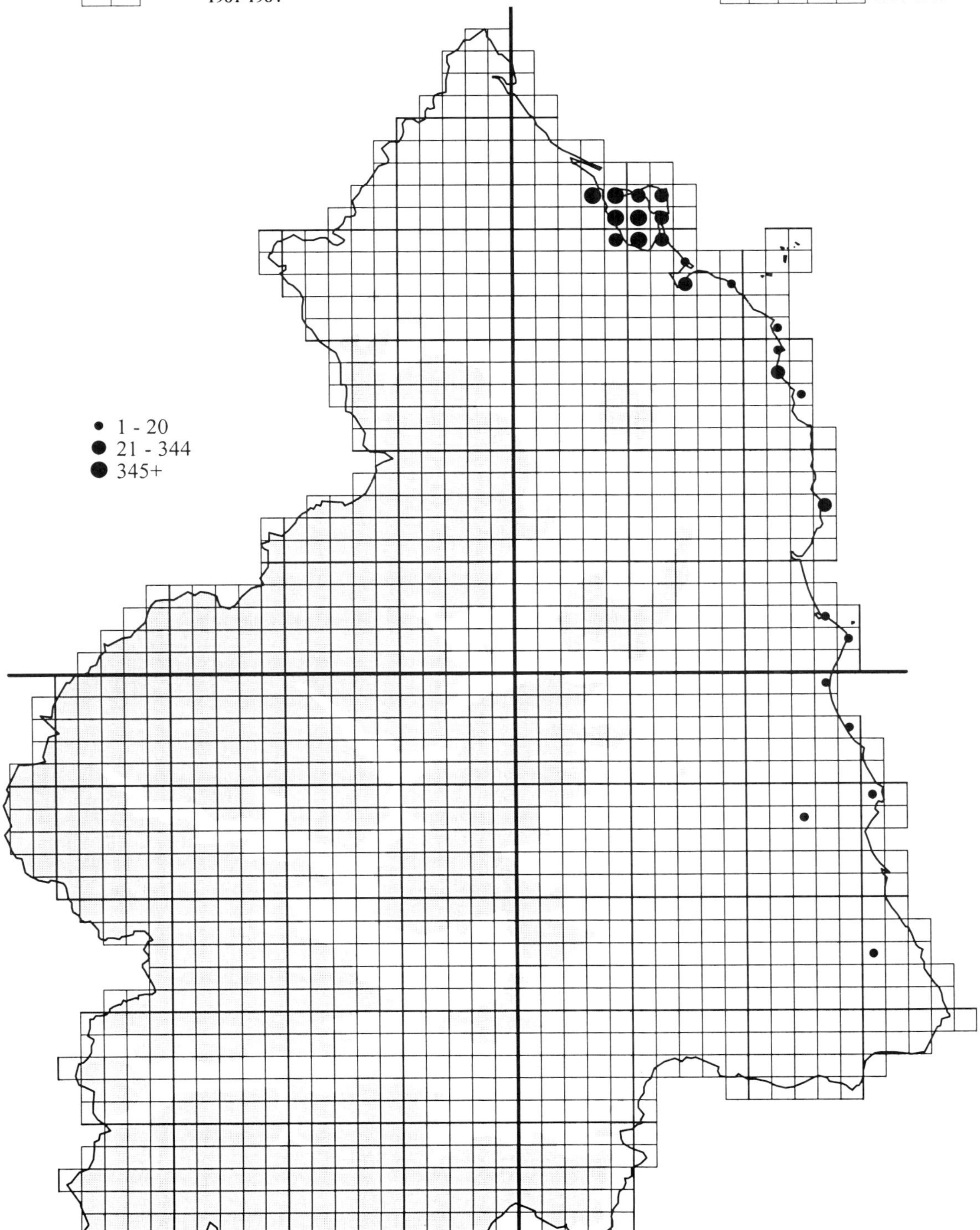

Brent Goose

SHELDUCK *Tadorna tadorna*

Bolam (1912) noted that 'in winter, the majority of the birds [Shelduck] leave us, though a few always remain'. This status appears to have changed somewhat as Galloway and Meek (1978) stated that up to 700 were regular at the Lindisfarne NNR between January and March, usually concentrated in Budle Bay. Currently, peak counts are routinely higher than this with the largest numbers found on the main mudflats at Lindisfarne. An increase in peak counts since the 1970s has levelled out somewhat in the 1990s, in line with the north west European population (Delany *et al.*, 1999).

The current atlas data demonstrate that Shelduck are still largely restricted to coastal areas in winter, with the majority of records over the survey period concentrated around the estuaries of the Rivers Blyth and Coquet and at Lindisfarne, together with moderate numbers around Druridge Bay. In the 1981-1984 national winter atlas survey (Lack, 1986), more ten kilometre squares were occupied in the south and on the coast in the north, but the overall distribution was similar to the current survey. In this survey 40 (2.8%) of the 1,432 tetrads surveyed were occupied by Shelduck with only four of these over 100 metres a.s.l.

The largest single count during the survey period was at Lindisfarne where 482 were in tetrad NU04V on 12 Dec 1998 although the total count on Lindisfarne NNR that day was 1,250. This species is monitored regularly at Lindisfarne, and larger peak counts have been recorded. The largest counts have coincided with the current survey period with 1,300 in December 1996 (Denny, unpublished data) and 1,319 in January 1998. During the 1990s peak counts have been above 1,000 every year (Denny, 2001). The number of bird-days, as shown in Appendix A, almost halved between 1991 and 1992, but has since recovered to an all time high in 1999. Lindisfarne is important as it contains ideal muddy intertidal feeding habitat for the species and, within the site, feeding distribution is correlated with the muddiest substrate areas to the south and west of the main channel (Denny, 2001). Most birds at Lindisfarne roost at high tide on the water in sheltered bays with particular concentrations at Elwick and Fenham Mill (Denny, unpublished data). Numbers of Shelduck at Lindisfarne build up during September, October and November, after departing the moulting grounds. They peak in December and fall in numbers thereafter, but hundreds may still be present in May.

Colour ringing suggests that at least some Shelduck are site faithful to Lindisfarne between winters and has demonstrated that some wintering at Lindisfarne moult in the Heligoland Bight area of the Waddensee (Denny, unpublished data). Other re-sightings have come from as far as Northern Ireland and north west France (S. Percival, pers. comm.), suggesting that some birds use Lindisfarne as a staging area. It is not known where wintering birds in Northumberland breed, although some are likely to breed locally. Indeed the breeding distribution as shown in *The atlas of breeding birds in Northumbria* (Day *et al.*, 1995) is almost identical to that of the current winter distribution pattern.

Peak counts in tetrads at coastal sites other than Lindisfarne during timed surveys included 65 in the Blyth Estuary (NZ28W) and 40 in the Coquet Estuary (NU20S), both in February 1998. Smaller numbers were well scattered at a number of localities along the coast as far south as Tynemouth. Away from the coast a maximum of 28 birds were counted at Caistron (NU00A) in January 1998, seven at Colt Crag Reservoir (NY97J) in November 1996 with odd birds at Grindon Lough (NY86D) and on the Milfield Plain (NT93L).

Despite being closely tied to intertidal mudflat habitat, the Shelduck is a widespread and common species in north west Europe (Cramp & Simmons, 1977). Britain holds 21% of the 300,000 Shelduck wintering in north west Europe (Delany *et al.*, 1999; Pollitt *et al.*, 2000) but in Northumbria, only at Lindisfarne do counts regularly peak at a level of national importance.

MATTHEW DENNY

Distribution by altitude

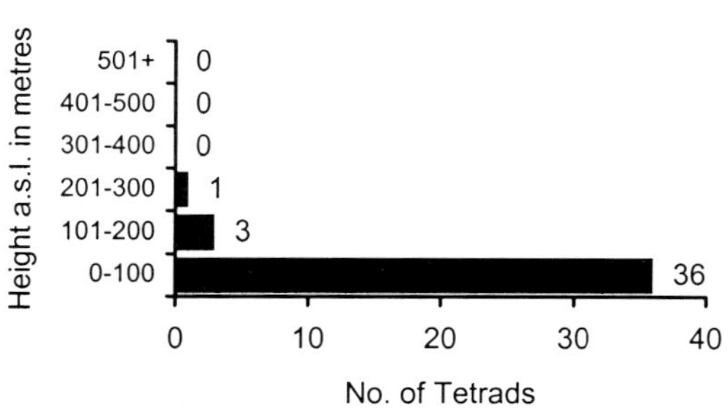

No. of tetrads in which recorded 40 (3%)

Tetrad Analysis	No. of tetrads
1-9 birds	21 (53%)
10-50 birds	11 (27%)
51+ birds	8 (20%)

Total No. of birds counted 2,092

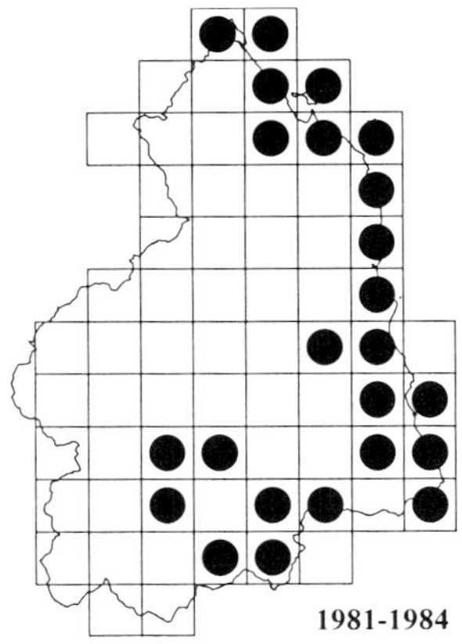

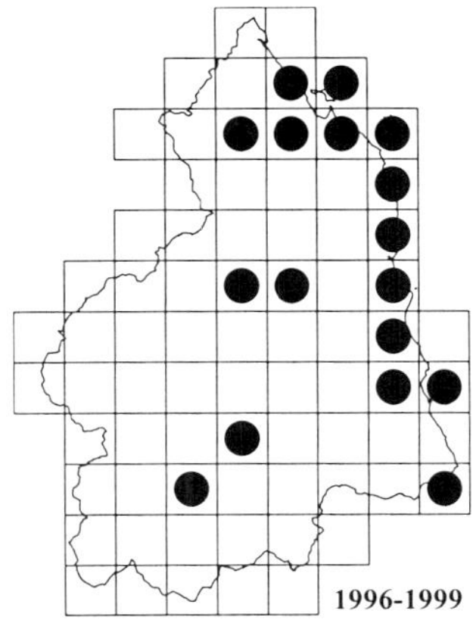

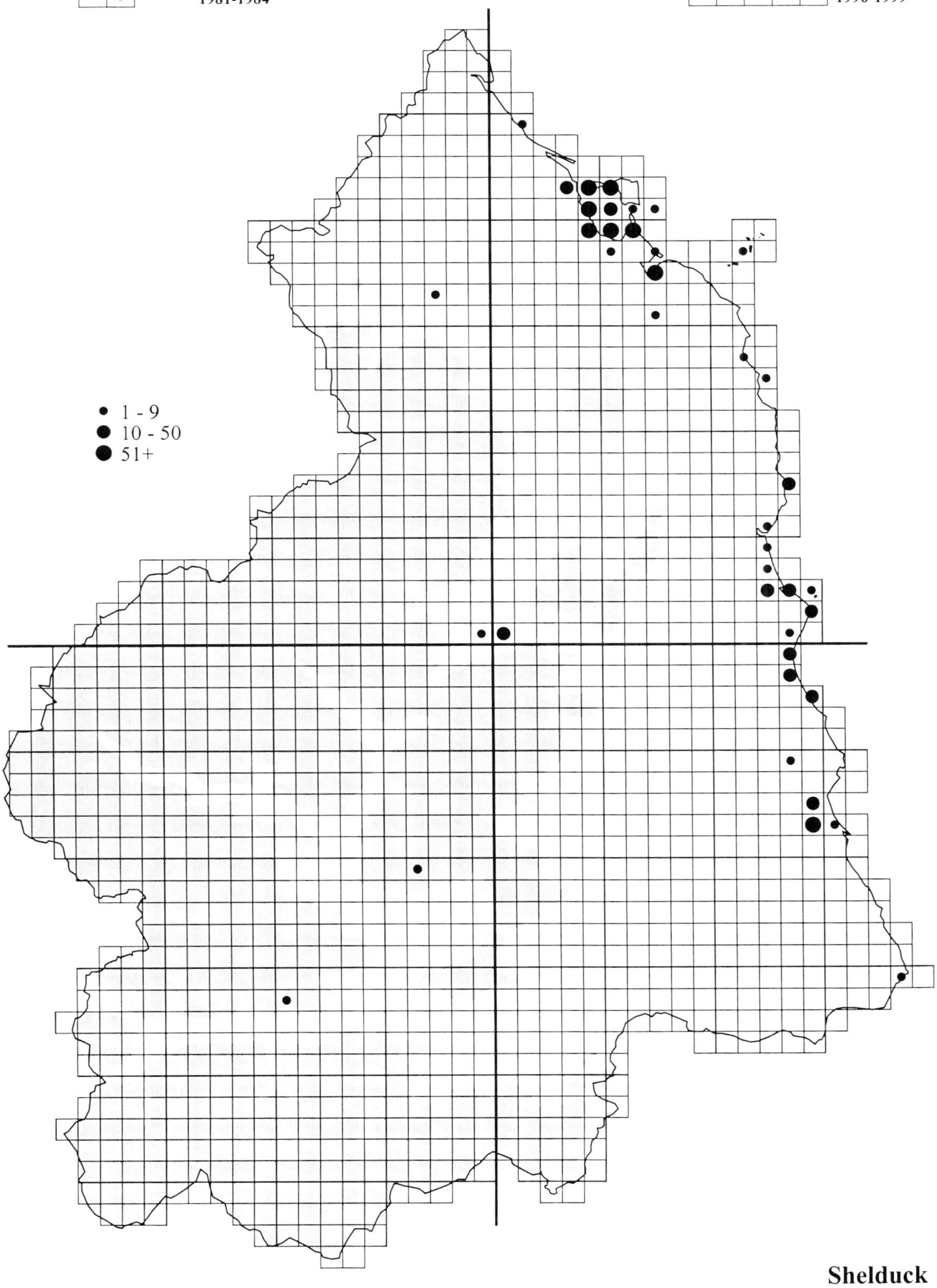

Shelduck

MANDARIN *Aix galericulata*

The Mandarin became established as a breeding resident in this country during the twentieth century. Its presence is due to both escapes and deliberate releases from wildfowl collections (Cramp & Simmons, 1997). In its natural range in Asia it is migratory, but the British population is resident, favouring slow-moving or standing fresh water fringed by thick overhanging foliage. It is primarily a lowland bird, nesting in hollow trees, tree roots and fallen logs, and in Northumberland has bred successfully in nest-boxes. In winter Mandarins may form flocks in which social play and display are a feature with many birds forming pairs between September and February (Lack, 1986).

The species is a very recent addition to Northumberland's avifauna. Bolam (1912; 1932) knew of no records with the first, according to Galloway and Meek (1978), being the unusual report of two Norwegian birds shot at Seaton Burn within thirty hours of leaving a wildfowl collection in Norway in 1962. Thereafter occasional males were recorded sporadically during the 1970s and 1980s, but from 1988, with the exception of 1992, birds have been reported annually, although not always in the winter months. Prior to the mid-1990s the origin of most birds is open to question, the majority being at coastal sites, but from 1994 when attempted breeding took place in the North Tyne Valley, a permanent nucleus was established in the county. At this site, near Ridley Stokoe (NY78M), birds are now regularly recorded, particularly in spring, as well as at other locations such as Kielder and Bellingham along the same river system.

During the winter atlas survey a flock of 31 Mandarin, including 19 males, was reported on the North Tyne near Ridley Stokoe in February 1999. Three birds, possibly part of this larger group, were also reported from the adjacent tetrad at Smalesmouth (NY78H) in January 1999. Away from the main area, single birds were present on the River Wansbeck at Morpeth (NZ18X) in December 1998 and again nearby (NZ28C) in February 1999. The increasing number of sightings throughout the year in the Linton/Warkworth Lane/Morpeth area (NZ28/NZ29), and the confirmed breeding at Bedlington Country Park in 1998 may relate to the formation of a second county breeding nucleus.

Indications are that the species is likely to expand in Northumberland and the number of winter sightings will therefore increase. Mead (2000) quoted a British population of about 7,000 individual birds, which represents a significant percentage of the world's population. As the Mandarin is now a declining species in the Far East the British population is likely to increase in global ornithological importance.

JOHN C. DAY

No. of tetrads in which recorded 4 (<1%)

Tetrad Analysis	No. of tetrads
1 bird	2 (50%)
2-3 birds	1 (25%)
4+ birds	1 (25%)

Total No. of birds counted 36

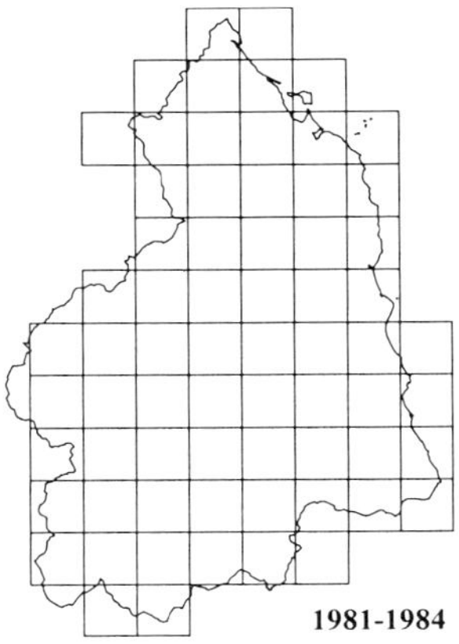

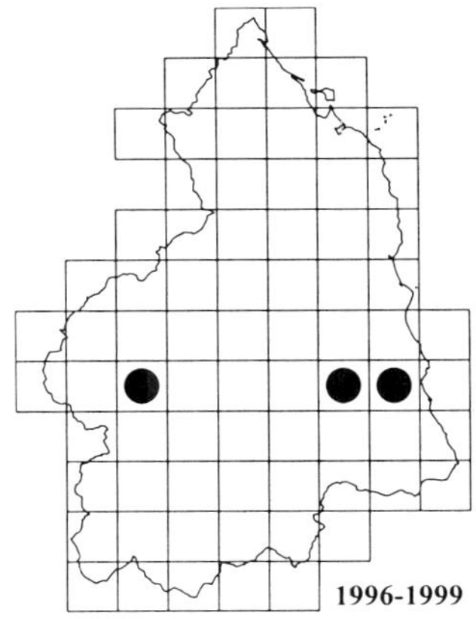

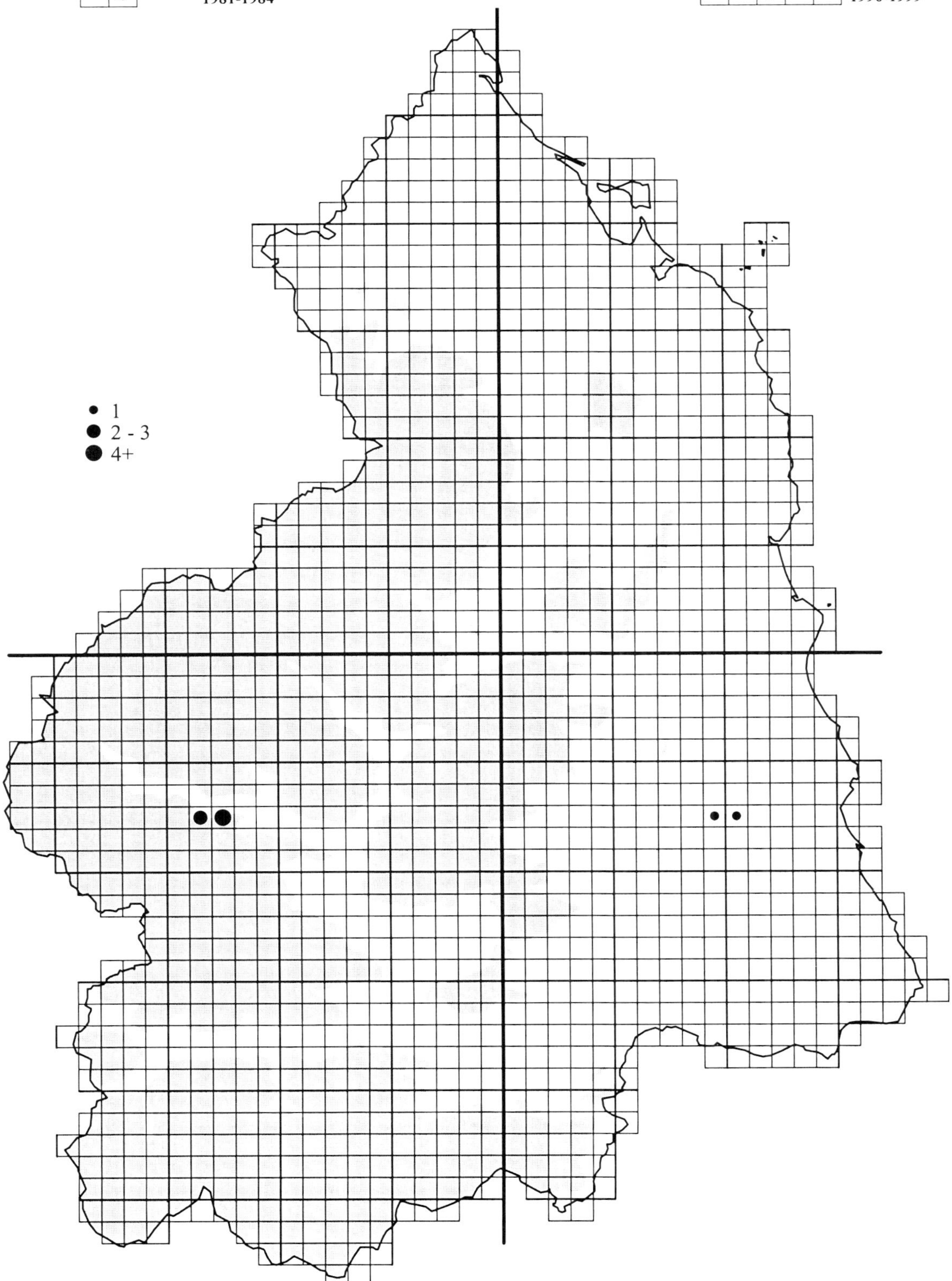

Mandarin

WIGEON *Anas penelope*

The Wigeon is well known to birdwatchers in Northumberland, particularly in the autumn and winter months when it occurs on many of the county's ponds, lakes and estuaries. Hancock (1874) described the species as a plentiful autumn and winter visitant and in more recent publications such as *Birds in Northumbria* and *Northumbrian Birds* (Kerr, 2001) its status is that of an abundant passage and winter visitor as well as an uncommon breeding species.

The main wintering grounds are Fenham Flats (NU14) and Budle Bay (NU13) and even before the establishment of the Lindisfarne NNR in 1964 huge numbers were present, with for example 20,000 counted in November 1948. Even larger numbers were recorded in the 1970s with 31,000 in November 1975 (Galloway & Meek, 1978). Peak counts occurred in October-December with generally less than 5,000 present by February indicating that many birds spent a relatively short period of time on the Reserve before moving on to other areas outside the county. In recent years the trend has continued with 14,000 counted in October 1999 but only 3,657 in November and 1,314 in December (*Birds in Northumbria 1999*). Wildfowling is a popular pastime on the Reserve and wintering numbers may well be affected by the disturbance caused by this activity. Concerns were raised initially in the mid-1980s resulting in the introduction of a limited shooting period and a review of punt gunning licences (*Birds in Northumbria 1985*). The subsequent establishment of a refuge, free from shooting, is to be welcomed and hopefully this will encourage more birds to linger throughout the winter. Lindisfarne NNR remains a site of national importance in Great Britain as it regularly holds more than 1% of the estimated British population (Pollitt *et al.*, 2000).

Away from Lindisfarne numbers are much lower in the winter months although the species is widely distributed throughout the county. Counts seldom exceed 600 at coastal ponds such as Druridge Pools (NZ29T), Cresswell Pond (NZ29X) and Hauxley (NZ20W), and inland sites including Derwent Reservoir (NY95W/NZ05B), and Grindon (NY86D) and Broomlee (NY76Z) Loughs.

The species favours lowland wintering sites with 60% of the 75 occupied tetrads during the survey period being below 100 metres a.s.l. and 85% less than 200 metres. However, wintering birds were present at three out of five upland sites where breeding was confirmed during fieldwork for *The atlas of breeding birds in Northumbria* (Day *et al.*, 1995). The winter distribution patterns shown in the 10km square maps indicate little change between the 1981-1984 and the 1996-1999 surveys.

Ringing recoveries indicate the diverse origins of the county's wintering population with records of birds marked in Iceland, Scandinavia and Russia (*Birds in Northumbria 1988, 1994, 1996*).

With a healthy wintering population and continued protection in sensitive areas, it seems likely that the Wigeon will continue to be a common sight in Northumberland during the winter months.

ROBIN HARVEY

Distribution by altitude

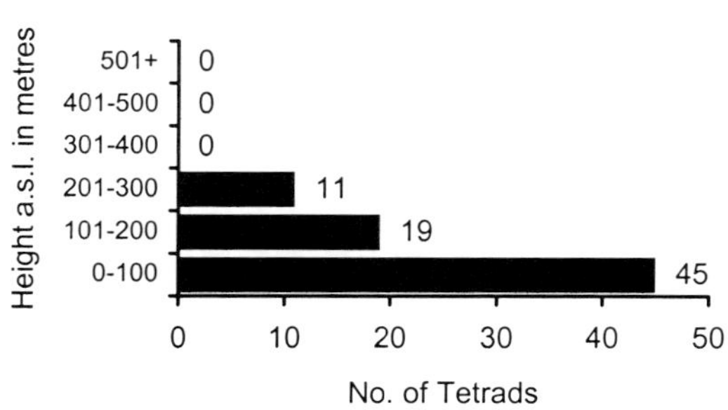

No. of tetrads in which recorded 75 (5%)

Tetrad Analysis	No. of tetrads
1-30 birds	39 (52%)
31-120 birds	21 (28%)
121+ birds	15 (20%)

Total No. of birds counted 7,910

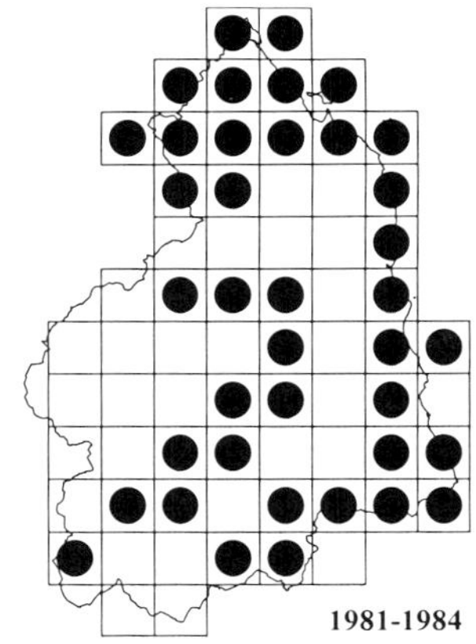

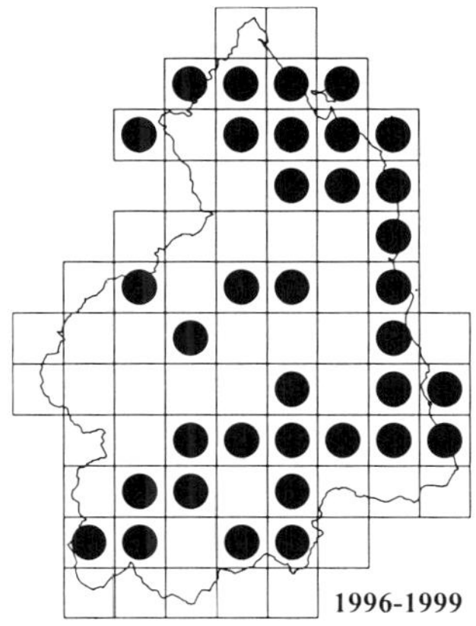

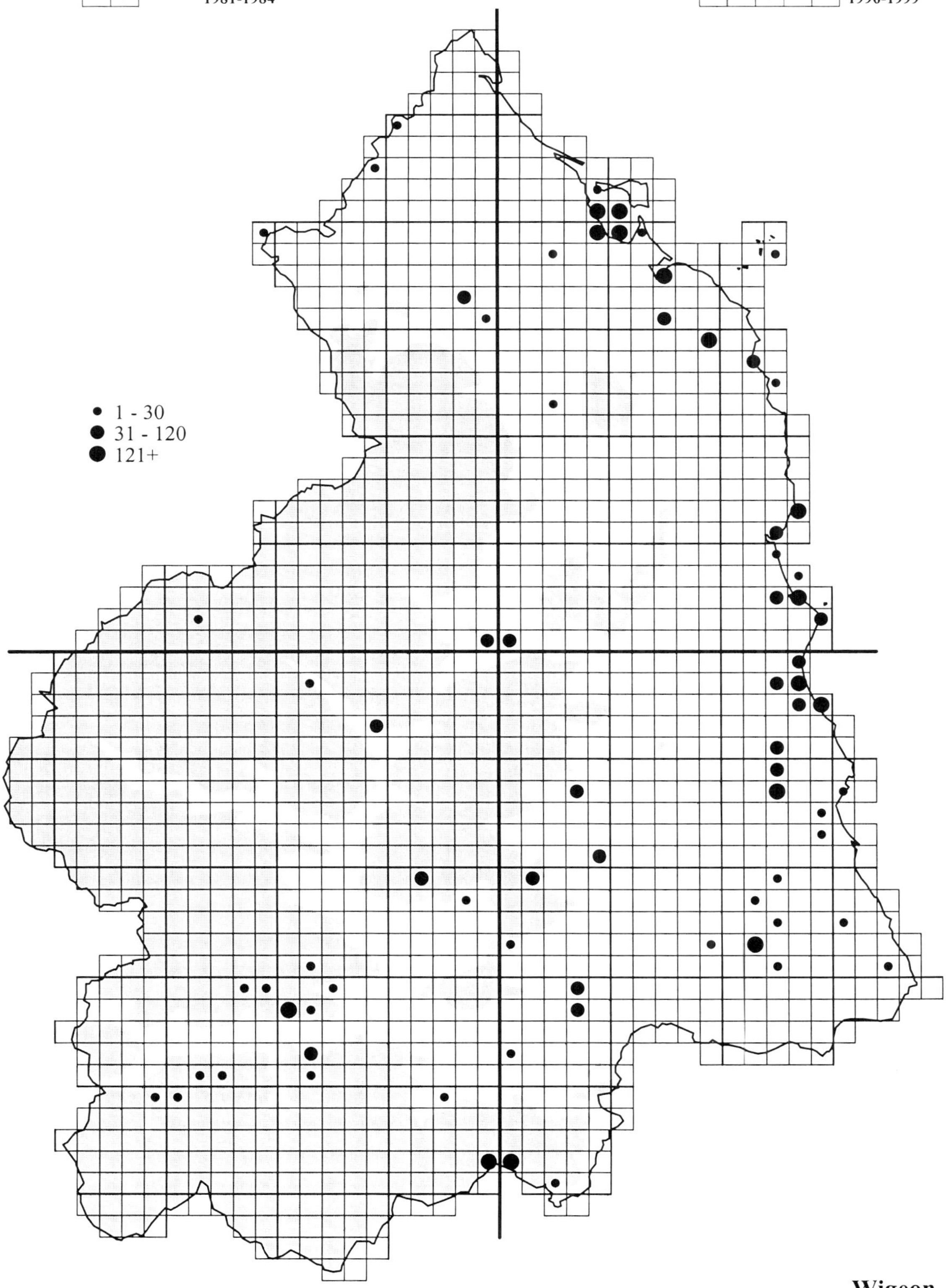

Wigeon

GADWALL *Anas strepera*

Within the county the Gadwall has increased both in number and distribution since Hancock (1874) cited 'only two examples of this casual visitant'. Bolam (1932) rated it as 'a rare winter and spring visitant, which has not yet been proved to nest here' and knew of only 12 records, some of them not fully authenticated. Confirmed breeding did not take place until 1965, with Galloway and Meek (1978) still describing it as 'an uncommon visitor and a casual breeding species' in the mid-1970s. More recently it has assumed the status of 'an uncommon breeder, and passage and winter visitor' (*Birds in Northumbria 1999*).

A slight change in distribution is evident between the current winter survey and the 1981-1984 national winter atlas survey, more being found in the northern half of the county in the current survey than previously. Despite this moderate shift, the totals of occupied 10km squares differ little (nine in the current survey against eight previously). Ten of the 16 occupied tetrads were found in the south east sector (NZ), reflecting the high density of suitable habitat in the form of lowland, often shallow, freshwater ponds. A strong bias towards lowland areas is demonstrated by a total of 14 (88%) occupied tetrads falling in the 0-100 metres a.s.l. band, with only single occupied tetrads in the 101-200 and 201-300 metre a.s.l. bands respectively.

Although only recorded in 16 tetrads within nine 10 kilometre squares during the current winter survey, numbers at several key localities were quite high. The grand total of maximum counts of the species over the three year period was 114. It should be noted that this is a maximum figure and such numbers may not be present in each individual winter. The largest concentrations involved 29 at Caistron (NU00A), 18 at East Chevington (NZ29U), and 12 at both Cresswell Pond (NZ29X) and Hauxley (NU20W), while five to eight were found in four other tetrads. Peak counts during the winter atlas period in 1981-1984 were only three at Big Waters (NZ27G) and Newton Pool (NU22M). This evident population increase is also apparent in the breeding population with, for example, ten broods being found at seven localities in 1999 (*Birds in Northumbria 1999*).

The annual WeBS counts revealed a population of 15,211 Gadwall in Great Britain in December 1998, including a remarkable 1,397 at Wraysbury Gravel Pits, Berkshire (Pollitt *et al.*, 2000). Compared with such figures the county population is not of any national significance as yet.

A preference for water bodies formed relatively recently, such as Caistron and East Chevington, and the increase in the number of apparently suitable 'flashes' formed by mining subsidence appear encouraging. The continued increase and expansion of Gadwall within the county, as with Britain as a whole (Mead, 2000), seems very likely.

GRAEME BOWMAN

Distribution by altitude

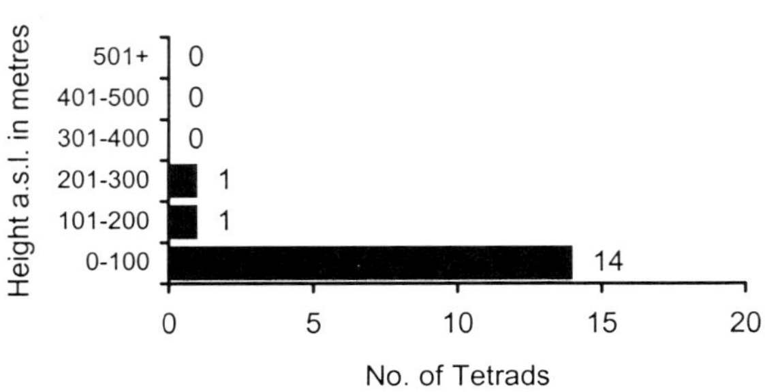

No. of tetrads in which recorded 16 (1%)

Tetrad Analysis	No. of tetrads
1-3 birds	8 (50%)
4-8 birds	4 (25%)
9+ birds	4 (25%)

Total No. of birds counted 114

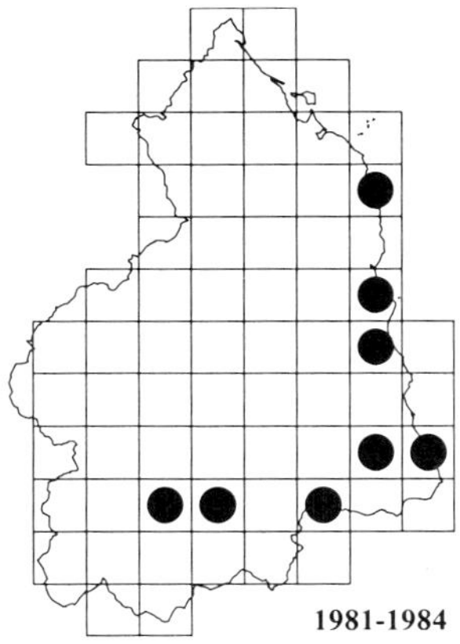

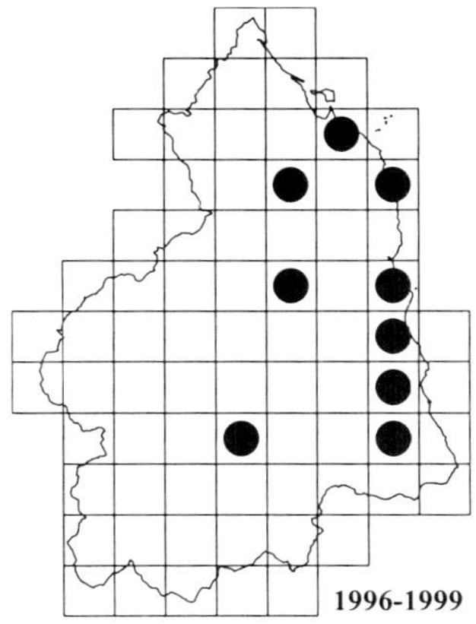

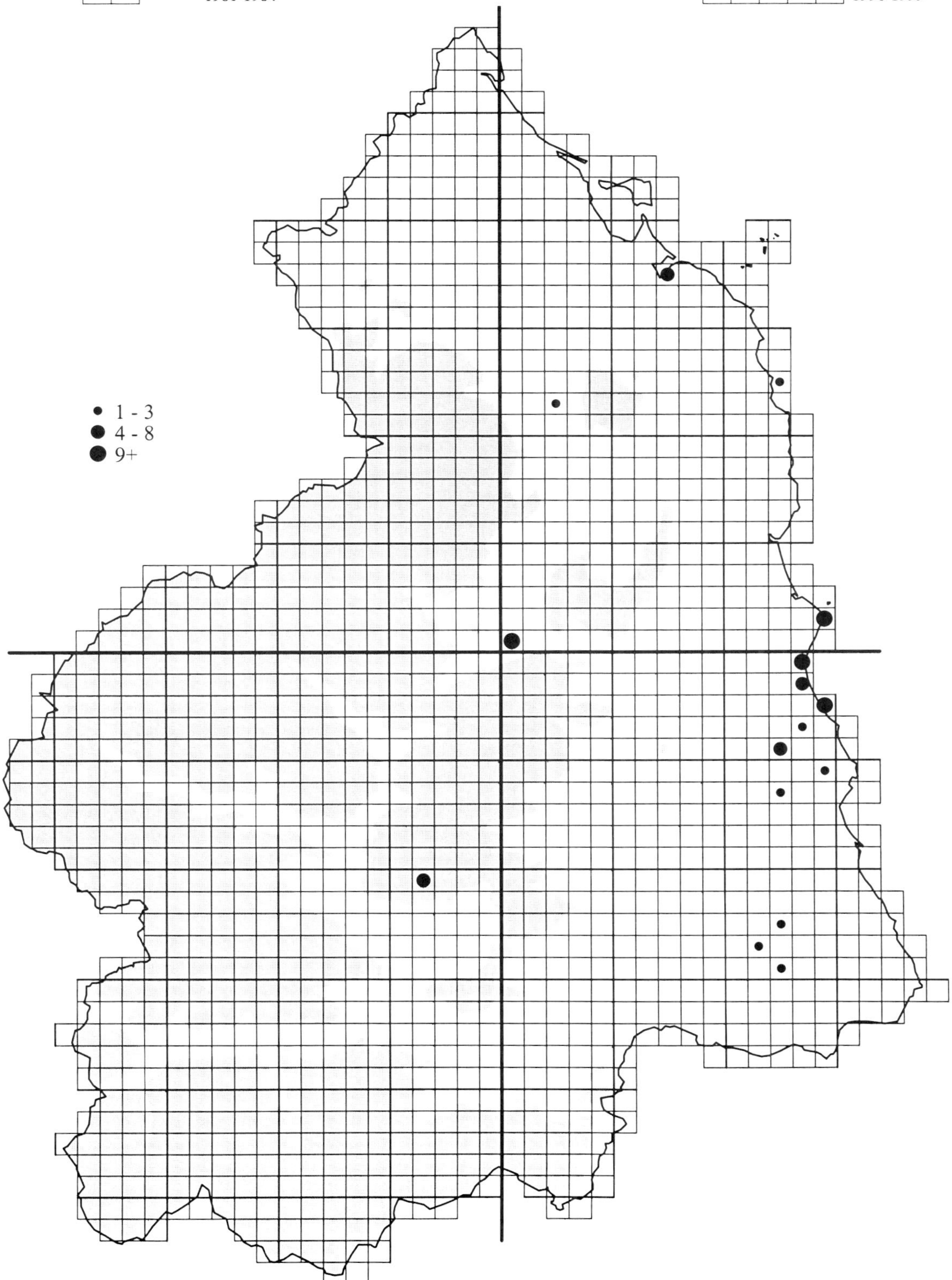

Gadwall

TEAL *Anas crecca*

Bolam (1932) regarded the Teal as 'a common resident, breeding in limited numbers' while Galloway and Meek (1978) described it as 'a common passage and winter visitor, but an uncommon breeding species'. A grand total of 7,691 was found by combining all maximum counts over the survey period. Despite the fact that this maximum figure may not have been present in each individual winter it is evident that the species falls into the 'common' category of 1,001-10,000 non-breeding individuals per year as defined by Galloway and Meek (1978).

Day *et al.* (1995) gave an annual county breeding population of around 60-80 pairs (with 20-40 additional non-breeding pairs) and there has been no evident increase since then. Clearly the bulk of those found in winter come from areas outside the county. *The atlas of wintering birds in Britain and Ireland* states 'immigrants come from a wide breeding range extending from the countries around the Baltic, through to north western Siberia. Several thousand Teals also come from Iceland' (Lack, 1986). Ringing recoveries have demonstrated birds originating in Scandinavia, the Baltic States and Iceland while an adult female ringed in the Rhone Estuary, France, in December 1957 was recovered near Wooler in December 1959. Movement between the county and Scotland and Wales has also been recorded (Galloway & Meek 1978).

Teal were recorded in a total of 44 ten kilometre squares in the current survey, closely matching a total of 45 in the 1981-1984 national atlas. In the upper half of the county there has been a slight shift eastwards, with some formerly occupied squares in the west now vacant. A total of 79 (64%) occupied tetrads were found within the 0-100 metres a.s.l. height range, with only 30 tetrads (24%) in the 101-200 metres a.s.l. band, and 14 tetrads in the next category of 201-300 metres a.s.l. As illustrated in *The atlas of breeding birds in Northumbria*, upland areas are favoured by nesting birds which tend to shun the coastal strip at this time. By contrast, wintering birds utilise lowland coastal areas and all but one 10km square that contain a section of coastline were occupied during the current survey. Furthermore, most counts in excess of 100 birds came from localities in the eastern half of the region.

The largest single concentrations recorded were 920 at Budle Bay (NU13M), 792 at Caistron (NU00A), 502 at Big Waters (NZ27G), with 500 at a high tide roost at Inner Farne (NU23C) and 480 at Grindon Lough (NY86D). Other favoured sites holding between 273-334 were Druridge Pools (NZ29T), near Fenton on the Milfield Plain (NT93R), Low Newton (NU22M) and Scotswood (NZ26B). The estuarine conditions such as those at Budle Bay are apparently favoured although some of the birds counted there may use the area as a safe roosting site and spend time feeding elsewhere. The Scotswood section of the River Tyne, which is tidal, was also favoured. Notable numbers using this locality appear to be a recent phenomenon, perhaps as a result of improved water quality. During the 1981-1984 national survey the largest single concentration in the county was 480 at Lindisfarne NNR in January 1983, significantly less than the peak counts found in the current survey.

The total number of birds counted in control tetrads was 153 in 1996/97, 163 in the following winter, and 790 in 1998/99. The dramatic increase in the final winter can largely be accounted for by the roost of 500 at the Farne Islands, mentioned above, where none had been recorded in the previous two winters. The 'missing' birds perhaps used the nearby Budle Bay section of Lindisfarne NNR instead. The only other significant change between the years was in the Alnmouth area (NU21K) where 14 and 28 in the first two winters respectively rose to 98 in the final winter. Teal are quick to react to cold and hard weather spells, and will readily move south and west to escape them although during the current survey period such conditions were infrequent.

A count in excess of 1,400 is needed to qualify for a site of national importance in Great Britain (Pollitt *et al.*, 2000) and no single site in the region reaches this figure. Collectively, however, the county population is not insignificant considering that the Great Britain WeBS total in January 1999 was 138,162.

GRAEME BOWMAN

Distribution by altitude

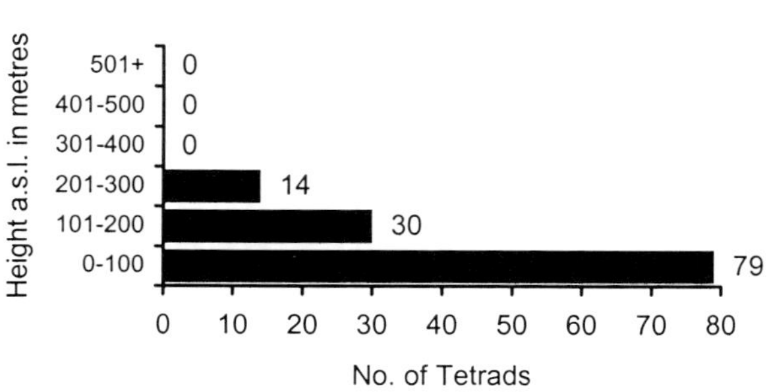

No. of tetrads in which recorded 123 (9%)

Tetrad Analysis	No. of tetrads
1-18 birds	68 (55%)
19-100 birds	38 (31%)
101+ birds	17 (14%)

Total No. of birds counted 7,691

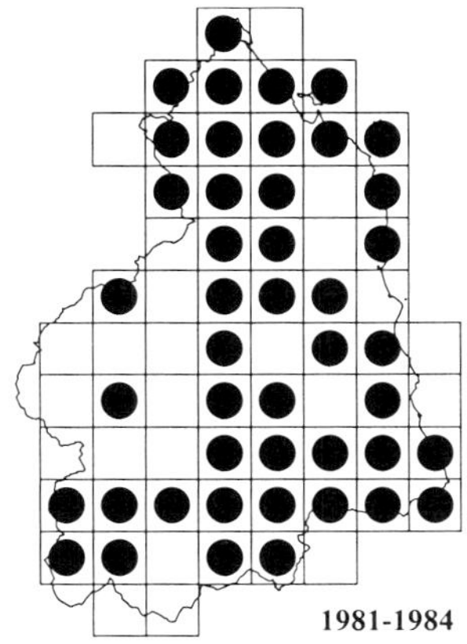

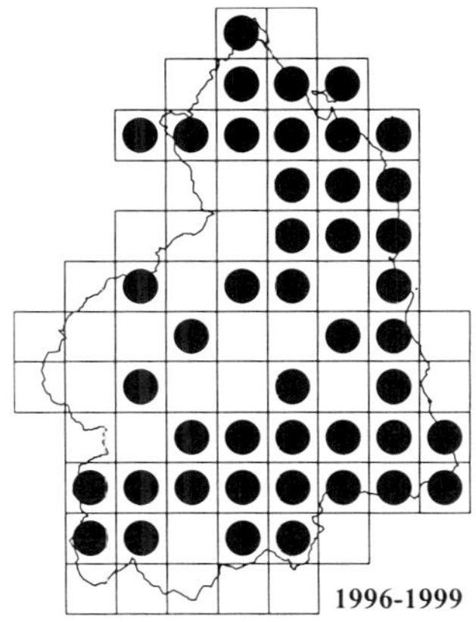

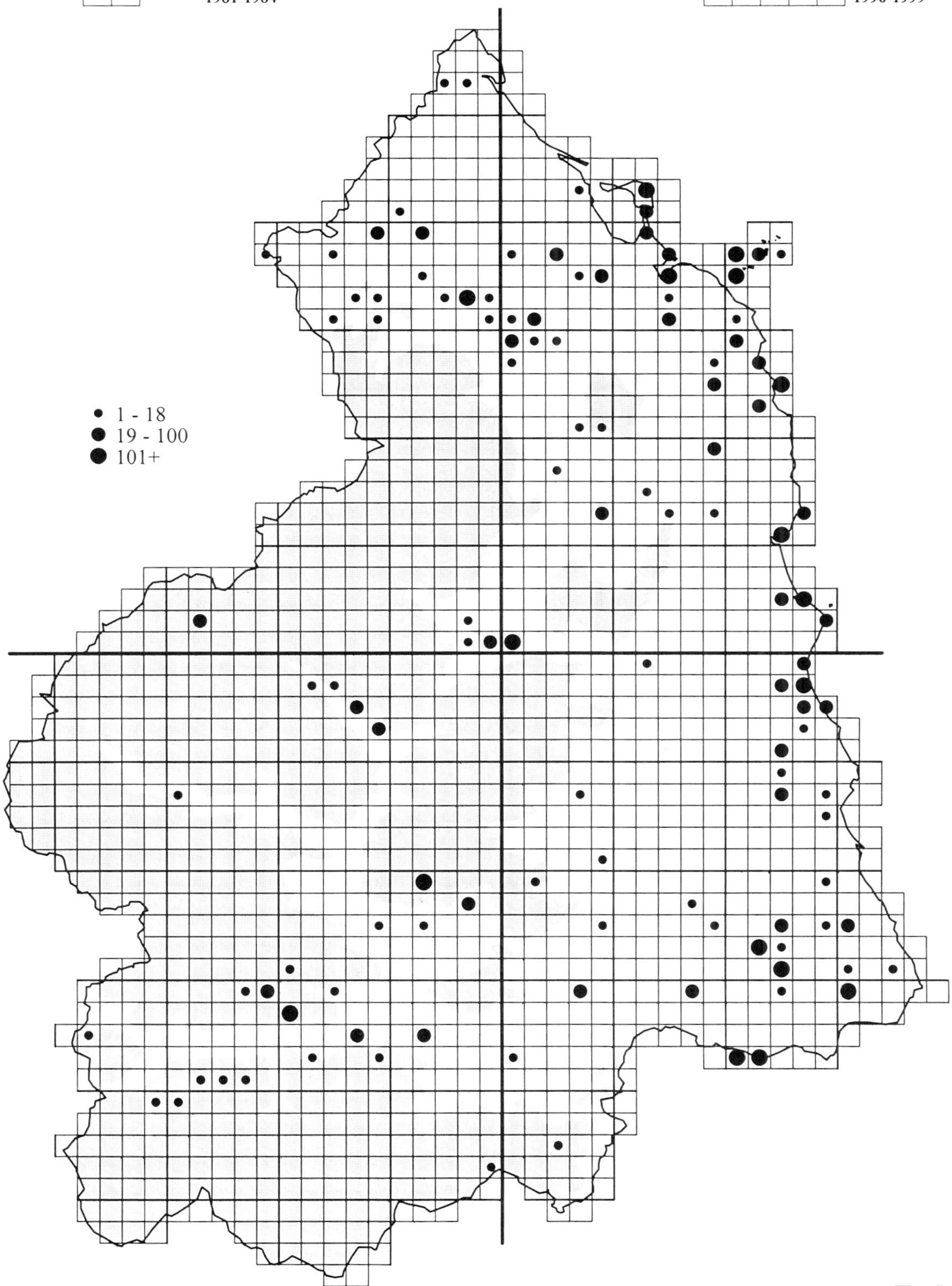

Teal

MALLARD *Anas platyrhynchos*

The Mallard was described by Bolam (1932) as 'a common resident' and nearly 50 years later by Galloway and Meek (1978) as 'an abundant passage and winter visitor, and a well-represented breeding species'. More recently it was classified as 'a common breeder and an abundant passage and winter visitor' (*Birds in Northumbria 1999*). The grand total of maximum counts over three winters was 11,092. This figure would place the species in the 'abundant' category of 10,000 non-breeding individuals per year according to Galloway and Meek. However, this is a maximum count and the actual total for each individual winter may have been lower than this.

The largest single concentrations during the current survey period were 604 at Big Waters (NZ27G), 508 at Caistron (NU00A), and between 233 and 357 at Bellasis Bridge (NZ17Y), Budle Bay (NU13M), Colt Crag Reservoir (NY97J), in Coquetdale (NT90R) and Linton Pond (NZ29K). Big Waters has become established as a favoured locality and in the previous national winter survey 700 were counted in December 1983. Other large counts during the previous survey period were 1,600 at Lindisfarne NNR in December 1981 and 1,400 in January 1982, with 900 at Derwent Reservoir in December 1982. Historically, the greatest counts within the region were 3,000 north of Holy Island in 1945 and 1,224 at Gosforth Park in December of that year (Galloway & Meek 1978).

A total of 1,255 pairs was recorded in *The atlas of breeding birds in Northumbria* (Day *et al.*, 1995) although the population was estimated as high as 1,500 pairs. Even allowing for a successful breeding season it is unlikely that the county breeding population could account for the numbers found in winter. Mallards are not wholly sedentary and young ringed in the county have been found in the Netherlands and Russia. Galloway and Meek stated 'ringing recoveries indicate that the winter immigrant population is of northern Eurasian origin'. Movement in and out of the region is also demonstrated by autumn coastal passage although this is typically much less conspicuous than that of Wigeon *Anas penelope* or Teal *Anas crecca*.

Variation in abundance between winters was not greatly significant as demonstrated by the control tetrads, which gave totals of 731, 640 and 787 for each of the successive winters respectively. A lack of prolonged hard weather is likely to have encouraged a relatively stable population and Mallard are anyway noted for tolerating spells of such conditions by 'sitting it out'.

Although Mallard are widely distributed there would appear to be some consolidation in winter when compared to the breeding season. The species was recorded in a total of 521 tetrads in *The atlas of breeding birds in Northumbria* compared to a total of 393 'occupied' tetrads in the current winter survey. It is likely that some small ponds and streams are deserted for larger lakes and rivers in winter. A preference for lower ground can be seen with over half of the 'occupied' tetrads (53%) at a height of 0-100 metres a.s.l., although six tetrads in the 301-400 metres a.s.l. range held birds. The heavily forested upland areas, with their limited amount of suitable habitat, are largely avoided. (In considering the winter totals it should be borne in mind that small numbers of hand-reared Mallard are still released annually on a number of shooting estates in the county. *Eds.*)

A maximum of 151,114 Mallard were recorded in Great Britain on the Wetland Bird Survey in December 1998 (Pollitt *et al.*, 2000). The WeBS threshold to qualify for a site of national importance in Great Britain is set at 5,000. There are no single sites in the region which approach this figure but the combined county population is more notable in a national context.

GRAEME BOWMAN

Distribution by altitude

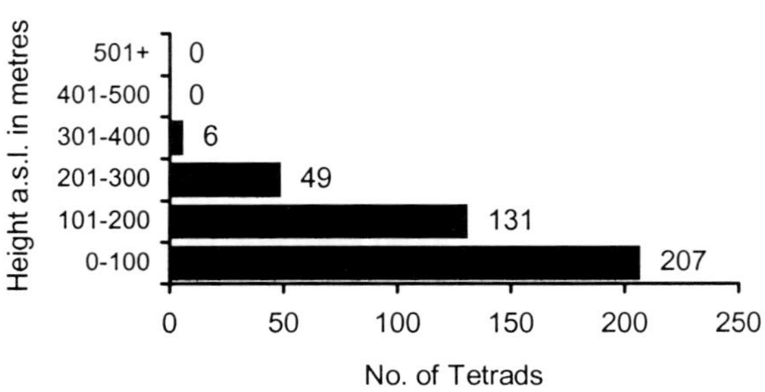

No. of tetrads in which recorded 393 (27%)

Tetrad Analysis	No. of tetrads
1-10 birds	200 (51%)
11-50 birds	134 (34%)
51+ birds	59 (15%)

Total No. of birds counted 11,092

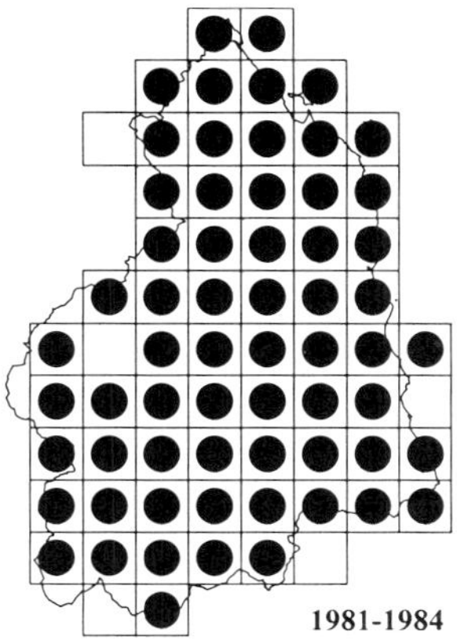

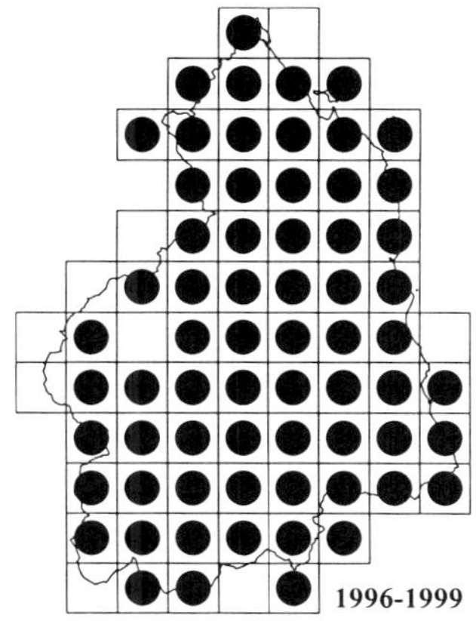

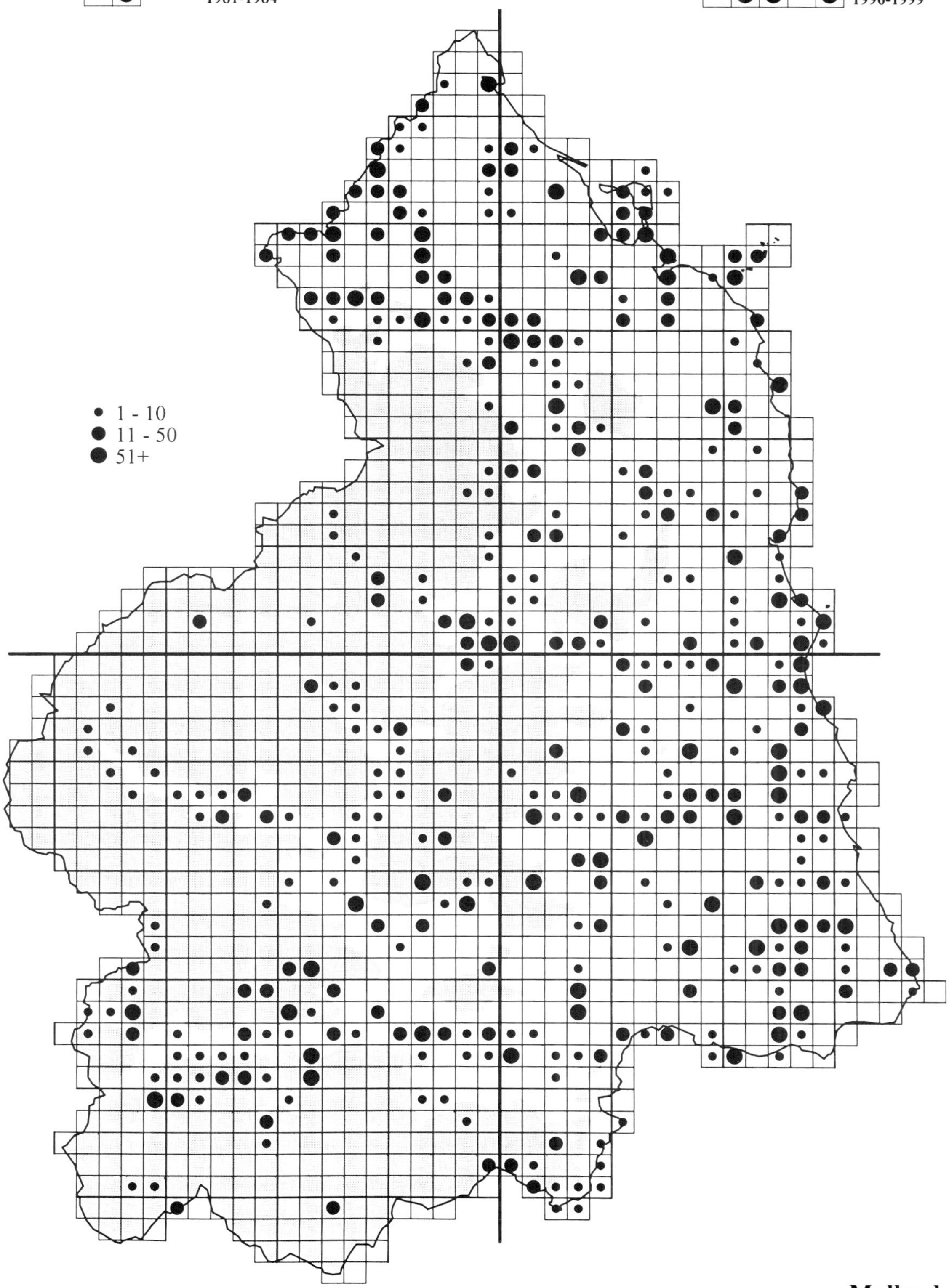

Mallard

PINTAIL *Anas acuta*

A 'rare resident' was how Hancock (1874) described the Pintail, and Bolam (1912) used the same description almost 40 years later, adding that it was a 'fairly regular autumn and winter visitant to the Northumberland coast, in small numbers'. Galloway and Meek (1978) stated 'a slow but steady increase ... most records come from places within ten miles of the coast and principally from Lindisfarne NNR and Holburn Moss, where flocks of 20 or more are not infrequent'.

Within the county it has a rather limited winter distribution. One area, Lindisfarne NNR, holds by far the largest concentration. During the current atlas period, peak counts for that reserve were 110 on 21st November 1998 and 87 in February 1999, whilst 62 was the largest figure for a single tetrad, at Tealhole Point, Fenham Flats (NU13E) in December 1998. The largest gathering ever recorded in the county was also at Lindisfarne NNR with 152 on 4th February 1996. Numbers away from this site rarely reach double figures and the next biggest counts during the present survey were of nine at both Grindon Lough (NY86D) and Druridge Pools (NZ29T) in January 1998.

Excluding the single counts covering the whole reserve of Lindisfarne, the grand total of maximum counts during the current survey period was 155 birds. As this is a maximum figure the actual numbers present in each individual winter may be less than this. Unfortunately the species was not recorded on any control tetrads so any yearly fluctuations are not readily apparent. However, a glance at the annual county bird reports for the period under review reveals peak counts at Lindisfarne NNR of 110 in winter 1998-99, only 35 in 1997-98, and 71 in 1996-97. The trend towards a generally increasing winter population is supported by a comparison of the peak counts during the 1981-1984 national winter atlas survey when Lindisfarne NNR held 71 in January 1982 and 42 in December 1983. The recent creation of a 'refuge', free from shooting and disturbance, in a section of the Lindisfarne NNR appears to have been beneficial.

With a negligible British breeding population, and only sporadic nesting historically within the county, almost the entire winter population comes from abroad, principally western Siberia and to a lesser extent Scandinavia and Iceland (Lack, 1986). An example indicating one source of origin involved a bird ringed in the Netherlands in September 1970 and recovered at Low Newton (NU22M) in November 1971 (Galloway & Meek, 1978). Dramatic fluctuations within Northumbria between years may be due to changes in breeding success or weather in the natal area, allowing birds to remain abroad or alternatively encouraging a westward movement.

In 'good' winters when numbers are high at Lindisfarne, an increasing trend in recent years (e.g. 125 in January and 102 in December 2000), the species just falls into the 'well-represented' category of 101-1,000 individuals but in leaner years an 'uncommon' status of 11-100 may be more fitting.

Pintail were recorded in only 25 of all tetrads surveyed spread across sixteen 10 kilometre squares, a slight fall from 18 ten kilometre squares in the 1981-1984 winter atlas. Almost half of the occupied tetrads (12 out of 25) were in the north east (NU) sector, with eight in the south east (NZ), five in the south west (NY) and none in the north west (NT). Dividing the county into western and eastern halves, 80% of occupied tetrads were in the eastern half, many of them on or close to the coast. Unsurprisingly, a clear preference for lowland areas was apparent, with 72% of occupied tetrads falling in the 0-100 metres a.s.l. band, compared to 24% between 101-200 metres a.s.l. and 4% between 201-300 metres a.s.l.

In national terms, this county does not currently hold significant numbers of the wintering population. The WeBS total for Great Britain in January 1999 was 26,783. The most favoured site, the Dee Estuary, held as many as 5,018 in winter 1998-99 (Pollitt *et al.*, 2000).

GRAEME BOWMAN

Distribution by altitude

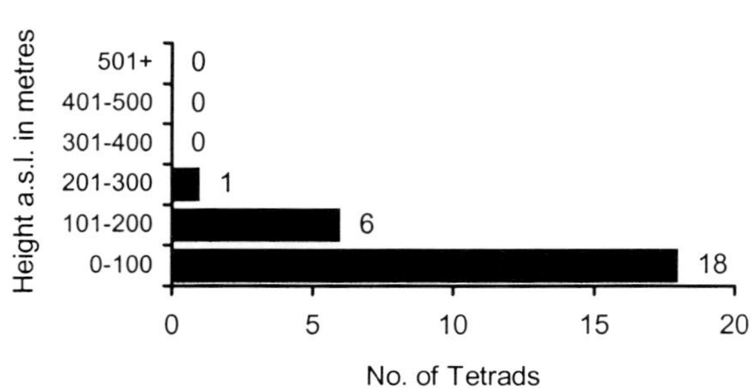

No. of tetrads in which recorded 25 (2%)

Tetrad Analysis	No. of tetrads
1-2 birds	12 (48%)
3-4 birds	7 (28%)
5+ birds	6 (24%)

Total No. of birds counted 155

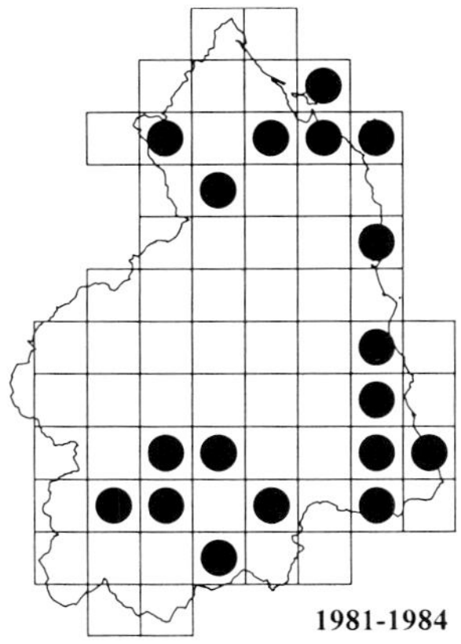

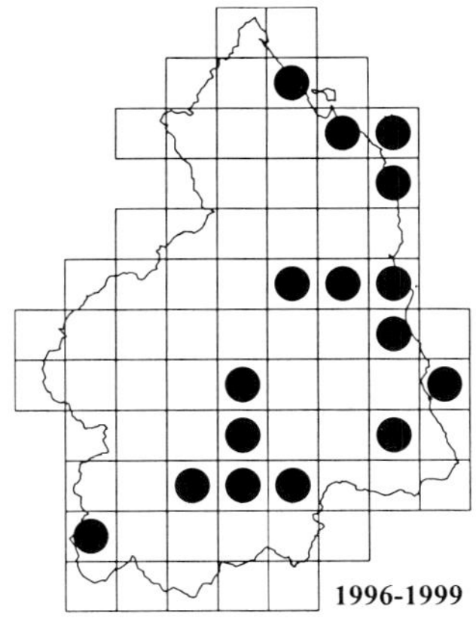

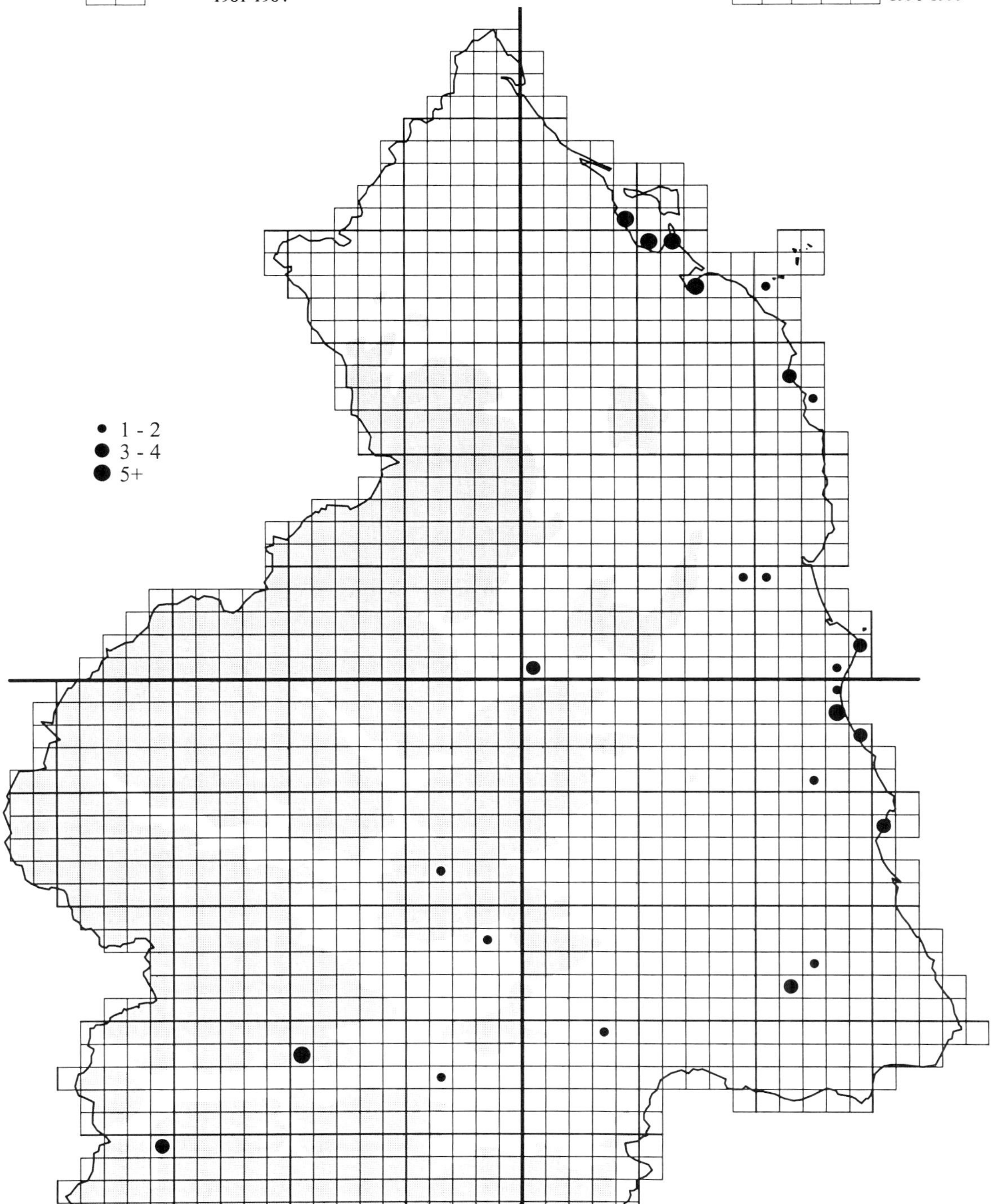

Pintail

SHOVELER *Anas clypeata*

The Shoveler was classified by Galloway and Meek (1978) as 'a well-represented passage and summer visitor, but less plentiful in winter; an uncommon breeding species'. The grand total of maximum counts over the current survey period was 140. Such a number may not be present in each individual winter but taking an average produces 47 per winter, which probably underestimates the true population. This mean figure would place the species in the 'uncommon' category as a wintering bird, i.e. between 11-100 non-breeding individuals, whereas the total of 140 would qualify for 'well-represented', i.e. between 101-1000 non-breeding individuals. Bolam (1912) stated that it had 'increased so much as to be now not uncommon in many parts of the district'. Nationally 'the breeding population ... apparently moves to France and Spain in the autumn, to be replaced by immigrants from as far east as western Siberia, many of which in turn move on southwards later in the winter.' (Lack, 1986).

As can be seen from the tetrad map there is a strong bias towards the coastal strip, with few being found well inland. Of a total of 22 occupied tetrads, 11 (50%) were in the south east (NZ). A preponderance of lowland, food-rich ponds and lakes in this area are clearly favoured by the surface-feeding Shoveler. The vast majority of occupied tetrads, 21 out of 22, were found in the 0-100 metres a.s.l. range with just one in the 101-200 metres a.s.l. bracket and none above these heights.

A slight change in distribution between the two winter atlases is apparent. There were 12 occupied 10km squares during the current winter survey compared to 18 during the 1981-1984 national winter atlas survey, with a noticeable contraction in inland localities.

The greatest numbers of Shoveler are typically found in September-October, for example 68 at Druridge Pools on 3rd October 1999, decreasing thereafter. There were only two counts in excess of 20 during the current survey, both of which were in February, with 29 at Druridge Pools (NZ29T) and 21 at Wallsend Swallow Pond (NZ36E), while Arcot Pond (NZ27M), Big Waters (NZ29G) and Cresswell Pond (NZ29X) produced peaks of 13-17, all in November. It is perhaps worth noting that all these peak counts occurred in either November or February and may have involved at least some late/early passage birds rather than prolonged winterers. The largest January counts during the survey period were of only four to five birds at two sites, Cresswell Pond and Budle Bay (NU13M). Galloway and Meek (1978) stated that 'in mild winters, many may remain into early December, but by the end of the year only small parties are in evidence'. The situation in the current survey period would seem similar. The species was too scarce to be recorded in any control tetrads. Interestingly, the largest count in this region recorded during the 1981-1984 national atlas survey was 16 at Wallsend Swallow Pond in December 1983.

The Wetland Bird Survey requires a threshold count of 100 or more to qualify for a site of national importance in Great Britain. One of the most productive sites, Burry Inlet, West Glamorgan, Dyfed, held 826 in January 1999, while the Somerset Levels held 485 in the same month (Pollitt *et al.*, 2000). In national terms, the numbers of wintering Shoveler within Northumberland, therefore, are not significant.

GRAEME BOWMAN

Distribution by altitude

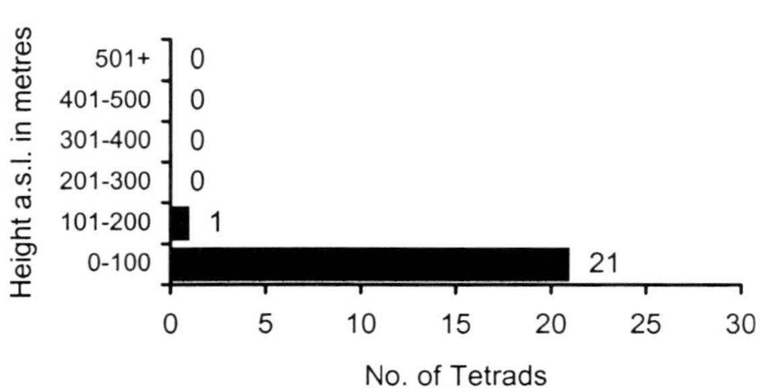

No. of tetrads in which recorded 22 (2%)

Tetrad Analysis	No. of tetrads
1-2 birds	10 (45%)
3-6 birds	7 (32%)
7+ birds	5 (23%)

Total No. of birds counted 140

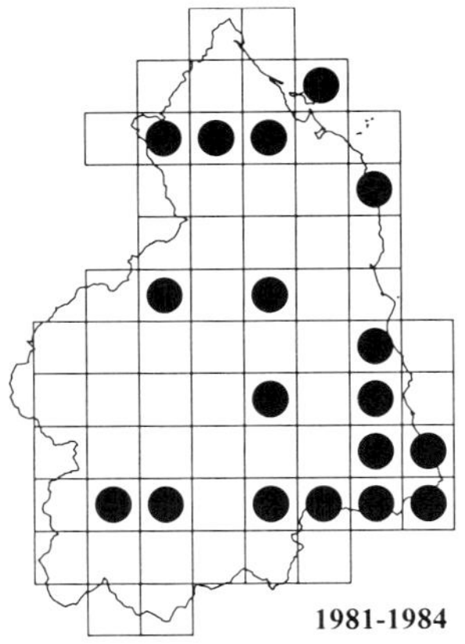

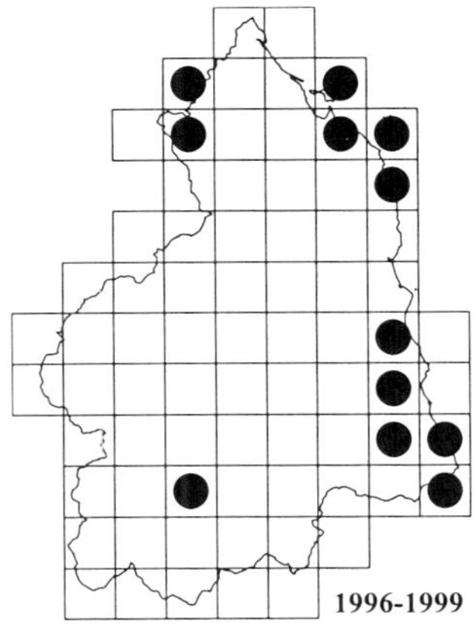

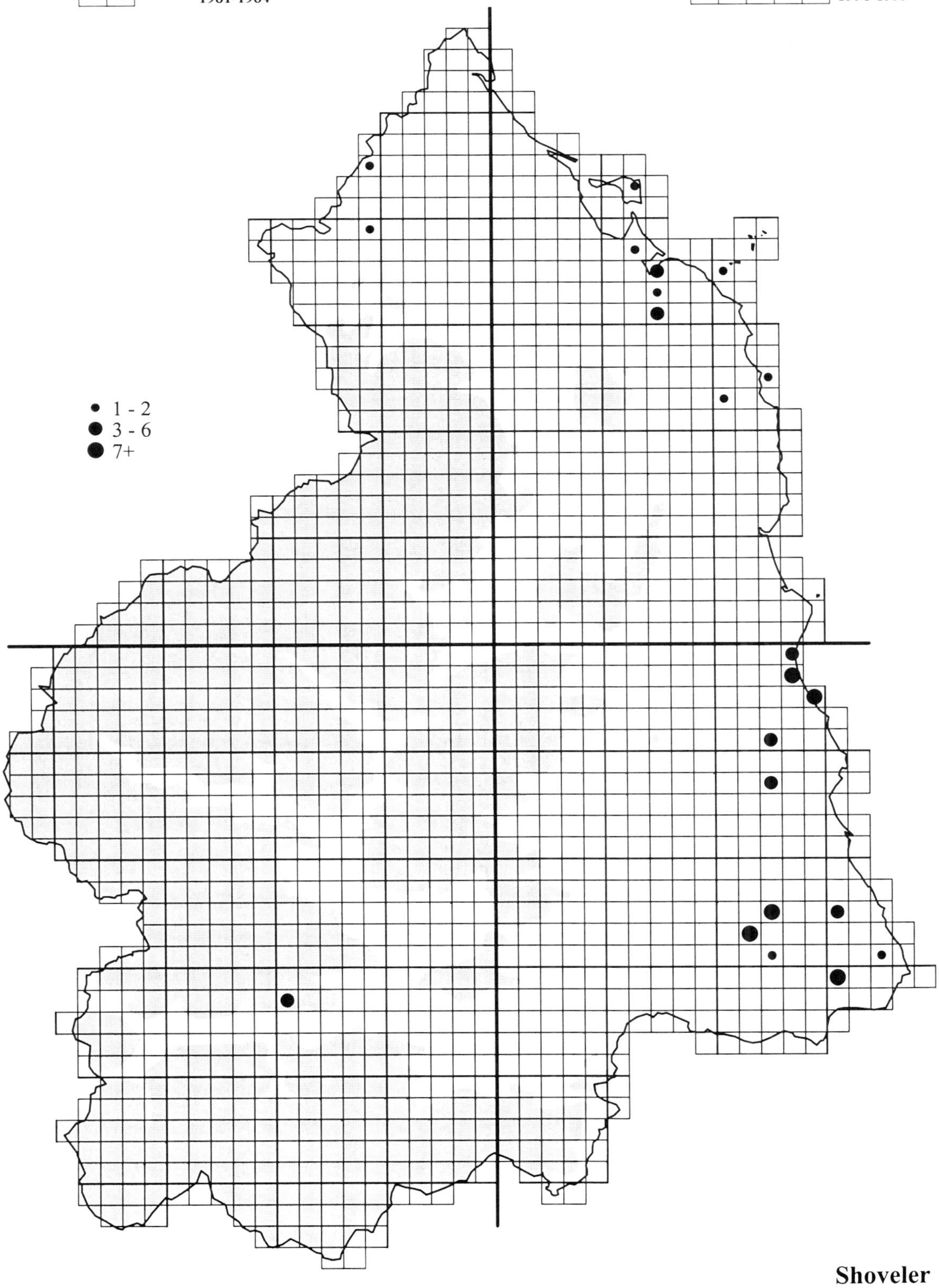

Shoveler

POCHARD *Aythya ferina*

'An uncommon breeder and a common passage and winter visitor' is how *Birds in Northumbria 1999* classified the Pochard, while Galloway and Meek (1978) described it as 'a common passage and winter visitor, but a rare breeding species'. Hancock (1874) called it 'a not uncommon winter visitant' and suspected it of nesting occasionally at Capheaton and Gosforth Park. Bolam (1912) said it bred 'in a considerable number of places' although it had 'only become thoroughly established as a nesting species within the last twenty years'. Galloway and Meek added 'Visitors begin to arrive in September ... and reach their peak between November and March, when parties of a hundred or more are seen regularly at Gosforth Park (252 were there on 6th November 1976). Large flocks, often well over a hundred, are also found, though somewhat irregularly, on many other waters'.

During the survey period, Pochard were found in 53 tetrads (4% of all those surveyed). In common with some other duck species over half (54%) of occupied tetrads were in the south east sector (NZ) of the county, reflecting a relative abundance of suitable feeding waters in this area. A total of 60% of occupied tetrads were in the 0-100 metres a.s.l. height range, with 26% and 13% in the 101-200 and 201-300 metres a.s.l. bands respectively. Optimum feeding quarters would appear to be concentrated in lowland areas, particularly along the coastal strip.

The grand total of maximum counts over the three winter period was 1,113. Such a total is unlikely to occur in one single winter but a typical winter population may not be much below this figure. Fluctuations between winters, as illustrated by counts from control tetrads, were not great, with respective totals of 35, 20 and 23 for the three successive winters. Care should be taken in reading too much into this, as only a small sample of six control tetrads was available. From the main survey the largest single counts were of 146 at Ladyburn Lake (NU20Q), 86 at Queen Elizabeth II Lake (NZ28Z) and 82 at Big Waters (NZ27G). Hauxley (NU20W), Holywell Pond (NZ37C), and Capheaton (NZ07J), Haggerston (NU04L) and Killingworth (NZ27Q) lakes all held peaks of 50-66. By contrast, peak counts during the 1981-1984 survey period were 448 at Hallington Reservoirs in January-February 1984, 400 at Whittle Dene Reservoirs in December 1981 and 350 at Big Waters in November 1981. The first two of these counts were probably attributable to hard weather being experienced at the time (*Birds in Northumbria 1981, 1984*). It seems likely that a lack of such conditions in the present survey would account for the relatively low maximum counts, at least to some extent.

Interestingly, the two sites that have held the largest all-time concentrations, Hallington Reservoirs (617 in November 1984) and Derwent Reservoir (565 in December 1976), did not feature at all in the current survey. Both of these sites are well inland and all those sites holding peak counts in the current survey are coastal, with the exception of Capheaton Lake. It may be inferred that immigrants from the east occupy suitable waters along the coastal strip and only move further inland when forced to. Three recoveries of birds ringed in eastern Europe, one in Russia and two in Latvia, indicate the origin of some of the visitors (Galloway & Meek, 1978).

It is not clear whether the average winter population across the county has recently (i.e. through the 1990s) declined, as might be suggested by generally lower peak concentrations, or whether the population is reasonably stable but scattered over a greater range of sites.

The Wetland Bird Survey 1998/99 noted that 'despite concerns in other parts of the wintering range, the long term trend in Great Britain of our second commonest diving duck has remained relatively stable for the last 20 years'. In December 1998 the WeBS total for Britain stood at 40,401 and the present threshold for national importance is 440 (Pollitt *et al.*, 2000). No single site within this county currently approaches that figure but collectively the wintering population is not insignificant.

GRAEME BOWMAN

Distribution by altitude

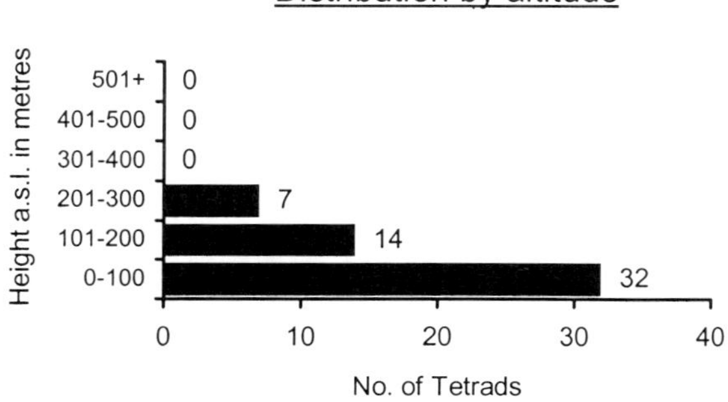

No. of tetrads in which recorded 53 (4%)

Tetrad Analysis	No. of tetrads
1-9 birds	26 (49%)
10-39 birds	17 (32%)
40+ birds	10 (19%)

Total No. of birds counted 1,113

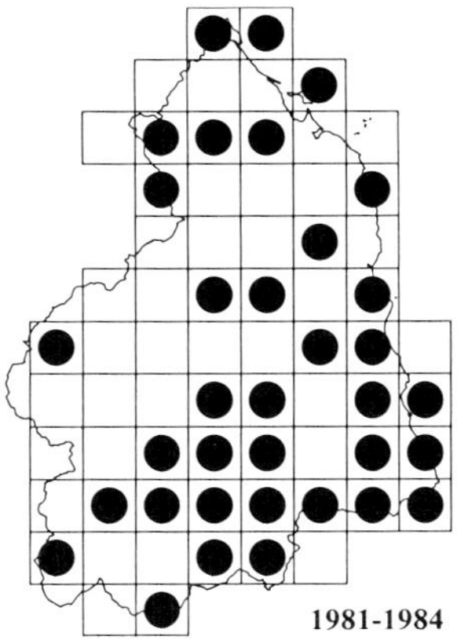

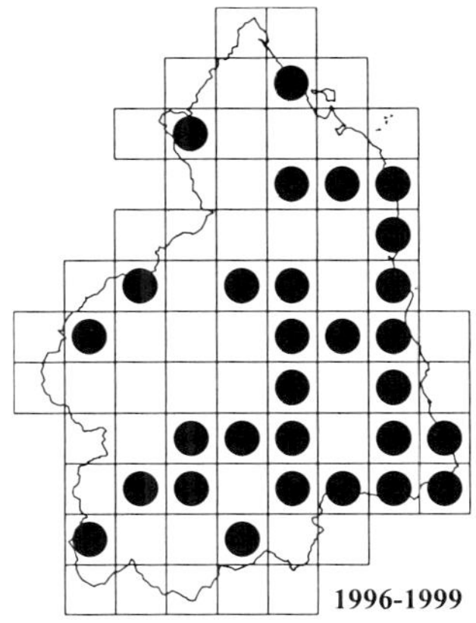

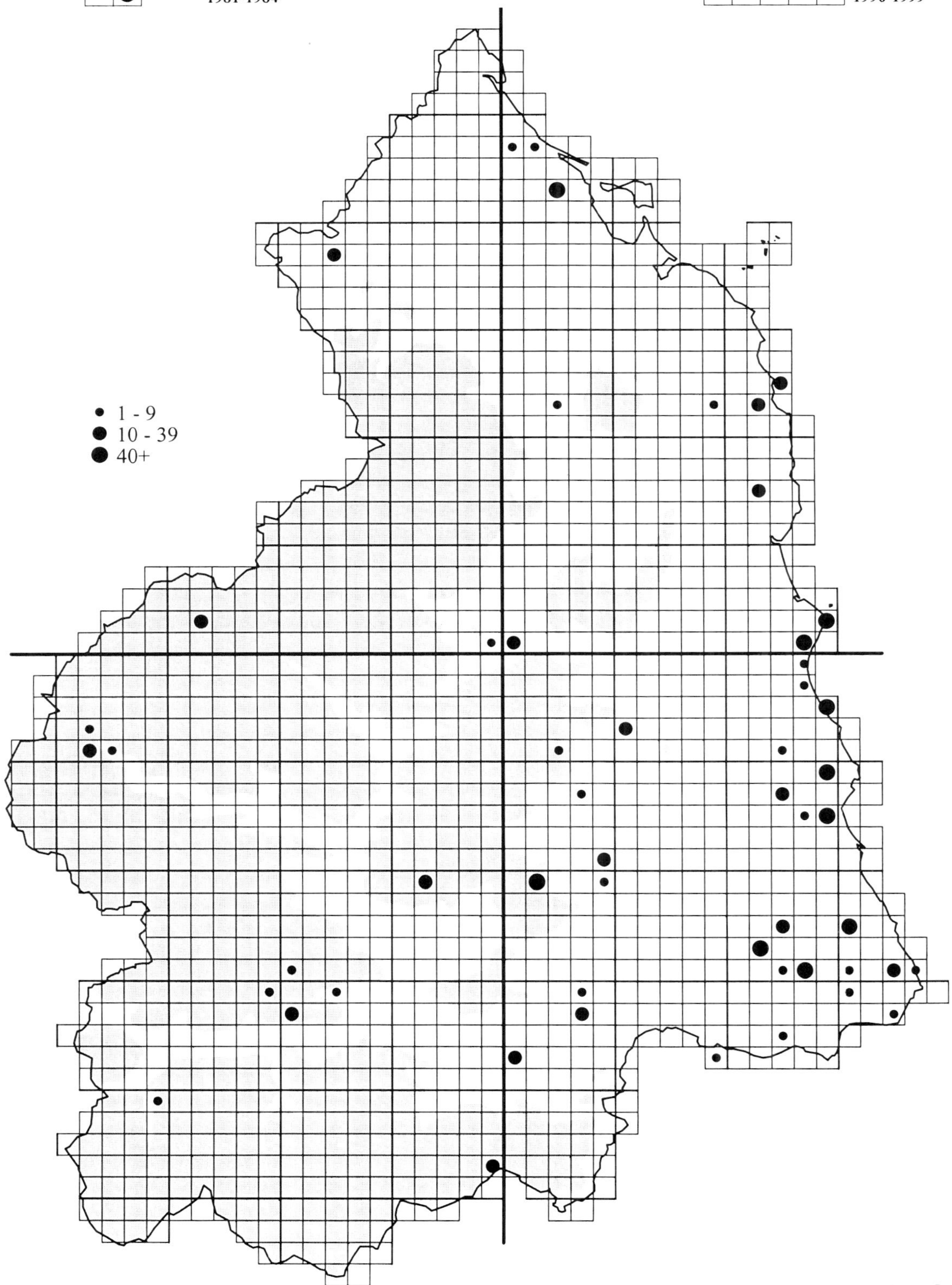

Pochard

TUFTED DUCK *Aythya fuligula*

The Tufted Duck is described as a common passage and winter visitor in *Birds in Northumbria*. The same status was also used by Galloway and Meek (1978) in their assessment of the species although they described fluctuations in the breeding population and hypothesized that the population had reduced significantly following an expansion in the early 1900s. They went on to suggest that the population was probably increasing in the county and this follows the national trend (Lack, 1986). In the UK, the Tufted duck is described by Lack (1986) as the commonest diving duck in Britain and Ireland. He also commented that numbers in the winter are greatly augmented by continental visitors.

In winter, non-breeding birds are mainly gregarious forming flocks of several hundred birds on freshwater habitats (Lack, 1986) although counts from Northumbria during the survey period are rather more modest with only one tetrad count of over 100 individuals on a site.

Nationally, only 5% of wintering Tufted Ducks were recorded on saline habitats during the previous national winter atlas (Lack, 1986), birds being predominantly recorded on still freshwater sites where they feed mainly on benthic animals. However, at a number of urban sites monitored during the local atlas period, Tufted Ducks were notable in the way they have adapted to the presence of humans and supplement their natural diets with human handouts. As with the national situation, most counts were from freshwater lakes and pools. However, during prolonged cold weather Tufted Ducks have been recorded in very large flocks on both the Tyne and Blyth estuaries, presumably as a result of their normal freshwater sites becoming icebound (pers. obs.). This indicates that they can change their habitat preferences in response to environmental conditions.

A total of 75 (84%) of all the tetrads, in which Tufted Ducks were recorded, were 200 metres a.s.l. or below indicating that they are predominately a lowland species during the winter.

A comparison of the breeding distribution (Day *et al.*, 1995) and the wintering distribution highlights remarkably few differences, suggesting that many local Tufted Ducks remain close to their breeding areas rather than moving large distances to wintering sites. However a summer estimate of 646 individuals, compared to the winter estimate of 1,285 individuals, suggests that there is a significant influx of birds during the winter period.

Since 1995 a number of Tufted Duck flocks on Tyneside have been monitored closely during the winter with regular counts between September and March each year and many birds have been caught and colour ringed (J. Coleman, unpub. data). The counts show that most immigration to the flocks occurs between December and February and is often precipitated by colder winter weather. Ringing has produced recoveries of two birds in Sweden and one in Eire indicating the possible origins of the immigrants. Further local recoveries and colour ring sightings of birds, in the breeding season, at a range of sites in the North East also highlight that these flocks do consist of a mixture of local and continental birds.

Despite the long distances that some birds travel to the region, Tufted Ducks do show some fidelity between winters with 48% of the birds colour-ringed in one year returning the following winter and 51% returning to the local area two winters after ringing.

JON COLEMAN

Distribution by altitude

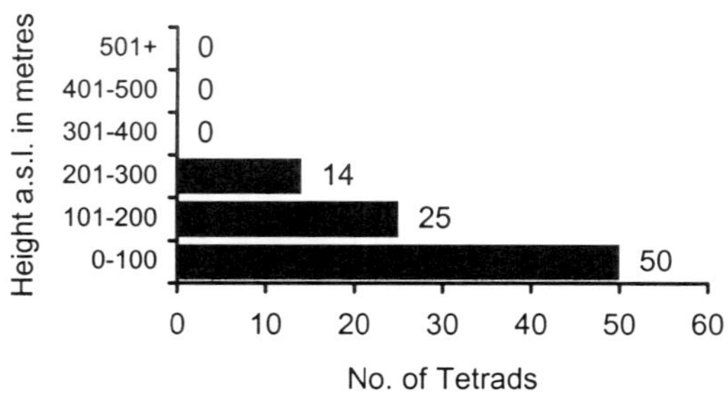

No. of tetrads in which recorded 89 (6%)

Tetrad Analysis	No. of tetrads
1-5 birds	48 (54%)
6-30 birds	26 (29%)
31+ birds	15 (17%)

Total No. of birds counted 1,285

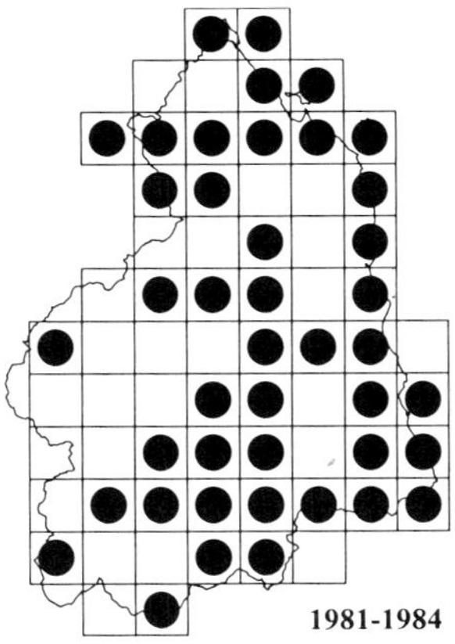

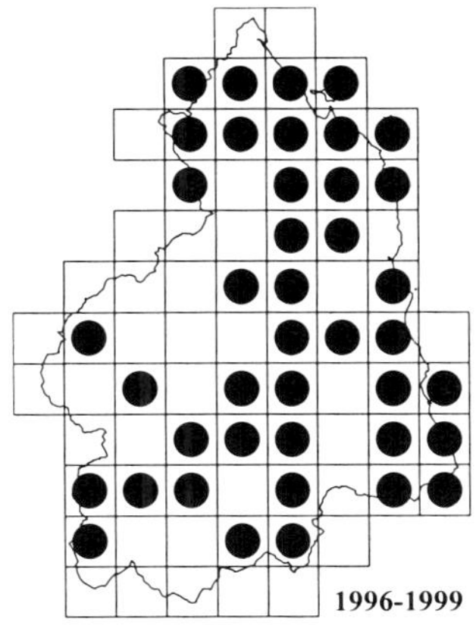

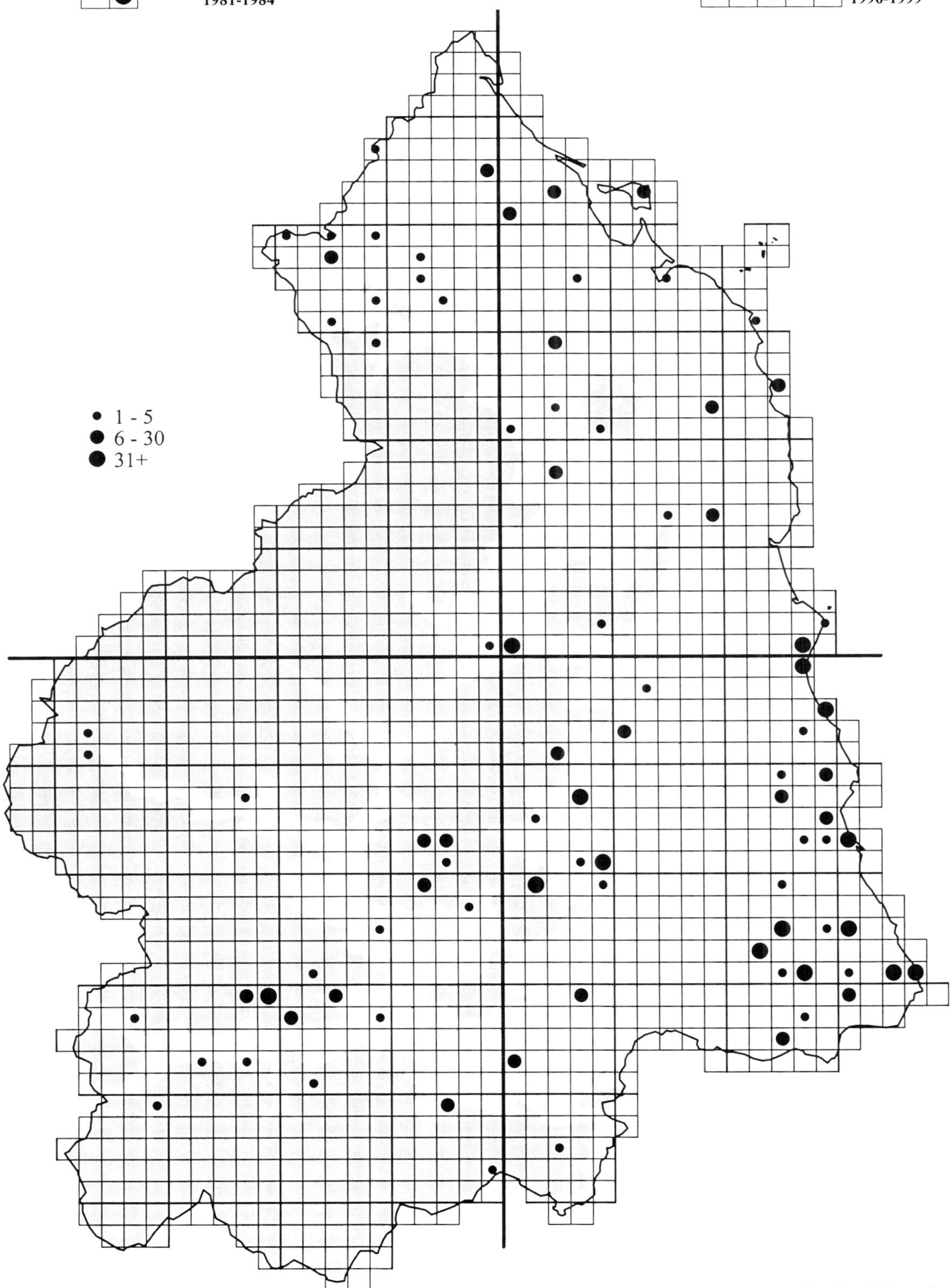

Tufted Duck

SCAUP *Aythya marila*

There is evidence to suggest that this robust diving duck wintered in much larger numbers in the county in the past as Bolam (1912) described it as an 'abundant winter visitant' and before him Chapman (1889) said that it was 'not infrequently met with'. The latter went on to suggest reliable wintering sites and added that often a 'company of Scaup will take up their quarters for the whole winter, and seldom leave the spot'. Galloway and Meek (1978) could not reaffirm the evidence collected by earlier commentators. Indeed they referred to the species becoming 'relatively scarce' and said that parties 'rarely exceeded ten and were widely scattered'. Lack (1986) confirmed this, stating that the British wintering population of 5,000 to 10,000 represented a 'considerable decrease' on the 1960s and 1970s when favoured feeding at sewage outfalls at Leith on the Firth of Forth could in some years produce counts of 30,000 at this site alone.

The number of wintering Scaup in Northumberland remains small, usually building up from mid-October and peaking in December and January. Autumn passage in suitable conditions can be pronounced and although increasingly recorded during the summer months, most wintering birds have departed by late March. In this current winter survey Scaup were recorded in 30 tetrads, the map confirming the winter distribution in the county as coastal or near coastal, some 86% (24) of tetrads being within 20 kilometres of the sea. Records away from this coastal plain were few, the furthest being a single bird at Grindon Lough (NY86D) approximately 60 kilometres inland.

The total of maximum counts during the current winter survey was 357, however, records were not evenly spread with 91% (328) occurring in the period January-February 1997, suggesting an obvious weather-related influx. Hancock (1874) in describing the species' status as 'abundant in severe winters' was aware of the effect of hard weather on numbers and Galloway and Meek (1978) stated large numbers occurred in the county in 1956 after the freezing of the Baltic, an area that is said to hold at least 50% of the estimated 310,000 Scaup wintering in north west Europe (Snow & Perrins, 1998). It is interesting to note that, during early January 1997, a record count of 804 Goldeneye *Bucephala clangula* occurred in the county, a species which also has its north west European wintering stronghold in the Baltic.

All counts of over ten birds during the current winter survey were made during January-February 1997, the maximum being 60 at Beadnell (NU22J). Outside this period the largest count was eight off Budle Point (NU13T). A variety of coastal habitats were used by the species including rocky reefs, estuaries and shallow sandy bays with numbers commuting to coastal pools such as Hauxley (NU20W) and Newton Pool (NU22M) on a regular basis.

A comparison of the two 10km square maps shows no evidence of any real decline in distribution since the 1981-1984 national winter atlas survey as during that period Scaup were recorded in 17 ten kilometre squares, two more than during the current winter survey. What the county winter atlas survey has shown is that, since Bolam (1932) described the species as 'one of the most numerous ducks upon the coast', it has undergone a distinct decline. Annual records warrant the status of 'well-represented' employed by Galloway and Meek (1978) but it remains very sporadic in its occurrence in winter, becoming most visible after hard weather on the near continent

CHRIS KNOX

Distribution by altitude

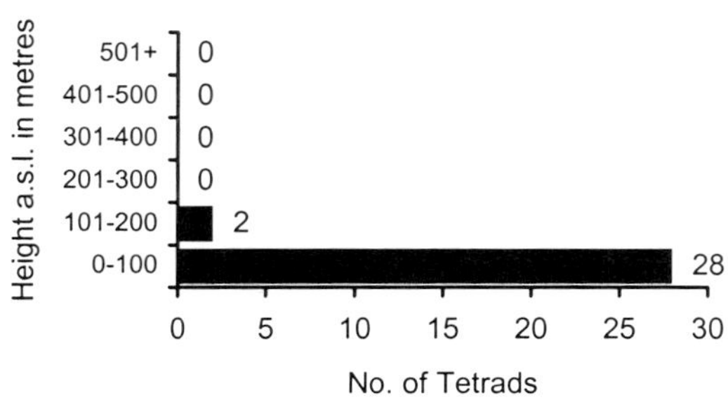

No. of tetrads in which recorded 30 (2%)

Tetrad Analysis	No. of tetrads
1-3 birds	15 (50%)
4-18 birds	9 (30%)
19+ birds	6 (20%)

Total No. of birds counted 357

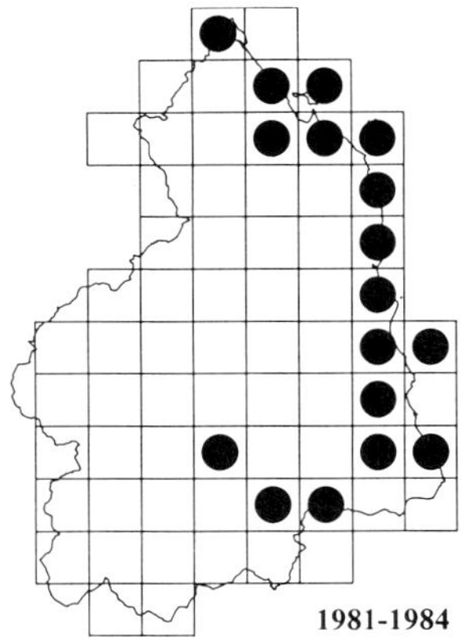

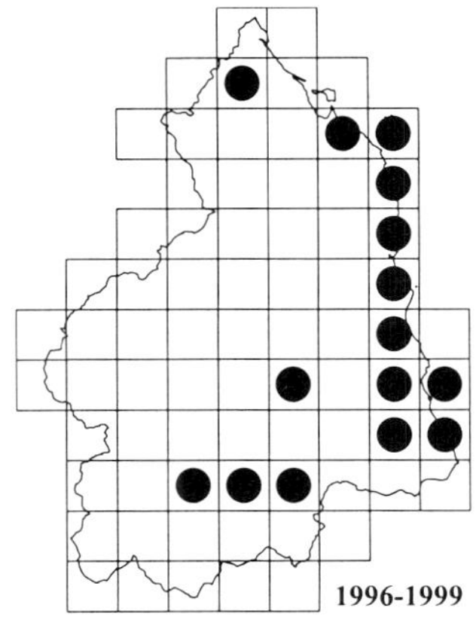

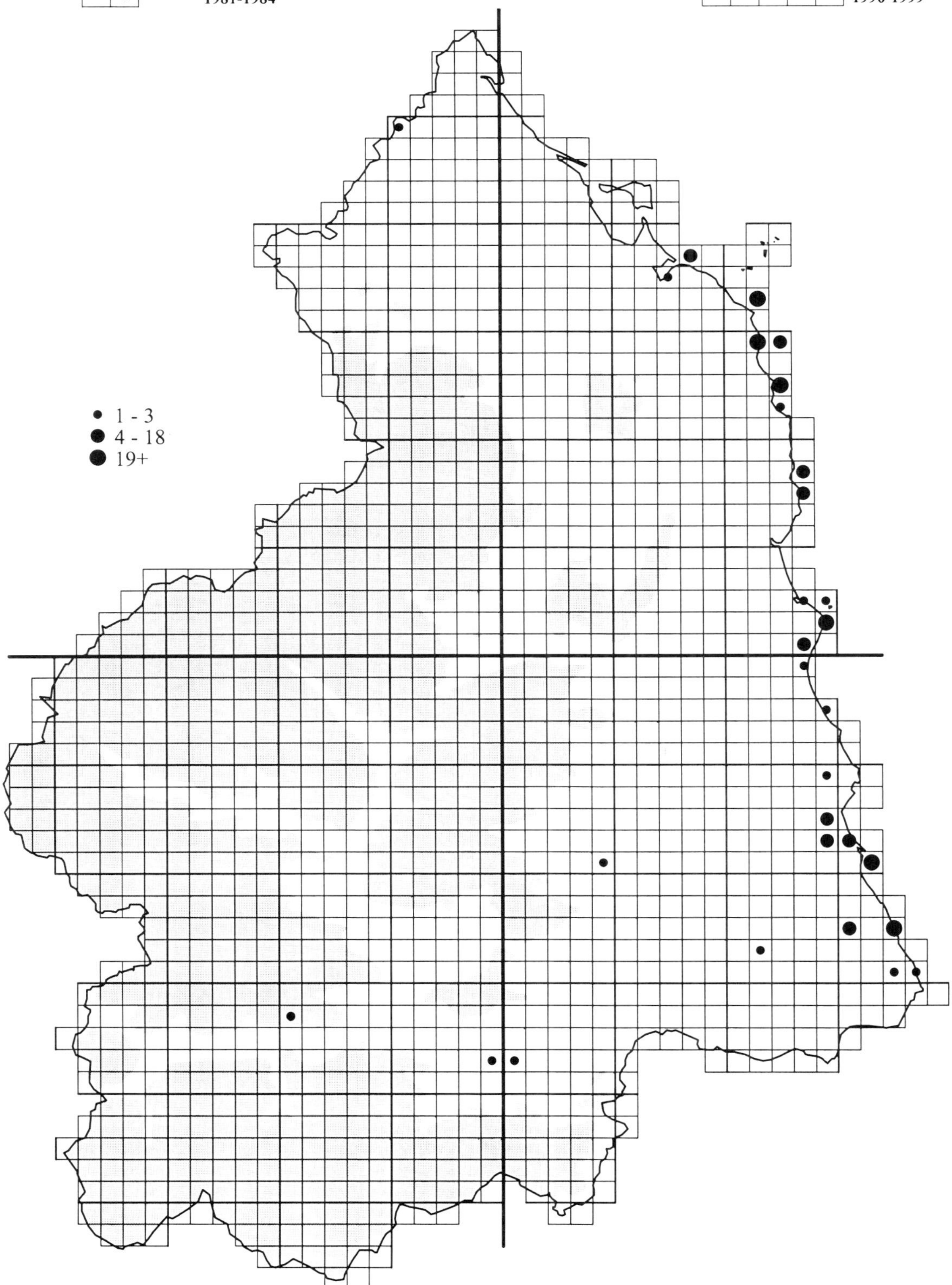

Scaup

EIDER *Somateria mollissima*

The Eider is the county's most famous bird being associated with St. Cuthbert and the protection he afforded it on the Farne Islands in the seventh century. It is now a common resident, breeding at two main localities, the Farnes and Coquet Island. During the breeding seasons (1996-1998) immediately prior to the current winter survey the number of nesting females on the Farnes was 1,912, 1,012 and 1,082. The 1996 total was the second highest ever, but the summer of 1997 had the lowest number since 1971 and, as a consequence of poor weather, very low productivity. On Coquet Island numbers ranged between 273 and 336 nests. Galloway and Meek (1978) said that during the late summer large gatherings of adults and young can be seen between Berwick and Amble but especially at the Lindisfarne NNR where 3,000 may be present between July and September, adding in their *Supplement* (1986) a huge count of 8,000 at that locality in September 1982. They also mentioned counts outside the breeding season indicating some 4,000 spread along the coastline.

The winter distribution as shown by the current survey extends along the entire coastline of the county with the highest densities in the north and numbers decreasing southwards from Beadnell but with some notable concentrations around the Coquet Estuary (NU20S) and in the Newbiggin-by-the-Sea to Blyth area (NZ38A-D). The highest counts came from the Farne Islands with two tetrads (NU23I & NU23C) holding about 3,400 birds in mid-November 1998 but it should be noted that it is not known how numbers might fluctuate here as winter progresses. Hawkey (1991) has already commented that during winter storms large flocks of up to 2,000 shelter in the lee of the islands. As expected, large concentrations were a feature of the coastline immediately opposite the islands and also around Holy Island and the Lindisfarne NNR. The tetrad at Holy Island harbour (NU14F) had a count of 606 and it would appear that a winter population of 1,000-2,000 may have been in the Lindisfarne area as a whole during the survey period. These numbers would seem to indicate a decline at this site when compared with published winter counts during the 1980s but may be a result of fluctuating breeding success in the county. Numbers north of Lindisfarne were lower but still with several hundred birds present. The winter population southwards from the Farnes was rather more thinly distributed but around the Coquet Estuary and adjacent coastline numbered several hundred birds, presumably originating from the Coquet Island colony. In the area between Newbiggin and Blyth there was a larger concentration of perhaps up to 1,000 birds. Between the Blyth and Tyne estuaries they are regularly reported but only in relatively low concentrations.

Although the majority of the population appears to be sedentary, Galloway and Meek (1978) have shown from ringing data that some birds disperse both north and south along the coast and occasionally cross the North Sea. It seems reasonable to assume that some birds wintering in Northumberland have originated from other east coast colonies, particularly those to the north, but the numbers involved remain unknown. Birds from both Denmark and Germany have been found in the county and thus a proportion may be of continental origin. Lack (1986) indicated that the British and Irish wintering population could be estimated at 72,000 and tabulated a total of 5,300 for Northumberland. However, to put these totals into context, the estimated European wintering population was thought to be about two million. A more recent estimate of the wintering population in the Western Palearctic of about three million birds was given by Hagemeijer & Blair (1997).

The cumulative effect of counts during this survey, with birds moving between feeding or roosting sites, and their reaction to adverse weather/sea conditions, means that the total of 9,904 is probably much higher than the average wintering population. There will no doubt be varying mortality affecting the population as the winter months progress, reducing the much higher numbers of late summer-early autumn, and this together with dispersal into and out of the region makes estimating a true winter figure difficult. A mid-winter population of between 4,000-9,000 may be a realistic range. Three sites in the county, the Farne Islands, Lindisfarne NNR and the Seahouses to Budle Point stretch of coastline are sites of national importance within Great Britain for Eiders (Pollitt *et al.*, 2000).

MIKE S. HODGSON

No. of tetrads in which recorded: 84 (6%)

Tetrad Analysis	No. of tetrads
1-36 birds	42 (50%)
37-150 birds	27 (32%)
151+ birds	15 (18%)

Total No. of birds counted: 9,904

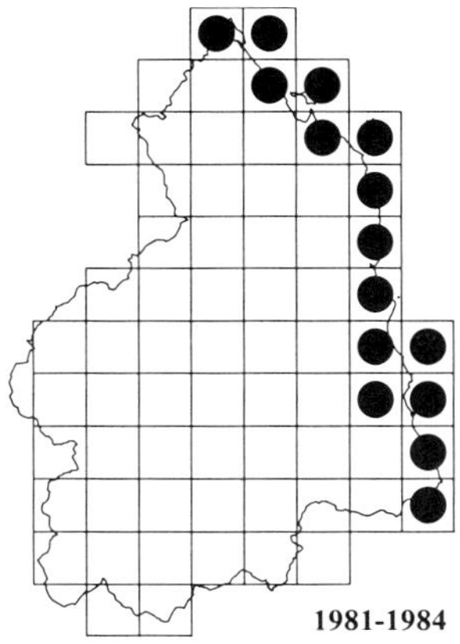

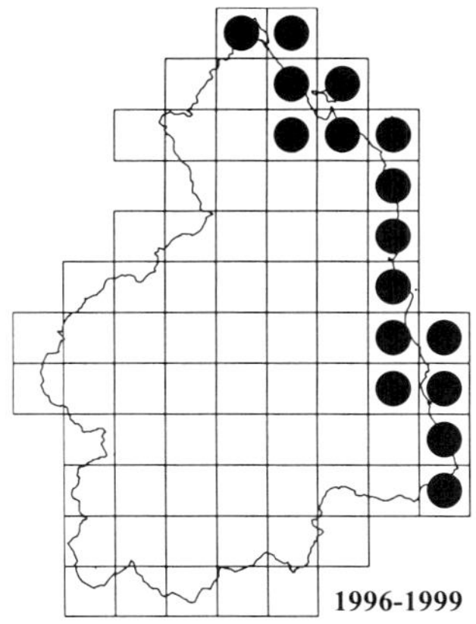

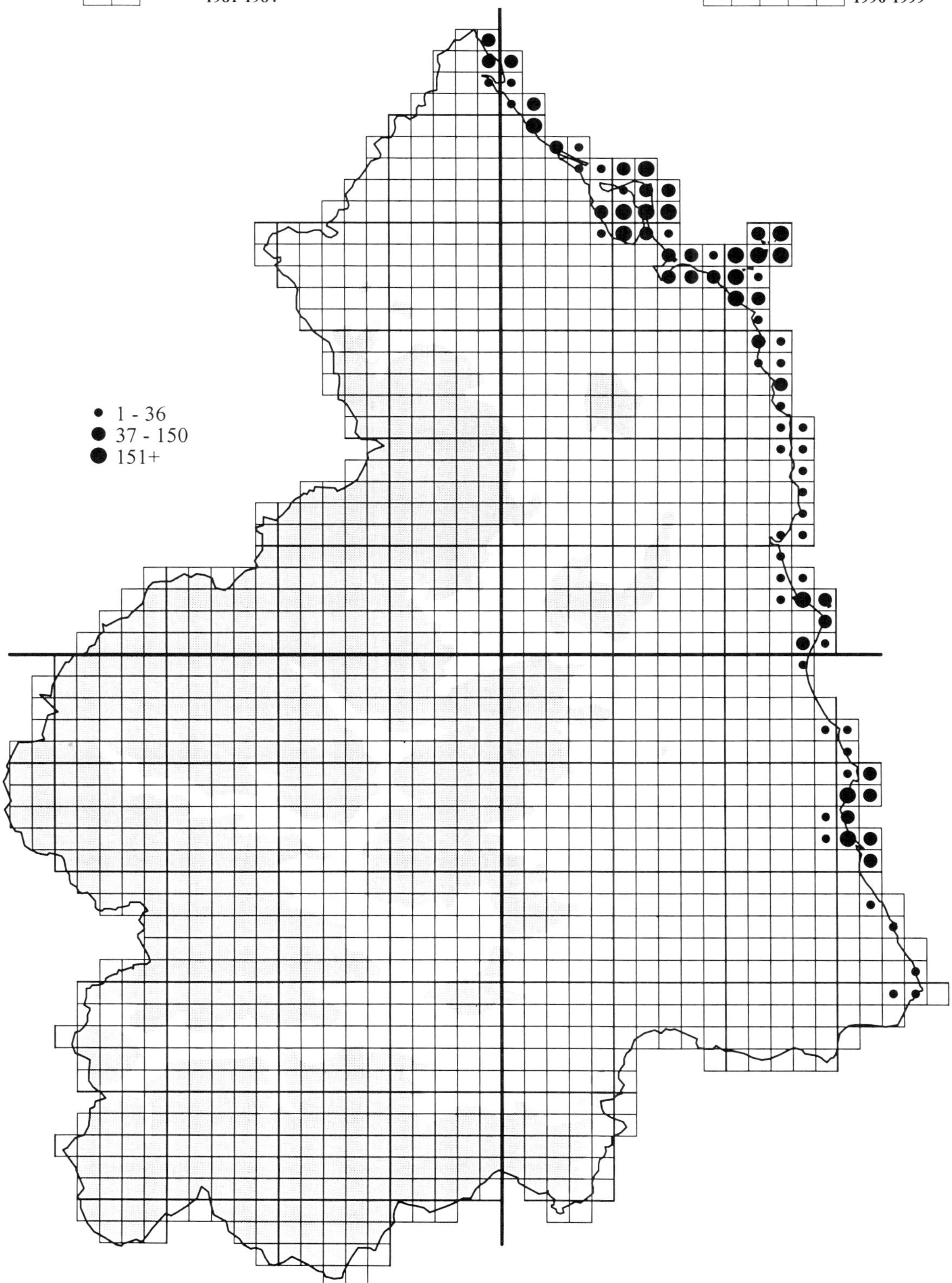

Eider

LONG-TAILED DUCK *Clangula hyemalis*

Bolam (1932) described this handsome species as a 'common passage migrant and winter visitant'. Galloway and Meek (1978) questioned this status, preferring to describe the species as 'well-represented' and added that 'it only occurs in numbers between Bamburgh and Holy Island'. Today, the stronghold of the species remains the north east of the county particularly the area around the Lindisfarne NNR, an area Prater (1981) regarded as having the largest English wintering population, representing some 1.6 % of the British total. The Long-tailed Duck prefers to stay well offshore and Chapman (1889) observed that the species was often found 'busily feeding miles from land'. Because of this, the species is best observed on calm days with a 'quiet' sea and it is on such days that the active nature of the species is apparent, continually diving, chasing and displaying. It is often possible to hear the 'yodelling' calls which have influenced a host of alternative names for the species including the common American name 'Old Squaw'.

Lack (1986) estimated that 20,000 winter in Britain and Ireland mainly on the Scottish east coast and around the northern and western isles. The Moray Firth has become Britain's most important site where monitoring of roost sites has regularly produced counts of 10,000-15,000. Approximately 500,000 winter in western European waters, the great majority around the Baltic and off North Norway. The earliest birds arrive in our region in late September-early October although they are never really apparent until November which is also a good month to see the species on passage. Although small numbers can remain until mid-May most Long-tailed Ducks have left the region by mid-April. Chapman's observation that 'most disappear during the early days of April - sometimes simultaneously with advent of the terns' still holds good today.

The tetrad map for the current winter atlas survey shows that the species was recorded in 30 (2%) of the tetrads surveyed with some 50% of them being confined to just three 10 kilometre squares (NU04, NU13, NU14) all in the favoured north east of the county. Occasionally wandering onto coastal ponds, Bolam's (1932) comment that 'small numbers annually follow our larger streams a long way inland' was not borne out during the current survey. The tetrad map confirms the essentially marine distribution of the species with a preference for soft sandy coves and bays, with shallows offshore. All areas with counts of over five birds shared this habitat. The total of maximum counts during the 1996-1999 period was 464, there being only three counts of over 50 birds, all recorded in the 10km square NU13. All three counts occurred during January which correlates with Bolam's (1932) observation that the species 'was most numerous after the New Year'. The largest count during the current winter survey was 98 off Ross Back Sands (NU13P), this perhaps representing an underestimate of numbers present, as annual county bird reports during the period show that this favoured area of the county can produce counts of up to 200 birds (*Birds in Northumbria 1996-1999*).

A comparison between the two 10km square maps shows that during the current winter atlas survey the species occurred in six fewer squares than during the 1981-1984 national winter atlas survey. Also during the earlier national survey the Long-tailed Duck was far less parochial in its distribution in Northumberland, occurring along the entire coastline between the River Tweed in the north and Tyne in the south. This reduced presence in the county may be explained by the species' notoriety in being difficult to monitor; if observation coincides with poor weather its preference for remaining well offshore makes it difficult to locate. An examination of peak counts for the species over the last three decades however, could suggest that smaller numbers are now wintering in the county. During the winters of 1974 and 1976 respectively, Galloway and Meek (1978) recorded peak counts of 500 whilst Martin (1993) noted that Lindisfarne NNR had a five-year average peak of 441 up to 1991. Since that year the annual county reports have failed to record counts of over 200 birds.

A reduction of birds wintering in the county contradicts the national picture where improved monitoring over recent years has amended Prater's estimate of 10,000 to a present figure of some 20,000-30,000 wintering in Britain (Martin, 1993). Nationally the Long-tailed Duck is threatened by oil pollution and exploitation of shellfish. At a local level, an increasing threat over the last decade has been disturbance in the north east of the county by watersports (pers. obs.). Once confined to the summer months, an increasing number of jet-skis and powerboats now use the area between Ross Back Sands and Stag Rocks on fine weekends during the New Year, taking disturbance further out to sea. Despite this, the Long-tailed Duck in Northumberland remains a 'well-represented' winter visitor

CHRIS KNOX

No. of tetrads in which recorded	30 (2%)

Tetrad Analysis	No. of tetrads
1-4 birds	15 (50%)
5-16 birds	9 (30%)
17+ birds	6 (20%)

Total No. of birds counted	464

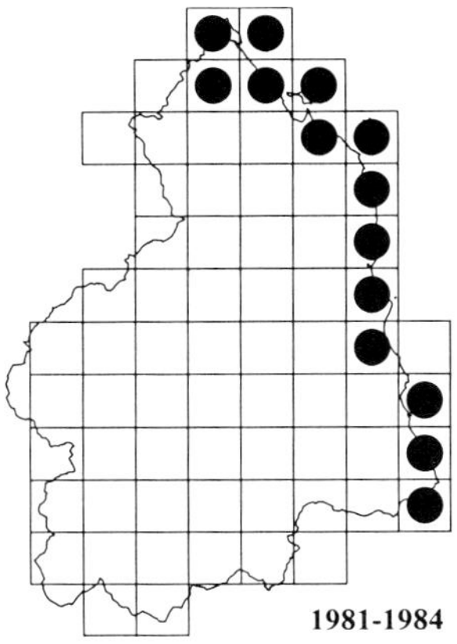

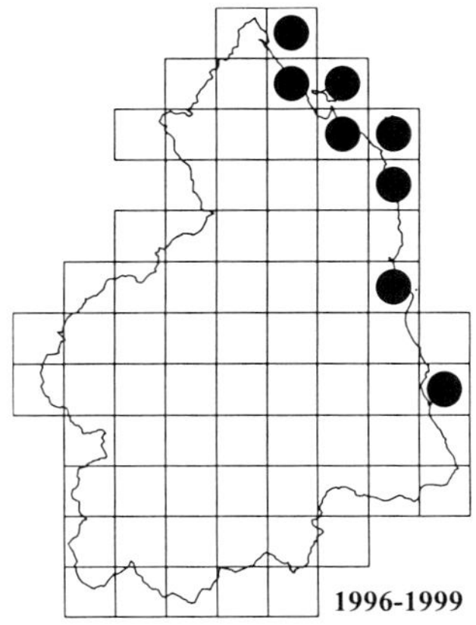

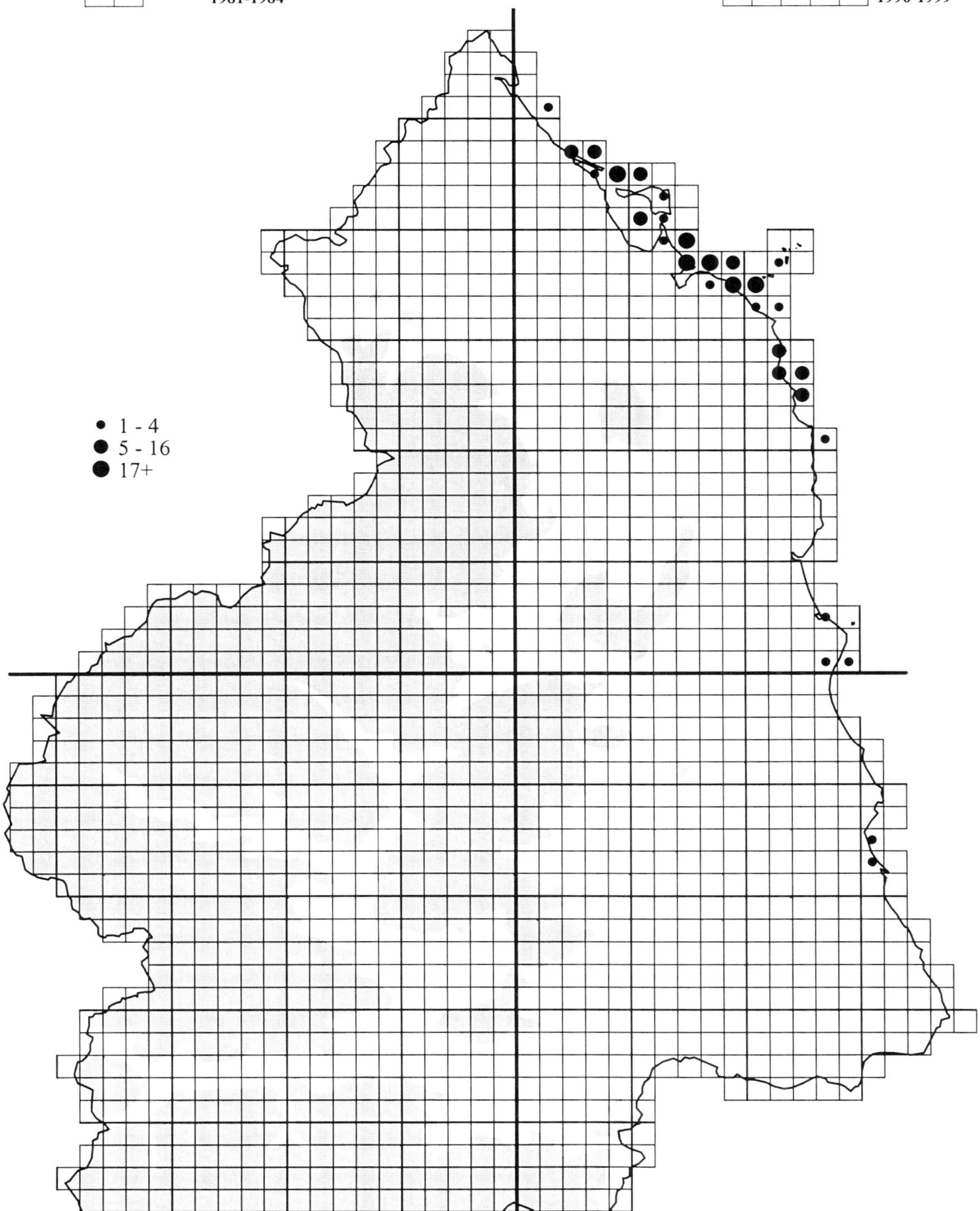

Long-tailed Duck

COMMON SCOTER *Melanitta nigra*

Bolam (1932) regarded the Common Scoter as 'a regular winter visitant and passage migrant on the coast, often in very large flocks; apt to be especially numerous during the first three months of the year'. Times have changed since then, and Galloway and Meek (1978), although acknowledging regular flocks in excess of 1,000 off the north east of the county in the early 1960s culminating in the record flock of 2,500 in January 1968 on Lindisfarne, described the Common Scoter's steady decline at the beginning of the 1970s. They noted that flocks failed to exceed 200 birds in number in 1970 and 1971. Numbers increased again from 1973/74 and in some years large gatherings were recorded, for example as many as 2,000 in January 1991 and February 1995 (Kerr, 2001). These fluctuations may be part of a longer term decline in numbers as it was noted that in the early 1970s the winter estimate of the western European population was 500,000, which indicated a considerable decline from 1952 when passage through Finland and the coast of West Germany was estimated to involve 1-1.5 million birds (Madge & Burn, 1988). Locally, Galloway and Meek similarly recorded a decrease in the size of a regular flock off Seaton Sluice between 1960 and 1973.

The present survey results indicate that the Common Scoter is widespread along the length of the Northumberland coast being recorded in some 36 tetrads. However, numbers do not seem to be back to the high point of the 1960s. The largest count in a single tetrad during the current survey was 700 at the end of January 1999 off Budle Point (NU13T), with counts of 540 off Spittal (NU05F) and 370 off Cambois/North Blyth (NZ38B) also being made. In total, 14 of the 36 occupied tetrads produced counts of 100 birds or more, representing 88% (3,324) of the total number of birds counted during the three winter periods. Common Scoters were distributed in every 10km square along the coast, with the exception of the marginal square NZ39 off Lynemouth and the Tyne Estuary. A comparison between the two smaller maps shows that in this survey birds were present in two more squares as compared to 1981-1984 although it should be pointed out that 78% of all the birds counted in the current survey were in the NU quadrant in the north east of the county.

One encouraging sign is the use of the offshore area between Newbiggin and North Blyth. Two tetrads here (NZ38B, NZ38D) produced counts in excess of 176 birds where none had been recorded in the 1981-1984 survey. There were also two inland sites that held Common Scoter during the current winter survey. These were Littlemill Nature Reserve (NU21I) where two birds were recorded in January 1999 and Big Waters NR (NZ27G) which held one in February 1999.

Coastal movement in autumn may indicate large passages of birds towards the wintering flocks in and around the Lindisfarne NNR or to the larger flocks off the east coast of Scotland, which were noted in the 1981-1984 national winter atlas survey with some sites in the Moray Firth holding up to 10,000 birds (Lack, 1986). The numbers of birds noted on autumn/early winter passage along the county coastline generally far exceed the counts made during the current survey, reinforcing the suggestion that many of these birds winter elsewhere.

The wintering numbers of Common Scoter recorded in the atlas fieldwork are perhaps an underestimate, bearing in mind the marine, and mobile, nature of the species, and it is likely that some birds or flocks were missed. What is clear however is that the Northumberland coast is still an important wintering site for the species and they should continue to enjoy the status of a common winter visitor.

SARAH BARRATT

No. of tetrads in which recorded — 36 (3%)

Tetrad Analysis	No. of tetrads
1-45 birds	18 (50%)
46-175 birds	11 (31%)
176+ birds	7 (19%)

Total No. of birds counted — 3,787

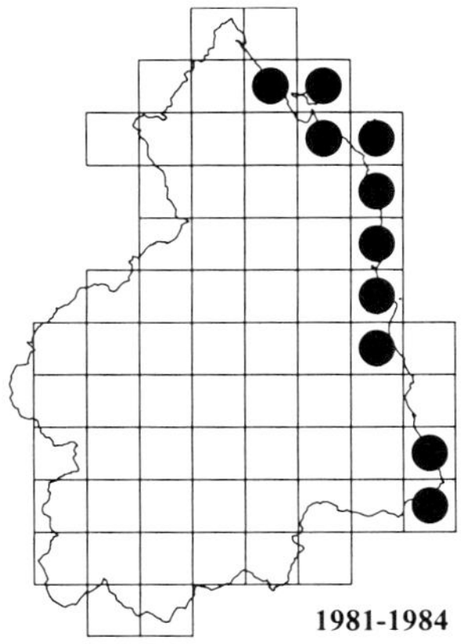

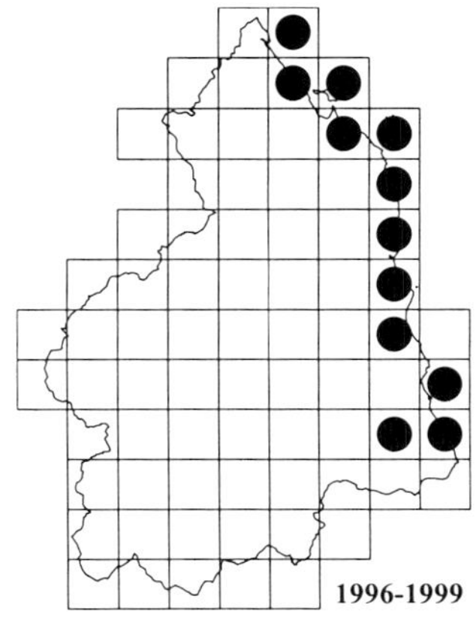

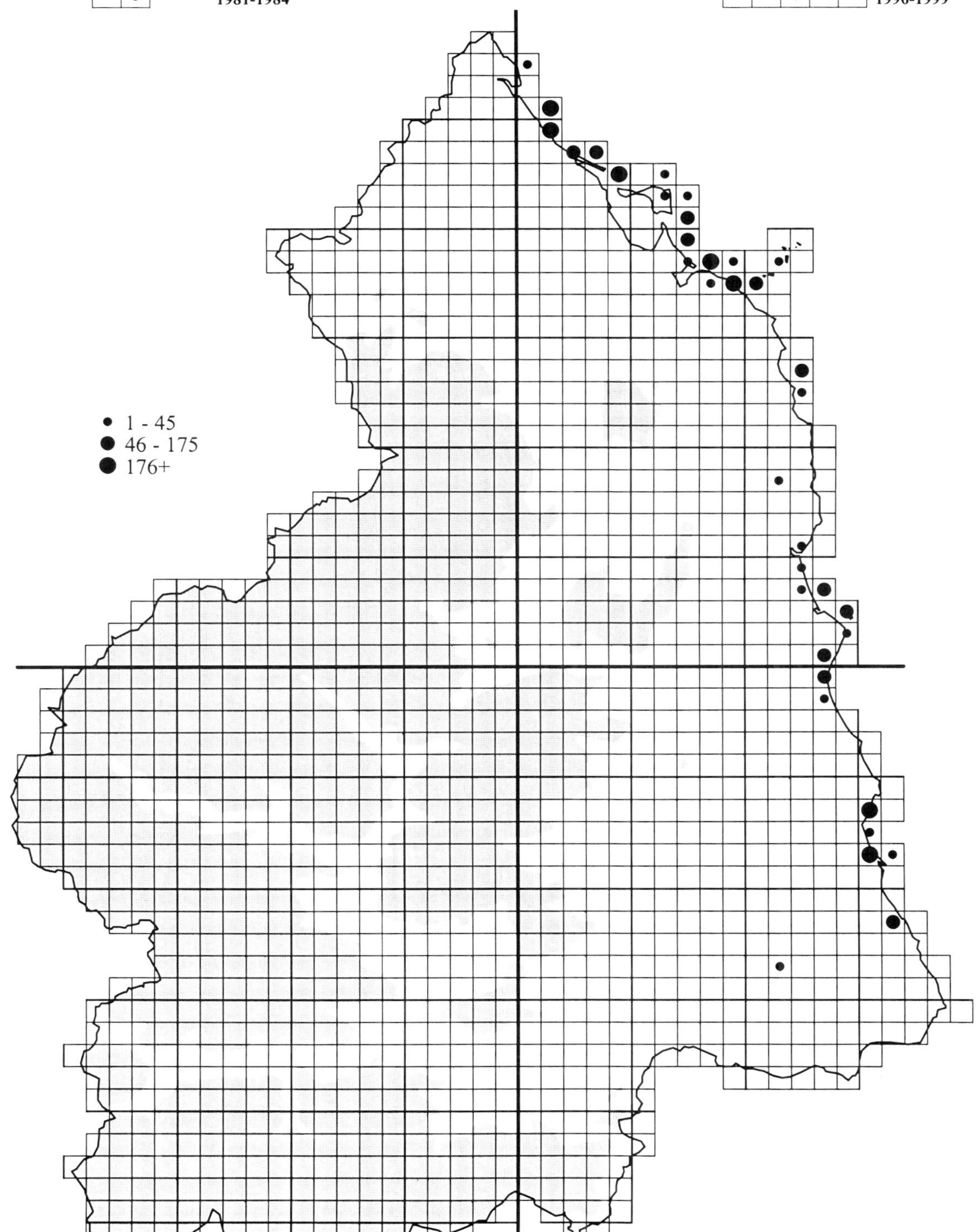

Common Scoter

VELVET SCOTER *Melanitta fusca*

The total wintering population of the Velvet Scoter in north west Europe was estimated by Snow and Perrins (1998) at one million birds which included 950,000 in the Baltic. Lack (1986), from fieldwork carried out for the national winter atlas in 1981-1984, described the species as comparatively rare around much of the coasts of Britain and Ireland, occurring most frequently, and numerously, along the North Sea coast. He estimated a normal wintering population for Britain and Ireland of 2,500-5,000 and indicated that gatherings of more than 50 were considered unusual although there were over 8,000 in the Moray Firth in early 1983. An apparent increase in the total population was thought to be a result of increased observer coverage rather than a genuine increase in the wintering population.

The status in Northumberland of this species was described by both Hancock (1874) and Bolam (1912) as a 'winter visitant' though not so common as Common Scoter *M. nigra*. More recently, Galloway and Meek (1978) felt that its status had 'changed very little, if at all, in the last hundred years' and described the Velvet Scoter as a well-represented passage and winter visitor. They stated that the total number of birds present at any one time rarely exceeded 50, but did report a record of approximately 100 off Bamburgh/Ross in the winter of 1973/74, an unusually high number on a national, as well as local, scale.

Its current status should now perhaps be re-considered as, during the three winters of this survey, there were only six records totalling 12 birds in 1996/97, four records totalling 18 birds in 1997/98 and two records totalling seven birds (including a flock of six) in 1998/99. All of the records were supplementary sightings, not a single bird being recorded during the timed visits, a further indication of the now genuine scarcity of this species in Northumberland during the winter months.

The thin distribution of wintering birds in the county is concentrated along the northern half of the coastline with only three records elsewhere during the survey period. There were six birds counted between Stag Rocks and the Megstone, Farne Islands (NU13Y) in January 1998, six in Embleton Bay (NU22L) in November 1998, and four birds off Holy Island (NU14L) and three off Budle Point (NU13T) in November 1996. Only two birds were seen off Ross Back Sands (NU13P) in February 1997 and a single bird there (NU13N) in January 1997. There were three records of single birds in Beadnell Bay (NU22I/J & NU22N) in November 1996, January 1998 and February 1999. Elsewhere, seven birds were located in the North Blyth/Cambois area (NZ38B), four in Newbiggin Bay (NZ38D) in January/February 1998 and one in Druridge Bay in January 1997. Passage birds, although not incorporated into the survey totals, are frequently seen during the late autumn and the early part of the winter period. They are almost certainly heading to the main wintering grounds on the east coast of Scotland, an observation that fits well with the statement in Galloway and Meek (1978) that the peak numbers of this species are recorded in October and November.

It is quite possible that the low wintering population in Northumberland is simply due to the availability of a far richer source of food a few hundred miles to the north and the drop in numbers may be an indicator of a decline in the quality of the inshore mussel-beds of the Northumberland coast. However, such a small wintering population is arguably insignificant and it would be unwise to draw any conclusions on population increase or decrease from such a limited sample of data.

The current survey shows that the larger wintering flocks are a distant memory and the status of the Velvet Scoter in Northumberland should be considered that of 'a common passage migrant' and, if the fieldwork of 1996-1999 is an indicator of the species' true status, at least 'an uncommon winter visitor'.

MARTIN KITCHING

No. of tetrads in which recorded	12 (<1%)

Tetrad Analysis	No. of tetrads
1-3 birds	7 (58%)
4-6 birds	4 (33%)
7 birds	1 (9%)

Total No. of birds counted	37

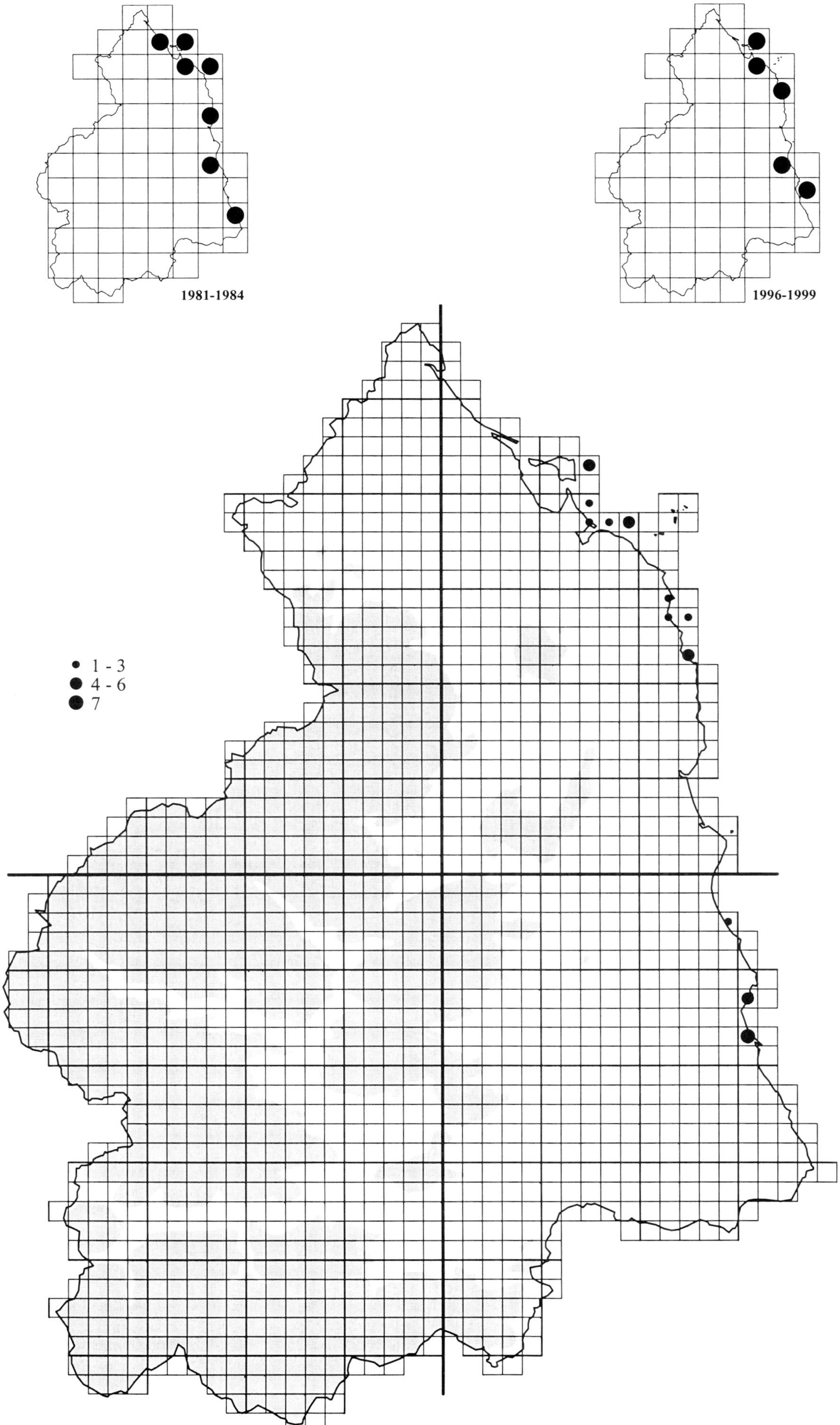

Velvet Scoter

GOLDENEYE *Bucephala clangula*

Bolam (1912) considered this common winter visitor to be highly palatable, fetching a higher price in game-shops than Scaup *Aythya marila* or Tufted Duck *A. fuligula*. Galloway and Meek (1978) approached it less gastronomically, describing the species as a 'well-represented passage and winter visitor', They further said that it often associated with Scaup in northerly autumn movements, was well distributed from October to March along the coast and had a particular preference for Tweedmouth. It could also be found regularly on inland waters, often on quite small ponds. The first birds usually arrive in September with the main influx in October and November.

Cramp and Simmons (1977) stated that Britain and Ireland are wintering areas for the breeding populations of Fenno-Scandia, north Germany, Poland, the Baltic States and north west Russia, and the recovery in the county of two birds ringed as young in Norway and Sweden would appear to confirm this (Galloway & Meek, 1978). Most birds have departed by early April with a few remaining until May. Bolam (1912) reported that solitary young individuals were present from April to June in the latter years of the nineteenth century while Galloway and Meek (1978) and recent records in *Birds in Northumbria* verify that some birds, mostly immatures, continue to occur in the summer months.

During the current winter survey most occupied tetrads (68%) were found below 100 metres a.s.l. and there were none occupied above 300 metres, although this may reflect the reduced availability of open water at such elevations. Single birds and small flocks were common, and larger flocks of up to 50 birds were regularly recorded. The largest counts were 804 at Tweedmouth (NU05B) in January 1997 and 350 in the adjacent Yarrow Slake area (NT95W) in January 1999. That large numbers of birds are already present in this area from late autumn was illustrated in October 1996 when 617 were counted on the Tweed (*Birds in Northumbria 1996*).

Goldeneye are reasonably faithful to coastal localities. Their presence was recorded in 17 of the 60 control tetrads with fairly consistent numbers appearing, in some squares, each winter, for example at Beadnell (NU22J) the three winter counts were 23, 17 and 37 birds, in the Castle Island area near the mouth of the River Wansbeck (NZ28X) there were 46, 43 and 28 and at East Chevington (NZ29U) seven, 25 and 37.

A direct comparison between the 10km square map of the 1981-1984 winter atlas survey and that for the current atlas reveals a small reduction in distribution, with six 10km squares vacated and two new squares occupied. Following the 1981-1984 national survey, the peak population for Great Britain was estimated at between 10,000-15,000 individuals (Lack, 1986), increasing to 17,000 for the period 1987-1992 (Stone *et al.*, 1997). This implies that the total of maximum counts of 3,109 birds in 152 tetrads in Northumberland represents a not insignificant proportion of the British wintering population.

Goldeneye can be found off the coast or along major rivers such as the Tyne and the Tweed, and also on most inland water bodies. This attractive duck feeds mainly during the day, flying between feeding sites and a regular night-time roost on either a tidal or diurnal cycle. Bolam wrote that they like to reach the sea to roost, and witnessed birds following every bend in the river as they flew up the Tweed after dawn and returning downstream before dusk. Pair formation begins in September and display parties form in December, with display becoming most intense during February and March and continuing on the breeding grounds. The species is known to be strongly attracted to sewage outfalls on the coast (Lack, 1986) and, formerly, feeding flocks of up to 80 birds were common at the mouth of the River Tyne. The recent advances in effluent treatment, however, has considerably improved and feeding flocks of more than 20 birds are now unusual (B. Pollinger, pers. comm.).

PHIL CHARLETON

Distribution by altitude

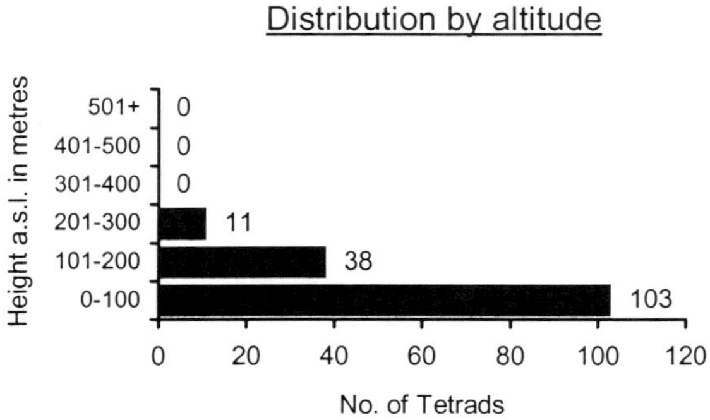

No. of tetrads in which recorded 152 (11%)

Tetrad Analysis	No. of tetrads
1-4 birds	83 (55%)
5-20 birds	43 (28%)
21+ birds	26 (17%)

Total No. of birds counted 3,109

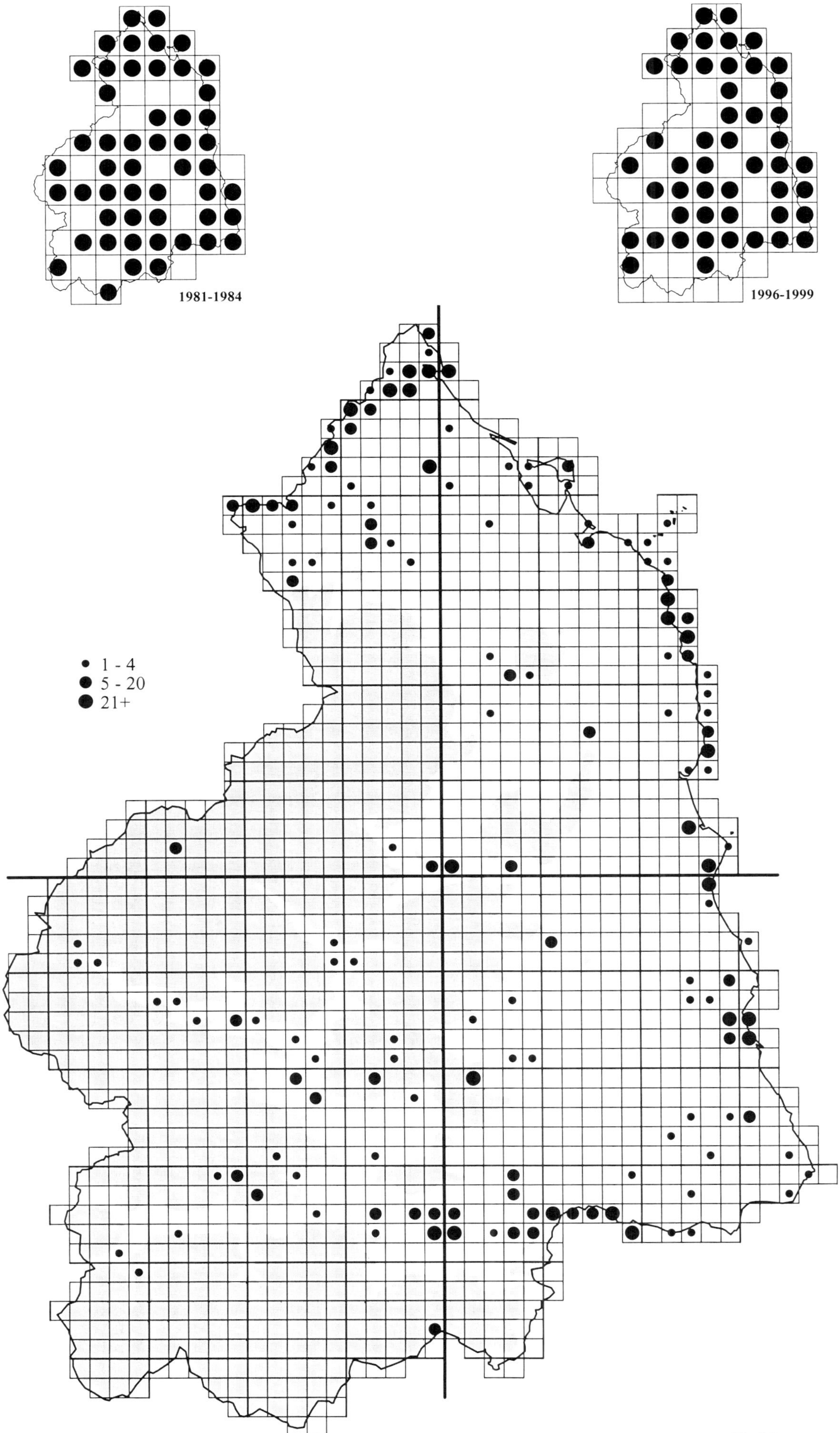

Goldeneye

SMEW *Mergellus albellus*

There can be few more evocative images of a northern winter than that of a drake Smew out on a grey, cold body of water. The fact that occurrences of males in particular are at best irregular only serves to add to their appeal among birdwatchers.

Originating from northern Russia, where the bulk of the population breed, Smew are an erratic winter visitor to the county. Most normally winter in the Netherlands with numbers in this country varying annually in response to severe local winter weather conditions on the near-continent. Nationally, it is by no means a numerous species, with an average wintering population of little more than 100 birds (Lack, 1986), though during cold weather influxes the overall total can well exceed the 400 mark. The bulk of this population is to be found in the south east of England, with Northumberland being very much on the periphery of its normal winter range. Preferring large bodies of lowland freshwater such as reservoirs and gravel pits, it is often to be found in the company of Goldeneye *Bucephala clangula* and Goosander *Mergus merganser* and is only rarely encountered on the open sea.

Within the county, the Smew has historically never been considered a numerous species, with only about thirty occurrences listed by Bolam up until 1932 and Galloway and Meek (1978) in *Northumberland's Birds* considering it to be a 'rare passage and winter visitor'. Nationally, Chandler (1984) considered the bulk of the wintering population to consist of immatures, a view previously alluded to by Selby (1831) who described the Smew in Northumberland as being 'very rare in the adult state'.

Comparing the tetrad map results of the current winter survey with the 1981-1984 winter atlas survey, the general spread of records within the county appears to have changed remarkably little, with most concentrated along the major river valleys and the mainly southern half of the lowland coastal plain. Wintering populations of seven to ten individuals were recorded during the period of the current survey and, although records were widespread, a detectable concentration could be found within the cluster of newly created wetlands in the Druridge Bay area, indicating a slight change in preference away from the more traditional Whittle Dene Reservoirs (NZ06T/U) and Tyne Valley localities. These primarily freshwater pools, such as East Chevington (NZ29U) and Druridge Pools (NZ29T), were not in existence during the period of the national winter atlas survey, being a product of the open-cast mining industry which transformed the area during the period 1980-1995, and have now become a key wintering area for this species in the county. Other localities favoured during the survey included the River Tweed in the Tweedmill area (NT84R) and the freshwater pools of south east Northumberland including Holywell Pond (NZ37C) and Marden Quarry (NZ37K).

Occurring from late November onward, Smew were typically encountered during the current winter atlas survey either individually or in small groups until departure in late March and early April. The largest group noted was of six at East Chevington on the 19th January 1997. Of a minimum of 23 individuals recorded in the county during the period of the survey, only two were adult drakes, the rest being 'redheads' i.e. females or unsexed first winter birds. There is evidence to suggest that sites attract regular returning individuals and this was strongly suggested at Holywell Pond (NZ37C) during 1997-1998 when a pair of wintering 'redheads' (one of which was sexed as a first-winter male) returned the following winter as an adult drake and female.

Considering the species' highly mobile nature, duplicate sightings will have undoubtedly occurred. However, there is no reason to assume that the status of Smew within the region has changed since the 1981-1984 survey and it should continue to be considered to be a rare winter visitor to the county.

ALAN CURRY

Distribution by altitude

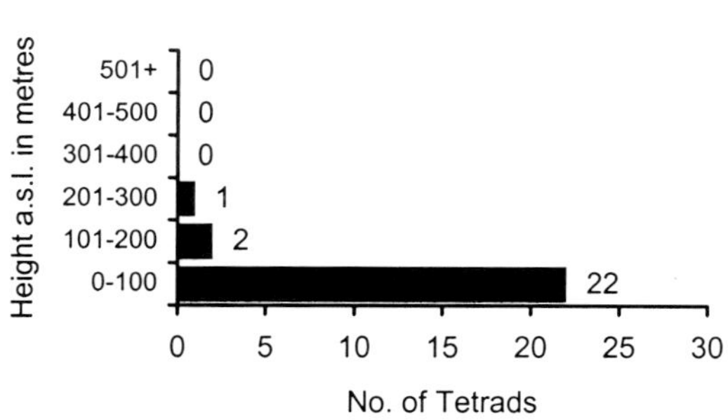

No. of tetrads in which recorded 25 (2%)

Tetrad Analysis	No. of tetrads
1 bird	15 (60%)
2-3 birds	5 (20%)
4+ birds	5 (20%)

Total No. of birds counted 53

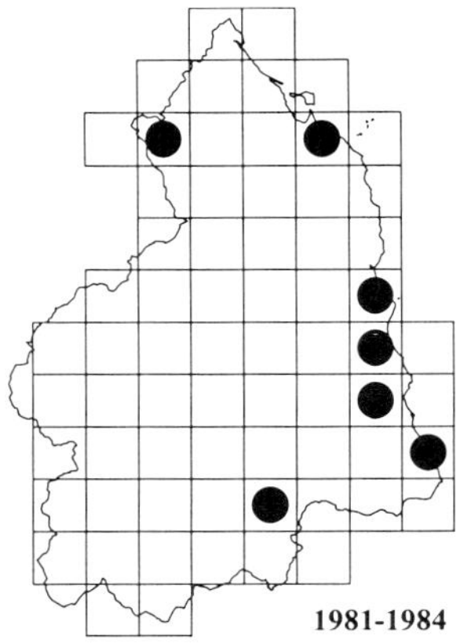

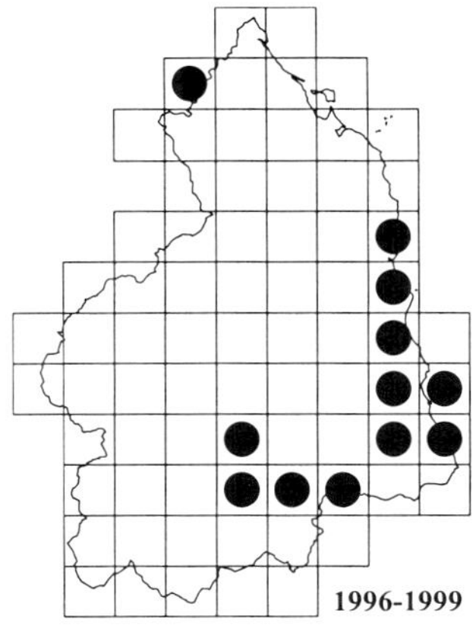

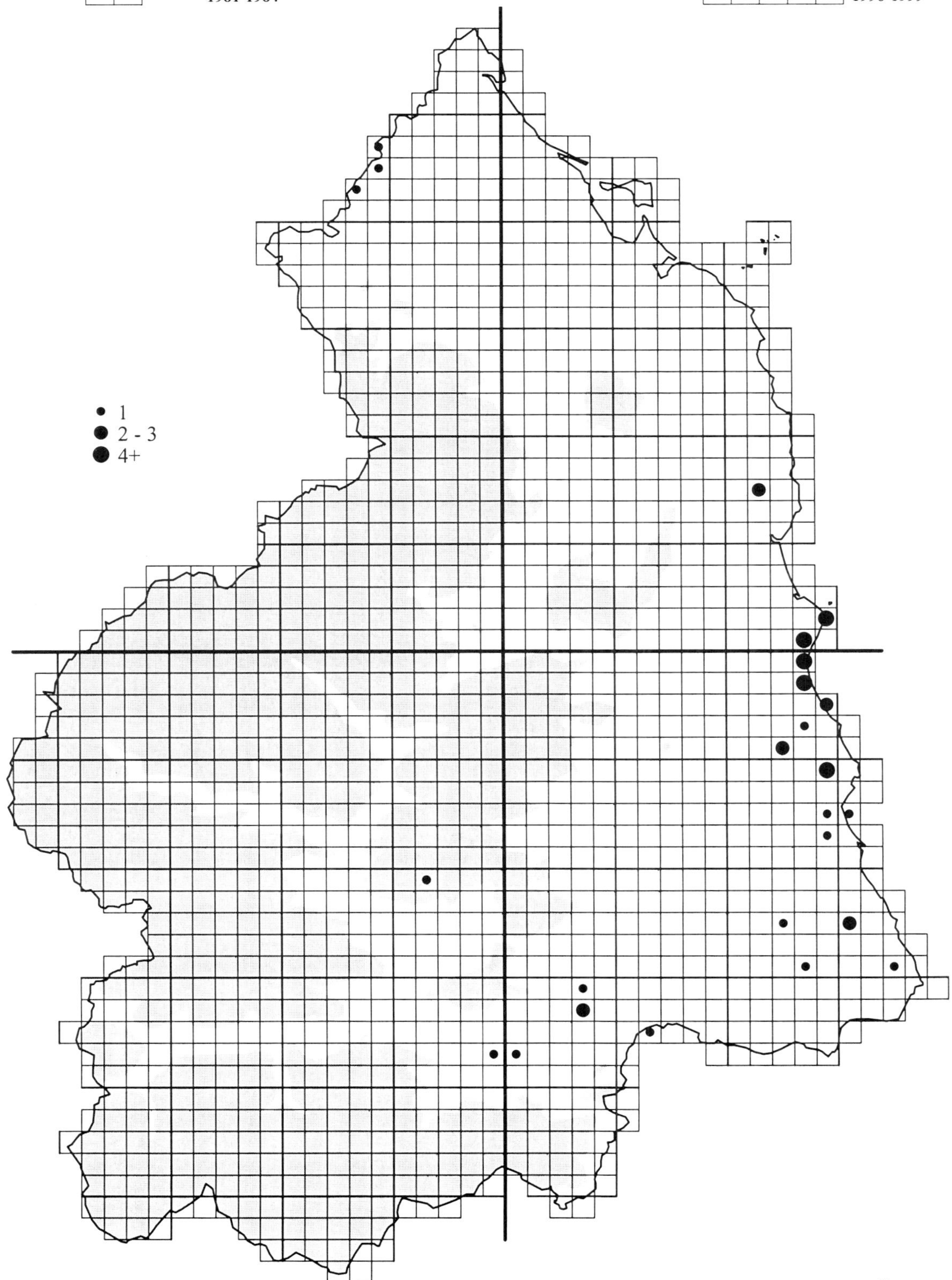

Smew

RED-BREASTED MERGANSER *Mergus serrator*

Most frequently encountered in small parties along sheltered sandy shorelines, the Red-breasted Merganser is a typical wintering species of the Northumberland coast and although it has bred occasionally (Day *et al.*, 1995) it is primarily a well-represented passage and winter visitor to the region.

Considered by Bolam (1912) to be 'common everywhere upon the coast, but much less frequently seen inland than the Goosander (*Mergus merganser*)', its current county status appears to have changed little. Data collected during the current county winter atlas survey found the Red-breasted Merganser to be present in a total of 57 tetrads and even allowing for the species' inherently mobile nature with duplicate counting inevitable, an average wintering population of between 100-150 individuals can be calculated within the county. This represents about 1.4% of the national wintering population of 11,000 birds as estimated by Lack (1986).

The tetrad map reveals the true maritime nature of the species and accurately reflects, in terms of distribution, the results of the 1981-1984 national winter atlas survey, with birds recorded along the full length of the Northumberland coastline and inland along the valleys of the Rivers Tweed and Tyne. The bulk of the records occurred within the Lindisfarne NNR (NU14A/F/K) and the large predominantly sandy bays at Spittal (NU05A), Beadnell (NU22I/J/N), Newton/Embleton (NU22M/L) and in the Druridge Bay area, for example at Druridge Bay Country Park (NU20Q) and East Chevington (NZ29U). In concurrence with Bolam (1912), inland records were very sparse during the current winter atlas survey, with four of the five occupied tetrads concentrated along the Tyne Valley. All these occurrences were of single individuals and it is likely that they were associating with the regular wintering Goosanders *Mergus merganser* in these areas. This coastal affiliation of the Red-breasted Merganser means that it comes into far less conflict with the fishing fraternity within the county than its unfortunate relative, the Goosander.

With little information as to the origins of Red-breasted Mergansers in Northumberland, it would be easy to surmise that the Northumbrian population consists of primarily Scottish-bred birds. However, Lack (1986) suggested that the majority of the Scottish and Irish population are to be found wintering around the coast close to their breeding areas, and given that northbound Red-breasted Mergansers are recorded frequently during autumn along the north east coastline, it is likely that a proportion of the wintering birds along the county coastline are of a Scandinavian origin.

Large concentrations were few and far between during the current survey, with an average group size numbering less than 20, although an exceptionally high accumulation of over 100 gathered off Spittal during January 1999. This impressive aggregation occurred at a time when other species such as Red-throated Diver *Gavia stellata* and Shag *Phalacrocorax aristotelis* were also concentrated in unusually high numbers at this locality, presumably taking advantage of high fish stocks in the mouth of the River Tweed (*Birds in Northumbria 1999*). It will be interesting to see if numbers of wintering Red-breasted Mergansers change in the next decade or so as Mead (2000) felt that the overall population was gradually increasing. Meanwhile, this handsome duck remains a well-represented winter visitor to Northumberland.

ALAN CURRY

Distribution by altitude

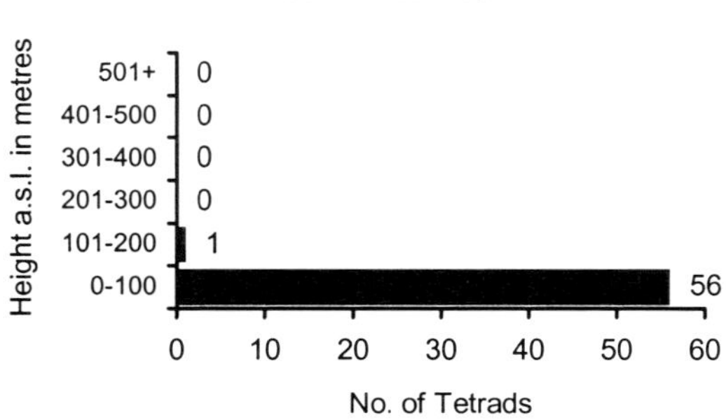

No. of tetrads in which recorded 57 (4%)

Tetrad Analysis	No. of tetrads
1-2 birds	28 (49%)
3-9 birds	18 (32%)
10+ birds	11 (19%)

Total No. of birds counted 351

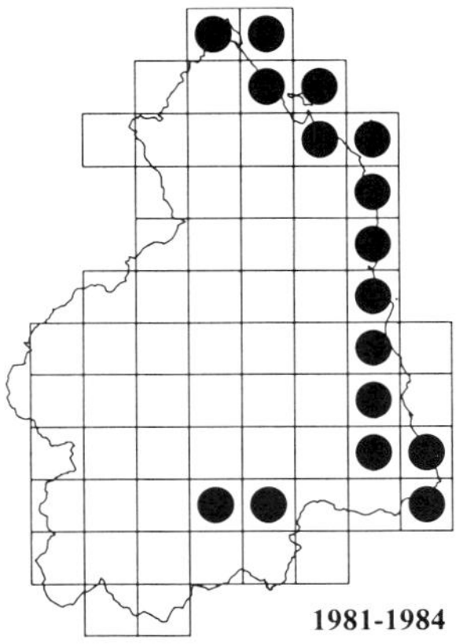

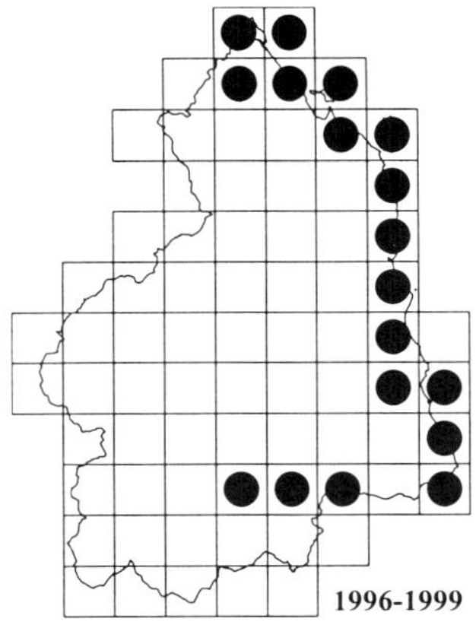

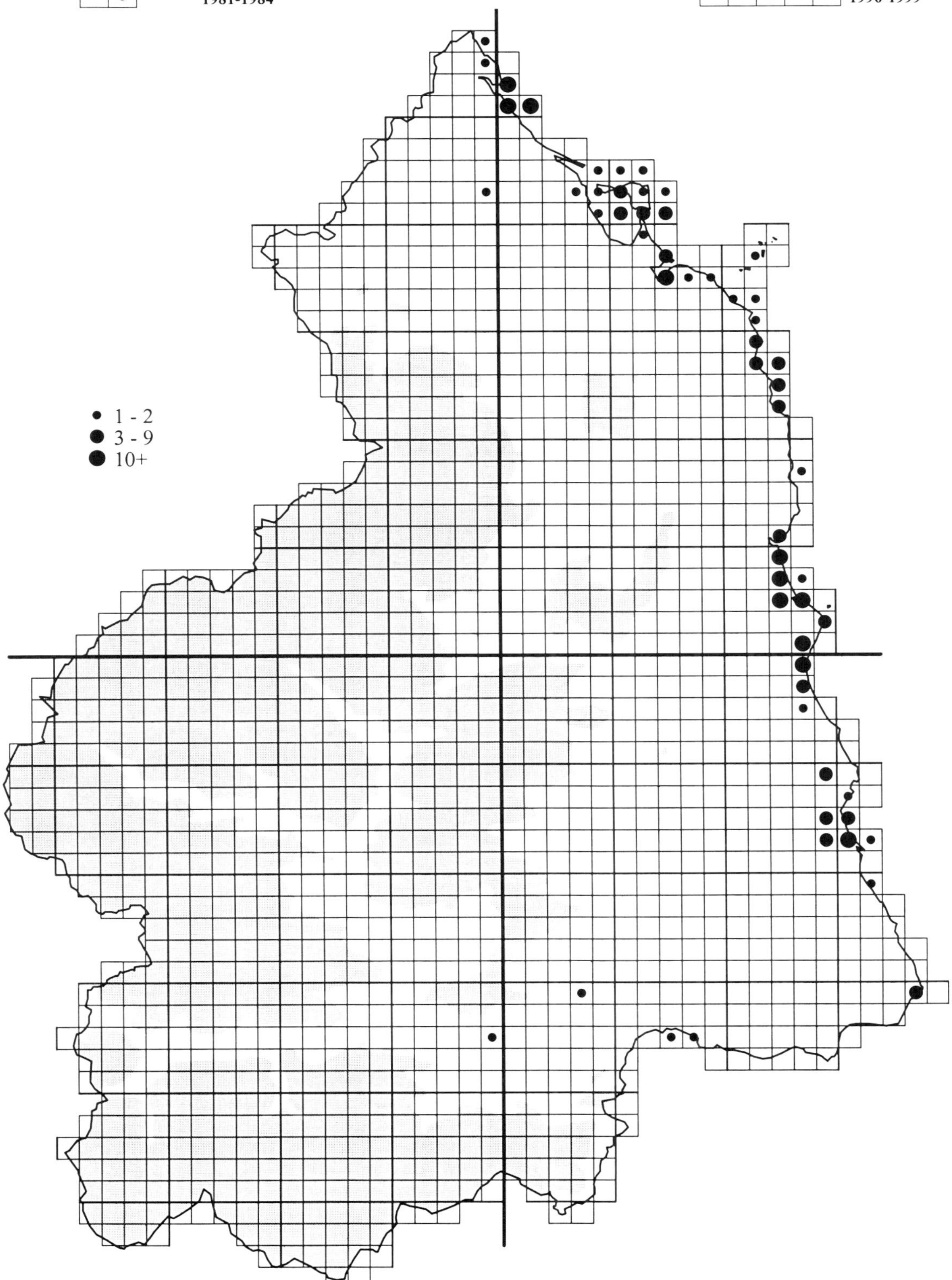

Red-breasted Merganser

GOOSANDER *Mergus merganser*

The Goosander may now be a familiar sight along the region's main rivers and on its reservoirs, but this has not always been the case. In fact Hancock (1874) only described the species as no more than 'an occasional winter visitant' and it was not until 1941 that the first confirmed breeding was established within the county (Galloway & Meek, 1978). Since that time, the Goosander has become a well-represented breeding species with an estimated population of 180 pairs (Day *et al.*, 1995) within the county. Unfortunately, with its dietary preference for small fish, it continues to fall victim to gamekeeper persecution and, as far as the breeding population is concerned, Cadwallender and Cadwallender (1998) indicated a significant population decrease (almost 36%) between two surveys in 1987 and 1997, which was considered due, at least in part, to illegal persecution.

In a study of Northumbrian Goosanders (Meek & Little, 1977) it was shown that most adults do not move far from their natal areas in winter, though juveniles are prone to a more widespread dispersal, suggesting that the majority of birds encountered during the current winter survey were of British origin. Goosanders are, however, occasionally forced into hard weather movements when feeding areas become frozen and it is not unreasonable to assume that occasional immigration from the continent must take place. Local movements during the day may also occur, with birds commuting between favoured feeding and roosting localities.

The tetrad map produced from the current survey data reflects the species' freshwater preferences, with few records from the coastal region. The bulk of these records are concentrated along the three main river valleys of the region with birds being recorded in a total of 168 tetrads, though because of the species' mobile nature duplicate counting must be inevitable. A total of 145 occupied tetrads (86%) were below 200 metres a.s.l. with the remaining 23 (14%) between 201-400 metres a.s.l. It can be calculated from data collected during the survey that the average wintering Goosander population in the county is probably between 250-300 individuals. This compares quite favourably with the estimated breeding population, suggesting the majority of the Northumbrian population may well be remaining within the region. Most encounters were of small groups though occasionally high concentrations were discovered such as 74 at Spittal (NU05A) during January 1999, 58 roosting at Farnley Haughs near Corbridge (NZ06B) on the 21st November 1996 and 41 at Whittle Dene Reservoirs (NZ06U) during December 1997. Of the medium sized counts (15-30 birds), five were located on the River Tweed during the three winter seasons with 29 birds roosting at Caistron (NU00A) in January 1997 and 17 at Big Waters (NZ27G) in February 1999.

Comparison between the current and the 1981-1984 ten km square maps shows a slight increase in the number of occupied squares in the present survey which may well be accounted for by increased observer coverage. Whilst some concern for the future maintenance of the Goosander population should be shown, it can still be considered a well-represented species in winter within the county.

ALAN CURRY

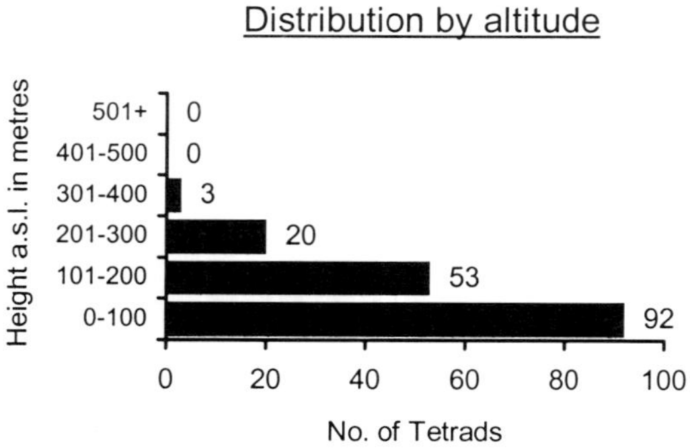

No. of tetrads in which recorded 168 (12%)

Tetrad Analysis	No. of tetrads
1-2 birds	100 (60%)
3-5 birds	39 (23%)
6+ birds	29 (17%)

Total No. of birds counted 829

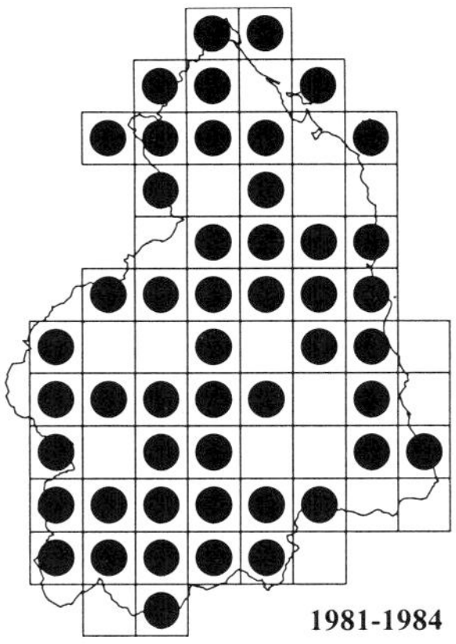

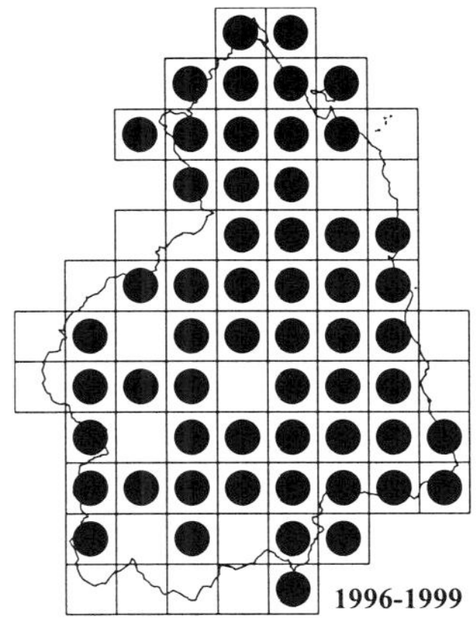

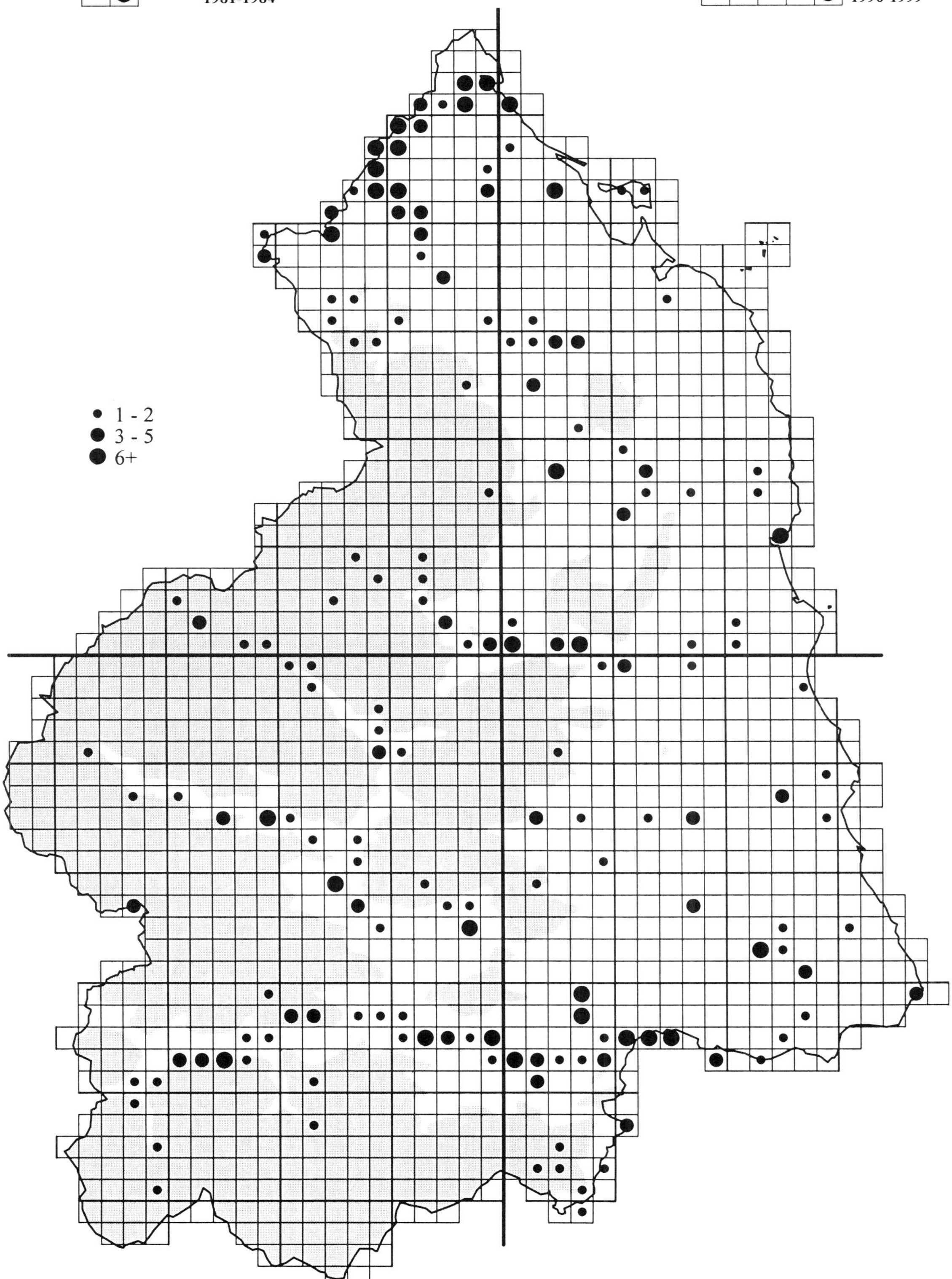

Goosander

RUDDY DUCK *Oxyura jamaicensis*

Galloway and Meek (1978) described this species as an extremely rare visitor with only one winter record of a bird remaining in the Holywell/Gosforth Park area from May into November 1974. This status had not changed by the time of their *Supplement* (1986). No birds were recorded during the 1981-1984 national winter atlas survey, although Lack (1986) estimated the national wintering population at that time as between 1,380 and 1,800 birds. However, since then there has been a significant expansion in the Northumberland population especially in the breeding season. It is therefore not surprising that there is now a small local wintering population, although some records may relate to late broods at breeding sites. An instance of this happening was four juveniles at Arcot Pond (NZ27M) during November 1997.

All birds recorded during this survey were on ponds and lakes below 200 metres a.s.l. The greatest concentration of records was around the Druridge Bay area with a maximum of 15 birds on Cresswell Pond (NZ29X) in November 1997, 11 on Druridge Pools (NZ29T) in January 1998, five on Ladyburn Lake (NU20Q) in November 1996 and three at Hauxley NR (NU20W) in January 1998. These four sites accounted for 51% of all maximum counts during the three winter periods. An unusual sighting in this general area involved a bird on the sea near the Coquet Estuary (NU20S). Several of the ponds used in winter are sites where Ruddy Duck have bred successfully, especially in the south east including Big Waters (NZ27G), Bothal Pond (NZ28N), Capheaton (NZ07J) where up to seven birds were found, Holywell Pond (NZ37C) and Wallsend Swallow Pond (NZ36E). Three birds were also seen on Killingworth Lake (NZ27Q) in November 1997, almost certainly having dispersed from a local breeding site. Inland winter records mainly of singles came from Branton Gravel Pit near Powburn (NU01N), Hallington Reservoirs (NY97T), Hartburn (NZ07T), Grindon Lough (NY86D), Kimmer Lough (NU11D), Rayburn Lake (NZ19B) and Whittle Dene Reservoirs (NZ06U). Ruddy Duck is now regarded as an uncommon breeding species in Northumberland but rare in winter. Whether this status will continue is, in part, dependent on the control measures being taken currently in other regions of the country in efforts to protect the European population of White-headed Duck *O. leucocephala*.

LINDSAY J. McDOUGALL

Distribution by altitude

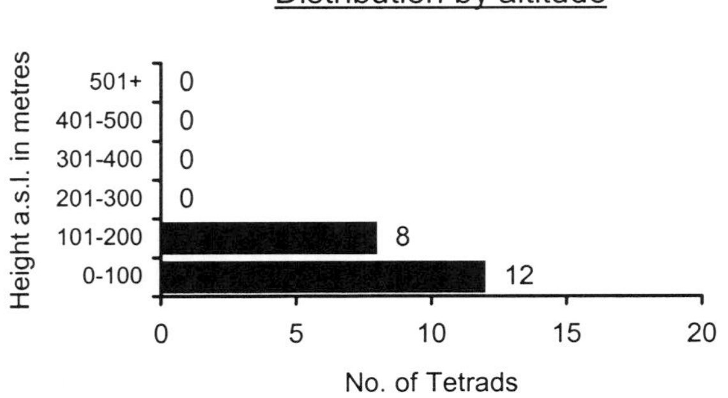

No. of tetrads in which recorded 20 (1%)

Tetrad Analysis	No. of tetrads
1 bird	11 (55%)
2-4 birds	5 (25%)
5+ birds	4 (20%)

Total No. of birds counted 67

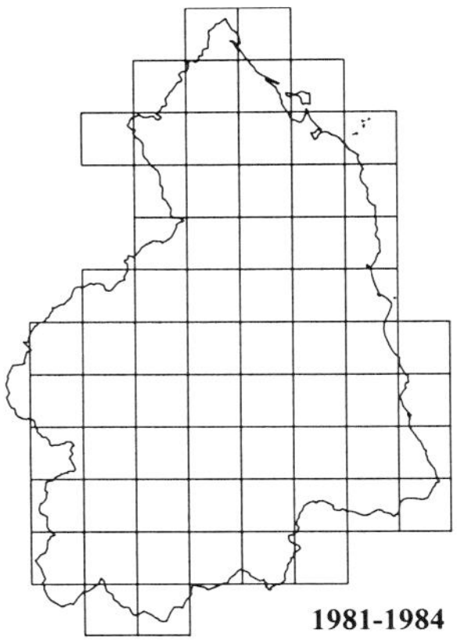

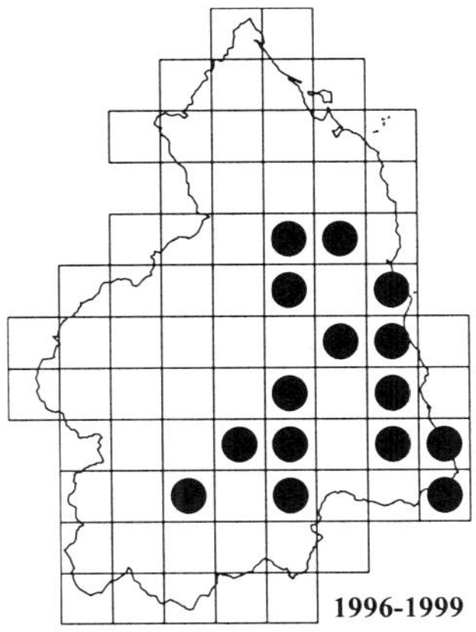

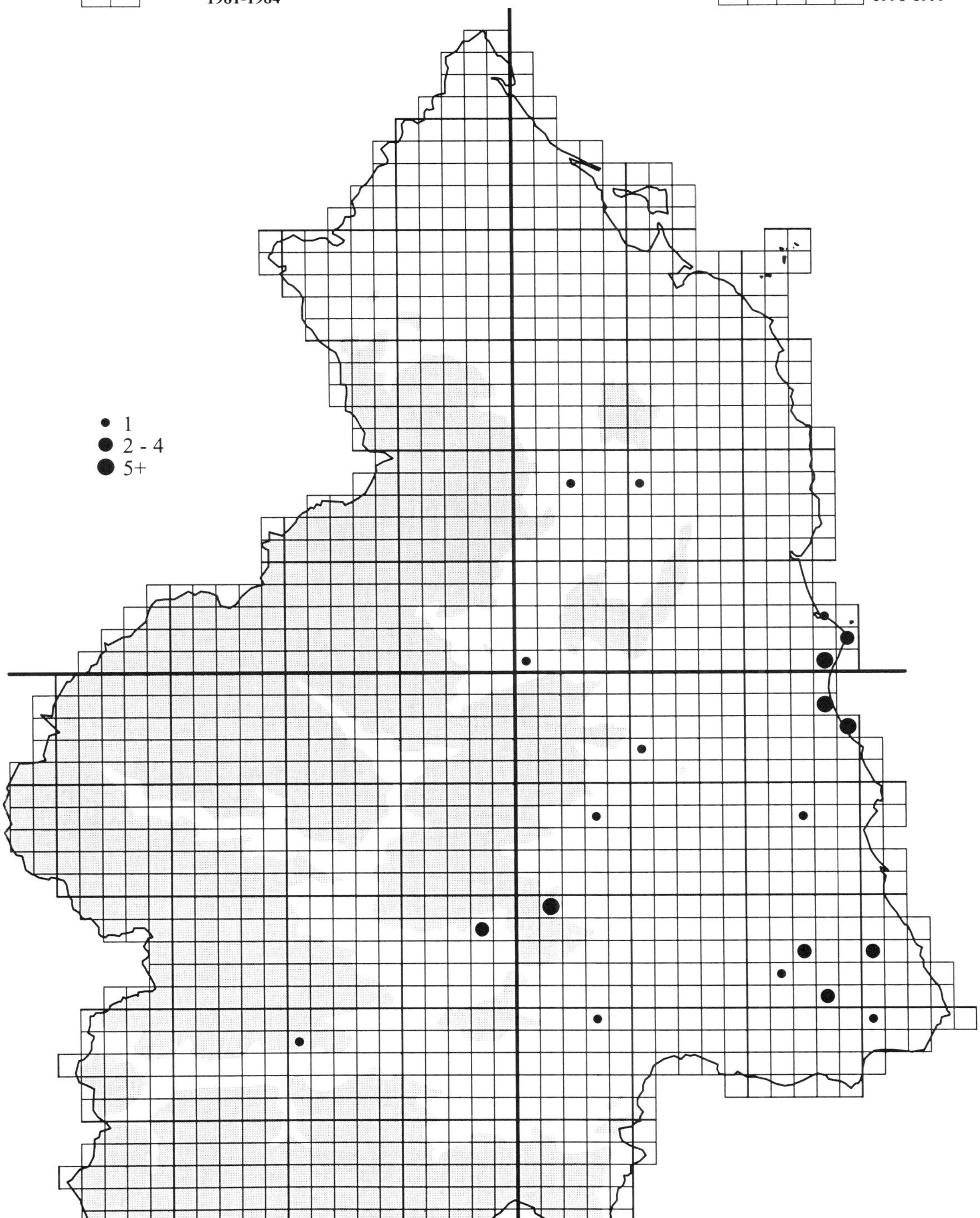

Ruddy Duck

WINTERING RAPTORS IN NORTHUMBERLAND

Bryan Galloway

Although 16 raptor species have been historically identified in Northumberland during the winter months, only ten species were recorded during the current survey. Those seen in previous winters between November and February were Honey Buzzard *Pernis apivorus*, White-tailed Eagle *Haliaeetus albicilla*, Marsh Harrier *Circus aeruginosus*, Osprey *Pandion haliaetus*, Hobby *Falco subbuteo* and Gyr Falcon *Falco rusticolus*, albeit in very small numbers or as isolated individuals.

Of the species reported during this survey, Red Kite *Milvus milvus*, Rough-legged Buzzard *Buteo lagopus* and Golden Eagle *Aquila chrysaetos* were predictably scarce, although some observers may have expected to see more of the Red Kite in view of the success of the reintroduction programmes that are on-going in both England and Scotland.

Censusing of raptors is more of a challenge in winter than in summer and there is no doubt that the two species of Accipiter, which are particularly secretive in their woodland haunts, were under-counted. Despite this difficulty, it was of interest to note that both seem to be increasing and it would be of little surprise that the Sparrowhawk *Accipiter nisus* has taken over from the Kestrel *F. tinnunculus* as our commonest bird of prey.

Of the remainder, the welcome return of the Common Buzzard *B. buteo* and the rapid increase in the population has surprised us all. It is difficult to understand why this has happened so quickly, but no doubt there has been a combination of factors such as a reduction in persecution, a good supply of food in the form of Rabbits *Oryctolagus cuniculus* and good productivity during the breeding period. Less of a surprise is the struggle that the Hen Harrier *C. cyaneus* has to endure as numbers are suppressed by illegal persecution activities. Northumberland offers ideal habitat for a species that would be a much more regular sight if it was left undisturbed in both winter and summer.

The changing fortunes of the falcons are not without interest. The Peregrine *F. peregrinus* population continues to increase slowly despite the apparent limitation of suitable nest sites. Twentieth century history has, however, shown that it is very vulnerable to the dubious direct and careless indirect activities of man. The Kestrel is still a regular sight in the county but recent reductions in the population in some breeding areas suggest that numbers may be on the decline. It is possible that it is suffering from the increase in the breeding populations of the three larger raptor species that share the same habitat. The Merlin *F. columbarius* also has its problems, especially in its breeding territory where it too is also struggling to cope with the increase in the larger species, especially the Goshawk *Accipiter gentilis*. Poor productivity is hence of local concern although the current national picture seems to be less of a problem. The winter population in the county is still encouraging but the future for our smallest raptor remains on a knife edge.

Raptors are particularly vulnerable and numbers have probably been influenced more by the direct intervention of man than any other group of species. Persecution, which gathered momentum in the nineteenth century, drastically reduced or eliminated several populations whilst late twentieth century policing coupled with reintroduction programmes has helped towards restoring numbers. However, changes in land use (e.g. increased afforestation) have, less directly, assisted some (Sparrowhawk and Goshawk) but hindered others (Kestrel and Merlin). Careless management of heather and agricultural intensification can reduce the choice of habitat for some specialist species and hence it is especially important that the populations of our raptors continue to be carefully monitored in both winter and summer to assist conservation groups with their action plans.

RED KITE *Milvus milvus*

In writing about this elegant raptor Bolam (1932) quoted the death, near Featherstone in 1869, of probably the last breeding Red Kite in Northumberland. As in many English counties before the nineteenth century, the species had been a not uncommon resident but declined dramatically as shooting estates and the resultant persecution increased after the agrarian revolution. Later sightings in the county, detailed by Galloway and Meek (1978), were extremely erratic and presumably of Welsh first-year birds, although continental stragglers cannot be ruled out.

From the mid-1990s the record changed dramatically, no doubt as a direct result of the re-establishment programmes in Scotland and England between 1989 and 1994, and the secondary releases in 1995-1996 (Evans *et al.*, 1997). Between 1991 and spring 1996 ten Red Kites were seen, including two Scottish wing-tagged birds, and a third with a tail-mounted radio transmitter. The ten showed no discernible pattern with one sighting in January, one in August and two in October, although the five in the March/April period may have been birds returning to Scottish natal or breeding areas.

The sightings during the three winter seasons of the atlas period relate to two winged-tagged birds, one of which was identified as being from central Scotland. Appropriately, from an historical perspective, the observation was in the Featherstone Castle area (NY66V) in December 1996. In all probability the same two birds were also seen on Ramshaw Fell (NY76A), in the adjacent tetrad, in January of the following year. A third Red Kite was also present near Fourstones (NY86Y) between 30 November 1996 and April 1997. No birds over-wintered during the 1997/98 or 1998/99 survey periods although there were four spring sightings in 1997 and three reports between June and October in 1998. In both years these records included wing-tagged birds, with the March 1997 bird displaying a blue wing-tag from the 1990 Scottish release programme.

The annual increase in reports, largely as a result of the re-introduction programmes, augurs well for more regular annual sightings and perhaps the possibility of breeding in Northumberland in the near future.

JOHN C. DAY

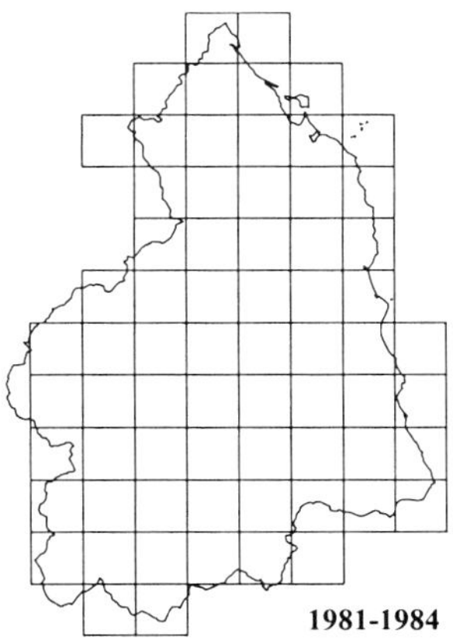

1981-1984

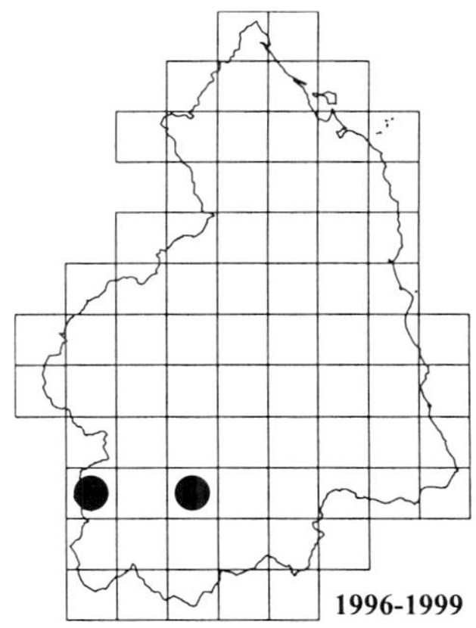

1996-1999

No. of tetrads in which recorded 2 (<1%)

Tetrad Analysis	No. of tetrads
1 bird	1 (50%)
2 birds	1 (50%)

Total No. of birds counted 3

HEN HARRIER *Circus cyaneus*

Bolam (1912) observed that the Hen Harrier 'still continues to visit us, at ever increasing intervals, during the winter months' and judging from the paucity of records up to the 1970s his prediction was right. On 20th December 1945 George Temperley watched a 'ring-tail' quartering the reeds at Broomlee Lough and commented on his record card that almost ten years to the day in 1935 a male had been seen at the same place, the implication being that none had been recorded there in between. Other single harriers were recorded at Crag Lough in the 1950s and Broomlee again in 1961 and 1963. Individuals also appeared irregularly in north Northumberland around Fenham Flats, at nearby Holburn Moss and on Ross Links.

It is probably true to say that, even though Hen Harriers were breeding in the newly planted Kielder uplands from 1957 and, by the winter of 1973/74, Galloway and Meek (1978) were able to refer to an upsurge in records to about 15 birds, it was probably only in 1978/79, when some 20 individuals were seen (Galloway & Meek, 1986), that wintering harriers became more obvious. In that winter, Northumberland was on the edge of a national influx involving over 750 birds, largely in south east England. Most were judged to have come from the continent and this was borne out by one found dead in February 1979 near Cramlington which had been ringed as a pullus on the Friesian Islands, Holland in 1977, although a juvenile male wing-tagged on mainland Orkney was seen at Holywell Pond in March 1979 (*Birds in Northumbria 1979*; Davenport, 1982). Since that winter, numbers have settled to a more normal level. The late Geoff Macfarlane estimated Northumberland's wintering population to be in the range of eight-ten birds in the early 1980s (pers. comm.) and that is valid today despite local increases in Dumfriesshire and occasional marked autumn passage/post-breeding dispersal.

Although Hen Harriers establish winter territories, they are highly mobile and opportunistic hunters, so the same individual may be encountered across a number of tetrads in one day. Harriers were found in 14 tetrads in winter 1996/97, 18 in 1997/98 and 17 in 1998/99, but this does not mean that there were 17 harriers present in 1998/99. Indeed, many of the records from NY65, NY66, NY75 and NY76 probably refer to the same birds (up to four gathered at a temporary communal roost at Coanwood Pond (NY65Z) in the winter of 1996/97). One of these, a juvenile female had been wing-tagged at Langholm, Dumfriesshire. Similar numbers have not been seen since, probably because of a combination of prey levels, which were unusually high in 1996/97, and possibly persecution.

During the current survey, by far the greatest number of records concern lone harriers, seen anywhere from Haltwhistle to Holy Island and Macfarlane's estimate would seem about right. However, a comparison between the two 10 km square maps reveals some interesting changes. They are now seen more frequently along the eastern fringes of the Cheviots where extensive heather regeneration has taken place, whereas they have become much scarcer at traditional coastal sites and the subsidence pools of south east Northumberland. Hen Harriers were recorded in only nine tetrads below 100 metres a.s.l. compared with 30 between 101 and 300 metres a.s.l. and ten over 301 metres.

continued overleaf

Distribution by altitude

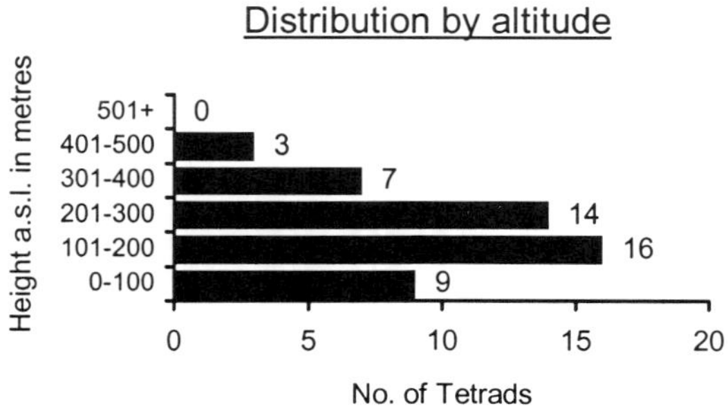

No. of tetrads in which recorded 49 (3%)

Tetrad Analysis	No. of tetrads
1 bird	43 (88%)
2 birds	4 (8%)
3+ birds	2 (4%)

Total No. of birds counted 58

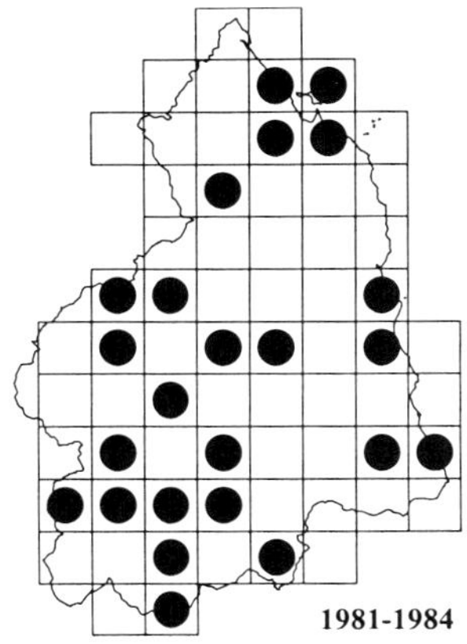

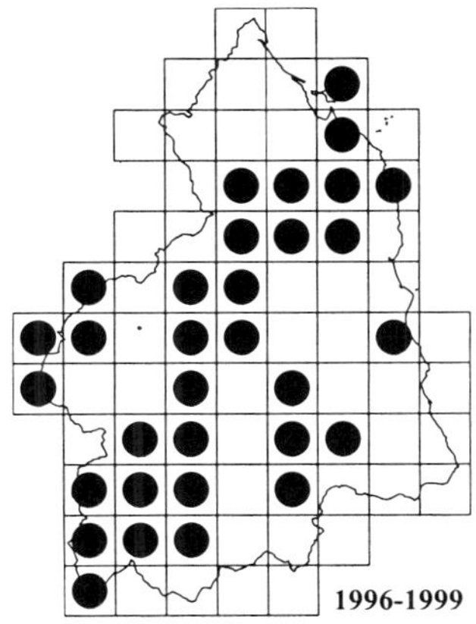

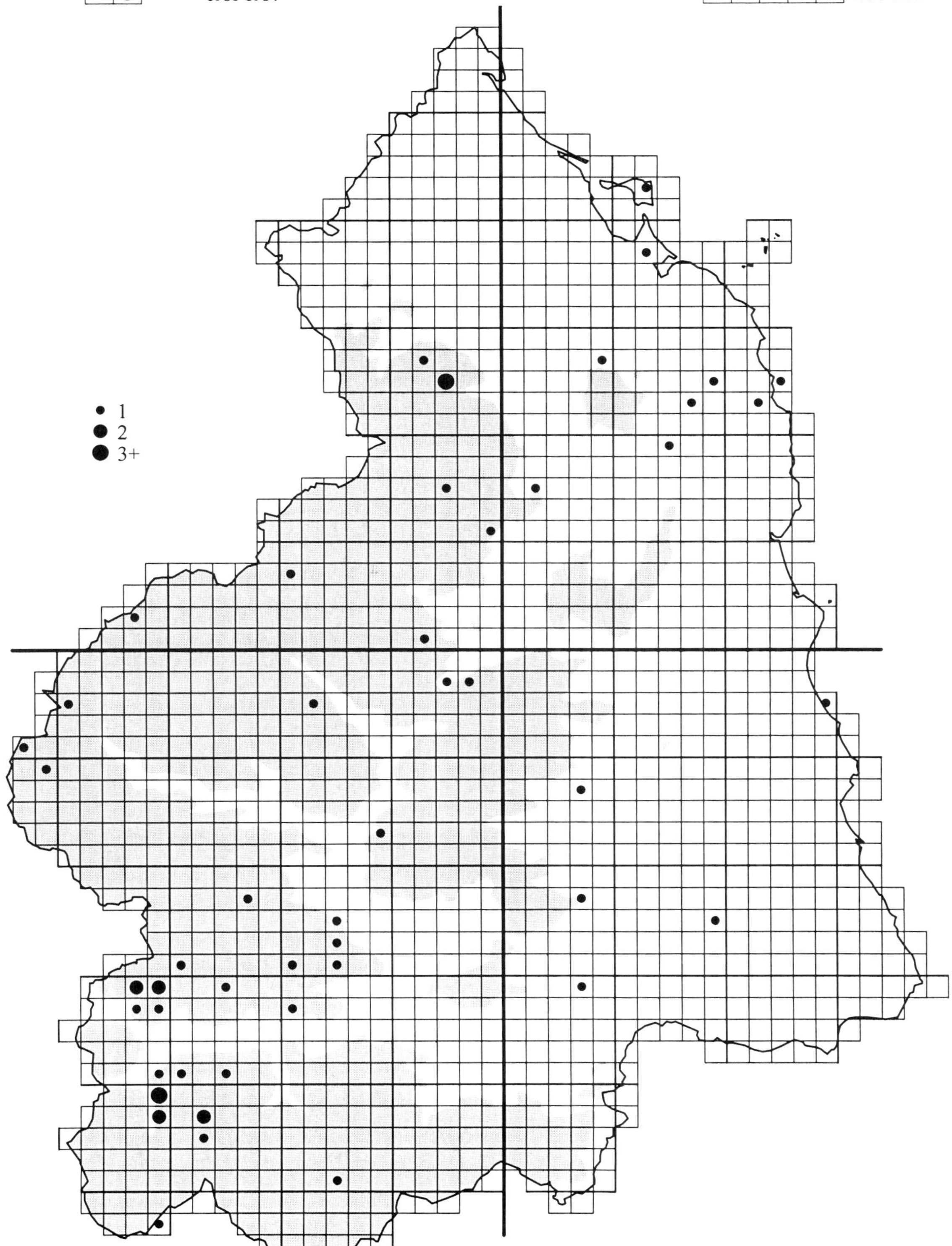

Hen Harrier

Hen Harriers are never easy to see in Northumberland and, because of the suspected level of persecution, it would be unwise to be too specific, but a watch at Grindon Lough (NY86D) and careful scanning from any road on or over moorland might be rewarding.

Many grouse moors were abandoned as un-commercial decades ago, as the decaying but still discernible shooting butts indicate. Hen Harriers did not make them un-commercial, since their demise came for the most part before the species' return so clearly documented by Watson (1977). But in the materialistic 1990s many of the ills which affect the game moor were blamed on the harrier especially after the Langholm report. In short, there is no room for complacency over the future of the Hen Harrier. With predictions that it will soon be extinct as a breeding species in England (The Independent 09.05.01) and only nine juveniles raised in 2000 on two protected moors, the county is dependent for wintering birds on the Scottish population (as evidenced from wing-tags) and occasionally continental immigrants. Even in Scotland many raptor workers are pessimistic about its future outside core areas like Argyll. Whether the fact that the North Pennines has recently been given European Union Special Protection Area status and the so-called CROW Act (Countryside and Rights of Way Act) will make any difference remains to be seen. However, the Hen Harrier is a survivor. It has come back from the brink once and may yet surprise us again.

MIKE HENRY

GOLDEN EAGLE *Aquila chrysaetos*

County records for the species have been deliberately vague and confidential over recent years to protect this vulnerable raptor. Its current status within the county is that of a rare visitor which has occasionally bred.

At the beginning of the twentieth century Bolam (1912) described it as 'once a resident on the Borders, but now only of very rare accidental occurrence'. Unfortunately for earlier data, the eighteenth and nineteenth century references to birds in the Cheviot massif and the Border uplands are not always clear as there seems to be some confusion with sightings and possible breeding records of White-tailed Eagle *Haliaeetus albicilla* (Rossiter, 1999).

By the time his *Catalogue* appeared in 1932 Bolam could add no further sightings of Golden Eagle in the county since 1912, and it was not until 1950 that a wandering bird was recorded on the Northumberland/Cumbria border. From that year sightings increased and Galloway and Meek (1978) were able to state that 'since 1968 its status has changed. Single immatures, or on occasions two together, have been seen almost every winter, and sometimes also in summer in the Cheviots, the Simonside Hills and the Kielder area'. One or two birds, often immatures, were recorded consistently in spring 'in the Border region' each year between 1979 and 1983, but there was then a gap until 1988. Thereafter, from 1991 to the end of the century, one or two juveniles or sub-adults have been seen annually, often throughout the year, in 'upland areas'.

The three winter atlas seasons of the current survey were no exception, with single birds being seen near the Scottish border in December 1997 and February 1999, although more unusual was one near Simonburn (NY87B) in February 1998.

As stated in *The atlas of breeding birds in Northumbria* (Day *et al.*, 1995) 'with suitable habitat, an adequate food supply, and where human interference is minimal, the species can survive'. As Forestry Commission management and farming land usage slowly change in the Northumbrian uplands the future for this magnificent bird is constantly improving. Hopefully, the Golden Eagle will become a more regular sight in the Border hills.

JOHN C. DAY

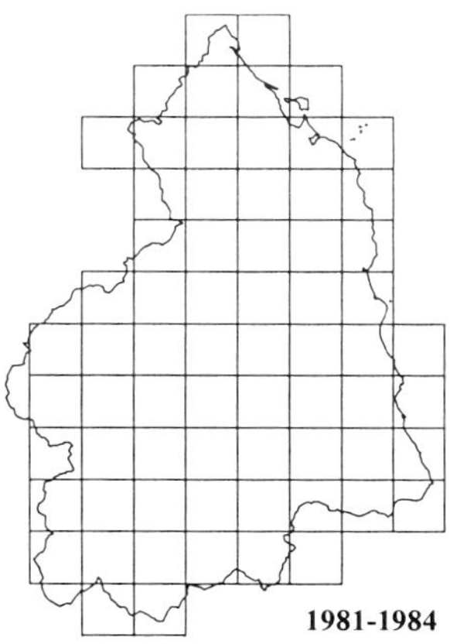

1981-1984

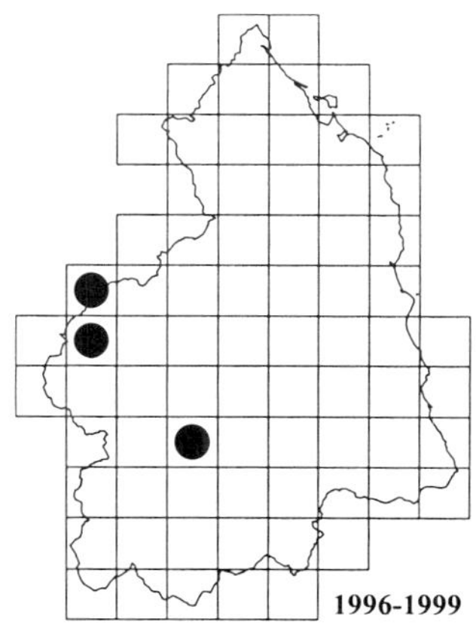

1996-1999

No. of tetrads in which recorded	3 (<1%)

Tetrad Analysis	No. of tetrads
1 bird	3 (100%)

Total No. of birds counted	3

GOSHAWK *Accipiter gentilis*

Galloway and Meek (1978) stated that there were only 14 records of Goshawk prior to one at Bamburgh in 1952 and all were in the nineteenth century in the time of Hancock and Bolam. During the winter of 1957/58 two were shot on pigeon shoots and late in 1969, when hawk keepers were releasing imported Goshawks into the Border Forest, single birds were seen at Rothbury and Blagdon. During the 1970s it became an increasingly regular sight in those western forests, albeit in very small numbers, and Day *et al.* (1995) and Petty and Anderson (1996) summarised events leading to the first breeding success this century in 1977.

The large forests of Northumberland provided ideal hunting and nesting habitat for this essentially sedentary raptor and with fledging success annually of over two young per nest it was of little surprise that some 20 years later the population had grown to 50 breeding pairs. Petty and Anderson suggested that because there was 'much unoccupied habitat to be colonised' the population should continue to grow slowly even taking into account the illegal persecution that clearly occurs.

The magnitude of the increase is clear from the comparison of the two 10km square distribution maps but it must be one of the most challenging species to census, especially over the early and mid-winter periods. Lack (1986) stated that 'Goshawks are rarely seen ... even in those areas where there are established populations' although they can sometimes be more obvious in late winter as they enter into 'prolonged display flights over nesting territories'. He also endorsed the opinion of other authors that 'Goshawks are sedentary birds and the distribution of winter sightings closely matches the breeding distribution'.

This certainly applies in Northumberland, as can be seen from the tetrad distribution map which shows that at least 50% of the individuals reported during the current survey were in the breeding stronghold so well researched by Petty and Anderson. The drive to explore more fragmented woodland areas on lower ground is confirmed by the sighting in that habitat of about 20% of the total of birds noted during the entire period. The survey produced 70 individual sightings spread over 59 tetrads and throughout the area most observations were of single birds but there were seven examples of tetrads containing two individuals, with three seen in each of Kielder (NY69G) and the Darden Burn areas (NY99T).

Taking into account the comments of Lack, there is little doubt that, because of its largely secretive nature, a significant proportion of the population was not detected in the survey. Looking at the results of the work of Petty and Anderson, who concluded a productivity of over two young per pair from a population of 50 breeding pairs, the number of individuals in the county in late summer of this very sedentary species would be in the order of 100 adults and 100 young. Immigrants from the expanding population in western Europe may occur in winter but Lack thought that these would be no more than of vagrant status and hence would not significantly alter the numbers. Allowing for a subsequent mortality of 30% per year, which can be no more than an estimate and is probably rather high, and a small exodus to adjacent regions, it is likely that in excess of 100 birds currently remain in Northumberland over the winter period. It thus should assume a winter status of well-represented, rather than uncommon as is presently used, albeit in the lower end of the range.

It has already been stated that Petty and Anderson predicted a growth in the breeding population in the county. Kerslake (1998) quoted 'it is steadily increasing' and Mead (2000) endorsed this view on a national scale commenting that 'further expansion expected to go ahead' despite illegal persecution problems. If this progress does continue then the Goshawk will be seen with increasing frequency in winter in the forest and woodland areas of Northumberland.

BRYAN GALLOWAY

Distribution by altitude

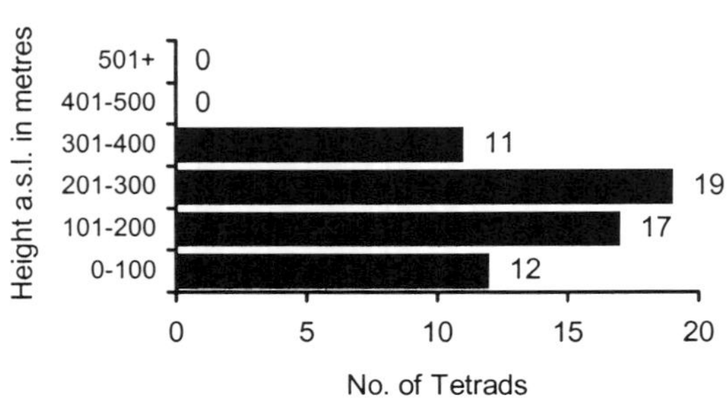

No. of tetrads in which recorded 59 (4%)

Tetrad Analysis	No. of tetrads
1 bird	50 (85%)
2 birds	7 (12%)
3 birds	2 (3%)

Total No. of birds counted 70

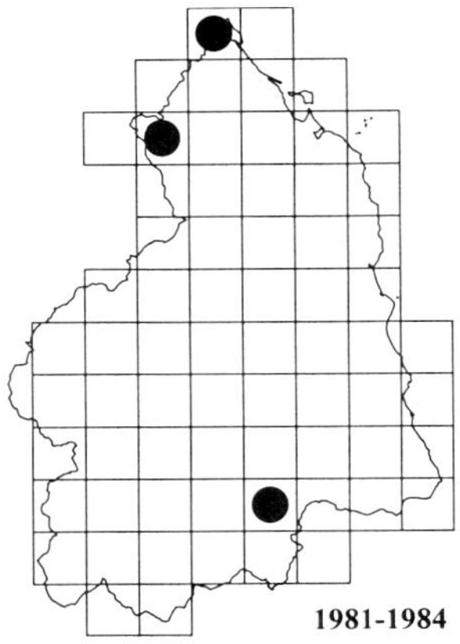

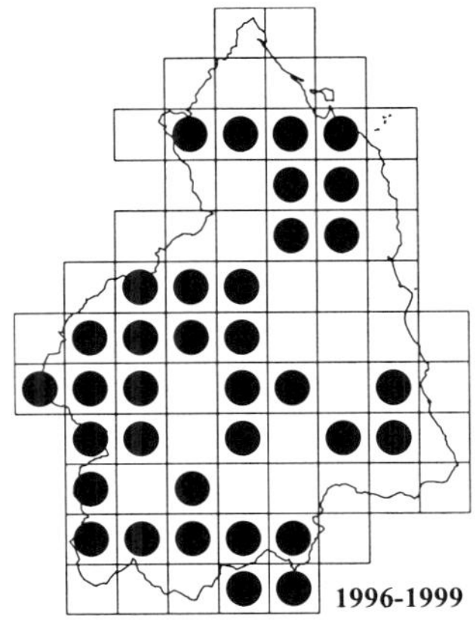

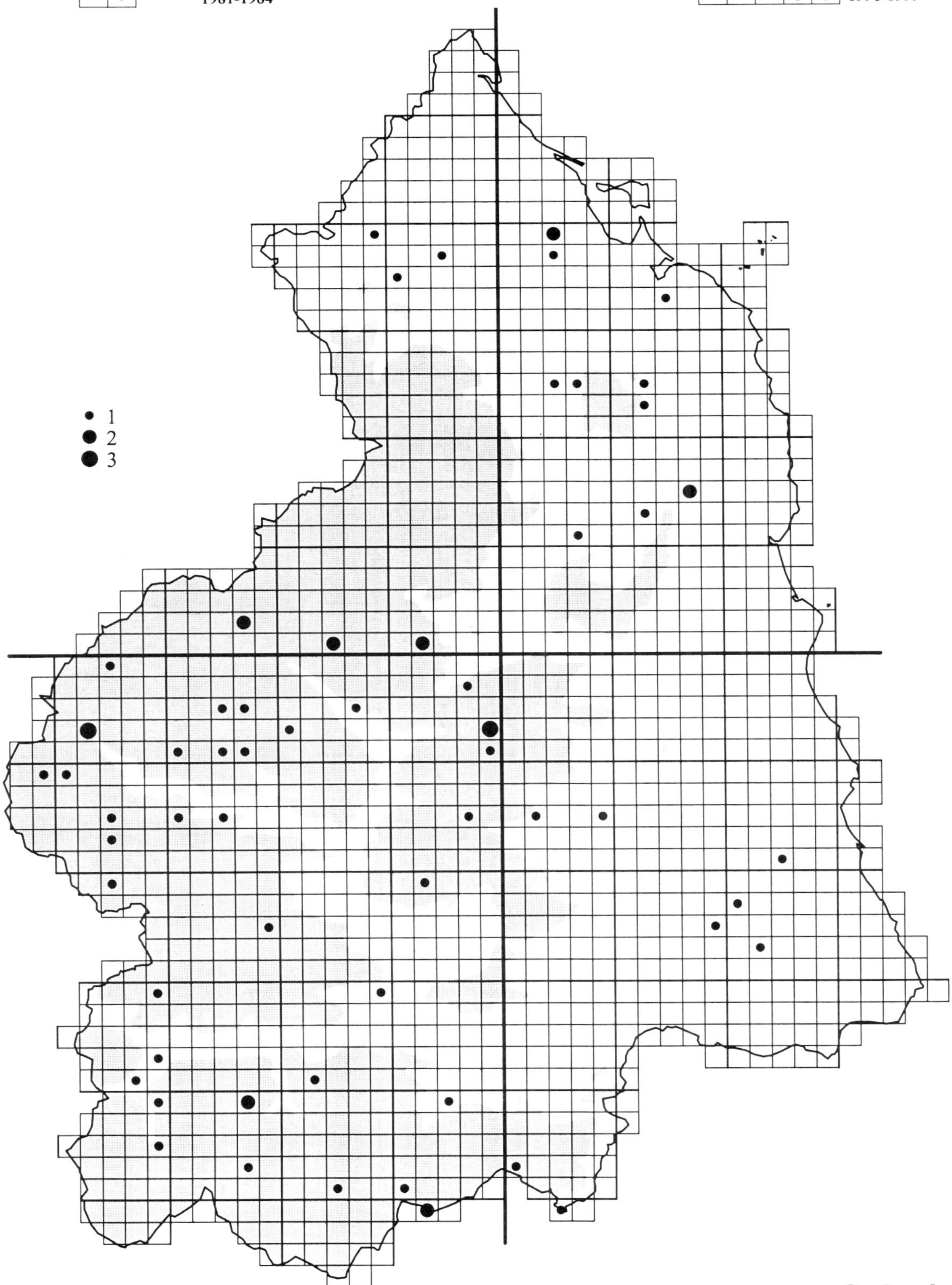

Goshawk

SPARROWHAWK *Accipiter nisus*

Previous authors indicated that the Sparrowhawk was always a common sight in the county until Galloway and Meek (1978) highlighted the catastrophic decline in numbers in the 1960s caused by the use of organochlorine pesticides. Thankfully, the Northumberland population did recover quite quickly after the ban on the use of such chemicals and since the mid-1970s it has assumed a status of well-represented in both summer and winter.

Galloway (1987) analysed the recoveries of 145 individuals that had been ringed as nestlings in the county and concluded that it was a remarkably sedentary species. Between 80% and 90% of those found were no more than 50km from the nest site and only 4% travelled more than 100km. This is consistent with the findings of Newton (1986) in various study areas throughout the UK.

Recoveries in the region of birds ringed in Dumfries and Galloway demonstrate that a proportion of the population in the county are winter visitors and it was probably from this nearby region, where Newton noted that 'Sparrowhawks survived in the greatest numbers through the height of the organochlorine era', that re-colonisation of the county occurred in the 1970s. Lack (1986) stated that some Scandinavian ringed birds had been recovered in winter in eastern Britain, confirming that another proportion are of continental origin, but none have been found in Northumberland. However, an adult male caught at Bamburgh on 4th November 1978 that had been ringed in western Germany in November of the previous year invites speculation. Was this individual a migrant passing through or was it going to spend the winter in Britain, possibly in Northumberland ?

The two 10km square maps show that there has been little change in distribution since the survey of 1981-1984. The tetrad map and supporting data demonstrate that it was encountered almost anywhere in the region up to about 200 metres a.s.l. with most no doubt being close to woodland, no matter how small, and in hedgerows and gardens. The majority of tetrad counts were of one or two birds but in 1997/98 four were seen in the Heaton/Jesmond Dene area (NZ26T) and five at Blagdon (NZ27D). An analysis of the control tetrad results suggests that the species may have been more plentiful during the winter of 1998/99.

Over 80% of the total of 430 individuals recorded were in areas below 200 metres a.s.l. The apparent absence from the large upland areas of the extensive Border Forest in the west can only be explained by difficulties in censusing, which was also the case during the county breeding survey of 1988-1992 (Day *et al.*, 1995), and there is probably no reason to believe that the population density in such areas during the period of this survey was any different from that in the lowlands. If this was to be true, then the number of Sparrowhawks wintering in Northumberland would be in the region of 700-800 individuals, confirming the well-represented status assessment that has prevailed since 1976.

Marchant *et al.* (1990) charted the national population recovery from 1974 and stated that 'further increase is likely as additional suitable sites become available' whilst Mead (2000) speculated that a 'full recovery seems likely'. Let us hope that toxic pesticides or something equally sinister have gone forever.

BRYAN GALLOWAY

Distribution by altitude

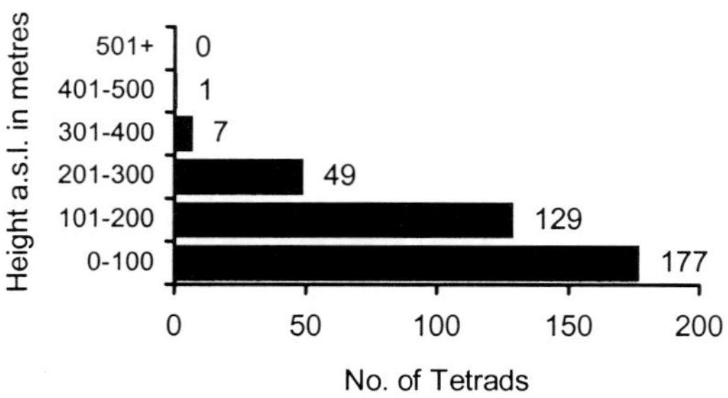

No. of tetrads in which recorded 363 (25%)

Tetrad Analysis	No. of tetrads
1 bird	311 (86%)
2 birds	40 (11%)
3+ birds	12 (3%)

Total No. of birds counted 430

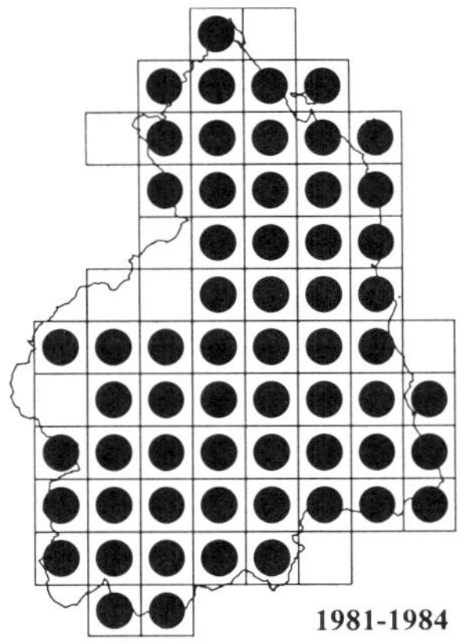

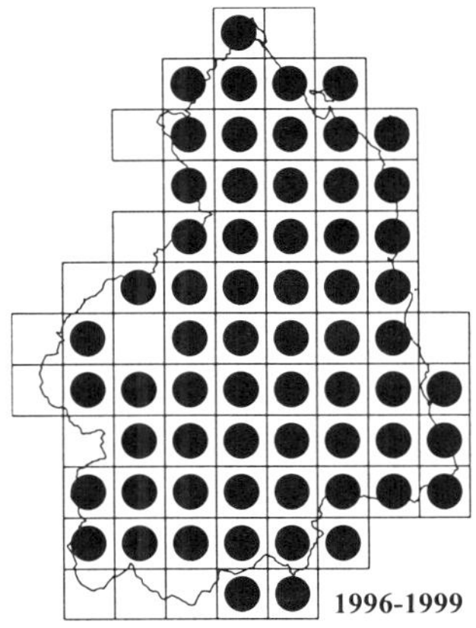

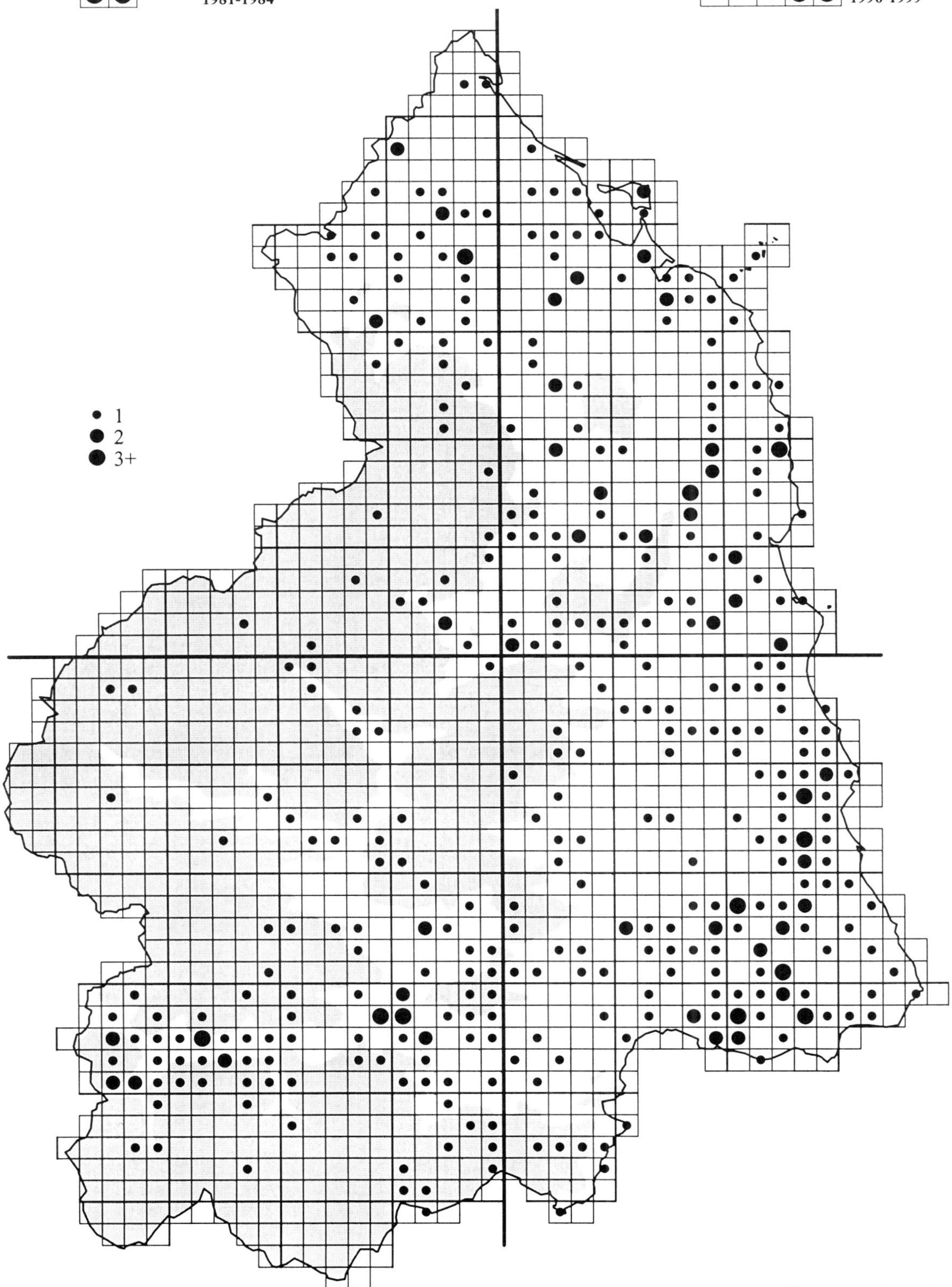

Sparrowhawk

COMMON BUZZARD *Buteo buteo*

In the eighteenth century, Wallis (1769) indicated that two types of buzzard occurred in Northumberland, the Common Buzzard and the Honey Buzzard *Pernis apivorus*. Wallis appeared to separate the species through specimens on cere and eye colour rather than in field observations. It would therefore appear that a number of specimens were available, making it likely that broad-winged hawks were already being shot on some scale at this time (Rossiter, 1999). Bolam (1932) provides anecdotal evidence for the greater abundance of the Common Buzzard in historical times commenting that 'in the days of our fathers, it had many nesting places, especially amongst the hills'.

In the late eighteenth and early nineteenth centuries, persecution intensified and a rapid national decline occurred with far less evidence for the abundance of the species in Northumberland. Wingate (1825) and Maddison (1830) included it in their lists but Selby (1831) noted that he had only occasionally met with it. The overall conclusion is that the Common Buzzard was scarce after 1800 and only survived on a very local basis into the 1830s and 1840s. For the next 150 years the species failed to gain any persistent foothold in the county except for two brief revivals. Bolam (1932) noted the speedy re-occupation of territories during the First World War when most of the gamekeepers were withdrawn from their usual occupations. McCavish (1971) reported that they were fairly common upon the moors near Kielder around the time of the Second World War.

In systematic breeding surveys, the species was found in six 10km squares (four with confirmed breeding) in the 1968-1972 breeding atlas (Sharrock, 1976) but was found to be completely absent in the 1983 national survey (Day *et al.*, 1995). The county breeding atlas survey of 1988-1993 was fortuitously timed in that it coincided with the start of a very rapid increase in Common Buzzard numbers. Regular breeding started in the South Tyne at Barhaugh Burn in 1988 and, in 1993, 14 pairs were confirmed breeding mainly in the south west but also in the north. Over the five-year period, pairs were recorded in 47 tetrads in 23 ten kilometre squares. The South Tyne was the stronghold, with breeding confirmed in six tetrads, mainly in the Slaggyford-Eals area. Numbers continued to rise rapidly in the mid-1990s with 43 broods totalling 85 young reported in 1997 (*Birds in Northumbria 1997*).

The current winter survey confirms the remarkable increase in numbers since the 1980s with reports from 50 (67% of the 75 surveyed) 10km squares as against 11 (17% of the 64 surveyed) in the 1981-1984 winter survey. As many as 240 tetrads were occupied compared to 47 in the 1988-1993 county breeding atlas. The species adapts to both lowland and upland habitat with 73 occupied tetrads at an altitude of 0-100 metres a.s.l. and 34 over 300 metres a.s.l.. Altogether 432 birds were counted with major concentrations in the South Tyne/Allen/West Allen area of the south west (71 tetrads, 162 birds, 2.28 birds per occupied tetrad) and the Lilburn/Glen/Till area north of the Cheviots (62, 120, 1.94). Smaller concentrations were found around Blagdon (12, 18, 1.5), Kielder Village (9, 15, 1.67) and Holburn (9, 13, 1.44). It remained largely absent from the Roman Wall area, the denser areas of coniferous woodland in the Border Forest and intensive arable agricultural areas in the south east and north of the county.

As this species is highly sedentary the counts should give a reasonable idea of the county population. A minimum figure for the breeding population is likely to be the number of tetrads with multiple birds, giving a total of 93 pairs. Alternatively, if it is assumed that for each pair two young are raised, as in 1997, and that one second-winter from the previous year survives, then 40% of the population is adult, indicating a population of 86 pairs. The county population over the atlas period would therefore appear to have been about 90 pairs. Colonisation has continued since, with 20 pairs in the Border Forest and a spread into areas such as Redesdale and Coquetdale.

B. N. ROSSITER

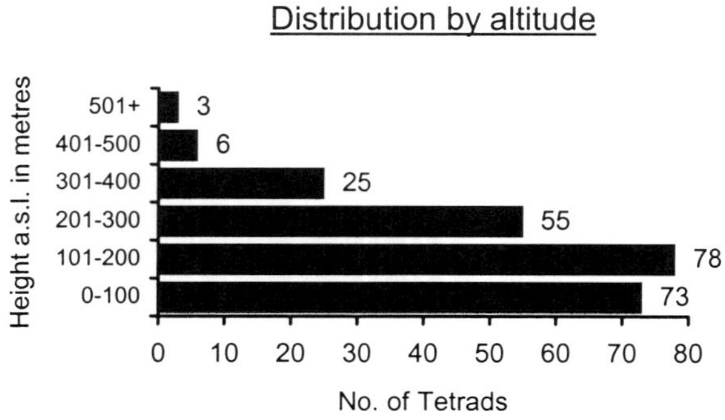

No. of tetrads in which recorded 240 (17%)

Tetrad Analysis	No. of tetrads
1 bird	147 (61%)
2 birds	53 (22%)
3+ birds	40 (17%)

Total No. of birds counted 432

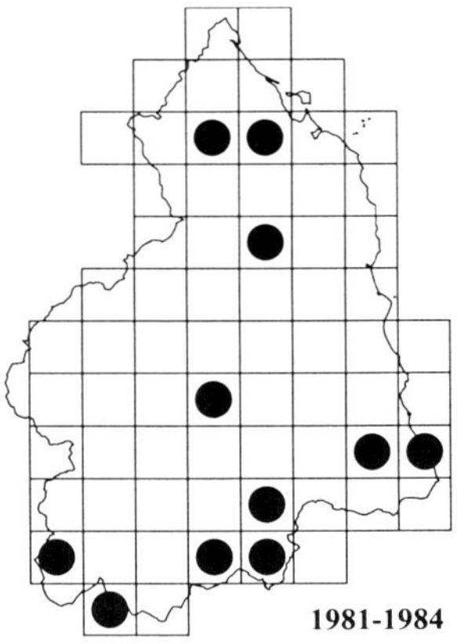

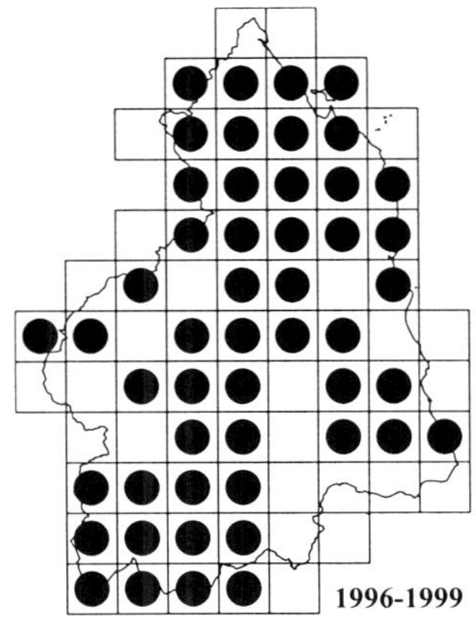

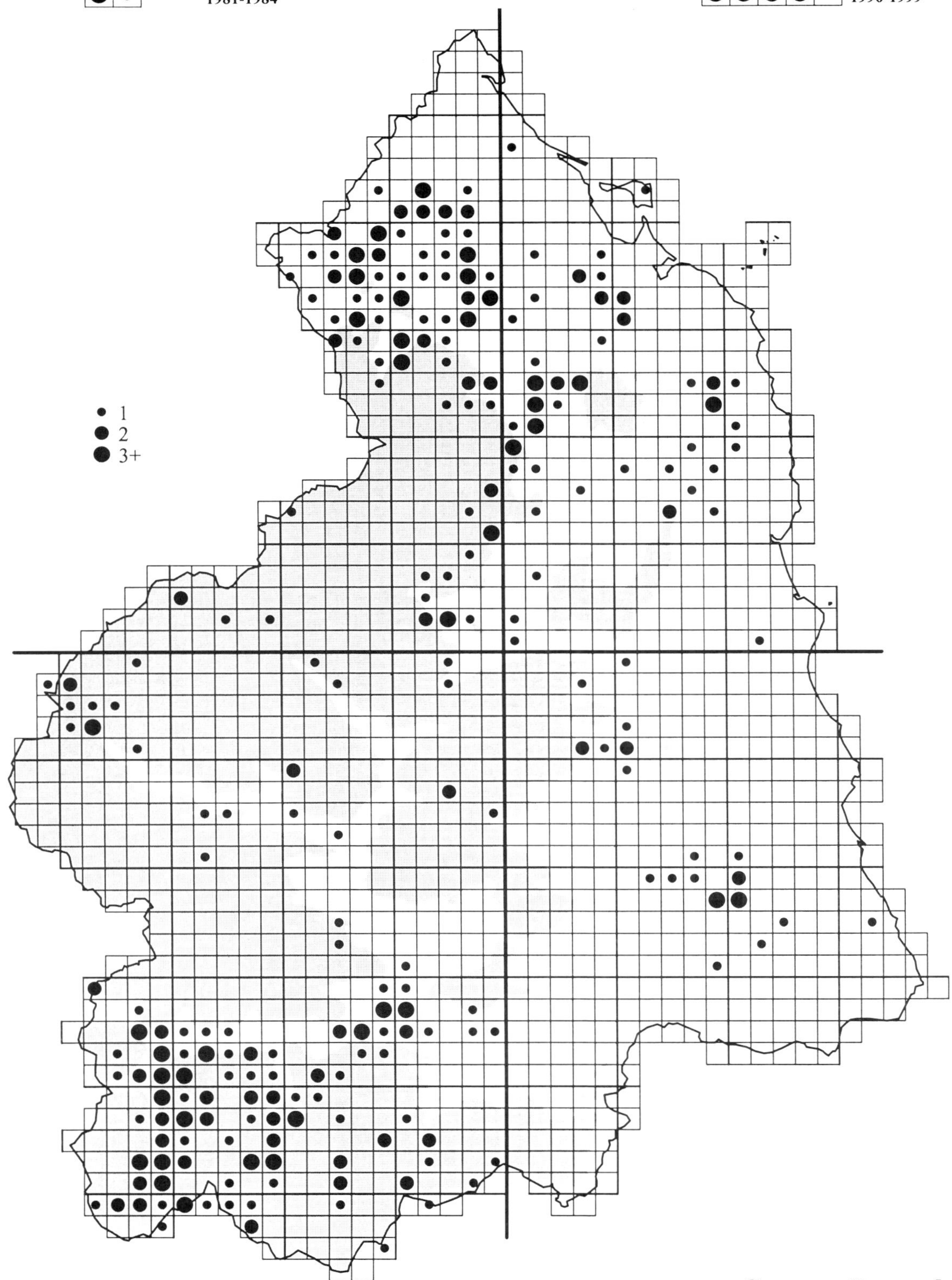

Common Buzzard

ROUGH-LEGGED BUZZARD *Buteo lagopus*

Although Rough-legged Buzzards were seen in eight tetrads during the current county winter atlas survey, they were recorded only in 1997 and 1998 (two spring passage birds were logged in 1999) and it is unlikely that more than four-five individuals were involved. One of these was a first winter bird which accounted for several sightings in the South Tyne area from late December 1997 until at least March 1998. This should be borne in mind when comparing the two maps. The current survey thus confirms the status of the Rough-legged Buzzard as a rare, not always annual visitor. It is extremely unlikely that any wintering individuals were overlooked as there is much greater observer awareness nowadays and the increasing population of Common Buzzards *Buteo buteo* is avidly checked for the rarer species.

In recent years the South Tyne Valley and Plenmeller Common areas have been the most productive sites for wintering Rough-legged Buzzards, with Eals Fell and Snope Common particularly attractive because they combine a high population of Rabbits *Oryctolagus cuniculus* with south west facing slopes providing an ideal updraught for hovering buzzards. Indeed, the only Rough-legged Buzzard of winter 1999/2000 appeared there on the 26th February (pers. obs.), a second calendar year bird.

In Bolam's day Rough-legged Buzzards seem to have been much more regular, with Horton and Doddington Moors in north Northumberland attracting sometimes 'several' annually. Hedgeley, a moor a little further south towards Alnwick, attracted a Rough-legged Buzzard 'over no fewer than fourteen winters' as R. Carr-Ellison reported in his Presidential Address to the Natural History Society of Northumberland and Durham in 1875. 'It seemed to feed mainly on moles and water rats; perhaps too on carrion. It never meddled with a Pheasant, and was never shot at, as we found it harmless' (Bolam, 1912). It is likely that 'lemming' years in the nineteenth century were more regular though, interestingly, Bolam explains invasion years by reference to 'vole plagues' in Northumberland and the Borders, especially between 1875 and 1887, with some 20-30 Rough-legged Buzzards having been 'obtained' at Dunbar alone in an earlier 'plague' between 1840 and 1842.

There has not been a good vole year in northern Scandinavia since 1982 and the Rough-legged Buzzard is one of the few raptors showing a strong negative tendency throughout the 1990s in annual counts from Falsterbo, Skåne, averaging 427 birds in 1996-1999 compared with 1,120 in 1986-1990 (Kjellén, 2000). Another is the Hen Harrier *Circus cyaneus*, also a vole specialist. It is, therefore, all the more surprising that the best Rough-legged Buzzard year in modern times was the winter of 1994/95 when up to 12 individuals (including three together in the Devil's Water/Beldon Burn area of Hexhamshire) were recorded as part of a national influx of at least 140 birds. These were thought to have originated from southern Norway after a good breeding season on the Hardangervidda, combined with ESE winds in late October. This influx was especially noteworthy for Northumberland because the county had hardly benefitted at all in the previous invasion years of 1966, 1973 and 1974 (Galloway & Meek, 1978). It seems safe to say that 1994/95 was probably the best winter for Rough-legged Buzzards in the twentieth century, and certainly the best since 1903! Unfortunately it occurred just a little too early for the current winter atlas survey, and Rough-legged Buzzard remains an exciting and unpredictable find for those who systematically scan the ridges of upland Northumberland. Britain is on the periphery of its wintering range at the best of times, and its occurrence here depends on a combination of factors such as breeding success and wind direction at the time of migration.

Of the eight sightings during this survey only one was near the coast, at Humford (NZ28Q) on 25th November 1997, and there is no history of the species wintering in dune slacks, coastal marshes and saltings in Northumberland as they do in Norfolk (Taylor *et al.*, 1999) or Kent (Lack, 1986).

MIKE HENRY

Distribution by altitude

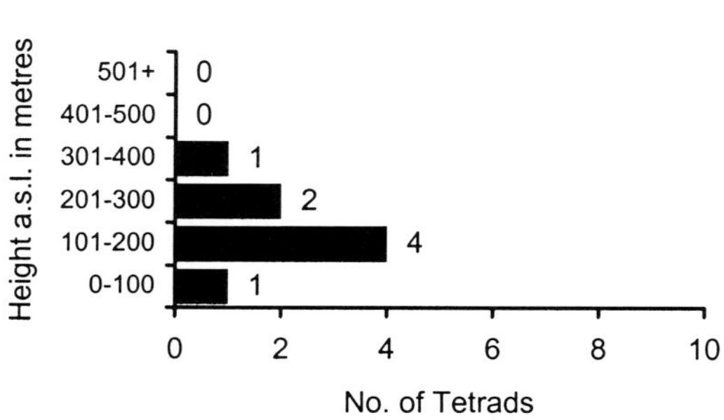

No. of tetrads in which recorded 8 (>1%)

Tetrad Analysis	No. of tetrads
1 bird	8 (100%)

Total No. of birds counted 8

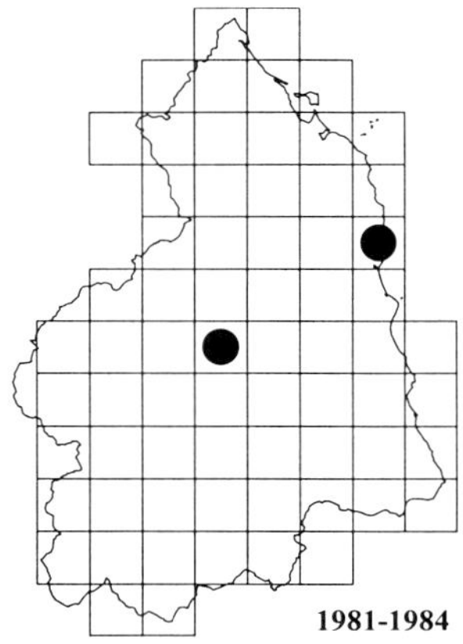

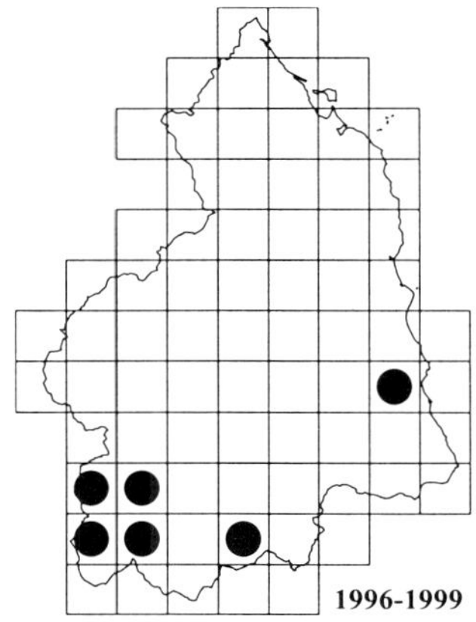

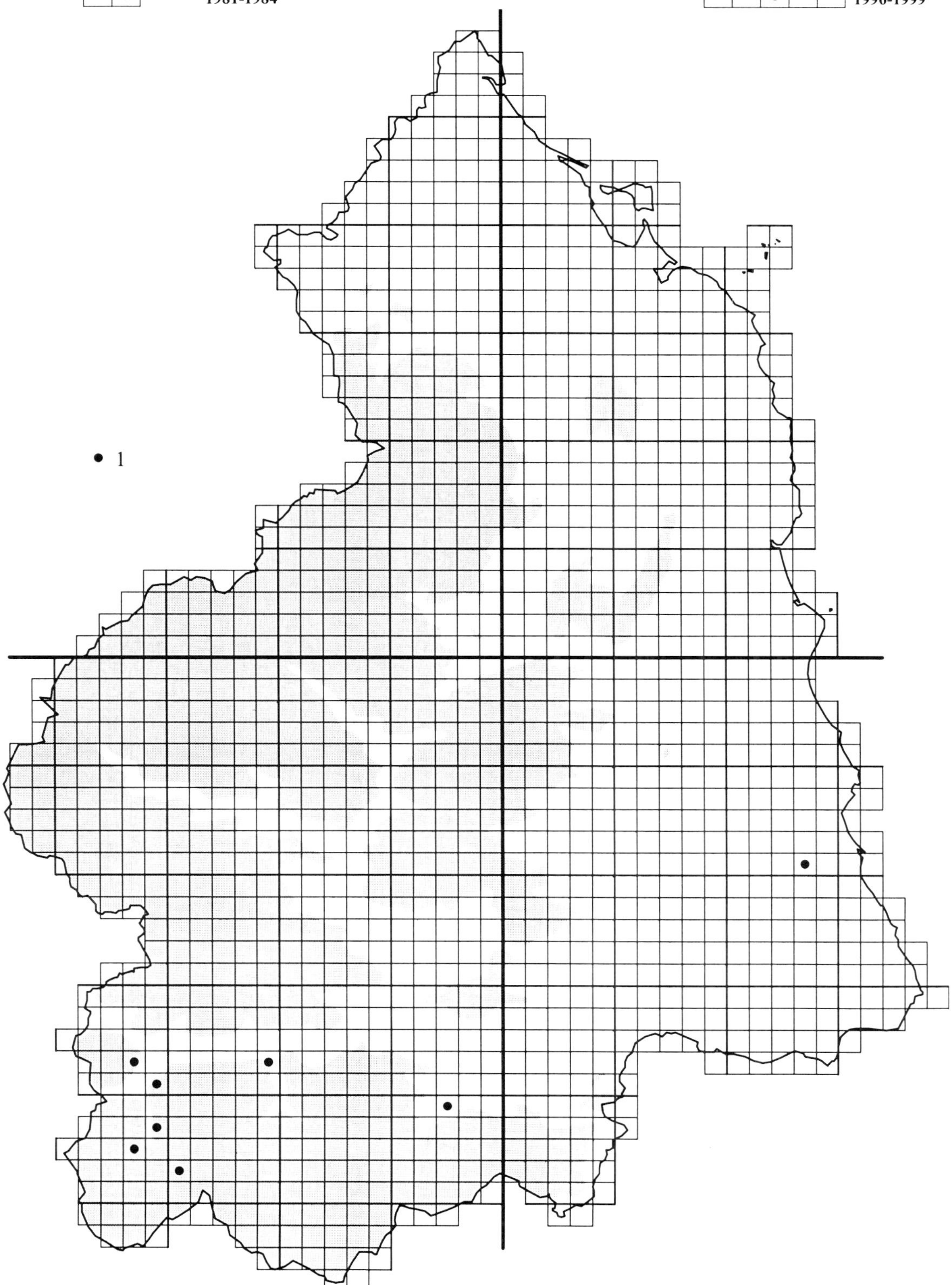

Rough-legged Buzzard

KESTREL *Falco tinnunculus*

Bolam (1912) described the Kestrel as a 'common resident' and inferred that the population increased in winter as a result of 'arrivals from abroad'. Galloway and Meek (1978) endorsed the assessment but added that a proportion of the breeding population, especially fledged juveniles, dispersed away from the region moving in a direction 'predominantly between south and south east'.

Galloway (1987) analysed the recoveries of 139 birds that were ringed as nestlings in Northumberland and showed that 58% had moved more than 50km from the nest site. In fact 14% moved more than 400km which took them into nearby Europe and in one case to North Africa. As such a large proportion leaves the area at the end of the breeding season, the Kestrel in Northumberland is hence better described as a partial migrant rather than a resident. This assessment is also given to the northern UK populations by Snow (1968), Village (1990) and Shrubb (1993).

Most writers since Bolam have also suggested that some north European birds spend the winter in the county but a foreign ringed Kestrel, which would help to confirm those opinions, has still to be recovered in Northumberland.

The two smaller distribution maps show that it was present in all but three 10km squares on the western extremity of the region during the current winter survey and that it may have been marginally more plentiful and widespread than in 1981-1984. There were 795 sightings, the majority of which refer to single birds per tetrad, although a maximum of four per tetrad was noted on ten occasions. The control tetrad analysis implies that they were twice as plentiful in 1997/98, with a count of 48 individuals, than in 1996/97 (24) or 1998/99 (20).

The tetrad distribution map suggests a preference for lower ground where the availability of food and safe roosting sites are better guaranteed. The analysis of occupied tetrads in relation to height a.s.l. confirms that this is the case with 552 (91%) of the occupied tetrads in the 0-300 metres a.s.l. range and only 56 tetrads above that height. When applied to all 1,432 tetrads in the survey, this shows 40-50% occupancy of all tetrads below 300 metres and 15-30% occupancy above that height. As shown in *The atlas of breeding birds in Northumbria* (Day *et al.*, 1995), there was a scarcity of records from the densely afforested tetrads in the west where the availability of food is extremely limited, especially in winter.

The current winter survey shows that the Kestrel is still a regular sight in the county but, in view of the comment by Mead (2000) that 'there is serious cause for concern' in relation to a decline in the UK breeding population, and because of the disappearance from many inland breeding haunts in Northumberland since the county breeding atlas fieldwork of 1988-1992, it may not be the case in years to come.

BRYAN GALLOWAY

Distribution by altitude

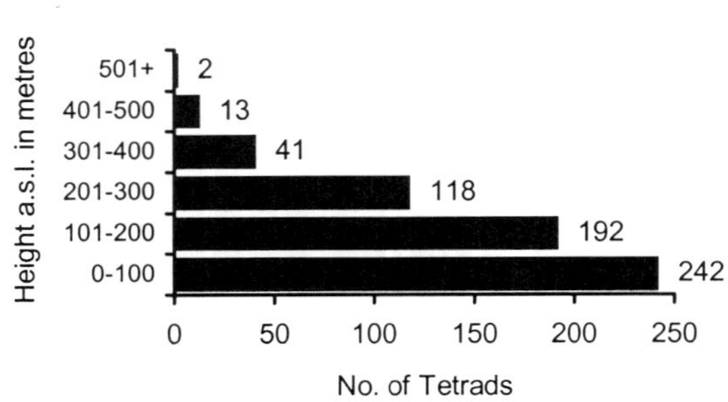

No. of tetrads in which recorded 608 (42%)

Tetrad Analysis	No. of tetrads
1 birds	459 (75%)
2 birds	121 (20%)
3+ birds	28 (5%)

Total No. of birds counted 795

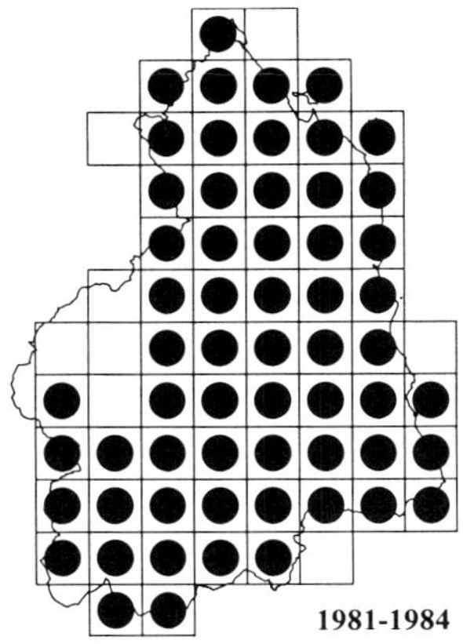

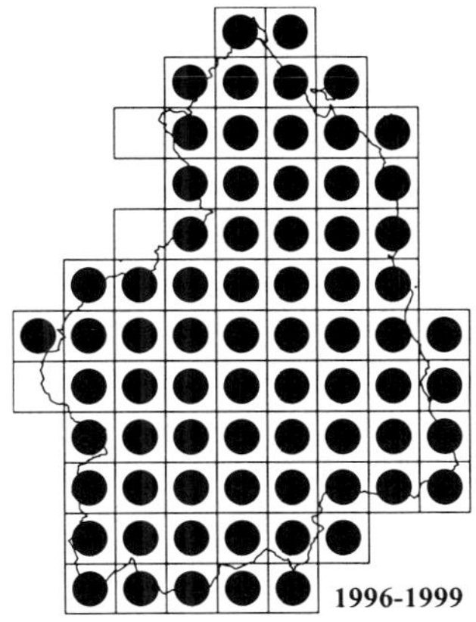

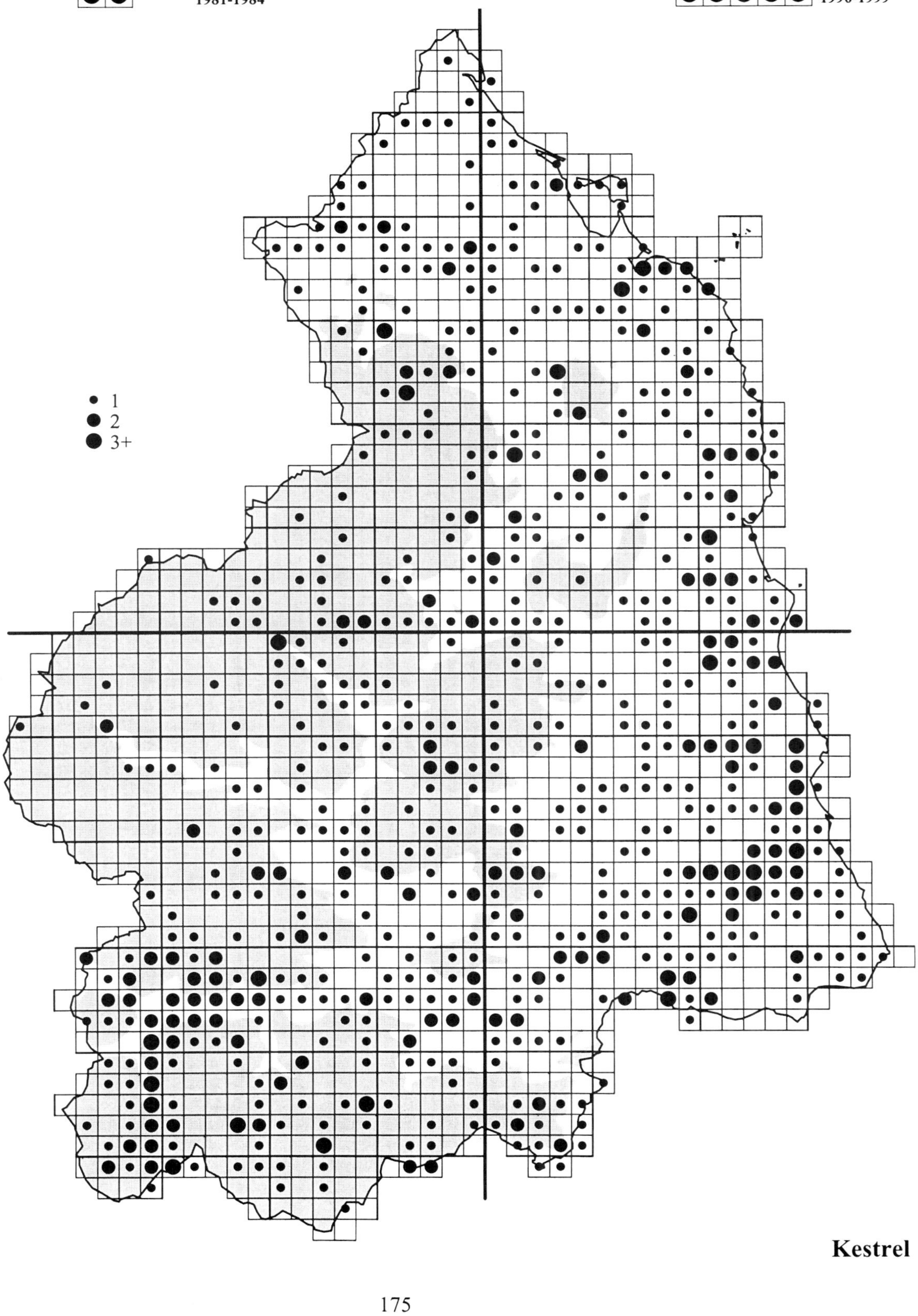

Kestrel

MERLIN *Falco columbarius*

Galloway and Meek (1978), referring to early authors and summarising the status of the Merlin, concluded that no more than 100 individuals spent the winter in the county. They also indicated that it was a visitor and indeed there is evidence from ringing returns that a proportion of our birds are from neighbouring regions (e.g. Cumbria and Yorkshire). Lack (1986) stated that Britain cannot be anything more than a minor wintering area for the large migratory Scandinavian populations and, as no continental ringed Merlin has ever been found in Northumberland, the suspicion of Galloway and Meek that 'some immigration from northern Europe' occurs in winter must remain no more than a suspicion.

Galloway (1987) analysed the recoveries of 75 individuals that had been ringed as nestlings in the county and showed that 60% had moved more than 50km from the nest site. As most of these were outside the recording area, the Merlin in Northumberland can be clearly described as a partial migrant.

Kerr (1989) examined the results of the 1981-1984 winter atlas survey and noted they occurred in 60% of the 10km squares that were visited. In addition, he analysed the results of the Northumberland winter surveys of 1986/87 and 1987/88 and found that of the 295 sightings, 28% were from well inland. Despite what seemed to be high counts, he suggested that because of their mobility some duplication of records must have occurred and the population may have been as low as 20-30 individuals.

In the current winter survey, 127 individuals were spread over 118 tetrads and the smaller 10km square maps show that it was more widely distributed than during the period 1981-1984. 28% of the sightings occurred at altitudes in excess of 100 metres a.s.l., which is remarkably similar to the conclusion reached by Kerr. On this higher ground they were found in only 4% of the 937 tetrads surveyed whilst in areas below 100 metres a.s.l., where 72% of the population was discovered, there was a tetrad occupation frequency of 17%. Most of the observations were of single birds per tetrad with the maximum of three being reported only at the Lindisfarne NNR (NU14G) and Tynemouth Golf Course (NZ36P).

As Kerr indicated, there will inevitably be some duplication of counts of the same individual, especially within the same tetrad or in adjacent tetrads, but his population assessment of 20-30 seems low compared with the present results. His conclusion may be explained by the fact that the summer of 1986 was a particularly poor year in the county for breeding success with only 52 young fledging. By contrast, the summer of 1996 was by far the best on record and 156 birds fledged. The years 1987, 1997 and 1998 were considered as average with some 70-80 juveniles being reared in each summer. As more birds were looking for winter haunts in 1996/97 and with a reasonable survival rate into the subsequent winters, it would seem that a population of 80-100 is more likely during the current survey. This is consistent with the past and present status assessments in *Birds in Northumbria* and with that arrived at by Galloway and Meek.

Ringing recoveries confirm that the majority of the wintering Merlins in Northumberland are of local origin. Hence its status is clearly dependent upon continued nesting success in the region which at times it struggles to maintain through weather problems, excessive heather burning and hostile campaigns against the Carrion Crow *Corvus corone corone*, which is a critically important nest provider on forest edges and in shelter-belt plantations. Although Mead (2000) stated that nationally it is 'doing quite well' the Merlin continues to be a species at risk (RSPB, 1996).

BRYAN GALLOWAY

Distribution by altitude

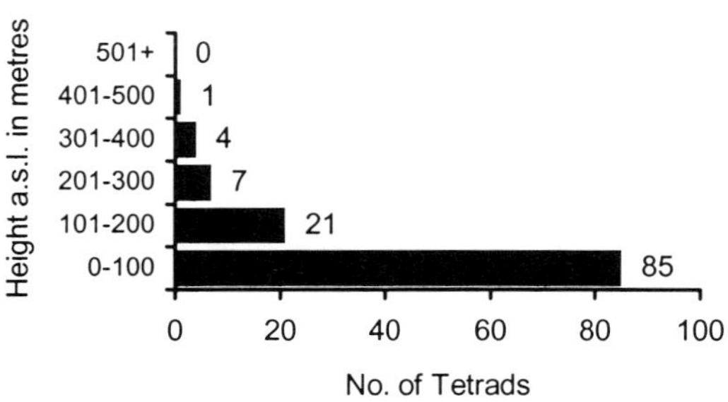

No. of tetrads in which recorded	118 (8%)
Tetrad Analysis	**No. of tetrads**
1 bird	111 (94%)
2 birds	5 (4%)
3 birds	2 (2%)
Total No. of birds counted	127

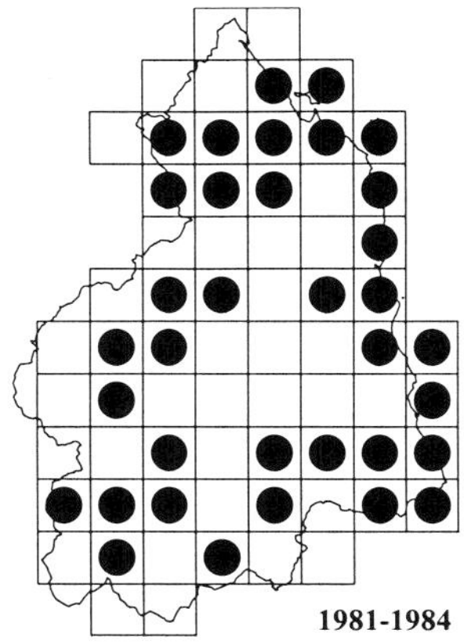

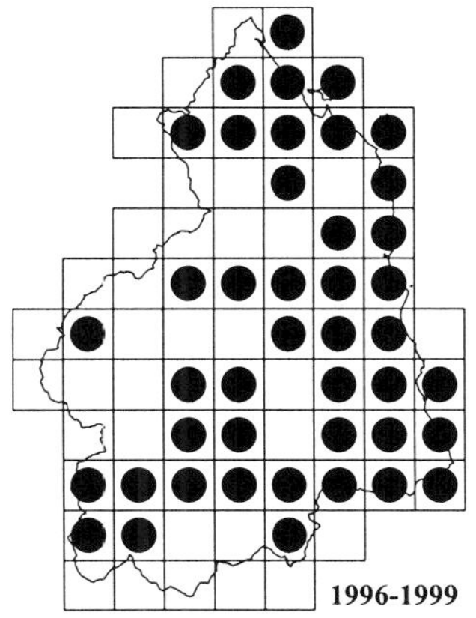

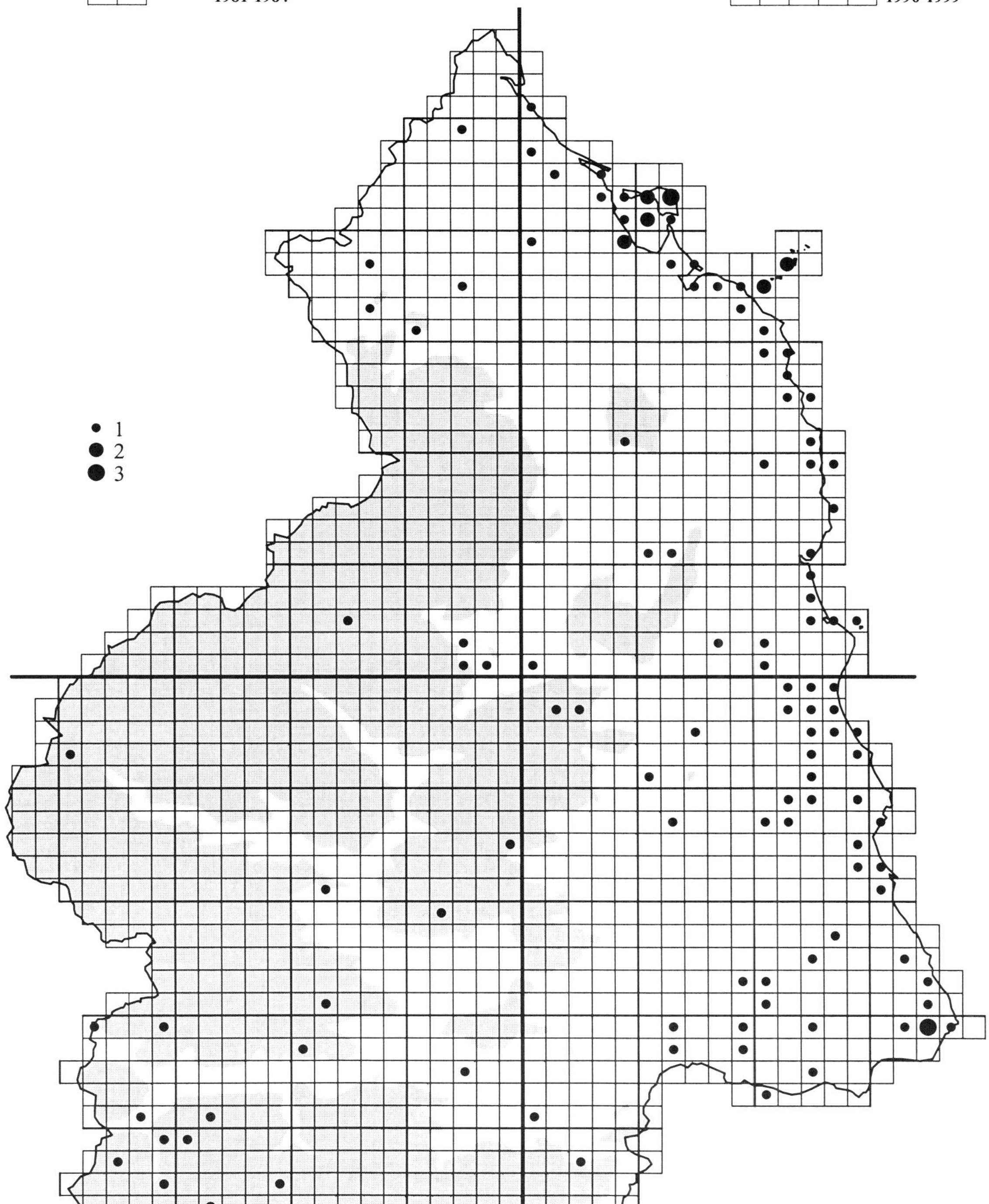

Merlin

PEREGRINE *Falco peregrinus*

Although Bolam (1912) considered the Peregrine to be a resident, he made very little reference to its winter status. Even Galloway and Meek (1978) could only comment that occasional birds wintered in the Lindisfarne NNR. Clearly there were few sightings to report upon and such was its status as it struggled for almost a century to cope with persecution initiated by the Victorians, the theft of eggs and young, the Second World War cull of the breeding population and the insidious effects of organochlorine poisoning in the 1950s and 1960s.

It was not until the 1980s that a significant population began to grow in the county. As well as at prospective inland breeding sites in the spring, it was increasingly reported throughout the region in winter and, during the period 1981-1984, it can be seen from the smaller map that it was located in 40% of the 10km squares surveyed. The present survey reveals a 63% occupancy of 10km squares with 158 individual birds spread over 145 tetrads. Most of the observations during the survey were of single birds per tetrad but three were at Sewing Shields (NY87A) in January 1999. Analysis of the control tetrads suggests that they might have been more plentiful in the last winter period of the survey.

Peregrines are well known for their mobility, especially during winter, in their search for prey and safe roosting sites, and there is no doubt that on more than one occasion the same individual has wandered through a number of adjacent tetrads and hence been double counted. It thus seems likely that less than 100 birds are present in the county during the winter which is consistent with the present 'uncommon' status assessment in *Birds in Northumbria*.

Although the coastal areas are a significant attraction, especially to birds in their first winter, with 44% of the individuals occurring in the altitude range 0-100 metres a.s.l., inland areas still provide enough winter food for those adults that are reluctant to vacate the 25-30 breeding sites. This is reflected in the tetrad distribution map.

Radcliffe (1980) investigated the origins of the UK winter populations but did not entirely agree with Mead (1973), who suggested that the lowland wintering birds came from Scandinavia. Although some 20 Peregrines of such origin have been recovered in Britain, including a male found injured at Bamburgh in February 1998 that had been ringed as a nestling in Finland in 1994, Radcliffe believed the essentially sedentary and growing UK population, most of which move no further than 150km away from the breeding areas, provided the majority of lowland records. In his analysis he also showed that three birds from nests in south west Scotland were subsequently found in Northumberland in the 1970s which is perhaps a clue to the origin of the re-population of the county underway at that time.

There are few recoveries of Northumberland-ringed Peregrines. All have moved within the range mentioned by Radcliffe except for a nestling from Redesdale that was found dead on a beach in the Canary Islands, 3,066km to the south, in March 1998, during its first winter. This is only one of three UK-ringed Peregrines that have been found abroad. Could this individual have come from parentage that originated from the highly migratory Scandinavian population? If so it suggests a wintering bird from this area of northern Europe remained to breed in Northumberland.

Ten years ago the UK breeding population of the Peregrine was over 1,000 pairs and as it continues to explore new nest sites (e.g. Blyth Power Station in 1999), Mead (2000) asked the question 'is 2,000 pairs the limit?' The proposed BTO national breeding census in 2002 should provide the answer.

The regions' Peregrines, which are incredibly resilient, are a truly wonderful sight at any time of the year. It is hoped that all of its major set-backs of the last 100 years are long gone.

BRYAN GALLOWAY

Distribution by altitude

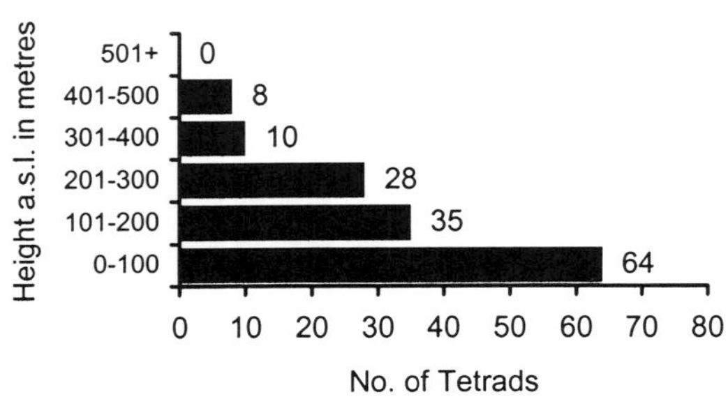

No. of tetrads in which recorded	145 (10%)
Tetrad Analysis	**No. of tetrads**
1 bird	133 (92%)
2 birds	11 (7%)
3 birds	1 (1%)
Total No. of birds counted	158

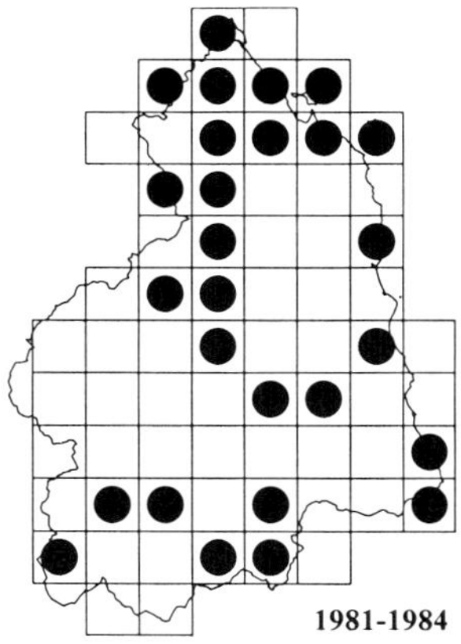

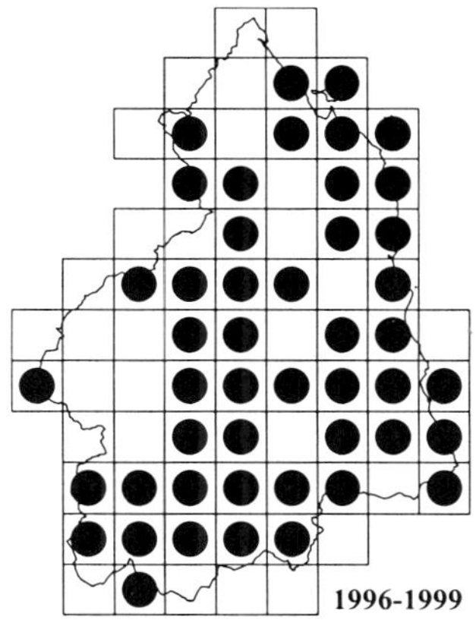

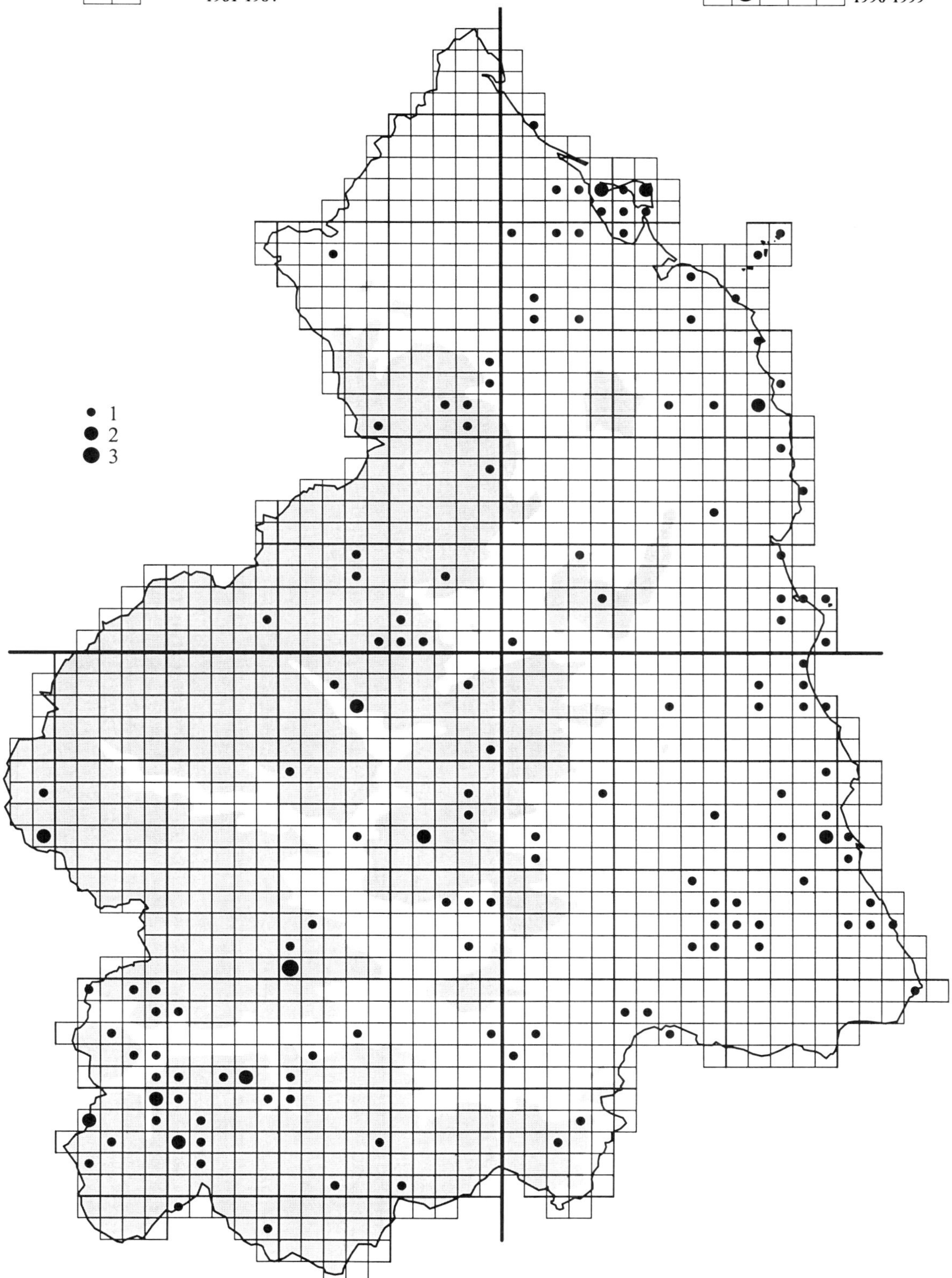

Peregrine

RED GROUSE *Lagopus lagopus*

Bolam (1912) described the Red Grouse as a 'well known resident more or less plentiful on all our moors ... on which heather grows', an assessment which needs qualifying only in the sense that there is far less heather moorland today than there was in his time, largely as a result of afforestation. The extensive coniferous plantations at Kielder, Redesdale, Wark, Thrunton, Slaley and Harwood occupy what was once moorland. However, where the heather *Calluna vulgaris* is healthy, and managed for grouse by rotational burning, grouse densities can be as high as almost anywhere in the country, with the exception perhaps of Yorkshire (Hudson, 1986).

Observers during the current survey found a grand total of 4,227 Red Grouse in 281 tetrads which correlates well with the 1,102 pairs located in the 260 tetrads during fieldwork for *The atlas of breeding birds in Northumbria* (Day *et al.*, 1995): indeed the distribution maps of the two surveys correspond almost exactly. A variation in the winter survey was the discovery of birds in the vicinity of Holburn Moss (NU03N) and the Doddington Law area (NU0A/B) where none had been recorded breeding. The correlation, in fact, is better than with the 1981-1984 ten km square winter atlas map, not because the species has extended its range eastwards, as appears the case, but because birds seem to have been missed for some reason during that survey. Almost two thirds of the 281 occupied tetrads were between 201 and 400 metres a.s.l., reflecting the altitude of heather moorland in Northumberland. A further 65 tetrads were over 400 metres a.s.l., with 13 over 500 metres a.s.l.

As might be expected, the highest tetrad counts came from the south west moors, especially the two extensive upland massifs of Geltsdale and Whitfield Moor on either side of the River South Tyne. Both are managed intensively for shooting. High tetrad counts included 166 on Ramshaw Fell (NY76A) in December 1996, after an exceptional season in which 10,000 birds were reported to have been bagged on two estates (*Birds in Northumbria 1996*) and 177 in two tetrads on Whitfield Moor (NY75C/H). Further south, Knarsdale Common (NY64P) held 116 in February 1997 and Hartleyburn Common (NY65T) 97 in December 1997. There were 105 in a tetrad on Whitfield Moor (NY75G) in January 1998 and 73 at Knarsdale Forest (NY65L) in December 1998. Snow cover often makes counting such flocks easier because they pack onto a slope free of snow. The south west has always been a stronghold of the Red Grouse but another contender is proving to be the east Cheviot Hills where, in the last decade or two, a major programme of heather regeneration and forest clearance has transformed the previously grassy uplands between the Harthope Burn and Newton Tors west of Wooler. 81 were counted near Yeavering Bell (NT92J) in January 1998 and, south of this area near Ilderton Dod (NT91Z), 44 in November 1997. Other managed moors in the Simonside Hills and the moors near Spylaw had tetrads which produced counts of 30 (NY99T) and 32 (NZ09P) respectively. These, however, are very much manipulated landscapes where predator control and heather management is designed to produce a harvestable surplus. Interestingly though, Red Grouse survive, sometimes in respectable numbers, in places where ruined, long abandoned, butts testify to the fact that they were once shot over. 12 birds were found on the Bewcastle Fells (NY58W), 15 on Deadwater Fell (NY69I) and ten on Kielderhead Moor (NT60W). The mosses north of the Roman Wall which are largely dominated by Cross-leaved Heath *Erica tetralix* still have a small relict population at places like Scotchcoulthard (NY77A) and Farglow (NY66Z).

Throughout its range in Europe the Willow Grouse, of which the Red Grouse *L. l. scoticus* is a subspecies, is thought to be in decline, though this has only been severe and measurable in marginal areas like Estonia, Latvia and Belarus (Hagemeijer & Blair, 1997). Although hard to quantify, there is undoubtedly a long term decline in Britain (Hudson, 1992) and ongoing studies continue to discover the mechanisms which trigger the six-seven year cycles which British grouse go through. However, there is so much invested in grouse moor management and it is such an important part of the economy of the uplands that Red Grouse and heather are likely to be features of the landscape for years to come especially as in some places, like the Northumberland National Park, active heather restoration programmes are taking place. These can only benefit the Red Grouse and ensure that the Glorious Twelfth endures!

MIKE HENRY

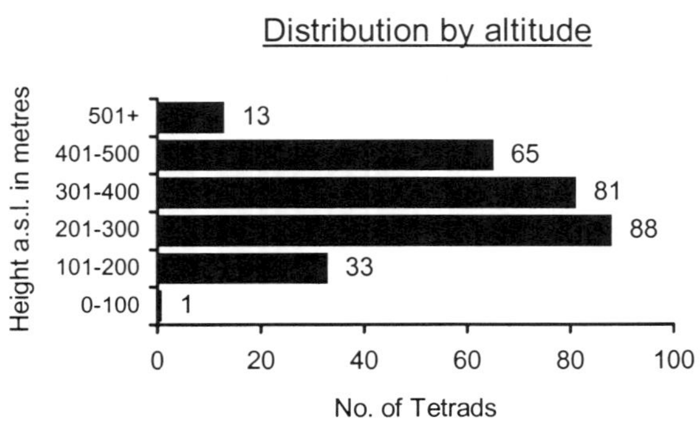

No. of tetrads in which recorded 281 (20%)

Tetrad Analysis	No. of tetrads
1-7 birds	151 (54%)
8-20 birds	70 (25%)
21+ birds	60 (21%)

Total No. of birds counted 4,227

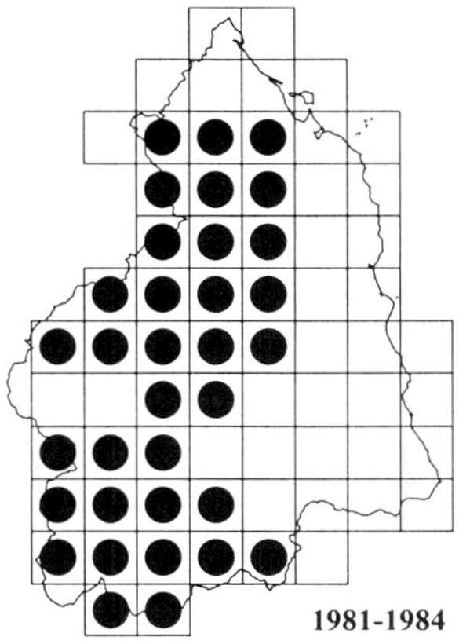

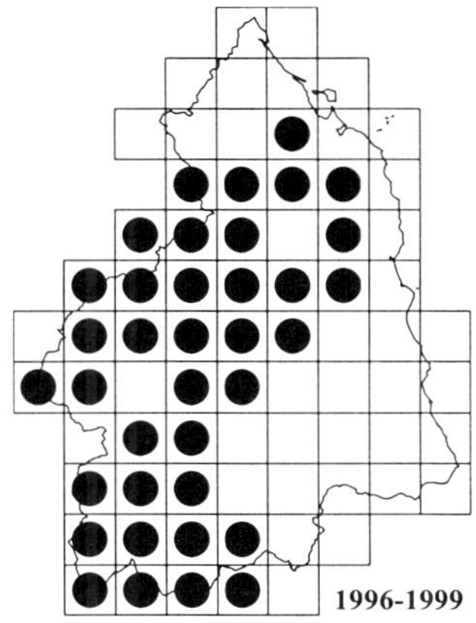

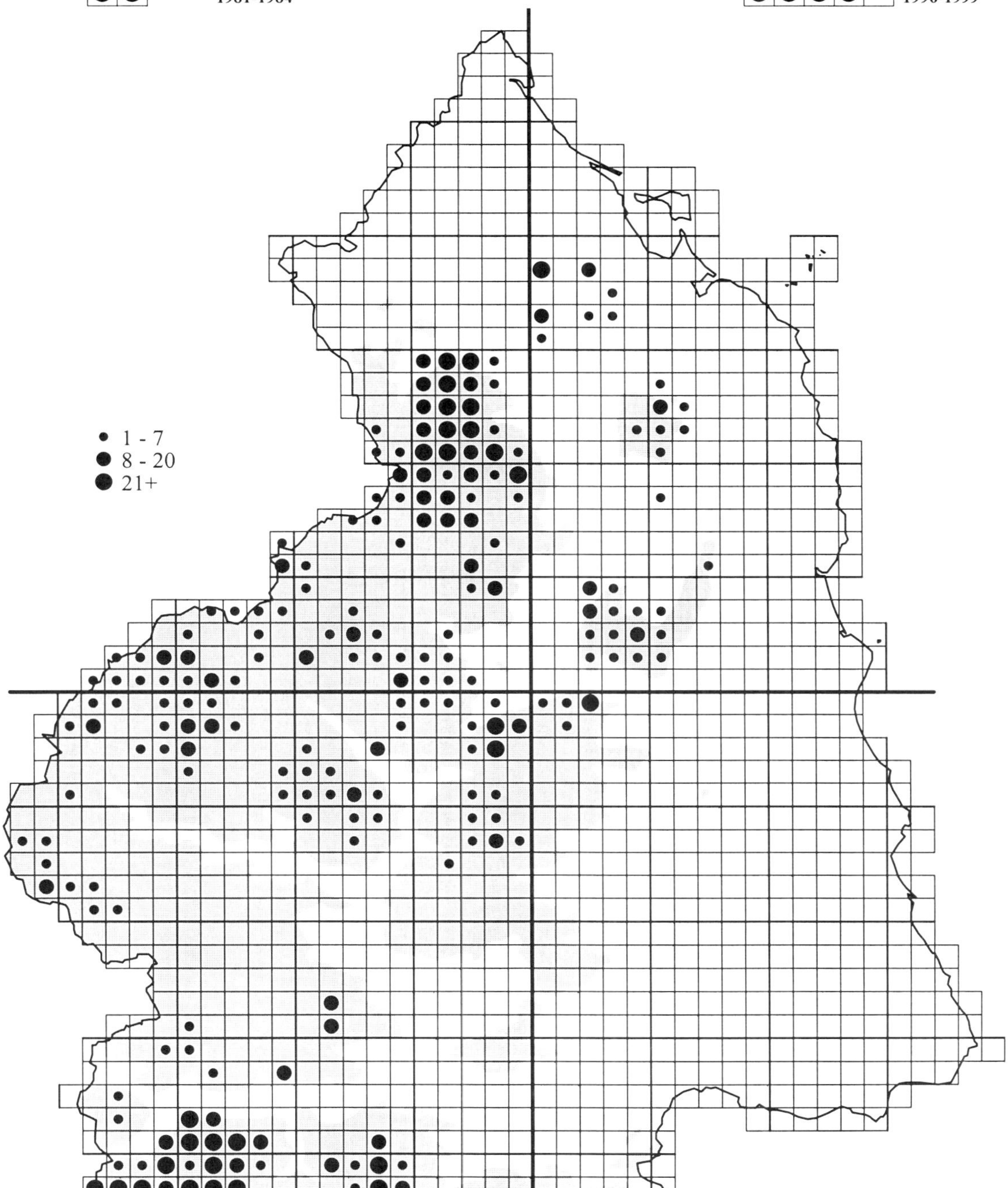

Red Grouse

BLACK GROUSE *Tetrao tetrix*

In the 1970s it was possible to drive under Blackcocks nipping hawthorn berries from the bushes along the road to the Gibbet near Elsdon. Those days are long gone, the current winter atlas detecting no Black Grouse in the Simonside Hills at all, but there are still places in the county where half a dozen black game can be seen in the tops of birches, willows or hawthorns.

Baines and Hudson (1995) documented a national decline and range contraction of 28% and in Europe the population has crashed in the Low Countries and north Germany (Hagemeijer & Blair, 1997). In southern Finland the population has declined by 80% since the 1940s and the same is believed to be true for southern Sweden (Svensson *et al.*, 1999). It would be surprising if Northumberland has escaped this downward spiral, since it too shows the factors commonly associated with the species' decline, namely the drainage of rushy hollows and blanket afforestation and overgrazing. In general these agricultural changes have affected much of the marginal land between 200 and 400 metres a.s.l., where over half the tetrads holding Black Grouse were found.

In the current winter atlas survey, 391 Black Grouse were counted in 65 tetrads, compared with 331 pairs in 101 tetrads found during fieldwork in 1988-1993 for the local breeding atlas (Day *et al.*, 1995). A superficial comparison of the two smaller 10km square maps may suggest little cause for concern, but a comparison with the breeding atlas map is more instructive. Since 1993 they seem to have disappeared from the Callaly area north of Rothbury (NU00), Elsdon and the western Simonsides (NY99), Kielder (NY69/NY79), Bellingham (NY88), Blanchland Moor (NY95) and the west Cheviot Hills (NT81). The species' strongholds in the county are now the Otterburn Ranges (NT80/NT90) in the north west, and the East and West Allen Valleys in the south west (especially NY74/NY84) and the Featherstone/Plenmeller Common areas just south of Haltwhistle (NY66/NY76). In the last area they have extended their range in the 1990s (pers. obs.) despite some habitat loss. Imaginative Countryside Stewardship schemes on farms like Whitwham (NY65) in the South Tyne are actively promoted by the RSPB which has also planted the lower slopes of Halton Lea Fell (NY65) with birch, willows and other native hardwoods specifically to encourage Black Grouse. Similar planting in the Cheviots by private landowners and under the auspices of the Northumberland National Park may also have beneficial results in the long run. Plenmeller Common, already mentioned as a stronghold, is currently being restored from opencast mining to its former glory of rushy sykes, peaty pools and rough grazing. Another area where the recent winter survey found evidence of Black Grouse increasing is Troughend Common in Redesdale, a population which is contiguous with the Otterburn core.

Most observations of Black Grouse in the 65 occupied tetrads were of less than ten but two extraordinary counts were of 95 near Allenheads (NY84S) in November 1996 with, only two months later, 80 on Ramshaw Fell (NY76A). Both these counts must have involved gatherings of almost the entire local population of the Upper Allen catchment area and the Plenmeller Common/Whitfield Moor areas. Equally interesting is the single bird recorded near Belsay (NZ07T) on 15th January 1997, well outside the usual area and possibly the nearest to Newcastle in modern times. It is alarming to witness the decline in the north of the county. The local breeding atlas referred to their disappearance from the Kyloe Hills and the moors above Eglingham. In the current survey, only five were located in the north of the county in suitable habitat near Wooler (NT92S). Since south east Scotland holds 10% of the estimated national population of 6,300 (Murray *et al.*, 1998) such discontinuity is worrying. However, Black Grouse can be hard to survey as from the tetrad map it would seem that there are none along Hadrian's Wall but they do exist in extremely low numbers at such sites as Muckle Moss and on the grasslands of Scotchcoulthard Waste and Thirlwall Common (pers. obs.).

Much effort and expense has been devoted to the Black Grouse over the last decade by, among others, the Game Conservancy and the RSPB. Initiatives have been launched and it is to be hoped that measures will be successful in helping preserve this sensitive species. It would seem that Northumberland still has a viable population, albeit fragmented into several distinct nuclei.

MIKE HENRY

Distribution by altitude

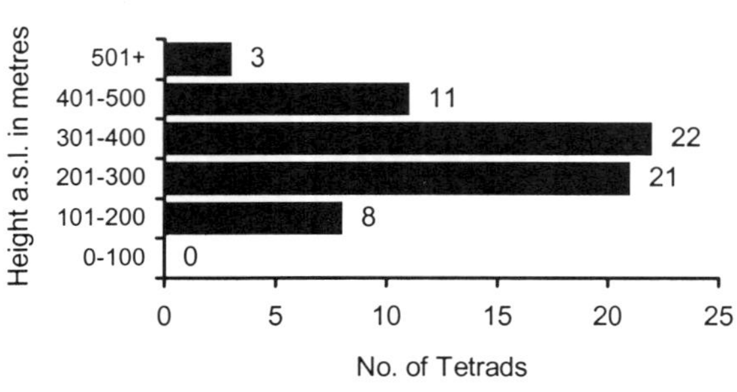

No. of tetrads in which recorded 65 (5%)

Tetrad Analysis	No. of tetrads
1-2 birds	35 (54%)
3-5 birds	17 (26%)
6+ birds	13 (20%)

Total No. of birds counted 391

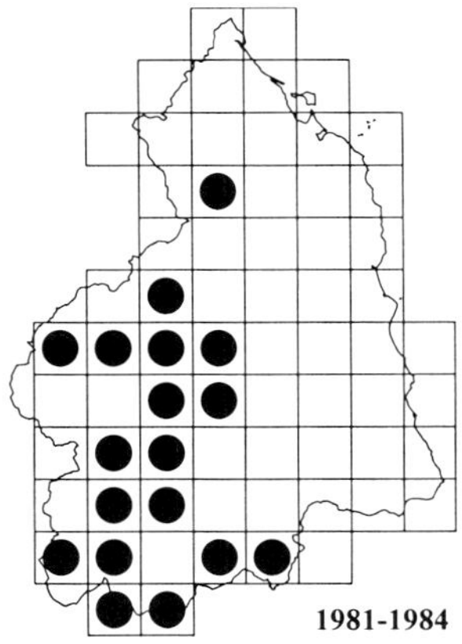

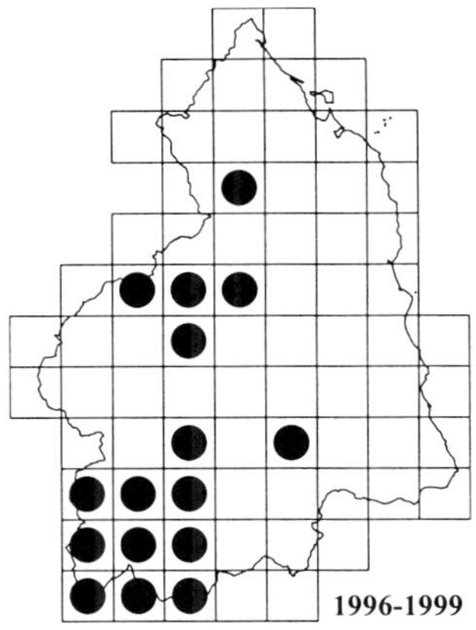

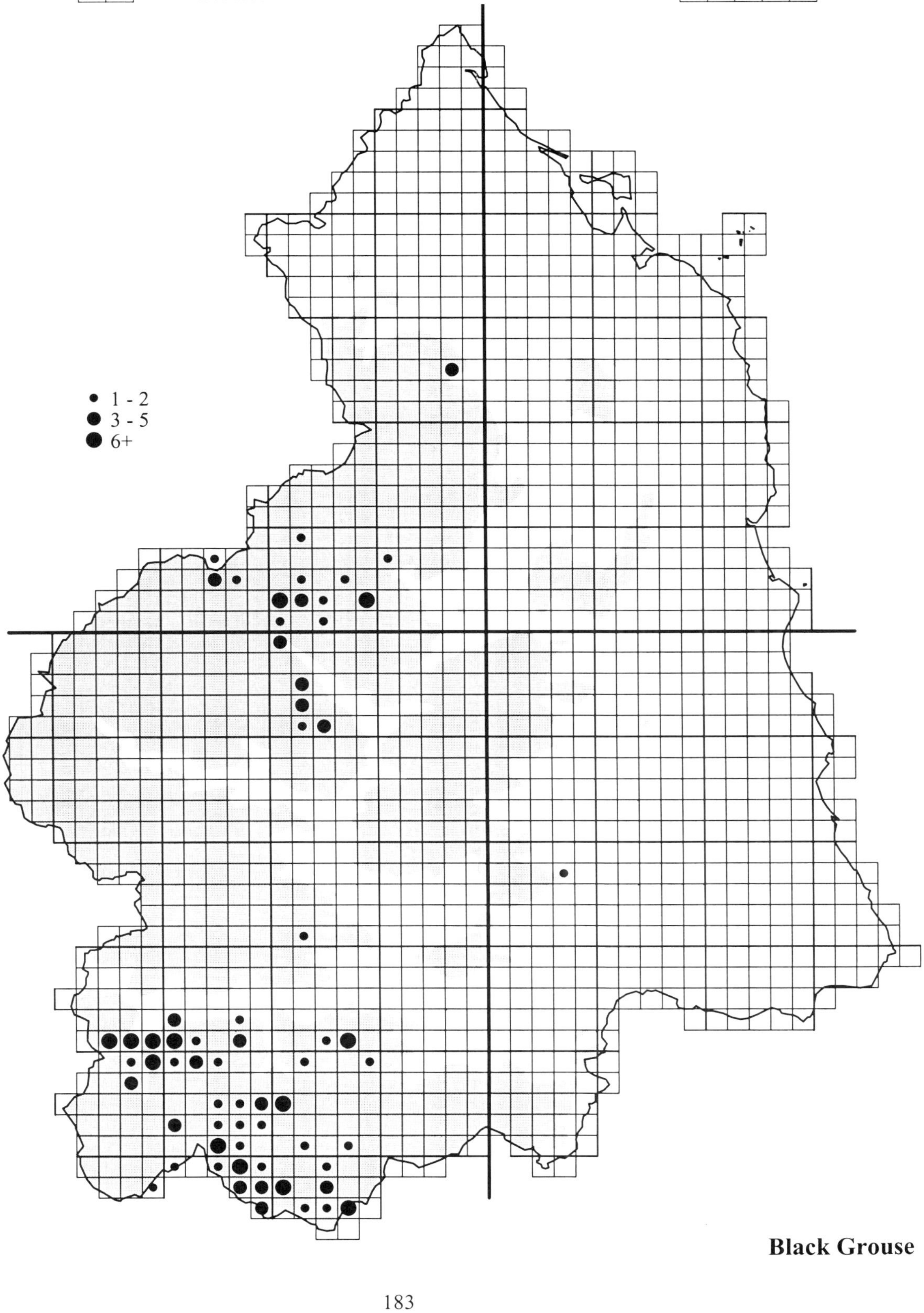

Black Grouse

RED-LEGGED PARTRIDGE *Alectoris rufa*

The Red-legged Partridge often promotes lively discussion among local birdwatchers as to whether it can be considered a genuine county species. This is largely due to its aversion to damp climates and areas of high rainfall and its reliance on large numbers being released for shooting purposes which helps it retain a tenuous footing in the county.

The species is not a native to Britain and was introduced from France and considered to be well established in the country by the 1930s. It is essentially a bird of open ground and needs low bushy vegetation for shelter with areas of short grass or bare ground for feeding. Normally it is associated with low intensity arable farming with a mixture of cultivated, uncultivated and fallow ground. In mainland Europe it also occurs on rocky mountain slopes up to 2,000 metres a.s.l. Recently, within the main range, very substantial declines have been documented among wild stocks since the 1970s due to the intensification of agriculture with the resulting degradation of its preferred habitat (Snow & Perrins, 1998).

Locally, it was introduced into the Scottish Border counties towards the end of the nineteenth century on a limited number of shooting estates and, according to Bolam (1912), as a result a few appeared in the Berwick-upon-Tweed area between 1889 and 1891. Later, in 1932, he stated that it 'has as yet scarcely maintained a footing'. More recently, Galloway and Meek (1980) said although further introductions had resulted in widespread sightings, it did not appear to be firmly established and they described the species' status as an uncommon introduced breeding resident.

The two winter atlas surveys of 1981-1984 and 1996-1999 show the number of occupied 10km squares in the county to be seven and 16 respectively but this is a reflection of artificial stocking rather than of a flourishing and expanding wild stock. As the numbers of Grey Partridge *Perdix perdix* decline, more shooting estates in both lowland and upland valleys are releasing large numbers of Red-legged Partridge for shooting purposes. This was evidenced by the reported release of 10,000 on an estate near Bellingham (*Birds in Northumbria 1999*) and by smaller numbers on other shooting estates (Eds.). For two or three years after the release of hand-reared birds, regular sightings occur at or near these vicinities but appear to be short-lived and reflect the survival rates of a species which prefers a warm, dry climate with little rainfall. Also in Britain, under these artificial conditions, it is normally sedentary with movements of less than one kilometre and its survival depends on avoidance of mammalian and avian predators.

Data collected for this atlas survey show that Red-legged Partridges were reported in 39 tetrads (3%) out of a total of 1,432 surveyed, with the number of birds seen being 311, an average of just less than eight birds per occupied tetrad. In *The atlas of breeding birds in Northumbria* (Day *et al.*, 1995) the number of tetrads in which the species was recorded was 36 from 1,410 surveyed, showing a similar distribution of summer and wintering populations. This is to be expected for a scarce and sedentary species. Although now appearing to be more scattered and widespread, the current distribution is still mainly concentrated in the north of the county around active shooting estates. The largest count during the survey was 39 at Ilderton (NU02A) with counts of 25 near Sharperton (NT90R) and Longwitton (NZ08U). The best areas to see this species are probably Caistron (NU00A), in the Milfield area (NT93F-H) and the Cheviot Valleys. It is clear that at present it continues to remain an uncommon species in the county dependent very much on large artificial releases into the wild.

ANDY D. McLEVY

Distribution by altitude

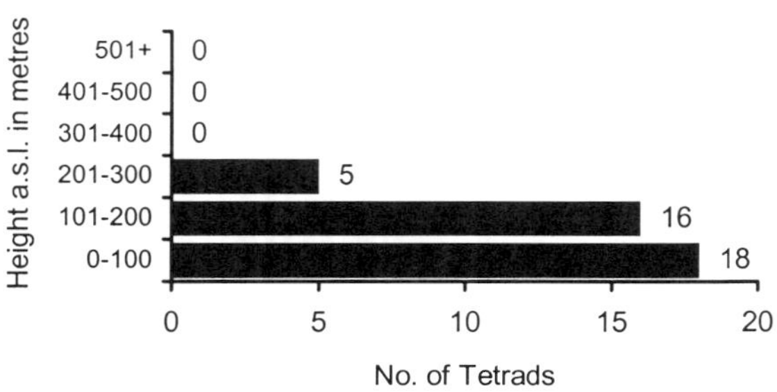

No. of tetrads in which recorded 39 (3%)

Tetrad Analysis	No. of tetrads
1-4 birds	20 (51%)
5-12 birds	11 (28%)
13+ birds	8 (21%)

Total No. of birds counted 311

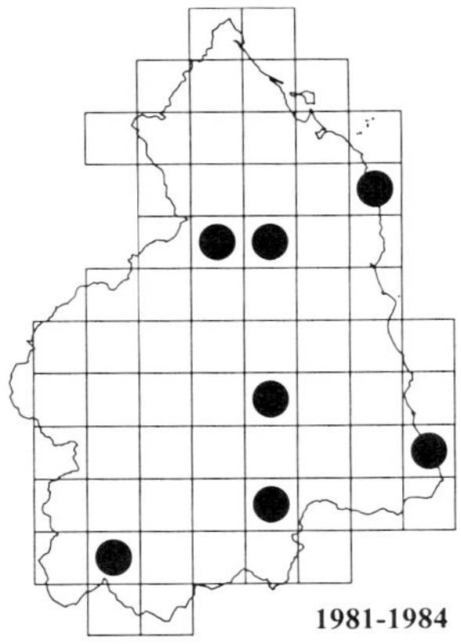

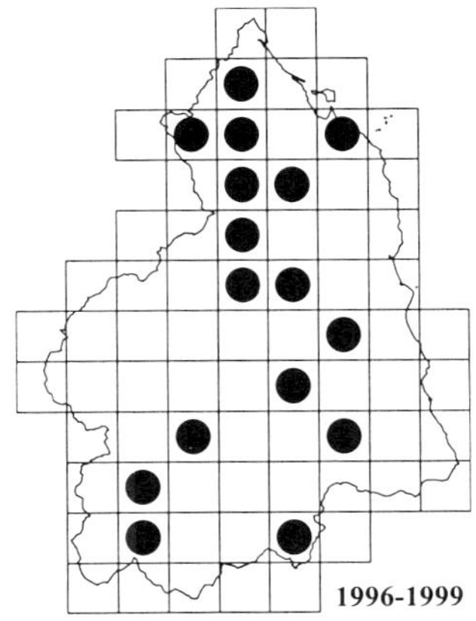

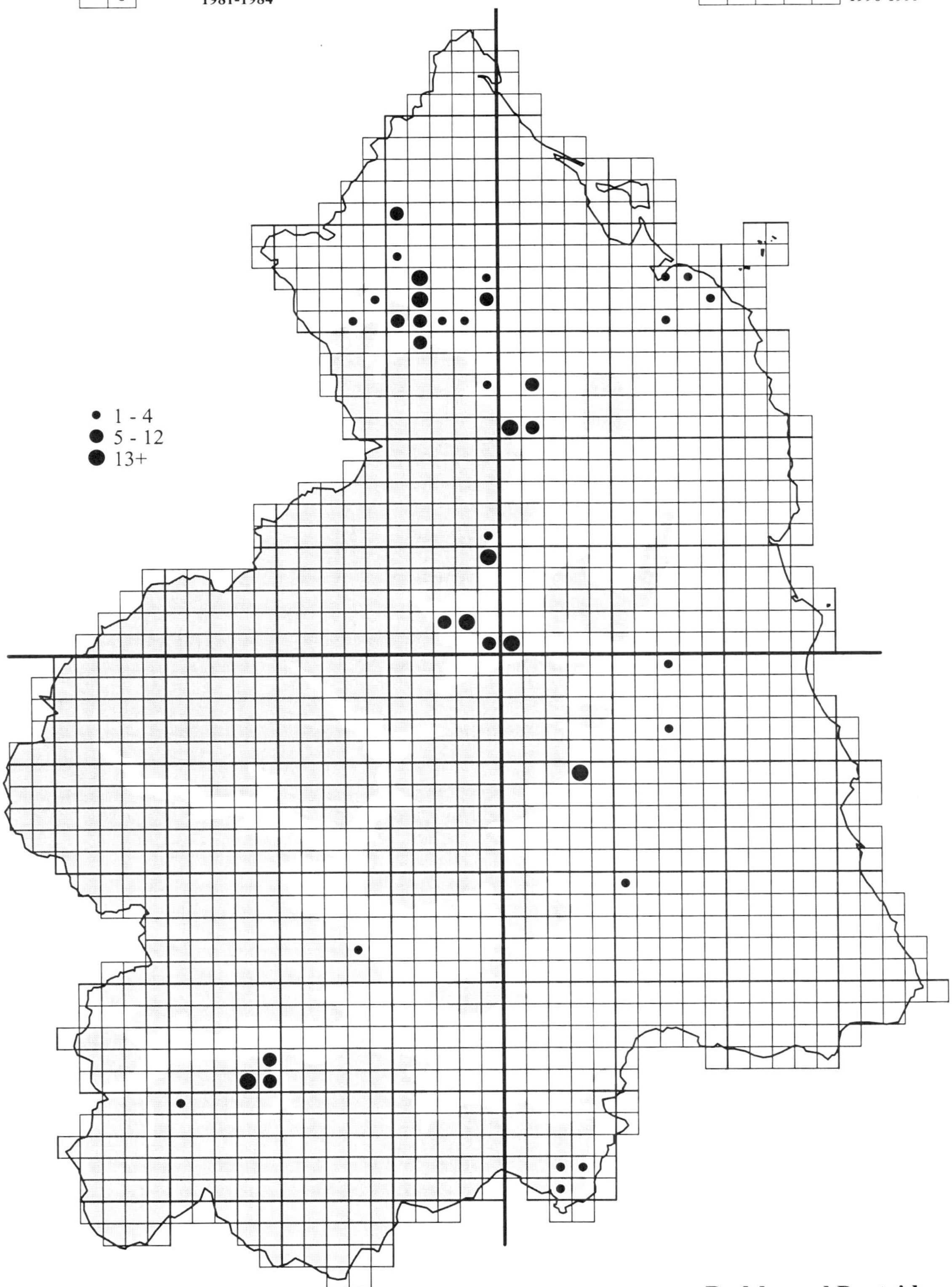

Red-legged Partridge

GREY PARTRIDGE *Perdix perdix*

Detailed game-bag figures of braces shot in the late nineteenth century, before the introduction of hand-reared birds, suggest a very healthy Grey Partridge population in suitable arable habitat (Bolam, 1912). Some twenty years later, however, he regarded the species as 'much less numerous than it was a few years ago, largely due to the decline of agriculture' (Bolam, 1932). The continued decline through the 1950s and 1960s was commented on by Galloway and Meek (1980) although they noted a slight recovery of the species' fortunes in the 1970s, particularly in arable areas.

The Grey Partridge is a very sedentary species related directly to cereal growing areas (Lack, 1986). At the beginning of winter family parties or coveys, usually two-five older birds with as many as eight young, forage and roost together, until pairing takes place and the covey disperses by the end of February. Stubble and ploughed fields are the favoured winter habitat, with fewer birds occupying grassy areas, although in Northumberland reasonably healthy populations survive in both marginal moorland areas and coastal sand dunes.

Over the three winters the survey recorded 2,151 birds in 312 tetrads and a comparison between the 1981-1984 ten kilometre square map and the later 1996-1999 map appears to show a slight expansion in the intervening period. In fact, as the current atlas data covered 75 ten kilometre squares as opposed to the 68 of the earlier survey, there is a decrease in occupied squares of 2% since the 1980s. This loss is also confirmed in comparing the breeding distribution map in *The atlas of the breeding birds in Northumbria* (Day *et al.*, 1995) with the latest winter tetrad map. Whilst occupying the same general areas, the species is much more thinly spread in the main agricultural plain and along the immediate coastal strip. Its absence from the marginal uplands can be partly explained by seasonal movement to lower land in winter, even though the three winters of the survey were far from severe, and other species such as Golden Plover *Pluvialis apricaria* and Meadow Pipit *Anthus pratensis* remained on higher ground for longer than usual. Only in the Tweed and South Tyne Valleys (NT83/93/94 and NY65/66/75/76) does the species seem to have held its own. The situation is even more alarming when considering that Grey Partridge are more easily seen and counted in winter than during the breeding season. Indeed analysis of control tetrad data for the 19 tetrads that held the species shows a steady reduction over the three winters from 6.8 birds per occupied tetrad in 1996/97 to 3.6 in 1998/99.

In the main survey 82% of all the tetrads in which Grey Partridge occurred were below 200 metres a.s.l. with 17% (54 tetrads) lying between 201 and 400 metres a.s.l. Numbers of birds per occupied tetrad ranged from one to five (165 tetrads), six to ten birds (86 tetrads) with 11 or more birds in 61 tetrads. The two largest counts were of 32 birds each near Ashington (NZ28U) and Newsham (NZ37E), but most counts, in all habitats, ranged from five to 12 birds.

Although attempts are being made in Northumberland by conservation agencies, the shooting fraternity and local farmers to improve the habitat for Grey Partridge, and so maintain the species' status as that of a common resident (just!), nationally it is in steep decline in most areas and remains a considerable cause for concern (Mead, 2000).

JOHN C. DAY

Distribution by altitude

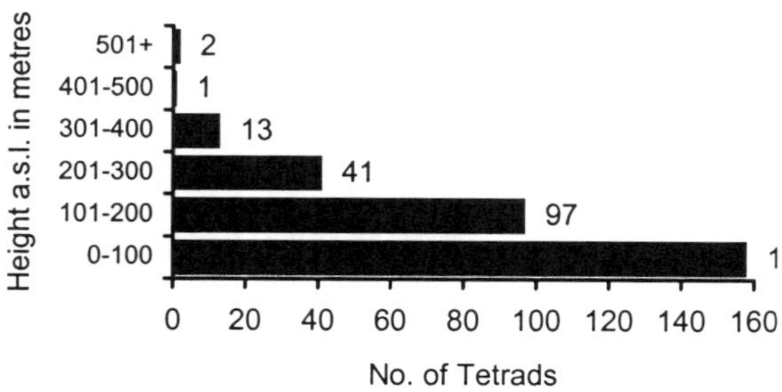

No. of tetrads in which recorded	312 (22%)
Tetrad Analysis	**No. of tetrads**
1-5 birds	165 (53%)
6-10 birds	86 (27%)
11+ birds	61 (20%)
Total No. of birds counted	2,151

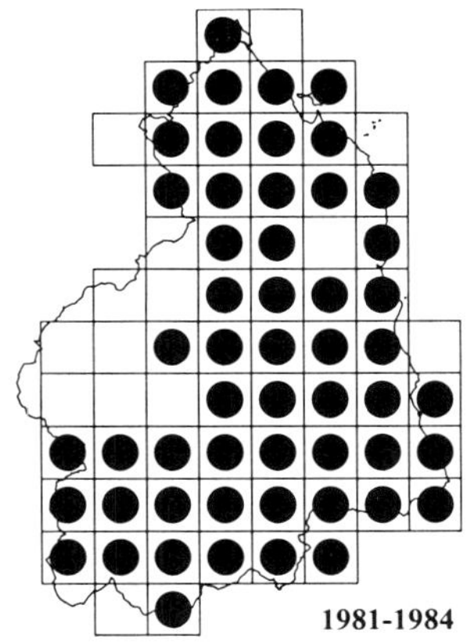

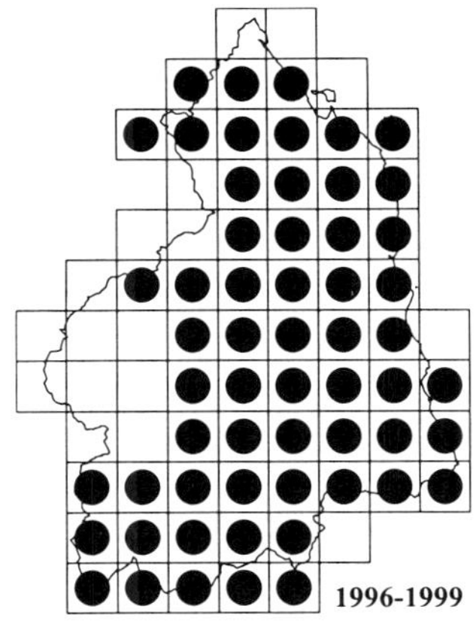

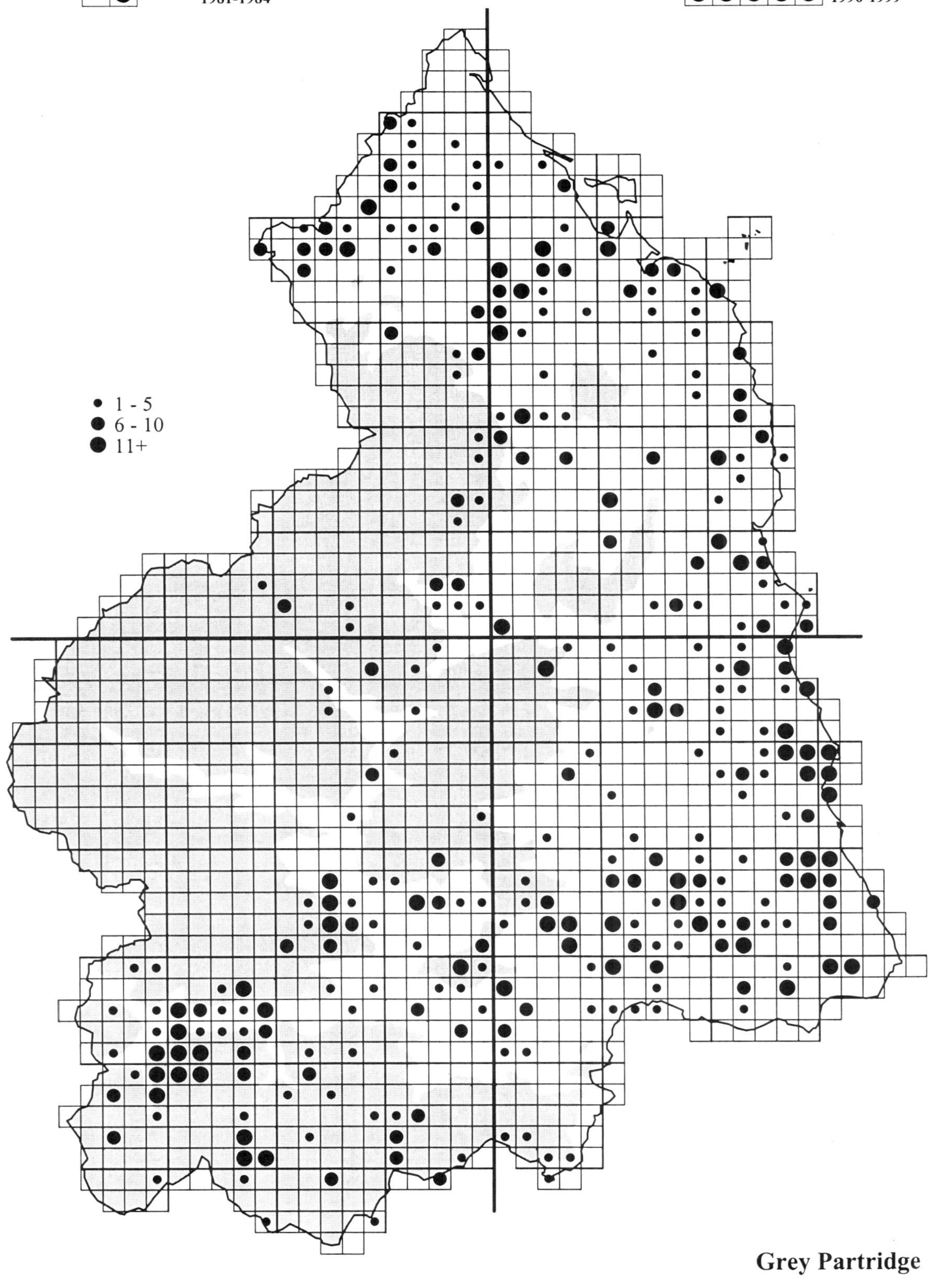

Grey Partridge

PHEASANT *Phasianus colchicus*

All local authors who have commented on the status of the species since Bolam's time (1912) have described the Pheasant as well-known, common or abundant. It is a bird of woodland, with a preference for those woods with a well-developed shrub layer. The structure of the wood is more important than the type of tree, with the length of the woodland edge also a significant factor in creating the ideal habitat (Hill & Robertson, 1988).

In winter, after most crops have been harvested, they often feed in open fields returning to adjacent woodland to roost. Early in winter small, but separate, groups of female and male birds feed independently, but by late February and early March, are likely to have broken up as males establish territories. Estimating numbers of the truly wild population, either nationally or locally, is however impossible due to the release of hand-reared birds on shooting estates. Lack (1986) commented on the big increase in the numbers of released birds in the 1970s and 1980s. He estimated a wild population of eight million birds nationally boosted by an annual release of 15 million birds. Of these hand-reared Pheasants he calculated that each winter 45% were shot and a further 20% died due to natural causes (including road casualties). By the last decade Mead (2000) reported over 20 million birds shot annually and made the point that the rearing of Pheasants was a significant rural industry with the habitats created being important for many other mammalian and avian species. Lack further commented that most birds were shot within 400 metres of their release point and that less than 1% dispersed more than two kilometres. This implies that Pheasants are largely sedentary but a comparison between the local breeding atlas map for Northumberland (Day *et al.*, 1995) and the current winter tetrad map shows a number of discrepancies, with fewer birds present on high ground in winter.

Hand-reared birds are most numerous during autumn and winter. They are usually released in July and August and shot from early November to 1st February. Research has shown that nearly one third of released birds die due to natural causes, including road casualties, and between 40 and 50% are shot. Of the remaining birds, many do not survive the winter but as March approaches surviving males begin to set up territories away from the immediate release areas. Game Conservancy Trust calculations estimate an average release density on keepered estates in Britain of 4.5 birds per hectare (Tapper, 1999).

Whilst there are 400 hectares in a tetrad, and the winter distribution map shows the species in 718 tetrads, it would be very unwise to undertake a simple calculation of hand-reared birds for the county using those figures. It is not known how much keepered land there is in the county and, even if it were, many shooting estates contain marginal land unsuitable for Pheasants, with numbers of birds released varying from year to year. The winter distribution map nevertheless shows distinct clusters of large (11+ birds) and medium sized (four-10 birds) dots, representing 138 and 202 tetrads respectively. All occur in areas of the county where shooting estates are active. A purely arbitrary calculation of one released bird for every two hectares x 200 hectares x 340 tetrads results in a total of 68,000 hand-reared Pheasants a year, always bearing in mind that about 30% will die before the shooting season. The confidential nature of data from shooting estates is understandable and obtaining an accurate figure for the county would be impossible, but the above total should probably be regarded as a minimum. Information on release figures for two large 'shoots' in the north of the county involves a total of 20,000 birds annually. Four medium sized estates in central Northumberland release a total of over 15,000 birds, and one very active estate in the south west releases on average 30,000 birds a year. Figures from a large number of other sizeable sporting estates were either not forthcoming or unobtainable, and no account has been taken of the many small estates and syndicates who may release only a few hundred birds annually.

The winter survey figure of 6,282 birds is therefore considerably short of the known numbers present in most winters. It is perhaps worth adding that in one control tetrad, on a shooting estate, the numbers of Pheasants counted over the three winter periods were 120, 250 and 200, and this was on an estate that was not approached for annual release figures. It is impossible to calculate the wild population numbers in the county although the north east is one of the areas listed by the Game Conservancy Trust as having a viable wild population.

JOHN C. DAY

Distribution by altitude

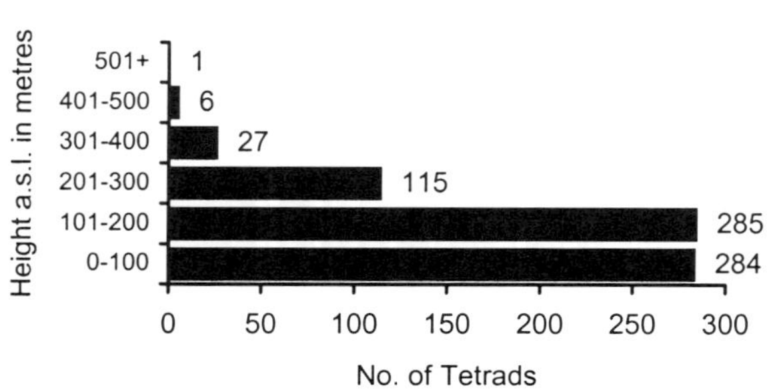

No. of tetrads in which recorded 718 (50%)

Tetrad Analysis	No. of tetrads
1-3 birds	378 (53%)
4-10 birds	202 (28%)
11+ birds	138 (19%)

Total No. of birds counted 6,282

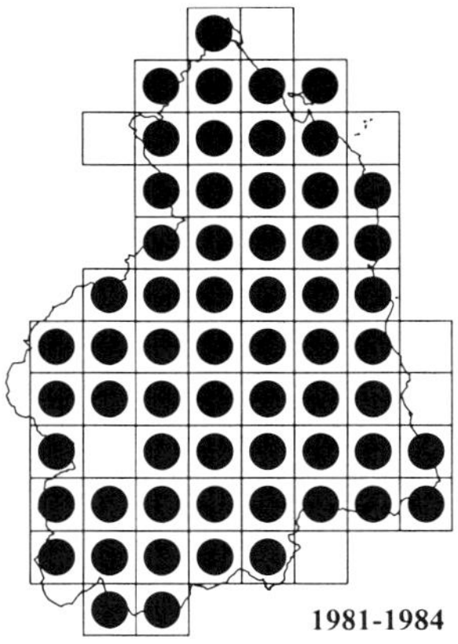

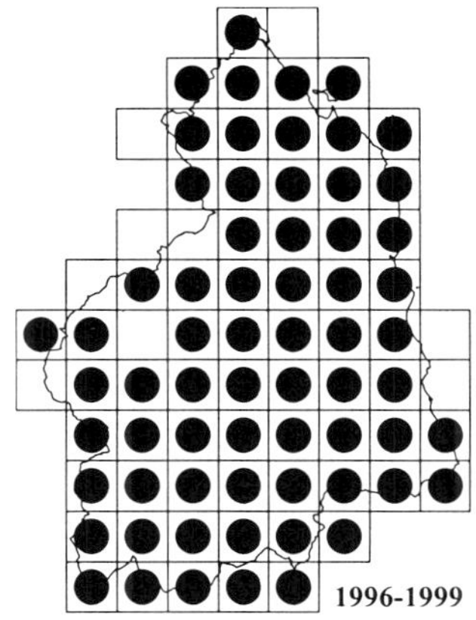

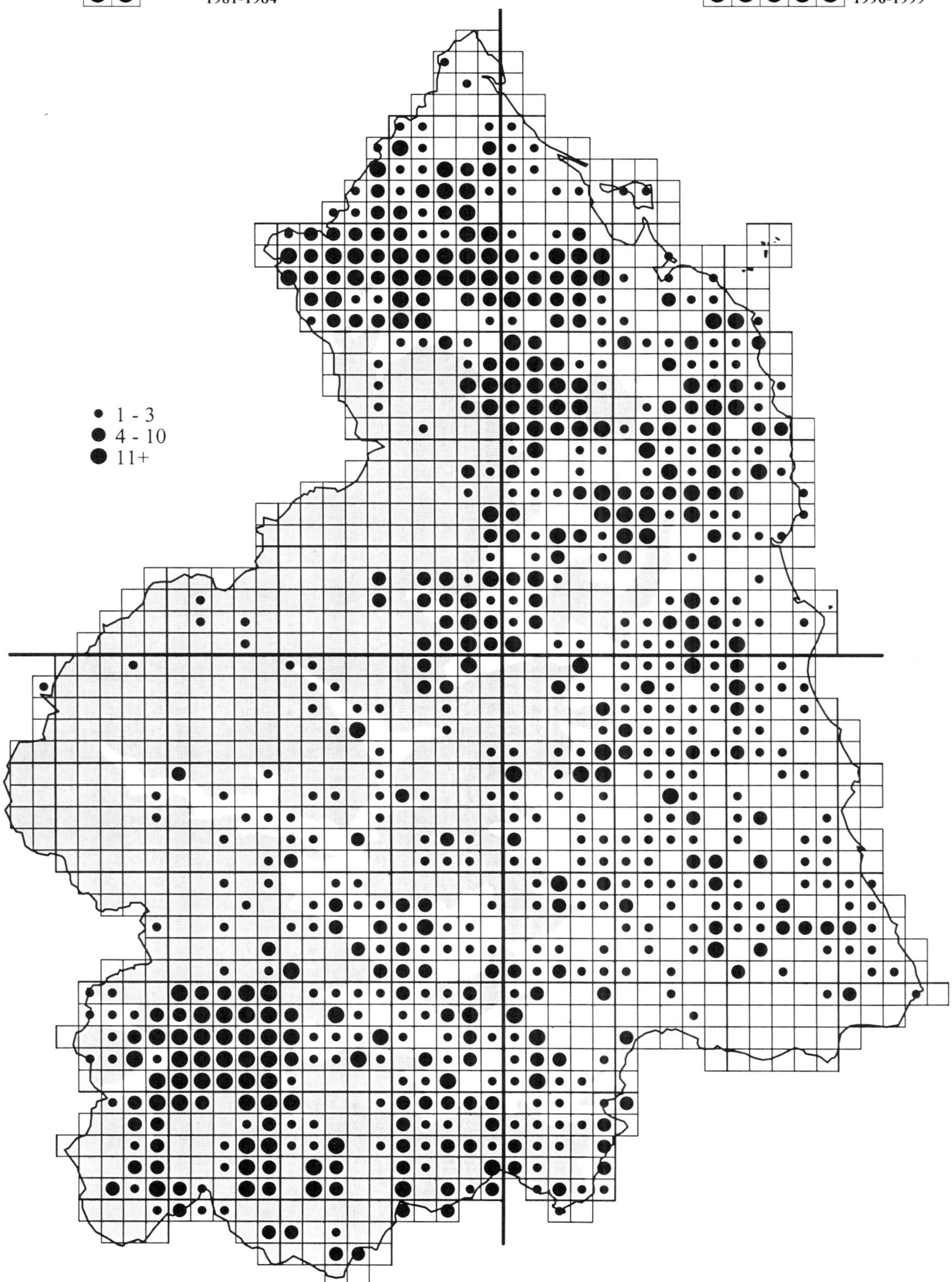

Pheasant

WATER RAIL *Rallus aquaticus*

This species is probably the most difficult bird to census with any accuracy. As Lack (1986) stated in *The atlas of wintering birds in Britain and Ireland* 'the Water Rail is ... elusive ... summer and winter alike. It is the prime skulker in dense wetland vegetation'. In spring and summer it is more often heard than seen in its breeding habitat and it is only in winter, when much of the vegetation has died back, that the patient observer may glimpse it hunting along the edges of ditches and ponds.

At the beginning of the twentieth century Bolam (1912) described it as 'a resident; but also to a large extent migratory, being always most numerous during winter'. Much of his account referred to the Water Rail in winter in which he said 'during the cold months, it is not uncommon, especially in the neighbourhood of the coast' and thought that it had 'increased considerably in numbers, as a winter resident, during recent years'. Of the species' activities in winter he stated that its 'sole idea of safety seems to be in hiding, and in very severe weather, when its usual haunts are frozen up ... I have frequently been amused at the shifts it will make in order to avoid taking wing ... At such seasons, it is sometimes forced to seek a living where common poultry are fed, or about cattle-sheds, or stackyards'. By 1932 Bolam was able to say that the species had increased in numbers as a resident and observed that in winter Water Rails were found in areas where they did not breed.

Evidence for the maintenance of this increase was no longer forthcoming by the 1980s according to Galloway and Meek (1980). They, however, elaborated on the Water Rail's winter status noting that 'immigrants, probably of continental origin, arrive in small numbers, mainly in October and early November'. They stated that 'such immigration results in winter gatherings at certain favoured locations, birds becoming more conspicuous during periods of hard weather when they are forced into the open to forage ... In recent years, the largest concentrations have been Gosforth Park [30 birds in January 1962 and 17 in February 1969], Prestwick Carr [27 in January 1968] and Bamburgh [15 in December 1962]'. Since those counts the greatest number recorded has been six at Gosforth Park in November 1995 and four at Holywell Pond (NZ37C) in February 1998 during the current survey.

In total, the current fieldwork over the three winter periods, accounted for 33 birds in 23 widely separated tetrads. Ten sightings were at inland localities, the remaining 23 at sites within twelve kilometres of the coast. The 'coastal' sites included Holy Island (NU14G), Low Newton (NU22M) and Cresswell (NZ29U) and Holywell Ponds each with two or more birds, with singles at Spindlestone (NU13L), Warkworth Dunes (NU20M), Hauxley (NU20W), Alnmouth (NU21L), on the Farne Islands (NU23I), Chevington Burn (NZ29U) and Druridge Pools (NZ29T). Whether these were all continental immigrants or wintering local birds is impossible to tell. The situation being all the more complex when the two birds at each of Gosforth Park (NZ27K) and Big Waters (NZ27G) are also considered. The inland observations were concentrated along the Tyne Valley and, with one exception, were all of single birds, the exception being two at Caistron (NU00A) in the Coquet Valley.

The winter tetrad distribution map bears little resemblance to the breeding distribution map for the county (Day *et al.*, 1995). In winter, birds were present in ten 10km coastal squares, but in the period for the local breeding atlas fieldwork only five of these were occupied. There is an even greater contrast with the inland sightings where only one 10km square held Water Rails in the breeding survey whilst they were present in eight 10km squares during the winter fieldwork. No doubt seasonal movement to lower-lying land, the mild winters over which the survey was conducted and the greater ease with which birds may be seen during colder weather account for some of the anomalies between the two county surveys.

The Water Rail is perhaps declining nationally (Mead, 2000). Certainly in Northumberland it has always been a rare breeding species and an uncommon passage and winter visitor.

JOHN C. DAY

Distribution by altitude

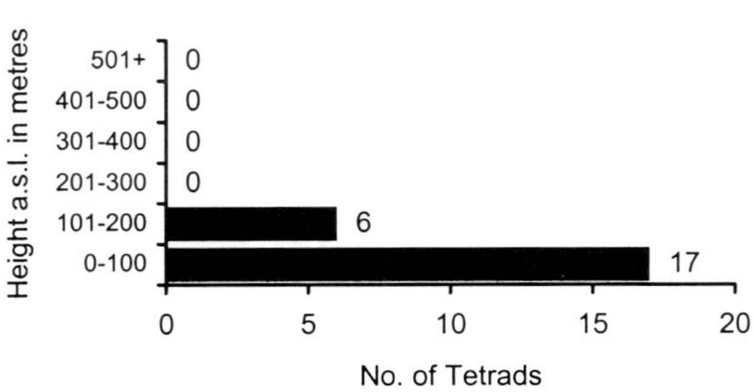

No. of tetrads in which recorded 23 (2%)

Tetrad Analysis	No. of tetrads
1 bird	16 (70%)
2 birds	5 (21%)
3+ birds	2 (9%)

Total No. of birds counted 33

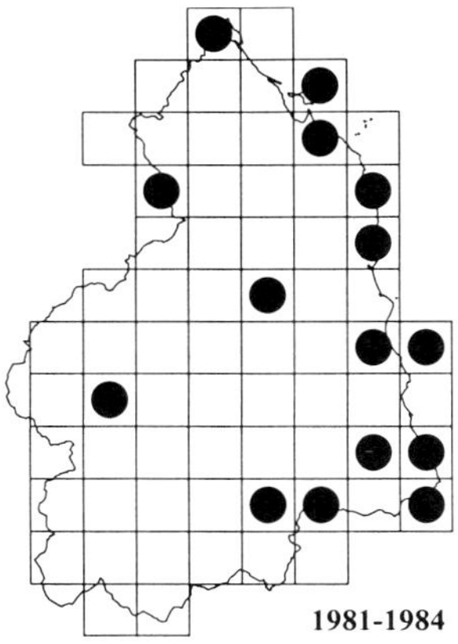

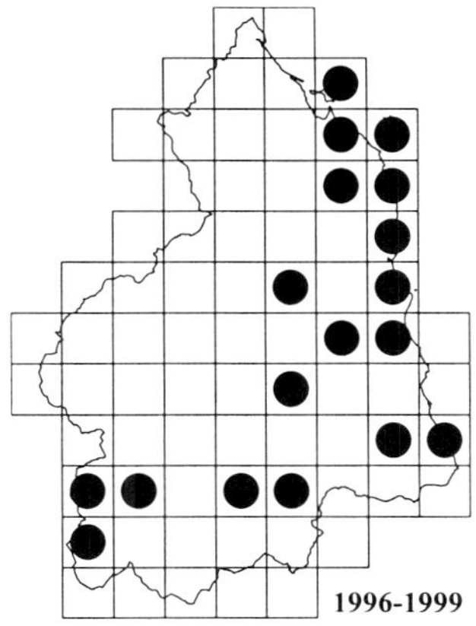

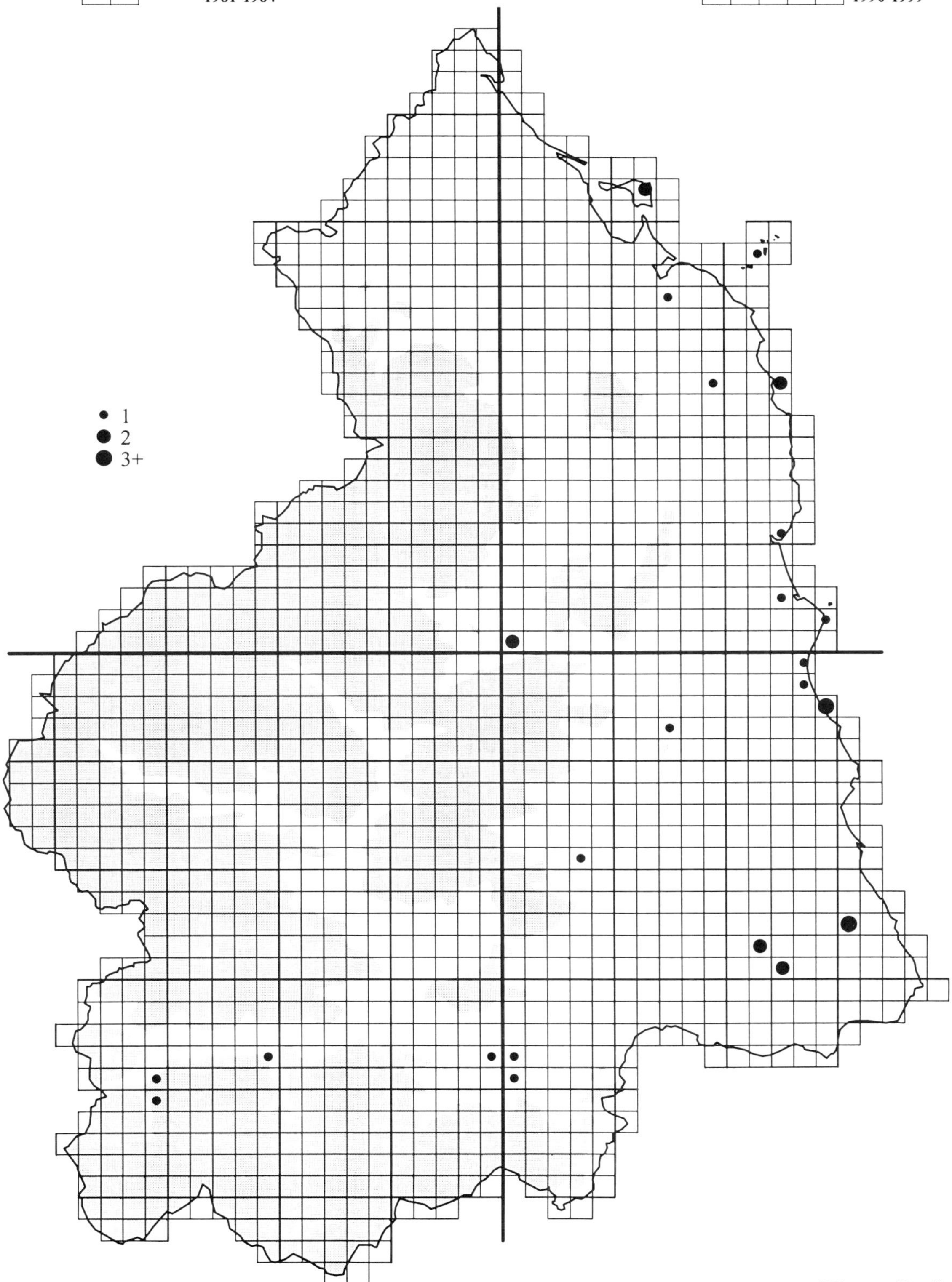

Water Rail

MOORHEN *Gallinula chloropus*

The Moorhen is a familiar bird of freshwater margins. It can readily be seen feeding in the open and will often betray its presence by its calls, even when concealed by vegetation. Moorhens are omnivorous and will take seeds, fruits and pondweeds as well as worms, fish and carrion. They are both adventurous and tenacious and are therefore able to thrive around a variety of water bodies. Their tolerance of human disturbance means that they are frequently found on urban park lakes and ponds.

Hancock (1874) described the 'Water Hen' as 'common everywhere in ponds and streams that abound with aquatic plants' while Bolam (1912) said it was 'a common resident in all lowland parts of the district'. These observations are endorsed by Lack (1986) who noted that 'the Moorhen is the commonest riparian bird in Britain and Ireland'. Gibbons *et al.* (1993) indicated that the breeding population in Britain and Ireland occupied an estimated 315,000 territories. There is, however, local variation in populations as the Moorhen struggles to survive in intensively farmed areas where habitats have been degraded by improved drainage and the filling-in of ponds, whilst in some areas predation by Mink *Mustela vison* is a significant problem. Breeding Moorhens in the UK are resident and sedentary, generally remaining within 20km of the nesting area. In autumn and winter they are joined by migrants from north west Europe, especially Sweden and Denmark. Severe winter weather can have a drastic effect on populations as was noted in the BTO Waterways Bird Surveys following the harsh winters of 1978/79 and 1981/82. However, most Moorhens are double or triple brooded and therefore the population are able to recover their numbers fairly rapidly.

Studies have shown that the Moorhen has a predominantly lowland distribution. This is demonstrated by the data collected during the current winter survey. Some 35% of all tetrads up to 100 metres a.s.l. were occupied. The proportion of tetrads occupied declines steeply with increased altitude, with 18% between 101 to 200 metres a.s.l., 6% between 201 to 300 metres and only 1.4% in the 301 to 400 metres range. These figures are no doubt also affected by the availability of suitable habitat during the winter months and the timing of counts. Indeed, counts in upland areas could be affected by the birds' behaviour. This is suggested from studies at Ladycross Nature Reserve, at a height of 365 metres a.s.l. in Slaley Forest. Here, Moorhens breed annually, but are very secretive and leave the site at the first autumn frosts, usually not returning until late February.

Wintering Moorhens often form small groups, though larger flocks can be seen, mainly in late autumn. Galloway and Meek (1980) noted that 'winter concentrations of up to eighty are not uncommon at favoured haunts such as Cresswell Ponds, Wallsend Swallow Pond and Holywell Ponds, while the last locality has on two occasions, in November 1968 and February 1976, attracted gatherings of a hundred'. In the current winter survey, the highest single tetrad count of 40 was recorded around the wetland nature reserve at Caistron (NU00A) in the Coquet Valley. Totals of 35 were counted around Wallsend Swallow Pond (NZ36E) and Warkworth Lane Pond (NZ29R) but by far the greatest number of records were of only one or two birds (in 149 tetrads) or between three and five birds (in 56 tetrads). A comparison between the two 10km square maps shows a patchier, but not dissimilar, distribution in the current survey, with 67% occupancy of all squares surveyed as opposed to 80% in 1981-1984. This would seem to confirm Mead's (2000) analysis that there has been a 'slight decline' but that the 'future seems assured'. The relatively sedentary nature of the species can also be noted in the control tetrad data with total counts of 52 in 1996/97 and 83 and 78 in the two succeeding winter seasons.

The results from the current survey confirm the winter status of the Moorhen in Northumberland remains that of a common resident.

KEN DAWSON

Distribution by altitude

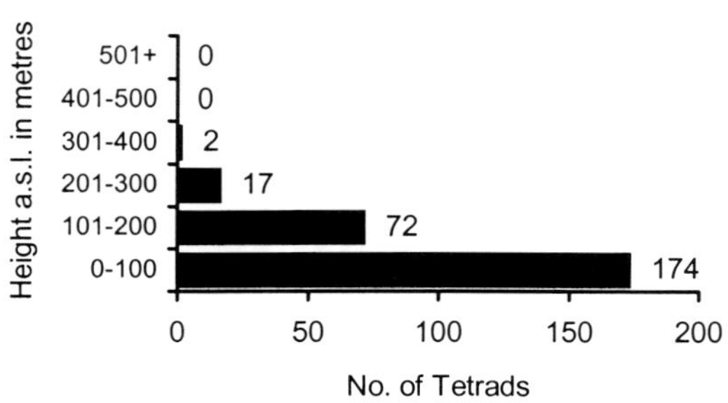

No. of tetrads in which recorded 265 (19%)

Tetrad Analysis	No. of tetrads
1-2 birds	149 (56%)
3-5 birds	56 (21%)
6+ birds	60 (23%)

Total No. of birds counted 1,144

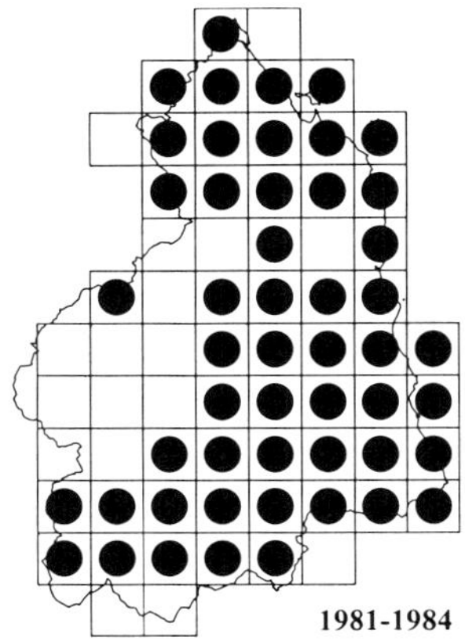

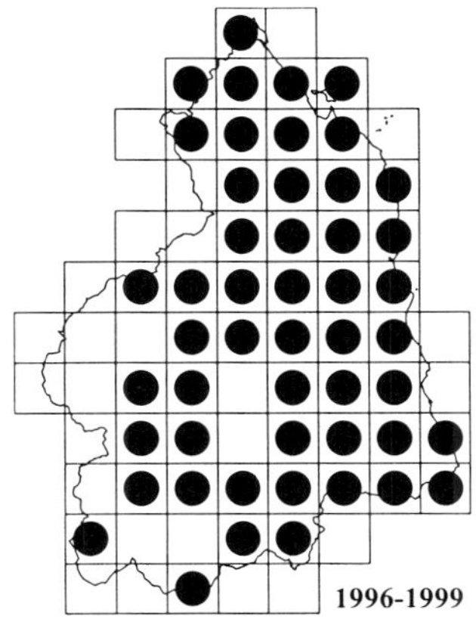

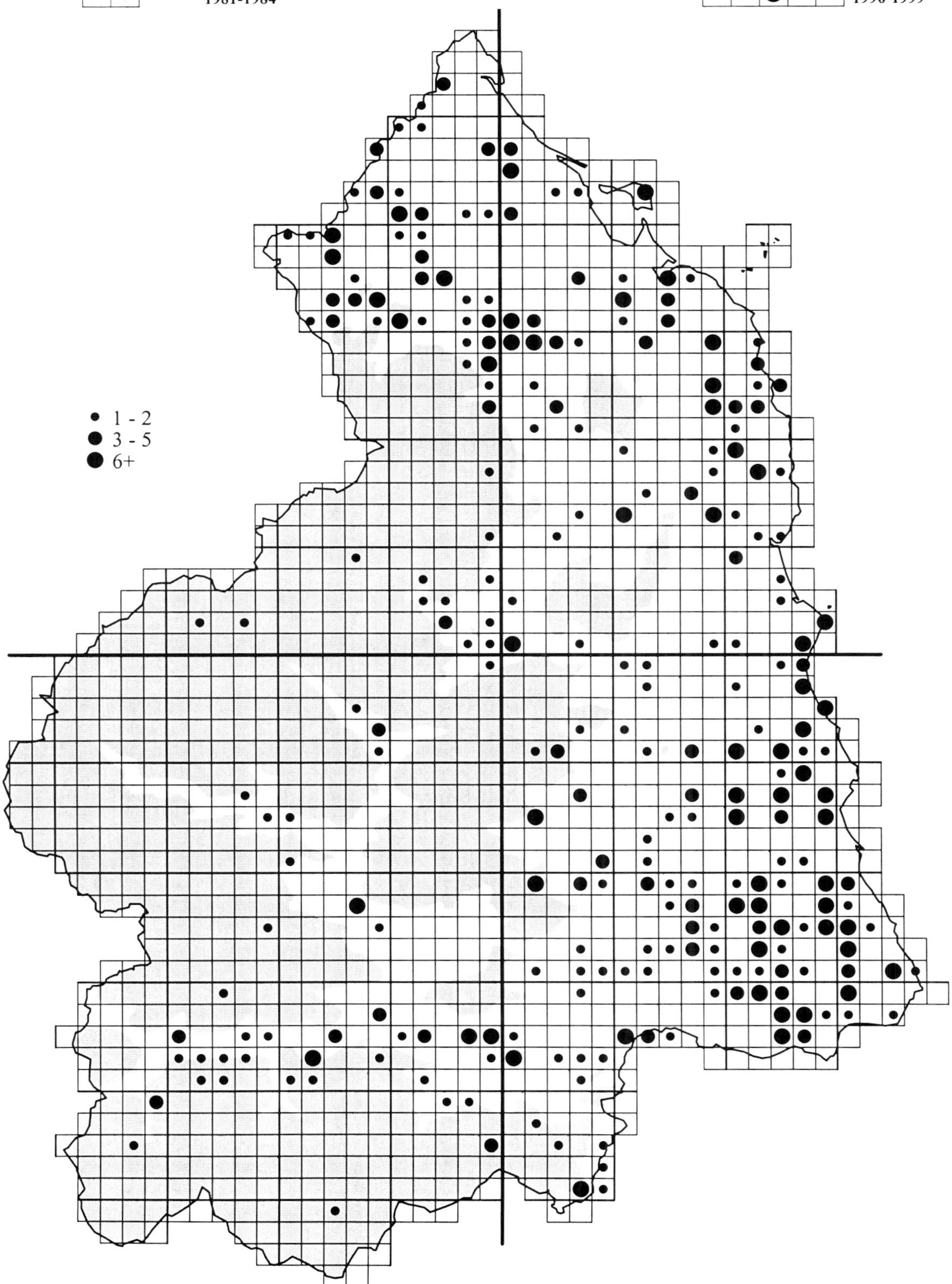

Moorhen

COOT *Fulica atra*

The status of the Coot within the county was described by Hancock (1874) as 'though common, is not so generally distributed as the Water Hen [Moorhen *Gallinula chloropus*]', while Bolam (1912) considered that it bred 'numerously on most of our larger sheets of water' and had 'increased considerably within the last twenty years'. By 1932 Bolam classed it as 'a common resident' which 'prefers a considerable extent of open water for nesting purposes'. Galloway and Meek (1980) described it as a 'common passage and winter visitor and well-represented breeding resident' and noted that hard winter weather, such as that experienced in 1947, can have a negative impact on the subsequent breeding population. In the 1981-1984 national winter atlas survey this suggestion was contradicted as it was thought that there are always non-breeders waiting to fill vacant sites (Lack, 1986). The British population trend according to Mead (2000) is relatively stable.

In Northumberland, and Britain as a whole, the winter population is swollen by immigrants which move west and south from as far east as Russia (Lack, 1986). An adult ringed at Abberton, Essex, on 19th December 1957 and recovered at Seghill on 23rd January 1958 is one of few ringing recoveries from the county but local movement between water bodies has been demonstrated by one ringed at Big Waters and recovered at Blagdon.

As Coots favour open waters and slow-moving rivers and are typically gregarious it seems likely that few were overlooked in the current survey. During the winter they may move from breeding sites to gather in large flocks with various wildfowl on selected ponds and lakes. A comparison of the distribution maps from *The atlas of breeding birds in Northumbria* (Day *et al.*, 1995), in which Coot were present in 135 out of 1,410 tetrads (10%), and this current survey shows a more concentrated pattern in the winter months with birds present in 99 out of 1,432 tetrads (7%). The grand total of maximum counts for the three-year winter survey was 2,730. It is perhaps unlikely that such a figure would be recorded in each individual winter but dividing the above total over three years produces an average of 910 per winter, which probably underestimates the true population. This mean figure would confirm the species' status as 'well-represented' as defined in Galloway and Meek, only falling slightly short of the 'common' category of 1,001 to 10,000 non-breeding individuals per year.

Within this current survey the largest single concentration was of 435 at Cresswell Pond (NZ29X) on 15th November 1997. Only two other counts exceeded 200, those of 231 at Capheaton Lake (NZ07J) in January 1998 and 223 at Big Waters (NZ27G) in December 1997, with 100-199 at a further five localities. Cresswell Pond was the most attractive locality for Coots during the survey. In addition to the above count it also held 420 in December 1998 and 371 in January 1999. During the 1981-1984 national winter atlas survey, peak counts were 650 at Big Waters and a total of 400 on the Northumbrian Loughs in December 1983, together with an unusually high count of 469 at the Tweed Estuary in December 1981. The latter occurred during a period of severe cold weather and probably included many birds driven off frozen inland waters. There were no such notable estuarine gatherings in the current survey, probably as a result of three relatively mild winters. Some previously popular wintering sites have, for unknown reasons, become much less attractive. Big Waters, regularly the most productive single site for Coot throughout the 1970s and 1980s, now rarely holds more than 150 birds. Fluctuations between years is confirmed by figures from the control tetrads, where in the winter of 1996/97 a total of 26 was recorded compared to 110 and 97 in the two succeeding winters.

In the 1981-1984 winter survey Coot were noted in a total of 45 ten kilometre squares in the county and, in this survey, in a total of 41 squares. From the tetrad map it can be seen that wintering Coots are reasonably well scattered, with a bias towards the east of the county, and particularly the NZ squares in the south east (48% of occupied tetrads were in this quarter). A large portion of the upland, heavily forested border regions completely lacked any records as would be expected due to the dearth of suitable eutrophic waters. Indeed the majority of occupied tetrads (67%) were found at an altitude of between 0-100 metres a.s.l. compared with only seven (7%) occupied tetrads in the 201-400 metres a.s.l. range. In a national context this county does not hold significant numbers of wintering Coot. The Wetland Bird Survey gave a winter count figure for Great Britain of 110,226 in December 1998, with Abberton Reservoir in Essex holding a massive 6,493 (Pollitt *et al.*, 2000).

GRAEME BOWMAN

Distribution by altitude

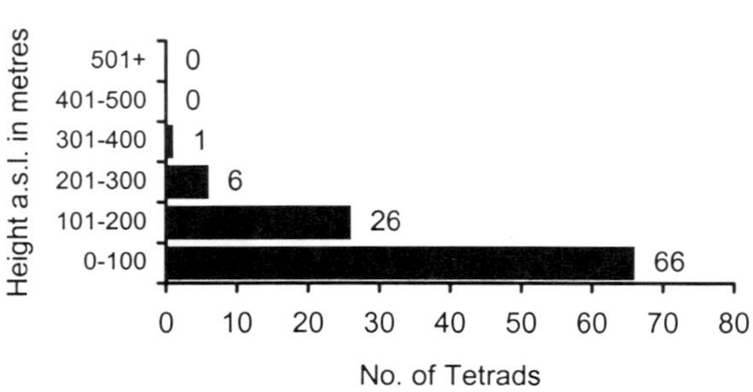

No. of tetrads in which recorded 99 (7%)

Tetrad Analysis	No. of tetrads
1-4 birds	50 (51%)
5-24 birds	27 (27%)
25+ birds	22 (22%)

Total No. of birds counted 2,730

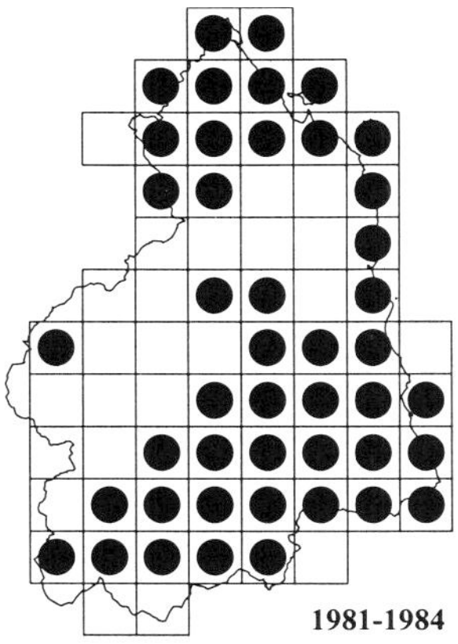

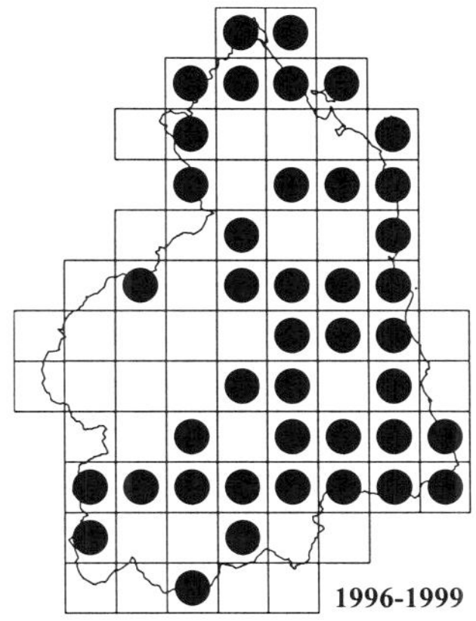

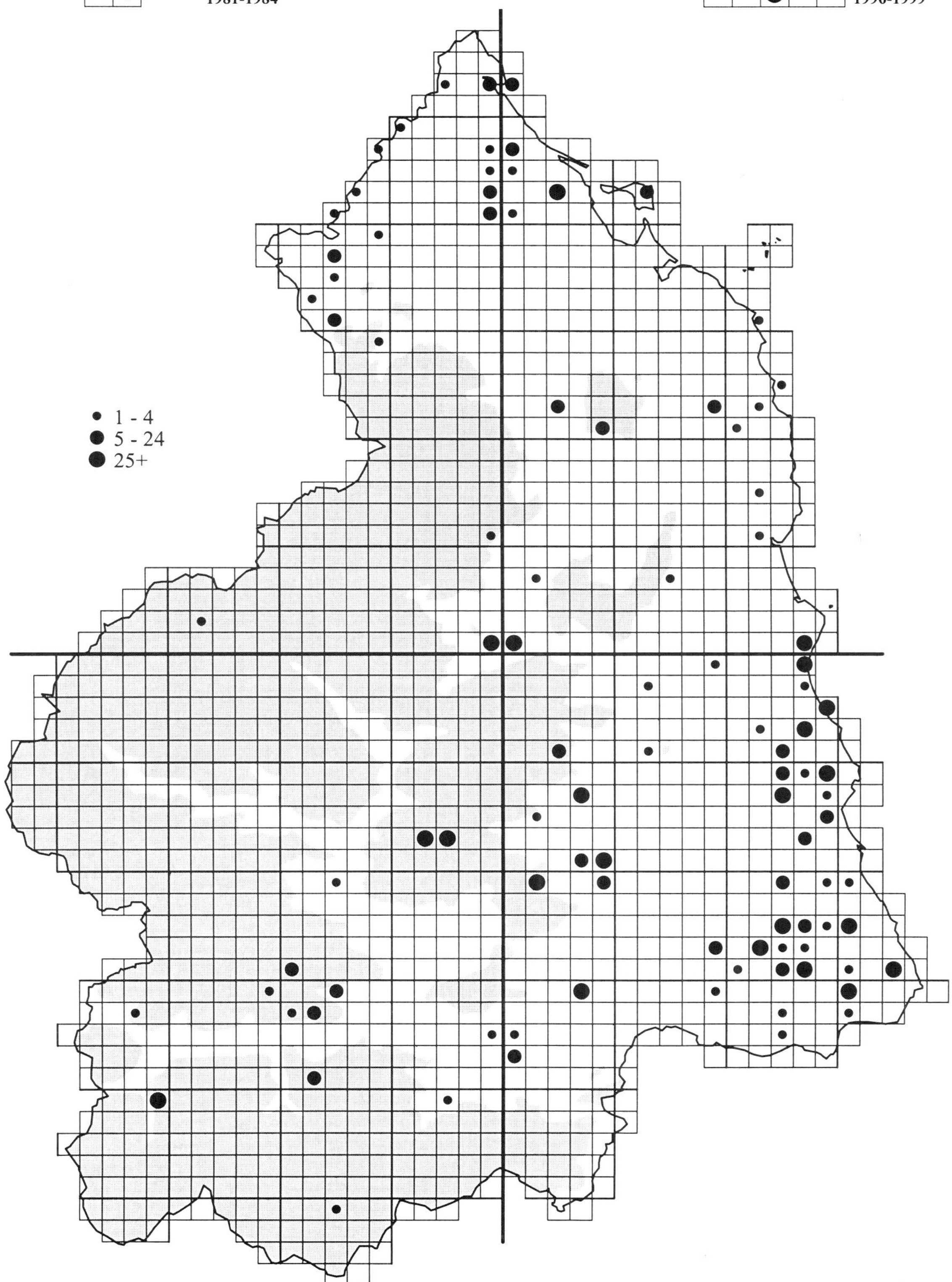

Coot

WINTERING WADERS IN NORTHUMBERLAND

Roger Norman

Up to one and three quarters of a million waders are present in Great Britain in a typical winter. Approximately 2% of these, around 35,000 birds, are in Northumberland and provide some of the best winter birdwatching in the region. The county has three key habitats for waders, the intertidal area at the Lindisfarne NNR, the open coast and five significant estuaries. Lindisfarne has vast expanses of mud and sand interspersed with tidal creeks. The open coast is characterized by a mixture of long sandy beaches and flat intertidal rocky shelves, these latter providing rich feeding among the seaweeds. The county's estuaries are relatively small in national terms with modest areas of intertidal mud. Only the Blyth and Tyne Estuaries have suffered the effects of major industrialization and adjacent high human population density. On a sixth estuary, the Wansbeck, a barrage near the mouth has been constructed, leading to the loss of most of its intertidal zone although a wildfowl site has developed on the freshwater impounded upstream of the barrage.

The importance of the county for wildfowl and waders is recognized by a number of major conservation measures. Both the Lindisfarne NNR and the Northumbria coast are designated as Ramsar sites and as SPAs, the coast having only recently been given that status after the end of the winter atlas period in February 2000. Also during the atlas fieldwork period a number of local sites were put forward as candidates for Special Areas of Conservation (SAC) status under the European Natura 2000 programme, although they will not come into being before 2003. Lindisfarne is internationally important for several species, including Grey Plover *Pluvialis squatarola*, Knot *Calidris canutus* and Bar-tailed Godwit *Limosa lapponica*. The Northumbria coast is internationally important for Purple Sandpiper *Calidris maritima* and Turnstone *Arenaria interpres*, and also for breeding Little Terns *Sterna albifrons*. The estuaries of the Tweed, Aln, Coquet and Blyth are designated as SSSIs. Various sites, including intertidal mudflats on the Tyne are designated as SNCIs and recently two high-tide refuges have been established on the river as part of sympathetic riverside redevelopment. The Farne Islands are designated as an SPA for their breeding birds, but hold significant numbers of 'rocky shore' waders in winter. A summary table of important sites and species numbers appears in Appendix J.

Numbers nationally of each species fluctuate from year to year and at a county level these fluctuations tend to be greater, partly because the 'sample' size is much smaller. However, long-term counting under the WeBS scheme shows that Lindisfarne holds on average over 60% of the county total, the open coasts about 22% and the five estuaries around 15%. Although birds are distributed generally along the open coast, there are a few particularly favoured areas. Berwick Little Beach, in the north of the county, with its large amounts of stranded wrack, and the shoreline between Budle Point and Alnmouth are very productive as is St. Mary's Island in the south of the county. Although all of the county's estuaries are relatively small, their narrowness has benefits in that it is relatively easy to observe and count the birds while they are feeding or resting at low tide. Whilst the south bank of the Tyne Estuary falls outside the club's recording area, the narrowness of the river means that single populations of waders and wildfowl utilize both banks as circumstances dictate. Taking both banks of the Tyne together, around 4,500 to 5,000 waders use this area of the river in a typical winter, making it the major estuary in the county. Many of these are Lapwing *Vanellus vanellus,* Golden Plover *Pluvialis apricaria,* and Redshank *Tringa totanus*.

Numbers on the River Tyne have increased rapidly in the last few years, paralleling the improvement of the river for migratory fish such as salmon and sea-trout. Rather more than half the birds occur up-river of the Tyne bridges, where significant intertidal areas have survived industrialization. For the best diversity of species, however, most birdwatchers would probably choose the Coquet where over 2,000 waders use the estuary in a typical winter. Flocks of Lapwing and Golden Plover are supplemented by nearly all the county's regular wintering species. The other estuaries, the Tweed, Blyth and Aln, normally hold smaller numbers of the commoner waders, typically 500 to 1,500 each winter, with the Tweed being notable for its wildfowl rather than wader interest. The county's farmland holds wintering flocks of 'field' or 'grassland' waders, principally Lapwing, many being concentrated in fields adjacent to the coast, often together with large concentrations of Golden Plovers. Whilst species that flock together in well-watched areas can be counted and their numbers assessed, a number of dispersed species are, of course, also present in the county. Birds such as Snipe *Gallinago gallinago*, Jack Snipe *Lymnocryptes minimus*, Woodcock *Scolopax rusticola* and Green Sandpiper *Tringa ochropus* can all escape regular counts. A targeted, 'dispersed species' survey, planned for 2002/2003 may throw more light on the numbers and distribution of such difficult-to-census birds.

Wader numbers at Lindisfarne, the open coast and on the estuaries all build up steadily from July through the autumn to reach their winter levels by November. Simple counts of birds mask the fact there is a substantial migration of birds through the county and it is probably only by November that some stability in the population is reached. Even then the influence of weather both in the county and elsewhere, such as on the near-continent, will affect flows of birds in and out of the county. From November through to January the total numbers of waders in the county is roughly constant before a steady decline is evident in February, which continues through March and April. As spring approaches, there is some movement of breeding birds back inland from the coast and flocks or individuals of various species, such as Oystercatcher *Haematopus ostralegus*, Lapwing, Golden Plover, Redshank and Ringed Plover *Charadrius hiaticula* occur on farmland and along river valleys in late February and early March.

In the past there has been a number of influences on our wintering waders. Wildfowling along the coast and at Lindisfarne has been prevalent since the 1800s. This is, of course, controlled now apart from illegal shooting which may take place along the shore. Human developments in the south east of the county resulted in heavy industrialization over the last 150 years with consequent major changes to the Blyth and Tyne Estuaries and much of the coastal plain. Recent habitat losses of intertidal mud have occurred with the barrage on the River Wansbeck and the development of a large car terminal on Jarrow Slake on the south bank of the River Tyne. Although, strictly speaking, this latter area is just outside the county boundary, it was a major component of the river's ecosystem. Hopefully, these will be the last habitat losses in the area. The general intensification of farming and urban sprawl has led to a slow attrition of small wetland areas away from the coast and estuaries, leaving the remaining wetlands and the need to conserve them more vital than ever. Increasing human recreational use of the long coastline, even in winter, leads to higher levels of disturbance along the shore.

There are a number of influences that will determine the future of the county's wintering waders. The wintering areas for most species already carry designations which recognize their importance for waders and also for wildfowl. These designations offer some protection against future threats. The county is lucky in that outside the south east corner there is unlikely to be much, if any, further industrial development. Estuary management plans have been established for the Tweed, Aln, Coquet and Blyth, which should assist in the conservation of the habitats and their birds. One recent change, the effect of which is still to be assessed, is the 'clean-up' of sewage discharges into the estuaries and along the coast. The reduction in nutrients entering coastal waters may lead to some redistribution of birds as the invertebrate population responds and hence food availability changes. Nutrient input to both the Blyth and Tyne Estuaries has markedly reduced recently and this may lead to a more varied invertebrate fauna.

On a broader canvas, any rise in sea levels due to a rise in global temperature will impact on waders directly by reducing both areas of mud and the time available for feeding between tides. It may also lead to a redistribution of wintering areas as fewer birds need to move west or south west to escape cold winters in Scandinavia or on the Waddensee.

OYSTERCATCHER *Haematopus ostralegus*

Large and bold in its black and white plumage and with a bright orange bill, the Oystercatcher is perhaps the most striking and familiar of our shorebirds. Whether busily seeking out and feeding on shellfish on rocky promontories or gathering in noisy and excitable piping parties, these unmistakable waders are to be found on virtually every stretch of the county's coastline.

Scott (1760) and Pennant (1771) recorded Oystercatchers on the Farne Islands, Hancock (1874) described them as abundant on the coast while Bolam (1912) agreed with that assessment and in 1932 wrote of their recent spread inland as a breeding species. More recently, Galloway and Meek (1980) described their winter status in the county as a common visitor.

The distribution map for the present survey demonstrates clearly that Oystercatchers were found in large numbers in every coastal tetrad, with the notable exceptions of short stretches north of Holy Island and in the south east between Blyth and Seaton Sluice. These are both areas with large expanses of sandy beaches which provide little or no rocky feeding areas so attractive to the species. The map also indicates that of the 130 tetrads where Oystercatchers were recorded, 51 of them were inland, indicating the ability of these strong and robust waders to find suitable feeding in areas far from the sea along the edges of the main river systems, principally the Coquet, Till, Tweed and South Tyne and in riverside fields.

The largest single coastal count during the survey was of 550 at the Lindisfarne NNR in January 1997 and the largest inland counts were 435 in the Coquet Valley around Caistron (NU00A) and 134 on the Tweed near Carham (NT73Z), both in the second half of February 1998. Both of these inland areas are well known and regular late winter and early spring staging posts for Oystercatchers moving to breeding areas, and perhaps to more distant nesting grounds in Scotland and Scandinavia, so it would be inaccurate to regard them as true winter gatherings.

The 10km square maps show little significant change between the 1981-1984 and 1996-1999 winter surveys although they appear to indicate some slight increase in records from the south west. In this current survey there was a maximum count of 5,128 birds over the three winter periods. In any given winter the total would be less than that and probably nearer to 3,000-3,500. This is partly confirmed by data from coastal WeBS counts showing a peak of 2,628 wintering Oystercatchers in January 1999 between Tynemouth and Berwick. This total included 1,371 at Lindisfarne NNR, the most important locality, with 282 between Beadnell and Howick Burn and 237 at St Mary's Island.

Lack (1986) believed that the vast majority of Oystercatchers wintering along the east coast of Britain were of Norwegian origin. There is one ringing recovery of a Norwegian bird at Holy Island but others have been shown by wing-tagging to be Scottish breeders. Lack estimated a national wintering population of about 300,000 birds, almost half the European total. The results of this current survey confirm the status of the Oystercatcher in Northumberland as a common winter visitor.

IAN KERR

Distribution by altitude

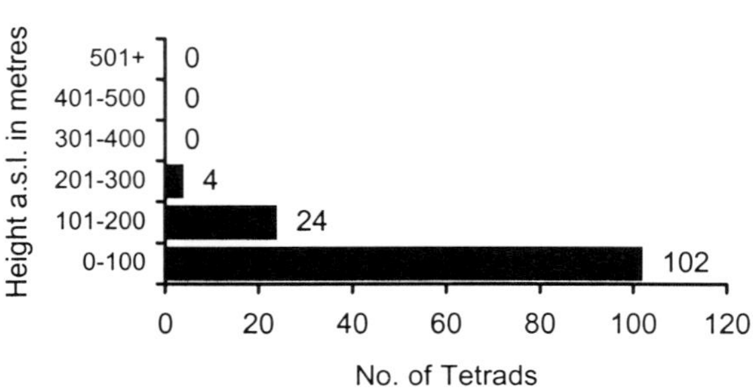

No. of tetrads in which recorded 130 (9%)

Tetrad Analysis	No. of tetrads
1-6 birds	63 (48%)
7-49 birds	36 (28%)
50+ birds	31 (24%)

Total No. of birds counted 5,128

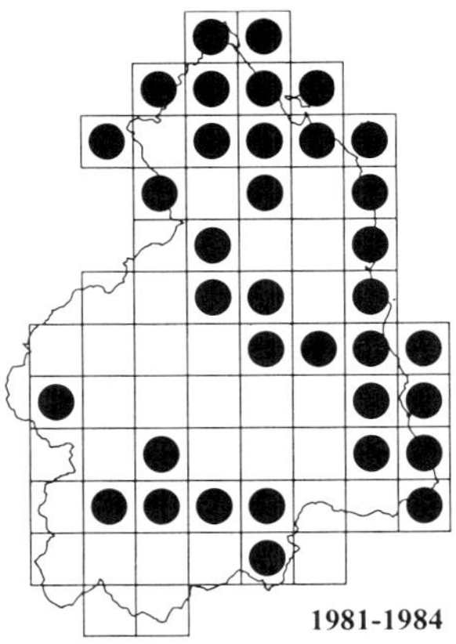

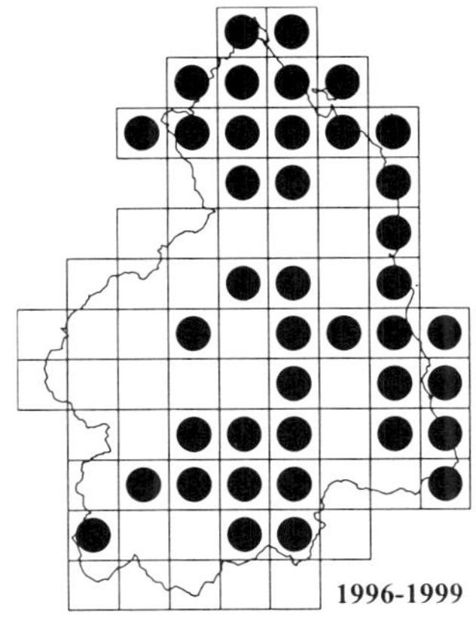

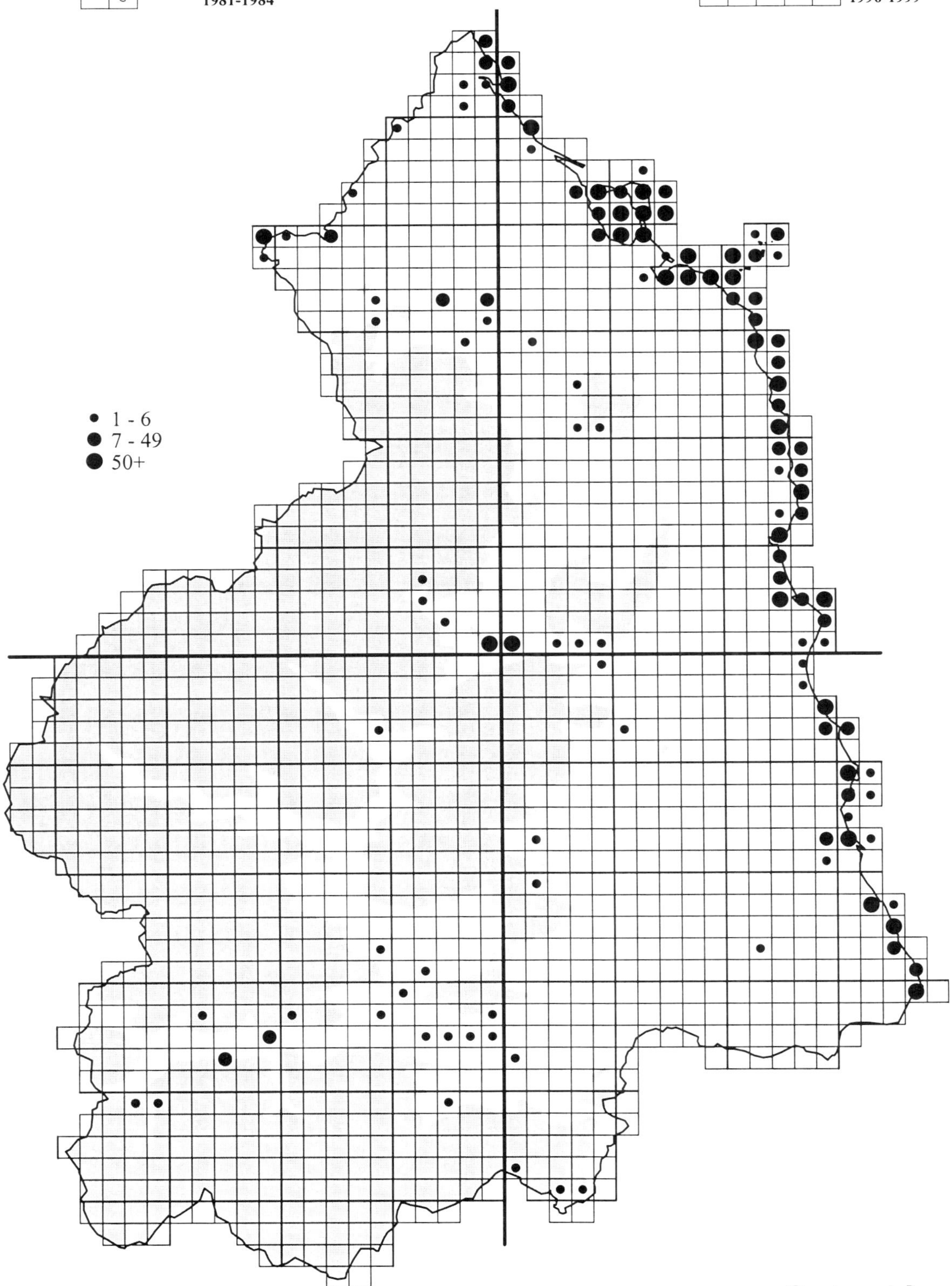

Oystercatcher

RINGED PLOVER *Charadrius hiaticula*

Daintily running along the beach, pausing momentarily and then running on, the Ringed Plover is one of the most familiar of our shorebirds. Its bold black head and breast markings blend so well against a background of sand and shingle, that this attractive little plover is often not noticed until it begins to move to pick prey in the form of worms or crustaceans from the surface or to flit away from intrusion.

The earliest indication of its local presence comes from bones found in excavations at the ninth and tenth century Anglo-Saxon farming settlement at Greenshiel, near the north shore of Holy Island, where they and other species which are still common in the area were presumably taken for food (Kerr, 1992). Pennant (1771) recorded it on the Farne Islands and both Hancock (1874) and Bolam (1912) knew it as a common resident along the coast with the latter author documenting the start of inland breeding. Galloway and Meek (1980) said that the Ringed Plover was a well-represented winter visitor with a population of around 900 birds, up to half of which may be found on the Lindisfarne NNR. They considered the winter numbers were made up of both local birds and immigrants from northern Europe. Lack (1986) estimated a total national wintering population of up to 35,000, most of them from the Baltic and the Waddensee area of Holland. He pointed out that Britain was on the northern edge of the wintering range with the species making up a much higher proportion of the wintering shorebird community in south west Europe and North Africa.

The current survey map clearly shows the importance of localities with wide sandy beaches including Ross Back Sands (NU13N), Bamburgh (NU13X), Beadnell Bay (NU22I), Low Newton (NU22M), Embleton Bay (NU22L), Alnmouth Bay (NU21K), Warkworth (NU20S) and Druridge Bay (NZ29/NU20), all areas most commonly associated with this species. During the survey, the only areas which provided counts of 100 or more were Fenham Flats (NU13E), Budle Bay (NU13M) and Beadnell Bay. However, some slightly higher winter totals are available although they extend beyond single tetrads. For example, 153 were present during a synchronised count on the Lindisfarne NNR in January 1998 and 168 were found on a WeBS count in feeding areas between Beadnell and the Howick Burn in December of that year.

The main map also clearly demonstrates the ability of this species to survive in winter inland in small numbers with, for example, 15 at Caistron (NU00A) and five in the extreme north west of the county at Carham (NT73Z). It is tempting to speculate that some at least of these birds may have been local breeders which decided to remain, the areas used coinciding with the inland nesting strongholds of the species. Others ventured short distances inland to take advantage of feeding opportunities with two each at Lemington on the River Tyne (NZ16X) and Burradon (NZ27R) and one near Woolsington (NZ17V).

Altogether during the current survey a total of 1,116 birds were counted in 49 tetrads, all but five of them along the coast, showing that the overwhelming majority of birds depend on a marine environment for their winter survival. The figures confirm the status of Ringed Plover in Northumberland as that of a well-represented winter visitor. The smaller 10km square maps show very little difference between the current wintering situation and that noted in 1981-1984, with the exception of the small numbers found in the extreme north west.

IAN KERR

Distribution by altitude

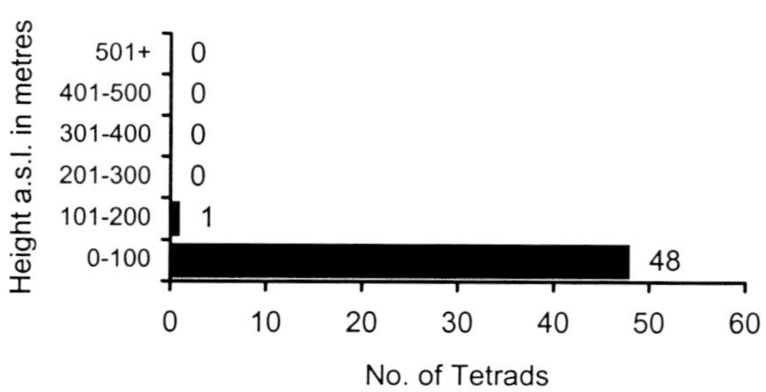

No. of tetrads in which recorded 49 (3%)

Tetrad Analysis	No. of tetrads
1-15 birds	26 (53%)
16-32 birds	13 (27%)
33+ birds	10 (20%)

Total No. of birds counted 1,116

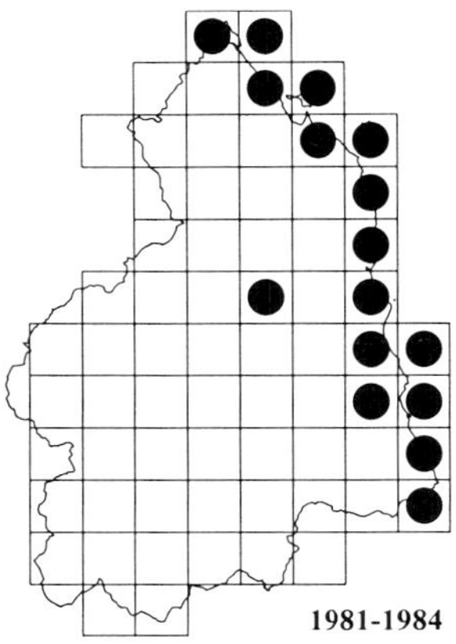

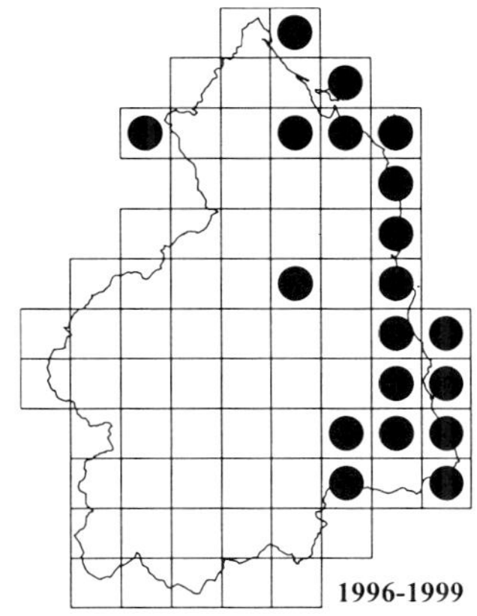

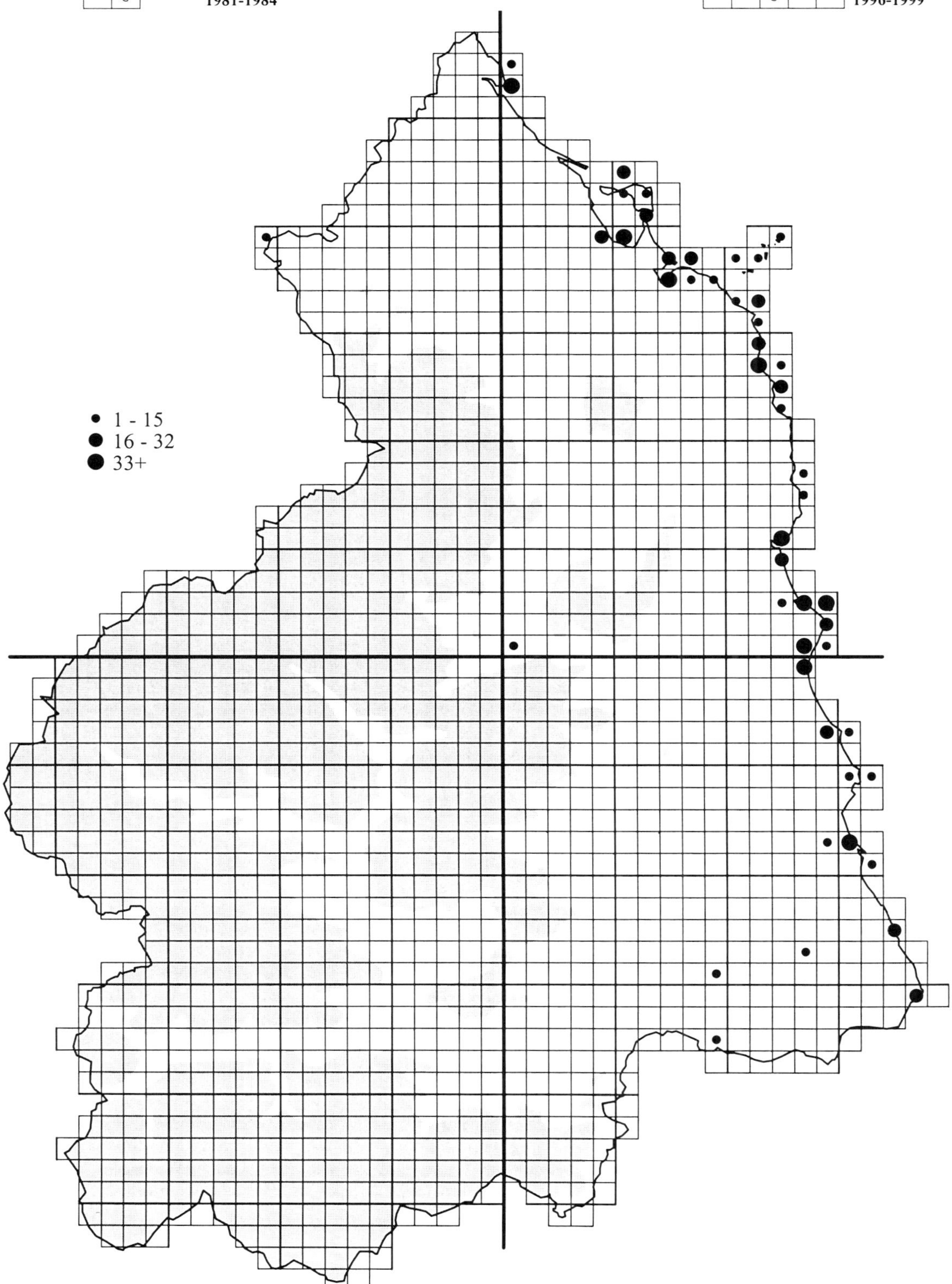

Ringed Plover

GOLDEN PLOVER *Pluvialis apricaria*

Tight and fast-flying flocks of Golden Plover, with their musical cries as they move between roosting and feeding areas, enliven any winter outing, particularly at the coast. Rich intertidal areas, such as those around Holy Island, Budle Bay and the Coquet Estuary, are used at low water, with large numbers of birds then exploiting feeding in coastal fields at other periods. Farmland in the low eastern half of the county and along the valleys of the main rivers also proves attractive for this species.

Lack (1986) said that wintering Golden Plover were found through much of lowland Britain, often associating with Lapwing *Vanellus vanellus* and the two species could be regarded as the 'grassland plovers'. He considered that most of the wintering population of between 200,000 and 300,000 in Britain and Ireland were from Iceland and Scandinavia. Locally, Bolam (1932) recognised that northern birds of the race *P. a. altifrons* comprised most of the wintering population, a fact still very apparent in late winter as birds begin to acquire their breeding plumage. Galloway and Meek (1980) described the species as 'an abundant winter visitor'.

The tetrad map shows clearly that the largest flocks are confined to the coast and the lower eastern half of the region. During the period of the current survey the largest concentrations were all in these areas, e.g. 6,000 at Lindisfarne NNR, 5,000 near St Mary's Island (NZ37M), 3,000 at Elswick (NZ26G) and 2,500 at Newbiggin (NZ38E). Older references exist of some very large winter numbers, including a wholly exceptional estimate of 50,000 on restored opencast mining land at Druridge Bay in November 1976, a vast concentration which has never been repeated (Galloway and Meek, 1980).

The map also shows that considerable numbers of Golden Plover winter further inland, particularly in the south west of the county, a few of them on apparently inhospitable areas up to 500 metres a.s.l. However, it would appear that in these western areas most of the birds are either on lower ground or in the valley bottoms, habitats which experience less harsh winter conditions except during periods of heavy snow and freezing temperatures. Small numbers of Golden Plovers may remain on high moorland throughout the year (Galloway & Meek, 1980) and this seems to have been confirmed during the current winter survey. An analysis of the 46 tetrads in the NY sector clearly shows that 15 of 25 squares visited in February contained parties of Golden Plover ranging from 16-200 birds, either commencing early passage or already on breeding territory.

The two 10km square maps indicate that there may have been some contraction in wintering distribution since 1981-1984. There appears to have been a retreat from some areas in the west and north west of the county although this has been balanced to some extent by more inland areas in the north east being regularly used by flocks.

Other data collected during the period of the current survey show some apparent sharp fluctuations in numbers. These may have been due to the weather conditions and/or the highly mobile nature of winter flocks, prepared to move quickly to new areas to exploit favourable feeding conditions. For example, during the survey, the monthly WeBS counts between Tynemouth and Berwick showed some very wide variations in numbers. These ranged from a high of 12,059 birds in November 1997 to only 361 in February 1999.

With some large concentrations, particularly in coastal and lowland localities, the current survey confirms that the Golden Plover in Northumberland remains an abundant winter visitor.

IAN KERR

Distribution by altitude

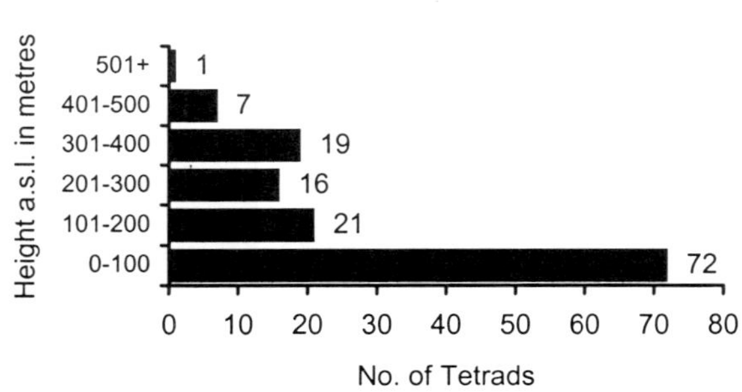

No. of tetrads in which recorded 136 (9%)

Tetrad Analysis	No. of tetrads
1-30 birds	68 (50%)
31-250 birds	40 (29%)
251+ birds	28 (21%)

Total No. of birds counted 42,586

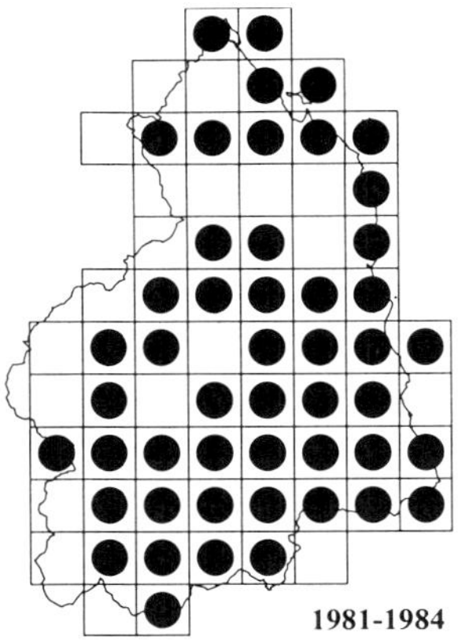

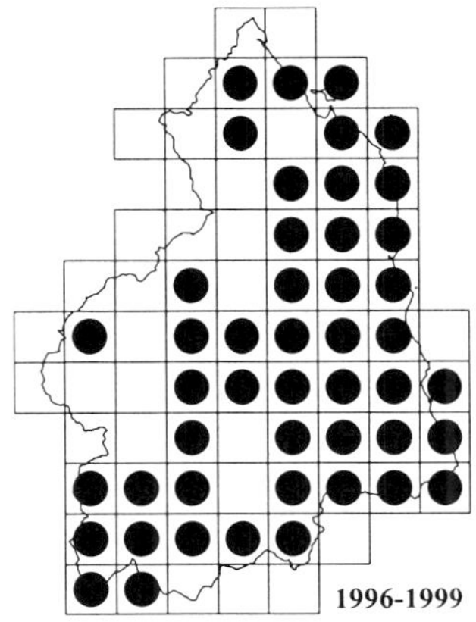

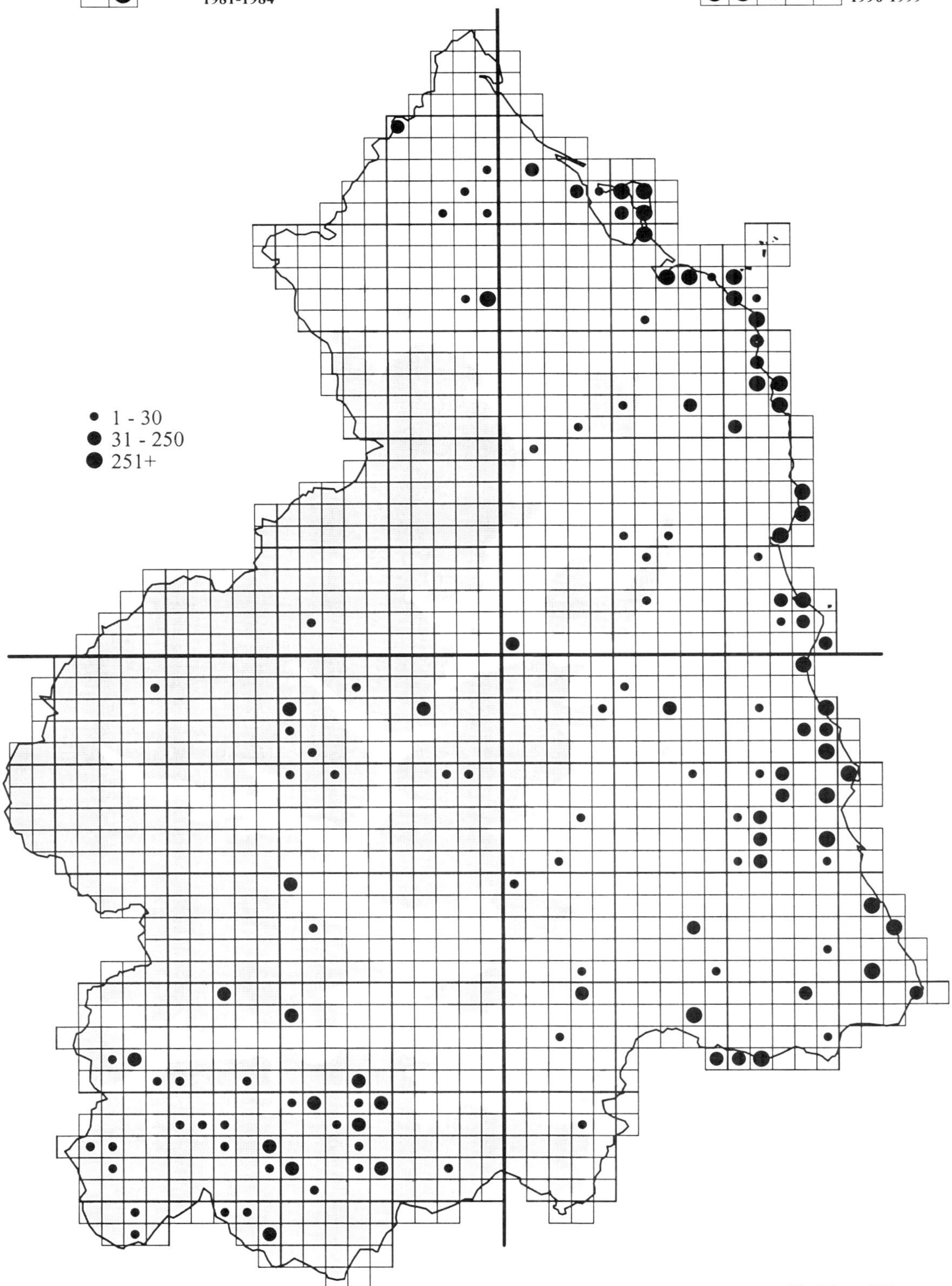

Golden Plover

GREY PLOVER *Pluvialis squatarola*

Unlike most other waders which feed in flocks, Grey Plovers are normally seen rather evenly spaced across the mudflats and similar areas, inclined to vigorously defend their territories. This appears to be a response to its technique of suddenly running forward to snatch unwary small prey items on the surface which would be quickly alerted and vanish if large numbers of feeding birds were involved. These plump robust plovers, which for a brief period after arrival on wintering grounds can sometimes be found in their glorious black and silver breeding plumage, also resort to feeding in coastal fields, again usually well spaced out.

The number of Grey Plovers arriving to winter in Britain from their breeding grounds in western Siberia appears to have fluctuated widely over the past century or so. Bolam (1932) recorded them only in small numbers. Lack (1986) said that the number of Grey Plovers wintering in Britain and Ireland had been increasing steadily since the 1970s, perhaps due to higher breeding success and less pressure from shooting. He believed that there was a wintering population of about 20,000 birds, more than one third of the European wintering total.

Locally, Galloway and Meek (1980), who described its status as a well-represented winter visitor, noted that numbers had increased considerably within the county to give a normal winter population of around 600, mainly centred on the Lindisfarne NNR. Since their assessment, the upward trend has continued with between 1,000 and 1,500 birds being present in some winters, although as many as 4,000 were found in January 1989, most of them at Lindisfarne (Kerr, 2001). Prater (1981) pointed out that Lindisfarne was of national importance for the species, holding over 1% of the British wintering population.

The tetrad map shows clearly the heavy concentrations in the Lindisfarne NNR around Holy Island, Fenham Flats and Budle Bay during the current survey and the generally small numbers occurring elsewhere along the coast. The species appears to be strictly confined to the coast, apart from the two individuals which strayed short distances inland in the south east corner of the recording area to the River Tyne at Scotswood (NZ26B) and Big Waters (NZ27G).

During the period of the current survey there was a peak of 2,950 at Lindisfarne in February 1998 (Cranswick *et al.*, 1999), indicating that the total counts revealed by the current atlas survey fieldwork show an underestimate of the possible peak winter population. Further evidence about the vital importance of Lindisfarne for the species was reinforced by the fact that during the same period fewer than 100 Grey Plovers were found along the entire coastline from Tynemouth to Berwick. Away from Lindisfarne, the only other significantly important local area for the species is the stretch of coastline between Alnmouth (NU21K), Boulmer (NU21S) and Howick (NU21T) where Grey Plovers have regularly wintered for many years, often moving on to coastal fields at high tide, enabling very accurate counts to be made. A peak of 154 was found during a WeBS count along this stretch in January 1998.

The distribution map indicates that during the current survey the species was found in a total of 48 tetrads, all but two of them on the coast, while the two smaller 10km square maps show there has been no change in the wintering areas being exploited by Grey Plovers since 1981-1984 and the species' status is that of a common winter visitor.

IAN KERR

No. of tetrads in which recorded	48 (3%)
Tetrad Analysis	**No. of tetrads**
1-5 birds	23 (48%)
6-80 birds	16 (33%)
81+ birds	9 (19%)
Total No. of birds counted	1,999

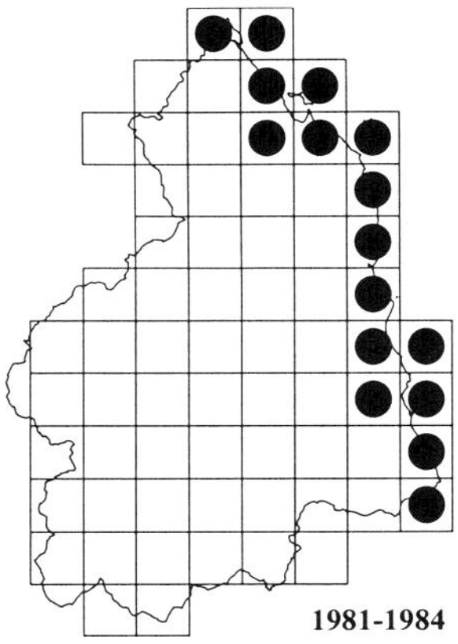

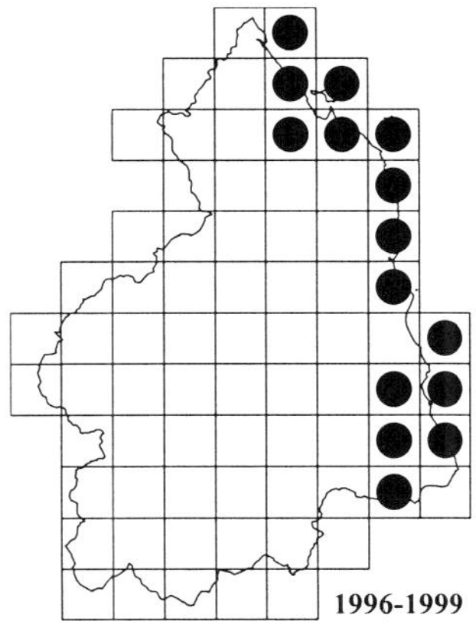

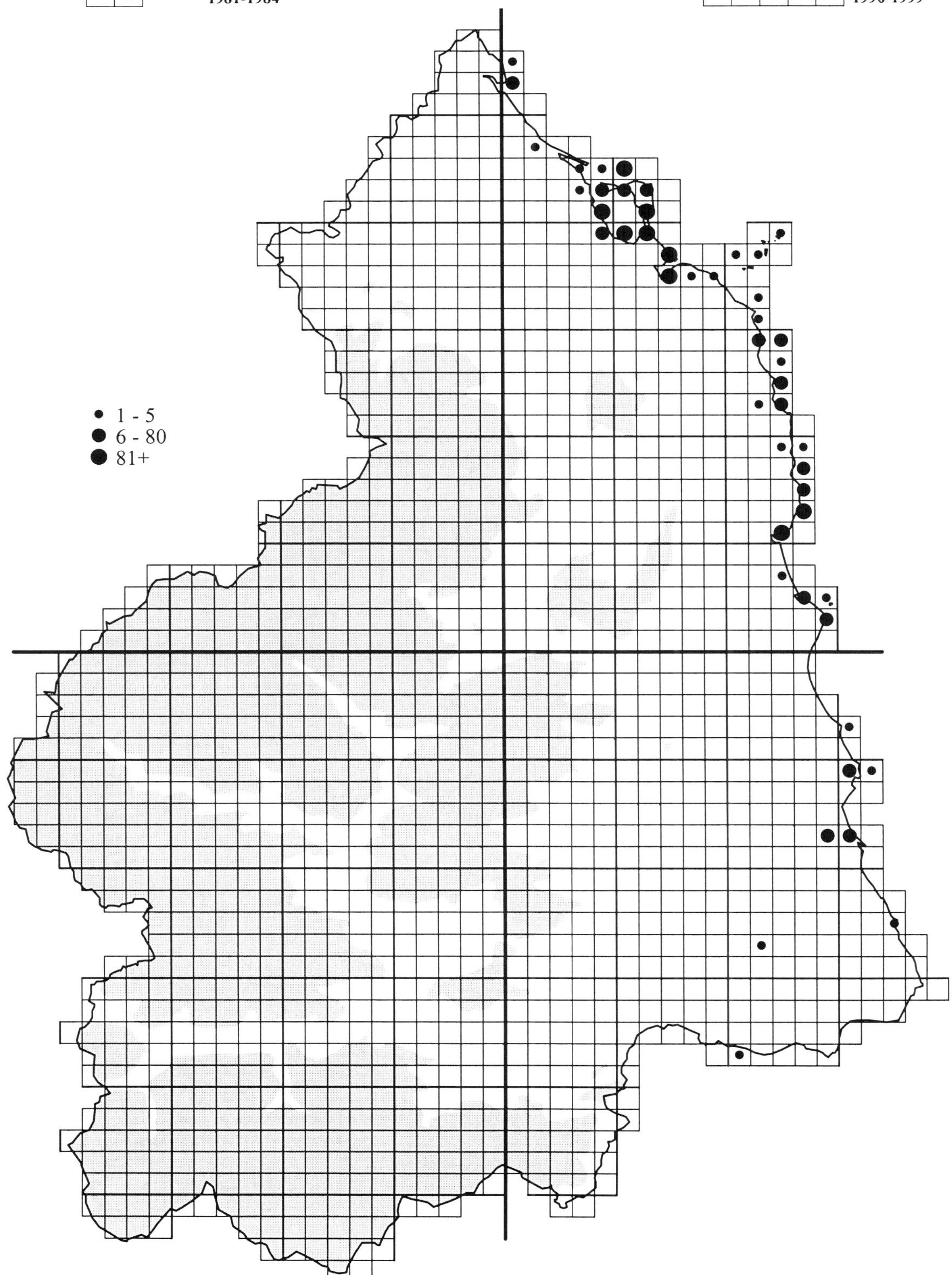

Grey Plover

LAPWING *Vanellus vanellus*

The Lapwing is the most widespread of Britain's waders, exploiting both coastal and inland habitats during winter for worms and other invertebrates, often feeding in association with Golden Plover *Pluvialis apricaria* and Black-headed Gull *Larus ridibundus*, the latter lurking to rob both of their food. Large flocks of these highly gregarious and distinctively plumaged birds are common throughout most of the country, a situation which appears to have continued for a long time.

Hancock (1874) and Bolam (1932) reported the species as common everywhere although, more recently, concern about a national decrease has been voiced over the past two decades (Marchant *et al.*, 1990) with agricultural changes being blamed for a decline in breeding success. The latter authors believed southern areas of Britain were worst affected and it was generally assumed that populations in northern areas were more stable. However, work in 1998 indicated a 43% decline in breeding pairs within Northumberland, a worrying indication that the region had fared little better than the rest of Britain (Cadwallender & Cadwallender, 1999).

Despite that concern, the tetrad map clearly confirms that Lapwings continue to exploit a wide range of winter habitats. Counts during the current survey showed a total maximum count of over 42,000 individuals in 273 tetrads. The vast majority of flocks were found either along the coast or in the eastern lowland half of the county on land up to 200 metres a.s.l. where they were exploiting both pasture and arable farmland. However, there were also 28 occupied tetrads lying between 201-300 metres a.s.l., eight between 301-400 metres and even three occupied areas in the 401-500 metres band, demonstrating the ability of the species to find food even in very harsh environments, provided the land remains without snow cover or frozen. The map shows that flocks were absent, as would be expected, only from the heavily forested areas and some of the highest and most inhospitable uplands of the west and north west, although some were still found in valleys in those localities. Most of those which did frequent higher ground were mainly in the south west where the base-rich substrate and a consequently higher density of invertebrate prey is more readily available than in other upland areas.

The two 10km square maps document some contraction in the wintering range of Lapwings since 1981-1984, particularly along the western side of the county. It is tempting to speculate that this decline fits in neatly with the findings of Cadwallender & Cadwallender with a lower overall Lapwing population withdrawing from some areas. However, when these numbers are considered, the vast majority of our wintering Lapwings are clearly immigrants. Lack (1986) believed that most were of Scandinavian, Dutch and German origin. He commented on the difficulties of establishing numbers because of the high mobility of Lapwings in response to feeding and weather conditions but considered the wintering population must be 1,000,000 or more. Local mobility is confirmed by data from control tetrads in this survey with numbers fluctuating considerably from year to year e.g. at Warkworth (NU20M) with counts of 1,210, 310 and 86 respectively over the three winter seasons. Rather surprisingly for such a common species, there are few records of large numbers arriving from the east in autumn, apart from a wholly exceptional movement of 20,000 arriving over St Mary's Island during a three-hour period in late October 1956 (Galloway & Meek, 1980).

During the current survey the single largest concentration was of 3,187 birds at the Lindisfarne NNR in December 1998 with other counts of 1,000-2,000 at Wallsend (NZ36E), Walbottle (NZ16T), Scotswood (NZ26B), Blyth (NZ28W), Woodhorn (NZ28Z), Druridge Pools (NZ29T), Boulmer (NU21S) and the Coquet Estuary (NU20M). The survey has shown that the Lapwing, despite the recent concerns about a decline, remains one of our most abundant winter visitors.

IAN KERR

Distribution by altitude

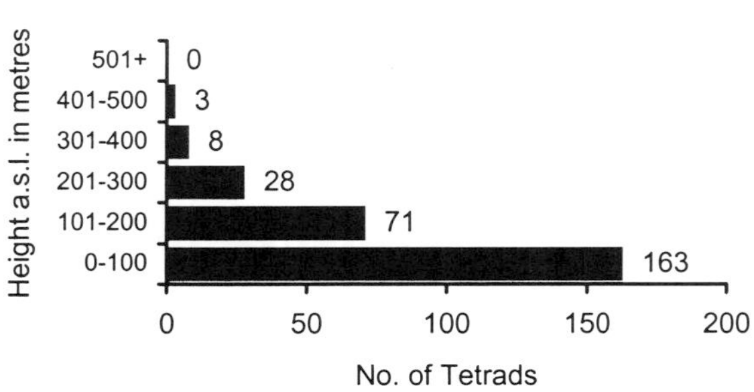

No. of tetrads in which recorded 273 (19%)

Tetrad Analysis	No. of tetrads
1-40 birds	135 (49%)
41-220 birds	85 (32%)
221+ birds	53 (19%)

Total No. of birds counted 42,360

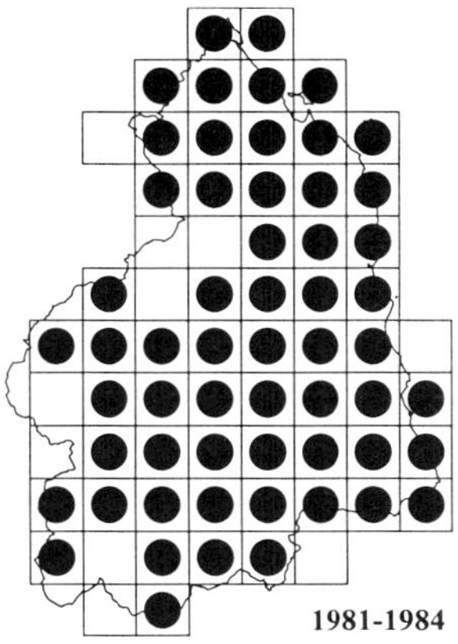

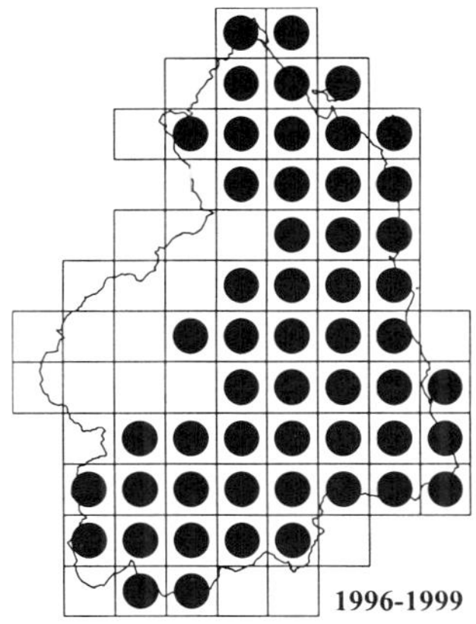

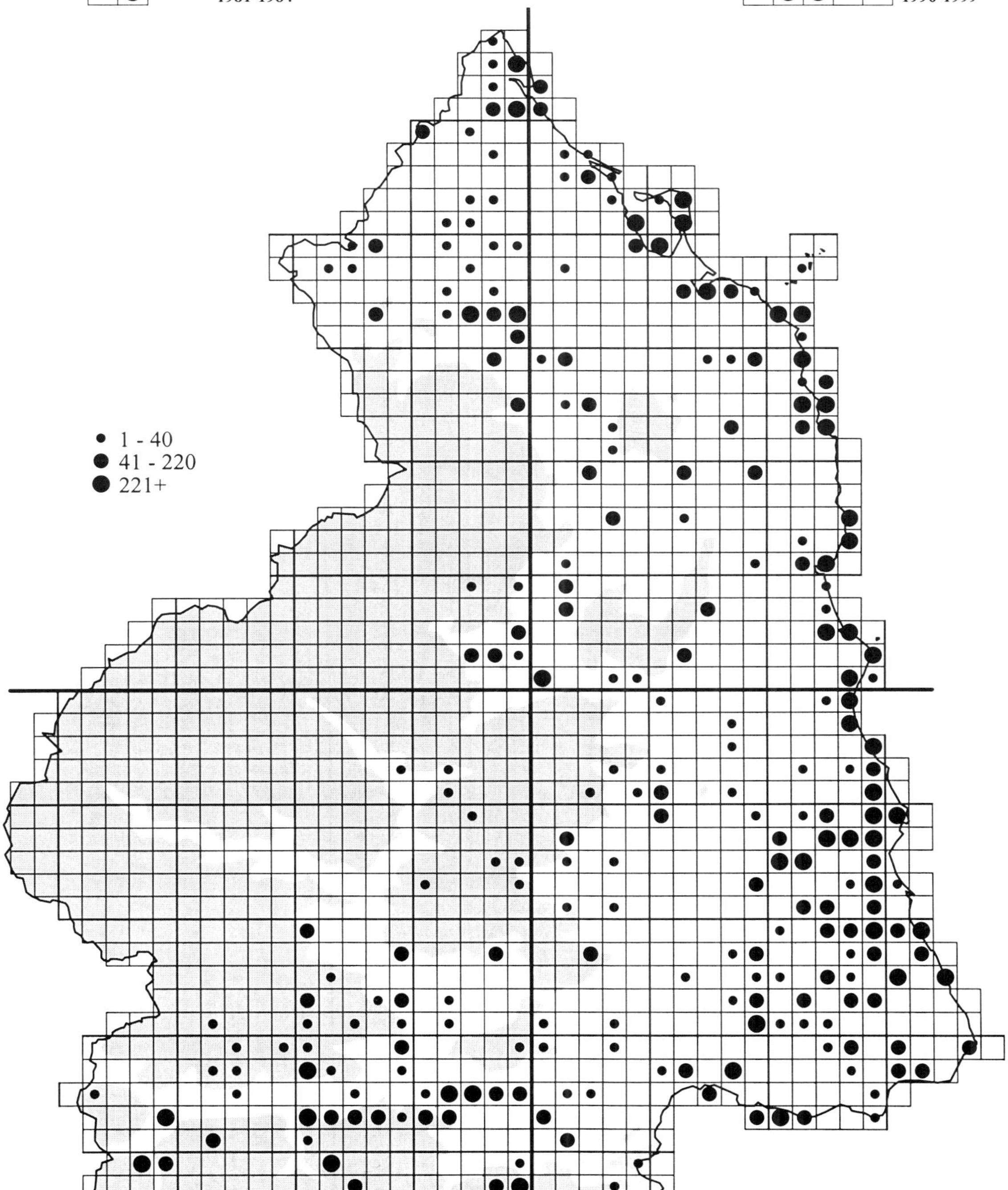

Lapwing

KNOT *Calidris canutus*

Lack (1986), in *The atlas of wintering birds in Britain and Ireland*, found the Knot to be widely dispersed in mid-winter and the current winter survey certainly confirmed a similar situation in the county. Galloway and Meek (1980) classified the Knot in Northumberland as an 'abundant passage and winter visitor' and, although acknowledging that spring passage seemed less conspicuous, confirmed that its status was much the same as that reported by Bolam (1932) who had commented that 'huge flocks' often arrived in October and November. Galloway and Meek further described the winter maxima at Lindisfarne NNR as having risen from 3,000-5,000 in the late 1940s and early 1950s to a normal 8,000-10,000 with, in 1974, a peak count of 14,500. The Seaton Sluice-St Mary's Island area was also identified as an important wintering locality with upwards of 1,000 present in most winters and 2,000 in early 1973. Up to 500 could also be found at other sites along the coast.

The majority of Knot wintering on the north east coast originate from Greenland and eastern Canada and nationally are supplemented by birds arriving in late winter from European wintering grounds before making their return journey to Iceland and the Arctic breeding areas. Signs of declining numbers were described by Lack (1986) who showed successive Birds of Estuaries Enquiry results in Britain and Ireland as 400,000 in 1971/72 falling to 230,000 in 1973/74. Poor breeding success was considered responsible. The WeBS report for 1998/99 (Pollitt *et al.*, 2000) indicates that the annual index for Knot fell to the lowest level for 15 years, with a Great Britain maximum of 234,978 birds.

The current winter survey revealed that Knot are still widely distributed along the Northumbrian coast, being found in all suitable areas. Outside the breeding season the Knot is gregarious by nature, having a specialised feeding requirement, predominantly in the intertidal zone on a small range of invertebrates, chiefly molluscs such as *Macoma* but also worms and crustaceans (Lack, 1986; Cramp, 1983). Although much reduced in numbers locally, their winter distribution may indicate that there are still suitable feeding areas along the whole county coastline. The main wintering site remains the Lindisfarne NNR and the peak count during the current survey was 4,625 in January 1997, with further totals of 4,540 in February 1997 and 4,040 in December 1998 being the only counts in the county above 4,000. Additional synchronised counts at this site, during January and December 1998, produced totals of 2,207 and 2,452 birds respectively, thus reinforcing the generally low levels. Although the survey identified a three-year maximum count of 11,788 wintering birds, the peak county total during the same period revealed by coastal WeBS counts reached only 5,542 in January 1997. The 1% threshold figure for a site of international importance is 3,500 birds and Lindisfarne is slightly above this, with an average of 3,543 during the five winters up to 1998-99.

Away from the main stronghold there were several counts of more than 500 birds, usually at what have historically been good sites. Some 500 were on the Aln Estuary (NU21K) and at Bondicarr (NU20V), 825 at Cresswell (NZ29W), 600 at Newbiggin (NZ38E), 561 at a North Blyth high-tide roost (NZ38B), 950 at Seaton Sluice (NZ37I) and 500 at St Mary's Island (NZ37M). The tetrad distribution map shows that much smaller numbers were in fact found in all but one 10km square along the coast. Indeed, there was even one inland record involving a single bird at Big Waters (NZ27G) on 1 January 1997. However, the winter status of Knot in Northumberland should now be considered as that of a common visitor reflecting the recent decline in numbers.

STEVE HOLLIDAY

No. of tetrads in which recorded	40 (3%)
Tetrad Analysis	**No. of tetrads**
1-60 birds	20 (50%)
61-500 birds	13 (32%)
501+ birds	7 (18%)
Total No. of birds counted	11,788

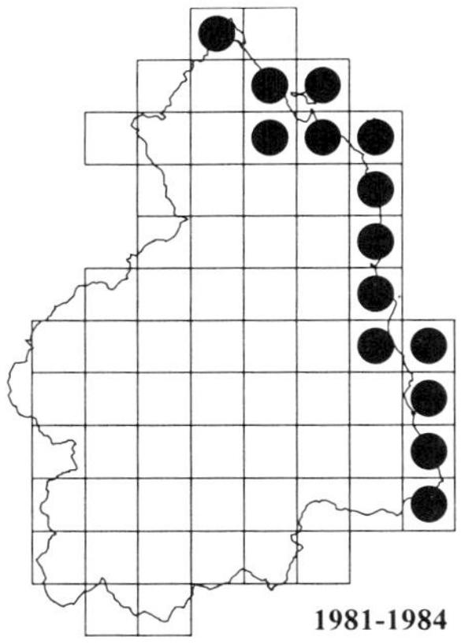

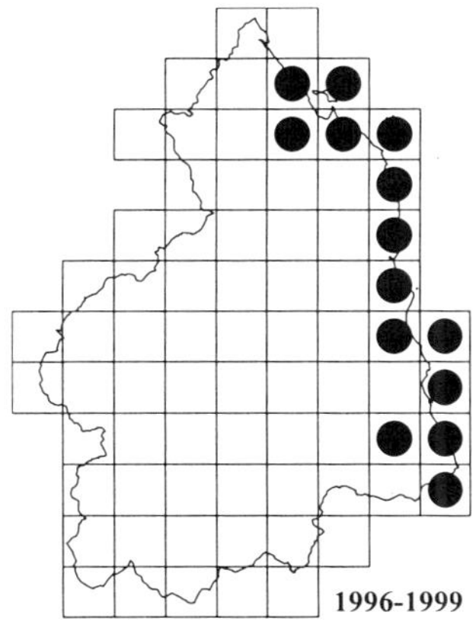

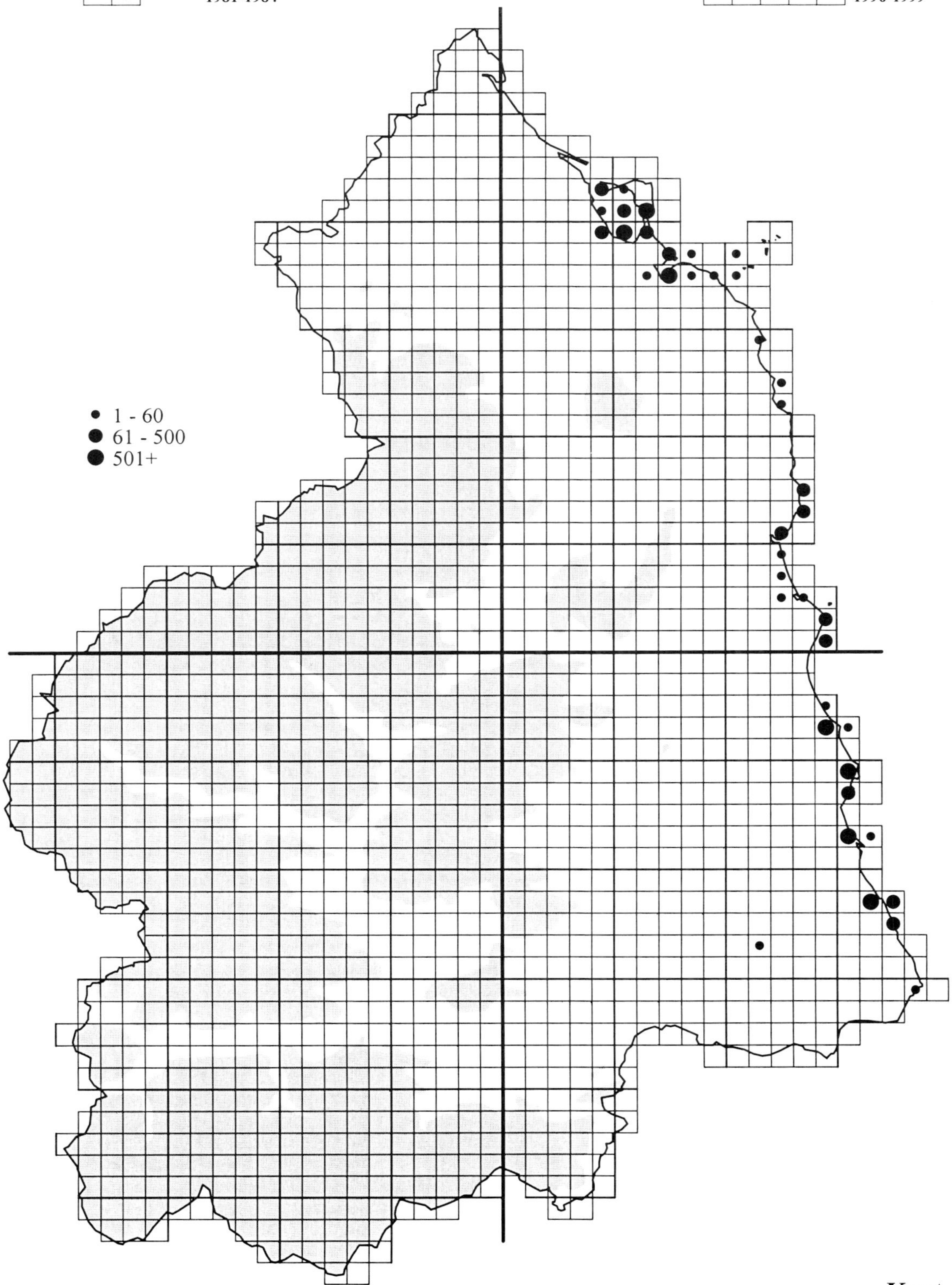

Knot

SANDERLING *Calidris alba*

The sparkling white plumage and clockwork-like following of the waves make this species a favourite of birdwatchers and non-birdwatchers alike. Their constant running is, of course, food-related and where it is abundant large groups of Sanderling can congregate. When following the tideline in this manner, they are seeking out small shrimp-like crustaceans *Bathyporeia* spp. and *Eurydice pulchra*. At other times their food may consist of small polychaete worms, such as *Nerine cirratulus* which is found within estuaries, or tiny mussels at low water and wrack-flies and sandhoppers at high water (Lack, 1986). Their preference for this type of food and associated habitat means that, within Britain, very few if any are found along cliff-bound shorelines, and consequently the north east coast of England provides an ideal wintering area. Although there are two main breeding populations, in Siberia and Greenland, the origins of the birds wintering in Britain are surprisingly still not certain, though believed to be primarily from the former area (Lack, 1986).

The Sanderling is a very familiar shorebird in the county at the present time, though this was not always the case. In the first half of the twentieth century Bolam (1932) considered it chiefly a passage migrant, with only a few remaining in winter. Galloway and Meek (1980) suggested a wintering population of around 350 with a count of 500 at Lindisfarne NNR in February 1948 being exceptional. The current winter survey, however, confirms the status, noted in *Birds in Northumbria 1999* as a well-represented winter visitor.

The 1981-1984 ten kilometre square map shows the species was found in 14 squares compared with 13 in the current county winter atlas survey and there is no significant difference in distribution between the two. Whilst the current survey shows total maximum counts of 1,701 birds along the coastline in the three winters, the peak monthly WeBS count during the period was only 758 in December 1998, with other high counts being 481 in November 1997, 449 in January 1998 and 488 in November 1998. Prater and Davies (1978) reported about 10,000 birds wintering in Britain and with winter counts remaining around average levels, despite marked fluctuations between years, (Pollitt *et al.*, 2000) the wintering numbers in Northumberland remain a significant percentage of the national population.

A more detailed look at the results of the current survey reveals a presence scattered all along the Northumberland coastline, although with some obviously favoured areas. The large expanses of beach in the Lindisfarne area hold particularly good numbers. However, totals here can vary, as demonstrated by counts from the control tetrad at Holy island (NU14G) with 250 in 1996/97, none in 1997/98 and 14 in 1998/99 and in the additional Lindisfarne NNR synchronised counts totalled only 36 in January 1998 and 156 in December 1998. A separate WeBS count at Lindisfarne NNR gave a total of 292 in January 1998. To the south of this stronghold are several other favoured stretches of coastline and during the survey period there were peaks of 85 at Low Newton (NU22M), 63 in Druridge Bay (NZ29U), 200 in the Cresswell area (NZ29W) and 140 at Newbiggin (NZ38E). The generally wide distribution is emphasised by the fact that there were ten other sites along the coast where more than 30 birds were found.

STEVE HOLLIDAY

No. of tetrads in which recorded 38 (3%)

Tetrad Analysis	No. of tetrads
1-20 birds	18 (47%)
21-60 birds	12 (32%)
61+ birds	8 (21%)

Total No. of birds counted 1,701

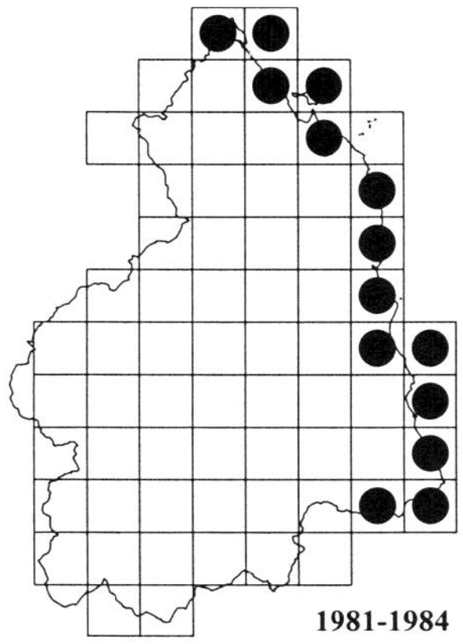

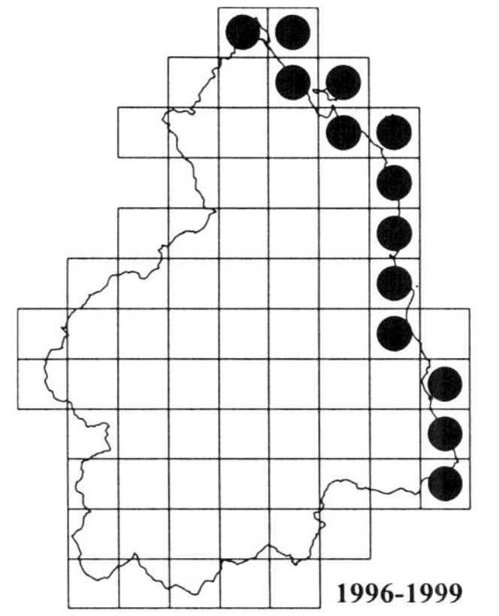

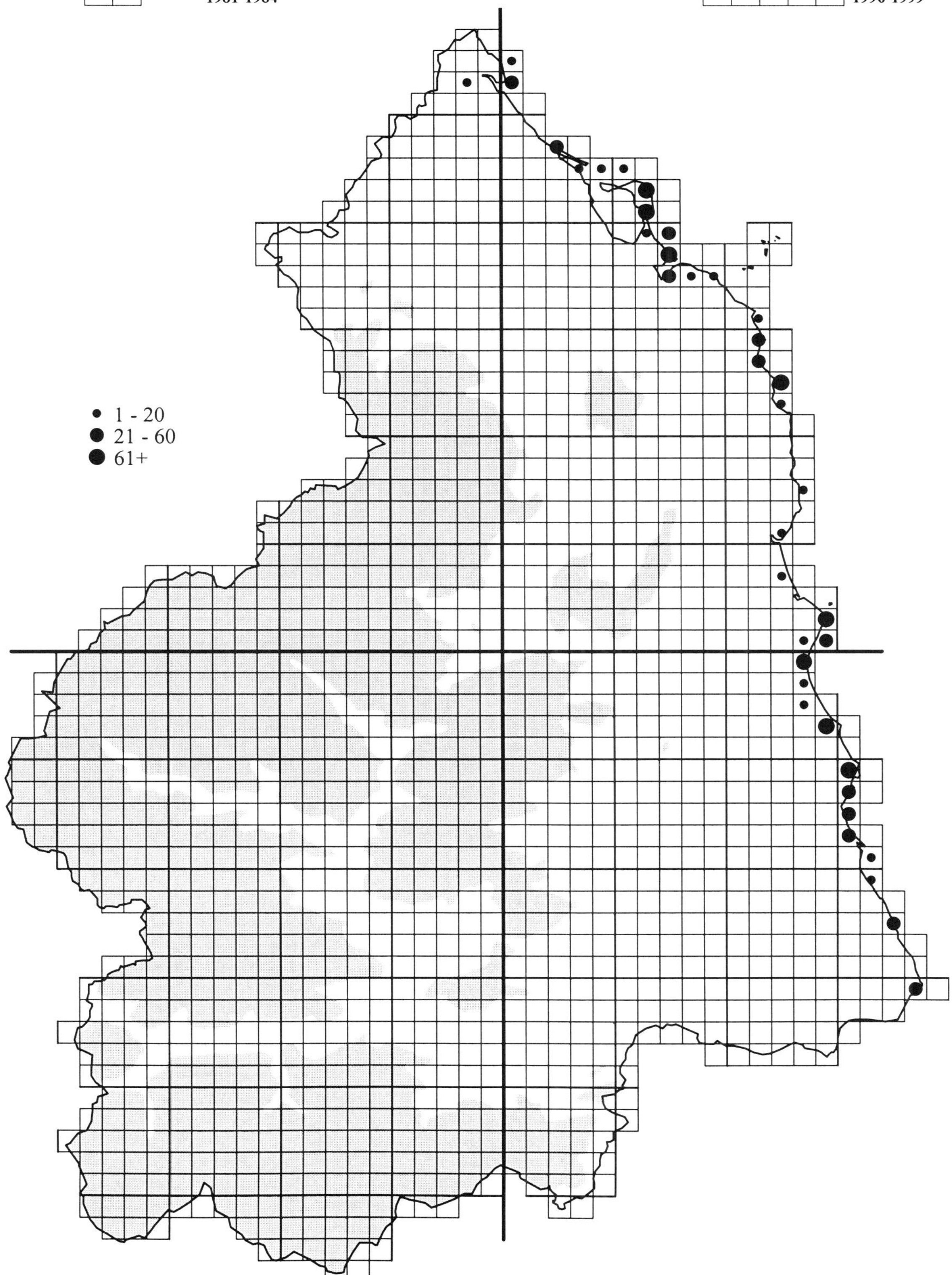

Sanderling

PURPLE SANDPIPER *Calidris maritima*

The Purple Sandpiper is almost exclusively maritime in winter. In the mid-nineteenth century Selby (1831) described it as 'common upon all our rocky shores. A winter visitant'. In 1912, Bolam considered that its status was virtually unchanged over the last 100 years and, more recently, Galloway and Meek (1980) reported it as a well-represented winter visitor with 480 present between Berwick and Tynemouth in February 1976.

The breeding distribution of Purple Sandpiper is from western Canada to central Russia and Eaton (2000) reports that our wintering birds come from two populations, a large, long-billed population, probably from arctic Canada, and a smaller, short-billed population from Greenland, Norway and Svalbard. Biometric data indicates that around 70% of our birds are of the short-billed race. The total east Atlantic winter population is estimated at 50,000 birds, with around 23,000 in Great Britain.

The tetrad map shows that the Purple Sandpiper has a discontinuous distribution along the county's coastline, being almost entirely dependent on rocky shorelines. The only surprise on the 10km square maps is the absence of records of birds at Cresswell (NZ29W), Boulmer (NU21R/S) and adjacent to the Scottish border (NT95X/Y). They feed almost exclusively in rocky areas, extracting periwinkles, dogwhelks, various intertidal snails and mussels and sometimes forage on rotting piles of storm-deposited wrack along the high-tide line. Roosts are at long-established sites such as Blyth East Pier (NZ38F) and Stag Rocks at Bamburgh (NU13S), and colour ringing studies have shown high site fidelity both within winters and from winter to winter (Atkinson *et al.*, 1978). One shift in population distribution from the time of Galloway and Meek appears to be from the previously favoured St. Mary's Island (NZ37M) as a roost and feeding area to Blyth East Pier and the adjacent rocky outcrops. Disturbance at St. Mary's Island has been suggested as the cause of the shift (Eaton, 2000).

The total number of 1,464 birds counted, being the sum of peak counts over the three winters of the atlas period, is probably an overestimate of the county's population. The actual population is mainly concentrated at three favoured areas, Stag Rocks at Bamburgh, the Farne Islands and Blyth East Pier. These three areas probably hold around 450-700 birds in mid-winter. A further 50-100 birds are thinly scattered along the entire coast on rocky outcrops. This suggests the true county population reaches a winter level in the region of 500-800 birds. Since this figure includes an estimate for birds on the Farnes, it appears that the population has not changed substantially since its assessment in the 1970s by Galloway and Meek (1980). Because the Purple Sandpiper is not well monitored by WeBS counts there are no national population indices available. Two specifically open-coast surveys have however been carried out, the 1984/85 Winter Shorebird Count and the 1997/98 Non-Estuarine Waterbird Survey. These indicated a decrease of 20.1% between surveys but it is unclear whether this apparent national decline has been reflected within the county.

As a result of the numbers of wintering Purple Sandpiper, together with those of Turnstone *Arenaria interpres* (and breeding Little Tern *Sterna albifrons*), the Government has now designated the rocky sections of the Northumberland and Durham coastlines between Spittal and Blackhall Rocks in Co. Durham as a Special Protection Area for Birds and a Wetland of International Importance under the Ramsar Convention. This area, with over 750 birds, holds about 1.6% of the wintering East Atlantic Flyway population. More than half of that occurs north of the Tyne in the area covered by this atlas. The habitat in our area for Purple Sandpiper now has appropriate levels of protection and the future for the species in the county will lie in other factors such as breeding success, or in global warming which may enable these birds to winter nearer their breeding areas.

ROGER NORMAN

No. of tetrads in which recorded 34 (2%)

Tetrad Analysis	No. of tetrads
1-16 birds	17 (50%)
17-45 birds	10 (29%)
46+ birds	7 (21%)

Total No. of birds counted 1,464

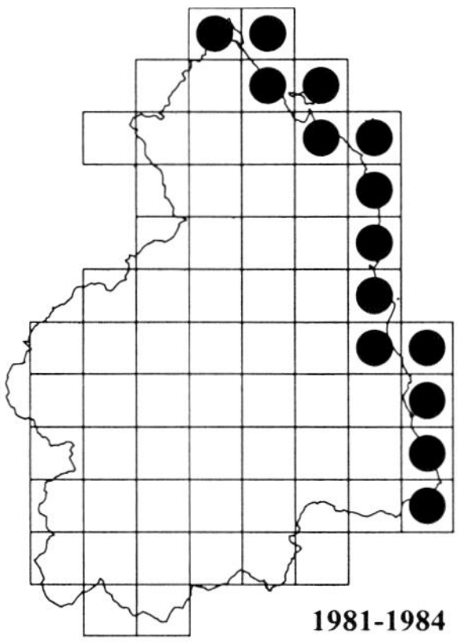

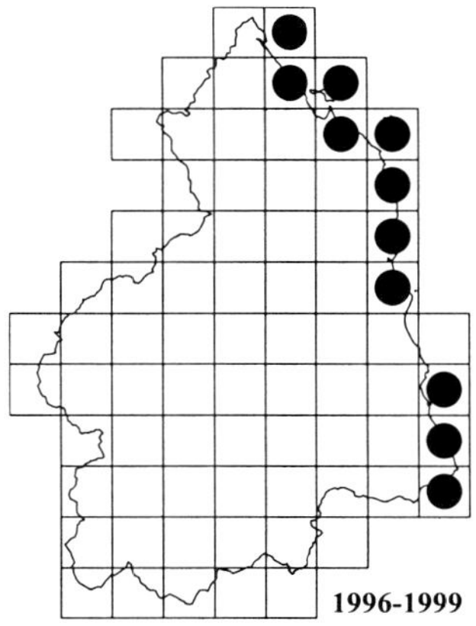

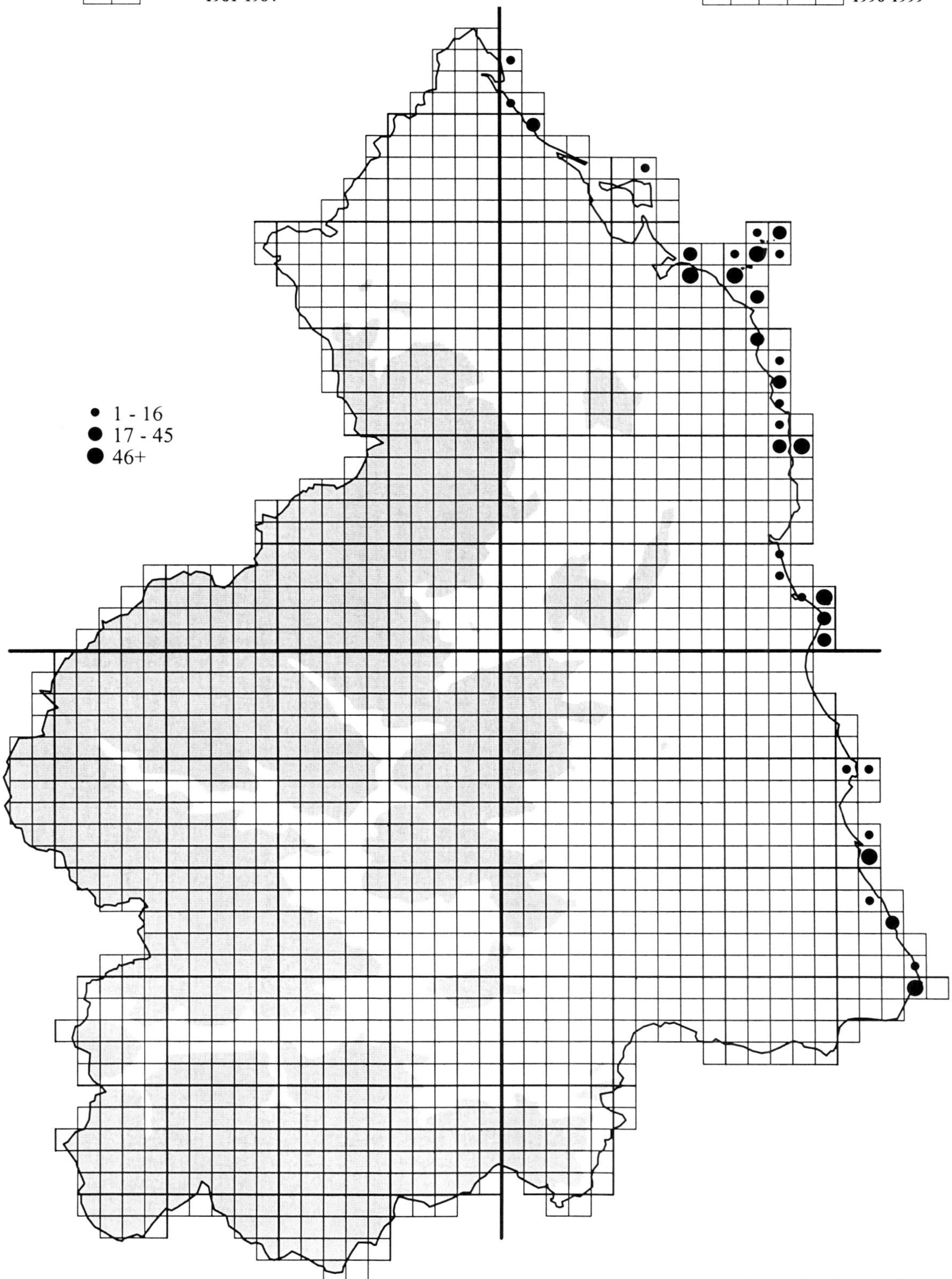

Purple Sandpiper

DUNLIN *Calidris alpina*

The Dunlin is our commonest small wader in winter. Bolam (1912) commented that 'In autumn and winter, the flocks on Fenham Flats are often beyond estimate'. The same is probably true today, although now we attempt to put numbers to such observations. Galloway and Meek (1980) reported that it was abundant, with the main wintering population at the Lindisfarne NNR where it reached an exceptional 31,700 in December 1978, and that in most years about 2,000 are also present between Budle Point and Tynemouth.

The Dunlin is a circumpolar species breeding mostly in the Arctic but also at lower latitudes in Western Europe. Our wintering birds, *C. a. alpina*, derive from northern Scandinavia and Russia, with the races *C. a. arctica*, (breeding in north-east Greenland) and *C. a. schinzii*, (breeding in Britain, south east Greenland, Iceland, the Baltic and the Netherlands), occurring on passage. Some areas, including the east coast of England, both gain and lose birds through the winter as moulted birds, many from the Waddensee, move westwards in October and November followed by eastward movement between February and April (Pienkowski & Pienkowski, 1983). For *C. a. alpina*, the wintering population in Great Britain is estimated at 530,000 out of a total European population of 1,400,000.

The 10km square maps show very little change over the fifteen years or so between the 1981-1984 national winter atlas survey (Lack, 1986) and this current survey. The tetrad map shows that Dunlin are almost completely maritime in winter with the main population concentrated at Lindisfarne which holds around 83% of the county's population. Apart from Lindisfarne, it is also present on almost all muddy areas of our coast with a few often feeding with Sanderling *C. alba* and Ringed Plover *Charadrius hiaticula* on sandy beaches and rocky outcrops. The map also indicates the tendency to use coastal ponds immediately behind the high tideline and coastal dunes, either for high tide roosting or for feeding. The favoured feeding areas are, however, on muddy stretches where small invertebrates can be found. Within each seasonally used area, individual birds tend to be faithful to particular sites both within and between years (Symonds *et al.*, 1984).

The total of 12,878 birds counted during the three winter periods of the survey would seem to be at the top end of estimates for the county's population when compared to the monthly WeBS counts. Those counts suggest that the winter population fluctuates between 5,000 and 12,500 with about 4,000 to 10,000 at Lindisfarne. The early years of systematic counting indicated an average peak at Lindisfarne of 14,000 (Prater, 1981), so clearly there has been a decrease at this site. A study of the figures for the other sites along the coast suggests a similar decrease. This would appear to be approximately in line with the UK population index, which reached its highest value of 140 in 1973/74, (1998/99=100) (Pollitt *et al.*, 2000). Despite this decrease, and other fluctuations in the index since 1973/74, there is no clear national long-term trend apparent since 1970/71 when the index started.

Although the numbers at Lindisfarne have declined since the late 1970s, the locality still holds a five-year peak average of 8,578 birds which indicates that it is a site of national importance for Dunlin, the threshold value being 5,300 (Pollitt *et al.*, 2000). With suitable protection in place at Lindisfarne and along the rest of our coast, the future for Dunlin lies in long-term factors outside the county, such as breeding success and coastal squeeze at its wintering sites due to sea-level rise.

ROGER NORMAN

Distribution by altitude

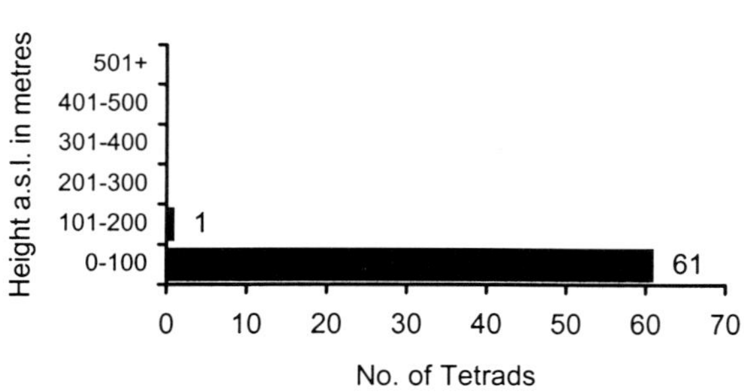

No. of tetrads in which recorded 62 (4%)

Tetrad Analysis	No. of tetrads
1-60 birds	31 (50%)
61-300 birds	19 (31%)
301+ birds	12 (19%)

Total No. of birds counted 12,878

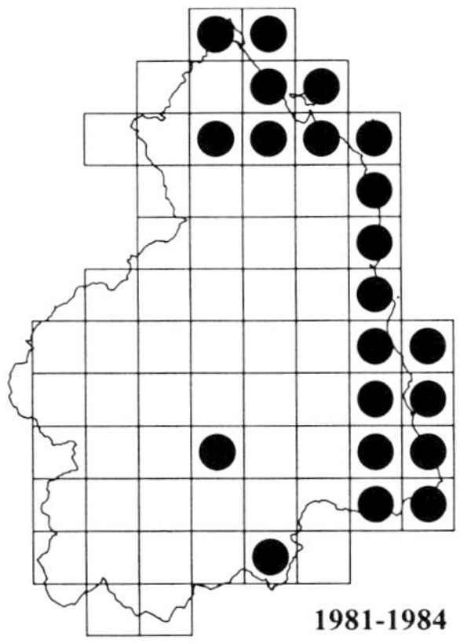

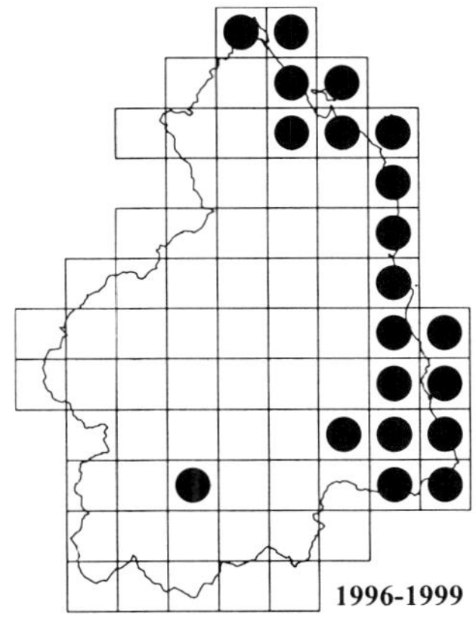

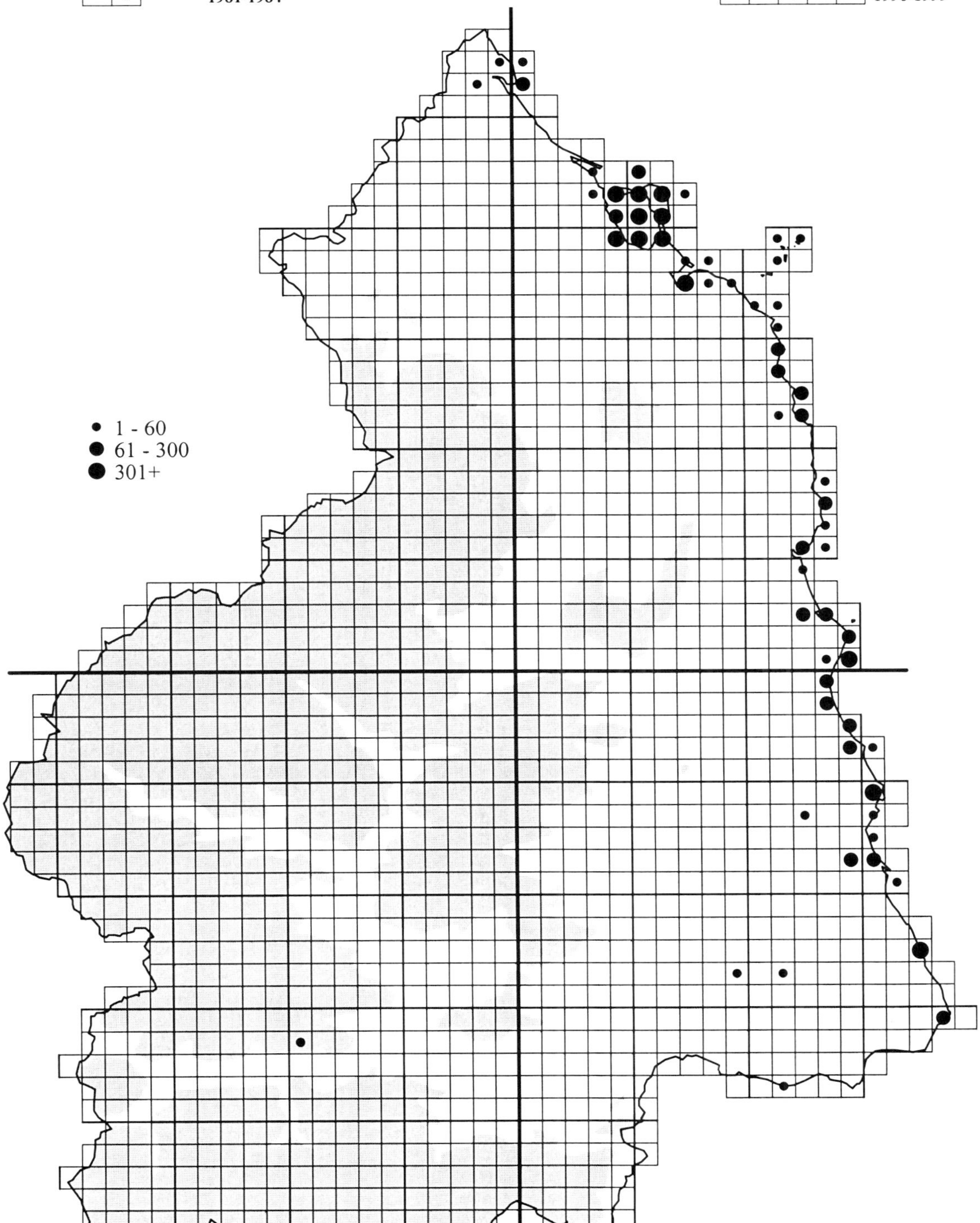

Dunlin

RUFF *Philomachus pugnax*

The Ruff was first found wintering in Britain in 1934/35, since when numbers have shown a steady increase. The 1981-1984 national winter atlas survey estimated a maximum British and Irish wintering population of about 1,400 birds with the main concentrations along the south coast and the eastern side of England. Further north, the Firth of Forth was the only regular site in Scotland, with other birds occurring infrequently on both Scottish coasts (Lack, 1986). Birds wintering in Northumberland are at the northern edge of their normal wintering range, not only in Britain but also in Europe. The county's first wintering Ruff appeared from 1971/72, being particularly noticeable in the Budle Bay-Monk's House Pool area where up to 14 could be found in the November to February period before the pool was drained (Galloway & Meek, 1980).

In Northumberland the species is regarded as an uncommon winter visitor, a status which is reinforced by the findings from the current winter atlas survey. Although found in four 10km squares in the survey, compared to six 10km squares in the 1981-1984 national winter atlas survey, there appears to be a slight upward trend in wintering numbers. The 1980s saw no more than eight birds in any winter, whereas 14 to 24 were reported in most winters during the 1990s.

The distribution map shows birds present in five tetrads with a maximum total of 28 individuals over the three winter periods. Although often found near the coast, the species is not an estuary bird, preferring to feed in flooded fields and wetlands. Short-term changes in conditions in the latter habitat, however, can mean that Ruff may be quite mobile at a local level. Such conditions are present in the Druridge Bay-Cresswell Pond area (NZ29T & NZ29X), where the current survey confirmed some 12 to 15 birds during each of the three winters, making it without doubt the county stronghold. Indeed, outside this survey some 30 birds were in this area during January 2001.

Away from this main site, the survey produced singles at three other locations namely, Fenham Mill (NU04V), on the River Tyne at Blaydon (NZ16W) and at Prestwick Carr (NZ17W). The latter site is particularly interesting as this represents the last definite breeding area in the county, prior to its draining in 1857 (Galloway & Meek, 1980). The largest ever flock in the county also occurred at Prestwick Carr with 150 in September 1986, although the favoured Druridge Bay area has since come close with 146 in September 1992 and 111 at nearby East Chevington in August 2000 (*Birds in Northumbria 1986, 1992 & 2000*).

STEVE HOLLIDAY

No. of tetrads in which recorded	5 (<1%)

Tetrad Analysis	No. of tetrads
1 bird	3 (60%)
2+ birds	2 (40%)

Total No. of birds counted	28

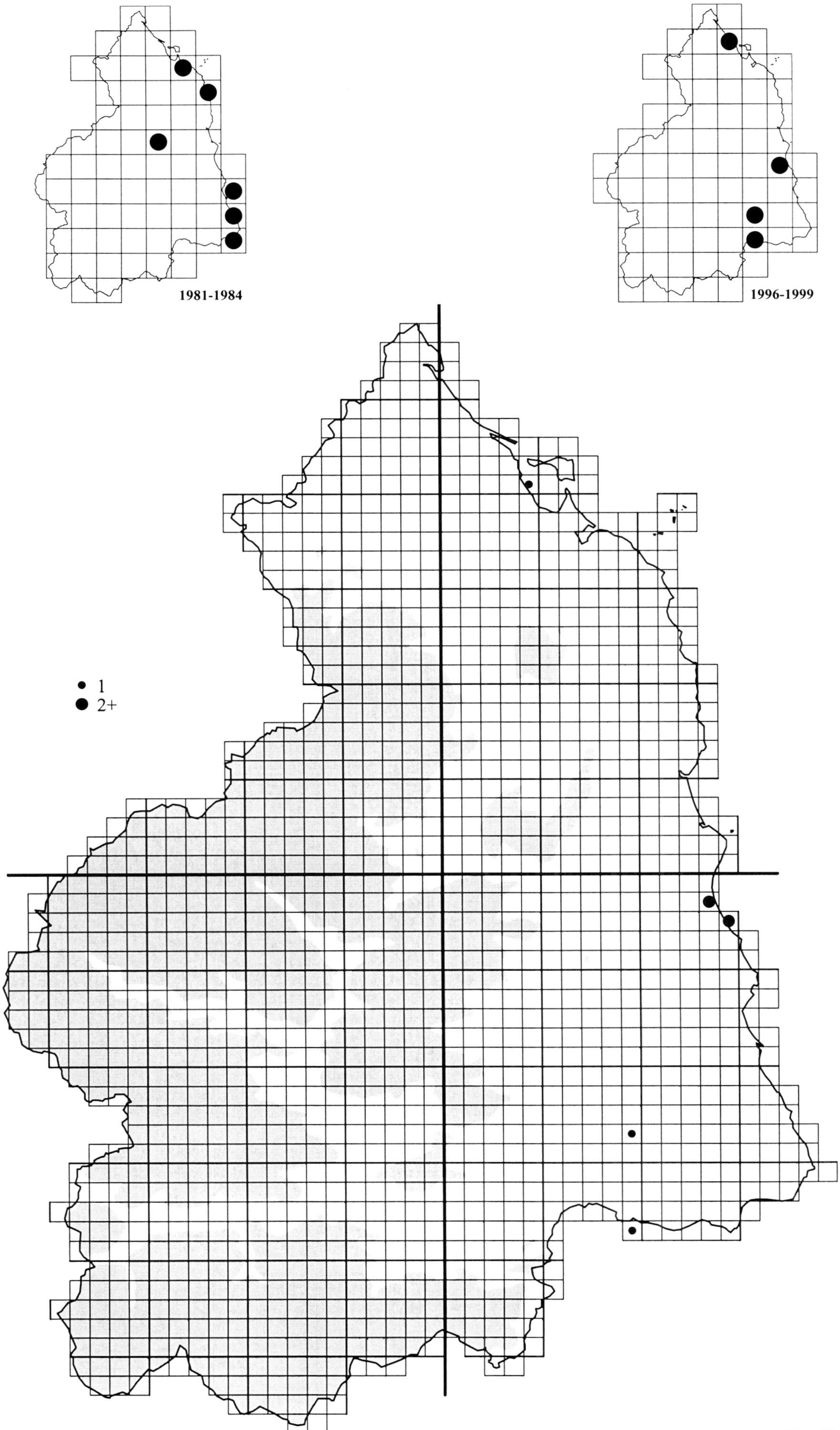

Ruff

JACK SNIPE *Lymnocryptes minimus*

Whilst Jack Snipe is correctly considered to be primarily a winter visitor to this country, its cryptic colouration, unobtrusive and silent nature, and 'difficult to flush' characteristics, make it probably one of the most overlooked and hence, under-recorded species. In addition, it has a preference for shallow, wet and muddy habitats, often with dense grass or low cover, i.e. a habitat not examined without purpose. The 1981-1984 national winter atlas survey considered that the British and Irish winter population may possibly number 100,000 birds, although the fieldwork suggested a much smaller number. There was no obvious geographical bias in Britain although it was shown to be largely absent from moorland and mountainous regions (Lack, 1986).

In Northumberland, the current winter survey found a maximum of 54 Jack Snipe in 19 ten kilometre squares, compared with its presence in 16 ten kilometre squares in the 1981-1984 winter atlas survey. An eastern bias is apparent which reflects the lowland nature of the habitat, all occupied tetrads being below 300 metres a.s.l. Just prior to the winter atlas survey period, a bird was found on moorland at 450 metres a.s.l. in the South Tyne in 1995 (*Birds in Northumbria 1995*). The species is regarded as an uncommon winter visitor, a status reaffirmed by this survey and remaining unchanged from earlier works (Galloway & Meek, 1980; Bolam, 1932). The vast majority of sightings involved single birds although two were noted at the Coquet Estuary (NU20S), Kirkley Mill (NZ17T) and Havannah Reserve (NZ27F) and four at Beal (NU04R). Two exceptional gatherings were found, seven on a limestone spring stream near Colwell (NY97S) and 13 at Preston Marsh (NU12X), the latter being a regular wintering haunt and the highest count in the county since 15 were found at Whittle Dene Reservoirs in November 1972. The only other higher count involved 'an unprecedented gathering of fifty at Holystone (presumably the area now known as Wallsend Swallow Pond) on 1 November 1952' (Galloway & Meek, 1980). The last decade produced several other significant counts which have included 11 with 50 Snipe *Gallinago gallinago* at Whiteside Law, near Haltwhistle in December 1990, nine at Whittle Dene Reservoirs in October-November 1991 and eight at Havannah Pond in November 1998 (*Birds in Northumbria 1990, 1991, 1998*).

The current winter survey also revealed singles further inland, in suitable wet habitat at Derwent Reservoir (NY95W & NZ05B), in the Slaley area (NY95X/Y), near Whitfield (NY75Y), Pundershaw (NY78V) and the Teppermoor area on the Roman Wall (NY87Q). Reports from wet moorlands are not without precedent, however, with singles noted on such ground at Sweethope Loughs and near Elsdon Gibbet in 1991 (*Birds in Northumbria 1991*).

Birdwatchers are consciously aware of favoured wintering areas for this species and so too, perhaps, are the birds. Galloway and Meek reported on ringing recoveries suggesting some degree of site fidelity, with one ringed at Bamburgh being caught there two years later while two ringed at Warkworth were retrapped there the following year. Another bird, which was ringed at Seaton Burn (now Big Waters) in December 1983, was also retrapped at the same site in October 1984 (*Birds in Northumbria 1984*).

STEVE HOLLIDAY

Distribution by altitude

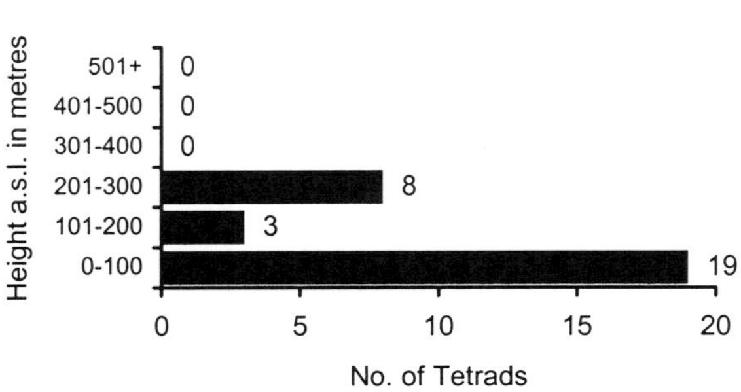

No. of tetrads in which recorded 30 (2%)

Tetrad Analysis	No. of tetrads
1 bird	24 (80%)
2-4 birds	4 (13%)
5+ birds	2 (7%)

Total No. of birds counted 54

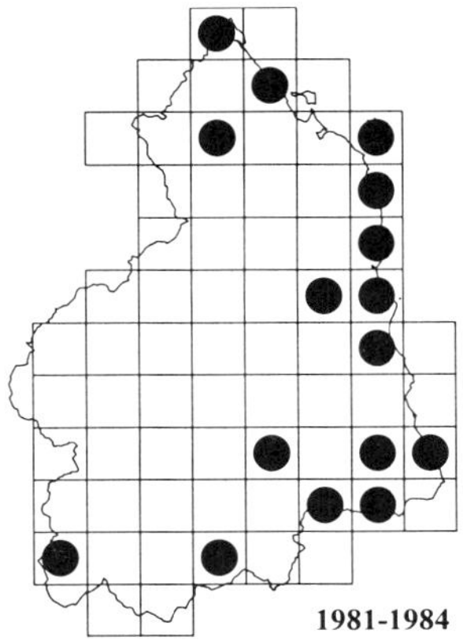

1981-1984

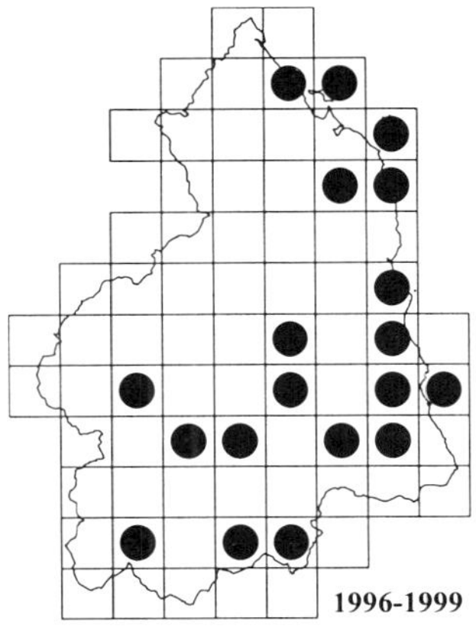

1996-1999

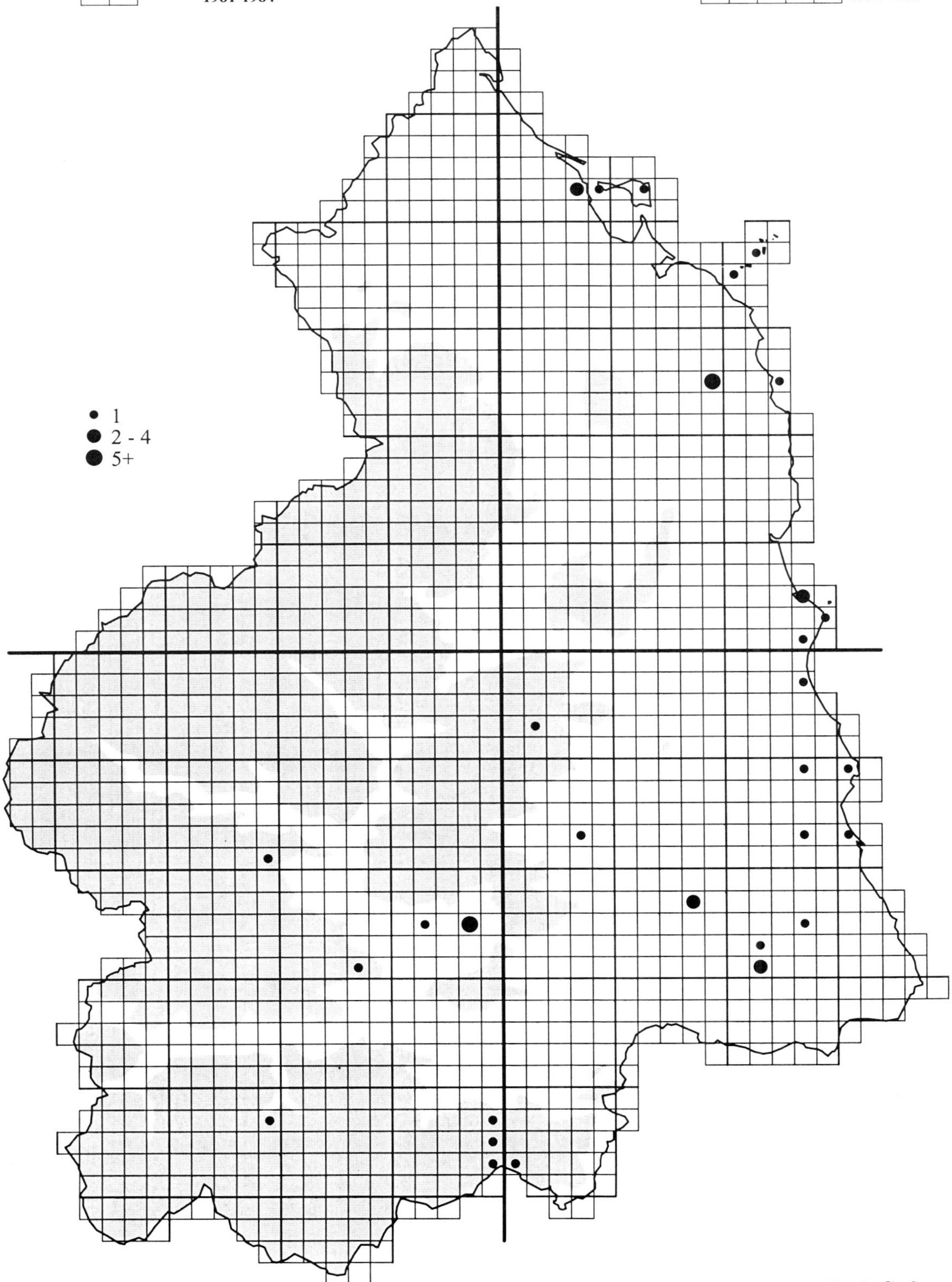

Jack Snipe

SNIPE *Gallinago gallinago*

Bolam (1912) recognised the Snipe as a 'common resident' being particularly numerous in the autumn and Galloway and Meek (1980) implied in their status assessment that between 1,001 and 10,000 birds were present in the county during the winter. Lack (1986) described the preferred winter habitat as 'inland and coastal marshes, bogs and stream sides' and 'temporary small, wet areas'. Such habitat can prevail throughout Northumberland in most years, especially if late autumn is accompanied by significant rainfall, but improved land drainage during the 1970s to support the intensification of arable farming has considerably reduced the choice that was once available.

Lack also quantified a staggering 20-30 million passing through north west Europe in late summer and went on to say that 'a large proportion which winter in Britain originate from countries around the Baltic Sea'. Galloway and Meek listed several recoveries of autumn and winter ringed birds moving to and from Northumberland which supported Lack's conclusions. Finland, Latvia, Estonia and Russia were the destinations of individuals marked in the county and a bird shot at Milbourne in January 1969 had been ringed in Helsinki. A programme of winter ringing at Big Waters, Killingworth and the Coquet Estuary during the 1960s and 1970s demonstrated that some individuals returned to the same feeding or roosting areas, presumably from their European breeding grounds, in successive winters. The onset of severe weather causes some birds to move south and west, as shown by locally ringed birds arriving in Devon and Morocco later in the same winter, but it can also result in further arrivals from the continent as was witnessed in December 1961.

Day *et al.* (1995) identified some 1,300 breeding pairs in the county but as it is suspected that most of these are largely replaced by continental birds in the winter, as evidenced by birds ringed in late summer moving to Eire, the statement made by Bolam that it is a resident is not strictly true. The 10km square distribution map from the current survey could suggest there is little change in the population from that which was discovered in 1981-1984, with 54 and 53 occupied squares respectively, but with a slight difference in distribution. However, it should be stressed that within the same 10km square a single sighting in only one of 25 tetrads is represented in the same way as 20 birds in each of 15 tetrads! Over the three winter periods a maximum total of 1,189 birds was counted, spread over 219 tetrads, and the greatest tetrad occupancy (19%) was between 0 to 200 metres a.s.l., although 13% of those in the range 201-300 metres a.s.l. attracted feeding or roosting Snipe. The majority of the 219 maximum counts were in single figures. Of the 25 in double figures, the highest was 88 in the Coquet Estuary (NU20S) and this was exceeded only by 100 at Newton Pool (NU22M) and 105 at Big Waters (NZ27G). Analysing the results from the control tetrads, low numbers in 1997/98 may have been weather-related as cold temperatures and significant snowfalls occurred during January.

The habits of the Snipe are such that it can be a difficult species to census and a hazardous walk through a winter bog or reed bed to detect its presence is a frequent requirement. There is probably no reason why it should not have been present in every 10km square in the county, except for those that comprise blanket forest. It is particularly surprising that it was not found (or reported) in NZ36 which contains Wallsend Swallow Pond and NU21 which contains the Aln Estuary. It is thus very likely that a significant under-count has occurred and that the population is well in excess of the 1,189 that were reported. Despite the difficulties, the population clearly does not approach 10,000 birds and the winter status, which is currently still summarised as common in *Birds in Northumbria*, remains unchanged.

Analysing the European status, Hagemeijer and Blair (1997) referred to a decline in the breeding populations in some northern countries, especially in Finland where a reduction of 33% occurred during the 1980s. If this was to continue, and also be paralleled in other nations around the Baltic Sea, we could expect to see a significant fall in the numbers wintering in the county. Mead (2000), commenting upon the future of the breeding population in the UK, wrote 'lowland outlook very poor with the restoration of wet areas to low intensity grazing the only hope'. This applies to Northumberland where the future status of the Snipe in both winter and summer depends to some extent upon how land drainage on farmland is managed. It is hoped that the current trend towards Stewardship schemes, and whatever might follow, will see a real reduction in land use for grazing and crop production and a return to more 'Snipe friendly' conditions. However, if Lack's estimate of birds shot is correct, can we really continue to justify the slaughter of 85,000 birds countrywide each year?

BRYAN GALLOWAY

Distribution by altitude

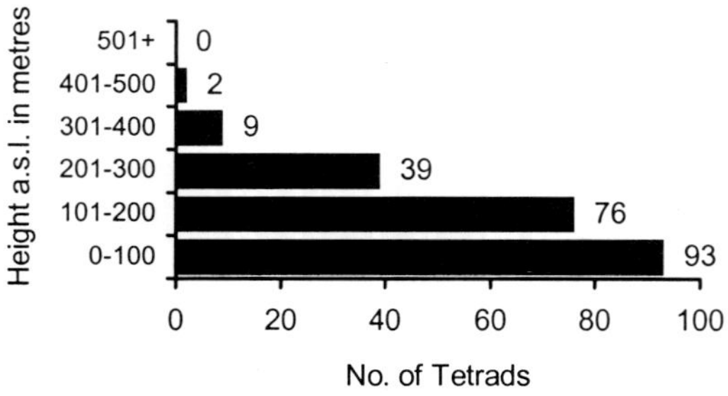

No. of tetrads in which recorded	219 (15%)
Tetrad Analysis	**No. of tetrads**
1 bird	96 (44%)
2-5 birds	80 (36%)
6+ birds	43 (20%)
Total No. of birds counted	1,189

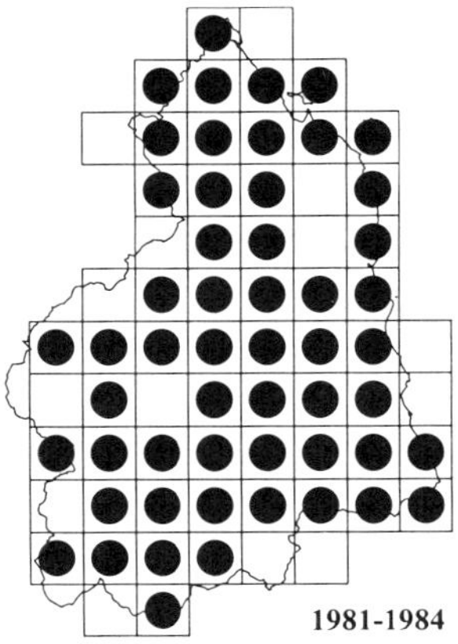

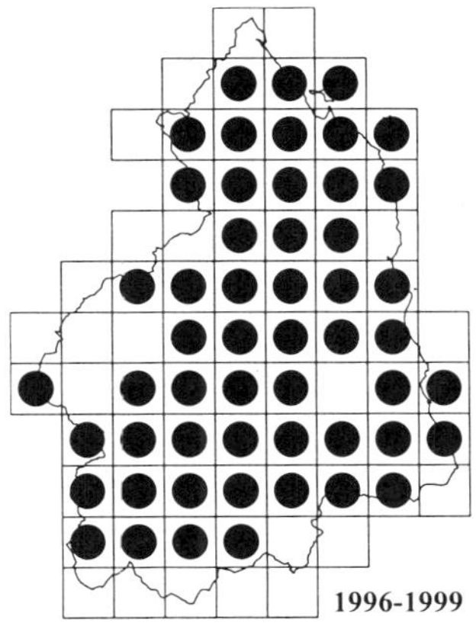

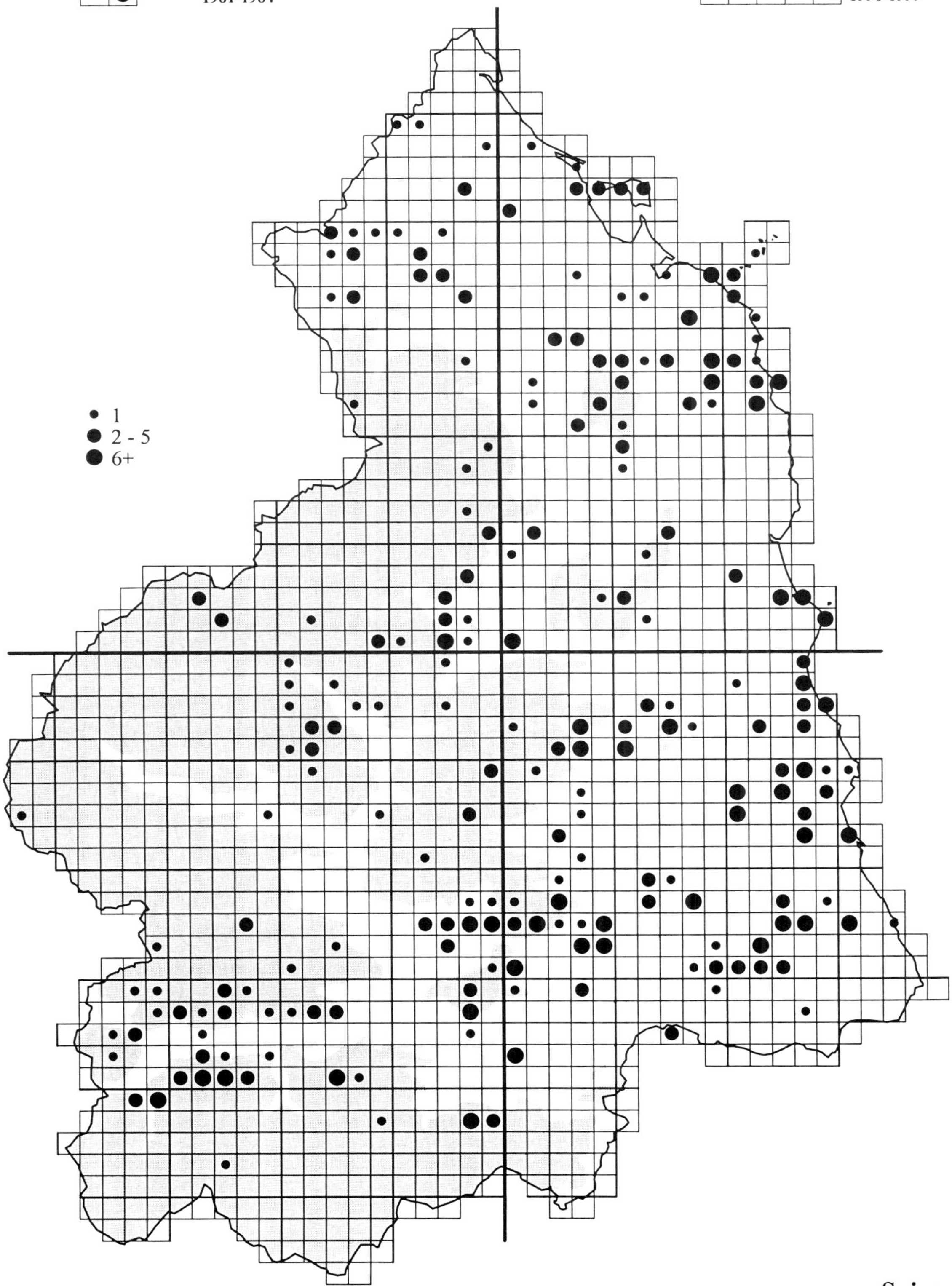

Snipe

WOODCOCK *Scolopax rusticola*

A comparison of the distribution of the Woodcock between this winter atlas map and the map in *The atlas of breeding birds in Northumbria* (Day *et al.*, 1995) confirms the status of the species as a well-represented resident species whose numbers are significantly increased by an influx of wintering birds. Bolam (1932) recorded the Woodcock as a numerous winter visitor and passage migrant with considerable fluctuations in numbers which were at least partly dictated by the weather. In the 1981-1984 national winter atlas survey (Lack, 1986) the species was described as being abundant in the coastal areas of Britain and Ireland with the birds being faithful to wintering areas, this having been confirmed by ringing studies.

The Woodcock roosts by day in dry areas of cover within woodland, venturing out between dusk and dawn to feed in damp or marshy areas where soft unfrozen ground is an essential requirement to enable the bird to probe for food. In the current winter survey, a majority (79%) of the wintering population occurred in tetrads below an elevation of 200 metres a.s.l. The generally sedentary nature of the resident population is confirmed in winter by the 57 occupied tetrads situated above 183 metres a.s.l. (600 feet), a figure similar to the number above that altitude containing Woodcock as shown in *The atlas of breeding birds in Northumbria*. The three winters of 1996-1999 in which survey work was carried out were relatively mild, which would have enabled birds to remain on their breeding territories. Nevertheless, some movement from favoured breeding areas to adjacent lower ground is apparent from inspection of the two local breeding and wintering maps. More severe winter conditions would certainly provoke larger-scale movements from these higher wintering areas to less harsh lowland localities. Furthermore, prolonged periods of cold may precipitate westerly movements away from Northumberland possibly terminating in Ireland or in south western counties of Britain. Similarly, some autumn passage migrants arriving in Northumberland move through to their regular wintering locations in these warmer regions, as ringing records have confirmed (Galloway & Meek, 1980).

The migrant wintering population originates mainly from Norway, Sweden and Finland (Lack, 1986) and may be augmented by birds from Russia. The local autumn influx usually peaks from mid-October to mid-November, during which time small numbers are seen regularly in coastal localities between Tynemouth and the Scottish border. Bolam (1912) recorded the association of migrant Woodcock with the influx of Redwing *Turdus iliacus*, Goldcrest *Regulus regulus* and Grey Crow *Corvus corone cornix*. The current winter atlas survey shows Woodcock remaining on the coast as well as on the coastal plains throughout the winter period with, for example, a maximum of six birds recorded at Bamburgh (NU13X) at the end of December 1996. At inland sites a concentration of 16 birds was recorded in three adjacent tetrads between Great Swinburne and Hallington (NY97H/M/S) in November/December 1996, with a further 13 birds in well-wooded areas to the east of Hexham in the Tyne Valley (NY96) during the December 1997-January 1998 period.

The Woodcock is a solitary and secretive species which is difficult to locate and there is little doubt that there will have been under-recording of its distribution and an under-estimation of the numbers occurring in the recording area. The overall total recorded for the current winter survey is 278 birds compared with the 136 pairs recorded in the local breeding atlas mentioned above. This comparison does not appear to reflect the significant winter influx and under-recording of this species is likely to have been a significant factor in the lack of correlation between the winter and summer populations.

The current winter survey shows an increase in the number of 10km squares containing Woodcock, compared with the 1981-1984 winter atlas survey, from 49 to 57. As the autumn influx is partly weather-dependent no conclusions can be drawn from this recorded increase in respect of long-term population trends, but the number of wintering birds appears to be at least stable, or possibly showing an increase, over the period between the two surveys.

EDDIE CRABTREE

Distribution by altitude

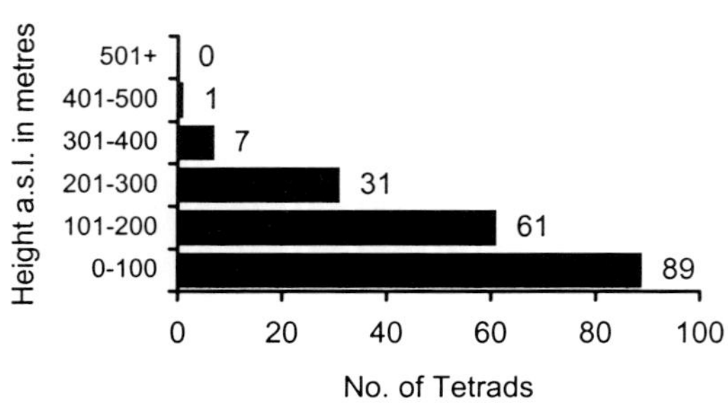

No. of tetrads in which recorded 189 (13%)

Tetrad Analysis	No. of tetrads
1 bird	144 (76%)
2 birds	23 (12%)
3+ birds	22 (12%)

Total No. of birds counted 278

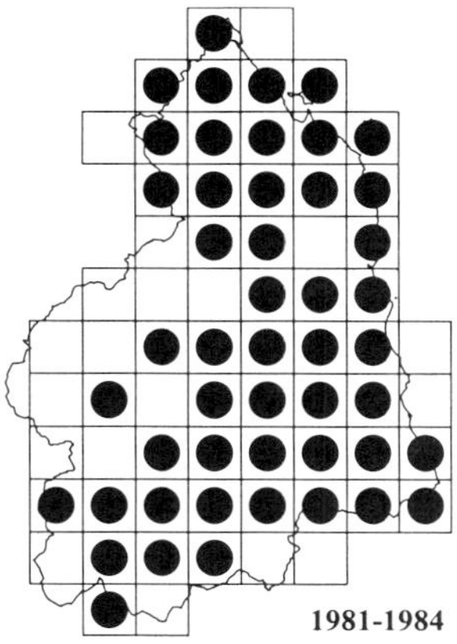

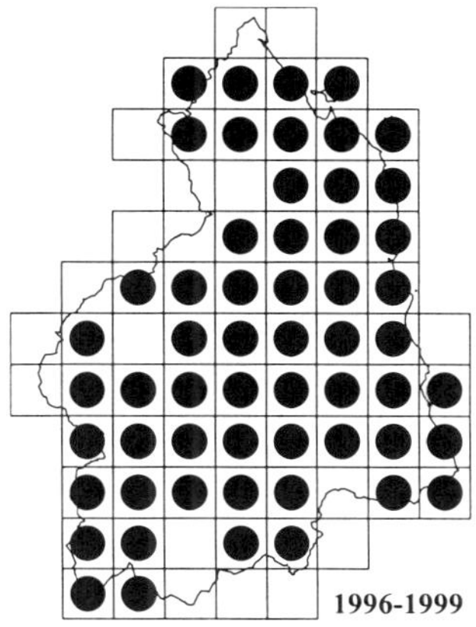

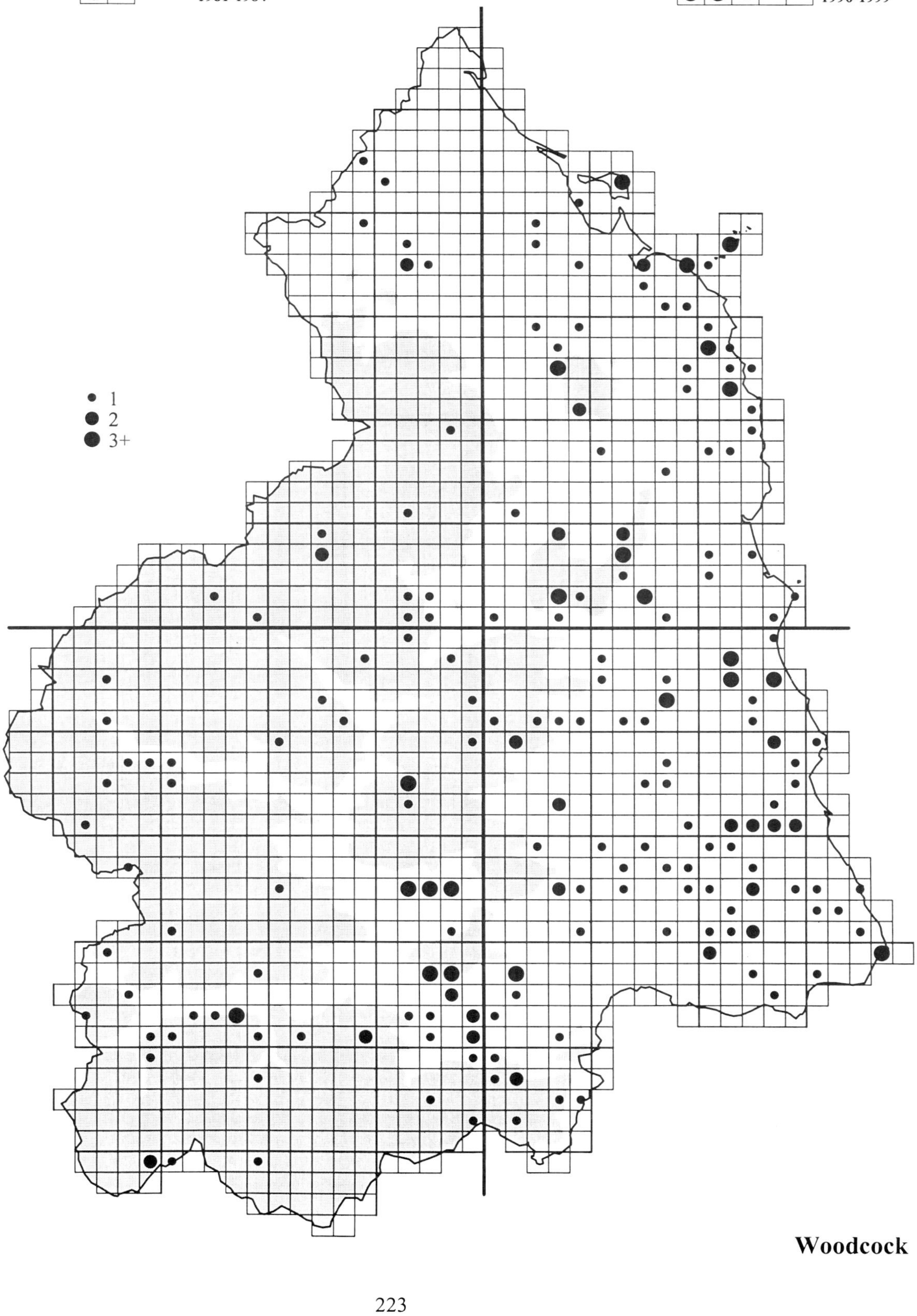

Woodcock

BLACK-TAILED GODWIT *Limosa limosa*

Bolam noted in 1932 that 'in recent years' he knew of only autumn or winter records of Black-tailed Godwit in the county and said 'its usual time of appearance now is in September and October'. He also mentioned an early winter record of one at Goswick on 1st January 1890. Galloway and Meek (1980) gave its winter status as an occasional visitor and added 'since 1968 birds have over-wintered regularly, one or two occurring in Lindisfarne NNR in most years'. The county annual reports for the 16-year period up to the current atlas fieldwork reveal an almost unchanged picture since then with, usually, between one and five birds in each winter period, many of the records coming from the Lindisfarne area. As many as nine were in the Budle Bay/Holy Island/Hoppen Kiln area in early 1988.

The current winter atlas survey resulted in birds being found in nine coastal tetrads, with maximum counts of 21 at the Coquet Estuary (NU20S) on 15th November 1996, although only 11 stayed to over-winter there, and a peak of 15 at Budle Bay (NU13M) on 22nd December 1996. More typically, only one-two were reported from the other seven tetrads spanning all three winter periods. It is interesting to note that none of the counts was made during timed visits, all coming from supplementary records, although this may have resulted in some duplicate counting.

Northumberland is not of significant importance for wintering Black-tailed Godwits as much larger numbers were recorded during the national winter atlas counts in 1981-1984 at various localities on the south east, south and west coasts of England and also in Ireland (Lack, 1986). Stone *et al.* (1997) indicated an estimated UK wintering population of 7,800 in 1989-1994.

The grand total of 46 counted during this latest survey should not be considered a normal winter population in the county as this total was inflated by exceptional numbers in the 1996/97 season. A more realistic average of less than ten individuals means that the Black-tailed Godwit remains a rare winter visitor to Northumberland.

MIKE S. HODGSON

No. of tetrads in which recorded: 9 (<1%)

Tetrad Analysis	No. of tetrads
1 bird	4 (44%)
2 birds	3 (34%)
3+ birds	2 (22%)

Total No. of birds counted: 46

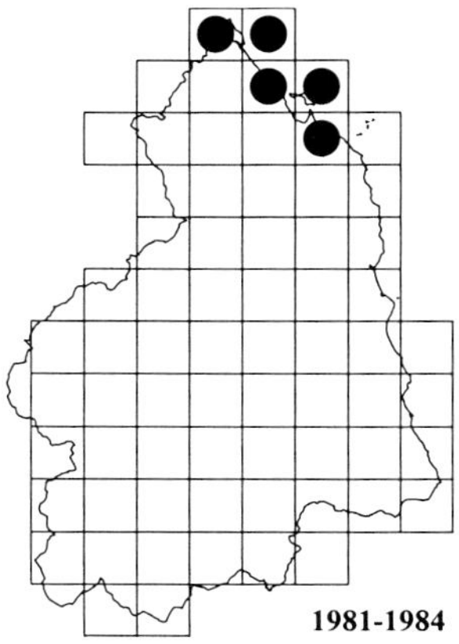

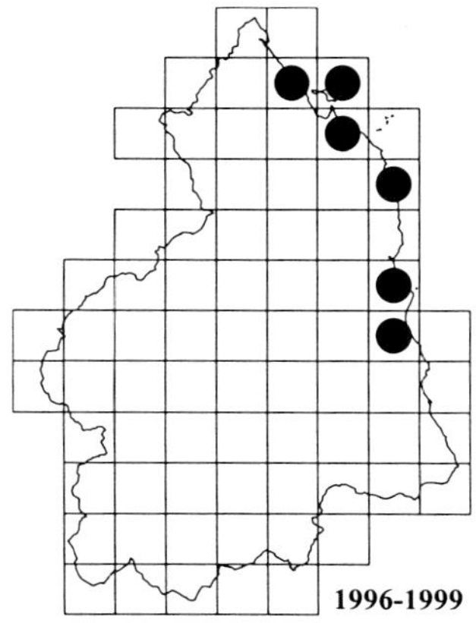

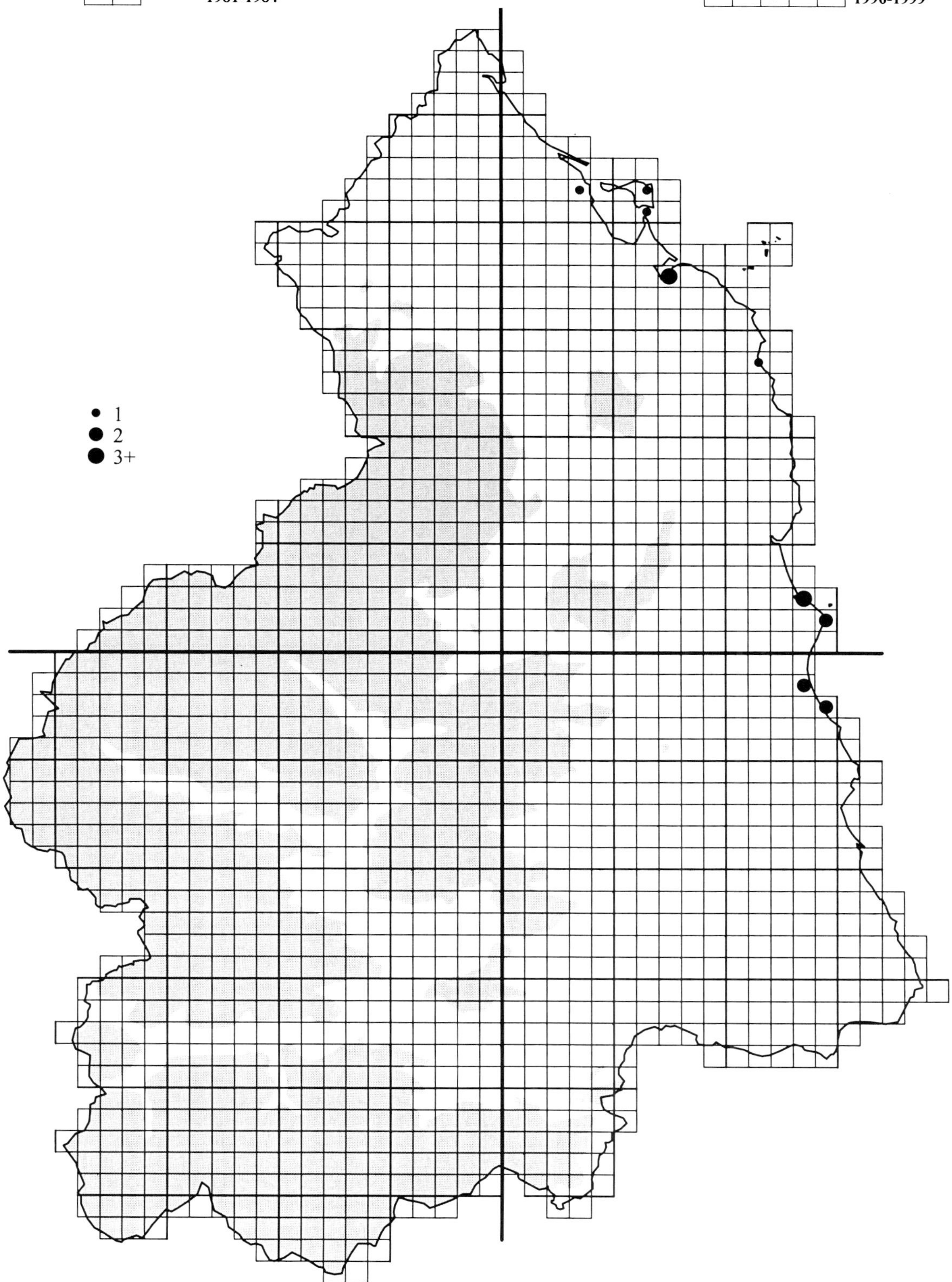

Black-tailed Godwit

BAR-TAILED GODWIT *Limosa lapponica*

The sight of a large flock of Bar-tailed Godwits banking and diving to escape a predator such as a Peregrine *Falco peregrinus* high over the mudflats is always one of the highlights of a winter visit to Lindisfarne NNR. Whether engaging in escape tactics or simply flighting in high and then spiralling down to a high-tide roost on the Black Law, St Cuthbert's Island or on the Goswick Sand Rig, these large and exciting waders really capture the atmosphere of the cold seasons on the Reserve.

Lindisfarne NNR appears to have always been the stronghold of the species. Bolam (1912) described it graphically as 'an abundant winter visitant and passage migrant to the slakes in the neighbourhood of Holy Island but of more uncertain appearance elsewhere along the coast'. His statement about its status in Northumberland was welcomed by Abel Chapman whose earlier claims about it remaining in winter had been doubted by the ornithological establishment of the era who regarded it as merely a passage visitor to Britain (Kerr, 1995).

Lindisfarne, which usually has a small non-breeding population in summer, sees the return in July and August of birds, often still in red breeding plumage. Numbers build up to an average wintering population of around 3,000 although 8,000 were present in late 1970, with 9,600 in February 1986 and 8,900 in January 1987. Bar-tailed Godwits are able to take advantage of feeding in both muddy and sandy conditions, their long bills enabling them to delve deeply to find rich food in the form of lugworms and similar marine prey.

Lack (1986) believed that the numbers of Bar-tailed Godwits wintering in Britain were governed by their breeding success in the Arctic and conditions in one of their other main haunts, the Waddensee area of Holland. He believed that many birds quickly moved across the North Sea in response to local conditions and estimated that the British wintering population was around 60,000 out of a European total of 100,000. Prater (1981) said that areas holding over 1% of the European population must be regarded as being of international importance, a statement which puts Lindisfarne very firmly into that category.

The distribution map from the current survey shows the major concentration of the species at Lindisfarne where rich feeding in the intertidal area provides the ideal winter habitat with only smaller numbers occurring elsewhere along the coast. Significantly, the small numbers found elsewhere, such as those at Boulmer (NU21R/S), are usually found in a muddy area of beach where conditions appear very similar to those at Lindisfarne. The importance of Lindisfarne was supported during the survey period by other data, including WeBS counts, which showed, for example, that in February 1998, of the 3,296 Bar-tailed Godwits found between Tynemouth and Berwick, no fewer than 3,225 were at Lindisfarne.

The tetrad map also clearly shows that the species is confined entirely to the coast in winter with no individuals straying even short distances inland. However, there are some inland records in winter. Galloway and Meek (1980) speculated that overland passage could occur through the Tyne Gap, a belief strengthened by a report of 43 flying east at Scotswood in December 1989.

The two smaller 10km square maps indicate that there appears to have been no change at all in the status or geographical spread of the species since 1981-1984, confirming the statements of earlier authorities that the Bar-tailed Godwit remains a common winter visitor to our shores.

IAN KERR

No. of tetrads in which recorded 35 (2%)

Tetrad Analysis	No. of tetrads
1-16 birds	17 (49%)
17-130 birds	11 (31%)
131+ birds	7 (20%)

Total No. of birds counted 4,951

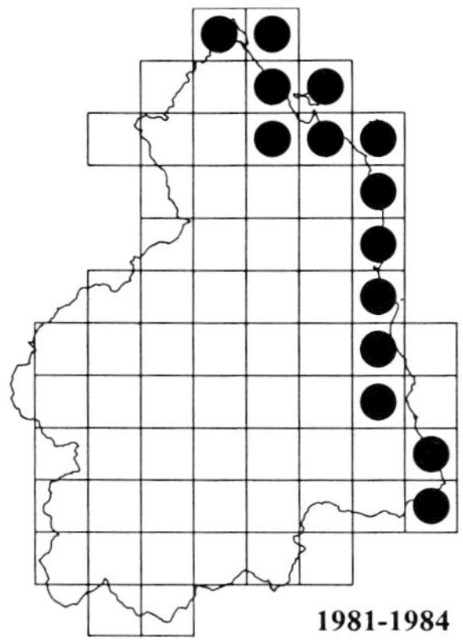

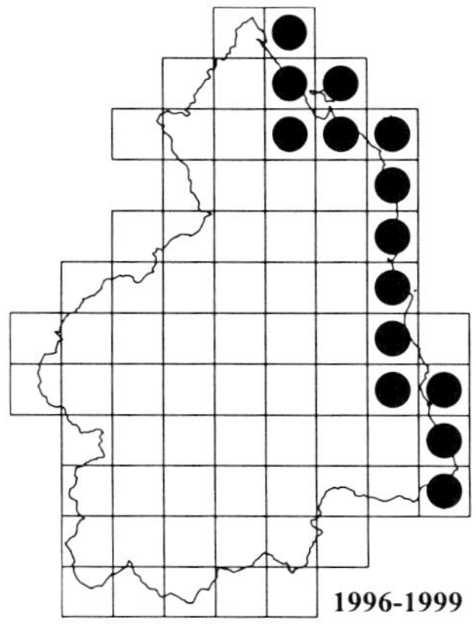

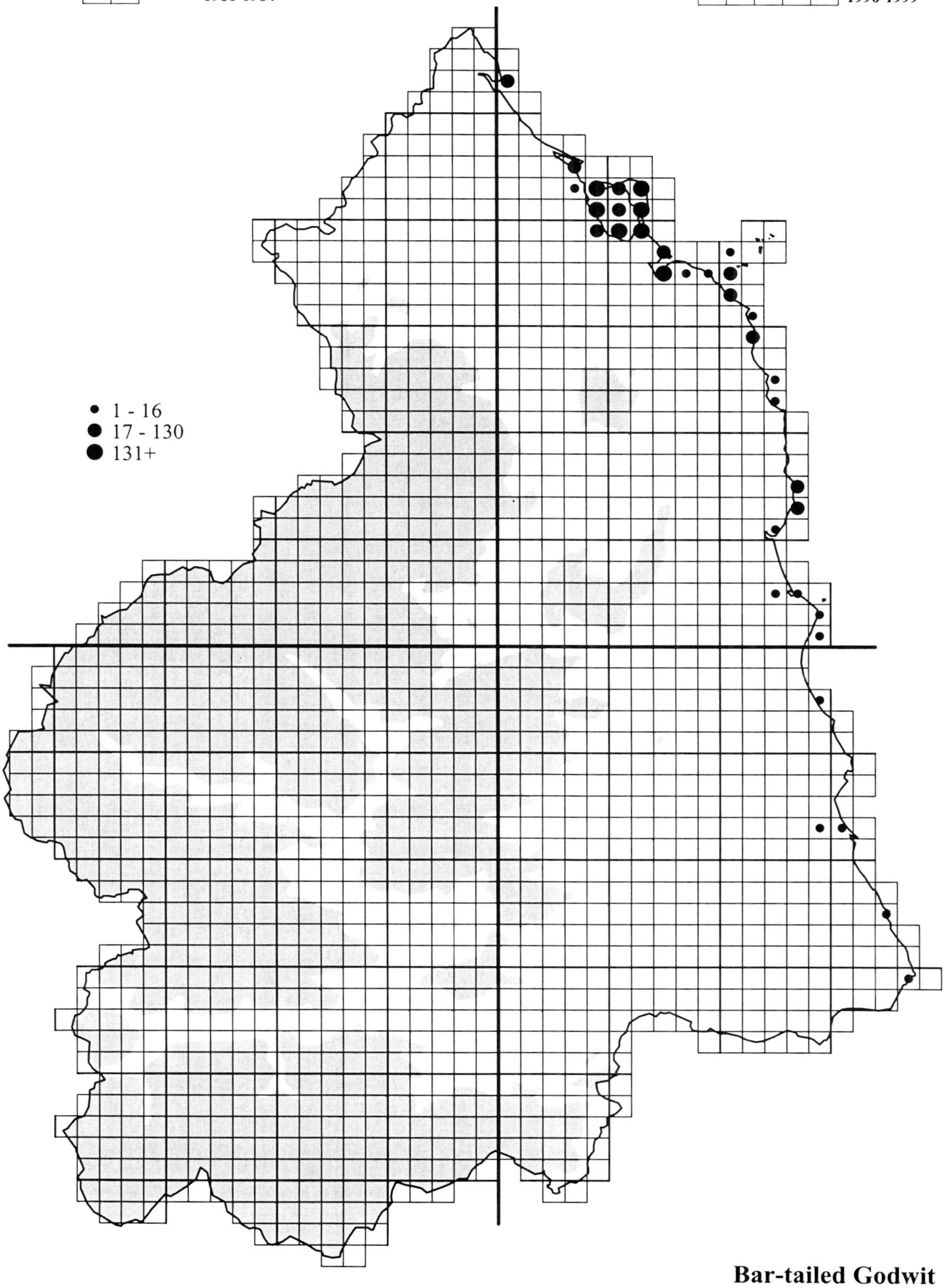

Bar-tailed Godwit

CURLEW *Numenius arquata*

Hancock (1874) and Bolam (1912) commented upon how common the Curlew was as a breeding species but made very little reference to its winter status. Galloway and Meek (1980) gave examples of juveniles that had been ringed in the summer, moving to Eire for the winter, and suggested that some breeding adults also made the same migration They referred to immigrants from Europe, quoting examples of recoveries of birds ringed in Finland and Norway as juveniles, as being the main source of our wintering populations which were to be found mainly in coastal areas. In summary they classified the Curlew as a common winter visitor.

Lack (1986) described the preferred winter habitat in Britain as 'the large estuarine mud flats, where they feed on worms such as ragworm, and crabs and molluscs' and indicated that numbers were at their highest early in the winter. The habitat at the Lindisfarne NNR fits Lack's description, and it is here where the largest gatherings can be found. The total maximum tetrad count for the period of the survey in the entire county was 8,315 individuals and over 3,500 were found at Lindisfarne and the adjacent farmland. However, as some duplication was suspected, single synchronised counts were organised in each of 1997/98 and 1998/99 and a total of 1,250 were found in both winters. Also the monthly WeBS counts for the area for each of the three winters produced maximum numbers ranging between 577 in 1996/97 and 1,420 in 1998/99. It thus seems that there was almost certainly an over-count in the Lindisfarne area.

The tetrad distribution map shows a concentration of Curlew at or near the coast, and of the 142 tetrads in which birds were found, 86% were in the altitude range 0-100 metres a.s.l. There seems little doubt that count duplication occurred in other areas, especially where significant sized flocks are shown in adjacent tetrads. Of the main areas of attraction away from Lindisfarne, 500 at the Farne Islands (NU23C), 325 at the Long Nanny (NU22I), 230 at Boulmer (NU21S), 153 at Alnmouth (NU21K) and 110 at Druridge (NZ29T) were the largest counts made, but 50-100 were also seen around Whitley Bay, especially at St Mary's Island (NZ37M) and near to Amble (NU20S) and Blyth (NZ38B). A few inland areas habitually attract flocks of Curlew in the winter, particularly the mid-reaches of the River Coquet between Caistron and Holystone (NT90L) where up to 200 were counted, and smaller gatherings of 15-40 near Coanwood (NY65Z), Doddington (NT93W), Fowberry (NU02I) and by the River Breamish at Beanley (NU01U). Some 40-70 birds were also present alongside the River Tyne in the Scotswood area of Newcastle (NZ16W & NZ26B/G).

A comparison of the 10km square maps suggests a wider distribution during the current survey when 36 squares were occupied compared with 31 in 1981-1984 whilst analysis of the control tetrad counts suggests that the Curlew was more numerous during the winter of 1998/99.

Taking into account the inevitable duplication of counts that has taken place as flocks move between roosting and feeding areas, especially at the coast where concentration variation is very much influenced by the movements of the tide, the winter population in Northumberland is probably no more than 5,000 birds. This is consistent with the current status classification in *Birds in Northumbria*, and with that arrived at by Galloway and Meek, as a common winter visitor. As Lack indicated that some 200,000 individuals were wintering in Britain and Ireland, Northumberland attracts only about 2.5% of the nation's population.

Hagemeijer and Blair (1997) reported a reduction in the breeding populations in Finland, Sweden and Norway, which are believed to be the countries of origin of most of our winter visitors and, as Mead (2000) speculated 'outlook not good at all' for the UK breeding population probably as a result of 'agricultural intensification', we might expect to see a reduction in winter numbers in Northumberland during the next few years.

BRYAN GALLOWAY

Distribution by altitude

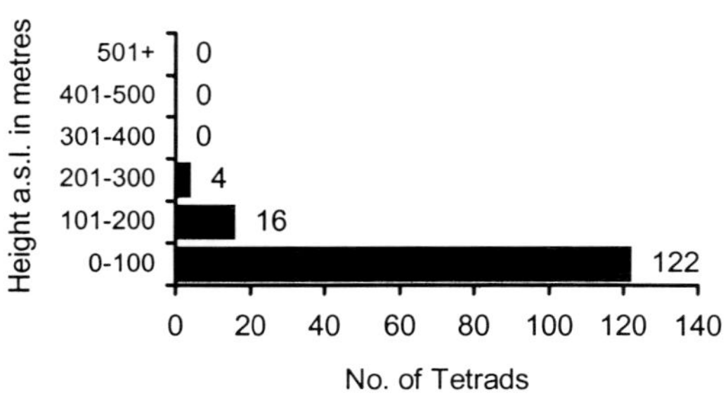

No. of tetrads in which recorded 142 (10%)

Tetrad Analysis	No. of tetrads
1-15 birds	71 (50%)
16-74 birds	42 (30%)
75+ birds	29 (20%)

Total No. of birds counted 8,315

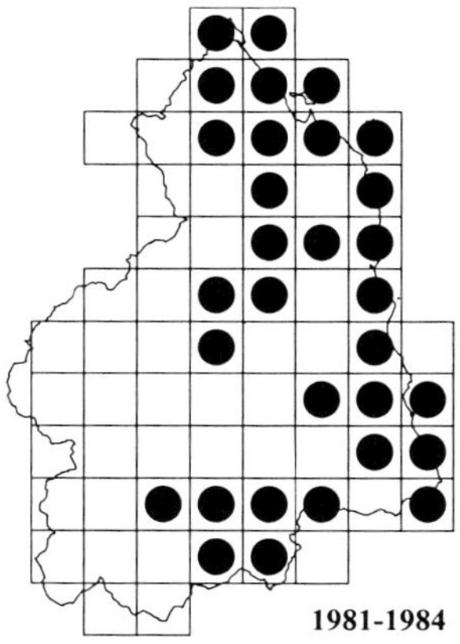

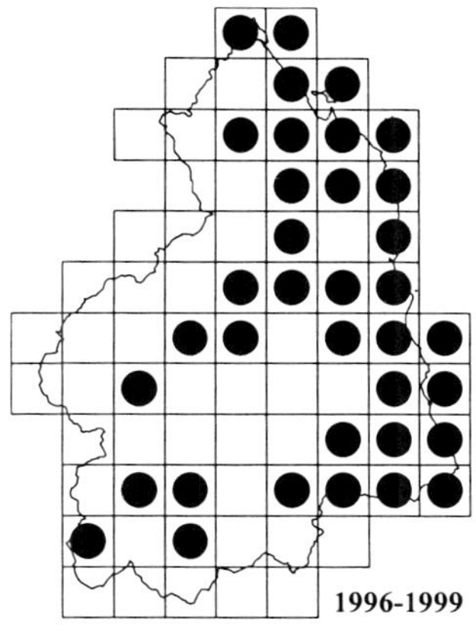

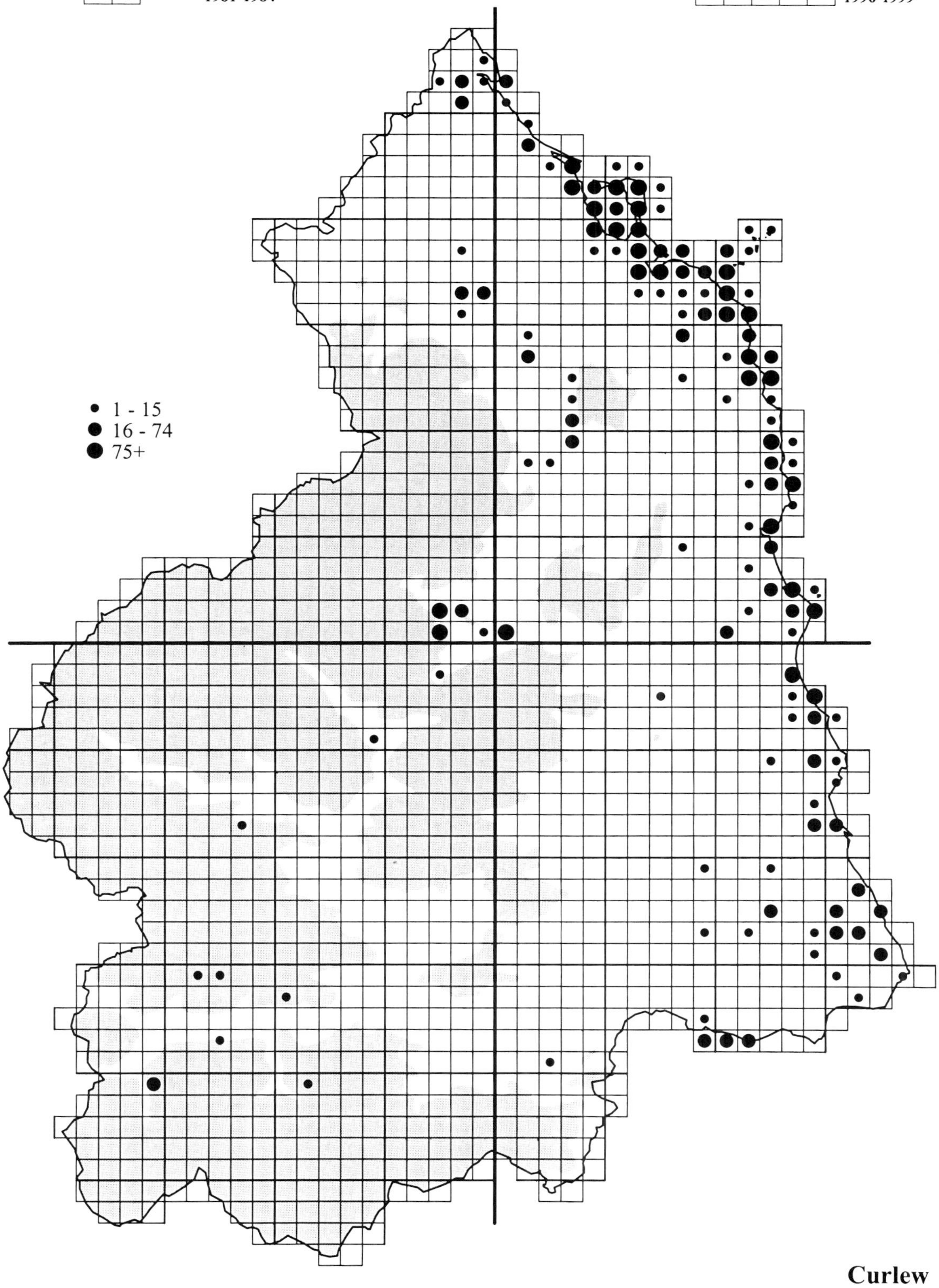

Curlew

SPOTTED REDSHANK *Tringa erythropus*

In Northumberland, this elegant wader is an uncommon passage migrant, more frequently encountered in autumn than in spring, and a rare winter visitor. Galloway and Meek (1980) noted a trend starting in the 1970s of one or two birds wintering at the Lindisfarne NNR, an area containing much soft, silty mud which Lack (1986) identified as being the preferred habitat of Spotted Redshanks wintering in Britain and Ireland.

At the time of the previous winter survey in 1981-1984, Spotted Redshanks were found in five Northumberland 10km squares, three of which were away from Lindisfarne. During this current survey all occupied tetrads, except one from Lindisfarne, were in the south east of the county with two being slightly inland. Although birds occurred in seven tetrads it is likely that, due to local movements, only four individuals account for these records. One found at Arcot Pond (NU27M) in October 1997 remained there until mid-December and was re-located at two sites in the Blyth Estuary (NZ28W & NZ38B) in January & February 1998 before returning to Arcot in March. The other inland record relates to a bird seen at Prestwick Carr (NZ17W) in November 1998. This site is perhaps not surprising as Bolam (1912), who regarded the species as a rare autumn visitant, recorded at least three birds shot there in late summer between 1830 and 1848. On the coastal ponds in January and February 1999, a single bird wintered in the Druridge Bay area, being seen at both Cresswell Pond (NZ29X) and Druridge Pools (NZ29T). The other record was a single bird found in the Holy Island area (NU14F) in November 1996.

It is unlikely that this species will ever become frequent in the county in winter. However, with the continuing run of mild winters it is probable that more records will occur especially if the species continues to show a liking for the shallow mining flashes of the south east of the county.

LINDSAY J. McDOUGALL

No. of tetrads in which recorded 7 (<1%)

Tetrad Analysis	No. of tetrads
1 bird	7 (100%)

Total No. of birds counted 7

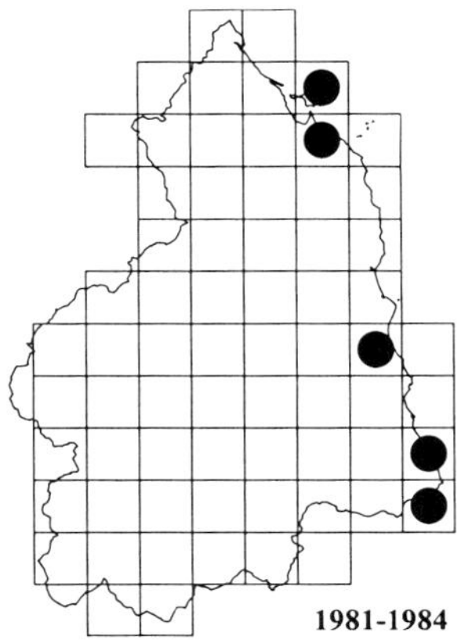

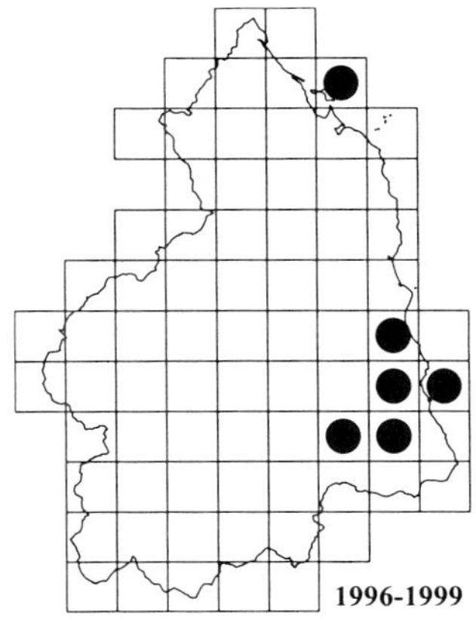

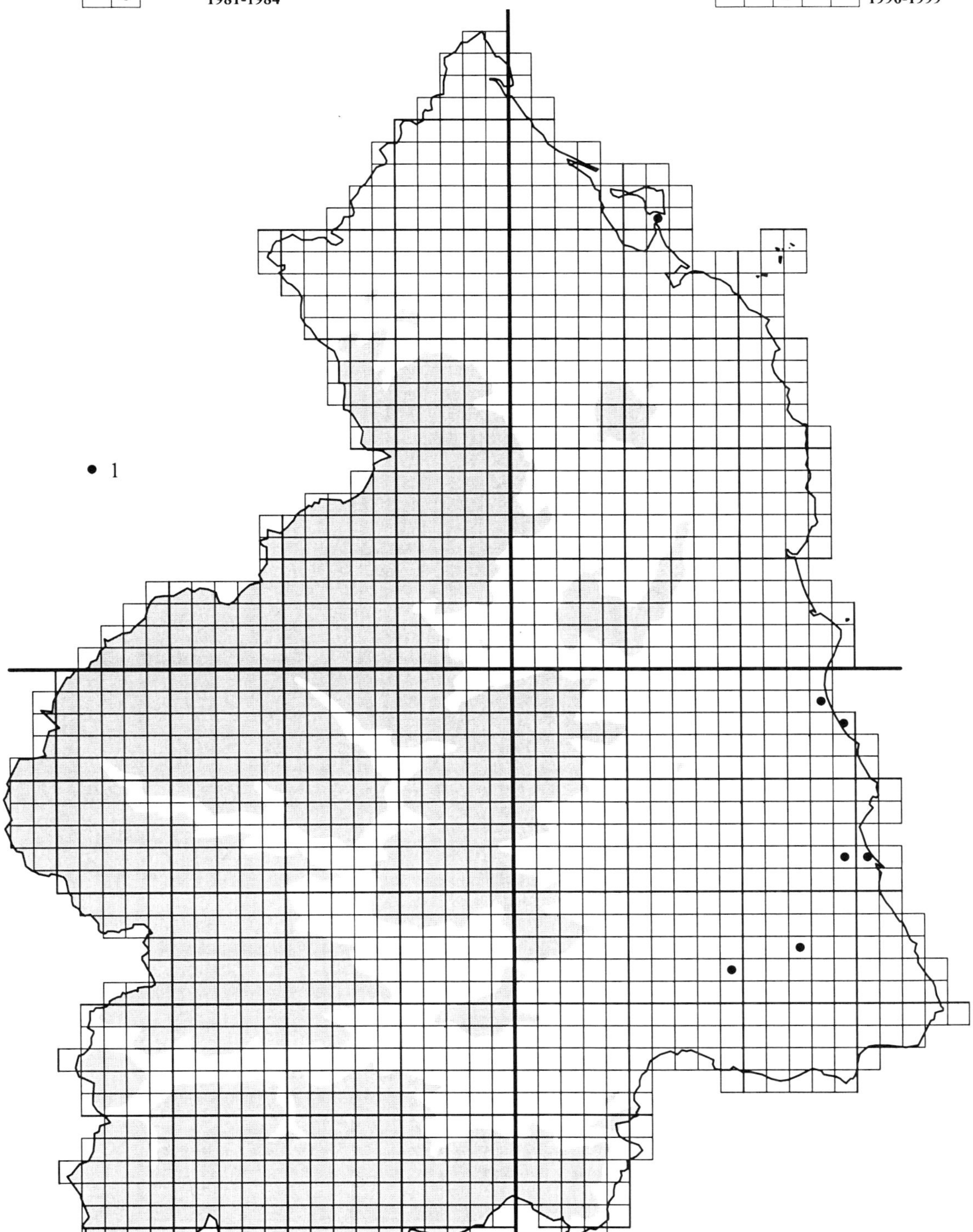

Spotted Redshank

REDSHANK *Tringa totanus*

Bolam (1912) referred to the Redshank as a 'common resident, always numerous on the coast in winter' and went on to say in 1932 that it had begun 'to appear in vast winter flocks upon the coast'. Evans (1966) concluded, after a period of extensive research, that both passage and winter visitors to the county were of Icelandic origin and referred to two examples of ringed birds moving between Iceland and Northumberland. He considered that none of the near-continental populations wintered in the region and also stated that some of the county's breeding birds moved to the nearby coast for the winter but others, as shown by ringing recoveries, moved south to locations as far ranging as Lincolnshire, the Isle of Wight, France and Portugal. Lack (1986) agreed with Evans and wrote 'many Icelandic birds move into Britain and Ireland in winter and it is likely that the majority of our wintering birds are of Icelandic origin'. Galloway and Meek (1980) referred to a Dutch ringed bird being found at Hauxley and hence were less certain but stated that 'whatever the origins' about 2,200 wintered on the Northumberland coast, including some 1,600 on the Lindisfarne NNR.

The results of the current survey confirmed that the Redshank in winter is very much a bird of the coastal areas. The tetrad map clearly shows this to be the case and an aggregate of 6,165 individuals was found in 129 tetrads across the county. Concern that there may have been some duplication prompted single synchronised counts in each of 1997/98 and 1998/99 in the principal wintering area at Lindisfarne, where a tetrad analysis suggested a population of 2,500. The results were 1,242 and 1,473 respectively, and with the WeBS count during the same period producing figures of 689 and 1,483, the suspected over-count was confirmed.

At other areas on the coast, double counting was in most cases thought to be less likely and an aggregate of about 1,800 resulted. This was largely made up of three-figure concentrations of 502 at the Blyth Estuary (NZ38B), 400 at St. Mary's Island (NZ37M), 300 at Boulmer (NU21S), 220 at Cresswell Pond (NZ29X), 120 at Newbiggin (NZ38E) and 100 at the Coquet Estuary (NU20S). The largest numbers found inland were of about 50 on the River Tyne in the Elswick area of Newcastle (NZ26G) and 16 near Parkend on the River North Tyne (NY87S). The control tetrad results together with the WeBS data from the same period indicate that the species was more plentiful during the winter of 1998/99.

The number of occupied 10km squares was 30 and is to be compared with 31 in the 1981-1984 winter survey. There is a slightly different distribution inland but, as only small numbers of birds were involved, the difference is not considered to be significant.

The Redshank in Northumberland in winter is clearly a species of the coast where there appears to be an abundance of food, probably in the form of *Hydrobia, Corophium* and nercid worms. The results of the current survey indicate a population of some 4,000 birds of which only about 200 manage to find sufficient food to survive inland. This overall total, which is to be compared with Lack's estimate of 100,000 for Britain and Ireland, is less than the aggregate tetrad count for reasons already discussed but is more than that estimated by Galloway and Meek. However, it continues to assume the status of common in winter, which is consistent with the assessment made by authors of *Birds in Northumbria.*

Mead (2000) stated that Redshanks were vulnerable to cold winter weather and land drainage, and that breeding areas in Britain were threatened because of increased grazing pressures. He also suggested that Mink *Mustela vison* and, surprisingly, Hedgehogs *Erinaceus europaeus* were significant predators of nests and young. His summary was that the outlook for the breeding population looked 'pretty poor in many traditional areas'. If Mead's predictions are fulfilled, we could see a decline in the numbers wintering in Northumberland.

BRYAN GALLOWAY

Distribution by altitude

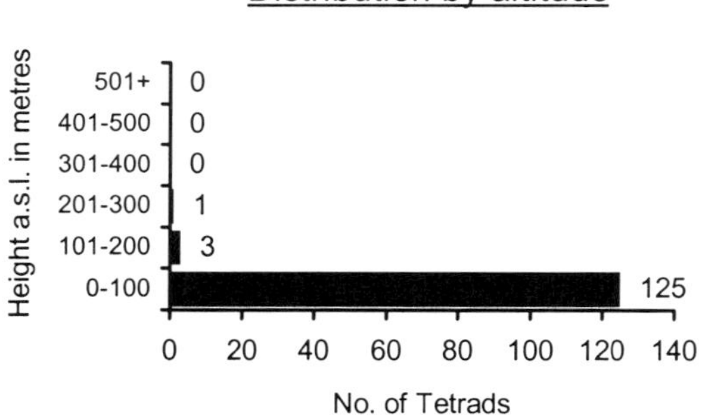

No. of tetrads in which recorded 129 (9%)

Tetrad Analysis	No. of tetrads
1-11 birds	65 (50%)
12-47 birds	37 (29%)
48+ birds	27 (21%)

Total No. of birds counted 6,165

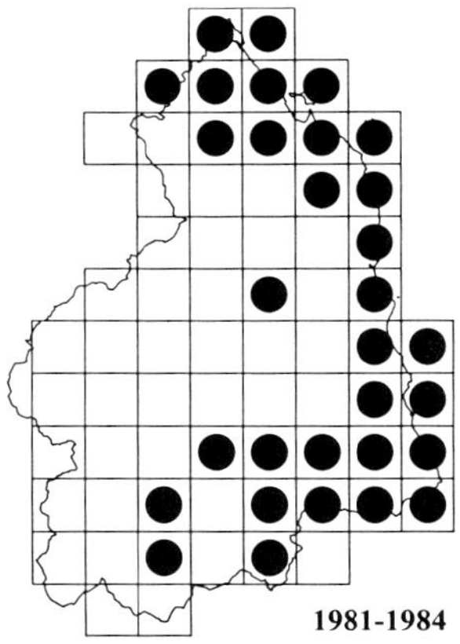

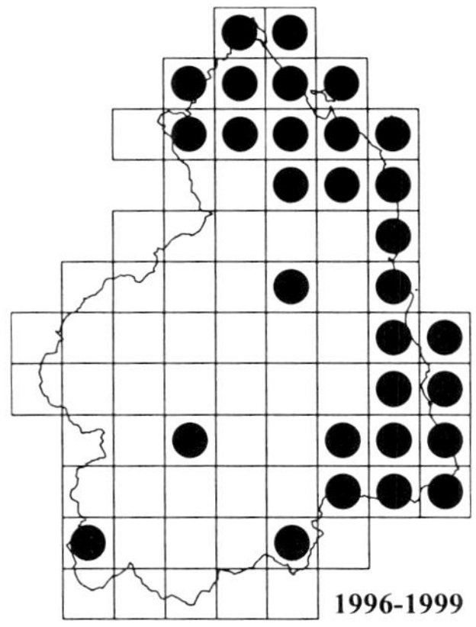

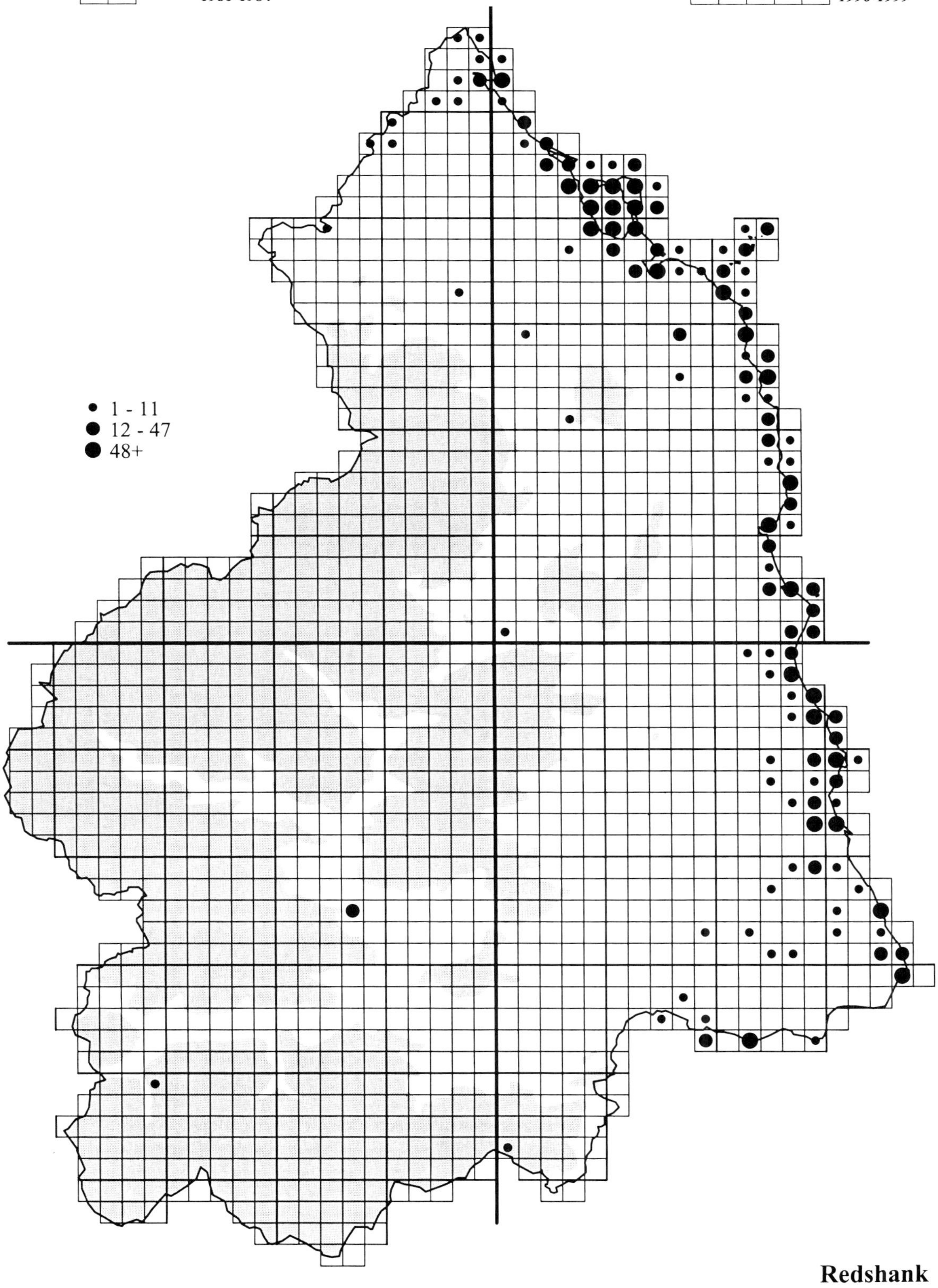

Redshank

GREENSHANK *Tringa nebularia*

Bolam (1912) said of the Greenshank 'a few always winter' and indicated Lindisfarne was a favoured area in the county. Twenty years later it appeared the situation was unchanged as he noted 'a few regularly spend the cold months at favourable coastal stations, particularly in the neighbourhood of Fenham Flats'. Galloway and Meek (1980) were unable to detect any variation in this wintering pattern and mentioned up to three at Lindisfarne and singles on the Aln and Coquet Estuaries and at Berwick.

Since then birds have been seen in ten winter periods between 1981/82 to 1995/96. In most of these winters only one-three have been noted but there was a remarkable count of 21 at Snook Point, Holy Island on 2nd February 1985, the largest ever winter gathering in the county (*Birds in Northumbria 1985*). Additionally, there were interesting inland sightings on the River Breamish at Powburn in January-March 1987, the first ever inland wintering record in the county, and on the River Till near Chillingham on 6th March 1992 (*Birds in Northumbria 1987; 1992*).

The results from this latest survey confirm that the Greenshank remains a rare winter visitor to Northumberland. Although six were present in Budle Bay (NU13M) on 22nd December 1996, only single birds were found, in November-December 1997, in the remaining three tetrads, at Fenham Mill (NU04V), the Tweed Estuary (NU05B) and near Longhirst (NZ28P). A single bird also wintered on the Tweed Estuary in 1998/99.

MIKE S. HODGSON

No. of tetrads in which recorded 4 (<1%)

Tetrad Analysis	No. of tetrads
1 bird	3 (75%)
2+ birds	1 (25%)

Total No. of birds counted 9

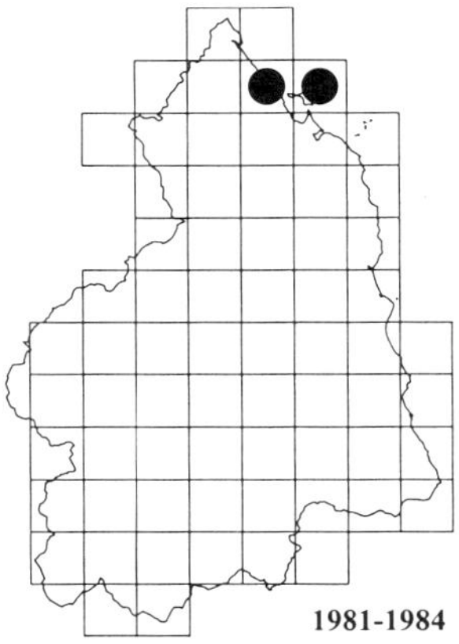

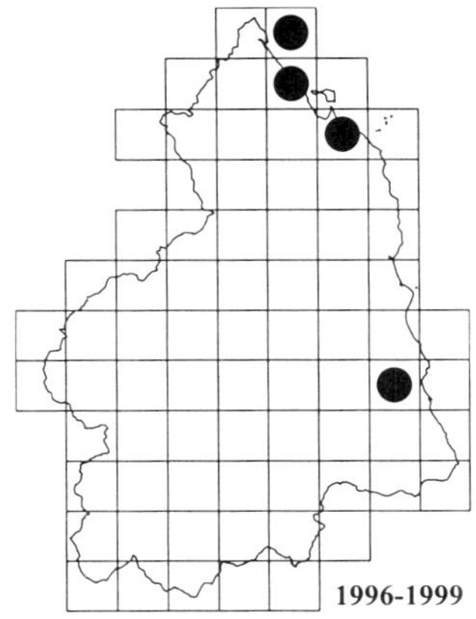

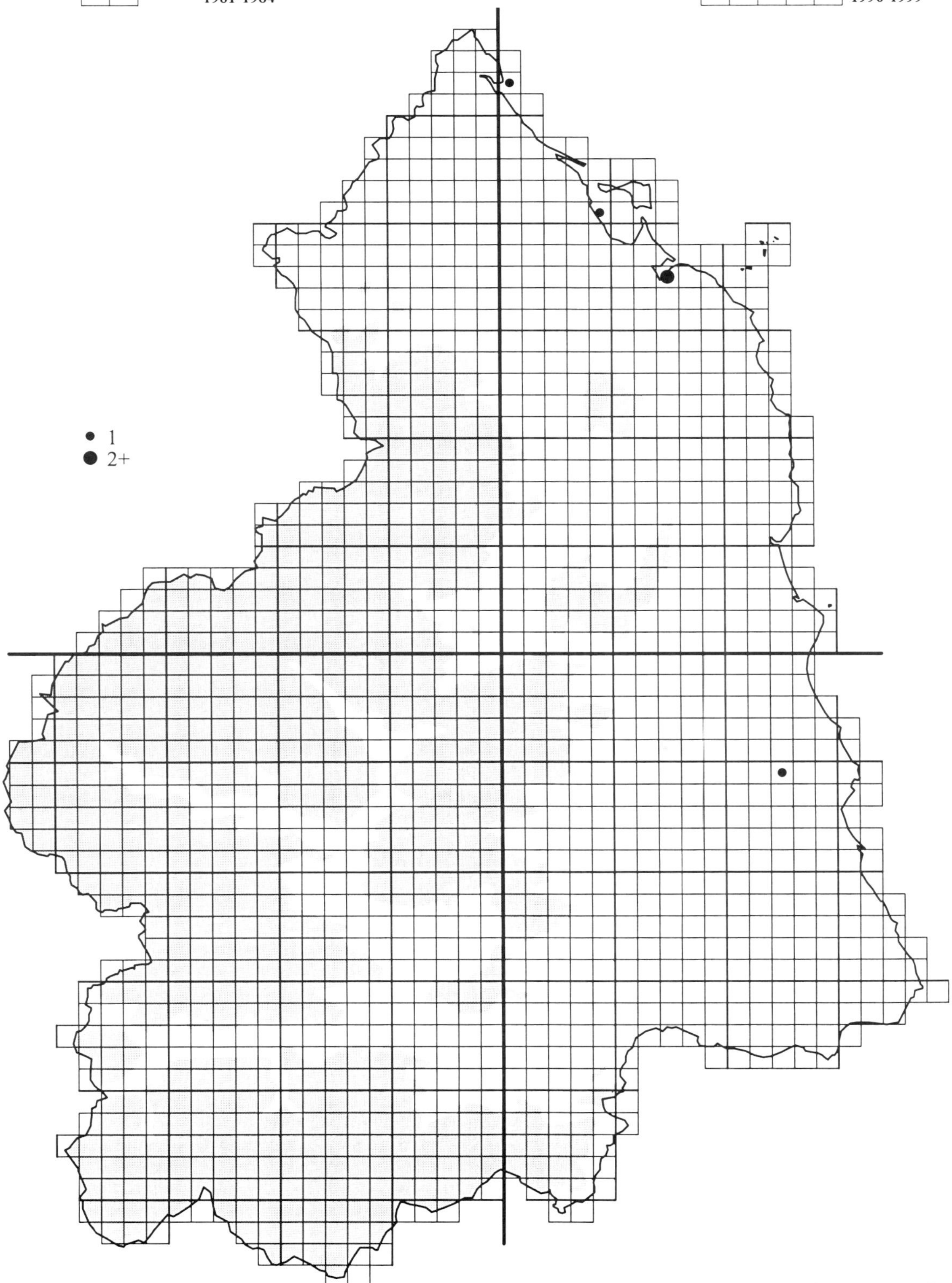

Greenshank

GREEN SANDPIPER *Tringa ochropus*

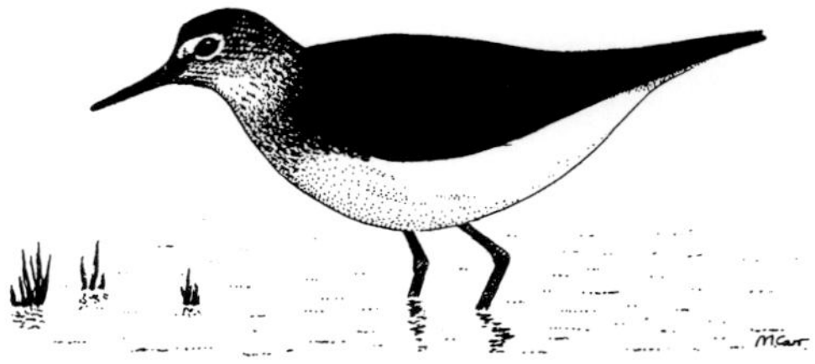

Never a common bird, the Green Sandpiper has been recorded in the county in small numbers almost every month of the year as either a migrant or over-wintering. Winter records tend to be from inland localities with birds favouring areas with standing or gently flowing freshwater, usually with saturated edges or margins (Smith *et al.*, 1992). They can, however, be secretive and easily overlooked unless flushed by the observer.

The trans-palearctic Green Sandpiper is monotypic, its breeding area is mostly confined to the boreal zone where it nests in trees, often using old thrush nests. Most of its range lies between the Arctic Circle and the Steppe zone (Hagemeijer & Blair, 1997). The European population winters in western and central Europe, the Mediterranean basin, Turkey, sub-Saharan and tropical Africa, with Britain and Ireland on the northern limits of its wintering range. In winter studies at a disused watercress farm maintained as a shallow lagoon in Hertfordshire, Green Sandpipers fed mainly on freshwater shrimp *Gammarus pulex* supplemented by small worms and small fish. Each bird would maintain an exclusive feeding territory by means of an elaborate display. Birds apparently roost away from the feeding areas (Lack, 1986).

In the nineteenth century, both Selby (1831) and Hancock (1874) considered the Green Sandpiper to be rare in Northumberland but in the early twentieth century, Bolam (1912) described it as an 'annual visitant in small numbers to be met with in every month, sometimes even in the depths of our hardest winters'. Galloway and Meek (1980) reported no change in status in the intervening years as small numbers still over-wintered with up to three at Whittle Dene Reservoirs and one or two elsewhere, mainly at inland sites.

Bankier (1994) suspected a decline in winter records from an average of 12 annually between 1973 and 1977 to five from 1978 to 1990 and less than four in subsequent years. Uncertainties about the cause of this decline, whether due to reduced observer coverage or a real reduction in numbers of birds, led to a new survey of the traditional wintering areas. Using historical sources such as Chapman (1907) and Bolam (1912), the 1992-1994 winter survey concentrated on the River Till and its tributaries, and the Glen, Breamish, Pow Burn and Wooler Water. The survey revealed seven and eight birds in each winter and Bankier concluded that no real decline had in fact occurred.

Another survey, organised in January 1996, which concentrated on the waterways not surveyed by Bankier, revealed only three birds, all in the Colwell-Great Whittingham area. Unfortunately low temperatures in January of that year resulted in a number of inland waters being frozen for long periods which may have had an adverse effect on numbers.

During the current winter atlas period, eight individuals were located in eight, mainly inland tetrads, at Chatton (NU02P), Doxford (NU12W), near Errington (NY97L), Colwell (NY97M), Whittle Dene Reservoirs (NZ06U), Great Whittingham (NZ07A), Rothley Lake (NZ09K) and near West Chevington (NZ29J) which suggests some consistency with Bankier's findings.

Lack (1986) considered the British and Irish winter population was in the order of 500-1000 birds but this represented a very small proportion of the western Palearctic breeding population. More recently from national WeBS data, Musgrove *et al.* (2001) have commented that while numbers on passage remained similar to previous years, the number of birds recorded in winter has increased. With this in mind, it is possible in future years that the Green Sandpiper may improve on its current winter status in the county from that of a rare visitor.

TOM A. CADWALLENDER

Distribution by altitude

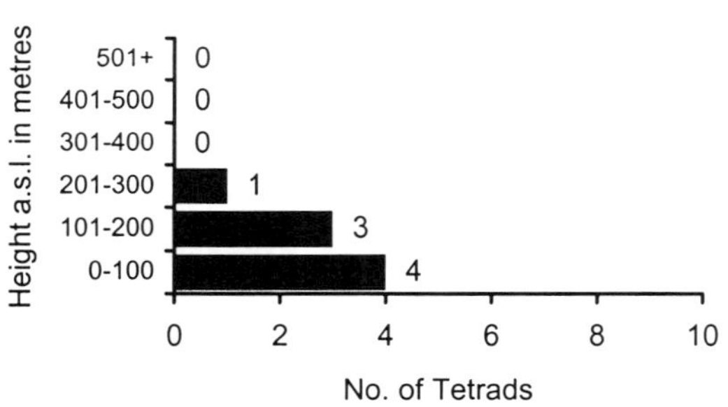

No. of tetrads in which recorded 8 (<1%)

Tetrad Analysis	No. of tetrads
1 bird	8 (100%)

Total No. of birds counted 8

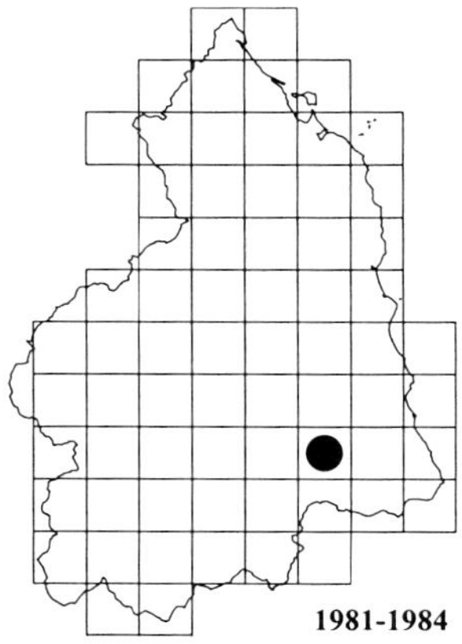

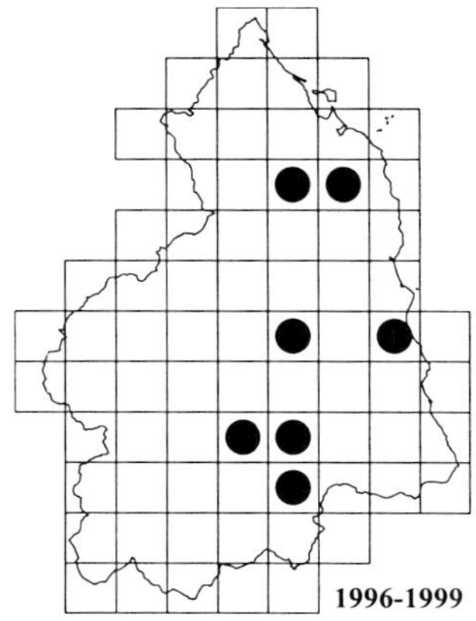

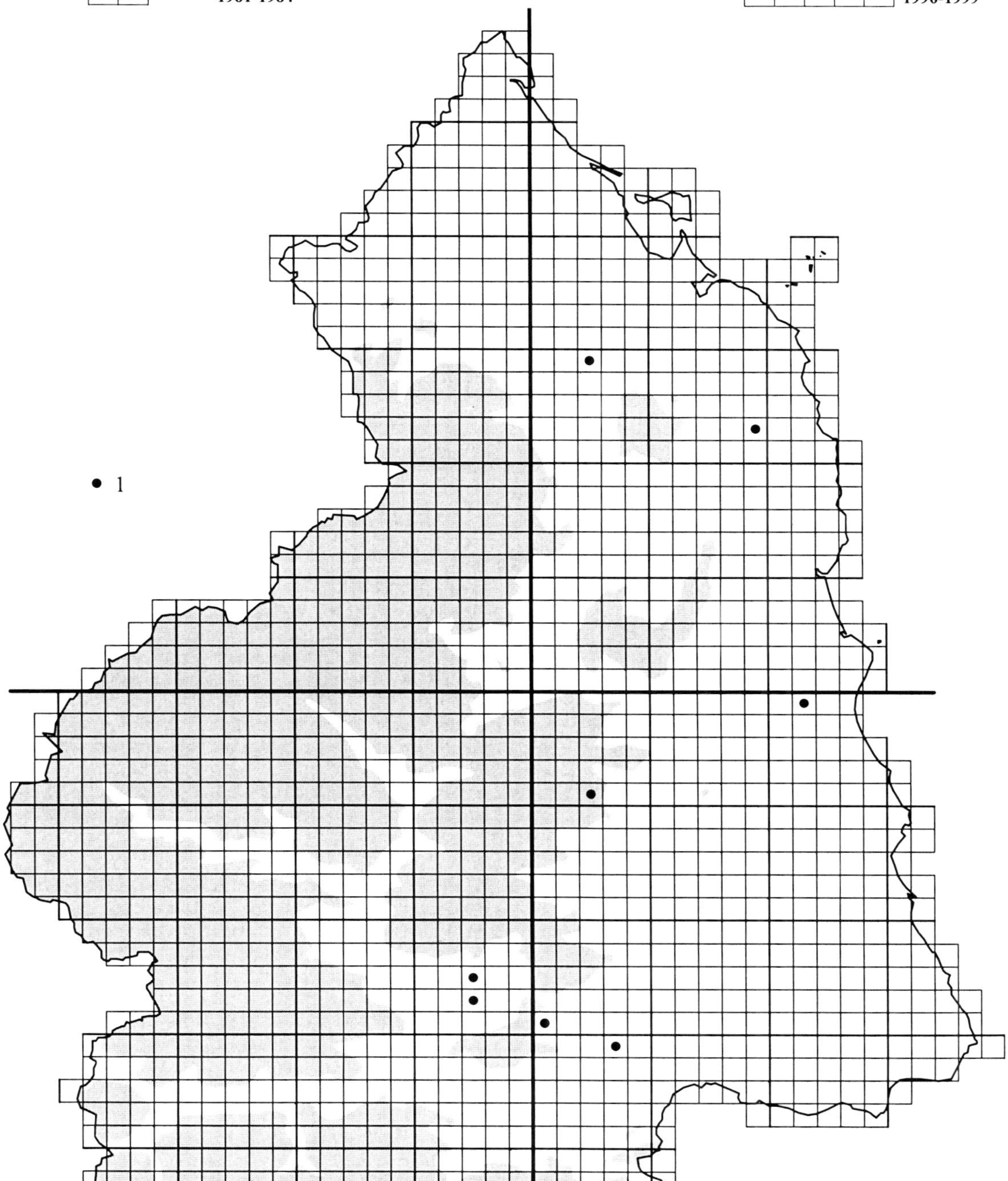

Green Sandpiper

TURNSTONE *Arenaria interpres*

Turnstones are almost exclusively coastal in winter. Bolam (1912) described them as 'a common autumn and winter resident where rocks intersect a sandy shore'. He further commented that 'Turnstones are usually very good eating, superior to most shore birds in that respect'. The same situation prevails today, at least as far as their distribution is concerned! Galloway and Meek (1980) reported that it is a common species, with a wintering population normally around 1,000-1,200 birds, but which reached 1,820 in mid-February 1976.

The breeding distribution of Turnstone is circumpolar, with our wintering birds coming from the Greenland/Canadian population although autumn passage birds are mainly from the Finnish/Northern Europe population. The wintering population in Great Britain is estimated at 64,000 out of a European wintering population of 70,000. Typically, 15% of winter flocks are juveniles although this depends on the annual breeding success (Metcalfe & Furness, 1985).

The two 10km square maps indicate no surprises with little change over the fifteen years between the two winter atlas periods. The tetrad map shows a wide distribution along the county's coastline, although with a number of obvious gaps. These coincide with stretches of sandy beach, such as those at Goswick and Druridge Bay. The map also indicates the tendency to use coastal ponds and fields immediately behind the high-tide line and coastal dunes which are utilised either for high-tide roosting or for feeding. The favoured feeding areas are, however, on wave-washed rocks and on stranded heaps of storm-deposited wrack with birds roosting normally on rocks or beach immediately above the high-tide line. Within each seasonally used area, individual birds tend to be faithful to particular sites both within and between years (Metcalfe & Furness, 1985).

The total number of birds counted during the atlas period was 1,847 which is almost certainly greater than the true county wintering population. A more accurate estimate may be taken from the monthly WeBS counts which cover the great majority of the coast from Berwick Little Beach to the mouth of the Tyne. These show peaks of 810, 1,359 and 1,506 for the three winters of the current survey. The last figure, for November 1998, includes 320 on the Farne Islands which were not counted for WeBS in the previous winters. These figures suggest that the population has not changed substantially since the assessment of Galloway and Meek in 1980 and appears to be generally in line with national trends, which show the United Kingdom population index in 1998/99 to be similar to that of the mid-1970s (Pollitt *et al.*, 2000). An apparent decrease between the 1984/85 BTO Winter Shorebird Count and the 1997/98 Non-Estuarine Waterbird Survey of 15.2% can be explained by an increase in the UK population in the 1980s followed by a steady decline.

As was stated for Purple Sandpiper *Calidris maritima* (q.v.), the Government has now designated the rocky sections of the Northumberland and Durham coastlines between Spittal and Blackhall Rocks in Co. Durham as a Special Protection Area for Birds and a Wetland of International Importance under the Ramsar Convention. The SPA, assessed at 1,739 birds, holds 2.5% of the wintering Western Palearctic population of Turnstone with more than half occurring north of the Tyne. This habitat for Turnstone, hopefully, now has appropriate levels of protection. The future for the species in the county will lie in other factors, such as breeding success and global warming, which may produce a shift in the wintering area for the species and should be monitored with interest.

ROGER NORMAN

No. of tetrads in which recorded: 63 (4%)

Tetrad Analysis	No. of tetrads
1-12 birds	31 (49%)
13-45 birds	20 (32%)
46+ birds	12 (19%)

Total No. of birds counted: 1,847

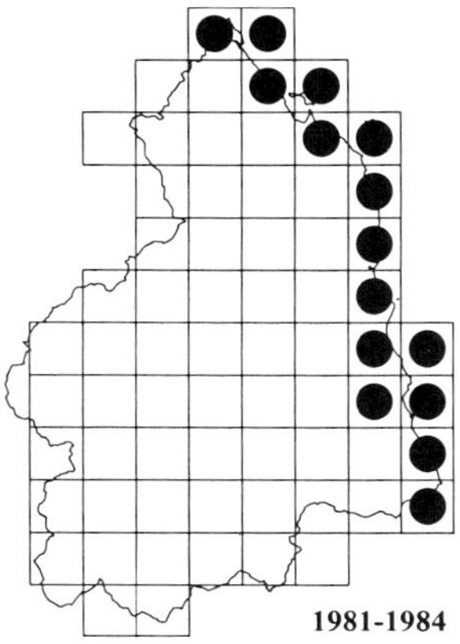

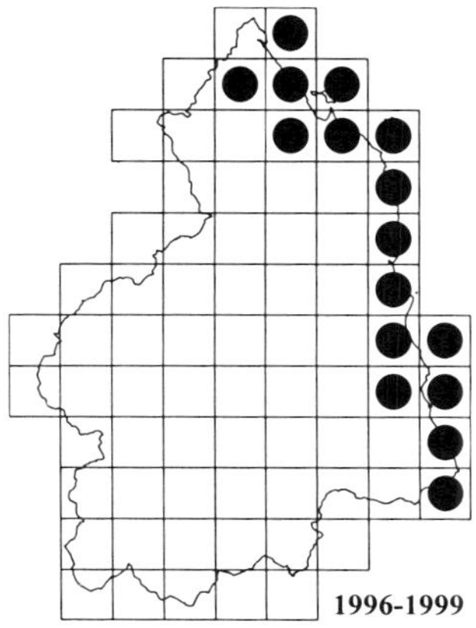

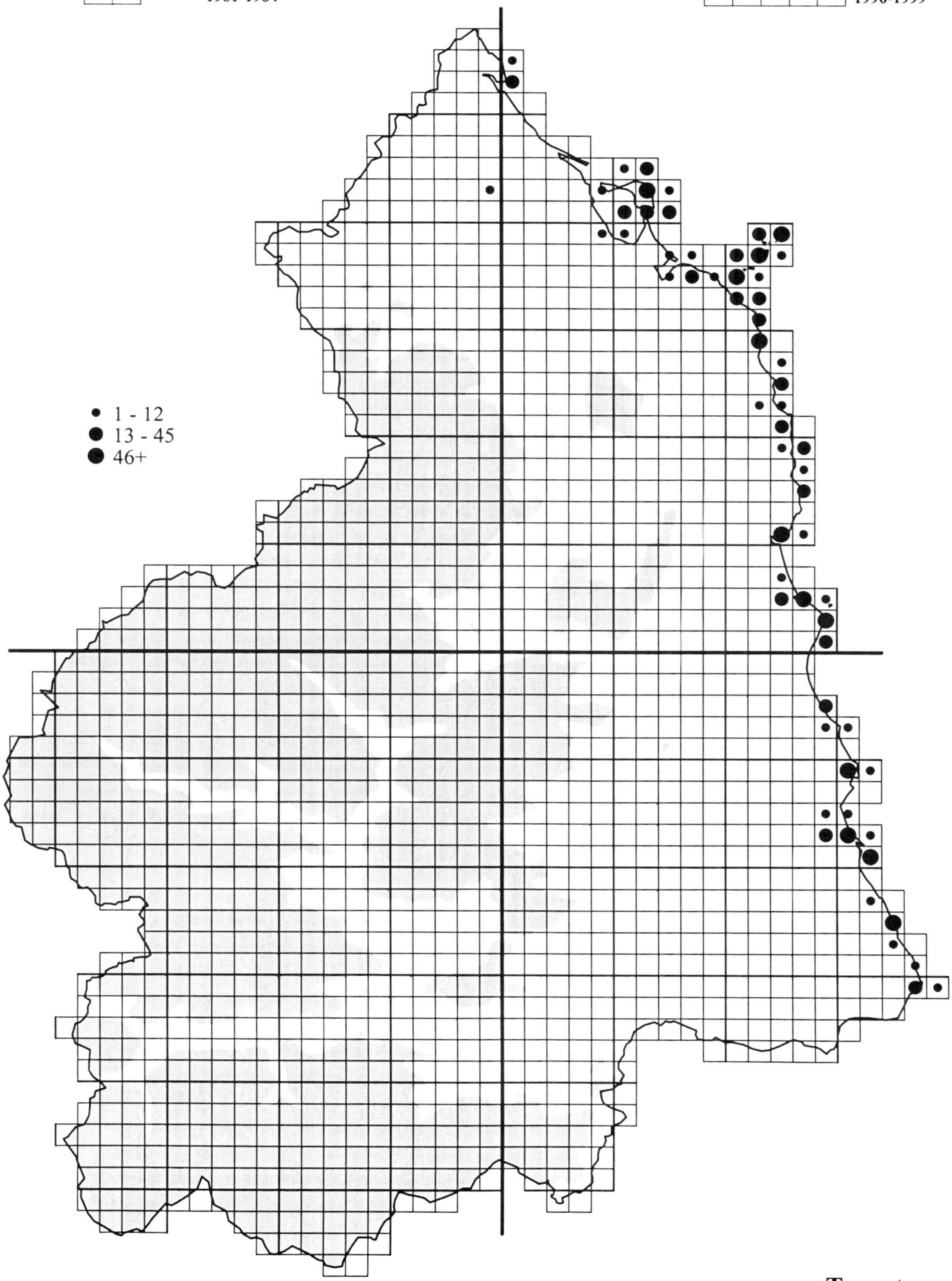

Turnstone

COMMON SANDPIPER *Actitis hypoleucos*

During the course of the three winter surveys the Common Sandpiper was only recorded on the River Tyne. It occurred in the Dilston/Corbridge area (NY96S/X) between December 1998 and February/March 1999 and, even though the sightings were reported in adjacent tetrads, it is almost certain that they refer to the same bird. In Northumberland the species is on the very northern limit of its wintering range and, although seasonal records nationally have increased, almost all of the estimated 100 wintering birds in England are at sites below a line drawn from the Humber to the Mersey (Lack, 1986). Whilst a common passage visitor and breeding species in Northumberland (Galloway & Meek, 1980), the Common Sandpiper is rare in winter (Kerr, 2001). Between 1938 and 1980 birds occurred in at least nine winters and in the last decade of the twentieth century were present during the winters of 1990, 1993, 1995 and the 'atlas winter' of 1998/99. The Tweed Estuary and the middle reaches of the River Tyne (Hexham to Corbridge) appear to be the favoured wintering areas.

JOHN C. DAY

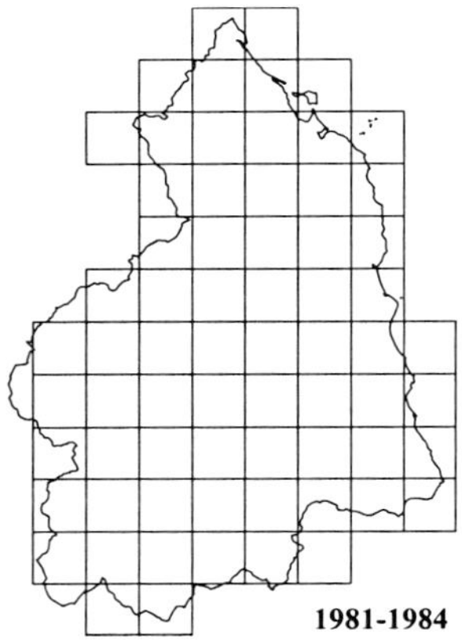

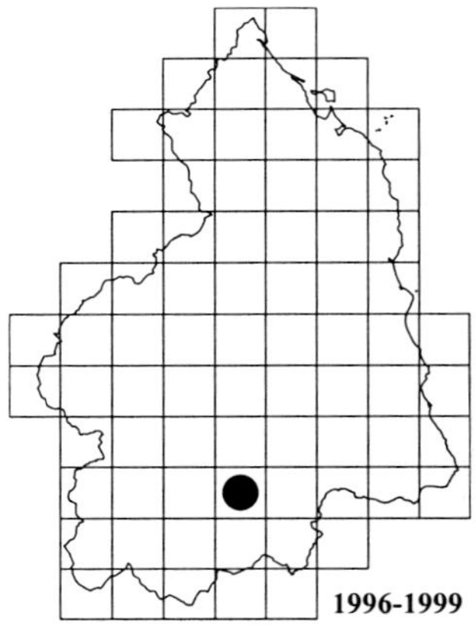

No. of tetrads in which recorded 2 (<1%)

Tetrad Analysis	No. of tetrads
1 bird	2 (100%)

Total No. of birds counted 2

WINTERING GULLS IN NORTHUMBERLAND

Nick Rossiter

Five, possibly six, species of gull are listed for Northumberland in Gardner-Medwin's account (1985) of *Birds: Ancient and Modern* from the eighteenth century, although the first mention in systematic lists was by Selby (1831; 1833) who in his *Catalogue* of 1831 recorded eight species including Black-headed *Larus ridibundus*, Common *L. canus*, Herring *L. argentatus*, Lesser Black-backed *L. fuscus*, Iceland *L. glaucoides*, Glaucous *L. hyperboreus*, Great Black-backed *L. marinus* and Kittiwake *Rissa tridactyla*. The commoner species are simply listed but the Iceland and Glaucous Gulls were clearly regarded as of more interest, being mentioned as very rare and an occasional visitor respectively. In his *Illustrations* of 1833, Selby gave more information. Most gulls were regarded as strictly coastal birds but with two exceptions. The Black-headed Gull bred inland but wintered on the coast. The Common Gull had more pronounced inland traits being 'accustomed to fly inland, feeding upon earth-worms, grubs and slugs'. Some of the complexities of gull plumages were already known, particularly the problems of identifying immature birds.

Little change seems to have occurred in the habits of the gulls by the 1870s (Hancock, 1874) although Little Gull *L. minutus* had been added to the county list as an autumn and winter visitor. Bolam (1912) mentioned the large roost of gulls on Goswick Sands. From analysis of its stomach contents, the predominant species, the Common Gull, fed mainly on earthworms. The tenth gull species to be recorded in the county was Ivory Gull *Pagophila eburnea* in 1887 (Kerr, 2001).

In the 1930s the Common Gull was recorded as wintering upon the coast in large flocks with some numbers found inland, particularly on migration (Bolam, 1932). The Glaucous Gull was regarded as an irregular winter visitant, sometimes present in moderate numbers, with immatures always in the majority. The Iceland Gull was thought to be always rarer than the Glaucous Gull but one had been recorded inland on the River North Tyne. The roving of the Great Black-backed Gull over the western moors in small parties was also recorded, particularly in the winter. The Herring Gull rarely ventured inland. The number of gull species recorded remained at ten although Perry was later to add Sabine's Gull *L. sabini* from a record at Holy Island in the 1920s (Kerr, 2001).

From the 1950s to the 1970s the first efforts were made to count gull roosts (Galloway & Meek, 1980). Some very large roosts were recorded on the coast in the Lindisfarne NNR area with 100,000 Black-headed Gulls in October 1956 and mixed flocks of Common/Black-headed Gulls of 40,000 in December 1974 and 53,000 in December 1975. Although roosts of Common Gulls inland were thought, usually, not to exceed 5,000, an estimated 35,000 were at Colt Crag Reservoir in January 1968. In the 1970s roosts of 4,000-5,000 Black-headed Gulls and 4,000-8,000 Common Gulls were found at Derwent Reservoir and Sweethope Lough. Great Black-backed Gulls also roosted inland in numbers, with 400 at Hallington Reservoirs and 100 at Catcleugh Reservoir in November and December 1973. Records of Bonaparte's Gull *L. philadelphia* and Mediterranean Gull *L. melanocephalus* in 1955, Ross's Gull *Rhodostethia rosea* in 1960 and Laughing Gull *L. atricilla* in 1975 (Kerr, 2001) increased the number of species recorded in the county to 15 by 1980.

Nationally roost strategies were changing in the 1960s, with very large movements of the five common species (Black-headed, Common, Herring, Lesser Black-backed and Great Black-backed) into inland urban areas (Hickling, 1967). This movement was attributed to the greater availability of food on landfill sites and the construction of new reservoirs which acted as safe overnight roosting sites.

The reasons for the movement inland in Northumberland at a similar time are less obvious. In the early nineteenth century there were no substantial reservoirs and a limited supply of loughs. The shortage of safe roosting sites inland ensured that all gulls returned to the coast to spend the night. This shortage was to be readily solved over the next century and a half by extensive reservoir construction (Rennison, 1982/83). The first reservoirs, comprising Whittle Dene (flooded 1848-1857), East Hallington (1872), Little Swinburne (1879), Colt Crag (1884), and West Hallington (1889/90), have been available for roosting in their present form for many decades without any changes. Yet there is little evidence for their use by gulls for roosting until the 1960s. Derwent Reservoir is different; this became available for roosting about 1967 and was an instant attraction to gulls of all types, at least partly because of the number of landfill sites in its vicinity. Hickling (1967) commented on the enthusiasm that gulls show for new reservoirs in suitable feeding areas. By contrast, the development of Kielder Reservoir in the 1970s has drawn gulls in very small numbers, presumably due to the lack of feeding areas in its vicinity. It would appear that the movement inland in Northumberland owed something to the timely construction of Derwent Reservoir but perhaps more to a change in behaviour learnt from birds wintering further south.

In the 1980s and 1990s gull roosts were counted more systematically and the highest counts in the 1990s are summarised below. The accompanying map of known gull roosts, classified as of major or minor importance, shows all the sites mentioned. Inland populations of Common Gulls were at very high levels, far exceeding those on the coast (Rossiter, 1996). Inland, 65,000 were at Hallington Reservoirs in October 1996, 48,000 at Derwent Reservoir in January 1998 and 41,000 at Colt Crag Reservoir in September 1993. On the coast, 14,000 were at Budle Bay in September 1993 and other roosts formed at Newton Haven, Alnmouth and the Tyne Estuary. Black-headed Gull numbers were relatively high inland in spring (Rossiter, 1999a) with roughly equal numbers on the coast in autumn and winter. Inland, 21,000 were at Scotswood in January and November 1997 and 17,000 at Hallington Reservoir in September 1992. Coastal roost sites included the Tweed Estuary, Budle Bay, Newton Haven, Alnmouth, Amble, Coquet Island, Blyth Estuary, St Mary's Island and the Tyne Estuary. Herring Gulls were generally commoner on the coast (Turner, 2000) with 5,000 at the Farne Islands in September 1992 and 3,600 in the Tyne Estuary in September 1999. However, in mid-winter large numbers could be found inland with 6,300 at Derwent Reservoir in January 1997 and 1,890 at Scotswood in December 1997. The picture is similar for Great Black-backed Gulls. On the coast, 6,000 were at the Farne Islands in October and November 1991, 1,800 in Druridge Bay in October 1995 with regular roosts also at Newbiggin, Amble, Blyth and the Tyne Estuary (Turner, 2001). Inland, 900 were at Derwent Reservoir and 240 at Hallington Reservoir in January 1991 (Rossiter, 2001a). Lesser Black-backed Gulls were scarce in mid-winter but a substantial autumn roost, a month before the winter atlas survey began, formed inland at Caistron, peaking at 970 in October 1996 (Rossiter, 1997).

The Tyne Estuary and other parts of the coast were again favoured by 'white-winged gulls' but, except in autumn, Iceland Gulls were now almost as common as Glaucous Gulls, in marked contrast to the picture in the nineteenth century. Mediterranean Gulls also became commoner in autumn and winter on the coast and inland and Little Gulls increased in numbers on the coast in summer and autumn. The first Ring-billed Gull *L. delawarensis* in 1985 (Kerr, 2001) increased the county gull list to 16.

More recently, gull taxonomy has been the subject of intense debate with the establishment, by some sources, of new species including the Yellow-legged Gull *L. cachinnans* as described later in the account for this form. Certainly gull identification has advanced and it is anticipated that, in conjunction with DNA studies, some more species will be established in the next few years.

Finally, one aspect of human activity that has favoured gull populations, landfill tipping, looks likely to be much less favourable in future. Proposed European legislation will ban the tipping of uncovered food waste. In areas where this has already happened, such as Hexham in 2000, there has been a dramatic reduction in the numbers of wintering large gulls, particularly Herring Gulls.

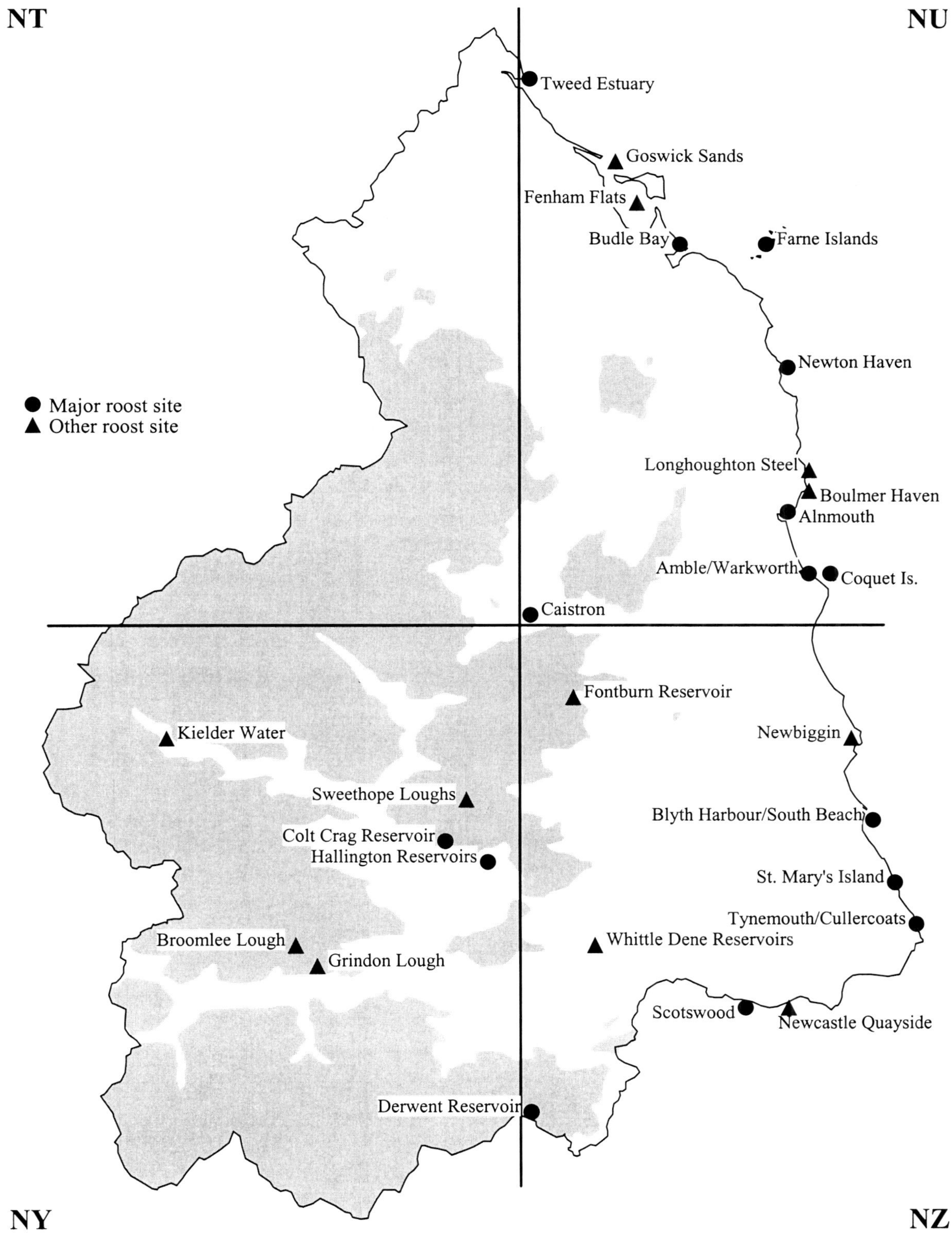

Location of gull roosts in Northumberland

MEDITERRANEAN GULL *Larus melanocephalus*

Galloway & Meek (1980) described the Mediterranean Gull as 'a rare visitor' and recorded the first occurrence in Northumberland as an adult bearing a ring at North Shields Fish Quay in March 1955. Since then the species has been increasingly well-recorded in the region during the winter, and the other seasons, although in small numbers. Many records over a period of years at well-frequented localities probably involve some returning individuals, best illustrated by the regularity of a metal-ringed adult at Craster each winter from December 1984 until at least 1999/2000.

In the current winter survey, single birds were recorded in 15 of the 18 occupied tetrads while the remaining tetrads held two to three as a maximum. Of these counts, three were at North Shields Fish Quay (NZ36U) in December 1996, three at Newbiggin (NZ38D/E) during 1997/98 and two at Druridge Pools (NZ29T) in December 1997. The majority of records were coastal, between North Shields Fish Quay and Holy Island, with six inland sightings. The coastal sites where individuals were observed during the survey included Blyth South Harbour and Estuary (NZ38F), North Blyth/Cambois (NZ38B), Ladyburn Lake (NU20Q), Amble (NU20S) and Craster (NU21U). Of the inland sightings, four were concentrated in the wetlands in the south east of the county at Wallsend Swallow Pond (NZ36E), Holywell Pond (NZ37C), Arcot Pond (NZ27M) and Big Waters (NZ27G). The other inland sightings were at the New Moor Tip near Ashington (NZ28U) with a more unusual record, 40km inland, at Derwent Reservoir (NZ05B).

Breeding Mediterranean Gulls in the Ukraine peaked at 336,000 pairs in 1983 (Ardamatskaya, 1999), this population showing a cyclic trend of peaks and troughs over an approximate 20-year period including a maximum of 72,000 breeding pairs during 1989-1998 constituting 'about 90% of the world population' (Rudenko, 1999). The breeding population in the Netherlands increased from ten pairs in 1980 to 410 pairs in 1998 and the Belgian population rose from up to 20 pairs until 1990 to at least 275 pairs in 1998 (Meininger & Flamant, 1999). The maximum number of breeding pairs in the UK has risen from five in 1986 to 54-65 pairs in 1998 (Ogilvie, 1999 and 2000). Of the wintering numbers, Lack (1986) noted that 'the December population is probably between 100 and 150 birds in Britain and Ireland'. Since then there has been a pronounced increase in numbers, the obvious example being those wintering in Kent at Folkestone, where numbers have risen from eight to 130 individuals between 1980 and 1998 (Henson, 1999). The country of origin of colour-ringed birds seen by Henson at Folkestone include the Netherlands, Belgium, France, Germany and Hungary. White (1993) recorded the increased status in Britain as 'believed to be in the region of 750-1,000 individuals recorded every year'. Henson (pers. comm.) mentions that British birds originate very largely from the Dutch and Belgian breeding areas, a fact confirmed by the colour-ringed bird seen at North Shields Fish Quay in October 1996 which had been ringed as a pullus at Antwerp, Belgium, in May of the same year.

A comparison of the two 10km square maps clearly shows a wider coastal distribution of this species in the current winter survey, with a little movement inland. Table 1 below shows the estimated total numbers recorded throughout the county during the three winter periods of the current survey.

Winter period	Totals by age group		
15th Nov - 28th Feb	1st winter	2nd winter	Adult
1996 / 97	2 - 4	1	4 - 5
1997 / 98	2	3	4 - 6
1998 / 99	0	1	5 - 7

Table 1 Numbers of wintering Mediterranean Gulls in Northumberland

The species has now been recorded in Northumberland in every month of the year, and still shows signs of increasing numbers. Its winter status is probably best described as borderline between rare and uncommon.

DANIEL M. TURNER

No. of tetrads in which recorded 18 (1%)

Tetrad Analysis	No. of tetrads
1 bird	15 (83%)
2-3 birds	3 (17%)

Total No. of birds counted 23

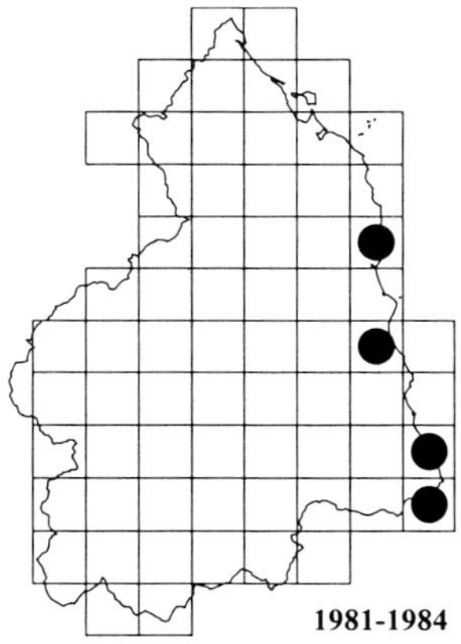

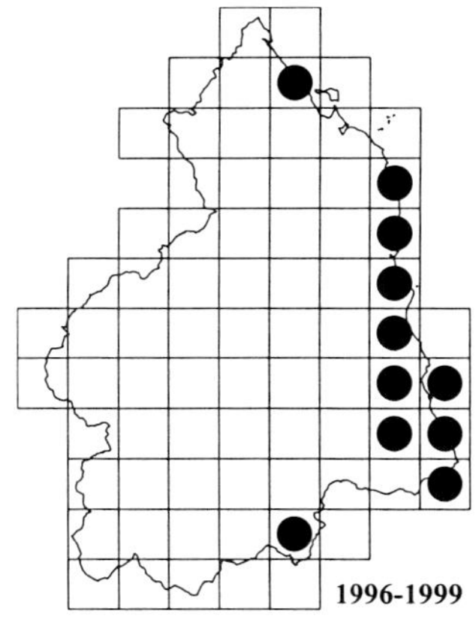

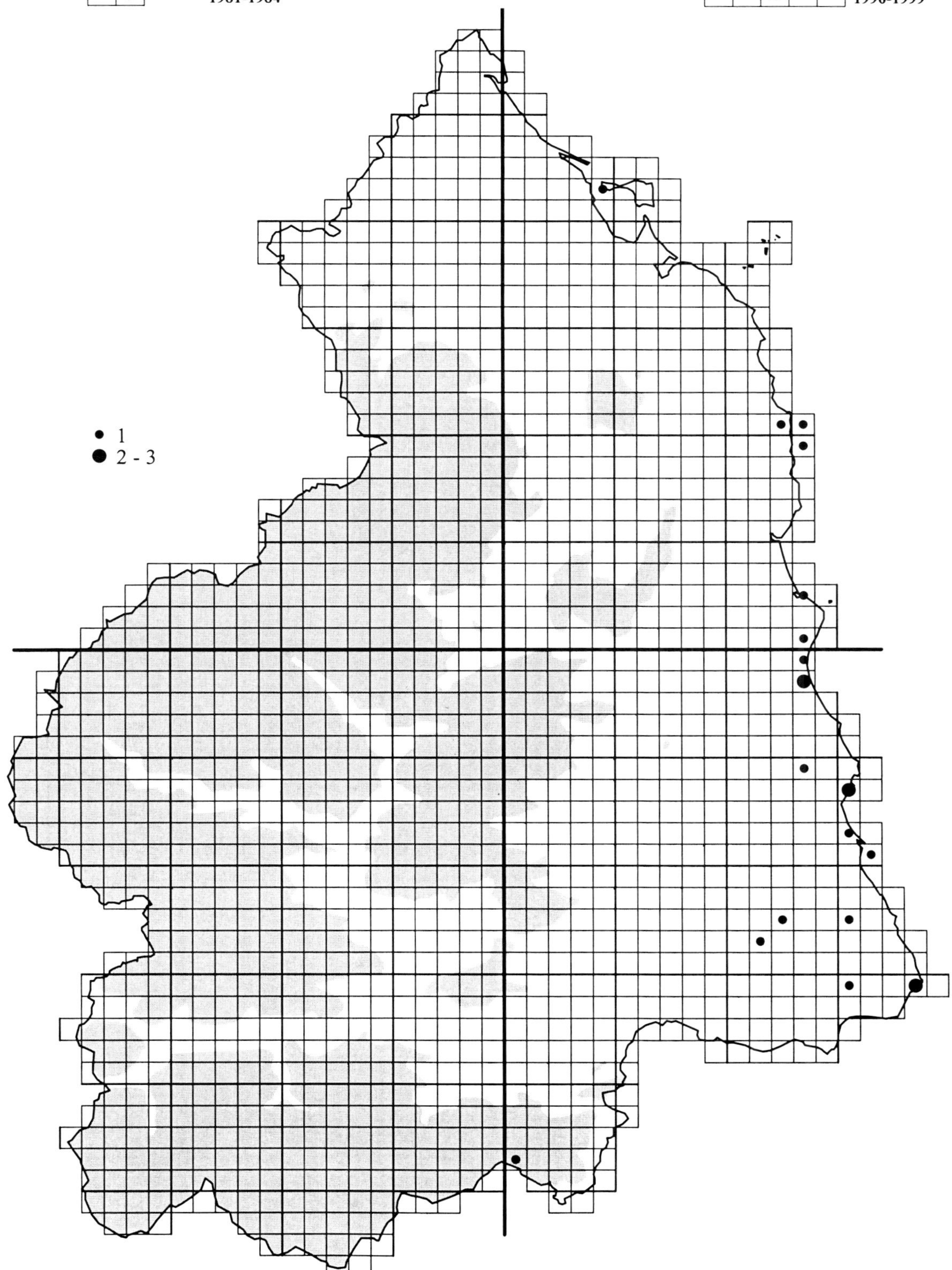

Mediterranean Gull

LITTLE GULL *Larus minutus*

This species was described by Hancock (1874) as 'an autumn and winter visitant', an assessment with which Bolam (1932) in his *Catalogue* agreed. Bolam indicated that for those records where dates of occurrence were known, some eight had been in January and three in December, and also mentioned a party of seven birds at Berwick on 2nd January 1930. Galloway and Meek (1980) said that, apart from 1953, the species had been recorded annually since 1945, and from the mid-1950s had been increasing in numbers. Much of the increase though was of passage birds in autumn and they said of winter sightings that they were 'now few and form a much smaller proportion of the total than in Bolam's time'.

Since 1981/82 up to the beginning of the current atlas survey, Little Gulls were recorded in every winter period but in most years only one-three individuals were involved. Records from the winters of 1990/91 and 1995/96 involved slightly higher numbers with about eight and ten birds respectively. The current survey produced a total of only nine birds with two in 1996/97, four in 1997/98 and three in 1998/99. As has come to be expected, all of the sightings were coastal with the exception of a first winter bird at Killingworth (NZ27Q) on 27th February 1997. From these rather sparse results it would appear that the Little Gull remains a rare visitor to Northumberland in winter.

MIKE S. HODGSON

No. of tetrads in which recorded 8 (<1%)

Tetrad Analysis	No. of tetrads
1 bird	7 (88%)
2 birds	1 (12%)

Total No. of birds counted 9

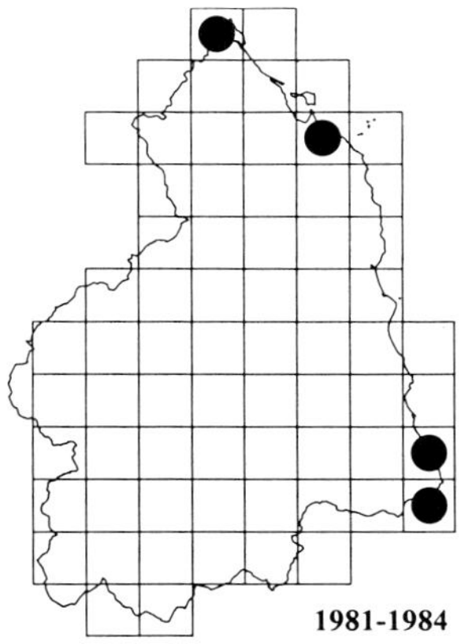

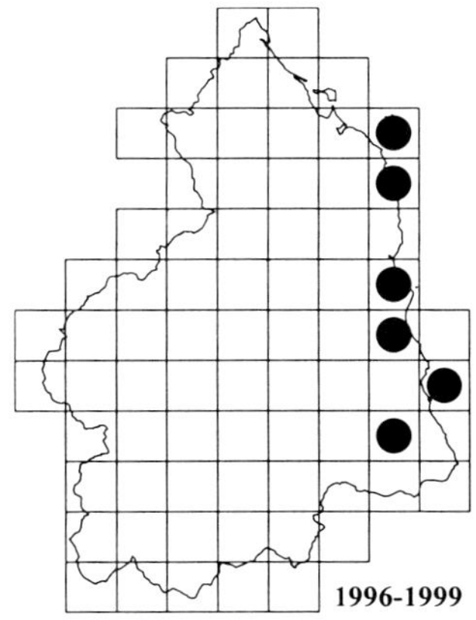

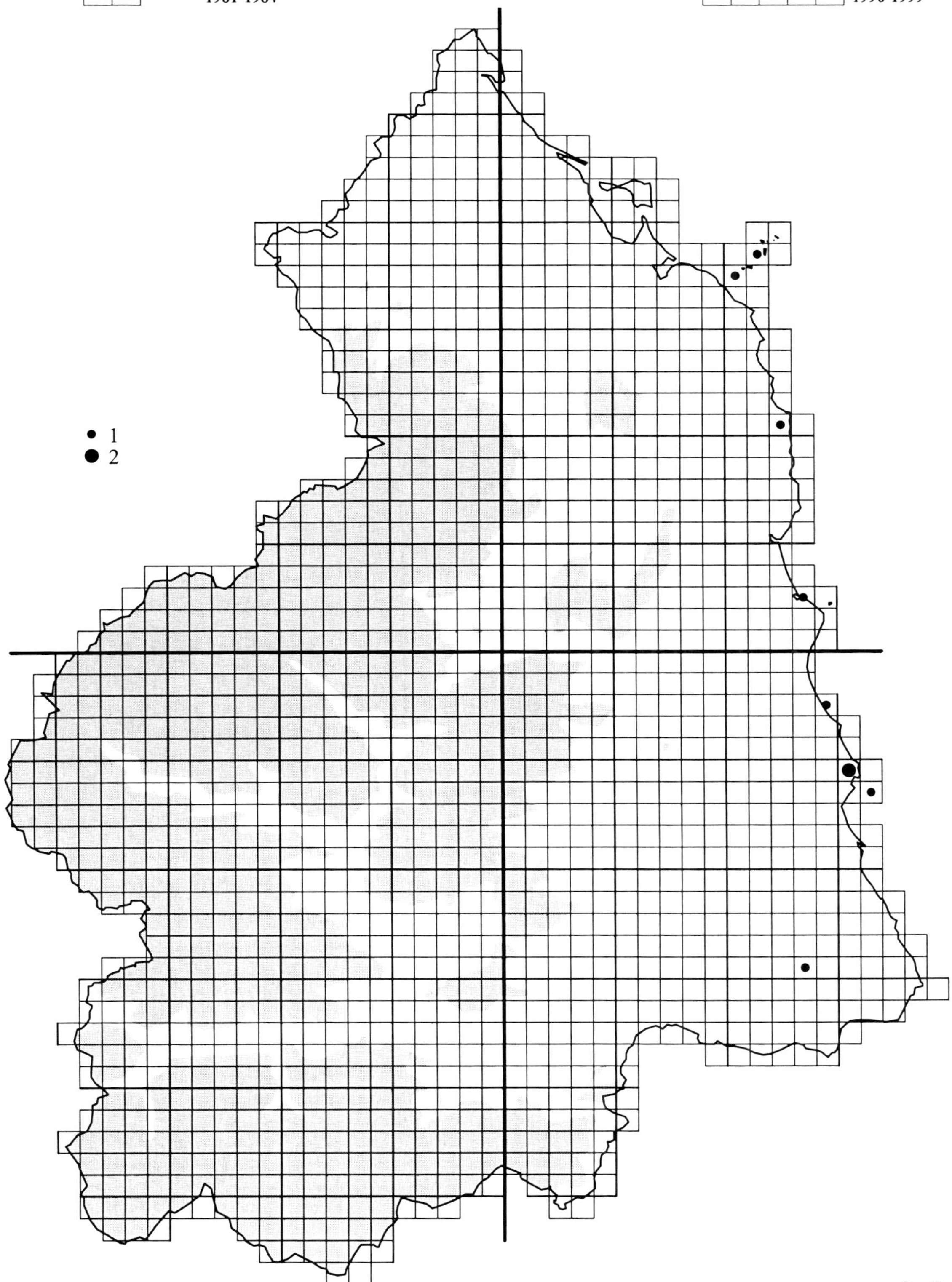

Little Gull

BLACK-HEADED GULL *Larus ridibundus*

Black-headed Gulls have been noted in numbers in Northumberland for some years, with Hancock (1874) describing the species as common and Bolam (1932) calling it an abundant resident. Galloway and Meek (1980) referred to it as an abundant winter visitor, with large concentrations of autumn arrivals by October and considerable flocks passing through the county in March and April. The same authors detailed a count of 100,000 on the Lindisfarne NNR in late October 1956 and a report of many thousands at St. Mary's Island in February 1976. Counts along the rest of the Northumberland coast suggested that the coastal wintering population of Black-headed Gulls was in the region of 4,000 birds. In addition large inland roosts were mentioned with up to 5,000 at Sweethope Lough in December 1977.

The tetrad map for the current county winter atlas survey suggests that the winter distribution for Black-headed Gull is still largely the same with concentrations along the coast but also inland, either following river basins (e.g. the River Tyne and River Coquet) or on low-lying inland areas to the east of higher ground. This predominantly low-level distribution is confirmed by the fact that 97% of the 487 occupied tetrads were below 200 metres a.s.l. This pattern of distribution is not unexpected, given that Black-headed Gulls in winter occupy a wide variety of habitats (Lack, 1986) ranging from estuaries and coastal marshes to grazing and ploughed land and tend to roost on open water either at the coast or inland.

Studies of ringing recoveries of Black-headed Gulls (Flegg & Cox, 1972) suggest that those breeding in Britain disperse in winter but, as the number of foreign recoveries is low, this dispersal remains largely within Britain and Ireland. Local ringing returns nevertheless include a number of foreign-ringed birds from Scandinavia and the Baltic with recoveries of locally ringed birds, usually first-years, from Holland, Spain and North Africa. Winter numbers are also increased by many immigrants from northern Europe (Cramp & Simmons, 1982). Comparison of the breeding distribution map in *The atlas of breeding birds in Northumbria* (Day *et al.*, 1995) with the current tetrad map shows a somewhat different pattern from that in winter. Breeding is concentrated in a relatively small number of tetrads (76), primarily in the south-west of the county and in scattered colonies on the coast. Apart from coastal sightings, there is almost a complete absence in winter of Black-headed Gulls in inland tetrads in which they breed. If the two smaller 10km square maps are compared however, the species did winter in the south west of the county in the 1980s. The reasons for the fluctuations are not clear, as there has been no widespread local change over the whole of that area and may be weather-related with birds dispersing more widely in milder conditions. There is also the possibility of a larger influx of European breeding birds in some years depending on weather conditions outside Britain. Further evidence that the number of Black-headed Gulls in Northumberland may vary from year to year is provided by data from the control tetrads. Of the 60 control tetrads monitored Black-headed Gulls were recorded in 33 (55%) accounting for 3,450 birds in the winter of 1996/97, 1,822 in 1997/98 and 2,497 in 1998/99. Numbers at roost sites in the county, some of which are regularly monitored in winter, are also prone to fluctuations from month to month and year to year. During the current survey the roost at Scotswood on the River Tyne (NZ26B) held most birds with a maximum of 21,000 in January 1997 and November 1997, 15,500 in November 1998 and 7,500 in January 1998.

The grand total of maximum counts in the current winter survey was 51,739 in 487 tetrads indicating that the winter status of Black-headed Gull should remain as an abundant visitor to Northumberland.

NEIL ANDERSON

Distribution by altitude

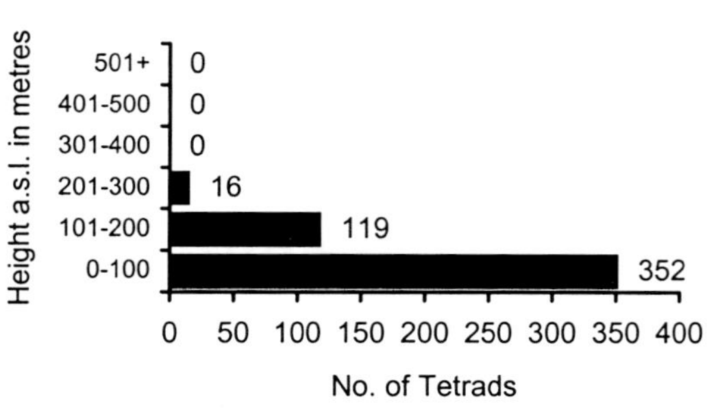

No. of tetrads in which recorded 487 (34%)

Tetrad Analysis	No. of tetrads
1-23 birds	241 (49%)
24-105 birds	148 (31%)
106+ birds	98 (20%)

Total No. of birds counted 51,759

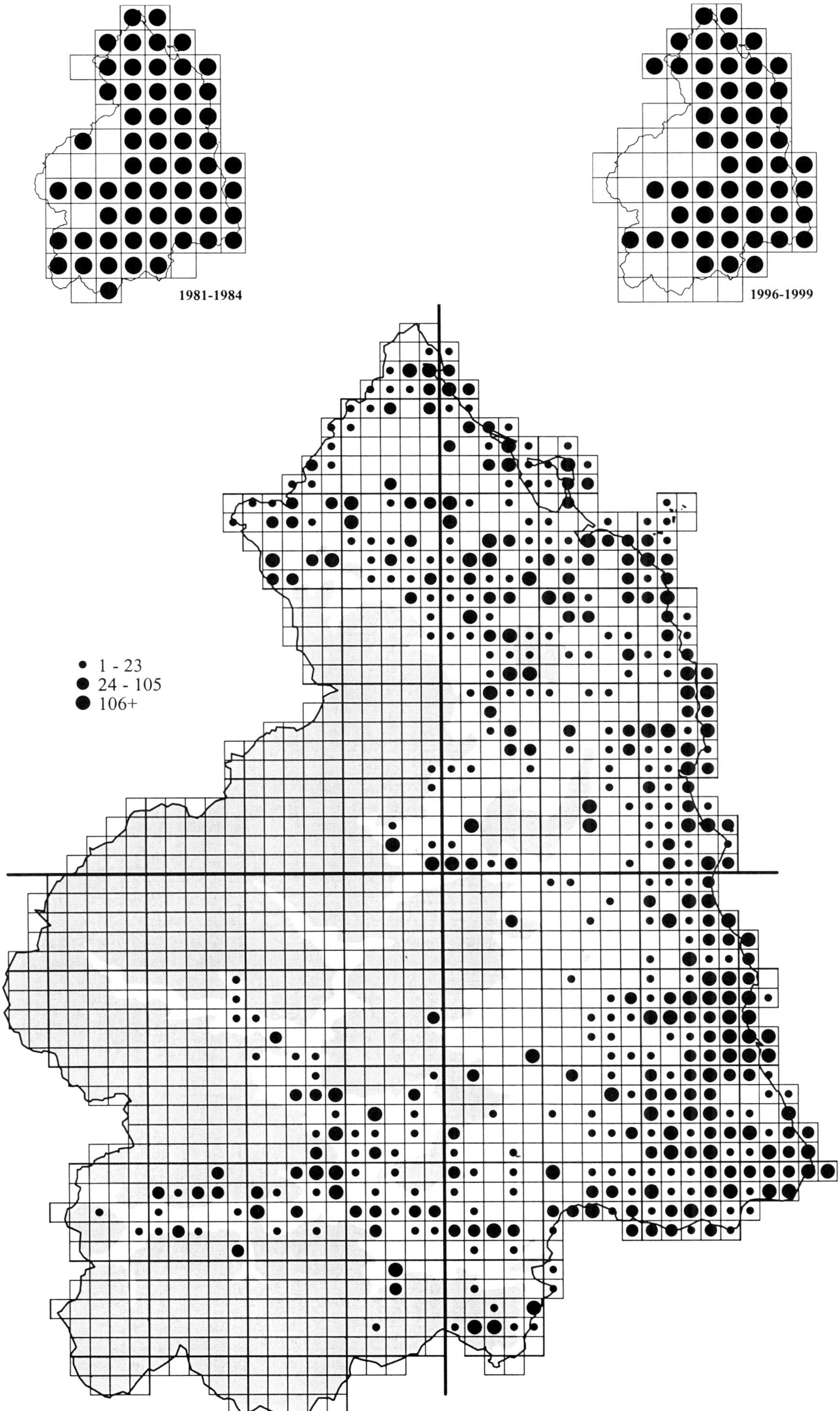

Black-headed Gull

COMMON GULL *Larus canus*

In the nineteenth century Selby (1833) thought the Common Gull was very widely distributed in Britain, including inland areas, almost throughout the year. Some forty years later Hancock (1874) did not note its presence inland, reporting only that the Common Gull was found in abundance on the whole Northumberland coast throughout the year. In turn Bolam (1932) regarded it as an abundant winter visitor and passage migrant, wintering upon the coast in large flocks, which were present from mid-August to April. By the 1970s the Lindisfarne NNR was a favoured roosting area, with a massive 53,000 present in December 1975 (Galloway & Meek, 1980), although numbers had begun to increase inland in the 1970s as part of a national trend (Hickling, 1977). Rossiter (1996), from a long-term study of roosting populations at mainly inland areas from 1983-1995, showed that substantial numbers (approaching 10,000 birds) returned at the end of July. Numbers then rose steadily through August to a plateau of 40,000-47,000 from September-November. Numbers fell sharply in winter, particularly in hard weather, to an average of around 16,000 in late January before increasing to 43,000 in late March. Few remained after mid-April. In Northumberland the species has, until recently, been regarded as a very rare breeding bird. Since the 1970s, however, a limited colonisation has taken place, particularly at industrial sites, with ten to 20 pairs found during the county breeding atlas survey (Day *et al.*, 1995).

The two 10km square winter atlas maps show a similar distribution pattern and frequency with 58 ten kilometre squares occupied in the early 1980s and 57 in the present survey. An obvious feature of the tetrad distribution map is the restriction to lowland areas with very few over 200 metres a.s.l. Indeed out of 603 occupied tetrads, 336 were below 100 metres a.s.l., 216 between 101 and 200 metres a.s.l. and only 51 above 200 metres. The Common Gull is absent from nearly all of Kielder Forest, the Cheviots and the moors of the North Pennines. The map also shows that it is very common inland with large numbers in pasture areas, adjacent to the uplands and on the coast. Intensive agricultural areas just inland of the coast and on the Tweed are less frequented. This gull shows a marked preference for feeding on well-grazed grassland (Lack, 1986).

Many feeding areas are close to the main roost sites such as the Derwent, Hallington and Colt Crag Reservoirs, Broomlee Lough, Kielder Reservoir, Budle Bay and other coastal locations. From personal observations, journeys to roost are as much as 30km in the north of the county to Budle Bay (NU13) from the Mindrum/Cornhill area (NT83) and the same in the south east to Hallington (NY97) from the Cramlington/Seaton Burn area (NZ27).

The highest winter tetrad counts were 2,500 at Tynemouth (NZ36U) and at Cullercoats (NZ37Q) on 7th February 1998, 1,716 at Fowberry (NU02I) on 28th December 1998 and 1,590 south of Lowick (NU03D) on 24th January 1998. However, much higher concentrations occurred at roosts with a peak of 66,000 in January 1998, including 48,000 at Derwent Reservoir on 24th (*Birds in Northumbria 1998*). The county population, from the long-term roost counts, appeared relatively high throughout the current atlas period, with few prolonged cold weather spells to drive the population further south as found in the longer-term study (Rossiter, 1996). The grand total of 61,880 recorded from the tetrad counts may over-state the wintering population to some extent but as many as 40,000-60,000 Common Gulls appeared to spend at least part of the winter in the county with a residual population of about 25,000 in the spells of hard weather.

Ringing studies show that the majority of wintering birds come from Norway (Radford, 1960) and the British Isles are particularly important as a wintering area for birds reared in north Norway (Haftorn, 1971), with some winter visitors also from Sweden and Finland (Kerr, 2001). Individuals that are darker and slightly larger are noted occasionally, showing the characteristics of the race *L. c. heinei* from Russia. In the current winter atlas, only one adult of this form was noted, at Tynemouth on 23rd January 1999 (*Birds in Northumbria 1999*).

B. N. ROSSITER

Distribution by altitude

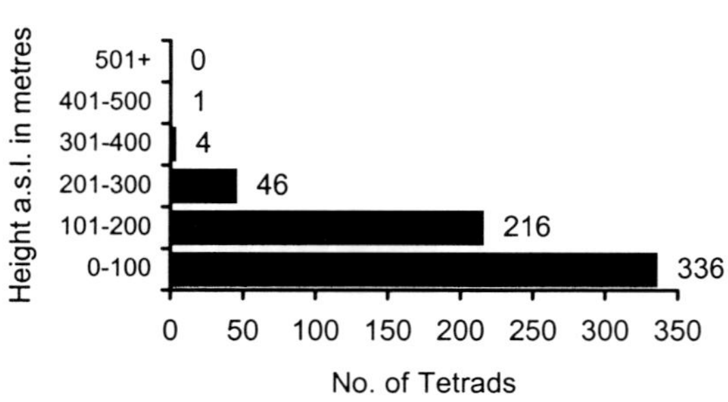

No. of tetrads in which recorded	603 (42%)
Tetrad Analysis	**No. of tetrads**
1-27 birds	303 (50%)
28-115 birds	180 (30%)
116+ birds	120 (20%)
Total No. of birds counted	61,880

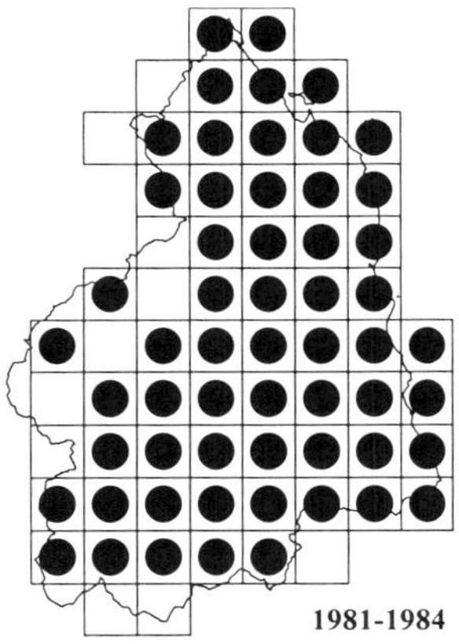

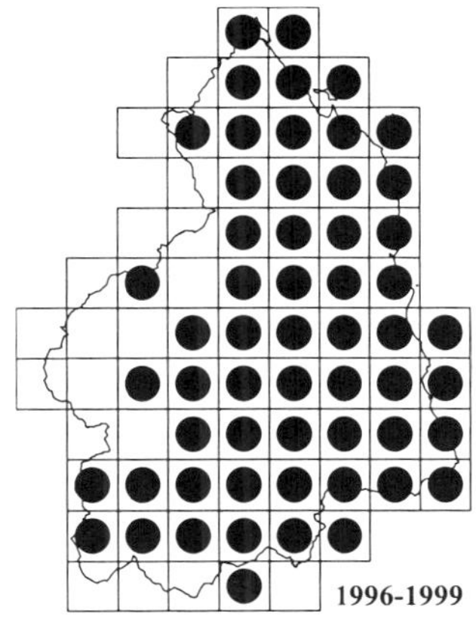

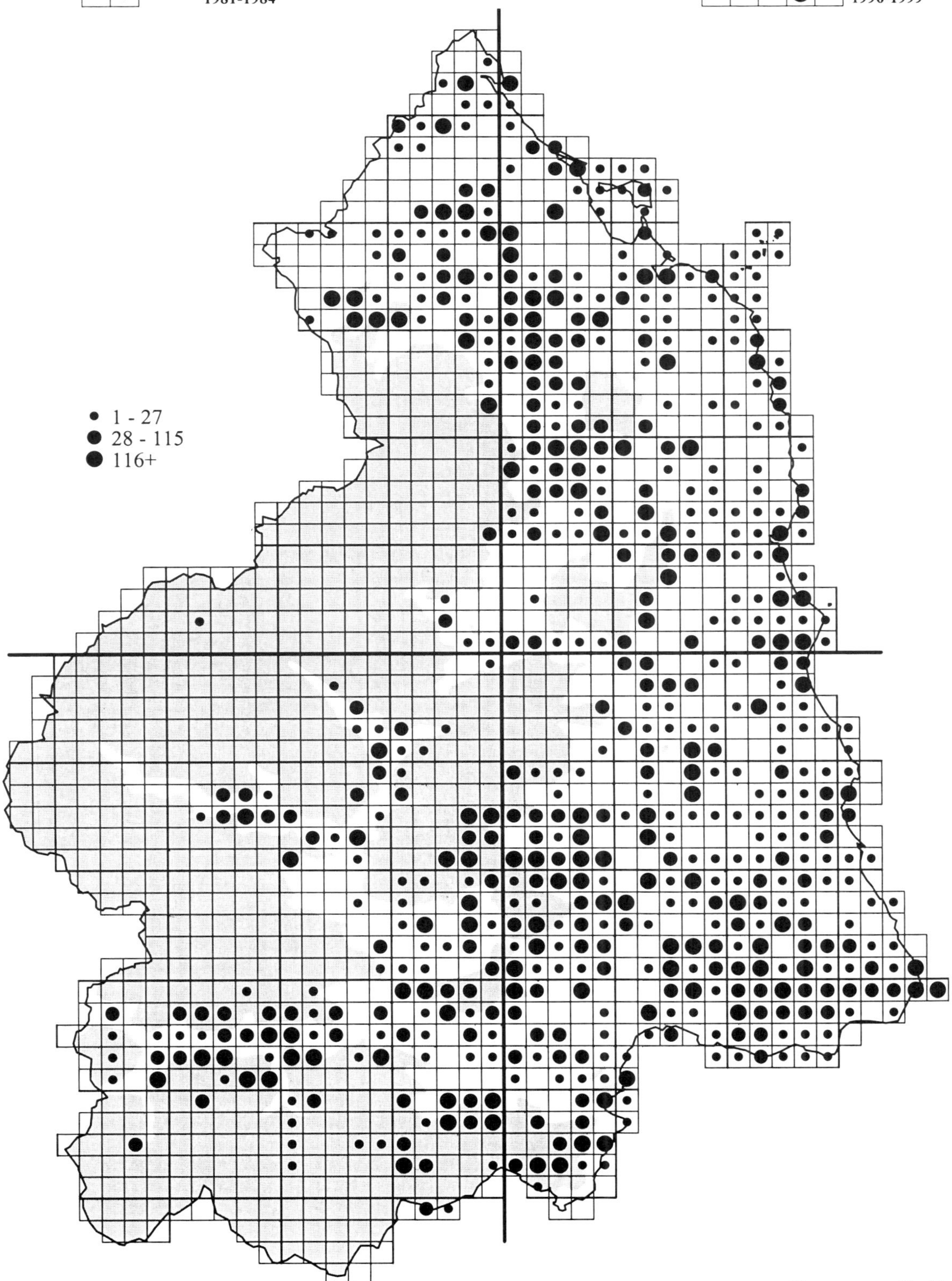

Common Gull

LESSER BLACK-BACKED GULL *Larus fuscus*

Bolam (1932) classified the Lesser Black-backed Gull of the British form *graellsii* as a summer visitor and passage migrant to the county with Galloway and Meek (1980) confirming this status, indicating that it was a common passage visitor and breeding species. The county's breeding population, based mainly at the Farne Islands, was thought to be stable at about 1,000 pairs from 1988-1992 (Day *et al.*, 1995).

This gull has been regarded as scarce in winter since the start of the twentieth century when gull identification became more soundly based. Bolam (1932) commented that some remained through the winter while Galloway and Meek (1980) said few birds remained to over-winter after late November. Even though Lack (1986) noted that numbers over-wintering in Britain had greatly increased, the species remained scarce in north east England and Scotland. Most birds that stay winter around landfill sites in the highly urbanised belt from south east to north west England, a very different habitat from the wild areas occupied in the breeding season. Rossiter (1997), in a long-term study of seasonal variations in gull numbers at roosts in Northumberland between 1983 and 1996, found that numbers of this species peak in September, decline slightly in October and fall very rapidly throughout November. During December to February, numbers are very low with an average total of about three adults found in each month. Immatures comprise 30% of the November roosts but less than 5% of the winter ones.

The picture shown by the current atlas is quite similar to that in the earlier national winter atlas with only a slight increase in the number of 10km squares occupied from 25 to 27. Geographically, there is some shift from the north of the county to the south west, with no records north of the Farne Islands and increased presence in the South Tyne Valley probably reflecting better coverage of this important migration route. The distribution within the 27 occupied 10km squares was sparse with a total of only 56 tetrads occupied, most of which (68%) were at low altitude within the range of 0-100 metres a.s.l.

All the higher counts in the current atlas were made in November. At the Farne Islands 102 were found at NU23I on 23rd November 1997 with 12 at NU23J and NU23N between 17th-27th November 1996. Other counts included 47 at Caistron (NU00A) and 16 at Broomlee Lough (NY76Z) on 23rd November and 25th November 1997 respectively. The only double-figure count outside November was 14 at Old Bewick on the River Till (NU02Q) on 6th February 1999. All other counts were of one to four birds with a concentration around Newcastle and North Tyneside where 16 tetrads were occupied in the four 10km squares NZ26, NZ27, NZ36 and NZ37. Other than the count above on the River Till, there was little evidence for any return migration in February. Overall, the current atlas confirms that very few over-winter but that significant numbers may still be found in November as the last of the summer visitors depart.

Bolam (1932) thought it probable that most of the birds wintering on the coast were of a Scandinavian form, and Rossiter (1997) found that the very small numbers that over-winter are more likely to be of the *intermedius* form from south and west Scandinavia. Analysis of county records for Lesser Black-backed Gulls in winter indicates that, of those which can be reasonably accurately identified, 44% of birds in December show characteristics of the form *intermedius*, 18% in January and 10% in February. Galloway and Meek (1980) reported that a pullus ringed in Norway at 59°N, within the *intermedius* zone, was found dead at Berwick on 2nd February 1974. In the three winters of the current winter survey, counts of adults showing characteristics of *intermedius* were two in 1996/97, 11 in 1997/98 and five in 1998/99 (*Birds in Northumbria*). The high totals suggest that this Scandinavian form is relatively common at this time. In support of this finding, Buckingham (1998) found that *intermedius* was actually commoner than *graellsii* between November-March in 1989/90 at reservoirs in west London.

B. N. ROSSITER

Distribution by altitude

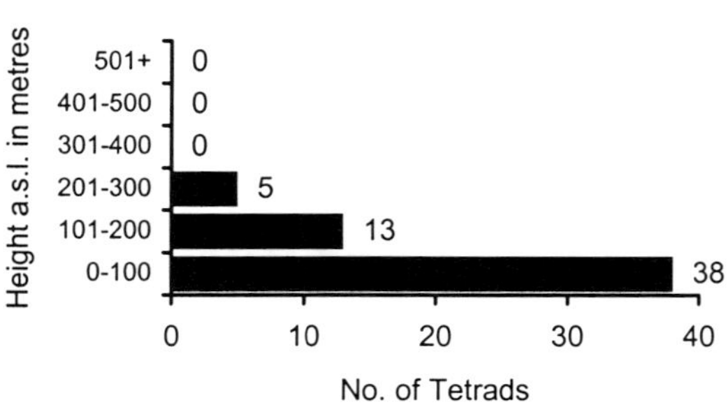

No. of tetrads in which recorded 56 (4%)

Tetrad Analysis	No. of tetrads
1 bird	27 (48%)
2-3 birds	19 (34%)
4+ birds	10 (18%)

Total No. of birds counted 291

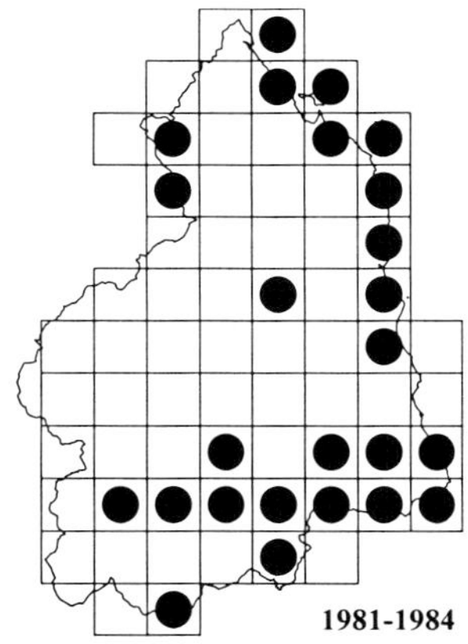

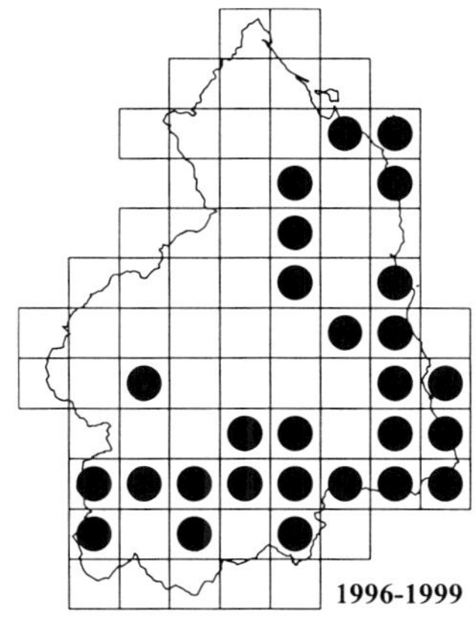

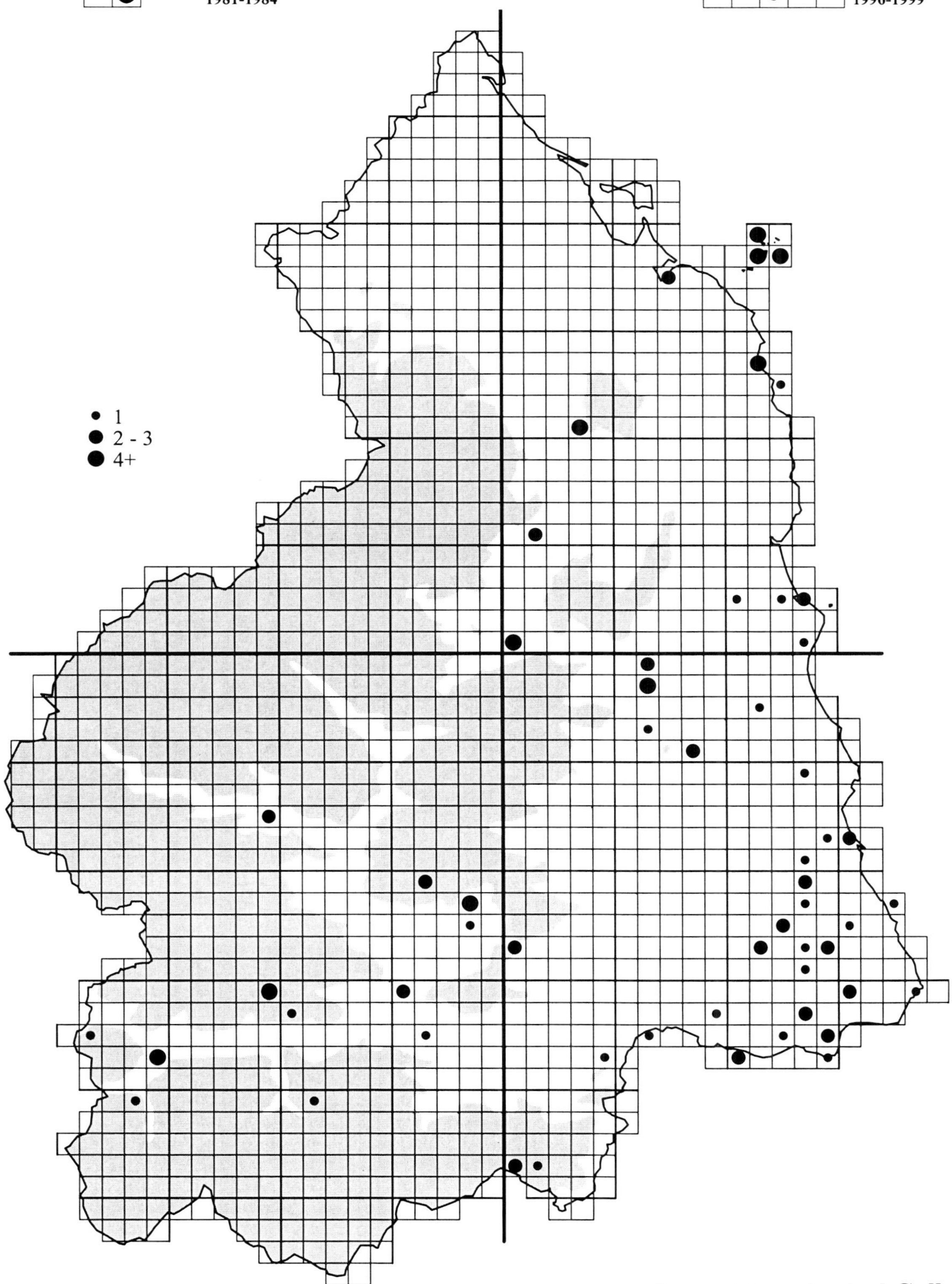

Lesser Black-backed Gull

HERRING GULL *Larus argentatus*

Bolam (1912) described the Herring Gull as 'another abundant species at all seasons'. It was still noted as 'an abundant passage and winter visitor' by Galloway and Meek (1980) who also recorded it as 'a common breeding species'. They mentioned 'wintering flocks numbering many thousands, especially on Lindisfarne NNR and the opencast mining area near Druridge'. Elsewhere on the coast they described it as common during the winter especially in sheltered harbours.

The tetrad distribution map shows that the majority of sightings in the current survey were at or close to the coast where most of the largest counts were also noted. Table 1 provides a summary of areas with large regular winter numbers in the county during the atlas survey period. P. Davey (pers. comm.) confirmed that the Lindisfarne figures do not reflect the much larger roosts to be found there in the evening. Evidence of east-west movement in northern England and south west Scotland is indicated by the sightings in the Tyne Gap area. This is supported by observations at North Shields Fish Quay of Herring Gulls which had been ringed on the Solway Firth (Turner, 1991).

Winter period 15th Nov-28th Feb	Ashington/ Widdrington Tips NU28	Derwent Reservoir NY95/NZ05	Tyne Estuary NZ36	Scotswood NZ26	Lindisfarne NU13/14	Blyth Estuary and Harbour NZ38
1996/97	3,000	6,300	1,200	460	280	565
1997/98	3,300	2,520	1,120	1,890	155	450
1998/99	10,000	975	1,100	240	312	700

Table 1 Maximum winter counts of Herring Gulls at popular roosting and feeding locations

Of the 314 occupied tetrads during the current winter survey, 240 (76%) were below 101 metres a.s.l., 61 (19%) were between 101 and 200 metres a.s.l. and the remainder between 201 and 500 metres a.s.l. There were 33 tetrads (11% of those occupied) with counts in excess of 100 birds, all but five of which were either at or within six kilometres of the coast.

A large proportion of the wintering individuals in northern England and southern Scotland have been shown to originate from Scandinavia (Coulson *et al.*, 1984). In that study approximately 24% of all adult Herring Gulls in Tyne and Wear, Co. Durham and Cleveland in the winter months were of the Scandinavian sub-species *L. a. argentatus*. In addition, between 71% to 82% of the Scandinavian adults caught during that study were sexed as female illustrating 'a marked inequality in the sex ratio of Scandinavian Herring Gulls wintering in NE Britain'. Further local evidence of the origins of some Herring Gulls in the region is provided by a breakdown of 417 uniquely identifiable colour-ringed birds seen in the North Shields Fish Quay area between December 1981 to December 1990. 371 had been ringed in Northumberland, Co. Durham and Tyne & Wear, 16 in Cleveland and Yorkshire, 29 in Scotland and one in Norway (Turner, 1991). The majority of these were ringed during the winter period.

Lack (1986) recorded the wintering total for Britain and Ireland to be 'perhaps in the region of half a million birds' and 'not one coastal square is without its attendant Herring Gulls'. He also showed that approximately one quarter of the wintering Herring Gulls were recorded inland. The minimum numbers of breeding pairs in Northumberland were 624 in 1997, 582 in 1998 and 548 in 1999 (*Birds in Northumbria 1997, 1998, 1999*) while Day *et al.* (1995) estimated the Northumberland breeding population as 'probably between 500 and 800 pairs in any one year'. Clearly the county wintering population is augmented by birds from elsewhere, the evidence suggesting principally Scotland and Norway/Scandinavia. The total counts of 26,919 during this winter survey will undoubtedly involve some over-recording. However, even allowing for this, the Herring Gull remains a common, if not abundant, species in the county during the winter. Nevertheless, a comparison of the two 10km square maps reveals an apparent slight contraction of winter distribution between 1981-1984 and 1996-1999.

DANIEL M. TURNER

Distribution by altitude

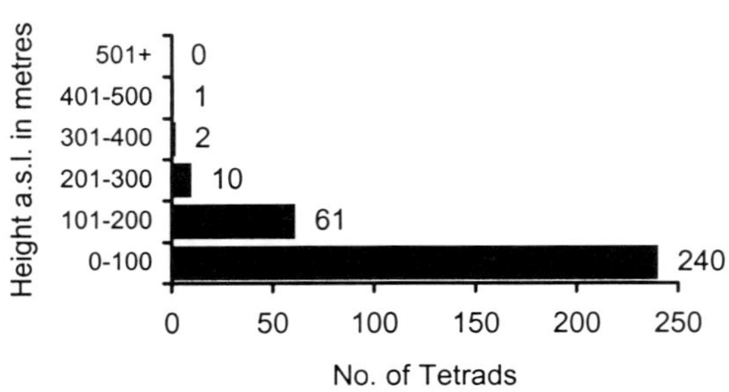

No. of tetrads in which recorded 314 (22%)

Tetrad Analysis	No. of tetrads
1-6 birds	152 (48%)
7-40 birds	99 (32%)
41+ birds	63 (20%)

Total No. of birds counted 26,919

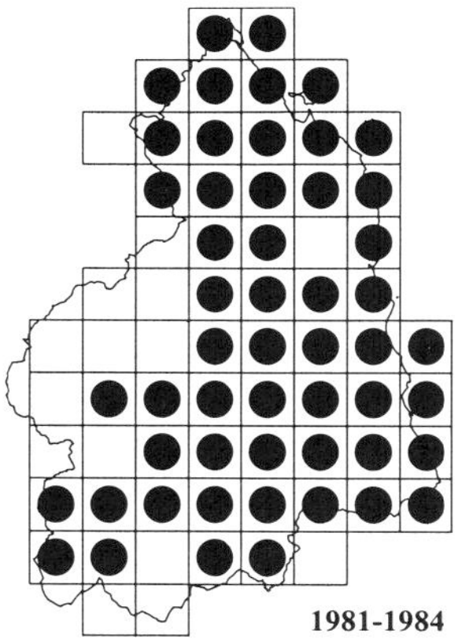

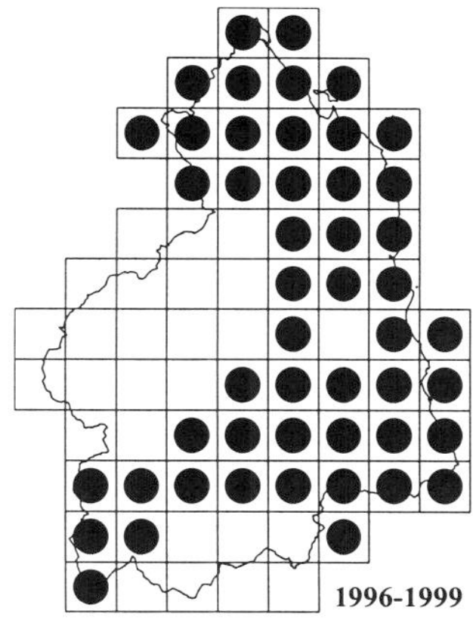

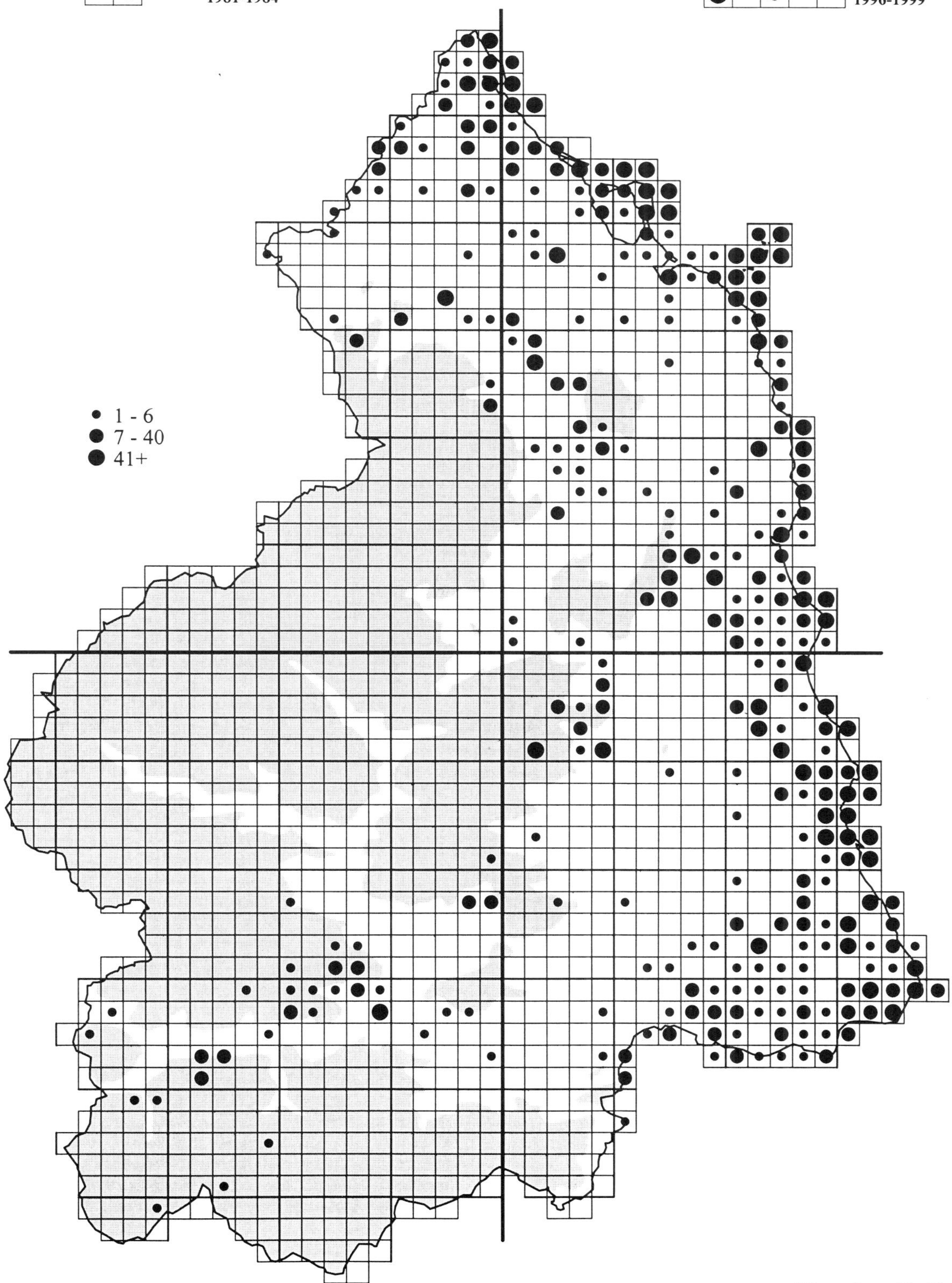

Herring Gull

YELLOW-LEGGED GULL *Larus cachinnans*

The County Records Committee, at the time of writing, regards the status and identification of this species to be provisional to some extent. The seasonal pattern found in Northumberland and the descriptions provided would suggest that the birds occurring in Northumberland in late summer and early autumn are mainly of the Mediterranean *michahellis* form as described in *British Birds* (Garner & Quinn, 1997). The first individual, a first-winter, resembling nominate *cachinnans* from the Middle East, sometimes called Caspian Gull (Garner & Quinn, 1997), was found in the county just after the end of the current atlas survey at Caistron on 17th October 1999. The position is complicated as there are a number of other forms of large gulls with yellow legs found on Atlantic coasts and in north east Europe and Asia which are subtly different from either of the two forms above. Those in north east Europe are described by Jonsson (1998) and those on the Atlantic coasts by Rossiter (2001b). There is also the possibility of hybrids and of intermediate and aberrant forms occurring.

In the current atlas survey period, a total of ten birds, all adult, was recorded in the county. Eight of these were found in November 1997 at the tail-end of an exceptional year for the species with over 60 present in August alone. The seasonal pattern for that year, showed significant numbers present only from May-November (*Birds in Northumbria 1997*), and the descriptions of the individuals involved suggest that all the birds present in November were of the Mediterranean *michahellis* form. Records came from Derwent Reservoir (NZ05B, maximum count three birds), Broomlee Lough (NY76Z, two birds) and Scotswood (NZ26B, two birds) and Caistron (NU00A, one) from 18th-27th November. None remained at these sites in December.

Later in the same winter there were two further records of adults. One was at Derwent Reservoir on 10th January 1998, the other in Budle Bay (NU13M) on 8th February. The latter was considered to be of the Mediterranean *michahellis* form. The description of the former suggests that it was a Yellow-legged Gull in the wider sense, possibly of an Atlantic form.

The 1997/98 winter was very exceptional in that as many as ten birds were recorded. Such counts followed the unprecedented influx in the late summer of 1997. No birds were recorded in the other two winters of 1996/97 and 1998/99. The evidence from the 1997/98 winter suggests that Yellow-legged Gulls of the Mediterranean *michahellis* form are unlikely to remain in Northumberland through the winter. In southern Britain individuals of the eastern nominate form show a greater propensity to over-winter (Garner & Quinn, 1997). Yellow-legged Herring Gulls from north east Europe are also potential visitors at this time.

B. N. ROSSITER

Distribution by altitude

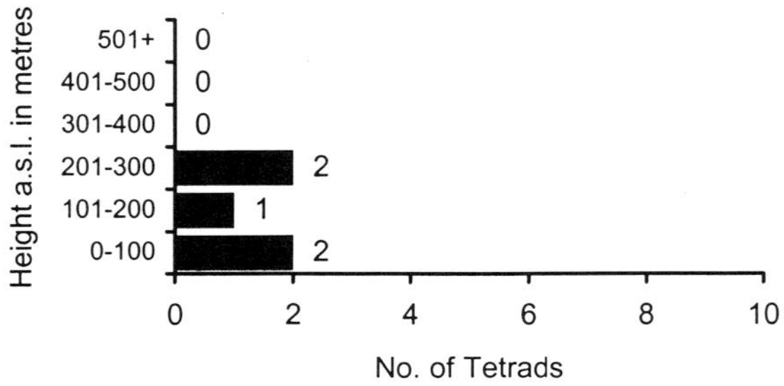

No. of tetrads in which recorded 5 (<1%)

Tetrad Analysis	No. of tetrads
1 bird	2 (40%)
2 birds	2 (40%)
3 birds	1 (20%)

Total No. of birds counted 9

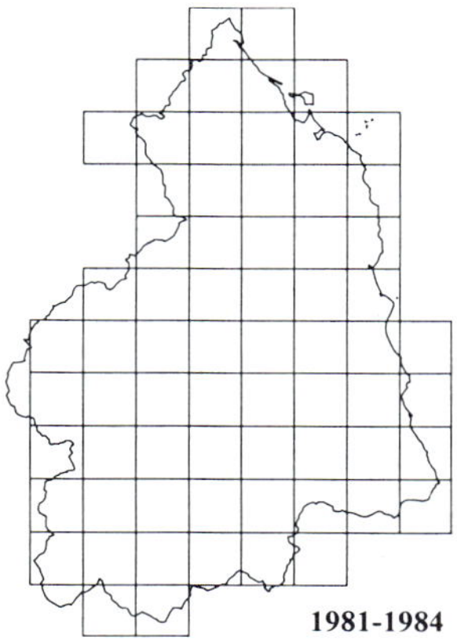

1981-1984

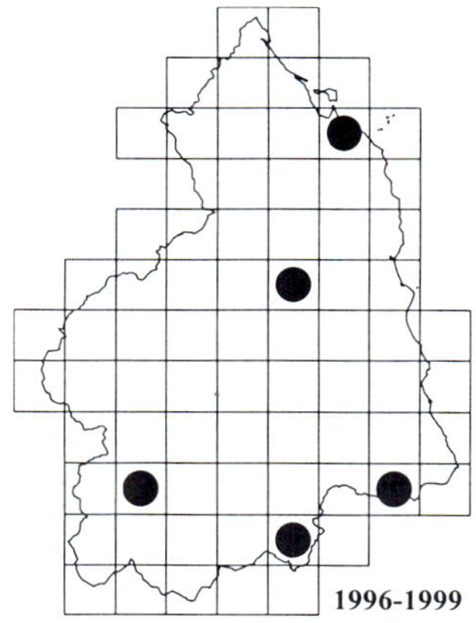

1996-1999

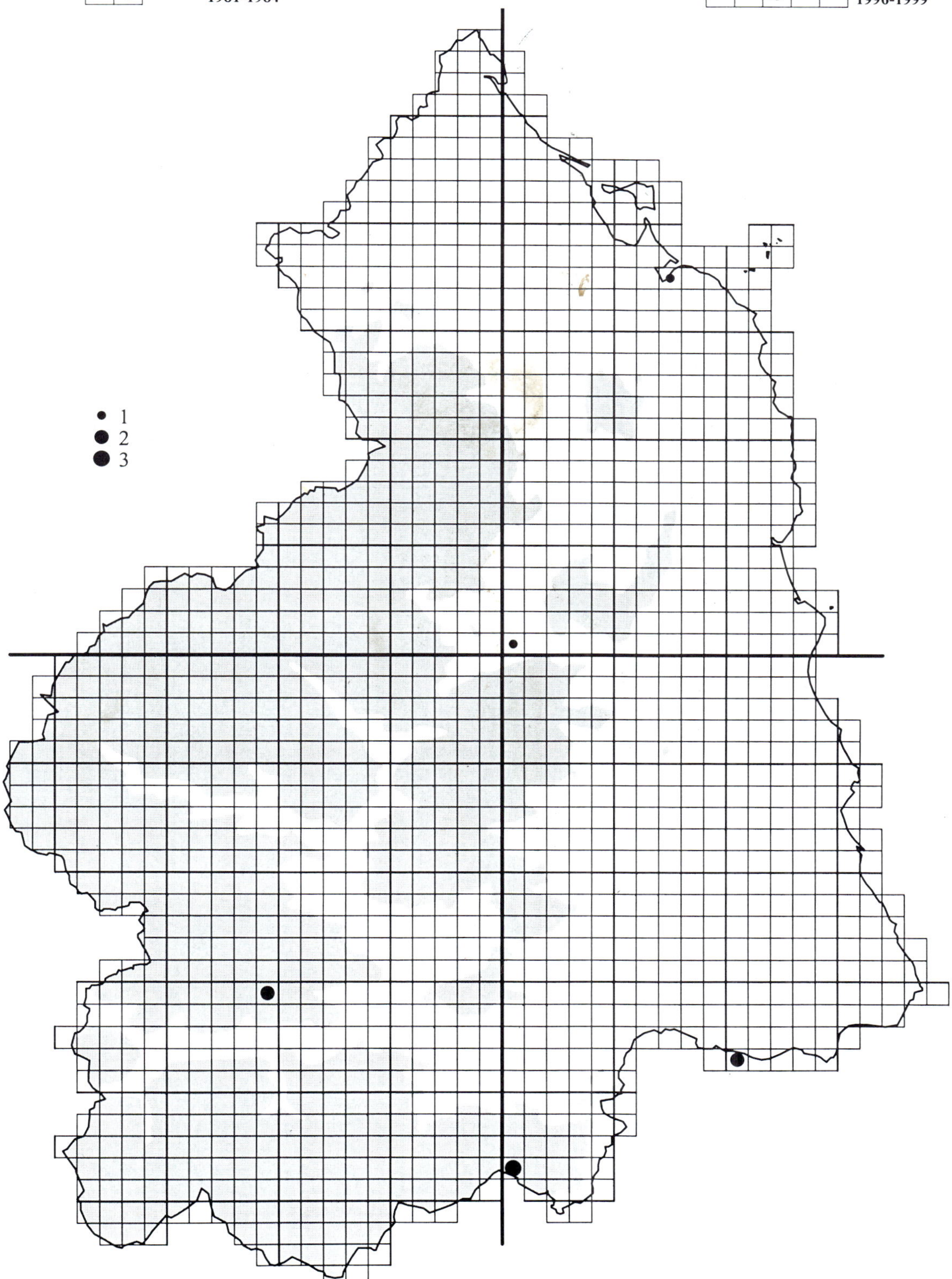

Yellow-legged Gull

ICELAND GULL *Larus glaucoides*

Bolam (1932) knew the Iceland Gull as 'a casual winter visitant' while Galloway and Meek (1980) categorised as it as 'a rare visitor' and went on to say none had occurred between 1932 and 1953 but that it had appeared 'in twenty-three of the next twenty-seven years'. The statistics from the current winter survey would suggest that its status should now fall between rare and uncommon. Table 1 shows the annual fluctuations in total numbers during the survey period, with immature birds generally outnumbering adults. Nevertheless the species is still less frequent than Glaucous Gull *Larus glaucoides* both locally and nationally (Lack, 1986). The affinity shown by some individual gulls for the same wintering location over a period of many years is demonstrated by an Iceland Gull at West Denton (NZ16Y). Initially seen there in March 1996 in first year plumage it continued to return in the following winters progressing through second and third year plumage to full adult in the winter of 1998/99 and subsequently.

Winter period	Totals by age group				
15th Nov-28th Feb	1st winter	2nd winter	3rd winter	Adult	Total
1996 / 97	6	1 - 2	1	1 - 2	9 - 11
1997 / 98	2 - 3	1 - 2	2	2 - 3	7 - 10
1998 / 99	1 - 2	1 - 3	0	2 - 3	4 - 8

Table 1 Numbers of wintering Iceland Gulls in Northumberland

The tetrad distribution map for this current survey shows a concentration of birds in the south east of the county, primarily on the coast with a few inland. Sites where there were records of more than one bird during a winter were as follows : North Shields Fish Quay/Tyne Estuary (NZ36U) with at least four birds in 1996/97, one in 1997/98 and two-four in 1998/99, and two birds at New Moor Tip, Ashington (NZ28U) in January 1997, Newbiggin (NZ38D/E) in 1997/98 and Amble in January 1998. All other sightings during the three winter periods were of single birds. Five of these were along the coast but more interesting were inland records at Holywell Pond (NZ37C), Wallsend Swallow Pond (NZ36E), Leazes Park (NZ26M), Scotswood (NZ26B), Bothal (NZ28N), Warkworth Lane (NZ29R) and the West Denton bird already mentioned above. At Derwent Reservoir (NZ05B/G), some 40 kilometres inland, a first winter bird was observed in January 1998 and an adult in January 1999.

The winter distribution map produced by Lack (1986) showed that inland records are not unusual, especially in the Midlands. The map also showed a scattered distribution around the British and Irish coastlines and he mentioned that 'in a normal year, Britain and Ireland may have as few as 70-80 Iceland Gulls but recent influxes have resulted in well over 250, even over 300 in 1983 and 1984'. He nevertheless felt that due to duplicate counting 'the higher figures could be slight overestimates'.

It is, on the whole, the eastern Greenland breeding population of nominate *L. g. glaucoides* that winter in Iceland and filter down to Britain and Ireland and other parts of Europe in smaller numbers (Cramp & Simmons, 1983; Snow & Perrins, 1998). It regularly winters in arctic Norway in small numbers (R. Henson, pers. comm.).

In Northumberland, the majority of winter birds arrive from December onwards, although stragglers on northward migration are seen into April and May. There are also occasional summer records and other early arrivals during the autumn in the county.

DANIEL M. TURNER

Distribution by altitude

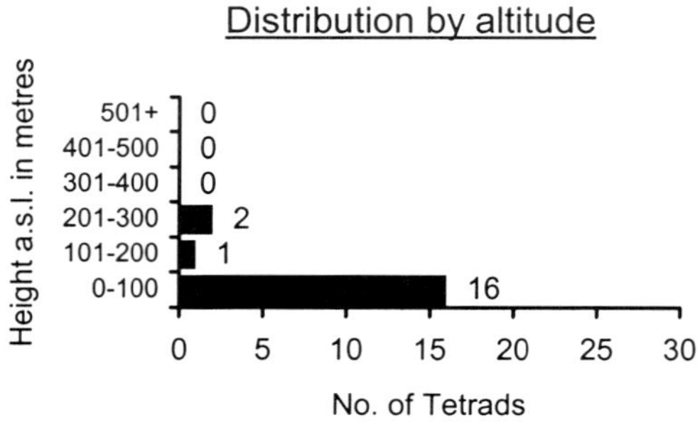

No. of tetrads in which recorded 19 (1%)

Tetrad Analysis	No. of tetrads
1 bird	14 (74%)
2 birds	5 (26%)

Total No. of birds counted 24

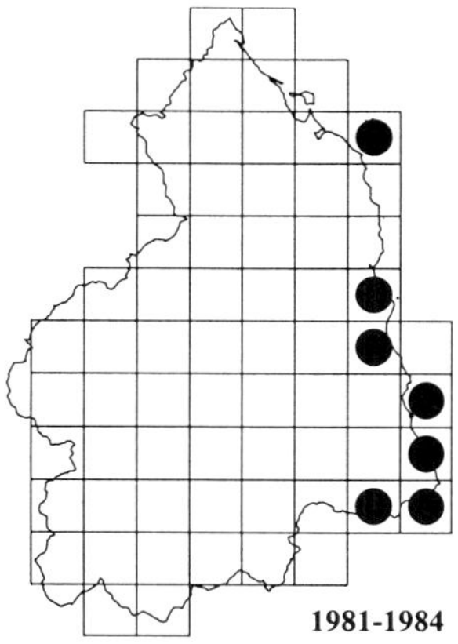

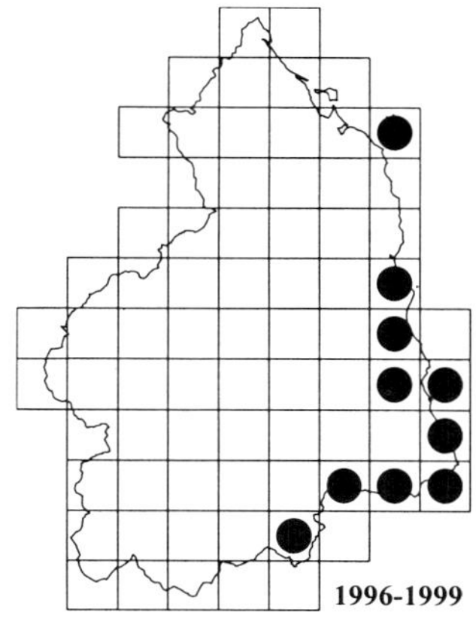

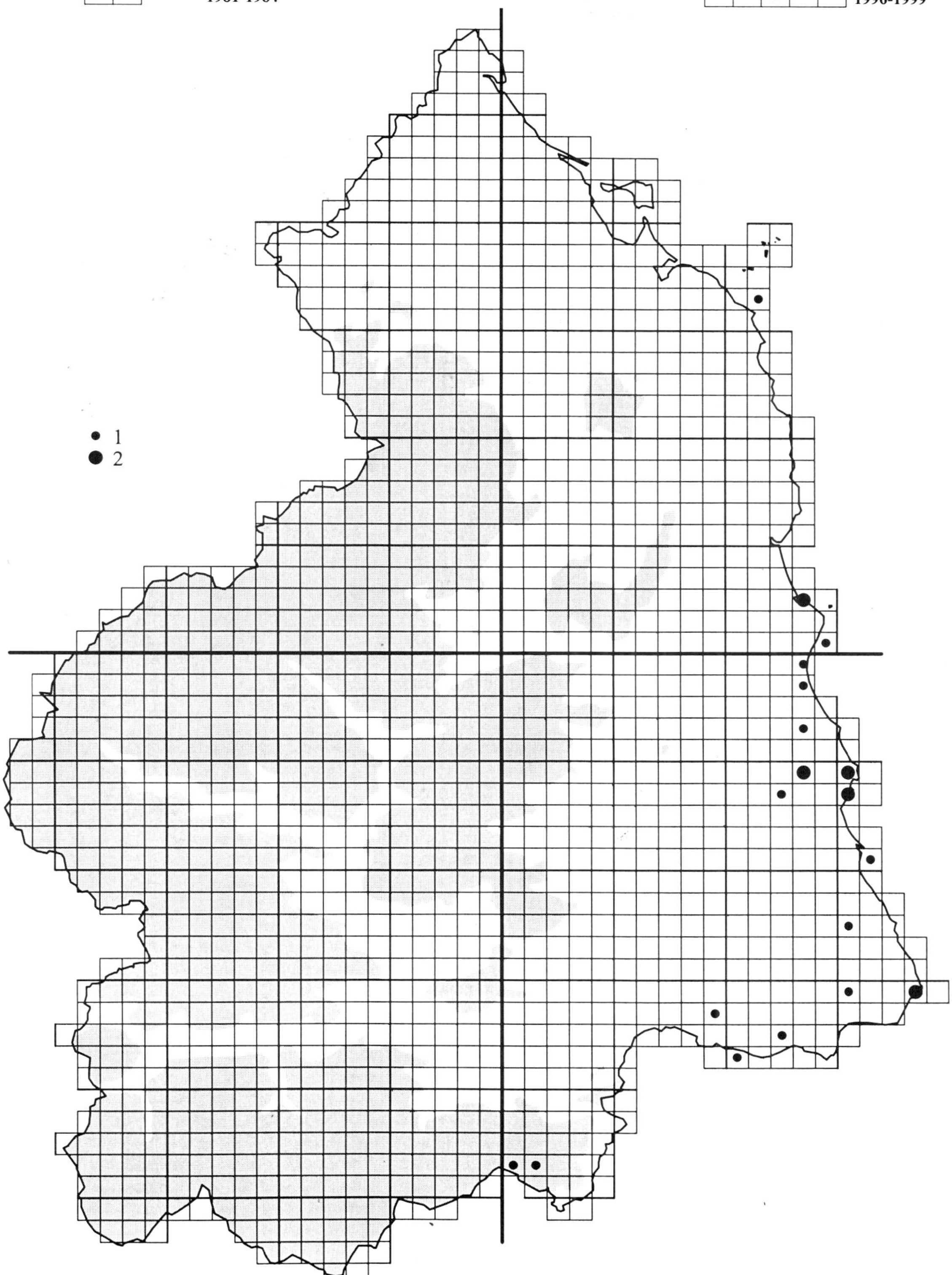

Iceland Gull

GLAUCOUS GULL *Larus hyperboreus*

Galloway and Meek (1980) described the Glaucous Gull as 'an uncommon passage and winter visitor', a status which still holds true today. Indeed its status remains almost unchanged after nearly 100 years as Bolam (1912; 1932) also knew the species as an irregular winter visitor, usually as single birds and mostly as immatures.

Comparison of the two 10km square maps shows a similar coastal distribution in both winter atlas periods, although there were a few additional inland records in the earlier survey in the south east. The current survey records birds from North Shields Fish Quay northwards to Holy Island with a fairly continuous spread, but with distinct concentrations of sightings along the southern half of the coast and in the north east. The two most favoured winter sites in recent years have been the North Shields Fish Quay/Tyne Estuary area (NZ36U) and Seahouses (NU23B/G) with up to six and four birds respectively during the survey period. Table 1 provides totals of wintering Glaucous Gulls in the county during 1996/97-1998/99.

Winter period	Totals by age group				
15th Nov-28thFeb	1st winter	2nd winter	3rd winter	Adult	Total
1996/97	5 - 7	2	0	4 - 6	11 - 15
1997/98	4 - 5	2 - 3	0	4 - 5	10 - 13
1998/99	7 - 10	4	1 - 2	4 - 6	16 - 22

Table 1 Numbers of wintering Glaucous Gulls in Northumberland

Using data from the current winter survey and other NTBC sources, two or more wintering birds were present at Holy Island (NU14G) and New Moor Tip, Ashington (NZ28U) in 1996/97, Amble (NU20S) with six in 1998/99 and two in January 1997, the Farne Islands (NU23) with three in November 1998 and Warkworth Lane (NZ29R) with two in December 1996. Not surprisingly therefore, some data on single birds shown on the tetrad distribution map may be explained by the movement of wintering individuals around the recording area. Glaucous Gulls can also be creatures of habit and this may explain the appearance of two adults at Seahouses and one to two adults in the Tyne Estuary over a period of many years.

Summarising the winter records for Britain and Ireland, Lack (1986) stated the species had 'a chiefly coastal distribution with a northerly bias' but also noted inland records 'close to Greater Manchester and central England'. Of numbers wintering in Britain as a whole he wrote that they ranged 'under 200 to 450-500, or sometimes rather more, each winter'.

Like the Iceland Gull *Larus glaucoides* the 'East Greenland population [of Glaucous Gull] is more migratory and largely winters in Iceland, though some may penetrate as far as Britain and Ireland' (Lack, 1986). With a mostly resident population of Glaucous Gulls in Iceland, some of the many Glaucous x Herring Gull *L. hyperboreus* x *L. argentatus* hybrids from there do reach Britain in winter. There are records of up to nine different birds (seen singly) showing characteristics of hybrids in the recording area between 1975 to 1999 (Galloway & Meek, 1980; *Birds in Northumbria 1975 to 1999*). Two of these hybrids were seen at Seahouses but the remainder were all in the Tyne Estuary/North Shields Fish Quay area.

Glaucous Gulls have been recorded in every month in the county with occasional birds over-summering. Birds can arrive from August, though the main arrival is between October and January with some seen on their return northerly passage well into April and May.

DANIEL M. TURNER

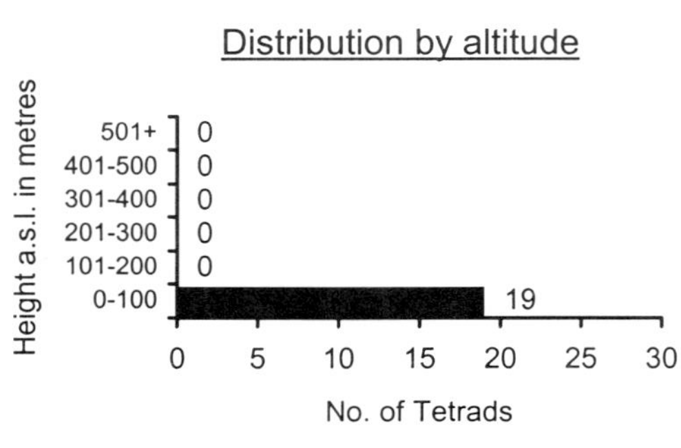

No. of tetrads in which recorded 19 (1%)

Tetrad Analysis	No. of tetrads
1 bird	13 (68%)
2 birds	4 (21%)
3 birds	2 (11%)

Total No. of birds counted 27

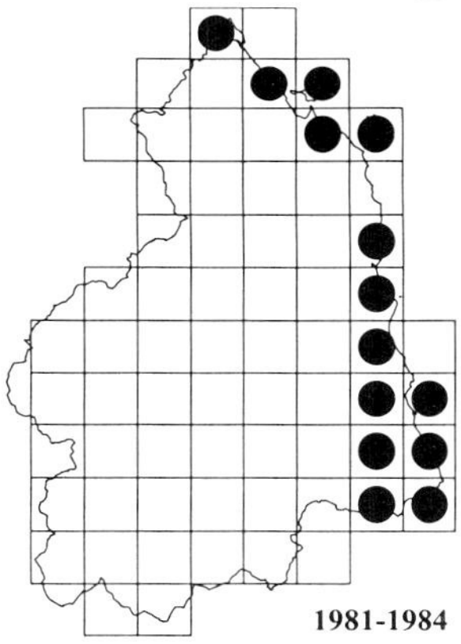

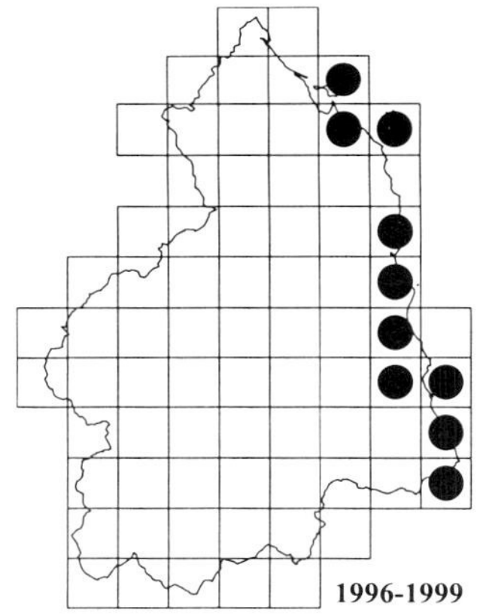

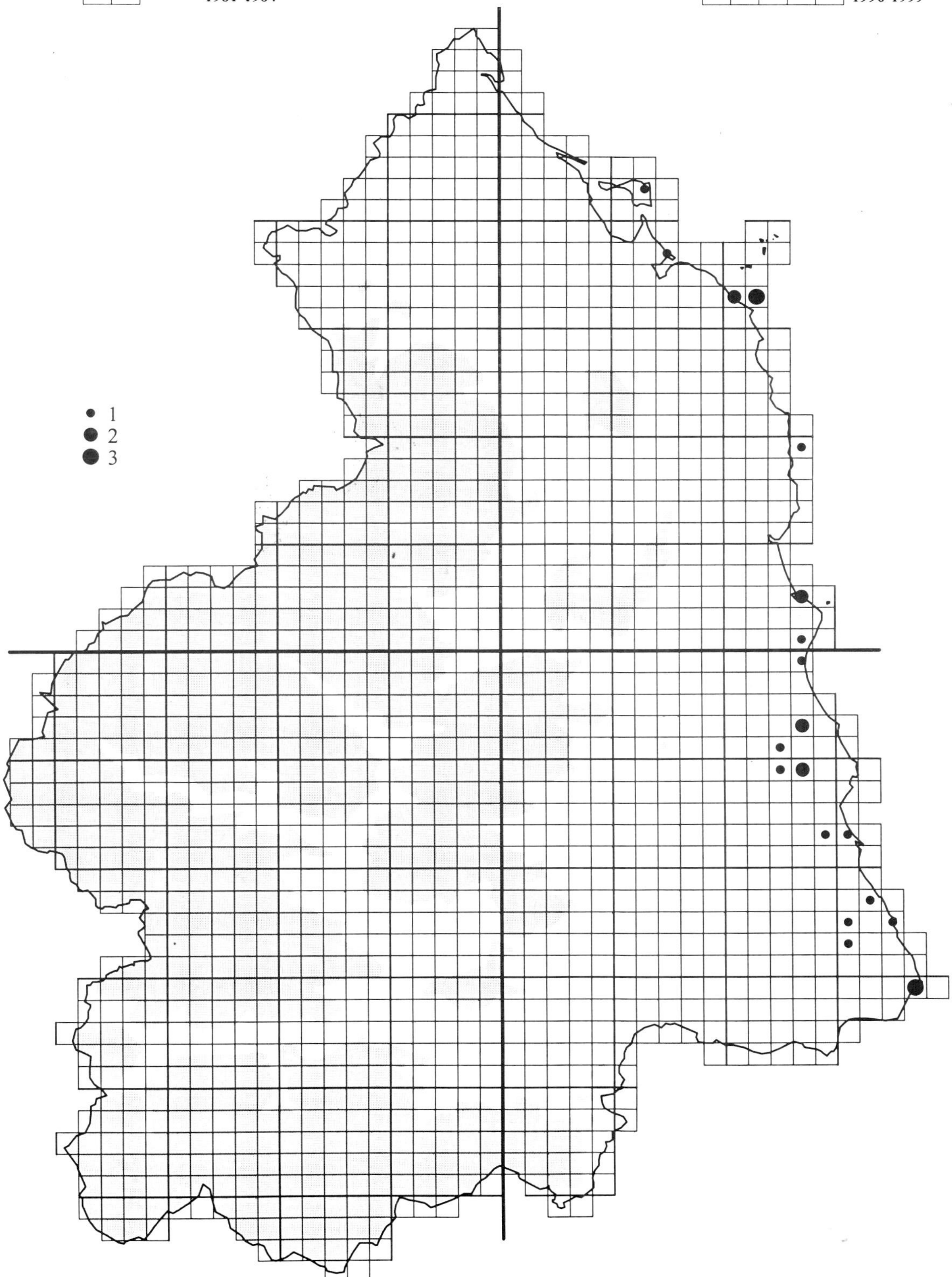

Glaucous Gull

GREAT BLACK-BACKED GULL *Larus marinus*

Bolam (1932) described the Great Black-backed Gull as 'common upon the coast in winter, and never wholly absent at any season. Over the western hills it likewise occurs throughout the year, in roving pairs or small companies, being, naturally, most frequent during the cold months'. More than 50 years later Galloway and Meek (1980) rated the species as a common passage and winter visitor and further said that 'very considerable numbers arrive from early autumn onwards'. They were able to re-affirm Bolam's earlier observation, noting that single birds and small parties could be found on remote moorlands throughout the winter and thought these birds might account for roosting flocks on inland reservoirs.

Information on the origins of Great Black-backed Gulls in North East England came from an intensive colour-ringing study, mainly in Co. Durham and Cleveland but also in Tyne & Wear and North Yorkshire (Coulson *et al.*, 1984). The results of this study strongly suggested that almost all Great Black-backed Gulls present during August-February were from the Norwegian breeding population. However, recoveries of nestlings ringed at Hoy, Orkney in June 1983 and Stronsay, Orkney in June 1987 and found at Blyth in January 1985 and Hexham in February 1988 respectively show that some birds in the county during the winter months originate from the Scottish breeding population.

The tetrad map for the current survey reflects the marine nature of this species, with just over half of the recorded sightings, and the largest numbers, in coastal or near-coastal areas. There were only eight counts of over 100 birds during the survey, the largest being 520 at Stobswood (NZ29H). The other seven counts were in widespread squares ranging between the Farne Islands (NU23I) and the Tyne Estuary (NZ36U). As this species is an opportunistic feeder, often reacting to the weather conditions and feeding out at sea, and therefore presenting a fluctuating picture, it is possible that numbers noted during timed visits were an underestimate. It was noticeable also that over half of the counts during this survey were of just one or two birds in a tetrad, particularly inland. Although few actual roost counts were included in the data collected, many of the birds were recorded in known resting or 'loafing' localities. The use of inland roost sites is still in evidence with 43 at Caistron (NU00A) in January 1999. In addition, records in the county annual bird reports, *Birds in Northumbria*, for the three winter periods show that both Derwent (NY95W, NZ05B/F) and Hallington Reservoirs (NY97S/T) regularly held roosting birds with maxima of 720 and 156 respectively in January 1997.

The survey also confirms the statements of earlier authors concerning its distribution over higher ground inland in winter with many records of singles or small groups in widespread areas. It is noticeable that the higher uplands around the Cheviot and the tree-clad Border Forest areas appear to be largely avoided, as is a broad swath of lowland lying between the coast and the uplands probably reflecting a lack of feeding opportunities. Many of the river valleys and other water courses contained a significant number of sightings, these presumably acting as natural flightlines both to and from the coast although B. Galloway has commented that he believes many of these birds spend the winter in these areas scavenging on sheep carcasses and dead salmon (pers. comm.). A direct comparison of the two 10km square maps shows that in the current survey they were not found in eight squares where they had previously been recorded. There would appear to be no apparent evidence for a major decline in numbers and the discrepancies may have been weather-related. Lack (1986) indicated that, although it was difficult to judge the extent to which our native population was augmented in winter by Scandinavian visitors, the British wintering numbers were of some international importance. Within the county it is a very rare breeder and, although much larger numbers are present in late summer and autumn presumably prior to onward dispersal, its status during the winter months remains that of a common visitor.

MIKE S. HODGSON

Distribution by altitude

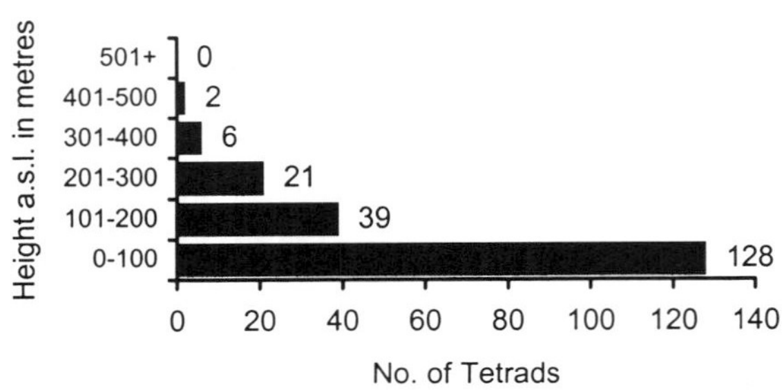

No. of tetrads in which recorded 196 (14%)

Tetrad Analysis	No. of tetrads
1-2 birds	99 (51%)
3-11 birds	53 (27%)
12+ birds	44 (22%)

Total No. of birds counted 3,914

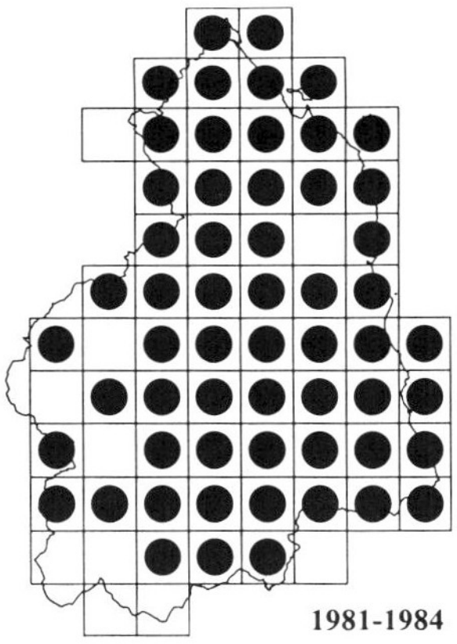

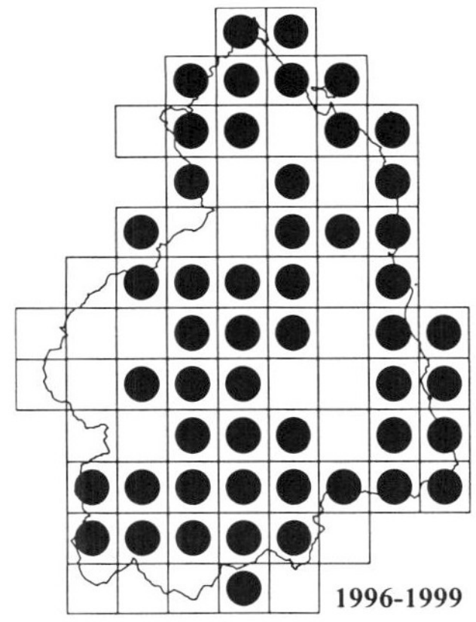

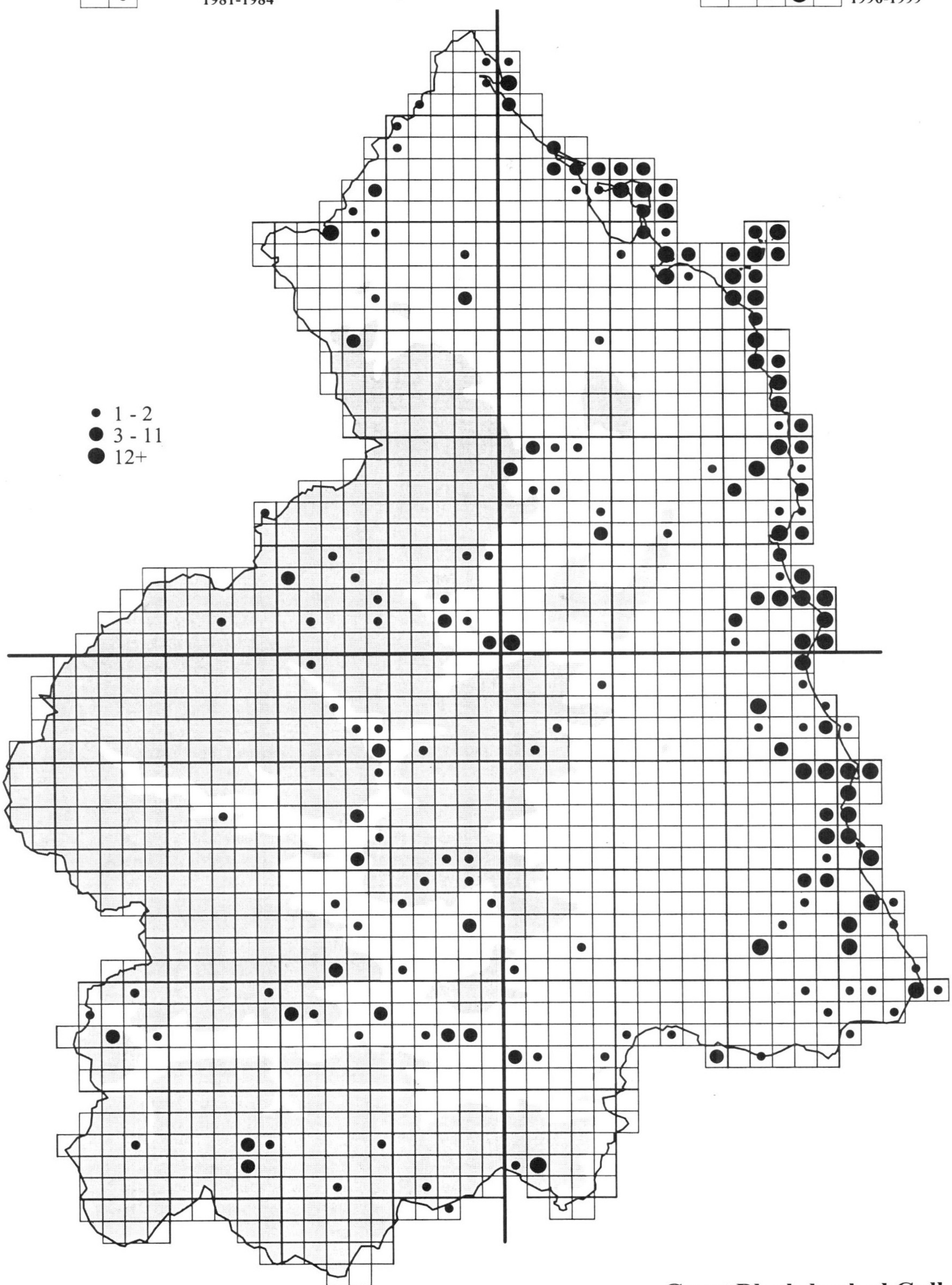

Great Black-backed Gull

KITTIWAKE *Rissa tridactyla*

The Kittiwake has been a breeding species in the county since at least the seventeenth century but comparatively little seems to have been written about its status during the winter. Bolam (1932) described it as a winter visitant and postulated that both local adults and their young moved south for the winter, their places being taken by birds from more northern latitudes. He also detailed a number of early ringing recoveries, showing the long-distance dispersal of nestlings marked on the Farne Islands, to Newfoundland, Labrador and the Davis Strait off Greenland. Coulson (1966) suggested, from an analysis of recoveries of birds ringed in the British Isles, that there were two groups of immatures; firstly those that disperse across the Atlantic and secondly those that remain near the European coast. Recoveries from the Farne Islands support this theory, although older birds have also been involved. Galloway and Meek (1980) said that the Kittiwake was a 'common winter visitor' but this may have been due to offshore passage noted in the winter months rather than large numbers of birds present along the coast for extended periods.

Nationally, Lack (1986) said that small numbers occur throughout the winter around harbours and fish docks but indicated this was rather a recent habit. He also said that, as the most pelagic of our breeding gulls, it was found in flocks right across the North Atlantic, north of 40°N, often hundreds of kilometres from land during the winter months. Because of the extensive winter movements it was thought that 'in winter ... perhaps, only 1,000 birds are within easy view around the coast'.

The tetrad distribution map for the current local winter survey conforms to the national picture, with relatively small numbers being recorded in only 17 coastal and two inland tetrads. The largest counts during the atlas period were 40 off Newbiggin-by-the-Sea (NZ38D), 34 at the Tyne Estuary (NZ36U), 25 at Marshall Meadows (NT95Y), 16 at North Blyth (NZ38B) and 14 at the Farne Islands (NU23N). The remaining 12 coastal tetrads produced counts of only one to five individuals. Birds occur occasionally inland usually as a result of weather or in more recent times on cross-country passage. Single birds were located at Caistron (NU00A) in February 1997 and, much nearer to the coast, at Holywell Pond (NZ37C) in February 1999.

With a overall total of only 157 birds counted during the current fieldwork, the winter status of the Kittiwake in the county is probably best described as well-represented.

MIKE S. HODGSON

No. of tetrads in which recorded 19 (1%)

Tetrad Analysis	No. of tetrads
1-2 birds	11 (58%)
3-14 birds	4 (21%)
15+ birds	4 (21%)

Total No. of birds counted 157

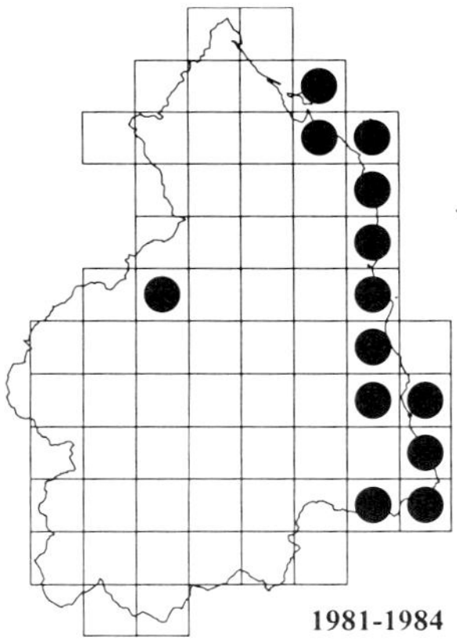

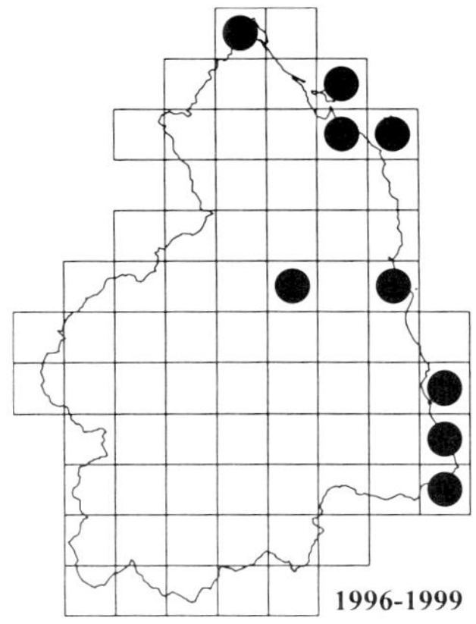

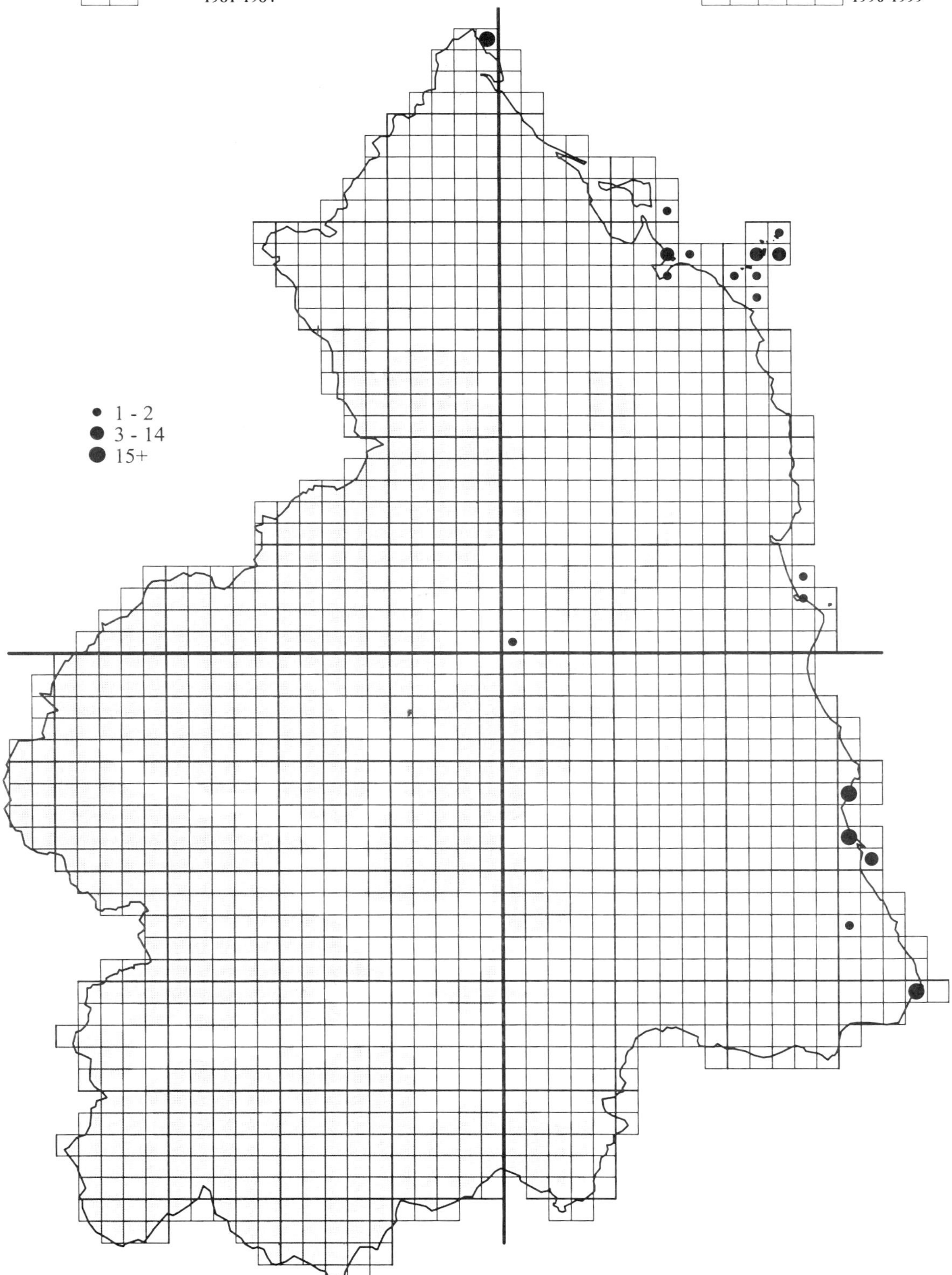

Kittiwake

GUILLEMOT *Uria aalge*

The Guillemot is a common breeding species in Northumberland although almost the entire population is centred on the famous Farne Islands colonies. Counts of breeding individuals here in the seasons immediately preceding the three winter periods were 28,650, 35,073 and 33,456 respectively.

Bolam (1932), commenting on its winter status, said it was 'perhaps, reinforced during winter by others bred farther north' while earlier (1912) he had noted that during stormy weather in winter it 'is frequently driven inland'. Galloway and Meek (1980) in their detailed account said that the breeding ledges were deserted by mid-August. They described its winter status as a common visitor and went on to note that birds returned to the breeding sites in strength in late October or early November and, provided the weather was not too stormy, might remain throughout the winter.

Sadly, Guillemots (and other auks) tend to be particularly obvious in the winter months when they are brought ashore dying or dead as a result of oiling or weather-related incidents. Indeed, Galloway and Meek reported that 'oiling incidents are almost annual, being especially noticeable in winter after periods of strong easterly winds'. They recorded a total of 1,160 dead on the county coastline in January 1970 and noted that hundreds came ashore between January-March 1978. In their supplement (1986) they said that 835 corpses were washed ashore in February 1983 but here starvation was the prime cause of death. Since then, such major incidents seem to be in decline, at least along our coastline, although the county annual bird reports highlight large mortalities in February 1986, February 1994 and again in March 1996. Thankfully, there were no major incidents of this type reported during the three winter periods of the current survey. Nationally, Mead (2000) suggested the British population had 'excellent prospects for the future' and that the main colonies in Scotland and 'North-east' England had been increasing rapidly.

A comparison of the two 10 km square maps shows that the distribution between the two winter surveys has remained virtually unchanged with only one, principally land-bound, square being unoccupied. These maps, however, mask the fact that during the current survey Guillemots were generally found at only very low density in inshore waters. The largest count was 200 birds feeding, with other seabirds, off Spittal (NU05A) in January 1999. There were only six occupied tetrads (13%) with counts of ten-19 and the remaining 39 tetrads (85%) contained between one-eight birds. The land-based survey methods used for both timed visits and supplementary recording will have had an effect on the numbers recorded as will any periods of unsettled weather, which would make counting from the shore difficult. The tetrad map shows that they are scattered right along the coastline of the county, with notable clusters at the mouth of the River Tweed and near the breeding sites on the Farne Islands. It should be borne in mind that no mid-winter counts around the latter area were available for this survey but it seems likely, in view of statements made above, that large numbers of returning breeding birds would have been present at some time during the winter months. Small number of birds were reported penetrating into various river mouths and estuaries but there were no real 'inland' records during the survey.

Although Guillemots disperse widely during the winter months, with first year birds moving farthest, most ringed birds found dead in Britain and Ireland in winter originate from the British and Irish colonies with a few, on the North Sea coasts, from further north and east (Lack, 1986). This is certainly true in Northumberland where there are a number of winter recoveries of birds from Scottish colonies and others from the Faeroe Islands and Denmark. There will presumably be, however, a large proportion of local breeding birds present in our area of the North Sea which, barring oiling incidents and large scale natural mortalities, remain undetected offshore during the winter. The numbers counted during this latest survey indicate that the species is at least well-represented in the county in winter.

MIKE S. HODGSON

No. of tetrads in which recorded 46 (3%)

Tetrad Analysis	No. of tetrads
1-2 birds	27 (59%)
3-5 birds	10 (21%)
6+ birds	9 (20%)

Total No. of birds counted 372

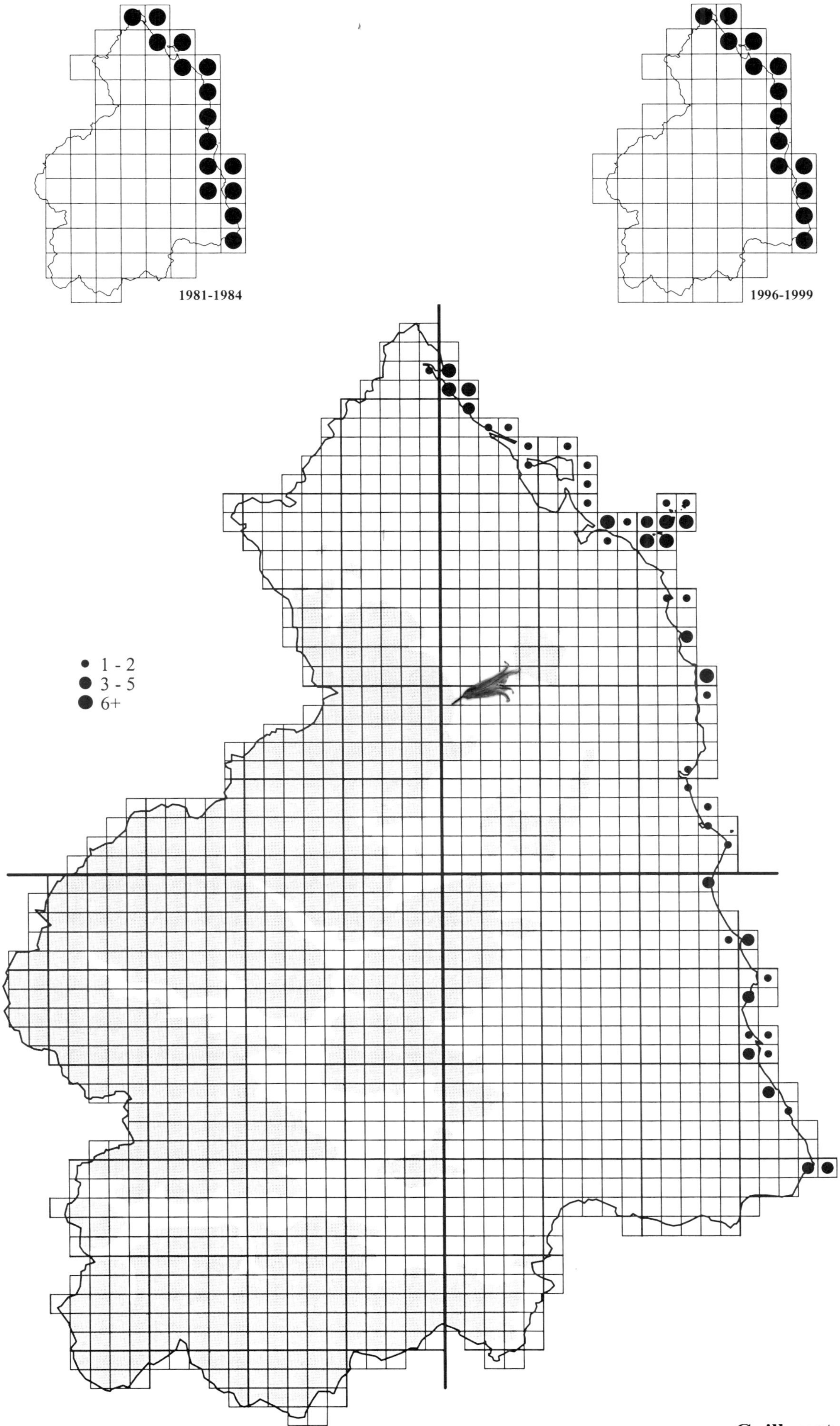

Guillemot

RAZORBILL *Alca torda*

A 'resident and winter visitant, common offshore during the cold months' was how Bolam (1932) described the status of Razorbill, adding 'like most of its kindred it is liable to be blown inland occasionally'. Galloway and Meek (1980), although not giving a specific winter status for the species, said that an oiling incident in January 1970 resulted in 149 being picked up dead on the Northumberland and Co. Durham coastline indicating that large numbers must be present at sea in winter. Sadly, like the Guillemot *Uria aalge*, it is mainly as a result of oiling or weather-related incidents off our coastlines that point to the true numbers of wintering Razorbills. This was graphically demonstrated in February 1983 when, following a period of prolonged storms, some 1,453 corpses were washed ashore, mainly of birds having succumbed to starvation (Galloway & Meek, 1986). In more recent times there seems to have been fewer incidents but in February 1994 a total of 52 was found along the Tyne and Wear coastline (Kerr, 2000).

Given the events outlined above, but with an overall total of only 42 birds counted during the three periods of the current survey, it seems likely that somewhat larger numbers must be present offshore in Northumberland during the winter than are currently reported. The survey methods employed probably accounted for some undercounting as tides, weather, state of the sea and availability of food would all affect the visibility of the species from the shore. Only 41% of the maximum counts were provided by timed visits, all other records coming from casual observations. The tetrad map shows a very thin and disjointed distribution along the whole of the coastline. The maximum count in any one tetrad was only ten off Budle Point (NU13T) in January 1999. All other maximum counts were of one to four birds and, as expected, the northern half of the coastline, particularly around the Farne Islands-Holy Island area, supplied the majority of winter sightings.

Lack (1986) said ringing had shown that birds from Russia, Norway and Iceland winter around Britain although he was unable to postulate any national winter population estimate. He also indicated that the distribution map produced from the 1981-1984 national winter atlas data understated the winter numbers at some north and east breeding areas. Locally there have been winter ringing recoveries from birds marked on both Handa and the Shiant Islands, Scotland, and a bird of the subspecies *A. t. torda* found dead at Embleton in March 1969 had been ringed on the White Sea coast of the former USSR. It would seem that many if not the majority of Razorbills wintering off our coastline do not originate from Northumberland. The county breeding population during the years of the current winter atlas only numbered between 172 and 196 pairs (or occupied nests) at three sites but it is not known with certainty where these birds disperse to after the summer. A comparison of the two 10km square maps shows that the winter distribution remains almost unchanged since the earlier survey in 1981-1984.

MIKE S. HODGSON

<u>No. of tetrads in which recorded</u> 17 (1%)

Tetrad Analysis	No. of tetrads
1 birds	6 (35%)
2-3 birds	8 (47%)
4+ birds	3 (18%)

<u>Total No. of birds counted</u> 42

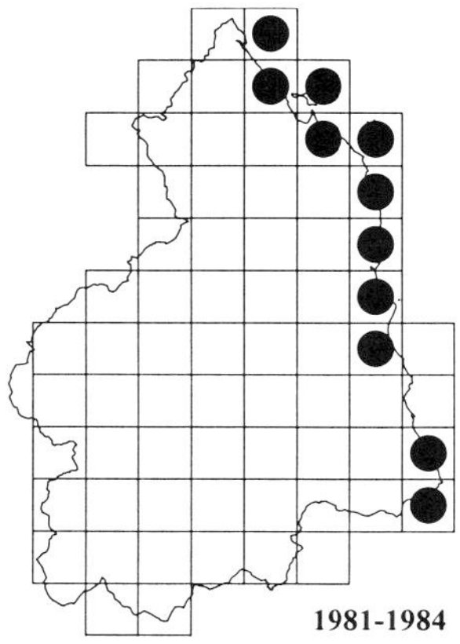

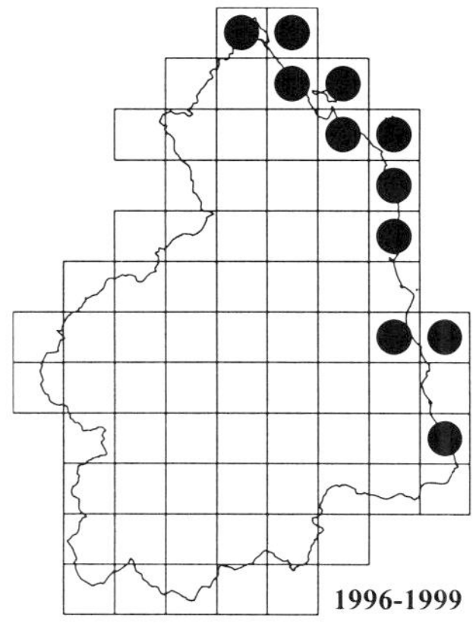

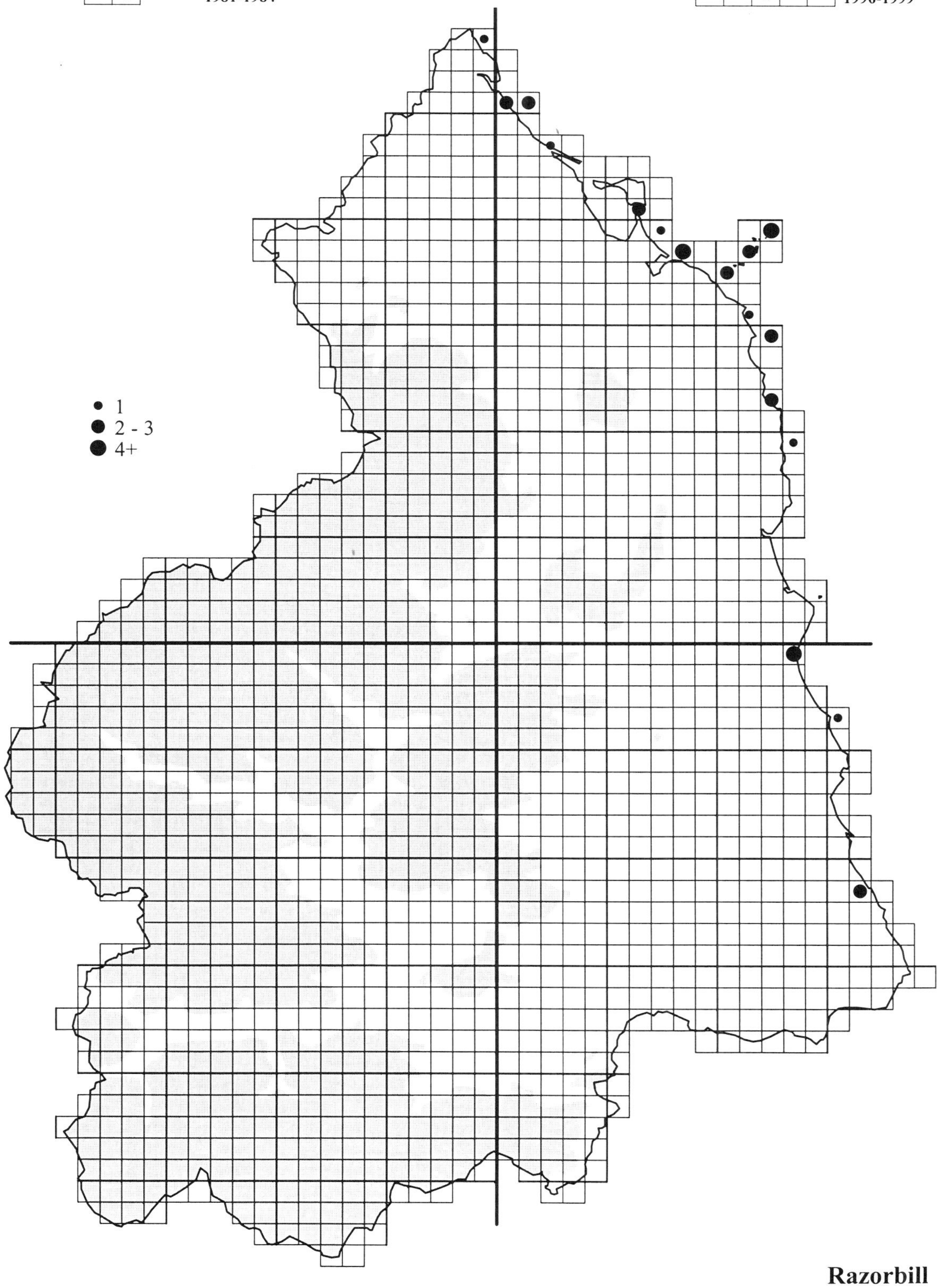

Razorbill

BLACK GUILLEMOT *Cepphus grylle*

Since Bolam's time, when he wrote that the Black Guillemot 'is strictly only a winter visitant to our coast' (Bolam, 1912), numbers have probably increased slightly. This phenomenon is comparatively recent for whilst Galloway and Meek (1980) regarded it as a rare visitor 'perhaps less common than in Bolam's time', Kerr (2001) noted that 'from the mid-1980s increased numbers [annually] ... including individuals in breeding plumage, but with most occurring in late autumn and early winter'. All commented on the species' concentration around the Farne Islands, where a rocky coastline provides its favoured habitat.

Black Guillemots were recorded in all three winter seasons of the survey with between two and five birds seen in the vicinity of the Farne Islands (NU23) each winter, and single birds sighted from the nearby mainland at Beadnell (NU22J) in January 1997 and at Stag Rocks, Bamburgh (NU13T), in January 1998. The numbers recorded, even allowing for duplicate counting in adjacent tetrads, may well be an underestimation. This was implied by Bolam in 1912 when he commented on the difficulty of counting 'blue water' birds from the mainland, and felt that it might be 'much less rare' than the limited sightings suggested. As evidence both in support of Bolam's suspicions and of the perceived increase in numbers on the Northumberland coast a count, made during stormy conditions round the Farne Islands in the winter of 1999/2000, which immediately succeeded the current survey, noted 12 individual birds. The observers stated however, that it could just as easily, under the prevailing conditions, be as many as 24 birds. The current increase in the number of birds and the presence of some throughout the year on the Farnes may perhaps portend successful breeding in the foreseeable future.

JOHN C. DAY

No. of tetrads in which recorded 5 (<1%)

Tetrad Analysis	No. of tetrads
1 bird	3 (60%)
2 birds	1 (20%)
3+ birds	1 (20%)

Total No. of birds counted 10

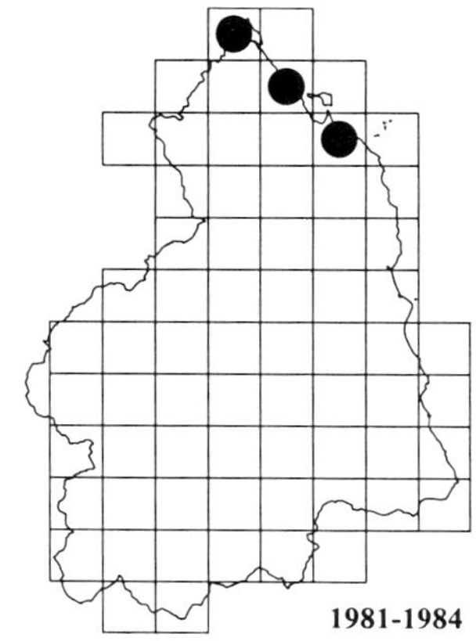

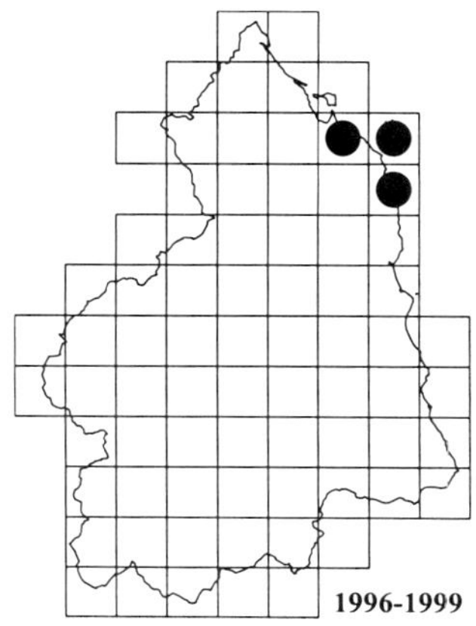

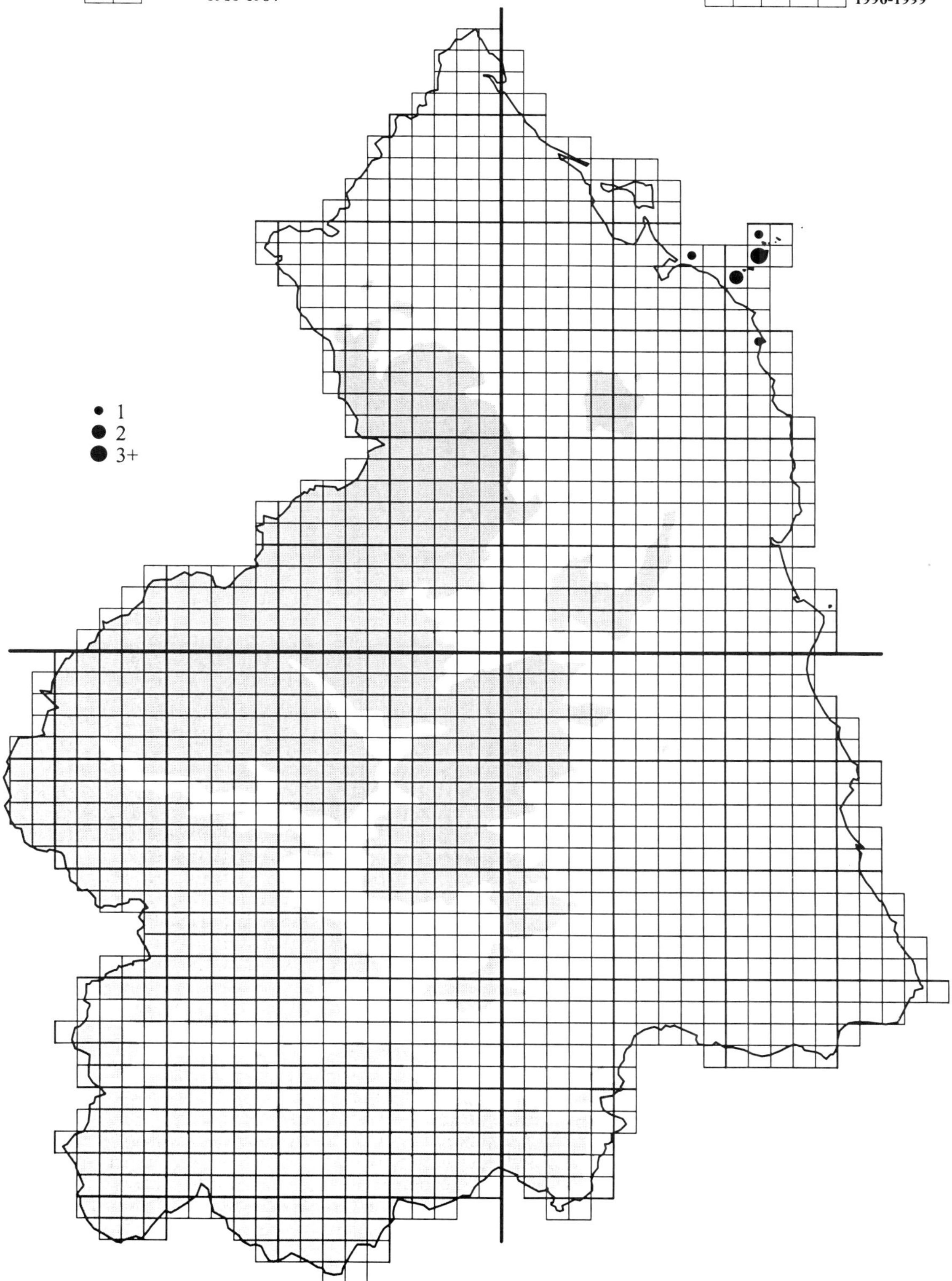

Black Guillemot

LITTLE AUK *Alle alle*

The Little Auk is a very numerous species, certainly numbering millions of pairs, within its breeding range in the high Arctic. Following the breeding season, birds have important wintering areas from the Barents Sea west into the Norwegian Sea, through the Denmark Strait to Davis Strait and south to the Grand Banks of Newfoundland (Snow & Perrins, 1998). However, Britain and Ireland are at the southern edge of its wintering range and the origins of the smaller numbers occurring around these coasts appear not to be known with any accuracy. Lack (1986) reported that they were widely distributed in the northern North Sea during the winter and thought these birds probably originated from colonies in Spitzbergen and further east. More recently, Parkin (2001) commented that, as far as was known, the northern North Sea, the Skagerrak and Kattegat were the most important wintering areas in the north-east Atlantic adding the 'origin of nearly 1 million wintering in North Sea is unknown'.

In Northumberland, the Little Auk's distribution and status seem to have remained largely unchanged for at least a century. In 1912 Bolam wrote that it was 'an irregular winter visitant, which sometimes comes to us in large numbers.....' while in 1932 he described it as 'a winter visitant, very erratic in its visits, in some seasons appearing on the coast in large storm-wrecked flocks and then liable, at times, to be blown inland'. Galloway and Meek (1980) concurred, saying that 'small numbers occur every winter, but in certain years there are considerable offshore movements, particularly in late autumn as northerly gales abate'. They also summarised the years since the mid-1800s when they were considered common or had shown heavy passages offshore. Since then considerable numbers were recorded in February 1983, November 1985, November 1987, November 1988, November/December 1990, January 1991 and January 1995. The movement in January 1995 was particularly heavy with counts on the 12th of 6,800 flying south at Cullercoats in one hour and 3,000 passing Seaton Sluice in only 30 minutes. The vulnerability of this species to both prolonged storms and oiling incidents is demonstrated by a number of records of birds found dead on the shore and elsewhere with a particularly large count by the RSPB of 115 corpses in February 1983 (*Birds in Northumbria* 1983).

The results for the current survey, shown by the tetrad map, are not unexpected as, during the three winter periods concerned, there were no exceptionally large passage movements. There was a period of strong passage during late October 1996 extending into early November but it was prior to the commencement of this survey. However, it is no coincidence that eight (62%) of the maximum counts made during the survey were in the period 15th-30th November 1996 and mainly clustered around the Farne Islands where good numbers were seen in the passage noted above. The two 10km square maps show well the disparate number of records between years as the large movements witnessed in 1983 would cloud the 'normal' winter distribution. It seems likely that many more Little Auks winter far out to sea from our coastline and therefore cannot be detected in a survey of this type unless some disaster, either bad weather or an oiling incident, brings the unfortunate corpses onto the shore. It seems appropriate then to continue to use Galloway and Meek's status for the Little Auk as an uncommon, but occasionally well-represented, winter visitor.

MIKE S. HODGSON

No. of tetrads in which recorded: 13 (1%)

Tetrad Analysis	No. of tetrads
1 bird	7 (54%)
2-8 birds	3 (33%)
9+ birds	3 (23%)

Total No. of birds counted: 95

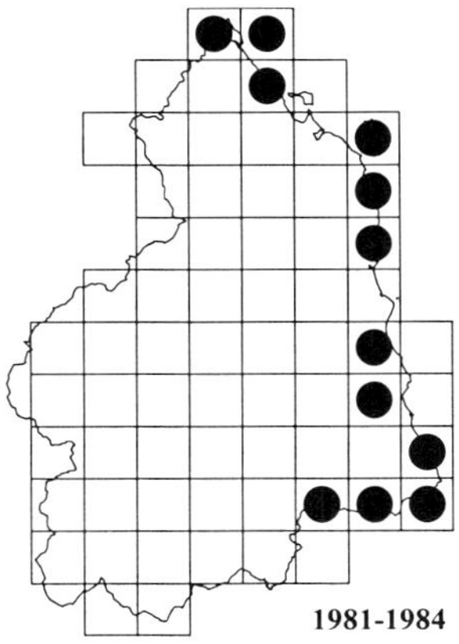

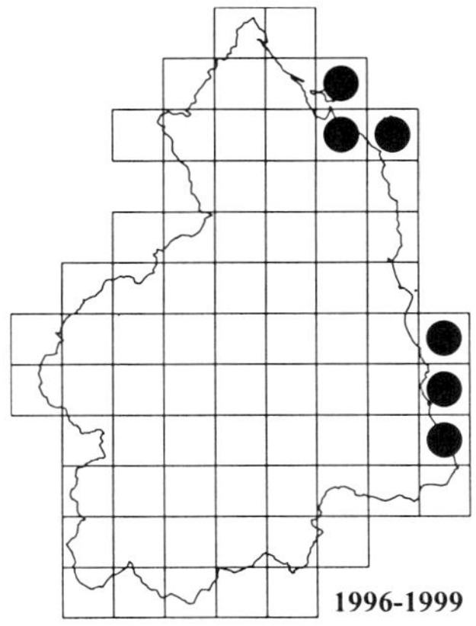

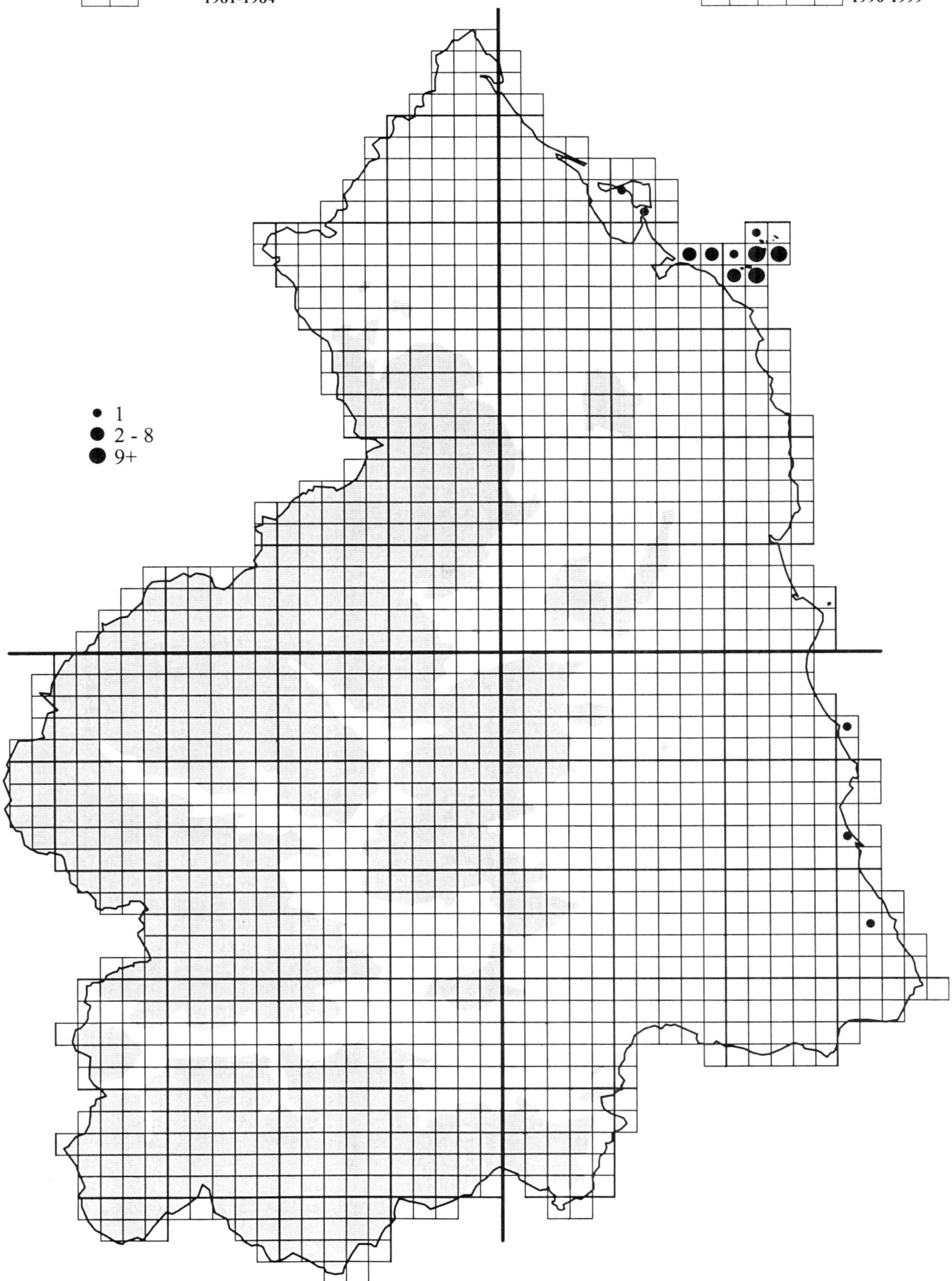

Little Auk

PUFFIN *Fratercula arctica*

The Puffin is the most numerous breeding seabird in the county (Day *et al.*, 1995) but with only two major sites at the Farne Islands and on Coquet Island. The most recent population count for the Farnes is for 1993, when there was an estimated 34,710 breeding pairs, while on Coquet Island the colony held 11,460 pairs in 1998. The breeding sites, however, are usually deserted by mid-August as birds disperse to the open sea. A glance at the tetrad distribution map for the current winter atlas survey shows quite clearly how scarce the species is in the inshore waters of Northumberland during the winter months. This thin winter distribution was also noted during the 1981-1984 winter survey and is clearly reflected in the two 10km square maps.

Harris (1984) said that the majority of Puffins winter in the open sea far from land and those reared in north east Britain do not move very far with most remaining in the North Sea. The results of the national winter atlas survey in 1981-1984 showed that Puffins were recorded in only 126 ten km squares in Britain and Ireland with most records coming from the east coast of Britain and around the Shetland Islands. Within that survey period the situation for the winters of 1981/82 and 1983/84, with virtually no records, were considered typical of a normal winter but the results for winter 1982/83 were atypical because of a major auk wreck in February 1983 (Lack, 1986).

Locally, Bolam (1932) considered the Puffin to be 'a resident, never altogether absent from the coast' and that 'the winter-flocks are largely composed of passage migrants from more northern latitudes, some of which doubtless remain off our coast as winter visitants'. More recently Galloway and Meek (1980) said it was an uncommon winter visitor and 'very few are noted in winter and during the major oiling incident in late January 1970 only eight were found dead on the shore'. Since then there have been only two notable counts, in the auk wreck in February 1983 mentioned above when 104 corpses were found and in February 1994 when 23 corpses were counted along the Tyne and Wear coastline. The post-breeding and winter dispersal from the Farne Islands is suggested, from ringing recoveries, to be within the North Sea basin with birds being found on the continental coast from southern Norway to south western France (Galloway & Meek, 1980).

With only 14 birds found in just six tetrads, the rather meagre results of the current survey were perhaps not unexpected and, thankfully, no major oiling or other incident increased the sightings during the three winter periods. Although well known and documented during the short breeding season, the Puffin remains an enigmatic species at other times of the year and much remains to be discovered about its life at sea. Although classified as an abundant breeding species in the county, in winter it currently can only be described as uncommon.

MIKE S. HODGSON

No. of tetrads in which recorded	6 (<1%)
Tetrad Analysis	**No. of tetrads**
1-2 birds	5 (83%)
3+ birds	1 (17%)
Total No. of birds counted	14

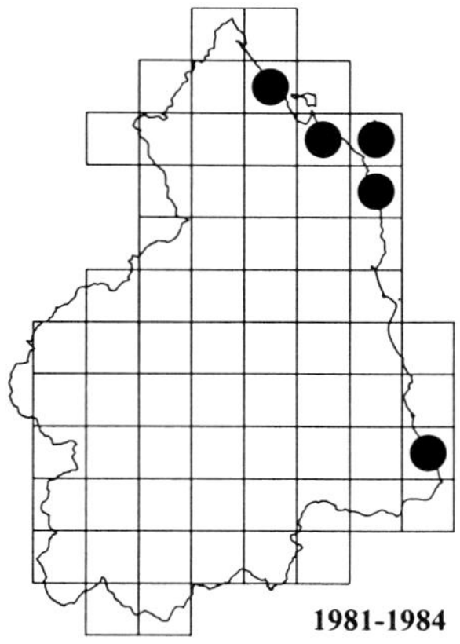

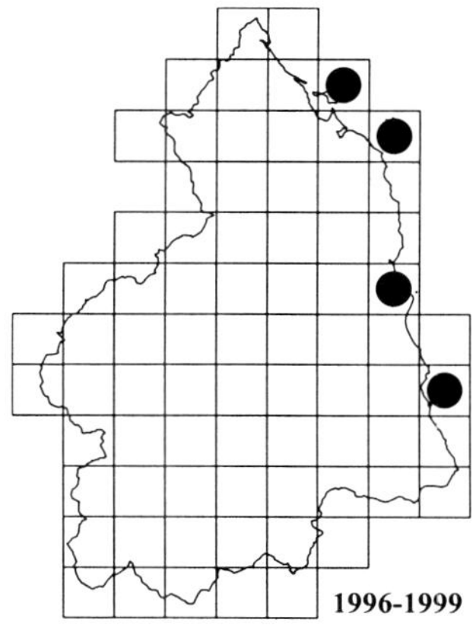

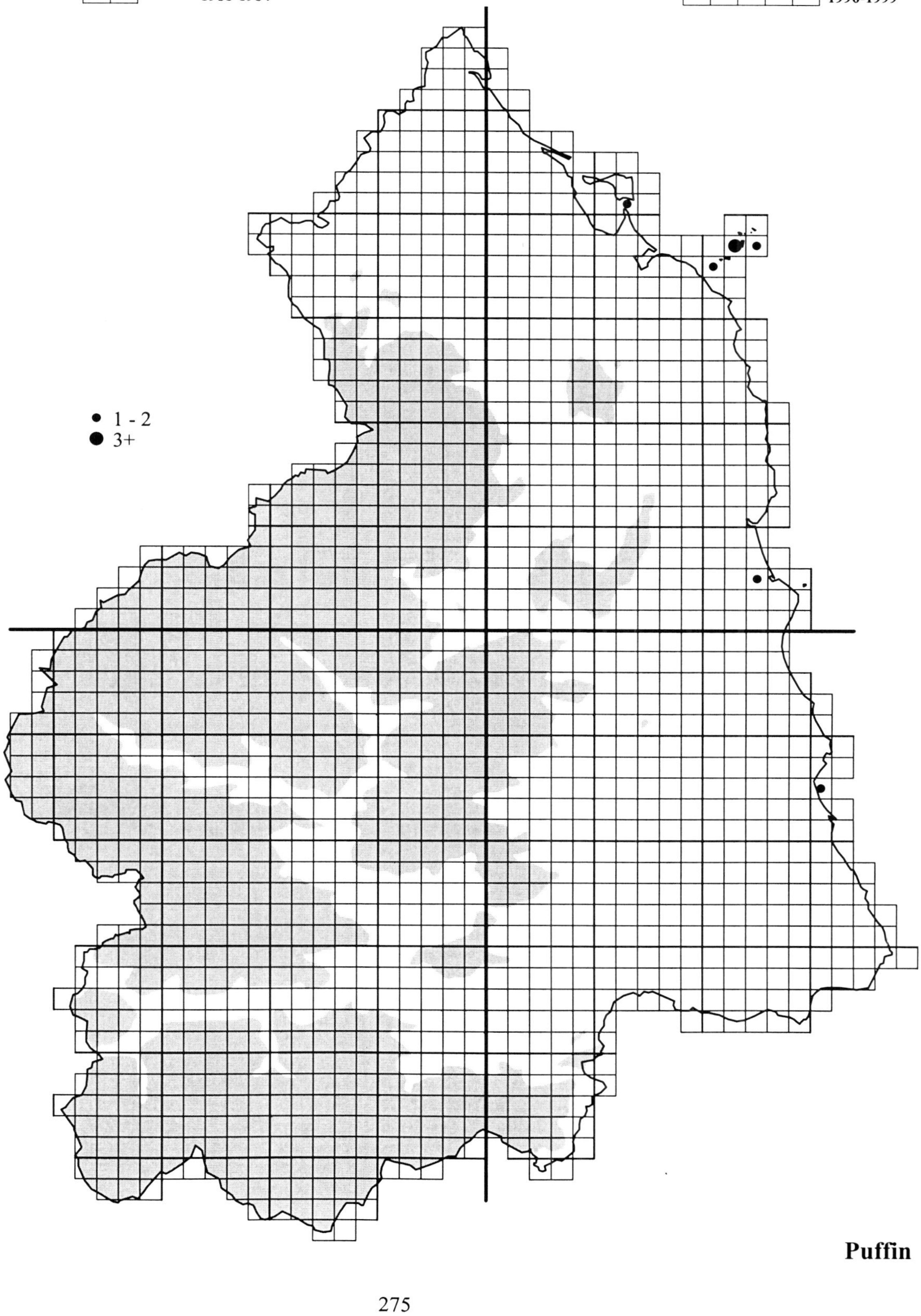

Puffin

FERAL PIGEON *Columba livia*

By the beginning of the twentieth century Bolam (1912) felt that it was impossible to definitely state that any coastal birds in Northumberland were pure Rock Doves, although he acknowledged that there could be exceptions on the Farne Islands and on isolated inland cliffs. Certainly, no later authors have been able to present conclusive evidence for the existence of genuine Rock Doves after Bolam's time. The descendants of the original Rock Doves are nevertheless widespread throughout Northumberland and Tyne and Wear, being particularly associated with human habitation. They are a gregarious species with a prolonged breeding season as indicated by two records during the current survey of young still in the nest in late January (*Birds in Northumbria* 1998). Feral Pigeons are essentially sedentary although post-breeding winter flocks may move short distances, particularly in agricultural areas, to find suitable feeding sites.

The tetrad distribution map for the species clearly shows that Feral Pigeons do not favour high ground or the conifer plantations in the west of the county; indeed, birds only occurred over 201 metres a.s.l. in 23 (6%) of the 390 occupied tetrads. Height above sea level was also shown to be significant in *The breeding birds of South East Scotland* (Murray *et al.*, 1998) where the species was found in 65% of all tetrads below the 200 metre contour. Equally apparent from the current winter map is the distribution of small (one-11) and medium (12-40) sized parties of birds in lowland rural habitat where they were frequently recorded feeding in stubble fields or where there were brassica crops. They were often to be identified in mixed flocks with Woodpigeon *C. palumbus*. Counts in excess of 41 birds (accounting for 20% of the occupied tetrads) also occur in low-lying agricultural areas, particularly near Rothbury (NT90 & NU00) and in the locality of Learmouth (NT83) as well as along the coastal plain between Berwick (NT95W) and Warkworth (NU20N). Further south large numbers were also present in the urban conurbation along the banks of the Tyne and in the triangle delineated by a line from Newburn (NZ16S), to Newbiggin (NZ38D) and North Shields (NZ36P). It was within this area that many of the largest counts were recorded with 1,500 in Heaton (NZ26T), 360 at Blyth, 300 in Newcastle City Centre (NZ26M) and 250 at Newbiggin.

A further feature of the map is the coastal distribution of the species. In many of the former cliff-breeding sites for Rock Dove there are still large populations of Feral Pigeon. Winter coastal counts of between 100 and 250 birds were noted at Tynemouth (NZ36U), Craster (NU21P), Holy Island (NU14G), the Farne Islands (NU23I), Berwick (NT95W) and Dunstan (NU22K).

Feral Pigeons were recorded in 390 tetrads (i.e. 27% of the 1,432 tetrads surveyed), and were present in 28 (47%) of the 60 control tetrads covered. The control data indicated some fluctuations in counts over the three seasons, for example in three coastal tetrads at Tynemouth (53, 21, & 101 birds), the Farne Islands (161, 89, & 68) and on Holy Island (60, 50, & 150). However, in most of the other control tetrads there was considerably more annual fluctuation in the numbers of wintering birds as indicated, for example, by counts in the Prestwick/Dinnington area (0, 180, & six birds), at Lilburn (19, 101, & 0), and Countess Park (0, 31, & 0). This is presumably as a result of the availability of food supplies.

The overall number of individual birds counted during the full survey was 14,121 which makes Feral Pigeon one of the most numerous birds of the winter count and indicates a status of an abundant resident, although it is much more restricted in its distribution than its close relative the Woodpigeon which was recorded in 849 tetrads.

JOHN C. DAY

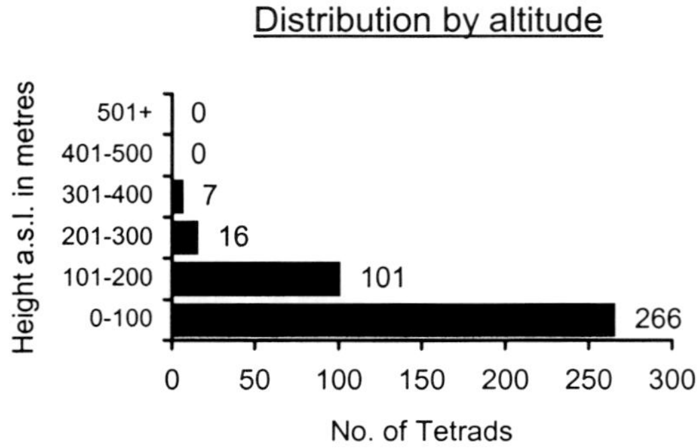

No. of tetrads in which recorded 390 (27%)

Tetrad Analysis	No. of tetrads
1-11 birds	194 (50%)
12-40 birds	118 (30%)
41+ birds	78 (20%)

Total No. of birds counted 14,121

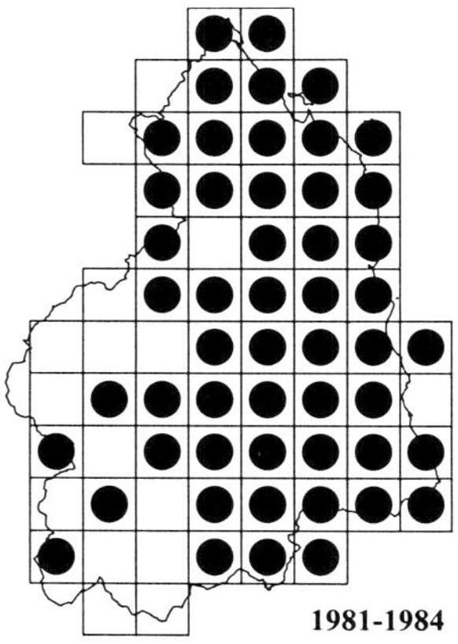

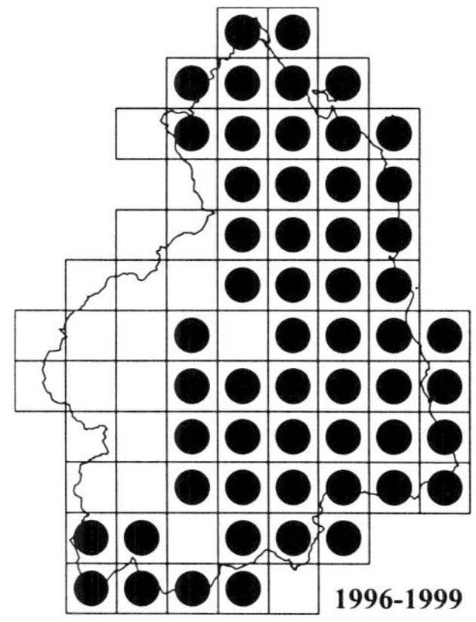

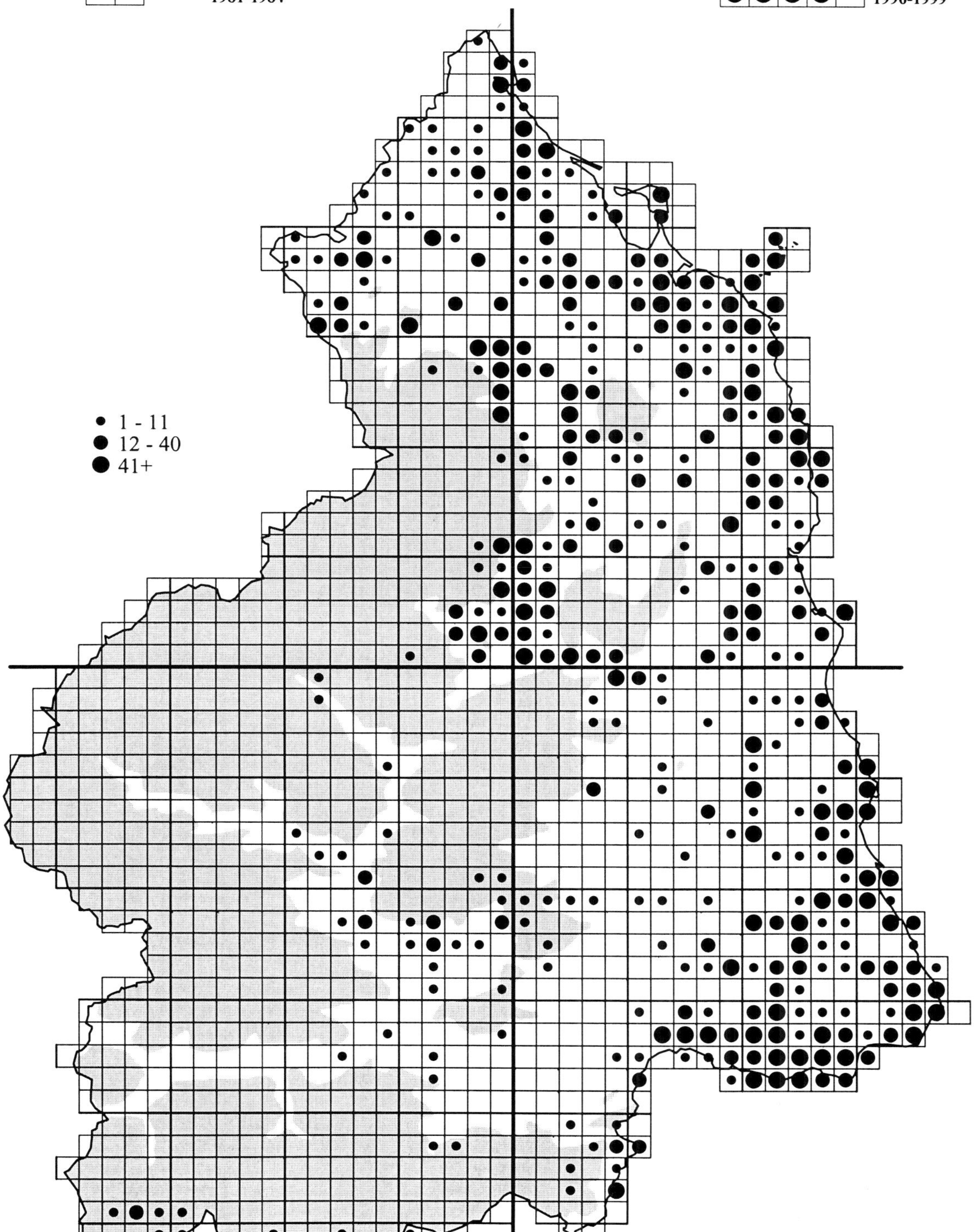

Feral Pigeon

STOCK DOVE *Columba oenas*

The Stock Dove is a relatively recent addition to the avifauna of Northumberland and its spread through the region during the late nineteenth century is well charted by Bolam (1912). He described it as 'now a common resident all over the district, where little more than thirty years ago it was unknown, even as a visitor'. He also gave evidence of small parties on winter migration at Emmanuel Head (50) in January 1891 and also at Berwick. Galloway and Meek (1980) found little evidence of Stock Dove arriving in significant numbers in autumn or winter, and the bird is considered a rarity on the Farne Islands (Walton, 2000).

The Stock Dove feeds in winter, mainly on weed seeds and grain from stubble, and on fallow and ploughed land later in the season. Its habitat preference is for areas of mixed farmland, with fewer birds in areas where pastoral or arable farming dominates (Lack, 1986). In our region birds have been seen feeding on Fat Hen *Chenopodium album* near Colwell, and in stubble fields near Newbiggin (*Birds in Northumbria 1990 & 1996*). There is overlap with the habitat of Woodpigeon *C. palumbus* but the two species select mainly different feeding habitats within the same area (Simms, 1971).

The tetrad map of this winter survey shows Stock Dove concentrations on the slopes of the river valleys of the south west near Whitfield (NY75S; 23 birds) and Plankey Mill (NY76V; 31), the River Tyne at Barrasford (NY97B; 54), and areas around the headwaters of the Rivers Pont and Blyth near Bavington (NZ07E; 44). They are also present in parks and remnants of farmland in urban areas such as that near Little Benton Farm (NZ26T; 30). Most records on timed counts were of less than ten birds, but counts of 20 to 50 were not uncommon, with an exceptional count of 100 at Cambois/Sandy Bay (NZ38C). A move to the edges of high ground in spring is suggested from a comparison with the tetrad map from *The atlas of breeding birds in Northumbria* (Day *et al.*, 1995). This is supported by data gathered for this survey showing 79% of occupied tetrads are below 200 metres a.s.l., with a marked drop in occupancy above this height. This movement is within the range of most ringing records, with only 11% exceeding 40 kilometres (Lack, 1986). Since 63% of all tetrads in the region visited during this survey lie within this height range (i.e. 0-200 metres), this is clearly the height at which the Stock Dove's preferred winter habitat is found. All control tetrad records also came from tetrads within this range.

Supplementary records were an important component of the total count of 1,768 birds, accounting for 24% of the maximum counts from the 245 tetrads containing Stock Dove. The species was found in 17% of all tetrads, a figure very close to the 19% found during the local breeding atlas survey. This confirms its 'retiring' nature in winter when it is not an obtrusive bird and often needs to be observed carefully to distinguish it from Feral Pigeon *C. livia*. The estimate of 1,000 pairs given in *The atlas of breeding birds in Northumbria* is not contradicted by the data from this survey and, within its preferred mixed farmland habitat, the Stock Dove appears widespread if rather thinly distributed. Future surveys will no doubt show whether the species is increasing in the area as Mead (2000) postulates, on a national scale, that 'modern agriculture does not yet seem to be a problem for this species'.

ANDREW BRUNT

Distribution by altitude

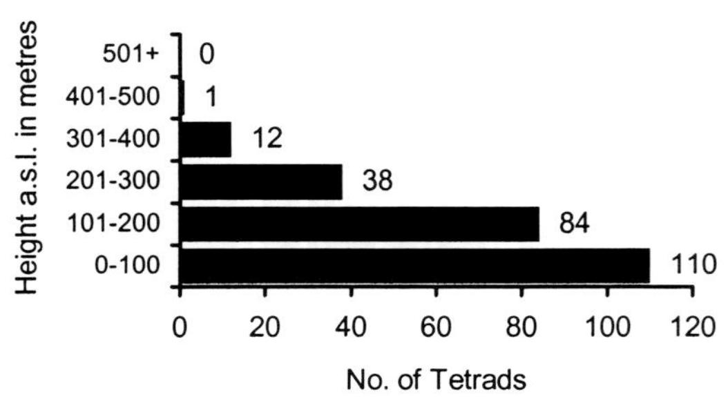

No. of tetrads in which recorded	245 (17%)
Tetrad Analysis	**No. of tetrads**
1-3 birds	125 (51%)
4-10 birds	70 (29%)
11+ birds	50 (20%)
Total No. of birds counted	1,768

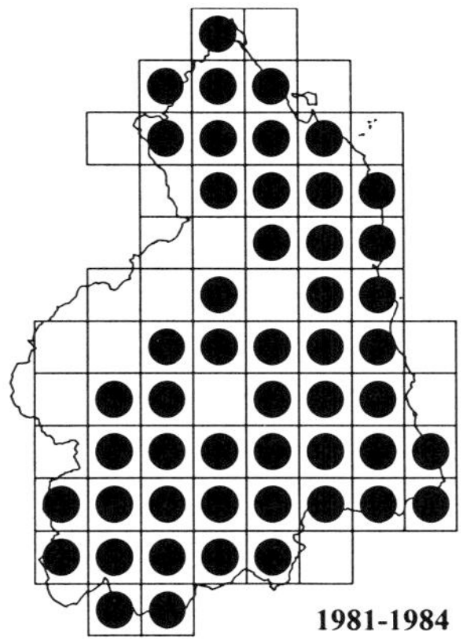

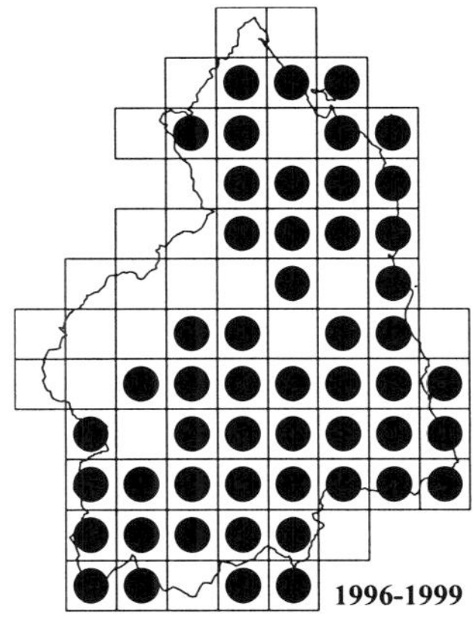

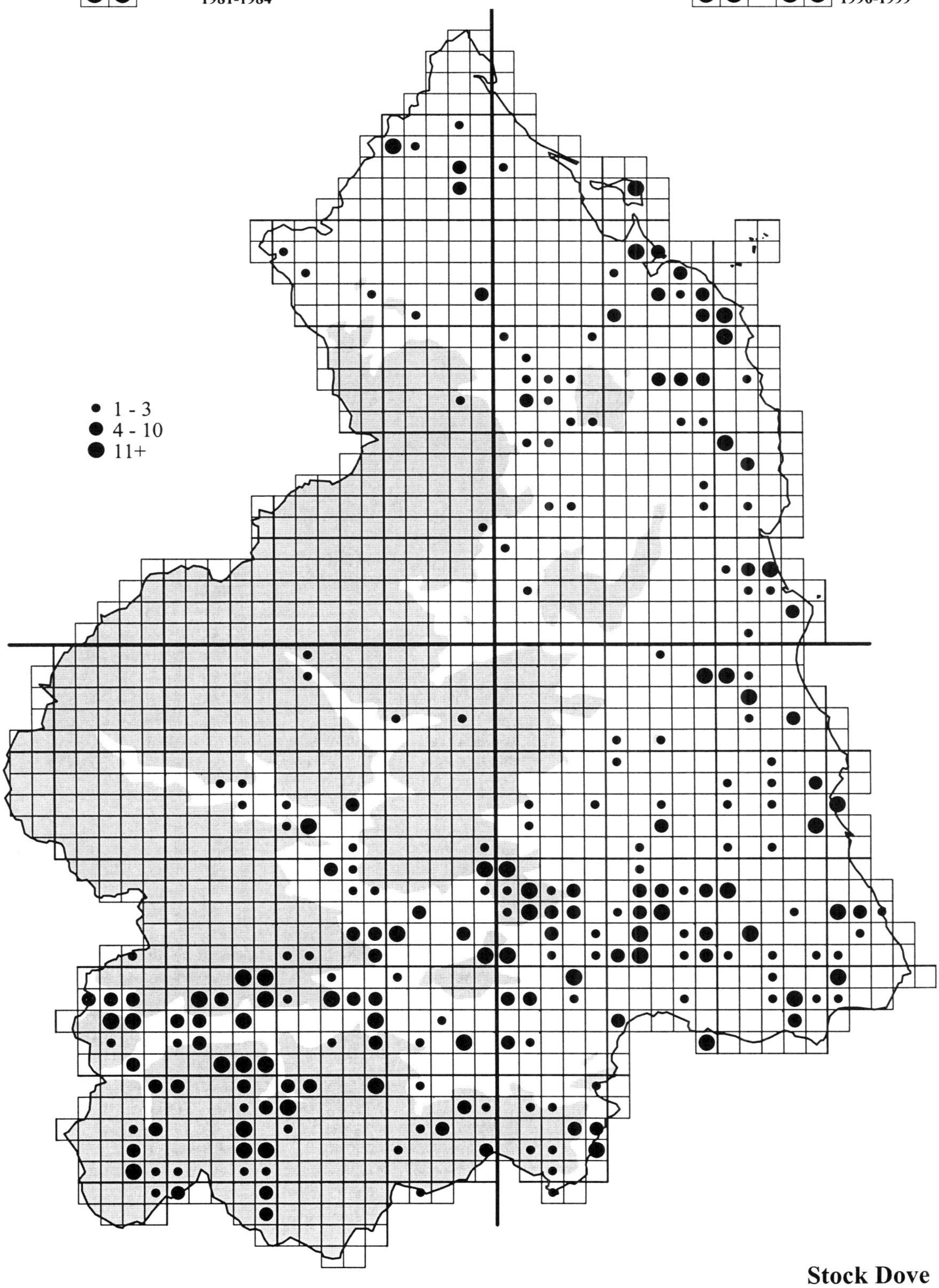

Stock Dove

WOODPIGEON *Columba palumbus*

The generally established opinion of the status of the Woodpigeon as a widespread and abundant species is confirmed by data collected for this atlas. Bolam (1912) believed it had historically always been common. He remarked that the large flocks attracted to winter crops (then turnip and clover) were already considered a serious problem by farmers in the late nineteenth century on farms around Berwick-upon-Tweed, and believed these crops to be a factor in the Woodpigeon's apparent population growth. He also gave evidence of large migration movements into the area. Writing in 1932, he connected a perceived decline in flocking with the agricultural depression of that time. There is no modern evidence suggesting our winter population contains a large proportion of migrants, with records from offshore islands involving only singles or small parties (Galloway & Meek, 1980).

The atlas of wintering birds in Britain and Ireland (Lack, 1986) supports the situation of a wide distribution with the largest winter concentrations in major arable farming areas. Locally, a comparison between the two 10km square maps shows little change in distribution between the winter surveys. Although Woodpigeons do take natural food in winter, large flocks are maintained by the feeding offered by stubble and cereal and oilseed sowings, with insects and disease now considered to cause less damage to Oilseed Rape *Brassica napus* than the Woodpigeon. The current winter tetrad distribution map shows the preference of this species for the agricultural areas along the River Tweed, the coastal plain, the south east and the Tyne Valley. The preference for lowland areas is confirmed by 409 (48%) occupied tetrads in the range 0-100 metres a.s.l. and 319 (38%) occupied between 101 to 200 metres a.s.l. Abundance falls at the higher altitudes with only 22 (2.6%) occupied tetrads in the range 301-400 metres a.s.l., four (0.4%) in the 401-500 metres range and none found above 500 metres. This is a considerable contraction from the middle and high altitude land occupied during the survey for *The atlas of breeding birds in Northumbria* (Day *et al.*, 1995) when 80% of tetrads surveyed were occupied compared with 59% in this survey.

The tetrads with the largest single winter counts were all in lowland arable areas, as for example 4,000 birds at East Learmouth (NT83T), 2,000 at Chesterhill near Waren Mill (NU13H), 1,968 at Christon Bank (NU22B), 1,000 near Corbridge (NY96S) and a huge count of 10,000 in the Horton/Brenkley area (NZ27C). The concentration of birds in feeding flocks may explain some of the zero counts in suitable lowland habitat such as at Stanton (NZ18J), Bolam (NZ08W) and South Charlton (NU12Q), though most of these were not in predominantly arable land. Some coastal tetrads with dunes or no appreciable cultivated land also lacked Woodpigeon, such as at Druridge (NZ29T), as did some wholly urban tetrads like Westerhope (NZ16Y). Woodpigeons were present during at least one count in 72% of the control tetrads. Some control tetrads showed a consistently high count over the three winters, such as the Swinhoe Lake area (NU03S) with 294, 500 & 400 birds and Spindlestone (NU13L) with 80, 117 & 420 where there was prime arable land. Those with consistently low counts were on higher ground, or with conifer cover, or mainly heather or rough grassland with no tilled fields as at Alnwick Moor (NU11K), Hawkhope (NY78E) and Shittleheugh (NY89S).

The difference between the count of 9,519 pairs in *The atlas of breeding birds in Northumbria* and the total of 117,165 during the current winter survey can be explained by the higher visibility of the Woodpigeon in winter. Whether resting in bare trees, seen in flight at distance or feeding amongst low vegetation, it is a relatively straightforward species to count. The proposed breeding figure of 40,000 to 80,000 pairs for the region is comparable with the grand total for this survey, with the control data suggesting that the timed visits were relatively accurate for this species.

ANDREW BRUNT

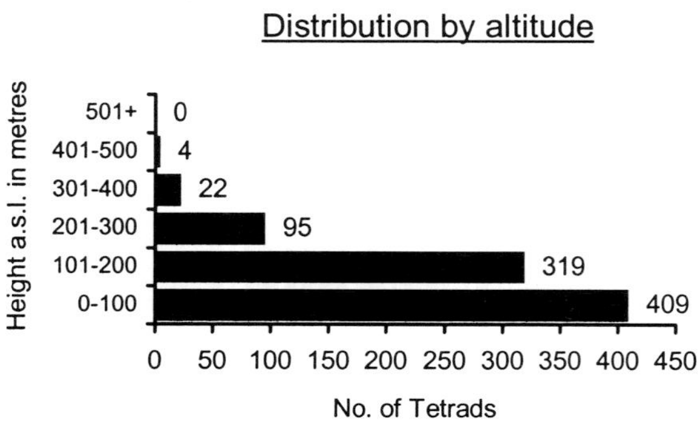

No. of tetrads in which recorded 849 (59%)

Tetrad Analysis	No. of tetrads
1-31 birds	421 (50%)
32-165 birds	259 (30%)
166+ birds	169 (20%)

Total No. of birds counted 117,165

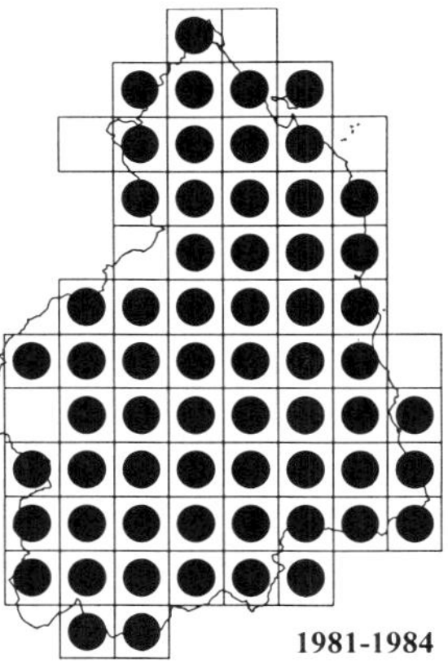

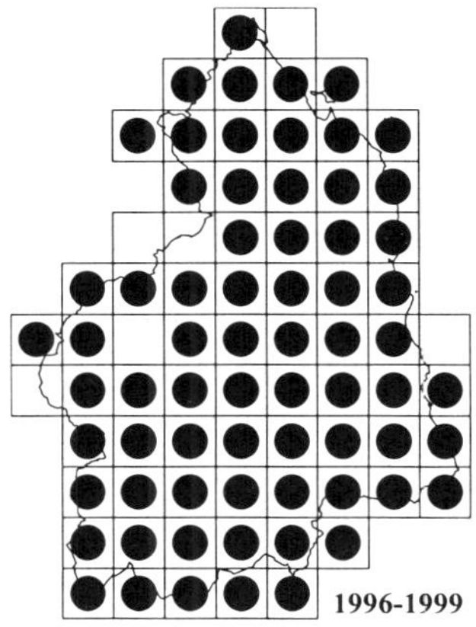

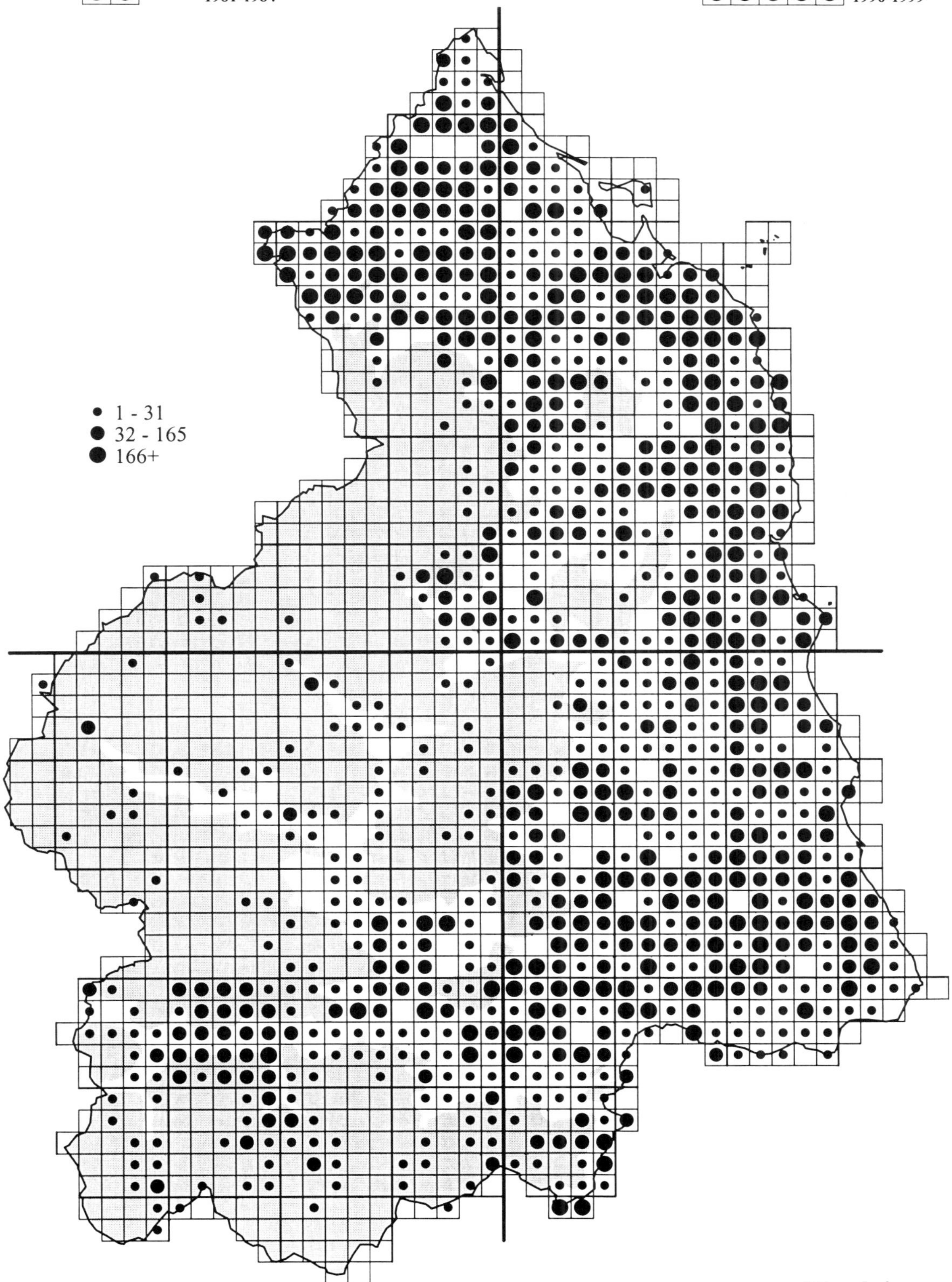

Woodpigeon

COLLARED DOVE *Streptopelia decaocto*

The Collared Dove is a relatively recent addition to the resident avifauna of the county and, following the first pair which was recorded at Ponteland in June 1958, it has now achieved the status of a common breeding bird. Galloway and Meek (1980) noted that by 1963 colonisation had continued and that it could be found at eight localities along the coast north to Bamburgh. A survey in 1967/68 (Macfarlane, 1973) revealed that it had 'colonised much of the coastal area between the Tyne and Embleton and inland as far as Alnwick, Morpeth and Ponteland' but also concluded that it did 'not appear to be colonising other areas of the county'. Galloway and Meek also observed that 'large gardens close to habitations remain the preferred habitat and it has not colonised woodland areas to any great extent'. Mead (2000) described the bird as 'the success story of the twentieth century' and furthermore 'definitely here to stay!'

During winter the Collared Dove depends upon cereal grains but will also feed upon small insects together with a variety of seeds and berries found both in the wild and in gardens. In adapting to a climate considerably cooler and moister than its original Asian homeland, the Collared Dove is most successful where there is a reliable source of food, with its current distribution being very much associated with human habitation. The BTO Garden Bird Feeding Survey records from the 1970s listed the Collared Dove as occurring in 60.1% of gardens and ranked it 12th in frequency. Recent records from the 1990s show that it is now recorded in 87.1% of gardens surveyed, however, its rank remains almost the same at 10th. Today it is a common sight, often perched on wires, particularly around farm buildings in arable areas as well as in villages, towns, suburbs and even the city centre.

The recent successful colonisation by this species is well illustrated at county level. In the 1981-1984 winter survey Collared Doves were recorded in 56% of the 10km squares as opposed to 65% of those in the recent winter survey. However, in the latter survey, the average number of birds recorded in control tetrads decreased from 9.6 per occupied square in 1996/97 to 6.6 in 1998/99, although this was perhaps due to birds finding and exploiting alternative sources of food in nearby tetrads. During the survey a total of 3,201 Collared Doves were recorded in 347 tetrads which represents 24% of the number surveyed. Of these, 335 (96.5%) were below 200 metres a.s.l. confirming its preference for lowland habitats. The tetrad distribution map shows the main concentrations to be in the south and east of the county with numbers declining significantly towards the west and none in the upland regions. The bird is fairly well represented in the main river valleys such as the Tyne and its tributaries and in some cases in the upper reaches. The coastal strip is undoubtedly the most frequented area with its milder winter climate, lowland habitat, concentrations of settlements and mainly arable farmland.

Being a gregarious bird, the Collared Dove tends to form sizeable flocks in winter, especially where there is a good supply of food such as spilt grain. The first record of this was a report of up to 30 birds at Gosforth Park in January 1965 and in the following year 52 were reported from Holywell (Galloway & Meek, 1980). County annual reports show this trend has continued, for example in 1976 it was reported that 'flocks of 200 are now regular in winter' and during the 1980s several flocks of over 100 individuals were noted, the largest being 344 at Brunton Lane in November 1989. The occurrence of communal roosts has also been noted with 300 birds recorded at Monkseaton in 1970. Winter roost sites are chosen which provide protection from predators as well as shelter from inclement weather and conifers, holly and thick ivy are especially favoured (Lack, 1986). In 1984, 150 were found roosting in a barn at Brunton and a well-watched roost site in North Shields regularly attracted up to 50 birds in the late 1980s. During this winter survey several counts of 50 or more birds were noted. The largest was 114 near Wylam (NZ16C) with 108 at Alndyke near Alnwick (NU21B), 90 at Berwick Hill (NZ17S), up to 67 between Amble and Warkworth (NU20M) and 59 at Cramlington (NZ27T).

Comparison of the breeding and wintering distribution maps of the county for Collared Dove shows that it is a relatively sedentary species with a stable population. In the 1988-1992 local breeding atlas survey they were recorded in 67% of the 10km squares visited (Day *et al.*, 1995) compared with 65% of those covered during the recent winter survey. The 1988-1992 breeding survey concluded that the total breeding population in the county was between 750 and 1,500 pairs and thus the 3,201 individuals recorded in the current fieldwork confirm its status as a common resident in Northumberland.

ALAN J. DAVIS

Distribution by altitude

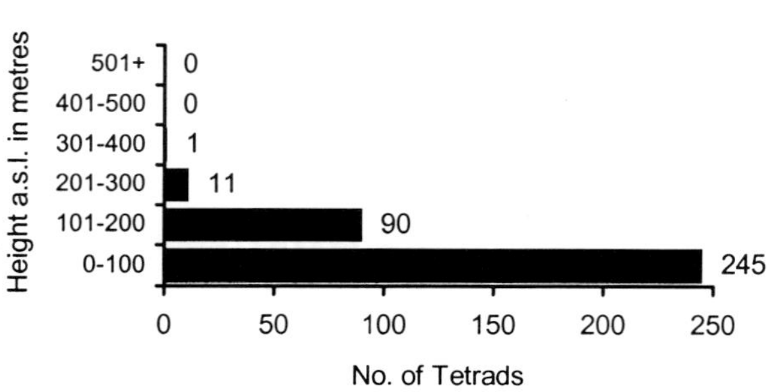

No. of tetrads in which recorded 347 (24%)

Tetrad Analysis	No. of tetrads
1-4 birds	186 (54%)
5-13 birds	96 (27%)
14+ birds	65 (19%)

Total No. of birds counted 3,201

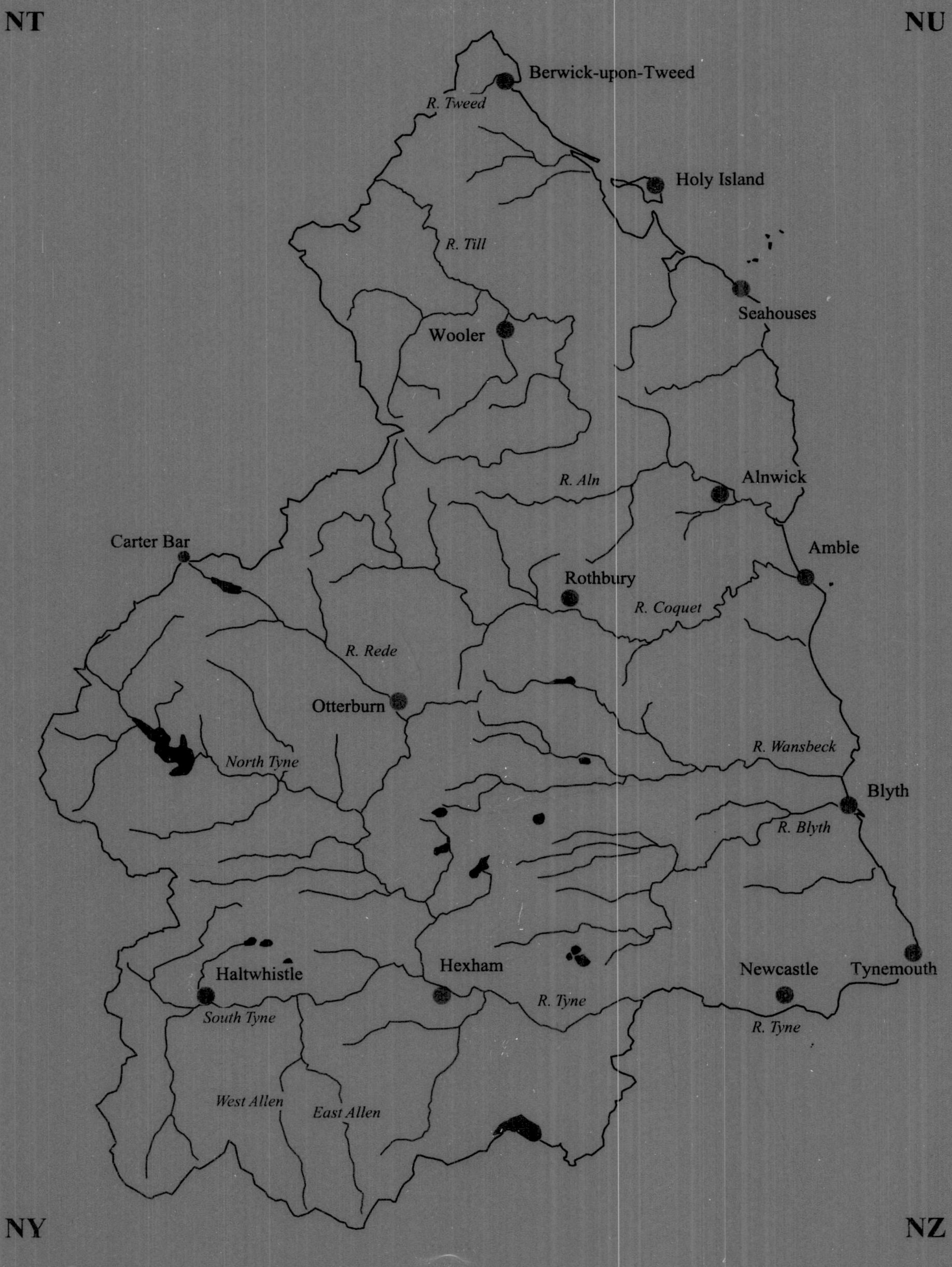

Atlas of Wintering Birds in Northumbria - General overlay for species distribution maps

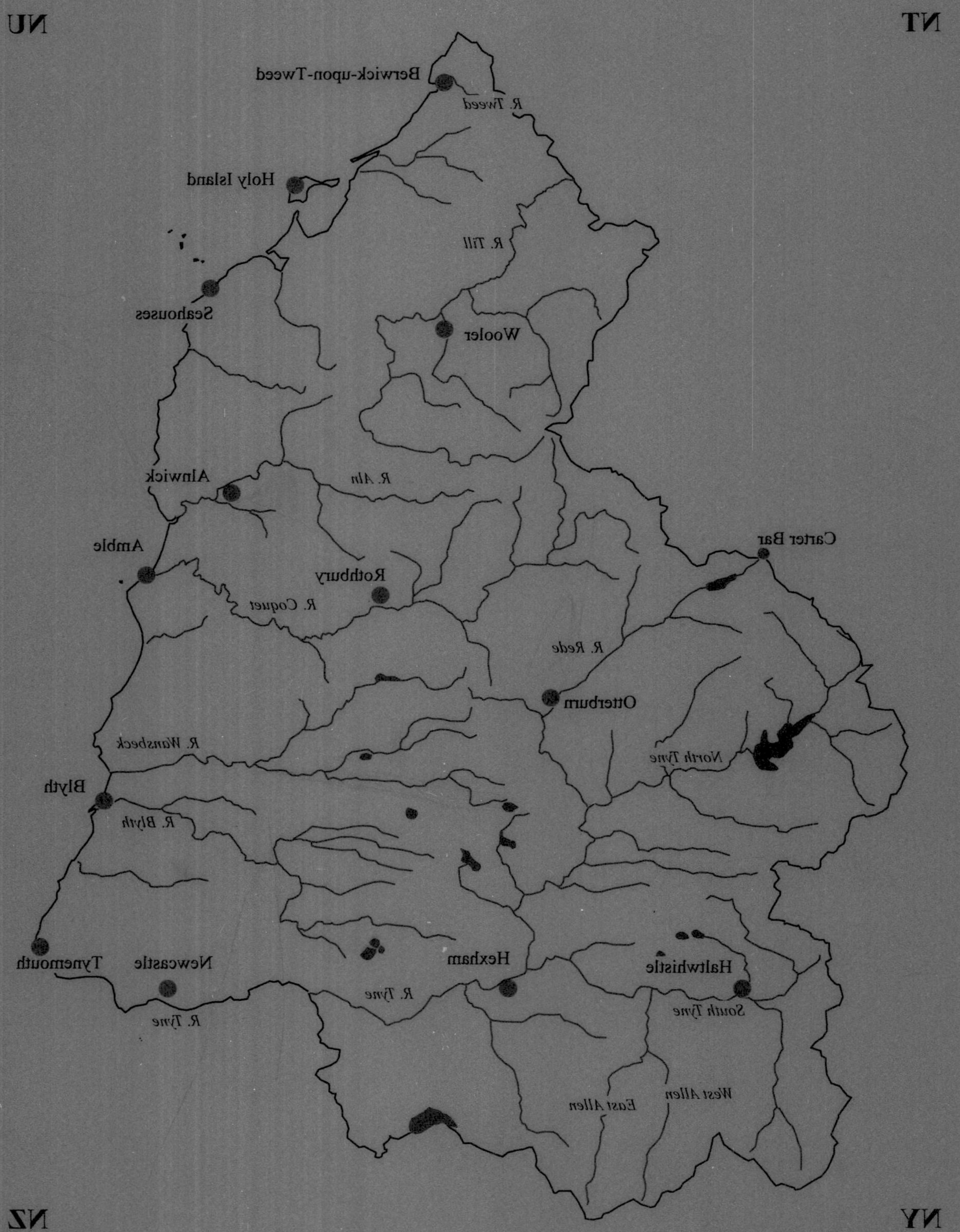

Atlas of Wintering Birds in Northumbria - General overlay for species distribution maps

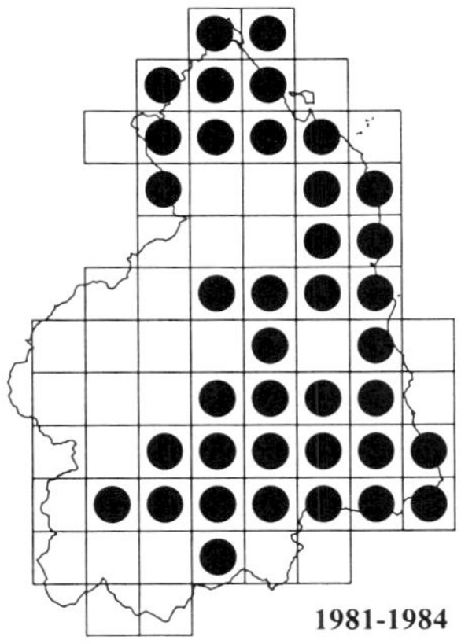

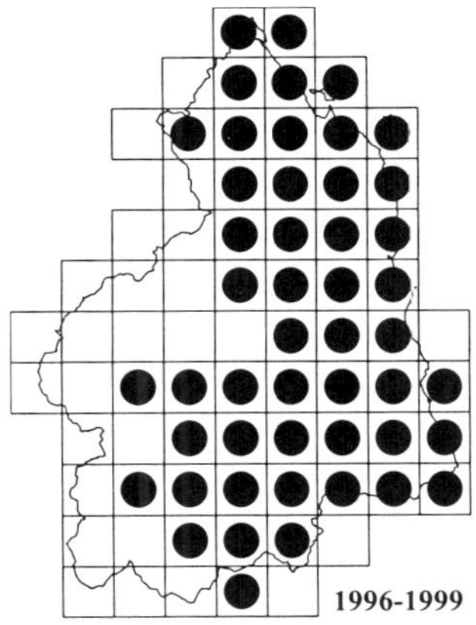

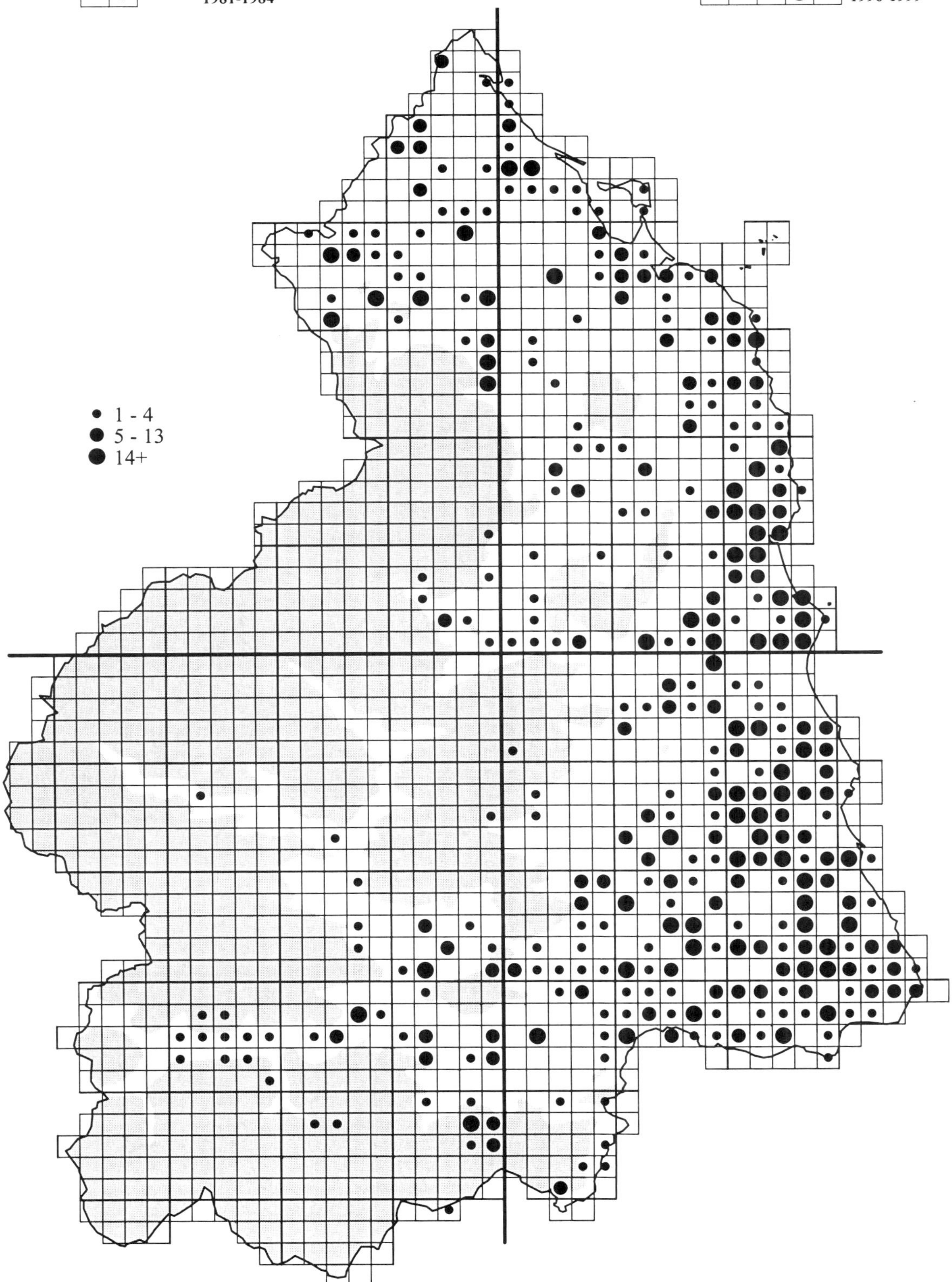

Collared Dove

BARN OWL *Tyto alba*

The Barn Owl is represented in every continent except Antarctica with 35 subspecies. In Europe two widespread forms occur and in Britain, at the extreme north west of its range, it is represented by the subspecies *Tyto alba alba*. Throughout most of Europe the Barn Owl favours rank open grassland habitats, particularly those associated with the banks of drainage ditches, rivers and hedgerows where high stocks of its preferred small mammal prey can be found. It normally avoids dune, heath, forest and all but the edges of mature woodland but exploits young tree plantations during their early years when voles can be abundant. In Britain, the Barn Owl favours low-lying regions because, as well as providing the most dependable food supply in harsh winters, they also hold a wide diversity of prey species. It also has a wide and scattered distribution at a relatively lower density than countries like, for example, France and Spain whose populations are in the region of 20-50,000 pairs and 50-90,000 pairs, respectively, compared to Britain's modest 4,400 pairs in the period 1982-1985 (Snow & Perrins, 1998).

The populations in the continental countries above are stable but in Britain a long term decline has occurred since the nineteenth century. In Northumberland, according to Hancock (1874), it was a common resident but suffered a slow decline due to illegal persecution. Later, Bolam (1912) said that it was formerly common throughout the district but now, at this time, was no longer a common species. However, by 1932, he was able to report a recovery in its numbers and it could be found over large areas of the county. This trend was maintained during the Second World War due to the decline in gamekeepering activities. Since the 1970s, there has been a marked decline in breeding numbers, especially in upland areas of the county, which can be attributed, in part, to the planting of large tracts of coniferous forest, changing the preferred open country habitat that the Barn Owl required. Allied to this, the destruction of known roosting sites, refurbishment of old buildings or removal of buildings altogether, along with the loss of many hollow trees, has increased this problem. Other factors are that during severe winters there can be high mortality, as experienced in 1946/47, 1962/63 and 1978/79, and many birds are also now found as road casualties each year. More recently, the status of the Barn Owl in the county was reported in *Birds in Northumbria 1983* as a well-represented breeding resident but by 1997 as an uncommon breeding resident.

The two 10 km square maps for the winter surveys of 1981-1984 and 1996-1999 show that there were 33 and 29 occupied squares respectively which suggests an even distribution throughout the county. In *The atlas of breeding birds in Northumbria* (Day *et al.*, 1995) the number of tetrads in which the species was recorded was 18. This contrasts quite strongly with data collected over three winters for this atlas which show there were 75 occupied tetrads with a maximum count of 81 birds. The distribution map shows the Barn Owl still favours the north of the county and the eastern coastal strip, especially in the south east and central areas. While birds appear to have been lost from the extreme south west they are being reported more often in central areas of Northumberland.

The number of occupied tetrads between 0 to 100 metres a.s.l. was 62, showing the species' distinct preference for low-lying habitats. However, while not surprising for an uncommon species, only six sightings occurred on timed visits, the other 75 being from supplementary data. As most Barn Owls remain paired throughout the winter and due to their largely sedentary nature and nocturnal habits, the numbers noted during the survey may represent an underestimate of the true population. Sightings of Barn Owl in the last ten years, nevertheless, appear to have remained constant with the possibility of a genuine increase. Although the county is not a stronghold for the Barn Owl, birdwatchers can still look forward to its ghostly form hunting over open rank grassland on a cold winter's afternoon, but, as with any uncommon species, can be elusive.

ANDY D. McLEVY

Distribution by altitude

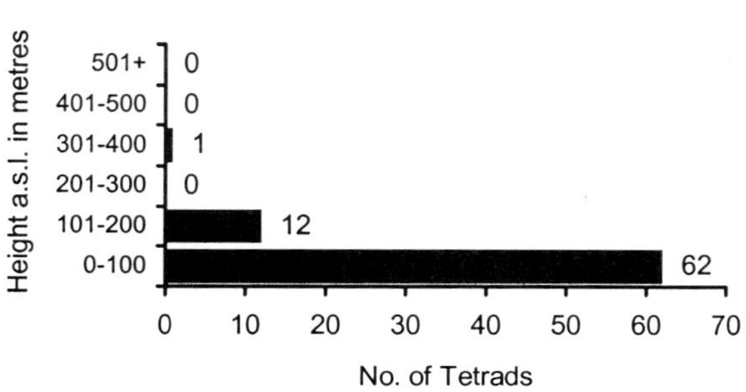

No. of tetrads in which recorded 75 (5%)

Tetrad Analysis	No. of tetrads
1 bird	71 (95%)
2+ birds	4 (5%)

Total No. of birds counted 81

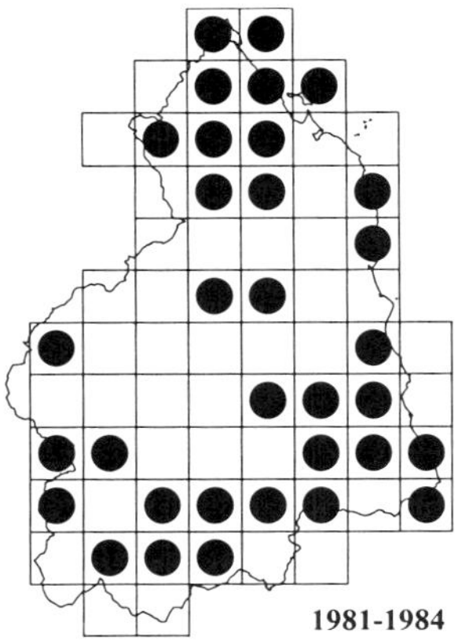

1981-1984

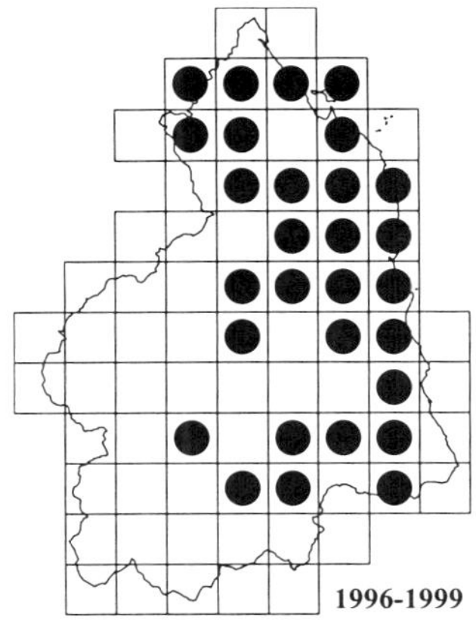

1996-1999

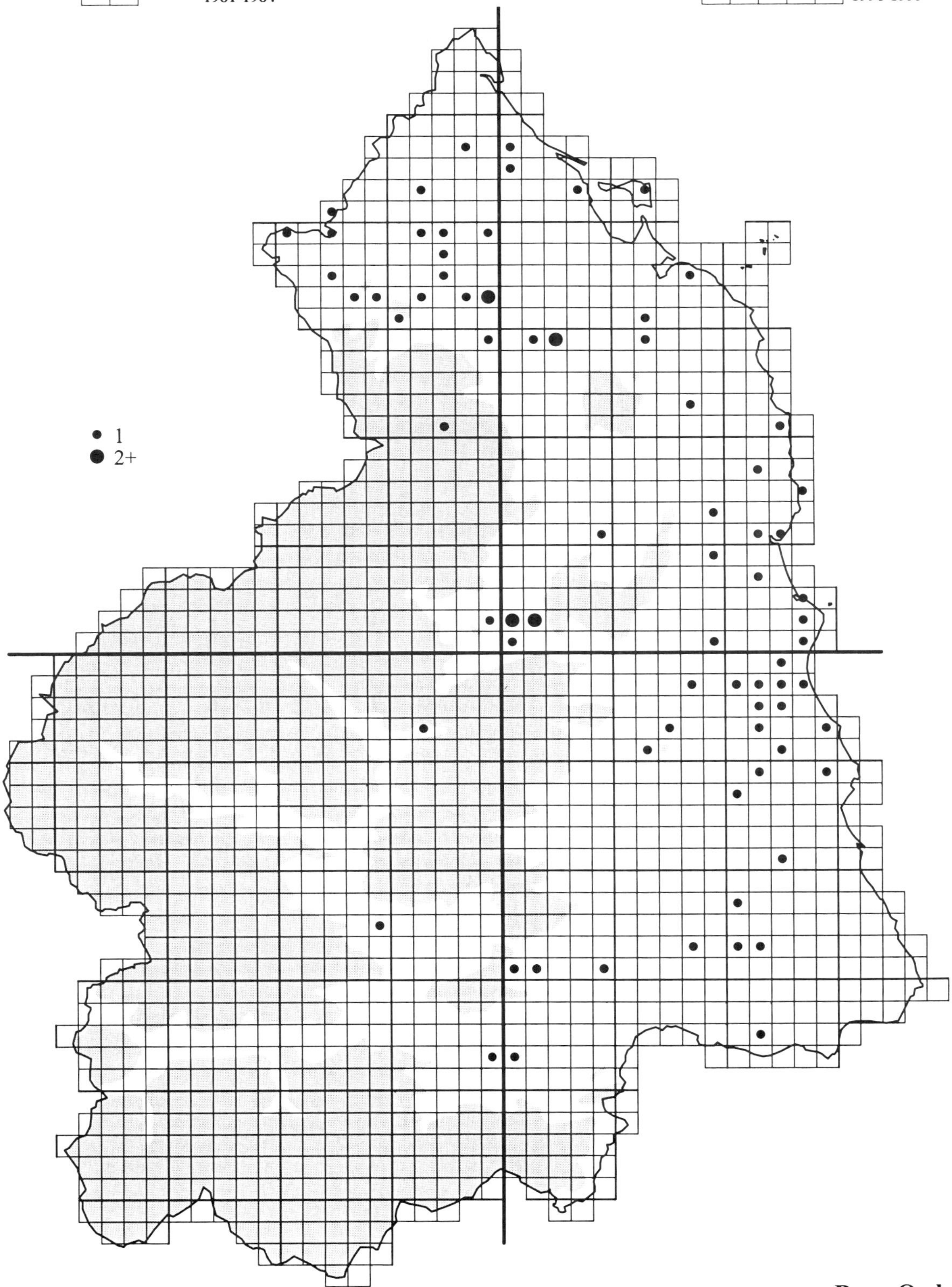

Barn Owl

LITTLE OWL *Athene noctua*

The introduction of this continental species into the British Isles has been well documented by a number of authors (e.g. Holloway, 1996). In Northumberland, Galloway and Meek (1980) said that by 1932 Bolam had listed seven county records although breeding was not confirmed until 1935. By the 1940s its distribution was described as 'thinly scattered over a wide area'. This description still holds good today based on the evidence of the current county winter atlas survey in which Little Owls were recorded in 40 tetrads. Galloway and Meek further stated that the species was an uncommon breeding resident and although there has been a slight increase in its range within the county, it is still not a common bird. Nationally, despite losses, the Little Owl is not experiencing any significant problems at the moment but Mead (2000) does forecast further losses in the future.

During the 1981-1984 winter survey the Little Owl was recorded in fourteen 10km squares. This figure rose to 23 during the current survey in which the majority of sightings fell roughly within a triangular area delineated by Newcastle, Greenhead and Warkworth. North of Warkworth, sightings were restricted to a narrow coastal strip as far as Bamburgh with some additional reports coming from the Coquet and Till Valleys and from the South Tyne and Derwent Valleys close to the border with Co. Durham. This area more or less corresponds to the distribution of Little Owl as it was described in the 1940s but with an additional further extension westwards that was later noted by Galloway and Meek and an extension southwards towards the border with Co. Durham. It also corresponds to the winter reports which have appeared in the Northumberland and Tyneside Bird Club Monthly Bulletins since 1988, apart from Holy Island where a bird remained for several weeks during the early winter of 1995.

The south east of the county has remained the stronghold of the species with the most frequent winter reports coming from the Druridge Bay area and its immediate hinterland around the settlements of Red Row, West Chevington and Widdrington (NZ29). It has also been regularly reported in the Blagdon-Dinnington (NZ27), Backworth-Earsdon (NZ37) and Kirkley (NZ17) areas as well as further west around Hallington (NY97). In none of these localities, though, could it be referred to as common. The reliance on trees for winter shelter, especially those in the hedge boundaries of agricultural land, as well as its lack of tolerance for the extremes of snow and ice, exclude the Little Owl from many upland areas. During the current winter survey 95% of occupied tetrads were below 200 metres a.s.l.

Whilst *The atlas of breeding birds in Northumbria* (Day *et al.*, 1995) shows 54 occupied tetrads compared to 40 during the current survey, the distribution is very similar. This is to be expected since Little Owls are largely sedentary. The pair bond appears quite strong and many adult birds roost at or close to the nesting place in winter (Lack, 1986). This is certainly the case in Northumberland where many winter sightings have been within a few kilometres of a known breeding site. Little Owls can be heard during the daytime, especially from February, when territories are being established, and can often be seen perched on a branch, post or building making them more easy to locate in winter than the other British owls. It is therefore unlikely that many birds will have been missed and the total of 51 recorded during the survey is probably a reasonably accurate reflection of the current situation. Ringing recoveries suggest that most birds do not travel very far and only a very small percentage leave the area. Even allowing for this, it would appear that, when compared to the breeding population estimate of between 50 and 100 pairs, losses in the county are greater than the 21% suggested by the BTO Breeding Bird Survey.

TONY BAKER

Distribution by altitude

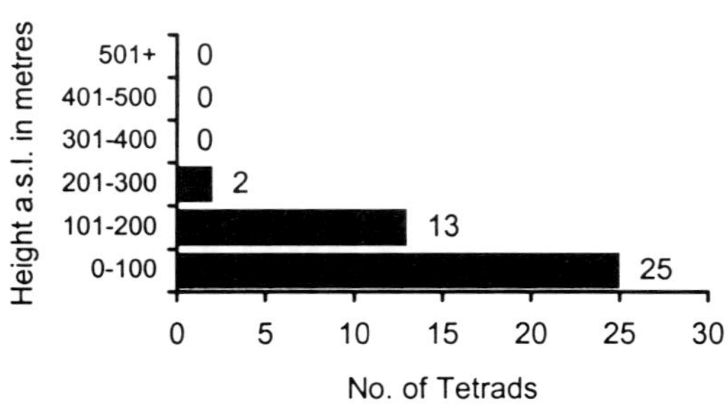

No. of tetrads in which recorded 40 (3%)

Tetrad Analysis	No. of tetrads
1 bird	29 (72%)
2 birds	11 (28%)

Total No. of birds counted 51

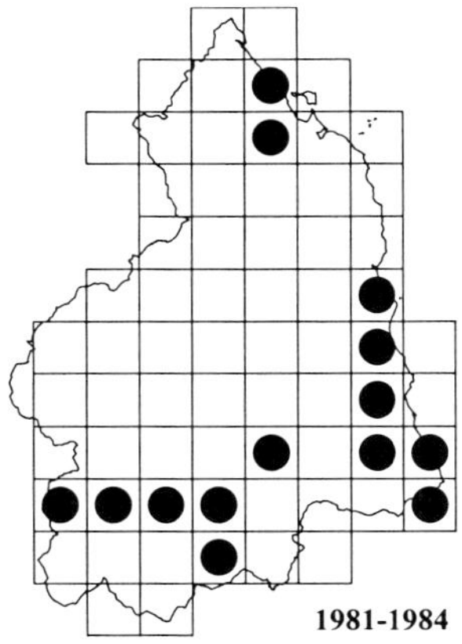

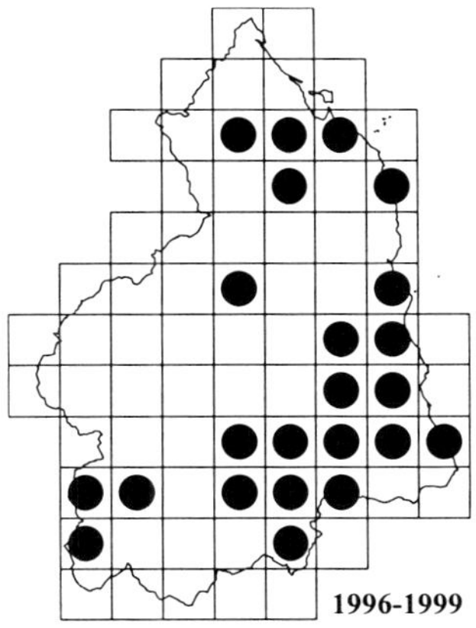

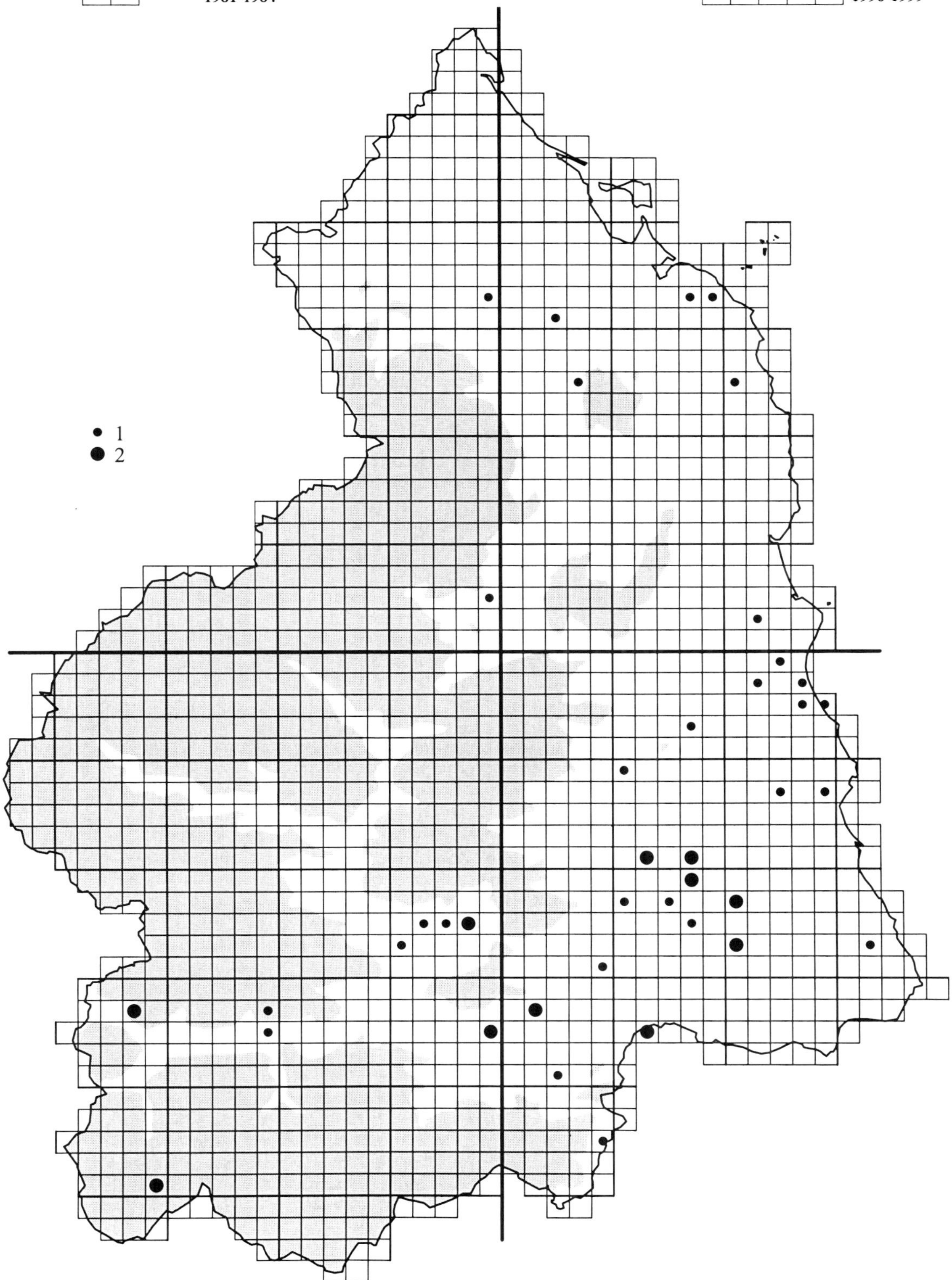

Little Owl

TAWNY OWL *Strix aluco*

The Tawny Owl is a well-represented resident in Northumberland being described by Bolam (1932) as 'a resident: the commonest and most generally distributed owl in the county'. Galloway and Meek (1980) said that 'woodlands and farmland in the lowlands are still the most favoured areas although smaller numbers nest in the uplands'. As with all nocturnal species there are problems using a methodology of timed daytime survey counts. The data presented in this current winter survey therefore probably represent an underestimate of the bird's abundance and distribution.

Tawny Owls do not form communal roosts in winter and roost either singly or in pairs, (Cramp, 1985) the adults remaining in their breeding territory having excluded their young in late autumn. The young birds either reside in nearby vacant territories or habitat unsuitable for breeding. The presence of roosting birds is sometimes betrayed by the mobbing behaviour of passerines. They are also often heard calling early in the morning or in the late evening and a number of the sightings included in this survey are from supplementary records obtained in these ways.

It is known that this species is sedentary in nature and therefore 'the winter and summer range overlaps considerably' (Lack, 1986). This has been confirmed within the county by a number of ringing recoveries from several long running nest-box studies. For example, a pullus ringed in 1994 at Falstone was recovered in the same locality in October 1996 and an adult female ringed at Slaley in April 1985 was found at Whitley Chapel in September 1999, a movement of only three kilometres.

The distribution of the Tawny Owl in this current winter atlas is similar to that shown in *The atlas of breeding birds in Northumbria* (Day *et al.*, 1995), as would be expected for such a sedentary species. There is however one difference, the local breeding atlas shows a concentration of birds in the woodland areas where there are large nest-box studies emphasising the fact that survey methodology can influence the apparent population of a nocturnal species.

The tetrad map shows the Tawny Owl is distributed widely throughout the county in winter. The majority of occupied tetrads (98%) were in the range 100 to 300 metres a.s.l. and this relates to the distribution of mature woodland. The map also indicates a concentration of records around the main areas of human habitation in the south east of the county. This bias is due to the majority of sightings being supplementary records (94 out of 107) and therefore concentrated in the areas with a strong observer presence. This concentration should not, therefore, be interpreted as representing a higher concentration of the Tawny Owl population in these areas but rather a likely under-recording in other areas.

Holloway (1996) claimed that Tawny Owl breeding populations have been broadly stable since the 1950s and this is likely to be reflected in winter populations in this county. There would, nevertheless, appear to be a slight decline in the status of this owl, as a comparison of the two 10km square maps shows 41 (60% of those surveyed) occupied squares in 1981-1984 and 37 (49%) in the current survey.

To calculate a winter population in the 1981-1984 national winter atlas survey, Lack (1986) used the criteria that an average pair raised 2.3 young, less than half of which survive the winter. Day *et al.* (1995) gave an estimated breeding population of between 500-900 pairs and using the same criteria, this would give an estimated total winter population of between 1,575-2,835 individuals, a figure considerably higher than the total counted during this winter survey.

ANNE MIDDLETON & MARTIN DAVISON

Distribution by altitude

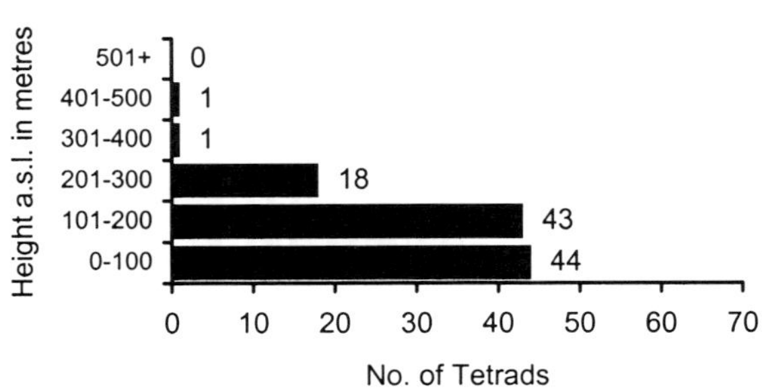

No. of tetrads in which recorded 107 (7%)

Tetrad Analysis	No. of tetrads
1 bird	81 (76%)
2 birds	23 (16%)
3 birds	3 (8%)

Total No. of birds counted 136

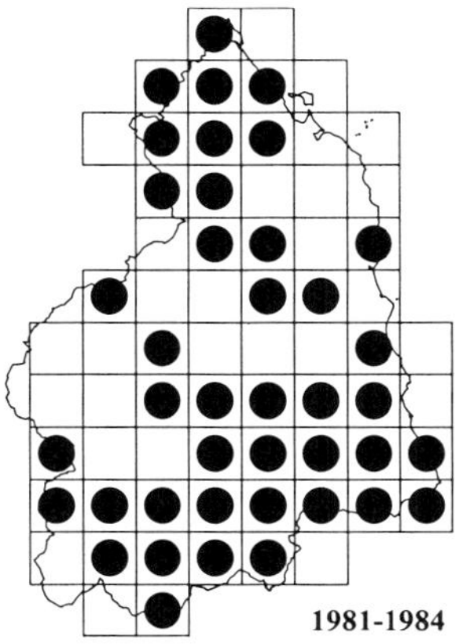

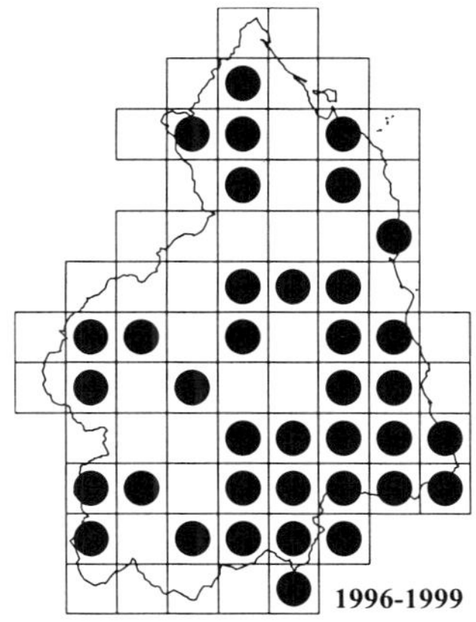

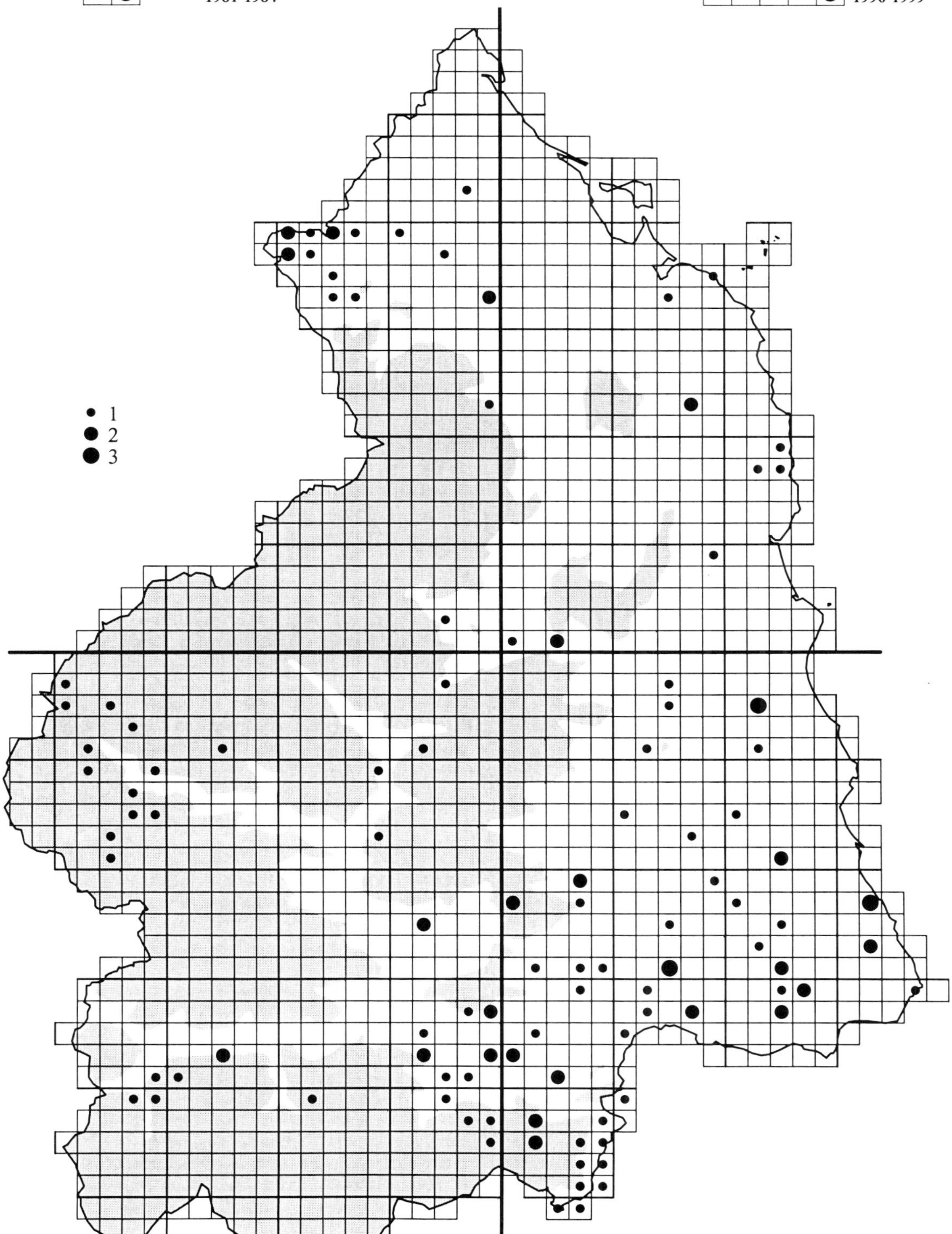

Tawny Owl

LONG-EARED OWL *Asio otus*

Bolam (1912) said that, in Northumberland, the Long-eared Owl 'appears to visit us regularly on migration' and by 1932 described it as 'a winter visitant' and commented that it was in evidence on the coast 'after the middle of September, throughout October, and, exceptionally, even during the depth of winter'. More recently, Galloway and Meek (1980) described it as an uncommon passage and winter visitor, a status that remains true today. The wintering population of Long-eared Owls in the county comprises immigrant birds in addition to the resident breeding population.

The Long-eared Owl is considered to be one of the most nocturnal of the medium-sized owls (Voous, 1988) and this has obvious implications for surveying the species. In particular, the current survey methodology of timed daytime counts mitigates against achieving accurate results, with the consequence that we are far from having complete data on the density and distribution of this bird. The resident population is thought to be largely sedentary and is found roosting in ones or twos in or near the breeding site. It is possible that there is some local movement out of the more upland breeding areas in winter. Immigrant birds from Fenno-Scandia enter Britain during late October to early December to winter in our milder climate. Ringing recoveries indicate the Scandinavian origin of immigrants to Northumberland, including one ringed at Hauxley in November 1970 and recovered in Sweden in May 1971, a bird ringed in Finland during October 1973 and found at Beadnell in January 1975 and an adult marked on Fair Isle in November 1976 identified in April 1977 at Widdrington.

Mikkola (1983) noted the Long-eared Owl is 'virtually unique amongst Palearctic owls in that it regularly forms communal roosts'. In Northumberland, roost sites are generally located in coniferous plantations, hawthorn thickets or overgrown hedges adjacent to good hunting areas such as rough grassland or young woodland. Bolam (1912) was familiar with this behaviour and said when covert shooting 'I have frequently seen a dozen or more Long-eared Owls driven out of a wood' and added that, at Ancroft in 1881, Long-eared Owls were 'numerous in every covert'. Although roosts of single birds are the most common in Northumberland, there are some records of large communal roosts that are generally assumed to consist of immigrant birds. These include 30 birds at Blagdon in December 1944, up to 15 at Gosforth Park, 12 at Prestwick Carr and, during a spell of cold weather in early 1979, 21 at Backworth (Galloway & Meek, 1980). The county annual bird reports show that during the 1980s there were nine roosts of three or more birds reported, with a maximum roost size of ten at Wallsend Swallow Pond in 1998. Throughout the 1990s however, there was only one roost exceeding three birds, involving six in a roost in 1990. These records, together with Bolam's observations, would seem to indicate that the number and size of communal roosts has declined in the county during the latter part of the twentieth century.

The difficulties of surveying a nocturnal species are shown by the fact that, of the 12 records during the current survey period, only one was from a timed survey visit. This indicates the records are likely to be skewed by a bias towards areas of higher observer activity and makes it impossible to say whether the distribution of most records (67%) from tetrads below 100 metres a.s.l. is an accurate representation or merely due to increased observer activity. The sedentary nature of the resident breeding population, however, would suggest that increased observer activity is the cause of this apparent distribution pattern. It is not possible, therefore, to make any meaningful comments on the current winter distribution of Long-eared Owls across the county, although a comparison between the 1981-1984 national winter survey and the current one shows an apparent large decline in the number of occupied 10km squares. The reduction in number and size of communal roosts together with a general decline in the number of winter records, particularly in the 1990s (see Appendix C), may indicate fewer immigrant birds arriving in autumn. It is tempting to speculate that this may be due to a succession of milder winters when birds have not been forced to move to Britain. Estimates from local fieldwork give a breeding population of 46-98 pairs in the county and, with an average fledging rate of 1.02 young/nest (Cramp, 1985), would give an early winter population of 139-296 birds. The total winter population for the county is therefore likely to exceed this estimate with the addition of an unknown number of winter immigrants.

ANNE MIDDLETON & MARTIN DAVISON

Distribution by altitude

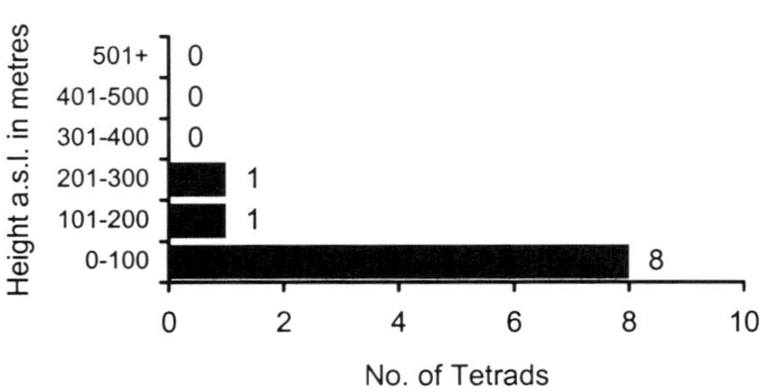

No. of tetrads in which recorded 10 (<1%)

Tetrad Analysis	No. of tetrads
1 bird	8 (80%)
2 birds	2 (20%)

Total No. of birds counted 12

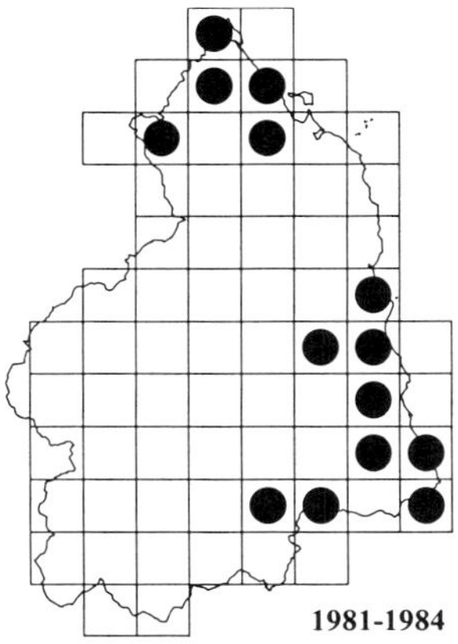

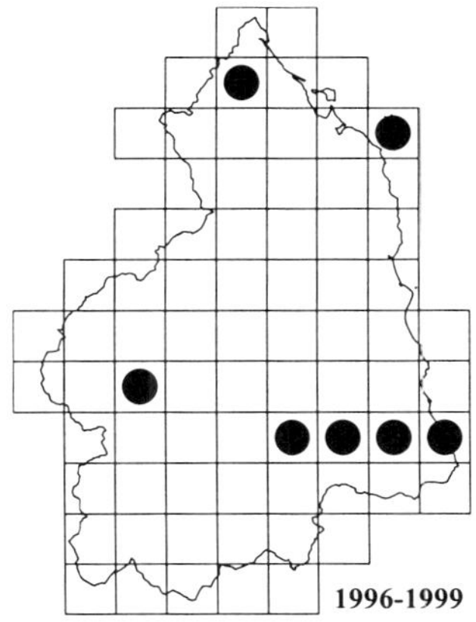

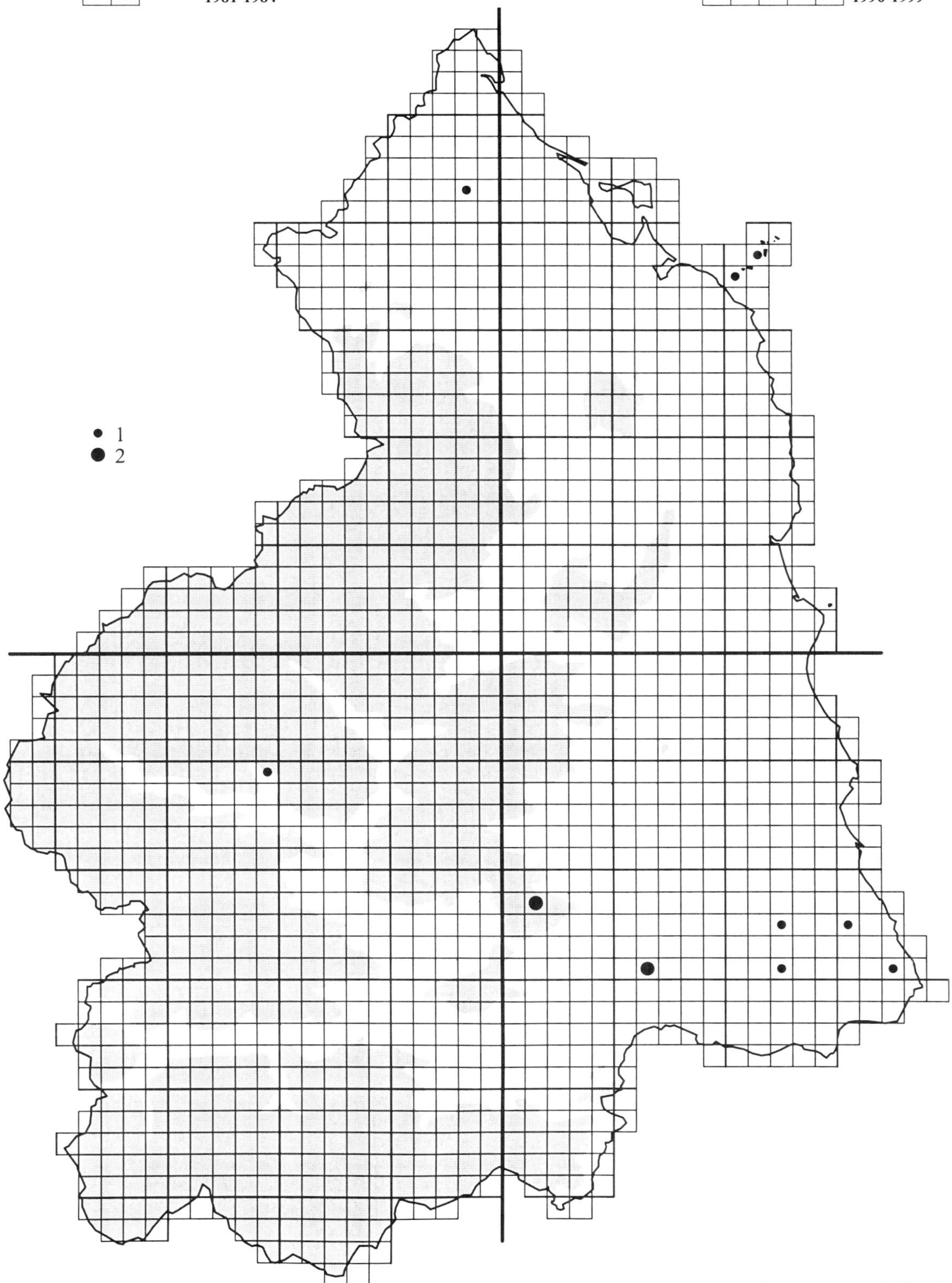

Long-eared Owl

SHORT-EARED OWL *Asio flammeus*

Galloway and Meek (1980) described the Short-eared Owl as a well-represented passage and winter visitor, but an uncommon breeding species. Well-represented means 100-1,000 birds, but it is unlikely that wintering numbers even approached 100 in any of the current winter atlas years. Even a superficial glance at the two 10km square maps shows a contraction of range between 1981-1984 and 1996-1999.

Short-eared Owls were found in 45 tetrads during the current survey and a breakdown shows that in 32 only one was located. Two or three occurred in six tetrads, four in five separate tetrads and in tetrads at Doddington Law near Wooler (NU03B) and Prestwick Carr (NZ17W) five and six birds respectively. These modern counts pale into insignificance, however, when compared with the 18 which roosted at Wallsend Swallow Pond in late 1971, or the 22 along a four mile stretch of the Tyne in November 1978. Over half the occupied tetrads (24) were below 100 metres a.s.l., which reflects the winter bias towards the coastal plain or the coast itself, with birds only being located in five tetrads over 300 metres a.s.l.. Some will undoubtedly be British-bred owls, moving down to coastal marshes, dunes, carrs and subsidence areas where prey is abundant, but others are from the continent. Short-eared Owls ringed in Finland, Norway, Sweden, Iceland, Belgium and Germany have been recovered in Britain (Lack, 1986), mostly in eastern counties. Ten Short-eared Owls appeared on the Farne Islands in autumn 1998 and one was watched coming in high from the east at Warkworth on 4th November 1998. Some are clearly exhausted, as they have been watched coming 'in-off' the sea at Seaton Sluice and Newbiggin, even as late as February, though as Bolam (1912) observed 'in autumn they usually arrive with the Woodcocks [*Scolopax rusticola*]'.

The nomadic nature of Short-eared Owls is classically illustrated by a pullus ringed in the Harbottle Hills in 1979 and found dead in the nest of a Rough-legged Buzzard *Buteo lagopus* in northern Sweden, 1,253 kilometres from its natal site (B. Galloway, pers. comm.). Because it is so nomadic, and responds to changes in land-use (afforestation, grazing pressure, etc.) and vole cycles, it is difficult to come to any conclusions about population trends. It is fair to say it does not appear to be as common as it was. Reference has already been made to Wallsend Swallow Pond (now largely surrounded by new housing) but other sites which used to be reliable for wintering Short-eared Owls seem no longer to be favoured, e.g. the dunes at Chevington which held nine birds in 1980 and Ross Links, where in the 1980s five-six were the norm, but in the current survey only one was recorded.

25 pairs were located in the Border Forest in 1985 (Kerr, 2001), with others on the southern moors, but few fledged broods were documented during breeding seasons between the winter atlas periods. To what extent poor breeding success is reflected in low wintering numbers is unknown but it could be that a species which benefited from afforestation in Northumberland and the Borders and enjoyed significant local increases in the mid-twentieth century is now in a period of contraction and decline. Persecution on grouse moors cannot be ruled out as a factor but there is at least one modern example of an incubating female being found frozen to death on its eggs after a heavy snowfall in May (W. Johnson, pers. comm.). Much more significant, however, must be vole numbers, as indicated in the *Borders Bird Reports*, where 15 territorial pairs in 1986 rose to 61 in 1991, only to fall back to 11 in 1995 (Murray *et al.*, 1998). Equally alarming for the future of the county's population is that the species appears to be declining nationally with sporadic vole years seemingly offering no long-term respite (Mead, 2000).

MIKE HENRY

Distribution by altitude

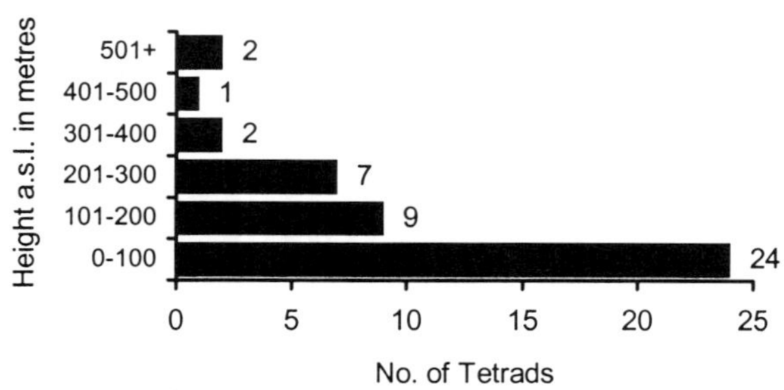

No. of tetrads in which recorded 45 (3%)

Tetrad Analysis	No. of tetrads
1 bird	32 (71%)
2-3 birds	6 (13%)
4+ birds	7 (16%)

Total No. of birds counted 77

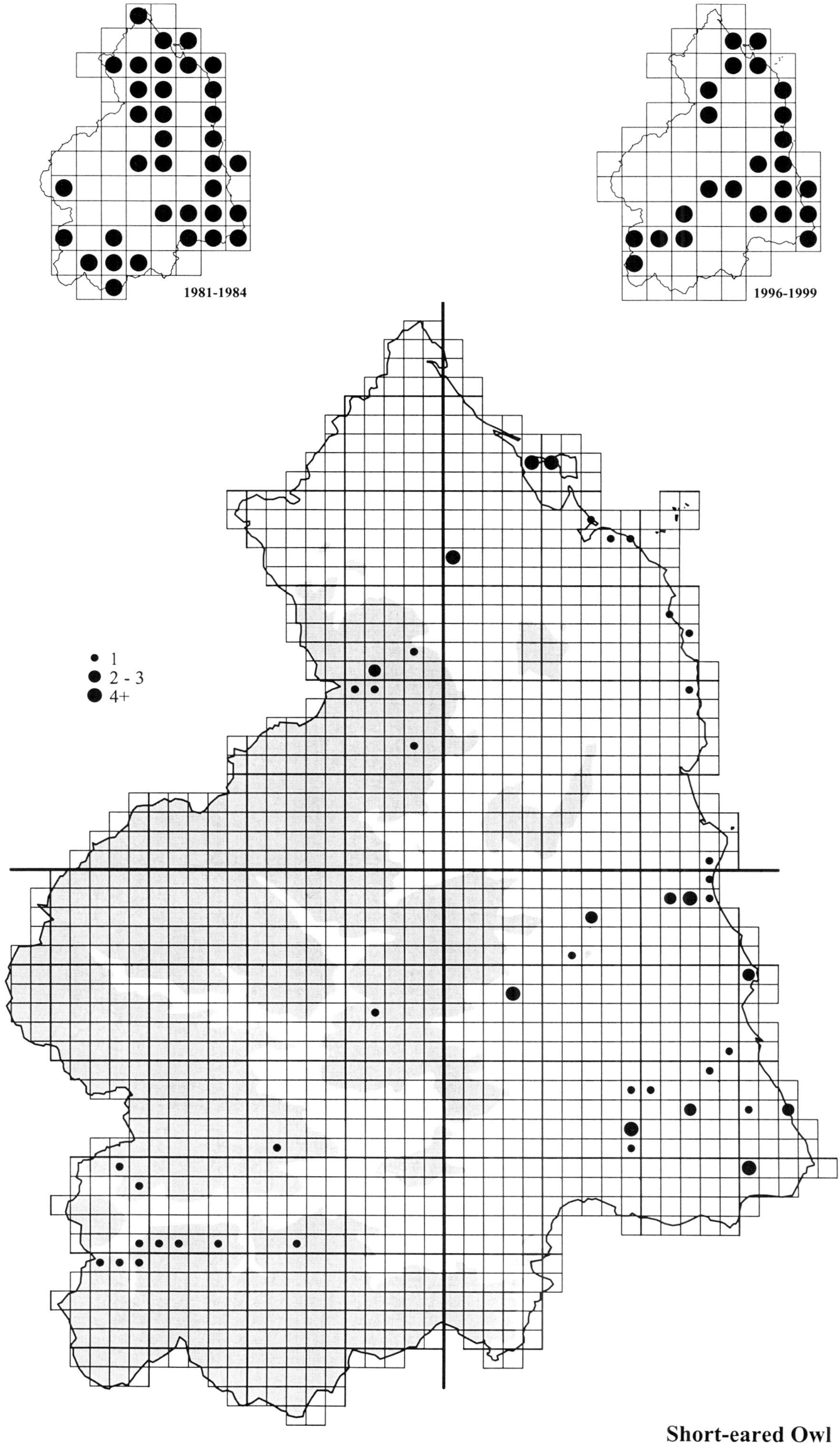

Short-eared Owl

KINGFISHER *Alcedo atthis*

The Kingfisher is a scarce resident in the UK with a fluctuating national population of about 3,600-6,000 pairs (Stone *et al.*, 1997), with overall populations sometimes dramatically influenced by winter severity (Lack, 1986). Indeed Lack's estimate of wintering birds in the mid-1980s was between 9,000 and 15,000 birds. More recently Mead (2000) quoted breeding estimates of 4,400 pairs in Britain and 1,700 pairs in Ireland.

In the recording area covered by this winter survey the Kingfisher is close to the northern limit of its breeding and wintering range. Bolam (1912) regarded it as 'not uncommon on many Border streams ... It breeds, occasionally at least on most of those which are at all suited to its habits' and indicated numbers had improved by the early 1930s (Bolam, 1932). For the next forty years, however, a series of severe winters lead to 'drastic decreases' with 'only two single birds ... reported [after the winter of 1962/63] up to the end of 1966' (Galloway & Meek, 1980). Comparatively mild winters saw a steady rise in numbers with birds back on most suitable waters although Galloway and Meek doubted that, even during peak periods such as the mid-1970s, there were ever more than 50 breeding pairs. Of wintering birds, like Bolam, they had noted an increase in numbers in coastal localities in most years. This coastal and countrywide increase since the early 1980s is clearly shown by comparing the two 10km square maps with ten (15%) of the squares surveyed in 1981-1984 occupied and 28 (37% of those surveyed) in the current fieldwork.

The atlas of breeding birds in Northumbria (Day *et al.*, 1995) suggested a possible breeding population of ten to 20 pairs. The figure of 78 sightings recorded in the current winter survey presumably included some young birds, and possibly winter visitors from other areas, and suggests a steady population increase which is perhaps to be expected given the run of mild winters during and between the breeding and winter atlas survey periods. The winter distribution in the county closely matches the breeding distribution, with the main concentration being in the south east. The most obvious difference, however, is the increase in the north of the county particularly in the Till Valley. This area was noted in the breeding atlas as particularly prone to winter freezing so will presumably have gained relatively greater benefit from the mild winters. There is also evidence of dispersal into habitats unsuitable for breeding with coastal records from Wellhaugh Point (NU20S), the Long Nanny (NU22I), St. Mary's Island (NZ37M), Cresswell Pond (NZ29X) and on the industrialised lower Tyne at Whitehall Point (NZ36N) and on the Tyne Estuary (NZ36U). Some occupied tetrads like those at Ogle (NZ17J) and near Ashington (NZ28P) also contain only very small burns, probably too small to support breeding pairs but able to hold single birds in winter. Despite this, the majority of occupied tetrads (including all those with two birds) were on the larger river systems in the county, with the courses of the River Blyth and the Ouse Burn being particularly evident on the map.

The Kingfisher is an uncommon resident in our area and is likely to remain so. Breeding sites are limited and the overall regional climatic conditions only marginal for the species. Even allowing for some over-recording on certain river stretches where there are adjacent riverside tetrads, the population is unlikely to exceed the 50 pairs postulated by Galloway and Meek unless there are lasting climate changes.

MICHAEL FRANKIS

Distribution by altitude

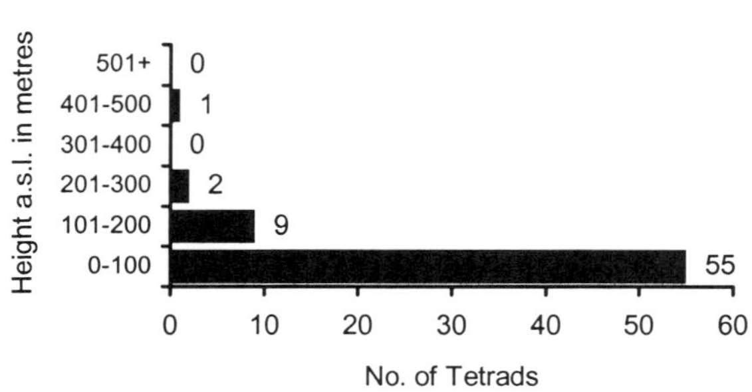

No. of tetrads in which recorded 67 (5%)

Tetrad Analysis	No. of tetrads
1 bird	56 (84%)
2 birds	11 (16%)

Total No. of birds counted 78

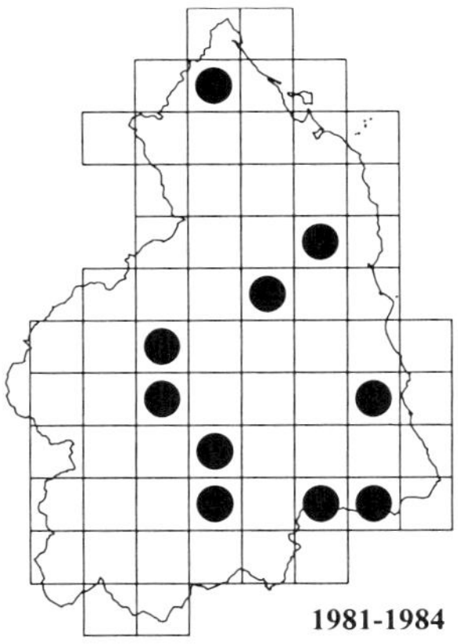

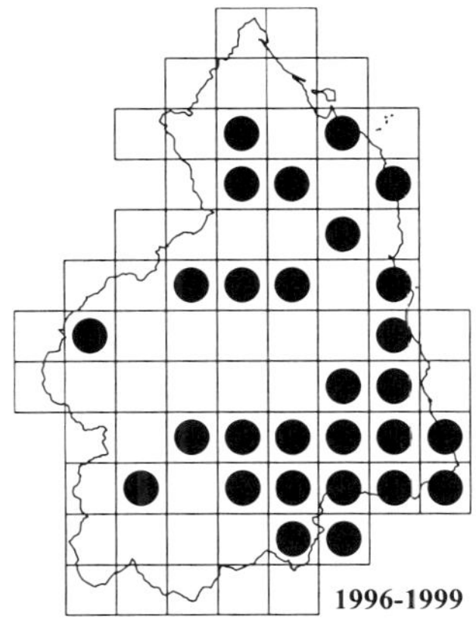

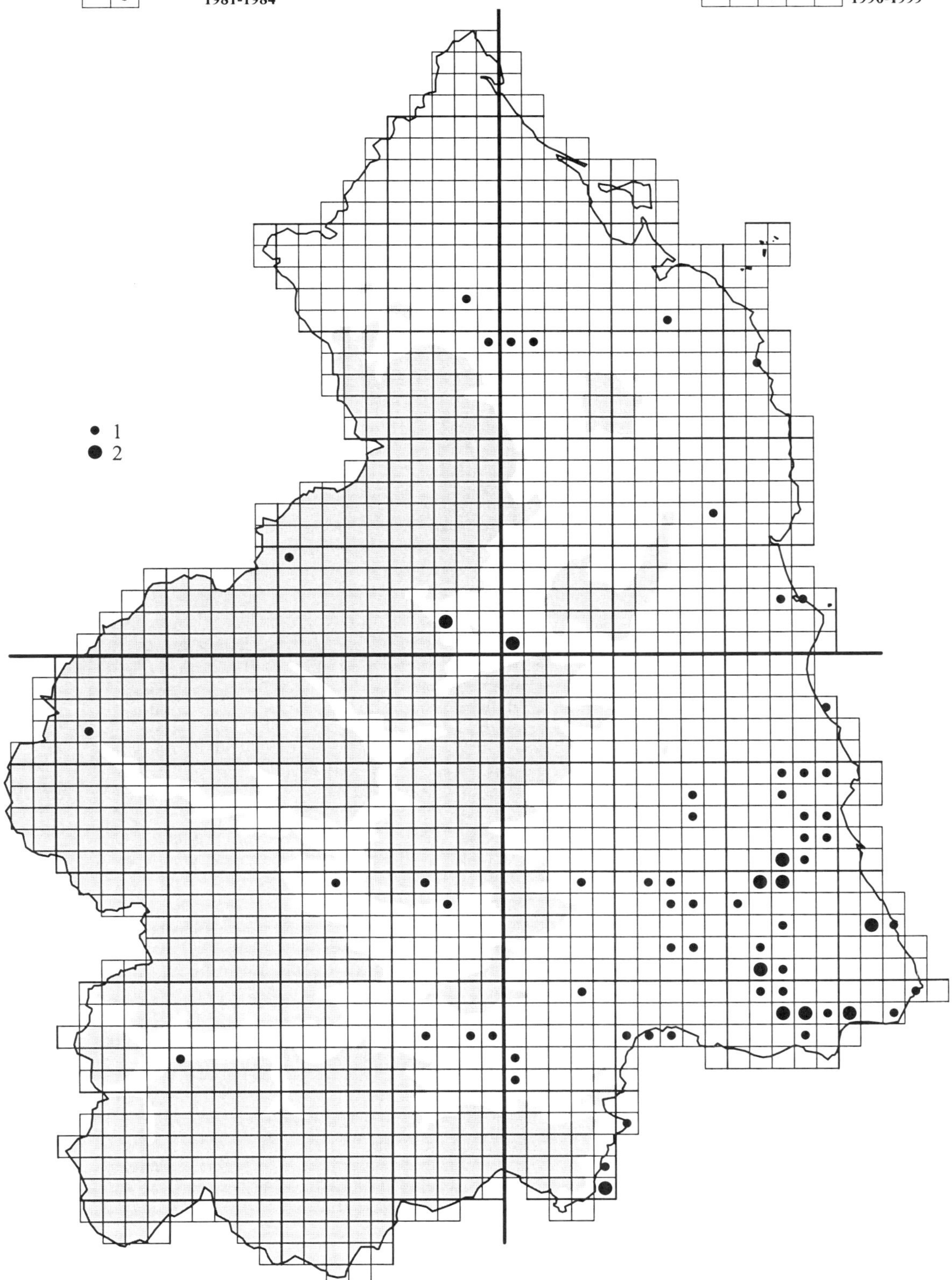

Kingfisher

GREEN WOODPECKER *Picus viridis*

The Green Woodpecker is a scarce resident in the British Isles with a fluctuating national population of about 15,000 pairs (Stone *et al.*, 1997), winter severity being cited as a significant factor controlling population levels (Lack, 1986). The county breeding population of about 113 pairs (Day *et al.*, 1995) is very low in this context and this is reflected in the density shown in both *The atlas of wintering birds in Britain and Ireland* (Lack, 1986) and *The new atlas of breeding birds in Britain and Ireland* (Gibbons *et al.*, 1993). The total of only 74 birds counted in this survey need not represent any decline as Green Woodpeckers are very secretive in winter and can be hard to find, even in ideal habitat.

Winter severity is clearly not the only factor affecting numbers as the abundance map in Gibbons *et al.* (1993) shows a substantially higher density in Scotland in Fife and southern Perthshire, an area with slightly colder winters than Northumberland. These Scottish localities, and other areas of Britain with high densities, are in regions with well-drained, light, sandy soils suitable for high populations of ants *Formica* spp. and *Lasius* spp., the main food of Green Woodpeckers. Ants do not form high population densities in the damp clay soils which predominate over most of Northumberland.

Within the county, the same determining factor can be picked out, with greatest numbers on the relatively dry sandy soils on the Lower Coal Measures and Longhoughton Grits with seven occupied tetrads in the Whittonstall/Minsteracres area (NZ05) and five in the Riding Mill/Bywell area (NZ06), and on the Fell Sandstones with five occupied tetrads near Chillingham (NU02). Conversely, Green Woodpeckers are very scarce or absent from the Middle Coal Measures, which are mostly overlain with a thick layer of damp glacial clays such as those in the former coal mining areas (NZ26 & NZ27).

There are some intriguing differences between the local breeding and winter maps. This is most evident in scarcity of birds, with only two occupied tetrads, in the northern Cheviot foothills (NT82Z, NT92E) in winter, compared with 12 occupied tetrads in summer between 1988-1992. Their presence in more winter tetrads (five, versus two in summer), a short distance east on lower ground in the Chatton/Newtown/Chillingham area (NU02), suggests the possibility of some short-distance migration from the cold Cheviot valleys to lower, warmer ground nearby. A similar effect is discernible, though less obvious, in the Coquet Valley, with fewer in winter in NY99 and NU00, but more in NU10 and NU20.

A comparison of the winter distribution between the two 10km square maps shows Green Woodpeckers to be present during both surveys in 45-46% of the squares surveyed. In this latest survey, however, there is a more pronounced distribution in the south and east of the county, with 89% of all occupied tetrads lying below 201 metres a.s.l. Nationally, the Green Woodpecker population may be increasing slightly (Mead, 2000) and certainly the recent mild winters in Northumberland do not appear to have reduced the overall local population. Despite the relatively low numbers found during this survey, the species probably remains a well-represented resident in our area.

MICHAEL FRANKIS

Distribution by altitude

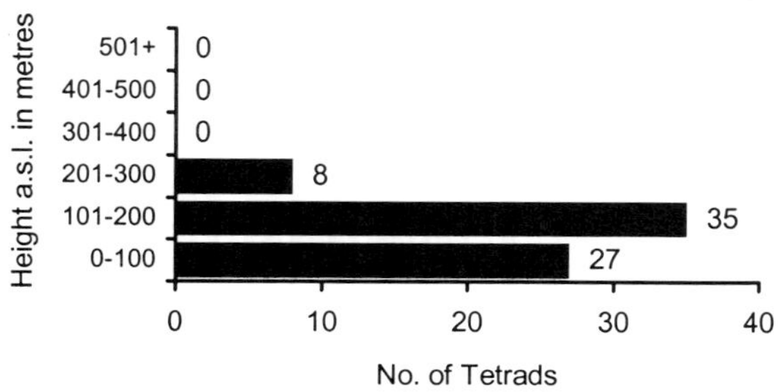

No. of tetrads in which recorded 70 (5%)

Tetrad Analysis	No. of tetrads
1 bird	66 (94%)
2 birds	4 (6%)

Total No. of birds counted 74

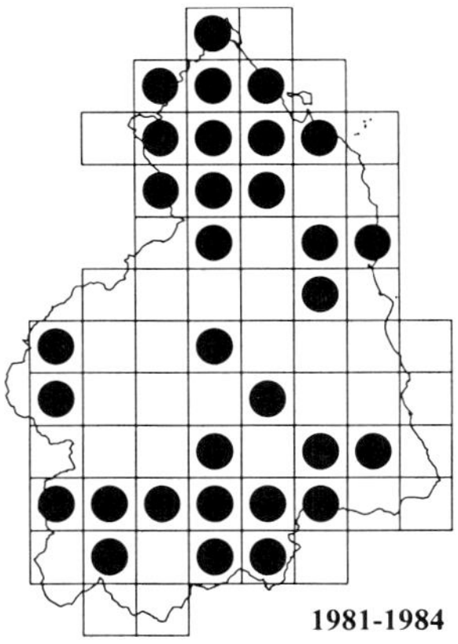

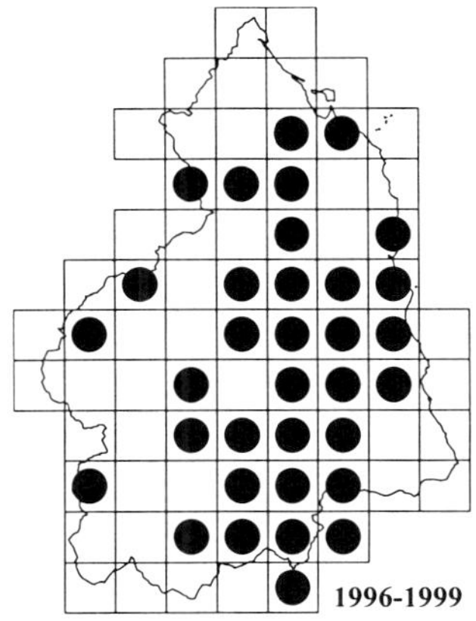

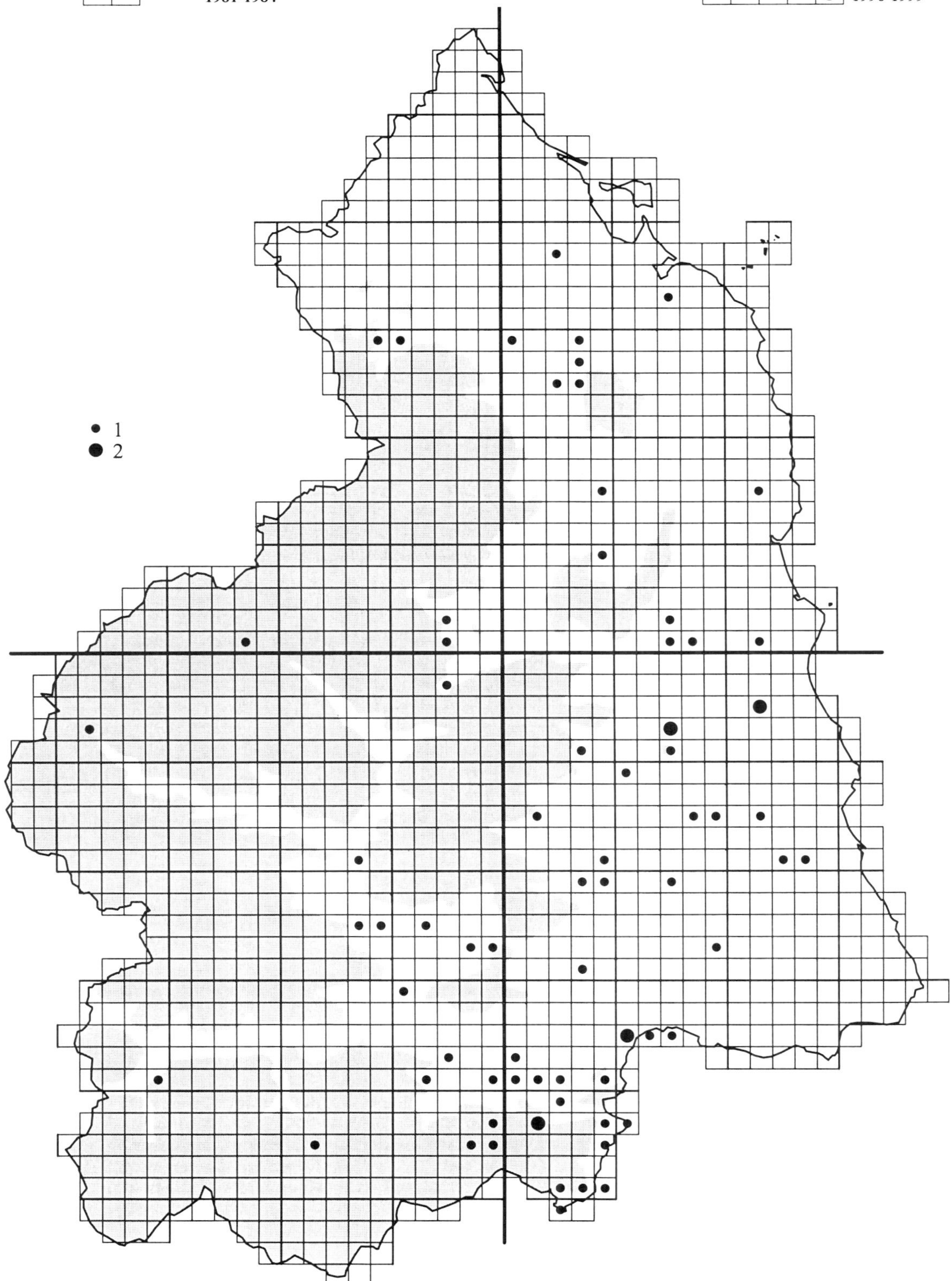

Green Woodpecker

GREAT SPOTTED WOODPECKER *Dendrocopos major*

In 1912 Bolam recorded that this species had only recently increased in numbers in the county after being relatively uncommon in the nineteenth century, although he suggested that the bird had re-colonised suitable areas in which they had formerly occurred. No theory is advanced for this fluctuation in status. Later records from Bolam (1932) indicate that the species was, by then, a not uncommon resident which may undertake local migratory movements during the winter period. This status was confirmed by Galloway and Meek (1983) who wrote that the bird was often found during winter in suburban and urban localities and could be seen feeding at bird tables.

In *The atlas of breeding birds in Northumbria* (Day *et al.*, 1995) it was suggested that nationally the species probably peaked in the late 1970s and early 1980s. However, the continuing increase from that period to the present time is well documented, for example, the BTO/JNCC/RSPB *Breeding Bird Survey 1999* (Noble *et al.*, 2000) reports a UK increase of around 42% between 1994 and 1999. It is likely that this is also paralleled in Northumberland in view of the significant increase in occupied tetrads from 213 mapped in *The atlas of breeding birds in Northumbria* to 274 in this winter atlas map. Although dispersal of pairs and juvenile birds may at least partly account for this recorded increase, it is noted that the current winter map shows 54 occupied 10km squares compared with only 47 in the 1981-1984 map, which seems to be further evidence of growth in the overall population. This may partly be accounted for by the presence of maturing coniferous plantations and an increasing supply of food at garden feeding stations.

The essentially sedentary nature of the species is revealed by comparison of the county breeding atlas tetrad map and the current winter map. There appears to be little winter movement out of the tetrads situated at altitudes above 183m (600ft) and both the breeding and winter atlas maps show around 60 occupied tetrads above this contour. Both maps demonstrate a concentration of birds in the south and south east of the county. As is to be expected, the well-wooded areas in the Tyne Valley to the east of Hexham are a stronghold of the Great Spotted Woodpecker, as are wooded areas in the corridor from Gosforth Park through Blagdon to Morpeth. A maximum tetrad count of seven birds was recorded in Stannington Vale (NZ27J) on the River Blyth in January 1997. Lower numbers and population densities are apparent in the northern half of the county.

The resident population of the race *D. m. anglicus,* which is confined to Great Britain, is augmented in most years by small numbers of migrant birds which appear on the coast, usually in October. Galloway and Meek (1983) stated that ringing had confirmed these to be of the nominate race *D. m. major* which, as described by Cramp (1985), breeds in Fenno-Scandia eastwards into Siberia, and is prone to eruptive behaviour. The presence of such migrants, which cannot be reliably separated in the field from the resident species, is perhaps illustrated by the number of coastal records shown on the winter map, in particular, the concentration to the west of Budle Bay in the 10 km squares NU03 and NU13.

The Great Spotted Woodpecker can be a secretive species which is sometimes difficult to locate, its presence often betrayed only by its distinctive call. Inevitably therefore, some under-recording of its distribution and under-estimation of the numbers occurring in the recording area will have occurred. The overall total recorded for the current winter survey is 362 birds in 274 tetrads and therefore the current winter population in the county may be of the order of 500-550 birds. As a comparison, it is noted that Day *et al.* (1995) suggested a breeding population within the range 250-300 pairs.

EDDIE CRABTREE

Distribution by altitude

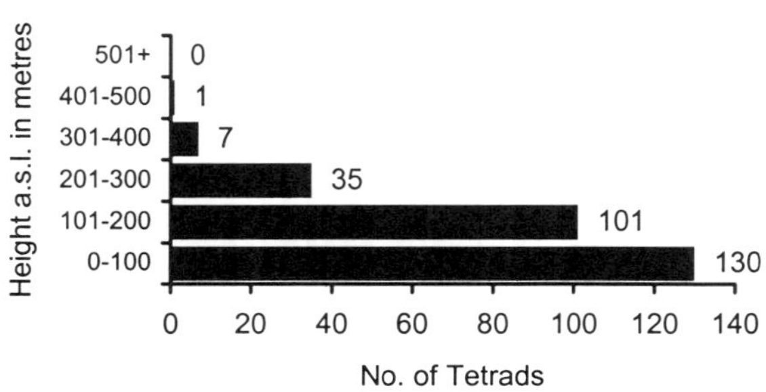

No. of tetrads in which recorded 274 (17%)

Tetrad Analysis	No. of tetrads
1 bird	207 (76%)
2 birds	51 (18%)
3+ birds	16 (6%)

Total No. of birds counted 362

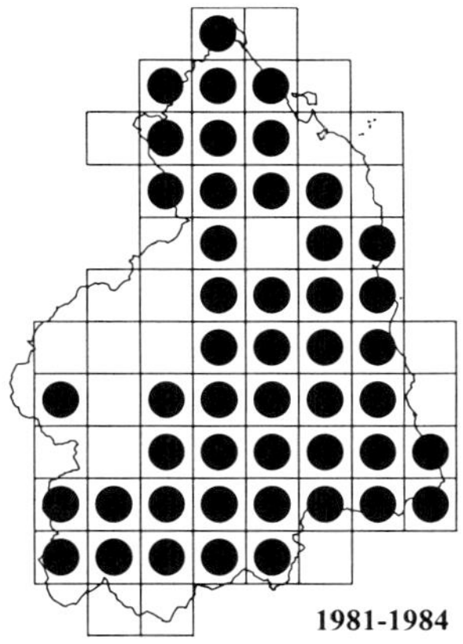

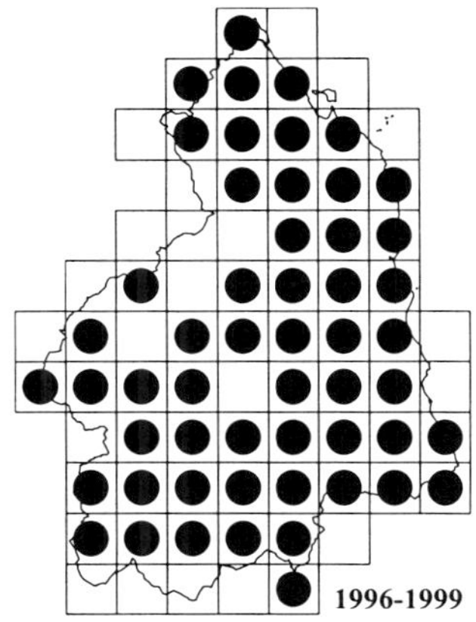

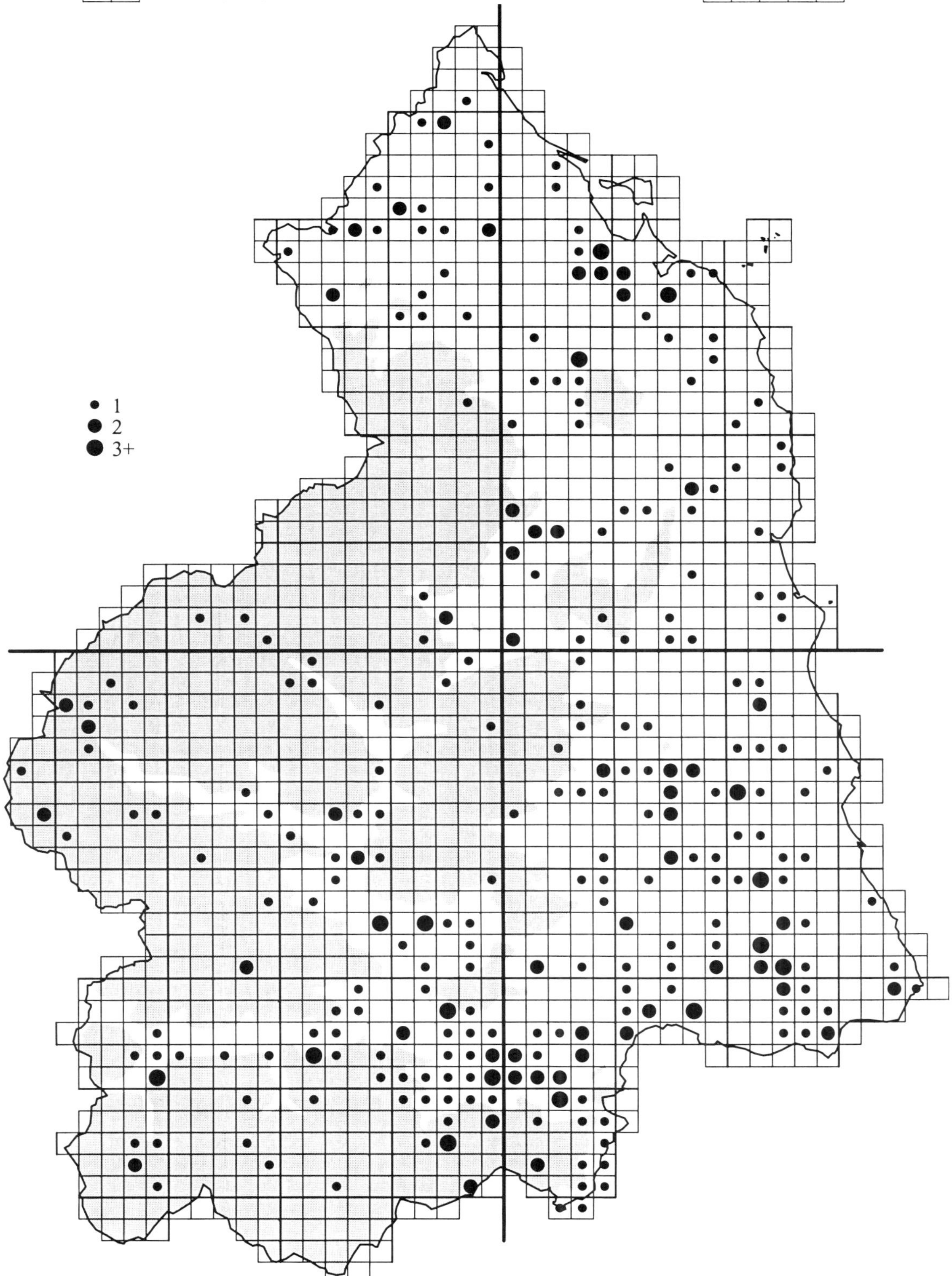

Great Spotted Woodpecker

LESSER SPOTTED WOODPECKER *Dendrocopos minor*

As there was only one sighting of Lesser Spotted Woodpecker during the whole of the winter atlas survey, it can only be assumed that its status continues to be that of a rare resident. This is hardly surprising as the species is on the very periphery of both its breeding and wintering range in the United Kingdom.

At the beginning of the twentieth century Bolam (1912) described it as 'a very rare casual visitant to Northumberland, which has not been observed in any of the other "Border counties" '. He noted four likely birds that had been 'collected' up to 1845, with a number of inadequately documented later records (Bolam, 1932). More frequent sightings, probably due to increased activity by birdwatchers, occurred from the 1950s to the early 1980s with Galloway and Meek (1983) able to describe it as 'a rare visitor which may have bred'. Possible breeding was indeed recorded at Nunnykirk in 1985, but the first conclusive evidence was not obtained until spring 1999 when a pair bred successfully in Hexhamshire (*Birds in Northumbria 1999*).

Whilst the species is sparsely distributed in the county, it is difficult to census accurately as it is both very silent and particularly elusive in winter, frequently feeding in the high canopy (Lack, 1986). An analysis of all county records throughout the year since 1980 gives an average of three sightings of either individual birds or pairs annually. In both the 1980-1989 and 1990-1999 decades there were 30 such observations. All were below 150 metres a.s.l., in open areas, where deciduous woodland predominated. Of all the annual records, 40% of the sightings occurred in the winter months, between November and February. Of these 24 records, sixteen (67%) were during the month of January, with November and December accounting for two (8%) sightings each and February for four (17%).

The geographic locations of winter records are very consistent as would be expected for a sedentary species. There were 14 winter records between 1980 and 1999 in the Tyne Valley (58%), four at Bolam Lake (17%), three at Gosforth Park (13%) and single sightings from Plessey Woods, Ford Castle and Bilton. It was from the last locality, near Alnmouth (NU21F) in February 1998, that the single winter atlas record was obtained, although another bird was observed three days before the census began in the same season, at Bolam Lake on 12 November 1997.

Whilst the number of annual sightings since 1980 has been consistently low, it is difficult to anticipate any future breeding or wintering trends. The Lesser Spotted Woodpecker may benefit from projected warmer winters, but this could be countered by wetter breeding seasons and, as Mead (2000) stated in relation to the national population, '[it is] in real trouble'. It would seem that the species is likely to have only a precarious toehold in Northumberland in the foreseeable future.

JOHN C. DAY

No. of tetrads in which recorded 1 (<1%)

Tetrad Analysis	No. of tetrads
1 bird	1 (100%)

Total No. of birds counted 1

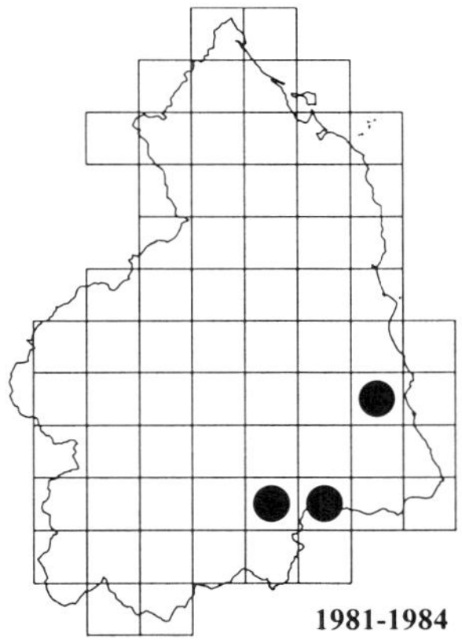

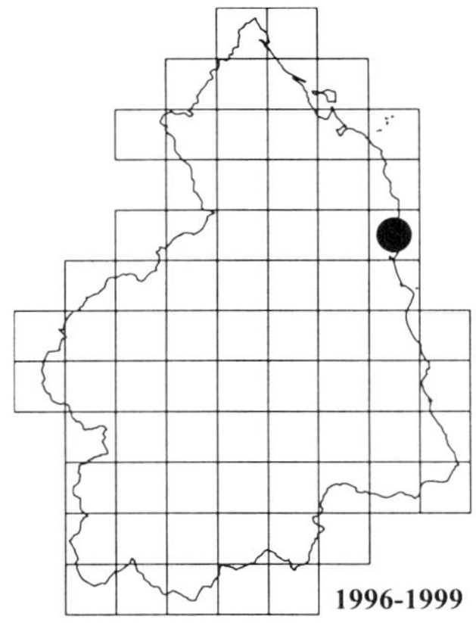

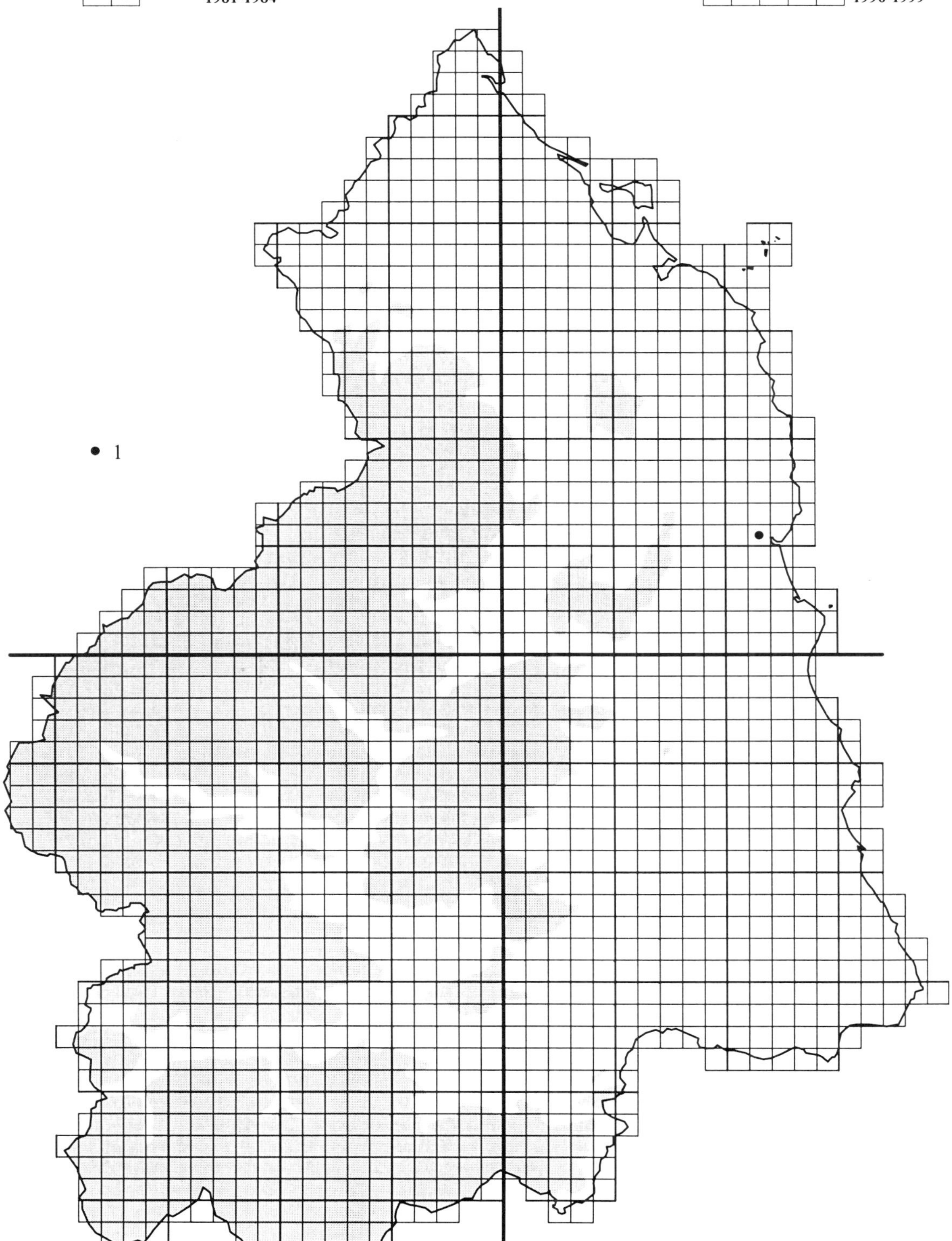

Lesser Spotted Woodpecker

SKYLARK *Alauda arvensis*

Bolam, writing in 1912, stated that the Skylark was 'an abundant resident over all our district'. However, when comparing data from *The atlas of breeding birds in Northumbria* (Day *et al.*, 1995) with this current survey it is clearly apparent that Skylark is much more thinly distributed in winter, occurring in only a quarter of the number of tetrads compared to those occupied during the breeding season. 77% of all these occupied tetrads in winter lie below 200 metres a.s.l. The number of individual birds counted in winter is also less than 20% of those present during the summer and represents a tiny proportion of the British wintering population. It is unlikely that any sizeable flocks were missed during this survey because of the obvious nature of the species. Galloway and Meek (1983) described Skylark as a common passage migrant, winter visitor and breeding species. There appears to have been no significant change in distribution since the 1981-1984 winter atlas survey as shown by a comparison of the two 10km square maps, however it might be more accurate to describe the status of Skylark as locally common in winter.

There is, in winter, movement away from the upland breeding areas of the Cheviot foothills, Coquetdale and North Pennines in the west of the county. Birds are even absent in the colder months from the river valleys in these areas. The majority of birds found inland at higher altitudes during this survey were seen in late February returning to, or already present, on breeding territories. Other upland records of note were eight at 260 metres a.s.l. at Glantless Hill, Edlingham (NU10I) in January 1999 and one at 520 metres a.s.l. near Catcleugh Reservoir (NT70S) in November 1998. A further interesting upland record is of two birds in the unlikely location of Harwood Forest (NY99V) in February 1997.

The peak concentration of the winter population is along the north Northumberland coastal plain, especially at the Lindisfarne NNR. The largest flock found was 400 at the Snook, Holy Island (NU14B) in January 1997. The Lindisfarne area also produced several other sizeable flocks, including 94 at Fenwick (NU04Q) in February 1998 and 200 at Holy Island causeway (NU04W) in January 1997. The two 10km squares (NU04 and NU14) which contain the National Nature Reserve held 32% of Northumberland's wintering Skylarks. The other important wintering area is around the urban fringe of the south east where conditions are usually milder and set-aside and stubble fields can often be found. Lack (1986) stated that in winter Skylarks feeding on arable farmland eat grain, weed seeds, leaves and frost-damaged vegetables. The 10km squares with the greatest number of occupied tetrads were Cramlington (NZ27) and Ashington/Bedlington (NZ28) with 16 and 14 squares respectively. These occupied squares, which represent 2% of all surveyed tetrads, have a considerable variety of suitable feeding habitats for wintering Skylark. Although the only large count in this area was 70 birds near Ashington (NZ28Z), these two 10km squares provided 10% of the total count. With a further 10% of the wintering birds being found along the coastal strip especially in the dunes between Whitley Bay and the Druridge/Cresswell area, the concentration of birds on low ground is clearly noticeable. They were recorded in 19 (32%) of the control tetrads visited but in only two of these were birds present in all three winters. The overall totals counted each winter, however, were fairly similar with 36, 58 and 52 birds respectively.

It is clear that for a viable wintering population of Skylarks to remain in Northumberland there must be no further degradation of habitat and the set-aside policy must continue.

LINDSAY J. McDOUGALL

Distribution by altitude

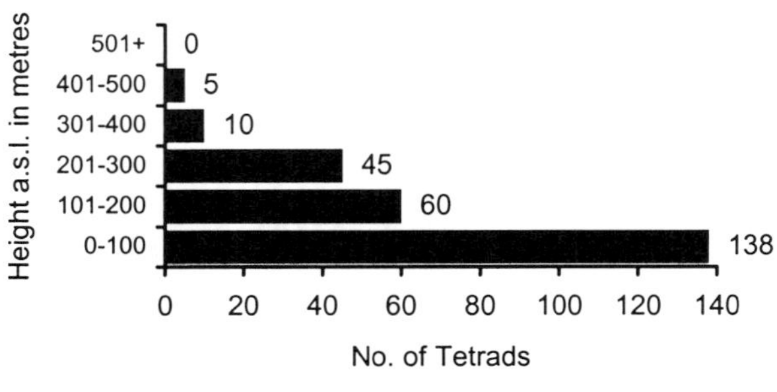

No. of tetrads in which recorded 258 (18%)

Tetrad Analysis	No. of tetrads
1-2 birds	126 (49%)
3-7 birds	67 (26%)
8+ birds	65 (25%)

Total No. of birds counted 2,919

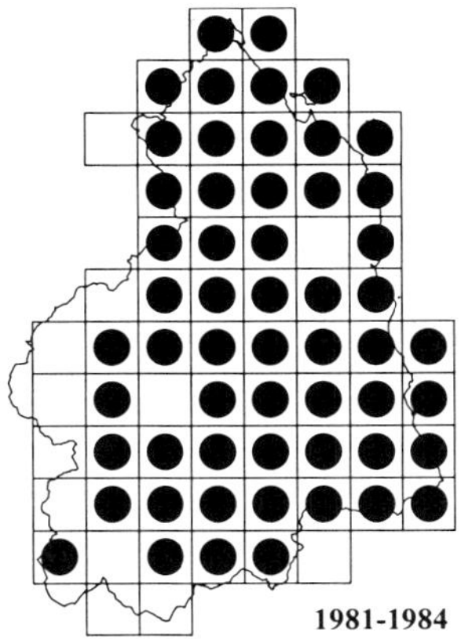

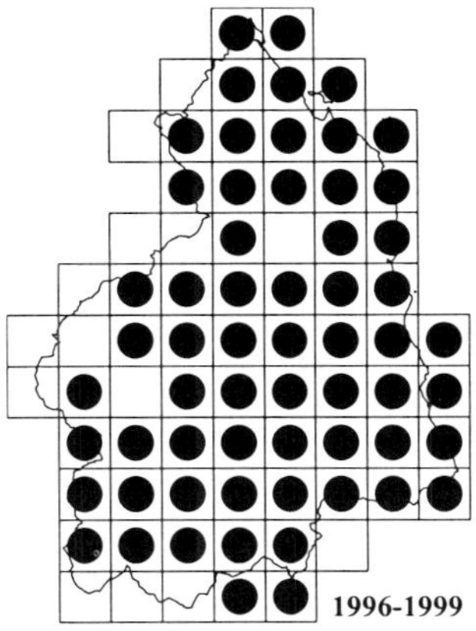

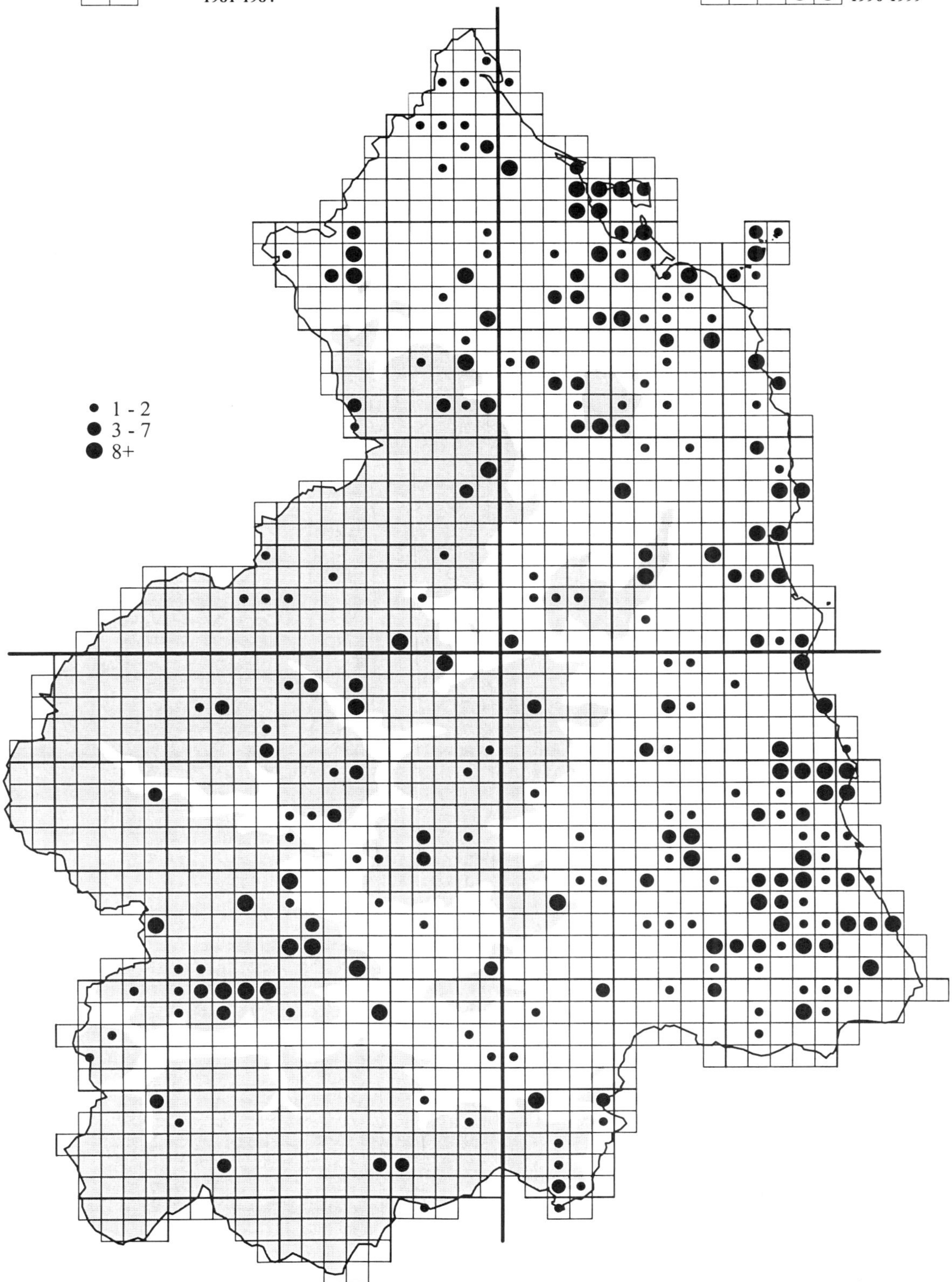

Skylark

SHORELARK *Eremophila alpestris*

Bolam (1932) described the Shorelark as 'a winter visitant, confined to the coast and only seen as a rule during severe weather, usually from December till February'. The occurrence of the species at that time was, to say the least, sporadic, with Bolam referring to only two records between 1912 and 1932. By the 1980s, Galloway and Meek (1983) noted that 'in recent years it has appeared in numbers in most winters' and described the species as an uncommon passage and winter visitor. They reiterated Bolam's comments that the species was 'certainly confined to the coast' and also stated that it occurred 'between mid-October and mid-May, in parties of up to twenty, although flocks of less than ten are more usual'. Only six individuals were recorded for the remainder of the 1980s and the species went unrecorded for the winter periods 1984/85, 1986/87, 1987/88 and 1988/89. With respect to the 1990s, prior to the current atlas survey, birds were recorded in each winter period, but only single individuals or groups of up to three were involved, apart from a single flock of six birds in the 1991/92 winter period. Since 1995, the species has been recorded as a rare winter visitor in *Birds in Northumbria*.

The Shorelarks that winter in Britain belong to the subspecies *flava* which breeds in northern Eurasia, from southern Norway, through Fennoscandinavia, north of the Arctic Circle, as far east as the Kolyma river (Snow & Perrins, 1998). It was stated in Lack (1986) that southern Scandinavia was colonised only two centuries ago and it was considered that it was from here that British birds originate, although there are no ringing recoveries to substantiate this. The Scandinavian population appears to have peaked around 1900 and has declined drastically since the 1950s (although less markedly in southern Norway), possibly due to reindeer overgrazing (Hagemeijer & Blair, 1997).

Results from the current survey confirm the affinity of this species for the coast. Six of the eight tetrads in which the species was recorded were coastal but, of the two inland tetrads, one, at Chattonpark Hill (NU02U), was on average below 100 metres a.s.l. whereas the other rather surprisingly held a flock of four individuals at a height of 600 metres a.s.l. on the south-west slopes of the Cheviot (NT81Z) on 30 January 1998. Whether these birds were wintering at this altitude or perhaps returning from the west coast (birds regularly winter on the Dee and Mersey estuaries) is open to speculation. Across western Europe as a whole, wintering birds are now virtually confined to coastal areas although in the past inland occurrences on farmland were much more common. This change in behaviour is presumably related to the loss of winter stubble fields (Hagemeijer & Blair, 1997). A direct comparison between the two smaller 10km square maps shows the species appearing to be more widespread during the current survey period, being present within seven squares as opposed to only three, all coastal, in the previous survey. This is perhaps merely a reflection of the paucity of records for the previous survey period. The numbers of individuals recorded for the winter periods 1996/97, 1997/98 and 1998/99 were three, 13 and eight respectively. The species should still be regarded therefore as a rare winter visitor and, given the decrease in the breeding population, may well become even rarer in the future.

Lack (1986) considered the British and Irish winter population to be less than 300 individuals for each of the three winter periods 1981/82, 1982/83 and 1983/84 but suggested that there could be a five-fold increase in years when the species is more numerous. Northumberland may well host somewhere in the region of 3% of the British and Irish wintering population.

MICHAEL J. CARR

Distribution by altitude

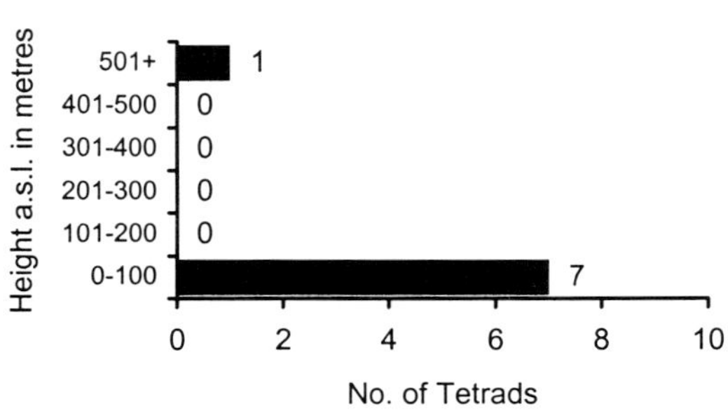

No. of tetrads in which recorded 8 (<1%)

Tetrad Analysis	No. of tetrads
1-2 birds	4 (50%)
3-4 birds	3 (38%)
5+ birds	1 (12%)

Total No. of birds counted 24

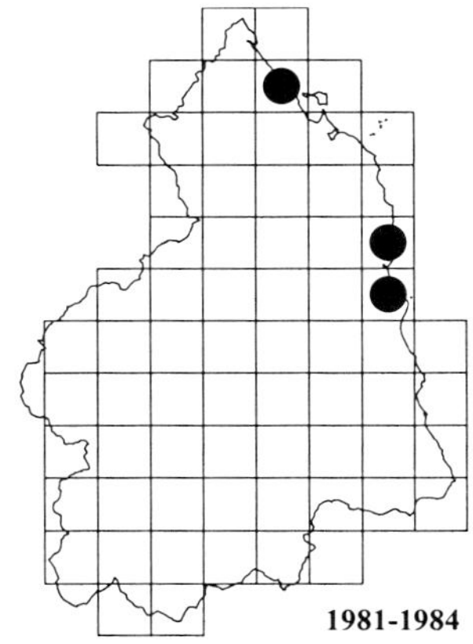

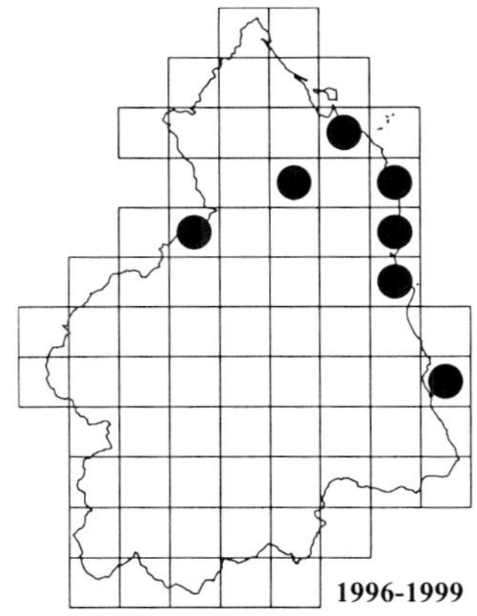

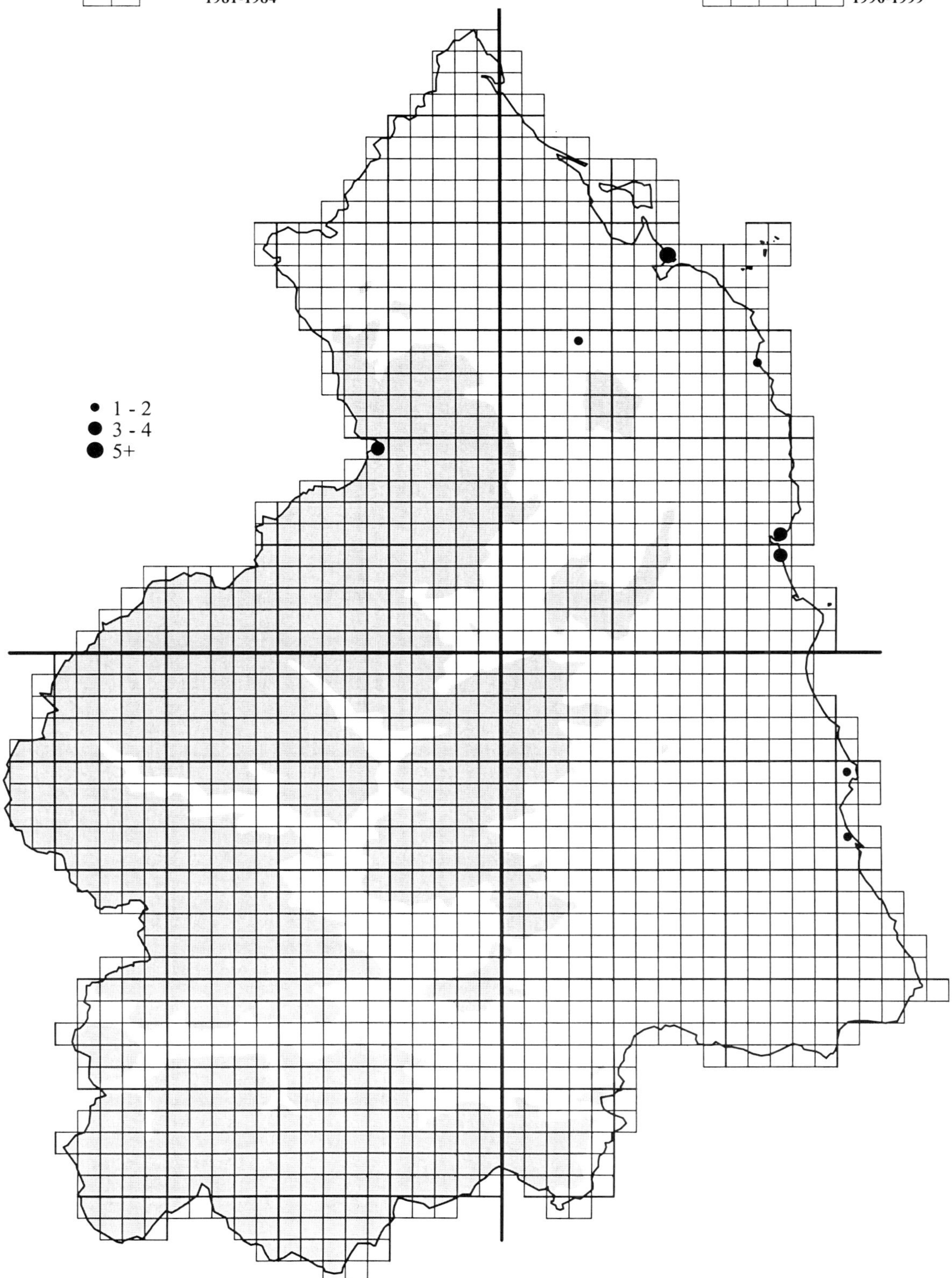

Shorelark

MEADOW PIPIT *Anthus pratensis*

Bolam (1932) considered that 'some of the visitors from the north remain here over the winter' and Galloway and Meek (1983) mentioned that 'the moors are not entirely deserted in winter' and cited a record of 19 individuals on the 18 December 1977 in the Simonside Hills. They further commented that birds would move away from areas in the grip of extreme cold weather, referring to the southerly movement at Seaton Sluice which involved 100 individuals on 31 December 1978 and 40 in as many minutes in early February 1980. They described the Meadow Pipit as an abundant passage visitor and breeding species. More recently small numbers have been recorded inland in most years. An exceptional record of 100 birds at 400 metres a.s.l. on Hexhamshire Common occurred on 22 December 1994. Records suggest that it was quite widespread within the region during the winter months and from 1992 the species has been described as a well-represented winter visitor. Hard weather movement was noted in January 1984, 1985 and 1987 and on 24th December 1995, the latter involving an unprecedented 1,500 birds moving south in 50 minutes at Druridge Bay (*Birds in Northumbria 1984, 1985, 1987, 1995*).

The origins of Northumberland's wintering birds are unclear. There is a marked emigration of breeding birds from late August to late October, with smaller numbers leaving some moorland areas as early as July (Galloway & Meek, 1983; *Birds in Northumbria*). Lack (1986) stated that 'very few ringed birds of proven British or Irish origin have been recovered here [Britain and Ireland] in December and January'. Although speculative, his comments imply that most, if not all, of our region's breeding birds could therefore move further south. Results of this current winter survey indicate that the size of the wintering population is only approximately 7-10% of the breeding population suggested in *The atlas of breeding birds in Northumbria* (Day *et al.*, 1995). From September, there is a considerable influx of birds from the north (Lack, 1986; *Birds in Northumbria*) but whether these originate from Iceland, Scandinavia or Scotland is unknown. The mid-winter population may therefore be a residual component of the breeding population or be a discretely different population comprised of more northerly breeding birds or some combination of both.

The results of the survey show the species to be widely distributed throughout the region, occupying approximately 24% of the available tetrads, although they were not recorded in any that averaged more than 500 metres a.s.l. There was however, no obvious preference exhibited between the other altitude categories. The percentage occupancy of the total number of tetrads available in each altitude category 0-100 metres, 101-200 metres, 201-300 metres, 301-400 metres and 401-500 metres a.s.l. was 21%, 18%, 35%, 27% and 33% respectively. Areas where the species appears to be absent tend to be those where either woodland or intensive agriculture predominate, as would be expected. Of the maximum counts for tetrads, the majority, nearly 92%, held between one and ten birds. Approximately 5% of tetrads had between 11 and 20 birds with the remaining 3% of tetrads containing 21 or more. There were two exceptionally high counts, both inland, with 130 birds recorded near Biddlestone (NT90P) and 66 in the Holystone Common area (NT90K). The totals of birds recorded in the control tetrads for 1996/97, 1997/98 and 1998/99 were 27, 88 and 35 and this may well indicate the transient nature of some of the winter population which, for the most part, would appear to be weather-related. The grand total of maximum tetrad counts was 1,689 birds. This perhaps suggests that the wintering population is in the order of 1,500 to 2,000 birds, therefore the status of the species should be classified as common rather than well-represented in winter.

A comparison between the 10km square maps shows that Meadow Pipits occurred in six squares in the current survey from which they were absent in the earlier survey and conversely have disappeared from four squares where they were previously recorded. The former scenario is almost certainly the result of the clear-felling of timber in two of the squares, both of which are in the Border Forest. Lack (1986) estimated the British and Irish mid-winter population to be in the region of 1 - 2.5 million birds, the Northumbrian population would therefore comprise less than 1% of this figure.

MICHAEL J. CARR

Distribution by altitude

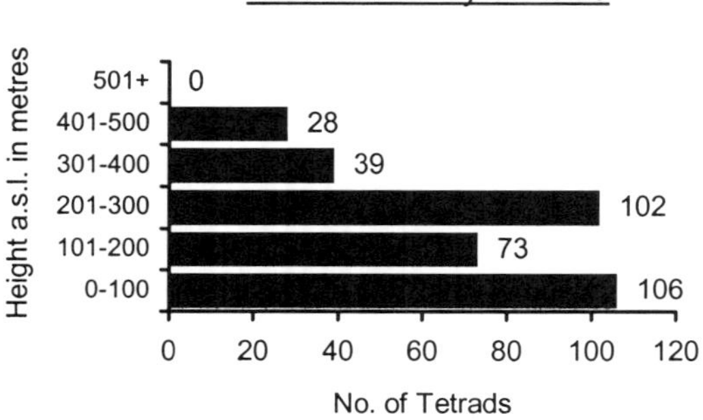

No. of tetrads in which recorded 348 (24%)

Tetrad Analysis	No. of tetrads
1-2 birds	201 (58%)
3-5 birds	80 (23%)
6+ birds	67 (19%)

Total No. of birds counted 1,689

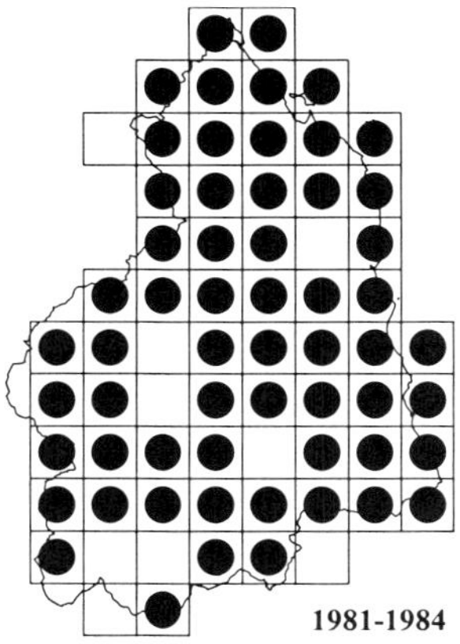

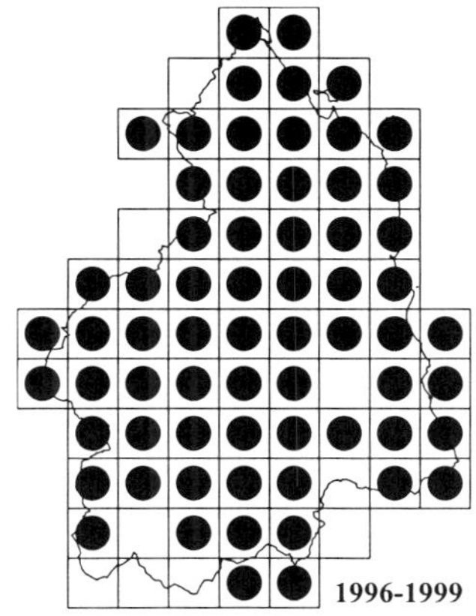

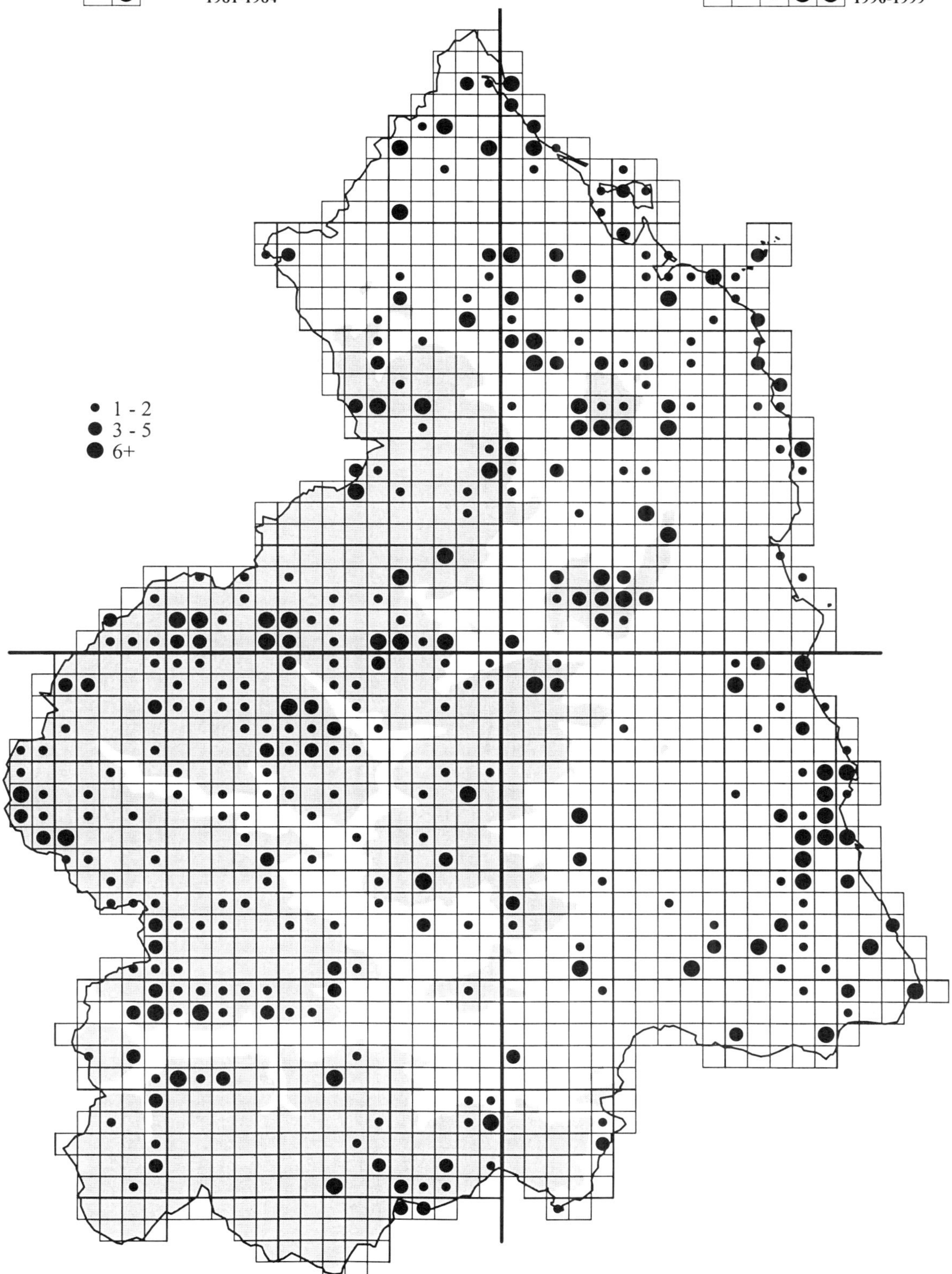

Meadow Pipit

ROCK PIPIT *Anthus petrosus*

Data collected over the three winters of fieldwork carried out for this winter atlas show a coastal distribution of Rock Pipits precisely as would be expected for a species specialised in living on rocky shores. In total, 262 individual birds were recorded in 54 tetrads, each of which contained some portion of coastline. This aligns well with Bolam (1912) who described the species as 'a common resident on all rocky portions of the coast, but strictly confined thereto and rarely straying more than a field's breadth from the shore'. This description of its distribution in the county does not appear to have changed significantly in the intervening period.

The species lives almost entirely on rocky shores, often backed by high cliffs, and feeds largely in the intertidal zone taking small molluscs, chironomid larvae and amphopods (Lack, 1986). This specialisation severely restricts the Northumbrian population to the relatively few tetrads which match such an exacting requirement. This is very clearly indicated by the distribution map which shows small numbers of birds in the majority of coastal tetrads except for those such as Druridge Bay (N29T/U) and Cheswick and Goswick Sands (NU04J/N/S/T) which include only sandy beaches. Population density is only significantly greater in the few tetrads with a particularly high ratio of rocky shoreline, such as Redshin Cove, Spittal (NU05A) and Stag Rocks, Bamburgh (NU13S) and especially offshore on the Farne Islands.

Rock Pipits were recorded in only seven control tetrads so the data on year-to-year consistency needs to be treated with some caution, although the results do show regular occupation of suitable tetrads in successive years. The numbers of birds recorded in control tetrads over the three years were much less consistent. Presumably this is due to the impact that the presence or absence of small flocks has on such a small sample size.

Comparison of the data recorded during this survey with the tetrad distribution map for breeding Rock Pipits given in *The atlas of breeding birds in Northumbria* (Day *et al.*, 1995) shows a marked increase in both numbers and occupation during the winter. Breeding data showed only 26 occupied tetrads with a confirmed, probable or possible breeding total of 56 pairs, compared with 54 occupied tetrads and a maximum of 262 individuals counted in the three winter periods. This difference is to be expected as small numbers of autumn passage birds stay to over-winter along stretches of the coast from which they are absent in summer (*Birds In Northumbria*; Galloway & Meek, 1983). There is a broad correlation between the tetrads with breeding pairs of Rock Pipits and those containing higher numbers of winter records such as the Farne Islands (NU23), Holy Island (NU14) and Coquet Island (NU20) indicating that these are probably the areas with the best habitat for this species.

In the most recent analysis of the status of Northumberland's birds, Kerr (2001) classified the Rock Pipit as an uncommon breeding resident, usually well-represented as a passage visitor. As Mead (2000) in his *State of the nation's birds* identified a potential decline in its British fortunes, it is hoped that the north east population can maintain its relatively strong foothold in the area. With a small but apparently stable wintering population limited to those tetrads which meet the precise habitat requirements of this species, it should perhaps best be described as well-represented in the county during the winter.

GEOFF LINKLETER

Distribution by altitude

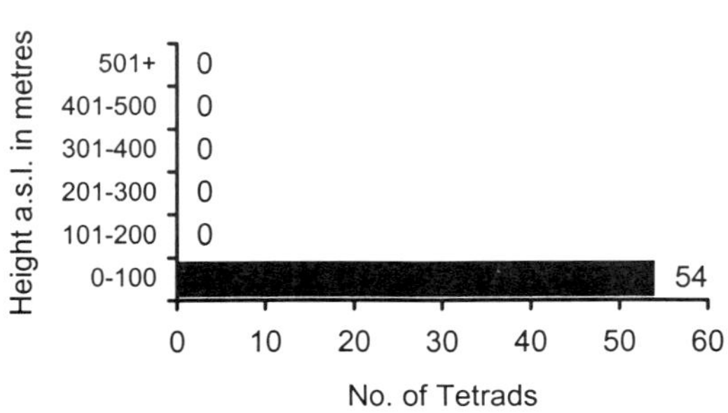

No. of tetrads in which recorded 54 (4%)

Tetrad Analysis	No. of tetrads
1-2 birds	28 (52%)
3-7 birds	15 (28%)
8+ birds	11 (20%)

Total No. of birds counted 262

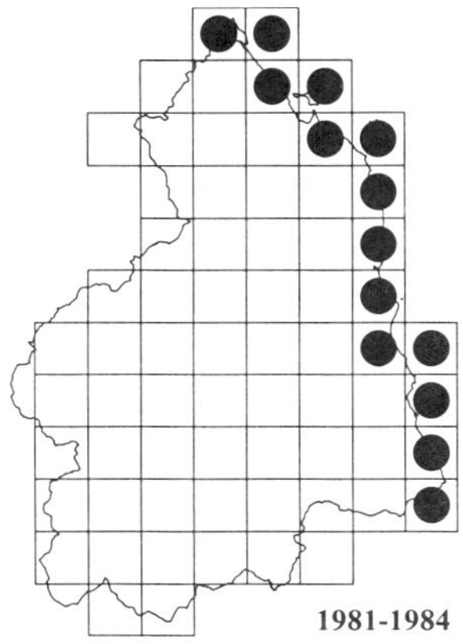

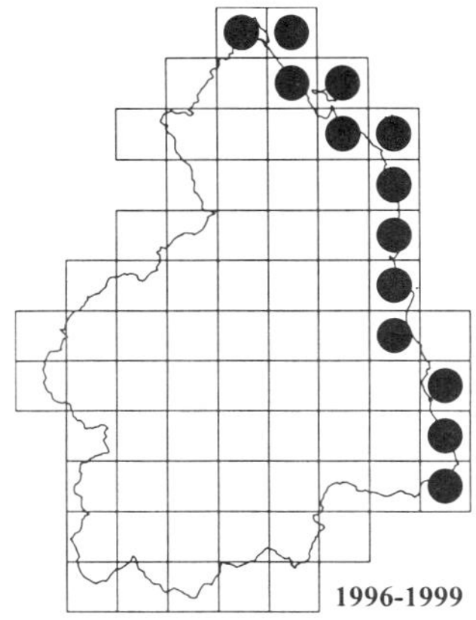

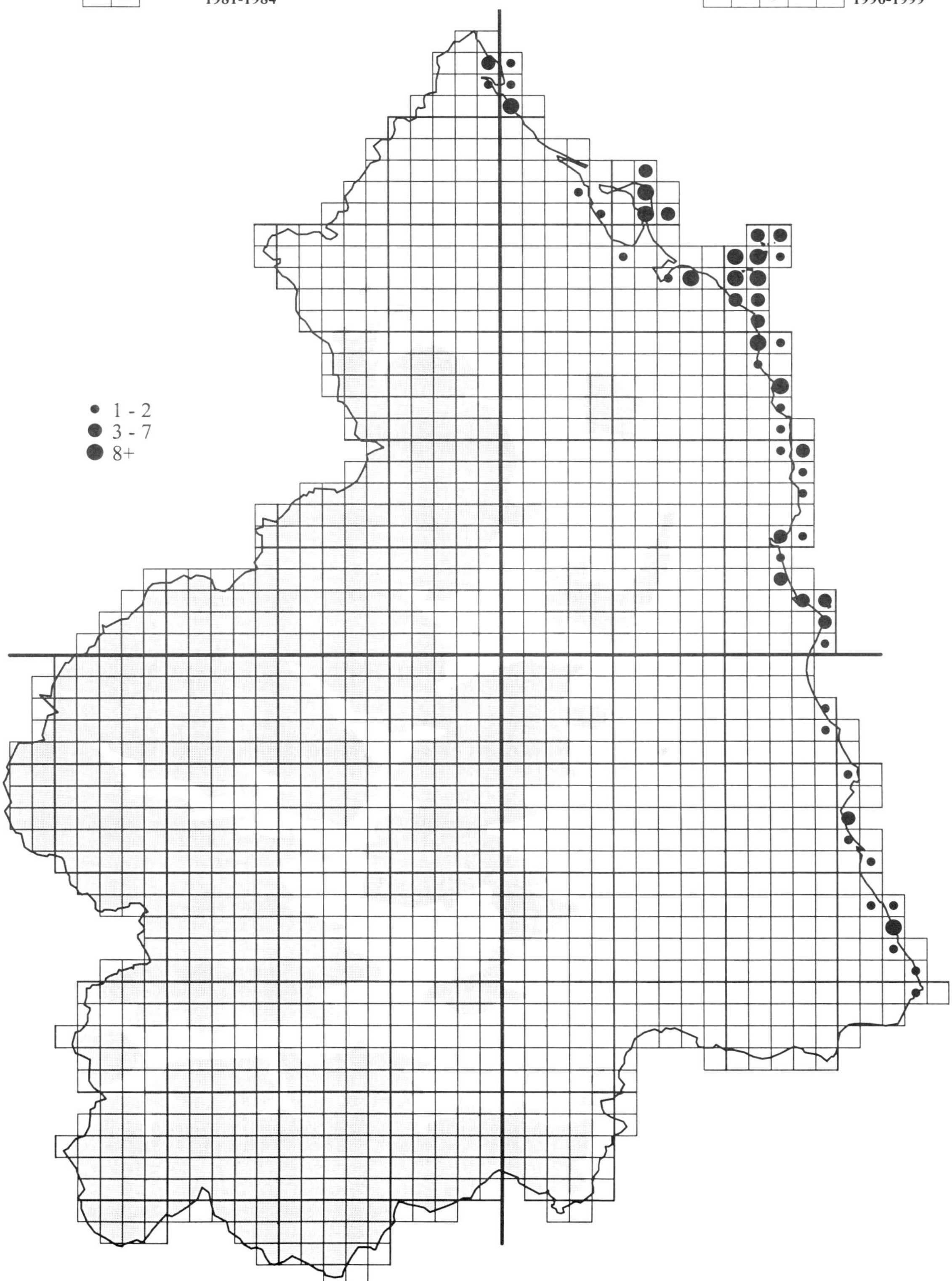

Rock Pipit

GREY WAGTAIL *Motacilla cinerea*

Bolam (1932) described the Grey Wagtail as 'a common resident, in limited numbers, throughout the county, our hill-burns being seldom without the presence of a pair or two, although the majority of those reared there move coastwards for the winter, some of them perhaps even quitting the country'. By 1983, Galloway and Meek referred to the species as an uncommon passage visitor and a well-represented breeding species. They too concluded that 'after breeding some birds disperse to the coast in July, and in winter individuals may sometimes be found in the centre of Newcastle or exploring suburban backyards'. Grey Wagtails provide a splash of colour to winter birding and are often first located by their sharp call. They retain a more marked attachment to water than their congeners and are often found in artificial situations such as sewage farms.

When comparing the distribution and numbers of birds between this winter survey and *The atlas of breeding birds in Northumbria* (Day *et al.*, 1995), the latter shows the breeding stronghold of the species to be along the waterways of the western uplands, whereas in winter this habitat is virtually deserted. Lack (1986) indicated that many birds from northern Britain move south to south west in the autumn, with some birds reaching Spain, Portugal or North Africa. In addition, some of the winter records in this country are of continental birds, although most recoveries or controls have been from southern Britain. In Northumberland, the Grey Wagtail is approaching the northern limit of its winter range in Britain whilst the stronghold is the south and south west of the country.

The overall winter total of maximum counts of 190 birds in this current local survey contrasts with an estimated county breeding population of 600-700 pairs (Day *et al.*, 1995). Clearly, even if a few birds were missed, a significant proportion of the breeding population migrates out of the county in winter. The tetrad map shows that in winter the species is a bird of lowland areas, with 94% of the occupied tetrads being below 200 metres a.s.l. The largest concentrations were recorded on lowland rivers and water bodies, with the highest counts being four birds at Corbridge (NY96X) and Whittle Dene Reservoirs (NZ06T), or favoured urban locations including three tetrads in Newcastle (NZ26M/N/T). There were only 11 counts of three or more birds during the survey. In winter the species is thinly but widely distributed throughout the county, being found in 10% of the tetrads that were surveyed, at a mean density of 1.33 birds per occupied tetrad.

Grey Wagtails were also recorded in a total of 15 control tetrads over the survey period and within these the mean number of birds per occupied tetrad in each winter period increased from 0.4 in 1996/97 to 0.66 in 1998/99. Compared with the 10km square map for 1981-1984, the present fieldwork shows the species occurred in three more squares and in one additional square not included in the previous analysis. In this survey, Grey Wagtails were not found in seven squares where they had previously been recorded but were present in 11 additional squares. Whilst no substantial conclusions can be drawn from such limited data, the distribution of the species during the winter period has actually remained relatively unchanged and there is little evidence to suggest that population numbers have altered since the 1981-1984 survey.

N. F. OSBORNE

Distribution by altitude

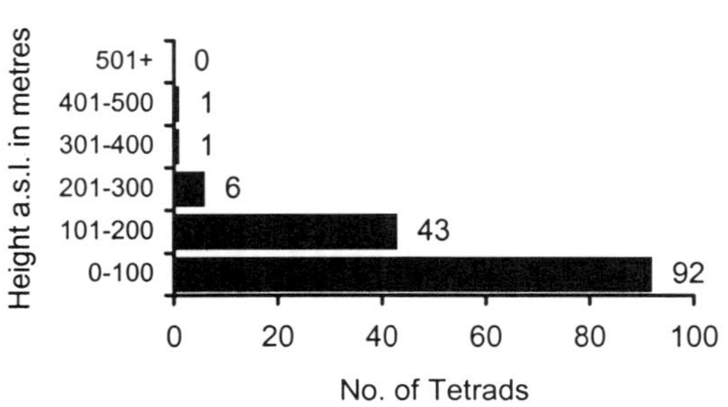

No. of tetrads in which recorded 143 (10%)

Tetrad Analysis	No. of tetrads
1 bird	109 (76%)
2 birds	23 (16%)
3+ birds	11 (8%)

Total No. of birds counted 190

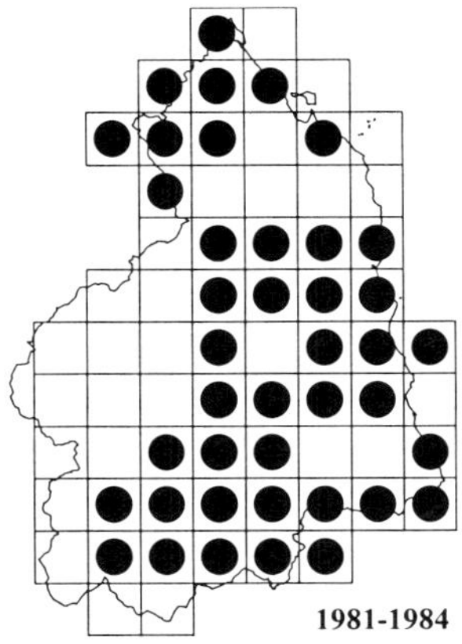

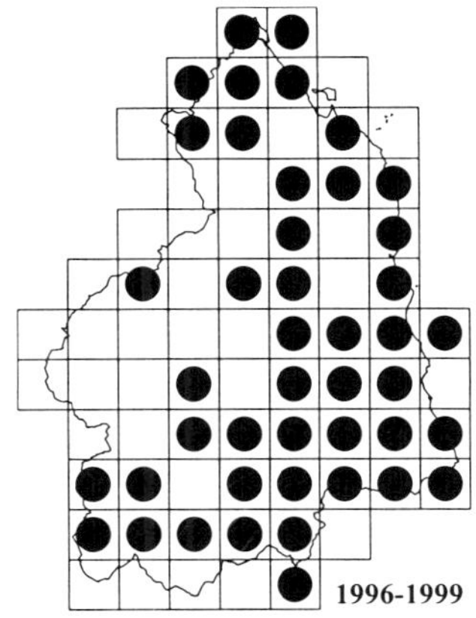

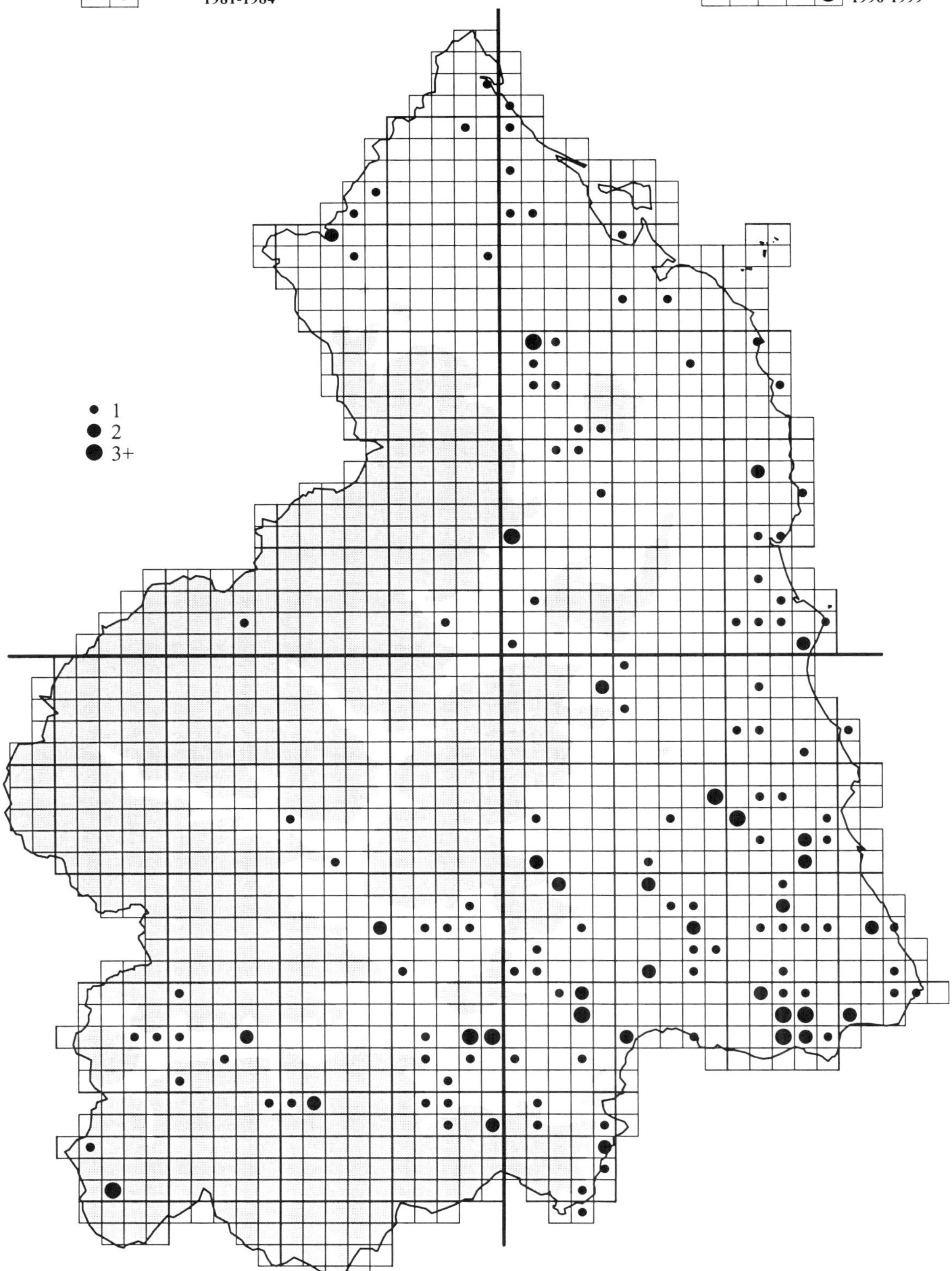

Grey Wagtail

PIED WAGTAIL *Motacilla alba yarrellii*

Galloway and Meek (1983) quoted Bolam's accurate statement of the status of *M. a. yarrellii* as being that of 'a common resident, though most of those which pass the summer with us depart in the autumn'. They also added a phrase to explain its abundance in summer as being due to 'a combination of drystone walls and running water'. The present survey work clearly demonstrates that this remains the case. Observers found 850 Pied Wagtails in 269, mostly lowland, tetrads. As the distribution map indicates, the uplands are largely abandoned in winter in favour of the coastal plains and river valleys. Well over half the tetrads in which Pied Wagtails were found (167) were below 101 metres a.s.l. and only four were above 300 metres. *The atlas of breeding birds in Northumbria* (Day *et al.*, 1995) shows an entirely different distribution pattern and a much higher summer population (1,861 pairs located in 891 tetrads and an estimated population of 2,500 to 4,000 pairs). By comparison, in winter the species is not common except where it roosts.

The departure from the upland areas to the coast and lowlands is marked in late summer and autumn by post-breeding flocks at places as diverse as Caistron, with, for example, 120 on 14th September 1996, and near Housesteads where 116 roosted at Broomlee Lough in September 1999 (*Birds in Northumbria 1996, 1999*). Some of these are simply staging posts but others, like the Old Post Office building in Alnwick, may be used throughout the winter as a communal roost for birds dispersing up to 12 kms to feed during the day.

Towns seem to be particularly favoured in winter, perhaps because they enjoy a slightly warmer micro-climate (Murray *et al.*, 1998) with the heat sources from industrial plants and buildings significant (Taylor *et al.*, 1999). During the atlas period large counts included 70 at Fawdon, Newcastle (NZ26J) in February 1997, 40 at Lynemouth (NZ29V) in January 1998, 60 at Wansbeck General Hospital, Ashington (NZ28Y) in January 1999 and 50 at Alnwick (NU11W) in February 1999. Other sites where such gatherings have been observed are British Gas at Killingworth, Morpeth Bus Station and Newcastle Airport. No communal roost in Northumberland, however, approaches in size those recorded by Mather (1986) in Yorkshire at Ferrybridge Power Station and York Railway Station or by Taylor *et al.* (1999) in Norwich City Centre. Indeed the largest roost in the region has been recorded just outside our recording area on the Team Valley Trading Estate in Gateshead which attracted up to 400 birds (Bowey *et al.*, 1993).

Many Pied Wagtails encountered in winter are single birds busily feeding on the tarmac of car-parks or garage forecourts, playing fields or on the flat roofs of industrial buildings. They are known to hold winter territories which they occasionally share with younger birds (Lack, 1986) and this has been the case in Fenham, Newcastle in recent winters (pers. obs.). Bolam (1912) was thus correct when he wrote 'a few odd birds, generally in adult plumage, may always be found in some favourite places, right through the winter'. He mentioned Berwick Little Beach as one such, and the tide wrack at places like Hauxley and Bondicarr continue to attract wintering wagtails with 14 at Hauxley Beach in December 1998.

Pied Wagtails are also flexible in their wintering strategies and will flock to sources of food, particularly during or after flooding, for example 50 at Prestwick Carr in November 1998. Only exceptionally are they found inland at high altitude as evidenced by one at 400 metres a.s.l. at Cottonshope Head on the Otterburn Ranges (NT80D) on 11 January 1998 and two at 350 metres on Spy Rigg in the Upper Irthing Valley (NY67X) in February 1998. There does seem to be a tendency to return to high ground earlier, especially if the weather is mild, and these records might represent the vanguard of such a movement. The return to the drystone wall country of Bolam's 'waterie-wagtail' is one of the indications of spring, but it is most marked in March and April when no drystone wall or inbye pasture is complete without its distinctive tail-wagger !

MIKE HENRY

Distribution by altitude

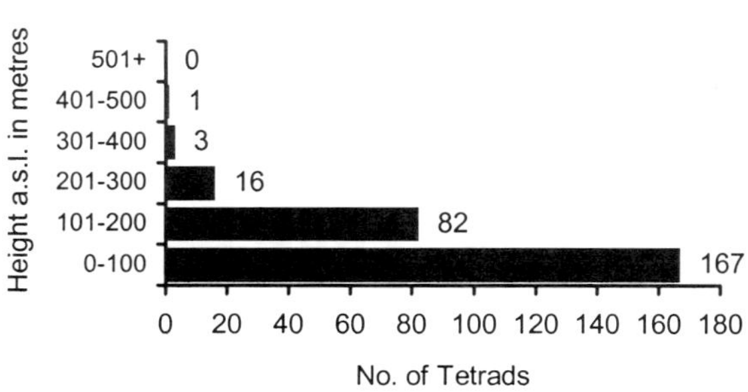

No. of tetrads in which recorded 269 (19%)

Tetrad Analysis	No. of tetrads
1 bird	144 (54%)
2-3 birds	76 (28%)
4+ birds	49 (18%)

Total No. of birds counted 850

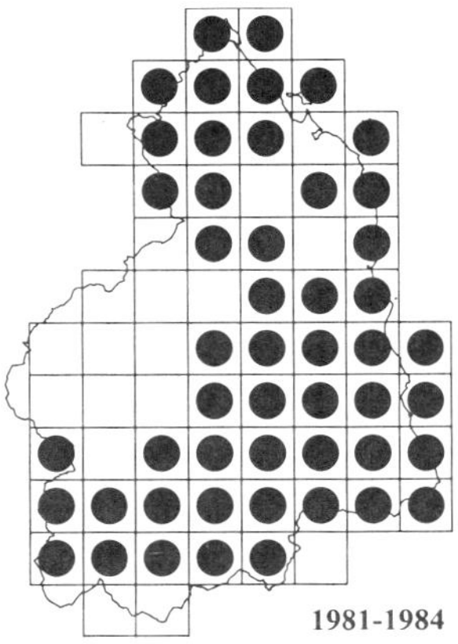

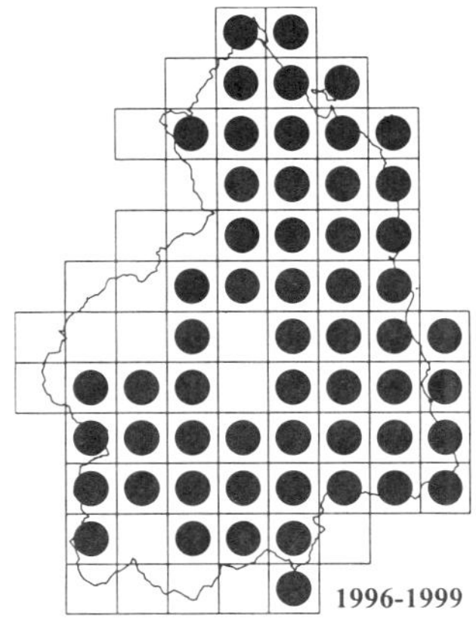

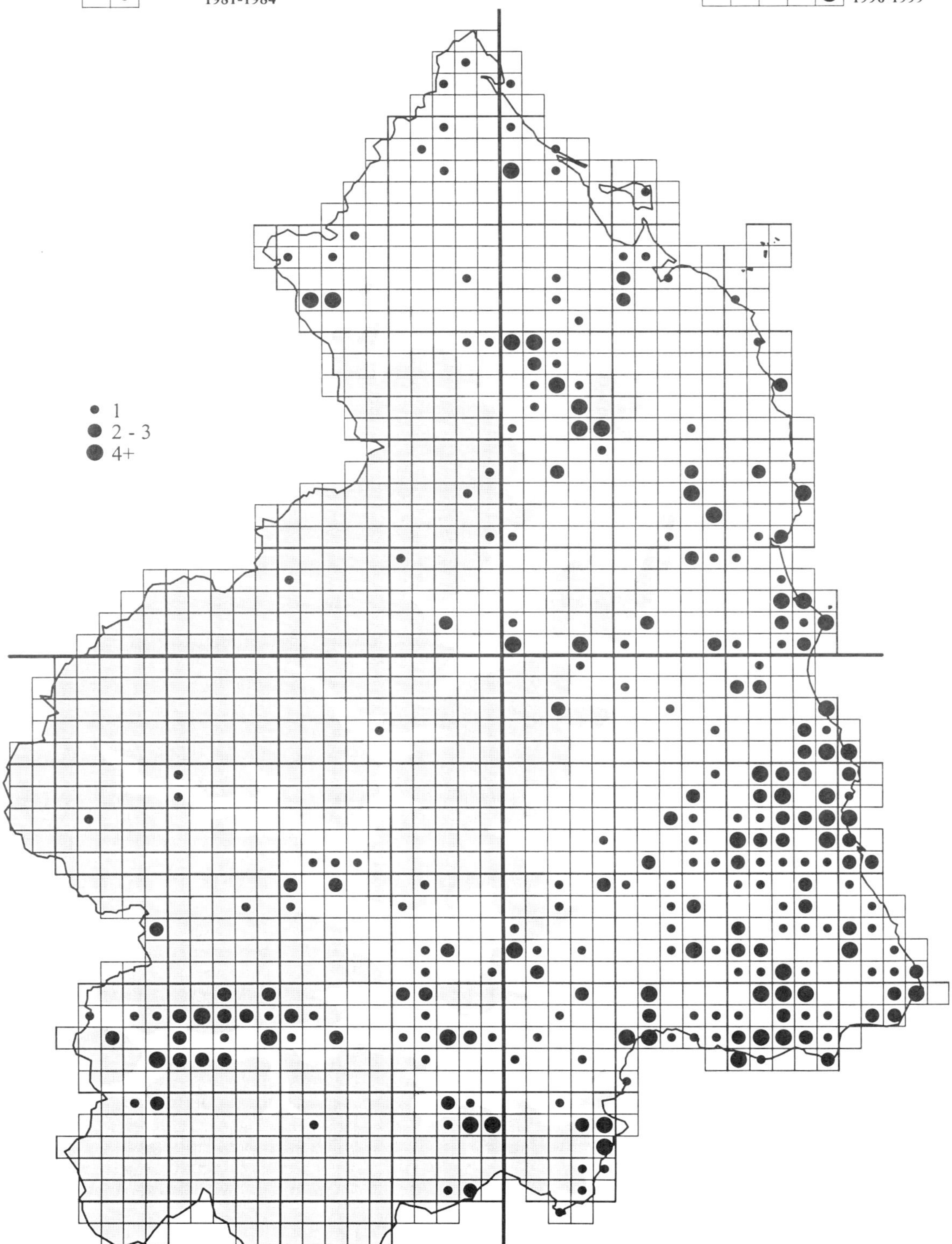

Pied Wagtail

WAXWING *Bombycilla garrulus*

In a season often devoid of avian treats the Waxwing can be relied upon to brighten up many a dull day. An exotically attractive species with a distinctive evocative call, erratic in occurrence, approachable and photogenic, few birdwatchers can resist it when the whereabouts of a flock becomes known.

Waxwings originate from Fennoscandinavia and Russia, and their occurrence in the region can vary widely from year to year. In some winters the total number of records may barely make double figures while in a good year many hundreds can be found. These good years are known as irruption years and are linked to the natural food cycle of the Waxwing within its natal range. The failure of the autumnal crop of its preferred food source, the Rowan berry *Pyrus asuparia*, will induce large scale movements into western Europe in search of winter sustenance. Arriving typically in November and December, these roving flocks frequently encounter hedgerows already stripped bare of their autumn berry crop and they invariably quickly descend upon the suburban areas in the south east of the county. Often coming together in large flocks, they take advantage of fruiting trees and shrubs such as Whitebeam *Sorbus aria* and Cotoneaster *Cotoneaster* and at times can be highly approachable in much disturbed places such as alongside dual carriageways and in supermarket car parks!

The current winter atlas survey confirms the statement of Bolam (1912) when he described the status of the Waxwing as a 'casual winter visitant' appearing 'in some winters in considerable flocks, in others only singly or in small parties'. Data collated during the current winter survey revealed a maximum count of 772 during the winter of 1996/97, this being an irruption year on a national scale, compared to only ten in 1997/98 and four in 1998/99. Though duplicate sightings of this highly mobile species undoubtedly occurred, the high totals within the county during the winter of 1996/97 were also reflected nationally with a monthly total of over 2,000 recorded during December, 1996 (Nightingale & Allsopp, 1997).

The tetrad map for the current survey also reflects the species' readiness to converge on the urban south east of the county with 28 of the 46 occupied tetrads located within this quadrant, with the bulk of the other records restricted to the coastal strip. With a couple of isolated records coming from the west of the county, such as near Chollerford (NY87V) and Allendale (NY85J), it may well be that these relate to birds in the process of relocating to the western side of the country or even further afield.

Some large concentrations were also noted during the current winter survey, with a peak count of 175 in the north of Cramlington (NZ27P) on the 1st December 1996 being a typical locality, but perhaps slightly more unusual were flocks of up to 70 in the Lowick area (NU03E) and 50 near Kyloe (NU03P) during November 1996.

Only in irruption years do Waxwings occur within Northumberland in significant numbers and it should therefore be regarded as a rare though occasionally well represented winter visitor, to be enjoyed where or whenever the opportunity arises!

ALAN CURRY

Distribution by altitude

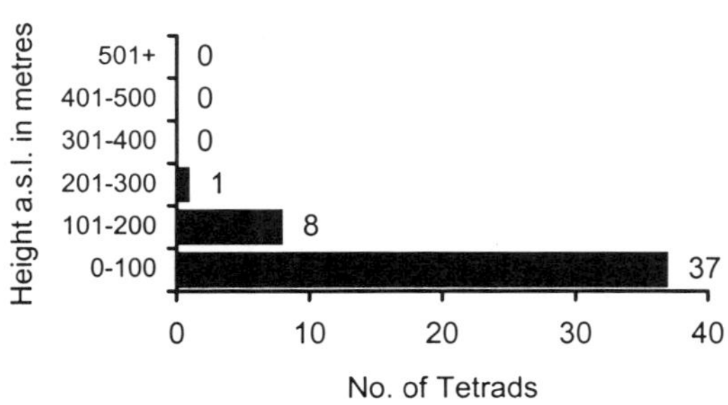

No. of tetrads in which recorded 46 (3%)

Tetrad Analysis	No. of tetrads
1-6 birds	23 (50%)
7-30 birds	15 (33%)
31+ birds	8 (17%)

Total No. of birds counted 772

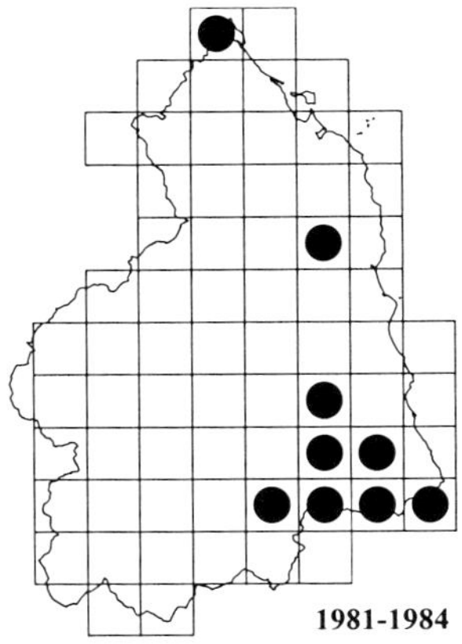

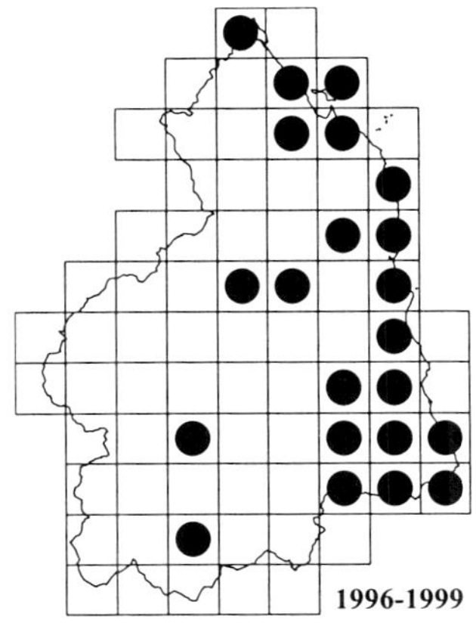

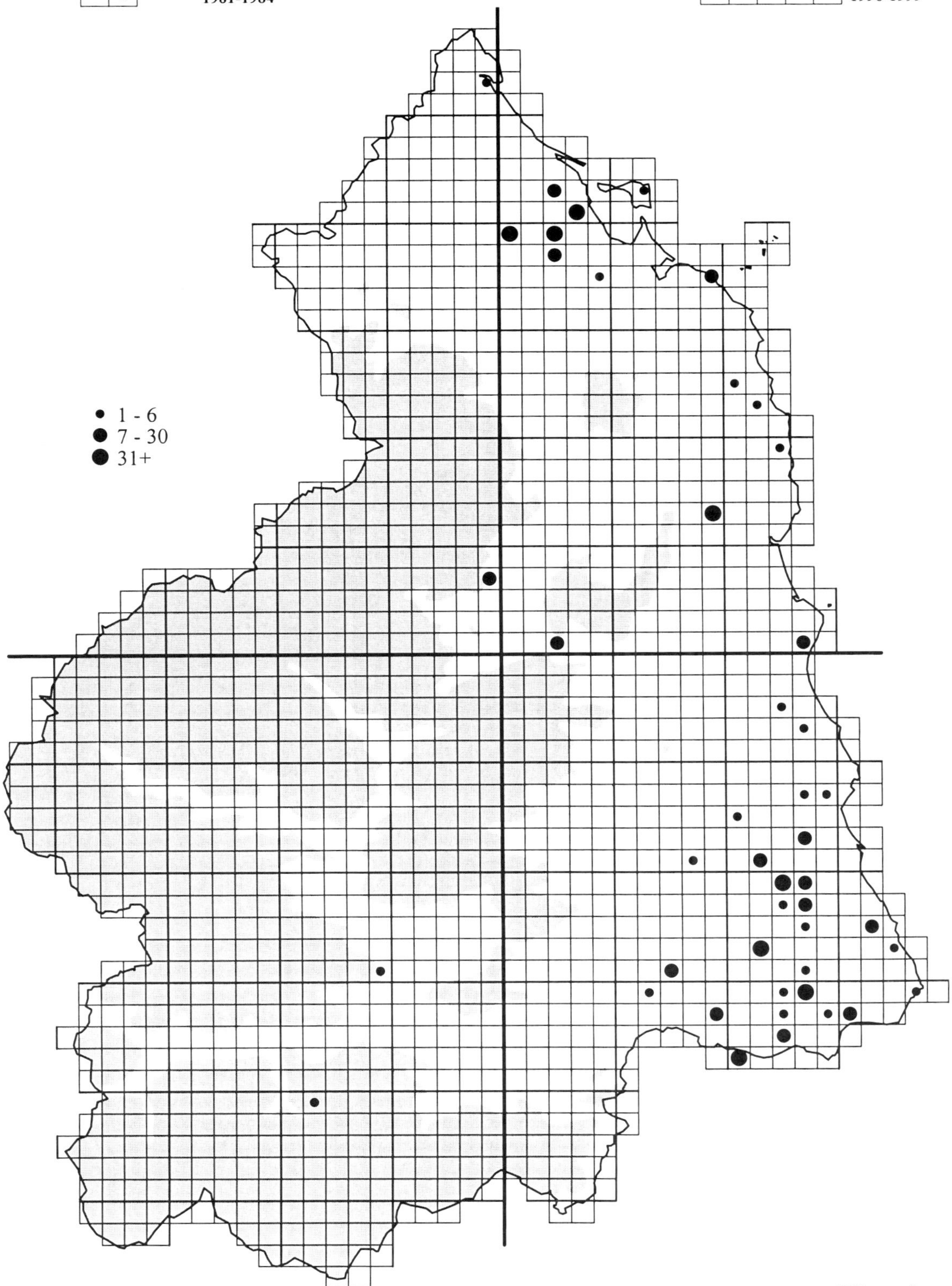

Waxwing

DIPPER *Cinclus cinclus*

The Dipper is a species which is characteristic of the waterways of Northumberland and in the nineteenth century was referred to as a constant resident by Hancock (1874). More recently Galloway and Meek (1983) described the species as a well-represented resident. In the survey for *The atlas of breeding birds in Northumbria* (Day *et al.*, 1995) a breeding population of between 250 and 300 pairs was estimated and, taken together with other national data, this led to the conclusion that Northumberland, along with the southern uplands of Scotland and the Pennines, forms the largest area of Dipper population density in the UK.

Dippers are unusual when compared to the majority of other species recorded during the current county winter atlas survey in that their breeding cycle is already well advanced by the end of the survey period in late February. Tyler and Ormerod (1994) reported that Dippers may start building or repairing nests during January and early February. This agrees with personal observations during an ongoing nine-year study of breeding Dippers in the catchment area of the River Coquet; indeed, eggs have been recorded as early as the beginning of March. This early breeding habit means that there will be some overlap between the winter and breeding distributions of Dippers during the period of the current winter survey and some records may refer to birds in breeding territories.

As expected, the distribution of Dippers shown on the tetrad map shows strong correlation with the presence of river systems and is similar to the breeding distribution. A noticeable difference however is the reduction in the number of records in the North Tyne Valley and the northern valleys of the Cheviots when compared to the breeding distribution. This may be evidence that Dippers in these areas move downstream from the more upland streams during the winter period as reported from studies in Wales (Tyler & Ormerod, 1994). This movement has also been noted in the Coquet study area where breeding territories on the Upper Coquet and its feeder burns are often deserted in winter and not re-occupied until late February.

Of the total of 226 tetrads recorded as containing Dippers, the vast majority (185 representing 82%) contained either one or two birds with only 19 (8%) containing four or more. These observations are consistent with the Welsh study area referred to above where it was shown that Dippers hold territories both within and outside the breeding season. Interestingly, of the nine records of six or seven birds recorded in a single tetrad, five of these (Shillmoor NT80Y, College Valley NT82Y, Harthope Valley NT92S and the River South Tyne NY76L/R) were in late January or early February 1997, suggesting that aggregations may have occurred during a spell of bad weather as Dippers have been recorded as reducing the size of feeding territories when river conditions prevent feeding in certain areas (Tyler & Ormerod, 1994).

Comparison of the current county winter survey with the 1981-1984 national winter atlas survey (Lack, 1986) suggests a broadly similar distribution, with the core areas of the uplands relatively constant but some small differences on the fringes. The maximum count total in the current study is 398 which for a resident species is low compared to the estimated population of 250 to 350 pairs from the 1988-1992 survey of breeding birds in Northumbria. Some fluctuation is also suggested by the control tetrads data, where numbers varied from 19 in 1996/97 to 11 in 1997/98, and also by the long-term River Coquet study where a decline in the number of pairs breeding in the study area has been noted since 1995. The Coquet study will continue to monitor these population changes and attempt to identify the underlying causes. However, the results of the current county winter atlas survey still identify the Dipper as a species which is well-represented within Northumberland.

NEIL ANDERSON

Distribution by altitude

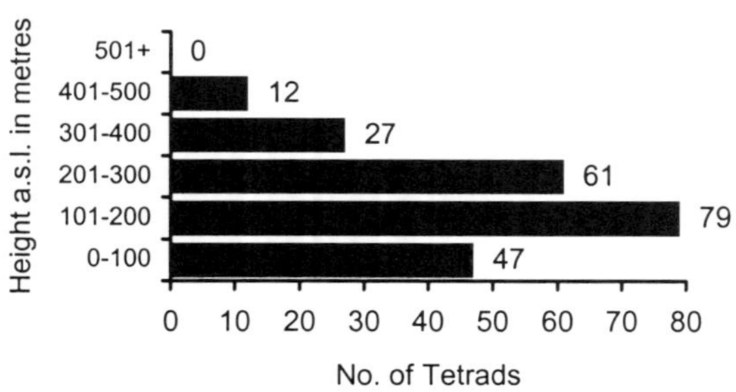

No. of tetrads in which recorded 226 (16%)

Tetrad Analysis	No. of tetrads
1 birds	136 (60%)
2 birds	49 (22%)
3+ birds	41 (18%)

Total No. of birds counted 398

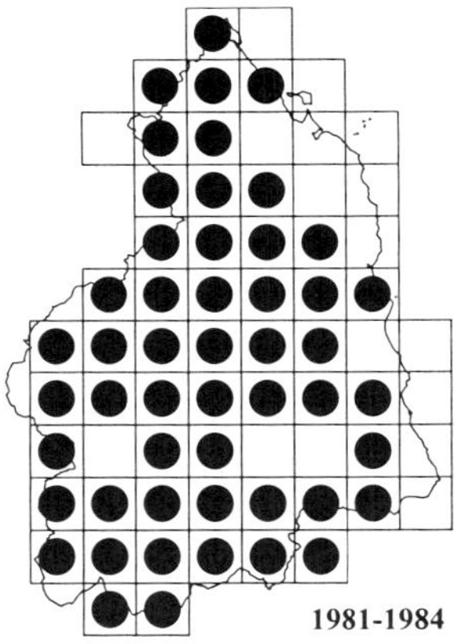

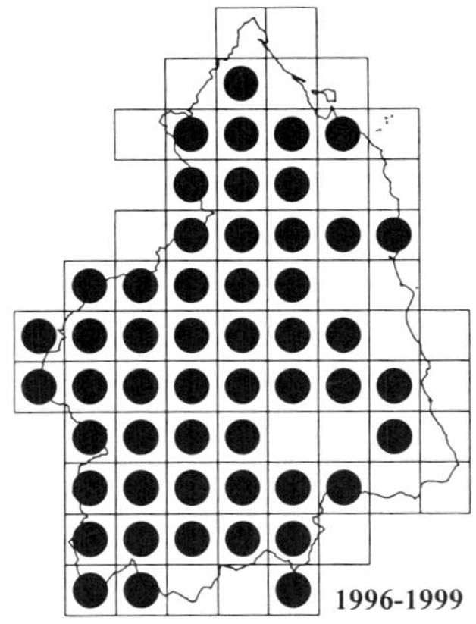

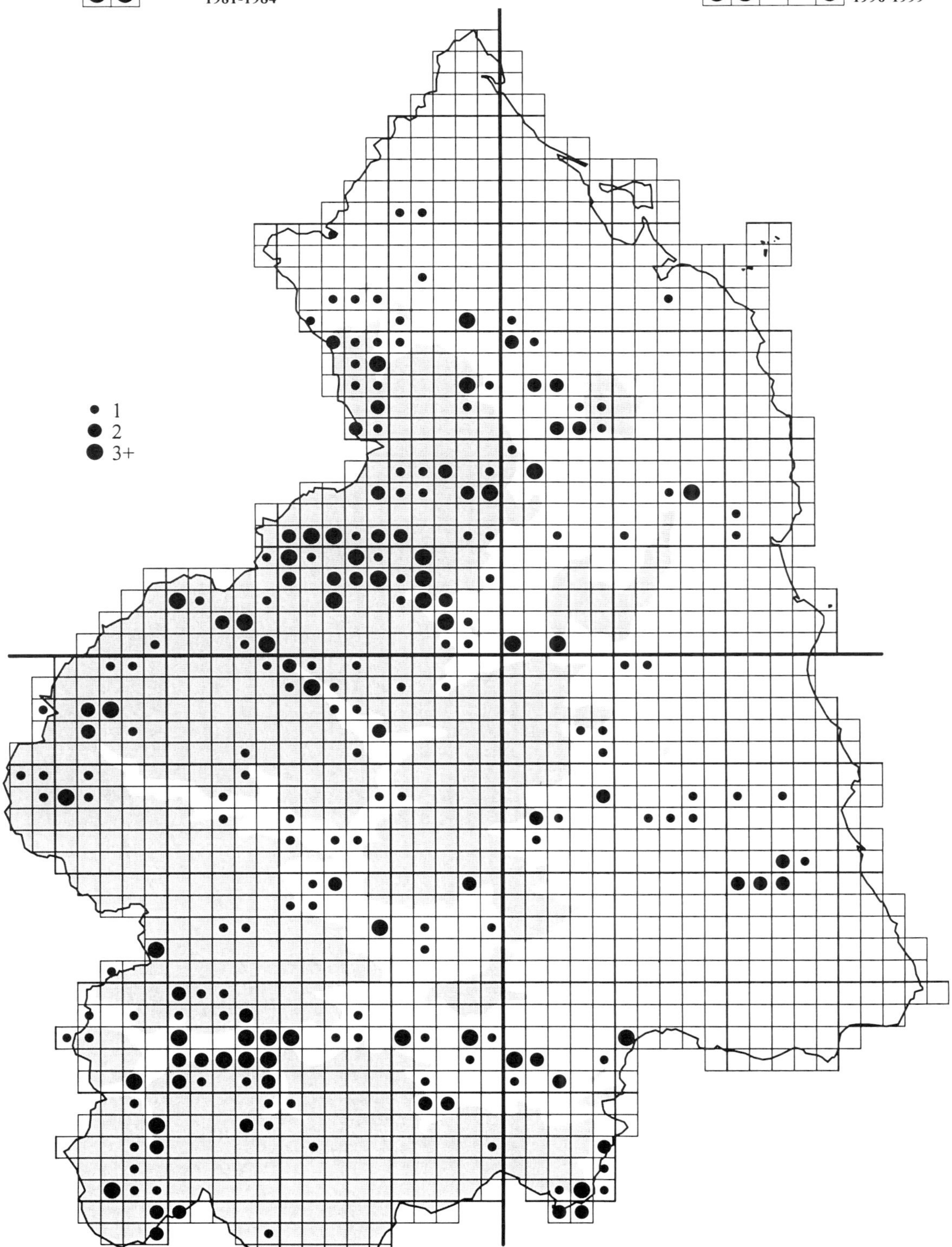

Dipper

WREN *Troglodytes troglodytes*

Judging by the data collected during the current county winter atlas survey, the Wren is one of the most widely distributed species in the area, having been recorded in 1,068 tetrads (75% of those covered). This would indicate that its status as a common resident, first noted by Bolam (1912) and later reinforced by Galloway and Meek (1983), has not changed. Mead (2000) stated that, nationally, the species is not experiencing any problems at the moment and this would seem to be true in the county.

The Wren was as widespread in the county during the winters of 1996-1999 as it was in 1981-1984, being recorded in virtually all 10km squares on both occasions. The percentage of occupied tetrads decreases with altitude, from over 80% of those below 201 metres a.s.l. to 25% in the range 401-500 metres a.s.l. Its wide distribution reflects the existence of suitable habitat with a variety of low cover and foraging opportunities of one sort or another throughout the county as well as the ability of the species to adapt. The higher concentrations during the survey were found in a variety of habitats, most notably the patches of deciduous woodland in the South Tyne Valley and its tributaries (NY76M; 25 birds, NY76S; 22, NY76L; 22), part of the coniferous forest of Kielder (NY68Y; 20), and those suburban areas of Newcastle near Gosforth Park (NZ26P; 20) and Jesmond Dene (NZ26T; 20). By contrast, birds were few or absent in the more exposed upland areas, in forested localities above 400 metres a.s.l. where breeding populations are relatively high, and in some of the lowland agricultural areas particularly in the north east of the county. The control tetrad data tend to confirm this distribution, with consistently higher numbers each year in broad-leaved woodland, e.g. Spindlestone (NU13L), Countesspark Wood (NY88Q), in parts of Redesdale and Wark Forests like Cottonshopeburn Foot (NT70V) and the Blackaburn area (NY77Z). There appear to be very few in exposed uplands like Allenheads (NY84S) or in some intensively farmed lowland agricultural areas, e.g. Fairney Flat near Berwick (NT95R).

As a small and agile bird, the Wren is able to forage in places inaccessible to other birds. Many of these sites are still available during snowy weather and it is possible for Wrens to feed and roost under a blanket of snow. In really severe weather they congregate to roost communally, seldom more than ten together but as many as 61 have been recorded (Snow & Perrins, 1998). In Northumberland, during the current survey, when relatively mild weather predominated there were no reports of such communal roosting. In 1991, however, the first 'white' winter for several years, birds were reported roosting in old Swallow *Hirundo rustica* nests, with 14 at Swarland and 17 at Matfen (*Birds in Northumbria 1991*). The Wren has a very high surface-to-volume ratio and relatively poor capacity to store winter fat. It is, therefore, very susceptible to winter weather severe enough to prevent efficient feeding and can suffer high mortality, but numbers do recover very quickly following one or two mild winters. The severe winter weather of 1978/79 drastically reduced the local population but by April 1980 it appeared to be recovering. Similarly, the population suffered as a result of the cold weather during parts of the 1980s but by 1990, following several milder winters, the population level was high once more (*Birds in Northumbria*).

Most breeding sites support fewer wintering birds and some exposed breeding habitats, such as remote uplands and moorlands, are completely deserted (Lack, 1986). A comparison between the current winter distribution map and the county breeding atlas map confirms this. The wintering Wrens were present in 1,068 tetrads (75% of those covered) whilst the breeding population was present in 1,169 (83%). A higher percentage of tetrads containing land above 183m a.s.l. was occupied in the breeding season, whilst a higher percentage of lowland tetrads was occupied in the winter months. This difference is clearly illustrated by two areas of quite high breeding density, Jesmond Dene and Kidland Forest. Whilst the former area also has one of the higher wintering densities, there were hardly any birds recorded in Kidland Forest during the winter survey. The movement away from high ground is most pronounced in the north west of the county. The overall wintering total for the three year survey of a minimum of 4,047 birds is considerably less than the 10,000 pairs suggested by Day *et al.* (1995). Though some Wrens may move south, ringing recoveries show that most only move short distances between summer and winter (Lack, 1986) and their populations tend to be sedentary (Snow & Perrins, 1998). Therefore, although many Wrens are territorial in winter and defend their feeding area with vigorous alarm calls and song, their preference to move around unobtrusively in thick undergrowth means that many birds were probably not recorded.

TONY BAKER

Distribution by altitude

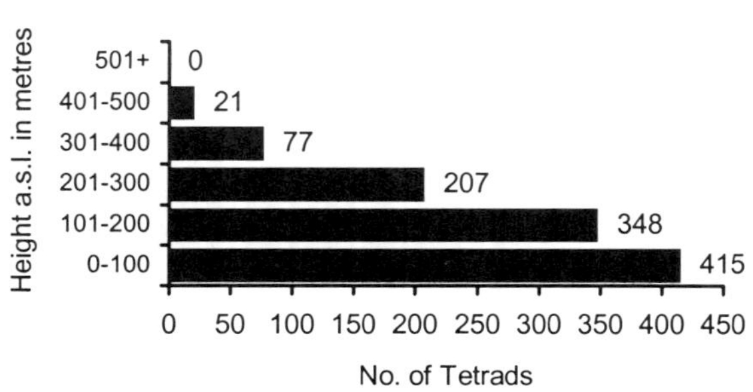

No. of tetrads in which recorded 1,068 (75%)

Tetrad Analysis	No. of tetrads
1-2 birds	481 (45%)
3-5 birds	366 (34%)
6+ birds	221 (21%)

Total No. of birds counted 4,047

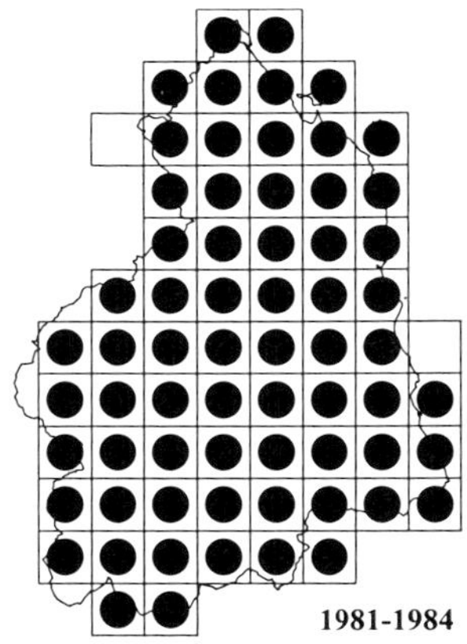

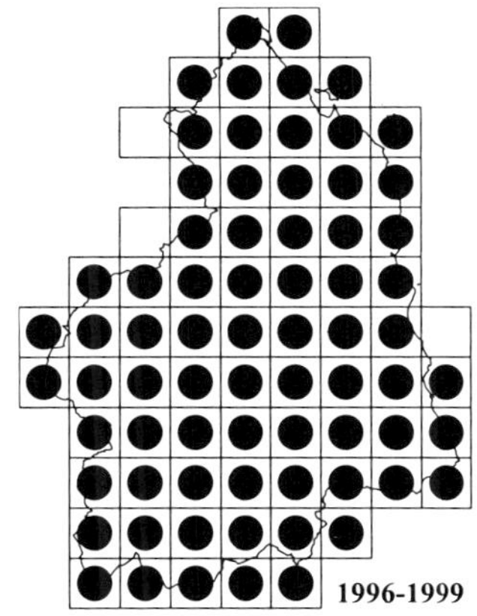

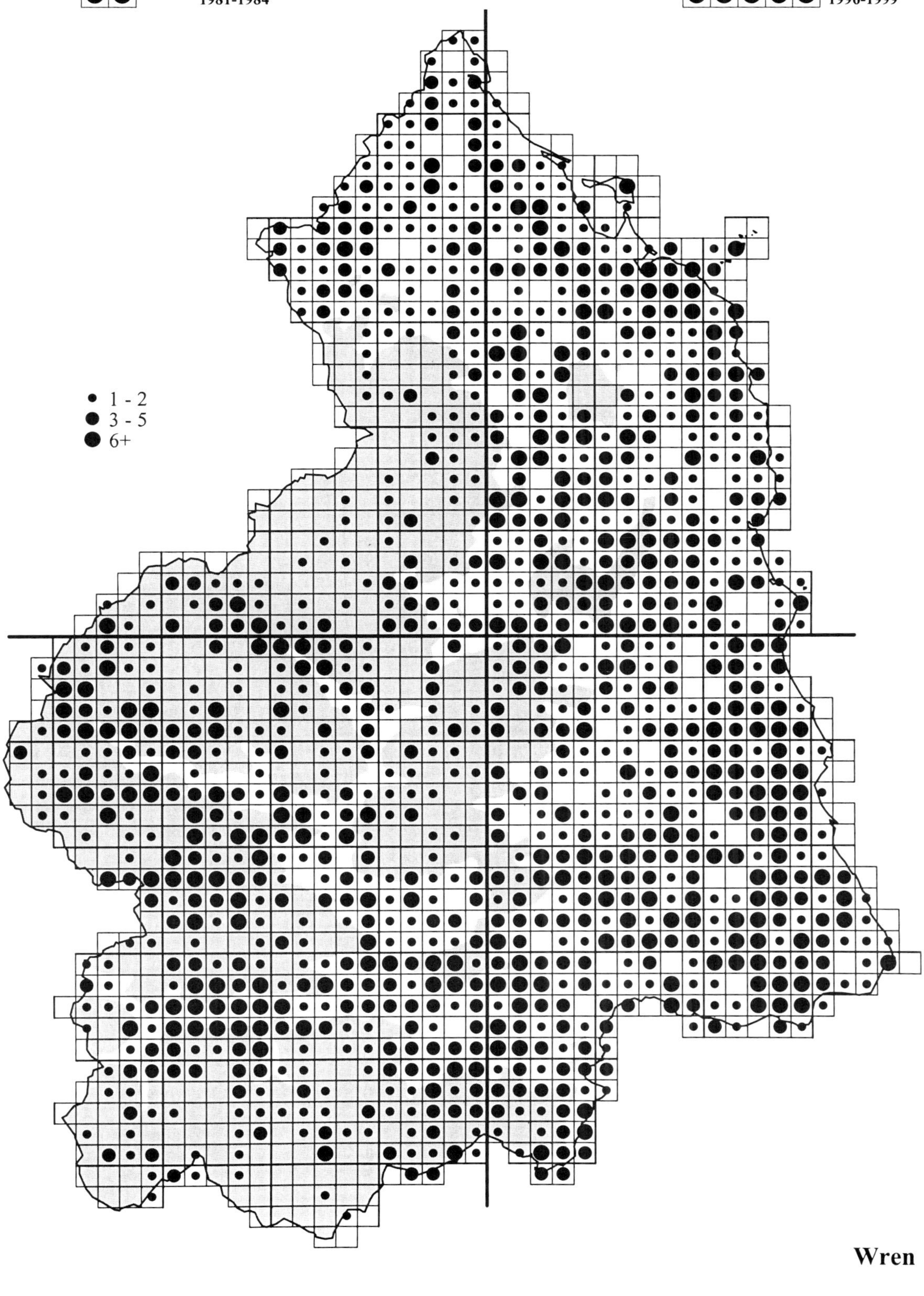

Wren

DUNNOCK *Prunella modularis*

Despite its shy, unobtrusive nature, the Dunnock is still one of the most common and widespread birds in the country and is found in a wide variety of habitats. Bolam (1912) observed that in Northumberland 'our birds are resident throughout the year, being never absent from their accustomed haunts, even during the severest weather, or in the remotest glens'. He also noted that the 'extraordinary numbers' seen in some eastern counties in autumn, were only rarely observed in Northumberland. Galloway and Meek (1983) described it as 'an uncommon passage visitor and an abundant breeding species'. They also commented that 'contrary to Bolam's observations, large numbers of passage visitors may be seen at the coast, especially in the autumn'. Records from *Birds in Northumbria* include small numbers seen during autumn on both the Farne Islands and other offshore islands as well as in other coastal regions. In October 1976, for example, a maximum of 25 were on the Farnes and 11 were found dead on the beach between Whitley Bay and Blyth, and, in 1983, 25 were recorded at Bamburgh also in October. Mead (2000) commented that whilst the Dunnock was 'still a common bird' it was undergoing an unexplained national decline.

During winter, the Dunnock is mainly solitary and gleans a wide variety of food from the ground, its diet consisting of a mixture of small seeds together with invertebrates such as beetles, spiders, earthworms, flies and springtails (Lack, 1986). The BTO Garden Bird Feeding Survey records from the 1970s list the Dunnock as occurring in 95.2% of gardens and rank it 6th in frequency. Recent records from the 1990s show that it is still recorded in 95.7% of gardens surveyed and its rank remains much the same at 7th. Undoubtedly, in urban areas, it is very much dependent upon small particles of food that fall from garden bird-tables and hanging feeders.

Its common and widespread status in the county is well illustrated in the 1981-84 winter survey, which recorded the Dunnock in 96% of the 10km squares surveyed compared with 95% of those visited in the recent winter survey. However, the average number of birds recorded in the control tetrads increased from 3.1 in 1996-97 to 4.3 in 1998-99, perhaps due to larger numbers of passage birds present in some years and also a series of mild winters. During this survey a total of 3,066 were recorded in 781 tetrads which represents 55% of the total number of tetrads surveyed. Of those occupied by Dunnocks, 674 (86%) were below 201 metres a.s.l. which confirms its general preference for lowland habitats. Recent records from *Birds in Northumbria* confirm that, as Bolam (1912) noted, the Dunnock is not entirely absent from upland regions, as in December 1999 two were recorded at 300 metres a.s.l. in the Otterburn Training area.

The current winter distribution map shows the main concentrations to be mainly in the east of the county with numbers declining towards the west and to some extent in upland regions. The bird is fairly well represented in the main river valleys such as the Tyne and its tributaries, and in some cases well into the upper reaches, and in suitably sheltered upland habitats. Some of the highest counts per tetrad were recorded in the Tyne Valley between Haltwhistle and Allenbanks (NY76) as well as in the urban area of Newcastle upon Tyne (NZ26). Comparison of the local breeding and wintering distribution maps for Dunnock confirms that it is a relatively sedentary species. In the 1988-1992 breeding atlas survey, they were recorded in 93% of 10km squares compared with 95% during the recent winter survey. Despite the difficulties of conducting an accurate census, the 1988-1992 breeding survey data indicated that the total breeding population of the Dunnock in the county was between 5,000 and 6,000 individuals (Day *et al.*, 1995). The 3,066 individuals recorded in the current winter survey perhaps again underlines the difficulty of counting such a shy and unobtrusive species.

ALAN J. DAVIS

Distribution by altitude

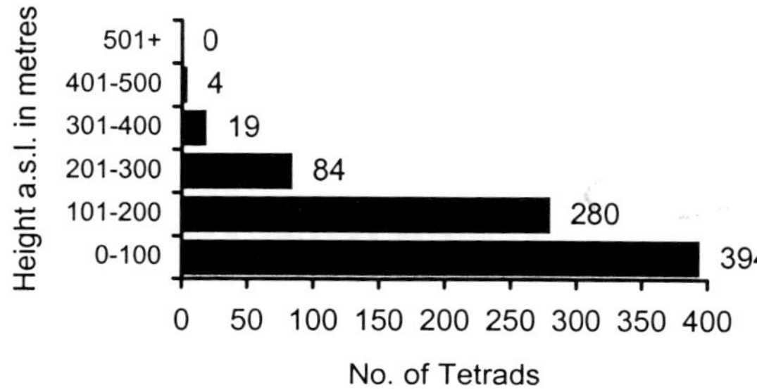

No. of tetrads in which recorded 781 (55%)

Tetrad Analysis	No. of tetrads
1-2 birds	357 (46%)
3-5 birds	249 (32%)
6+ birds	175 (22%)

Total No. of birds counted 3,066

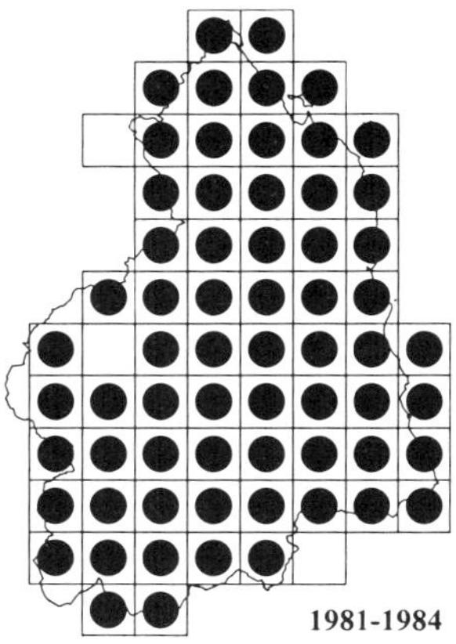

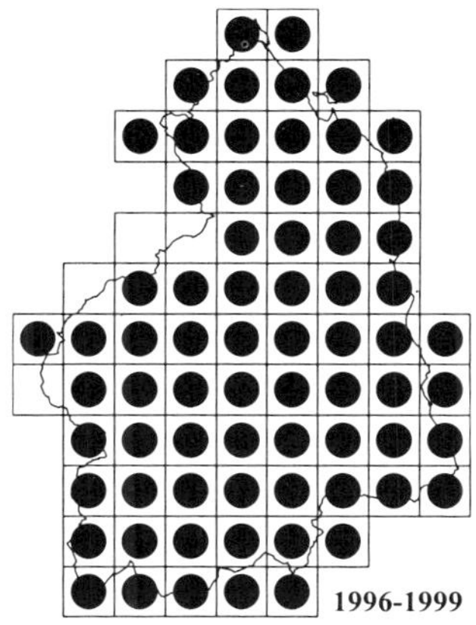

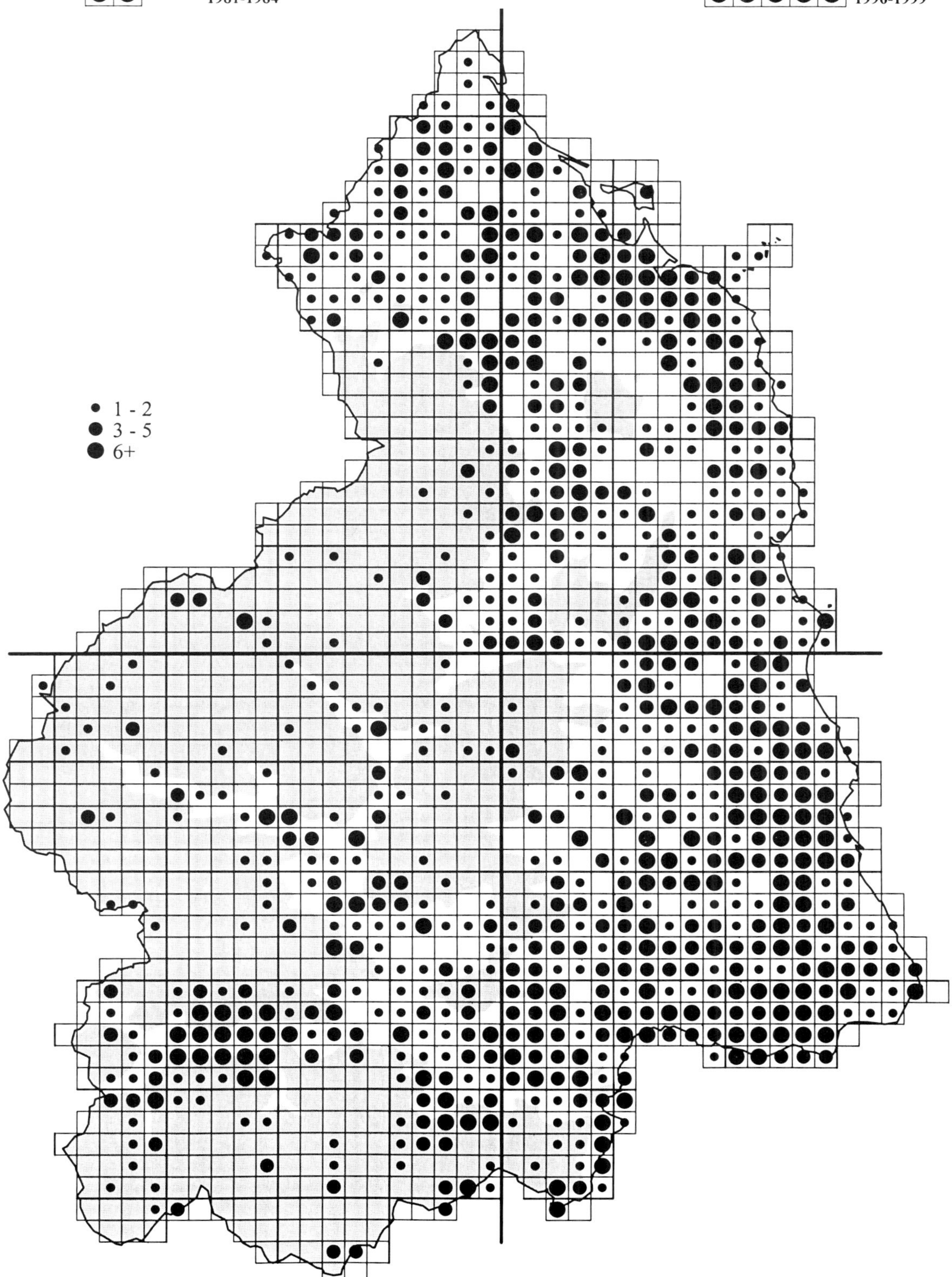

Dunnock

ROBIN *Erithacus rubecula*

The Robin was recorded in the current winter survey in virtually all of the 10km squares in Northumberland, just as it had been during the previous winter survey of 1981-84, and appears as widespread today as when it was first described as a common resident by Bolam (1912). This status was later confirmed by Galloway and Meek (1983). Nationally, Mead (2000) considered the future prospects of Robin to be good, the loss of hedges in arable areas being more than compensated for by the increase in gardens due to housing developments. After Blackbird *Turdus merula* and Blue Tit *Parus caeruleus*, the Robin is the most commonly recorded bird in gardens during winter, being noted in over 99% of gardens taking part in the BTO Garden Bird Feeding Survey.

Its wide distribution within the county is a result of a willingness to live in a broad range of habitats, usually within the vicinity of some mature trees but particularly where good ground cover exists (Lack, 1986). The majority of their food consists of invertebrates caught on the ground. Vegetable food such as fruit, though more important in winter, rarely accounts for more than 10% of energy intake. Therefore, a dependence on ground-living prey makes the Robin vulnerable to periods of snow. Following severe weather in the winter of 1981/82, it was reported in *Birds in Northumbria 1982* that numbers of Robins were low in rural areas. However, Mead (2000) commented that Robins are better at avoiding losses than many species and quickly recover after one or two milder winters.

Within the survey area there is a strong link between altitude and the occurrence of Robin during the winter, with more than 80% of the occupied tetrads being below 201 metres a.s.l. This results in Robins being more widespread in the eastern half of the county and particularly in the south east. However, whilst the highest density was recorded in the south east at Bedlington Country Park (NZ28Q) with 44 birds counted, the majority of higher densities recorded were all in the south west, for example along the wooded streams and in gardens and scrub between Henshaw and Bardon Mill in the South Tyne Valley (NY76S) with 38 and the small patches of woodland and wooded streams near Steel in Hexhamshire (NY95J) with 31.

Nationally, the winter and breeding distribution maps look very similar but at county level, when the distribution is plotted by tetrads rather than 10km squares, there are some important differences related to altitude. In Northumberland, the number of occupied tetrads in winter with land over 183 metres a.s.l. is more than 20% less than during the breeding season, with the greatest decrease occurring in the north west. Conversely, the number of occupied lowland tetrads increases in winter but by less than 10%. Galloway and Meek (1983) commented upon this and linked it to extreme weather movements. The occurrence of relatively mild winters during the current survey suggests that this is a seasonal movement which occurs anyway. Lack (1986) suggested that these seasonal changes are because many birds move into habitats which are unsuitable for breeding such as reed beds and suburban areas without mature vegetation. Locally wintering Robins were present in 966 tetrads (68% of those covered) whilst the breeding population was present in 1,064 (76%) (Day *et al.*, 1995). This would suggest that, as well as moving to lower ground, some birds leave the county altogether during the winter.

The strictly territorial behaviour of Robins, their confiding nature and distinctive warble will have ensured that a high proportion of the birds in the region was recorded during the survey. Though ringing recoveries indicate that some passage birds do remain in the county, the majority presumably move quickly through and the overall wintering total for the three-year survey of 5,329 birds is unlikely to have been considerably inflated by any such arrivals. Nevertheless, the control tetrad data demonstrates a reasonably stable wintering population with occupied tetrads in 1996/97, 1997/98 and 1998/99 holding an average of 4.8, 5.1 and 5.5 birds respectively. Since very few British birds winter abroad, the difference between the overall winter total and the estimated breeding population of 5,000 pairs could be a result of birds moving further than the 5km which Lack (1986) suggested most Robins may move between breeding and wintering grounds.

TONY BAKER

Distribution by altitude

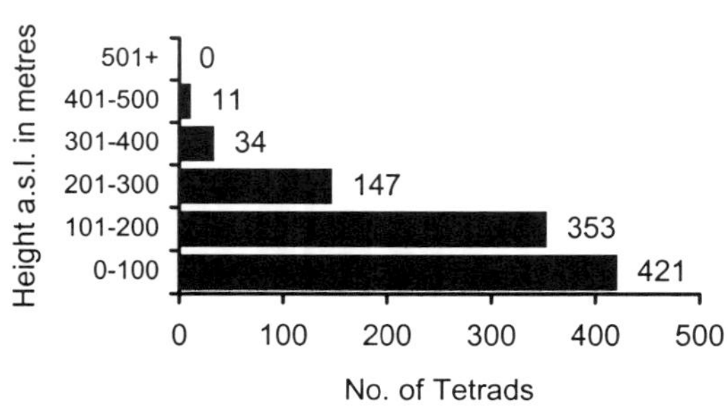

No. of tetrads in which recorded 966 (68%)

Tetrad Analysis	No. of tetrads
1-3 birds	435 (45%)
4-8 birds	345 (36%)
9+ birds	186 (19%)

Total No. of birds counted 5,329

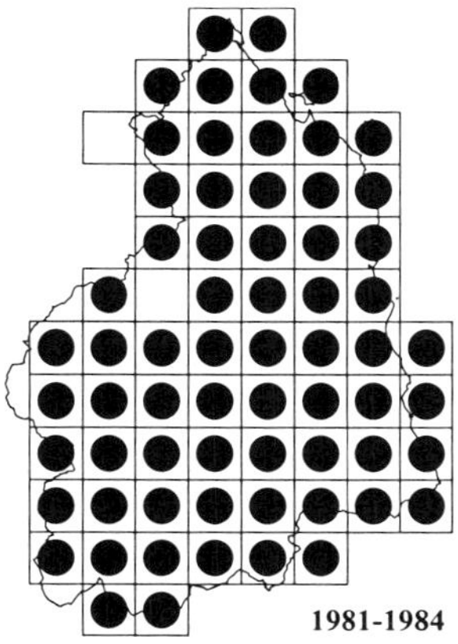

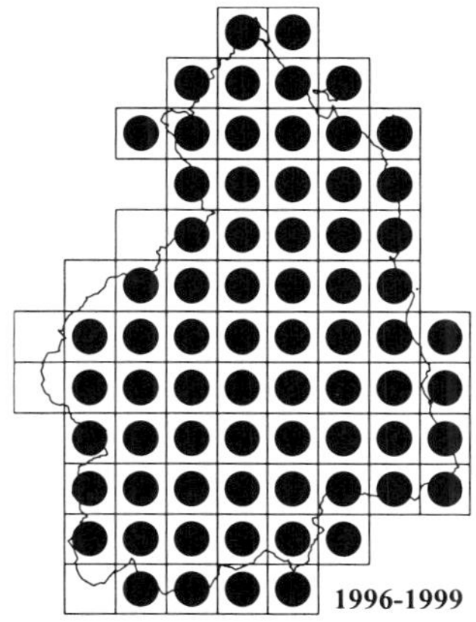

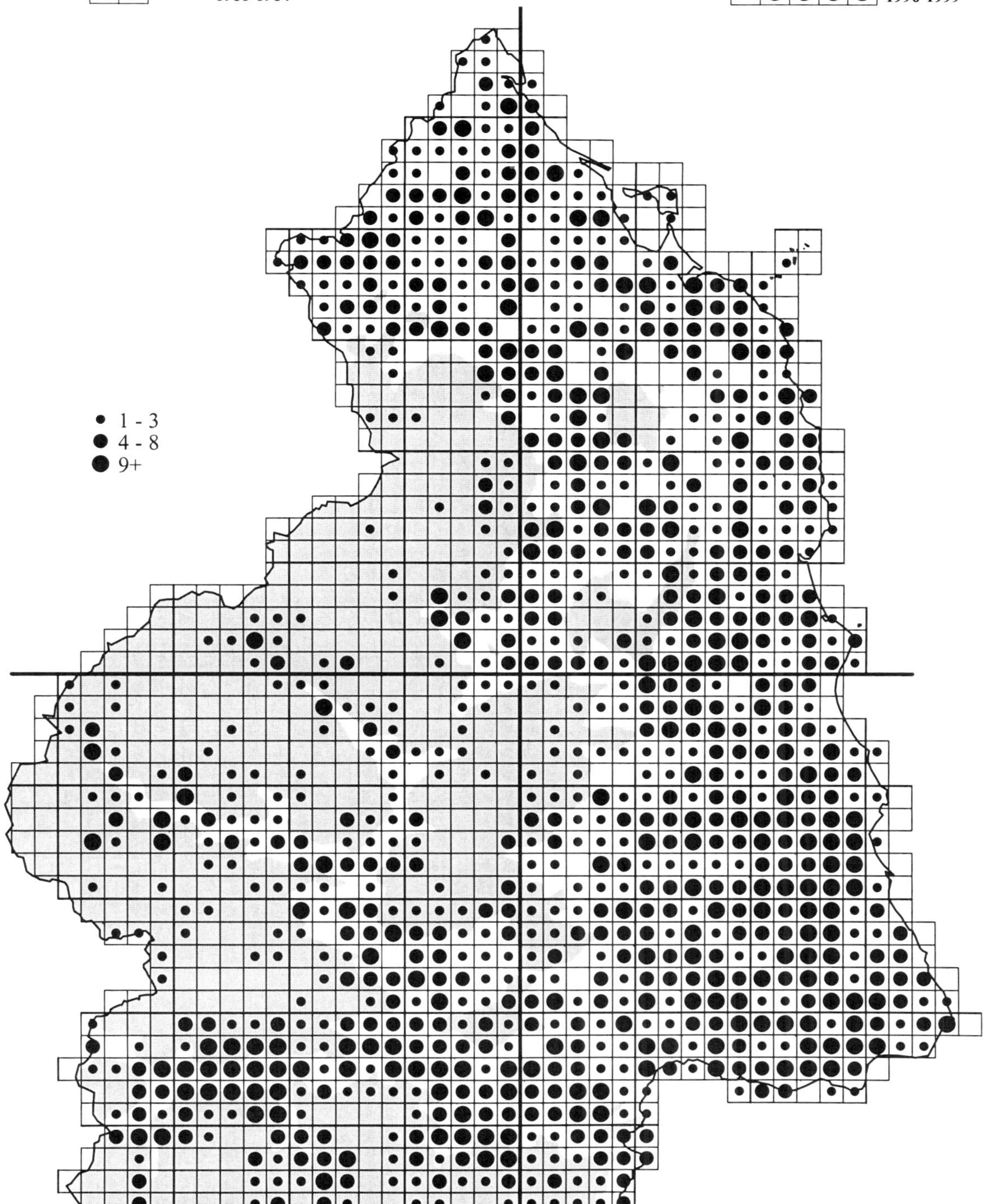

Robin

BLACK REDSTART *Phoenicurus ochruros*

A comparison of the two small 10km square maps confirms that wintering Black Redstarts are more common now than in the 1980s. In the last decade, two or three birds have been recorded between mid-November and the end of February in most years, whilst previously only one and sometimes two wintering birds were reported in occasional years.

The Black Redstart nevertheless seems to be a comparatively recent addition to the county's avifauna. As early as 1912 Bolam described it as a 'casual visitor, which has only very rarely occurred in the district', and noted wintering birds at Berwick in December 1893 and St. Mary's Island in November 1903. By 1932 he was able to say that it had become 'a winter visitant which has occurred with some frequency since 1912', and by the mid-1980s Galloway and Meek (1983) described it as 'an uncommon passage and rare winter visitor' that was 'most numerous on passage, especially in March, April, May and October when the majority occur on the coast'. They stated that between 20 and 30 were reported in most years, including inland records, with the possibility that pairs may have bred.

After the main autumnal passage small numbers of Black Redstarts may remain throughout the winter, usually in coastal habitat (Lack, 1986). In the south of England, where the species has bred consistently since 1923, some wintering birds remain near their urban breeding sites, but most prefer cliffs and beaches. Lack was of the opinion that many wintering east coast birds were of continental origin and quoted a number of ringing returns for birds from Central Europe.

The current atlas survey recorded a minimum of eleven over the three winter seasons, with two birds in 1996, singles on the Farnes in 1997, seven individuals in 1998 and two in January and February 1999. All were in typical coastal locations including Holy Island (NU14F), Beadnell (NU22J), North Blyth (NZ38B) and Tynemouth (NZ36U), with birds present on the Farne Islands (NU23) in November of both 1997 and 1998. Two birds were identified as first-winter males and two as females.

As milder winters seem likely to continue, and the breeding range slowly expands (Mead, 2000), there may be an increase in both annual and winter sightings in the county in succeeding years.

JOHN C. DAY

Distribution by altitude

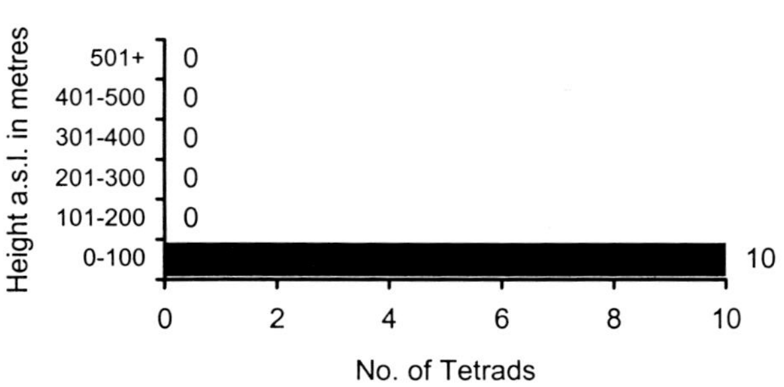

No. of tetrads in which recorded 10 (>1%)

Tetrad Analysis	No. of tetrads
1 bird	9 (90%)
2 birds	1 (10%)

Total No. of birds counted 11

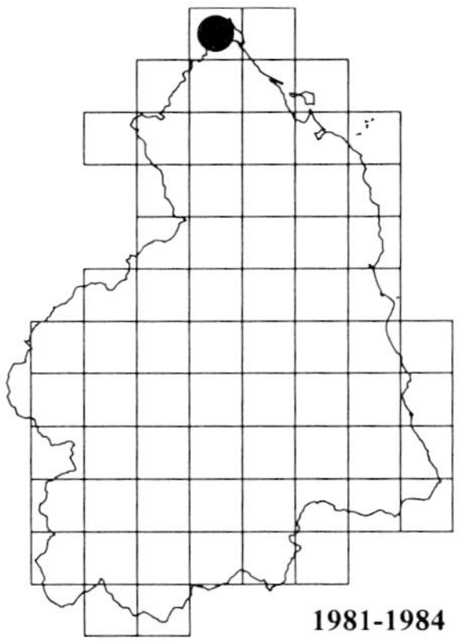

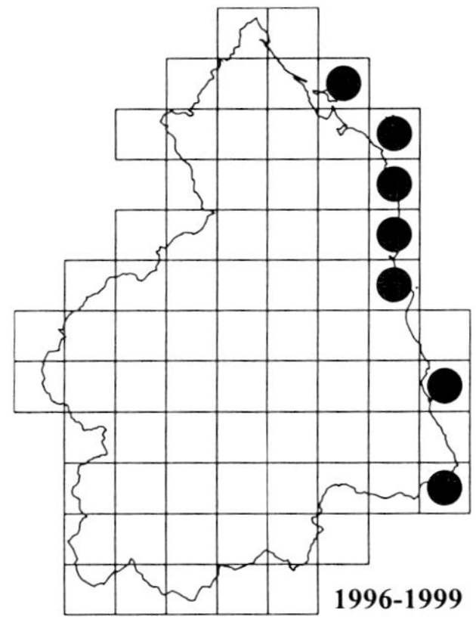

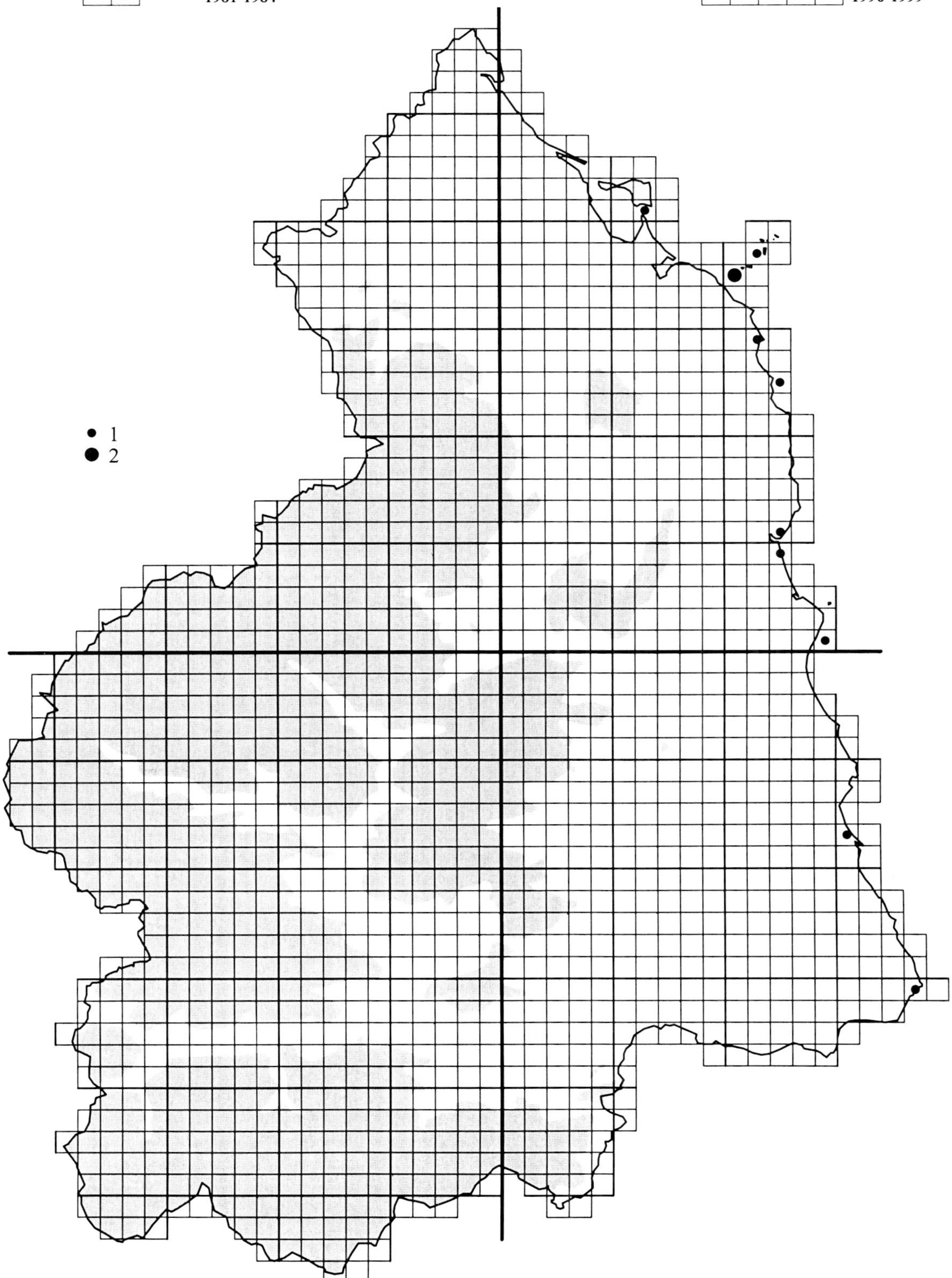

Black Redstart

STONECHAT *Saxicola torquata*

Bolam (1912) knew the Stonechat as 'a partial resident ... widely distributed over the district' and some twenty years later commented on its winter status when he said it was 'a typical resident ... it is to be found in scattered, stay-at-home pairs braving even the most severe winters on our lonely moors, where almost its sole feathered companions are the Grouse, or perhaps a Wren. It likewise winters, in small companies, or solitary pairs, about our seaside links and similar places'. He was certainly aware that breeding numbers were prone to fluctuations and commented 'old records suggest that the species may always have shown a similar tendency to fluctuate in numbers'. Galloway and Meek (1983) documented the fortunes of the species as a breeding bird up to the 1980s but, following the severe winters of 1978/79 and 1981/82, numbers were at a low ebb. Data collected for the local breeding atlas between 1988 and 1992 (Day *et al.*, 1995) showed the species had not appeared to have made a significant recovery, with only 13 occupied tetrads (1% of those surveyed) containing a maximum of 13 pairs.

A comparison of the two 10km square maps shows a marked change in the winter distribution of the Stonechat since 1981-1984 when only 16% of the squares visited were occupied against 27% in the current survey. It should be borne in mind, however, that the fieldwork methodology, involving tetrad-based visits, employed in this last survey would be far more conducive to locating scattered pairs and individuals, particularly inland. The tetrad distribution map indicates that the winter strongholds are scattered along almost all of the coastline although there is a noticeable gap north of Holy Island. The largest population concentrations are to be found in the eminently suitable habitat along Druridge and Alnmouth Bays; indeed 43% of the occupied coastal tetrads were in these two areas. Inland there were 15 occupied tetrads, all containing either only one or two birds, which presumably reflects the continuing changing fortunes of the species which has already been outlined by previous local authors. The maximum count was seven in the Buston Links area (NU20P), with six at East Chevington (NZ29U) and five in the adjacent tetrad at Druridge Links (NZ29T), but the vast majority of counts (82%) were of one to three birds. There is some evidence, albeit from a very small sample, for a rather consistent population over the three winters, as two coastal control tetrads produced counts of four, four and three and two, two and two respectively.

Lack (1986) said that in Britain the winter range of the Stonechat was broadly similar to its breeding range and that pairs occupy territories during the winter which, at times, may be much larger than in the summer. A few birds migrate south, as indeed do Stonechats on continental Europe. He estimated the British winter population overall was unlikely to differ widely from that during the breeding season (estimated at 30,000-60,000 pairs in 1972). Following a steady downward trend since 1972, Gibbons *et al.* (1993) gave a British breeding population of only 8,500-21,500 pairs. More recently, Mead (2000), after commenting on the declines in the last century, pessimistically said 'we may be about to lose more'.

In Northumberland, there is a distinct increase in numbers of Stonechats reported during the autumn months which probably results from post-breeding dispersal of local birds combined with some immigration into the county. The more widespread distribution during the current winter survey will have been assisted, no doubt, by a slight upward turn in the number of breeding pairs located in the county since 1993. During 1995, for example, at least five pairs were confirmed breeding on the coast while another ten breeding pairs represented the highest population level inland since the 1970s (*Birds in Northumbria 1995*). The continuation of rather mild winters may well be beneficial to continuing population expansion but even one severe winter can cause large losses. At the moment the Stonechat's status still varies between rare and uncommon.

MIKE S. HODGSON

Distribution by altitude

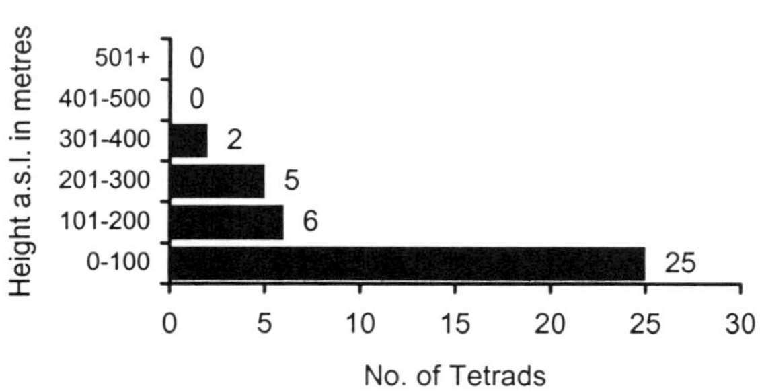

No. of tetrads in which recorded 38 (3%)

Tetrad Analysis	No. of tetrads
1 bird	16 (42%)
2-3 birds	15 (40%)
4+ birds	7 (18%)

Total No. of birds counted 82

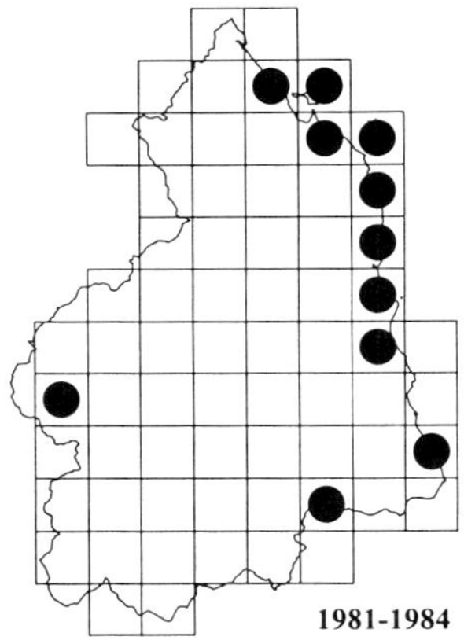

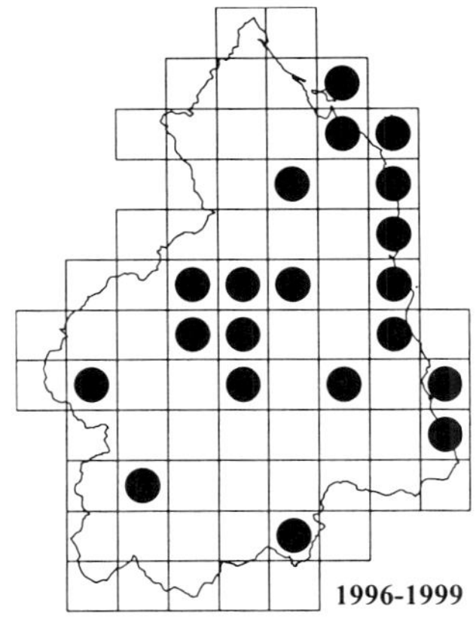

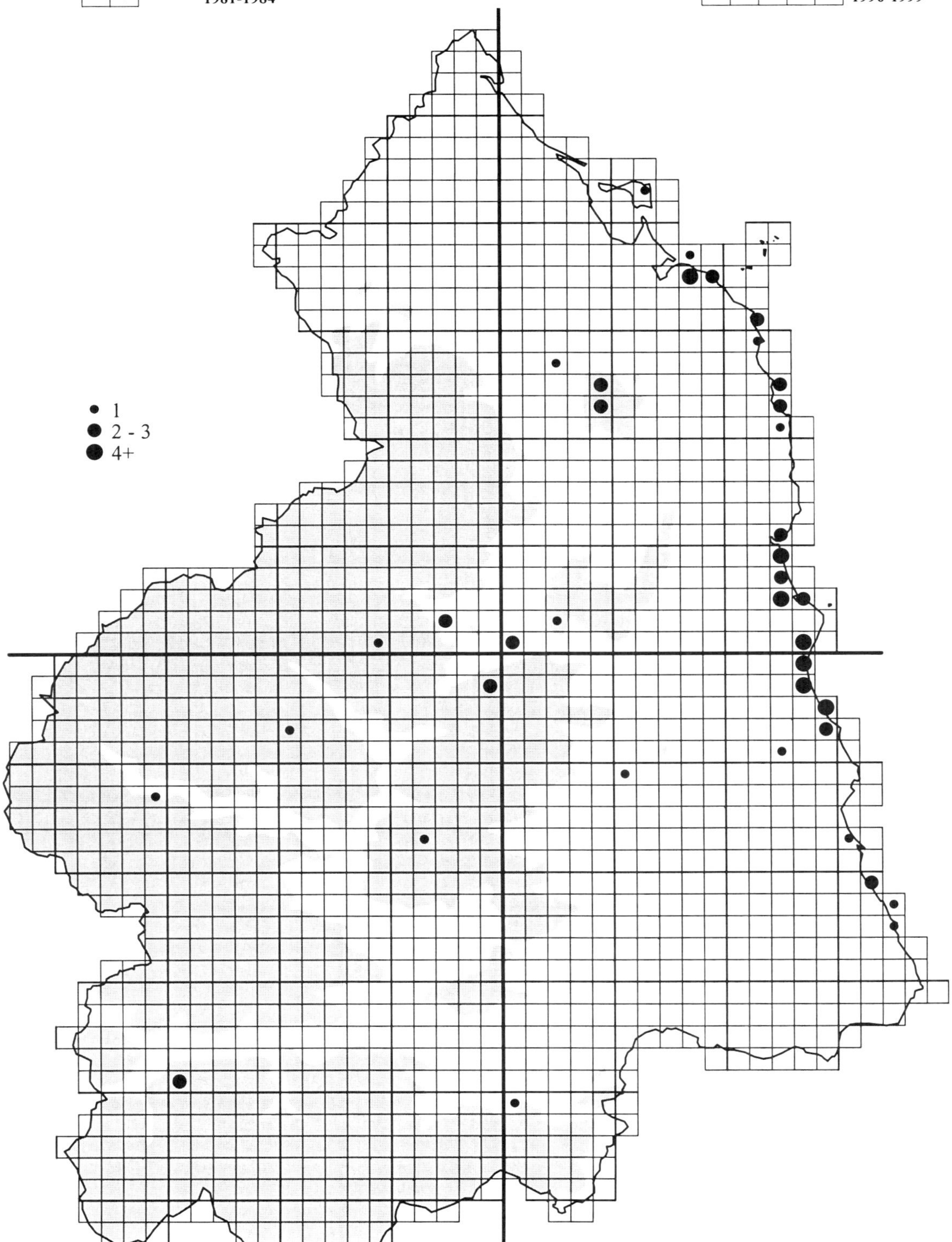

Stonechat

RING OUZEL *Turdus torquatus*

Bolam (1932) said of the Ring Ouzel in Northumberland that 'individuals encountered during the winter months are, probably, chiefly belated birds-of-passage, though now and then one or two would appear to elect to pass the winter here'. Galloway and Meek (9183) in their review of this mainly summer visitor to the county said that birds at Berwick in January 1895 and near Chillingham in February 1975 could be considered as true winter occurrences. More recently Kerr (2001) added another at Marden Quarry, Whitley Bay in January 1990 and a remarkable four individuals in January-February 1996 at Holy Island, North Shields, Red Row and Morpeth.

The birds breeding in northern Europe and Britain are known to winter in southern Spain and north west Africa (Snow & Perrins, 1998). Lack (1986) listed only four 10km squares in Britain and Ireland that held Ring Ouzels, and in each case only single birds, during the winters of 1981-1984.

During the three winter periods of this current survey a further four birds were located, at Elford (NU13V) on 8th December 1996, at the Wansbeck Estuary on 18th November 1997, in the College Valley (NT82Y) on 28th February 1998 and at Parmentley (NY75R) on 21st February 1999. The first two may well relate to lingering passage migrants on or near the coast but the latter two, both well-inland, must surely refer to true wintering birds.

Although the sample size is small, the fact that small numbers were found in the preceding winter and during this current survey may indicate a series of milder winters has allowed birds to remain much further north than normal. Might this trend continue in the light of the potential consequences of global warming ?

MIKE S. HODGSON

Distribution by altitude

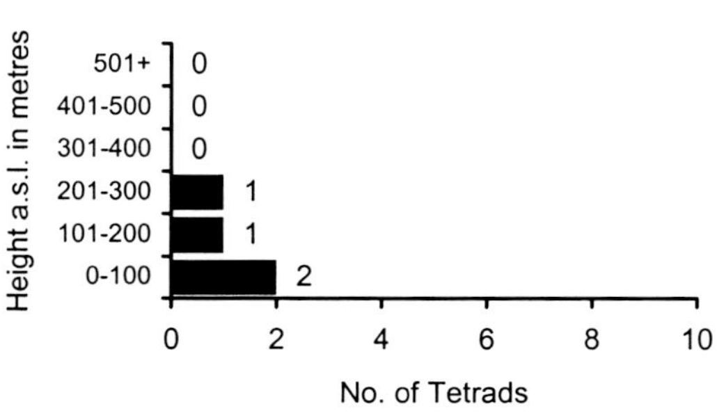

No. of tetrads in which recorded 4 (<1%)

Tetrad Analysis	No. of tetrads
1 bird	4 (100%)

Total No. of birds counted 4

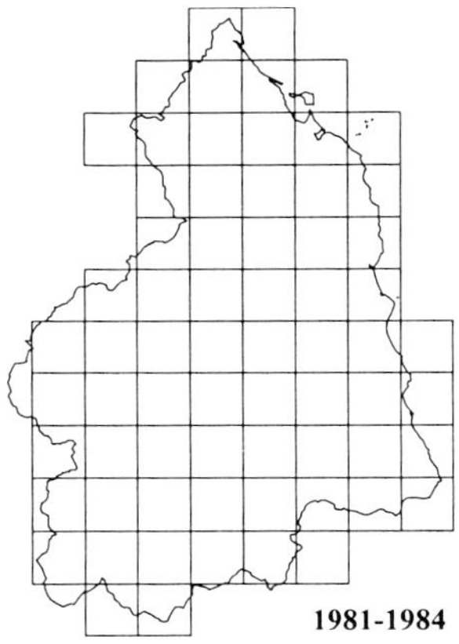

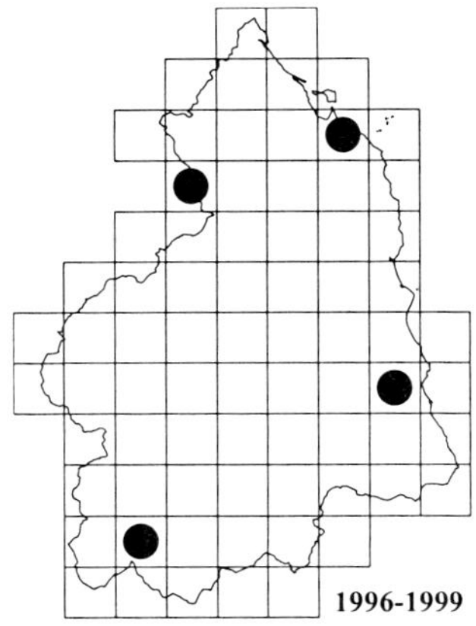

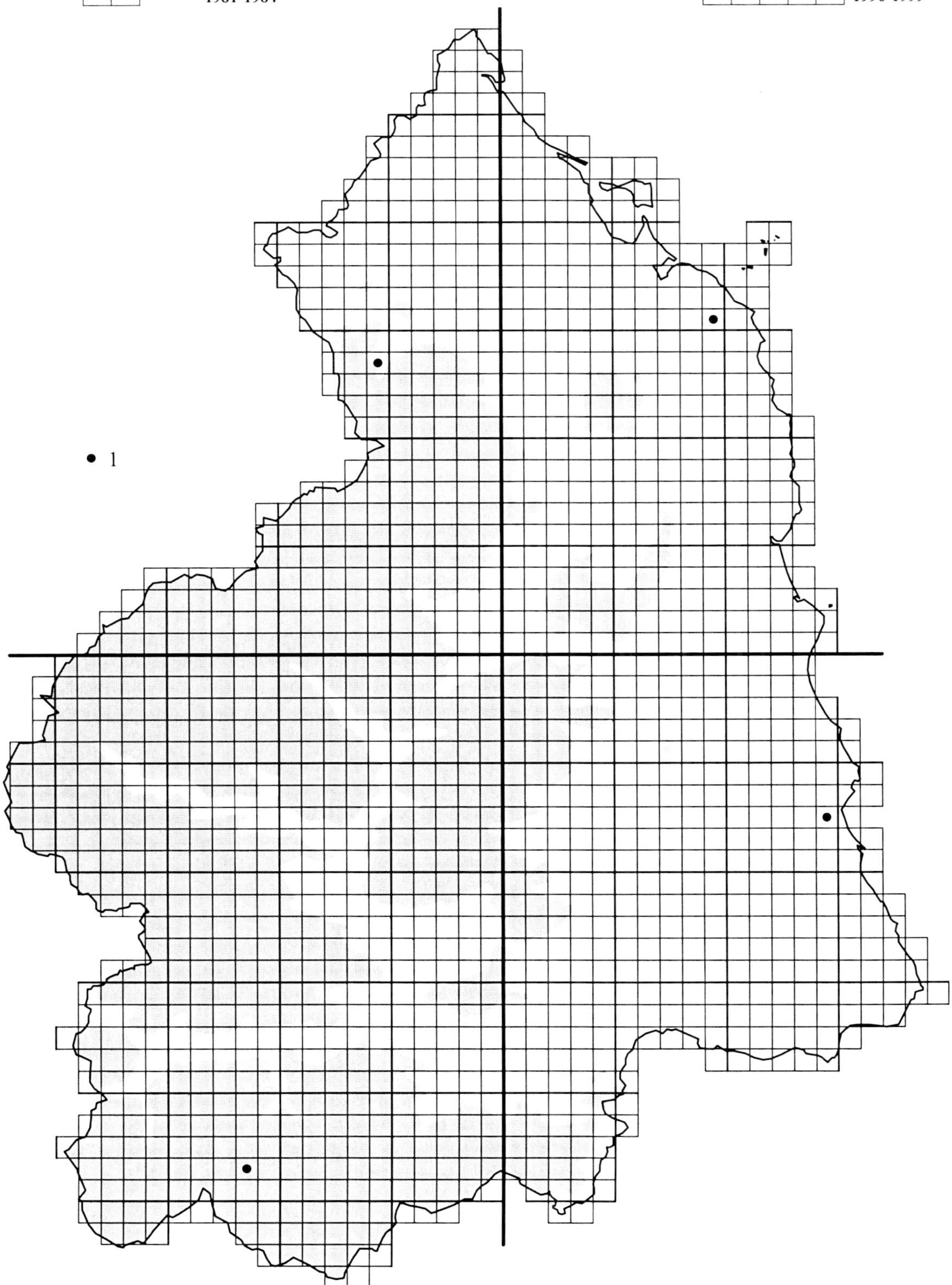

Ring Ouzel

BLACKBIRD *Turdus merula*

The Blackbird is one of the most familiar bird species occurring in Great Britain and was recorded by 97% of observers taking part in the BTO's Garden Watch scheme during winter 2000/2001. It was seen in more gardens than any other species. Clement and Hathway (2000) detail the north west European mainland to be the major source of winter migrants into Great Britain. This has been confirmed many times from ringing recoveries, whilst many birds ringed in Northumberland in winter have been recovered in Scandinavia, Estonia and Germany.

In Northumberland Kerr (2001) classified the Blackbird as an abundant resident, passage migrant and winter visitor. This does not represent any change from the status accorded the species by Bolam in 1912. However, despite a large wintering population, Blackbirds were only found in 67% of the tetrads surveyed with a marked absence from higher ground and much of the west except in the river valleys. An analysis of distribution by altitude showed that 89% of all tetrads in the ranges 0-100 metres and 101-200 metres a.s.l. were occupied, decreasing to 43% between 201-300 metres, 21% between 301 and 400 metres and only 7% in the 401-500 metres a.s.l. range.

It is clear when comparing results with data from the local breeding atlas (Day *et al.*, 1995) that there is some movement away from the higher altitude breeding locations in winter, as 75% of all tetrads were found to be occupied during the breeding season as opposed to 67% in the current survey. At higher altitudes Blackbirds were mainly found nesting around villages and in deciduous woodland. One lowland area where birds were absent during the breeding atlas survey work was the former opencast area immediately to the west of Druridge Bay. However, the completion of restoration work, and its associated planting, lead to Blackbirds occupying this area by the time of the winter fieldwork.

Like the earlier county breeding survey, the greatest concentration of birds in winter was around the Tyneside/south east Northumberland conurbation. Some 2,435 (22%) of the total number of birds counted occurred in 83 tetrads covered by the four ten kilometre squares of NZ26 (Newcastle upon Tyne), NZ27 (Cramlington), NZ28 (Ashington/Bedlington) and NZ37 (Whitley Bay). Clement and Hathway (2000) observed that the species feeds both on the ground and in trees and bushes so that an urban environment provides much suitable feeding habit with its many gardens, parks and school grounds. These are often planted with such berry-bearing species as Hawthorn *Crataegus laevigata*, Honeysuckle *Lonicera* sp., Cotoneaster *Cotoneaster* sp., Elder *Sambucus nigra* and Guelder Rose *Viburnum opulus*, all of which are readily consumed by Blackbirds in winter.

Away from the main wintering population, the ten kilometre square in the Haltwhistle area (NY76) produced counts totalling 655 birds representing 6% of the overall total in the three winter periods, while the Bardon Mill area (NY76S) provided the peak count of 103 birds. A high concentration of garden feeding stations was noted in this latter area perhaps increasing its appeal to Blackbirds. (S. Hingston pers. comm.*)*. No other inland ten kilometre square came near to matching these numbers although many contained similar habitats. Blackbirds were recorded in 51 of the 60 control tetrads covered during the survey period. Their high winter numbers remained remarkably consistent in many of these tetrads, displaying overall an average per occupied tetrad of 13 in 1996/97, 12 in 1997/98 and 11 in 1998/99.

Perhaps the most unfortunate bird found in the survey was one that was seen dead in the talons of a Peregrine *Falco peregrinus* in Upper Coquetdale! Despite this, all the trends suggest that the Blackbird will continue to be an abundant and familiar species in Northumberland during the winter.

LINDSAY J. McDOUGALL

Distribution by altitude

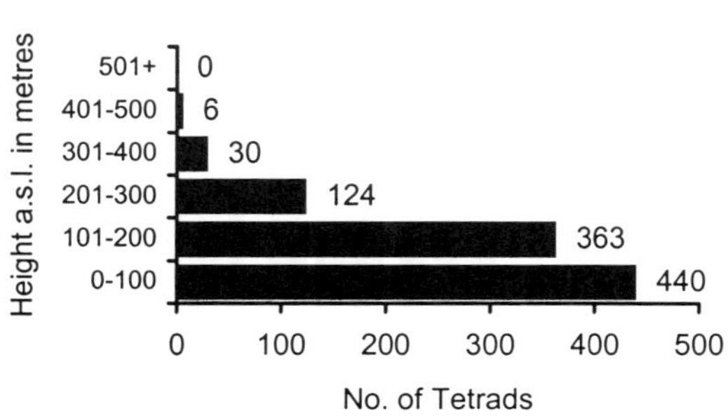

No. of tetrads in which recorded 963 (67%)

Tetrad Analysis	No. of tetrads
1-8 birds	509 (53%)
9-16 birds	256 (26%)
17+ birds	198 (21%)

Total No. of birds counted 11,107

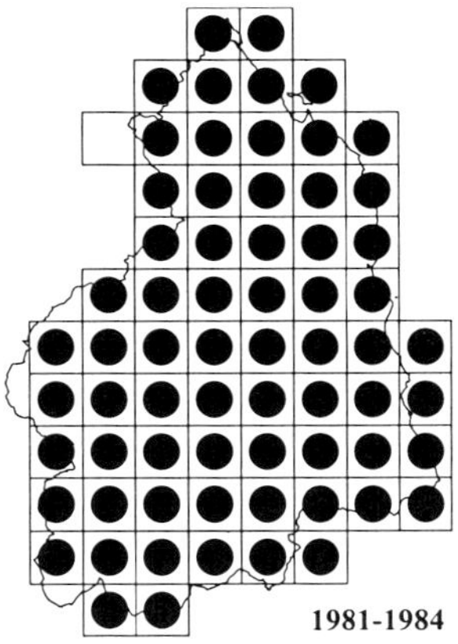

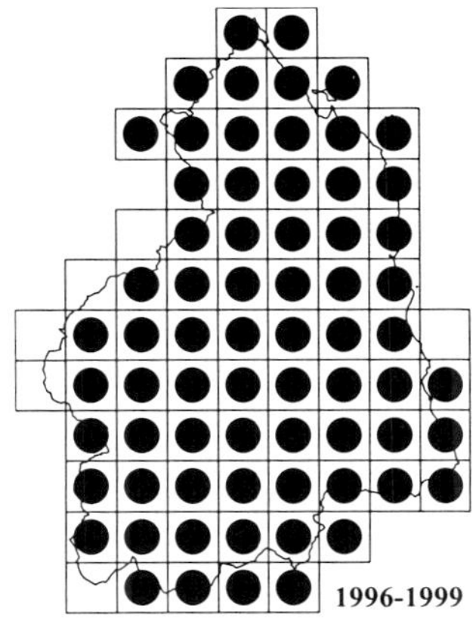

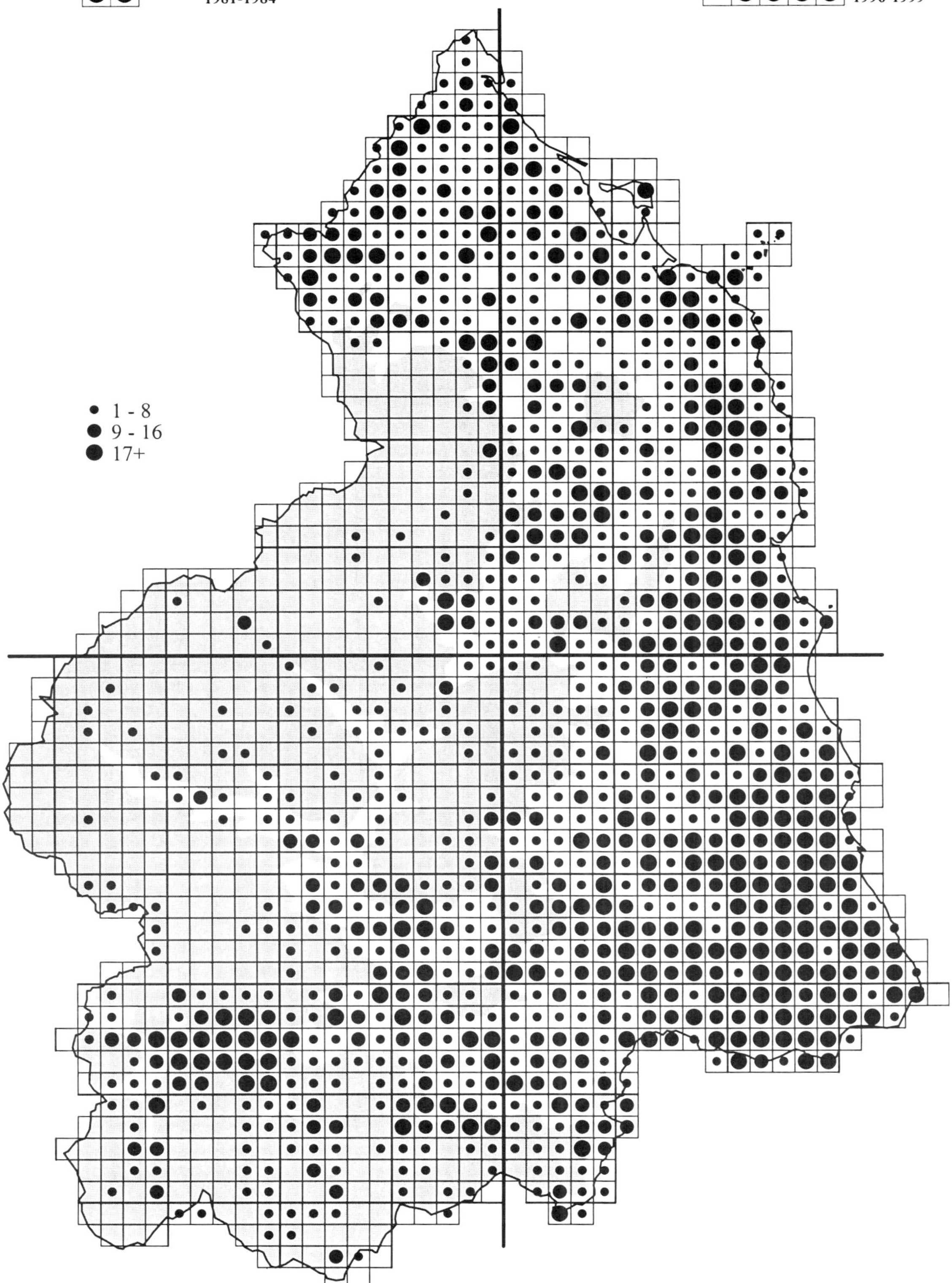

Blackbird

FIELDFARE *Turdus pilaris*

Locally, Hancock (1874) described the Fieldfare as 'an abundant winter visitant, arriving in October and not departing till late in spring' and this description has remained true throughout the twentieth century. Indeed Galloway and Meek (1983) were able to be even more specific in extending its status to one of 'an abundant passage and winter visitor which may have bred'.

Ringing recoveries (though very few in number) correlate with the view expressed by Cramp (1988) that most of our birds come from northern Sweden and Norway. Norman (1994) said 'They move in a south-west direction into Britain, Ireland, central Europe, South-west France, North-west Spain and Portugal and rarely to North-west Italy'. Studies in Scandinavia indicate that the time of departure of Fieldfare populations depends upon the abundance of the Rowan *Sorbus aucuparia* fruit crop there (Tyrvainen, 1975) although birds can remain well into the winter if food supplies are adequate but, when the temperature drops and food becomes scarce, migration to this country commences.

Fieldfares usually arrive from mid-September and reach a peak in October/November. On their arrival birds move rapidly inland and take up winter quarters. By December most are to be found in the upper river valleys, lower moorland slopes and pastureland, where they remain until either hard weather or a diminishing food supply forces them to move on. This current winter survey shows a marked preference for the south west of the county, where, in the NY quadrant which consists mainly of Hexhamshire, the South Tyne and West and East Allendales, 44% of the total was found. Flocks usually avoid land over 450 metres a.s.l. and coniferous plantations (except for roosting) and feed gregariously, often associating with Starlings *Sturnus vulgaris* and Redwings *Turdus iliacus* on alluvial river plains and lightly wooded pasture land. The largest and most frequent counts were recorded around Harbottle and Alwinton (NT90), Bellingham (NY88), Haltwhistle (NY76), the Matfen area (NZ07) and the central Northumbrian plain, most of which lies below 250 metres a.s.l.

During the period of the survey, count/flock numbers varied greatly in size but in most instances numbers recorded were much higher than those of Redwing. Many instances were recorded of flocks of more than 350 and in one exceptional case of 1,500. Whilst survey returns gave a total number of Fieldfare in each tetrad this was not necessarily a figure relating to flock size. Nevertheless, tetrad counts provide an interesting density figure that is overall much higher than that for Redwing. In 219 tetrads (44%) there were counts of between five and 39 birds and in a further 130 tetrads (25%) between 40 and 90 individuals. Greater numbers, between 100 and 299, were also counted in 25% of the tetrads where the species was present, with 25 tetrads (5%) holding between 300 and 1,000. These high numbers probably indicate the reluctance of Fieldfare to move on, in comparison to Redwing, as they remain in these areas until either the food supply is exhausted or excessive hard weather arrives. If either of these occur, they move further south in the country seeking shelter and fresh food supplies. As spring migration calls, Fieldfares gather in large flocks to begin the return to Scandinavia, usually in March/April, though some delay their departure until May.

The winter feeding habits of Fieldfares, and the benefit to the farming community, were commented upon by Lack (1986) as was their high mortality, in comparison with Blackbird *Turdus merula*, in severe winters. Whilst Bolam (1912) made reference to local winter fatalities there was no evidence for this during the current fieldwork, all three winter periods being comparatively mild. Analysis of control tetrad data indicates both the itinerant nature of the species and, presumably, the availability of suitable food. Out of a total of 42 control tetrads in which Fieldfares were located they were present in only two tetrads in comparable numbers in each of the three winter visits, these being Sharperton/Holystone (NT90L) with 20, 90 and 30 being counted and in the Ramshaw Fell area (NY76A) with 33, 87 and 74.

Of the 1,432 tetrads visited during this atlas survey, Fieldfares were present in 609 (43%). The survey produced a maximum count of 43,977 birds but, since some of these would have been recorded more than once, it seems a total of 15,000-20,000 might give a more accurate picture of the wintering numbers of the species in Northumberland.

MICHAEL BELL

Distribution by altitude

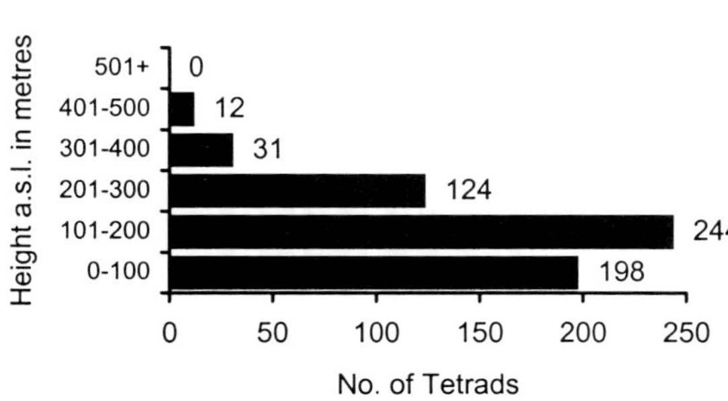

No. of tetrads in which recorded 609 (43%)

Tetrad Analysis	No. of tetrads
1-30 birds	297 (49%)
31-100 birds	190 (31%)
101+ birds	122 (20%)

Total No. of birds counted 43,977

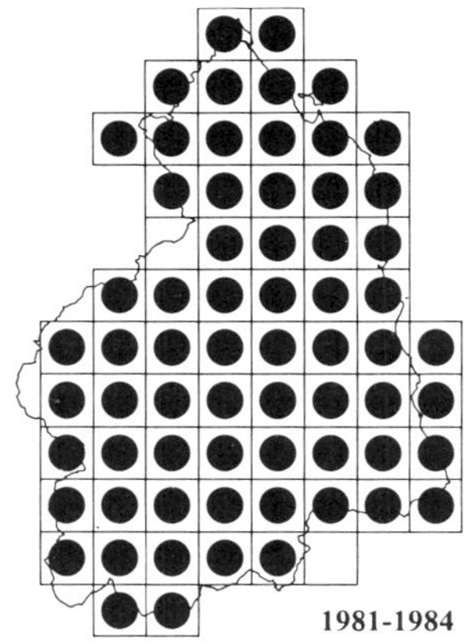

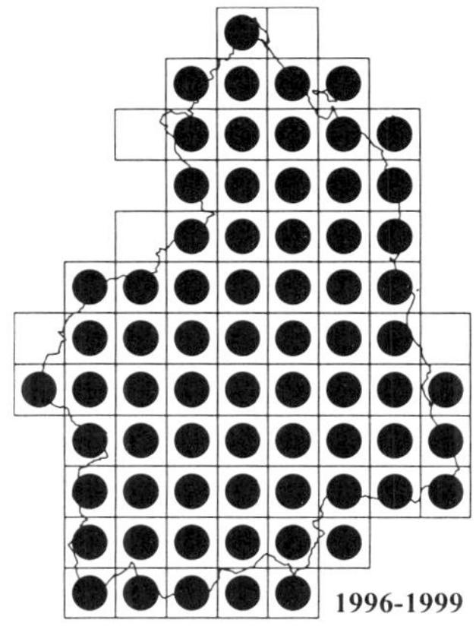

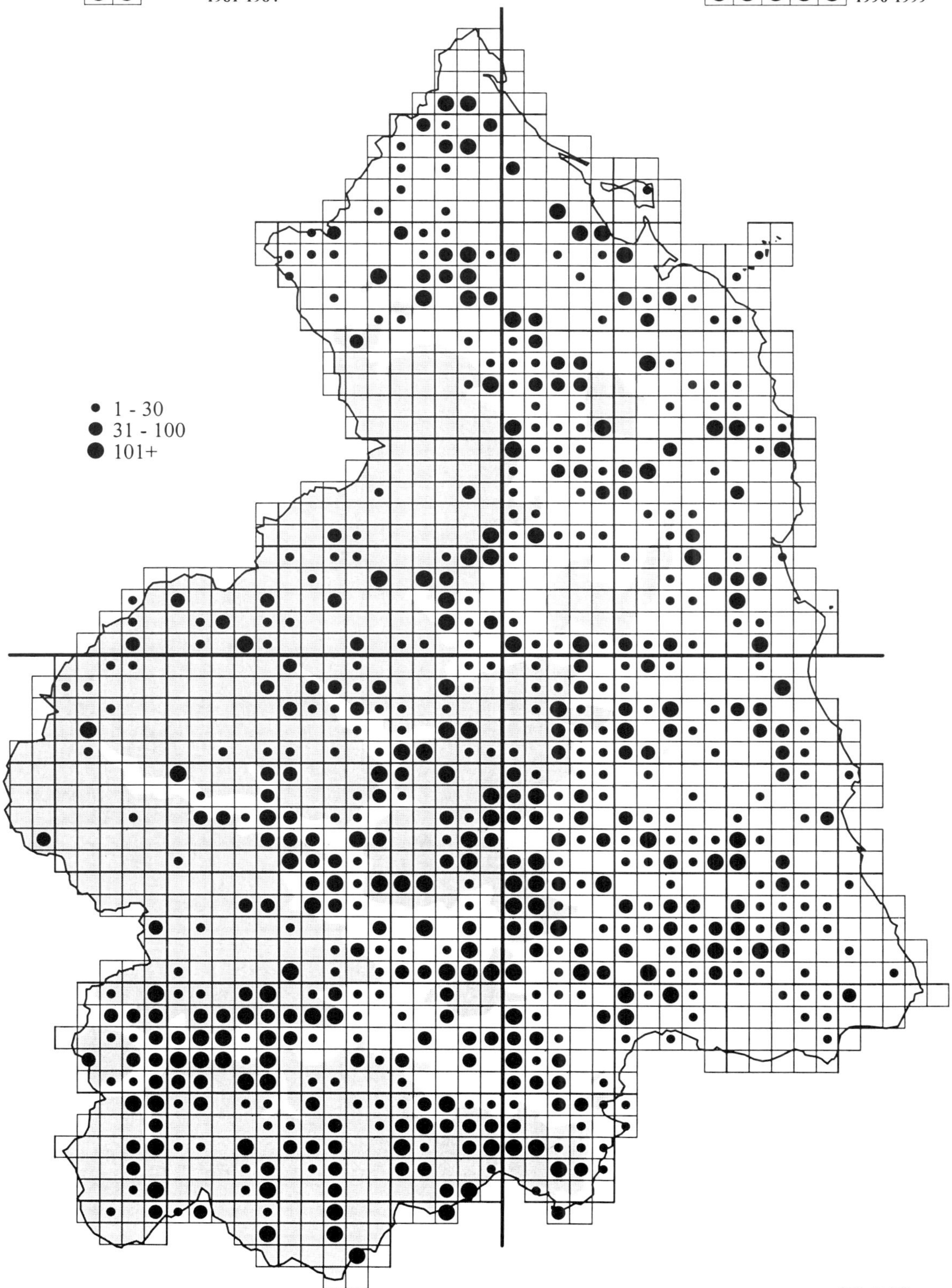

Fieldfare

SONG THRUSH *Turdus philomelos*

Bolam (1912) described the Song Thrush as a well-known resident. Over 70 years later Galloway and Meek (1983) confirmed this status, describing it as a common breeding resident and passage visitor. Since the mid-1970s the Song Thrush has been in a long-term national decline and despite recent increases, Mead (2000) identified the species as one of conservation concern and uncertain future. In Northumberland, however, it was recorded in most of the 10km squares in this current survey, as it had been during the 1981-1984 national winter survey.

In winter, Song Thrushes feed on earthworms, weather permitting, and fruits but unlike other thrushes they also feed on large or medium-sized snails, especially in harsh weather when they can be seen breaking open the shells by hammering the snail against a stone or other hard surface. Song Thrushes are particularly vulnerable to cold weather but past losses have generally been made good after several mild winters. The severe winters of the late 1970s and early 1980s were responsible for some reduction in numbers nationally but weather conditions alone do not account for its continued decline thereafter. Other factors such as changes in agricultural practices, food supply and the ability of young birds to survive the winter also need to be examined.

British Song Thrushes are partial migrants, with the proportion of the breeding population that migrate increasing the further north one moves. In Northumberland this results in a significant proportion of the breeding population leaving the county in winter. This probably accounts for the absence of birds in the upland areas where they would be vulnerable to lower temperatures and makes the species very much a lowland bird during the winter months. Indeed, 89% of the tetrads they were recorded in lay below 201 metres a.s.l. However, by February, birds are already starting to return to breeding sites on higher ground as illustrated by three of the larger counts during the survey near Ordley (NY95J, NY95P) with 11 and 22 birds and near Carterway Heads (NZ05K) with 12 birds respectively. The Song Thrush, though, does not confine itself to broad-leaved woodlands, favouring any type of habitat with trees and bushes (for breeding) as shown by smaller numbers present in coniferous plantations during the survey, most notably in the Kielder Forest area. The south east part of the county has the largest winter population of Song Thrushes with counts of nearly half the birds recorded during the survey and, therefore, not surprisingly almost half the tetrads with four or more birds. The highest density was in and around Newcastle with Wallsend (NZ26Y) holding 11 birds, the area to the south of Gosforth Park (NZ26P) with ten and the Jesmond Dene area (NZ26T) with 11 producing the biggest counts. The latter area was also the only one to consistently record higher than average counts for occupied control tetrads over the three-year survey period.

The Song Thrush was recorded in 443 tetrads (31%) during the current winter survey compared with 963 tetrads (68%) in the local breeding atlas survey (Day *et al.*, 1995). The major difference is in those tetrads containing land above183 metres a.s.l., 60% being occupied during the breeding season but only 15% in winter. The decrease in the number of occupied tetrads in the lowland areas is much less and the highest densities of both breeding and wintering birds are in and around Newcastle.

Day *et al.* (1995) suggested that a county breeding population of 2,659 pairs might be on the low side due to the difficulty of surveying extensive coniferous habitat and this same difficulty is probably relevant to the current winter survey. Lack (1986) stated that, overall, 48% of adults and 64% of first year birds migrate with a higher proportion than this in the north. The winter population in the county may be boosted by late autumn immigrants and to a lesser extent by early spring passage birds but ringing returns noted in *Birds in Northumbria* tend to confirm that the majority of winter arrivals move on. Considering that the Song Thrush is visually less conspicuous in winter, the total of 1,007 birds recorded during the current winter survey may reasonably correlate to the breeding population numbers when long-term decline trends and more recent increases as suggested by Mead (2000) are also taken into consideration.

TONY BAKER

Distribution by altitude

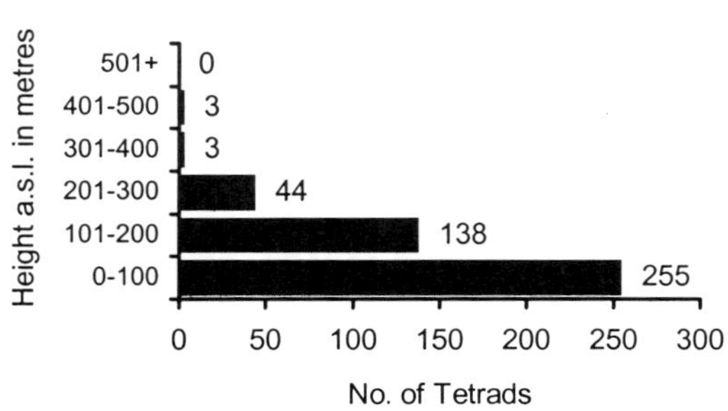

No. of tetrads in which recorded 443 (31%)

Tetrad Analysis	No. of tetrads
1 bird	227 (51%)
2-3 birds	148 (34%)
4+ birds	68 (15%)

Total No. of birds counted 1,007

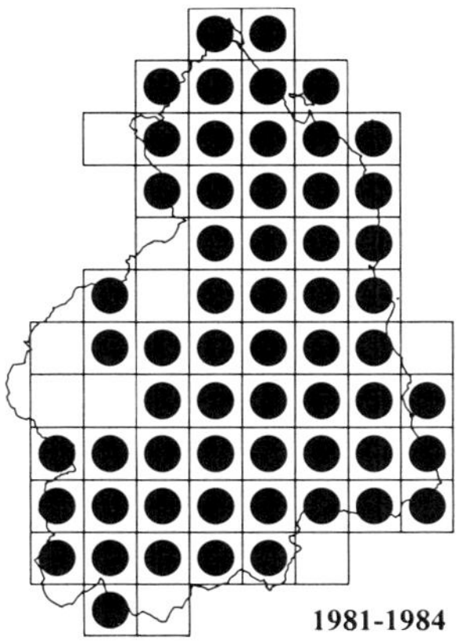

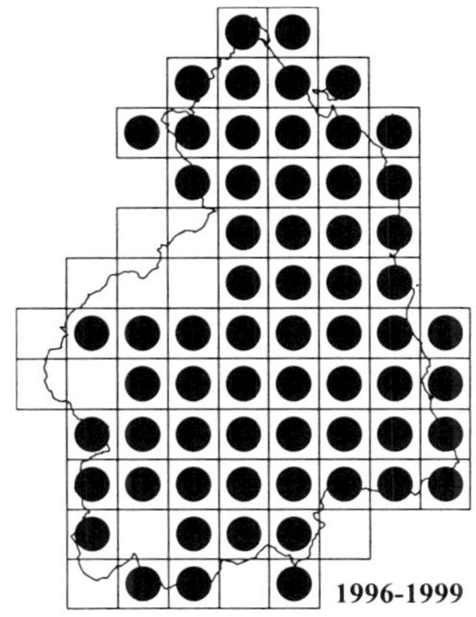

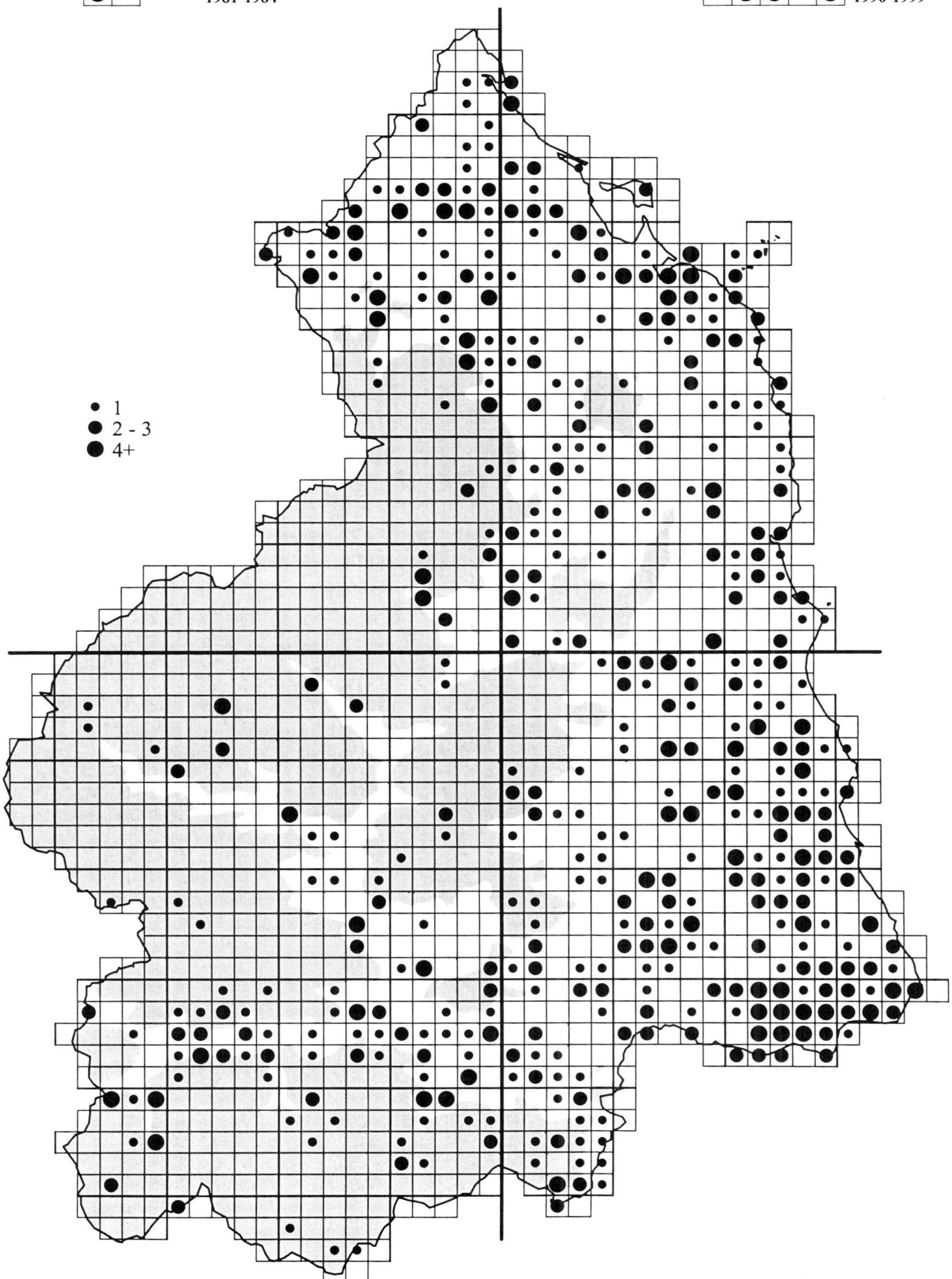

Song Thrush

REDWING *Turdus iliacus*

The arrival and passage of large numbers of thrushes through the county is an annual autumn spectacle. The birds which arrive in Northumberland are mainly of the Eurasian race that winter south of Scotland, coastal Norway, the south east Baltic and in areas around the Mediterranean, Black and Caspian Seas. At the beginning of the twentieth century Bolam (1912) wrote that it was 'a common and regular visitant' and there is nothing to suggest that this status has changed, other than occasional breeding records in recent years (Day *et al.*, 1995).

The autumn movement out of Sweden, Norway and Finland occurs between late September and mid-November. These nocturnal migrants are usually plentiful during the first three weeks in October, and for the most part quickly move on, many remaining for less than 24 hours. Perhaps even more than Fieldfares *Turdus pilaris*, Redwings tend to be nomadic in winter, moving widely in response to weather conditions and availability of food. Few remain later in the winter, as the species is well known to be vulnerable to cold weather. The largest count in a single tetrad during the survey was 500 birds at Kirkheaton (NZ07D). This count was perhaps unusual as an analysis of tetrad numbers during the three winter seasons demonstrates that the number in each tetrad, whilst not necessarily referring to one flock, nevertheless gives some idea of the size of parties present or passing through during the winter months. In all, there were 370 tetrads in which between five and 500 birds were recorded. The breakdown of these statistics indicates that in 263 tetrads (70%) there were between five and 39 birds, 70 tetrads (19%) held between 40 and 99, 34 tetrads (10%) between 100 and 299 with only three tetrads (0.8%) containing in excess of 300 birds. Tetrad counts were usually of a much lower order than those recorded for Fieldfare (*q.v.*). Nor do Redwings always return to the same areas in winter, as ringing has shown that they can be here one year and in the Balkans the next. Data from the 39 control tetrads in which they were recorded during the survey appear to confirm the erratic occupation of wintering areas, as 17 were apparently occupied in only one winter, 17 in two winters and only five in all three winter periods, while total counts of 450, 526 and 261 respectively seem to indicate that they were much scarcer in the last season. However, because of the small data set, it would perhaps be best to treat these figures with caution.

The Redwings that remain in our county are usually found on much lower ground than that used by Fieldfares. This is exemplified by the fact that over the three winters, 6% of the total maximum counts were recorded in the north west quadrant (NT), where there are the Cheviot Hills and large areas of coniferous forest, compared to the south east quadrant (NZ) where 44% of the maximum total was located. Small flocks were recorded throughout the coastal plain and along the North and South Tyne Valleys, numbers becoming smaller the nearer the Scottish border. Emigration can take place from late February, especially in mild winters, and passage may extend into April but only a few linger until May (Galloway & Meek, 1983).

In mild winters Redwings forage much in open fields for earthworms but, unlike Fieldfares, in cold weather they regularly feed on the ground in woodland. As fruit eaters, on arrival in this county they feed in flocks on hedgerow haws, though Richards (1977) recorded that new arrivals on Holy Island appeared largely to eat snails. Stomach analysis has shown that 86% of fruit eaten consists of Hawthorn.

Of the 1,432 tetrads surveyed during this winter atlas, Redwings were recorded in 511 (36%). The survey produced a maximum total count of 14,442 birds. Taking into account the fact that many of the Redwings present in November and December often move out of our county, it seems reasonable to speculate that a total of 10,000 would give a fairly accurate picture of the winter population of this species in Northumberland, even allowing for some duplication of counts in neighbouring tetrads. As the annual wintering total for Great Britain has been various estimated at one million by Lack (1986) and later at 750,000 by Stone *et al.* (1997), the Northumberland population is not insignificant.

MICHAEL BELL

Distribution by altitude

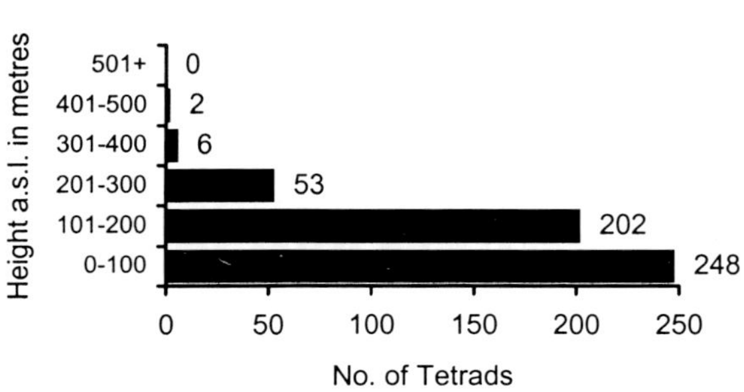

No. of tetrads in which recorded 511 (36%)

Tetrad Analysis	No. of tetrads
1-10 birds	251 (49%)
11-39 birds	153 (30%)
40+ birds	107 (21%)

Total No. of birds counted 14,442

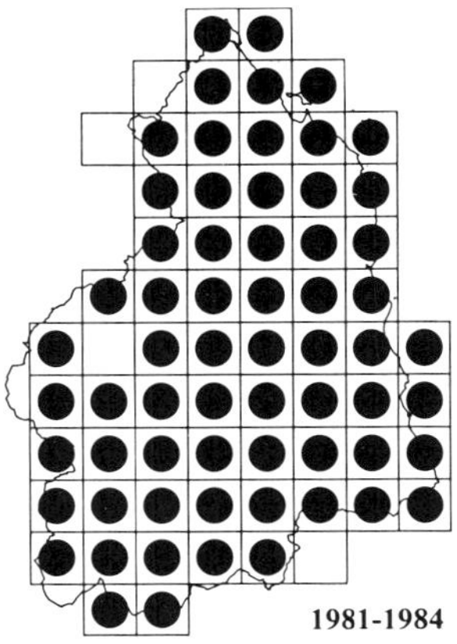

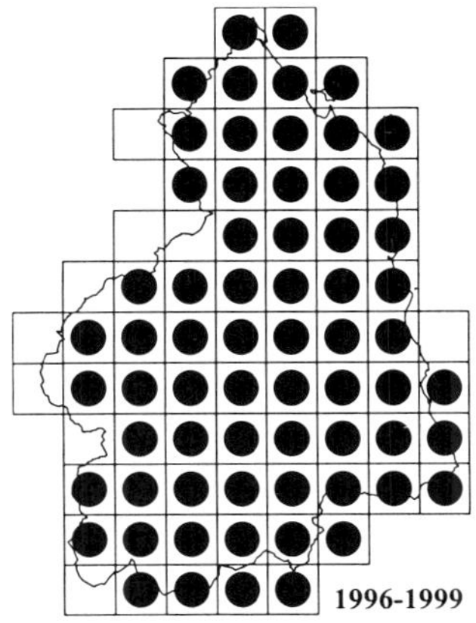

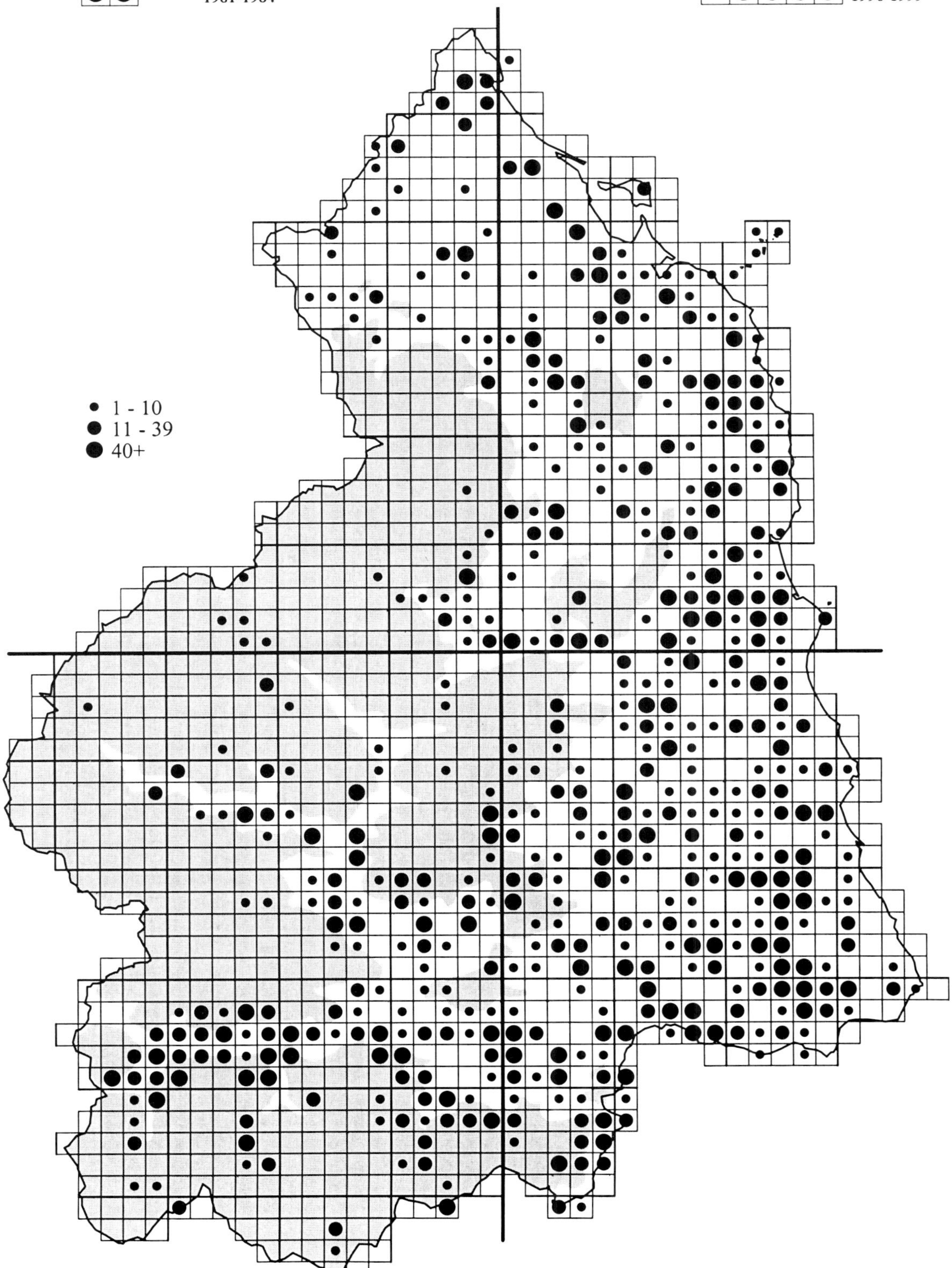

Redwing

MISTLE THRUSH *Turdus viscivorus*

During the nineteenth century the Mistle Thrush spread northwards through England and into Scotland and has now become one of the most widely distributed species in Britain. In Northumberland, Selby (1831) noted that 'this species within the last ten or fifteen years has become very common' and by 1932 Bolam regarded it as 'a resident, common and well-known throughout the county' whilst Galloway and Meek (1983) referred to it as 'a well represented passage visitor and common breeding resident'. More recently, Mead (2000) described the bird nationally as being 'on a downwards pointing roller coaster' due perhaps to its poor winter survival rate.

During the winter months the Mistle Thrush is highly dependent upon fruit-bearing trees and shrubs including Hawthorn *Crataegus monogyma*, Buckthorn *Rhamnus catharticus* and Holly *Ilex aquifolium*. Once located, a supply of fruit can be vigorously defended throughout the winter especially by established pairs. In milder winters they, together with other thrushes, exploit alternative food supplies such as earthworms. The BTO Garden Bird Feeding Survey records from the 1970s list the Mistle Thrush as occurring in 34.6% of gardens and rank it 14th in frequency. Recent records from the 1990s show that it is now recorded in only 23.2% of gardens surveyed and its rank has dropped to 26th. This decline is in keeping with the national trend. Locally, the two 10km square maps imply a relatively unchanged distribution for the species as both the 1981-1984 winter survey and this latest survey recorded Mistle Thrushes in 92% of the squares. However, the average number of birds recorded in the control tetrads decreased from 4.0 in 1996/97 to 2.8 in 1998/99.

During the winter survey a total of 2,852 Mistle Thrushes was recorded in 788 tetrads which represents 55% of the number surveyed. Of these, 613 (78%) were below 201 metres a.s.l. and 747 (95%) below 301 metres a.s.l., thus confirming its preference for more lowland habitats in winter. The tetrad distribution map shows the main concentrations to be in the south and east of the county with numbers declining towards the west and in upland regions. The bird is nevertheless fairly well represented in the main river valleys, such as the Tyne and Rede and their tributaries, and in some cases into especially sheltered upper reaches. The urban areas of the south and east are well frequented with their milder winter climate and abundance of suitable food supplies.

Like other thrushes, the Mistle Thrush tends to form small flocks in winter, especially where there is a good supply of fruiting trees and shrubs. Galloway and Meek (1978) noted that large winter flocks were, however, unusual and a record of 28 at Wallington in February 1980 was one of the largest recorded. The county annual reports record exceptional flocks of 120 at Howick in October 1989 and a similar number in the same area in 1998 (*Birds in Northumbria 1989, 1998*). The extent to which this is unusual is illustrated by the fact that in the recent winter survey, counts of ten or more were noted only in 32 tetrads and counts in excess of 20 in only six.

Comparison of the breeding distribution map in *The atlas of breeding birds in Northumbria* (Day *et al.*, 1995) and this winter map shows that there are relatively sedentary lowland and urban populations with more exposed upland areas being deserted during the winter months. Winter populations may increase to some extent with the arrival of small numbers of birds in autumn from continental Europe and recent records that may support this include 35 birds in off the sea at Bamburgh in October 1994 (*Birds in Northumbria 1994*). In the 1988-1992 local breeding survey, Mistle Thrushes were recorded in 95% of the 10km squares compared with 92% during the recent winter survey. The breeding survey also indicated that the total population of the Mistle Thrush in the county was about 1,315 pairs and thus the 2,852 individuals recorded in the current winter survey confirms the status of this species as a common resident in Northumberland.

ALAN J. DAVIS

Distribution by altitude

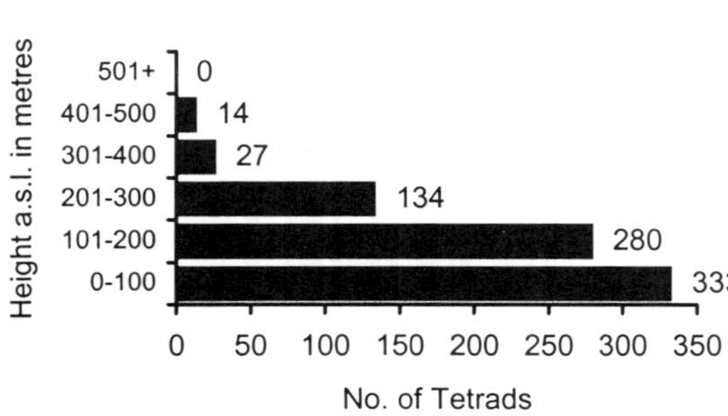

No. of tetrads in which recorded 788 (55%)

Tetrad Analysis	No. of tetrads
1-2 birds	402 (51%)
3-5 birds	245 (31%)
6+ birds	141 (18%)

Total No. of birds counted 2,852

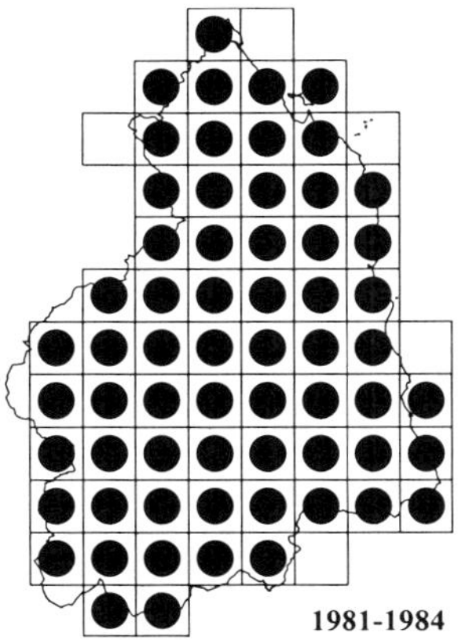

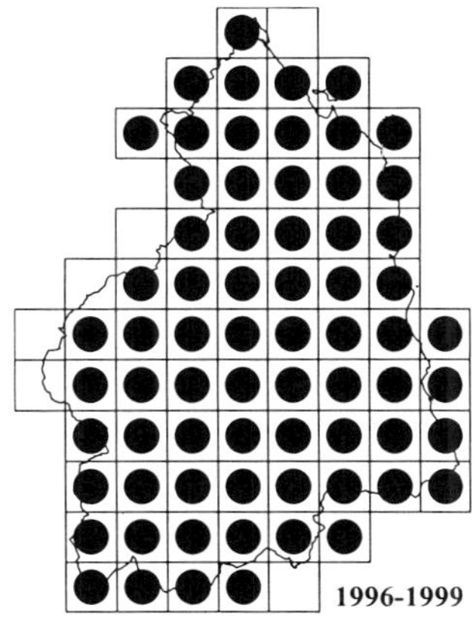

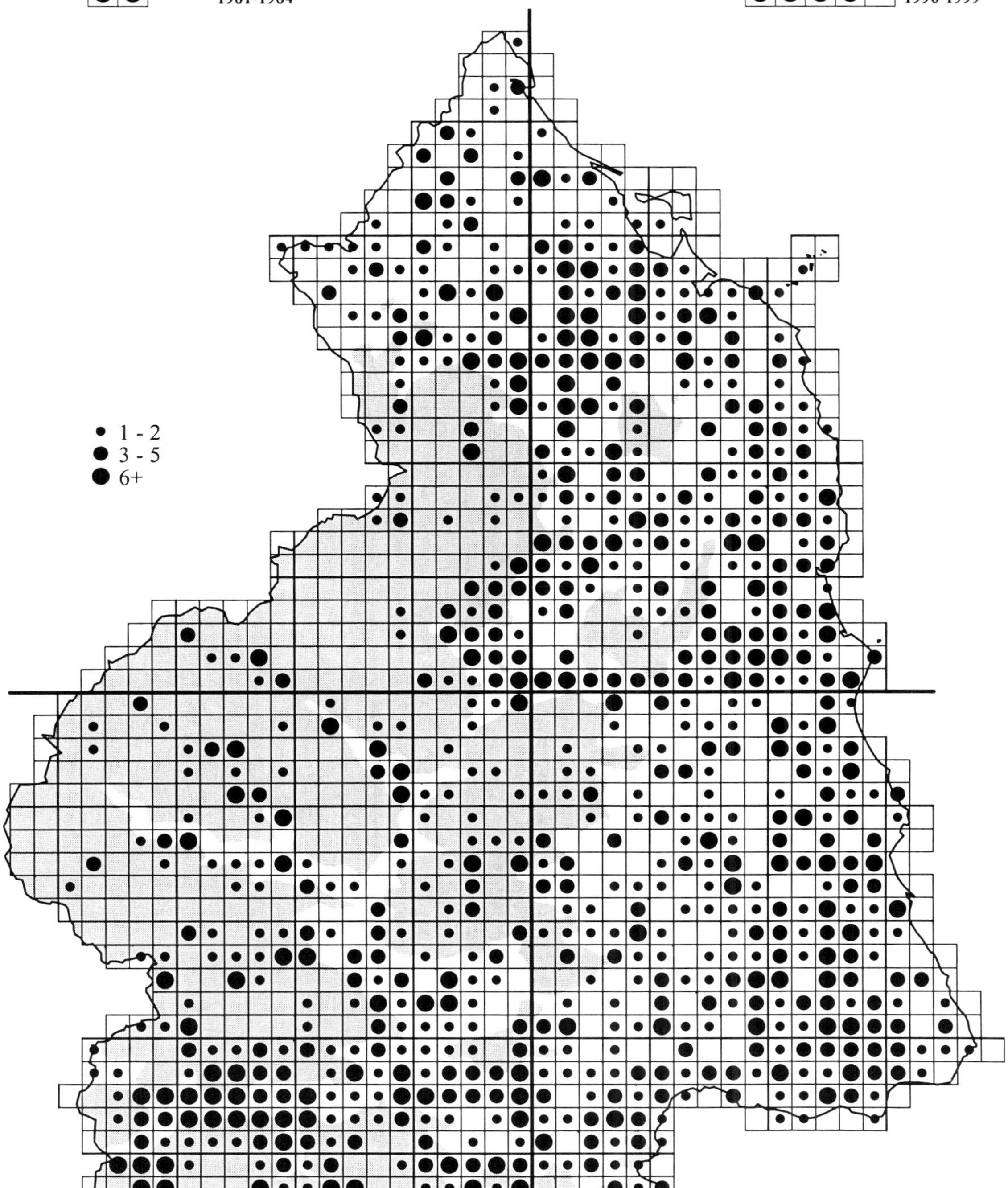

Mistle Thrush

BLACKCAP *Sylvia atricapilla*

Despite its inconspicuous appearance and skulking habits, the Blackcap is well known for its forceful song and as a breeding bird throughout the county. Its status as a winter visitor and the origin of individuals involved, however, has only recently been established and explained. Bolam (1912) remarked that individuals appear occasionally to winter in the district, although his only example of a truly wintering bird in Northumberland was one at Powburn in March 1909. Later he mentioned a male at Twizell House which was found dead on 9th January 1921 (Bolam, 1932). The next bird, in 1943, was reported by Galloway and Meek (1983) who went on to observe that 'since 1948 Blackcaps have been seen in most years between December and February ... Many of the birds reported have been feeding at bird tables in urban, and especially suburban areas'.

It has been established that wintering Blackcaps in Britain are of continental origin, probably from breeding populations in southern Germany and Austria (Lack, 1986; Mason, 1995). Ringing records reveal 95 recoveries in winter of Blackcaps ringed during the breeding season on the continent but no recoveries of British breeders (Bertold & Terrill, 1988). Whilst the highest numbers of records are in January and February, wintering Blackcaps arrive along the east coast during late autumn, giving rise to individuals seen in November in typical woodland and scrub habitats. During this time their diet consists of natural food such as insects and berries (Lack, 1986). It is only in late winter and during cold spells that they take refuge in gardens and depend upon food provided at bird tables. It is at this time that they are most easily seen and recorded.

The presence of a wintering population in the county was demonstrated by the 1981-1984 winter atlas survey which recorded Blackcaps in 34% of the 10km squares compared with 27% of those in the recent winter survey. Whilst the number of 10km squares in which Blackcaps were recorded seems to have declined slightly, the distribution remains very much unchanged. During the recent survey, maximum counts revealed a total of 57 Blackcaps in 43 tetrads representing 3% of the number surveyed. Virtually all of these were in lowland habitats with 81% of occupied tetrads being below 100 metres a.s.l. The main distribution of sightings was along the coast and in the urban and suburban areas of the Tyne Valley, Newcastle upon Tyne and North Tyneside. During the three years of the survey, the monthly distribution of records mirrors the national pattern. Of the 57 records, 13 were in November, 14 in December, 23 in January and only seven in February. Records from *Birds in Northumbria 1972-1999* confirm that the majority of individuals are recorded in January, mainly from gardens and regular wintering habitats such as Jesmond Dene. Nationally there seems to be a fairly constant sex imbalance with 40% of records being females (Lack, 1996). However, the recent local winter survey recorded 17 males and 20 females with 20 unspecified.

The location of records during the three winter periods fits the pattern of birds arriving on the coast in late autumn and moving inland to urban and suburban areas as the winter progresses. In nine tetrads where Blackcaps were recorded in November, eight were on or within 10km of the coast at such places as the Farne Islands, Alnmouth and Newbiggin. In December, six records were from tetrads in coastal areas. However, three were 10-20 km and four 20-30 km from the coast, suggesting a gradual move inland. In January, birds were recorded from a total of 17 tetrads and, whilst some were still in coastal areas, three were from tetrads 30-40 km from the coast and two from tetrads over 40 km away, all mainly along the Tyne Valley. Finally in February, Blackcaps were only recorded from four tetrads, all of which were in urban or suburban areas and generally closer to the coast. It is therefore likely that the total number of Blackcaps wintering in the county is much less that the total number of records as the same individuals may be reported in different months and in different locations. Undoubtedly Blackcaps find that, unlike their breeding grounds in continental Europe, our milder climate and availability of alternative food sources provide a suitable habitat in which to spend the winter and far preferable to a long migration to Mediterranean regions. As a result, the Blackcap has become a welcome and more regular sight during the winter in suitable parts of the county.

ALAN J. DAVIS

Distribution by altitude

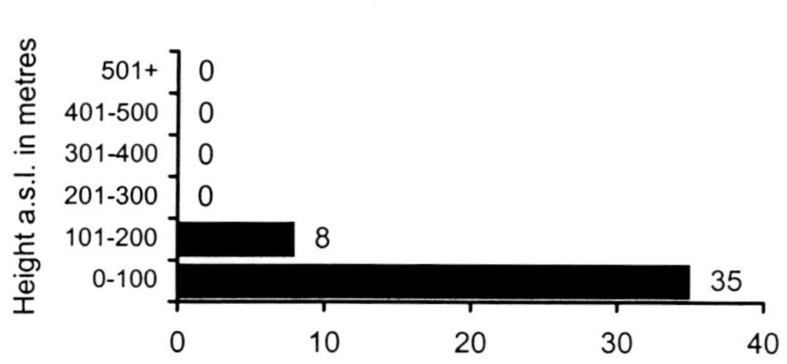

No. of tetrads in which recorded 43 (3%)

Tetrad Analysis	No. of tetrads
1 bird	32 (74%)
2 birds	8 (19%)
3 birds	3 (7%)

Total No. of birds counted 57

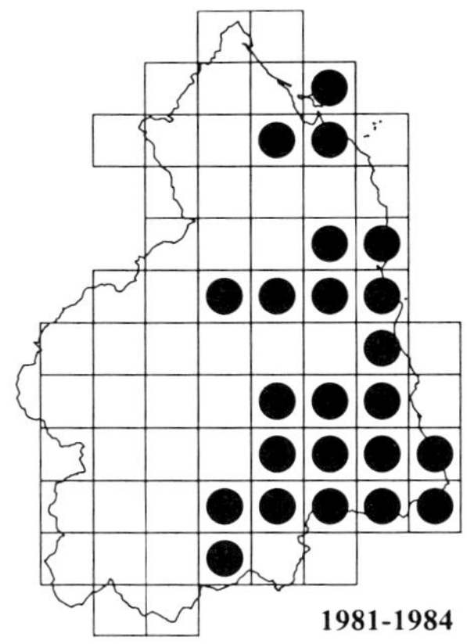

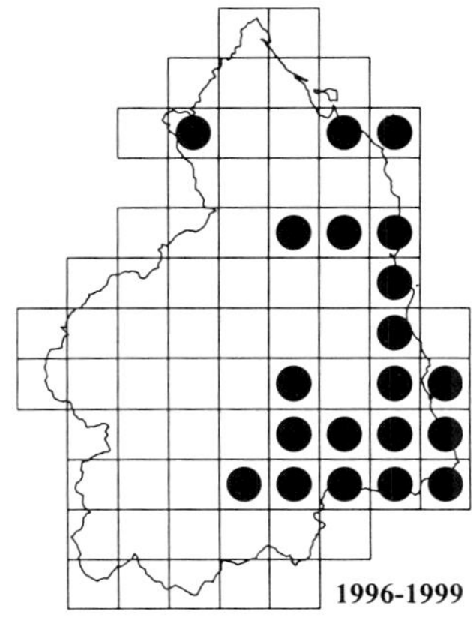

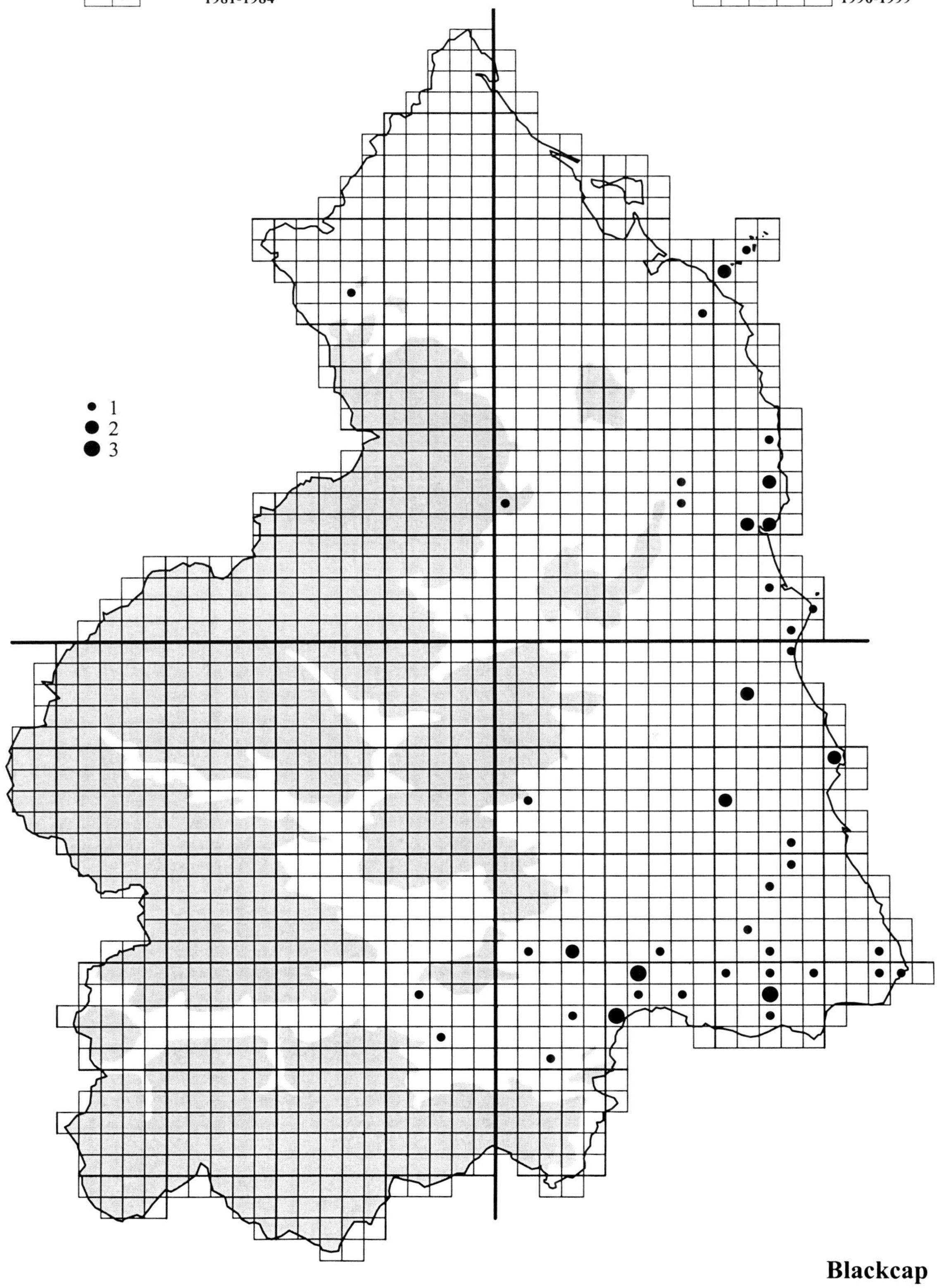

Blackcap

CHIFFCHAFF *Phylloscopus collybita*

In Northumberland, the Chiffchaff is a well-represented breeding summer and passage visitor which is rare in winter (Kerr, 2001). Autumn passage usually begins during August and continues throughout September and October. Lingering birds or late visitors are reported annually during November and even into December, usually in single or occasionally in double figures and, as in November 1988, in three figures when a late influx of around a hundred birds was reported along the coast. In most years, in addition to these late visitors, a small number remains in the county throughout the winter. Locally, Bolam (1932) referred to birds at Berwick and Cullercoats in winter and Galloway and Meek (1983) mentioned rare but regular winter sightings. Chiffchaffs were recorded in 20 out of the 24 winters between 1975/76 and 1998/99, usually between one and four individuals although there were possibly up to ten in 1996/97, up to nine in 1980/81 and up to eight in 1986/87 and 1997/98 (*Birds in Northumbria 1975-2000*). During the current winter survey a maximum of 44 Chiffchaffs was recorded in 36 tetrads. They were present down the length of the coast, and just inland, from Spittal in the north to Tynemouth in the south as well as in and around Newcastle, with a couple of reported sightings further west. The earlier records were mostly on the coast, suggesting late passage birds whilst later records, including the wintering birds, tended to be further inland. Although wintering birds have been recorded on or near the coast, and November birds are regularly recorded from inland sites in the south east, this is a general pattern to emerge from the last 24 winters.

Wintering Chiffchaffs must be able to find sufficient food and adequate shelter in order to survive. In parts of the country, sheltered areas such as thick hedgerows, thornscrub or reedbeds provide a micro-climate which offers a degree of protection against freezing night temperatures (Clement, 1995). In Northumberland this protection is largely provided by suburban gardens. Additionally, because they retain an entirely insectivorous diet through the winter, Chiffchaffs are often reported close to areas of water, which are warm enough to sustain insect life. In Northumberland, for example, this makes the gardens of Wideopen, with their close proximity to Big Waters, or the gardens of Morpeth adjacent to the sewage works, potentially attractive sites. However, whilst there are regular wintering sites in southern England, where average temperatures are higher, there are no identifiable regular sites in Northumberland. Birds have been recorded as far north as Berwick, as far south as Ebchester and as far west as Hexham, nearly always in suburban gardens or near to water, e.g. near Wallsend Swallow Pond (NZ26Z) where up to four birds over-wintered in 1996/97.

Apart from a single case in Ireland where a ringing recovery indicated a wintering bird of local origin, there is no other evidence to suggest that it is primarily local birds that over-winter. Analysis of the records in southern England reveals that most Chiffchaffs arrive at the wintering site in the middle or at the end of November, suggesting late or delayed passage (Clement, 1995). In Northumberland, because there are no regular wintering sites, it is not possible to make this analysis. On two occasions though, birds have been reported in December and remained at the same site throughout January and February at Marden Quarry in 1988/89 and Wallsend Swallow Pond in 1996/97, which may suggest late passage birds. Whilst the majority of late and wintering birds are of the nominate race, they are sometimes joined by other late autumn migrants belonging to the Scandinavian race *P. c. abietinus* and the Siberian race *P. c. tristis*. The first definite English record of a *tristis* individual was one shot on Holy Island in November 1923. Since the 1980s most county records of *tristis*, *abietinus* and those classed only as 'eastern' birds have been in November. Exceptions to this during the current survey include an *abietinus* reported in the Castle Island area (NZ28X) on 27th December 1996 and a *tristis* at Wallsend Swallow Pond in February 1997.

A comparison of the two 10km square maps would suggest a considerable increase in the distribution and numbers of wintering Chiffchaffs in the county, with 10% of squares occupied between 1981-1984 as opposed to 24% during the current survey. Nationally the numbers of wintering Chiffchaffs in Britain have increased during the past 30 years (Clement, 1995). According to Lack (1986) the vast majority of wintering Chiffchaffs, which may be around five hundred in a normal year in Britain and Ireland and more than a thousand in milder winters, are concentrated south of a line from the Wash to the Mersey. The Northumberland winter population, therefore, usually forms less than 1% of this total.

TONY BAKER

Distribution by altitude

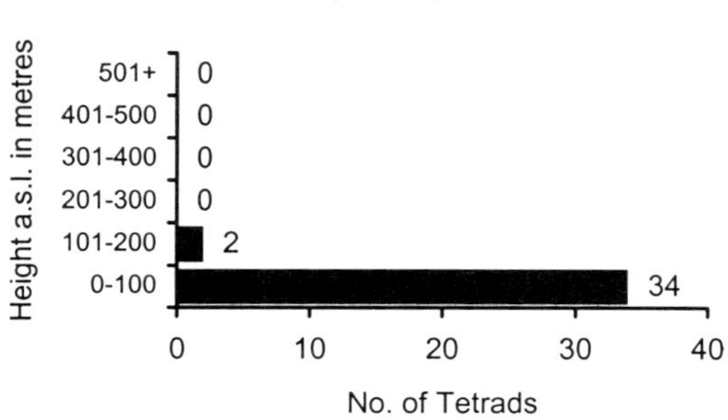

No. of tetrads in which recorded 36 (3%)

Tetrad Analysis	No. of tetrads
1 bird	32 (89%)
2 birds	2 (6%)
3+ birds	2 (5%)

Total No. of birds counted 44

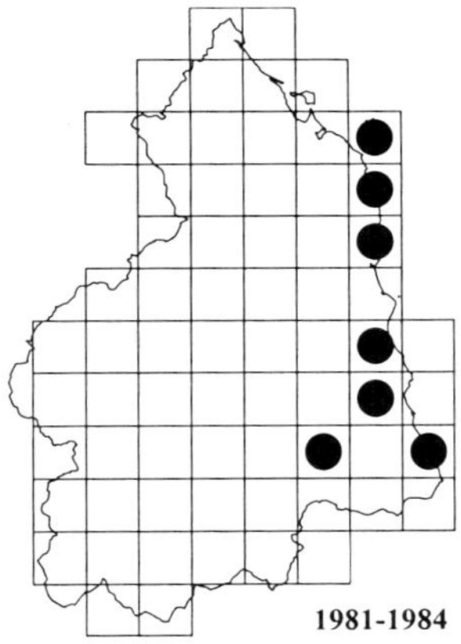

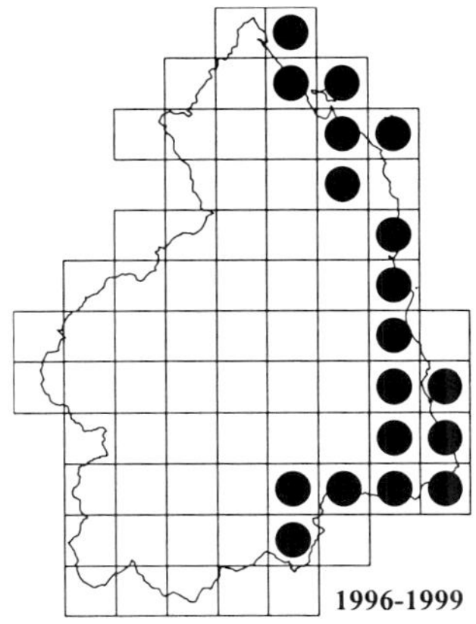

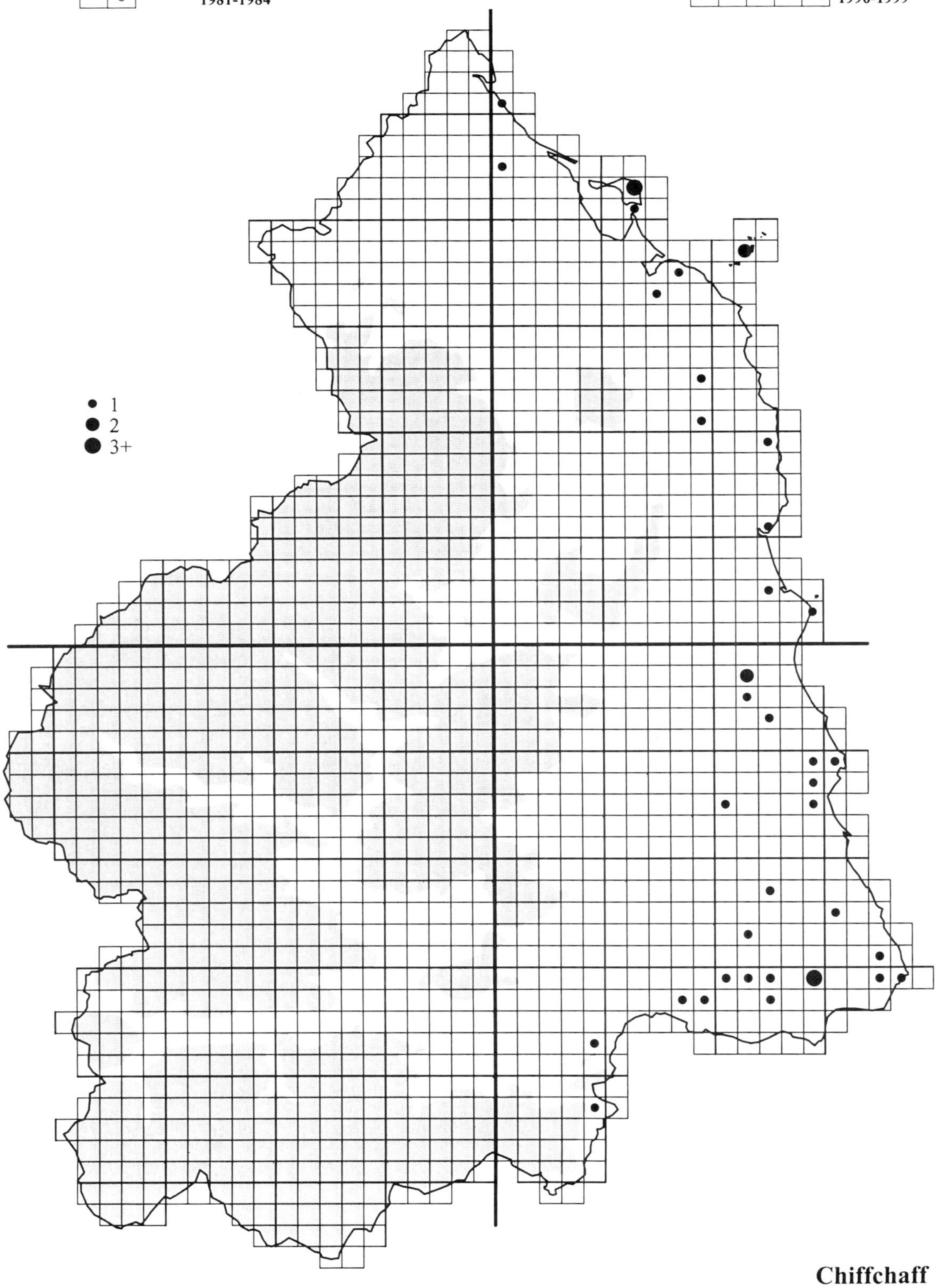

Chiffchaff

GOLDCREST *Regulus regulus*

Over the three seasons of this winter atlas survey, a grand total of 3,817 Goldcrests was recorded in 747 tetrads. Galloway and Meek (1983) quoted Selby, who in 1831 had written that the Goldcrest was 'common in all our plantations, particularly those abounding in larch and fir'. They further commented that 'these words have remained true for a hundred and fifty years although today it is probably even more common as a breeding species'. There is certainly a discrepancy in numbers of Goldcrests between *The atlas of breeding birds in Northumbria* (Day *et al.*, 1995) and those of this survey, with 3,713 breeding pairs compared to 3,817 individuals during the winter period. In fact the estimated breeding population in Northumberland was given as between 50,000 and 75,000 pairs! It must be noted, however, that Goldcrests prove harder to survey in the winter period, particularly in dense coniferous areas, and this will no doubt account for some under-recording.

Whilst the Goldcrest is probably most noticeable, and the subject of considerable interest, during autumn 'falls' on the coast, it is usually found in small foraging flocks in coniferous forests during the winter period. Bolam wrote in 1932 that the Golden-Crested Wren is a 'common resident wherever fir woods prevail'. The winter atlas data reinforce his findings some 70 years later, in that individuals predominate in the now well established coniferous forest in Northumberland.

Goldcrests were well recorded throughout the Kielder (NY68) and Redesdale (NT70) Forests, around Minsteracres (NZ05), and in the Thrunton Wood area (NU00), all of which contain extensive conifer forest. The control tetrad data collected also confirmed its status in coniferous woodland with, for example, maxima of 25 individuals in one tetrad in the Harwood Forest (NY99V) and 12 at Hawkhope in the Kielder Forest (NY78E). Overall in the county the species is well-represented and was found in 68 out of a possible 75 ten kilometre squares. Few were found in some coastal areas like Craster and Beadnell due to an absence of suitable habitat. Elevation is also a factor in winter distribution with fewer birds being found over 300 metres a.s.l. and more tetrads occupied in the lowland agricultural areas than is the case during the breeding season. During the survey period they were found in 650 tetrads between 0 and 300 metres a.s.l. representing 87% of the total of 747 occupied tetrads. Thus the species remains loyal to coniferous forests, which in Northumberland have been the subject of vast expansion as reported by Galloway and Meek (1983). They also commented on the devastating effects on the Goldcrest population of severe winters, such as those of 1945/46, 1962/63 and 1978/79. In that we are experiencing a series of milder winters, it will be interesting to see whether this will lead to an increase in the population, alongside habitat improvement. A comparison between the findings of this survey and those in *The atlas of wintering birds in Britain and Ireland* (Lack, 1986), as shown in the two 10km square maps, suggests a slightly broader distribution in the 1990s. The Goldcrest is more catholic in its choice of winter habitat as compared to its breeding territories with birds being found in parkland and gardens such as those in the Hexham, Corbridge and Wall areas (NY96).

During the entire survey period, the maximum count for one tetrad was 46 birds at Broomfield Fell (NZ09Q), an isolated conifer plantation near Rothbury. A further 105 tetrads held between ten and 39 birds although the overall average in occupied tetrads was just over five birds. The predominance of smaller groups supports the statement by Snow and Perrins (1998) that many Goldcrests 'maintain exclusive winter territories, which they apparently defend against neighbouring groups'. Autumn influxes of Goldcrest are usual in September and October with ringing recoveries indicating that most birds are from Scandinavia and the Baltic states. It is not clear whether these birds winter in the county although they may account for some of those that over-winter in the lowland agricultural areas. The Goldcrest remains an abundant resident and passage visitor in the county (Kerr, 2001) and the alarm expressed by Mead (2000) that the population is 'declining badly' does not seem to apply in Northumberland.

ALAN JANES

Distribution by altitude

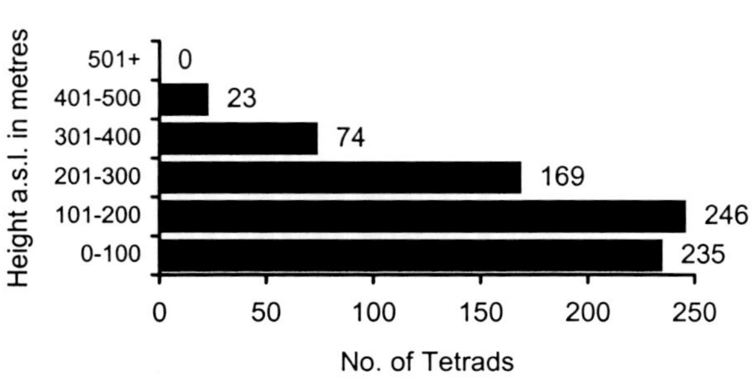

No. of tetrads in which recorded 747 (52%)

Tetrad Analysis	No. of tetrads
1-3 birds	390 (52%)
4-7 birds	210 (28%)
8+ birds	147 (20%)

Total No. of birds counted 3,817

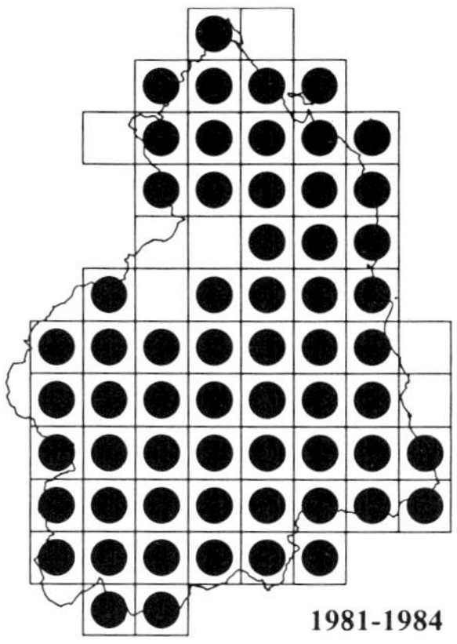

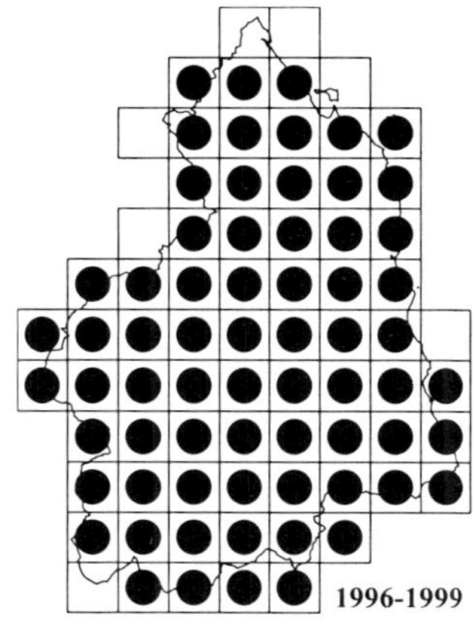

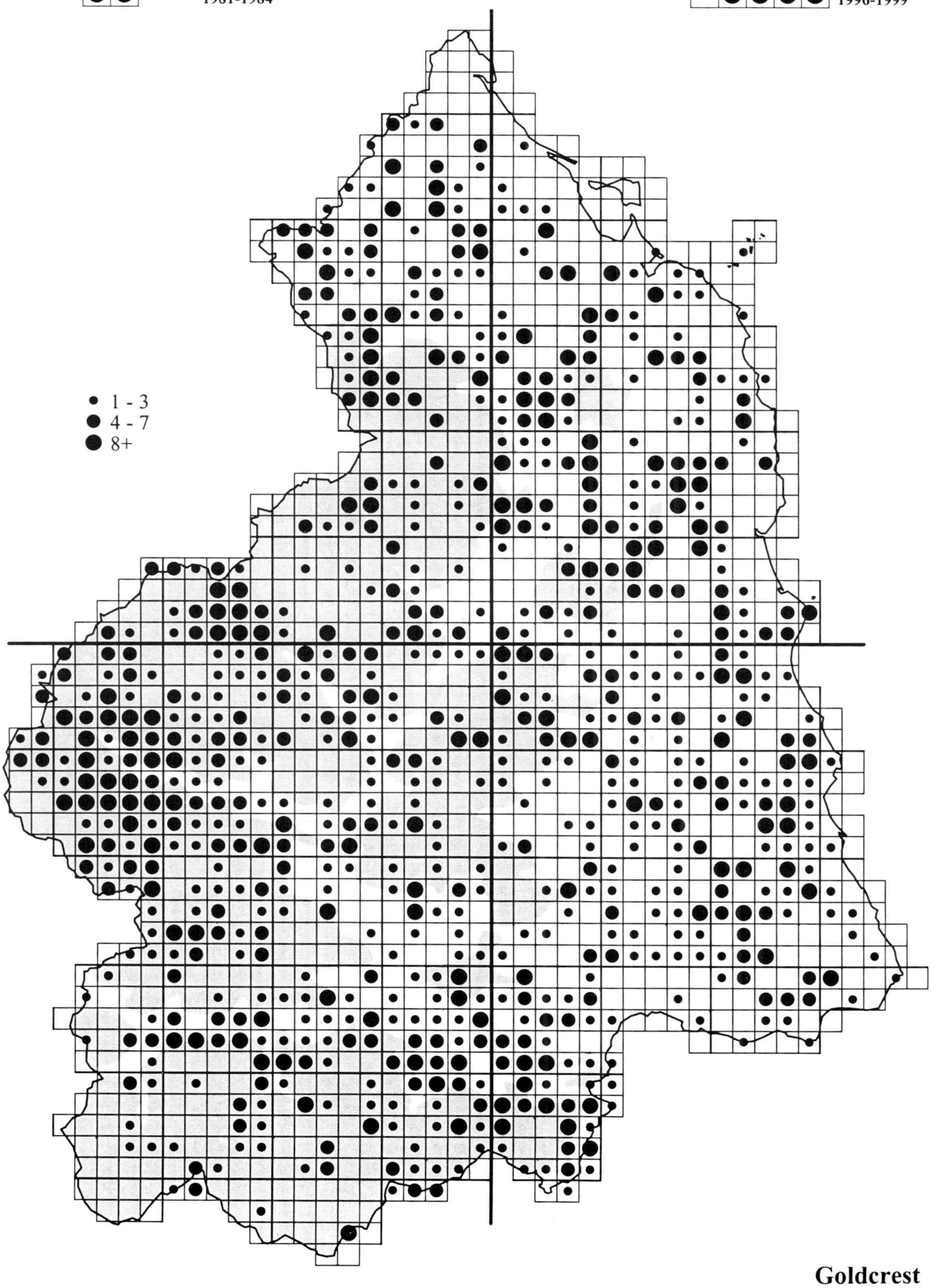

Goldcrest

FIRECREST *Regulus ignicapillus*

Whilst Firecrests have bred in the south of England since 1962, Britain marks the most northerly point of its wintering area (Lack, 1986). East coast birds in the northern counties nevertheless appear to be of continental origin rather than from southern England, and to be very much a twentieth century phenomenon. Writing in 1912 Bolam stated that 'so far as I am aware it has not occurred in the Border counties'. He listed the first authenticated record on Holy Island in October 1912, with further autumn sightings in 1923 and 1927, and one spring record for the county in 1924 (Bolam, 1932). According to Galloway and Meek (1983), no more were recorded until the 1950s, and those virtually all on either spring or autumn passage, with the latter period accounting for 86% of the sightings. With only two exceptions, all of the records quoted by them were of coastal birds.

This trend continued into the late 1980s and included an increase in spring sightings, together with evidence that a few Firecrests were over-wintering. The pattern continued with birds recorded in each year in the 1990s with only 1995 and 1996 lacking autumn or winter reports. Migrating birds in Northumberland typically favour coastal scrub, where they may be very approachable. This was certainly the case during the winter atlas survey with birds located at Craster (NU21P) in January and November 1997, St. Mary's Island (NZ37M), also in November 1997, and Newbiggin (NZ38E). In the last instance a Firecrest was present from 14 December 1997 through to 25 February 1998. An early winter bird was also found a little inland at Newham (NU12U) in November 1998, and a probable over-wintering bird was in the Holywell Dene area (NZ37H) from 6 January to 13 February 1999.

The pattern of spring and autumn passage has continued in the two years since the survey and will presumably be repeated as mild winters continue. Specifically during the atlas survey, Firecrests occurred in five different tetrads and, whilst the recording methodology involved listing the maximum number of birds in each tetrad *at any given time* (which was one in all instances), it only gives a total of five separate birds when there were in fact two different Firecrests in the Craster tetrad in the January and November of 1997.

JOHN C. DAY

Distribution by altitude

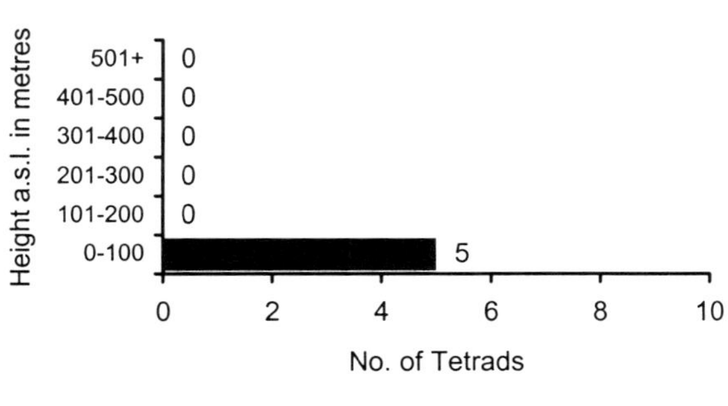

No. of tetrads in which recorded 5 (>1%)

Tetrad Analysis	No. of tetrads
1 bird	5 (100%)

Total No. of birds counted 5

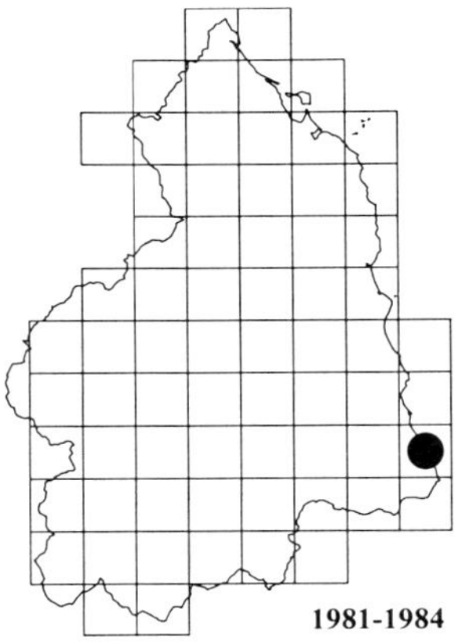

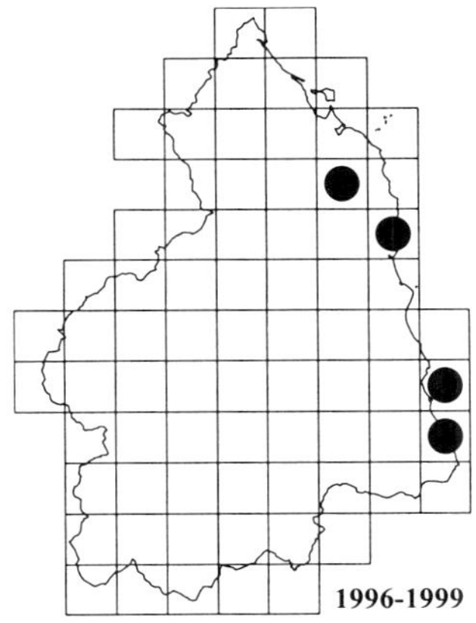

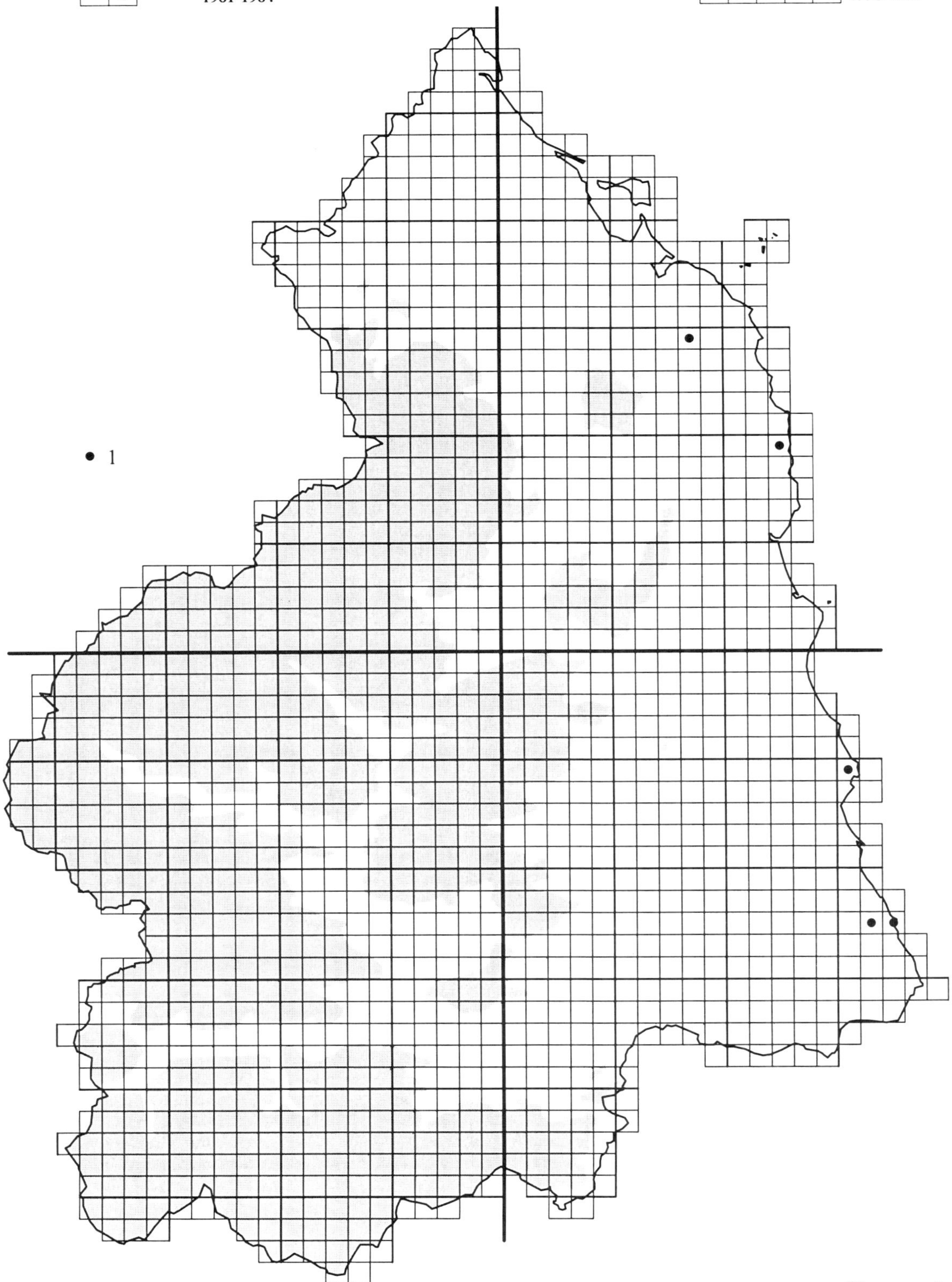

Firecrest

LONG-TAILED TIT *Aegithalos caudatus*

The winter atlas data gives a total count of 3,293 Long-tailed Tits in 342 tetrads. Galloway and Meek (1983) quoted Bolam, who wrote in 1932, that the Long-tailed Tit is 'a well-known resident; seldom numerous, but nesting in many places throughout the county, and found during the cold months in roving bands of a score or two together'. In the 1960s Macfarlane (1973) confirmed that there were small numbers over much of the county, with the possible exception of the north. The winter survey total compares quite well with a breeding survey total of 272 pairs, as noted in *The atlas of breeding birds in Northumbria* (Day *et al*., 1995), although it was estimated that the breeding population was probably nearer 300-500 pairs together with a comment that this species can be 'remarkably inconspicuous in its breeding territories, particularly in large tracts of woodland'. The gregarious and mobile nature of the species outside the breeding season makes them easier to survey in winter. In addition they would appear to inhabit less inhospitable zones in the county, such as lowland deciduous or mixed woodland which are easier to census than vast tracts of conifers.

Bolam (1912) described the Long-tailed Tit in autumn and winter as moving about in flocks, often accompanied by other Tits, Goldcrests and Creepers, visiting gardens and hedgerows in quest of food, and not infrequently straying into the neighbourhood of our large towns. His view is corroborated in results from ten kilometre squares such as that in which Ashington, Morpeth, Bedlington and Blyth (NZ28) are located, where 17 of the 25 tetrads held Long-tailed Tits. But on continental immigration his views are somewhat more contentious. Bolam deduced that single birds at Goswick Links in 1883 and on Holy Island in 1903, when other migrants like Rough-Legged Buzzards *Buteo lagopus*, Goldcrests *Regulus regulus* and the like were numerous, suggested immigration. Galloway and Meek (1983) however, doubted this claim, saying that there was insufficient data to support immigration, their view being that coastal records are explained through 'autumn wandering' which has since been confirmed by ringing recoveries.

A comparison of the occupied squares on the smaller 10km square maps reveals a more widespread distribution of Long-tailed Tits compared to the previous winter survey between 1981-1984. It is likely that, because of its largely insectivorous diet, the recent sequence of relatively mild winters may have lead to a net increase in numbers. A detailed analysis of tetrad data reveals that the species has a preference for lowland areas below 200 metres a.s.l. and 291 (85%) of the 342 occupied tetrads were in this height range. Distribution is widespread in the south east of the county and in the river valleys and deciduous woodlands in the south west. They are more sparsely distributed in the north but there are notable numbers from some areas, such as those around Bamburgh and Belford (NU13) and Norham and Duddo (NT94). Long-tailed Tits were well-represented in deciduous woodland areas, such as those at Ponteland and Belsay (NZ17), and in areas of slightly higher land where wooded valleys provide suitable habitat as in the Halton Lea Gate and Slaggyford region (NY65). The highest count was in the tetrad that included Hartford Hall (NZ28K) with 47 birds. The peripatetic nature of wintering Long-tailed Tits is highlighted by the control tetrad data. Whilst the species was recorded in 27 (45%) of the 60 control tetrads visited over the three winter periods, they were only present in 11 in the first winter and 15 and 16 respectively in the following two winters. Numbers fluctuated dramatically with, for example, successive counts of 23, seven and none at Whinney Hill near Netherwitton (NZ19G) and six, none and ten at Hulne Park (NU11S). In fact, Long-tailed Tits were present in all three winters in only four of the occupied control tetrads.

Whilst Long-tailed Tits are particularly prone to severe winter weather (Mead, 2000) the recent series of mild winters has done nothing to diminish their status as a common species in Northumberland.

ALAN JANES

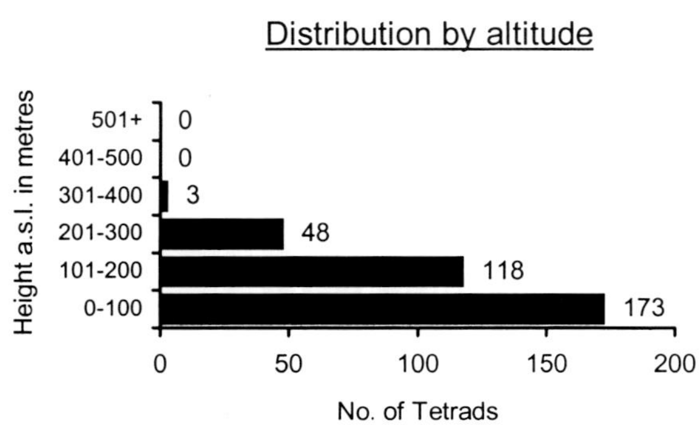

No. of tetrads in which recorded 342 (24%)

Tetrad Analysis	No. of tetrads
1-7 birds	175 (51%)
8-15 birds	103 (30%)
16+ birds	64 (19%)

Total No. of birds counted 3,293

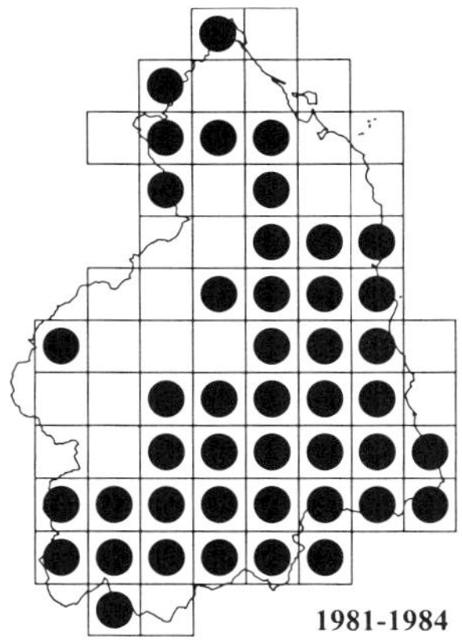

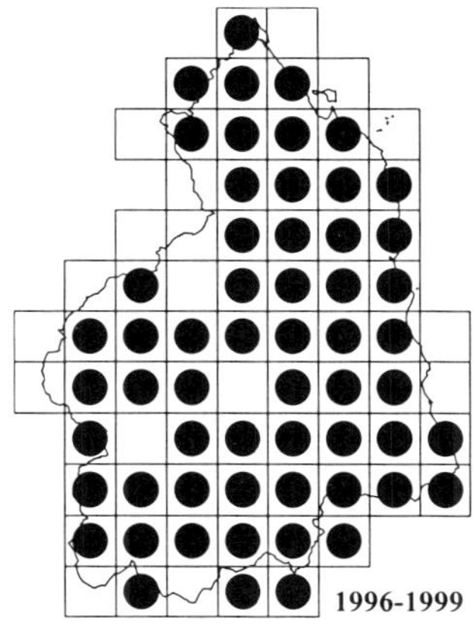

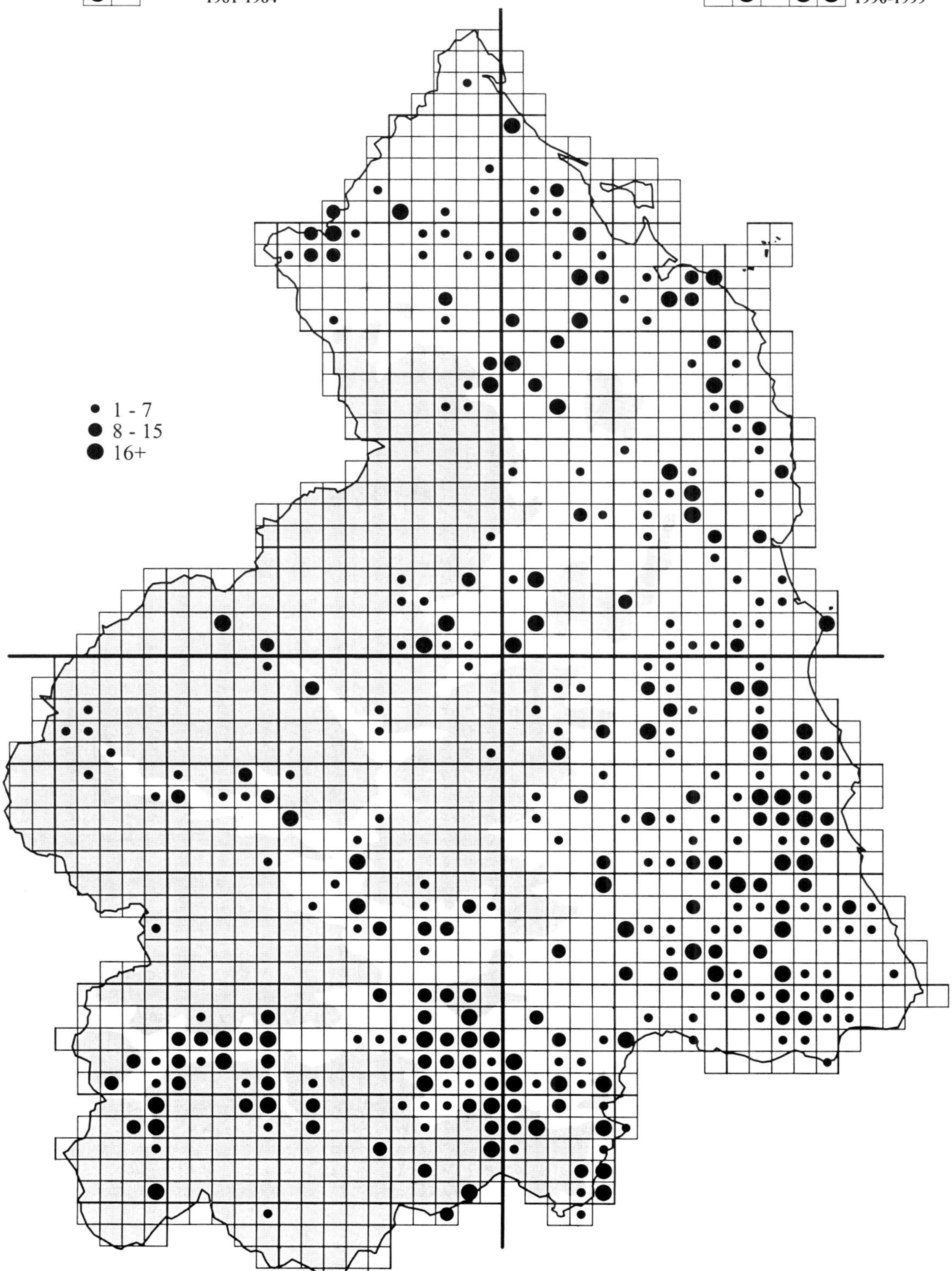

Long-tailed Tit

MARSH TIT *Parus palustris*

Galloway and Meek (1983) described the Marsh Tit as well-represented in the county and quoted Macfarlane (1973) who had stated that it was 'a somewhat scarce and local breeding species but perhaps more widespread than Willow Tit [*Parus montanus*]'. The distribution and numbers of this species counted during the winter atlas period show that it can still be described as such, with a total of 218 birds being recorded in 109 tetrads.

The tetrad map clearly shows the distribution of birds in the deciduous woodland areas in the county. Marsh Tits are associated with large, mature deciduous woodlands with Oak *Quercus* sp. and Beech *Fagus sylvatica* (Harrap & Quinn, 1996). Beech-mast is particularly important in the winter (Cramp & Perrins, 1993) and good shrub and field layers are needed as they use these niches within a wood more than other tits (Fuller, 1982). The map reflects the distribution of these beech and oak woodlands in the middle sections of the Wansbeck, Coquet and Aln valleys, the woodland around Craster and the Tweed Valley. They are also found in the North Tyne Valley around Bellingham, and the South Tyne Valley tributaries. In the last area, the valleys of the South Tyne, West Allen and Devil's Water are all clearly marked on the map running north/south and there certainly seems to have been an expansion here since the local breeding atlas survey (Day *et al.*, 1995). This possibly results from the good beech-mast year of 1998 as, in years of high seed production, Marsh Tits colonise new areas of woodland. The highest counts for this survey came from Cupola Bridge (NY75Z; 12 birds), Muggleswick Gorge NNR, Crooked Oak (NZ04P; seven), the Shawdon Hall area near Glanton (NU01X; seven) and Shipley near Alnwick (NU11N; six). The lack of records in the Gilsland area, on the border, is surprising, considering how common the species is in Cumbria. The Marsh Tit's slightly more upland distribution compared with Willow Tit is illustrated by the number of occupied tetrads within the higher altitude groups, 54% of the occupied tetrads being above 100 metres a.s.l. in comparison with 42% for Willow Tit.

Although the population has declined by 21% nationally in CBC plots between 1993 and 1998 (and by 66% since 1968), there has conversely been a recorded increase of 23% in BBS squares between 1994 and 1999. The atlas data reflect this discrepancy. The comparison of distribution in 10km squares between this winter atlas survey period and the last, shows a reduction by three squares overall (Marsh Tits were not recorded in seven 10km squares in this period but were seen in three in which they were not recorded in the last). But comparison with the tetrad maps in Day *et al.* (1995) shows an increase in the species' distribution. As Marsh Tits are highly sedentary and are the most site-faithful of all passerine species (Lack, 1985) and only 13% of all ringing recoveries are over 10km from the ringing site (Toms & Clark, 1998), it would seem reasonable to compare the distribution maps between this survey and the local breeding atlas. Marsh Tits were recorded in 109 tetrads during the winter survey period and in 85 in the breeding season, which would appear to indicate a 25% increase. Further comparison between the two Northumberland atlases shows there is only a 20% overlap in the number of tetrads in which the species was recorded between the winter and summer maps. This would indicate that the species is in some way overlooked by the survey methodology of the atlas and that the population of Marsh Tits is in fact much larger than is suggested in Day *et al.* (1995). As this species is very vocal and easily located, any reason for it being overlooked is most likely to be attributable to its low population density with winter territories of up to 4.6 ha. (Cramp & Perrins, 1993). In Northumberland there was a very low average number per occupied tetrad of only two birds and this is further highlighted when the data from control tetrads are examined. Of the nine control tetrads in which Marsh Tits were recorded, they were found in only two tetrads in every year and recorded only once in five tetrads. However, some change in the winter distribution may be due to supplementary feeding in gardens. In some areas of the north east there is evidence to suggest that this has maintained populations in areas where the species was only occasionally seen, especially where black sunflower seeds are provided (Armstrong, 1999).

A total of 218 birds was counted during this winter atlas survey, a figure which compares well with the count of 108 pairs recorded for the county breeding atlas. However, taking into account the small overlap in distribution between the two surveys, it seems likely that the Northumberland wintering population is in the region of 350 birds.

STEPHEN WESTERBERG

Distribution by altitude

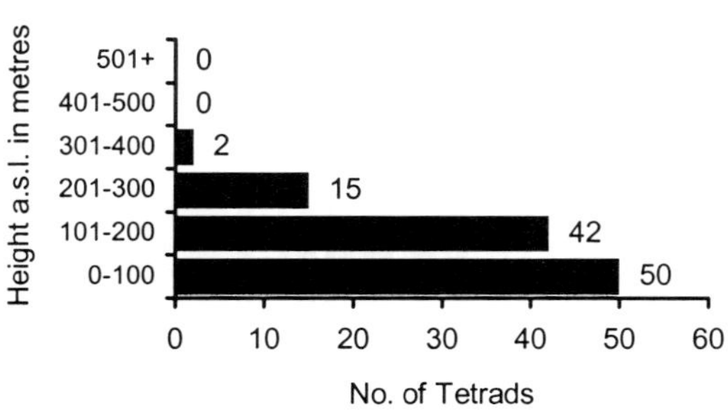

No. of tetrads in which recorded 109 (8%)

Tetrad Analysis	No. of tetrads
1 bird	61 (56%)
2-3 birds	31 (28%)
4+ birds	17 (16%)

Total No. of birds counted 218

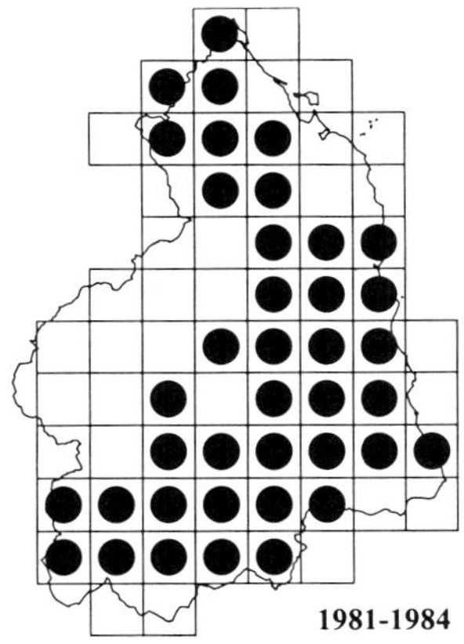

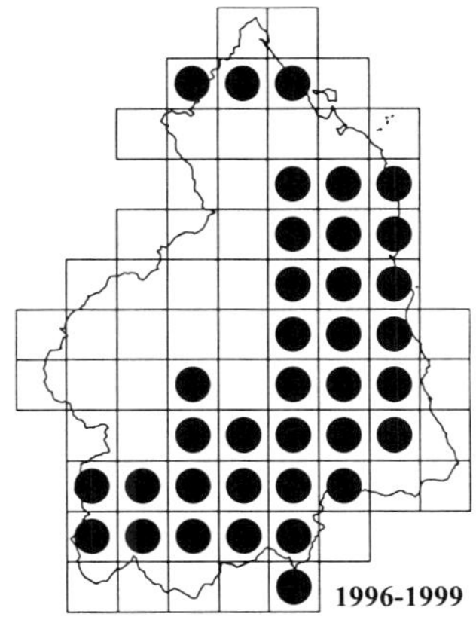

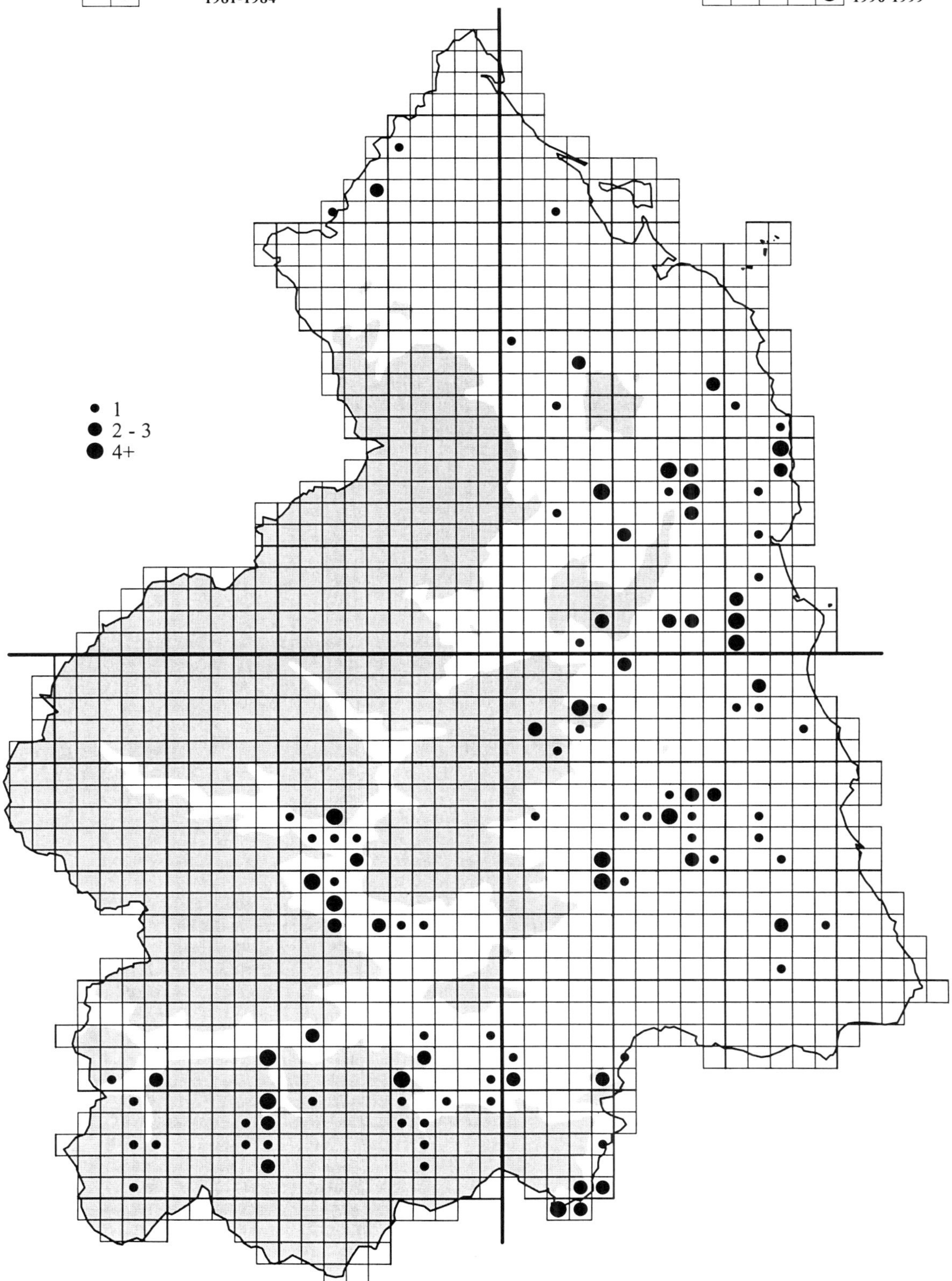

Marsh Tit

WILLOW TIT *Parus montanus*

Early comparisons of the range and population of this species with the present day are difficult since Willow Tit was only recognised as a distinct species in 1897 (Lack, 1986). In fact, the difficulty of identification of Marsh Tit *P. palustris* and Willow Tit still causes some problems and every atlas account for the species mentions this fact. Galloway and Meek (1983) described the Willow Tit as well-represented, principally in the south-east of the county, but scarce in the north. As with Marsh Tit this statement would appear to be generally true today as is evident from the tetrad map. Since the Willow Tit population in Northumberland is on the northern edge of its range in Britain it can be expected to be fairly scarce in the north of the county. Just north of the border the population is believed to number only about ten pairs (Murray *et al.*, 1998), mainly in the Tweed Valley.

Willow Tits are found in damp woodlands, carrs and lowland conifer forests (Lack, 1986) and in winter also on heathland and in hedgerows (Harrap & Quinn, 1996). They mainly forage in the herb and shrub layers, reflecting the birds' preference for smaller, less mature woodlands, such as those in which the species occurs at Plenmeller, in the Hexham area and the wooded areas from Gosforth Park to the Blyth Valley. The lowland distribution is highlighted by the fact that all the records were from areas below 300 metres a.s.l. (two Marsh Tit tetrads were above 300 metres) and 88% of occupied tetrads were below 200 metres. Maximum counts in tetrads were five near Swarland (NU10M) and Prestwick Carr (NZ17W) and four near Oakwood (NY96N), Rothley Lakes (NZ09K) and the Blyth Valley woodland near Bedlington (NZ28L).

Nationally, there has been a decline in the population of Willow Tits, but mainly in secondary habitats for the species, while in damp woodland the population has remained stable (Siriwardena, 2001). This would also seem to be true for Northumberland. The number of records in *Birds in Northumbria* shows a comparative decline in the population in the county. However, there was an increase in the number of tetrads recorded between the local breeding and winter surveys, from 79 to 89. The maps indicate a slight expansion in the range of this species in the north of the county. This expansion has occurred just inland from Newton-by-the-Sea, Spindlestone and in the Tweed Valley. Conversely there appears to be a loss of birds from the Threestoneburn area, Fontburn, Hartburn and Hulne Park. Willow Tits, like Marsh Tits, are sedentary, with only 17% of national ringing recoveries showing movements over five km (Toms & Clark, 1998). The comparison with the summer tetrad atlas also reveals a very small overlap between the summer and winter distributions. As with Marsh Tit, there was only a 20% overlap in tetrads between the two surveys and, as Willow Tits are also found at low densities, it would appear that here again the limited time spent in the field stipulated by the survey methodology may mean that birds were overlooked and that the population is higher than is apparent from the tetrad counts. In none of the control tetrads were birds recorded in every year.

The count of 154 birds during this winter survey is slightly lower than would be suggested by the 95 pairs recorded in the local breeding atlas survey (Day *et al.*, 1995). When the small degree of overlap in tetrads between the two surveys is taken into consideration, a total population of about 250 birds may be estimated.

STEPHEN WESTERBERG

Distribution by altitude

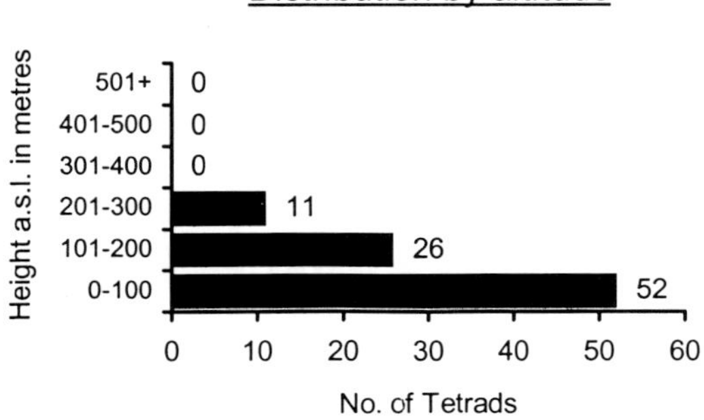

No. of tetrads in which recorded	89 (6%)
Tetrad Analysis	**No. of tetrads**
1 bird	50 (56%)
2 birds	21 (24%)
3+ birds	18 (20%)
Total No. of birds counted	154

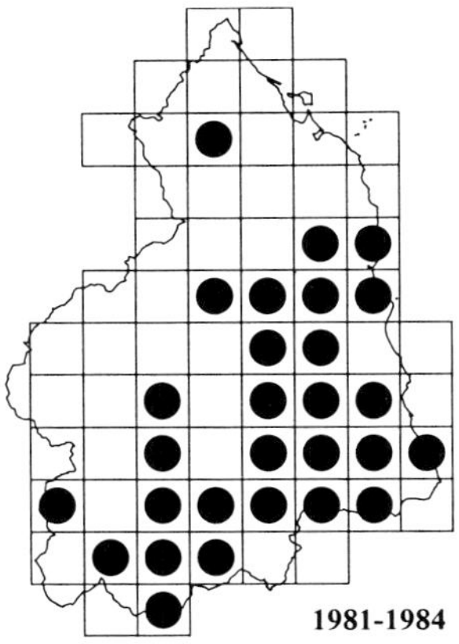

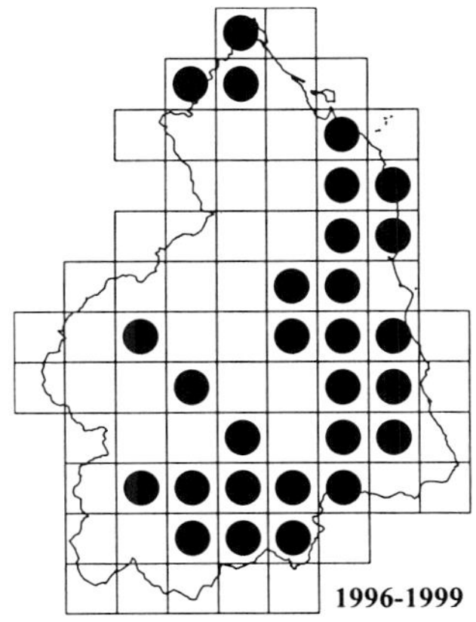

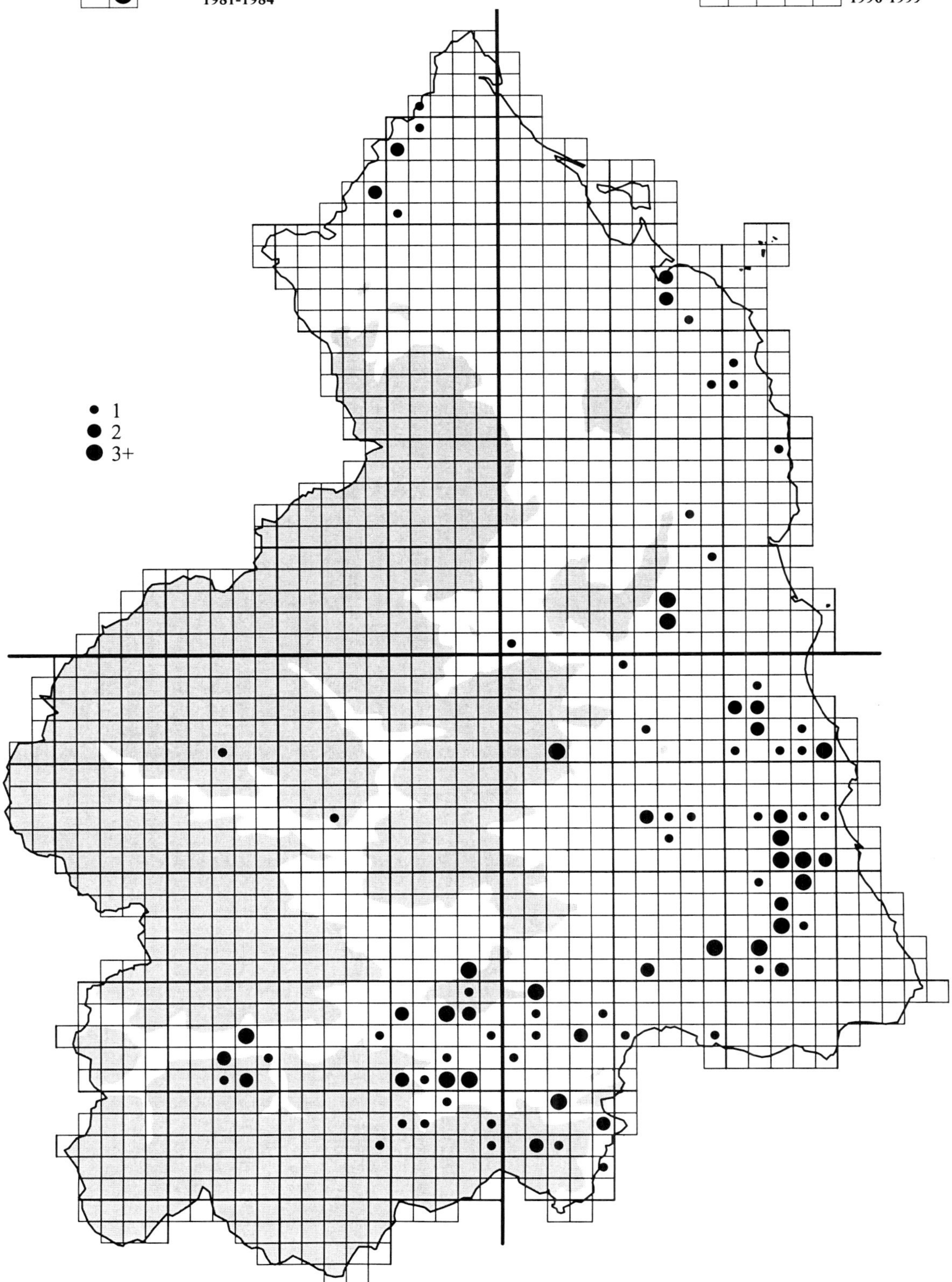

Willow Tit

COAL TIT *Parus ater*

The current winter atlas survey produced a total count of 5,838 Coal Tits found in 881 tetrads. As early as 1831 Selby wrote that the Coal Tit was then a very common bird in Northumberland, a fact that he attributed to 'the extensive plantations, particularly of the fir tribe'. More than a century later Galloway and Meek (1983) were able to say that it 'is now probably much more common than ever before as the expansion of the border forests has enabled it to colonise what were once remote moorland areas'. The winter total compares with 2,580 breeding pairs which were recorded in *The atlas of breeding birds in Northumbria* (Day *et al.*, 1995) although the breeding population was estimated at between 30,000 and 90,000 pairs. It was indicated, however, that there would be considerable fluctuation in the population in response to availability of food resources and the severity of winters. As noted with Goldcrest *Regulus regulus*, the winter survey results probably represent an underestimate as Coal Tits often feed high up in conifer trees and whilst they can be located by call, numbers can prove difficult to assess in tall stands.

The tetrad distribution map shows that whilst the Coal Tit in winter is not limited to conifer forest, higher densities are to be found there. Lack (1986) commented on the Coal Tit's ecological characteristics including its narrow bill adapted for picking insects from between conifer needles which reduce the need for altitudinal migration that occurs in Great Tit *Parus major* and Blue Tit *Parus caeruleus*. He further described the Coal Tit as subordinate to these two species in mixed flocks but, within its preferred habitat, it is found in higher densities. Therefore, as one would expect, Coal Tits were well-represented in conifer plantations especially in the Kielder (NY68/NY69) and Wark (NY77) Forests. The species is also represented, though in smaller numbers, in areas with mixed woodland and where there are smaller but more isolated conifer stands, such as Minsteracres (NZ05) and the Cambo/Scots Gap (NZ08) area. The largest count in any one tetrad was 130 at Kyloe Wood (NU03P).

The distribution map clearly shows that by far the greatest density of occupancy is in those upland areas of the county, primarily in the west and south west, where conifer woodland predominates. As Coal Tits are well-adapted to this habitat it is not surprising that they maintained their numbers in each of the three winter periods in which control tetrads were surveyed. Nevertheless, a comparison between the local breeding distribution map (Day *et al.*, 1995) and the current winter map reveals 658 occupied tetrads in the former and 881 in the latter. This disparity may be partly explained by some seasonal movement as Galloway and Meek (1983) commented that in 1963 flocks of up to 100 were at Dipton and 40 at Blagdon in January and February, but by the summer there had been a marked reduction in numbers. In addition, the appearance in the last few decades of many small lowland conifer plantations has provided further suitable winter habitat. The proliferation of wind-breaks and plantations on reclaimed opencast sites, as well as recreational planting and conservation management have all resulted in conifer planting away from the upland areas and the inevitable expansion of the Coal Tit into new localities. That 64% of all occupied tetrads in winter lie below 201 metres a.s.l. is therefore to be expected.

Subject to the vagaries of severe winter weather, the Coal Tit should long remain a common, or even abundant resident in Northumberland, particularly as the national trend clearly shows a steady increase in the population (Mead, 2000).

ALAN JANES

Distribution by altitude

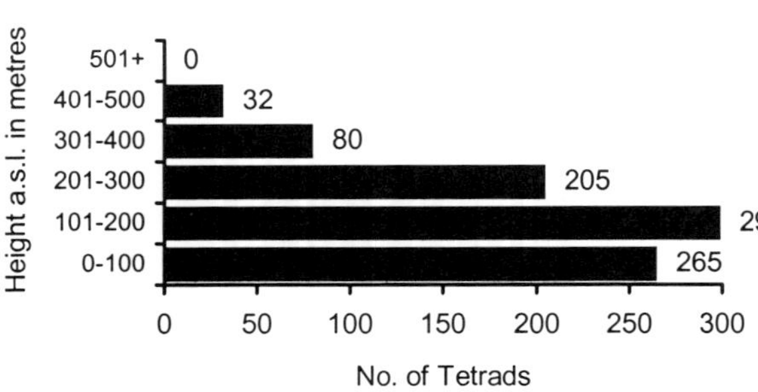

No. of tetrads in which recorded 881 (62%)

Tetrad Analysis	No. of tetrads
1-3 birds	416 (47%)
4-9 birds	290 (33%)
10+ birds	175 (20%)

Total No. of birds counted 5,838

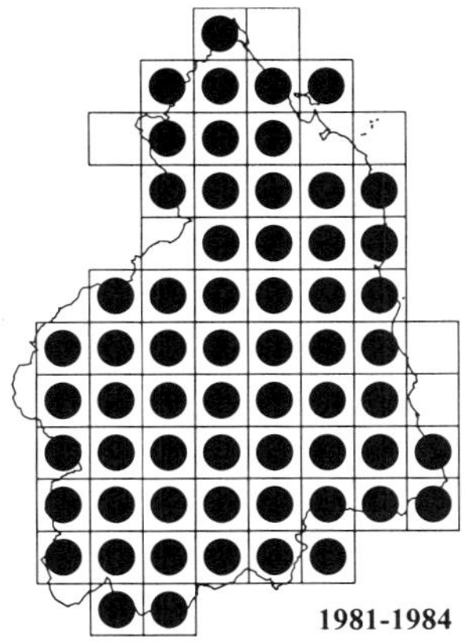

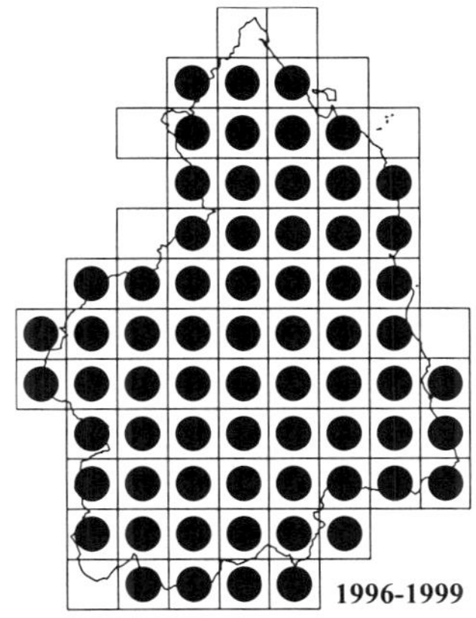

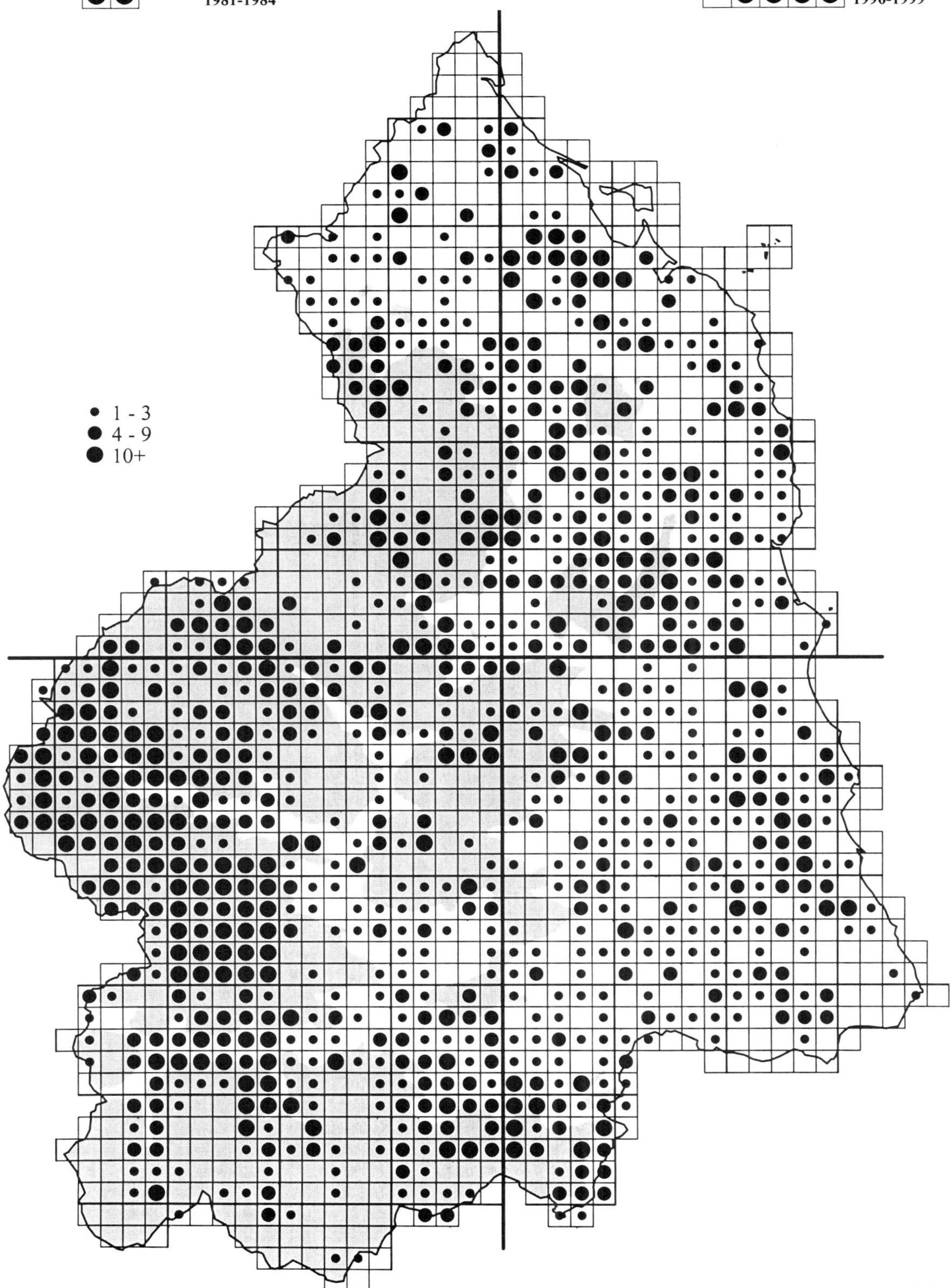

Coal Tit

BLUE TIT *Parus caeruleus*

Data collected over three winters for this atlas clearly show that the Blue Tit is one of the commonest and most numerous species in the area surveyed. In total 14,126 individual birds were counted in 1,004 tetrads. Its status as a common resident does not appear to have altered in the last hundred years with both Bolam (1912) and, more recently, Galloway and Meek (1983) commenting on the size of the breeding and wintering populations. Nationally the Blue Tit is the commonest of the British titmice (Mead, 2000).

In winter the species is gregarious, often associating with other members of the tit family as well as with Nuthatch *Sitta europaea*, Goldcrest *Regulus regulus* and Treecreeper *Certhia familiaris*. These wintering parties are most frequently observed in broad-leaved woodland, although Blue Tits may join Coal Tits *Parus ater* and Goldcrests in coniferous habitats in some winters (Barnes, 1975). Flocks of foraging birds are usually most numerous in the morning with birds dispersing later in the day. Within the flock there is little competition for food as each species occupies a distinct niche, the agile Blue Tit feeding in the canopy at the extremities of branches. Mixed woodland with Beech *Fagus* sp., Oak *Quercus* sp. and Birch *Betula* sp. are favoured habitats and in this current survey many tetrads with a large proportion of this type of habitat held sizeable numbers of Blue Tit e.g. Bardon Mill (NY76S) with 152 birds counted, Gunnerton (NY97C) with 81, Plankey Mill (NY76W) with 55 and Stannington Vale (NZ27J) with 42. In contrast numbers in tetrads where conifers predominated were much lower e.g. Sidwood (NY78U) and Greenlee Farm (NY77Q) both four birds, Thrunton (NU00Y) two and Slaley (NY95M) with three.

This finding is confirmed by the control tetrad data, with consistently higher numbers of Blue Tits each year in broadleaved woodland, e.g. Holystone (NT90L), Spindlestone (NU13L) and the Featherstone (NY66V) and Jesmond Dene areas (NZ26T), than in the coniferous and upland areas such as Alnwick Moor (NU11K), Bewshaugh (NY69B), Blakehopeburnhaugh (NY79Z) and Harwood area (NY99V). Small flocks consisting solely of Blue Tits may also occur but rarely do they exceed more than 30 individuals (*Birds in Northumbria 1997, 1998*). In winter, the Blue Tit is the commonest species at garden bird-tables (Perrins, 1979) and in Northumberland there is a marked movement to these localities which is apparent from many of the tetrad returns.

In the area surveyed, the species was widely distributed in all habitats, particularly below 200 metres a.s.l. (794 tetrads). They were also found along many inland river valleys with deciduous woodland up to 300 metres a.s.l. (169 tetrads). Their absence was most evident on land above 300 metres and in the extensive conifer plantations of the Kielder, Wark and Redesdale Forests. When present in these areas, it was often near hamlets and farms where bird-tables were maintained, e.g. Kielder Village, Falstone and Byrness. More detailed coverage in the current fieldwork recorded Blue Tits in some of the marginal 10km squares where they were not seen in the 1981-1984 winter atlas survey, but the only significant difference between the two surveys is the paucity of records for the species in NT81, an exposed upland area on the Scottish border.

A more significant comparison of the distribution of Blue Tit can be made between this wintering atlas map and that in *The atlas of breeding birds in Northumbria* (Day *et al.*, 1995). There is a remarkable correlation between the distribution of the breeding and wintering populations. The former occupy 899 tetrads (64% of those covered), the latter 1,004 tetrads (70%). The similarities are perhaps not surprising when ringing data from Northumberland sites over the last ten years are examined. Winter ringing has taken place at a number of sites, e.g. Big Waters, Bolam, Matfen, Sandhoe, Spindlestone, and Swarland and, of sixty birds recovered or controlled, the average distance travelled was under 19 kilometres. Only five other birds had moved any greater distance averaging 65 kilometres each. Although some coastal passage is recorded in most autumns (Galloway & Meek, 1983), the local ringing returns confirm the national pattern of the Blue Tit as a primarily sedentary species.

The overall wintering total for the three year survey of a minimum of 14,126 birds makes interesting comparison with the breeding population estimate of between 5,000 and 10,000 pairs in the county's recording area.

JOHN C. DAY

Distribution by altitude

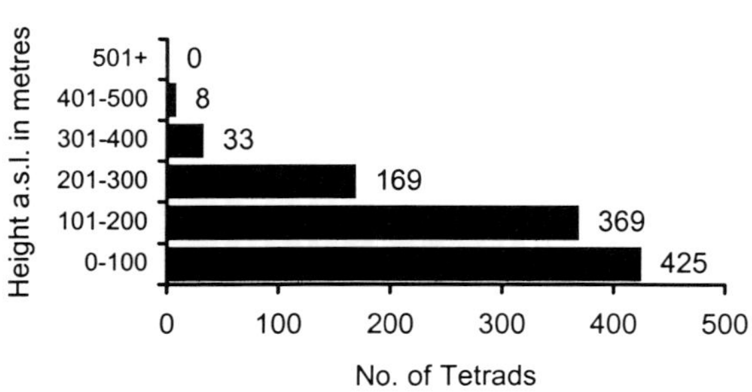

No. of tetrads in which recorded 1,004 (70%)

Tetrad Analysis	No. of tetrads
1-10 birds	515 (51%)
11-20 birds	263 (26%)
21+ birds	226 (23%)

Total No. of birds counted 14,126

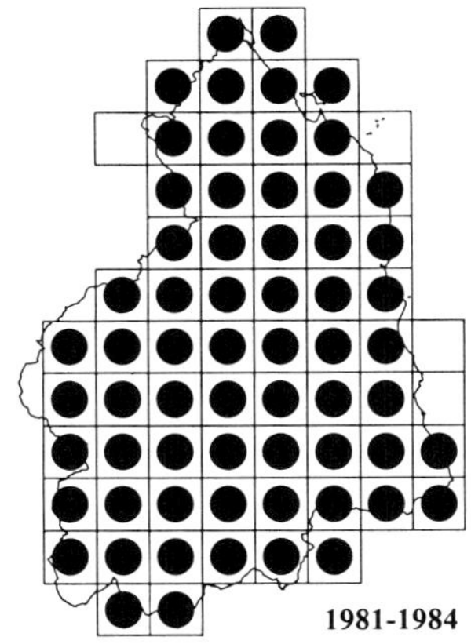

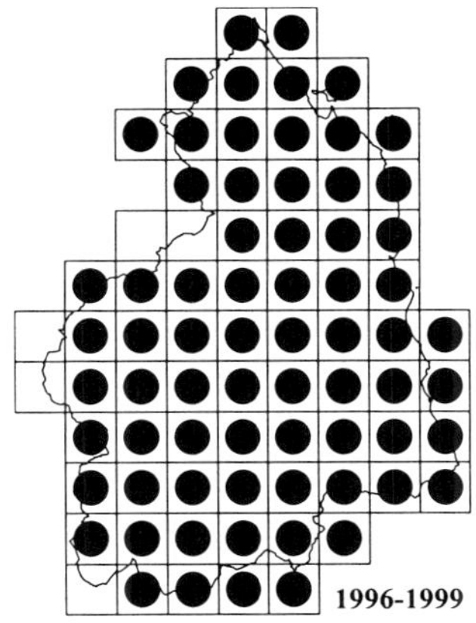

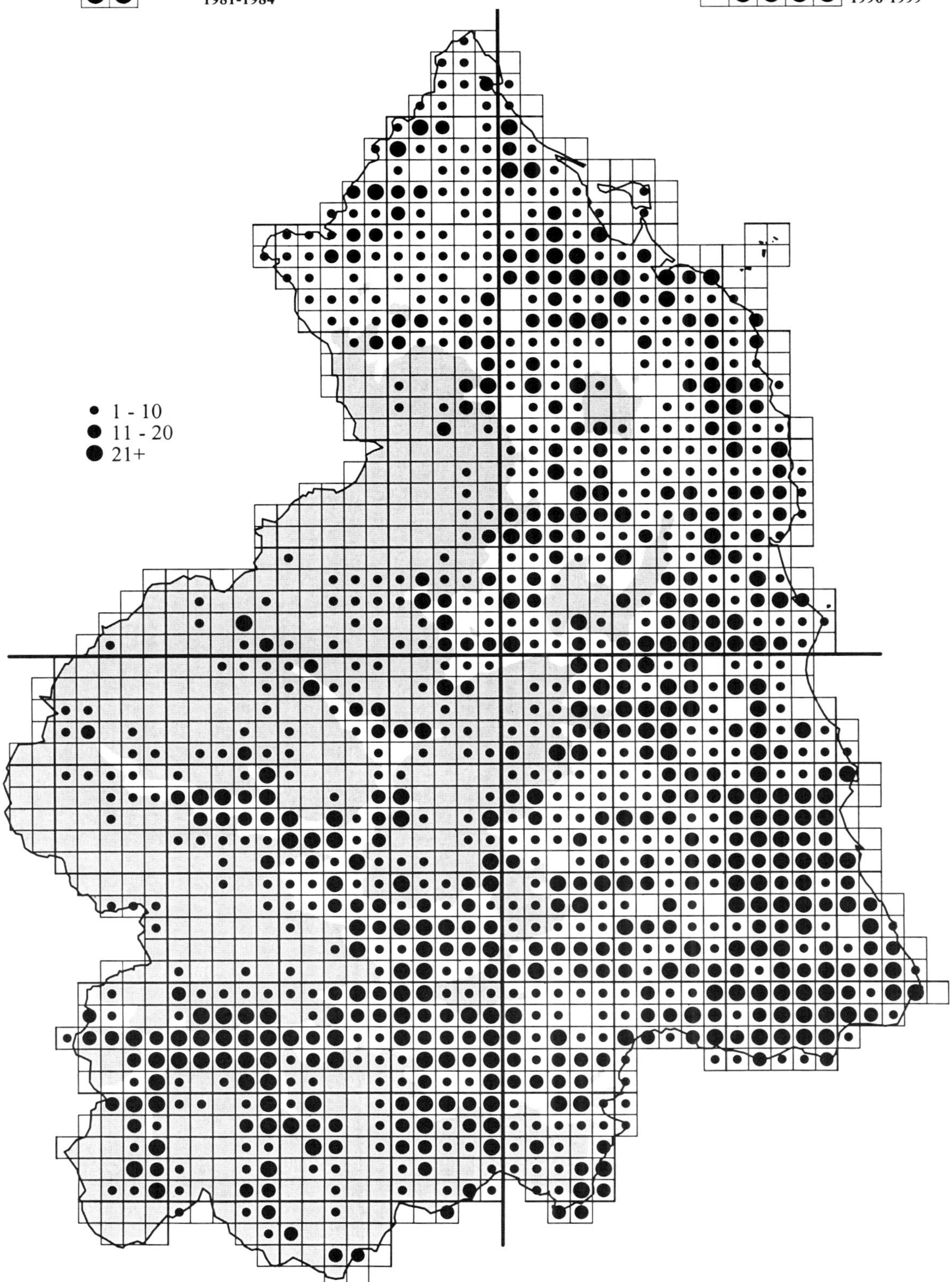

Blue Tit

GREAT TIT *Parus major*

The statement by Bolam (1912) that the Great Tit is 'almost as common throughout the district as the Blue Tit', which was later repeated by Galloway and Meek (1983), is not wholly supported by recent statistics. *The atlas of breeding of birds in Northumbria* (Day *et al.*, 1995) concluded that there were more than twice as many breeding pairs of Blue Tit than Great Tit and, in this present winter survey, Great Tits were outnumbered by nearly four to one (14,126 : 3,727). In considering these figures, it should be borne in mind that in winter the Blue Tit is more gregarious, and hence more obvious, than the Great Tit. This collective habit is further demonstrated by county-wide ringing returns produced by the Northumbria Ringing Group, in which only 29 ringed Great Tits were controlled or recorded in the decade 1990-2000 compared with 50 Blue Tits.

Normally in winter the species shows a preference for deciduous woodland and suburban gardens (Barnes, 1975) and is predominantly a ground feeder, being less agile than many of its close relatives. This is particularly the case where Beech-mast *Fagus sylvaticus* is available, although Yew *Taxus baccata* and Hazel *Corylus arellana* are also important winter food sources. In suburban areas where winter bird-tables are maintained the Great Tit tends to be more 'sedentary' than the Blue Tit (Barnes, 1975), this source of food helping to maintain population levels in the colder months. Nationally, the Great Tit population seems to be stable although global warming may be causing changes in spring weather that coincides and interferes with the breeding cycle (Mead, 2000).

In Northumberland, the Great Tit should continue to be regarded as a common breeding resident, its sedentary nature being confirmed by the above ringing returns which indicate that 26 of the 29 birds controlled averaged movements of less than 11 kilometres. Further confirmation of the species' sedentary nature is provided by comparison between the local breeding atlas map and the winter distribution map, in which there are no significant differences. Nor does the pattern of winter occupancy appear to have altered in this current survey from that of the previous winter survey of 1981–1984 (Lack, 1986).

The more detailed tetrad distribution for the species on the accompanying map clearly shows that neither the higher land (over 180 metres a.s.l.) nor the extensive coniferous forests in the west of the county are favoured. Great Tits are usually present in lowland agricultural habitat where there is woodland, but not in barren areas devoid of copses or with closely cut hedges. Also, as stated by Lack (1986), they are more thinly distributed on the immediate colder coastal belt and in the lower reaches of upland valleys in winter. Examples of this pattern of distribution between mid-November and March in Northumberland are widespread. Tetrads with mature deciduous woodland such as Jesmond (NZ26N) recorded 15 Great Tits ; Gosforth Park (NZ27K) 22 ; Belsay Hall (NZ07Z) 30 and the Bardon Mill area over 90 birds. The cooler coastal sites held far fewer numbers of the species, e.g. Yarrow Slake (NT95W) only two birds ; Fenwick (NU04Q) two ; Fenham Mill (NU04V) one ; Foxton (NU21K) one and Newbiggin (NZ38E) one. More evidence for the sedentary nature of Great Tits comes from the data collected in the control tetrads where, over the three winter seasons, numbers remained reasonably constant, for example at Countess Park (NY88Q) eight, six and eight birds; Wallington (NZ08H) seven, five and three and the Heaton Park area (NZ26T) with 16, 22 and 17.

Overall, Great Tits were recorded in 732 tetrads (cf. Blue Tits in 1,004) and of these 613 (84%) were below 200 metres a.s.l., with winter presence in only 17 (2%) of the occupied tetrads above the 300 metre contour. In spite of the apparent decrease in numbers the status of Great Tit in Northumberland in winter still remains that of a common resident.

JOHN C. DAY

Distribution by altitude

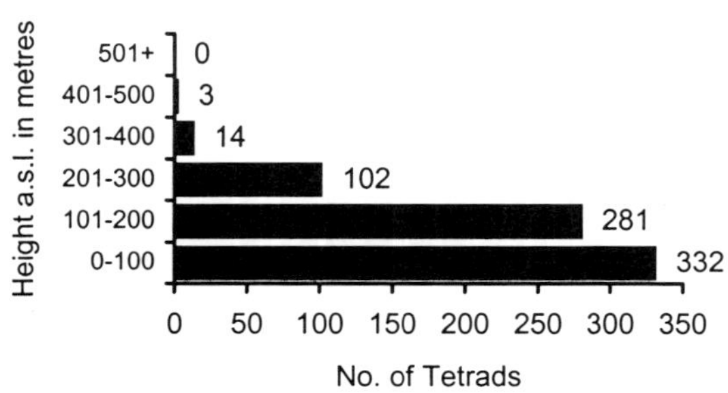

No. of tetrads in which recorded	732 (51%)
Tetrad Analysis	**No. of tetrads**
1-3 birds	377 (52%)
4-7 birds	199 (27%)
8+ birds	156 (21%)
Total No. of birds counted	3,727

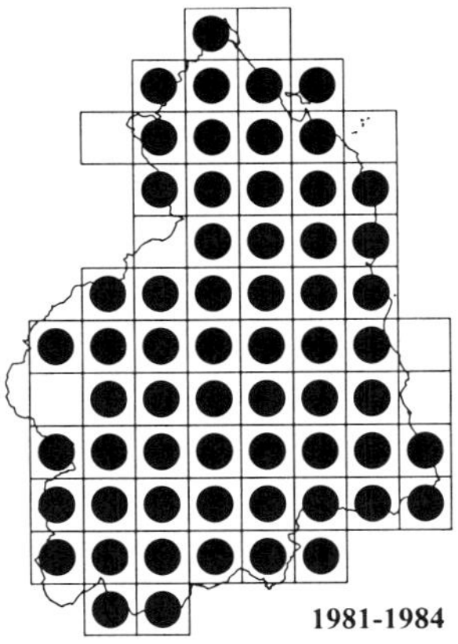

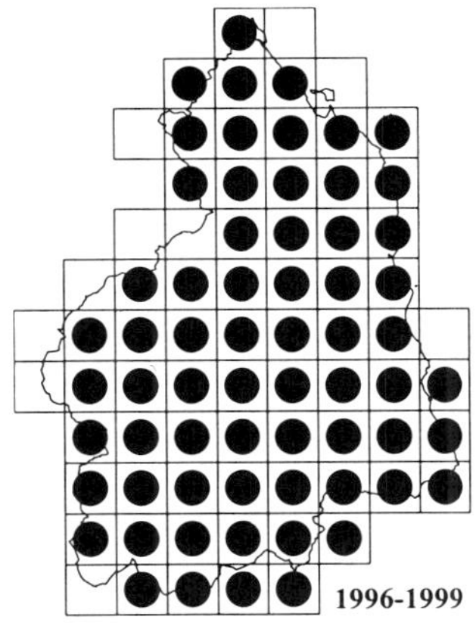

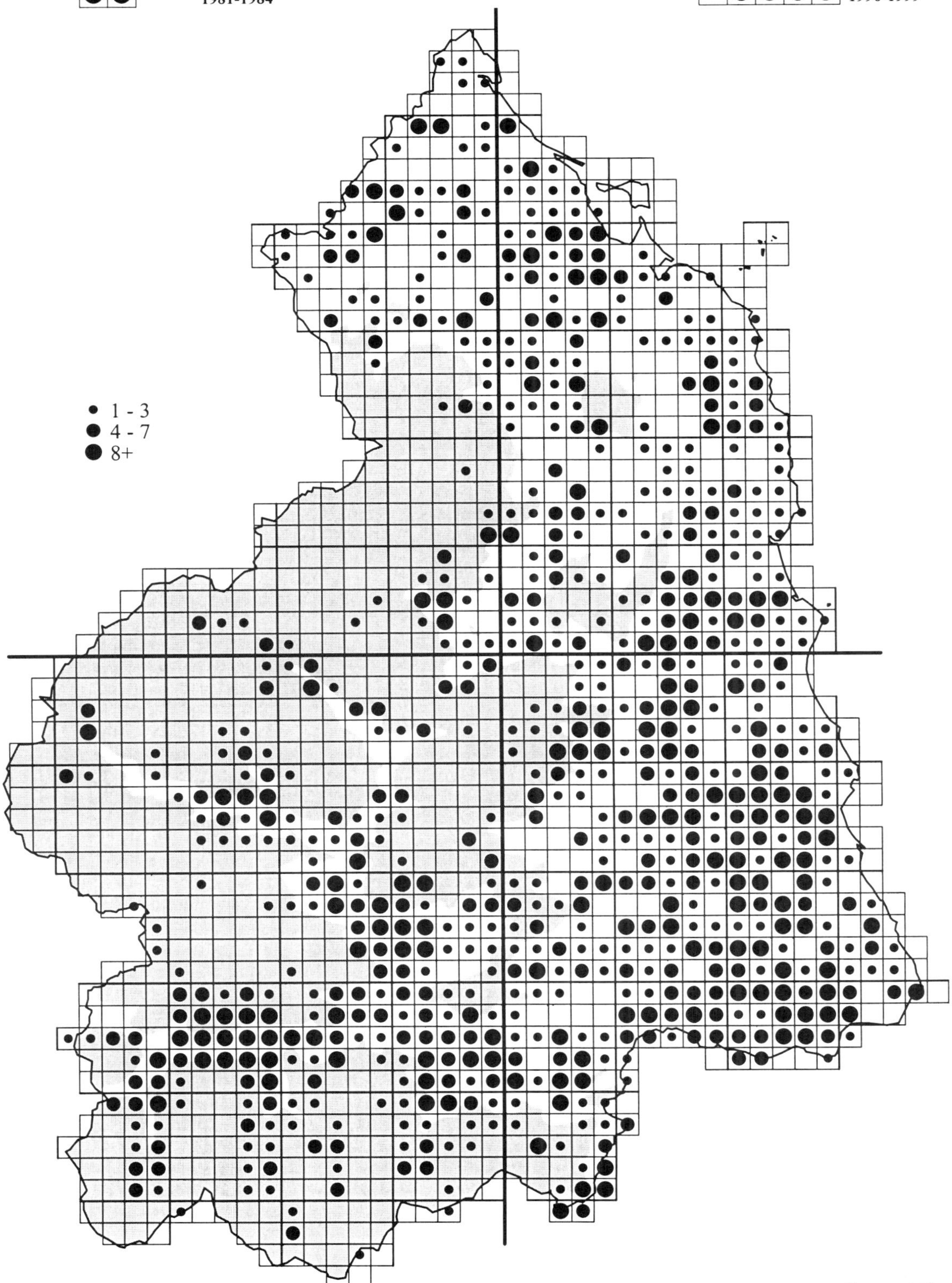

Great Tit

NUTHATCH *Sitta europaea*

The ringing calls of Nuthatches are now a familiar sound in a widespread number of localities in the county on a cold, bright winter's day. This situation, however, has only been reached following a marked period of northward and westward expansion during the last 40 years. Since the first modern confirmed breeding record in 1964, they have spread throughout the county. The rate of expansion can be roughly judged by the number of 'new' localities in which they were reported, with 14 between 1961-1970, 22 in 1971-1980, 33 in 1981-1985 (Hodgson, 1986) and a further 13 in 1986-1989 (*Birds in Northumbria 1986-1989*).

The tetrad map for this winter atlas shows that the main distribution, and therefore the bulk of the population, is along the Tyne Valley and other lowland areas and river valleys in the south and south west of the county. This, unsurprisingly for such a sedentary species, mirrors the main area of breeding distribution during 1988-1992 (Day *et al.*, 1995) and reflects the availability of suitable woodland habitat. Similar lowland areas in the south east and, to some extent, the north east are also occupied. However, birds were recorded at a fairly low density almost throughout their range in the county, with 83% of occupied tetrads apparently containing only one or two birds. The largest single count was 14 in the Prospect Hill area, south of Corbridge (NY96W). Nine were found in woodland south east of Hexham (NY96L), eight at Sandhoe (NY96T) and Wallington Hall (NZ08H) and six at each of Jesmond Dene (NZ26N), Belsay Castle (NZ07Z) and Hexham (NY96G). In the relatively sparsely occupied northern half of the county, there were only single counts of four and three birds, all others being only one or two. Visits to control tetrads during the three winter periods indicated that the number per occupied tetrad rose from 1.6 in 1996/97 to 2.8 in 1998/99. Caution should be exercised in interpreting these figures as the sample size, at 7.7% of all occupied tetrads, was fairly small. The species' preference in the county for lowland areas with suitable deciduous woodland is confirmed as nearly 87% of all occupied tetrads had an average height below 201 metres a.s.l.

The continuing spread is illustrated by a comparison of the two 10km square winter maps which show that they were reported in 21 more squares during the current survey, while only one square, a marginal coastal area, recorded in the earlier survey showed an absence. The major range expansion within the county between the two winter surveys has been into the north east, although some new areas in the south west have now been occupied.

Pairs defend territories year-round and young birds settle in territories of their own very early in life. Such permanent pair territories are rarely found in small birds of temperate latitudes (Matthysen, 1998). As movement into new areas seems to be a result of short-distance dispersal from natal sites, coupled with the fact that birds are at a low density on the northern edge of their range within Britain, it is not surprising that colonisation of the county is a relatively slow but steady process. Population density varies from site to site and birds may be absent from apparently suitable areas (Gibbons *et al.*, 1993), a situation which exists in the northern half of Northumberland but one that may change in the coming decades. The winter weather throughout the period of the current survey was not particularly harsh and it is not known how a prolonged period of severe weather might affect the local population. Nuthatches, however, will readily come to bird-tables and other artificial food sources which have no doubt helped establish healthy and viable 'population centres', particularly in the south of the county.

The atlas of breeding birds in Northumbria (Day *et al.*, 1995) revealed a total of 144 pairs in 98 tetrads, although it was acknowledged that it can be difficult to locate breeding Nuthatches within the constraints of timed visits, and therefore an estimated overall population of perhaps 200 pairs was given. This current winter survey found a total of 330 birds in 168 tetrads reinforcing the trend of continued colonisation. It is again likely some birds will have been missed due to the timed-visit survey methodology and some scattered areas of woodland habitat may not have been visited, but the results are encouraging for continued population growth.

MIKE S. HODGSON

Distribution by altitude

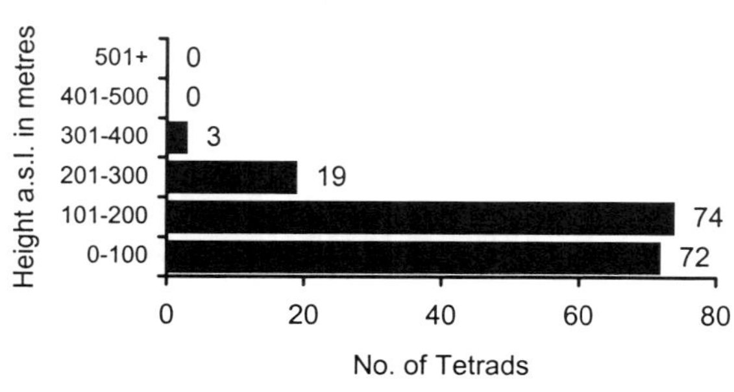

No. of tetrads in which recorded 168 (12%)

Tetrad Analysis	No. of tetrads
1 birds	85 (51%)
2 birds	54 (32%)
3+ birds	29 (17%)

Total No. of birds counted 330

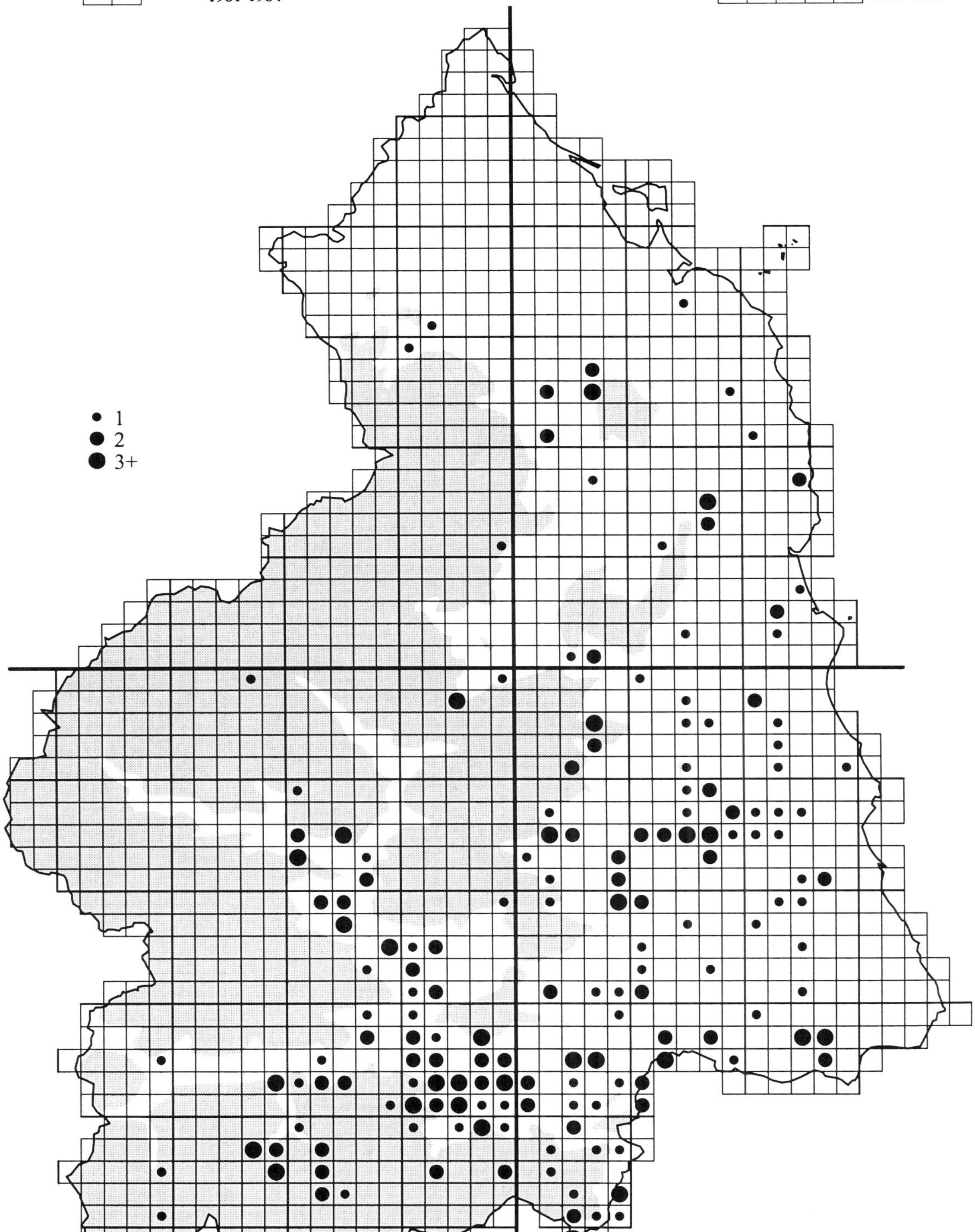

Nuthatch

TREECREEPER *Certhia familiaris*

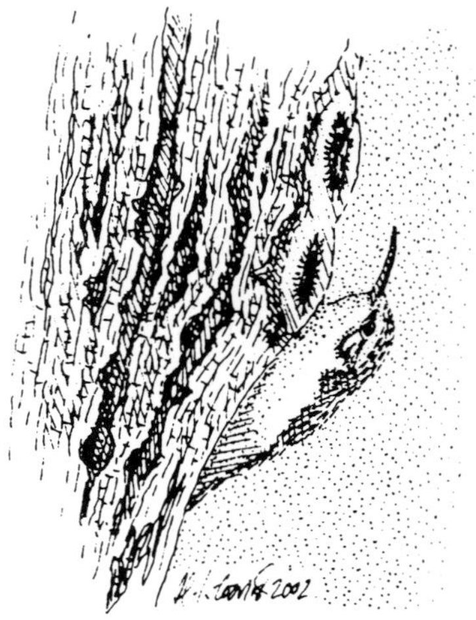

Bolam (1912) described the Treecreeper as being met in winter 'in the wake of a band of tits, hunting hedgerows at a considerable distance from trees' and again, in 1932, 'In winter it is a roving species readily attaching itself to the gypsy-like bands of titmice and similar birds that wander through the woods'. This has indeed been the usual description of the species' winter habit. However, recent research in the Holywell Dene area (Henderson, 1989) shows that the birds are 'usually to be found feeding solitarily'. Of 142 tit flocks observed, only 16% were found to contain Treecreepers. The solitary nature of this species is reflected in the analysis of the tetrad records throughout this survey. Single birds were recorded in 56% of tetrads visited while two were found in only 28% and three in 10%. In only two tetrads, at Caistron (NU00A) and Burnmouth, West Allen (NY75Z), was the maximum number of six birds recorded on any one visit.

Cramp & Simmons (1993) describes this species as 'strictly arboreal ... predominantly found in mature broad-leaved trees', the British race *britannica* being considered 'sedentary' with individuals rarely moving more than 20 km and there being 'no evidence for any marked descent from uplands' in winter (Lack, 1986). The breeding and winter distributions in Northumberland confirm this, Treecreepers being found in all areas of suitable woodland but rarely if ever above 300 metres a.s.l. They were found in 29% of tetrads between 0 and 200 metres a.s.l. and in 13% of those between 201 and 400 metres a.s.l. but there were no records higher than this. The map shows the Treecreeper to be well, if thinly, spread over the eastern part of the county but penetrating far up into the major river systems of the North and South Tyne and the Rede. Those 10km squares showing major concentrations (over 20 birds counted) were Hexham (NY96), Whittonstall (NZ05), the mid-Wansbeck Valley (NZ18) and Bardon Mill (NY76) where there is an abundance of suitable habitat.

Although there is considered to be no evidence of immigration into Britain from the continent (Lack, 1986), there are occasional instances of birds showing the characteristics of the northern race *C. f. familiaris* at coastal locations. Bolam (1912) noted two at or near Berwick in the winter of 1903 and wrote (1932) that they were 'occasionally found at such places as Holy Island'. This situation has not changed in the intervening years and singles or very small numbers are recorded in almost every winter along the coast with Holy Island, Bamburgh, Hauxley and Druridge Bay being the favoured localities.

Ringing recoveries (Flegg, 1973) show that the Treecreeper is one of our most sedentary of birds but that it can suffer in cold and wet winters. Cold weather movements and consequent population changes were evident in the hard winter of 1979 when up to six were found in Holywell Dene, while between September and November 1985 up to 18 were found along the Northumberland coast. Following the coldest February on record in 1986, they were 'noticeably absent from coastal areas' (*Birds in Northumbria 1986*). This dependence upon winter temperatures is perhaps also demonstrated by the slight change in average numbers per occupied control tetrad observed in the current survey when there was a marginal increase from 1.5 (1996/97) to 1.8 (1997/98) following the warmest February on record in 1997.

The Treecreeper can be difficult to locate due to its high-pitched call which is given most frequently early in the year between February and April and consequently it may be under-recorded. The 525 birds recorded in the current survey therefore match well with the 339 pairs noted in the local breeding survey, also considered to be an under-estimate (Day *et al.*, 1995). Nationally the Treecreeper population is considered to be 'fluctuating with no long-term trend' (Baillie *et al.*, 2001) and Mead (2000) expressed no concern in his statement 'still vulnerable to winter cold but otherwise set fair'.

MIKE R. SMITH

Distribution by altitude

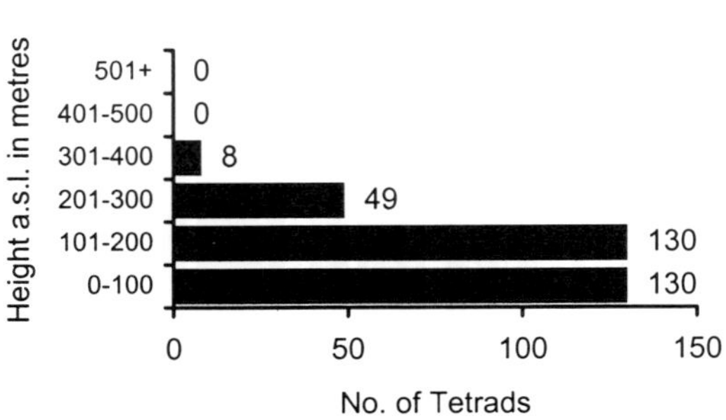

No. of tetrads in which recorded 317 (22%)

Tetrad Analysis	No. of tetrads
1 bird	179 (56%)
2 birds	90 (29%)
3+ birds	48 (15%)

Total No. of birds counted 525

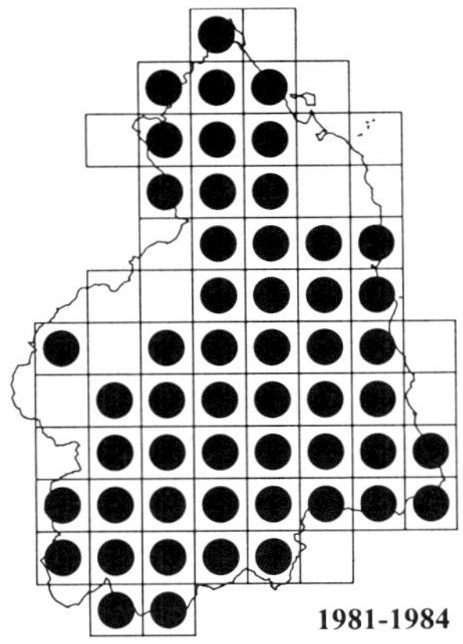

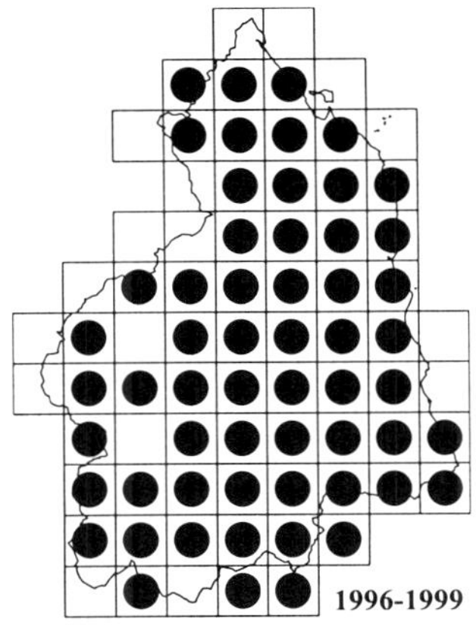

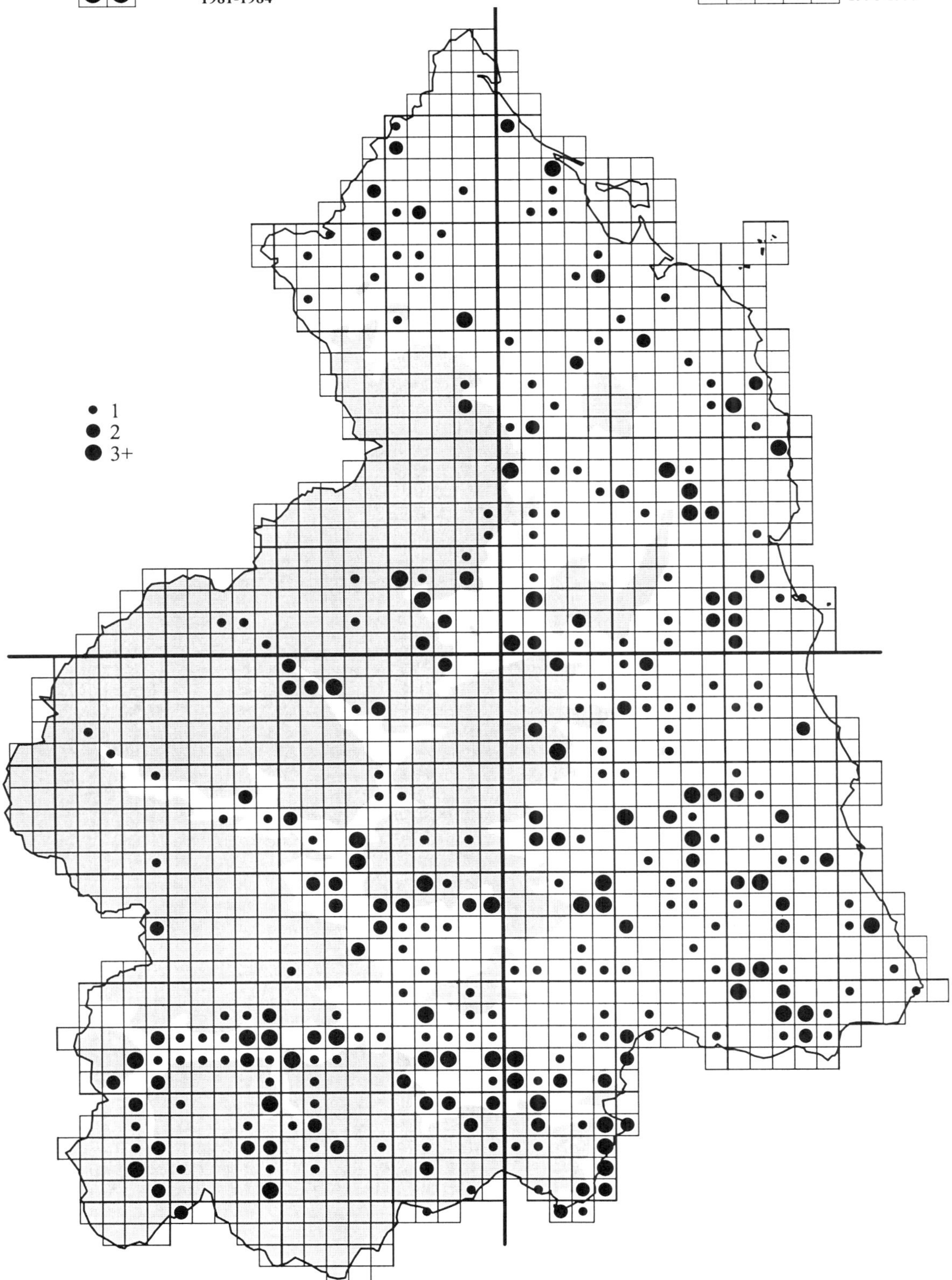

Treecreeper

GREAT GREY SHRIKE *Lanius excubitor*

Both Selby (1831) and Bolam (1912) regarded the Great Grey Shrike as an 'irregular' winter visitor. It occurred most winters, occasionally in good numbers, although in other years none occurred at all. Galloway and Meek (1983) stated that the wintering population 'seldom exceeds ten or a dozen birds' and that 'lowland areas with tall hawthorns are much favoured, while clear-felled areas within the border forests have been increasingly used during the 1970s. Certain wintering haunts may be used for several years in succession, but whether by the same individuals, or by different birds attracted to particularly suitable habitat, is not known'. More recently lowland areas have been less frequented, with most records coming from the Border Forest clear-felled sections, the winter population not normally exceeding five birds. In spring, (late March/April, but occasionally into May) there is usually a light coastal passage, which may include undetected local wintering birds.

This species is now much scarcer in winter than in the 1970s. Analysis of the data in *Birds in Northumbria 1970-1999* shows that between January-February 1970 and the 1978/79 winter period there were 60 records, with an average of six birds per winter period. As these data do not include information from mid-November-December 1969, the total may have been more. This contrasts with 19 records from the 1979/80-1988/89 and 1989/90-1998/99 winter periods, giving only an average of 1.9 birds per winter period. Whether this is due to fewer observers birdwatching at inland localities or fewer birds during the winter is not known. However, following the influx of autumn 1998, when five birds were seen along the coast, three were found during the winter period 1998/99, so the wintering population may be linked to the number of migrants in the preceding autumn.

During the 1981-1984 winter atlas survey, Great Grey Shrikes were found in nine widespread 10km squares, mainly in the south west quarter of the county, with birds in squares that contain land over 183 metres a.s.l. In the current winter survey birds were only recorded in three tetrads, all in the south west of the county and all in areas over 183 metres. It is quite probable that more birds were present during the survey period, especially in the Border Forest and perhaps Harwood Forest (NY99/NZ09) and the Slaley area (NY95), where there are vast areas of suitable habitat, most of which are relatively inaccessible. Typical habitat includes plenty of hunting perches, from which the birds can adopt the 'sit and wait' method of searching for prey. It must also include a reasonable amount of cover, in case there is danger. Great Grey Shrikes have a large winter territory, which they rigorously defend from other shrikes, so birds will be widely dispersed during the winter months. Probably, the secretive nature of the species may have played a part in its non-detection, as the four sightings in the current winter survey at Plashetts Burn (NY69R), near Kielder Village (NY69M), in Redesdale (NY79Z) and near Sweethope Loughs (NY98G) were from supplementary records rather than from timed visits.

IAN FISHER

No. of tetrads in which recorded	4 (<1%)
Tetrad Analysis	No. of tetrads
1 bird	4 (100%)
Total No. of birds counted	4

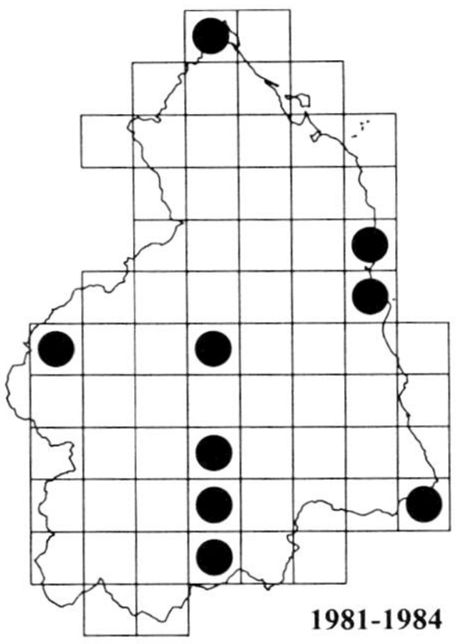

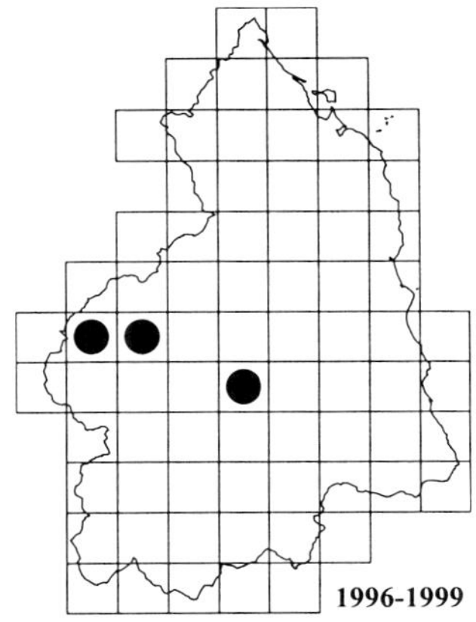

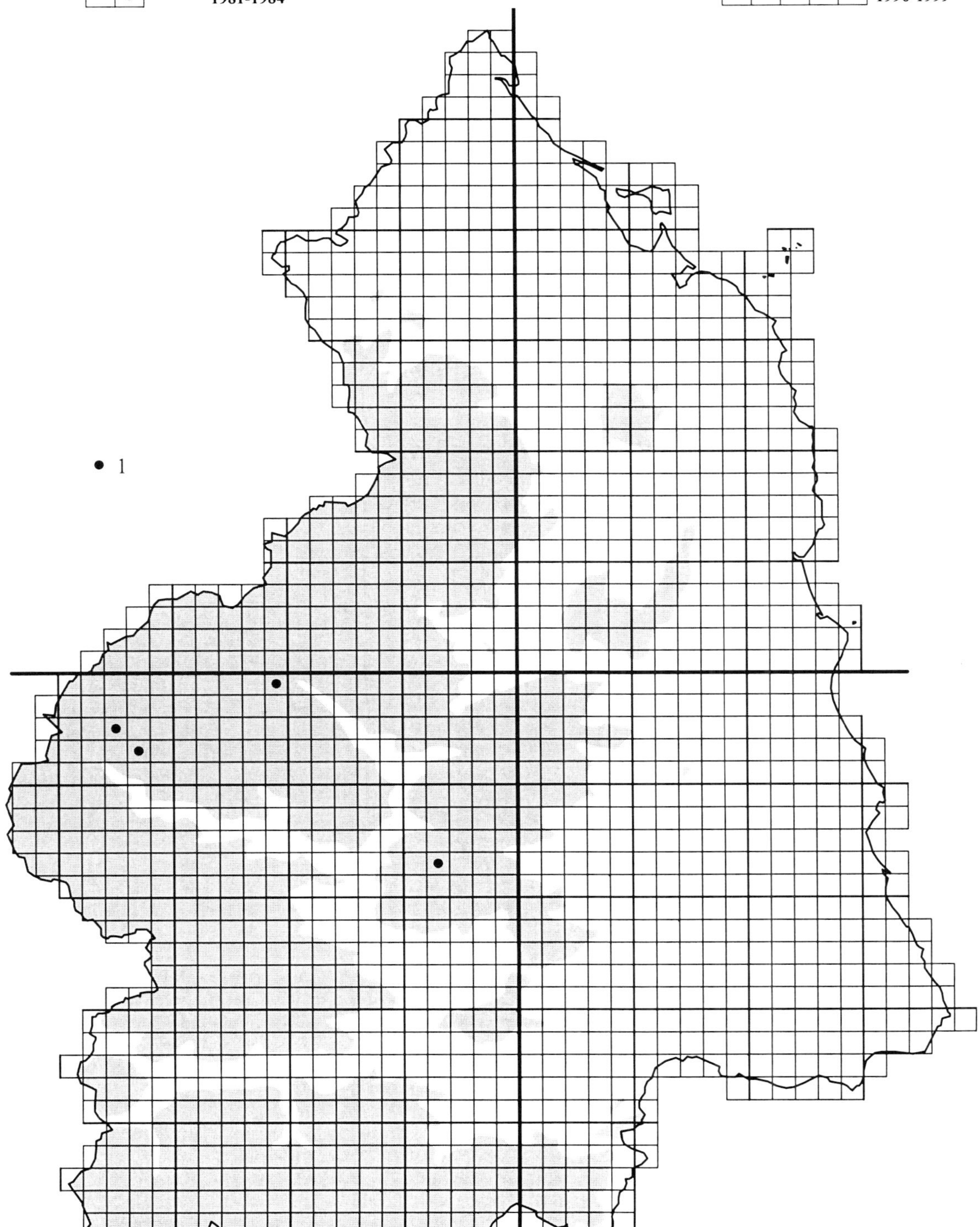

Great Grey Shrike

JAY *Garrulus glandarius*

Although the Jay has suffered a long history of persecution, Wallis, as early as 1769, was able to write that 'despite all persecution it has endured, ... it has never been entirely absent from the county'. A century later Hancock (1874) wrote that it was 'nearly annihilated' and laid the blame fairly and squarely upon the activities of gamekeepers. Contemporary winter records were few, e.g. one shot at Coupland Castle in 1878 and only two within living memory in Glendale, one seen at Detchant in 1879, one trapped at Harehope Hill in 1883 and one near Berwick in a snow storm in the winter of 1890/91 (Bolam, 1912). One of the few good things to come out of the First World War was the almost complete cessation of persecution and the Jay was consequently able to spread considerably throughout England and Scotland. By 1932 Bolam was able to report two or three pairs in the Haggerston Castle area in December 1931 where they had long been absent.

Being almost exclusively arboreal by nature, the Jay can be found in most types of woodland but favours oaks *Quercus* spp., having developed a taste for acorns. Indeed it has been credited with being responsible for the spread of oak woodland as a result of its habit of burying acorns as winter food (Lack, 1986). The tetrad distribution map shows the Jay to be well distributed throughout the lower-lying areas of the county, with concentrations in suitable habitat in the Tyne Valley around Hexham and Stocksfield (NY96 & NZ06) with maximum counts of 34 and 25 birds respectively, the Gosforth Park area (NZ27) with 26, the Wansbeck Valley (NZ28) with 21 and Whittonstall (NZ05) and the Kyloe/Swinhoe areas (NU03) with totals of 19 birds each. With the exception of the Holystone 10km square (NT90), there are very few records of Jays in the higher land to the west and height analysis of tetrad records reveals that no birds were found above 400 metres a.s.l. Out of the total of 169 occupied tetrads throughout the county, no fewer than 157 were below 200 metres a.s.l., which represents only 17% of the total of 902 tetrads below this level, demonstrating clearly how thinly spread the species is.

Confirmation of the sedentary nature of the Jay is given by comparison with the distribution map in the current survey with that in *The atlas of breeding birds in Northumbria* (Day *et al.*, 1995), the only significant difference being a move in winter from the upper reaches of the North Tyne Valley. Birds were recorded in 152 tetrads compared to the 169 of the present survey. Hard winters can however produce influxes of birds from the continent as was noted in 1897 (Bolam, 1912) when, in the north of the county, many survived 'until the following Spring when they were shot'. In the same year many were seen in the south of the county for the first time. Writing in 1932, Bolam mentioned this influx as well as those of 1901, 1917 and 1931 but doubted whether any birds were from the continent. More recently in 1983, when the main food crop failed in continental Europe, birds were to be found in larger than normal numbers throughout Britain. In Northumberland small numbers were recorded on the coast with a peak in late October, small flocks being noted until the end of the year (Galloway & Meek, 1986). Between October and December 1993 there was a similar occurrence (*Birds in Northumbria 1993*).

Outside the breeding season, Jays do not move far, generally less than 10 km (Lack, 1986), but roam through suitable woodland seeking food. They are most vociferous at this time but generally can be difficult to locate and to count reliably. For this reason they may well be under-recorded but the total number in the current survey of 321 birds compares reasonably with the estimated population of 207 breeding pairs (Day *et al.*, 1995).

Nationally, Lack (1986) notes the steady increase in Jay numbers during the past century, especially since the 1940s and, in his account *The state of the nation's birds*, Mead (2000) wrote 'Woodland Jays, at least, seem to be doing well'. In Northumberland too, this certainly seems to be the case.

MIKE R. SMITH

Distribution by altitude

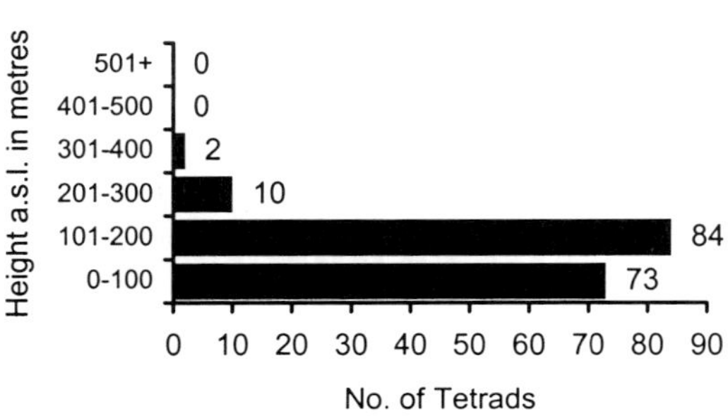

No. of tetrads in which recorded	169 (12%)
Tetrad Analysis	No. of tetrads
1 bird	84 (50%)
2 birds	50 (29%)
3+ birds	35 (21%)
Total No. of birds counted	321

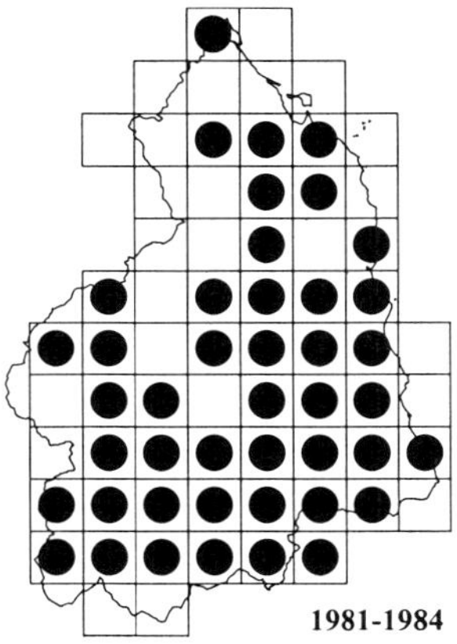

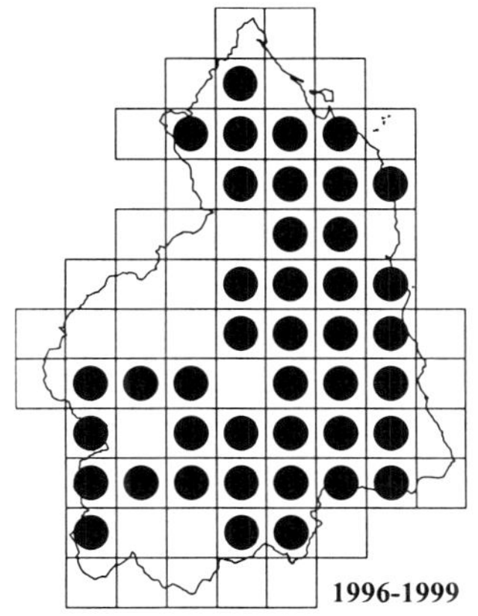

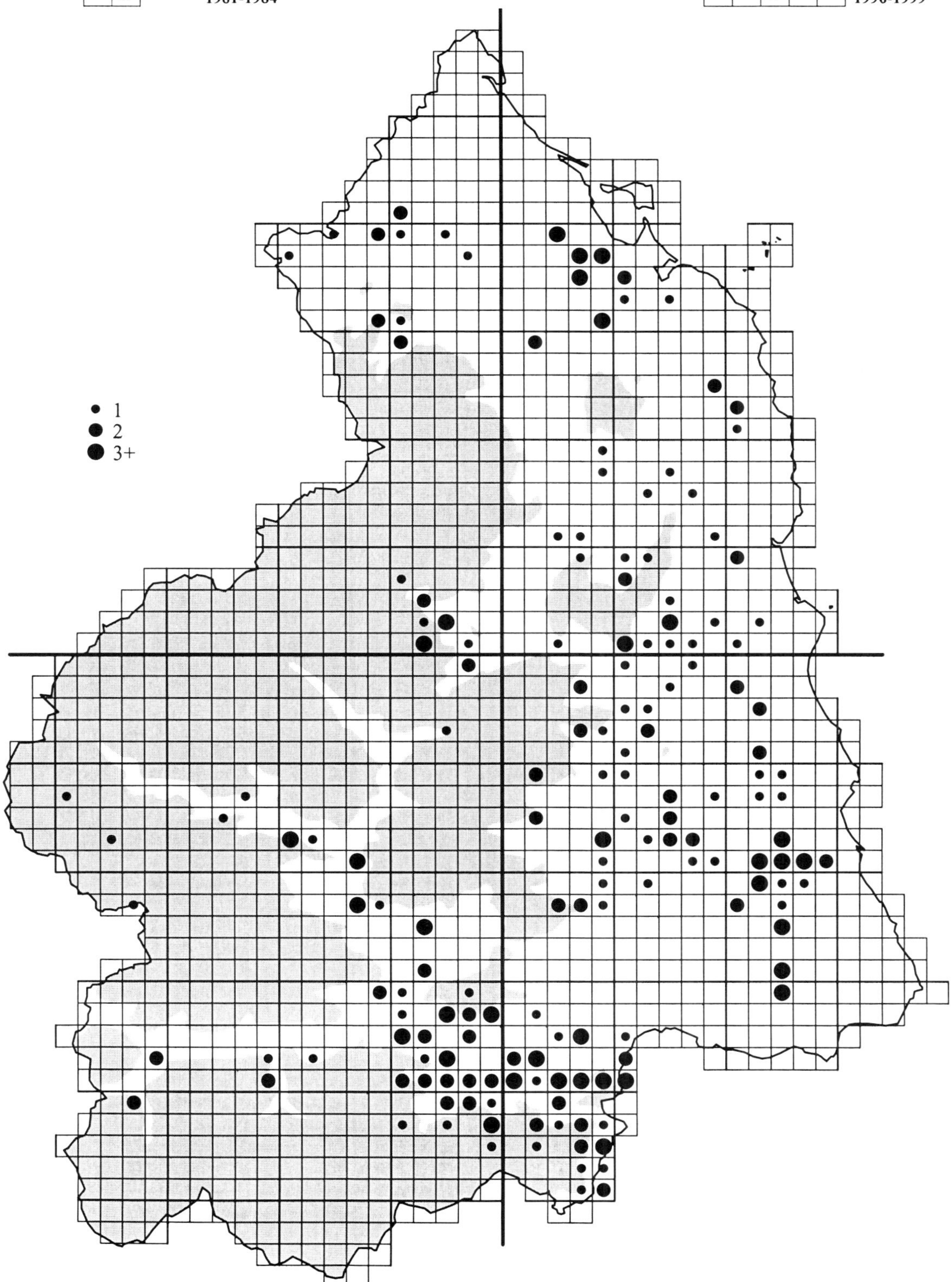

Jay

MAGPIE *Pica pica*

With its unmistakable plumage and harsh voice, the Magpie is now a very familiar and noticeable bird throughout the county. As early as 1912, Bolam described it as 'a resident, almost exterminated in many places, but still fairly common in others'. Later, in 1932, he considered that its numbers in any given area were 'dependent only upon the exigencies of game-preserving'. Galloway and Meek (1983) observed that increases noted in the 1940s could be attributed to the decline in gamekeeping during the Second World War and that it seemed 'to be most numerous in agricultural areas with tall hedges and scattered woodland'. They also noted that it was an increasingly frequent visitor to urban gardens. Mead (2000) described the bird as having a stable population following a big increase and suggested that the 'outlook seems excellent for a very well adapted species for modern living'.

During winter, the Magpie depends upon a mainly vegetarian diet supplemented by the occasional small mammal and the opportunity to scavenge on road-kill victims. Like other members of the corvid family, the habit of food hoarding is an important aspect of their feeding ecology. In addition, their spread into urban areas has led them to exploit bird feeding stations in gardens. The BTO Garden Bird Feeding Survey records from the 1970s list the Magpie as occurring in 29.4% of gardens and rank it 17th in frequency. Recent records from the 1990s show that it is now recorded in 71.7% of gardens surveyed, and that its rank has moved up to 12th. This is all in keeping with its well-documented national population increase and range expansion.

These trends are also evident at the local level where, in Northumberland, the 1981-1984 winter survey recorded Magpies in 76% of the 10km squares compared with 79% in the recent winter survey. In addition, the average number per occupied tetrad recorded in the control squares increased from 4.6 in 1996/97 to 5.5 in 1998/99. In total, during the recent survey, 2,720 Magpies were counted in 535 tetrads (37% of the number surveyed). Of these, 463 (87%) were below 200 metres a.s.l. confirming its preference for lowland habitats. The tetrad distribution map shows a concentration in the south and east of the county with numbers declining significantly to the west and north. The species is well-represented in the main river valleys of the Tyne and its tributaries and the climate of the coastal strip is undoubtedly a factor encouraging wintering birds to stay in the north of the county.

The Magpie is generally monogamous and pairs remain together throughout the year. However, during winter months, flocks start to form and communal roosting is quite common. In the 1970s, flocks of between ten and 20 birds were noted with a maximum of 40 at Slaley in January 1976. During the 1980s, an increase in roosts and large gatherings were recorded with 138 at Stocksfield in February 1983 being the largest count. Groups and roosts were also noted in areas where the species had previously been scarce such as 30 at Seaton Burn in November 1986 and 19 at Arcot in December 1987. Large roosts became a feature of the 1990s with numbers at Big Waters (NZ27G) steadily increasing to a reserve record of 85 in February 1999. In addition the expansion north and south west, as well as onto moorland edges, was confirmed by two at Coanwood in January 1997 (*Birds in Northumbria 1972-1999*). This recent winter survey recorded nine groups of 30 or more birds, mainly in the south east of the region, around the fringes of the urban zone. They included counts of 45-63 at Throckley (NZ16N), Wallsend Swallow Pond (NZ36E) and near Corbridge (NZ06B), with 30-40 at Heddon-on-the-Wall (NZ16I), Cramlington (NZ27T), Bedlington (NZ28R), Marden Quarry (NZ37K) and Medburn (NZ17F).

Adult Magpies are very territorial throughout the year and seldom move more than 0.5km even if they change territories. Immature birds up to 2 years old spend most of their time within 2km of their natal area and a survey of birds ringed as chicks found that 80% of recoveries were within 5km of the nest. (Lack, 1986). In the 1988-1992 county breeding atlas survey, Magpies were recorded in 73% of the 10km squares visited (Day *et al.*, 1995) compared with 79% during the winter survey. The slight increase is no doubt due to population growth and range expansion over the last decade. Day *et al.* (1995) concluded the total breeding population in the county was in the range of 750-1,000 pairs. Thus the overall wintering total for this survey is not an unreasonable indication of the current status of Magpie in Northumberland.

ALAN J. DAVIS

Distribution by altitude

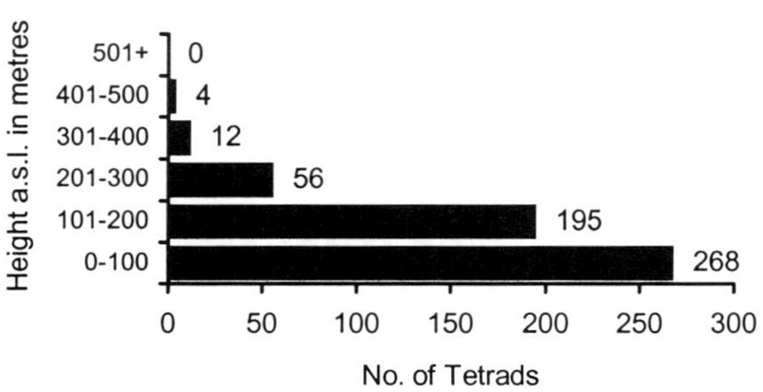

No. of tetrads in which recorded 535 (37%)

Tetrad Analysis	No. of tetrads
1-2 birds	246 (46%)
3-6 birds	185 (35%)
7+ birds	104 (19%)

Total No. of birds counted 2,720

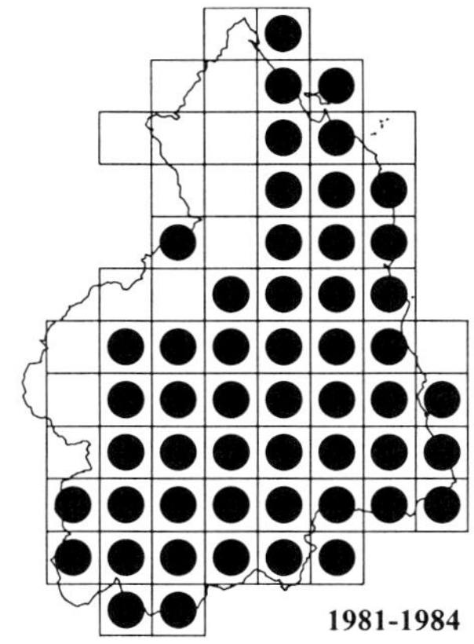

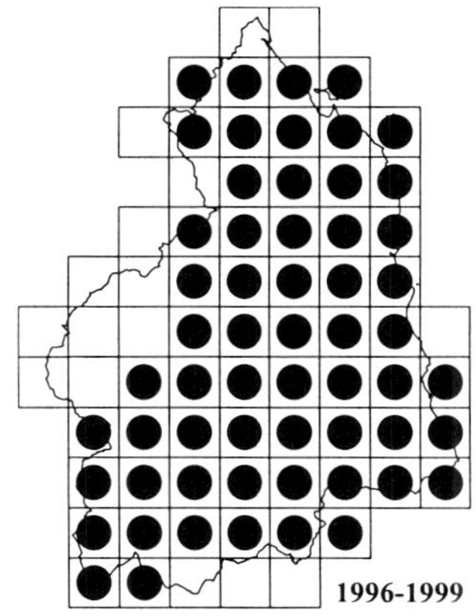

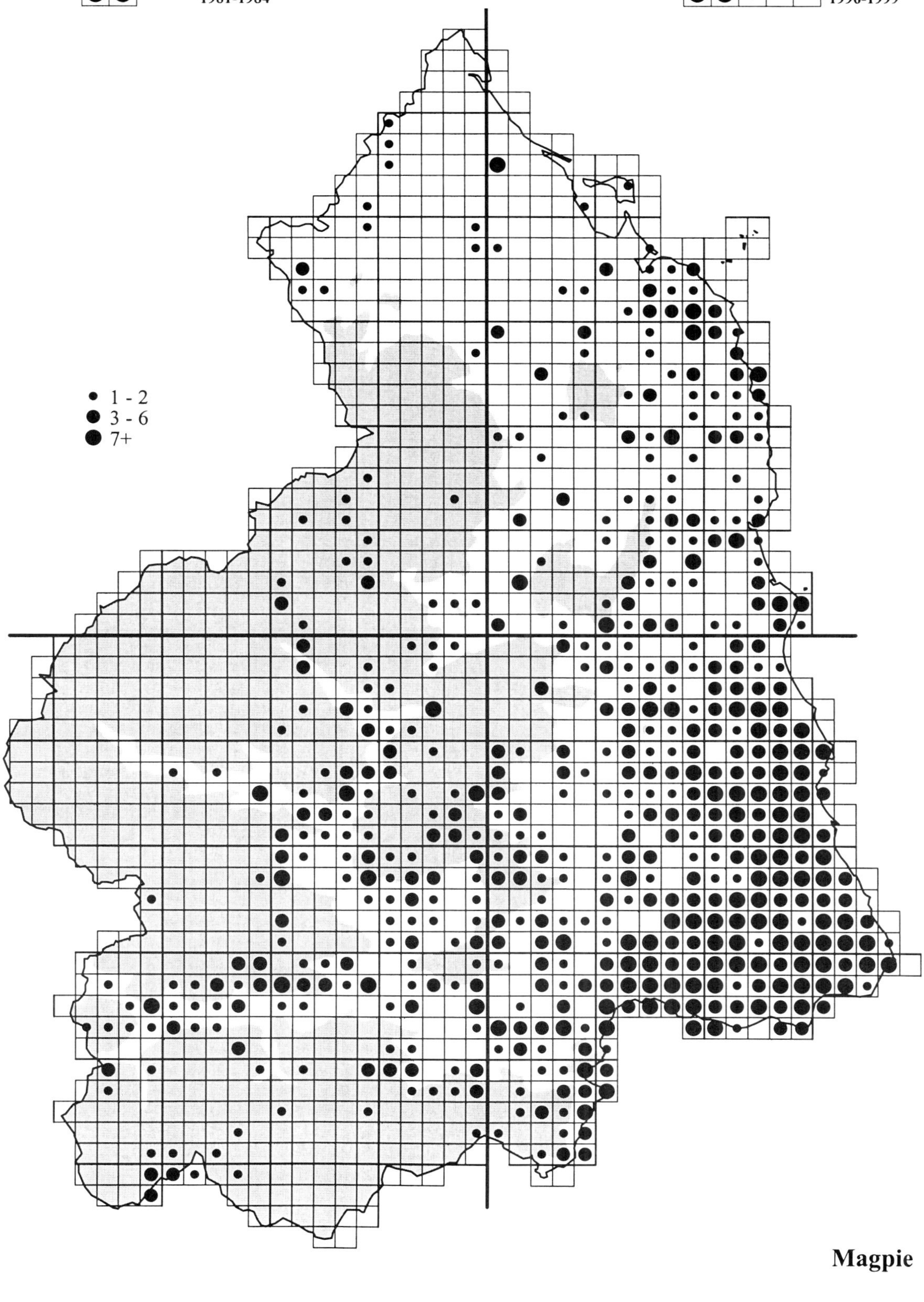

Magpie

JACKDAW *Corvus monedula*

In Northumberland, the adaptable and gregarious Jackdaw was historically described as a 'very common resident' by Hancock (1874) and as a 'common resident ... increased greatly in living memory' by Bolam (1912). The increase in the species continued throughout the UK during much of the twentieth century and received a boost during the Second World War due to the expansion in arable farming. Hagemeijer and Blair (1997) suggested that the British population has continued to grow since 1975 in contrast to much of Europe where populations have more or less stabilised. The reasons for the continued growth are not clear as it coincided with progressive agricultural intensification and without an improvement in the availability of nest sites. They also indicated that in Britain adults are remarkably sedentary whereas in continental Europe, particularly in northern regions, the species undergoes extensive south westerly movements in autumn. Of interest during the survey period was a single bird showing the characteristics of the eastern race *C. m. soemmerringii* at Druridge Pools (NZ29T) on 4th February 1997.

Snow and Perrins (1998) stated that although the species is frequently gregarious outside the breeding season, life-long pair-bonds are formed in the first year and the pair is the basic unit within flocks. In the sedentary parts of the range, pairs will continue to visit nest-sites almost throughout the year. Records of Jackdaw in *Birds in Northumbria* published during the 1990s do not suggest that the species migrates in significant numbers between the county and Scandinavia and this conclusion corroborates the findings of Galloway and Meek (1983).

Over the three winters during which data were collected for this atlas, a total of 56,117 were counted in 866 tetrads, 60% of those covered during the fieldwork. The altitudinal distribution of the species during the winter months makes an interesting comparison with that during the breeding season. *The atlas of breeding birds in Northumbria* (Day *et al*., 1995) recorded breeding pairs in 747 (53%) of the tetrads surveyed and demonstrated that, as a breeding bird, the Jackdaw was effectively absent from land above 250 metres a.s.l. in the recording area. Although the species is more widely distributed in winter, the altitudinal range remains very similar with 97% of the records from land up to 300 metres a.s.l. The winter range mirrors the breeding range very closely. The species is found predominantly on agricultural land although its flexibility in diet also allows it to spread into urban areas and along the main river valleys onto higher ground. It is largely absent from moorland and very densely forested areas. The survey confirmed the gregarious nature of the species although some 82% of the maximum counts recorded were of less than 100 birds. Three very large counts were reported with 1,000 birds near Ashington (NZ28U) and Caistron (NU00A) in January and February 1997 respectively and 5,000 at a pre-roost gathering near Rudchester (NZ16E) in November 1997. In addition, there were counts in 11 tetrads of between 375 and 800 birds. Many sizeable counts were made in adjacent tetrads in the same survey period and some duplication cannot be ruled out. Similarly, the presence of large flocks, over successive winters, in tetrads that lie in close proximity might also mean that winter numbers have been exaggerated, bearing in mind the Jackdaw's highly sedentary nature. The survey methodology has further exacerbated the findings by taking the maximum count over the three winter seasons for each tetrad.

The true wintering population is therefore difficult to estimate. Some 5,100 breeding pairs have been reported in the recording area (Day *et al*., 1995) and, in the absence of major post-breeding movements, the wintering population might be expected to be of a similar order of magnitude. Given that the wintering flocks may be expected to move around as optimum feeding areas and climatic conditions vary, multiple counting of wintering birds as suggested above, seems inevitable, but it is extremely hard to gauge the extent of this. Analysis of the 43 control tetrads occupied by the species showed a remarkable consistency in total numbers over the three seasons with 1,778, 1,811 and 1,814 birds respectively, producing an overall average of 44 per occupied tetrad each winter. If this average were to be maintained over all the occupied tetrads, nearly four times the breeding population estimated in 1995 would be present in the recording area! Whilst such a large influx could hardly go unreported, a crude calculation of the number of breeding pairs plus, say two surviving fledged young per pair, and an expansion of the species, as noted by Mead (2000), suggests that a figure of between 25,000-30,000 wintering birds in Northumberland would not be unreasonable.

BRIAN SYKES

Distribution by altitude

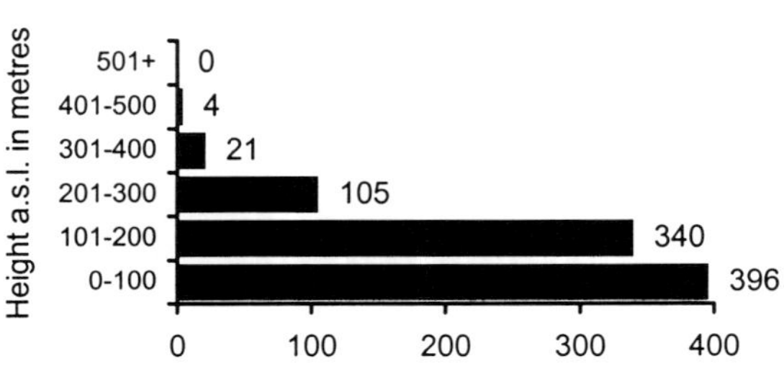

No. of tetrads in which recorded 866 (60%)

Tetrad Analysis	No. of tetrads
1-30 birds	434 (50%)
31-85 birds	258 (30%)
86+ birds	174 (20%)

Total No. of birds counted 56,117

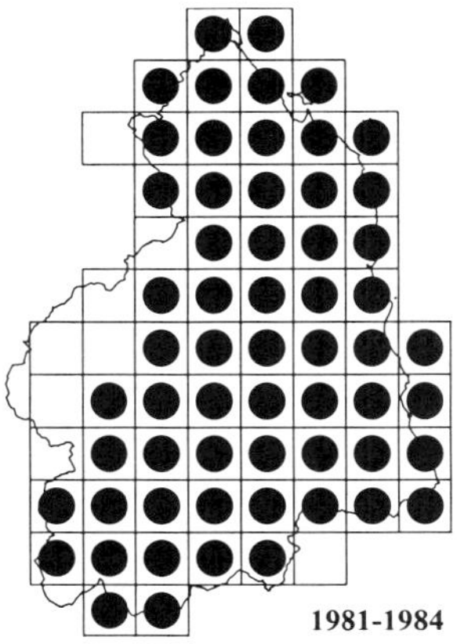

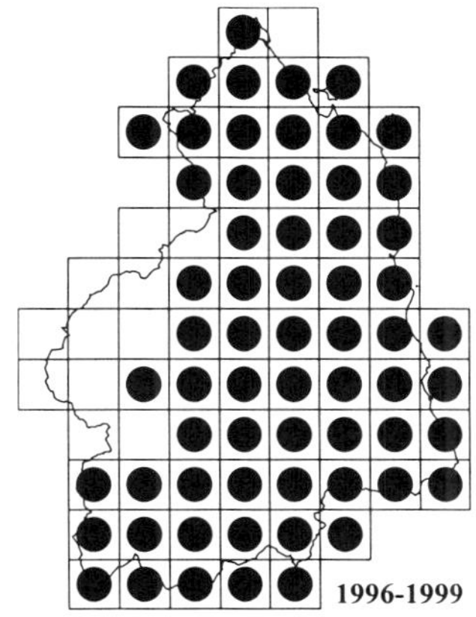

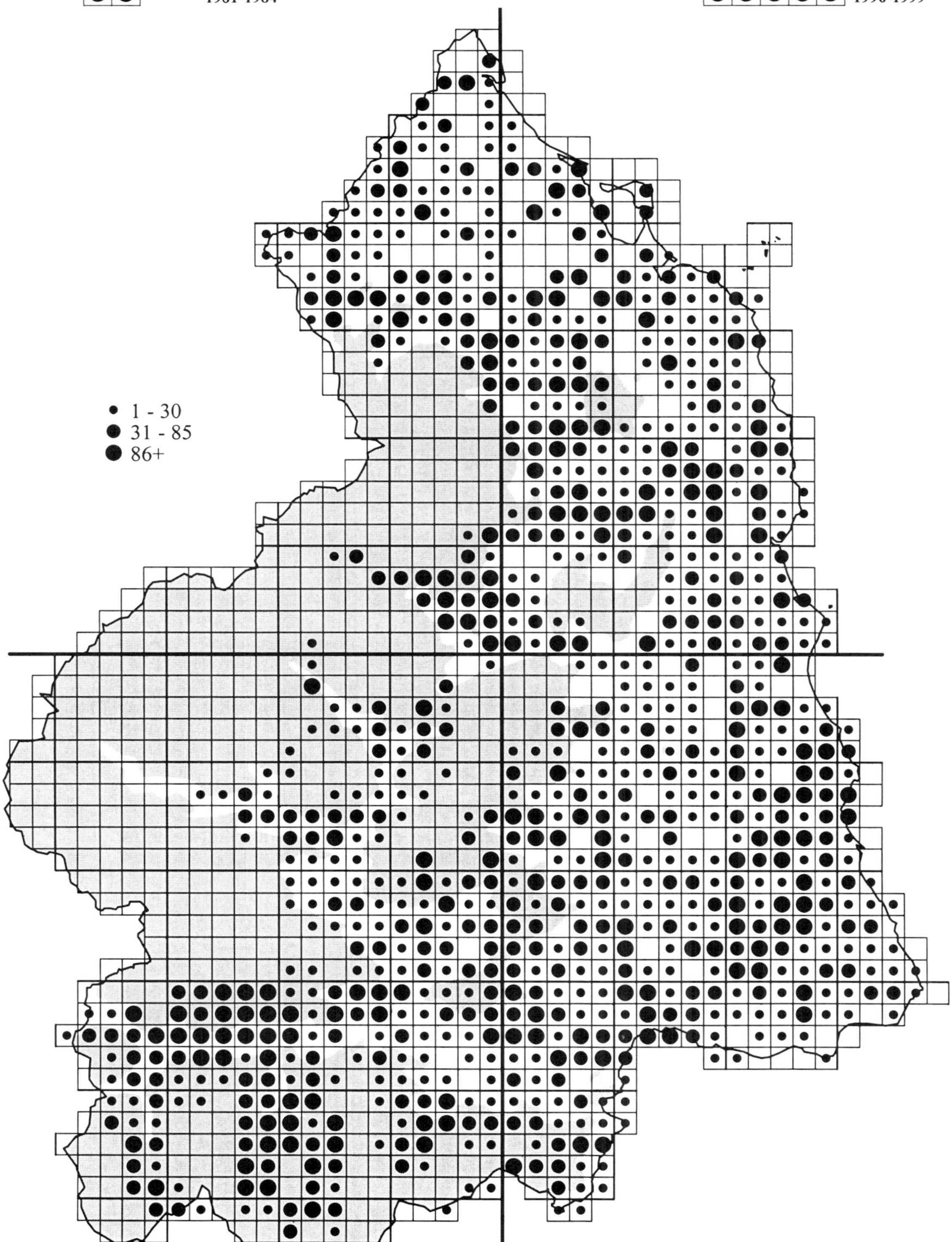

Jackdaw

ROOK *Corvus frugilegus*

Galloway and Meek (1983) gave a fairly comprehensive history of the Rook's changing fortunes in Northumberland, since the time of Hancock, and outlined the results of a number of local breeding surveys. They showed some rookeries had attained considerable age in the county, quoting Smail (1882-84), who named a number of colonies that were 'old' in 1877 and indicated that others probably dated back to the late eighteenth century. Bolam (1912) believed that winter numbers were increased as a result of large scale autumn immigration but Galloway and Meek could show no recent evidence of such coastal movements and this situation remains today.

The most recent breeding survey in the county in 1996 revealed that 350 tetrads contained rookeries, representing 26% of those visited. A total of 27,016 nests were counted with the bulk of the population in the NU and NZ sectors. These results identified an apparent decline since the previous 'one season' survey in 1980, and indicated that, at present, the results from Northumberland do not reflect the national upward trend (Cadwallender & Cadwallender, 1997). The results of the local breeding atlas fieldwork between 1988-1992 produced confirmed or probable breeding in 402 tetrads (29% of those surveyed) with a grand total of only 17,034 pairs counted (Day *et al.*, 1995), but the survey methodology was not felt to have been conducive to obtaining accurate population figures for this species.

A comparison of the 10km square winter distribution maps would seem to indicate little change between the two, with 61 squares occupied in both 1981-1984 and 1996-1999. However, it should be borne in mind that these represent a rate of 90% and 81% occupancy respectively of the total of squares visited, suggesting some decline in the years between the two surveys. A more interesting comparison can be made between the local breeding atlas and the current winter survey tetrad maps. Whilst superficially these are broadly similar in terms of overall distribution, there were over 300 more occupied tetrads in winter presumably reflecting the movement of feeding and roosting birds during that season. Many of these additional tetrads are along the lowland coastal plain where the bulk of the breeding population is found, but there are noticeable concentrations in the south west of the county, suggesting favourable wintering conditions in that area at least during the three periods of this survey. As expected, the bulk of the population was found at relatively low altitude with 751 (85%) of occupied tetrads falling in the range of 0 to 200 metres a.s.l., 106 (12%) in the range 201 to 300 metres a.s.l. and only 23 (3%) above 300 metres. The data from control tetrads showed that Rooks were found in 42 (70%) of the squares involved and, reflecting its widespread distribution in some areas, were noted in 30 (71%) of these in all three winter periods. Numerically, the control tetrad total counts seemed to indicate a fairly stable population in the first two winters but perhaps show a slight decline in the third with 3,247 birds in 1996/97, 3,077 in 1997/98 and 2,717 in 1998/99.

In winter, Rooks, often together with large numbers of Jackdaws *Corvus monedula*, form large communal roosts usually in traditional sites. Birds may gather from many kilometres around to attend these roosts (Coombs, 1978; Lack, 1986). Certainly large flocks at dawn and dusk are a regular sight throughout many areas of the county on a winter's day, but only a few of the counts gathered for the current survey were noted as being from pre or post roost gatherings, or indeed from the roosts themselves. The largest counts of 2,000 birds came from Alnwick (NU11W) in November 1998 and the Buston Barns area (NU20I) in January 1999. 1,600 were near Hetton Hall (NU03G) in December 1997 and 1,100 at Holburn Grange (NU03M) in January 1997. Other large counts involved three tetrads with 1,000, 21 with 500-950 and 291 tetrads holding between 100-495 birds. The vast majority of counts were much lower with between one-99 birds in 561 tetrads (64% of those occupied). There is a suggestion from some data that a number of the larger counts from adjacent or reasonably close tetrads, within the same winter period, may indicate an element of over-counting. However, with a resident breeding population of around 27,000 pairs, each rearing an average of two young, then the grand total counted during the survey of 99,737 would appear to be a not unreasonable estimate of the early winter population. Even so, as the Rook is acknowledged as a good 'indicator' species, continued monitoring of the population seems advisable in order to detect any changes in the fortunes of this, and perhaps other species, in the county.

MIKE S. HODGSON

Distribution by altitude

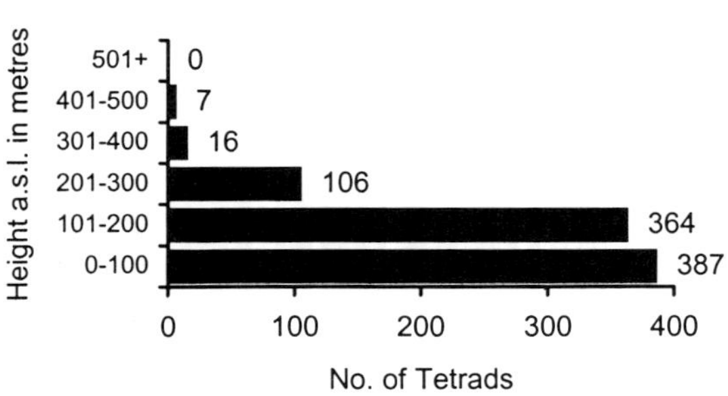

No. of tetrads in which recorded 880 (61%)

Tetrad Analysis	No. of tetrads
1-60 birds	438 (50%)
61-170 birds	271 (31%)
171+ birds	171 (19%)

Total No. of birds counted 99,737

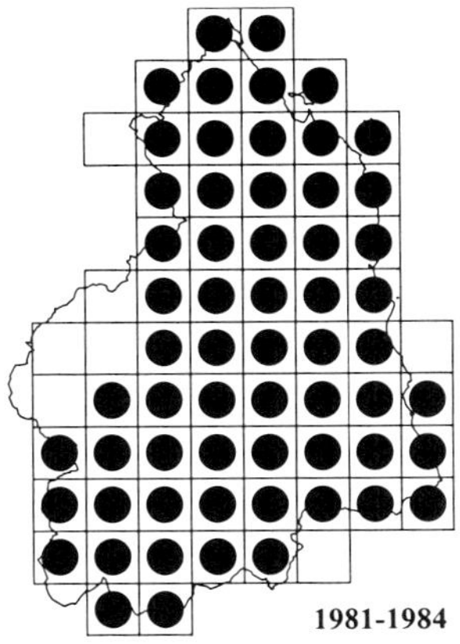

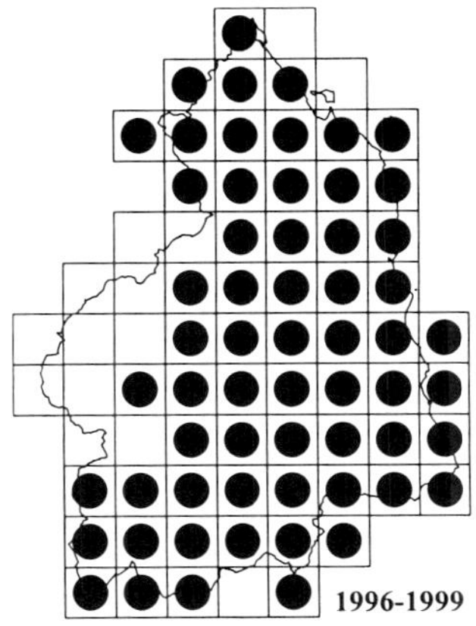

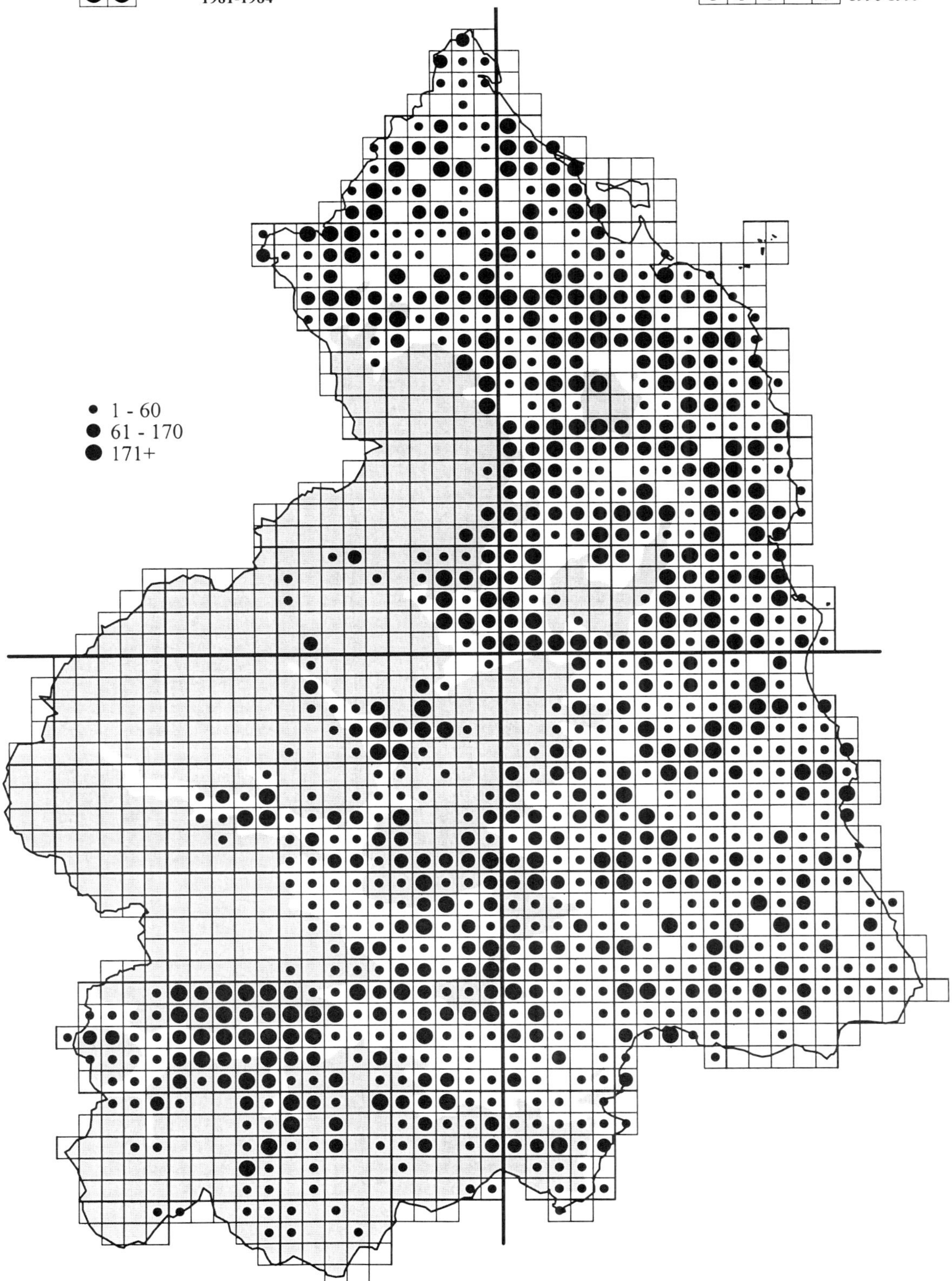

Rook

CARRION CROW *Corvus corone corone*

As one of the most visible groups of birds in Britain, the crow family is a good indicator species of the state of the environment. Carrion Crows, in particular, are found in every habitat, from the coastal shore to mountain tops, dense woodland, through farmland, to the centre of towns. In fact they occur anywhere where there is a good food supply and a tolerance level from humans who don't regard every member of the crow family as vermin. Both Hancock (1874) and Bolam (1932) were concerned about the persecution of crows, and the effect on the population but, since the Second World War when gamekeeping declined, numbers of crows have gradually increased. They are still considered by some gamekeepers to be a serious predator of game birds and, by farmers, to be responsible for lamb deaths. Despite legal control measures, over the last 35 years there has been a four-fold increase in the British population shown by the Common Bird Census index (Mead, 2000).

With its catholic taste in food, it is no surprise that the Carrion Crow is the most widespread species to be recorded in the county during the current winter atlas survey, being present in 1,180 out of the 1,432 tetrads. Its feeding habits will take it to ploughed and stubble fields, roadside verges (for casualties), the shoreline and, of course, rubbish tips. Holyoak (1968) listed 26 items of food taken from gizzards of 234 crows in an agricultural area in southern England. Of these, grain, live small mammals (March-August), wild-plant seeds, and carrion were the most important food items, with earthworms featuring highly from January to April. In Argyllshire, a study on the effect of Hooded Crows on sheep farming found that between November and February stomach contents contained 62% carrion, 27% grain, 6% small mammals and 5% beetles. In winter, communal roosting is quite normal. Sometimes the normally solitary and sedentary breeding Carrion Crow will join Rooks *C. frugilegus* and Jackdaws *C. monedula* to form large assemblies of roosting birds. They will roost in quite dense woodland at night, although it is thought that Carrion Crows do not travel quite as far as Rooks and Jackdaws to do so (Coombs, 1978).

During the winter atlas fieldwork, the largest concentrations were 164 at Widdrington tip (NZ29M) in December 1997, 156 near Bywell (NZ06L) in February 1999, 152 each at Harlow Hill (NZ06Z) and near Mordington on the Scottish border (NT95M) in January 1999. A further 30 tetrads held 50 or more birds but, as befits its normally solitary nature, over 50% of the records were of between one and seven birds.

No Carrion Crows were recorded in tetrads over 500 metres a.s.l. but 41% of tetrads between 401 and 500 metres a.s.l. were occupied rising to 93% of all tetrads below 200 metres a.s.l. The 10km square with fewest birds reported was NY79 which includes the north eastern area of Kielder Forest and Emblehope Moor. It only held three birds in two tetrads suggesting that altitude and the dense expanse of conifer forest are probably the reasons for the dearth of birds. In the control tetrads the highest total count of birds was 681 in the 1997/98 season, having been 539 in the previous winter period. Nevertheless the tetrad average for occupancy over the three winters was reasonably stable at 10.5, 13.6 and 12.2 birds. A comparison with the county breeding distribution map (Day *et al.*, 1995) confirms the sedentary nature of Carrion Crows although, as already noted, some birds leave higher bleak moorlands and the blanket conifer areas in the winter months.

Although the total of 13,860 birds achieved during the current survey may include some duplication of counts in adjacent tetrads, the local breeding atlas estimate of 3,716 pairs, each of which could produce an average of 1.5 young per year, also gives a potential winter population in the region of 13,000 birds. Whilst this could imply the winter population consists wholly of our resident birds, and that its status remains stable, there is a possibility of some originating from the continent. Both Bolam (1932) and Galloway and Meek (1983) noted apparent arrivals on the coast in autumn.

continued overleaf

Distribution by altitude

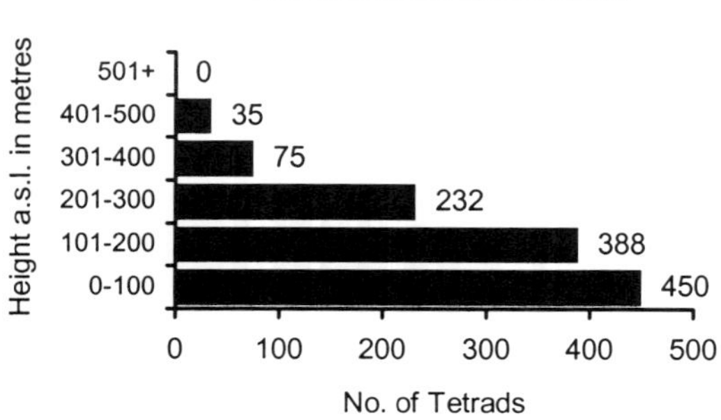

No. of tetrads in which recorded 1,180 (82%)

Tetrad Analysis	No. of tetrads
1-7 birds	598 (51%)
8-17 birds	369 (31%)
18+ birds	213 (18%)

Total No. of birds counted 13,860

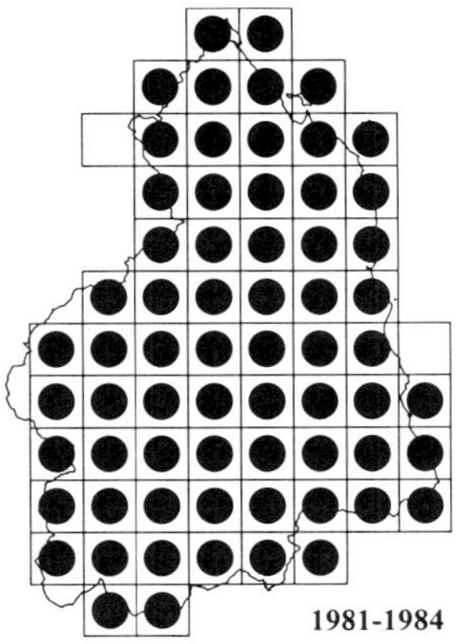

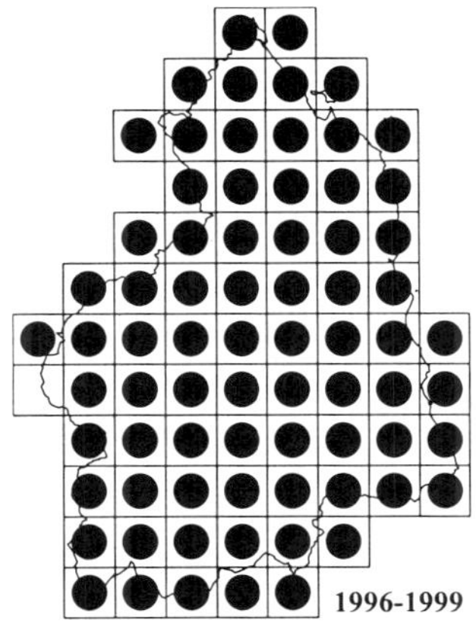

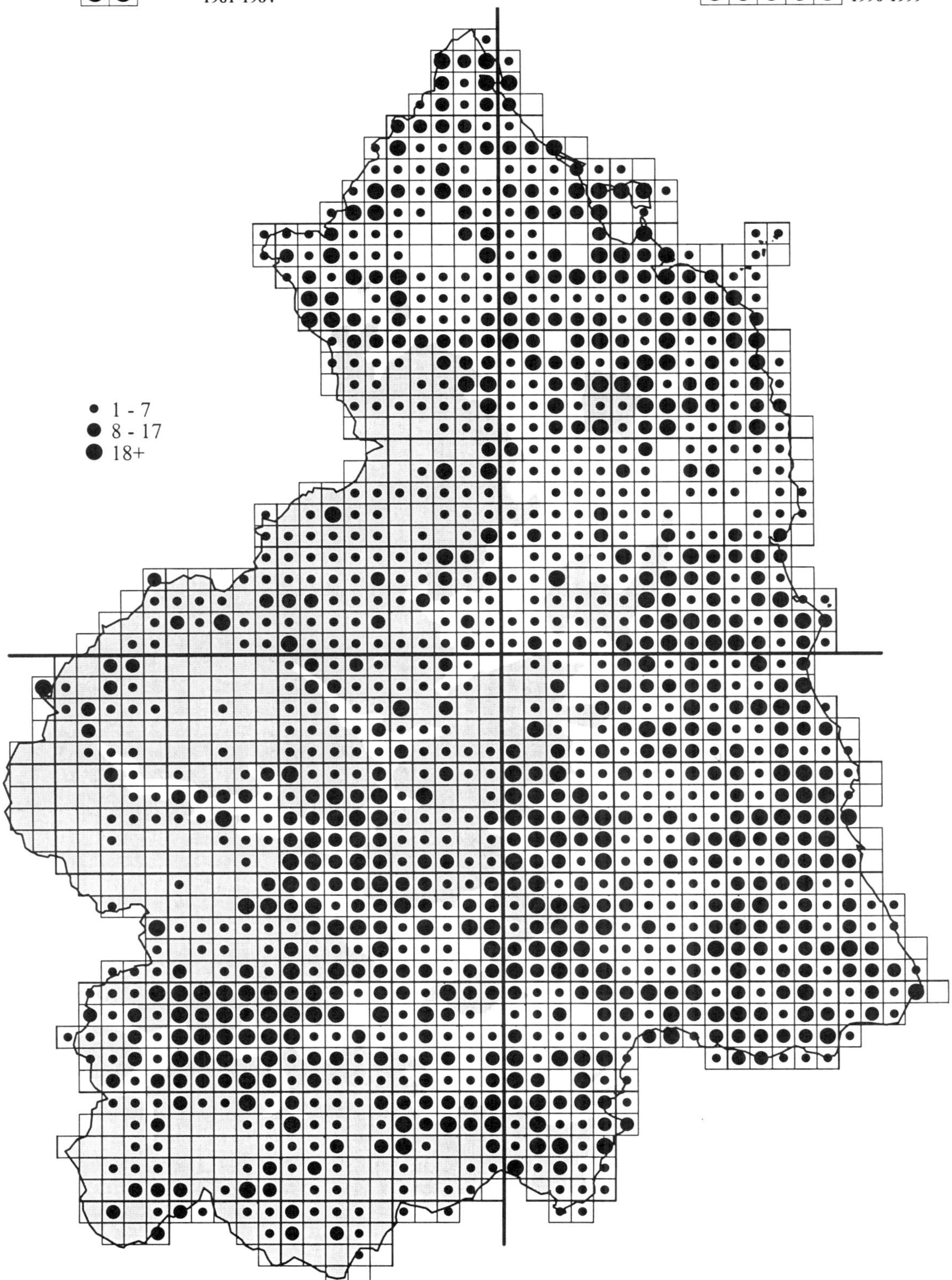

Carrion Crow

HOODED CROW *Corvus corone cornix*

The Carrion Crow *Corvus corone corone* and Hooded Crow *C. c. cornix* are thought to have developed in isolation during a separation caused by the last ice age (Coombs, 1978) and they and their hybrids have bred all over Britain at least since records began. Because the hybrids are generally fertile birds, the two subspecies are still regarded as one species. The Carrion Crow is predominant in Northumberland with records of Hooded Crow diminishing over the past 40 years. The Scottish area of the hybrid population of *C. c. corone* and *C. c. cornix* has been moving further away from Northumberland to the north and west over the last 70 years (Mead, 2000), though some are still breeding in the hills south of Edinburgh (Murray *et al.*, 1998). Up until 1979 breeding occasionally occurred in Northumberland (Galloway & Meek, 1983).

By the 1980s, the Hooded Crow was regarded as an uncommon passage and winter visitor, occasionally reaching the well-represented status (Galloway & Meek, 1983). Bolam (1912) had recorded flocks of up to 100 Hooded Crows arriving at Berwick in the autumn, and although later records of winter flocks included 80 in Budle Bay in November 1948 and 50-60 in Whitley Bay, Blyth and Seaton Burn in 1960, since then the number of sightings has diminished dramatically. Only two birds were recorded over the three winter seasons of the survey. In December 1997, one was well inland at Greenleighton (NZ09G), the other, in January 1999, in a more typical coastal location near Beadnell (NU22J). Even allowing for other occasional sightings at different times during the three years of the data collection, the status of this subspecies should probably now be amended to that of a rare passage and winter visitor in the county.

MURIEL L. CADWALLENDER

POSTSCRIPT : Since these accounts were prepared the BOURC has recommended that Carrion Crow and Hooded Crow be treated as separate species (Knox *et al.*, 2002)

No. of tetrads in which recorded 2 (<1%)

Tetrad Analysis	No. of tetrads
1 bird	2 (100%)

Total No. of birds counted 2

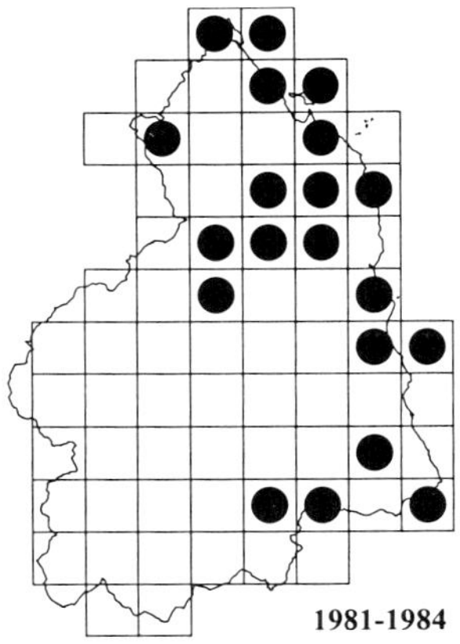

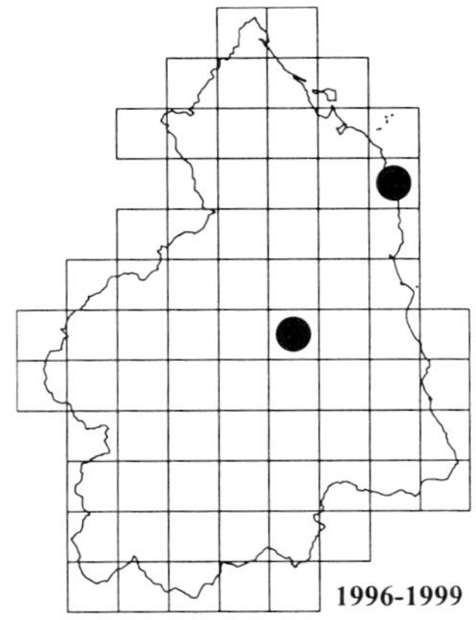

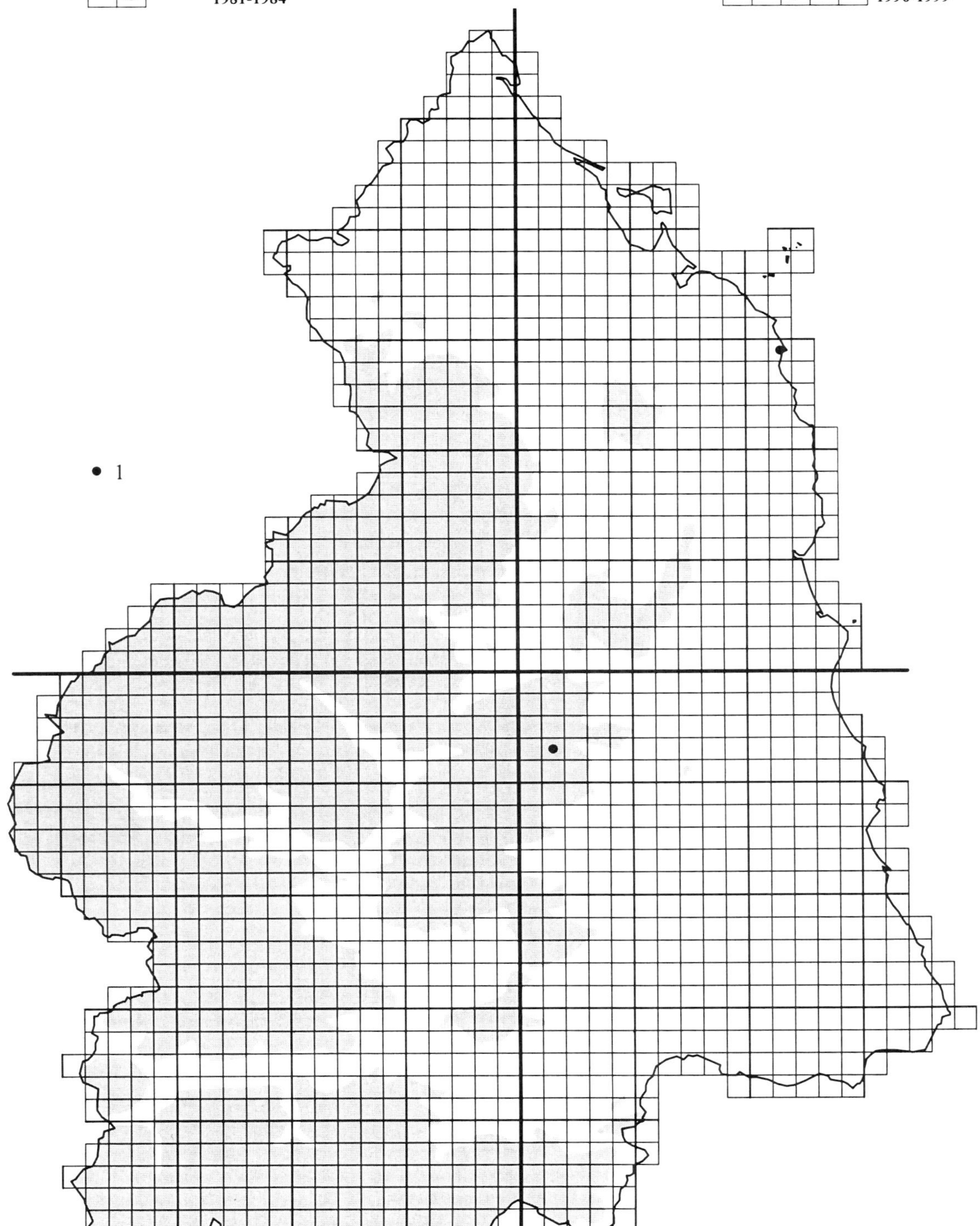

Hooded Crow

RAVEN *Corvus corax*

The winter distribution of the Raven has received little attention from previous authors. In particular, the habit of communal roosting seems to have gone unrecorded before Bolam (1912) referred to seeing flocks of up to seven birds together in the winter. With breeding numbers locally remaining low throughout the twentieth century, Galloway and Meek (1983) added little to the wintering knowledge except for a record of a bird on Holy Island in January 1979 following exceptionally hard weather. Harle (1984) however, added a further record of 17 birds having been seen on the moors at Warksburn in 1937 but *Birds in Northumbria* (1984-1997) charts very low levels of records throughout the year. It is not until the early 1990s that breeding success shows signs of a slight increase with subsequent additional sightings throughout the year.

It is important to note that to understand the winter distribution of Ravens, there is a need to consider its breeding distribution. In his monograph, Radcliffe (1997) commented on the fact that it is a rather sedentary species and established pairs appear to remain largely attached to their breeding territories throughout the year. The breeding range should therefore mirror the wintering distribution for territory holders, especially for records of birds in January and February when breeding behaviour starts in earnest. However, groups of non-breeders may also be present in the winter in the uplands when numbers increase following successful breeding seasons and when relatively local immigration occurs. In this last instance, Radcliffe (1997) noted movement of birds from the Lake District to the North Pennines.

It is no surprise to find that the great majority of sightings in this current winter survey are of birds in upland habitat above 183 metres a.s.l. as illustrated by the tetrad map. In fact, no birds were found in tetrads with average heights lower than 101 metres a.s.l. or above 500 metres. Additionally, almost 11% of tetrads between 401 metres and 500 metres were occupied. The total occupied tetrads noted over the three winter periods of the survey totalled 29, but care needs to be exercised in interpreting these results. For instance, adjoining tetrads were often counted on the same day or within a few days of each other and may well have contained 'double counted' territorial pairs, given that 23 of the 29 records were noted in January or February, effectively the start of the breeding season. Reports of two-three breeding pairs in the late 1990s, just over the border in Scotland (M. Henderson, pers. comm.) could go some way to explaining the concentration of records along the Border Ridge. One significant record of seven birds on 9th January 1999 in the Halleypike Lough area (NY87A) represents the first sizeable winter flock in over 60 years.

Since the publication of *The atlas of wintering birds in Britain and Ireland* (Lack, 1986), the county total of nine occupied 10km squares has almost doubled to 17. Lack suggested that breeding and wintering distribution should be almost identical and uses this to illustrate a contraction in the range of Ravens in Britain at this time. By comparing national winter atlas records with the results of the first national breeding atlas (Sharrock, 1976), he showed a potential loss of a quarter of occupied 10km squares in the intervening period. Clearly the current local survey shows an increase in real terms and a turn around in the fortune of Ravens in our area during the last years of the twentieth century. However, it is clear that despite this increase, the county still falls a long way short of Lack's average estimate of 12 birds per occupied 10km square for Britain.

E. JOHN STEELE

Distribution by altitude

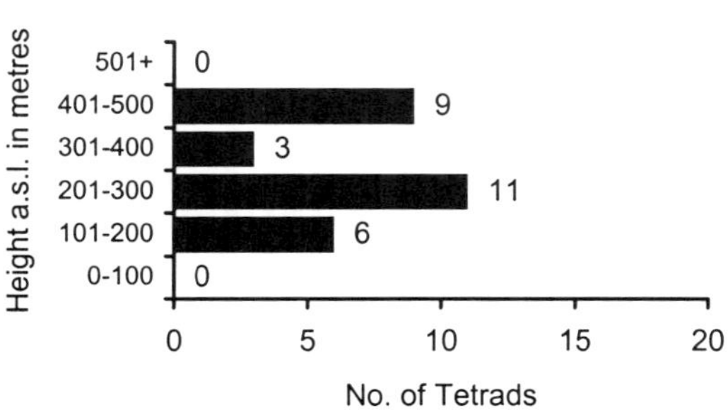

No. of tetrads in which recorded 29 (2%)

Tetrad Analysis	No. of tetrads
1 bird	13 (45%)
2 birds	14 (48%)
3+ birds	2 (7%)

Total No. of birds counted 51

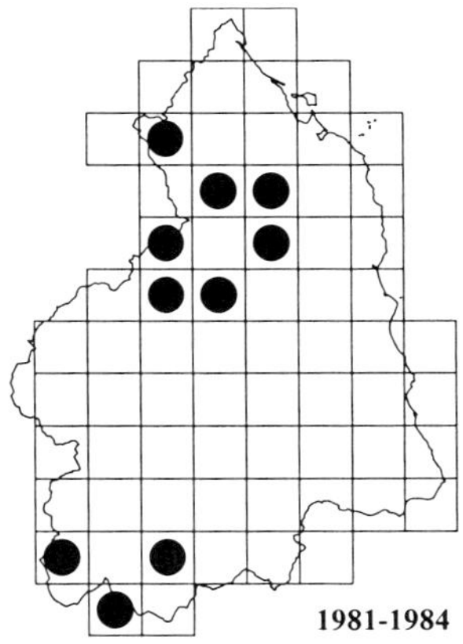

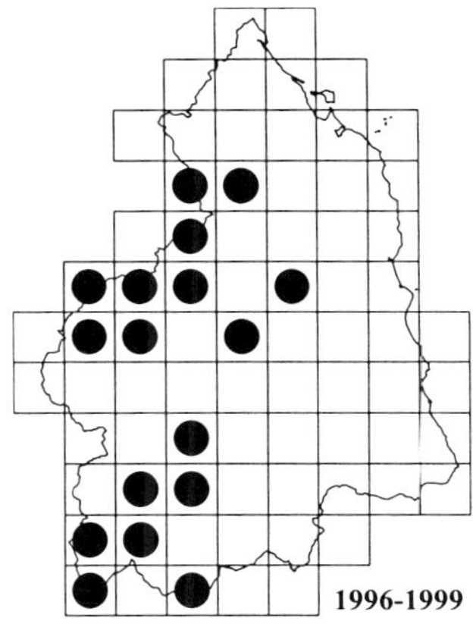

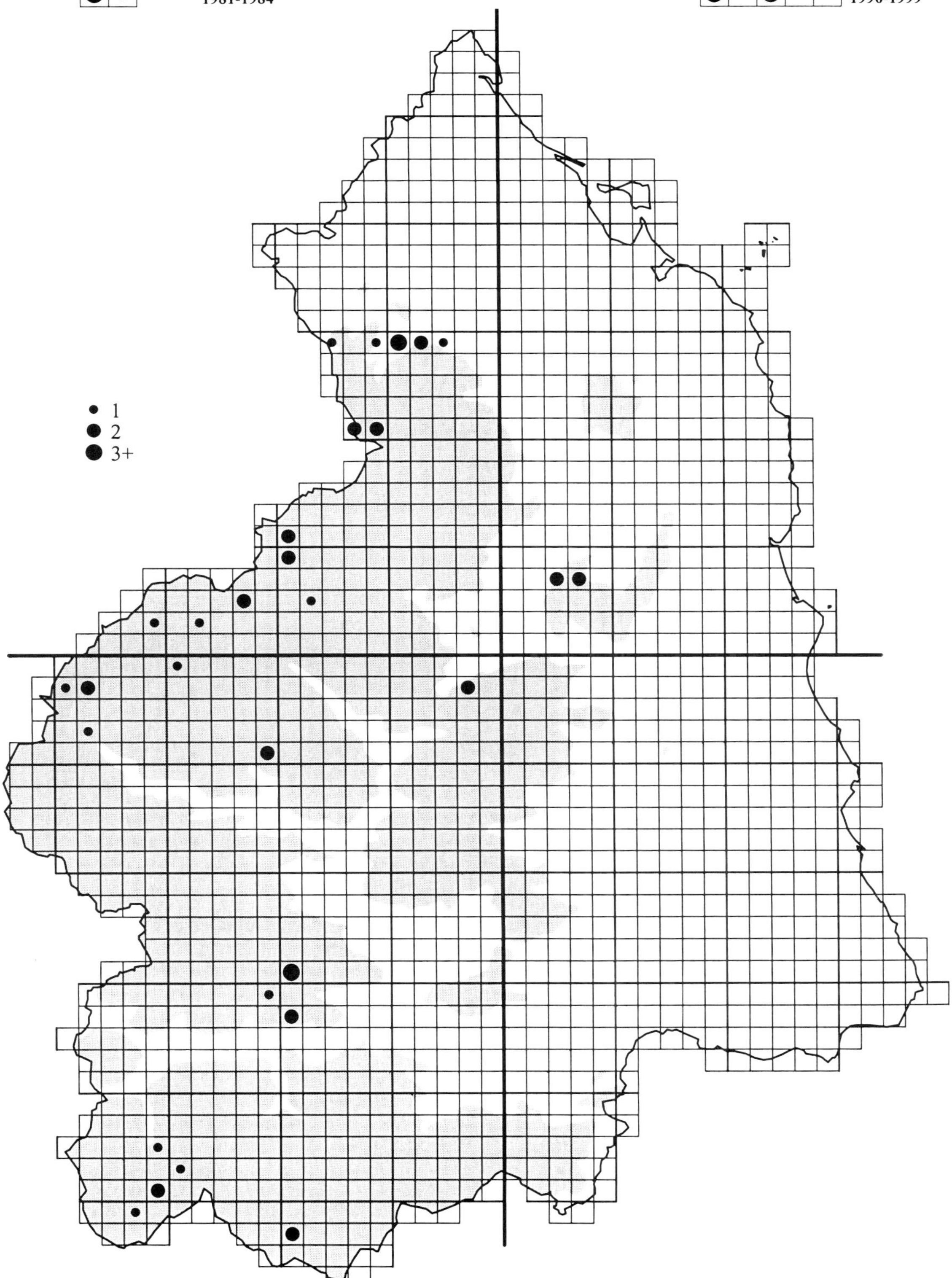

Raven

STARLING *Sturnus vulgaris*

Bolam (1912) was most loquacious about the status of the Starling, stating that it was 'abundant at all seasons, but especially numerous ... during autumn and winter ... Where they have all come from, how they manage to find a living, and where the increase is going to stop, are questions more easily asked than answered'. He described huge winter flocks at Doxford and Cheswick and felt 'its [the Starling's] numbers have more than quadrupled within the last quarter of a century'. His comments were still valid when he published his *Catalogue* in 1932 and confirmed in the 1980s by Galloway and Meek (1983). Indeed the latter authors described large roosts of between a million and a million and a half birds in some years with regular flocks of up to 16,000 in Newcastle City Centre in the late 1960s and early 1970s. Data in *Birds in Northumbria* throughout the 1980s indicate that the trend in Newcastle continued with as many as 100,000 noted in 1984 but, during the early 1990s, they disappeared from the city centre although smaller flocks were present elsewhere in the county. The reason for their desertion of Newcastle City Centre is probably a combination of the campaign to place wire mesh on the ledges of buildings and a considerable contraction in the breeding range in north western Europe which has seen a corresponding decline in the numbers wintering in south western France, Spain and North Africa (Feare & Craig, 1998).

Despite the dramatic decline in the Newcastle roost, the Starling was still abundant in the winter survey area with a huge total of 108,207 being counted. The species was present in 54% of all tetrads. However, it was less widespread than in the local breeding atlas survey when Starlings were present in 66% of surveyed tetrads (Day *et al.*, 1995). Birds tended to move away from higher ground in the winter, especially in the Cheviots, with the few remaining at higher altitude often found in areas of improved pasture that supported grazing animals. An example is the four tetrads in the Allendale/Catton area (NY85) each of which contained more than 150 birds. However, only 16% of all occupied tetrads were above 200 metres a.s.l.

The greatest concentration of birds was found in the urban south east where continental migrants probably augment the resident population. Here the six 10km squares of Newcastle (NZ26), Cramlington (NZ27), Ashington/Bedlington (NZ28), Tynemouth (NZ36), Whitley Bay (NZ37) and Blyth (NZ38) produced combined counts of 24,799 birds including a roost of 5,000 at Blyth South Harbour (NZ38A/F). This area contains much grassland and cultivation which provides the source of invertebrates that are a significant proportion of winter diet (Feare & Craig, 1998) while gardens in suburban areas provide an additional food supply. Other significant roosts and counts, away from the south east of the county, included 15,000 at Holy Island (NU14G) in November 1997, 6,000 at Longhorsley (NZ19M) in January 1999 and 10,000 at Swarland (NU10R) in February 1999. A total of 3,000 was also noted at East Ord (NT95V) in November 1996 with other large gatherings of 2,300 near Chatton (NU02J) and 1,000 near Haltwhistle (NY66W). Evidence from visits to the control tetrads indicates the species' preference for suitable feeding areas. No more than one bird was found at the predominantly scrub/wetland habit of Arcot (NZ27M) whilst seasonal counts varied between 70 and 1,200 in the Lilburn (NU02M), Holy Island (NU14G) and Beadnell (NU22J) tetrads, all of which have large expanses of suitable feeding areas.

The atlas of breeding birds in Northumbria estimated a county breeding population of 10,000-20,000 pairs, far less than the 108,000 individuals recorded in the winter survey. Even allowing for large scale immigration of continental birds, the count may be rather high due to duplication of numbers in adjacent tetrads in the same season. An example of this being in the Blyth area where 5,000 were noted in NZ38A in December 1998 and the same total in NZ38F the following February. On a smaller scale, similar discrepancies could be detected in a number of 10km squares, e.g. NU10, NZ06, NZ07 and NZ27.

Until the decline in winter flock sizes in the early 1990s, ringing recoveries clearly indicated the European origin of some of our wintering Starlings, with birds found in Scandinavia, the Baltic States and the Low Countries, but overall, as numbers have declined, so too have the number of ringing recoveries. Even so, as long as invertebrate-rich feeding areas are available, the Starling ought to remain an abundant resident and winter visitor to our area, although Mead (2000) stated that 'recent losses are very worrying - is the Starling going to disappear just as quickly as it arrived two centuries ago?'.

LINDSAY J. McDOUGALL

Distribution by altitude

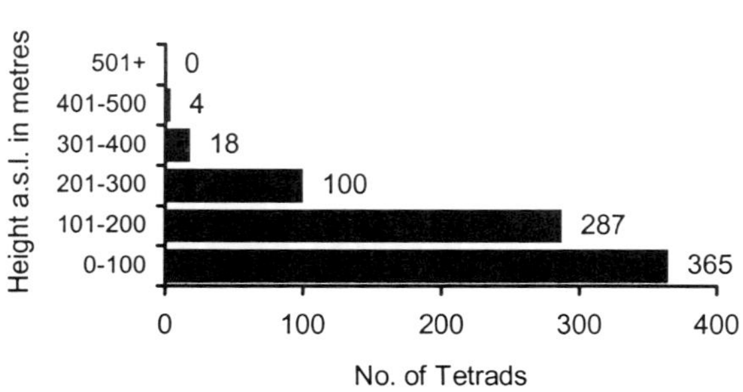

No. of tetrads in which recorded 774 (54%)

Tetrad Analysis	No. of tetrads
1-37 birds	387 (50%)
38-125 birds	233 (30%)
126+ birds	154 (20%)

Total No. of birds counted 108,207

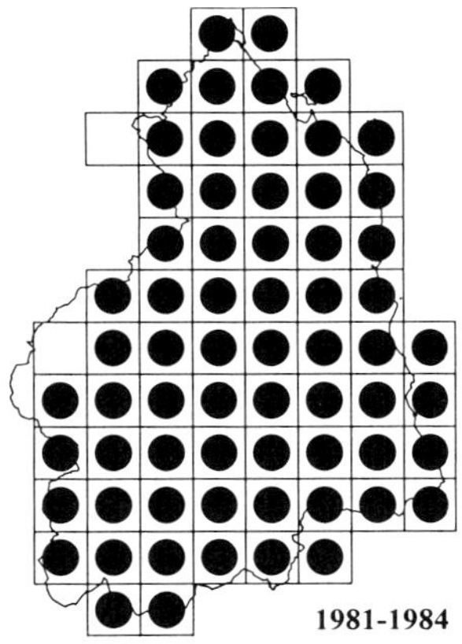

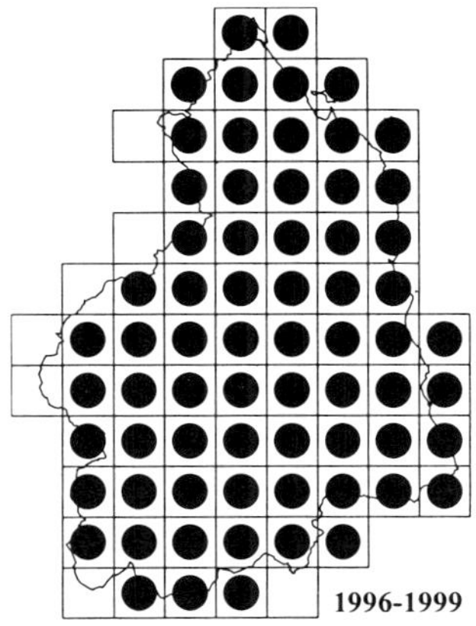

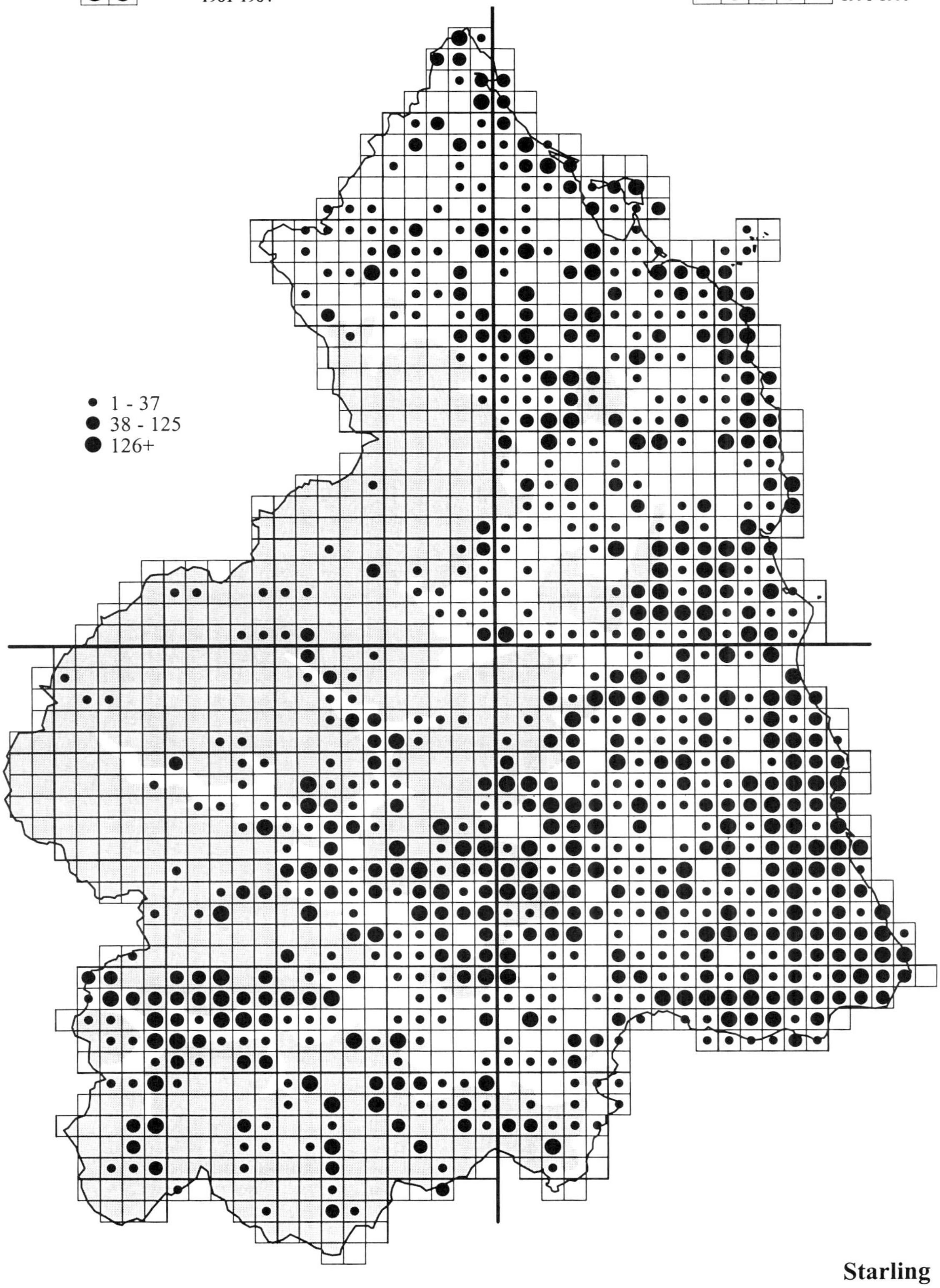

Starling

HOUSE SPARROW *Passer domesticus*

Describing the House Sparrow, Hancock (1874) stated that 'this very common resident is almost everywhere associated with the dwellings of man, but is rare in wild and elevated situations'. Bolam (1932) agreed with this, adding that it was 'abundant in all corn growing districts'. The survey work carried out for this atlas has confirmed this is still an extremely numerous species that is widely recorded in all areas which include a significant amount of human habitation. A maximum total of 12,533 individual birds was recorded in 639 tetrads with distribution still very much in accordance with Hancock's statement.

The rapid spread of urban and suburban areas has undoubtedly increased the population of House Sparrows in Northumbria since Hancock's time, reaching a peak in the 1970s (Summers-Smith, 1988). However, at a national level there is now concern that, while still an abundant species, the population of House Sparrows is probably decreasing. This decrease was described by Marchant *et al.* (1990) as significant but was regarded much more bleakly by Mead (2000) who stated that it was 'seriously declining'.

During the winter period, House Sparrows flock together in highly social groups comprising both adults and young birds. These feed largely on vegetable matter, traditionally weed seeds and un-harvested grain but in highly urban areas they are very dependent on feeding in gardens especially on bread and seeds at bird feeders (Summer-Smith, 1998). The declining population is thought to be due to improvements in agricultural efficiency reducing the weed population and to winter cereals limiting the amount of stubble available for foraging. This is borne out by the survey results with the highest counts being in some of the more marginal agricultural areas such as Longframlington (NU10F) with a count of 137 birds, Hetton Steads (NU03I) 130 birds, Scremerston and near Cheswick (NU04E/H) with 121 & 125 respectively and Gunnerton (NY97C) with 102 whereas more intensively farmed areas often have lower counts. Highly urbanised tetrads such as those on Tyneside (e.g. NZ26 & NZ27) have much lower counts than the peak farmland numbers, with typically ten to 50 birds, but are consistent over much larger areas. Altitudinal analysis of the distribution of the occupied tetrads shows 90% being below 200 metres a.s.l. This, of course, closely reflects the distribution of urban population centres.

In spite of Bolam's (1932) comments that 'our home bred stock is augmented by arrivals from flocks abroad in autumn' the majority of the population is highly sedentary and Summers-Smith quoted that 95% never move more than 5 kilometres from where they hatched. This is confirmed by data collected from control tetrads, some of which show a high degree of consistency of counts from year to year. In two rural areas the control tetrad counts over the three successive winters were at Ancroft (NU04C) 31, 36 and 26 birds and at Holystone (NT90L) 13, 11 and ten. In the semi-rural habitat of Prestwick (NZ17W), numbers were 30, 27 and 28 and in Heaton (NZ26T), in urban Newcastle, the counts were 33, 43 and 35. Comparison with *The atlas of breeding birds in Northumbria* (Day *et al.*, 1995) shows a very close correlation between tetrads with proven, possible or probable breeding and tetrads with wintering populations. The total number of tetrads in which the breeding atlas recorded pairs was 687 compared with 639 occupied in this winter atlas. Similarly, the total number of breeding pairs recorded in the breeding atlas was 6,334 which correlates closely with the total maximum count of 12,533 birds in the present survey. They were, however, not present in four 10km squares in winter where they had been recorded in the breeding atlas survey and were less evident in a number of lowland agricultural areas and in some tetrads in the 201-300 metres a.s.l. range.

In summary, the population of House Sparrows in Northumbria is large and distributed as expected but requires future monitoring to confirm if it is in long-term decline as is believed to be the case at a national level. Numerically, it currently remains an abundant resident.

GEOFF LINKLETER

Distribution by altitude

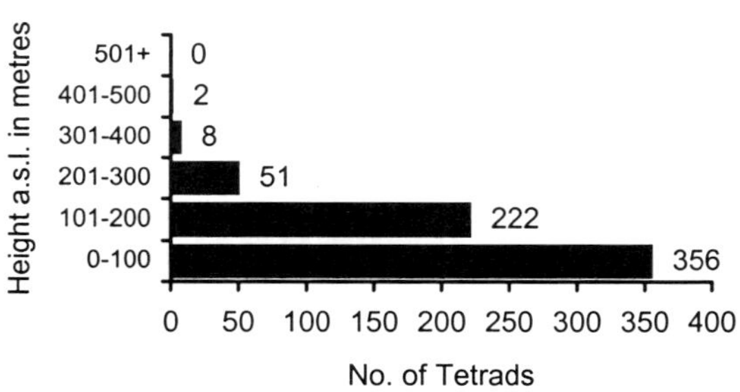

No. of tetrads in which recorded 639 (45%)

Tetrad Analysis	No. of tetrads
1-12 birds	332 (52%)
13-29 birds	165 (26%)
30+ birds	142 (22%)

Total No. of birds counted 12,533

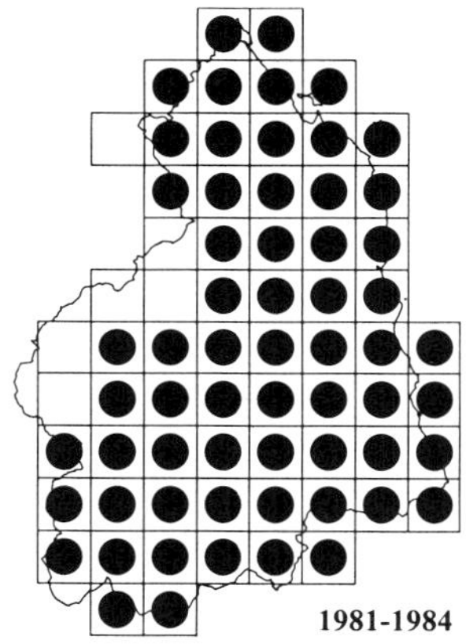

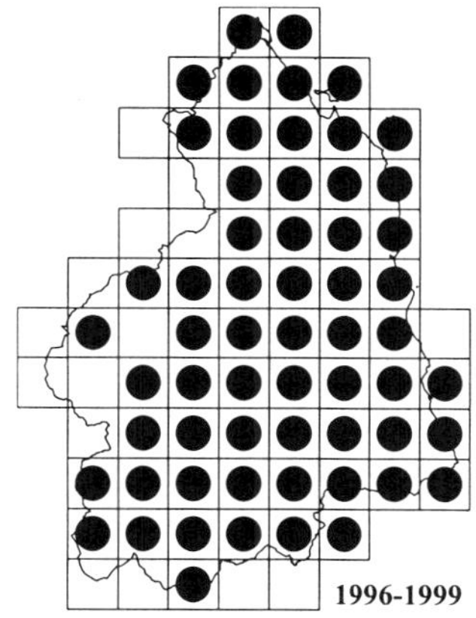

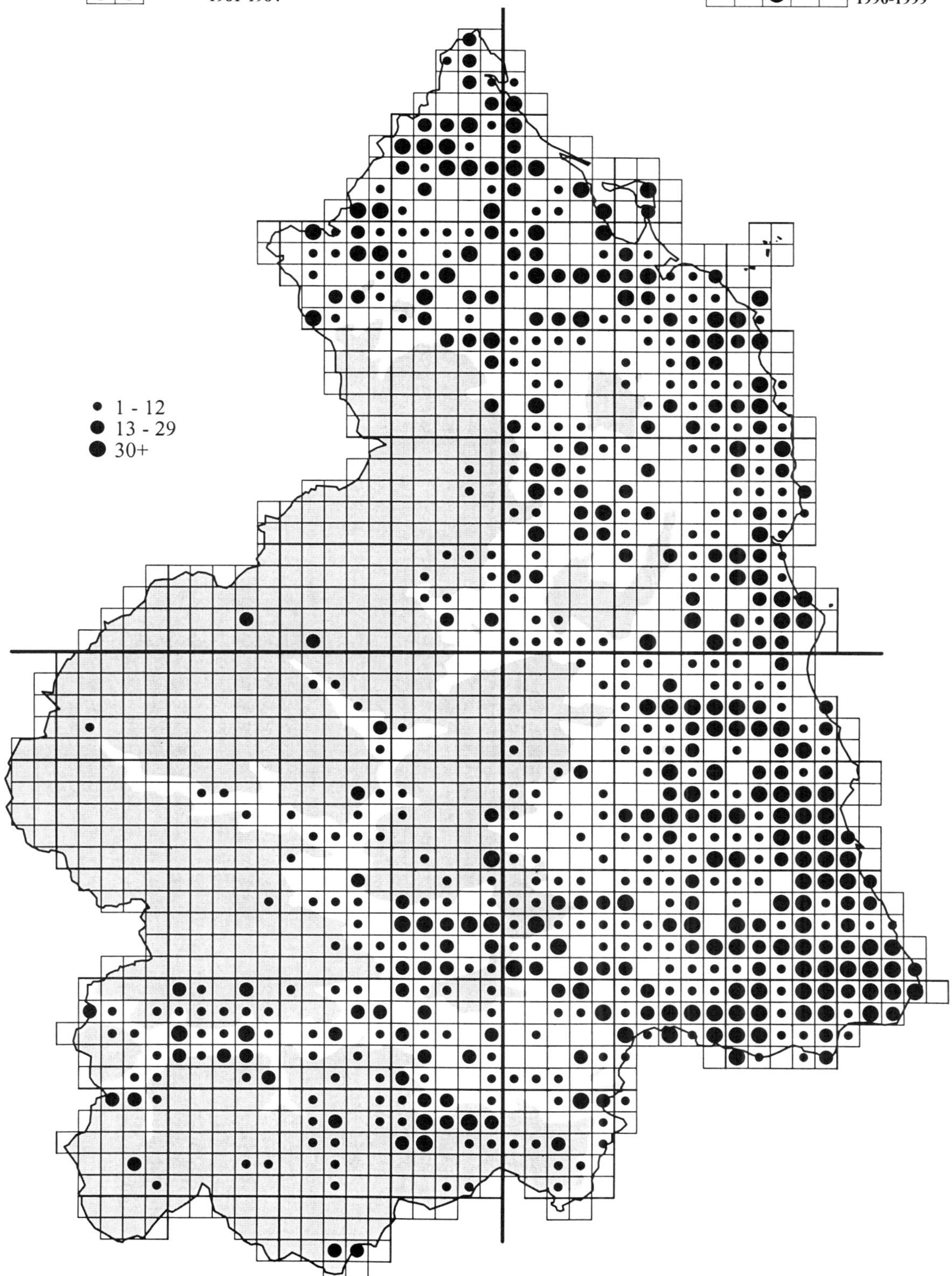

House Sparrow

TREE SPARROW *Passer montanus*

Over the long term, the UK population of Tree Sparrows has suffered from significant fluctuations which are not easy to explain. After a high population at the beginning of the twentieth century, many places experienced a decrease and range contraction which had become very significant by 1930. Then, in the late 1950s and early 1960s the population began to increase, reaching a plateau which remained relatively constant until 1976/77, before commencing the current decline. These trends fail to mirror any of the major factors such as agricultural decline and recovery, organochloride pesticide problems or Dutch Elm disease which affected other farmland species (Marchant *et al*., 1990; Summers-Smith, 1998).

The Northumberland population reflects these trends. Selby (1831) wrote that it was frequently seen in parts of Durham, but he had not been able to find it in Northumberland. Bolam (1912), however, was able to describe its expansion northwards, stating that on the Borders it had been virtually confined to the coast up to 1884 but subsequently had 'penetrated westwards in a manner that is remarkable'. Writing in 1932, he regarded it as a local resident, even into the 'Highlands of Redesdale'. By the 1940s, it had again declined and was deemed rare enough for individual colonies to be listed in the county bird reports. Within another 30 years, however, Galloway and Meek (1983) were describing an expanding population with coastal flocks reaching as many as 500 birds in the winters of 1975/76 and 1976/77. Since those dates, the pattern has been reversed and the county annual bird reports record a steady population decline.

In the UK during the winter, Tree Sparrows largely specialise in feeding on the seeds of grasses and small annual weeds. The tetrad distribution map shows a wintering population primarily in low-lying agricultural areas, as would be expected from the historical data and the availability of suitable feeding habitat. The maximum count recorded during the current survey was 120 at Druridge (NZ29T) and only a further seven tetrads gave counts of more than 50. They were at Fenwick (NU04Q) with 70 birds, Swinhoe (NU22E) with 65, Embleton Mill (NU22F) and Brenkley (NZ27C) with 58 each, near Hepscott (NZ28H) and Big Waters (NZ27G) with 60 each and 50 at Beal (NU04R). An additional 22 tetrads contained between 20 and 43 birds all of which were in the flatter agricultural plain below 100 metres a.s.l., where 75% of all occupied tetrads were to be found.

A comparison of the two 10km square maps indicates a marked reduction in occupied squares with the population retreating eastwards into the areas originally colonised and presumably offering the premium habitat. It is postulated that this is in part due to agricultural herbicides reducing the weed population on which this species largely depends for food (Summers-Smith, 1998), but this is unlikely to explain the total extent of the change. Further evidence of this winter decline comes from the control tetrad data, for whilst Tree Sparrows were only present in six of the 60 tetrads involved, the occupancy average per tetrad over the three winter seasons was five, eight and two birds respectively. The 1988-1992 10km square distribution map for the local breeding atlas (Day *et al*., 1995) also shows a closer affinity to this latest winter map than the earlier 1981-1984 survey. The tetrad breeding survey map shows 173 occupied tetrads as opposed to 117 in this survey which implies a considerable contraction for a species which is supposed to be sedentary. Over the three winter seasons the maximum tetrad counts involved 1,689 birds which is somewhat short of the population that could be expected from the estimated 1,000 breeding pairs in the county. The difference may be partly explained by the relatively secretive nature of the species and the fact that three mild winters have provided large areas of suitable feeding habitat which are not easy to survey. However the statistics on the Tree Sparrow in Northumberland are interpreted, the species, whilst technically attaining the status of well-represented, appears to be fast declining as a breeding resident and consequently winter numbers are also falling.

GEOFF LINKLETER

Distribution by altitude

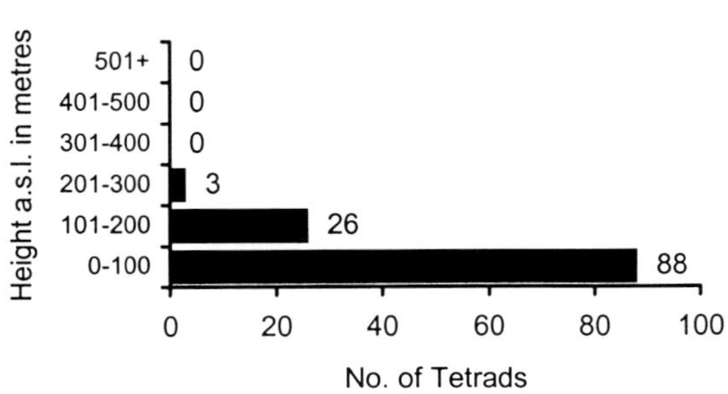

No. of tetrads in which recorded 117 (8%)

Tetrad Analysis	No. of tetrads
1-7 birds	61 (52%)
8-24 birds	33 (28%)
25+ birds	23 (20%)

Total No. of birds counted 1,689

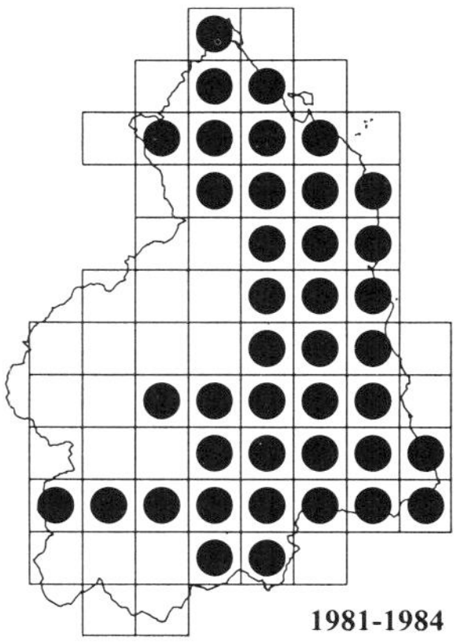

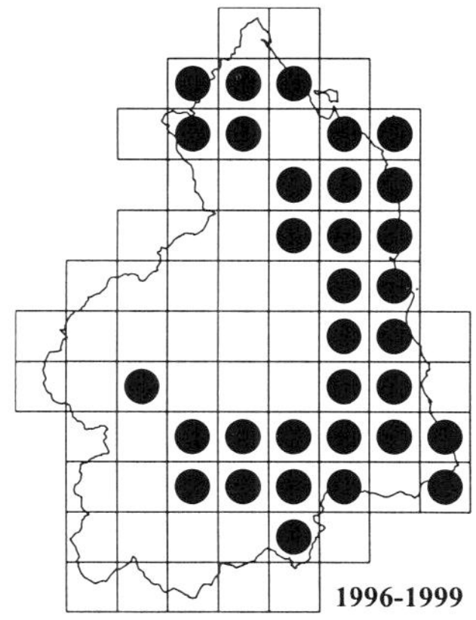

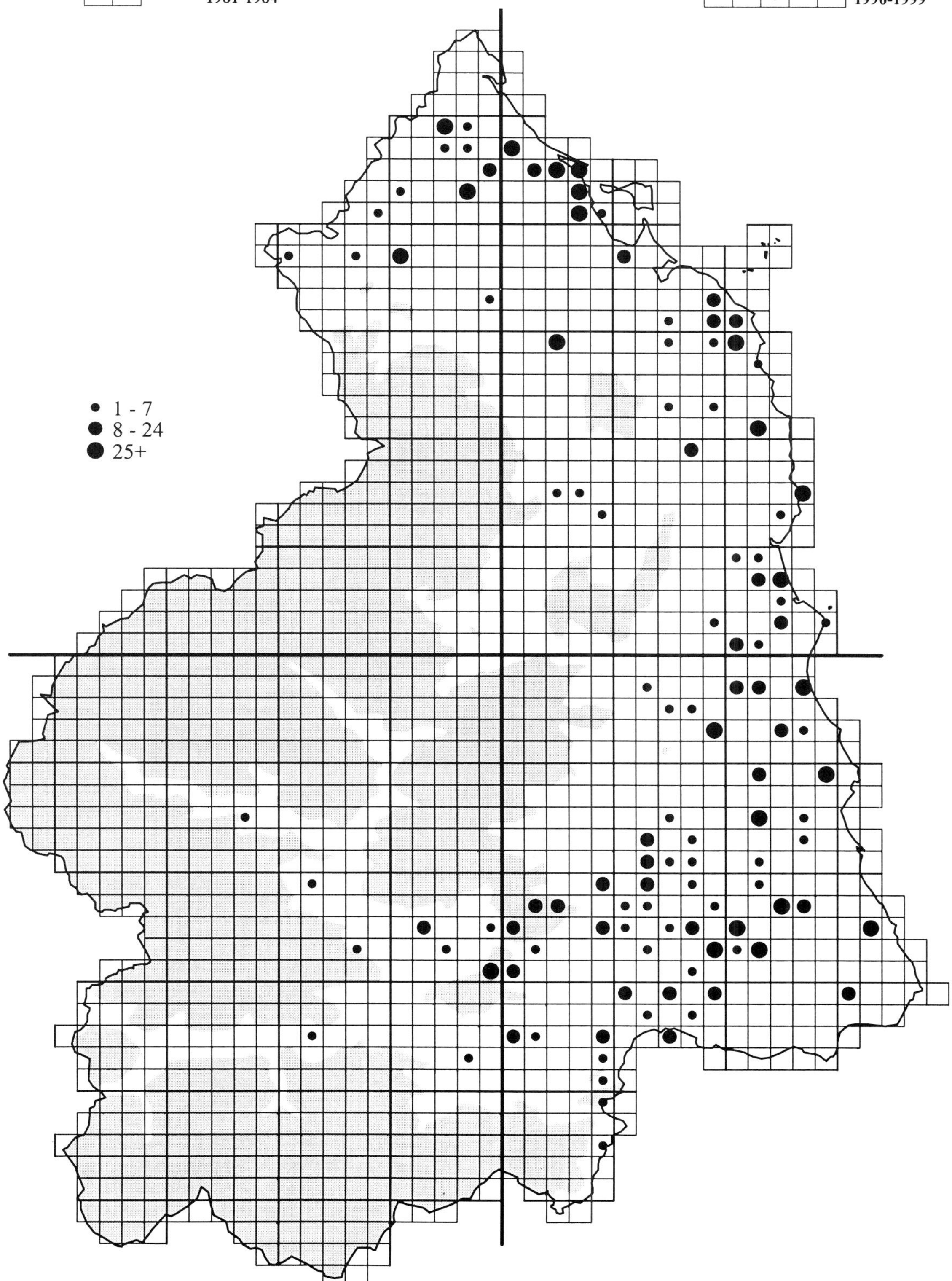

Tree Sparrow

CHAFFINCH *Fringilla coelebs*

The Chaffinch is the commonest European finch and is one of our best known birds. It was recorded by Thomas Bewick (1797) as a lively bird, which, together with its elegant plumage, gave rise to the saying 'as gay as a Chaffinch'. Locally, Bolam (1932) knew the species as a migrant which appeared on the coast in both spring and autumn, believing that 'the bulk of them are of foreign origin, many of them no more than birds of passage, though others from abroad winter here'. Galloway and Meek (1983) described the Chaffinch as 'a common passage and winter visitor and abundant breeding resident'.

The subspecies, *F. c. gengleri* breeding in Britain is different from the nominate *F. c. coelebs* to which our winter visitors belong, with the latter tending to be slightly longer and paler. During the winter period the two subspecies have differing behaviour patterns. British Chaffinches are very sedentary and are normally found close to their breeding territory, feeding on a wide range of whatever seed is locally available. The adults roost singly or in pairs within their old territory and first-year birds in small groups of two-three. Ringing recoveries indicate that 90% move no further than five kilometres from their birthplace and the rest less than 50 kilometres (Newton, 1972). Recoveries of Northumberland-ringed birds are broadly in line with these parameters. The immigrants are mostly from Fenno-Scandia but some also come from Denmark and Northern Germany. They arrive mainly in October having travelled through Denmark and the Low Countries to enter Britain at the south east corner but, with easterly winds, some may take a more direct route across the North Sea. In early March and mid-April they depart on a broad front across the North Sea (Newton, 1972). Birds ringed in Northumberland during the autumn and winter periods have been recovered in March of the following year on the East and West Friesian Islands and at sea west of Esbjerg, Denmark. Further examples of birds of continental origin in the county are an adult female ringed in January 1972 and recovered at Kueluage Frey, Norway in April 1973, an adult male ringed at Seaton Delaval in October 1976 and controlled on Heligoland, Germany in March 1978 and one caught at Schiermonnikoog, West Friesian Islands in October 1977 and controlled at Gosforth Park in January 1979. Continental birds mainly form large flocks and can wander widely in search of local abundance of food. They often have a more restricted diet in which seeds of a few common weeds and cereals predominate. At times, especially in hard weather, they may be joined by their British cousins sexes of which are usually present in equal numbers. Ringing returns show that hens migrate further than cocks so that the sexes tend to form separate flocks. In northern Britain cocks out-number hens. At night they form large communal roosts in woodland and scrub (Newton, 1972).

During the present winter survey, the Chaffinch was recorded in 1,048 tetrads (73%) and in 73 (96% of those surveyed) ten kilometre squares compared to 66 (97% of those surveyed) in the 1981-1984 national winter survey. Lack (1986) said that 'there is a noticeably high density of wintering birds on land between 300-800m, covering much of Scotland and NE England'. The tetrad distribution map for the local winter survey would appear to contradict this as 95% of the occupied tetrads were below 300 metres a.s.l. A comparison with the tetrad distribution map for the local breeding survey (Day *et al.*, 1995), where the species was recorded in 1,256 tetrads (89% of those surveyed), shows that quite extensive areas of high ground are deserted in winter.

Newton (1972) gives flock sizes of immigrants usually between 50-100 birds and in this respect the county compares favourably with 50 or more being recorded on numerous occasions. The largest single tetrad count during the current survey was 500 near Caistron (NU00A) on 22 December 1996. There were 11 counts of between 201 to 333 birds and 158 counts between 50 to 200 but the vast majority of counts (84%) were much smaller. Larger flocks, however, have been recorded in the county with, for example, 800 present at Brinkburn in December 1976. The control tetrad data indicate that, overall, numbers may have been reasonably consistent over the three winter periods of the survey with total counts of 1,551, 1,161 and 1,145 birds respectively.

The number of immigrants is not easily calculated but it seems likely that, together with a breeding population in excess of 15,000 pairs and their young, the overall winter population in the county could be in the range of 80,000-200,000 birds making it one of our commonest wintering species with a widespread distribution.

F. D. MIDDLETON

Distribution by altitude

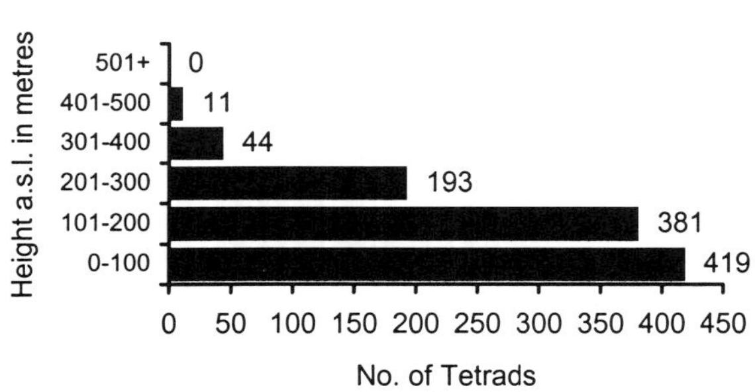

No. of tetrads in which recorded 1,048 (73%)

Tetrad Analysis	No. of tetrads
1-16 birds	541 (52%)
17-39 birds	272 (26%)
40+ birds	235 (22%)

Total No. of birds counted 31,621

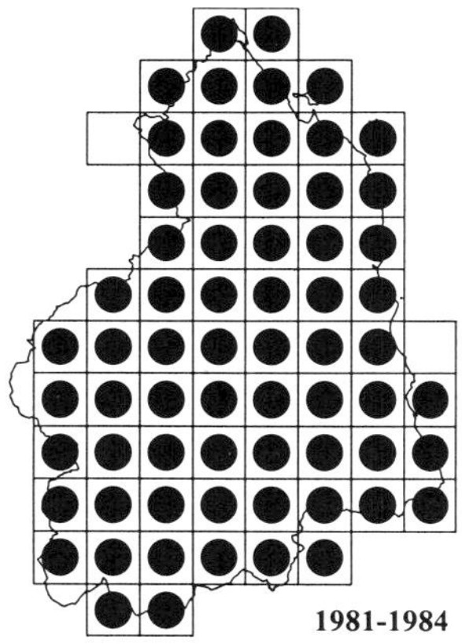

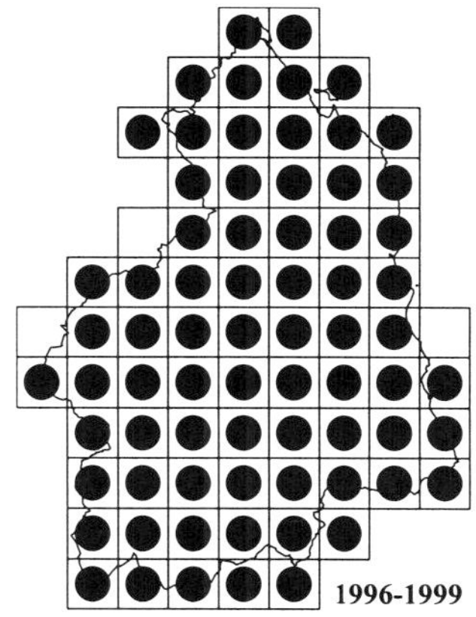

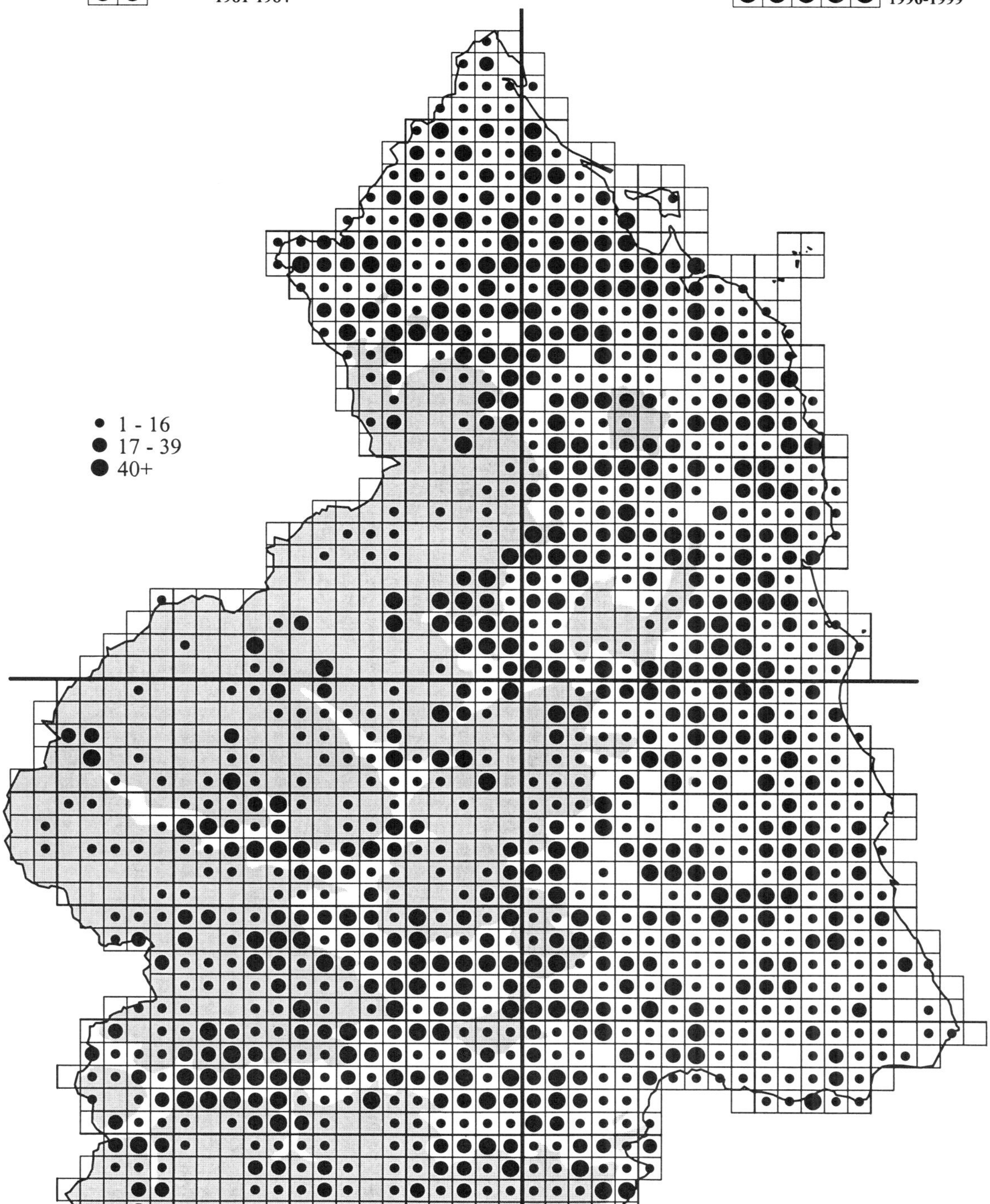

Chaffinch

BRAMBLING *Fringilla montifringilla*

Bolam (1932) described the Brambling in Northumberland as a 'common winter visitant, reaching us in flocks about the middle of October ... and departing in early spring'. Galloway and Meek (1983) confirmed this status, commenting on the numbers remaining to winter in the county as 'apparently dependent upon the availability of beech mast'.

Although the Brambling is a very widespread and numerous species in Northern Europe, it is a winter visitor to Britain in comparatively small and variable numbers. It is perhaps the most highly migratory of the finches and is the only one that vacates completely, in autumn, its European breeding grounds in the sub-arctic and boreal zones (Newton, 1972). Wintering numbers vary widely perhaps between 50,000 and 2 million birds, patchily distributed over much of Britain in areas where Beech *Fagus* occurs, beech mast being its preferred winter food (Cramp & Perrins, 1994). Influxes of Brambling fluctuate each year, therefore, depending on the beech mast crop in differing locations and feeding conditions in its main continental winter quarters. Ringing has shown the British wintering birds originate mainly from the Fenno-Scandian breeding population, reaching us either across the North Sea directly or via Denmark and the Low Countries. Birds ringed in Northumberland have been recovered on Fair Isle in 1998, at Goes, Zeeland, Holland in 1992 and at Jipelle, Liege, Belgium in 1964, confirming this pattern of migration.

The Brambling in its winter quarters is predominately a ground feeder and often flocks like its near relative the Chaffinch *Fringilla coelebs*. Its strong deep bill enables it to feed on a wide range of seeds up to the size of beech mast (competition with the Chaffinch for this food source being avoided as it is unable to extract the beech seed). In the event of beech mast not being available, particularly towards the end of winter, it is frequently found feeding in farmland on cereal and weed seeds where it co-exists with the Chaffinch. Like so many birds it has learnt to take advantage of peanuts and seed feeders provided in gardens and, in January 1996, a flock of 500 was recorded feeding in a Stocksfield garden (*Birds in Northumbria 1996*). Roosts are usually in clumps of evergreen, like Rhododendron *Rhododendron* sp., young conifers, brambles and other scrub. On the Continent roosts containing millions of birds have been recorded but in Britain, at best, numbers reach only a few hundred (Newton, 1972). In the late 1960s, at Belsay, 200 or more regularly gathered to roost in Rhododendrons (Galloway & Meek, 1983). A more unusual record was noted by Bolam (1912) who said 'I have seen it, in mixed flocks with Redwing and Fieldfares, preparing to pass the night amongst rough 'white grass', *Nardus stricta*'.

The tetrad map reveals a very widespread distribution throughout the county during the three winter periods of this survey. Although known as the 'Mountain Finch' in earlier literature (Bewick, 1797; Bolam, 1932), in its Northumbrian winter quarters it was located in only five tetrads above 300 metres a.s.l. Most of the occupied tetrads, some 120 out of 147, fell in the range between 0 and 200 metres a.s.l. Notwithstanding the fact that the survey shows the species to be widespread, if thinly distributed in the county, it is invariably in small numbers. A total of 78 occupied tetrads held only one-two birds and only 29 produced counts of more than 15 individuals. The maximum counts recorded during the survey were 300 at Mosswood (NZ05Q) in February 1998, 200 at both Kennels (NT83R) in January 1999 and Middleton Hall (NT92X) in February 1999 and 102 at Kirknewton (NT93A) in January 1997. A comparison of the two 10km square maps, however, shows a very similar distribution pattern between the national winter survey in 1981-1984 and the current local fieldwork. They were recorded in 54 (72% of those surveyed) squares in the latest survey as opposed to 48 (71%) in the earlier survey. The rather limited data collected from the control tetrads tend to confirm the fluctuations in numbers between winter periods with total counts of 77, 22 and three and it was interesting to note that, out of 12 control tetrads occupied, none held Bramblings in all three winters.

Although the variability of numbers located in the county in winter makes it difficult to assess an 'average' population, the total count of 2,273 made during this latest survey indicates that the status of the Brambling in Northumberland can still be described with some confidence as at least a well-represented and, in some years, common winter visitor.

F. D. MIDDLETON

Distribution by altitude

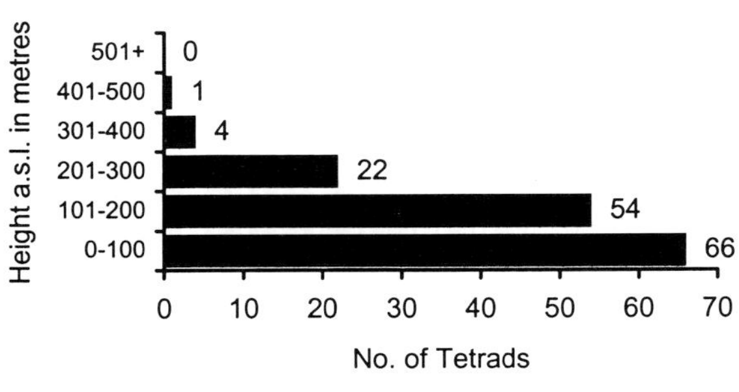

No. of tetrads in which recorded 147 (10%)

Tetrad Analysis	No. of tetrads
1-2 birds	78 (53%)
3-14 birds	38 (26%)
15+ birds	31 (21%)

Total No. of birds counted 2,273

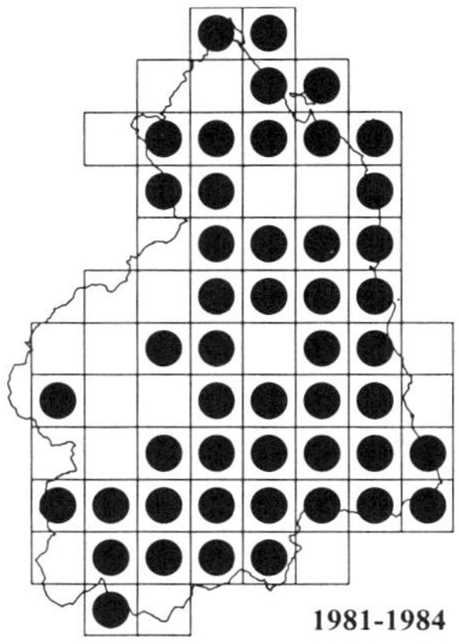

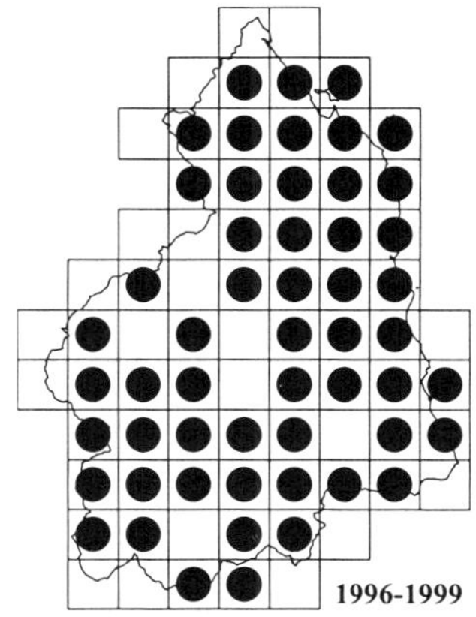

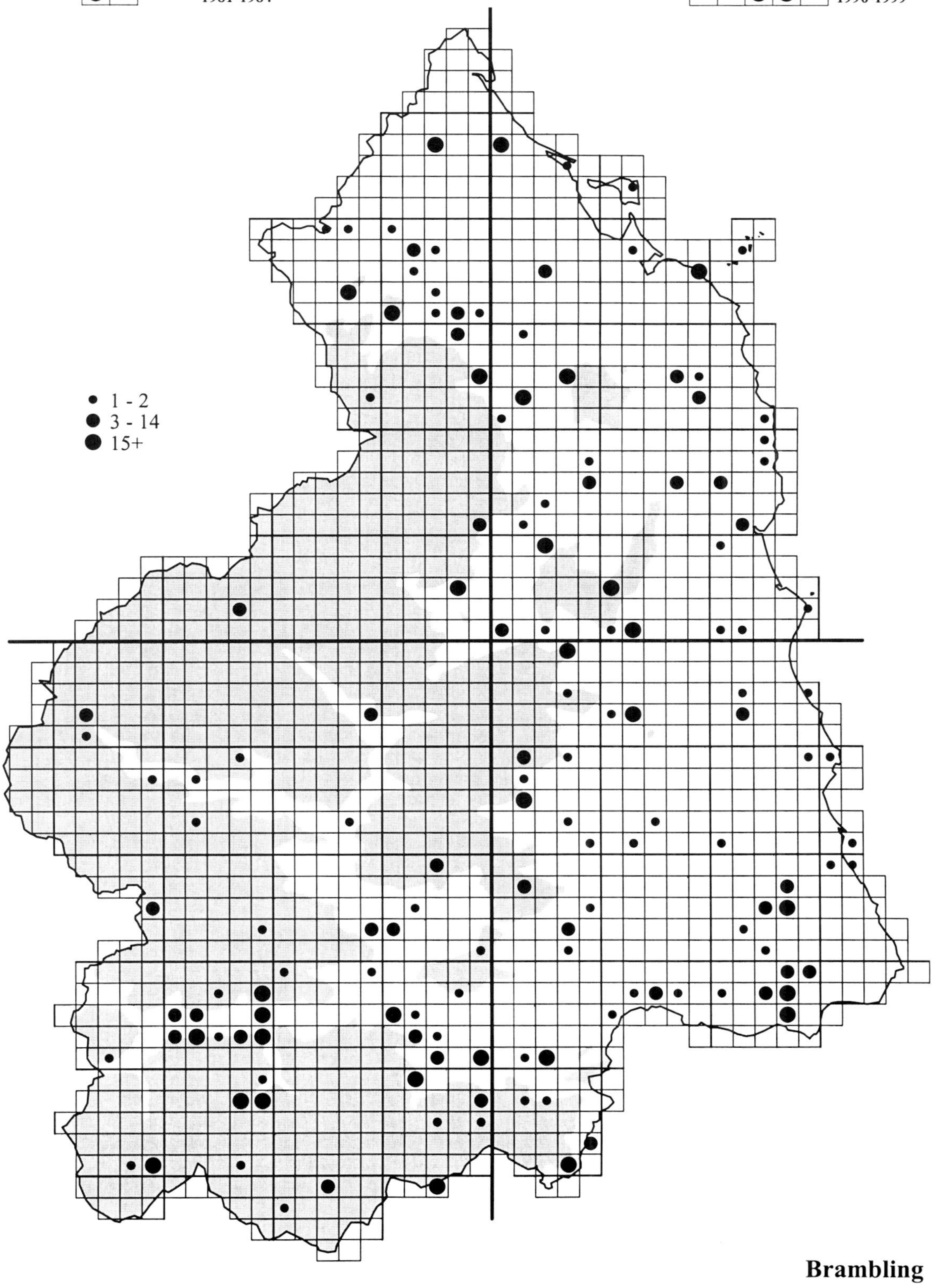

Brambling

GREENFINCH *Carduelis chloris*

Counts collected over the three winters for this atlas confirm that the Greenfinch is a familiar and common species in the recording area. In total 4,398 were noted in 495 tetrads. Its status as a common breeding resident, and also a passage visitor, has been corroborated for over 125 years by, respectively, Hancock (1874), Bolam (1932) and more recently Galloway and Meek (1983), although it did suffer a decline during the pesticide era of the 1950s and 1960s.

In winter, the species is gregarious, forming small to sizeable flocks and often associates with other *Carduelis* finches such as Goldfinch *C. carduelis*, Linnet *C. cannabina* and Twite *C. flavirostris*. The number of birds in these noisy feeding flocks and communal roosts tends to increase as food supplies become patchy. Gatherings of over 1,000 individuals have been found in the county in the past, particularly during the harsh winters of 1963 and 1971. However, a series of mild winters during the current survey period meant that flock numbers remained low, only exceeding 100 birds at Hepburn (NU02S), Hazelrigg near Belford (NU03L), Holy Island (NU14G) and Ingoe Moor (NZ07N).

Arable farmland is the species' preferred winter habitat where it can feed on cereal seeds and the seeds of weeds which form much of its diet. Seeds from un-harvested or feral plants of Oilseed rape *Brassica napus* are now readily taken. In scrub and wooded localities, seeds from the hips of Wild Rose *Rosa* and Brambles *Rubus fruticosus* are favoured while coastal flocks feed on the seeds of plants growing on saltmarsh or plunder Sea-Buckthorn *Hippophaë rhamnoides* or Wild Rose thickets in sand dunes (Newton, 1972). A more recent adaptation, probably due to the intensification of farming practices and use of agro-pesticides during the 1950s and 1960s, is the appearance of Greenfinches in suburban gardens where they are now a familiar winter sight clinging, sometimes precariously, to the peanut feeders. As natural seed stocks decline and are not replenished until late spring, so Greenfinches take greater advantage of this readily available artificial food supply.

The Greenfinch is a partial migrant, with recoveries of locally ringed autumn and winter birds indicating that they may move as far away as Aberdeenshire, Ayrshire, Cheshire and Norfolk (Galloway & Meek, 1983). Recent records also relate to birds controlled in Northumberland that were ringed in Norway, and others going in the opposite direction (Kerr, 2001). Its winter distribution in the county is virtually identical to that recorded during the local breeding atlas survey (Day *et al.*, 1995), with perhaps an even more biased trend to the lowland east and coastal belt. Its preference for lowland farmland, coastal and urban habitats is borne out by the fact that the densest populations were observed in the built-up south east and the rich agricultural lands of the northern coastal plain and the Tweed catchment area. Indeed, 90% of the occupied tetrads in this survey were below 200 metres a.s.l. Between the two local winter atlas surveys the Greenfinch appears to have maintained a stable presence in the area, being found in 79% (1981-1984) and 81% (1996-1999) of the available 10km squares respectively, as was also the case during the local breeding atlas survey (1988-1992) with 80%. The average number of birds present each winter in control tetrads also remained consistent at 7.0, 6.8 and 7.1, although the average number in all the occupied tetrads was slightly higher with 8.9 birds. The overall total of 4,398 birds for the three winter periods of this survey is probably an under-representation, bearing in mind a likely breeding population of between 3,000-3,500 pairs in the county.

DEE McKEOWN

Distribution by altitude

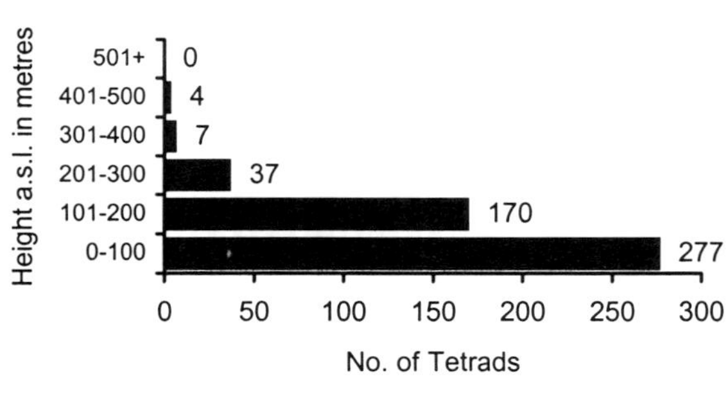

No. of tetrads in which recorded 495 (35%)

Tetrad Analysis	No. of tetrads
1-4 birds	266 (54%)
5-11 birds	128 (26%)
12+ birds	101 (20%)

Total No. of birds counted 4,398

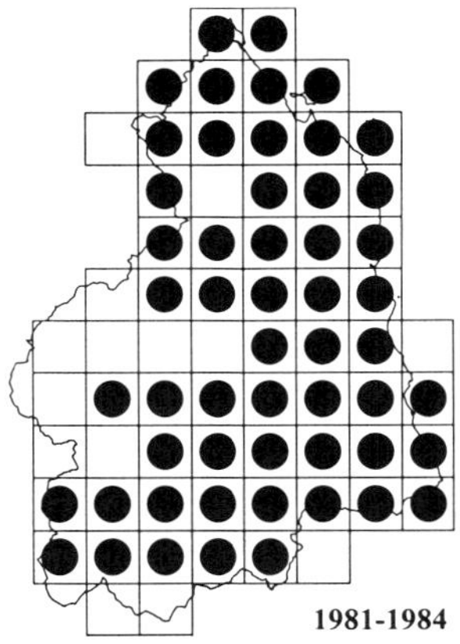

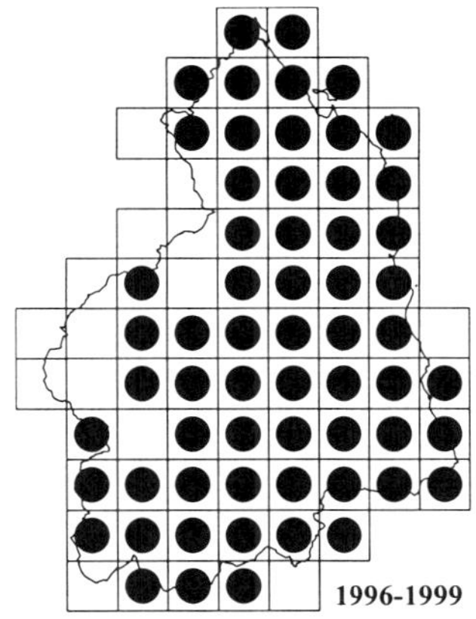

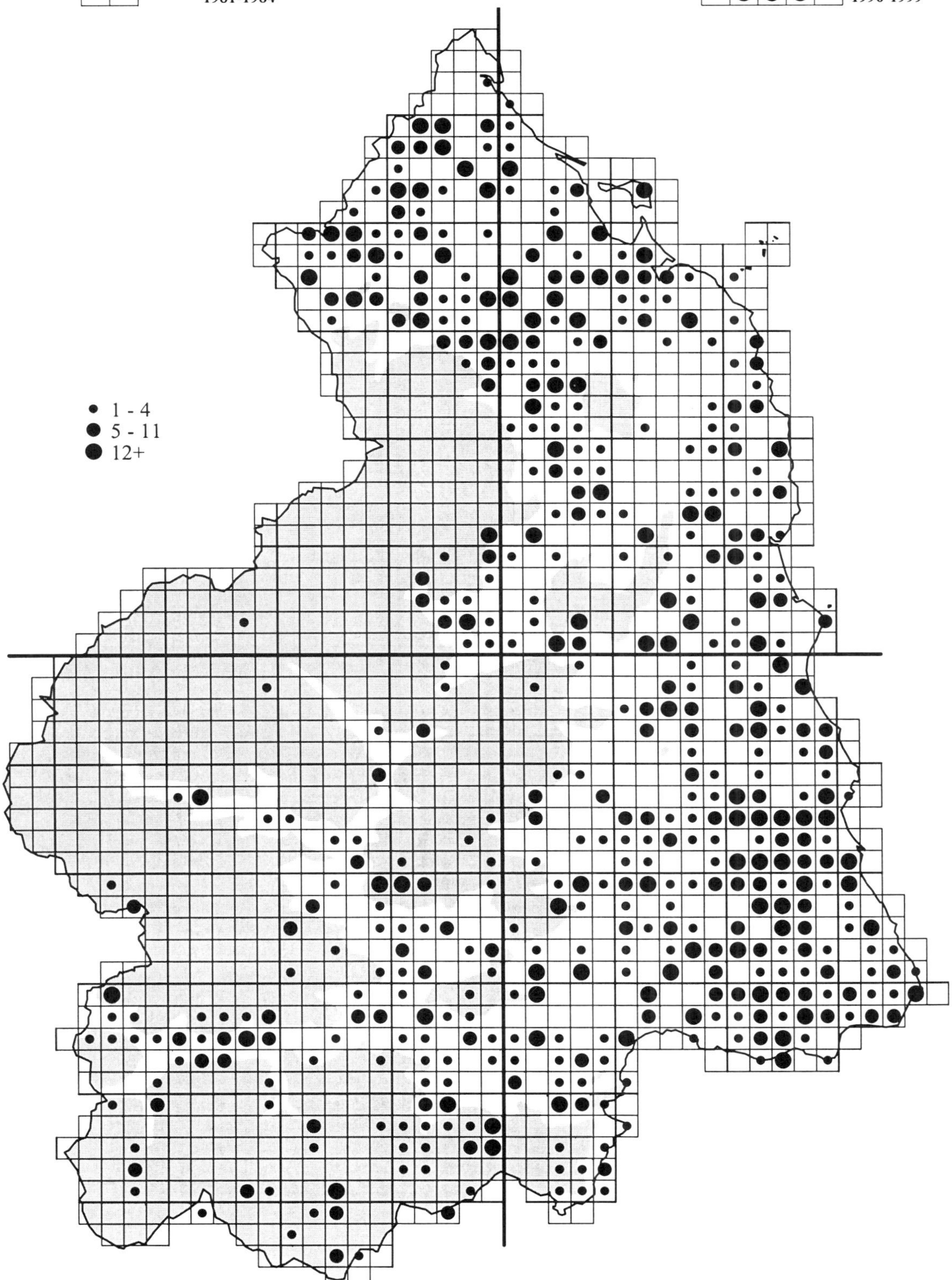

Greenfinch

GOLDFINCH *Carduelis carduelis*

In the nineteenth century, Hancock (1874) described the Goldfinch as a casual visitor. Bolam (1912; 1932), however, observed that its numbers were increasing, a situation that continued enabling Galloway and Meek (1983) to describe it as a common resident. Mead (2000) listed the bird, nationally, as a recovering species and predicts that its immediate future is bright.

Goldfinches, more than any other finch, specialise in feeding on the seeds of plants in the family *Compositae*, especially the larger seeds of thistles, burdocks and teasels, as well as the smaller seeds of some of the more abundant weeds. They also feed in woodlands, on Birch *Betula* sp., pine and Alder *Alnus* sp. seeds, when other food is not available. Goldfinches feed gregariously throughout the year, concentrating wherever suitable seeding plants occur, but become more widely distributed as winter progresses and some food sources become scarce. They are the only finches with bills slender enough to reach teasel seeds which lie at the bottom of narrow tubes and because of their specialised foods, often feed alone and not with other finches in winter.

During the current winter atlas survey, Goldfinches were recorded in 431 tetrads. Over 80% of these were below 201 metres a.s.l., thus confirming the species as predominantly a lowland bird in Northumberland, although its continued spread westwards results in an increasing number of reports from higher ground. By day they roam the countryside from one feeding site to another and at night roost communally, usually in thick deciduous scrub or evergreens. The size of flocks varies with the food supply. The largest flocks form in autumn when food is plentiful and the year's population is at its highest but, as winter progresses, the flocks are mostly of less than ten (Lack, 1986).

There is considerable evidence of continued expansion as well as increase in numbers in the county. During the current survey they were recorded in 87% of the 10km squares compared with only 79% during the 1981-1984 winter survey. The average number of birds per occupied control tetrad during the period of the survey more than doubled from 4 to 8.9. Charms of between 15 and 100 birds were regularly reported in the late 1970s and early 1980s, and one of 168 was recorded at a regular roosting site in a holly tree at Matfen in 1978. Whilst the harsh winter weather of much of the 1980s led to a reduction in reported charm size, regular reports of between ten and 50 birds were still being made. Since the late 1980s and the onset of milder winters, the size of charms has continued to rise almost annually with 300 reported on set-aside at Longhoughton in 1998 and near Alnwick Castle in January 2000. More than twice the number of charms of 30 or more birds have been reported in the last five winters, since the start of the atlas survey in 1996, than were reported in the previous eight winters. They have been reported from the River Tyne right up to the River Tweed and, with one exception, on land below 250 metres a.s.l. The largest cluster of reports is around Hauxley, Druridge and Cresswell (NU20/NZ29) with smaller clusters around Beadnell, Low Newton and Embleton (NU21/NU22) and Prestwick Carr, Big Waters and Arcot (NZ17/NZ27).

The distribution maps for breeding and wintering Goldfinches are very similar, 33% and 30% respectively of tetrads being occupied. The movement westwards into land above 183 metres a.s.l. referred to in *The atlas of breeding birds in Northumbria* (Day *et al.*, 1995) has continued, with winter reports showing a spreading out from the major river valleys. Wintering birds occupied fewer tetrads below 183 metres a.s.l., notably in and around Newcastle where some of the breeding population will have dispersed in search of food. The overall wintering total for the current survey of 4,216 birds is quite an increase on the 850 to 1,750 pairs suggested in the local breeding atlas, especially as many leave Britain each year to winter on the continent (Lack, 1986). Due to the fact that they roam the countryside in search of food, it is likely that some will have been counted more than once. However, whilst it would appear from the maps that some have left the county, recent mild winters, coupled with a possible increase in the availability of food through changes in agricultural practice such as set-aside, will have meant fewer birds migrating than perhaps was once the case. Mead (2000) noted the increased use being made of garden bird feeders by Goldfinches since the 1970s, although such reports in the county are few but have been increasing since 1999. In addition, winter flocks may have grown in size as the breeding population has expanded and together these factors are probably responsible for the current healthy situation.

TONY BAKER

Distribution by altitude

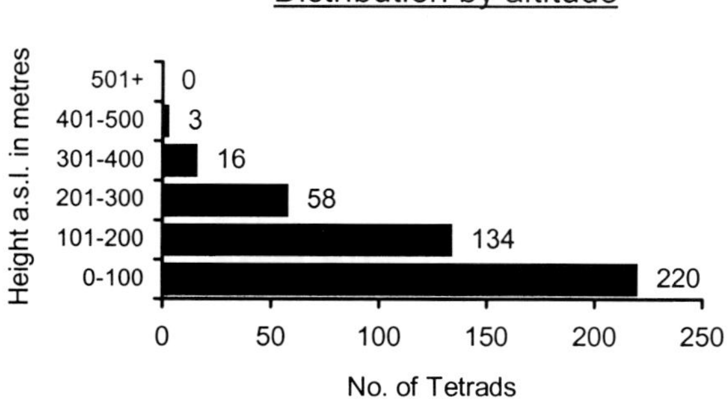

No. of tetrads in which recorded 431 (30%)

Tetrad Analysis	No. of tetrads
1-4 birds	219 (51%)
5-13 birds	126 (29%)
14+ birds	86 (20%)

Total No. of birds counted 4,216

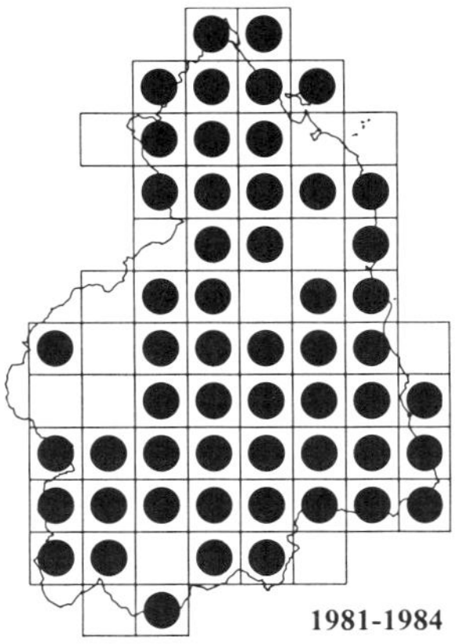

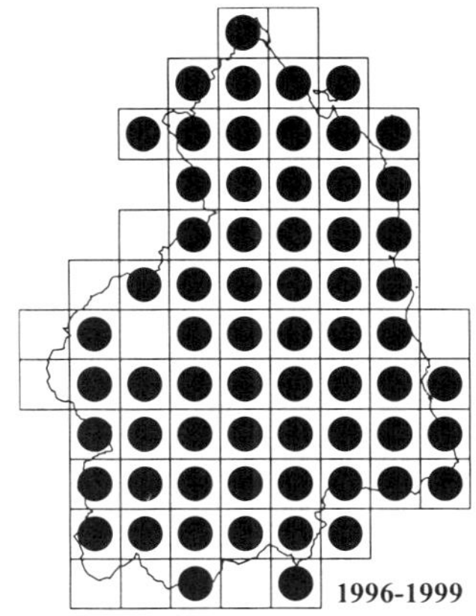

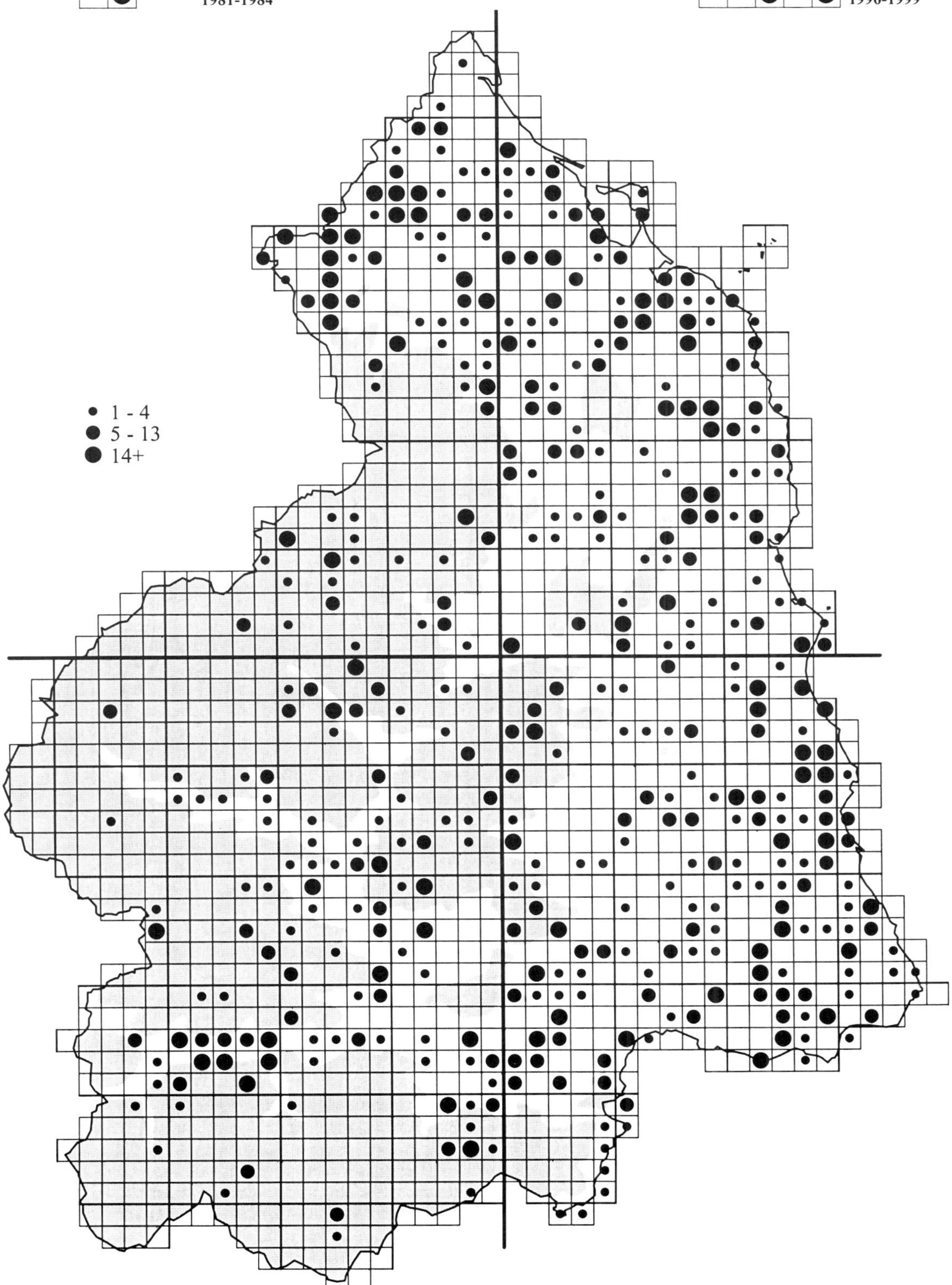

Goldfinch

SISKIN *Carduelis spinus*

This dapper bird is one of the smallest European finches and 'to most of Britain is still a winter visitor only' (Newton, 1972). Previously it was recorded in Northumberland as a 'winter visitant' by Bolam (1932) who went on to say that 'gathering together in larger flocks - often of 50, sometimes twice that number - these spend some months in woods ... and usually disappear about March or April'. In addition, he also suspected that it might have bred. Half a century later, Galloway and Meek (1983) described the Siskin as a 'well represented passage and winter visitor and breeding species'.

British breeding Siskins are 'greatly out-numbered by Continental birds' entering the country by the same routes as the Chaffinch *Fringilla coelebs*. These birds arrive between September and early November and depart between mid-March and mid-May. Ringing recoveries have shown that some of the immigrants to Britain come from Fenno-Scandia and others from the montane areas of central and eastern Europe (Newton, 1972). Birds ringed in Northumberland have been subsequently recovered in Belgium, Denmark and Germany.

A comparison of the winter and breeding distribution of Siskins is complicated by the arrival of continental birds (Lack, 1986). The immigrant birds, unlike the Chaffinch, do not have differing behaviour patterns whilst in this country. Local movements certainly occur within the county and also within Britain as birds move out of their breeding areas in the coniferous forests. A comparison between the local breeding survey map (Day *et al.*, 1995) and the tetrad map for the present winter survey demonstrates the movement away from the Border Forest and this is also supported by numerous local ringing returns. Ringing controls also show that a considerable number of Scottish Siskins from the Grampian and Highland Regions spend the winter period in the county or on passage to the more southerly parts of Britain. Some Northumberland-breeding birds also move south with movements of between 350-450 kilometres being not uncommon.

During the current survey, Siskins were found in 315 tetrads (22% of those surveyed) and the map indicates that they are widely distributed in winter throughout the county. Of the occupied tetrads, 212 (67%) were below 200 metres a.s.l., 96 (30%) were between 201 and 400 metres a.s.l. and only seven (3%) above 400 metres.). There were 13 tetrad counts of 100 or more with the largest being 300 at Dukesfield (NY95N) in January 1997. Of the remaining counts, 114 tetrads (36%) held 11-90 birds but 188 tetrads (60%) contained one-ten birds. The control tetrad data collected would seem to indicate that they were perhaps more numerous in the winter of 1996/97 as total counts were 267, 192 and 145 respectively for the three winter periods. However, it should be noted that none of the control tetrads held Siskins in all three winters. A comparison of the two 10km square maps indicates a slight range expansion since the 1981-1984 national winter survey with birds located in 59 (79%) of the squares surveyed as opposed to 49 (72%) in the earlier survey.

Siskin feed mainly in winter on Alder *Alnus* sp., first from cones and later on the ground. They may also be seen in Birches *Betula* sp. or Larches *Larix* sp. with Redpoll *Carduelis flammea* (Lack, 1986). In late winter and early spring when their main food has perhaps become scarce they have adapted, like many species, to garden feeding where they now feed readily on peanuts and fat. The 1981-1984 national winter atlas survey reported that 'during winter Siskins form flocks of up to 50, occasionally more' and 'roost in flocks of similar size to the feeding groups, in conifers, thorn scrub, alders or reed beds' (Lack, 1986). The Siskin is an irruptive finch whose movements are dictated by the abundance of food. Consequently there can be great fluctuations in the numbers wintering in the county in any year and their origin can differ from one year to the next.

The atlas of breeding birds in Northumbria (Day *et al.*, 1995) estimated that there are now at least 10,000 breeding pairs, although the number can be greatly exceeded in exceptional years. Should all the breeding birds and surviving juveniles remain in the county, this would indicate a minimum wintering population in excess of 40,000, considerably higher than that indicated by the total count of 6,724 in this survey. In a winter where there is a large influx of continental migrants, the overall wintering population could well be swollen to perhaps 50,000+, even allowing for some movement of the breeding birds.

F. D. MIDDLETON

Distribution by altitude

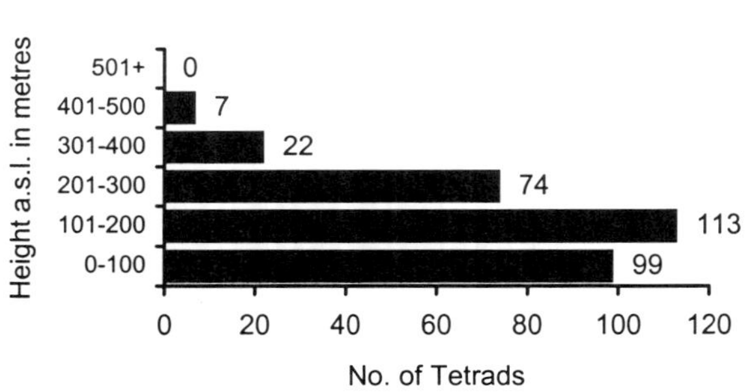

No. of tetrads in which recorded	315 (22%)
Tetrad Analysis	**No. of tetrads**
1-6 birds	157 (50%)
7-30 birds	95 (30%)
31+ birds	63 (20%)
Total No. of birds counted	6,724

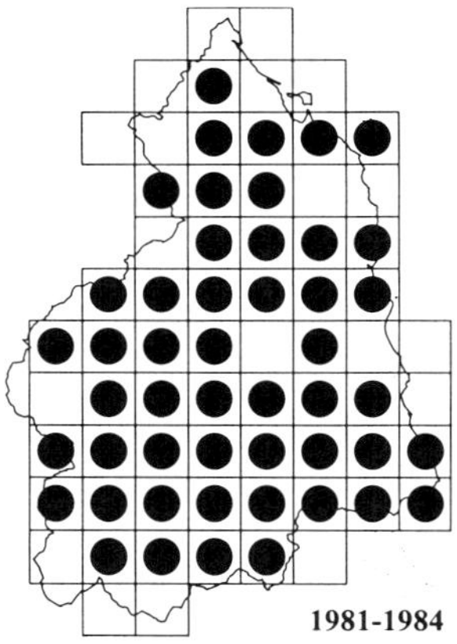

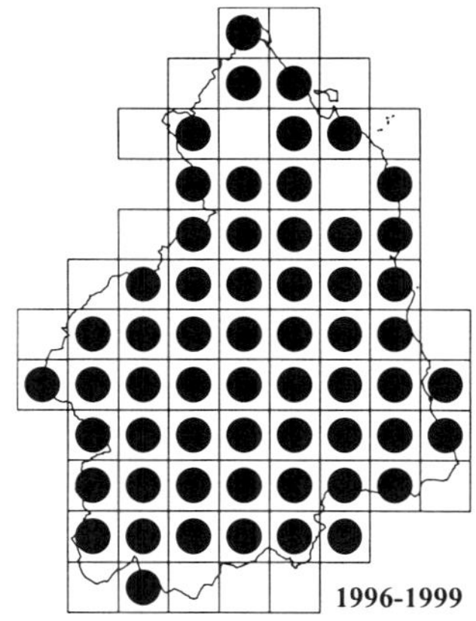

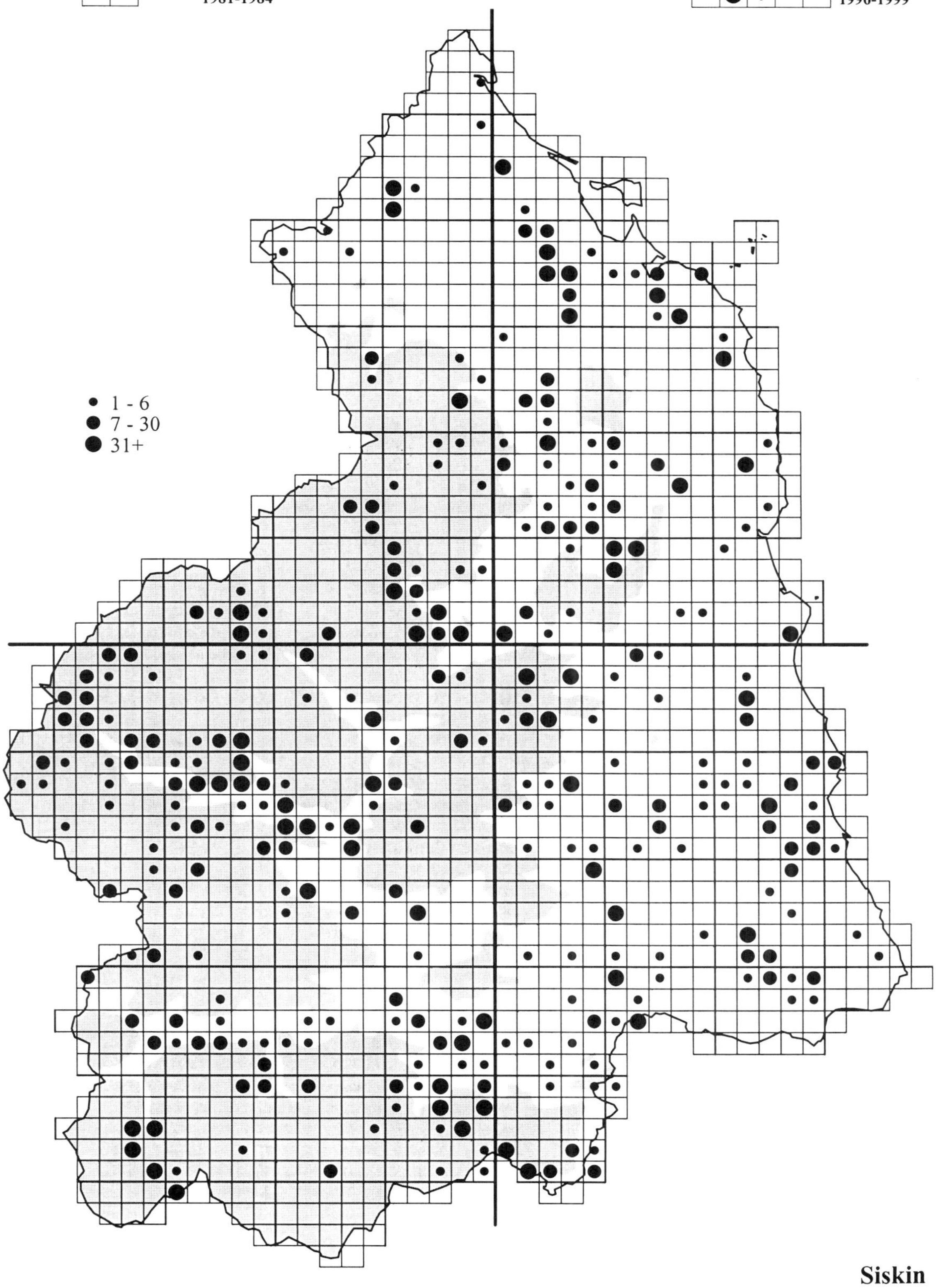

Siskin

LINNET *Carduelis cannabina*

The Linnet in Northumberland is a familiar species on farmland and scrub in summer and was described as 'common' by both Selby (1831) and Bolam (1932). In winter however, it can prove more difficult to find as whole populations can congregate in a few flocks. Of its status in winter, Bolam (1912) described it as 'perhaps most abundant on the coast ... after the arrival of immigrant flocks'. Galloway and Meek (1983), whilst agreeing with its summer status, found little to support Bolam's contention of large scale foreign invasions. They stated, on ringing evidence, that the sizeable coastal flocks in autumn and winter were of British origin.

Winter movement to lower-lying land along the coastal plain is very evident in comparing the winter tetrad map with that in *The atlas of breeding birds in Northumbria* (Day *et al.*, 1995). Altitudinal movement is obvious with the species virtually absent from the county's low moors and upland river valleys. Statistically for the whole of the county, 51% of all tetrads were occupied in the breeding season whilst in winter the figure falls to 13%. Linnets in winter are almost totally absent from the south west quadrant (NY) and the upland areas of the Cheviot (NT). Even in lowland agricultural areas and along the coastal plain (NU & NZ), whilst widespread, their distribution is patchy.

During the winter months Linnets are largely confined to open country, particularly lowland farmland. This is because of a specialist diet of small weed seeds taken from the ground. Prior to the 1950s there was a bountiful supply of exposed seed on our cultivated land. This was diminished by the intensive use of agro-chemicals, especially during the 1950s and 1960s, which resulted in the Linnet, as well as a number of other common farmland bird specialists, experiencing a massive national decline. However, there are signs that the species is adapting to late twentieth century agricultural practices in the county, where the introduction of Oilseed Rape *Brassica napus* may be helping to compensate for the loss of traditional food sources. Recently introduced agricultural set-aside policies, such as the Countryside Stewardship Scheme, are hopefully a step in the right direction in further encouraging the spread of this colourful finch. Birds are also colonising waste ground in suburban and industrial areas, especially in the south east.

Linnets are gregarious and may often be observed in flocks of up to 200 or more. They frequently associate and roost with other finches and buntings although remaining as an independent sub-unit. During the current atlas survey, 9,750 birds were counted in 182 tetrads. These finch flocks are a feature of coastal and lowland Northumberland during the winter and some 73 (40%) of occupied tetrads held between 30 and 300 birds during the survey period, although larger counts included 350 at Cramlington (NZ27N), 400 near Glanton (NU01M) and 500 on Holy Island (NU14G) with a very large flock of 700 at Beal (NU04K) in January 1997.

The national decline of the Linnet population (Mead, 2000) is evident on a local scale in Northumberland. A comparison of the two 10km square maps shows a decrease in occupied squares from 71% during 1981-1984 to 63% in the current survey. Further support is provided by an analysis of returns in the annual county bird report *Birds in Northumbria* which suggests a decline in flock sizes over the last twenty years. Lastly, data from the control tetrads show a wide discrepancy in occupancy over the three winter seasons with averages of 44, 90 and 16 birds per occupied tetrad. Whilst this can be partly explained by flock mobility and availability of food sources, the pattern of annual figures shows very little continuous stability. Given the large area of suitable habitat on the county's long coastline and the broad agricultural plain, there is plenty of wintering territory for Linnets. Whether the total of 9,750 birds counted is an accurate reflection of the winter population is debatable as it was estimated that the county breeding population was about 4,000 pairs and, as implied by ringing returns, at least part of the population moves away from the area to the continent.

DEE McKEOWN

Distribution by altitude

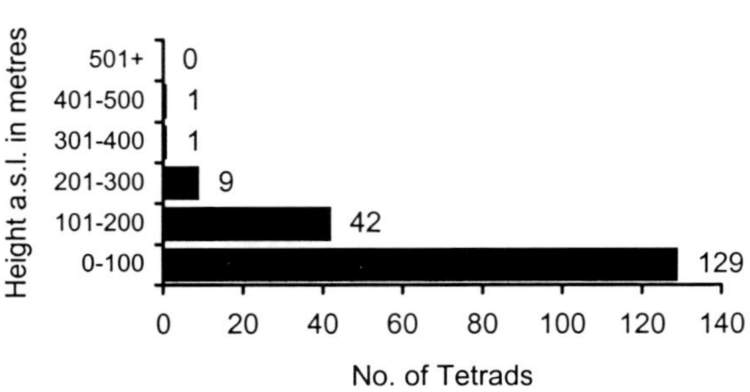

No. of tetrads in which recorded 182 (13%)

Tetrad Analysis	No. of tetrads
1-20 birds	95 (52%)
21-80 birds	52 (29%)
81+ birds	35 (19%)

Total No. of birds counted 9,750

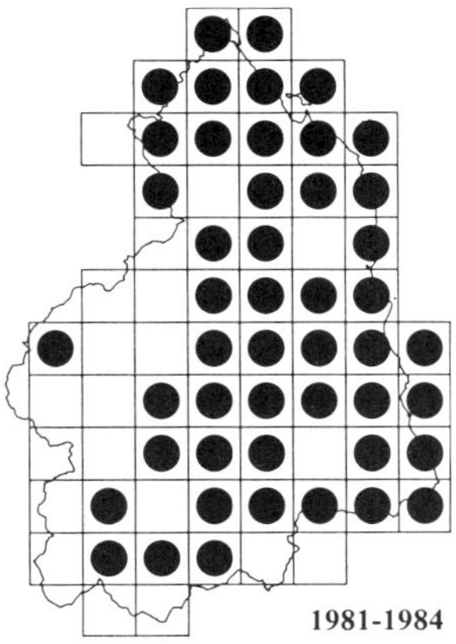

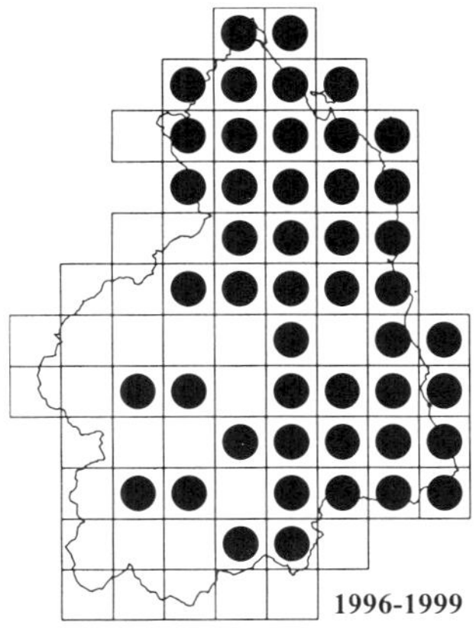

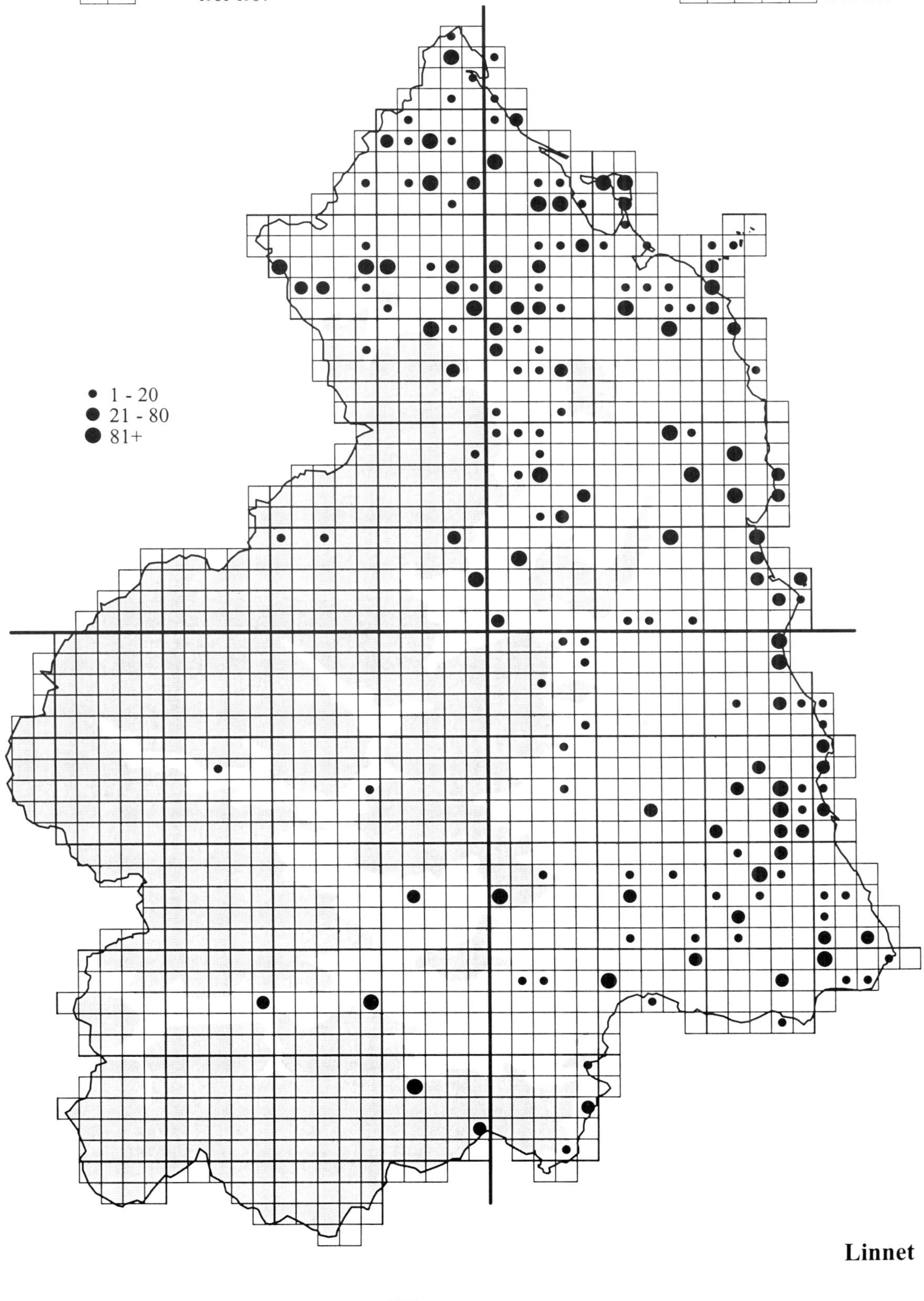

Linnet

TWITE *Carduelis flavirostris*

Hancock (1874) referred to the Twite in Northumberland as 'resident ... not uncommon' while Bolam (1932) also noted its status as a breeding bird and commented that 'as a winter visitant, the Twite reaches the coast pretty regularly in September and October, often in large flocks, which commonly penetrate to the foothills of the Cheviots'. Galloway and Meek (1983) classified the species as a well-represented passage and winter visitor which formerly bred. They also mentioned that 'between 1932 and the late 1960s only very small numbers were reported from anywhere in the county ... during the 1970s, however, wintering flocks were reported much more regularly, the favourite areas being Lindisfarne NNR, the Coquet Estuary, Hauxley (where reclaimed opencast mining area provided an ideal food source) and Druridge'. Respective maxima for these localities were 60, 97, 130 and 80'. They further commented that small numbers were still occasionally found inland. There was a drop in numbers of birds during the early to mid-1980s, the largest flock recorded being 50 birds at the Coquet Estuary. Since 1988, more flocks containing higher numbers, often in excess of 100 birds, have been recorded. The largest flock on record involved 210 birds during the winter period 1992/93 at Druridge which had become the most important site in the county, followed by the Lindisfarne NNR. During this period the ability of the Coquet Estuary and Hauxley to hold birds had declined. Since the early 1980s, birds have continued to be largely confined to coastal areas with the occasional records coming from inland sites (*Birds in Northumbria 1983-1996*). There has been little change concerning the arrival and departure of wintering birds since Bolam's time, with the majority of birds appearing in October and November and disappearing by early March.

The origin of birds wintering in Northumberland seems unclear: they may be birds which breed in either Scotland or Scandinavia or a combination of both. Of the local population since at least the 1930s, there have only been sporadic instances of the species attempting to breed (Day *et al.*, 1995; Kerr, 2001).

The total of maximum counts for the survey period was 1,485 and even accounting for some duplication arising from the mobility of flocks, the status of the species remains that of a well-represented winter visitor. There continues to be a marked preference for the coast as 18 of the 22 tetrads in which the species was recorded were coastal. Two of the tetrads, which held 40 and 60 birds respectively, were in the central Cheviots (NT80H/NT80U) at an average altitude of about 350 metres a.s.l. and a further tetrad on Chatton Moor (NU02X) with seven birds is just over 220 metres. This confirms previous authors' comments that the species occasionally ventures into upland areas. The survey reveals that the most important areas for Twite are the Lindisfarne NNR and Druridge Bay.

Direct comparison between the two 10km square maps shows little difference in coastal distribution but a large change in the inland distribution of the species. With respect to this, it can be assumed that it is merely a reflection of the sporadic nature of inland occurrence. The apparent similarity in coastal distribution masks significant changes revealed by the tetrad information and that gleaned from the references above, in particular, the demise of the importance of the Coquet Estuary and Hauxley for the species and the greater importance of Druridge Bay. Hauxley's previous importance was related to the large expanses of annual plants provided by open-cast mining, the cessation of which and subsequent reclamation has, on the whole, eliminated this 'wasteland' habitat. Finding an explanation for the changes in the preference of the species for Druridge as opposed to the Coquet Estuary is more problematical. The reason presumably relates to a combination of human disturbance (which has increased at both sites, although the relative importance is hard to quantify) and habitat change.

Lack (1986) considered the wintering population of Britain and Ireland to be in the region of 100,000 to 150,000 birds. The Northumberland population therefore represents less than 1% of the national total but still remains of local significance.

MICHAEL J. CARR

Distribution by altitude

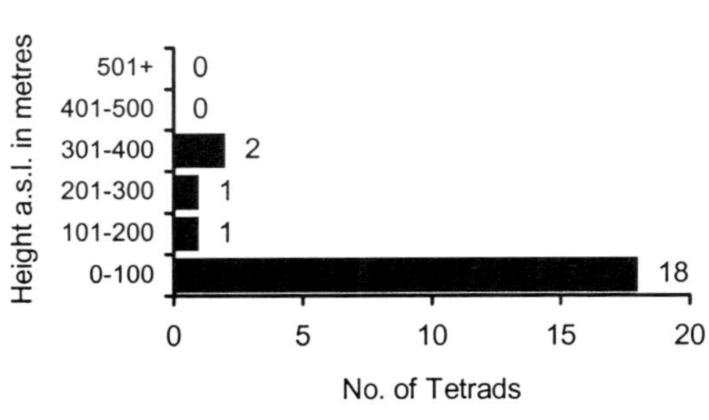

No. of tetrads in which recorded 22 (2%)

Tetrad Analysis	No. of tetrads
1-40 birds	11 (50%)
41-100 birds	6 (27%)
101+ birds	5 (23%)

Total No. of birds counted 1,485

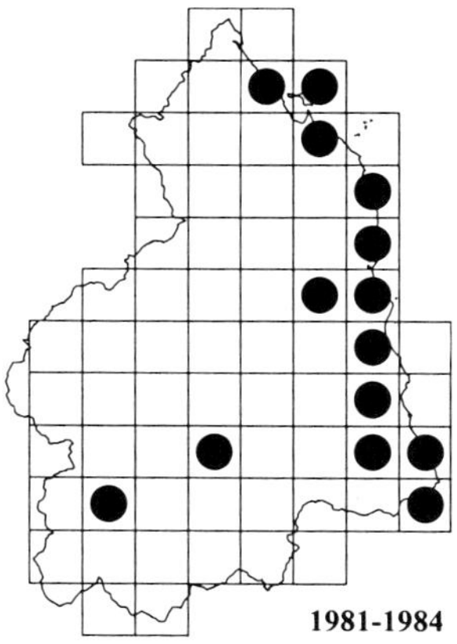

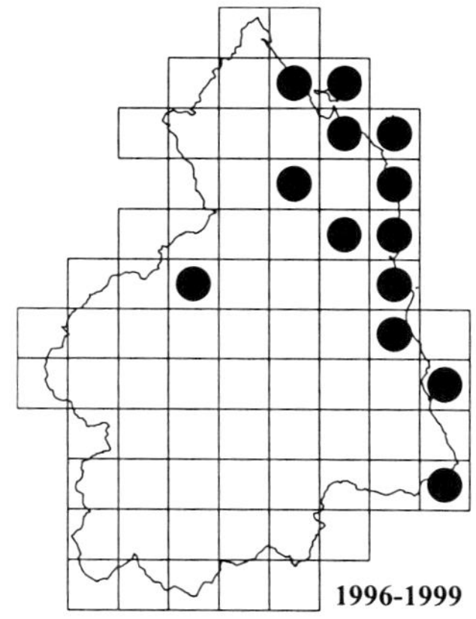

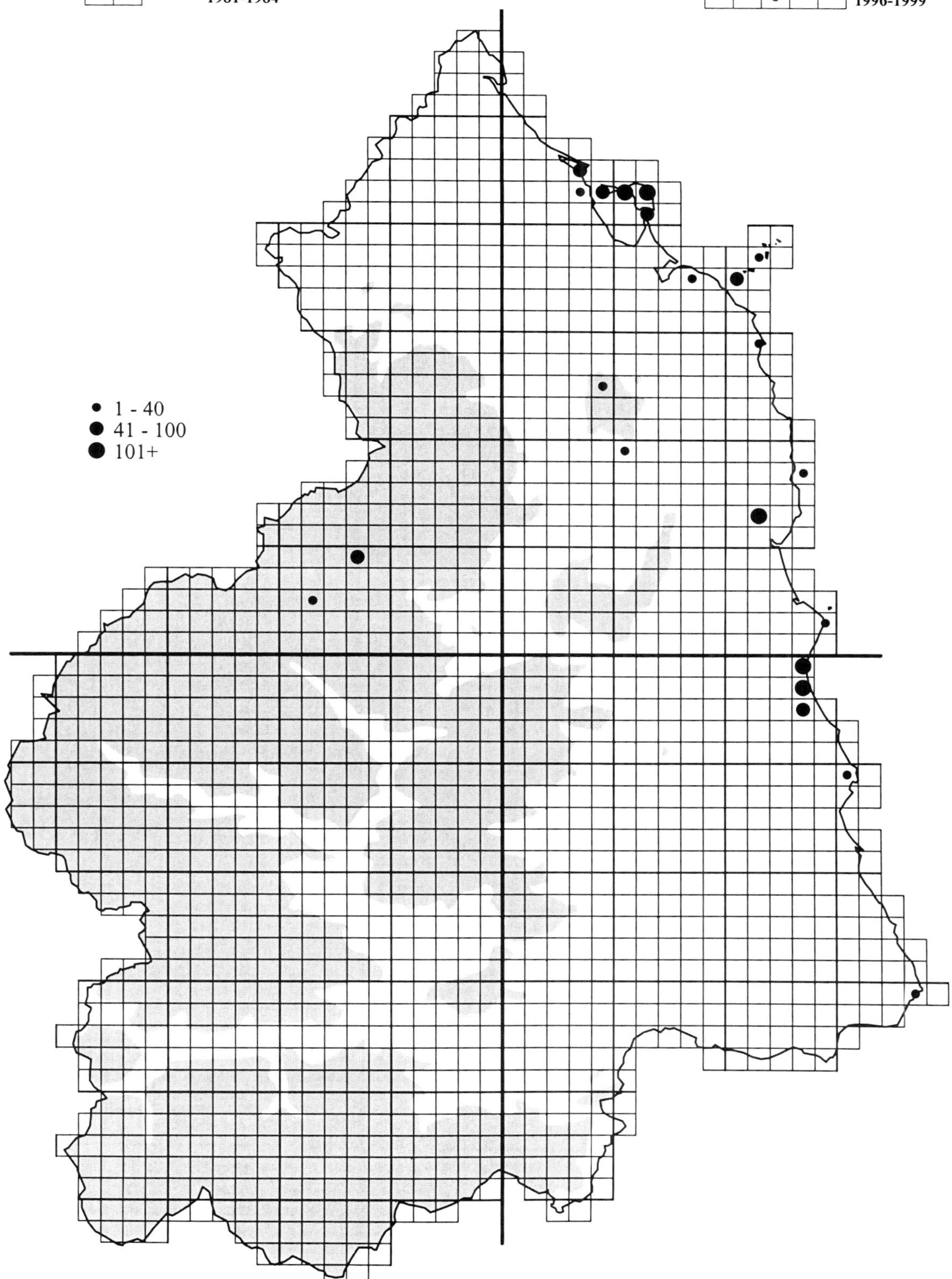

Twite

LESSER REDPOLL *Carduelis cabaret*

Bolam (1932) knew the Lesser Redpoll as 'a resident, winter visitor and passage migrant' and went on to say of its winter status that it was 'always most in evidence during the colder months when it gathers into considerable flocks to wander widely over the country'. Galloway and Meek (1983) however, noted a distinct change in occurrence, saying 'at least in recent years, it is largely absent from the county in winter'. They described how a good crop of Alder *Alnus glutinosa* in the winter of 1976/77 allowed many to over-winter in the Kielder area and then experience a very good breeding season. A poor crop the following winter meant that few Redpolls were seen.

Data collected over the three winter periods covered by this current survey show that Lesser Redpolls are still widely, but thinly, distributed throughout the county but do not generally occur in very large numbers in any region. Only three tetrads contained relatively large numbers with 100 birds in both the Dye House area (NY95J) and at the Queen Elizabeth II Country Park (NZ28Z), and 110 in the Happy Valley area (NT92X). These widely spread tetrads all contain suitable feeding habitat including younger plantations or recent re-stocking where quick growing tree species can provide good crops of seeds. A total of 15 tetrads produced counts of 30-60 with a further 25 holding ten-25 birds. The remaining 101 occupied tetrads (72%) held maximum counts of less than ten birds. The rather nomadic winter nature of the Lesser Redpoll in the county was to some extent confirmed by data provided from the control tetrads. They were recorded in only five of these and in only one in more than one winter. Numbers were also low with seasonal totals of 12, zero and 21.

Comparison with the data collected for the local breeding atlas in 1988-1992 (Day *et al.*, 1995) shows a significant difference in occurrence with only 36% of tetrads occupied during the breeding season continuing to be inhabited in the winter. This compares well with the 1981-1984 national winter atlas where Lack (1986) estimated that 30-70% of Lesser Redpolls emigrate after breeding. The tetrads which contained birds during the breeding season but not in winter are broadly those which, while they may contain suitable feeding reserves, are exposed to extremes of the weather. This is confirmed by an altitudinal analysis, as only 17 (12%) of the occupied tetrads in winter were above 300 metres a.s.l.

The UK population as a whole has undergone several medium term fluctuations, with populations dipping during the 1920s or possibly earlier in the northern part of the country, followed by a build up with a preference shown for new conifer plantations, this expansion continuing throughout the 1970s. The population has subsequently declined and is now thought to have reduced to the level of the late 1960s (Marchant *et al.*, 1990). In Northumberland, the status of the Lesser Redpoll, as described by earlier authors, suggests that the local population has largely followed the national trend. However, the population reduction in the last 20 years is difficult to explain. It is unlikely that suitable habitat has greatly reduced since the 1980s, as that lost through the maturing, and in some cases subsequent felling, of plantations, is likely to have been replaced by the significant amount of re-stocking of forestry and other areas.

With an overall total of 1,554 birds counted during the current survey, the Lesser Redpoll maintains a status of a common winter visitor but the fortunes of the species in the county could well merit a more detailed study, especially in light of the comments made by Mead (2000) who said 'Redpolls ... have increased rapidly in the past - let's hope they do it again'.

GEOFF LINKLETER

Distribution by altitude

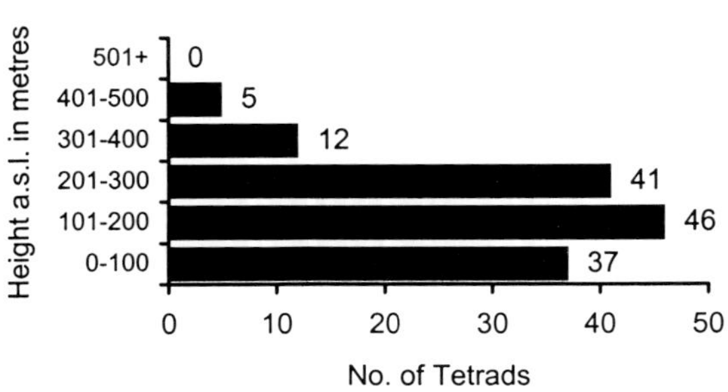

No. of tetrads in which recorded 141 (10%)

Tetrad Analysis	No. of tetrads
1-4 birds	77 (55%)
5-15 birds	39 (27%)
16+ birds	25 (18%)

Total No. of birds counted 1,554

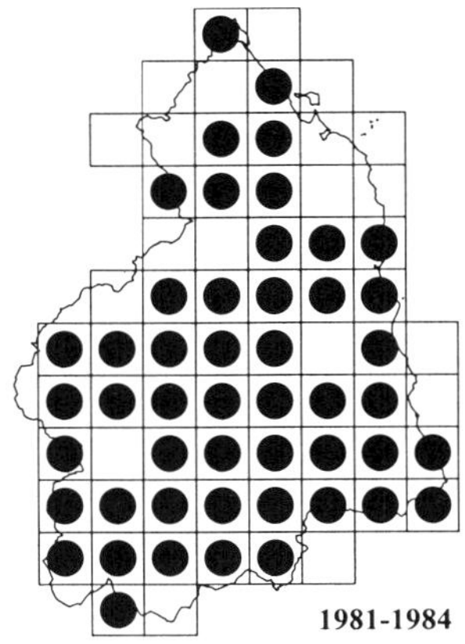

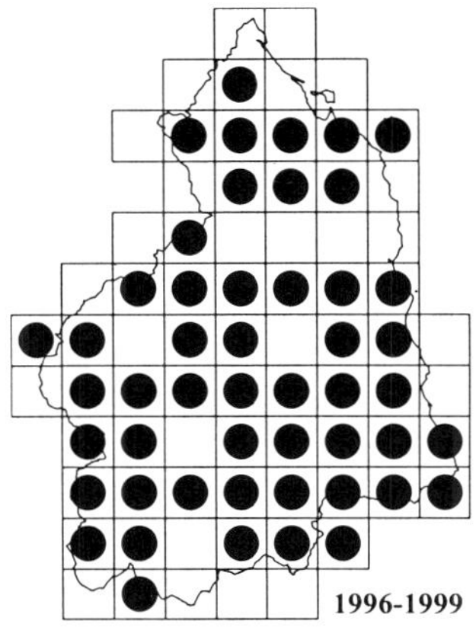

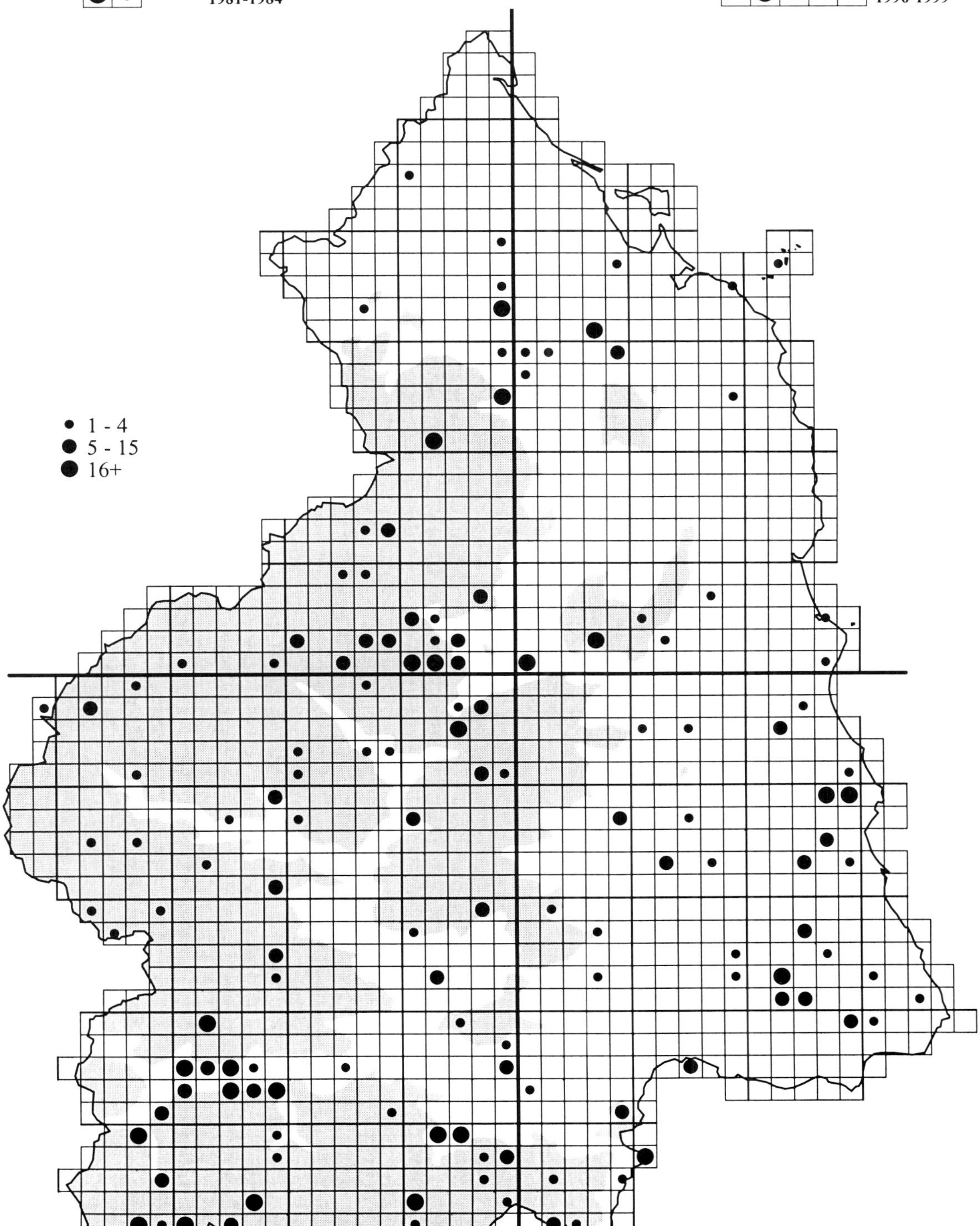

Lesser Redpoll

MEALY REDPOLL *Carduelis flammea*

In August 2000 the BOU announced that with effect from 1st January 2001 two sub-species of Common Redpoll *C. flammea*, the Mealy Redpoll *C .f. flammea* and the Lesser Redpoll *Carduelis cabaret*, would be treated as separate species. Whereas the Lesser Redpoll is a breeding resident and passage and winter visitor in Northumberland, the Mealy Redpoll in western Europe is both a short distance migrant and also a long distance migrant from its more northern and eastern breeding areas. In winter Mealy Redpolls move mainly south east away from their breeding grounds, but the movement and winter range varies from year to year (Snow & Perrins, 1998). Hence, they appear in Britain in most winters, though only rarely in significant numbers, and then mainly on the east coast.

Bolam (1932) described the Mealy Redpoll as 'a winter visitant, and passage migrant; not rare, but very irregular in its appearance, sometimes coming in considerable flocks, in other years altogether absent or scarcely noticed'. Galloway and Meek (1983) noted that from Bolam's era until 1946 none were recorded, but they reported influxes in autumn 1972 and again in 1975. The same authors noted another major arrival in November 1984 (Galloway & Meek, 1986). Kerr (2001) also recorded a recent influx in 1995, when large numbers arrived along the coast.

Between these main influxes, small numbers were reported annually and this pattern was repeated in the results from the current winter survey where one to three birds were recorded in only five tetrads with the maximum count of six individuals in a tetrad at Druridge Bay (NZ29T) in January 1998. These records are split virtually evenly between the years of the survey giving an average annual total of only four.

Although based on a small set of data, the distribution map shows that birds can be found either in coastal locations or inland in forested areas. It is presumed that in the former case the birds are living in an area close to their point of arrival, especially as these records are often earlier in the winter. In the inland tetrads it would be expected that birds would find habitat with good numbers of seed bearing trees such as Birch *Betula* sp., Spruce *Picea* sp. or Larch *Larix* sp. which are the main winter food of the species. This is confirmed by the fact that the majority of inland tetrads where Mealy Redpolls were found also contained high populations of Lesser Redpolls which feed on similar tree seeds.

Direct comparison of the distribution with the national winter atlas (Lack, 1986) is difficult, as Mealy Redpoll was not treated as a separate species, the only comment being the qualitative statement that it occurs most winters on the east coast, but only exceptionally in large numbers. This again mirrors the current findings.

Mealy Redpolls leave the UK for their breeding grounds in early spring and were not recorded in *The atlas of breeding birds in Northumbria* (Day *et al.*, 1995), the only potential breeding record in the county being one, with a brood patch, trapped at Seaton Delaval in June 1976 (Galloway & Meek, 1983). The current winter status of Mealy Redpoll in the county is hence believed to be unchanged as an irruptive visitor, its occurrence in any given winter being largely independent of conditions in our region, being governed by food supply and breeding success in northern and eastern Europe.

GEOFF LINKLETER

Distribution by altitude

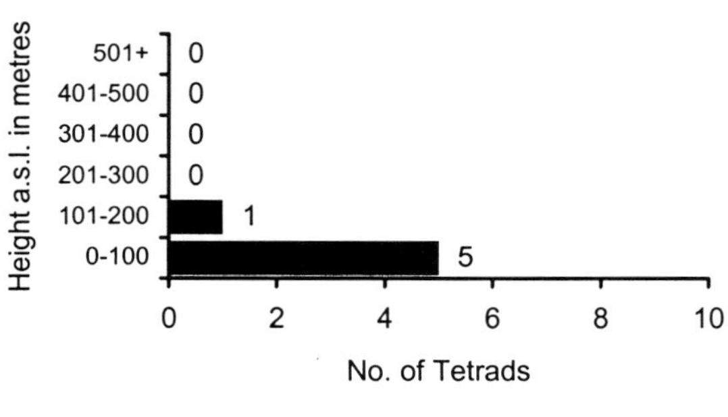

No. of tetrads in which recorded — 6 (<1%)

Tetrad Analysis	No. of tetrads
1-2 birds	3 (50%)
3 birds	2 (33%)
4+ birds	1 (17%)

Total No. of birds counted — 17

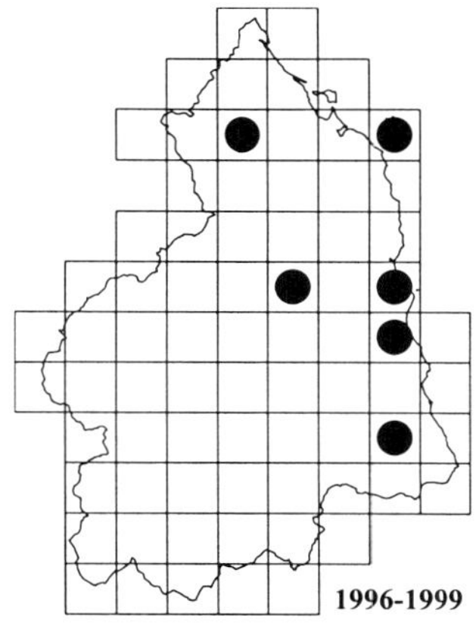

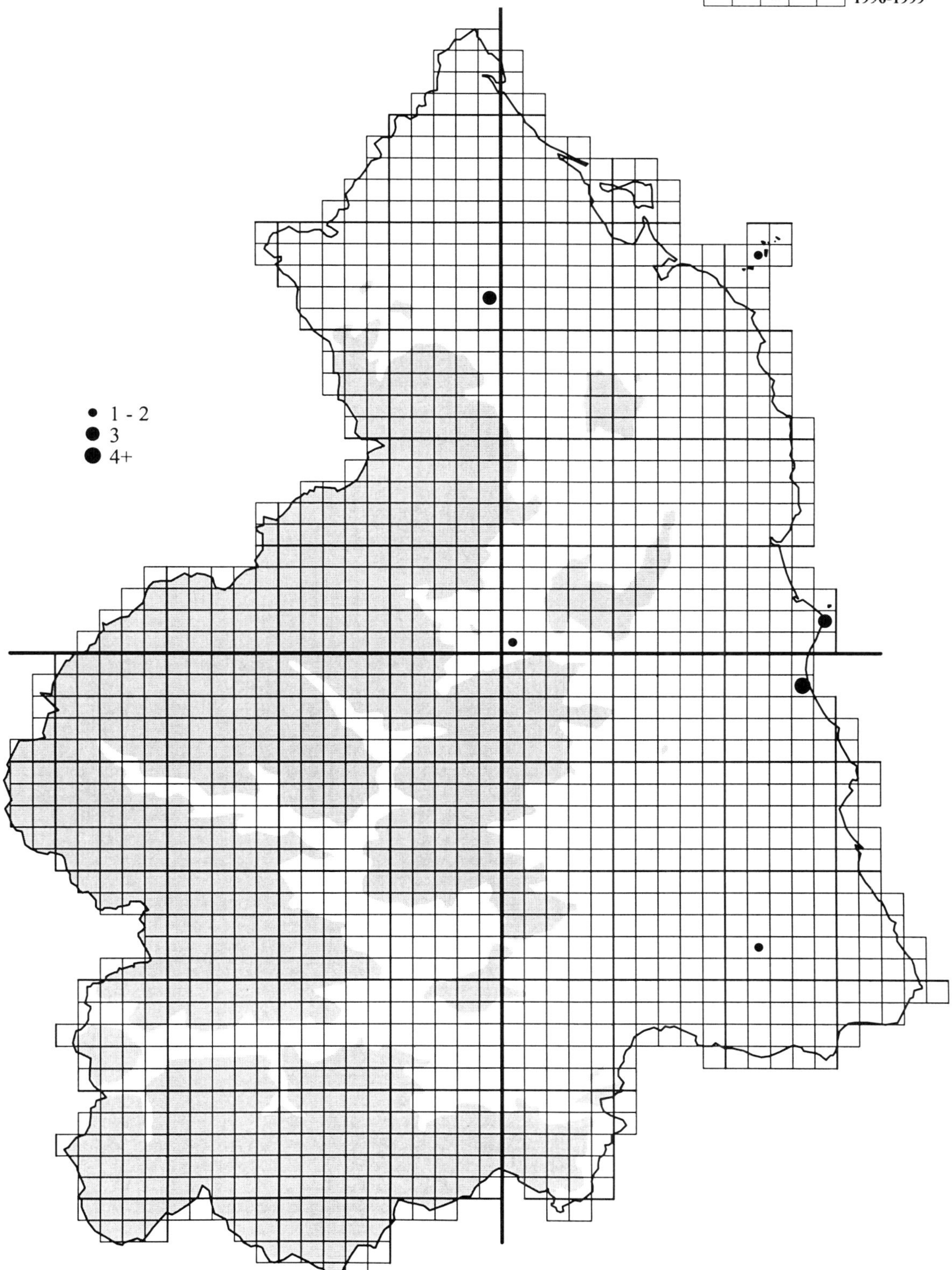

Mealy Redpoll

CROSSBILL *Loxia curvirostra*

Northumberland has a large and nomadic Crossbill population. The species is almost totally reliant on conifer seeds for food (Lack, 1986) and therefore restricted to the conifer plantations of the county. These areas include the Border Forest and those at Slaley, Harwood, the Simonside and Kyloe Hills and this is reflected on the tetrad distribution map for the current survey. The species is a sporadic breeder, capable of breeding throughout the year. Its peak breeding seasons are during October-December and February-April (Day *et al.*, 1995) both of which fall partially within the current winter survey periods. This means that, unlike most species in this atlas, it is impossible to discuss a wintering population without reference to breeding.

Bolam (1932) knew the species as a relatively rare breeder whose population was augmented by immigrants arriving in good numbers in 'invasion years'. The establishment of large coniferous plantations throughout the twentieth century means there is now a much larger resident population in the county. This population, however, can still be greatly enhanced by immigrants from Scandinavia in invasion years. The invasion year of 1990 enjoyed what was estimated to be the largest population of Crossbills ever seen in the county. Results from a point count census conducted in November-December 1990 at Kielder Forest suggested that there might be as many as 40,000 Crossbills in 34,000 hectares of forest (Jardine, 1991).

The breeding cycle of Crossbill is related to the availability of the conifer seeds on which they live almost exclusively (Newton, 1972). The availability of the conifer seed varies from year to year, the cone crop of upland spruce forests being particularly variable, with years of high abundance and others with virtually no crop. The smaller cone crop of larch and pine plantations is, however, more reliable. When there is a good cone crop in the large upland forests of the county the birds breed there successfully in large numbers. In years when this crop fails however, the birds disperse into lowland larch and pine plantations. This dispersal from upland forests in the county is recorded in Galloway and Meek (1983) who noted there were 70 pairs of Crossbills at Kielder Burn in February 1975 but none in the same area during the following winter of 1975/76. Breeding birds then again occupied the area in the winter of 1976/77. During this current survey there appears to have been a similar movement of birds out of the upland spruce forest due to a lack of available food in the winter of 1997/98 as indicated by control tetrad data. In the winter of 1996/97, with a high spruce cone abundance, there were ten control tetrads in upland areas which recorded Crossbills. This dropped to only one in 1997/98 when the cone crop was low-medium, but rose to six in 1998/99 when the crop increased. An invasion of Crossbills during the summer of 1997 (*Birds in Northumbria 1997*) did not lead to a significant increase in breeding birds during the winter of 1997/98, due to the low abundance of food in the upland forests. A large number of immigrant birds presumably wintered that year in the lowland plantations, along with the county's resident birds. Although there were only two lowland control tetrads, at Swinhoe (NU03S) and Riding Mill (NZ06A) which recorded Crossbills, they were both occupied initially in the winter of 1997/98.

Due to their breeding strategy, Crossbills can be seen from autumn onwards in small family parties. As the winter progresses, and the cone crop becomes depleted, these family groups join together to form larger flocks in areas where there is still food available. In addition, when occupying the lowland larch and pine plantations, they are further concentrated into larger flocks, due to the more isolated nature of these plantations compared to the broad, relatively unbroken, sweep of the upland spruce forests. During this survey the largest counts, in predominately upland areas, were 100 at Broomlee (NY76Z) and three counts of 30 in the Kielder Forest area (NY68T, NY69M, NY78C), whereas in the mainly lowland areas there were nine counts of 40 or more. The distribution of Crossbill appears to have expanded since the 1981-84 winter survey with the number of occupied 10km squares increasing from 24 to 46. The irruptive behaviour of the species makes it difficult to accurately determine if this is a true increase in distribution, however, this probably reflects a real trend as more habitat has become available with the coniferous plantations in the county maturing.

ANNE MIDDLETON & MARTIN DAVISON

Distribution by altitude

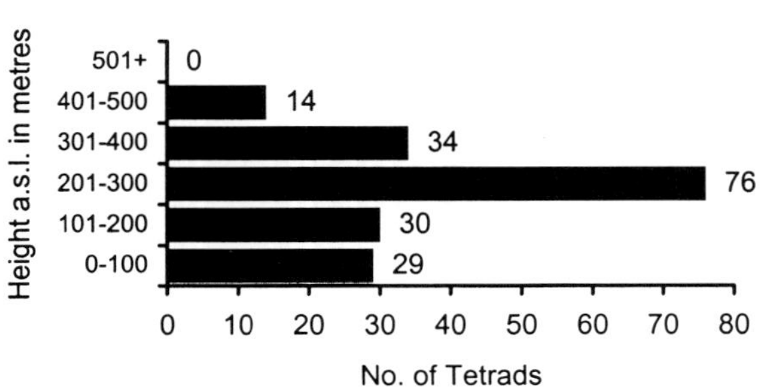

No. of tetrads in which recorded 183 (13%)

Tetrad Analysis	No. of tetrads
1-6 birds	94 (51%)
7-16 birds	55 (30%)
17+ birds	34 (19%)

Total No. of birds counted 2,103

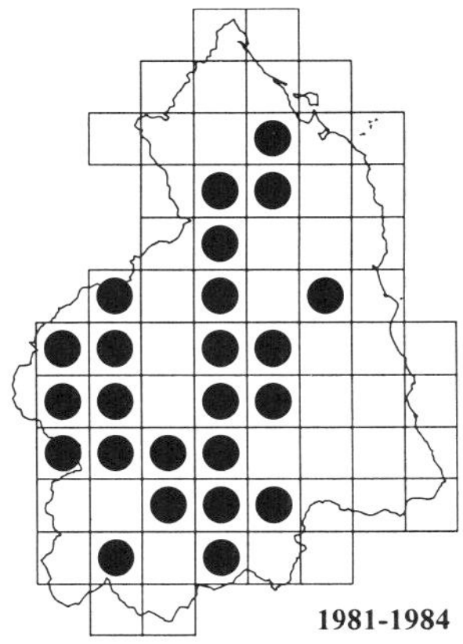

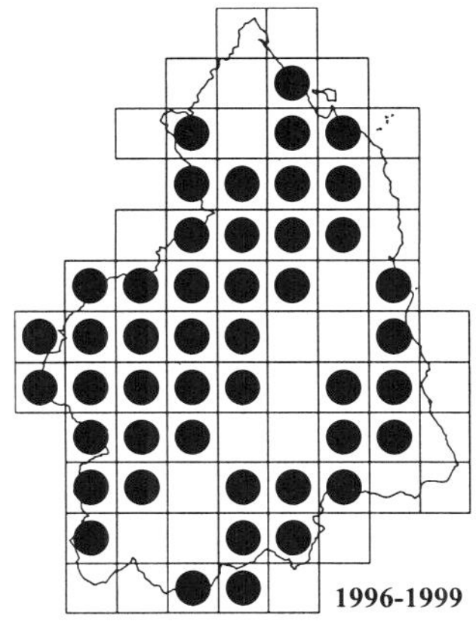

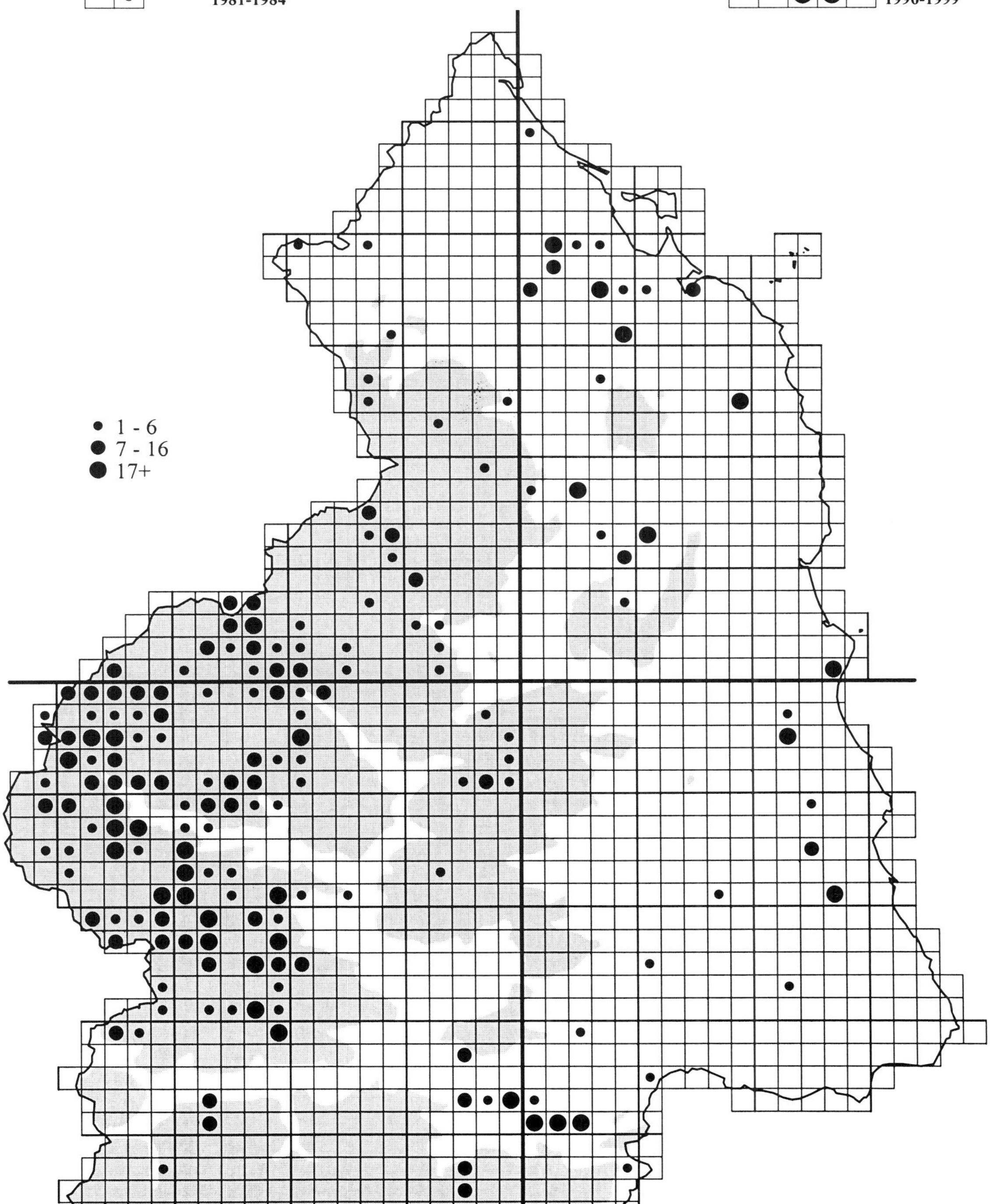

Crossbill

BULLFINCH *Pyrrhula pyrrhula*

At the beginning of the twentieth century, Bolam (1912) regarded the Bullfinch as 'a well-known resident, breeding in all Border counties, but nowhere very abundant'. Of the species in winter, he was more informative stating that 'it is sometimes conspicuous when the ground is all under snow, and most other birds have left'. He noted that 'as a rule, our native Bullfinches [*P. p. pileata*] spend the winter in pairs, or small family parties', and remarked on larger, more brightly coloured, birds sometimes seen on the coast. He added little more in his *Catalogue* (Bolam, 1932) still regarding the Bullfinch as 'seldom numerous'.

Some 50 years later, Galloway and Meek (1983) felt that the species had increased considerably since the 1930s, in particular spreading to the moorland fringe and the coniferous plantations in the west of the county. Of the latter habitat, they specifically stated that 'the forests have, in fact, become its stronghold in the county'. Winter flocking was also commented on, with an exceptional gathering of 120 birds at Arcot Hall in January 1963 being the largest ever recorded in Northumberland. The theme of winter flocking was also referred to by Kerr (2001) who stated that 'most winter flocks involve ten to 20 birds', and quoted a gathering of 50 to 60 birds at Kielder Castle in late autumn 1992. He too, like Galloway and Meek, noted the occurrence, mostly on the coast in October, of the larger northern form *P. p. pyrrhula*.

Whilst there is some evidence in Northumberland of birds moving to the milder coastal plain in winter, Lack (1986) regarded the Bullfinch as essentially a resident, with ringing recoveries showing that not many moved more than a few kilometres. In winter, the species is never easy to see, despite the male's garish plumage. Its presence is often betrayed by the flash of a white rump as pairs are flushed from a hedgerow or thicket, or by their soft contact calls. In Northumberland they seem to occur in low densities almost anywhere where there is an adequate amount of mixed woodland, parkland, scrub or marginal land.

During the winter atlas survey, 77% (317) of all the occupied tetrads were below 200 metres a.s.l. Just over half of the 411 tetrad records related to one or two birds, with 126 tetrads (30%) holding between three and five birds and, whilst not necessarily relating to single wintering parties, a further 73 tetrads held between six and 30 birds. An analysis of the larger groupings highlights the importance of the coniferous habitat in the west of the county with tetrads in Kielder (NY59 & NY69) holding 17, 18 and 26 birds, in Upper Coquetdale (NT80 & NT90) 17 and 22, and a tetrad in Harwood Forest (NY99V) with 30 birds. Their presence each winter in all habitats, however, is obviously determined by food supply as very few of the control tetrads had records for Bullfinches on all three visits. A single bird of the northern race was noted on Holy Island in November 1996.

A comparison between the winter tetrad map and the map in *The atlas of breeding birds in Northumbria* (Day *et al*., 1995) shows a much denser distribution at this scale in winter. This is particularly the case for the Border Forest, the Tyne Valley, the south east agricultural plain and the Tweed and Till valleys. Indeed, the current winter distribution as indicated by the10km square map shows Bullfinches in 85% of the squares, whilst they were only present in 79% in the breeding season between 1988 and 1992.

Although declining alarmingly on a national scale (Mead, 2000), the Bullfinch in Northumberland seems to be bucking the trend, as destruction of suitable habitat has been less intensive and the widespread conifer plantations have produced a very sizeable new habitat. Because of the wide range of suitable habitat and the species' shy nature, the survey total of 1,528 birds in the county is probably conservative. The supposition in the local breeding atlas that there may be as many as 1,000 breeding pairs is perhaps nearer the true number.

DEE McKEOWN

Distribution by altitude

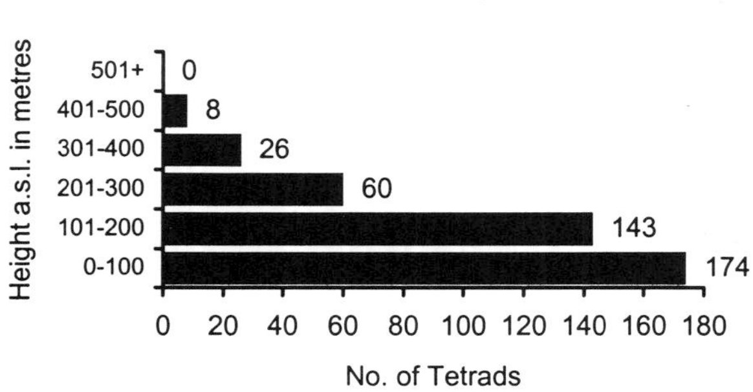

No. of tetrads in which recorded 411 (29%)

Tetrad Analysis	No. of tetrads
1-2 birds	212 (52%)
3-5 birds	126 (30%)
6+ birds	73 (18%)

Total No. of birds counted 1,528

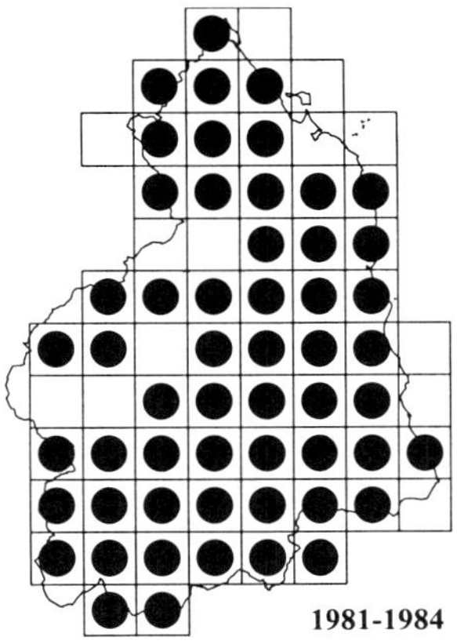

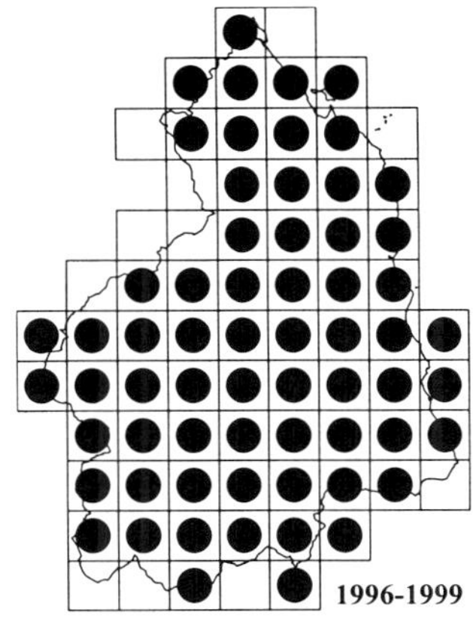

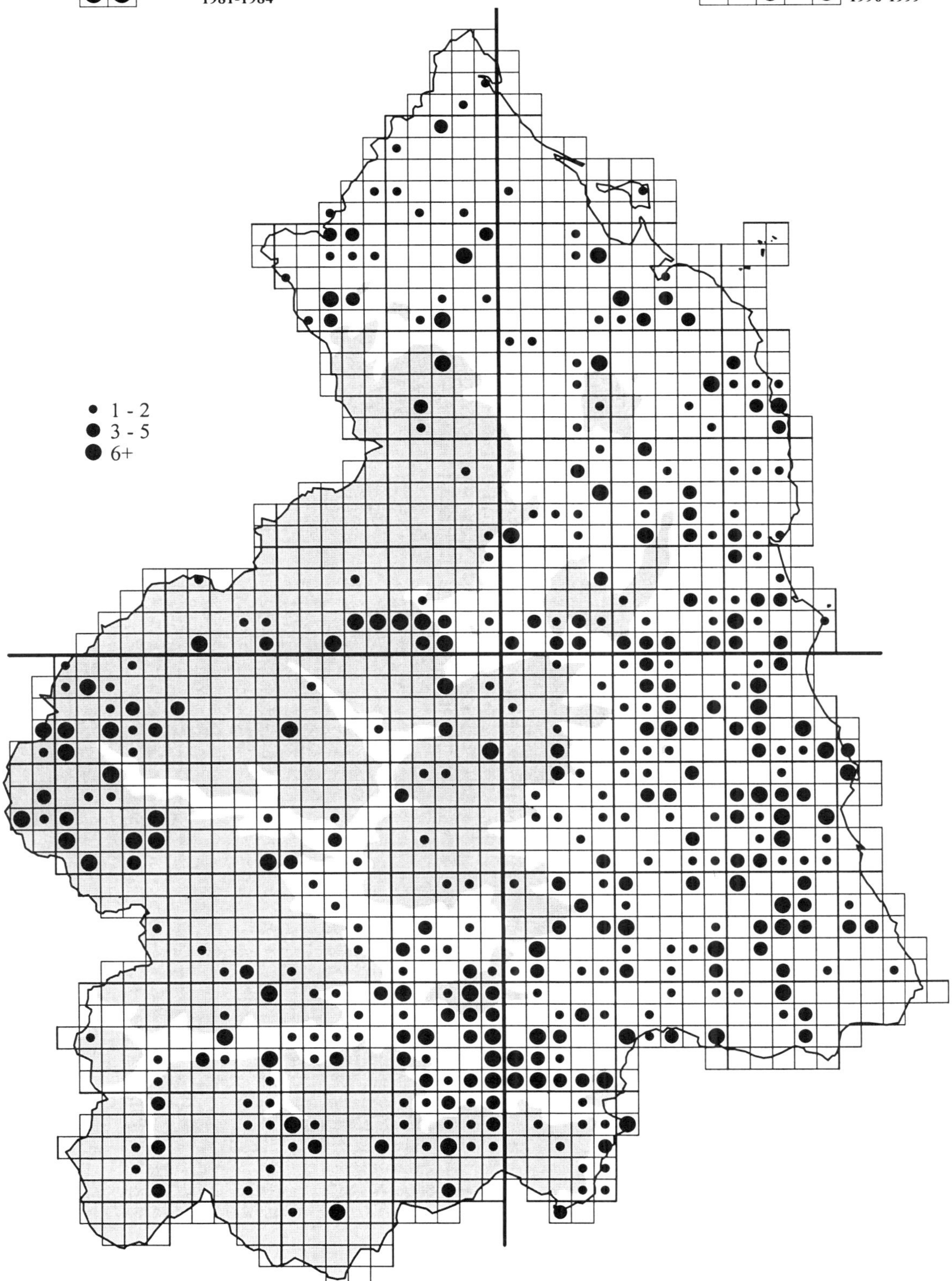

Bullfinch

HAWFINCH *Coccothraustes coccothraustes*

In *The atlas of wintering birds in Britain and Ireland* (Lack, 1986) the account for Hawfinch commences by stating that 'studying Hawfinches in winter is only marginally easier than in summer. They remain notoriously self-effacing and even when the woods they inhabit are leafless they easily escape notice'. As Northumberland is on the periphery of the Hawfinch's range, its extremely thinly distributed population gives the species a high level of ornithological interest.

In the county, the Hawfinch was first recorded by Prideaux Selby (1831), with Hancock (1874) describing it forty years later as a 'rare casual visitant'. Bolam (1912) reported the first instance of breeding in 1884 and noted an expansion which was still continuing in the early 1930s (Bolam, 1932). Significantly, almost all of Bolam's reports and those of later observers link sightings to ornamental parkland where planted exotic trees and shrubs give a much higher diversity of food species than found in native woodland. Frankis (1996) demonstrated the strong relationship between such habitats and the limited success of Hawfinch in Northumberland in both breeding and winter records.

During the current winter survey, Hawfinches were found in five tetrads, with sightings only from supplementary records rather than timed visits. This sadly emphasises the continued decline of the species in the county noted earlier by Frankis (1996). This decline has been found elsewhere in eastern Britain from Aberdeen to Kent, but not in western England, where numbers have increased slightly (UK Hawfinch Study Group, pers. comm.). Mead (2000) expressed considerable concern for the species in his *State of the nation's birds*.

The tetrad distribution map suggests a moderate inland trend but avoiding high ground, with no coastal areas occupied. This matches the areas of the county with the warmest spring weather which indicates a possible reason for the decline. The survey years, and several preceding, were noteworthy for a series of unusually cool, wet springs due to a high incidence of north-east winds in April-June. As good tree seed crops are strongly related to warm settled weather at this time of year, the result has been a series of poor crops on the eastern side of Britain, thus reducing winter feeding options for Hawfinches. Although not proven, this may well account for the observed decline in the species in the absence of any evidence for other significant changes in their parkland environment.

The highest winter count was, perhaps predictably, from Hulne Park (NU11R), the largest area of ornamental park planting rich in exotic species in Northumberland, where a peak of 15 birds was located on 19th January 1997. Smaller numbers were also noted there on many other dates. The next largest group was six at Newbiggin Hall near Blanchland (NY94P) on 5th December 1998, in a deep valley well protected from cold north-east winds. Four were at another favoured site at the Northumberland National Park Offices in Hexham (NY96G) in February 1997, with singles also near Gunnerton (NY97C) and Linden Hall (NZ19N) on 11th and 19th January 1997 respectively.

If further evidence of the decline of the species in Northumberland is needed, a comparison of the two 10km square maps clearly illustrates the point. If the trend towards cold wet springs persists, the Hawfinch may be in danger of disappearing from the area.

MICHAEL FRANKIS

Distribution by altitude

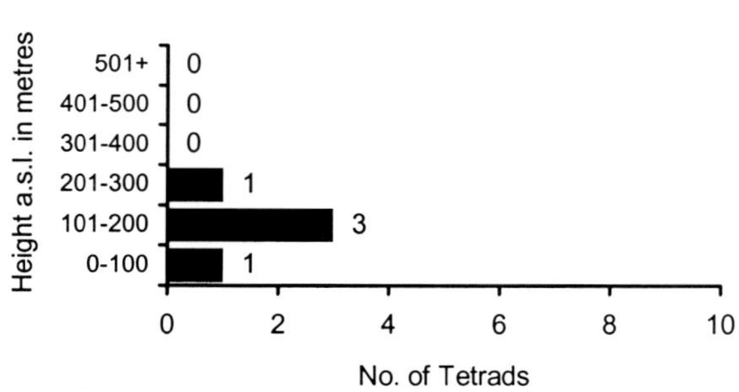

No. of tetrads in which recorded 5 (<1%)

Tetrad Analysis	No. of tetrads
1 bird	2 (40%)
2-6 birds	2 (40%)
7+ birds	1 (20%)

Total No. of birds counted 27

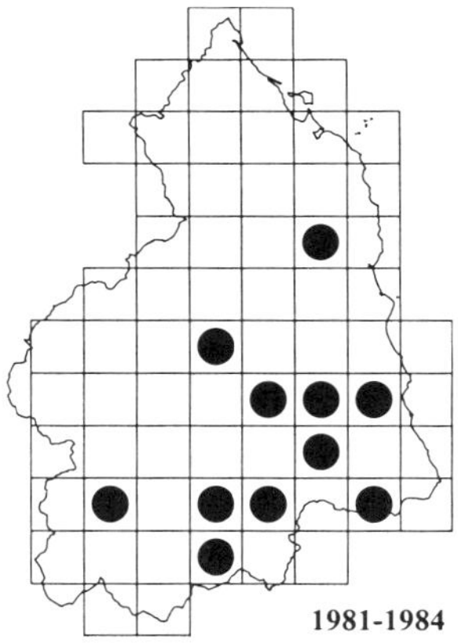

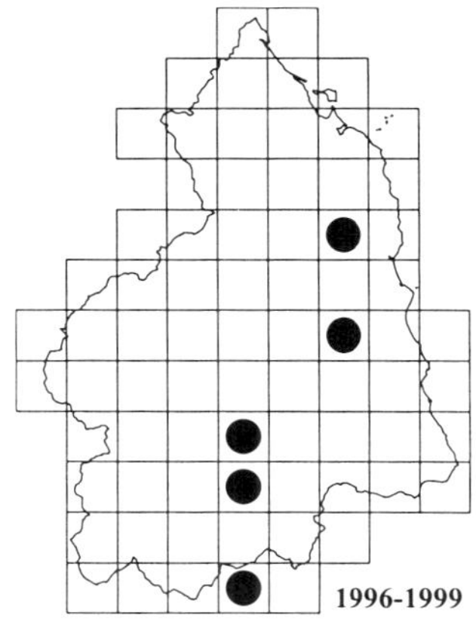

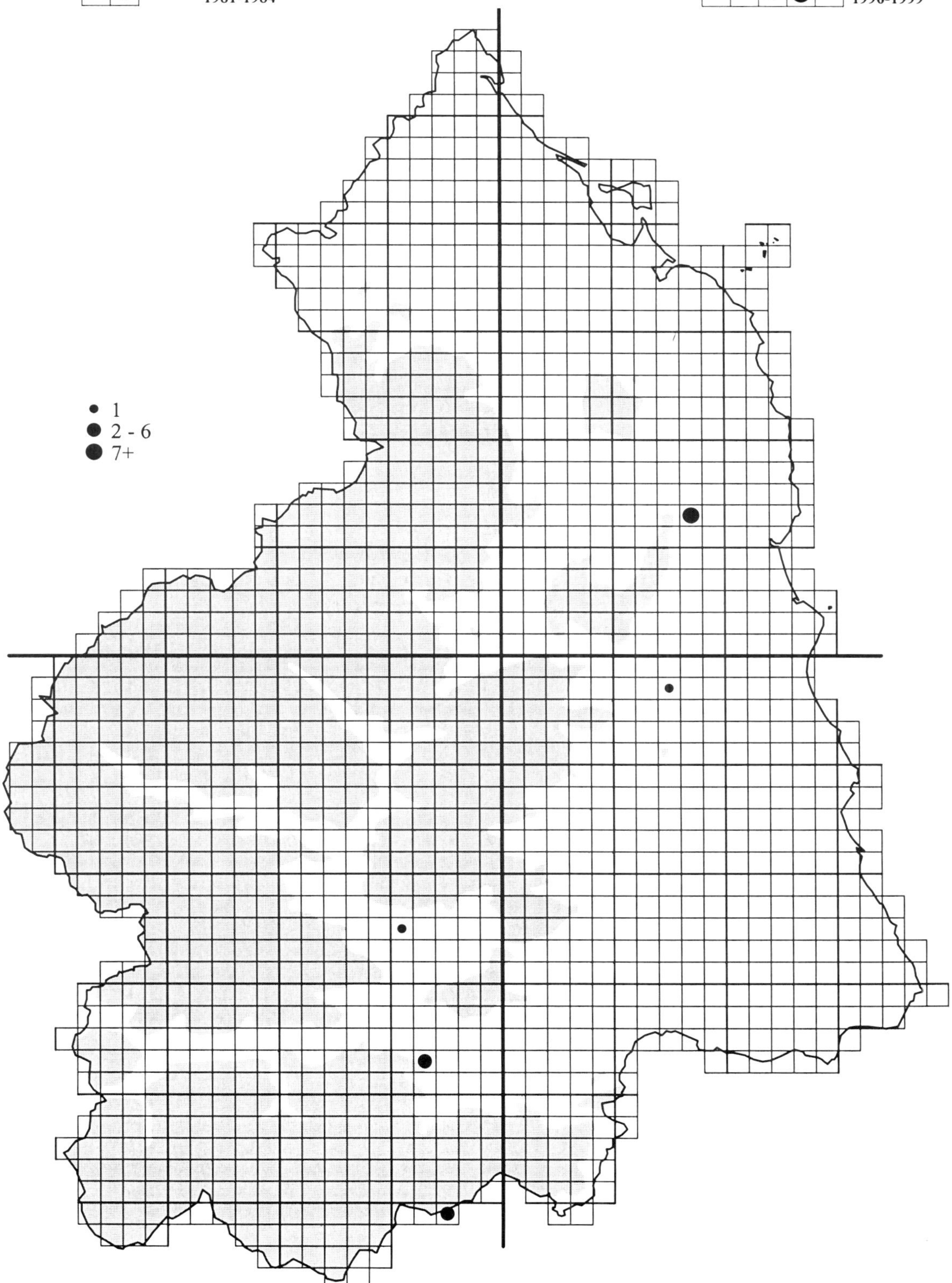

Hawfinch

LAPLAND BUNTING *Calcarius lapponicus*

Bolam (1912) described the species as 'a rare casual visitant which, up until 1892, had been but seldom noticed in Britain'. Twenty years later he was able to refer to only three years when it had been recorded between 1892 and 1932 (Bolam, 1932). Galloway and Meek (1983) mentioned the next record was not until 1952, after which they noted that the species occurred annually and classified its status as an uncommon passage and winter visitor. The increase in records was largely attributed to the greater awareness of recorders to the distinctive flight call. They also noted the affinity of the species for coastal areas. Lapland Buntings usually occur either singly or in small flocks of less than ten birds. However, in some winters, larger flocks of up to 40 birds have been reported, with exceptional gatherings of 97 and 60 in 1986 and 1987 respectively (both in the Lindisfarne NNR area). There has been a recent decline in the number of records, and with fewer birds, during the 1990s, the majority of which were coastal. Most birds arrive during October and November and leave by April (*Birds in Northumbria* 1983 to 1999).

Birds wintering in Britain appear to originate from both the Scandinavian and Greenland breeding populations of this circumpolar species. The presence of birds in Britain is reliant upon drift migration, since neither of these populations migrates in directions likely to bring them to Britain. Greenland birds travel south west to winter in North America, whereas Scandinavian birds head south east into south central Asia (Lack, 1986; Snow & Perrins, 1998). Birds wintering in Northumberland are perhaps most likely to be predominantly of Scandinavian origin, with their appearance a consequence of the weather conditions they are subjected to during migration.

The tetrad map for the current survey confirms the association of the species with coastal areas, only one record concerning a single individual coming from a non-coastal tetrad near Windy Gyle (NT81S) some 490 metres a.s.l. It is also apparent from the map that there is a marked preference for the Lindisfarne NNR (NU03, NU04 & NU14) and Newbiggin (NZ38) areas. The number of individuals recorded for the three winter periods 1996/97, 1997/98 and 1998/99, was seven, 16 and 36 respectively. Six of the coastal sightings were of single birds, four of small parties of between two and seven birds, with one count of 25 on Holy Island (NU14G). The status of the species, when viewed as an average over the three winter periods, still remains that of an uncommon winter visitor.

A comparison between the two 10km square maps, suggests that the species is not as widespread along the coast now as it was previously. If this is the case, then areas which no longer appear to support Lapland Buntings may not do so as a result of either higher disturbance or lower habitat quality caused by current agricultural practices (e.g. lack of winter stubble fields), or a combination of both. Rough grassland and stubble are the favoured winter habitat of this wary species.

Lack (1986) considered the British and Irish wintering population to be in the order of 200 to 500 individuals, which could be 'increased several-fold in peak years'. Birds wintering in Northumberland may well represent something in the region of 3%-7% of the national population.

MICHAEL J. CARR

Distribution by altitude

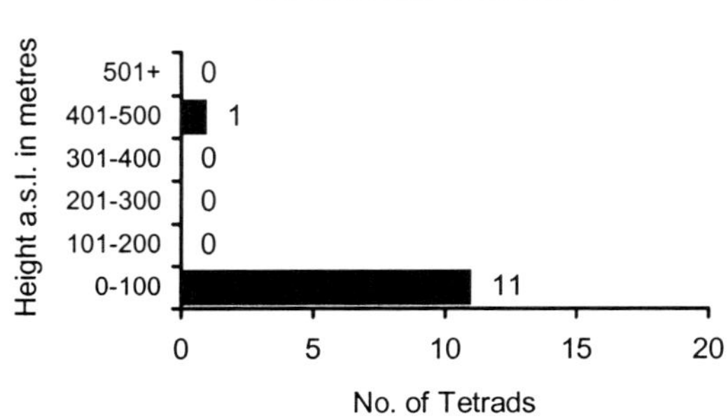

No. of tetrads in which recorded 12 (>1%)

Tetrad Analysis	No. of tetrads
1 bird	7 (58%)
2-7 birds	4 (34%)
8+ birds	1 (8%)

Total No. of birds counted 48

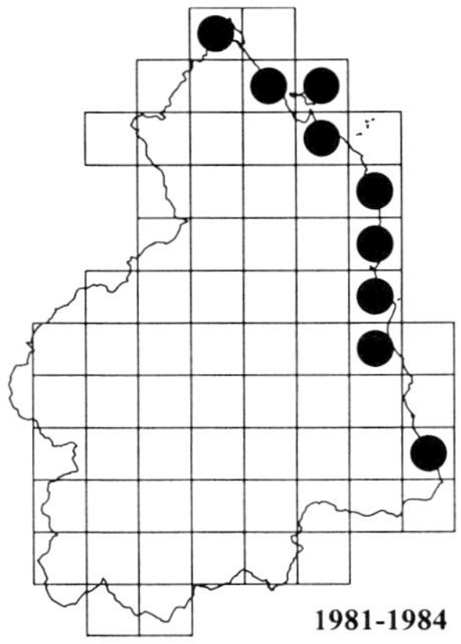

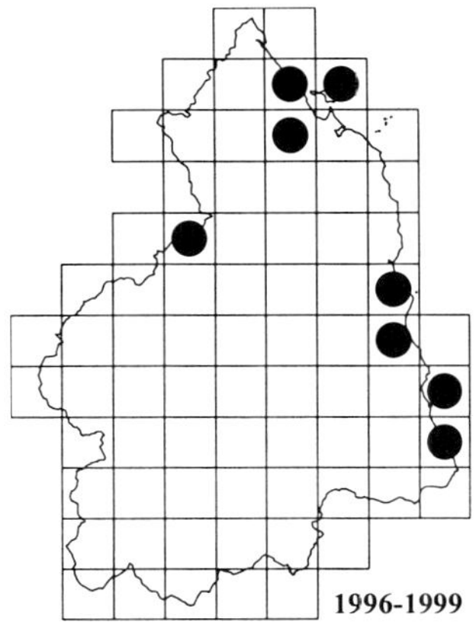

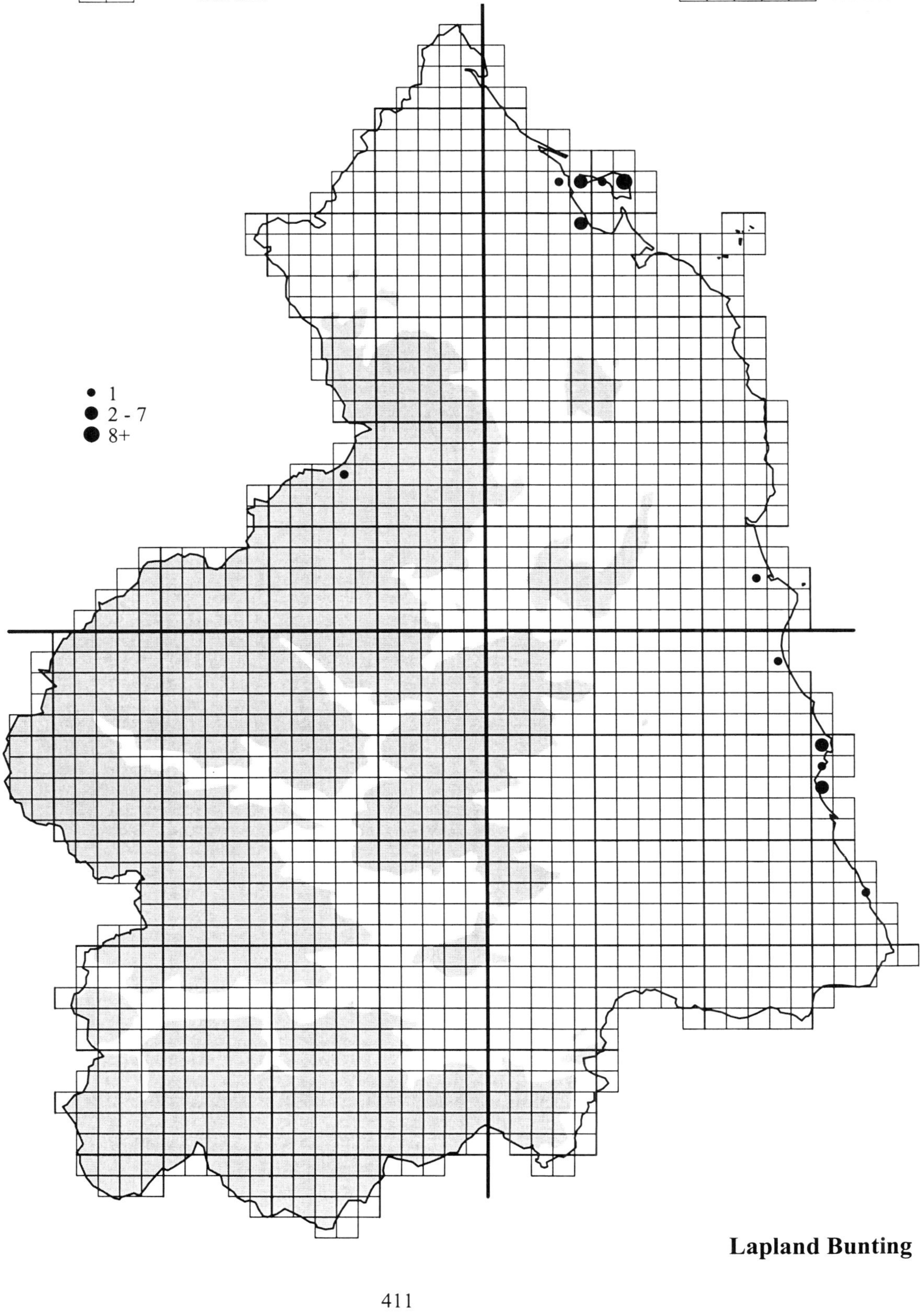

Lapland Bunting

SNOW BUNTING *Plectrophenax nivalis*

Bolam (1912) described it as 'an abundant winter visitant over the whole district, usually arriving in flocks during October and November and remaining until the end of February'. Interestingly, he also noted that small numbers arrived in September and some lingered well into spring with severe weather bringing in flocks of thousands. More recently, Galloway and Meek (1983) regarded the Snow Bunting as far less abundant but mirrored Bolam's movement pattern for the species. They recorded only six incidences where numbers exceeded 300. All were coastal encounters, centred on the Lindisfarne NNR and Druridge Bay, with one exception, that of a flock of 300 on Hedgehope in mid-February 1972. Between the early 1980s and the mid-1990s the county bird report, *Birds in Northumbria*, documented annual counts for most years of under 200 birds. However, a peak total in 1989 exceeded 500 birds, with Hauxley and Ross Back Sands holding flocks of 200 and 150 respectively. During these two decades, the vast majority of birds were seen at coastal or lowland sites with numbers in the uplands rarely exceeding 30 in most years.

There can be few winter birding spectaculars more exciting than a blizzard of white flickering buntings against a cold grey sky. Gregarious, they often allow an observer a close approach even with single or small groups of birds. However, this has almost certainly meant that birds have gone undetected in fieldwork for this atlas and in previous years, particularly in the vast expanses of suitable upland terrain. In winter the Snow Bunting is found in open habitats with short vegetation where they prefer to pick seed from the ground or low plants. Therefore saltmarsh, sand dunes and stubble fields typify the preferred lowland areas with wind-swept grass and heather moorlands typical of their upland haunts where rushes *Juncus* sp. are thought to be an important food in this habitat. Cramp and Simmons (1994) and Lack (1986) have pointed to the widely fluctuating annual numbers wintering in this country. As these birds originate from North America, Iceland and Scandinavia, it is thought that numbers reflect winter weather patterns on this global scale as well as at a regional and local level.

The 1996-1999 atlas fieldwork has shown a substantial increase in numbers recorded annually despite the fact all the winters were relatively mild. It is clear that upland records have increased markedly and probably more accurately reflect the distribution and numbers in this habitat than those in Lack (1986) and pre-1996 records would suggest. Clearly, few birders regularly spent time in the uplands in winter prior to the current fieldwork, biasing the records towards the coastal areas. Those who do frequent such places are firmly of the opinion that the species has been significantly under-recorded in upland habitats. The three winter seasons amassed a total count of 1,800 birds with a number of significant highlights. In 1997 a flock of 90 near Chew Green (NT70Y) in Upper Coquetdale was the highest upland count since 1972, only to be surpassed in 1998 by 100 birds at Sundaysight (NY88I/J). In all, nearly 1,000 Snow Buntings were recorded in 1998 with some 300 recorded from the uplands and 380 from tetrads near Bamburgh (NU13W) and Monk's House (NU23B). These gross figures need to be treated with some caution however, as flocks can be very mobile and counts in adjacent tetrads may involve the same birds. Numbers aside, the fact remains that exactly half of the occupied tetrads were at a height of over 100 metres a.s.l.

Ringing recoveries in the county for Snow Buntings have been quite limited. Records of a bird moving from Cleveland to Cambois between January and February 1990 were followed by a colour-ringed bird found at Chevington on 17th February 1996. This had been ringed at Salthouse, Norfolk in December 1995 so that both records infer a northerly movement up the east coast in early spring. Intriguingly, an adult male ringed at the same Norfolk site on the same day as the Chevington bird appeared at Newbiggin in January 1998! Spring and autumn passage of this kind has been well documented by Cramp and Simmons (1994).

It remains unclear whether or not we have a permanent wintering population within the county because of the fluctuating numbers and the mobility of flocks and individuals. However, it is clear that Northumberland has an international responsibility for the species, with numbers averaging approx. 450 per year, representing 4.5-3% of the estimated UK wintering population of 10,000-15,000 (Lack, 1986).

E. JOHN STEELE

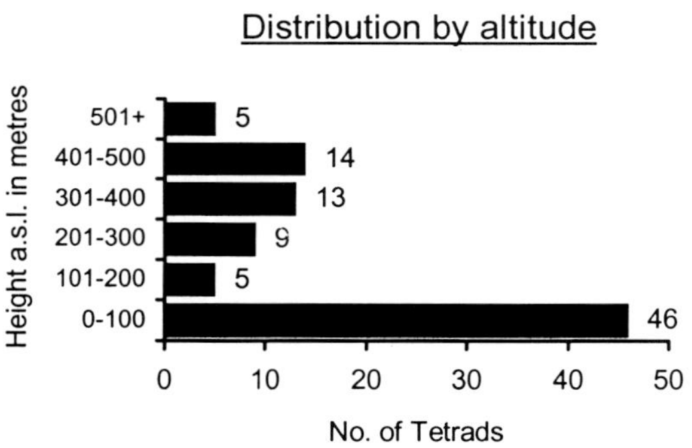

No. of tetrads in which recorded 92 (6%)

Tetrad Analysis	No. of tetrads
1-5 birds	46 (50%)
6-30 birds	29 (32%)
31+ birds	17 (18%)

Total No. of birds counted 1,800

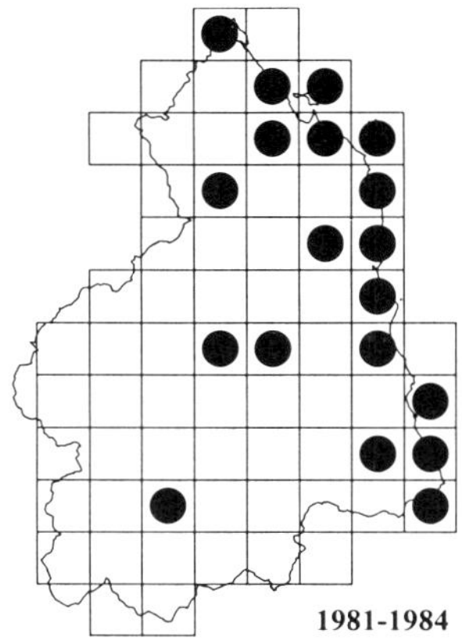

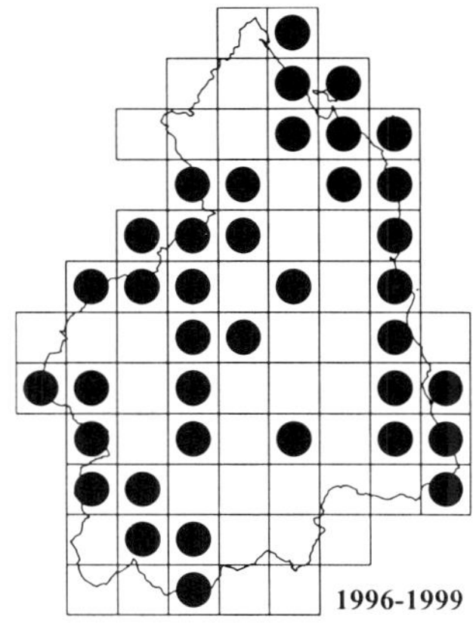

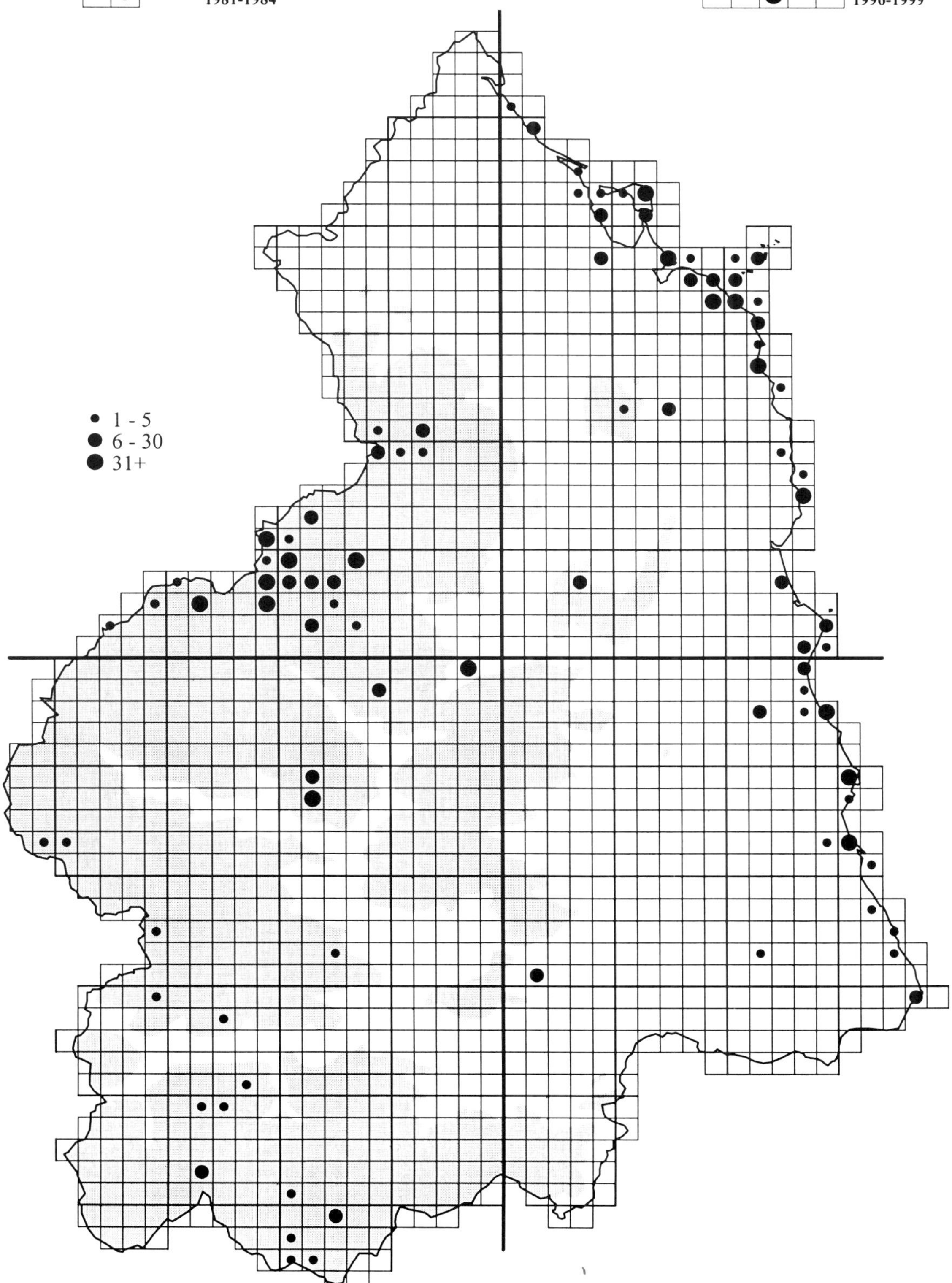

Snow Bunting

YELLOWHAMMER *Emberiza citrinella*

With its brightly coloured plumage and distinctive song, the Yellowhammer is a familiar bird of farmland areas throughout the county. In the past, according to Bolam (1912) it was 'an abundant resident all over the district'. However, by 1932, he considered that it was 'showing some indications of growing scarcer since so much land went out of cultivation'. Contraction of its range appears to have continued, for, in the late 1960s, according to Macfarlane (1973) it was 'confined to the principal river valleys in higher areas and absent over much of the afforested west and ... rather scarce in South Tynedale'. Nevertheless, Galloway and Meek (1983) still regarded it as 'common in most agricultural areas' although they noted a decline in some local breeding census areas in the 1970s. In describing its status nationally at the end of the twentieth century, Mead (2000) said it was 'another species in dire straits and still falling: out of control?'

During winter the Yellowhammer's diet consists mainly of cereal grains and other large grass seeds. Winter stubble fields, areas of set-aside, farmyards and places where cattle are fed provide suitable food sources where flocks may gather. In addition, garden and other feeding stations may also attract regular gatherings, with records from the BTO Garden Bird Feeding Survey for the 1990s showing that it was recorded in 12.6% of gardens surveyed. This is perhaps a response to the reduction in traditional food supplies as a result of changing agricultural practices. The well documented national decline in population is also evident at county level as the 1981-1984 winter survey recorded Yellowhammers in 74% of the 10km squares compared with 60% of those in the recent winter survey. In addition, the average number of birds recorded in the control tetrads decreased from 11.1 in 1996/97 to 9.5 in 1998/99.

During this latest survey, a total of 7,641 Yellowhammers was recorded in 451 tetrads, representing 32% of the number surveyed. Of the occupied tetrads, 428 (95%) were below 200 metres a.s.l. confirming the species' preference for lowland habitats. The winter distribution map shows the main concentrations to be in the east of the county with numbers declining significantly towards the west. The bird is fairly well represented in the lower reaches of the main river valleys of the Tyne and its tributaries, although the coastal strip is undoubtedly the most frequented area with its milder winter climate, lowland habitat and mainly arable farming.

In winter the Yellowhammer tends to form flocks in suitable areas and, nationally, ringing studies have found that adults seldom move more than 5 kilometres from their breeding territories (Lack 1986). In Northumberland, large flocks of between 100-200 birds were regularly recorded in the 1970s and 1980s and during particularly severe winters, such as that of 1992/93, in flocks in excess of 200. Communal roosts were also noted by Galloway and Meek during the 1980s with upwards of 150 birds in some suitable localities. Unfortunately, counts during the current winter survey appear to reflect the continued decline of the species in the county. The largest count, an exception, was of 320 in the Swinhoe area (NU22E). Other large counts were 150 at Fenwick (NU04Q) and 131 near Callerton (NZ16P) with only three other counts of over 100 birds during the whole of the survey period. More typical were the 118 tetrads (26%) in which between 15 and 50 birds were noted. Comparison of the breeding and wintering distribution maps for Yellowhammer shows that it is a relatively sedentary species with birds moving down from the upper reaches of river valleys and the lower slopes of upland regions in the colder months. In the 1988-1992 local breeding atlas survey they were recorded in 76% of the 10km squares visited (Day *et al.*, 1995) compared with 60% during the recent winter survey. The reduction is no doubt due to the previously described population decline over the last two decades and its tendency to form flocks in winter. Galloway and Meek suggested that the presence of birds along the coast and on offshore islands in October and again in April and May could indicate that not all birds wintering in the county are of local origin and Lack (1986) suggested that ringing recoveries of individuals trapped in eastern England are in fact Scandinavian birds migrating along the coast in small numbers.

In *The atlas of breeding birds in Northumbria*, it was concluded that the total population was in the range of 4,000-5,000 pairs. The potential wintering population can be calculated on the basis of each pair producing two young surviving to mid-winter and an annual adult mortality rate of 46% (Lack 1986). This would indicate a county wintering population in excess of 12,000 and thus the 7,641 recorded in the current survey may illustrate the extent to which the species has declined in recent years.

ALAN J. DAVIS

Distribution by altitude

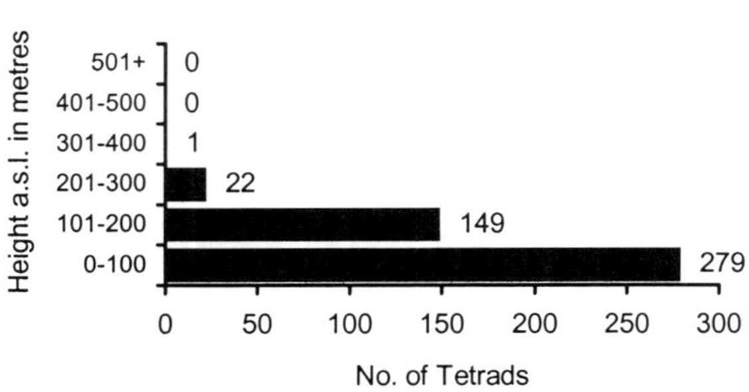

No. of tetrads in which recorded 451 (32%)

Tetrad Analysis	No. of tetrads
1-8 birds	230 (51%)
9-25 birds	126 (28%)
26+ birds	95 (21%)

Total No. of birds counted 7,641

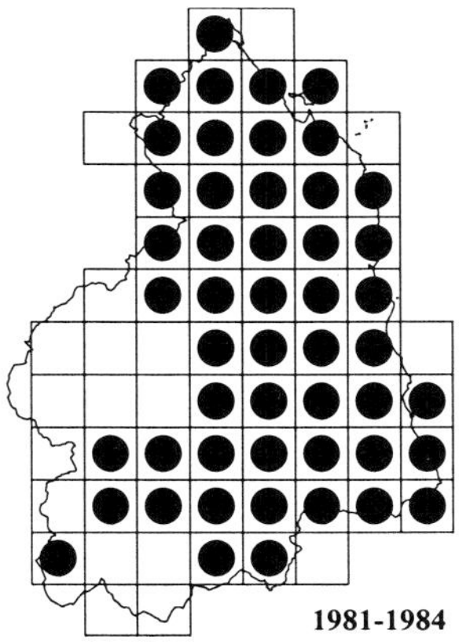

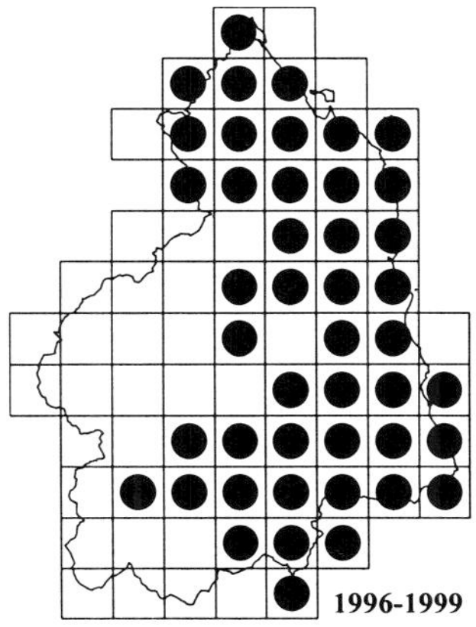

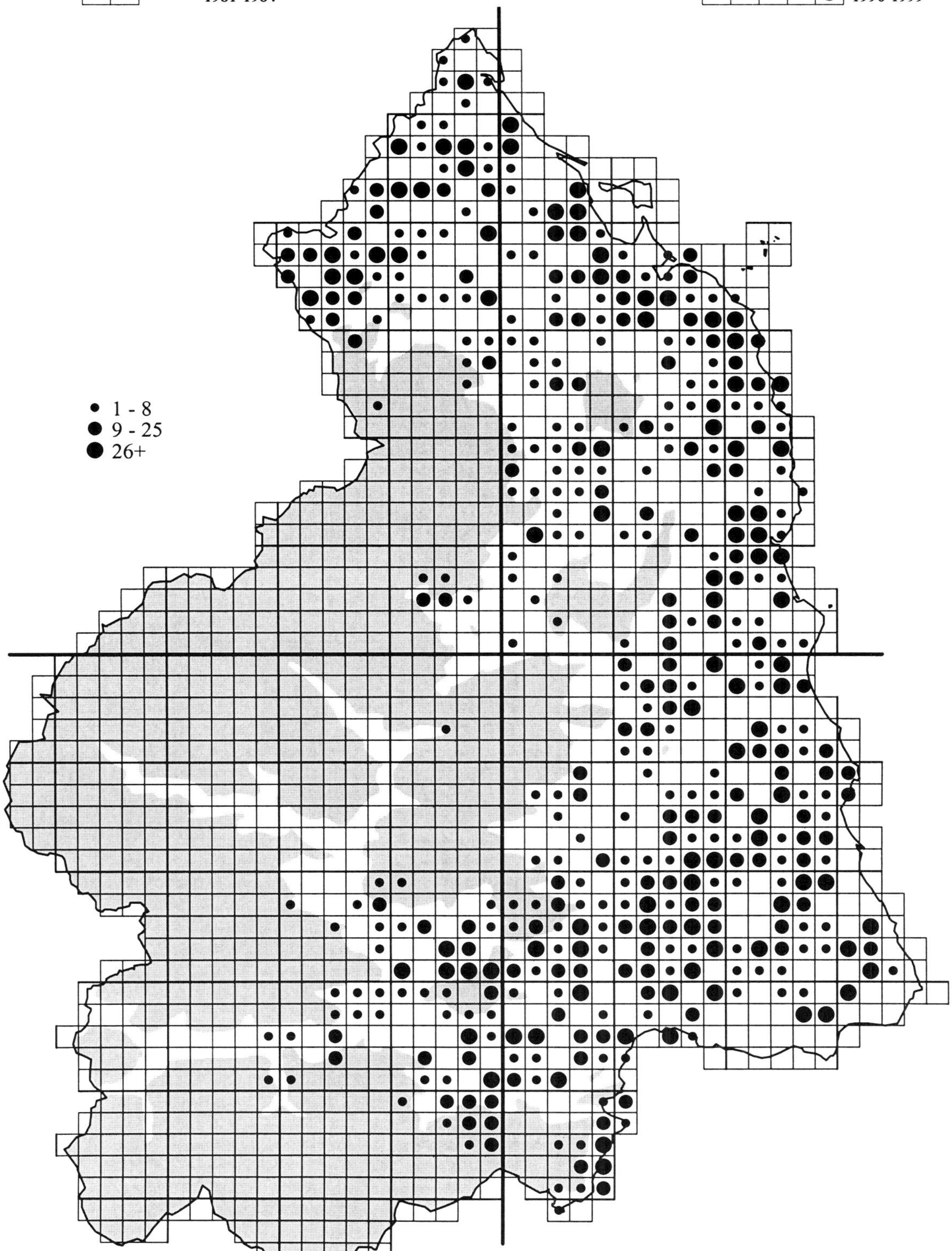

Yellowhammer

REED BUNTING *Emberiza schoeniclus*

The Reed Bunting, as its name implies, is principally, although not exclusively, a bird of marshy habitats. In the summer months, it is a familiar sight breeding in damp scrub and reed beds throughout much of lowland Britain but also expanding into drier areas and onto higher ground, where it may be found in young conifer plantations. The characteristic 'black-headed' males advertise their presence with a loud, repetitive song which they deliver from the tallest reed stems and exposed perches.

In winter, Reed Buntings are much less conspicuous. Their affinity with the wetland habitat is also less obvious as small groups roam widely over adjacent farmland and waste ground in search of food, often associated with flocks of Yellowhammers *Emberiza citrinella*, finches and sparrows. The Common Bird Census (CBC) and Waterways Birds Surveys, organised jointly by the BTO and the Nature Conservation Council, over the last forty years or so, reveal marked fluctuations in numbers. Despite the Reed Bunting's ability to adapt to new environments, it is still sensitive to cold winters and has declined as a result. The recent emphasis by some farmers towards less intensive land use, including the established practice of set-aside, where fields are left uncultivated and unmanaged, will no doubt help the Reed Bunting in winter. Food supply and weather are the main factors governing the population. Lack (1986) indicated that, from ringing results within Britain, it was probable that about 40% of female Reed Buntings and 80% of males move no more than 5 kilometres between summer and winter. Comparisons between the current winter atlas map and that in *The atlas of breeding birds in Northumbria* (Day *et al.*, 1995) would appear to confirm the Reed Bunting's local status as a mainly sedentary species.

Reed Buntings were recorded in 178 (12%) of the 1,432 tetrads surveyed during the three winter periods compared with 252 tetrads (18%) from 1,410 occupied during the local breeding survey. This apparent disparity may be due in part to some local movement from breeding sites but there is little evidence to suggest large numbers congregate in any particular areas. Indeed, of the 178 tetrads occupied, only 17 (10%) held more than ten birds. Further analysis of current survey results also reveals that 123 tetrads (69%) held less than four birds. From these findings it seems that in tetrads where Reed Buntings were found they were usually at a low density and, as a result, it is likely some birds could have been overlooked. There is no evidence to suppose there has been any significant decline in numbers since the completion of the breeding atlas in 1992.

Comparing the 10km square winter distribution map for 1981-1984 with the current atlas reveals 16 'new' squares occupied during the recent survey, the majority of these on higher ground, with a particular prevalence in Upper Coquetdale, e.g. in the Ridleeshope area (NT80I) at over 300 metres a.s.l. with 25 birds. By contrast nine squares had apparently been deserted during the current period. They include the Harbottle/Harwood (NZ09) ten kilometre square as well as low-lying farmland between Morpeth (NZ18) and Alnwick (NU11). The main concentration of records is in the south east of the county with a distinct paucity from some upland regions and also the Border Forest. Large areas of north Northumberland are likewise poorly represented. Much of this is mirrored in the local breeding atlas further emphasising the sedentary nature of the species. In keeping with this south east bias, the largest counts were made near Widdrington (NZ29N) with 30 birds, Newbiggin (NZ38E) 35 birds and the Little Benton Farm area (NZ26T) holding 50, the latter on an abandoned wheat field.

Lack (1986) stated that, from ringing, it was indicated that less than 1% of British breeding birds move abroad in winter. A somewhat greater, though still small, number of foreign breeding birds spend the winter in Britain, these coming mainly from western Scandinavia. Other western Scandinavian birds migrate along the east coast of Britain to winter further south in continental Europe. In Northumberland there is obvious evidence of light coastal passage, as commented on by Galloway and Meek (1983) who said that 'passage of continental birds, chiefly in October, adds considerably to the size of late autumn flocks and roosts'. Whether or not these birds spend the winter in the county is unclear. There is however at least one record of a probable over-wintering bird of Scandinavian origin which was controlled at Big Waters in March 1991 having been ringed at Vest Agder, Norway, in October 1989 (*Birds in Northumbria 1993*).

MICHAEL RICHARDSON

Distribution by altitude

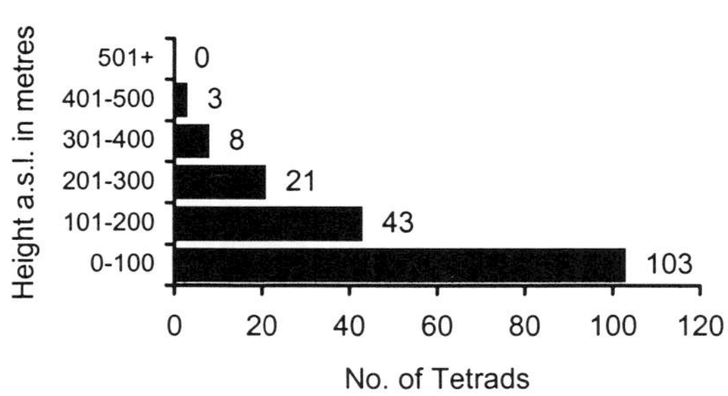

No. of tetrads in which recorded 178 (12%)

Tetrad Analysis	No. of tetrads
1-2 birds	108 (61%)
3-5 birds	34 (19%)
6+ birds	36 (20%)

Total No. of birds counted 746

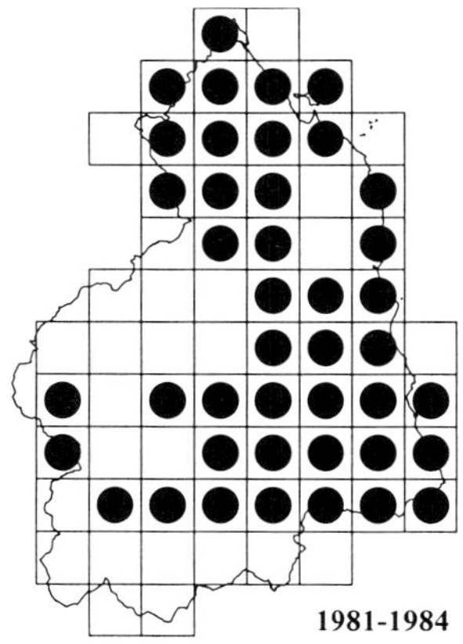

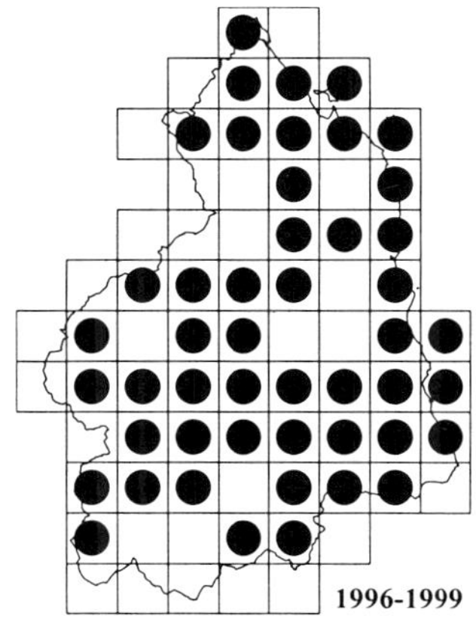

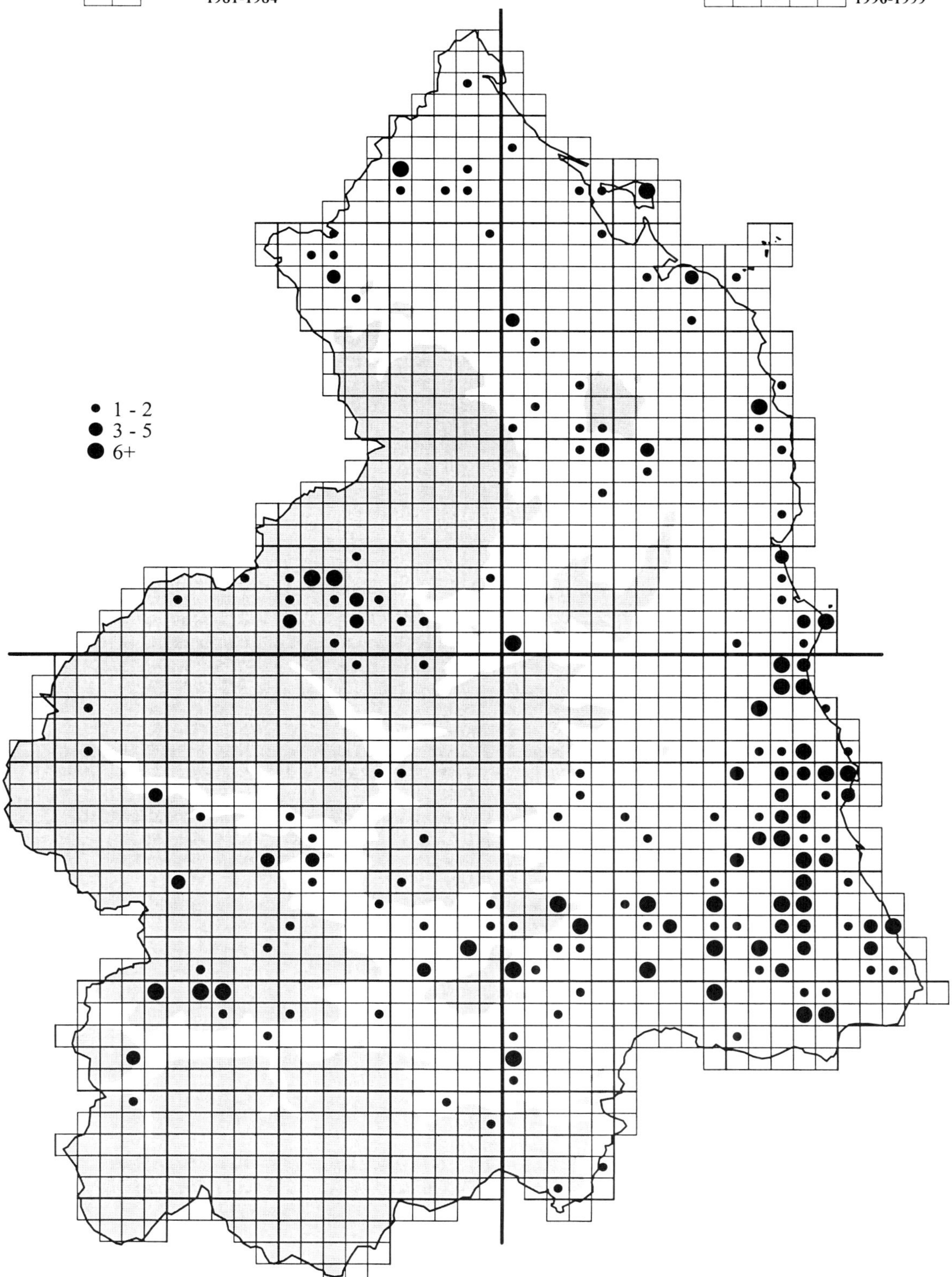

Reed Bunting

CORN BUNTING *Miliaria calandra*

Nationally, changing farming practices have had a dramatic effect on the population of Corn Buntings, particularly during the winter period. Their association with cereal crops during the breeding season is well documented. In winter, Corn Buntings are often dependent on cereal stubbles which have become scarcer over the last 30 years owing to a major change from spring to autumn sowing of crops (Donald & Evans, 1994). The distribution of arable farmland, therefore, restricts the penetration and range of Corn Bunting in Northumberland to low-lying farmland of the coastal plain and the Tyne Valley. In their habitat and diet studies on the South Downs, West Sussex, Brickle and Harper (2000) found a preference for cereal stubbles in early winter, but subsequently cattle feed and then spring-sown cereals were utilised. Indeed, spring-sown cereals may be particularly valuable due to long stubbles and abundance of food in the form of surface grain when first sown. Lack (1986) has also shown that Corn Buntings roost communally in winter, favouring reed beds or gorse and similar low scrub, and tend to feed in flocks. This communal activity helps the birds find food which may be very locally distributed.

Writing in 1912, Bolam was able to describe the Corn Bunting as 'a common resident, most numerous, perhaps, along the coast, breeding in rough grass and corn-fields, to which it also resorts with Larks ... in flocks, in winter'. He also considered that 'in autumn, our native stock is reinforced from abroad'. To perhaps support this view, Temperley (1942) recorded arrivals of large numbers at Beadnell and Seahouses during November 1941. There is, however, no recent evidence to support the theory of large-scale immigration, although there are occasional records of small parties of possibly coasting birds (Galloway & Meek, 1983). During the 1960s and early 1970s Galloway and Meek reported winter flocks of over 100 birds at a number of traditional sites such as Seaton Delaval, Bamburgh and Druridge Bay, with an exceptional roost of approximately 300 at Wallsend Swallow Pond in 1965.

By the mid-1980s both breeding population numbers and winter flock sizes were causing national and local concern. A BTO survey carried out during the winter of 1992/93 indicated a dramatic decline. It clearly showed that many of the traditional farmland areas which had held wintering flocks during fieldwork for *The atlas of wintering birds in Britain and Ireland* (Lack, 1986) were no longer attracting Corn Buntings. Local evidence for this decline during the 1990s was apparent as very few flocks were recorded. Only the Druridge Bay area regularly held two to three small groups, with the largest of 23 at Warkworth Lane in 1994. The only other regular sites where flocks reached double figures were East Fleetham, Beadnell, East Flodden and Boulmer (*Birds in Northumbria*).

The decline, and the possible imminent disappearance, of the Corn Bunting from the county is highlighted by the findings of the current survey. The two 10km square maps clearly show a dramatic reduction in the number of squares occupied in winter from 28% in 1981-1984 down to 9% in 1996-1999. Even more serious was the grand total of 28 birds in only seven tetrads. Four of these records were of single birds, at the coastal sites of Buston Links (NU20P) and Craster (NU21P), whilst the others were in adjacent inland tetrads at Corbridge (NY96X) and Thornbrough (NZ06C). Two birds were also noted at North Sunderland (NU23A) but the only evidence for winter flocking was gatherings of five at Widdrington (NZ29L) in January 1998 and 17 at the traditional site of East Fleetham (NU22E) in February of the same year.

Nationally, Mead (2000) described the British population trend as being in 'severe decline' and wondered whether the species will survive in Britain. Certainly, the alarming figures produced by this survey for wintering birds and those described by Cadwallender and Cadwallender (2000) for breeding birds in Northumberland provide little cause for optimism. The status of the species in the county is currently that of an uncommon resident; it is in considerable danger of rapidly becoming a rare resident!

TOM A. CADWALLENDER

Distribution by altitude

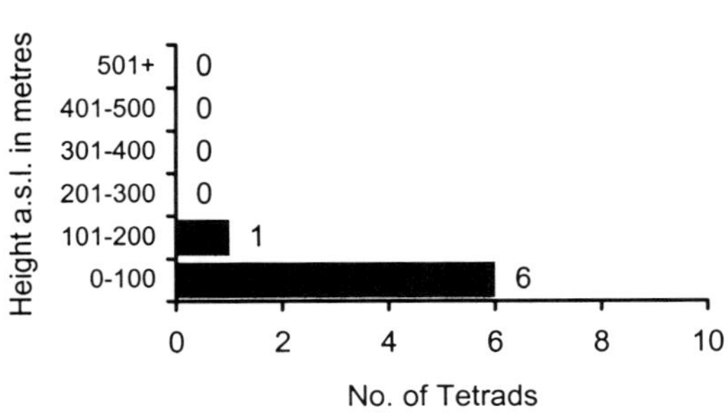

No. of tetrads in which recorded 7 (<1%)

Tetrad Analysis	No. of tetrads
1 bird	4 (57%)
2-5 birds	2 (29%)
6+ birds	1 (14%)

Total No. of birds counted 28

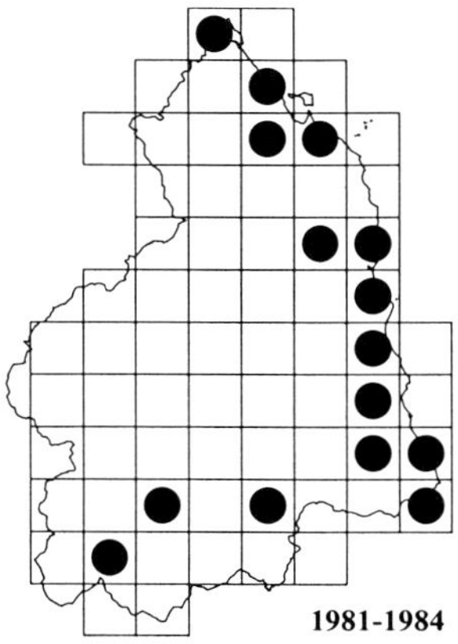

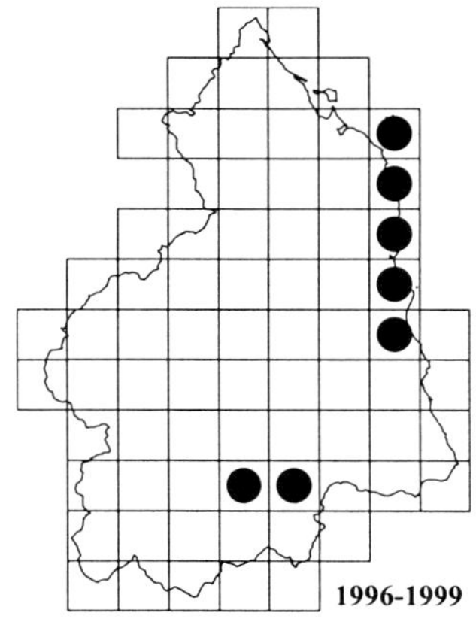

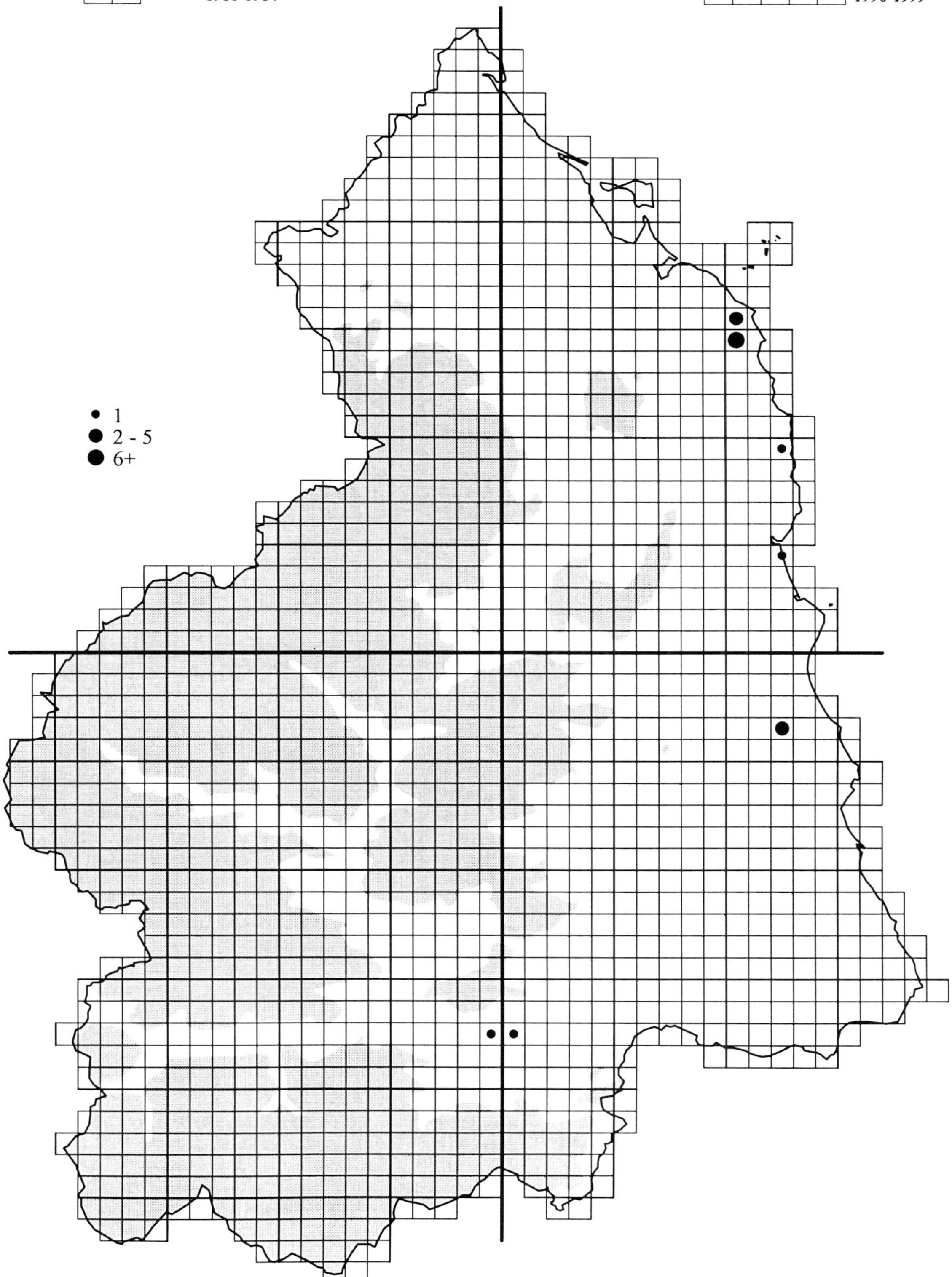

Corn Bunting

RARITIES AND OTHER SPECIES

One of the delights of birdwatching is the finding of an unexpected or rare species and this is arguably even more agreeable when it occurs during survey work. A number of rare, scarce or out-of-season species were indeed found during the three winter periods of this atlas survey although most details were received as supplementary records rather than from timed visits to tetrads.

BLACK-NECKED GREBE *Podiceps nigricollis*

Bolam (1932) described this species as 'a winter visitant, of irregular appearance upon the coast', while Galloway and Meek (1978) as well as describing initial breeding efforts in the county, noted that 'the Holy Island-Bamburgh area is the favourite wintering haunt, but numbers never exceed seven'. The species remains rare in winter in the county and during the current survey only two birds were found, at Cambois (NZ38B) and off Stag Rocks (NU13T) on 7th and 31st January 1998 respectively.

STORM PETREL *Hydrobates pelagicus*

A single bird was found dead on the Farne Islands (NU23P) on 29th November 1996. Although an active ringing programme with the aid of tape lures has now established quite considerable numbers offshore during the late summer months, the species remains difficult for land-based observers to detect and remains rarely recorded during the winter. The Atlantic population migrates as far south as waters off southern Africa between October-February (Hagemeijer & Blair, 1997).

SNOW GOOSE *Anser caerulescens*

Two birds were at Holywell Pond (NZ37C) on 4th/5th and 20th/21st January 1997 but had been seen sporadically since the previous August. A party of three birds, two adults and a juvenile, were at Ford (NT93N) on 16th February 1998. Although the origins of these birds is not known with any certainty, most records are considered to relate to escapes.

AMERICAN WIGEON *Anas americana*

A drake was at Cresswell Pond (NZ29X) on 20th November 1998 while other drakes were at Linton Pond (NZ29K) and Lindisfarne NNR (NU13E) on 12th and 17th February 1999 respectively. Despite the rarity of this species, these three winter records are not unprecedented as singles were seen at Holywell Pond in February/March 1962 and at Cresswell Pond and Druridge Pools in December 1991

GREEN-WINGED TEAL *Anas carolinensis*

This small North American duck was previously regarded as a sub-species of Teal *Anas crecca* but was accorded full species status by the BOU in 2001 just after the main winter atlas period. A drake was present at Cresswell Pond (NZ29X) between 8th and 11th January 1998 and Druridge Pools (NZ29T) between 27th January and 1st February 1998. What was presumably the same individual re-appeared at Cresswell Pond in October 1998 and remained into 1999. Although the number of sightings has increased during recent years, this species remains a very rare visitor to the county.

GARGANEY *Anas querquedula*

A drake at Newton Pool (NU22M) between 15th and 26th February 1999 was the earliest-ever spring record in the county.

BLUE-WINGED TEAL *Anas discors*

A female at Holywell Pond (NZ37C) on 5th January 1997 was the first to be found in the county in mid-winter.

LONG-BILLED DOWITCHER *Limnodromus scolopaceus*

One was at Cresswell Pond (NZ29X) on 15th November 1998 although it had first been seen at East Chevington on 8th August. Both previous records of this species in the county involved birds which arrived in the autumn and made protracted stays into the early winter months, at Killingworth Lake between September and November 1959 and at Cresswell Pond between October and December 1964.

POMARINE SKUA *Stercorarius pomarinus*

On 26th November 1996 three birds were seen in the vicinity of the Farne Islands (NU23C/D) and another was off Craster (NU21U) on 23rd November 1998. Although occasionally involved in some numbers in late autumn movements, the species remains rare in Northumberland in winter.

ARCTIC SKUA *Stercorarius parasiticus*

A single bird was in Beadnell Bay (NU22N) on 28th November 1998 but, like the preceding species, Arctic Skua is rarely noted in the winter months.

GREAT SKUA *Catharacta skua*

One was seen at the Farne Islands (NU23D) on 30th November 1997.

LAUGHING GULL *Larus atricilla*

One circled the gull roost at Hallington Reservoirs (NY97S) on 20th February 1999. The most famous Laughing Gull in the county was an individual that arrived in the Newcastle General Hospital area in January 1984 where it was regularly seen, particularly in the winter months, until March 1987, occasionally visiting one or two localities such as the Tyne Estuary, Big Waters and Jesmond Dene.

WATER PIPIT *Anthus spinoletta*

A single bird seen at Caistron (NU00A) on 24th November 1996 was the only record during the current winter survey. Kerr (2001) indicated that 14 had occurred during the winter months since the mid-1980s.

PIED WHEATEAR *Oenanthe pleschanka*

A female was present at Tynemouth Haven (NZ36U) between 8th and 14th December 1998. During this week-long stay its diet was supplemented by mealworms provided by a kindly birdwatcher!

DESERT WHEATEAR *Oenanthe deserti*

A male was present on Bamburgh Golf Course and nearby beach (NU13S) between 9th and 15th December 1997 and may have been the same individual which was seen, but not positively identified, on Holy Island in late November.

YELLOW-BROWED WARBLER *Phylloscopus inornatus*

There was one record of this species within the survey dates during the current Winter Atlas period; a single bird at Prior's Park, Tynemouth (NZ36U) on 17th November 1996. This undoubtedly refers to a late passage migrant rather than a potential wintering bird. This is almost certainly the case for the previous four records in late autumn/early winter between 1951-1995 (16th/17th November 1974 Holywell Dene, 17th November 1984 Prior's Park, 20th November 1984 Prior's Park and 28th November - 2nd December 1985 Farne Islands), while a fifth bird, trapped and ringed at Fenwick, on 14th/15th December 1957 was exceptionally late. To date there has been no evidence that Yellow-browed Warbler has ever wintered in the county although this has been recorded in other parts of Britain.

DUSKY WARBLER *Phylloscopus fuscatus*

One, found at Newbiggin (NZ38E) on 16th-21st November 1997 was a late migrant.

ESCAPES AND OTHER EXOTICA

It would seem inevitable that during a winter survey conducted over several years a number of escaped or exotic species would be encountered by fieldworkers. This proved to be the case, although remarkably few records were received. Records of **Helmeted Guineafowl** *Numida meleagris* and **Ostrich** *Struthio* sp. have not been included in detail for obvious reasons but at least it shows that observers were being thorough! Likewise, records of pigeons *Columba* circling known lofts are excluded, as this traditional hobby is still widespread and enthusiastically pursued in the county. Many of the following observations, which are included for completeness, were extracted from the county annual bird reports.

Records of wildfowl can be problematical when attempting to determine their origins. A number of records of Mallard described as 'domesticated' were received and these too were excluded from the atlas data. A female **Wood Duck** *Aix sponsa* was recorded as being present at Leazes Park, Newcastle (NZ26M) during June-December 1996 and again during 1997-1999. **Muscovy Duck** *Cairina moschata*, a species which has bred in the wild in the county, were seen at Ladyburn Lake (NU20Q) in November/December 1996, a pair at Big Waters (NZ27G) between September and December 1997 with a male there in 1999. Others were at Wooler (NT92Z) on 6th January 1999 and near Bywell (NZ06L) on 1st February 1999. A **Chiloe Wigeon** *Anas sibilatrix* was at Ladyburn Lake on 21st January 1997. More exotic species included a **Harris's Hawk** *Parabuteo unicinctus* at Big Waters on 16th November 1997 and a **White-cheeked Bulbul** *Pycnonotus leucogenys* in a Walbottle garden (NZ16T) in November/December 1997. Finally, many birders had the opportunity to see a **Patagonian Conure** *Cyanoliseus patagonus* in the Marden Quarry area (NZ37K) between April 1996 and January 1998.

APPENDIX A Shelduck at Lindisfarne NNR

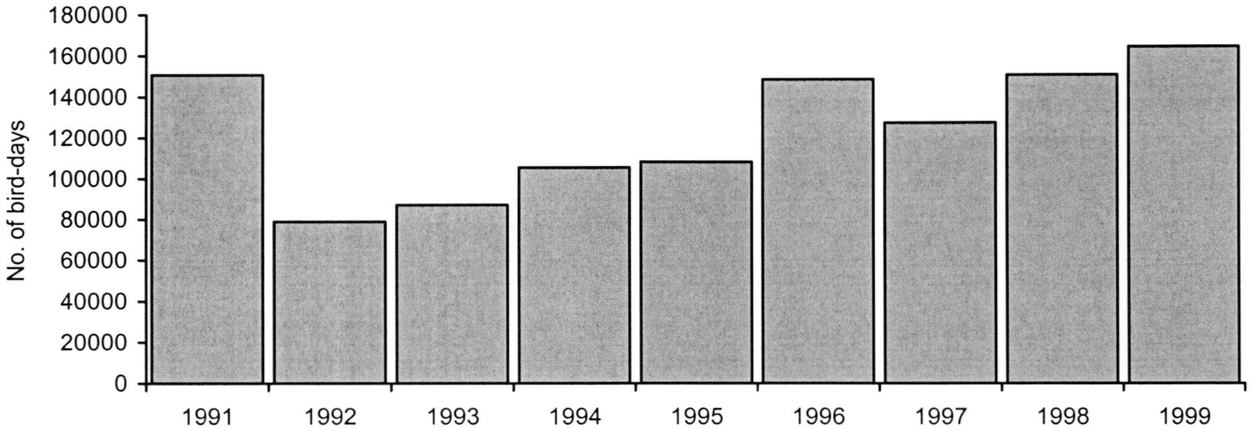

The bar chart shows the number of Shelduck 'bird-days' recorded at Lindisfarne NNR each 'winter' (1 Sept. to 31 Mar.) between 1991 and 1999 (Source : Denny, 2001). Note that 'bird-days' were calculated by multiplying each count with the number of inter-count days and summing these over the winter period.

APPENDIX B Pale-bellied Brent Geese at Lindisfarne NNR

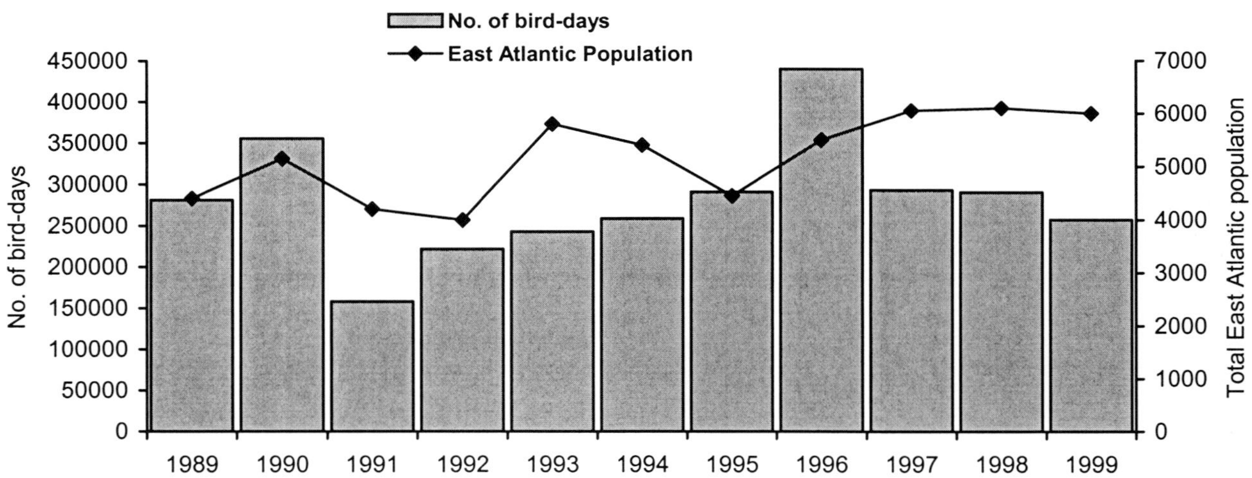

The bar chart shows the number of pale-bellied Brent Goose 'bird-days' recorded at Lindisfarne NNR each 'winter' (1 Sept. to 31 Mar.) between 1989 and 1999 together with the total east Atlantic population estimates (Source : Denny, 2001). Note that 'bird-days' were calculated by multiplying each count with the number of inter-count days and summing these over the winter period.

APPENDIX C Long-eared Owl numbers

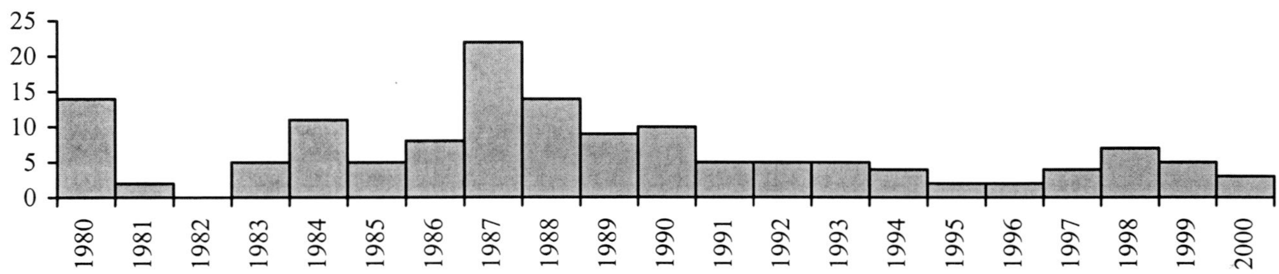

Long-eared Owl records between 15th November - 28th February 1980-2000 (Source : *Birds in Northumbria*)

APPENDIX D Control Tetrad analysis 1996/97 - 1998/99

10 KM	TETRAD	No. of Species 1st winter	No. of Species 2nd winter	No. of Species 3rd winter	No. of New Species 2nd winter	No. of New Species 3rd winter	Running Total 1st winter	Running Total 2nd winter	Running Total 3rd winter
NT70	**R**	23	19	22	4	3	23	27	30
NT70	**V**	12	17	20	10	4	12	22	26
NT80	**K**	11	10	2	4	1	11	15	16
NT82	**W**	7	9	9	4	1	7	11	12
NT83	**P**	29	36	28	14	1	23	43	44
NT84	**W**	25	22	27	8	7	25	33	40
NT90	**L**	38	32	37	2	3	38	40	43
NT91	**V**	20	25	19	12	5	20	32	37
NT94	**J**	31	28	21	6	2	31	37	39
NT95	**R**	12	29	23	20	5	12	32	37
NU00	**Q**	28	29	27	7	7	28	35	42
NU02	**M**	23	28	37	11	12	23	34	46
NU03	**S**	23	34	40	17	4	23	40	44
NU04	**C**	27	29	23	9	3	27	36	39
NU10	**Z**	28	21	no visit	5	no visit	28	33	no visit
NU11	**K**	12	21	20	11	4	12	23	27
NU11	**S**	27	28	27	7	4	27	34	38
NU12	**W**	32	22	28	8	3	32	40	43
NU13	**L**	33	35	32	10	5	33	43	48
NU14	**G**	45	55	39	16	3	45	61	64
NU20	**M**	44	41	53	7	10	44	51	61
NU20	**P**	28	29	32	9	11	28	37	48
NU21	**K**	46	37	44	7	4	46	53	57
NU22	**J**	39	43	47	11	6	39	50	56
NU23	**C**	25	21	29	11	10	25	36	46
NU23	**I**	31	45	28	20	2	31	51	53
NY65	**Z**	29	37	32	11	5	29	40	45
NY66	**V**	30	23	28	3	6	30	33	39
NY67	**X**	13	16	16	9	5	13	22	27
NY69	**B**	6	5	7	2	3	6	8	11
NY76	**A**	21	28	28	8	5	21	29	34
NY77	**Z**	11	9	11	3	4	11	14	18
NY78	**E**	7	18	11	13	1	7	20	21
NY79	**Z**	8	3	7	1	1	8	9	10
NY84	**S**	13	8	15	2	5	13	15	20
NY87	**A**	14	23	16	13	4	14	27	31
NY88	**Q**	36	25	24	5	1	36	41	42
NY89	**F**	3	4	5	2	2	3	5	7

APPENDIX D (continued)

10 KM	TETRAD	No. of Species 1st winter	No. of Species 2nd winter	No. of Species 3rd winter	No. of New Species 2nd winter	No. of New Species 3rd winter	Running Total 1st winter	Running Total 2nd winter	Running Total 3rd winter
NY89	**S**	23	21	27	9	4	23	32	36
NY95	**Y**	29	25	26	6	1	29	35	36
NY96	**H**	34	36	37	9	6	34	43	49
NY97	**V**	26	21	23	5	6	26	31	37
NY98	**G**	11	7	6	4	1	11	15	16
NY99	**L**	16	11	14	4	2	16	20	22
NY99	**V**	8	5	8	2	3	8	10	13
NZ05	**M**	16	18	23	12	5	16	28	33
NZ06	**A**	29	23	27	4	4	29	33	37
NZ07	**A**	25	25	28	7	4	25	32	36
NZ08	**H**	23	24	27	9	5	23	32	37
NZ09	**K**	20	24	29	12	6	20	32	38
NZ16	**T**	30	26	27	2	2	30	32	34
NZ17	**W**	36	37	36	8	5	36	44	49
NZ18	**H**	13	22	23	11	8	13	24	32
NZ18	**M**	38	38	33	7	3	38	45	48
NZ19	**G**	27	25	20	6	2	27	33	35
NZ26	**T**	36	40	38	8	3	36	44	47
NZ27	**M**	28	29	43	10	10	28	38	48
NZ28	**X**	48	49	49	10	5	48	58	63
NZ29	**U**	30	34	35	10	8	30	40	48
NZ36	**U**	39	38	38	3	3	39	42	45
NZ37	**E**	19	25	18	13	1	19	32	33
NZ38	**E**	39	38	no visit	12	no visit	39	51	no visit

APPENDIX E Summary of Control Tetrad visits 1996/97 - 1998/99

Species which were recorded in more than one year and in more than two tetrads. Maximum number of tetrads = 60

Species	No. of Tetrads in which recorded	Total Counts 1996/97	Total Counts 1997/98	Total Counts 1998/99
Red-throated Diver	5	24	8	9
Great Northern Diver	3	1	1	3
Little Grebe	11	18	11	14
Fulmar	5	136	71	282
Cormorant	13	63	67	96
Shag	6	629	234	792
Grey Heron	31	26	39	46
Mute Swan	17	42	60	25
Greylag Goose	7	232	426	4
Canada Goose	3	3	10	35
Shelduck	6	22	14	48
Wigeon	6	20	90	154
Teal	13	153	163	790
Mallard	37	731	640	787
Pochard	6	35	20	23
Tufted Duck	11	24	53	55
Eider	10	1153	599	1481
Common Scoter	5	12	10	121
Goldeneye	17	126	225	190
Red-breasted Merganser	8	27	28	31
Goosander	18	21	45	40
Hen Harrier	4	3	1	1
Goshawk	7	4	1	4
Sparrowhawk	28	15	14	21
Common Buzzard	9	5	7	14
Kestrel	43	24	48	20
Merlin	5	3	1	3
Peregrine	9	1	4	11
Red Grouse	8	217	173	104
Black Grouse	6	109	16	11
Grey Partridge	19	82	32	36
Pheasant	43	222	478	337
Moorhen	26	52	83	78
Coot	11	26	110	97
Oystercatcher	12	179	465	457
Ringed Plover	8	49	91	35
Golden Plover	7	792	899	487
Grey Plover	4	32	95	38
Lapwing	22	2746	1513	945
Sanderling	6	252	33	137
Purple Sandpiper	5	39	33	127
Dunlin	9	536	438	194
Snipe	18	16	7	18
Woodcock	11	7	5	3
Bar-tailed Godwit	3	8	49	259
Curlew	14	456	328	537
Redshank	14	180	249	340
Turnstone	7	183	170	268
Black-headed Gull	33	3450	1822	2497
Common Gull	41	728	1004	1612
Lesser Black-backed Gull	3	1	103	1
Herring Gull	25	679	616	993
Great Black-backed Gull	17	69	154	241
Kittiwake	3	6	5	6
Guillemot	5	30	12	6
Razorbill	3	2	6	0
Feral Pigeon	28	832	1022	662

APPENDIX E (continued)

Species	No. of Tetrads in which recorded	Total Counts 1996/97	Total Counts 1997/98	Total Counts 1998/99
Stock Dove	12	69	18	25
Woodpigeon	43	1892	1407	3291
Collared Dove	26	145	140	125
Kingfisher	3	1	1	2
Green Woodpecker	3	1	0	2
Great Spotted Woodpecker	24	16	21	13
Skylark	19	36	58	52
Meadow Pipit	29	27	88	35
Rock Pipit	7	56	52	23
Grey Wagtail	15	6	8	10
Pied Wagtail	18	20	27	19
Dipper	15	19	11	16
Wren	58	165	208	256
Dunnock	50	97	135	149
Robin	54	192	238	295
Stonechat	4	6	6	8
Blackbird	51	595	589	504
Fieldfare	42	1545	740	922
Song Thrush	34	32	58	47
Redwing	39	450	526	261
Mistle Thrush	49	128	118	101
Goldcrest	46	189	165	250
Long-tailed Tit	27	85	105	155
Marsh Tit	9	11	11	6
Willow Tit	10	13	7	6
Coal Tit	48	307	259	196
Blue Tit	53	747	645	518
Great Tit	45	188	192	191
Nuthatch	13	16	27	17
Treecreeper	24	21	24	23
Jay	13	13	16	21
Magpie	33	115	126	144
Jackdaw	43	1778	1811	1814
Rook	42	3247	3077	2717
Carrion Crow	58	539	681	649
Starling	47	1644	2966	1409
House Sparrow	36	549	600	630
Tree Sparrow	6	14	38	5
Chaffinch	52	1551	1161	1145
Brambling	12	77	22	3
Greenfinch	36	204	191	165
Goldfinch	37	84	77	177
Siskin	22	267	192	145
Linnet	12	397	360	95
Redpoll	5	12	0	21
Crossbill	12	61	42	59
Bullfinch	36	67	68	84
Snow Bunting	3	2	0	4
Yellowhammer	25	222	247	142
Reed Bunting	13	31	28	23

APPENDIX F **Lindisfarne NNR Synchronised count 17th January 1998**

	NU03 Z	NU04 R	NU04 S	NU04 V	NU04 W	NU14 A	NU14 B	NU14 F	NU13 E	NU13 J	NU13 M	NU13 N	**TOTALS**
Red-throated Diver								6		1			**7**
Red-necked Grebe						2		11					**13**
Slavonian Grebe								1					**1**
Fulmar								40					**40**
Cormorant				1		1		24					**26**
Shag								6					**6**
Grey Heron								3			1		**4**
Mute Swan			3		2					5			**10**
Whooper Swan				4									**4**
Greylag Goose			17								2		**19**
Barnacle Goose							2						**2**
Brent Goose	287	200		61		270	10	37	147	209			**1,221**
Shelduck	42	8		479	29		60		400	106	190	5	**1,319**
Wigeon	160					440			250	30	662		**1,542**
Teal		8						27		30	208		**273**
Mallard	25									48	215	7	**295**
Pintail													**0**
Eider	2					169		472	190	133	12	7	**985**
Long-tailed Duck						10		1		2			**13**
Goldeneye											3		**3**
Red-breasted Merganser		1		1			4	6		1	12		**25**
Sparrowhawk				1									**1**
Kestrel		1						1					**2**
Merlin			1	1	1								**3**
Peregrine							1	1					**2**
Grey Partridge		6							8				**14**
Oystercatcher	25	4		42		55	13	209	120	244	136		**848**
Ringed Plover							3	18	120			12	**153**
Golden Plover								170			50		**220**
Grey Plover				118			56	8	150	42		150	**524**
Lapwing			22	46				270			750		**1,088**
Knot							32	5	1300	500	220	150	**2,207**
Sanderling			11									25	**36**
Dunlin				104			319	57	2000	1460	134		**4074**
Jack Snipe		1			1								**2**
Snipe					2		1						**3**
Bar-tailed Godwit	60	7		273		100	37	360	870	44	83	70	**1,904**
Curlew	20	10	281	111	29		115	91	320	228	44		**1,249**
Redshank	50	7		101	56		26	75	625	152	130	20	**1,242**
Turnstone								10			4	3	**17**

APPENDIX F (continued)

	NU03 Z	NU04 R	NU04 S	NU04 V	NU04 W	NU14 A	NU14 B	NU14 F	NU13 E	NU13 J	NU13 M	NU13 N	**TOTALS**
Black-headed Gull				12			3	4		26	138		**183**
Common Gull		1	41	1			8	2		40	42	1	**136**
Herring Gull			2	17	14		11	49		11	48	3	**155**
Great Black-backed Gull		1					3			4	13		**21**
Puffin								1					**1**
Feral Pigeon				18							8		**26**
Collared Dove				3									**3**
Short-eared Owl					1		3						**4**
Skylark		80		2	124		70		5	40			**321**
Meadow Pipit							2						**2**
Rock Pipit		1		1				7					**9**
Wren			1	2					2		1		**6**
Dunnock				1					3		1		**5**
Robin				2			1				2		**5**
Blackbird				2					2		7		**11**
Song Thrush			1										**1**
Mistle Thrush				1									**1**
Blue Tit				4							22		**26**
Great Tit				1							2		**3**
Magpie											1		**1**
Jackdaw			15	150				20			3		**188**
Rook			112	150									**262**
Carrion Crow		29	15	14	23		7	6		28	28		**150**
Starling			51	117	18		9			20			**215**
House Sparrow				11							1		**12**
Chaffinch				48							27		**75**
Greenfinch											8		**8**
Goldfinch				6									**6**
Linnet		1		6			10	4		12			**33**
Twite		35					4						**39**
Lapland Bunting		1			1								**2**
Totals	**671**	**402**	**573**	**1,912**	**301**	**1,047**	**810**	**2,002**	**6,512**	**3,416**	**3,208**	**453**	**21,307**

APPENDIX G **Lindisfarne NNR Synchronised count 12th December 1998**

	NU03 Z	NU04 R	NU04 S	NU04 V	NU04 W	NU14 A	NU14 B	NU14 F	NU14 G	NU13 E	NU13 J	NU13 M	NU13 N	**TOTALS**
Red-throated Diver								1	2				2	**5**
Red-necked Grebe								1					1	**2**
Slavonian Grebe								2					9	**11**
Fulmar									7					**7**
Cormorant			2			11		16	4					**33**
Shag								33	3				5	**41**
Grey Heron									2		1			**3**
Mute Swan		5		4	10						13	4		**36**
Whooper Swan		48												**48**
Pink-footed Goose												30		**30**
Greylag Goose			80	100						1			1	**182**
Barnacle Goose														**0**
Brent Goose	238	43		963	207		197	122	60	562	344			**2,736**
Shelduck	74	26		482	85	4	10	1		336	7	225		**1,250**
Wigeon	7			770	8					810	4	950		**2,549**
Teal								27	106			570	20	**723**
Mallard								43	2	20	68	150	80	**363**
Pintail				8						62				**70**
Eider			9	56		17		606	15		7	10	2	**722**
Long-tailed Duck			2						1				1	**4**
Common Scoter													35	**35**
Goldeneye		3		2	1				3			2		**11**
Red-breasted Merganser		1		1	2	4		7	2			1	1	**19**
Sparrowhawk		1		1					1					**3**
Kestrel		2	1		1				1			1		**6**
Merlin		1	1		1		1	1	1					**6**
Peregrine					2				1	1				**4**
Red-legged Partridge												3		**3**
Grey Partridge		6								4				**10**
Pheasant							1		1				3	**5**
Moorhen		2							8					**10**
Coot									12					**12**
Oystercatcher	3	37		4	50	30	11	356	121	49	51	52	5	**769**
Ringed Plover	20						7	23	6				20	**76**
Golden Plover		50			1			100			3500	2250		**5,901**
Grey Plover	60	3	4	57	20		11	162		204	300	52		**873**
Lapwing		18		300			1	104	94	370		2300		**3,187**
Knot	162			9	230					1410	86	550	5	**2,452**
Sanderling								137	9		6		4	**156**
Dunlin	520	11	2	170	350		162	308	350	1330	270	900		**4,373**

APPENDIX G (continued)

	NU03 Z	NU04 R	NU04 S	NU04 V	NU04 W	NU14 A	NU14 B	NU14 F	NU14 G	NU13 E	NU13 J	NU13 M	NU13 N	**TOTALS**
Jack Snipe														**0**
Snipe		3	1		3							1		**8**
Woodcock				1										**1**
Bar-tailed Godwit	130	10		1	840		1	302	320	148	526	75	70	**2,423**
Black-tailed Godwit		1												**1**
Curlew	12	361	36	126	31	4	7	33	328	187	58	60	15	**1,258**
Redshank	40	585	29	137	14	5	24	86	97	176	57	207	16	**1,473**
Turnstone	1				3			33	18	2		1		**58**
Black-headed Gull		133	630	10	8	3		17	30		1	20		**852**
Common Gull			133	1	1				10		2		3	**150**
Herring Gull			231	14		4	1	18	40		2		2	**312**
Great Black-backed Gull			7		1		3	11	20			2	12	**56**
Guillemot					1									**1**
Little Auk							1 (dead)							**1**
Puffin														**0**
Feral Pigeon				27					60			20		**107**
Collared Dove		1							4					**5**
Stock Dove													3	**3**
Woodpigeon				72									2	**74**
Short-eared Owl							4							**4**
Skylark		6	3	15			6		1					**31**
Meadow Pipit				1	1		4			3			1	**10**
Rock Pipit								3	11					**14**
Wren		2		3				1	1			1		**8**
Dunnock				1					2	1				**4**
Robin		1		2					1					**4**
Blackbird				4					4			5		**13**
Song Thrush														**0**
Mistle Thrush		1												**1**
Blue Tit		2		3					1			4		**10**
Great Tit		1												**1**
Magpie				2										**2**
Jackdaw		50	105	6					70			10	2	**243**
Rook		150	452	600								200		**1,402**
Carrion Crow		61	11	18	10		28	3	29		8	20	6	**194**
Starling									40					**40**
House Sparrow		9		30					10			1		**50**
Tree Sparrow				2										**2**
Chaffinch				21										**21**
Greenfinch												1		**1**

APPENDIX G (continued)

	NU03 Z	NU04 R	NU04 S	NU04 V	NU04 W	NU14 A	NU14 B	NU14 F	NU14 G	NU13 E	NU13 J	NU13 M	NU13 N	**TOTALS**
Goldfinch									2					**2**
Linnet		7					51	14	12					**84**
Twite							22		10					**32**
Lapland Bunting		1												**1**
Snow Bunting				10				15	3				17	**45**
Yellowhammer		3												**3**
Reed Bunting		1												**1**
Totals	**1,267**	**1,642**	**1,739**	**4,024**	**1,881**	**82**	**552**	**2,571**	**1,933**	**5,676**	**5,311**	**8,678**	**326**	**35,682**

APPENDIX H **Coastal WeBS Counts during the Winter Atlas period**

nc = no count

OYSTERCATCHER

	Nov-96	Dec-96	Jan-97	Feb-97	Nov-97	Dec-97	Jan-98	Feb-98	Nov-98	Dec-98	Jan-99	Feb-99
Berwick Little Beach	12	30	30	nc	43	55	60	32	30	50	25	58
Tweed Estuary	3	nc	4	3	19	4	15	0	6	7	16	15
Spittal to Cocklawburn	41	120	97	142	150	57	84	36	124	nc	70	93
Lindisfarne NNR	1401	1008	1489	1175	723	1251	1160	1360	580	933	1371	1181
Budle Point to Seahouses	92	147	151	59	99	101	78	55	84	60	139	78
Seahouses to Beadnell	118	94	159	114	137	162	214	153	202	207	77	65
Beadnell to Howick Burn	148	173	nc	207	216	nc	122	nc	155	200	282	nc
Howick Burn to Boulmer	25	46	35	9	127	79	45	88	53	23	29	38
Boulmer to Alnmouth	41	44	81	104	56	88	97	nc	95	156	52	81
Aln Estuary	0	0	0	3	0	22	4	6	0	2	0	2
Coquet Estuary	35	41	59	58	9	41	50	12	47	17	37	nc
Amble to Chevington	146	102	nc	61	38	112	nc	97	100	114	50	nc
Chevington to Cresswell	16	14	47	10	12	1	31	17	25	26	nc	48
Cresswell to Newbiggin	68	158	nc	85	137	161	99	nc	nc	88	119	nc
Newbiggin to Cambois	57	nc	22	27	80	124	nc	33	64	nc	79	94
Blyth Estuary	140	169	171	136	17	nc	5	7	10	13	18	109
Blyth to Hartley Point	15	76	nc	nc	nc	69	nc	nc	45	12	nc	nc
St. Mary's Island	35	nc	36	nc	96	66	49	139	93	127	237	160
Tynemouth, N.Pier to North Shields Fish Quay	9	30	53	22	53	47	54	53	30	21	27	30
TOTALS	**2,402**	**2,252**	**2,434**	**2,215**	**2,012**	**2,440**	**2,167**	**2,088**	**1,743**	**2,056**	**2,628**	**2,052**

RINGED PLOVER

	Nov-96	Dec-96	Jan-97	Feb-97	Nov-97	Dec-97	Jan-98	Feb-98	Nov-98	Dec-98	Jan-99	Feb-99
Berwick Little Beach	80	85	10	nc	0	0	20	52	0	120	0	0
Tweed Estuary	0	nc	0	0	23	0	0	0	0	0	0	0
Spittal to Cocklawburn	0	0	0	3	0	32	50	5	0	nc	0	0
Lindisfarne NNR	36	10	39	36	6	20	116	0	56	15	78	80
Budle Point to Seahouses	18	20	9	35	58	0	6	19	10	12	40	0
Seahouses to Beadnell	31	12	3	1	0	0	2	0	10	19	28	27
Beadnell to Howick Burn	47	54	nc	43	42	nc	85	nc	119	168	78	nc
Howick Burn to Boulmer	0	0	1	0	7	0	0	0	12	24	12	12
Boulmer to Alnmouth	8	13	0	3	2	5	0	nc	22	0	3	6
Aln Estuary	0	0	0	0	0	0	0	0	0	0	0	0
Coquet Estuary	6	6	35	0	0	0	0	0	0	0	0	nc
Amble to Chevington	79	46	nc	15	7	35	nc	21	33	54	36	nc
Chevington to Cresswell	0	0	0	0	0	23	0	0	0	2	nc	1
Cresswell to Newbiggin	25	2	nc	11	31	51	1	nc	nc	3	0	nc
Newbiggin to Cambois	33	nc	14	17	4	25	nc	0	13	nc	14	1
Blyth Estuary	0	0	0	0	1	nc	0	0	2	0	0	2
Blyth to Hartley Point	0	5	nc	nc	nc	0	nc	nc	0	7	nc	nc
St. Mary's Island	11	nc	30	nc	15	21	21	11	43	32	13	32
Tynemouth, N.Pier to North Shields Fish Quay	1	2	10	8	12	0	12	16	0	2	16	4
TOTALS	**375**	**255**	**151**	**172**	**208**	**212**	**313**	**124**	**320**	**458**	**318**	**165**

APPENDIX H (continued)

GOLDEN PLOVER

	Nov-96	Dec-96	Jan-97	Feb-97	Nov-97	Dec-97	Jan-98	Feb-98	Nov-98	Dec-98	Jan-99	Feb-99
Berwick Little Beach	0	0	0	nc	0	0	0	0	0	0	0	0
Tweed Estuary	0	nc	0	0	0	0	0	0	0	0	0	0
Spittal to Cocklawburn	15	0	0	0	0	0	0	0	0	nc	0	0
Lindisfarne NNR	315	2604	917	650	2580	1050	1429	950	4990	2385	270	19
Budle Point to Seahouses	750	100	151	256	20	60	290	350	0	0	30	0
Seahouses to Beadnell	8	0	610	0	255	32	800	0	400	50	0	0
Beadnell to Howick Burn	149	616	nc	252	600	nc	0	nc	0	711	100	nc
Howick Burn to Boulmer	1	160	1	0	1400	105	5	20	375	10	180	9
Boulmer to Alnmouth	0	0	0	42	315	23	0	nc	0	0	0	0
Aln Estuary	0	0	0	0	325	0	26	0	106	0	0	0
Coquet Estuary	0	575	400	0	21	36	308	654	1100	281	220	nc
Amble to Chevington	500	0	nc	0	0	0	nc	0	0	0	0	nc
Chevington to Cresswell	0	0	50	0	40	0	0	0	0	40	nc	0
Cresswell to Newbiggin	0	0	nc	0	0	0	0	nc	nc	0	0	nc
Newbiggin to Cambois	0	nc	0	0	3	0	nc	0	0	nc	0	28
Blyth Estuary	4	0	0	0	0	nc	400	0	13	0	6	0
Blyth to Hartley Point	0	0	nc	nc	nc	0	nc	nc	0	0	nc	nc
St. Mary's Island	1600	nc	3000	nc	6500	3000	1200	75	1500	725	1000	305
Tynemouth, N.Pier to North Shields Fish Quay	0	0	4	0	0	0	0	0	0	0	0	0
TOTALS	**3,342**	**4,055**	**5,133**	**1,200**	**12,059**	**4,306**	**4,458**	**2,049**	**8,484**	**4,202**	**1,806**	**361**

GREY PLOVER

	Nov-96	Dec-96	Jan-97	Feb-97	Nov-97	Dec-97	Jan-98	Feb-98	Nov-98	Dec-98	Jan-99	Feb-99
Berwick Little Beach	4	0	1	nc	0	0	0	3	0	0	0	0
Tweed Estuary	0	nc	0	0	1	0	0	0	0	0	0	0
Spittal to Cocklawburn	4	1	0	0	0	1	0	4	2	nc	0	0
Lindisfarne NNR	988	732	1465	1530	894	680	1432	2950	646	997	1067	1106
Budle Point to Seahouses	8	8	0	1	0	0	0	0	2	0	0	0
Seahouses to Beadnell	13	18	29	38	26	28	45	24	24	31	36	16
Beadnell to Howick Burn	9	6	nc	22	10	nc	7	nc	1	31	9	nc
Howick Burn to Boulmer	1	13	17	3	13	5	36	15	15	0	21	13
Boulmer to Alnmouth	2	18	106	58	14	74	118	nc	11	93	30	21
Aln Estuary	0	0	0	0	0	0	0	0	0	0	0	0
Coquet Estuary	2	2	31	4	1	0	1	6	2	1	1	nc
Amble to Chevington	2	7	nc	18	0	0	nc	0	1	9	16	nc
Chevington to Cresswell	0	0	0	0	0	0	0	0	0	1	nc	0
Cresswell to Newbiggin	8	0	nc	3	0	13	27	nc	nc	0	0	nc
Newbiggin to Cambois	2	nc	0	9	0	0	nc	0	0	nc	0	0
Blyth Estuary	1	18	10	8	0	nc	15	13	12	4	14	4
Blyth to Hartley Point	0	0	nc	nc	nc	0	nc	nc	0	0	nc	nc
St. Mary's Island	0	nc	0	nc	1	1	0	0	0	1	0	0
Tynemouth, N.Pier to North Shields Fish Quay	0	0	0	0	0	0	0	0	0	0	0	0
TOTALS	**1,044**	**823**	**1,659**	**1,694**	**960**	**802**	**1,681**	**3,015**	**716**	**1,168**	**1,194**	**1,160**

APPENDIX H (continued)

LAPWING

	Nov-96	Dec-96	Jan-97	Feb-97	Nov-97	Dec-97	Jan-98	Feb-98	Nov-98	Dec-98	Jan-99	Feb-99
Berwick Little Beach	0	0	0	nc	0	0	0	0	0	0	0	0
Tweed Estuary	0	nc	540	14	700	420	350	350	221	250	170	0
Spittal to Cocklawburn	100	23	0	0	400	2	0	0	90	nc	0	0
Lindisfarne NNR	320	527	713	560	1729	575	620	120	1306	641	1066	108
Budle Point to Seahouses	650	170	468	345	325	840	189	0	63	75	150	30
Seahouses to Beadnell	3	260	840	0	594	1010	1071	163	332	692	0	5
Beadnell to Howick Burn	20	85	nc	35	779	nc	30	nc	0	271	242	nc
Howick Burn to Boulmer	88	150	300	0	250	862	190	130	480	0	70	23
Boulmer to Alnmouth	0	713	360	300	878	400	178	nc	120	410	350	0
Aln Estuary	620	121	277	479	551	413	640	0	785	285	483	17
Coquet Estuary	0	630	474	350	129	1000	1000	500	370	493	787	nc
Amble to Chevington	250	0	nc	0	0	0	nc	0	0	48	0	nc
Chevington to Cresswell	0	0	0	0	0	0	40	0	0	530	nc	0
Cresswell to Newbiggin	0	0	nc	0	0	0	0	nc	nc	0	0	nc
Newbiggin to Cambois	0	nc	0	0	0	0	nc	0	0	nc	0	0
Blyth Estuary	315	0	541	108	4	nc	618	44	157	35	5	0
Blyth to Hartley Point	3	0	nc	nc	nc	0	nc	nc	0	0	nc	nc
St. Mary's Island	152	nc	350	nc	465	600	358	233	330	118	75	12
Tynemouth, N.Pier to North Shields Fish Quay	0	0	0	1	0	0	0	0	0	0	0	0
TOTALS	**2,521**	**2,679**	**4,863**	**2,192**	**6,804**	**6,122**	**5,284**	**1,540**	**4,254**	**3,848**	**3,398**	**195**

KNOT

	Nov-96	Dec-96	Jan-97	Feb-97	Nov-97	Dec-97	Jan-98	Feb-98	Nov-98	Dec-98	Jan-99	Feb-99
Berwick Little Beach	0	0	0	nc	0	0	0	0	0	0	0	0
Tweed Estuary	0	nc	0	0	0	0	0	0	0	0	0	0
Spittal to Cocklawburn	0	0	0	0	0	0	0	0	0	nc	0	0
Lindisfarne NNR	973	1412	4625	4540	823	1365	3218	1152	1355	4040	2580	1385
Budle Point to Seahouses	0	0	20	12	0	0	0	4	0	0	0	0
Seahouses to Beadnell	2	0	11	0	0	0	0	0	0	0	0	0
Beadnell to Howick Burn	0	1	nc	0	0	nc	0	nc	0	0	0	nc
Howick Burn to Boulmer	0	0	40	0	0	0	56	40	8	13	0	0
Boulmer to Alnmouth	2	0	1	2	2	0	142	nc	0	0	0	570
Aln Estuary	0	0	0	0	0	0	0	0	0	0	0	0
Coquet Estuary	14	0	135	0	0	0	1	57	2	0	0	nc
Amble to Chevington	8	300	nc	140	0	82	nc	300	0	12	520	nc
Chevington to Cresswell	0	0	350	0	0	0	40	0	0	0	nc	0
Cresswell to Newbiggin	0	89	nc	438	0	41	139	nc	nc	100	110	nc
Newbiggin to Cambois	300	nc	310	310	0	0	nc	80	0	nc	8	16
Blyth Estuary	0	16	18	0	0	nc	0	0	0	0	0	0
Blyth to Hartley Point	0	18	nc	nc	nc	450	nc	nc	0	0	nc	nc
St. Mary's Island	0	nc	32	nc	121	191	0	31	144	141	57	550
Tynemouth, N.Pier to North Shields Fish Quay	0	0	0	0	0	0	1	0	0	1	0	0
TOTALS	**1,299**	**1,836**	**5,542**	**5,442**	**946**	**2,129**	**3,597**	**1,664**	**1,509**	**4,307**	**3275**	**2,521**

APPENDIX H (continued)

SANDERLING

	Nov-96	Dec-96	Jan-97	Feb-97	Nov-97	Dec-97	Jan-98	Feb-98	Nov-98	Dec-98	Jan-99	Feb-99
Berwick Little Beach	50	3	30	nc	0	15	11	56	33	60	2	2
Tweed Estuary	0	nc	0	0	10	0	0	0	18	0	0	0
Spittal to Cocklawburn	4	23	15	20	3	2	20	20	25	nc	0	45
Lindisfarne NNR	93	73	80	38	115	120	292	16	10	236	23	97
Budle Point to Seahouses	59	38	5	11	41	0	1	17	4	4	17	0
Seahouses to Beadnell	26	1	0	21	69	7	68	0	78	78	81	21
Beadnell to Howick Burn	17	77	nc	30	118	nc	30	nc	110	83	69	nc
Howick Burn to Boulmer	0	0	0	0	0	0	0	0	0	2	0	0
Boulmer to Alnmouth	1	0	4	0	0	0	0	nc	0	8	6	1
Aln Estuary	0	0	0	0	0	0	0	0	0	0	0	0
Coquet Estuary	3	0	0	0	0	0	0	0	0	0	0	nc
Amble to Chevington	19	2	nc	21	95	53	nc	0	61	51	28	nc
Chevington to Cresswell	28	0	18	14	27	74	27	16	132	140	nc	39
Cresswell to Newbiggin	5	12	nc	0	2	50	0	nc	nc	70	56	nc
Newbiggin to Cambois	25	nc	0	2	0	0	nc	0	0	nc	0	0
Blyth Estuary	0	0	0	0	0	nc	0	0	0	0	0	0
Blyth to Hartley Point	4	0	nc	nc	nc	0	nc	nc	2	12	nc	nc
St. Mary's Island	0	nc	1	nc	0	10	0	0	3	0	10	10
Tynemouth, N.Pier to North Shields Fish Quay	33	0	13	2	1	9	0	18	12	14	3	33
TOTALS	**367**	**229**	**166**	**159**	**481**	**340**	**449**	**143**	**488**	**758**	**295**	**248**

PURPLE SANDPIPER

	Nov-96	Dec-96	Jan-97	Feb-97	Nov-97	Dec-97	Jan-98	Feb-98	Nov-98	Dec-98	Jan-99	Feb-99
Berwick Little Beach	0	0	0	nc	0	0	0	0	0	0	0	0
Tweed Estuary	0	nc	0	0	0	0	0	0	0	0	0	0
Spittal to Cocklawburn	0	0	0	0	0	0	0	25	0	nc	0	8
Lindisfarne NNR	3	0	0	2	0	0	0	0	0	0	18	0
Budle Point to Seahouses	135	108	56	144	46	88	149	71	175	120	274	120
Seahouses to Beadnell	16	1	3	44	43	10	48	28	46	49	53	10
Beadnell to Howick Burn	34	10	nc	2	14	nc	6	nc	40	3	23	nc
Howick Burn to Boulmer	0	0	0	0	0	0	0	0	0	5	0	0
Boulmer to Alnmouth	8	0	2	2	1	0	1	nc	0	0	0	1
Aln Estuary	0	0	0	0	0	0	0	0	0	0	0	0
Coquet Estuary	0	9	11	0	0	0	10	0	1	0	4	nc
Amble to Chevington	3	5	nc	12	3	4	nc	17	27	29	21	nc
Chevington to Cresswell	0	0	0	0	0	0	0	0	0	0	nc	0
Cresswell to Newbiggin	0	7	nc	0	4	0	0	nc	nc	0	1	nc
Newbiggin to Cambois	26	nc	3	6	0	2	nc	0	67	nc	180	52
Blyth Estuary	0	0	0	0	0	nc	0	12	1	0	0	0
Blyth to Hartley Point	1	0	nc	nc	nc	3	nc	nc	0	3	nc	nc
St. Mary's Island	3	nc	0	nc	1	3	1	0	1	1	3	18
Tynemouth, N.Pier to North Shields FishQuay	1	6	1	3	8	7	0	17	9	6	0	46
TOTALS	**230**	**146**	**76**	**215**	**120**	**117**	**215**	**170**	**367**	**216**	**577**	**255**

APPENDIX H (continued)

DUNLIN

	Nov-96	Dec-96	Jan-97	Feb-97	Nov-97	Dec-97	Jan-98	Feb-98	Nov-98	Dec-98	Jan-99	Feb-99
Berwick Little Beach	176	120	220	nc	0	34	20	82	185	15	5	0
Tweed Estuary	11	nc	6	0	121	0	0	4	29	0	0	0
Spittal to Cocklawburn	0	0	0	5	0	0	0	0	11	nc	37	0
Lindisfarne NNR	4512	5468	10364	8307	3966	4199	6039	5140	5936	6291	9880	5155
Budle Point to Seahouses	1	8	28	92	23	6	0	9	0	24	10	9
Seahouses to Beadnell	115	105	150	172	39	121	18	40	13	56	27	24
Beadnell to Howick Burn	41	69	nc	135	198	nc	161	nc	79	122	165	nc
Howick Burn to Boulmer	14	38	240	0	280	31	150	121	132	15	33	119
Boulmer to Alnmouth	31	116	220	176	82	248	154	nc	21	458	45	132
Aln Estuary	0	0	7	17	26	2	0	0	0	0	0	0
Coquet Estuary	144	120	459	265	67	224	387	384	11	29	19	nc
Amble to Chevington	28	73	nc	63	143	88	nc	35	48	226	131	nc
Chevington to Cresswell	1	0	204	0	0	0	1	3	0	7	nc	0
Cresswell to Newbiggin	16	371	nc	82	68	462	320	nc	nc	41	60	nc
Newbiggin to Cambois	11	nc	0	46	31	0	nc	14	27	nc	26	0
Blyth Estuary	51	14	166	97	40	nc	241	156	60	13	127	117
Blyth to Hartley Point	0	0	nc	nc	nc	0	nc	nc	0	0	nc	nc
St. Mary's Island	11	nc	250	nc	35	400	148	87	246	400	206	348
Tynemouth, N.Pier to North Shields Fish Quay	7	39	33	208	2	119	90	259	17	63	42	220
TOTALS	**5,170**	**6,541**	**12,347**	**9,665**	**5,121**	**5,934**	**7,729**	**6,334**	**6,815**	**7,760**	**10,813**	**6,124**

BAR-TAILED GODWIT

	Nov-96	Dec-96	Jan-97	Feb-97	Nov-97	Dec-97	Jan-98	Feb-98	Nov-98	Dec-98	Jan-99	Feb-99
Berwick Little Beach	0	0	0	nc	0	0	0	0	4	1	0	0
Tweed Estuary	0	nc	0	0	0	0	0	0	0	0	0	0
Spittal to Cocklawburn	0	0	0	0	0	9	0	0	0	nc	5	0
Lindisfarne NNR	1809	2850	2770	2854	2154	2181	2649	3225	2946	1646	3086	1787
Budle Point to Seahouses	3	3	8	2	0	1	8	0	1	0	4	7
Seahouses to Beadnell	30	53	85	27	16	59	74	55	67	60	40	99
Beadnell to Howick Burn	12	15	nc	16	17	nc	18	nc	5	10	19	nc
Howick Burn to Boulmer	0	0	1	0	17	7	25	4	27	0	0	2
Boulmer to Alnmouth	0	0	21	12	1	9	33	nc	6	46	43	12
Aln Estuary	0	0	0	0	0	0	0	0	0	0	0	0
Coquet Estuary	5	0	16	3	5	10	11	3	2	0	9	nc
Amble to Chevington	4	3	nc	0	1	1	nc	7	6	0	0	nc
Chevington to Cresswell	0	0	0	0	0	0	0	0	0	0	nc	0
Cresswell to Newbiggin	0	1	nc	0	0	0	0	nc	nc	0	0	nc
Newbiggin to Cambois	0	nc	0	3	0	0	nc	0	0	nc	0	0
Blyth Estuary	0	5	1	0	0	nc	2	2	3	0	1	0
Blyth to Hartley Point	0	0	nc	nc	nc	0	nc	nc	0	0	nc	nc
St. Mary's Island	1	nc	0	nc	1	1	1	0	0	2	0	0
Tynemouth, N.Pier to North Shields Fish Quay	0	0	1	0	0	0	0	0	0	0	0	0
TOTALS	**1,864**	**2,930**	**2,903**	**2,917**	**2,212**	**2,278**	**2,821**	**3,296**	**3,067**	**1,765**	**3,207**	**1,907**

APPENDIX H (continued)

CURLEW

	Nov-96	Dec-96	Jan-97	Feb-97	Nov-97	Dec-97	Jan-98	Feb-98	Nov-98	Dec-98	Jan-99	Feb-99
Berwick Little Beach	0	0	0	nc	0	0	0	0	0	0	0	3
Tweed Estuary	6	nc	7	5	14	5	7	23	1	0	17	3
Spittal to Cocklawburn	1	6	18	3	13	4	4	2	6	nc	3	2
Lindisfarne NNR	500	397	198	577	445	660	1330	731	742	1215	1420	729
Budle Point to Seahouses	38	45	83	0	130	94	1	86	105	185	15	0
Seahouses to Beadnell	9	14	9	50	6	37	9	9	38	35	0	60
Beadnell to Howick Burn	103	114	nc	318	111	nc	53	nc	5	162	15	nc
Howick Burn to Boulmer	67	75	51	0	120	230	380	190	140	74	97	37
Boulmer to Alnmouth	0	18	6	4	1	24	18	nc	25	34	6	9
Aln Estuary	61	98	56	106	36	137	51	105	51	13	49	24
Coquet Estuary	16	10	3	15	21	16	22	6	42	17	91	nc
Amble to Chevington	0	62	nc	0	2	6	nc	5	1	6	3	nc
Chevington to Cresswell	0	0	41	0	1	1	1	0	6	29	nc	0
Cresswell to Newbiggin	1	6	nc	1	2	23	0	nc	nc	3	2	nc
Newbiggin to Cambois	0	nc	6	0	1	4	nc	1	3	nc	3	2
Blyth Estuary	16	56	9	64	53	nc	26	41	54	68	46	68
Blyth to Hartley Point	0	1	nc	nc	nc	0	nc	nc	0	1	nc	nc
St. Mary's Island	2	nc	62	nc	24	93	42	32	8	48	8	3
Tynemouth, N.Pier to North Shields Fish Quay	0	2	3	3	1	1	1	1	1	6	5	0
TOTALS	**820**	**904**	**552**	**1,146**	**981**	**1,335**	**1,945**	**1,232**	**1,228**	**1,896**	**1,780**	**940**

REDSHANK

	Nov-96	Dec-96	Jan-97	Feb-97	Nov-97	Dec-97	Jan-98	Feb-98	Nov-98	Dec-98	Jan-99	Feb-99
Berwick Little Beach	17	32	40	nc	62	132	72	17	31	84	20	56
Tweed Estuary	110	nc	182	158	196	384	129	233	244	107	15	73
Spittal to Cocklawburn	8	8	17	7	32	25	10	15	36	nc	11	2
Lindisfarne NNR	984	844	867	901	1119	1207	689	967	1459	1483	1576	491
Budle Point to Seahouses	30	48	21	49	81	33	35	89	86	6	32	26
Seahouses to Beadnell	38	41	71	61	81	138	163	105	17	177	8	32
Beadnell to Howick Burn	47	73	nc	68	151	nc	104	nc	57	177	109	nc
Howick Burn to Boulmer	39	42	25	5	48	100	79	124	93	27	48	34
Boulmer to Alnmouth	147	132	51	34	93	62	62	nc	315	243	120	32
Aln Estuary	11	23	21	23	51	90	15	32	87	8	114	21
Coquet Estuary	17	62	13	35	56	133	84	61	74	71	52	nc
Amble to Chevington	31	56	nc	29	163	104	nc	46	71	135	41	nc
Chevington to Cresswell	1	22	18	25	19	0	41	3	41	70	nc	0
Cresswell to Newbiggin	12	18	nc	25	40	88	122	nc	nc	131	130	nc
Newbiggin to Cambois	54	nc	26	35	50	81	nc	6	20	nc	46	44
Blyth Estuary	200	169	98	86	168	nc	121	163	228	91	196	133
Blyth to Hartley Point	1	39	nc	nc	nc	9	nc	nc	24	11	nc	nc
St. Mary's Island	24	nc	170	nc	159	139	56	243	229	42	93	42
Tynemouth, N.Pier to North Shields Fish Quay	11	38	69	42	105	128	97	95	137	110	35	79
TOTALS	**1,782**	**1,647**	**1,689**	**1,583**	**2,674**	**2,853**	**1,879**	**2,199**	**3,249**	**2,973**	**2,646**	**1,065**

APPENDIX H (continued)

TURNSTONE

	Nov-96	Dec-96	Jan-97	Feb-97	Nov-97	Dec-97	Jan-98	Feb-98	Nov-98	Dec-98	Jan-99	Feb-99
Berwick Little Beach	36	31	2	nc	5	54	2	27	105	30	20	40
Tweed Estuary	32	nc	13	4	65	0	0	1	28	0	0	3
Spittal to Cocklawburn	16	26	12	18	12	12	15	40	17	nc	13	0
Lindisfarne NNR	137	98	52	148	82	171	230	93	84	148	242	32
Budle Point to Seahouses	120	89	118	129	144	84	71	61	190	0	85	176
Seahouses to Beadnell	37	52	55	145	201	92	177	139	141	199	0	116
Beadnell to Howick Burn	89	70	nc	35	176	nc	0	nc	57	30	96	nc
Howick Burn to Boulmer	10	23	3	0	72	43	53	38	45	12	14	9
Boulmer to Alnmouth	161	121	83	112	151	70	53	nc	243	122	127	40
Aln Estuary	0	0	0	0	0	0	0	0	0	0	0	0
Coquet Estuary	13	11	14	8	1	4	9	14	7	0	5	nc
Amble to Chevington	32	62	nc	103	180	71	nc	54	103	75	98	nc
Chevington to Cresswell	3	0	20	3	6	0	1	2	8	0	nc	0
Cresswell to Newbiggin	7	78	nc	4	46	9	21	nc	nc	42	34	nc
Newbiggin to Cambois	34	nc	23	4	71	66	nc	10	39	nc	31	11
Blyth Estuary	51	18	20	27	3	nc	2	24	11	15	15	30
Blyth to Hartley Point	24	8	nc	nc	nc	14	nc	nc	18	16	nc	nc
St. Mary's Island	3	nc	25	nc	123	165	20	95	68	22	36	30
Tynemouth, N.Pier to North Shields Fish Quay	5	18	10	30	21	34	30	35	22	29	3	25
TOTALS	**810**	**705**	**450**	**770**	**1,359**	**889**	**684**	**633**	**1,186**	**740**	**819**	**512**

APPENDIX I The status of important sites for Wildfowl in Northumberland based on WeBS Surveys

KEY : I = International status; S = significant numbers; c = candidate; N = National status; O = no longer meets requirement; p = proposed; X = exceeds national threshold in some years; * = important site but below threshold number

These relate to November-February counts unless otherwise stated

SITE	SPECIES	1996/97	1997/98	1998/99	1999/2000	International/ National threshold figure
LINDISFARNE NNR	Pink-footed Goose	-	-	X	O	2,250
(Ramsar site, SPA	Greylag Goose(Icelandic)	I	*I	*I	O	1,000
& cSAC)	Pale-bellied Brent Goose	I	I	I	I	50
	Shelduck	N	N	N	N	750
	Wigeon	N	N	N	N	2,800
	Eider	N	N	N	N	750
	Long-tailed Duck	*N	*N	*N	O	230
	Common Scoter	N	*N	N	*N	275
TWEED ESTUARY	Mute Swan (July/Aug)	N	N	N	N	260
(SSSI & pSAC))	Goldeneye	N	N	N	N	170
TWEED VALLEY						
Kelso-Coldstream	Whooper Swan	N	N	N	*N	55
	Goldeneye	N	*N	N	N	90
	Goosander	N	N	N	N	170
FARNE ISLANDS	Eider	-	-	N	*N	750
(SPA & cSAC)						
HOLBURN MOSS	Pink-footed Goose (Oct)	*I	I	I	*I	2,250
(Ramsar site & SPA)	Greylag Goose (Icelandic)	I	*I	*I	O	1,000
NORTHUMBRIA COAST						
(Ramsar site & SPA)						
Seahouses-Budle Point	Pale-bellied Brent Goose	-	Nil	*I	*N	50/25
(SSSI & cSAC)	Long-tailed Duck	*N	*N	Nil	*N	230
	Eider	N	*N	N	*N	750
Alnmouth	Eider	-	-	S	-	750
(SSSI & cSAC)						

APPENDIX J The status of important sites for Waders in Northumberland based on WeBS Surveys

KEY : I = International status N = National status X = exceeds national threshold in some years
S = significant numbers O = no longer meets requirement * = important site but below threshold number
c = candidate

These relate to November-February counts unless otherwise stated

SITE	SPECIES	1996/97	1997/98	1998/99	1999/2000	International/ National threshold figure
LINDISFARNE NNR (Ramsar site, SPA & cSAC)	Golden Plover	N	N	N	N	2,500
	Grey Plover	I	I	*I	*I	1,500
	Knot	I	I	I	*I	3,500
	Dunlin	N	N	N	N	5,300
	Bar-tailed Godwit	I	I	I	I	1,000
	Curlew	-	N	N	N	1,200
	Redshank	-	-	X	-	1,100
FARNE ISLANDS (SSSI, SPA & cSAC)	Purple Sandpiper	-	-	N	-	210
NORTHUMBRIA COAST (Ramsar site & SPA)						
Seahouses-Budle Point (SSSI & cSAC)	Purple Sandpiper	*N	*N	N	N	210
Howick to Beadnell (SSSI & cSAC)	Purple Sandpiper	-	-	-	S	210
Cambois to Newbiggin (SSSI)	Purple Sandpiper	*N	*N	*N	*N	210
St. Mary's Island (SSSI)	Golden Plover	N	N	*N	*N	2,500

APPENDIX K Number of Breeding (either possible, probable or confirmed) and Wintering species by tetrad. (Breeding data source - Day *et al.*, 1995)

		Breeding 1988-92	Winter 1996-99
NT60	F	7	1
	K	15	7
	L	5	4
	Q	9	7
	R	4	4
	S	no count	1
	V	9	4
	W	9	4
	X	15	3
	Y	17	6
NT70	A	11	7
	B	18	6
	C	25	13
	D	14	2
	F	12	6
	G	37	28
	H	31	12
	I	15	6
	K	14	4
	L	25	21
	M	14	6
	N	16	5
	Q	29	19
	R	32	30
	S	17	11
	T	17	8
	V	27	26
	W	32	15
	X	22	12
	Y	8	3
	Z	9	5
NT71	V	11	3
	W	6	3
NT73	Y	15	18
	Z	26	14
NT80	A	17	10
	B	15	13
	C	12	10
	D	12	10
	E	12	10
	F	24	10
	G	16	9
	H	10	7
	I	18	6
	J	13	3
	K	21	16
	L	11	6
	M	10	12
	N	20	11
	P	13	12
	Q	20	5
	R	41	12
	S	10	5
	T	29	13
	U	22	17
	V	12	7
NT80	W	24	7
	X	17	16
	Y	39	16
	Z	25	4
NT81	A	15	6
	B	15	1
	F	31	7
	G	11	2
	H	4	0
	K	32	7
	L	20	6
	M	6	1
	Q	26	10
	R	17	12
	S	24	6
	T	no count	3
	V	27	7
	W	18	9
	X	22	9
	Y	23	5
	Z	5	3
NT82	M	no count	0
	N	8	2
	P	19	7
	Q	19	4
	R	17	9
	S	19	5
	T	28	6
	U	26	16
	V	18	5
	W	24	12
	X	30	13
	Y	40	24
	Z	46	22
NT83	C	30	17
	D	17	25
	E	41	30
	F	29	19
	G	26	28
	H	29	21
	I	37	29
	J	31	30
	K	28	34
	L	44	37
	M	21	20
	N	49	48
	P	24	58
	Q	30	15
	R	31	41
	S	24	17
	T	30	36
	U	37	34
	V	27	29
	W	39	35
	X	22	18
	Y	26	25
	Z	21	37
NT84	K	34	23
	Q	21	20
	R	31	26
	V	24	21
	W	29	40
	X	42	23
	Y	32	23
NT90	A	26	17
	B	27	6
	C	50	13
	D	41	12
	E	31	8
	F	61	25
	G	44	15
	H	66	41
	I	44	32
	J	32	5
	K	22	23
	L	50	59
	M	35	26
	N	32	17
	P	26	19
	Q	34	34
	R	29	29
	S	24	21
	T	25	20
	U	27	19
	V	35	38
	W	27	28
	X	13	19
	Y	36	24
	Z	22	24
NT91	A	27	5
	B	16	2
	C	9	8
	D	17	3
	E	15	4
	F	36	5
	G	19	2
	H	28	9
	I	19	3
	J	8	4
	K	8	1
	L	15	2
	M	32	3
	N	34	7
	P	17	5
	Q	30	10
	R	24	17
	S	32	20
	T	41	15
	U	15	7
	V	36	43
	W	24	8
	X	32	12
	Y	35	20
	Z	29	11

APPENDIX K Number of Breeding (either possible, probable or confirmed) and Wintering species by tetrad. *continued*

		Breeding 1988-92	Winter 1996-99
NT92	A	10	1
	B	29	7
	C	9	5
	D	11	3
	E	41	19
	F	31	7
	G	22	9
	H	10	3
	I	30	5
	J	40	12
	K	53	12
	L	24	12
	M	22	4
	N	17	9
	P	43	20
	Q	70	4
	R	36	20
	S	41	23
	T	41	26
	U	26	34
	V	40	4
	W	37	28
	X	50	38
	Y	34	33
	Z	31	35
NT93	A	30	36
	B	20	12
	C	19	25
	D	17	22
	E	16	28
	F	31	32
	G	14	26
	H	26	37
	I	26	27
	J	28	36
	K	24	24
	L	37	29
	M	27	33
	N	29	26
	P	29	29
	Q	45	33
	R	30	42
	S	28	29
	T	40	25
	U	29	17
	V	25	23
	W	28	44
	X	28	18
	Y	30	23
	Z	34	30
NT94	A	56	36
	B	16	30
	C	37	22
	D	36	40
	E	53	33
	F	25	29
	G	17	27
NT94	H	19	11
	I	20	22
	J	19	41
	K	48	21
	L	36	21
	M	25	21
	N	25	18
	P	19	31
	Q	18	24
	R	26	28
	S	18	19
	T	17	20
	U	34	17
	V	28	24
	W	25	29
	X	50	24
	Y	22	26
	Z	23	21
NT95	F	21	16
	K	28	16
	L	24	24
	M	18	14
	Q	18	23
	R	21	37
	S	22	18
	T	25	15
	V	18	18
	W	30	44
	X	26	23
	Y	25	14
NU00	A	75	95
	B	56	24
	C	46	18
	D	33	21
	E	38	18
	F	48	25
	G	50	26
	H	27	26
	I	23	28
	J	34	17
	K	61	38
	L	39	18
	M	26	8
	N	17	13
	P	36	19
	Q	25	42
	R	30	20
	S	10	6
	T	34	9
	U	19	11
	V	47	19
	W	35	18
	X	35	10
	Y	40	12
	Z	42	17
NU01	A	41	25
NU01	B	31	22
	C	27	7
	D	47	29
	E	23	28
	F	31	37
	G	25	24
	H	22	22
	I	20	26
	J	34	24
	K	16	32
	L	17	29
	M	31	19
	N	53	41
	P	26	31
	Q	26	25
	R	36	28
	S	44	28
	T	49	26
	U	57	31
	V	44	27
	W	43	33
	X	42	30
	Y	34	20
	Z	34	34
NU02	A	56	32
	B	34	9
	C	37	12
	D	32	27
	E	35	50
	F	50	24
	G	37	31
	H	38	40
	I	36	36
	J	30	52
	K	46	27
	L	37	37
	M	25	46
	N	20	21
	P	38	23
	Q	34	54
	R	28	29
	S	29	45
	T	16	26
	U	31	23
	V	31	37
	W	19	12
	X	20	15
	Y	18	12
	Z	23	27
NU03	A	35	29
	B	15	16
	C	21	23
	D	25	26
	E	24	21
	F	29	26
	G	21	19
	H	25	15

APPENDIX K Number of Breeding (either possible, probable or confirmed) and Wintering species by tetrad. *continued*

Tetrad		Breeding 1988-92	Winter 1996-99
NU03	I	17	26
	J	24	22
	K	39	24
	L	29	26
	M	24	28
	N	33	36
	P	18	22
	Q	29	30
	R	17	15
	S	42	46
	T	18	18
	U	22	25
	V	26	29
	W	28	17
	X	34	32
	Y	22	36
	Z	16	39
NU04	A	34	17
	B	28	17
	C	31	42
	D	34	32
	E	28	30
	F	45	23
	G	31	18
	H	19	27
	I	38	27
	J	32	20
	K	34	26
	L	35	32
	M	25	29
	N	16	20
	Q	39	21
	R	43	61
	S	11	30
	T	0	6
	V	28	52
	W	18	38
	X	0	16
NU05	A	39	42
	B	47	42
	C	16	20
	F	0	13
NU10	A	37	27
	B	32	13
	C	32	19
	D	40	10
	E	50	23
	F	31	24
	G	40	24
	H	32	18
	I	32	10
	J	52	14
	K	36	31
	L	41	28
	M	45	27
	N	45	24
NU10	P	30	21
	Q	40	32
	R	30	27
	S	35	23
	T	40	20
	U	26	24
	V	46	27
	W	38	28
	X	39	24
	Y	31	22
	Z	32	34
NU11	A	30	24
	B	44	28
	C	28	20
	D	31	20
	E	45	22
	F	31	23
	G	35	32
	H	27	29
	I	44	22
	J	39	24
	K	25	27
	L	23	15
	M	53	17
	N	41	27
	P	34	20
	Q	32	23
	R	42	32
	S	52	44
	T	34	14
	U	30	24
	V	32	22
	W	39	39
	X	37	24
	Y	28	24
	Z	32	21
NU12	A	28	14
	B	19	7
	C	24	8
	D	22	10
	E	23	11
	F	31	19
	G	19	11
	H	22	12
	I	18	14
	J	31	23
	K	31	13
	L	26	25
	M	26	10
	N	30	27
	P	28	30
	Q	31	20
	R	30	25
	S	29	28
	T	32	23
	U	26	27
	V	32	26
NU12	W	33	48
	X	28	45
	Y	22	18
	Z	34	34
NU13	A	31	30
	B	37	33
	C	40	35
	D	22	39
	E	14	26
	F	38	33
	G	24	25
	H	30	35
	I	31	32
	J	11	30
	K	42	32
	L	48	59
	M	36	83
	N	11	53
	P	3	15
	Q	30	30
	R	42	30
	S	36	71
	T	6	36
	V	43	35
	W	32	34
	X	51	63
	Y	0	8
NU14	A	0	24
	B	16	40
	C	0	19
	F	22	59
	G	35	85
	H	0	19
	K	0	21
	L	0	19
NU20	A	33	38
	B	43	38
	C	21	31
	D	30	27
	E	33	39
	F	30	34
	G	27	30
	H	33	30
	I	32	35
	J	26	25
	K	28	29
	L	26	23
	M	41	76
	N	40	62
	P	25	53
	Q	45	75
	R	43	31
	S	33	65
	T	0	15
	V	15	37
	W	46	82

APPENDIX K Number of Breeding (either possible, probable or confirmed) and Wintering species by tetrad. *continued*

		Breeding 1988-92	Winter 1996-99
NU20	X	19	23
NU21	A	35	21
	B	43	22
	C	32	24
	D	24	22
	E	23	24
	F	50	47
	G	24	25
	H	39	33
	I	32	39
	J	41	24
	K	52	74
	L	36	27
	M	36	21
	N	67	38
	P	48	56
	Q	0	13
	R	31	35
	S	25	50
	T	4	27
	U	5	28
NU22	A	44	29
	B	40	33
	C	42	29
	D	37	25
	E	32	32
	F	40	32
	G	42	47
	H	46	35
	I	55	62
	J	37	72
	K	44	45
	L	43	43
	M	53	85
	N	0	25
	P	0	10
	Q	0	9
NU23	A	34	33
	B	24	45
	C	23	61
	D	5	33
	F	36	53
	G	0	33
	H	12	18
	I	23	70
	J	12	25
	N	0	20
	P	8	26
NY58	S	15	4
	T	11	4
	U	11	6
	W	14	6
	X	9	8
	Y	14	10
	Z	17	7

		Breeding 1988-92	Winter 1996-99
NY59	Q	9	5
	V	17	6
	W	8	2
	X	no count	3
	Y	6	10
NY64	I	5	no count
	J	5	2
	M	10	no count
	N	9	1
	P	16	5
	T	6	2
	U	8	5
	Y	29	12
	Z	40	19
NY65	B	3	no count
	C	3	1
	F	7	1
	G	10	4
	H	9	4
	I	6	2
	J	4	no count
	K	11	15
	L	15	5
	M	11	4
	N	25	10
	P	48	22
	Q	29	26
	R	40	28
	S	48	34
	T	31	19
	U	45	40
	V	40	36
	W	27	14
	X	55	39
	Y	41	19
	Z	51	63
NY66	C	no count	6
	F	15	0
	G	15	13
	H	25	21
	I	53	22
	J	41	14
	K	35	18
	L	19	15
	M	33	29
	N	26	21
	P	24	15
	Q	53	25
	R	49	28
	S	40	30
	T	50	21
	U	14	12
	V	37	48
	W	31	39
	X	29	28
	Y	20	14

		Breeding 1988-92	Winter 1996-99
NY66	Z	16	15
NY67	J	14	5
	K	no count	2
	N	23	14
	P	17	8
	Q	37	12
	T	32	16
	U	16	5
	V	23	9
	W	25	11
	X	36	27
	Y	26	9
	Z	18	7
NY68	A	20	1
	B	14	11
	C	20	5
	D	17	5
	E	34	8
	F	16	7
	G	12	3
	H	12	11
	I	20	7
	J	18	10
	K	11	4
	L	15	7
	M	18	14
	N	21	9
	P	25	11
	Q	8	4
	R	13	4
	S	18	12
	T	15	13
	U	13	7
	V	13	9
	W	12	3
	X	22	10
	Y	32	18
	Z	23	9
NY69	A	14	5
	B	19	11
	C	27	13
	D	26	13
	E	21	6
	F	21	21
	G	40	33
	H	15	20
	I	22	12
	J	19	4
	K	19	14
	L	13	7
	M	20	15
	N	24	12
	P	26	11
	Q	19	12
	R	18	11
	S	26	7

APPENDIX K Number of Breeding (either possible, probable or confirmed) and Wintering species by tetrad. *continued*

		Breeding 1988-92	Winter 1996-99
NY69	T	23	5
	U	20	16
	V	18	11
	W	15	4
	X	17	5
	Y	19	8
	Z	18	5
NY74	E	40	32
	J	29	13
	P	23	5
	S	38	no count
	T	13	3
	U	27	13
	X	29	3
	Y	23	18
	Z	40	15
NY75	A	20	11
	B	29	10
	C	18	6
	D	17	4
	E	35	30
	F	19	6
	G	18	4
	H	23	4
	I	12	5
	J	26	17
	K	22	10
	L	18	6
	M	28	6
	N	14	2
	P	12	4
	Q	32	22
	R	38	31
	S	26	23
	T	31	24
	U	18	24
	V	31	19
	W	40	30
	X	42	27
	Y	36	29
	Z	40	29
NY76	A	26	38
	B	24	46
	C	26	41
	D	9	27
	E	16	24
	F	16	30
	G	32	48
	H	17	34
	I	17	34
	J	16	25
	K	21	26
	L	24	52
	M	27	36
	N	19	41
	P	16	28
NY76	Q	26	40
	R	35	35
	S	23	39
	T	30	27
	U	38	32
	V	25	37
	W	45	41
	X	31	43
	Y	23	34
	Z	39	41
NY77	A	15	14
	B	15	7
	C	13	5
	D	10	7
	E	13	8
	F	23	9
	G	20	6
	H	13	10
	I	16	5
	J	20	8
	K	19	5
	L	12	5
	M	20	11
	N	15	8
	P	11	6
	Q	15	9
	R	18	4
	S	25	13
	T	21	15
	U	16	7
	V	21	8
	W	18	12
	X	26	13
	Y	27	22
	Z	19	11
NY78	A	20	5
	B	18	5
	C	28	10
	D	27	25
	E	22	21
	F	16	6
	G	18	11
	H	25	19
	I	36	22
	J	15	6
	K	27	5
	L	15	14
	M	37	28
	N	23	26
	P	13	6
	Q	17	8
	R	36	10
	S	29	23
	T	34	20
	U	20	15
	V	26	18
	W	18	8
NY78	X	44	34
	Y	38	18
	Z	35	24
NY79	A	21	5
	B	18	4
	C	15	6
	D	13	3
	E	12	4
	F	16	7
	G	17	4
	H	20	6
	I	10	1
	J	16	4
	K	17	20
	L	26	6
	M	18	12
	N	15	4
	P	15	5
	Q	28	15
	R	20	7
	S	21	3
	T	22	4
	U	9	7
	V	19	10
	W	18	6
	X	20	3
	Y	14	9
	Z	21	12
NY84	C	14	2
	D	36	16
	E	13	9
	H	17	3
	I	14	1
	J	16	7
	L	12	1
	M	46	13
	N	56	13
	P	36	23
	R	7	1
	S	22	20
	T	10	3
	U	11	1
	X	13	2
	Y	11	0
	Z	10	1
NY85	A	10	2
	B	19	6
	C	19	17
	D	36	22
	E	35	25
	F	16	10
	G	27	16
	H	41	24
	I	38	21
	J	20	37
	K	37	28

APPENDIX K Number of Breeding (either possible, probable or confirmed) and Wintering species by tetrad. *continued*

		Breeding 1988-92	Winter 1996-99
NY85	L	28	21
	M	20	19
	N	21	21
	P	19	3
	Q	17	2
	R	12	4
	S	15	5
	T	12	2
	U	14	4
	V	17	1
	W	15	6
	X	18	26
	Y	28	13
	Z	19	23
NY86	A	61	17
	B	72	19
	C	32	27
	D	38	62
	E	22	16
	F	71	26
	G	66	35
	H	33	33
	I	40	33
	J	22	22
	K	30	14
	L	58	19
	M	58	38
	N	21	28
	P	28	33
	Q	21	7
	R	27	25
	S	40	31
	T	25	28
	U	27	26
	V	26	15
	W	27	28
	X	32	26
	Y	32	37
	Z	19	28
NY87	A	30	37
	B	13	9
	C	20	19
	D	23	19
	E	27	17
	F	29	18
	G	14	8
	H	10	15
	I	26	19
	J	27	25
	K	9	12
	L	17	19
	M	33	21
	N	37	26
	P	39	34
	Q	22	11
	R	36	30
	S	43	28

		Breeding 1988-92	Winter 1996-99
NY87	T	48	33
	U	36	20
	V	37	23
	W	34	26
	X	60	34
	Y	32	28
	Z	23	20
NY88	A	42	21
	B	40	25
	C	41	40
	D	27	6
	E	24	17
	F	33	17
	G	24	33
	H	27	12
	I	15	7
	J	9	3
	K	35	20
	L	41	28
	M	30	21
	N	17	11
	P	10	9
	Q	37	42
	R	32	34
	S	25	18
	T	26	12
	U	11	5
	V	33	11
	W	47	21
	X	30	25
	Y	39	23
	Z	29	25
NY89	A	31	16
	B	24	14
	C	24	15
	D	31	14
	E	37	21
	F	9	7
	G	13	12
	H	19	13
	I	45	36
	J	40	26
	K	20	7
	L	21	15
	M	28	14
	N	33	25
	P	14	6
	Q	27	9
	R	38	23
	S	43	36
	T	28	12
	U	29	11
	V	34	25
	W	46	41
	X	51	23
	Y	34	14
	Z	26	10

		Breeding 1988-92	Winter 1996-99
NY94	D	6	no count
	E	35	7
	J	31	15
	P	29	27
	U	10	no count
NY95	A	31	18
	B	37	25
	C	28	23
	D	32	24
	E	30	24
	F	15	8
	G	22	25
	H	44	28
	I	42	26
	J	49	36
	K	30	22
	L	19	5
	M	36	19
	N	20	30
	P	69	51
	Q	37	25
	R	30	2
	S	23	23
	T	38	36
	U	37	32
	V	56	8
	W	44	33
	X	44	36
	Y	52	45
	Z	34	33
NY96	A	20	27
	B	33	18
	C	29	42
	D	36	25
	E	20	31
	F	39	33
	G	36	43
	H	39	58
	I	29	26
	J	23	26
	K	41	29
	L	34	27
	M	27	32
	N	23	33
	P	20	24
	Q	33	21
	R	22	34
	S	32	51
	T	20	37
	U	19	27
	V	40	31
	W	30	41
	X	33	59
	Y	24	28
	Z	20	19

APPENDIX K Number of Breeding (either possible, probable or confirmed) and Wintering species by tetrad. *continued*

		Breeding 1988-92	Winter 1996-99
NY97	A	41	31
	B	34	29
	C	31	23
	D	32	28
	E	24	20
	F	49	38
	G	39	28
	H	57	57
	I	34	19
	J	29	42
	K	19	16
	L	29	25
	M	34	34
	N	26	18
	P	22	18
	Q	27	21
	R	31	25
	S	27	37
	T	37	40
	U	21	17
	V	27	37
	W	34	18
	X	35	22
	Y	29	28
	Z	35	23
NY98	A	21	8
	B	22	9
	C	19	11
	D	33	23
	E	14	13
	F	24	11
	G	39	25
	H	20	11
	I	19	7
	J	19	6
	K	32	17
	L	28	17
	M	20	7
	N	12	10
	P	22	16
	Q	22	13
	R	27	17
	S	11	14
	T	17	6
	U	14	6
	V	22	17
	W	18	10
	X	29	23
	Y	23	15
	Z	18	4
NY99	A	26	15
	B	32	18
	C	26	7
	D	22	3
	E	12	1
	F	23	17
	G	39	16

		Breeding 1988-92	Winter 1996-99
NY99	H	21	4
	I	44	6
	J	38	7
	K	23	6
	L	33	22
	M	27	15
	N	43	32
	P	33	17
	Q	23	17
	R	27	12
	S	14	1
	T	22	20
	U	39	21
	V	30	17
	W	20	6
	X	14	2
	Y	13	4
	Z	31	18
NZ04	P	48	35
	U	40	24
NZ05	A	38	no count
	B	53	30
	C	32	16
	D	40	18
	E	40	16
	F	54	13
	G	47	27
	H	41	26
	I	47	28
	J	29	16
	K	41	36
	L	35	23
	M	42	37
	N	37	16
	P	44	31
	Q	35	40
	R	42	32
	S	37	25
	T	39	30
	U	36	22
	V	41	37
	W	43	48
	X	61	51
	Y	43	37
	Z	39	31
NZ06	A	46	41
	B	59	73
	C	28	25
	D	38	20
	E	31	23
	F	32	36
	G	26	31
	H	22	40
	I	28	24
	J	21	22
	K	53	41

		Breeding 1988-92	Winter 1996-99
NZ06	L	38	34
	M	24	27
	N	24	23
	P	23	21
	Q	37	26
	R	46	28
	S	41	21
	T	54	25
	U	58	56
	V	50	25
	W	50	34
	X	43	26
	Y	31	28
	Z	29	19
NZ07	A	27	38
	B	15	21
	C	25	27
	D	25	24
	E	24	18
	F	44	38
	G	24	30
	H	31	22
	I	27	28
	J	54	40
	K	30	19
	L	35	24
	M	22	22
	N	27	31
	P	30	28
	Q	46	44
	R	34	33
	S	30	25
	T	30	30
	U	46	32
	V	40	30
	W	37	20
	X	34	26
	Y	31	19
	Z	47	41
NZ08	A	23	17
	B	34	19
	C	28	20
	D	21	17
	E	33	22
	F	40	25
	G	43	18
	H	49	45
	I	27	27
	J	30	19
	K	28	21
	L	38	14
	M	32	22
	N	28	22
	P	40	19
	Q	33	25
	R	33	28
	S	29	22

APPENDIX K Number of Breeding (either possible, probable or confirmed) and Wintering species by tetrad.

continued

		Breeding 1988-92	Winter 1996-99
NZ08	T	40	37
	U	28	31
	V	26	46
	W	42	22
	X	36	19
	Y	36	22
	Z	26	21
NZ09	A	30	20
	B	22	7
	C	19	6
	D	11	2
	E	26	6
	F	24	8
	G	41	16
	H	32	15
	I	15	10
	J	28	8
	K	33	39
	L	43	19
	M	28	18
	N	33	13
	P	32	9
	Q	25	19
	R	50	20
	S	26	20
	T	28	16
	U	27	20
	V	34	24
	W	33	21
	X	27	18
	Y	29	23
	Z	31	17
NZ15	D	20	35
	E	11	22
NZ16	A	33	22
	B	27	24
	C	56	55
	D	34	21
	E	42	22
	H	55	39
	I	38	40
	J	30	29
	M	46	39
	N	35	25
	P	35	28
	S	35	29
	T	47	44
	U	43	21
	W	no count	29
	X	21	34
	Y	21	28
	Z	30	38
NZ17	A	42	32
	B	35	26
	C	32	36
NZ17	D	36	30
	E	35	29
	F	50	33
	G	40	24
	H	33	33
	I	32	21
	J	31	34
	K	30	34
	L	30	33
	M	27	35
	N	60	33
	P	34	34
	Q	32	25
	R	44	45
	S	23	34
	T	34	41
	U	29	31
	V	38	36
	W	38	61
	X	37	41
	Y	34	31
	Z	37	27
NZ18	A	17	16
	B	20	21
	C	37	36
	D	21	12
	E	18	24
	F	28	36
	G	31	26
	H	33	33
	I	20	15
	J	33	24
	K	25	20
	L	26	30
	M	25	48
	N	32	31
	P	21	18
	Q	18	42
	R	25	32
	S	55	39
	T	38	35
	U	29	27
	V	26	34
	W	25	20
	X	35	31
	Y	32	30
	Z	27	26
NZ19	A	34	19
	B	40	40
	C	22	29
	D	27	25
	E	43	38
	F	24	33
	G	25	35
	H	22	27
	I	22	32
	J	25	35
NZ19	K	37	29
	L	29	33
	M	34	45
	N	29	29
	P	28	25
	Q	24	26
	R	17	29
	S	23	32
	T	31	23
	U	21	25
	V	19	15
	W	25	17
	X	15	16
	Y	21	15
	Z	25	18
NZ26	B	22	32
	C	24	25
	D	19	26
	E	39	36
	G	17	35
	H	26	25
	I	26	24
	J	36	35
	L	12	16
	M	37	45
	N	47	45
	P	44	48
	R	13	18
	S	39	37
	T	43	51
	U	32	43
	W	17	28
	X	30	30
	Y	35	41
	Z	46	34
NZ27	A	26	36
	B	34	30
	C	35	37
	D	38	38
	E	35	38
	F	32	46
	G	81	100
	H	49	25
	I	30	29
	J	31	40
	K	68	68
	L	27	30
	M	63	83
	N	32	47
	P	43	43
	Q	29	43
	R	25	33
	S	39	52
	T	33	44
	U	35	51
	V	27	26
	W	33	30

APPENDIX K Number of Breeding (either possible, probable or confirmed) and Wintering species by tetrad. *continued*

		Breeding 1988-92	Winter 1996-99
NZ27	X	31	35
	Y	37	24
	Z	44	38
NZ28	A	28	35
	B	19	21
	C	34	46
	D	33	45
	E	27	23
	F	33	30
	G	26	33
	H	27	41
	I	39	36
	J	25	32
	K	34	47
	L	33	36
	M	33	40
	N	35	71
	P	31	53
	Q	40	55
	R	25	45
	S	29	40
	T	31	34
	U	29	51
	V	22	44
	W	31	73
	X	42	70
	Y	18	46
	Z	20	63
NZ29	A	32	30
	B	43	25
	C	37	21
	D	30	43
	E	18	24
	F	26	24
	G	51	46
	H	39	53
	I	39	48
	J	27	28
	K	27	51
	L	34	31
	M	33	28
	N	19	38
	P	37	36
	Q	37	34
	R	65	63

		Breeding 1988-92	Winter 1996-99
NZ29	S	34	36
	T	49	73
	U	16	68
	V	28	36
	W	36	39
	X	33	69
NZ36	C	6	14
	D	32	33
	E	63	56
	I	32	26
	J	31	24
	N	22	26
	P	18	31
	U	32	83
	Z	0	7
NZ37	A	35	29
	B	55	40
	C	52	76
	D	43	25
	E	33	37
	F	30	26
	G	42	32
	H	67	42
	I	40	49
	J	4	17
	K	40	64
	L	25	28
	M	26	54
	N	2	16
	Q	12	32
	R	0	4
NZ38	A	18	31
	B	17	59
	C	9	36
	D	17	44
	E	22	66
	F	0	25
	G	0	10
	I	0	5
	J	0	13
NZ39	A	11	23
	B	0	25

BIBLIOGRAPHY

ANDERSON, G.Q.A. (1999). Feeding habitat selection by pale-bellied Brent Geese *Branta bernicla hrota* at Lindisfarne National Nature Reserve, U.K. Unpublished Ph.D. thesis. University of Sunderland.

ANON. (1909). *A guide to the birds of Holy Island.* Andrew Reid & Co. Ltd. Newcastle upon Tyne.

ARDAMATSKAYA, T.B. (1999). Breeding sites of Mediterranean Gull *Larus melanocephalus* in the countries of the former Soviet Union. *In* Meininger, P.L., Hoogendoorn, W., Flamant, R. & Raevel, P. (eds.) *Proceedings of the 1st International Mediterranean Gull Meeting, Le Portel, Pas-de-Calais, France, 4-7 September 1998.* EcoNum, Bailleul: 19-24.

ARMSTRONG, A.L. (2003). *Birds in Durham* [1999]. Durham Bird Club.

ATKINSON, N.K., DAVIES, M. & PRATER, A.J. (1978). The winter distribution of Purple Sandpipers in Britain. *Bird Study* 25: 223-228.

BAILLIE, S.R., CRICK, H.Q.P., BALMER, D.E., BASHFORD, R.I., BEAVEN, L.P., FREEMAN, S.N., MARCHANT, J.H., NOBLE, D.G., RAVEN, M.J., SIRIWARDENA, G.M., THEWLIS, R. & WERNHAM, C.V. (2001). *Breeding birds in the wider countryside: their conservation status 2000.* BTO Research report No. 252. BTO. Thetford.

BAINES, D. & HUDSON, P.J. (1995). The decline of the Black Grouse in Scotland and N. England. *Bird Study 42*: 122-131.

BANKIER, A.M. (1994). Green Sandpipers in Northumberland. *Birds in Northumbria 1993*: 100-102.

BARNES, J.A.G. (1975). *The titmice of the British Isles.* David & Charles. London.

BATTEN, L.A., BIBBY, C.J., CLEMENT, P., ELLIOTT, G.D. & PORTER, R.F. (1990). *Red data birds in Britain.* T. & A. D. Poyser. London.

BENN, S. (comp.) **(2001).** *Slavonian Grebe newsletter 2000.* RSPB/SNH.

BERTOLD, P. & TERRILL, S.B. (1988). Migratory behaviour and population growth of Blackcaps wintering in Britain and Ireland: some hypotheses. *Ringing and Migration 9*: 153-159.

BEWICK, T. (1797). *History of British birds Vol. 1.* Hodgson. Newcastle.

BIBBY, C.J., BURGESS, N.D. & HILL, D.A. (1992). *Bird census techniques.* BTO/RSPB. Academic Press. London.

BOLAM, G. (1912). *The birds of Northumberland and the Eastern Borders.* H.H. Blair. Alnwick

BOLAM, G. (1932). A catalogue of the birds of Northumberland. *Trans. Natural History Society of Northumberland, Durham, and Newcastle upon Tyne Vol. VIII.*

BOWEY, K., RUTHERFORD, S. & WESTERBERG, S. (1993). *Birds of Gateshead.* Gateshead Metropolitan Borough Council.

BRICKLE, N.W., & HARPER, D.G.C. (2000). Habitat use by Corn Bunting *Miliaria calandra* in winter and summer. *In* Aebishcher, N.J., Evans, A.D., Grice, P.V. & Vickery, J.A. (eds.) *Ecology and conservation of lowland farmland birds.* BOU. Tring: 156-164.

BRITTON, D. & DAY, J.C. (1995). *Where to watch birds in Northeast England.* Christopher Helm. London.

BRODIN, N. (2001). *A biodiversity audit of the North East.* English Nature. Harrogate.

BUCKINGHAM, D.L. (1998). Variation and occurrence of *intermedius* Lesser Black-backed Gulls in southern England. *British Birds* 91: 60-62.

BUCKLAND, S.T., BELL, M.V. & PICOZZI, N. (1990). *The birds of North-East Scotland.* North-East Scotland Bird Club. Aberdeen.

CADWALLENDER, T.A. & CADWALLENDER, M.L. (1997). Rooks in Northumberland 1996. *Birds in Northumbria 1996*: 116-126.

CADWALLENDER, T.A. & CADWALLENDER, M.L. (1998). The Sawbill survey 1997. *Birds in Northumbria 1997*: 126-129.

CADWALLENDER, T.A. & CADWALLENDER, M.L. (1999). Breeding Lapwing survey 1998. *Birds in Northumbria 1998*: 126-129.

CADWALLENDER, T.A. & CADWALLENDER, M.L. (2000). Breeding Corn Bunting survey 1999. *Birds in Northumbria 1999*: 149-154.

CHANDLER, R.J. (1981). Influxes into Britain and Ireland of Red-necked Grebes and other waterbirds during winter 1978/79. *British Birds 74*: 55-81.

CHANDLER, R.J. (1984). Proportions of adult male Smews and Red-breasted Mergansers in England and Wales in 1978/79. *British Birds* 77: 479-481.

CHAPMAN, A. (1889). *Birdlife of the Borders; records of wild sport and natural history on moorland and sea.* Gurney & Jackson. London.

CHAPMAN, A. (1907). *Birdlife of the Borders.* 2nd ed. Gurney & Jackson. London.

CLAUSEN, P. & BUSTNES, J.O. (1998). Flyways of North Atlantic light-bellied Brent Geese *Branta bernicla hrota* reassessed by satellite telemetry. *Norsk Polarinstitutt Skrifter* 200: 235-249.

CLAUSEN, P., FREDERIKSEN, M., PERCIVAL, S.M., ANDERSON, G.Q.A. & DENNY, M.J.H. (2001). Seasonal and annual survival of East-Atlantic pale-bellied Brent Geese *Branta bernicla hrota* assessed by capture-recapture analysis. *Ardea* 89: 101-111.

CLAUSEN, P., MADSEN, J., PERCIVAL, S.M., ANDERSON, G.Q.A., KOFFIJBERG, K., MEHLUM, F. & VANGELUWE, D. (1999). Svalbard pale-bellied Brent Goose *Branta bernicla hrota. In Goose populations of the Western Palearctic. A review of status and distribution.* J. Madsen, G.S. Cracknell & A.D. Fox (eds.). Wetlands International Publication No. 48. Wageningen, Netherlands.

CLAUSEN, P., MADSEN, J., PERCIVAL, S.M., O'CONNOR, D. & ANDERSON, G.Q.A. (1998). Population development and changes in winter site use by the Svalbard light-bellied Brent Goose *Branta bernicla hrota*, 1980-1994. *Biological Conservation* 84: 157-165.

CLAUSEN, P. & PERCIVAL, S.M. (1998). Changes in the distribution and habitat use of Svalbard light-bellied Brent Geese *Branta bernicla hrota*, 1980-1995: driven by Zostera availability? *Norsk Polarinstitutt Skrifter* 200: 253-276.

CLEMENT, P. (1995). *The Chiffchaff.* Hamlyn. London.

CLEMENT, P. & HATHWAY, R. (2000). *Thrushes.* Christopher Helm. London.

COLEMAN A.E., COLEMAN J.T., MINTON C.D.T. & COLEMAN P.A. (2001). A 39 year study of the Mute Swan. Ardea (in press).

COLLINGE, W.E. (1924-27). The food of some British wild birds: a study in economic ornothology. 2nd edition. Privately published. York.

COOMBS, F. (1978). *The Crows.* Batsford. London.

COULSON, J.C. (1966). The movement of the Atlantic Kittiwake with special reference to age. *Bird Study 13*: 107-115.

COULSON, J.C., BUTTERFIELD, J., DUNCAN, N., KEARSEY, S., MONAGHAN, P. & THOMAS, C. (1984). Origin and behaviour of Great Black-backed Gulls wintering in northeast England. *British Birds* 77: 1-11.

COULSON, J.C., MONAGHAN, P., BUTTERFIELD, J., DUNCAN, N., THOMAS, C.S. & WRIGHT, H. (1982). Variation in the wing-tip pattern of the Herring Gull in Britain. *Bird Study* 29: 111-120.

COULSON, J.C., MONAGHAN, P., DUNCAN, N., FURNESS, R.W., SHEDDEN, C.B., & THOMAS, C. (1982b). The geographical variation of the Herring Gull *Larus argentatus* within Britain and in northern Europe; a biometrical approach. *Ibis* 125: 412-417.

COULSON, J.C., MONAGHAN, P., BUTTERFIELD, J.E.L., DUNCAN, N., ENSOR, K., SHEDDEN, C. & THOMAS, C. (1984). Scandinavian Herring Gulls wintering in Britain. *Ornis Scand. 15*: 79-88.

CRAMP, S. (ed.) **(1985).** *The birds of the Western Palearctic Vol. IV.* OUP. Oxford.

CRAMP, S. (ed.) **(1988).** *The birds of the Western Palearctic Vol. V.* OUP. Oxford.

CRAMP, S. & PERRINS, C.M. (eds) **(1993).** *The birds of the Western Palearctic Vol. VII.* OUP. Oxford.

CRAMP, S. & PERRINS, C.M. (eds) **(1994).** *The birds of the Western Palearctic Vol. VIII.* OUP. Oxford.

CRAMP, S. & SIMMONS, K.E.L. (eds) **(1977).** *The birds of the Western Palearctic Vol. I.* OUP. Oxford.

CRAMP, S. & SIMMONS, K.E.L. (eds) **(1983).** *The birds of the Western Palearctic Vol. III.* OUP. Oxford.

CRAMP, S. & SIMMONS, K.E.L. (eds) **(1994).** *The birds of the Western Palearctic Vol. IX.* OUP. Oxford.

CRANSWICK, P.A., POLLITT, M.S., MUSGROVE, A.J. & HUGHES, R.C. (1999). *The Wetland Bird Survey 1997-98: wildfowl and wader counts.* BTO/WWT/RSPB/JNCC. Slimbridge.

DAVENPORT, D.L. (1982). Influxes into Britain of Hen Harriers, Long-eared Owls and Short-eared Owls in winter 1978-9. *British Birds 75.* 309-316.

DAY, J.C. & CHARLTON, D.B. (1979). The Otterburn Estate. *The Adjutant 9*: 3-9.

DAY, J.C., HODGSON, M.S. & ROSSITER, B.N. (eds.) **(1995).** *The atlas of breeding birds in Northumbria.* Northumberland & Tyneside Bird Club. Newcastle-upon-Tyne.

DELANY, S., REYES, C., HUBERT, E., PIHL, S., REES, E., HAANSTRA, L. & VAN STRIEN, A. (1999). *Results from the International Waterbird Census in the Western Palearctic and Southwest Asia 1995 and 1996.* Wetlands International Publication. Wageningen. Netherlands.

DENNY, M.J.H. (2000). 'Black Brant' - An addition to the county list. *Birds in Northumbria 1999*: 165-166.

DENNY, M.J.H. (2001). Waterfowl disturbance: effects of hunting in a coastal ecosystem. Unpublished Ph.D. thesis. University of Sunderland.

DONALD, P.F. (1997). The Corn Bunting *Miliaria calandra* in Britain: a review of current status, patterns of decline and possible causes. *In* Donald, P.F. & Aebischer, N.J. *The ecology and conservation of Corn Buntings Miliaria calandra.* UK Nature Conservation No. 13. Joint Nature Conservation Committee, Peterborough.

DONALD, P.F. & EVANS, A.D. (1994). Habitat selection of Corn Buntings in Winter. *Bird Study 41*: 199-210.

EATON, M. (2000). Studies on Purple Sandpipers *Calidris maritima* at Blyth 1996-1999. *In* Holliday, S. *Blyth Birds.* Kingston upon Hull: 140-152

ELKINS, S. (1983). *Weather and bird behaviour.* T. & A.D. Poyser. Calton.

EVANS, F. (1967). Local sea fogs on the Northumberland coast. *Proc. University of Newcastle-upon-Tyne Philosophical Society 1*: 162-169.

EVANS, I.M., DENNIS, R.H., ORR-EWING, D.C., KJELLÉN, N., ANDERSSON, P., SYLVÉN, M., SENOSIAIN, A. & CARBO, F.C. (1997). The re-establishment of Red Kite breeding populations in Scotland and England. *British Birds 90*: 123-138

EVANS, P.R. (1966). Wader migration in north-east England. *Trans. Natural History Society of Northumbria 16*: 126-151.

FEARE, C. & CRAIG, A. (1998). Starlings and Mynahs. Christopher Helm. London.

FEIGE, D (ed.) **(2000)**. *Working for wildlife: the Northumberland biodiversity action plan.* Northumberland County Council. Morpeth.

FLEGG, J.J.M. (1973). A study of Treecreepers. *Bird Study 21*: 287-302.

FLEGG, J.J.M. & COX, C.J. (1972). Movement of Black-headed Gulls from colonies in England and Wales. *Bird Study 19*: 228-240.

FRANKIS, M. P. (1996). The status of the Hawfinch in Northumberland. *Birds in Northumbria 1995*: 119-124.

GALLOWAY, B. (1987). Dispersal of small raptors from Northumberland nest sites. *Birds in Northumbria 1986*: 91-93.

GALLOWAY, B. & MEEK, E.R. (1978). Northumberland's Birds. *Trans. Natural History Society of Northumbria 44 Pt.1.*

GALLOWAY, B. & MEEK, E.R. (1980). Northumberland's Birds. *Trans. Natural History Society of Northumbria 44 Pt.2.*

GALLOWAY, B. & MEEK, E.R. (1983). Northumberland's Birds. *Trans. Natural History Society of Northumbria 44 Pt.3.*

GALLOWAY, B. & MEEK, E.R. (1986). *Supplement to Northumberland's Birds.* Northumberland & Tyneside Bird Club.

GARDNER-MEDWIN, D. (1985). Early bird records for Northumberland and Durham. *Trans. Natural History Society of Northumbria 54*: 5-22.

GARNER, M. & QUINN, D. (1997). Identification of Yellow-legged Gulls in Britain, Part 1. *British Birds 90*: 25-62.

GIBBONS, D.W., REID, J.B. & CHAPMAN, R.A. (1993). *The new atlas of breeding birds in Britain and Ireland: 1988-1991.* T. & A D. Poyser. London.

GRANT, P.J. (1986). *Gulls a guide to identification.* Second edition. T. & A.D. Poyser. Calton.

HAGEMEIJER, E.J.M. & BLAIR, M.J. (1997). *The EBCC atlas of European breeding birds: their distribution and abundance.* T. & A.D. Poyser. London

HANCOCK, J. (1874). A catalogue of the birds of Northumberland and Durham. *Trans. Natural History Society of Northumberland, Durham and Newcastle upon Tyne 6.*

HARLE, B. (1984). The Raven *Corvus corax* in Northumberland. *Trans. Natural History Society of Northumbria 52*: 19-23.

HARRAP, S. & QUINN, D. (1996). *Tits, Nuthatches and Treecreepers.* Christopher Helm. London.

HARRIS, M.P. (1984). *The Puffin.* T. & A.D. Poyser. Calton.

HAWKEY, P. (1991). The birds of the Farne Islands. *Trans. Natural History Society of Northumbria 55*: 155-192.

HENDERSON, I.G. (1989). The exploitation of tits *Parus* species, Long-tailed Tits *Aegithos caudatus* and Goldcrest *Regulus regulus* by Treecreepers *Certhia familiaris*: a behavioural study. *Bird Study 36*: 99-104.

HENSON, R. (1999). Mediterranean Gulls *Larus melanocephalus* at Folkestone, England. *In* Meininger, P.L., Hoogendoorn, W., Flamant, R. & Raevel, P. *Proceedings of the 1st International Mediterranean Gull Meeting, Le Portel, Pas-de-Calais, France, 4-7 September 1998.* EcoNum, Bailleul: 131-133.

HICKLING, R.A.O. (1967). The inland wintering of gulls in England 1963. *Bird Study 14*: 104-113.

HILL, D. & ROBERTSON, P. (1988). *The Pheasant.* BSP Professional Books. Oxford.

HODGSON, M.S. (1986). *The spread of the Nuthatch in Northumberland.* Mimeographed report. Privately published.

HOLLIDAY, S. (2000). *Blyth birds.* Steve Holliday. Kingston upon Hull.

HOLLOWAY, S. (1996). *The historical atlas of breeding birds in Britain and Ireland: 1875-1900.* T. & A.D. Poyser. London.

HOLYOAK, D. (1968). A comparative study of the food of some British Corvidae. *Bird Study 115*: 147-153.

HUDSON, P.J. (1986). *The Red Grouse: biology and management of a wild game bird.* Game Conservancy. Fordingbridge.

HUDSON, P.J. (1992). *Grouse in space and time.* Game Conservancy. Fordingbridge.

HUDSON, R. (1964). Recoveries in Great Britain and Ireland of birds ringed abroad. *British Birds* 57: 583-596.

JARDINE, D. (1991). 1990 - The year of the Crossbill. *Birds in Northumbria 1990*: 103-106.

JOHNSON, G.A.L. (ed.) **(1995).** Robson's geology of North East England 2nd ed. *Trans. Natural History Society of Northumbria 56 Pt. 5.*

JONSSON, L. (1998). Yellow-legged Gulls and Yellow-legged Herring Gulls in the Baltic. *Alula 4(3)*: 74-100.

KERR, I. (1989). The Merlin in winter in Northumberland. *Birds in Northumbria 1988*: 91-94.

KERR, I. (1992). *Lindisfarne's birds.* 2nd ed. Northumberland & Tyneside Bird Club. Newcastle-upon-Tyne.

KERR, I. (1995). Letters from our ornithological past. *Birds in Northumbria 1994*: 98-99.

KERR, I. (2001). *Northumbrian birds.* Northumberland & Tyneside Bird Club. Newcastle-upon-Tyne.

KERSLAKE, L. (ed.) **(1998).** Red data book for Northumberland. *Trans. Natural History Society of Northumbria 58 Pt. 2.*

KIRBY, J., DELANY, S. & QUINN, J. (1994). Mute Swans in Great Britain: a review, current status and long term trends. *Hydrobiologia 280*: 467-482

KJELLÉN, N. (2000). *Fåglar i skåne 1999.* SK.O.F.

KNOX, A.G., COLLINSON, M., HELBIG, A.J., PARKIN, D.T. & SANGSTER, G. (2002). Taxonomic recommendations for British birds. *Ibis 144*: 707-710

LACK, P. (1966). *Population studies of birds.* OUP. Oxford.

LACK, P. (1986). *The atlas of wintering birds in Britain and Ireland.* T. & A.D. Poyser. London.

LLOYD, C., TASKER, T.L. & PARTRIDGE, K. (1991). *The status of seabirds in Britain and Ireland.* T. & A.D. Poyser. London.

MACFARLANE, L.G. (1973). *The status of the breeding birds of Northumberland in 1967-1968.* Mimeographed report. Tyneside Bird Club.

MADDISON, D. (1830). *An historical and descriptive account of Prestwick Carr and its environs.* W. Orange. North Shields.

MADGE, S.C. & BURN, H. (1988). *Wildfowl - an identification guide to the ducks, geese and swans of the world.* Christopher Helm, London.

MADSEN, J., REED, A. & ANDREW, A. (1996). Status and trends of geese (*Anser* sp. and *Branta* sp.) in the world: a review, updating and evaluation. *Gibier Faune Sauvage 13*: 337-353.

MANLEY, G. (1935). Some notes on the climate of North-East England. *Quarterly Journal of the Royal Meteorological Society 61*: 405-410.

MARCHANT, J.H., HUDSON, R., CARTER, S.P. & WHITTINGTON, P. (1990). *Population trends in British breeding birds*. BTO, NCC. Tring.

MARTIN, B.P. (1993). *The wildfowl of the British Isles and NW Europe*. David & Charles. Newton Abbot.

MASON, C.F. (1995). *The Blackcap*. Hamlyn. London.

MATHER, J.R. (1986). *The Birds of Yorkshire*. Croom Helm. London.

MCCAVISH, W.L. (1971). *Birds of the Kielder Forest*. Frank Graham. Newcastle-upon-Tyne.

MEAD, C.J. (1973). Movements of British raptors. *Bird Study 20*: 259-286.

MEAD, C. (2000). *The state of the nation's birds*. Whittet Books. Stowmarket.

MEEK, E.R. & LITTLE, B. (1977). Ringing studies of Goosanders in Northumberland. *British Birds 70*: 273-283.

MEININGER, P.L. & FLAMANT, R. (1999). Breeding populations of Mediterranean Gull *Larus melanocephalus* in the Netherlands and Belgium. *In* Meininger, P.L., Hoogendoorn, W., Flamant, R. & Raevel, P. *Proceedings of the 1st International Mediterranean Gull Meeting, Le Portel, Pas-de-Calais, France, 4-7 September 1998*. EcoNum, Bailleul: 47-54.

METCALFE, N.B. & FURNESS. R.W. (1985). Survival, winter population stability and site fidelity in the Turnstone *Arenaria interpres*. *Bird Study 32*: 207-214.

MIKKOLA, H. (1983). *Owls of Europe*. T. & A.D. Poyser. Calton.

MURRAY, R.D. (ed.) **(1999)**. *Scottish bird report for 1997*. SOC. Edinburgh.

MURRAY, R.D., HOLLING, M., DOTT, H.E.M. & VANDOME, P. (1998). *The breeding birds of South-East Scotland*. S.O.C. Edinburgh.

MUSGROVE, A.J., POLLITT, M.S., HALL, C., HEARN, R.D., HOLLOWAY, S.J., MARSHALL, P.E., ROBINSON, J.A. & CRANSWICK, P.A. (2001). *The Wetland Bird Survey 1999-2000: wildfowl and wader counts*. BTO/WWT/RSPB/JNCC. Slimbridge.

NEWTON, I. (1972). *Finches*. Collins. London.

NEWTON, I. (1986). *The Sparrowhawk*. T. & A.D. Poyser. Calton.

NIGHTINGALE, B. & ALLSOPP, K. (1997). The ornithological year 1996. *British Birds 90*: 538-548.

NOBLE, D.G., BASHFORD, R.I. & BAILLIE, S.R. (2000). *The Breeding Bird Survey 1999*. BTO Research Report 247. British Trust for Ornithology, Thetford.

NORMAN, D. (1994). *The Fieldfare*. Hamlyn. London.

NORTHUMBERLAND COAST MANAGEMENT PLAN (1993). Northumberland County Council. Morpeth.

NORTHUMBERLAND NATIONAL PARK PLAN (1984). First review. NNP. Hexham.

NORTHUMBERLAND NATIONAL PARK PLAN (1998). Draft second review. NNP. Hexham.

OGILVIE, M. (ed.) **(1999)**. Rare breeding birds in the UK in 1996. *British Birds 92*: 120-154.

OGILVIE, M. (ed.) **(2000).** Rare breeding birds in the UK in 1998. *British Birds 93*: 358-393.

PARKIN, D. (2001). Little Auk. *BWP Update 3*: 175-201.

PENNANT, T. (1771). *A tour in Scotland 1769*. J. Monk. Chester.

PERCIVAL, S.M., SUTHERLAND, W.J. & EVANS, P.R. (1996). A spatial depletion model of responses of grazing wildfowl to availability of intertidal vegetation. *Journal of Applied Ecology 33*: 979-992.

PERCIVAL, S.M. & ANDERSON, G.Q.A. (1998). Habitat use and site fidelity of Svalbard light-bellied Brent Geese *Branta bernicla hrota* at Lindisfarne: exploitation of a novel food resource. *Norsk Polarinstitutt Skrifter 200*: 295-301.

PERRINS, C. (1979). *British Tits*. Collins. London.

PERRY, R. (1946). *A naturalist on Lindisfarne*. Lindsay Drummond Ltd. London.

PETTY, S.J. & ANDERSON, D.I.K. (1996). *Population growth and breeding performance of Goshawks in the English/Scottish Borders during 1987-1996*. Forestry Commission Research Division. Roslin, Midlothian.

PIENKOWSKI, M.W. & PIENKOWSKI, A.E. (1983). WSG project on the movement of wader populations in western Europe: eight progress report. *Wader Study Group Bull. 38*: 13-22.

POLLITT, M.S., CRANSWICK, P.A., MUSGROVE, A.J., HALL, C., HEARN, R.D., ROBINSON, J.A. & HOLLOWAY, S.J. (2000). *The Wetland Bird Survey 1998-1999: wildfowl and wader counts*. BTO/WWT/RSPB/JNCC. Slimbridge.

PRATER, A.J. (1981). *Estuary birds of Britain and Ireland*. T. & A.D. Poyser. Calton.

PRATER, A.J. & DAVIES, M. (1978). Wintering Sanderlings in Britain. *Bird Study 25*: 33-38.

RADCLIFFE, D.A. (1980). *The Peregrine Falcon*. T. & A.D. Poyser. Calton.

RADCLIFFE, D.A. (1997). *The Raven*. T. & A.D. Poyser. Calton.

RENNISON, R.W. (1982-83). The impounding reservoirs of the Newcastle and Gateshead Water Co., 1845-1905. *Trans. Newcomen Society 54*: 44-47.

RICHARDS, A.J. (1977). Predation of snails by migrant Song Thrushes and Redwings. *Bird Study 24*: 53-54.

ROSSITER, B.N. (1996). Seasonal variations in Common Gull numbers. *Birds in Northumbria 1995*: 124-127.

ROSSITER, B.N. (1997). Seasonal variations in Lesser Black-backed Gull numbers. *Birds in Northumbria 1996:* 133-136.

ROSSITER, B.N. (1999). Northumberland's birds in the 18th and early 19th centuries : the contribution of John Wallis (1714-1793). *Trans. Natural History Society of Northumbria 59*: 93-136.

ROSSITER, B.N. (1999a). Seasonal variations in Black-headed Gull numbers. *Birds in Northumbria 1998*: 145-148.

ROSSITER, B.N. (2001a). Seasonal variations in Great Black-backed Gull numbers. *Birds in Northumbria 2000*: 153-155.

ROSSITER, B.N. (2001b). Characteristics of Atlantic Yellow-legged Gulls. http://www.nrossiter.supanet.com/ylg/

RUDENKO, A.G. (1999). Mediterranean Gull *Larus melanocephalus* in the Black Sea Reserve: population trends and breeding success. *In* Meininger, P.L., Hoogendoorn, W., Flamant, R. & Raevel, P. *Proceedings of the 1st International Mediterranean Gull Meeting, Le Portel, Pas-de-Calais, France, 4-7 September 1998*. EcoNum, Bailleul: 121-130.

SCOTT, G. (1760). *Select remains of the learned John Ray, M.A. and F.R.S.* J. Dodsley & J. Walter. London.

SELBY, P.J. (1831). A catalogue of the birds hitherto met with in the counties of Northumberland and Durham. *Trans. Natural History Society of Northumberland, Durham and Newcastle upon Tyne 1*.

SELBY, P.J. (1833). *Illustrations of British ornithology*. 2nd edition. 2 vols. W.H. Lizars. Edinburgh.

SHARP, J.I. (1993). *The climate of Newcastle-upon-Tyne*. University of Newcastle. Dept. of Geography. Seminar papers Series No. 64.

SHARROCK, J.T.R. (1976). *The atlas of breeding birds in Britain and Ireland*. BTO. Tring.

SHRUBB, M. (1993). *The Kestrel*. Hamlyn. London.

SIMMS, E. (1971). *Woodland birds.* Collins. London.

SIRIWARDENA, G.M. (2001). Why are 'brown tits' declining?. *BTO News No. 235*: 24.

SMAIL, J. (1882-84). Rooks and rookeries. *Hist. Berwickshire Naturalists Club 10*: 159-184.

SMITH, K.W., REED, J.M. & TREVIS, B.E. (1992). Habitat use and site fidelity of Green Sandpipers *Tringa ochropus* wintering in southern England. *Bird Study 39*: 155-164.

SNOW, D.W. (1968). Movements and mortality of British Kestrels. *Bird Study 15*: 65-83.

SNOW, D.W. & PERRINS, C.M. (1998). *The birds of the Western Palearctic. Concise edition. Vol. 1.* OUP. Oxford.

STONE, B.H., SEARS, J., CRANSWICK, P.A., GREGORY, R.D., GIBBONS, D.W., REHFISH, M.M., AEBISCHER, N.J. & REID, J.B. (1997). Population estimates of birds in Britain and in the United Kingdom. *British Birds 90*: 1-22.

SUMMERS-SMITH, J. D. (1988). *The Sparrows.* T. & A.D. Poyser. Calton.

SVENSSON, S., SVENSSON, M. & TJERNBERG, M. (1999). Svensk fågelatlas. *Vår Fågelväuld* supplement. SK.O.F. Stockholm.

SWAN, G.A. (1993). *Flora of Northumberland.* Natural History Society of Northumbria. Newcastle-upon-Tyne.

SYMONDS, F.L., LANGSLOW, D.R. & PIENKOWSKI, M.W. (1984). Movements of wintering shorebirds within the Firth of Forth: species differences in usage of an intertidal complex. *Biological Conservation 28*: 187-215.

TAPPER, S. (1999). A question of balance. Game Conservancy Trust. Fordingbridge.

TARDIVEL, N. (1984). *Winter bird survey 1977-1980.* Kent Ornithological Society.

TASKER, M.L., WEBB, A., HALL, A.J., PIENKOWSKI, M.W. & LANGSLOW, D.R. (1987). *Seabirds in the North Sea.* NCC. Peterborough.

TAYLOR, M., SEAGO, M., ALLARD, P. & DORLING, D. (1999). *The birds of Norfolk.* Pica Press. E. Sussex.

TEMPERLEY, G.W. (1942). Ornithological report for Northumberland and Durham for 1941. *Naturalist 67*: 71-77.

TOMS, M.P. & CLARK, J.A. (1998). Bird ringing in Britain and Ireland in 1996. *Ringing and Migration 19*: 95-168.

TURNER, D.M. (1991). Colour-ringed Herring Gulls (*Larus argentatus*) in the North Shields Fish Quay area. *N. & TBC Monthly Summary June 1991.*

TURNER, D.M. (2000). Comparison of gull numbers at Blyth South Harbour and the Tyne Estuary during 1999. *In* Holliday, S. *Blyth Birds*. Kingston upon Hull: 120-139.

TURNER, D.M. (2001). Seasonal variation in numbers of immature Great Black-backed Gulls in the mouths of the rivers Tyne and Blyth during 1999 and 2000. *Birds in Northumbria 2000*: 149-152.

TYLER, S. J. & ORMEROD, S. (1994). *The Dippers.* T. & A.D. Poyser. London.

TYRVÄINEN, H. (1975). The winter irruption of the Fieldfare *Turdus pilaris* and the supply of rowan-berries. *Orn. Fenn. 52*: 27-31.

VILLAGE, A. (1990). *The Kestrel.* T. & A.D. Poyser. London

VOOUS, K.H. (1977). List of recent Holarctic bird species. *Ibis 119*: Pt.1. 223-250: Pt.2. 376-406.

VOOUS, K.H. (1988). *Owls of the Northern Hemisphere.* Collins. London.

WALLIS, J. (1769). *Natural history and antiquities of Northumberland, and of so much of the county of Durham as lies between the rivers Tyne and Tweed; commonly called north bishopric. Vol. 1.* W. & W. Strahan. London.

WALTON, J. (comp.) **(1997)**. Birds on the Farne Islands in 1996. *Trans. Natural History Society of Northumbria 57.* 93-113.

WALTON, J. (comp.) **(2000)**. Birds on the Farne Islands in 1999. *Trans. Natural History Society of Northumbria 60.* 37-58.

WATERS, R.J., CRANSWICK, P.A., MUSGROVE, A.J. & POLLITT, M.S. (1998). *The Wetland Bird Survey 1996-97; Wildfowl and Wader Counts.* BTO/WWT/RSPB/JNCC. Slimbridge.

WATSON, D. (1977). *The Hen Harrier.* T. & A.D. Poyser. Berkhamsted.

WESTERBERG, A. (1994). North-east England regional water bird survey - the January 'Blitz'. *Birds in Northumbria 1993*: 104-109.

WHEELER, D. (1984). The July 1983 'heatwave' in North East England. *Weather 39*: 178-182.

WHEELER, D. (1988). Some observations on the memorable weather in North East England during September 1986. *Trans. Natural History Society of Northumbria 55*: 47-54.

WHITE, S. (1993). Here to Stay. *Birdwatch* 2, Number 4: 18-22.

WINGATE, J. (1825). Ornithology. *In* Mackenzie, E. *An historical, topographical, and descriptive view of the County of Northumberland.* 2nd ed. Mackenzie & Dent. Newcastle upon Tyne. Vol. 1: 114-121.

Many references have been made to the county annual bird report *Birds in Northumbria* and, for the sake of completeness, a full bibliographical list is provided. All were published by the Northumberland and Tyneside Bird Club (formerly the Tyneside Bird Club), each yearly report normally being published during the following calendar year.

Birds in Northumbria 1972	Galloway, B., Meek, E.R., & Armstrong, I.H.
Birds in Northumbria 1973	Galloway, B. & Meek, E.R.
Birds in Northumbria 1974	Galloway, B., Hodgson, M.S. & Meek, E.R.
Birds in Northumbria 1975	Galloway, B., Hodgson, M.S. & Meek, E.R.
Birds in Northumbria 1976	Galloway, B., Hodgson, M.S. & Meek, E.R.
Birds in Northumbria 1977	Galloway, B. & Meek, E.R.
Birds in Northumbria 1978	Galloway, B. & Hodgson, M.S.
Birds in Northumbria 1979	Heavisides, A. & Hodgson, M.S.
Birds in Northumbria 1980	Heavisides, A. & Hodgson, M.S.
Birds in Northumbria 1981	Heavisides, A. & Hodgson, M.S.
Birds in Northumbria 1982	Heavisides, A., Hodgson, M.S. & Kerr, I.
Birds in Northumbria 1983	Hodgson, M.S. & Kerr, I.
Birds in Northumbria 1984	Hodgson, M.S. & Kerr, I
Birds in Northumbria 1985	Hodgson, M.S., Johnston, A.J. & Kerr, I.
Birds in Northumbria 1986	Hodgson, M. S., Johnston, A.J. & Kerr, I.
Birds in Northumbria 1987	Hodgson, M.S., Johnston, A.J. & Kerr, I.
Birds in Northumbria 1988	Bradshaw, C., Hodgson, M.S., Johnston, A.J. & Kerr, I.

Birds in Northumbria 1989	Bradshaw, C., Hodgson, M.S., Johnston, A.J. & Kerr, I.
Birds in Northumbria 1990	Hodgson, M.S., Johnston, A.J., Kerr, I. & Rossiter, B.N.
Birds in Northumbria 1991	Jardine, D., Johnston, A.J., Kerr, I. & Rossiter, B.N.
Birds in Northumbria 1992	Jardine, D., Johnston, A.J., Kerr, I., McKeown, D. & Rossiter, B.N.
Birds in Northumbria 1993	Kerr, I. (ed.)
Birds in Northumbria 1994	Johnston, A.J. & Kerr, I. (eds.)
Birds in Northumbria 1995	Johnston, A.J. & Kerr, I. (eds.)
Birds in Northumbria 1996	Bowman, G. & Hodgson, M.S. (eds.)
Birds in Northumbria 1997	Bowman, G. & Hodgson, M.S. (eds.)
Birds in Northumbria 1998	Bowman, G. (ed.)
Birds in Northumbria 1999	Bowman, G. (ed.)
Birds in Northumbria 2000	Bowman, G. (ed.)

----------oOo----------

Index of English Bird Names

Species main entry only

----------oOo----------

Index of Scientific Bird Names

Species main entry only

----------oOo----------

THE NORTHUMBERLAND & TYNESIDE BIRD CLUB

Registered Charity No. 517641

The Northumberland & Tyneside Bird Club, formerly the Tyneside Bird Club, was formed in 1958. Membership currently stands at 260 and is open to anyone who has a beneficial interest in ornithology. The club aims to provide members with news of local ornithological interest through monthly bulletins, an annual report and other occasional publications. All members are encouraged to submit their records to the County Recorder for inclusion in these publications.

The club also undertakes to encourage and instruct members in various ornithological activities by means of indoor meetings held monthly between September and April, and field outings throughout the year.

Although bird ringing is not an official club activity some members operate ringing stations at Bamburgh and Hauxley, providing additional information for club publications.

Various subscription rates for membership exist including junior, ordinary, family and institutional categories. Further details may be obtained from the Honorary Secretary.

Honorary Secretary :

Alan Watson
3 Green Close
Whitley Bay
Tyne & Wear
NE25 9SH

County Recorder :

Ian Fisher
74 Benton Park Road
Newcastle upon Tyne
NE7 7NB